VOLUME 2

THE PAPERS OF JOSEPH HENRY

November 1832–December 1835

The Princeton Years

Henry's galvanic battery, with detail of the plates and interchangeable connectors.
Transactions of the American Philosophical Society, 1837, n.s. 5:plate 22.

The Papers of
JOSEPH HENRY

Editor: NATHAN REINGOLD
Assistant Editors: Arthur P. Molella and Michele L. Aldrich
with the assistance of James M. Hobbins
and Kathleen Waldenfels

November 1832–December 1835
The Princeton Years

SMITHSONIAN INSTITUTION PRESS
CITY OF WASHINGTON
1975

Published in the United States by the Smithsonian Institution Press.
Distributed in the United States and Canada by George Braziller, Inc.;
and throughout the rest of the world by Feffer and Simons, Inc.

Designed by Crimilda Pontes.
Produced in the United States by Heritage Printers, Inc.

ENDPAPERS: *A modern view of Nassau Hall—in Henry's day the center of college activities. Courtesy of the Princeton University Archives.*

Smithsonian Institution Press Publication Number 6112

Library of Congress Cataloging in Publication Data

Henry, Joseph, 1797–1878.
The papers of Joseph Henry . . .

Includes bibliographical references.

CONTENTS: *v. 1. December 1797–October 1832: the Albany years.*
v. 2. November 1832–December 1835: the Princeton years.

1. Science—Collected works.
2. Science—History—Collected works.
3. Smithsonian Institution—Collected works.
I. Reingold, Nathan, ed.

Q113.H43 537'.092'4 72–2005
ISBN 0–87474–164–5 (V. 2)

CONTENTS

ILLUSTRATIONS

INTRODUCTION

With the move to Princeton in November 1832, Joseph Henry began a new phase in his social and professional life. His years as a teacher and a researcher at Princeton, until his appointment to the Smithsonian in 1846, will be documented in this and four subsequent volumes of the *Henry Papers*. These years, marked by important scientific investigations and new professional friendships, start with the family's arrival in the small town that was to be home for fourteen years. A bright, ambitious Professor of Natural Philosophy has new environments in which to earn "the reputation of a scientific man": the town of Princeton, its modest but rising College of New Jersey, and, most important, Philadelphia, a metropolis with notable cultural organizations. Two environments remained unchanged: the world of science and research, an abstraction embedded in literature and in an oral tradition, and the most intimate environment of all, that of Henry's immediate family. While these environments are discussed separately in this introduction, in the documents they are often intertwined.

The volume opens, then, with a domestic interlude, establishing the family in a new area. Family letters reappear throughout the volume, notably Joseph Henry's letters to his brother James in Albany. While important as sources for Henry's opinions, actions, and personal traits, they often contain information on his professional development. For social historians, Joseph Henry's letters to James Henry are revealing of daily domestic life in Jacksonian America. Space limitations prevent the printing of all the family letters. Those in this volume and the remainder in the Smithsonian Archives have much information on the various activities of the women in the family—nursing, kitchen supervision, and child rearing. Present academics may note with envy that, on an initial salary of $1,000 a year plus a rent-free house (raised to $1500 by the end of 1835), the Henrys were able to employ at least one live-in servant and hire women for part-time tasks. (The family also received some funds from the estate of Harriet Henry's father.)

Perhaps not unique, Henry's expressed concern and involvement with the routine of domesticity was atypical for males of his day. A self-trained observer of natural phenomena, he carefully noted the landmarks of his children's life—weaning, walking, using table utensils, and forms of play. His wife Harriet added similar comments on family life. In his later years

Joseph Henry often seemed an austere statesman of science. Intimate glimpses of the younger Henry in these documents are of a proper but rather warm and tolerant father and husband.

Only professional interests loom larger than family life in the surviving Henry letters. That great obsession of his contemporaries, politics, appears occasionally in casual observations. Although he describes his reactions to such leading politicians as Henry Clay and Andrew Jackson on their visits to Princeton and comments on the great issues of the day, he was preoccupied with his teaching and his research. He did not form firm political opinions or involve himself in political activity. Henry's religious stance reflects an ambivalence similar to that of his politics: while he apparently attended Presbyterian services in Princeton, Henry did not make the formal declaration of faith that sealed church membership until later in life.

Princeton was a small, well-established, college town at the time of Henry's arrival. White settlers had begun farming in the area during the seventeenth century, and they gradually clustered to form the nucleus of a town. In the late eighteenth century the town was the site of an important battle of the American Revolution (January 3, 1777) and the meeting place briefly for both the fledgling state legislature and the American Congress. Thereafter its historical landmarks were religious and educational in nature, connected with the College and the Seminary situated there. In 1832–1835, Princeton had around eleven hundred residents plus about three hundred and fifty students from out of town. Princeton incorporated as a borough in 1813 and became a township in 1837.[1]

By 1832, Princeton was beginning a new phase of economic development. Construction on the Delaware and Raritan Canal, which had its office in the town, started that year and was completed in 1834. Stagelines out of Princeton north toward New York and south to Philadelphia continued to attract passenger traffic until eclipsed by the railroad in 1839, but the canal became and remained for some time the preferred means for cheap transportation of goods. With the arrival of the canal, small shops catering to local needs were joined by small businesses which marketed goods at some distance. The Princeton Bank incorporated in 1835 to provide these newer ventures with capital and to rationalize the real estate transactions of the town and surrounding farmlands.[2]

Princeton's single largest business continued to be education. In 1834,

[1] *Hageman, 1*:1, 9; 2:1–3. For the full citation of *Hageman* and other works in the Introduction to which we have assigned short titles, see the List of Short Titles. In the text, these works will be cited in full the first time they appear. Thomas F. Gordon, *A Gazetteer of the State of New Jersey* (Trenton, 1834), pp. 177, 221, 239.

[2] *Hageman, 1*:8, 252–255; 2:20–21. Gordon, *Gazetteer*, p. 221. *Princeton Courier and Literary Register*, January 25, 1833. *Princeton Whig*, August 29, 1834, and October 2, 1835.

Princeton was the home not only of the College and the Theological Seminary, but also of three classical schools, two schools for girls, and three or four common schools. Most of these were ephemeral institutions, but Edgehill High School, founded in 1829, endured long after the Henrys left. Princeton's second most important cultural institutions were its churches. The Presbyterian congregation, with a large church building and a separate meetinghouse for blacks, had existed since the eighteenth century, and far outnumbered those of other faiths. An Episcopal group built its church in 1833. According to its historian, John Hageman, while other towns were investing in manufacturing enterprises Princeton invested capital in educational and religious institutions.[3]

Princeton, then, differed a great deal from Albany. As state capital, Albany devoted an extraordinary amount of energy to politics, and its activity in that sector influenced national affairs. The same could hardly be said of Princeton.[4] Albany supported much larger and more numerous businesses, although, as in Princeton, the nature of that business remained first-stage processing of forest and agricultural products. The cultural heritage of Albany differed owing to the strong Dutch influence. Finally, as an intellectual center, Albany lacked the nucleus of the College, but sported a vigorous, productive, diversified set of organizations such as the Albany Institute. To match these Henry had to go to Philadelphia or New York, particularly the former.

The history of the town of Princeton was intimately connected with that of the College. Evangelical Presbyterians seeking a school to train their clergy and to educate their laymen had obtained a charter to create the College of New Jersey in 1746. The College met at Elizabeth and Newark before moving to Princeton as its permanent home in 1754. Nassau Hall was built for classes and student quarters. The first group of College Presidents sided with the evangelical faction of the divided colonial churches, but John Witherspoon, brought over from Scotland in 1768 and President until his death in 1795, was acceptable to both the new and the orthodox persuasions. During the American Revolution, Witherspoon found much of his time taken up by Congressional and diplomatic duties for the new nation; also, students interrupted or deferred their education to join the military (usually on the American side), dropping enrollments considerably. Nassau Hall was damaged by both American and British troops. Witherspoon managed to rebuild the College after the war. Overall, his

[3] *Hageman, 1*:15, 254; 2:221–222. Gordon, *Gazetteer*, p. 221.

[4] The town's most enduring newspaper during the Henrys' life there, the *Princeton Whig*, emblazoned its politics on the masthead, but the town elected Democratic officials on several occasions.

administration was characterized by the widening of Princeton's function from training clergy to educating for any walk of life, be it business, law, politics, or the church.[5]

During Samuel Stanhope Smith's tenure as President (1795–1812), the Trustees reasserted their authority and tried to direct the school back to training churchmen. From a student body that expected the school to reflect the era's ideology of responsibly exercised freedom, they sought meek, pious behavior. The efforts of the President and Trustees culminated in the heavy-handed suppression of a student riot in 1807, after which College enrollment—and, with it, student-fee income—dropped drastically. The term of Smith's successor, Ashbel Green (1812–1821), was marred by a similarly mishandled outbreak in 1817. Early nineteenth-century Princeton possessed overzealous Trustees, overworked professors, oversupervised students, and an undercapitalized endowment. Ironically, church dissatisfaction with affairs at the College had led to the establishment of a separate Theological Seminary in the town in 1812, taking away the main motive for severe disciplinary policies. Despite the creation of the Seminary, clergy still held a majority of posts on the College Board of Trustees, a control they kept through Henry's years there and afterwards. They also continued to elect fellow clergymen as Presidents.[6]

The combination of bad policy, poor teaching, and little money resulted in the dismally low enrollments of the first six years of James Carnahan's presidency, which ran from 1823 until 1854. By the time Joseph Henry arrived at Princeton in November 1832, the College's fortunes were on the upswing. Although the potential for severe repression of student misconduct remained, Carnahan, Vice President John Maclean, and the faculty came to distinguish between harmless student merriment and seriously disruptive behavior, to censure the first but to reserve harsh penalties or dismissal only for the second. Appalled at the pitiful state of College finances, the alumni had raised $20,000 in 1831 to increase the endowment, and even tried a campaign, albeit unsuccessful, for $100,000 three years later. Maclean persuaded the Trustees that a building program and new faculty appointments would increase student enrollments and fees—that is, to earn money, the College had first to spend it. Earlier, Philosophical Hall and the Library (later Stanhope Hall) had been built to supplement the classroom space of overpopulated Nassau Hall. Student quarters were expanded by the addition of East College (1834) and West College (1836), and faculty houses were increased in number as well. Henry and Maclean convinced the Trustees to renovate and expand Philosophical Hall in 1834.

[5] *Wertenbaker*, pp. 15–79.

[6] Ibid., pp. 87, 118–175, 239.

The faculty grew from a low of one professor and two tutors (plus the President and Vice President, who taught in addition to their other duties) during Green's administration to nine professors and two tutors in 1835. Tutors oversaw freshmen and sophomore recitations in the classics, aided students in understanding class materials, and monitored student behavior. The library remained the most seriously inadequate facility during Henry's years at Princeton; he was often driven to the American Philosophical Society for scholarly reading. The students frequently found the stock of their literary societies' libraries more satisfactory than the College bookshelves for popular literature and for works on contemporary issues.[7]

The courses were presented in two terms, a winter session of twenty-two weeks from November until April and a summer one of nineteen weeks (after five weeks' vacation) which terminated with a late September commencement.[8] Before being released in mid-August, the seniors faced examinations on all the material covered in their three or four years at the school; the three lower classes took tests at the end of each year to determine their fitness for promotion. Professors also held midterms and quarterly examinations in their courses. Princeton examinations were partially written and partly oral. The recitation system still governed teaching methods, especially for the freshman and sophomore classes in classics. The professors, however, had begun to use lecturing, class discussion, and essay writing as means of instruction by the time Henry arrived in 1832. Laboratory demonstrations by Torrey and Henry enlivened the science courses. Princeton possessed an important source of education outside the classroom in its two literary societies, the Whig and Cliosophic groups, which held formal debates and informal discussions over current political affairs and great moral issues. Whig and Clio also provided a social life for the students and maintained discipline among their members. Few holidays existed for student recreation; the Fourth of July and commencement occasioned festivities, but Christmas passed quietly at the College. The students did have a few hours free each school day for taking walks or exercising in games.[9]

Three factors in the composition of the Princeton student body deserve mention here: regionalism, career choices, and wealth. Much has been made of the number of Southerners who attended Princeton, especially by those seeking to explain the College's attitude during the Civil War. Dur-

[7] Ibid., pp. 131, 175–254. *Laws of the College of New-Jersey; Revised, Amended and Adopted by the Board of Trustees, April 1832* (Princeton, 1832) spelled out the duties and regulations for students, teachers, and administrators, but Wertenbaker indicates that the faculty and officers enforced the rules on student behavior flexibly.

[8] In 1844, the college year was altered to end with a June commencement. *Wertenbaker*, p. 249.

[9] *Wertenbaker*, pp. 97–98, 101, 134, 184–214.

ing the 1832–1835 period, however, twice as many students came from the middle states (225 from New York, Pennsylvania, Delaware, and New Jersey, of which 113 were from New Jersey alone) as from the South (108 from Virginia, Maryland, the Carolinas, Mississippi, the District of Columbia, Georgia, and Alabama).[10] Southerners hardly dominated the College, although their proportions were doubtless higher than at distant Harvard or Yale. Of the seniors in the classes of 1833, 1834, and 1835, a plurality (thirty-six) of the 136 graduates went on to a theological seminary. Twenty became teachers or physicians, and at least twenty spent a significant portion of their lives in public service, as judges, politicians, civil servants, or military officers.[11] Princeton had earned a reputation as a school for the sons of wealthy people, but it is difficult to assess the accuracy of that image. The minimum fixed fees for the year in 1835 were $121.50, assuming that the student dispensed with a room servant, lived in the cheapest quarters, and qualified for the reduced board offered to "pious and indigent young men, who have a view to the gospel ministry." The student still faced the costs of books, clothes, travel, furniture, and lights.[12] Wertenbaker suggests that some of the wealthy students at the school misled outsiders with their extravagant clothes, elegantly barbered hair, and profligate spending habits.[13]

The Princeton curriculum in 1832–1835 matched that of other American liberal arts colleges, such as Brown, Columbia, Union, Harvard, and Yale. Each year, the Princeton student found much of his class time devoted to studying Greek and Roman classics (freshmen and sophomores also received instruction in French). The student likewise faced some mathematics each year, from algebra for freshmen, into descriptive and analytic geometry and trigonometry during the middle years, and through integral calculus as seniors. What would now be called social sciences and humanities courses varied for each class: sophomores took history, juniors had courses on phi-

[10] Thirteen others came from the Midwest and New England. The count was taken from the *Princeton Annual Catalogues*, 1833 to 1836, inclusive, with seniors, juniors, and sophomores counted for the first year, and sophomores thereafter. Freshmen were omitted because so many students entered Princeton with advanced standing; the sophomore class was frequently three times that of the freshmen. James McLachlan, editor of *Princetonians: A Biographical Dictionary* (in progress), kindly loaned unpublished data from his personal research files at the Princeton Library, showing a significant nongraduate population in the Princeton student body. His data on a sample of the nongraduates associated with the classes of 1832 through 1836 suggests that they came from the South and middle states in virtually the same proportions as the students in our calculations. *Wertenbaker* (pp. 265–270) assesses the relevance of Southern students for Princeton's attitudes before and during the Civil War.

[11] The careers of sixty seniors are not given in the *Princeton Catalogue*. McLachlan's sample from the classes of 1832–1836, inclusive, shows the following career choices: thirty clergy, twenty-nine lawyers and politicians, six physicians, five each of landowners, merchants, and teachers, and four engineers.

[12] For yearly expenses at the College, see *Princeton Annual Catalogue*, 1836, p. 17.

[13] *Wertenbaker*, pp. 192–193.

losophy, Christianity, and natural theology, and seniors took a potpourri of economics, logic, ethics, belles-lettres, and constitutional law. Scientific courses also had a place in the curriculum. Sophomores were exposed to a variety of applied topics (mensuration, surveying, navigation, and nautical astronomy), while juniors took mechanics, natural history, or architecture, depending on what was offered. Seniors heard Joseph Henry's lectures on natural philosophy and took John Torrey's chemistry course, spending a great deal of their last year on study and work in these two subjects.[14] Other liberal arts colleges might differ from Princeton in the order in which topics were taught or in the classical authors chosen for study. Collectively, their curricula contrasted sharply with those of the technical schools such as West Point or Rensselaer Polytechnic Institute, where science dominated at the expense of the classics.

While Henry's research credentials weighed heavily in his recruitment, his chief duty at Princeton was to his students. As Professor of Natural Philosophy, Henry gave a two-term course in the subject required of all Princeton seniors.[15] In addition he took over John Torrey's chemical course in the 1833 summer session and, for his first five years at the College, delivered a brief course of lectures in architecture. His natural philosophy lectures averaged about three a week with as many recitations. But his academic schedule was evidently flexible, allowing him to double up lectures when he needed research or travel time. It appears that Henry often tried to compress most of his natural philosophy course into the winter session in order to leave the summers relatively free for his own work.

Henry rarely mentioned classroom concerns in his correspondence, except as a constant burden and obstacle to his "favourite pursuit," laboratory research. Yet he was clearly a hard-working and conscientious teacher. Before he left Albany, he was told to expect to spend one to two hours a day in the classroom. While his formal schedule probably amounted to that, Henry found himself spending substantially more time on his teaching, especially in the initial years when new lectures had to be developed. Henry regarded teaching as his first responsibility and reconciled himself to squeezing his scientific research into vacation periods and other breaks in his academic schedule.

By all accounts, Henry was one of Princeton's most innovative and inspiring professors. He worked hard at keeping his lectures informed with current knowledge and abundantly illustrated with experiments. His emphasis on experimental demonstration in his natural philosophy course

[14] *Princeton Annual Catalogues*, 1833–1836.

[15] Princeton catalogs give the following senior enrollments: 1832–1833: 43; 1833–1834: 37; 1834–1835: 53; 1835–1836: 68. *Princeton Annual Catalogues*, 1833–1836.

was an important innovation at Princeton and a technique just taking hold in physics courses at other American liberal arts colleges.[16] Henry was also a leading advocate of the lecture method at the College,[17] insisting that his students maintain careful notes and submit them to him weekly. Preparing lectures with a full complement of experimental demonstration proved arduous and time consuming, especially with the shortage of mechanical assistants. Henry pointed out to his students that "the lectures cost much trouble and labour: 3 hours before, 1 during, 1 after, 2 in putting up [the apparatus]. The class must labour in accord."[18] His efforts were appreciated by the students who remembered Henry as a demanding but captivating lecturer.[19]

For the content of Henry's natural philosophy lectures during his first three years at Princeton, there is little contemporary documentation. Though many of his lecture notes are preserved, they are often disorganized and fragmentary, and most appear to date from a later period. What Henry actually delivered to his classes is best recorded in a collection of student notebooks preserved at Princeton and elsewhere. The best and most fully developed of the surviving notebooks date from the latter part of Henry's teaching career. A detailed consideration of what Henry taught will be reserved for later volumes of this series in light of this fuller documentation.[20] Like most professors, Henry drew the bulk of his lectures from textbooks, encyclopedias, and other standard contemporary sources, organizing his topics according to conventional patterns. Since they usually do not reflect Henry's original ideas, unlike his experimental notes, neither his own nor his students' lecture notes will be published in full in these volumes.

Two incomplete sets of natural philosophy notes survive from the 1835–1836 academic year.[21] These early lectures contain the basic outlines of the physics course Henry developed over the next decade. Often described in the Princeton catalog as a course in mechanics and physics, the natural philosophy lectures moved methodically from the general properties of matter and force to their specific manifestations in heat, electricity, and so

[16] Stanley M. Guralnick, "Science and the American College, 1828–1860" (Ph.D. dissertation, University of Pennsylvania, 1969), p. 110.

[17] *Maclean*, 2:314.

[18] In Box 18 of the Henry Papers, Smithsonian Archives, folder entitled "Introductory Remarks and First Lecture." The item was quoted and pointed out to us by Charles Irwin Weiner, "Joseph Henry's Lectures," p. 63.

[19] Among the many rave reviews of Henry's teaching, see the respectful remarks tendered by the seniors upon his departure to Europe, dated February 13, 1837, Henry Papers, Smithsonian Archives. To be printed in volume 3 of this series.

[20] A model course is reconstructed and extensively analyzed by Weiner, "Joseph Henry's Lectures," still the best guide to Henry's natural philosophy course at Princeton.

[21] Those of John Miller and Aaron B. Belknap, in Rare Book and Manuscripts Library, Princeton University.

forth.[22] To impress physical concepts upon his students, Henry illustrated them with numerous concrete and often fascinating examples. The human body, for instance, was used to show basic mechanical principles. Other examples were taken from areas of technology that Henry himself found interesting. Attention to recent findings, especially on electricity and magnetism, mitigated the rather conventional nature of Henry's early physics syllabus. For example, his 1835–1836 electrical lectures treated Wheatstone's 1834 experiment on the velocity of electricity, which Henry also explored in one of his scientific notebooks.[23]

The documents on Henry's teaching are too sparse at this point to disclose any significant interplay between Henry's lectures and his original research. Though hired to teach, Henry went to Princeton for the sake of his research. Plainly, it was Henry's scientific reputation that made him so attractive to Princeton Trustees bent on refurbishing the reputation of their College. Other faculty members enjoyed scholarly reputations and the College clearly perceived pedagogical benefits in scholarship.[24] Still, Princeton made no visible effort to alleviate Henry's load relative to other professors, beyond assigning him mainly senior classes.

In addition to devoting a substantial amount of his working day to teaching, Henry spent a significant amount of time renovating and equipping his place of research. The move to Princeton resulted in a significant gap in Henry's laboratory studies. Although Henry hoped for an improved scientific situation at Princeton, existing laboratory apparatus and facilities at the College proved severely deficient for teaching as well as research. Several years later Henry reflected with some bitterness on what he found on his arrival:

> Before I was called to the chair of Natural Philosophy in this Institution no lectures had been given on the subject nor experiments shown to the class for many years. The apparatus was not only very deficient in quality but also the articles in a very bad state of preservation.[25]

Henry complained of having to spend an inordinate amount of time just bringing the quality of the apparatus to a basic level. In refurbishing the apparatus, Henry was clearly unimpressed with the backing Princeton was willing to give. Chronic shortages of help often compelled him to hire his own laboratory assistants or to resort to unreliable student volunteers.

[22] According to Miller's notes, Henry covered these topics in order: somatology, statics, dynamics, hydrostatics, hydrodynamics, pneumatics, heat, electricity, magnetism, galvanism, light, and sound.

[23] Printed at the end of this volume, [ca. 1835].

[24] *Wertenbaker*, pp. 220–221.

[25] Joseph Henry to [Princeton Trustees?, ca. 1838], Henry Papers, Smithsonian Archives.

The College also apparently dragged its feet in reimbursing him for purchases of new instruments.[26]

Despite the obstacles, Henry hoped to develop one of the finest physical research laboratories in the country. He took full advantage of the transition to prepare himself for a whole new assault on the electrical problems that had engaged him in Albany. While leaving no record of sustained experimentation in his Philosophical Hall laboratory until August 1834, Henry's correspondence shows him going vigorously about the construction of three impressive scientific instruments: a large galvanic battery with adjustable output, powerful new induction coils, and an electromagnet of unprecedented strength. The novel design and large dimensions of the new apparatus strained the resources of the Princeton area, which lacked the diverse craft shops, materials, and other industrial and commercial advantages of Albany. Henry encountered considerable delay, for example, in locating a shop capable of producing the large zinc sheets he needed for battery plates. As Henry mentioned to Silliman in 1834, just fitting up the battery "cost me nearly all my leisure time for a year past."[27] Easier to deal with was a host of lesser apparatus—small coils, various iron and steel magnets, iron tubes and shields, and magnetic needles.

For much of this equipment, Henry traveled south to Philadelphia. Philadelphia had been the major American city in the eighteenth century, serving as the political, economic, and intellectual center of the colonies and the new nation, but it lost its primacy in the nineteenth century. Shortly after 1810, New York surpassed Philadelphia in population, although Philadelphia remained the second largest American city, with 161,410 residents in 1830 and 231,702 in 1840. Washington had become the nation's political headquarters; New York drew away part of the growing Western trade via the Erie Canal, and Baltimore drained much of the rest through the Susquehanna River. Andrew Jackson's successful war against the Second Bank of the United States ended Philadelphia's financial supremacy, causing capital in the city's banks to drop over a third. Philadelphia instituted several changes to counteract its loss of economic mastery. It eventually developed a transportation system in the Pennsylvania Railroad which competed with those networks to the north and south. It exploited the state's mineral wealth, notably the coal deposits. And it became a manufacturing center, with especially innovative ironmaking and machine industries.[28] The institutions Henry visited and the people he met were often

[26] See Allen G. Shenstone, "Joseph Henry's Bills, 1832–1837–1844–1865," *The Princeton University Library Chronicle*, 1967, *28*:150–155.

[27] Henry to Silliman, October 1, 1834, printed below.

[28] Edwin T. Freedley, *Philadelphia and Its Manufactures: A Handbook Exhibiting the*

involved in bringing about these changes, especially the third. In Philadelphia, Henry found mechanics who had access to the materials he needed and the expertise in manufacturing that Princeton lacked. He visited mechanical exhibitions and spent time with the mechanics, picking up valuable or just interesting information on new processes. Characteristically, Henry focused upon the "philosophical" component of the devices and processes he observed there. As in Albany, Henry's associations with practical men and their work reflected an unquestioned belief in the scientific origins of all significant technological achievement.

Philadelphia's array of cultural institutions also drew Henry to the city. He was particularly interested in Peale's Museum, the Franklin Institute, and, of course, the American Philosophical Society. In touring Peale's Museum, Henry found the scientific apparatus of special interest; he experimented with one of the magnets there in May 1835. The Franklin Institute, organized in 1824, published the abstract of one of his papers in January 1835, well in advance of its appearance in the Philosophical Society *Transactions*. The Institute was to sponsor research projects in meteorology, strength of materials, and steam boiler explosions, all areas in which Henry became involved. The iron industrialists and the scientific instrument makers congregated at the Franklin Institute along with notable academic scientists, such as Henry's friend Alexander Dallas Bache, making the group a collective expression of much that lured Henry to the city.[29] Through these and other institutions, Henry also came into contact with Philadelphia medical men, many with scientific interests and a devotion to research.

The American Philosophical Society provided the chief outlet for Henry's scientific investigations and publications at Princeton. Although aware of the Society's scientific decline in recent decades, Henry was deeply honored by his election in January 1835 and became one of its most active and productive participants. Along with a core of like-minded members,

Development, Varieties, and Statistics of the Manufacturing Industry of Philadelphia in 1857 (Philadelphia, 1858), pp. 22, 94–97, 104, 130, 342, 397; Samuel Bass Warner, Jr., *The Private City: Philadelphia in Three Decades of Its Growth* (Philadelphia, 1968), pp. 51, 69, 71, 77; Louis Hartz, *Economic Policy and Democratic Thought: Pennsylvania, 1776–1860* (Cambridge, Massachusetts, 1948); Ellis P. Oberholtzer, *Philadelphia: A History of the City and Its People, A Record of Two Hundred and Twenty Five Years* (Philadelphia, [1912]), 2:185; *American Almanac and Repository of Useful Knowledge for the Year 1848* (Boston, 1847), p. 213; Bruce Sinclair, *Philadelphia's Philosopher Mechanics: A History of the Franklin Institute, 1824–1865* (Baltimore, 1974), pp. 73, 83–84, 290–294, 323; Edward Digby Baltzell, *Philadelphia Gentlemen: The Making of a National Upper Class* (Glencoe, Illinois, 1959), pp. 90, 101–104; J. Thomas Scharf and Thompson Westcott, *History of Philadelphia, 1609–1884* (Philadelphia, 1884), pp. 2235–2236.

[29] Sinclair, *Franklin Institute*, passim; Warner, *Private City*, pp. 117–118; Scharf and Westcott, *History*, pp. 1927–1928, 1967–2099; and Freedley, *Manufactures*, pp. 96, 185, 397.

he hoped to revitalize the Society to fit his specialized and professional needs. Through the contributions of Henry and a few of his most productive colleagues, the Society experienced a marked, though relatively short, scientific revival during the 1830s, especially in the physical and geophysical subjects of greatest concern to Henry. Individuals such as A. D. Bache and Robert Hare complemented Henry's interests, provided him with an appreciative audience, and, during the 1830s, helped turn the APS *Transactions* into a leading American journal of physical science.

In turn the Society nurtured Henry's scientific reputation. Although later overtaken by more specialized journals, the *Transactions* was still a prestigious publication with worldwide distribution. It was true that Henry was continually frustrated by its snaillike publication schedule, but he could still make his discoveries a matter of record in the biweekly meetings of the Society. Certain members who were particularly zealous in guarding Henry's scientific priorities did their best to hasten publication of his results.

Henry also greatly valued the American Philosophical Society for its extensive holdings in recent and past scientific literature, especially in view of the Princeton library's early deficiencies. Aspiring to international eminence, the Society exchanged publications with scientific and learned societies throughout the world.[30] Henry rarely made a trip to Philadelphia without "posting up" on current knowledge at the Society's library.

Yet, as an ambitious young physicist, Henry was aware of the limitations inherent in a general learned society from an older tradition. For more informal, specialized criticism, Henry and several scientific friends formed a small secret group known only as the "club," centered in Philadelphia. We know very little about this ephemeral organization except that it was to meet three or four times a year to provide "mutual support and instruction."

Philadelphia offered Henry a national stage and rich incentives for the pursuit of research. Yet, with the interruptions of the move to Princeton, reestablishing the active research and publication schedule he had maintained in his last years in Albany was no easy matter. Once settled at the College, Henry began to move forward again in the areas that made his early scientific reputation: terrestrial magnetism, including related topics like the aurora borealis, and electromagnetism, particularly self-induction.

The transfer south posed far fewer obstacles to the continuation of Henry's terrestrial magnetic observations than to the studies in electricity.

[30] On the development of the Society's library holdings, see Richard H. Shryock, "The Library of the American Philosophical Society," *Proceedings of the American Philosophical Society*, 1960, *104*:398–403.

The former could proceed without special new apparatus or elaborate physical plant. In fact, visits to the Albany area in the period after the move offered excellent opportunities for comparative magnetic readings and for contact with observers in Albany, West Point, and other sites north of Princeton. Terrestrial magnetism and related phenomena continued to engage and fascinate Henry well into the Princeton years. His priority in these investigations was the collection and correlation of data, gleaned primarily from the northeastern regions of the United States and Canada. There was an extensive European literature for comparison. Although Henry speculated occasionally about the probable origins of the earth's magnetism, he generally regarded as premature any attempt at a broad theoretical synthesis of the field.

At Princeton, Henry continued to read intensively on terrestrial magnetism and constantly strove to refine his instruments and observational techniques. To ensure comparable data, for example, he took readings from the best magnetic needles available and then exchanged the instruments with observers in America and abroad. Henry also tried his hand at fashioning improved apparatus. Among other devices, Henry attempted the construction of a gigantic magnetic needle some six feet in length, possibly inspired by the great German scientist and mathematician C. F. Gauss. Apparently the project was never fully realized.

Despite the abundant evidence of his continued involvement in terrestrial magnetism at Princeton, the fact remains that Henry produced no significant new publication in the field. It fell to colleagues like A. D. Bache to incorporate Henry's results in their publications. Henry's long-standing geomagnetic concerns were not necessarily waning in this period, but his scientific priorities clearly lay elsewhere—in electromagnetic research, then the leading edge of electrical science.

Once Henry had equipped his laboratory, he began serious electromagnetic research at the first break in his teaching schedule. Unlike the active give-and-take of his terrestrial magnetic observations, Henry worked in relative isolation on electromagnetic problems. No one at the College, except possibly John Torrey and Henry's brother-in-law Stephen Alexander, was fully conversant with his laboratory experiments. In fact, few Americans were doing original research in the areas of electromagnetism Henry had marked for investigation. He enjoyed fruitful interchanges in Philadelphia, New York, and New Haven, but his main inspiration was the European literature, which he carefully monitored for experimental results and ideas. Consequently, technical discussion of electromagnetic issues are uncommon in Henry's early Princeton correspondence. Henry as yet had no significant contacts with the leading European investigators in his field; Sturgeon, Faraday, Ampère, Roget, and other Europeans were silent colleagues.

Yet, his activities and solitary ruminations in the laboratory are solidly documented. Beginning with what appears to be his first major experimental effort at Philosophical Hall, Henry maintained a detailed laboratory record, preserved in three volumes among his papers in the Smithsonian Archives. Entitled the "Record of Experiments," Henry's laboratory notes cover his most important researches at Princeton and, later, at the Smithsonian Institution. Early entries from the "Record" printed in this volume provide a running commentary on his laboratory efforts and on the scientific publications he produced through 1835.

A comprehensive and intimate working record, the notebooks illuminate both the routine and the significant. Details of Henry's work habits, research schedule, and approach to experimental problems give a rounded picture of Henry as a working physicist, at the same time suggesting a great deal about the daily pursuit of physical science in a nineteenth-century academic setting. The experimental notebooks also fully document the train of electrical discoveries that firmly established Henry as the foremost American electrical physicist of his generation. When the "Record" began, Henry stood at the threshhold of the most creative and productive decade of his scientific career.

The majority of the entries from the "Record of Experiments" given in this volume deal with Henry's further explorations of self-induction, a discovery he announced in Albany in 1832. The notebooks pick up the subject approximately where he left it at that time. The experimental efforts documented below culminated in two major publications, inaugurating Henry's five-part "Contributions to Electricity and Magnetism."

Basic to the renewed investigation of self-induction were the electrical instruments Henry constructed for his Princeton laboratory. The powerful galvanic battery had convertible circuitry which allowed Henry to vary the types and strengths of currents applied to his induction apparatus. Early entries depict Henry exploring the varied capabilities of the battery, whose construction he described in the first of his "Contributions to Electricity and Magnetism."[31] Complementing the battery were Henry's unique induction coils, lengths of thick insulated copper ribbon which he generally wound into flat spirals. As early as 1832 Henry had observed that when a long wire was disconnected from its galvanic source, sparks and shocks appeared at the point and instant of disjunction. He found that winding the

[31] "Contributions to Electricity and Magnetism. No. I.—Description of a Galvanic Battery for Producing Electricity of Different Intensities," *Transactions of the American Philosophical Society*, 1837, n.s. 5:217–222.

conductor into a spiral enhanced the effect, while, at Princeton, he learned that ribbon coils elicited the most powerful shocks and sparks of all. The second of his "Contributions"[32] was a careful analysis of the conditions most conducive to sparks and shocks from extended conductors and coils.

Following the recitation of experimental results in Henry's article was a well-developed but tentatively given theory of self-induction, discussed below in conjunction with numerous documents in our text. As Henry's research progressed, self-induction began to rival his earlier discoveries in magnetoelectricity in theoretical importance. In self-induction, Henry saw an opportunity for integrating a wide range of galvanic and magnetic phenomena upon the basis of known laws in static electricity. As in Albany, Henry's principal and most explicit theoretical inspiration continued to be the French electrodynamicist André-Marie Ampère.

Ample theoretical speculation can be found in Henry's publications, in his correspondence, and in various scientific notes. Significantly, however, the actual laboratory results given in the "Record of Experiments" are virtually devoid of the specific theoretical propositions that emerge so clearly in his publications. In its early portions, the "Record of Experiments" is a terse rendering of experimental setups and results, making it difficult to draw any meaningful conclusions about the interplay of theory and experiment in the process of discovery, at least at this stage of Henry's researches.

The "Record of Experiments" also reveals avenues of Henry's electromagnetic research that failed to lead to any major scientific publication. A sequence of entries in August 1834 shows sustained experimentation on the magnetism of coils, with special concern for the screening powers of iron. Other experiments dealt with the relative strengths and inductive powers of iron and steel magnets as well as electromagnets. Researches of this sort run as a subtheme in the "Record of Experiments" and were apparently once destined for publication. The effort toward publication aborted, yielding to articles on induction.

On related themes Henry constructed the largest and most powerful electromagnet of his career. Lifting nearly two tons, the magnet attracted wide publicity and confirmed his reputation as the builder of the world's strongest electromagnets. Henry was convinced by the success of his apparatus that electromagnetic power knew no theoretical limit. Yet, as original research, the electromagnet represented more a capstone of an older line of investigation than a vital component of ongoing research.

[32] "Contributions to Electricity and Magnetism. No. II.—On the Influence of a Spiral Conductor in Increasing the Intensity of Electricity from a Galvanic Arrangement of a Single Pair, &c.," *Transactions of the American Philosophical Society*, 1837, n.s. 5:223–231.

Questions of priority in discovery continued to plague Henry at Princeton. By far the most serious challenge came from Michael Faraday, who had already overshadowed his most important results in Albany. The work of Henry and Faraday continued to reveal astonishing chronological and theoretical parallels. Henry's recorded experiments in self-induction began in August 1834; Faraday's laboratory *Diary* takes up the subject in October of the same year.[33] Though their investigations emerged independently as natural outgrowths of their separate studies of mutual induction and magnetoelectricity, they mapped out much of the same experimental territory. According to a familiar pattern, Faraday appeared in print just as Henry was bringing his experiments to a conclusion, forcing Henry into intensive research and hasty publication.

The striking and persistent parallels in the experimental programs of the two physicists invite some preliminary comparisons. Both in manuscript and in print, Faraday emerges as the more methodical and analytical experimentalist. Henry, for instance, took the identity of mutual and self-induction effects virtually for granted; Faraday insisted on a careful point-by-point demonstration of their equivalence. In part, these were differences of scientific style. As a more recent entrant to science, Henry was less experienced and perhaps less sophisticated in the laboratory. (His experiments become notably more complex in later portions of the notebook.) It should also be remembered that Faraday enjoyed an unencumbered research schedule at the Royal Institution. Teaching and priority pressure may have forced Henry into producing less-than-thorough publications.

While Henry incorporated some of Faraday's earlier results in explaining self-induction, he evidenced no visible concern for distinctive Faradian notions like the "electrotonic state" and nascent field theory. Viewed in terms of their lifework, Henry, with his conventional Ampèrian allegiances, followed a quite different tradition from the heterodox Faraday. Yet, in their approaches to self-induction at least, these distinctions are not altogether clear. The ideas of both physicists were still in flux and in the process of formation. Their rather expansive publications on self-induction reflect this early uncertainty and reveal their close similarities as much as their contrasts. Despite differences in terminology, for example, Henry and Faraday both seemed to conclude that, during the uninterrupted current flow, self-inductive wires entered into a peculiar intermediate state.[34] Moreover,

[33] Thomas Martin, ed., *Faraday's Diary*, 8 vols. (London, 1932–1936), 2:330.

[34] See Faraday's formulation in "Experimental Researches in Electricity. 9th Series. 15. On the Influence by Induction of an Electric Current on Itself:—And on the Inductive Action of Electric Currents Generally," *Phil. Trans.*, 1835, pp. 41–56, sections 1114–1115.

Henry saw no reason that all of Faraday's results could not be subsumed along with his own under the theories of Ampère.

Henry's discoveries in self-induction clearly deserved international recognition as central contributions to electromagnetic science. Although conscientiously following the latest European results in his field, his own writings were slow to disseminate abroad. Recurring priority problems with Faraday, who remained fairly ignorant of Henry's work, reinforced his sense of isolation as a physicist working in America. Vociferous advocates of Henry's reputation such as A. D. Bache urged an aggressive stance toward Faraday. Yet, in his early career, Henry remained a reluctant competitor, hesitating even to send Faraday and other Europeans reprints of his first two "Contributions." The next few years would see an extension of his transatlantic associations and a growth in his European reputation. At Princeton, as in Albany, Henry's deepest commitment was to "speculative science"—to scientific research pursued for its own sake without special regard to practical application. If Henry was pursuing anything, it was a recognized role in this international enterprise.

* * * * *

The editorial work on this volume of *The Papers of Joseph Henry* was supported by the Smithsonian Institution, supplemented by generous grants from the National Endowment for the Humanities and the American Philosophical Society. Preliminary work benefited from funds from the National Science Foundation. The staff of the Henry Papers is most grateful for this financial assistance, tendered in all cases with flexibility and liberality. Working with the Joint Committee of our sponsoring institutions is a great pleasure.

Of inestimable benefit to our research is the presence of the surviving volumes of Joseph Henry's Library. We are greatly indebted to the heirs of Gilbert H. Grosvenor for their courtesy in depositing this valuable collection with us. Melville Bell Grosvenor and Joseph Marion Jones, in particular, have thoughtfully considered our needs. Every time we open a Henry volume, we are aware of our obligation to the Grosvenors.

We are especially conscious of many kindnesses received from our Smithsonian colleagues—too many for any complete enumeration. Nancy Powars and Crimilda Pontes of the Press have instructed us in the making of books. As the largest single user of his collections, the staff of the Henry Papers has inflicted a fair number of burdens on Richard Lytle, the Institution's Archivist. We appreciate his cheerful unflappability. Jack Marquardt of the Library has tended our bibliographical fevers. We again express our indebtedness to the advice received from many of the curators of the National

Museum of History and Technology. Their presence has lightened our burden.

Similarly, the second volume of *The Papers of Joseph Henry* could not have come into existence without the cooperation of an enormous number of archivists, librarians, and historians in institutions all over the United States and a number of foreign countries. Their names are too many for enumeration, and we have not figured out any fair standard for selecting a significant number for particular mention. Instead, we in the Henry Papers wish to thank all who answered our letters, suffered our telephone calls, and guided us on visits to their institutions. (In our annotations we have sometimes cited such individuals as our sources.) Several institutions require particular mention in the context of this volume. Alexander Clark and Edith Blendon of the Princeton University Library were very helpful. Murphy Smith of the American Philosophical Society Library has greatly aided us. The New York State Library—particularly James Corsaro—is a principal source of information. On a number of occasions A. M. McMahon, the Archivist of the Franklin Institute, did some rather extensive hunts for this volume.

While the Smithsonian Archives is the largest single source of our documents, this volume is much the richer for manuscripts made available to us by the following institutions:

Alderman Library, University of Virginia
American Philosophical Society Library
Duke University Medical Center Library
Eisenhower Library, Johns Hopkins University
Firestone Library, Princeton University
Gray Herbarium Library, Harvard University
Harvard University Archives
Historical Society of Pennsylvania
Massachusetts Institute of Technology Archives
National Archives and Records Service
New York Botanical Garden Library
Princeton University Archives
St. Andrews University Library, Scotland

Beverly Jo Lepley has kept our office running, no matter what. For one year Maxine Benson, a National Historical Publications Commission Fellow, worked with us. She contributed much to the closing stages of volume one and to the opening stages of this volume. Philip Pauly, a University of Maryland student, did splendid work as a graduate assistant for a semester.

For many years the Henry Papers has benefited from the assistance of volunteers from the Smithsonian Associates. They prepared the transcription of documents, a necessary initial step. We thank them all for their great contribution to our endeavor.

NOTES ON STYLE

Our practices are generally similar to those of other editorial projects, particularly to those of the Adams Papers. The nature of our documents and our personal inclinations have resulted in a few departures from the style of that great project, and these are noted below. In preparing this volume we followed an expanded and revised version of the style manual prepared prior to the editing of volume one. Copies of the revised manual are available to scholars interested in the editing of historical documents. Here a few points necessary for the reader's understanding are presented.

Organization

Documents are given in chronological order. If a specific date is not given or is not ascribable, the document is placed at the end of the dated documents from the nearest unit of time to which it can be tied. For example, if only the year can be determined, the document will appear at the end of all the items of that year. If the month and year are available but not the day, the document will appear after the fully dated documents of that month and year. Where the year is in doubt, the item will normally appear in an appendix.

Preliminaries to the Documents

Preliminaries to the documents are title, provenance note, and (sometimes) an introductory headnote.

The title briefly signals what is to come. In the case of correspondence, if Henry is the author of the letter, we simply indicate to whom he is writing:

TO BENJAMIN SILLIMAN, SR.

or we note the name of the person writing to Joseph Henry:

FROM BENJAMIN SILLIMAN, SR.

If Henry is neither the author nor the recipient, both parties are specified:

BENJAMIN SILLIMAN, SR., TO ROBERT HARE

In the case of noncorrespondence items, we prefer using the titles given on the originals. If the title is lacking or if the given title is noncommunicative, the editors will devise a suitable title, usually with an explanatory footnote. "RECORD OF EXPERIMENTS" will be used for entries from Henry's three-volume laboratory notebook. Entries from his various reading and lecture notebooks will be titled HENRY NOTEBOOK ENTRY.

The provenance note, immediately following the title, briefly gives the location of the original and, if necessary, the nature of the document being published (i.e., "draft," "retained copy," etc.). If these matters are too complicated for the provenance note, we normally provide additional pertinent details in a footnote. In the provenance note and in footnotes, we will refer to Henry's lecture and reading notebooks by the numbers (enclosed in brackets) which were assigned when they were entered into the project's control system (e.g., notebook [7171]). The use of such traditional abbreviations as "ALS" and the like are avoided. When the particulars of authorship or handwriting are historically significant, these are elaborated in a footnote if not clear from the title and provenance note.

In a few instances an explanatory headnote, immediately after the provenance note, will introduce a document. Where important items are not suitable for publication in a work of this nature, the headnote, often expanded in size, stands in their stead.

Date and Place

Date and place are usually placed at the top, right-hand side preceding the body of the text, regardless of location in the original. Missing dates are supplied in brackets as an editorial insertion. If the place is lacking, it is only supplied or discussed in a footnote if of some historical significance. Where the dating is not obvious or hinges on a matter of moment, this too becomes the subject of a footnote.

Texts

Our general practice is to hew as close to the original as possible, so long as the meaning is reasonably clear to a modern reader. A few revisions, mostly specified below, are made silently in the interest of clarity. We prefer to retain the original and to aid the modern reader in this respect by means of our annotations: only rarely do we make changes or insertions indicated by using square brackets, [ ]. "Sic" does not appear in our texts; barring human error, a reader must assume that any strange usage in print is a faithful transcription of the original.

Mary Henry, our subject's daughter, bequeathed a nasty problem to this project. Shortly after her father's death Mary Henry began working toward the preparation of a biography. In her possession were most of Joseph

Henry's personal papers. To this she added items gathered from friends and relatives, as well as documents culled from the official archives of the Smithsonian Institution. Mary Henry's efforts eventually progressed to the point where she had prepared a partial text which included original documents and transcriptions done by herself and her cohorts. Her text and its associated materials were largely the basis upon which Coulson based his biography of Joseph Henry. Although posterity owes Mary Henry thanks for efforts to preserve her father's literary remains, many of her actions resulted in irreparable damage to many Joseph Henry manuscripts. For example, in a number of cases she removed part of a book or transcribed a few pages, carelessly losing the entire volume. A neat trick of Mary's was to remove items from groups of documents and, in the process, to lose some and hopelessly disorder and scatter the remainder. The transcriptions she prepared for the contemplated biography are another vexation she inflicted on posterity. Almost invariably they omit an undisclosed amount of text, frequently passages of great interest. The transcribing is inaccurate at times and often corrects the language to conform with later standards, sometimes changing meanings. Unfortunately, many of the originals were lost, because, we think, of careless handling by Mary Henry and her aides. Many of these faulty, unique copies are quite important. We have decided to use them in our edition, signaling their nature by the expression "Mary Henry Copy" in the provenance note. From the numerous instances where both the copy and the original survive, we are convinced these are not fabrications, that the omissions were short-sighted but not acts of suppression, and that the surviving texts are reliable enough for use. Here and here alone, in the absence of any evidence to the contrary, we resolve textual uncertainties by opting for modern usage. There seems little point in trying to recapture Henry's archaisms.

Only in the few cases where the original paragraphing causes confusion in modern print have we made changes. Grammatical usage, punctuation, and spelling are usually faithfully preserved. The biggest exception is our decision to start each sentence with a capital letter and to end with appropriate punctuation. Punctuation that is obviously intrusive is removed; ubiquitous dashes are converted to modern commas and periods, and a few commas and periods are inserted silently where absolutely necessary for clear understanding. Only in a few egregious cases do we silently correct slips of the pen. Where the reading is doubtful or where meaning is otherwise unclear, we give an editorial insertion in square brackets, [ ]. Where these insertions are offered tentatively, we indicate our uncertainty by placing a question mark within the bracket. If the entire insertion is tentative, the question mark is placed immediately after the opening bracket,

[? March 6, 1832]; if only one element is uncertain, the question mark is placed immediately afterward to indicate our doubt, [March 6?, 1832]. When the insertions arise from matters of moment, they will receive amplification in footnotes. A special case are entries from Henry's "Record of Experiments." The unique format of these entries called for special treatment which is explained in the headnote to the entry of August 15, 1834.

In a number of documents there are interlineations, canceled matter, variant texts, marginalia, and even footnotes by the original author. The first are silently brought into line unless there is some point in their position. In that event we generally use a footnote to elucidate the significance, retaining the original position only in exceptional cases. If canceled matter or variant versions of expressions have historical, psychological, or stylistic significance, we place them immediately preceding the text in question in italics within angled brackets:

celebrated <*mathematical*> philosophical school at Alexandria.

Marginalia of significance are inserted into the text at the proper points with suitable comments in footnotes. Author's footnotes are given symbols other than arabic numerals which are reserved for editorial annotations.

Where one or two words are illegible or missing, we have so indicated by inserting suspension points enclosed in square brackets, [. . .]; if more than two words, we will, in addition, give an explanatory footnote, estimating, where possible, the number missing. Where a reasonable reconstruction is possible, we do so as an editorial insertion within square brackets.

Abbreviations occur frequently in the documents. If clear to the modern reader, they are retained. Otherwise the term is spelled out. The ampersand is used in place of the many variant forms occurring during Henry's lifetime. A particular problem to many readers unfamiliar with past usages is abbreviations involving raised letters, a practice quite common in Henry's generation and at least as far back as the seventeenth century. The writer would retain the first letter or letters of a word, giving the last letter or letters of the word in a raised position with or without a marking underneath:

Jany or Jan$^{\underset{..}{r}y}$ for January

A reader aware of this practice should have no trouble understanding such abbreviations which we leave unchanged. Some raised letter abbreviations are likely to cause trouble. Sch^{dy} for Schenectady is not exactly obvious. In such cases we simply spell out the word without comment.

Signatures or initials at the close are given as in the original, usually without any commentary. Draft or retained copies generally lack these, as will our printed versions without any further notice. Where the recipient's name appears at the bottom left of the last page of an original letter, this is silently omitted as repeating information already given in the title. Dates at the end are also suppressed as redundant unless we silently shift their position to supply the missing dating at the start. We have retained closing matter of this nature only where meaning is conveyed. In the love letters exchanged by Joseph Henry and his wife Harriet, the closing salutations tell us something about the sentiments of the correspondents and are, therefore, given.

Editorial footnotes are numbered consecutively within each entry. We follow the citation form of the 12th edition of the *Manual of Style* of the University of Chicago Press with one important exception. We prefer the ISIS form in citing the periodical literature. Of less moment, perhaps, are two other preferences. The Editor does not relish the current tendency to suppress capitalization and to use the lower case in titles of officials, names of institutions, and publications. We capitalize. There is also an antipathy here against the tendency to run abbreviation-wild. We think readers should not have to approach each footnote as an exercise in decoding. Except for a few standard usages (e.g., n.d., ibid., etc.), everything is given in full or nearly so. The principal exceptions are the items below for which we consistently use short titles or standard abbreviations.

LIST OF SHORT TITLES

Academy Seventy-fifth Anniversary	*The Celebration of the Seventy-fifth Anniversary of the Founding of the Albany Academy, October 25, 1888* (Albany, 1889).
"Alexander Genealogy"	Unpublished Alexander Family Genealogy by Robert Gaylord Lester in the Henry Papers files.
Biographical Directory of the American Congress	*Biographical Directory of the American Congress, 1774–1949* (Washington, 1950).
Burke's Index	Edmund Burke, compiler, *List of Patents for Inventions and Designs Issued by the United States from 1790–1847, with the Patent Laws and Notes of Decisions of the Courts of the United States for the Same Period* (Washington, 1847).
Columbia Alumni	M. Halsey Thomas, compiler, *Columbia University Officers and Alumni, 1754–1857* (New York, 1936).
"Contributions I: Battery"	Joseph Henry, "Contributions to Electricity and Magnetism. No. I.—Description of a Galvanic Battery for Producing Electricity of Different Intensities," *Transactions of the American Philosophical Society*, 1837, n.s., *5*:217–222.
"Contributions II: Spiral Conductor"	Joseph Henry, "Contributions to Electricity and Magnetism. No. II.—On the Influence of a Spiral Conductor in Increasing the Intensity of Electricity from a Galvanic Arrangement of a Single Pair, &c.," *Transactions of the American Philosophical Society*, 1837, n.s., *5*:223–231.
"Contributions III: Electro-Dynamic Induction"	Joseph Henry, "Contributions to Electricity and Magnetism. No. III.—On Electro-Dynamic Induction," *Transactions of the American Philosophical Society*, 1839, n.s., *6*:303–337.
"Contributions IV: Electro-Dynamic Induction"	Joseph Henry, "Contributions to Electricity and Magnetism. No. IV.—On Electro-Dynamic Induction," *Transactions of the American Philosophical Society*, 1843, n.s., *8*:1–35.
"Contributions V: Induction from	Joseph Henry, "Contributions to Electricity and Magnetism. No. V.—On Induction from Ordinary

Ordinary Electricity; Oscillatory Discharge"	Electricity; And on the Oscillatory Discharge," *Proceedings of the American Philosophical Society,* January 1841–June 1843, 2:193–196.
Coulson	Thomas Coulson, *Joseph Henry: His Life and Work* (Princeton, 1950).
Cullum	G. W. Cullum, *Biographical Register of the Officers and Graduates of the United States Military Academy, at West Point, New York,* rev. ed., 2 vols. (New York, 1879).
DAB	*Dictionary of American Biography*
DNB	*Dictionary of National Biography*
DSB	*Dictionary of Scientific Biography*
Hageman	John F. Hageman, *History of Princeton and its Institutions,* 2d ed., 2 vols. (Philadelphia, 1879).
Henry Papers	Nathan Reingold, editor, *The Papers of Joseph Henry* (Washington, 1972)
Herringshaw	Thomas William Herringshaw, *Encyclopedia of American Biography of the Nineteenth Century* (Chicago, 1905).
Howell and Tenney	George Rogers Howell and Jonathan Tenney, editors, *History of the County of Albany, N.Y., from 1609 to 1886* (New York, 1886).
Hun, "Albany Academy"	Henry Hun, "A Survey of the Activity of the Albany Academy" (unpublished manuscript, 1922–1935, Manuscript Division, New York State Library and Archives of the Albany Academy).
King	W. James King, "The Development of Electrical Technology in the 19th Century: 1. The Electrochemical Cell and the Electromagnet; 2. The Telegraph and the Telephone; 3. The Early Arc Light and Generator," *United States Museum Bulletin No. 228* (Washington, 1962), pp. 231–271, 273–332, 333–407.
Maclean	John Maclean, *History of the College of New Jersey, 1746–1854,* 2 vols. in 1 vol. (1877; reprint ed., New York, 1969).
Munsell, *Ann. Alb.*	Joel Munsell, compiler, *Annals of Albany,* 10 vols. (Albany, 1850–1859).
Munsell, *Coll. Alb.*	Joel Munsell, compiler, *Collections on the History of Albany, from Its Discovery to the Present Time, with Notices of Its Public Institutions and*

	Biographical Sketches of Citizens Deceased, 4 vols. (Albany, 1865–1871).
Nason	Henry B. Nason, editor, *Biographical Record of the Officers and Graduates of the Rensselaer Polytechnic Institute, 1824–1886* (Troy, 1887).
Phil. Mag.	The well-known London journal which began as *The Philosophical Magazine* in 1798 and appeared under various titles throughout Henry's life. See Henry Carrington Bolton, *A Catalogue of Scientific and Technical Periodicals, 1665–1895. . .*, 2d ed. (Washington, 1897), pp. 445–446.
Phil. Trans.	*Philosophical Transactions of the Royal Society of London.*
Poggendorff	J. C. Poggendorff, compiler, *Biographisch-Literarisches Handwörterbuch Zur Geschichte Der Exacten Wissenschaften.*
Princeton Annual Catalogue	*Catalogue of the Officers and Students of the College of New-Jersey* (Princeton).
Princeton Catalogue	*General Catalogue of Princeton University, 1746–1906* (Princeton, 1908).
Reynolds, *Alb. Chron.*	Cuyler Reynolds, compiler, *Albany Chronicles: A History of the City Arranged Chronologically* (Albany, 1906).
Roberts	Edward Howell Roberts, compiler, *Biographical Catalogue of the Princeton Theological Seminary, 1815–1932* (Princeton, 1933).
Silliman's Journal	Benjamin Silliman, editor, *American Journal of Science and Arts* (New Haven, 1818–).
Sprague, *Annals*	William Buell Sprague, *Annals of the American Pulpit*, 9 vols. (New York, 1857–1869).
Union Catalog	*Union University: Centennial Catalog, 1795–1895, of the Officers and Alumni of Union College in . . . Schenectady, N.Y.* (Troy, 1895).
Weiner, "Joseph Henry's Lectures"	Charles Irwin Weiner, "Joseph Henry's Lectures on Natural Philosophy: Teaching and Research in Physics, 1832–1847" (Ph.D. dissertation, Case Institute of Technology, 1965).
Wertenbaker	Thomas Jefferson Wertenbaker, *Princeton, 1746–1896* (Princeton, 1946).

THE PAPERS OF JOSEPH HENRY

TO JAMES HENRY[1]

Family Correspondence, Henry Papers, Smithsonian Archives

New York Nov. 7th 1832

Dear James

Mother and Nancy will doubtless be anxious to hear from Harriet and the Boy how they got to New York. Harriet was somewhat unwell during the night but not near as bad as she was before we left Albany. Aunt[2] declaired that our Boy was the best behaved child among all the number aboard the boat which ammounted to nearly a doz. We arrived about 5 oclock and have taken up our quarters at a Miss Van Antwerps[3] in Barcaly Street No. 50 a relation, very distant however, of the Family. They were much pleased to see us and would not suffer Stephen[4] and myself to go to a Public House as we had intended. The boat with the furniture has not yet arrived. We expect to see it to day sometime but cannot tell at what hour. We will endeavour to leave N.Y. tomorrow but perhaps will not be able to depart until the next day.

Your Brother[5]

[1] After going to Princeton, Henry kept in close touch with family, friends, and colleagues in Albany. He corresponded regularly with his brother James, but, with rare exception, only Henry's side of the exchange survives among his papers. How his letters to his brother found their way to the Henry Papers in the Smithsonian Archives is not known, but we conjecture that the letters were handed down to James's daughter Agnes and eventually added to Joseph Henry's papers in the course of Mary Henry's collecting activities.

[2] Henry, his wife Harriet, and son William were accompanied to Princeton by Harriet's mother Maria Alexander and her mother's sister Nancy Connor. Since Henry and Harriet were first cousins, Aunt could indicate either Nancy or Maria. Henry's mother Ann Alexander Henry remained in Albany with Henry's brother James and sister Nancy.

[3] Perhaps Margaret Van Antwerp (1788–1867). Although the New York City Directory for 1832–1833 does not list a Miss Van Antwerp, it does list a Simon Van Antwerp at 50 Barclay. Margaret Van Antwerp had a brother of that name. *New York Genealogical and Biographical Record*, April 1948, *79*:53. The Van Antwerps (variantly spelled Van Antwerpen) were a prominent and prolific New York family; Henry was distantly related through the maternal side of his wife's family. See typed notes on Henry's ancestry in Family Correspondence, Henry Papers, Smithsonian Archives.

[4] Henry's cousin and brother-in-law Stephen Alexander. See *Henry Papers, 1*:115n.

[5] On the verso is a penciled note, apparently a reminder jotted down by James: "Mr. Orr says 20 shillings of the money you paid him is in the bundle of Bismuth & Antimony [if] you will examinate it." Orr, of Orr and Gibson, was an Albany brass founder. Albany City Directory, 1832–1833. Henry presumably requested the material for the chemical course he would deliver that summer for John Torrey, who would be away in Europe. In his letter of November 24, 1832, below, Henry acknowledges receipt of the packet, containing the elements and the money. Shillings and other foreign currency circulated freely in the United States until suppressed in 1857. (Information courtesy of Vladimir Clain-Stefanelli, National Museum of History and Technology.) The references to the transaction indicate that 1832 shillings were worth about twelve and one-half cents.

James Henry (In great haste)
P.S. Stephen sends you a paper which is all the information we can give relative to the election.[6]

[6] President Andrew Jackson was seeking re-election. Albanians probably had special interest in Jackson's new running mate, Martin Van Buren, former U.S. senator, governor of the state, and head of the Albany Regency. Henry was writing on the last day of a three-day election period. As vote counting was a slow process, only partial local results would have been available at the time.

FROM JAMES R. WILLSON[1]

Copy, Henry Papers, Smithsonian Archives

Albany 1832 Nov. 8th

Dear Sir

I have just received your Aurora Borealis & Occultations & have read the pamphlet with much gratification.[2] It is a valuable addition to the stock of facts on a very obscure philosophical topic. It shall soon be prepared for a legitimate deduction.

I observed both the Aurora of April 19th 1831 & the occultation of Dec. 9th. Much disturbance of the needle is not to be expected in the polar Seas,

[1] The note below Wilson's signature and Henry's file note on the verso of the letter, "Dr. Wilson (copy per James) *Aurora borealis 1832*," indicate that James Henry received the original letter in Albany and sent this copy to Princeton.

"Jas R. Wilson" is probably James Renwick Willson, D.D. (1780–1853), a Reformed Presbyterian minister who had charge of a small church and classical academy in Albany from 1830 to 1833. His name was probably Willson but it appears as Wilson in local sources and directories. Possibly James Henry altered the spelling in making his copy.

James Renwick Willson graduated from an academy in Canonsburg, Pennsylvania, was Principal of an academy at Bedford, Pennsylvania, from 1809 to 1815, and then pastor at Coldenham and Newburgh, New York. Moving to Albany in 1830, he was coeditor of the *Albany Quarterly*, a publication of the Albany Historical Society. He returned to Coldenham in 1833.

There is no other evidence of the astronomical work referred to in his letter or of further contact with Henry. He is known to have had continuing interests in natural history and chemistry, and his son records that he studied medicine in early life. Sprague, *Annals*, 9:39–45; *Howell and Tenney*, p. 376; Albany City Directory, 1831–1832; Munsell, *Ann. Alb.*, 1:255.

[2] The reference is to two articles appearing as an appendix in *An Abstract of the Returns of Meteorological Observations Made to the Regents for the Year 1831. Annual Report of the Regents of the University of the State of New York* (Albany, 1832). The first article (pp. 107–119), written by Henry, was "On a Disturbance of the Earth's Magnetism, in Connection with the Appearance of an Aurora Borealis, as Observed at Albany, April 19, 1831," which also appeared in *Silliman's Journal*, April 1832, 22:143–155. (See *Henry Papers*, 1:404–405.) The second (pp. 120–121), on "Observations of Lunar Occultations of the Planets and Fixed Stars, 1831," was a brief report by Henry's brother-in-law Stephen Alexander, who mentions corroborating observations by Henry.

near the centre of magnetic power. The moon certainly has an atmosphere. I infered it from the Dec. occultation.[3]

Why does cold weather succeed aurora?

Yours truly
Ja^s^ R. Wilson

The above is a copy of a letter addressed to you through the Post office.

[3] The observations of December 9 concerned the occultation of Jupiter and its satellites by the moon. Any distortion of the planet's image as it passed the limb of the moon gave possible evidence of a lunar atmosphere.

TO JAMES HENRY

Family Correspondence, Henry Papers, Smithsonian Archives

New York Nov 8th 1832

Dear James

I send you the book I spoke of by Mr Richard De Witt.[1] I took it with me to N.Y. in order to copy part of an article on magnetism which it contains. It belongs to the State Library. I got it from Wm Seymour's brother the book binder[2] by means of an order from Mr Wright the comptroler.[3] You may return it either to Seymour or to the State Librarian.[4] You need

[1] Richard Varick DeWitt (1800–1868), son of Simeon DeWitt and a Union College graduate (see *Henry Papers, 1*:62). We have no further information on the borrowed book. In place of "De Witt" Henry originally wrote "Yates" but then crossed it out. He probably was thinking of Richard Yates for whom see below, Henry to James Henry, December 1, 1832, footnote 8).

[2] William Seymour (1793–1867), an Albany native, learned the trade of bookbinder with his uncle, Benjamin D. Packard. After a period as a partner in the firm of Van Vechten and Seymour he opened his own bindery on the corner of State and North Market streets. A lifelong Democrat, he was very active in politics, holding such offices as Collector of the Port, Alderman, Supervisor, City Chamberlain, and others. In 1831 William Seymour was joined by his brother Timothy as a partner in the bindery, and the business remained W. & T. Seymour, "plain and fancy bookbinders," until 1838. Timothy Seymour then headed the firm himself for the next two years before removing to Bethlehem, New York, south of Albany. Albany City Directories, 1830–1841; Munsell, *Coll. Alb.*, *3*:367–368.

[3] Silas Wright (1795–1847), Comptroller of New York from 1829 to 1833 and later Governor of the State, 1845–1847 (see *Henry Papers, 1*:414 and *DAB*). In 1824 the Comptroller, Secretary of State, and Attorney General had been added to the State Library's Board of Trustees, joining the Governor, Lieutenant-Governor, Chancellor, and Chief Justice of the Supreme Court, who comprised the Board when the Library was founded by the Legislature in 1818. Edgar A. Werner, *Civil List and Constitutional History of the Colony and State of New York* (Albany, 1889), p. 248.

[4] James Maher (1780–1852) was State Librarian at this time. A native of Ireland, Maher had immigrated to Albany at an early age. During the War of 1812 he gained renown as Captain of the "Irish Greens," a volunteer corps he had helped organize in Albany. State Librarian for many years, he was active in politics as well and was chosen repeatedly for the Common Council. Albany City Directory, 1832–1833; Munsell, *Ann. Alb.*, *4*:368–369; *Howell and Tenney*, p. 147.

not mention that I took it with me to N.Y. as some remarks might be made on that acc[ount].

We will probably start this afternoon. All well. In great haste

Your Brother
Joseph

Write me and direct to
Princeton N.J.

TO JAMES HENRY

Family Correspondence, Henry Papers, Smithsonian Archives

Princeton Nov 13th 1832
Tuesday afternoon

Dear James

We arrived safely and all in good health at the place of our destination on Friday evening a little after dark and took up our Lodgings for the night at one of the public houses. The family all except myself left New York on Thursday afternoon at one o'clock in the Steamboat Napoleon. I was left behind by being detained in having the furniture carted from the tow boat. The steamboat started just as I arrived at the warf with the two last cart loads. I remained in New York until the next morning and arrived at New Brunswick about half past ten o'clock where I found Stephen on the warf waiting my arrival. The Ladies were near by in the Steamboat Hotel. After being left in New York I visited Mr McMullen's.[1] I was so much engaged that I could find no leisure to do so before. The family are all well.

[1] Although John McMullen seems to have been a close personal friend of Henry's, he has proved a somewhat elusive figure. He is listed in New York City Directories as a grocer from 1832 to 1838 and as a teacher from 1843 to 1846. He disappears from the city directories until the mid-1850s when several John McMullens are listed, making his occupation difficult to ascertain; the two most likely listings are for a school proprietor and a commission merchant.

Several tantalizing references to McMullen exist in the Family Correspondence, Henry Papers, Smithsonian Archives. In a letter to James Henry of August 23, 1845, Henry reports on a visit to the McMullens in New York: "Henry James appeared to be much taken with John and it appears by your letter that they have concluded the bargain. I think the situation will give John a fine chance of seeing the world and in every respect will be pleasant provided he can properly manage the *boy*." Unfortunately, we have no idea what sort of arrangement Henry James, Sr., was thinking about. The James family remained on this side of the Atlantic. Letters from 1847 and 1848 comment on John McMullen's activities in Europe. From correspondence between Henry and McMullen in 1849 and 1850 about accounts for the purchase of instruments we suspect that McMullen may have ordered or purchased philosophical apparatus for Henry while in Europe.

Although lack of biographical information on John McMullen has made it difficult to identify his family, it seems to have consisted

We found our house[2] had been thouroughly cleaned and put in complete repair. It is much better and more convenient than the Ladies [thought]. They are much pleased with it and not disappointed with the place. Harriet was so anxious to see the house that she visited it with me by moon light on the evening of our arrival. We have not yet become settled but would have been nearly so had we not been obliged to leave two of our boxes at New Brunswick and as these contain the Screws of our beadsted and the head board of another we have not yet put up but one bead stead. The boxes are expected this evening so that tomorrow we will probably be nearly prepaired to commence living in something like a civilized manner. The furniture came remarkably safe. The only article which has received any dammage is the old side board and this can be easily repaired with a few nailes and a little glue.

The frame of the large looking glass came apart but both glasses were safe although they received pretty rough usage on the passage. The large tables were not in the least injured and only one plate broken among all the crockery. Harriet is just at this momment trying her *musical box* and finds it but little out of tune.

We have been much favoured with pleasant weather. It has been almost as warm as summer the whole time since our arrival. I have not yet commenced my duties in the college but will begin on Friday next.

I shall be ingaged for this winter only on three days in a week and about 2 hours in the day. We are all considerable better of the colds with which we were afflicted when we left Albany. The boys cough is much better and he appears to be in good health although he requires all the time which Aunt can spare from her meals to attend him. We have received the Gazette of Friday and learn by it that you had something of a riot on the last day of the election.[3] When you write give us some more of the particulars. I am very anxious to hear from Mother. You must be particular in giving an account of her health and whether our departure had a bad effit on her. If she should get much worse write me and I will indeavour to procure leave of absence to visit her before the river closes.

---

of Lucinda, Jane, and Lewis, probably his wife, sister, and brother. New York City Directories, 1839–1846, list a Lewis McMullen, hardware merchant, at the same home address as John McMullen. Gay Wilson Allen, *William James, a Biography* (New York, 1967), p. 20.

[2] A sketch of the location of Henry's first Princeton house appears below in Henry's letter to James Henry, February 9, 1833.

[3] The riots, resulting in some bloodshed, erupted on the last day of the three-day gubernatorial and presidential elections in Albany (November 5 to 7). On November 9, the anti-Jacksonian *Albany Gazette* accused the Regency of buying the votes of hastily naturalized Irish immigrants and inciting them to riot, with the design of intimidating "native" voters. Denying these accusations, the politically opposed *Argus* (November 10) laid the bully tactics and bloodshed at the door of the opposition coalition party of Henry Clay.

Aunt wishes me to request Nancy to give Susan Shankland[4] one or two of the plants as a keep-sake for her. Remember us to Mr. McArthur,[5] Dr Frank,[6] Mr. Sammons,[7] Mr. Bullions[8] and all who may enquire for us. Tell Mother & Nancy that Harriet and myself do not forget them but that we now miss the priviledge of seeing them when we please as we did in Albany.

Your Brother

P.S. W McCammon[9] has arrived and is boarding in our family. You have promised to write me once a week. Do not fail to do so. J.H.

N.B. The remainder of the furniture has just arrived.

Motherinlaw lost her band box on board the Ohio. Will you call and inquire for it. Miss Van Antwerp of N.Y. promised to send to the boat the next time she came to NY and may have got it before this time. Write me if Mr DeWitt has given you the book belonging to the state library and if any person has spoken to you in reference to any business which I may have forgot.

[4] See *Henry Papers, 1*:284n.

[5] The Reverend Samuel McArthur; *Henry Papers, 1*:399n.

[6] We have determined that "Dr. Frank" was actually Dr. Francis N. Selkirk (1809–1849), a physician friend of the Henry family. He was licensed to practice medicine by the Albany County Medical Society. In 1838, Selkirk went to Texas to seek his fortune. The attempt aborting, Selkirk returned home but never successfully established himself in the medical profession. Sylvester D. Willard, *Annals of the Medical Society of the County of Albany, 1806–1851. With Biographical Sketches of Deceased Members* (Albany, 1864), pp. 324–325. *Henry Papers, 1*:452n. Henry may have used the nickname "Dr. Frank" to distinguish him from his brother Dr. Joseph Selkirk.

[7] Stephen Sammons (1814 or 1815–1879), son of New York congressman Thomas Sammons, attended the Albany Academy from 1832 to 1834. From one of the Mohawk Valley's leading families, Sammons later became a high-ranking member of the Know-Nothing Party and, in 1850, District Attorney of Montgomery County. Apparently his political prospects were once considered hopeful. He served as a Major in the Civil War, following the military tradition of his family. Henry Hun, "A Survey of the Activity of the Albany Academy" (unpublished manuscript, 1922–1935, Manuscript Division, New York State Library and Archives of the Albany Academy), hereafter cited as Hun, "Albany Academy." Obituary in *Fulton County Republican*, September 4, 1879, p. 3; E. A. Werner, *Civil List and Constitutional History of the Colony and State of New York* (Albany, 1889), p. 511.

Although we have no direct evidence, Samuel McArthur, Francis N. Selkirk, and Stephen Sammons may have boarded with the Henry family in Albany.

[8] The Reverend Peter Bullions (*Henry Papers, 1*:129n).

[9] William McCammon (?–1881) had studied at the Albany Academy, entering in 1822. Henry evidently offered McCammon living accommodations and instruction at Princeton in exchange for his mechanical assistance in the laboratory. See Henry to James Henry, below, March 2, 1833; and a letter of Henry's [ca. 1838], possibly to the Princeton Trustees, Henry Papers, Smithsonian Archives. It is noted in the *Catalogue of the Officers and Students of the College of New-Jersey* (Princeton, New Jersey; hereafter cited as *Princeton Annual Catalogue*), 1833, pp. 12–13, that by applying to individual lecturers, young men not enrolled at Princeton could be granted the privilege of attending college lectures, which may have been the arrangement between Henry and McCammon. A machinist by trade, McCammon later manufactured pianos in Albany. *Howell and Tenney*, pp. 601–602. *Academy Seventy-fifth Anniversary*, p. 83.

November 24, 1832

TO JAMES HENRY

Family Correspondence, Henry Papers, Smithsonian Archives

Princeton Nov 24th, 1832
Saturday evening

Dear James

Your litter of last saturday[1] was received on Wednesday or thursday. The paper was received last evening although it arrived the night previous. I would have answered your letter sooner but have been so much engaged that I could not well spare the time. I will if possible write every saturday afternoon or evening hereafter and make it a rule to do so. By your note on the margin of the paper I learn that Mother is not as well as when you last wrote. I wish when you again write that you would give a particular account of her health and should she get much worse write me immediatly and if it be possible I will come to Albany. We will have a vacation[2] in College of two week to commence in about four weeks or less from this time and should the river happen to continue open until that time I will visit mother. I find my situation here as pleasant as I had any reason to expet. My duties in College occupy only about 5 hours in each week and these are in the last three days Thurs. Frid. & satur. The other part of the time I am almost intirely disconnected with College and am only required to attend at the Chapel every evening at 5 o'clock. The immediate government of the students devolves on the Tutors who room in the College building.[3] I find however sufficient employment at present in preparing two lectures a week and in reviewing my studies for the three recitations. On the receipt of your letter before the last[4] I opened the bundle of bismuth and found the money you mentioned. It consisted of two one dollar bills and 4 shillings in silver. The bills were considerably chafed but not so much so as to prevent their passing as current money. If you can spare the money I wish you would pay Mr Orr[5] and charge the ammount to me.

Aunt is happy to learn that her plants are in such good hands as those of Mr. McArthur. He must cultivate a taste for flowers as nothing will tend

[1] Not found.

[2] This was an unusual vacation (from December 19 to January 3) occasioned by opening the College a month early because of the cholera in the preceding August (Minutes of the Faculty of the College of New Jersey, October 11 and December 19, 1832, Princeton University Archives). Henry saw the same epidemic interrupt academic schedules in Albany at the same time. See *Henry Papers, 1*: 441–454 passim.

[3] Nassau Hall, then the students' and tutors' residence, as well as the center of most college activities. T. J. Wertenbaker, *Princeton, 1746–1896* (Princeton, 1946), p. 39 (hereafter cited as *Wertenbaker*). For the tutors' involvement in student discipline, see below, Faculty Minutes of January 8, 1833, footnote 2.

[4] Also not found.

[5] William Orr, the Albany brass founder mentioned above in Henry's letter to James Henry of November 7, 1832, footnote 5.

more to recommend him to the Ladies and I hope in a few years to see him a married man. I told Dr Ten Eyck that he might have the *Globe ball* which I left at Mother's. I am pleased that he has called since my departure. Give him my respects when you next see him and tell him I will write when I get a little more settled. I promised Mr Bullions that I would write to him after I had been three weeks in Princeton. He gave me that to be settled in. Tell him I have not forgotten my promis.[6] We have found much difficulty in getting stoves and having the house affairs put in proper order. Stephen went last week to New York and purchased two stoves one the smalest patern of Dr Nott's stove[7] and the other a Cooking stove. The Nott stove does excedingly well but the cooking article we will be obliged to return. This has caused some confusion and made it very unpleasant for Motherinlaw who has worked very hard as she had no other help than William.[8] She engaged a black wooman at New Brunswick on our passage to Princeton but she cannot leave the place where she is now engaged for some weeks to come. I am pleased to hear that business is so good with you and hope that you have engaged with Anthony[9] for another year. I suppose that Mother and Nancy will wish to hear something particular about the Boy. He is just at this moment making considerable noise on account of his mother's undressing him and because he wishes to go downstairs into the room below where he has been for some hours past. He manifests a great dislike to be confined in one room and immediately makes for the door as soon as it is opened.

He has learned to walk a few steps and can stand alone for a second or two. He is however something of a coward and does not like to trust himself much to his feet but prefers gowing on all fours as usual. He begins al-

[6] As this sentence appears as an interlineation in the original, Henry probably added the comment later.

[7] The 1826 product of the inventive genius of Eliphalet Nott, this design was the first to make practical the burning of anthracite coal for home heating. But this stove was of more than practical interest to Henry, as he became concerned with Nott's theoretical approaches (see below, Joseph Henry to Harriet Henry, December 13, 1832) as well as Nott's patent troubles (for the first mention of which see below, Jackson to Henry, January 8, 1833). Nott's development of the stove design from principles of heat is treated in Codman Hislop, *Eliphalet Nott* (Middletown, Connecticut, 1971), pp. 255–271.

[8] William Bannard (1820–1904), often referred to as "English William" or "William the English boy." William Bannard lived with the Henrys, performing duties ranging from gardening to recording meteorological observations for Henry. Born in England, he came to the United States with his parents in 1832. He graduated from Union College in 1844 and from the Princeton Theological Seminary in 1847. Ordained in 1848, he was the Pastor of churches in New York and New Jersey. He was "a gentleman of scholarly attainments . . . of a modest and retiring disposition, but of substantial worth." Alfred Nevin, ed., *Encyclopaedia of the Presbyterian Church in the United States of America* (Philadelphia, 1884), p. 55. Edward Howell Roberts, comp., *Biographical Catalogue of the Princeton Theological Seminary, 1815–1932* (Princeton, 1933), p. 136 (hereafter cited as *Roberts*).

[9] Anthony Gould, Albany book seller, for whom see *Henry Papers, 1*:446n.

most to talk and has lately got into a habit of crying out quite loud *pa* and *Aunt* and this he does when any person passes the window. I have not had much time to attend to the news of the day but learn that it is settled that *Andrew the First*[10] is to continue his reign for an other term if he do not die or resign in favour of Mr V. B. will.[11] I hope the "*Union will be preserved*"[12] and that no civil commotion will ensue to desturbe those who are no sharers in the spoils. I am sorry that Uncle Thomas[13] has lost his election. It would doubtless have been very gratifying to his feelings to have been chosen. I hope Catherine has been more successful in *her* election.[14] You must fill your letter and give as much news as you can. Every trifling thing concerning Albany is now to us a matter of interest. Harriet says she will write to Nancy next week.

Tell Mother that Harriet and myself long very much to see her and that her Likeness[15] stands on the Mantle tree directly infront of our bed and that I never go to sleep without thinking of her. I know that Nancy and yourself will give her every comfort you can bestow and that she will have every attention necessary in a bodily point of view. Still I am not without my fears that our removal may have acted unfavourable on her health. She would certainly have been entertained with the visits of the Boy had we staid and must now miss him and us very much. I hope she will be spaired

[10] Henry is writing soon after a presidential campaign in which Andrew Jackson was reelected in the face of the banking challenges of Nicholas Biddle and the nullifying, states' rights assertions of Jackson's own Vice President, John C. Calhoun. In both cases, and in others, Jackson's aggressive use of federal and presidential powers caused his opponents to dub him "King Andrew the First."

[11] Physically and emotionally drained by his first administration, President Jackson spoke confidentially of a plan to resign. He wished first to vindicate himself by an overwhelming victory in November 1832. Then, according to the plan he discussed several times with his running mate Martin Van Buren, Jackson would retire to the Hermitage and "Mr V. B." would become President. Repeatedly Van Buren discouraged this plan, preferring his own election to the presidency over ascending to it without a mandate. Jackson's plan, which he had apparently abandoned by the time of his reelection, never became public knowledge in this period. Marquis James, *The Life of Andrew Jackson* (New York and Indianapolis, 1938), p. 593; further information from Sam B. Smith, Editor, *The Papers of Andrew Jackson*, Hermitage, Tennessee.

We can only speculate on how Henry may have heard of Jackson's contemplated resignation. We suspect Henry caught wind of it from one of his Albany friends, a number of whom were friends of Van Buren or political associates of his in the Albany Regency. See volume one of *The Papers of Joseph Henry*.

[12] This political rhetoric seems to be derived from Andrew Jackson's famous toast at the April 13, 1830, Thomas Jefferson birthday celebration: "Our Federal Union: it must be preserved."

[13] Thomas Alexander (1775–1842), Henry's half-uncle. Unpublished Alexander Family Genealogy by Robert Gaylord Lester in the Henry Papers files (hereafted cited as "Alexander Genealogy").

[14] Catherine Alexander (1804–1886), daughter of Thomas Alexander, married William Robb on November 14, 1832 ("Alexander Genealogy"). Robb was apparently a wealthy political dabbler, about fifty-six years old at the time of the marriage (Henry to Harriet Henry, December 19, 1832, Family Correspondence, Henry Papers, Smithsonian Archives).

[15] Probably a reference to the Ezra Ames miniature, painted circa 1829, of Ann Alexander Henry. It is reproduced in *Henry Papers, 1*: opposite p. 248.

until spring as Harriet and myself with the Boy will be up if we live in April. Dr Wing[16] informed me before I left Albany that if she took no sudden cold he saw no fear of immediate danger in her case. I hope there may be none yet.

Tell Nancy that she must forgive me for neglecting to purchase a copy of the "*Domestic Housewife*"[17] for her as I promised. I had so much to attend to on the day of our departure that I entirely forgot it until I was in N.Y.

My respets to Frank, Sammons & though last not lea[s]t Mr McArthur. I send Mr Sammons a Catalogue of Princeton College. Do not fail to write every week at least and as often besides as you chose.

Your Brother

P.S.[18] Your answers are very good only write a little more. I mean fill you sheet as I have done with any thing that may occur at the time.

[16] Dr. Joel A. Wing, Albany physician, for whom see *Henry Papers, 1*:50.

[17] We have found no publication by that name, but perhaps Henry is referring to one of Lydia Maria Child's books. Her *Frugal Housewife* (Boston, 1829) changed its name to *American Frugal Housewife*, 8th ed. (Boston, 1832). In all, the book went through thirty-three editions by 1870. Lydia Maria Child also published a spinoff of the *Frugal Housewife*, namely *Domestic Economy* [? Boston, 1830], which consisted of revisions of passages containing recipes and housekeeping suggestions.

[18] This postscript was written along the length of the left margin of the opening page.

TO JAMES HENRY

Family Correspondence, Henry Papers, Smithsonian Archives

Princeton Dec 1st 1832 Saturday Evening

Dear James

Your third letter was received on wednesday and you probably received my letter[1] about the same time as it was written on the same evening as yours. It however did not leave this place until sunday evening as the mail closes at 6 o'clock P.M. on saturday and not again until the same time on sunday. I hope my letter will have relieve[d] Mother's anxiety concerning our health and that she will be assured that we are very far from forgetting her or any member of the family.

Your letter relieved our fears in some respets on account of Mother's

[1] Probably the letter of November 24, 1832, above. James Henry's letters of the period, as explained previously, have not survived.

health but we are certain that she is very weak and liable to be affected by every change of atmosphere. You must not fail to write me should she become dangerously ill & I will immediatly leave all other engagements to visit her. I informed you in my last that we have a vacation in college to commence in about 3 weeks but I think I can so arrange my duties as to be able to leave here for Albany on saturday two weeks from this. I hope the river will remain open or at least partially so as a journey to Albany by land at this season of the year will be rather unpleasant but be this as it may I have concluded that it is my duty to visit Mother and shall accordingly make the journey should health and life be spaired. We are all well at present. The boy was unwell the first part of the week probably on account of having taken some cold but appears entirely recovered. Harriet I think enjoys better health than she has done for more than a year past. Motherinlaw is tolerably well but complains of the work which she has to attend to and indeed she has some reason for we have as yet no other healp than William the English Boy and there has been much to be done in the way of getting things in order. We are now however pretty well settled except that there is as yet no stove put up in the Kitchen. The cooking stove we purchased did not answer the purpose but the Merchant has consented to take it back on our paying for the cleaning &c. Aunt is quite well and seams contented with her new residence. She says however that you must tell her friends in Albany that she did not sufficiently value their society until she came to this land of strangers. I hope she and Motherinlaw will find some persons here withwhom they can associate in a pleasant manner and that before the spring they will cease to consider themselves amoung strangers. Stephen will probably entre the Theological seminary in a few weeks as he has been making some preparation in the way of purchasing the necessary books and calling on the Professors &c.

He has a prospect of being connected with this college at some future time but will not engage at present in any thing else than his Theological studies. I believe it is not his intention to become a constant preacher but he engages in the study to render himself better qualified for a Profership in a College.[2] The College of N.J. is at present in a flourishing state and the number of students greater than at any period for a number of years past. In 1830 according to the published catalogue (a copy of which I sent to Mr Sammons), the senior class consisted of but 20 members. The same class has now 42. The whole number of students is rising of 130. Few of these are

[2] In this period clergymen quite commonly served as college teachers in American institutions. Stephen Alexander's theological studies were analogous to the medical studies of some other American scientists—they provided access to occupations which might allow a young scientist to earn a living and do research.

from the state of N.Y. except some from N.Y. city. The majority are natives of N.J. and the southern states. In looking over the catalogue of all the persons who have been attached to the Institution I find a number from albany (not lately however) among these are the Rev. Mr. Kirk,[3] V. P. Douw,[4] P. S. Henry,[5] J. V. Henry,[6] John Porter,[7] Richard Yates[8] (the cashier) and Wm. Walsh.[9] Albanians have got out of the fashion of sending their sons here of late but I hope they will reestablish the custom now that I am connected with the Institution.

This place is certainly much warmer than Albany or the season has become remarkably mild. We have had no weather as cold since we came here as we had in Albany a few days before we started. The thermometer has stood some days past at 58° in the shade and there has been no appearance of snow unless on one day about two weeks since when Stephen saw a few spits which have been blown from one of the flurries you have had at Albany. Harriet promised and intended to write to Nancy this week but she has been so much engaged in ironing, it being the washing week, that she could find no leisure. She says that she sat down with the intention of commencing a letter but was detered from writing by not being able to find a

[3] Edward Norris Kirk (1802–1874), Princeton B.A. 1820, A.M. 1825; attended the Princeton Seminary, 1822–1826; Amherst D.D. 1855. From 1826 to 1828 Kirk was an agent of the American Board of Commissioners for Foreign Missions, becoming ordained in the latter year. From 1829 to 1835 or 1837 (depending on the source) he was Pastor of the Fourth Presbyterian Church, Albany. An Evangelical, Kirk corresponded with Charles Finney and toured the countryside. In 1834 he held a great revival in Jefferson County, New York. Cross describes him as directing an evangelical training school "which bred Albany perfectionists." After leaving Albany, he was Secretary of the Foreign Evangelical Society (1839–1842) and Pastor of the Mt. Vernon Congregational Church, Boston, Massachusetts (1842–1874). David Otis Mears, *Life of Edward Norris Kirk, D.D.* (Boston, 1877); F. B. Hough, *American Biographical Notes* (Albany, 1875); Whitney R. Cross, *The Burned-over District: The Social and Intellectual History of Enthusiastic Religion in Western New York, 1800–1850* (Ithaca, 1950), p. 195; *Roberts*, p. 24.

[4] Volkert P. Douw (1789?–1869) received a B.A. from Princeton in 1809. He spent the rest of his life as a hardware merchant in Albany. *Princeton Catalogue*, p. 121. Munsell, *Ann. Alb.*, *4*:61.

[5] Peter Seton Henry. See *Henry Papers, 1*:74.

[6] John Vernon Henry. See *Henry Papers, 1*:11.

[7] John C. Porter (1807–1820) entered the Albany Academy in 1815. After receiving the Princeton B.A. in 1824, Porter was at the General Theological Seminary in New York from 1825 to 1828, receiving deacon's orders. He then accepted posts in the South. In 1830 when Rector of Trinity Church, Natchez, Porter drowned. Munsell, *Ann. Alb.*, *9*:218–219; *Princeton Catalogue*, p. 137; *Academy Seventy-fifth Anniversary*, p. 77.

[8] Richard Yates (d. 1855), son of John W. Yates (1769 or 1770–1828), for whom see *Henry Papers, 1*:34. Richard Yates entered the Albany Academy in 1815 and was an 1824 graduate of Princeton. He served as Cashier of the New York State Bank and Treasurer of the Albany Academy (1828–1836), positions his father had held previously. *Academy Seventy-fifth Anniversary*, pp. 16, 68, 78; *Princeton Catalogue*, p. 138. According to Munsell, *Ann. Alb.*, *7*:322, in March of 1855 "Richard Yates, late of Albany, committed suicide in California by shooting himself through the head."

[9] William Walsh (1802–1854), Princeton B.A. 1825, A.M. 1832, was an attorney. *Princeton Catalogue*, p. 139; Munsell, *Ann. Alb.*, *6*: 344.

pen; or a knife to make one (poor woman!). I forgot to state in my last letter that Stephen brought the stray band-box from N.Y. Miss Van Antwerp had sent to the steam boat Ohio and found it. You have probably been put to some inconvenience in searching for it. Harriet bids me say that she has been home sick several times and wishes much to see her relations in Albany. Should the Misses Mead[10] call again tell them we miss the society of their family very much and that our Ladies dispair of ever finding any in Princeton with whom they can associate on such terms of intimacy and friendship. Did I understand you aright when you said Dr Powers[11] intended to give me a visit? Does he intend comming to Princeton?

Do not fail to write at least every week and be assured that I will not suffer a saturday to pass without letting you hear from us. N.B. The Boy received the kiss which Mother requested should be given him for her. If it were not in the Winter I would bring Harriet and the boy with me to Albany but the season will not permit. I hope Mother and they will be alive and well enough to meet next April when we have our spring vacation. Tell Mr. Furguson[12] and the rest of my Friends that I hope to see them in Albany

[10] Probably referring to Charlotte and Louisa, the two oldest daughters of John Meads of Albany, a cabinetmaker. Louisa married Stephen Alexander in 1836. Their brother, Orlando, was a friend of Joseph Henry's. See footnote 1 of Joseph Henry to James Henry, May 17, 1833, below.

[11] Titus Powers. See *Henry Papers, 1*:331.

[12] James Ferguson (1797–1867) was born in Scotland and brought to this country in 1800. His early years were spent in Albany where he was associated with Simeon DeWitt. An engineer and surveyor, Ferguson worked on the Erie Canal and on the international boundary surveys following the Treaty of Ghent. Ferguson belonged to the Albany Institute (originally a corresponding member of the Second Department); after DeWitt's death he was asked to deliver the eulogy but declined. In 1838 Ferguson delivered the annual address to the Institute, on scientific institutions.

From 1833 until 1847 Ferguson was in the Coast Survey. During Hassler's superintendency he was, in effect, the second ranking member of the Survey. In the latter year Alexander Dallas Bache, Hassler's successor, forced Ferguson out, alleging that the work done in the Chesapeake and Delaware Bays was erroneous, a view upheld by Benjamin Peirce in what we might now designate a grievance proceeding. In 1847 Ferguson was hired by Maury in the Naval Observatory (where he remained until his death). This event undoubtedly contributed to the coolness between Maury and Bache. When Sears C. Walker became embroiled with Maury over the interpretation of LeVerrier's work on Neptune, Bache reciprocated by giving Walker a place in the Survey. In the dispute between Ferguson and Bache, Henry was awkwardly placed between two friends, one going back to his Albany years. Whatever the technical merits or demerits of Ferguson's work, the suspicion lingers that the Bache-Ferguson enmity arose from the latter's disappointment at not succeeding Hassler and Bache's desire to rid himself of a hostile subordinate. In the Walker contretemps, Henry had no doubt as to where he stood. The relationship with Maury will receive extensive treatment in later volumes.

But if the transfer to the Naval Observatory was an administrative disappointment to Ferguson, it was a boon scientifically. From 1851 to 1862 the first series of the *Royal Society Catalogue of Scientific Papers* lists eighty-five articles by Ferguson. Largely forgotten today, Ferguson was the most prolific American astronomer of the pre-Civil War period. The papers are brief reports of observations of asteroids, comets, and stars, devoid of any sophisticated mathematics or theory construction. Although not impressive to the modern eye, Ferguson's contributions were very much part of an active research tradition in observational or practical astronomy, bringing him a measure of professional recognition. In

in about 2 or three weeks. Give my warmest love with Harriets to Mother and Nancy and be assured for yourself that I remain

Your affectionate
Brother

Motherinlaw Aunt & Stephen send love to yourself Mother & Nancy also to Shankland's family.

P.S. I send a no. of the Princeton Courier.[13] When you find it convenient send me a copy of the evening Journal. The New York Observer of to day contains a very severe article on Mr B. F. Butler relative to his splash on the subject of the Missionaries and Georgia.[14]

1854 and 1860 the French Academy of Sciences awarded him medals for discovery of asteroids.

Just before his death, Ferguson again placed Henry in an uncomfortable position. With the departure of Charles Henry Davis from the Naval Observatory, many astronomers hoped to have a civilian succeed to the directorship. When Ferguson asked Joseph Henry to support his candidacy, Henry evaded the issue. Refusing to back any individual, he ended up endorsing four astronomers (including Ferguson) as possibilities for the civilian head of the observatory.

Appleton's Cyclopaedia of American Biography (New York, 1888), 2:433. *Herringshaw*, p. 356. *Transactions*, Albany Institute, *1*, Part 2, Appendix:71, 2:275. Ferguson to T. R. Beck, December 13 and 15, 1834, Albany Institute Correspondence, 1795–1840, Library, Albany Institute. Albany City Directories, 1818–1841. *Memorial of James Ferguson, Late First Assistant in the Survey of the Coast: Presented in the Senate by Hon. Thomas H. Benton, July 19, 1850* (Washington, 1850). Henry to Ferguson, May 1, 1867, Private Letterpress Copy, Henry Papers, Smithsonian Archives. Simon Newcomb, *Reminiscences of an Astronomer* (Boston, 1903), p. 111.

[13] The weekly *Princeton Courier and Literary Register* existed from 1831 to 1835. It was founded by William D'Hart, publisher, and Bernard Connolly, printer. The paper supported Jackson's cause. Varnum Lansing Collins, *Early Princeton Printing* (Princeton, 1911), pp. 24, 29.

[14] Benjamin Franklin Butler was well known to Henry from Albany. See *Henry Papers, 1*: 412. *DAB*. At this point in his career Butler was Attorney General of the United States. The *New-York Observer*, a religious weekly newspaper, on December 1, 1832, printed a letter (p. 192) from "No Politician" attacking Butler's criticisms of the two missionaries jailed by the State of Georgia. This casual reference of Henry's refers to a notable event in the constitutional history of the United States. President Jackson supported those in the southern states and elsewhere who wanted the Indians moved beyond the Mississippi. These tribes had treaties guaranteeing them lands and, so they thought, a measure of independence. When Georgia extended its laws over the Cherokees, Chief Justice Marshall in 1831 declined to intervene in *Cherokee Nation* v. *Georgia* (5 Peters 1). Georgia passed a law requiring whites resident in Cherokee country to obtain a state permit and to take an oath of allegiance to the State. Eleven missionaries refused, receiving a sentence of four years in the penitentiary. Nine then accepted pardon. The remaining two appealed to the Supreme Court where their position was sustained by Marshall in *Worcester* v. *Georgia* (6 Peters 515). Georgia declined to appear as it considered the case an infringement of states' rights. More important, Jackson declined to enforce the Court's judgment. "No Politician" saw this as an attack on religion and a blow to missionary efforts.

HARRIET HENRY TO [NANCY HENRY]

Mary Henry Copy, Memoir,[1] Henry Papers, Smithsonian Archives

Princeton Dec. 5th. 1832.

My dear sister:[2] . . . Our sail to New York was a comfortable one. . . . . We remained in New York a day and a half and then proceeded to New Brunswick . . . We remained in New Brunswick one night and a part of the next day, reached here after dark. Our house was better than we expected to find it; it had been painted throughout and the rooms neatly papered &c. It is comfortable and quite convenient, there are two rooms on a floor with a hall between. One of these rooms is our parlour. It has four windows, two in the front and two in the rear. It is a very pleasant handsome room. The other is our dwelling room, it has two closets in it, one on each side of the chimney. Directly back of it is the kitchen, quite a spacious one. The upper part of the house is very pleasant and convenient. We have three large rooms with closets and clothes presses attached, and one small bedroom over the hall. Our situation is a very pleasant one; directly in front of us is the college green, in which are a number of elms and poplar trees; on one side of us is the college; on the other or nearly so is the library. Back of [us] is a fine large yard and a large garden, where we can raise vegetables enough for our family. . . . Princeton I think must be a very pleasant place in Spring or Summer when the trees are in foliage but a long time must elapse before it will appear pleasant to us as our home. . . . We have received some calls from the ladies of the college and seminary. Last evening the President[3] called with his daughter, who seems quite pleasant and interesting but we do not expect to form as pleasant and valuable acquaintances here as those we have left. We all agree in saying that we did not value our friends sufficiently when we were with them. They certainly never appeared so dear to us as at present. Scarcely an hour passes that we do not speak of you or wish we were with you. I did so most heartily this morning when I read James' account of Ma Ma's[4] illness. I felt you required a sister in aid as

[1] Although materials collected by Mary Henry for the proposed biography of her father are scattered throughout the Henry Papers, a major portion of them as preserved in five boxes in the Henry collection in the Smithsonian Archives. Unfortunately, many of the items are scraps in seemingly random order. Some are Mary Henry's own prose; some are copies, or copies of extracts, of Henry letters. "Mary Henry Copy, Memoir," will be used to designate copies from this particular body of documents.

[2] The ellipses in this text are as given by Mary Henry's copyist.

[3] James Carnahan (1775–1859), *DAB*. See *Henry Papers, 1*:18.

[4] The text has this crossed out and the word "Mother's" written in above. We assume Harriet Henry used the familiar term in referring to her mother-in-law but that her daughter Mary preferred the more formal usage.

well as in name, one who would be pleased to assist you in nursing, for you must be nearly worn out with fatigue and anxiety.

The climate here is much warmer than in Albany; the grass in front of us is quite green, and there is no appearance of frost in the ground. Yesterday morning I heard birds sing.

I cannot bear to think of staying here all winter from you all. Tell mother we will take care of the boy. I wish he could be with you to cheer you up, as he does us, we have found him a great source of amusement. I hope we shall all live until Spring, and meet with joy.

Yours as ever Harriet.

TO JAMES HENRY

Family Correspondence, Henry Papers, Smithsonian Archives

Princeton Dec. 8th 1832
Saturday afternoon 3 o'clock

Dear James

Nancy has probably received Harriets Letter[1] and consequently you will scarcely expect another from me at this time but if I were not to write the omission would be a breach of promis. I therefore send this principally as a sample of my punctuality a virtue you will perhaps say I have only lately acquired. To this I would answer "*better late than never.*" My last letter you probably did not receive until a day after the usual time as it did not leave the office until monday evening although it was written on saturday[2] but just as it was finished we were alarmed by the cry of *fire fire*—from the students of the college. One of the chimneys accidently caught fire and sent forth an abundance of sparkes. This with the bustle so much pleased the young gentlemen that several of them set fire to their chimneys to prolong the sport. Although there was much noise yet no harm was done and the chimneys were well cleaned. The only effect of consequence was that my letter to you did not reach the post office on saturday evening and as it was not thought advisable to send it on sunday it remained until monday. I informed you in my last that I had concluded to visit mother during our vacation. I am glad to see the wether so mild and warm for this season of the year. I shall start next week and hope still to reach Albany by water. We had no snow on saturday last athough during the whole day there was a strong wind from the north west. On Mondy morning there was a slight

[1] See above, December 5, 1832.

[2] See above, December 1, 1832.

fall of snow on the ground which disappeared during the day. We have had pleasant weather since until this morning when it commenced raining and stil continues to do so. I do not insert this account of the weather merely to fill my letter but that you may have an opportunity of comparing the state of the atmosphere here and at Albany. A comparison of this kind is quite interesting to me and may be so to you. It certainly would be interesting to you were you in Princeton instead of Albany.

I have sent every morning to the office since the receipt of your letter expecting and fearing a letter from you relative to Mothers health. I trust you will write immediatly should she be taken suddenly worse. She must have failed very fast since we left Albany. I have made arrangements to leave next week although the vacation does not commence until the week after. I am not certain that I shall be able to be in Albany next saturday but if nothing unusual occurs I will hope to see [our?] Mother the begining of the week after. I regret to hear that Joseph Selkirk [is] in such a poor state of health. He is one of the most amiable members of the Family & his loss would be regretted by all his acquances.[3]

I had heard something relative to the persons who had taken the Rain Gague but did not know that it had been payed for &c. It was intended I presume only as a boyish piece of fun without any malecious motive.[4]

I have been very much employed this [. . .][5] in preparing my lectures on Mech[anics and?] in attending to my recitations. My duties are some what more arduous on account of my never having before lectured on this subject[6] and also because the apparatus is much out of order and repair. If you

[3] Selkirk had been in failing health for several months; see *Henry Papers, 1*:452. He died early in 1833. See below, Joseph Henry to James Henry, January 30, 1833.

[4] Since 1825, when the Board of Regents began requiring each academy in the state to submit annual meteorological reports, Henry and T. R. Beck had been making the observations and compiling the necessary data (see *Henry Papers, 1*:106–107). When the Albany Academy's rain gauge was stolen in 1832, Beck had offered a reward for the detection of those responsible. He subsequently received a note from "a former scholar" dated October 17, 1832 (now in the Joseph Henry Personal Papers, Smithsonian Archives) informing him that "the persons engaged in it are now out of the Academy." According to the informant (who stated that he wished no reward, nor did he want to involve anyone in trouble), four students, whom he identified by name, had taken part in the escapade. One of them "had a small gague & he wished to have a correct scale & so they were about to take the scale alone when they heard your door open & being terrified they took the whole." This account would seem to substantiate Henry's theory that the thieves had acted "without any malecious motive"; indeed, the boys apparently were attempting, however unwisely, to satisfy the requirements of scientific precision and accuracy which we presume their instructors had tried to inculcate.

[5] Approximately one word has been obliterated here by a hole in the letter.

[6] Although one of Henry's courses in 1831 at the Albany Academy was described as encompassing mechanics in addition to differential and integral calculus, astronomy, and descriptive geometry (*Henry Papers, 1*:190), he apparently had not lectured on mechanics in any more than a cursory fashion. As de-

see Mr Bullions tell him I shall probably take charge of my letter to him myself and not trust so important a communication to the Post.[7]

Give my respects to Mr Mc.[8] The Doctor[9] Mr Sammons[10] and all whom I should remember. Tell mother the boy is quite well and begins to show some little signs of temper although in general he is quite gentle and well behaved. Give my love to mother and Nancy. They will be convinced that I have not forgotten them when I come to visit them. We are all well.

I rem^{n}
Your Brother

veloped and codified during his Princeton tenure, the second part of his Natural Philosophy course, "Rational & Physical Mechanics," included sections entitled "Friction," "Machines & Mechanical Power," "Dynamics," "Bodies on Inclined Planes," "Motion on Curves," and "Central Forces." Five of the fourteen mechanics lectures discussed practical applications of the scientific principles involved, and Henry frequently suggested improvements in existing practices. See Charles Irwin Weiner, "Joseph Henry's Lectures on Natural Philosophy: Teaching and Research in Physics, 1832–1847" (Ph.D. dissertation, Case Institute of Technology, 1965), pp. 71–75, especially pp. 74–75 (hereafter cited as Weiner, "Joseph Henry's Lectures"). Two incomplete printed copies of this part of Henry's syllabus, "Part II. Rational and Physical Mechanics," survive in Henry's Library. Unlike Part I, Part II is undated and apparently was never published.

[7] We do not know what confidential information Henry may have had in mind for the long-promised letter to Bullions. Since he is making plans for a trip back to Albany, when he presumably will see Bullions (and did so, in fact), perhaps he is speaking facetiously, especially in light of his earlier comments on punctuality.

[8] Probably the Reverend Samuel McArthur.

[9] Most likely Dr. Francis N. Selkirk.

[10] Stephen Sammons.

NOTE ON CONVERSATION WITH CHILTON[1]

Miscellaneous Manuscripts,[2] Henry Papers, Smithsonian Archives

New York Dec 11th 1832

In a conversation Mr Chilton he informs me that the best kind of Lacker[3] is made by desolving seed Lack in strong alcohol.

[1] It is unclear whether Henry is referring to George Chilton (*Henry Papers, 1*:295) or his son. James R. Chilton (ca. 1809–1863) received an M.D. from the New York College of Physicians and Surgeons in 1833 and apparently practiced medicine in New York City at least occasionally. He assisted his father as a commercial chemist until 1836, when he continued the business on his own following his father's death. Chilton was also involved in the sale and manufacture of philosophical apparatus, the focus of Joseph Henry's contacts with him. Although Chilton did not author any articles on science, his services were undoubtedly valued by the research community. From 1848–1851 he was a member of the American Association for the Advancement of Science. New York City Directories, 1837–1863; *Columbia Alumni*, p. 206; *Silliman's Journal*, 1863, 2d ser. *36*:314.

[2] This item is from Box 28, in the folder "Unsorted material." Henry had a habit of noting down information acquired in conversation or reading, often in notebooks. This note is on a separate sheet. To the frustration of his editors, Henry was not consistent in such notetaking; to their relief, he often conscientiously dated these notes and clearly differentiated his views from those in his sources.

[3] Henry's interest in lacquer was under-

To purify mercury place the metal on a plate and pour over it a quan[ti]ty of diluted sulphuric acid; let the article stand a few days. Or the same may be efected by shaking the mercury in a bottel after the manner of Priestly.[4]

He proposes to heat the barometer tube in filling it with mercury and then dip the end into purifyed mercury contained in a dish under a receiver of an air pump in which a vacuum has been formed.

t the tube *b* the receiver and c the plate of mercury

In making barometers he has observed the regular fact that if the tube be cleaned by a swab made by cotton on the end of a fine wire [and] if the end of the wire is allowed to come in contact with the sides of the tube so as to make a slite scratch [and] if the tube be laid asid for an hour or so it will be observed to crack in a longitudinal or spiral direction. This I explain on the same principle as the bursting of Prince ruperts drops.[5]

He also mentioned to me an interesting experiment. Take a globe nearly filled with water and on the top of the water place a small quantity of turpentine tinged with some substance. On whirling the globe rapidly on the table the colored turpentine will descend through the axis of the globe and be indicated in its descent by the tinge of colour. This is a very interesting experiment.

standable. In his "Electricity" lecture notebook (No. [23894]), he noted in the section on insulation and conduction that "gum lac is the most perffect of all insulators 10 times better than pure silk." This notebook, although undated, was probably used in preparing lectures during Henry's first years at Princeton.

[4] Henry may have already known of Joseph Priestley's method from Faraday's *Chemical Manipulations* (London, 1827), p. 443; Henry's copy was probably acquired in Albany. Priestley's account, according to Faraday, originally appeared in section xvi of the "fourth volume" of *Experiments and Observations on Different Kinds of Air* (more exactly, the *Experiments and Observations Relating to Various Branches of Natural Philosophy* . . . , 3 vols. [London, 1779], *1*:151–153).

Priestley's method was particularly recommended for removing lead and tin impurities. It was suitable for small quantities of the liquid metal. The agitation produced an easily separable "black coagulated part" by reaction with the air. We suspect that purified mercury was important for electrical experiments, as well as in the barometer and thermometer discussed below.

[5] Named after their supposed discoverer, Prince Rupert of Bavaria (1619–1682; *DNB*), a Stuart who participated in the early years of the Royal Society. These are droplets of glass produced by letting drops of molten glass fall into water. Those surviving have the properties of unannealed glass. When touched at the tapered end, they burst into powder with explosive force. Bigelow, perhaps Henry's source, ascribed the effect to "permanent and strong inequality of pressure" in the drops. Henry implies a flaw in the annealing process. Jacob Bigelow, *Elements of Technology* . . . (Boston, 1829), pp. 451–452.

He propounds the following question. What use is there in expelling the air from the top of the thermometer.[6]

[6] Henry's noting without comment does not tell us either his answer or Chilton's purpose in making this query. During the eighteenth-century development of the thermometer, there was a suspicion that air introduced errors in the readings of liquid-in-glass thermometers, although, as Middleton notes, the supposed disturbing effect of air pressure on the expansion of the liquid was in general overestimated and "was to hamper the progress of thermometry" at least until the end of the century. W. E. K. Middleton, *A History of the Thermometer . . .* (Baltimore, 1966), p. 82. By the mid-eighteenth century, a Royal Society Commission recommended removing the air from mercury thermometers. *Encyclopaedia Britannica*, 8th ed., s.v. "Thermometer." We suspect that Henry found the practice routine. Faraday in the *Chemical Manipulations* (p. 135), simply says of the mercury thermometer, "It should not include air."

TO HARRIET HENRY

Family Correspondence, Henry Papers, Smithsonian Archives

Albany Dec. Thursday 13th 1832
11 o'clock A M

My Dear Harriet

I arrived at home this morning about ½ past nine and found Mother quite easy. She was much pleased to see me and regretted much that it was not possible for you and the boy to visit her. She would be much gratified to see you both before she *departs* but knows that she cannot expect it. She has failed much since we left Albany but is more comfortable this week than she was at the time James wrote. She is lying in the room with the bed placed in the North west corner almost before the door of the bedroom. This arraingement is much more pleasant than that of having her in the bed-room. Her apetite has returned and she eats rather more than usual. Her fever also has not been so high for two days past but no dependance can be placed on her present state of health as it is affected by every change of weather. She has not been out of the room-door since we left Albany. I have been conversing with her during the last hour. She spoke quite strong but now feels considerably exhausted by the exersion. She has made a great many inquiries about the boy as well as the whole family. She cannot forget the circumstances of her telling him on some occasion that he could not have the *watch* to play with and that he never afterwards expressed a desire for it as he had always before done. She thinks he was wise enough to understand her and like a good boy obeyed her wishes. Aunt Jennet Uncle James' wife[1] is here. She came up on monday and will probably remain the remainder of the week. Mrs. Shankland is better and called at Mother's on tuesday. She was alone and appeared although not well cheerful. Mr[s] Shankland has not taken any of Aunts plants. She says [she] cannot attend to them this winter and fears they would freeze.[2]

Stephen Hase[3] has been down from Galway lately and says that all our relatives are well except Uncle Thomas who is recovering from the effect of an accident which happened [to] him at the raising of a neighbours building. A piece of timber in falling struck him on the head and nearly deprived him of life. He lay for some time senseless but has I believe received no very perminent injury. I have not yet left the house and consequently have not seen any of your acquaintances. I was obliged to remain in N.Y. yesterday. We did not get to the city until nearly ½ past 6 oclock on Tuesday. [We] were very detained on account of some injury the boat had sustained in her passage from N.Y. in the morning by running against another boat in the thick fog. I had not time before the starting of the boat to call on Mrs Van Pelt[4] and deliver the message concerning the black woman; it will therefore be necessary for you to write to the lady on the subject by the mail & do not forget to pay the postage.

I was much surprised a short time after the starting of the boat and while ascending the cabin stairs to hear my name called by a female voice. On turning round I recognized Mrs. Solomons[5] who was on her passage to N.Y. and without an escort. She requested me to settle her passage and appeared quite pleased that we had met. I spent considerable time in conversation with her and was both pleased and edifyed by her reminissences of Princeton College. She has a sister living in the city of N.Y. and her nephew was waiting anxiously for her arrival on the warf. I called at Miss Van antwerps yesterday morning found all well. The whole family of ladies were busily engaged in fabricating different articles of apparrel. Miss V. wishes to know how much money was given her by your mother and also by Stephen: you must mention the ammounts in your letter to me that I may settle the business on my return. I called at Gasskins[6] in refference to the

[1] Jannet Jolly Alexander (ca. 1767–1844) was the wife of Henry's half-uncle James Alexander (1767–1850). "Alexander Genealogy."

[2] The last two sentences of this paragraph appear in the margin of the first page.

[3] Stephen Hays (d. 1862) was married to Joseph Henry's first cousin Lydia Alexander (1802–1894). "Alexander Genealogy."

[4] Not identified. Nor have we identified the black woman.

[5] Susan Salomans, daughter of Princeton President Samuel Stanhope Smith (1750–1819, *DAB*), "occupied a prominent place in Princeton society." John F. Hageman, *History of Princeton and its Institutions*, 2 vols., 2d ed. (Philadelphia, 1879), 2:268 (hereafter cited as *Hageman*).

[6] J & C Gascoigne (James B. and Charles), New York City hardware merchants, offered both imports and, "direct from the manufacturers, hardware in the greatest variety." New York City Directories, 1831–1833.

stove—he has no cooking stovs for wood but has been an agent for selling James'[7] patent. He requested me to go to James' store in Water Street and choose such a size as I supposed would answer and said that he would send it as soon as possible to N. Brunswick. I called at James' but was informed that there was none to spare to Mr. Gasskins. They appeared willing however to sell one to me or said they would be able to do so in a few days. I called at several places but found that the large kind of cooking stove for wood is a very scarce article; there is none of Postlys Patent[8] in the market, they have sold all that were manufactured last summer and have a great demand for more. I returned to the store of Gasskins and he agreed to procure one of James patent or some other and to send it on as soon as possible. He requested that you would send the stove to N.Y. as quick as possible as he may perhaps have a chance of selling it. When you write give me a particular memorandum of every thing you wish me to attend to both here and in New York.

I had a very pleasant passage up the river although the boat was much crowded. Among the passengers was Mr Cill[9] of Albany who resids in the white House near the academy. Also Mr McIntire,[10] Mr Yates[11] (Henry I believe), Mr. J. Randall[12] the engineer of the Owego rail road and last

[7] William T. James held two patents for improvements in stoves (1815 and 1824). He was a stove manufacturer in New York City. New York City Directories, 1831–1833; Edmund Burke, comp., *List of Patents for Inventions and Designs Issued by the United States from 1790 to 1847, with the Patent Laws and Notes of Decisions of the Courts of the United States for the Same Period* (Washington, 1847), pp. 136, 138 (hereafter cited as *Burke's Index*).

[8] Charles Postley, who held two stove patents by this time (1814 and 1815), was an iron founder at an establishment near James's in New York City. He patented another improved cooking stove in 1843. New York City Directories, 1831–1833; *Burke's Index*, pp. 136, 141, 144.

[9] We have been unable to find a Mr. Cill. Henry may be referring to Bennington Gill whom he mentions in the next document.

[10] Archibald McIntyre (1772–1858), whom Henry knew as a trustee of the Albany Academy (*Henry Papers, 1*:10), was probably traveling on business relating to his iron mining company. McIntyre had been involved in an unsuccessful ironworks near Lake Placid, New York, from 1809 to 1815. In 1826 he joined a partnership to develop newly discovered beds near Lake Sanford in the Adirondacks. McIntyre handled the Albany end of operations, assuring steady flows of supplies and cooperation from the state legislature on acquisition of title and building of a road. In 1848 the ore from McIntyre's mine was used by a New Jersey firm to produce the first high quality steel produced in America. However, the floods of 1856, the financial panic of 1857, and McIntyre's death in 1858 led to a precipitous decline in the business. Harold Hochschild, *The MacIntyre Mine: From Failure to Fortune* (Blue Mountain Lake, New York, 1962), pp. 1–8; Arthur Masten, *The Story of Adirondac* (Syracuse, 1968), pp. 18–143.

[11] Henry Yates (1770–1854), the treasurer and a trustee of Union College, was a lawyer who was active in Schenectady and state politics. A partner in the firm of Yates and McIntyre, he was instrumental in the running of the state lottery which also involved Eliphalet Nott. See below, Henry to James Henry, February 23, 1835, especially footnote 4. Codman Hislop, *Eliphalet Nott* (Middletown, Connecticut, 1971), p. 186 and passim; Munsell, *Ann. Alb., 6*:325.

[12] John Randel, Jr. (1785 or 1786–1865), a native of Albany, began there a long and productive career as a surveyor and engineer. Daniel H. Calhoun, *The American Civil Engineer: Origins and Conflict* (Cambridge, Mas-

though not least Dr Nott. I never before had an opportunity of conversing with the Dr and therefore took the liberty of introducing myself. He was extremly communicative and we became quite intimate. He inducted me into all his views on the subject of heat and payed me the compliment to say that I more readily caught his idea than any other scientific person with whom he had ever talked.[13] I have now a much higher opinion of his stoves than ever and have his consent to explain the philosophy of them to my class—with his views of heat.[14] He gave me a very pressing invitation to come to see him and offered to show me all his plans of future operations on heat and steam.

Mr Yates was also very polite. Said we were relatives[15] and would be hap-

---

sachusetts, 1960), p. 112, states that Randel is a significant example of the unyielding "surveyor-engineer with strong local interests" in the midst of changing standards of engineering in the nineteenth century. Randel did turnpike surveying in the Albany area as early as 1805. Next he laid out the Manhattan street grid and later he did levels for a projected Delaware-Raritan canal in New Jersey. Then he returned to Albany, where he worked on the plans for the east end of the Erie Canal, vehemently advocating that the Canal should bypass Troy and come directly to Albany (hence Calhoun's characterization). He later served as engineer for the Ithaca and Owego Railroad and several other railroad projects. Calhoun, pp. 109–113; Munsell, *Coll. Alb.*, *3*:256.

Randel was an early member of the Society for the Promotion of Useful Arts in Albany, but he never joined its successor, the Albany Institute. He and Henry undoubtedly met in the Albany surveyors' circles, in which Henry had gained considerable experience in the mid-1820s (see *Henry Papers*, *1*:xxv–xxvi, 97–105). One of their infrequent contacts concerned a topic of perennial interest to Henry and was noted by him at some unknown date:

> Mr John Randall informed me that in his measure of the Island of New York he made use of iron bars of 20, 30 and 50 feet long and that two bars were always on the ground at the same time that the other was adjusting and being carried ahead. The expansion of these bars by heat was determined by placing them in a long trough and pouring boiling water on them and noting the temperature by three thermometers placed at equal distances along the rod; when these thermometers stoo[d] at the same degree the division of the Pyrometer was noted.
>
> He informed me that the expansion according to these experiments gave a difference between summer and winter in the City of N.Y. of between three and four feet in a mile; a very important quantity where the value of land is as great as it is in N.Y.

(Henry Notebook [7169], p. 23, Henry Papers, Smithsonian Archives.)

[13] Henry circled the second half of this sentence, beginning with "and payed me the compliment," and noted in the margin "This is only for your eye."

[14] Henry was always delighted to see the use of scientific principles as the basis for improvements in the "useful arts;" mere tinkering impressed him less. Despite his enthusiasm for Nott's philosophical approach, Henry does not seem to have included Nott, by name or implication, in his lectures on heat in his Princeton natural philosophy course. Neither the surviving student notebooks nor Henry's own lecture notes make any such references. Subsequent letters in this volume will discuss Henry's involvement with Nott's patent claims.

[15] Maria Connor Alexander (1769–1852), wife of Alexander Alexander (1765–1809), was Harriet Henry's mother and Joseph Henry's aunt as well as mother-in-law. She was a fourth generation descendant of Joseph Yates (d. 1730), an Englishman who emigrated to Albany in 1664. Joseph Yates was the head of the numerous prolific generations from which Henry Yates was descended. See Munsell, *Coll. Alb.*, *4*:184y–184z; typed notes on the Henry ancestry in the Family Correspondence, Henry Papers, Smithsonian Archives.

py to see me allways when I came to N.Y. Both gentlemen made several inquiries concerning the Family.

I have not yet seen any of Mr McCammons relatives except his younger brother whom I met in the street on my way from the steam boat. Tell him his mother has been several times at our house inquiring concerning him. Also that one of his acquaintances was buried about two weeks since the oldest son of Mr. Laton[16] of the furnace; it is supposed that he was injured at the time the engines were tried in the park[17] before McCammon left albany[;] he was never well afterwards. Stephen has probably seen General Jacksons proclamation.[18] It produced a great sensation in N.Y.

I am obliged to close as the mail closes in a short time. Nancy sends her love to all. Mother has fallen asleep after her exersion in talking with me.

As ever My Dear Wife
Your
Husband

I did not rest well on board the boat and consequently am rather out of sorts to day.[19]

[16] Thomas Layton, listed as a furnaceman in the Albany City Directories, 1833–1835.

[17] We have found no elucidating accounts of this incident.

[18] President Andrew Jackson's response to South Carolina's "Ordinance of Nullification" (November 24, 1832) was his "Proclamation to the People of South Carolina," delivered December 10 and his proposal to Congress for passage of the "Force Bill."

[19] Henry appended this note in the left margin of the last sheet.

TO JAMES HENRY

Family Correspondence, Henry Papers, Smithsonian Archives

New York Friday [December 21, 1832]
12 o'clock

Dear James

I arrived safely at about 7 o'clock this morning and conclude from the temperature that I did wisely in starting as I did on Thursday evening. We passed through considerable ice between Albany and Hudson and I think it quite probable that the river is frozen across this morning at Albany.

I did not see Mr Hammond or Mr Dean although I called at their office[1] for that purpose. Give my respects to them and tell them that I called.

[1] In 1832 Jabez Hammond and Amos Dean, attorneys and counsellors at law, were maintaining offices at 67 State Street in Albany (Albany City Directory, 1832–1833). Hammond (1778–1855), for whom see *Henry Papers, 1*: 98–99, had been practicing law in Albany fol-

Also tell Judge Conkling[2] that I will call on him when I next visit Albany that my short stay prevented my do[ing] so at this time. It is probable that a letter will arrive in Albany for me to day or tomorrow from Harriet.[3] You must take it from the office and open it as it will give you the news from Princeton.

I had quite pleasant companions down last evening. Old Gruttenden[4] Dr. James[5] Gill the hardware merchant[6] Mr McIntire[7] and some others. I hope mother was not made worse by my departure. It was a very great trial to my feelings and must have affected her some although she did not appear as much affected as I feared she would.

I shall remain in N.Y. to day & leave tomorrow morning at half past six and will then unless something unusual prevents reach Princeton about one o'clock.

I stop at the American and find it a very plesant house.[8] I have not yet visited Mr McMullens[9] but will indeavor to call either this afternoon or this evening.

I forgot to speak to you about the coat I got from Tailor. I will settle with you for it when I next come to Albany.

If Samuel Pruyn should not call on you in the course of next week you had better call on him. The ammount he is to pay is $50.[10]

---

lowing a term in Congress (1815–1817) and four terms as Senator in the New York Assembly (1818–1821). Amos Dean (1803–1868) studied law with Hammond, his maternal uncle, after being graduated from Union College in 1826. He was instrumental in the organization of the Albany Medical College in 1839 and served as Professor of Medical Jurisprudence for over twenty years. In 1851 he helped establish the Department of Law of the University of Albany (unofficially known as the Albany Law School), becoming a member of its faculty. A prolific writer, Dean is represented by three books and three pamphlets in the Henry Library. *DAB*.

[2] Alfred Conkling.

[3] Not found.

[4] We have no information on "Old Gruttenden." Henry may, however, be referring either to Leverett Cruttenden, an Albany tavern keeper, or Robert Cruttenden, master of the steamboat *Constellation*, also an Albany resident. Albany City Directory, 1832–1833.

[5] Perhaps Dr. John James (1789–1859), at that time a practicing physician in Albany. A graduate of the College of Physicians and Surgeons in New York, James was an older brother of Edwin James, botanist with the Stephen H. Long expedition to the Rocky Mountains in 1820. Albany City Directory, 1832–1833; Amasa J. Parker, ed., *Landmarks of Albany County, New York* (Syracuse, 1892), p. 186.

[6] Bennington Gill, of Gill, Cooper, and Company, dealers in hardware and stoves at 10 Green Street, Albany. Albany City Directory, 1832–1833.

[7] Probably Archibald McIntyre, for whom see above, Joseph Henry to Harriet Henry, December 13, 1832.

[8] The American Hotel at 229 Broadway. New York City Directory, 1832–1833.

[9] John McMullen, for whom see above, Joseph Henry to James Henry, November 13, 1832.

[10] In 1832 Samuel Pruyn (1799–1862) was a member of the firm of William White and Company, brewers, in Albany (Albany City Directory, 1832–1833). During his lifetime he was a bank director, supervisor, and "inspector of the penitentiary from its inception" as well, according to Munsell, *Coll. Alb.*, 2:101. It appears that he also was less than prompt in paying his debt, the exact nature of which is

Do not fail to write every saturday and be particular in delivering any little message which mother may wish to send.

I remain as ever
Your Brother.

P.S. I was much gratifyed by the conversation which I had with old Mr. Gould[11] relative to yourself. He said he is perfectly satisfyed and also that there was a good opportunity in the store for you to make valuable acquantances and to establish a character which will be of great use to you through life. The old man is perhapse [a] little singular in some of his notions but it will be to your interest to [keep] him your friend as far as possible. JH

unknown to us, for Henry inquired about the matter in several subsequent letters (see below, Joseph Henry to James Henry, January 1, 1833; January 7, 1833; and February 12, 1834). Indeed, just prior to his European trip in 1837, Henry still was making financial arrangements concerning "a note I hold against Samuel Pruyn" (Joseph Henry to James Henry, February 8, 1837, Family Correspondence, Henry Papers, Smithsonian Archives).

[11] William Gould (1774–1846), who came from New Jersey to Albany in 1809 and established a prosperous legal bookstore (Munsell, *Ann. Alb.*, *10*:368). His nephew Anthony Gould, for whom see *Henry Papers*, *1*:446, joined him as a partner in the store after having served as a clerk for several years.

FROM JOHN MILLINGTON[1] AND JACOB GREEN

Henry Papers,[2] Smithsonian Archives

N° 207 Pine Street Philadelphia
31st December 1832.

To Dr J. Henry
Albany

Sir

I beg to apprize you that I have been residing as above during the last 6 months with the intention of establishing a Manufactory and Sale Store

[1] Millington (1779–1868) was an Englishman who was variously an engineer, patent agent, science teacher, and scientific instrument maker. He attended Oxford but left before obtaining a degree. Millington presumably had a medical degree but never practiced. Prior to 1817 he was Professor of Natural and Experimental Philosophy at Guy's Hospital in London. Active in various London scientific societies, he authored several scientific articles and two popular scientific works. In 1829 and 1830 he was in Mexico working for a firm leasing silver mines. By 1832 Millington had come to Philadelphia. He joined the faculty at William and Mary in 1835, leaving it in 1848 and going to the University of Mississippi. In 1853

for all kinds of Philosophical, Mechanical, and Chemical apparatus, on a larger and more comprehensive scale than any thing of the kind that has ever been attempted in the United States. It being my intention to keep on hand a large assortment of almost every article that can be asked for by men of science of the most perfect forms and constructions, made on my own premises and under my immediate inspection by first rate workmen who I have engaged, and to prepare all the nicer chemical tests reagents and other articles with my own hands; and I have already made great progress in my establishment and am beginning to get together a tolerably large assortment which will increase with each week. I can further add, from the experience I have already got, that I shall be able to furnish Instruments fully equal in accuracy and workmanship to any that have been imported from London or Paris, at prices considerably under those at which they have ever been obtained in this country. Among other articles I find it necessary to possess a good scale of chemical equivalents, and with this view I had prepared one in manuscript, and was about to put it into the hands of an engraver, when I accidentally mentioned the circumstances [to] my friend Dr Jacob Green[3] Professor of Chemistry in Jefferson college here, when he shewed me that which you have already Published in conjunction with M^r L C Beck[4] and mentioned to me that he thought you had some stock of them on hand, and that you might probably have no objection to making me your agent for the sale of them, or that you might perhaps be inclined to sell me the plates and stock on hand at a fair rate.[5] With a view to ascertain these points I therefore trouble you with the present letter, and have deferred the engraving of my own scale (which is rather more full of substances than your own) untill I may receive your answer which I shall be glad to have as early as may be convenient. Indeed I write at the suggestion of Dr Green which must be my apology to you for the present application.

I was originally initiated in the business I am now undertaking in one of the first manufacturing houses in London, and having held the Professorship of Natural Philosophy in the Royal Instit^e of Great Britain in

---

he accepted a post at the Memphis Medical College where he remained until 1859 or 1860. We know of only one co-authored scientific article done in the United States and an 1839 civil engineering text. *DAB*, *DNB*, and information from Silvio Bedini's forthcoming biographical dictionary of American mathematical practitioners.

[2] Jacob Green wrote his note to Henry one day later on the third sheet of Millington's letter. Henry's file notation on the cover reads "From Prof. Millington & Dr Green—1833."

[3] See *Henry Papers, 1*:322–323.

[4] See *Henry Papers, 1*:191–195 and passim.

[5] Henry's response to this letter has not been found, but a second letter from Millington, dated February 22, 1833, appears below. See especially the second paragraph and footnote 7 to that letter.

London for upwards of 16 years,[6] I am tolerably conversant with the use, perfections and imperfections of all Instruments, besides which I am personally acquainted with all the best makers in Europe and consequently whether I import apparatus or make it, at home, I can pledge myself that whatever I do supply shall be unrivalled in point of excellence.

I remain Sir
your very obed^t^ Servt
John Millington

[6] An exaggeration. Millington did lecture at the Royal Institution from 1815 to 1829. From 1817 to 1829 he was Professor of Mechanics (without salary) at the Royal Institution. (Information supplied by the Archivist of the Royal Institution.)

❧ 1833 ❧

Philad. Jany 1st 1833

My dear Sir

At my request my friend Professor Millington has addressed this letter to you. The establishment for Philosophical apparatus which he has opened in this city will no doubt be considered highly interesting & valuable to all who lecture on the Physical sciences. As I wish it to be as complete as possible, I hope you will comply with his request respecting your *Scales*. Should your college be desirous of extending their apparatus, they can do it on more reasonable terms by applying to him than to any one else. Have you done any thing further on electro magnetism? I congratulate you on your removal from the North to more temperate regions.

yours truly
Jacob Green

TO JAMES HENRY

Family Correspondence, Henry Papers, Smithsonian Archives

Princeton New Years day
1833 10 o'clock A.M.

Dear James

Your letter was received this morning while we were at the breakfast table and at the most proper time to wish us a *happy New Year* as you intended it should. We are sory to hear that Mother has had so bad a turn and that Nancy is unwell. I hope she has some person with her for if not she must be very lonely now that Mr McArthur and Mr Sammons have left. Perhaps Miss Raymond[1] is still with her. We are all well and have become quite familiar with our house and the appearance of things within the College yard but the town appears quite strange yet and not at all like home. The weather has been remarkably mild and pleasant since my return. The thermometer stood yesterday in the shade at 46°. We have had no appearance of snow this winter except on one morning and that before I went to Albany. This morning is rainy but gives appearance of [c]learing off.

Our cooking stove which has been so long expected arrived in Princeton last night but the Kettle still remains at New Brunswick. We will however most probably receive it this week.

Harriet is much obliged to you for setling her bill with Mr. Martin[2] and will pay you with interest when she comes to albany. In my last letter I informed you that I intended to send Mr William Gould a copy of Judge Southards address[3] on the death of Judge Ewing but on inquiring I found that the postage would cost more than the worth of the pamphlet on account of its not being a periodical. I therefore concluded not to send it. I however will forward another address of the same person which will cost in postage much less.

Stephen is much engaged in his Theological Studies: he attends two recitations at the seminary daily and as the building is about 3/4 of a mile from our house the walk affords him good exercise. The *boy* is quite well and appears to improve daily. He understands almost every thing that is said to him (or at least so says *Aunt*) and is very expert in expressing his wants in the language of signes. He is very cowardly about walking but can stand and walk alone if he has hold of his own apron as he then supposes he has some thing to support him.

The vacation in College is not yet ended. We commence opperations again on Friday. The halls of the College appear very lonely and deserted now in comparison to what they did in *term* time. You must call on Pruyn if he does not call on you but I expect he will give you the money in the course of a few days. Perhaps Mother would like occassionally a glass of ail. If so you can ask Pruyn to send you on my account half a barrel. *After-*

[1] Unidentified.

[2] A name too common to pin down. Perhaps the Robert Martin referred to in the letter of November 14, 1833, below (footnote 7).

[3] Samuel Lewis Southard, *An Eulogium upon the Hon. Charles Ewing, Late Chief Justice of New Jersey* (Trenton, 1832). A copy of this pamphlet, perhaps a presentation copy from the Mayor of Trenton, survives in Henry's Library.

noon 3 o'clock This has been so far rather a dull New Year. It is not the custom here as in Albany for friends and acquaintances to call on each other. Besids this the day has been rainy and unpleasant. I presume that you did not forget to call at the office of the Gazette and inform them that our paper had failed to come twice as we received the paper for Friday last with your letter and this is the first one we have reced since the 23^d of Dec. so that it has miscarried or has not been sent since I first went to Albany.

Give our wishes of a happy New Year to Mother and Nancy and tell them Harriet and myself would have been happy to have had an oportunity of eating a New Year's dinner at Mother's but as this was impossible we endeavoured to content ourselves with hoping that mother and Nancy's health did not prevent you all from seeing your friends and enjoying yourselves as usual on this day.

I remain as ever Your
Brother

FROM EDWARD HENRY COURTENAY[1]

Henry Papers, Smithsonian Archives

U.S. Military Academy
West Point Jany 3rd 1833.

My dear Sir

I had the pleasure to receive your letter of the 26 Ult^o.[2] expressing the hope that I had not abandoned the idea of preparing a translation of Boucharlat's Mechanics.[3] My leisure hours have been, for some time past, de-

[1] Courtenay (1803–1853) was born and raised in Maryland. He received his scientific training at the U.S. Military Academy at West Point, being commissioned in 1821. Courtenay served in various teaching positions at the Academy in Engineering and in Natural and Experimental Philosophy, resigning his professorship in the latter in 1834. He then taught mathematics at the University of Pennsylvania (1834–1836) and later at the University of Virginia (1842–1853). From 1836 to 1842 Courtenay worked as an engineer in the construction of the Erie Railroad, Fort Independence, and the Dry Dock of the Brooklyn Navy Yard. See Charles K. Gardner, *A Dictionary of All Officers . . . in the Army of the United States* (New York, 1860), p. 128, and *Herringshaw*, p. 254.

As correspondence to follow indicates, Courtenay and Henry soon became close professional colleagues. In the coming spring Henry visited the Academy and worked with Courtenay on experiments in terrestrial magnetism. Henry was delighted when his friend joined the faculty of the University of Pennsylvania.

[2] Not found.

[3] Edward H. Courtenay, *An Elementary Treatise on Mechanics* (New York, 1833). Courtenay's text was "Translated from the French of M. Boucharlat, with additions and emendations, designed to adapt it to the use of the cadets of the U.S. Military Academy." A copy of this work, presented to Henry by the author, survives in Henry's Library. It contains unusually frequent annotations through-

voted to the work; and it is now in a very forward state. It is my intention to have it ready for our next class, and it will therefore certainly appear before the 1st September, the commencement of our academic term. I am highly gratified to learn that you deem the work suitable to your purposes, as the prospect of its being adopted as a text-book in your Institution, affords the hope that it will be favourably received elsewhere.

There are many inaccuracies in the original, which I have endeavoured to correct in the translation; the bulk of the work will be slightly increased by the addition of some subjects which seem to form a necessary part of a course of Mechanics, and some few omissions have been made, but these changes will not affect in the slightest degree the general character of the work. I hope sincerely that the period at which the book is to appear may be such as to suit your convenience, & I am induced to believe that this may be the case, as your term commences somewhat later than ours.[4]

We shall hail with pleasure the appearance of a translation of Boucharlats Calculus,[5] or indeed, that of any work which is calculated to advance the cause of Mathematical Science, towards which purpose the efforts of those connected with the Academy are constantly directed.

I hope you have found your new duties as agreeable as you had anticipated. It will always afford us pleasure to see you, & to offer you any facilities in the prosecution of your researches which the means of our institution will supply.

Very Respectfully & Truly
Your's
Edward H. Courtenay

I should be pleased to learn whether you will require the work before the 1st September.

---

out the book, indicating that Henry worked through much of the calculus himself.

[4] In 1833 the Princeton winter session began in early November, and Henry declared his intention of using Courtenay's *Mechanics* in the "ensuing term" (see below, Courtenay to Henry, October 19, 1833). However, Courtenay's *Mechanics* is first listed as a text in the *Princeton Annual Catalogue*, 1835, covering the 1834–1835 academic year. According to the *Catalogue* (p. 12), the text was assigned for the Juniors in the summer session (May through September).

[5] J.-L. Boucharlat, *Élémens de calcul différentiel et de calcul intégral* (Paris, 1813). There survives in the Henry Library a sparsely annotated copy of the fourth edition (Paris, 1830). Courtenay's *Treatise on Differential and Integral Calculus* (New York, 1855) was published posthumously, but no mention is made there of any direct derivation from Boucharlat's original.

January 7, 1833

TO JAMES HENRY

Family Correspondence, Henry Papers, Smithsonian Archives

Princeton Monday Jany
7th 1833

Dear James,

The paper containing the Governor's Message[1] was received this morning. I have perused it with considerable interest and think the message a very creditable production. I find in it however no allusion to the *Farm* in the Hudson.[2] Mr Bloodgood's speech is also tolerably well done and makes a promise of economy.[3]

We are all well and nothing of interest to Mother Nancy or yourself has occurred, unless it be that the *Boy* on the day he was 15 months old walked *alone* across the floor from one side of the room to the other. He however became frightened in some way or other and did not attempt the same fete again until to day and then not without some forcing. The weather has been most remarkably mild for this season of the year. The thermometer in our yard and in the shade stood on saturday at 66° degrees and on sunday at 62° but to day it is down to 40° and appears to be growing colder. I have not heard how far the Hudson is closed by ice below Albany, but I suppose that the ice does not extend further down than Hudson, [New York].

We have received the *Kettle* in good order and the Ladies were much pleased with the exchange.

[1] Governor William Marcy's message of January 2, 1833, discussed the recent cholera epidemic, penitentiaries, lotteries, the militia system, the quality of teachers for common schools, and the county poorhouse system. In regard to agriculture and agricultural societies Marcy felt that "general intelligence and individual enterprise . . . have carried the art as far, perhaps, as could be reasonably expected without a better knowledge of the sciences. . . . We may reasonably expect great advantages from the cultivation and diffusion of the sciences connected with this art. . . . " *New York Assembly Journal*, 56th Session, 1833, pp. 9–27.

William Learned Marcy (1786–1857) graduated from Brown in 1808 and then worked as a lawyer and newspaper writer in Troy, New York, where he was an active supporter of the Jefferson party. He moved to Albany in 1823, becoming State Comptroller until 1829, a judge (1829–1831), and Governor (1833–1838). Since Martin Van Buren was in Washington during those years, Marcy headed the New York branch of the Jacksonian party, known as the "Albany Regency." Beginning in 1840, Marcy held a succession of national offices. His tenure as Secretary of State (1853–1857) was marked by several diplomatic accomplishments. (*DAB*.) Marcy's name will appear frequently in volume three of *The Papers of Joseph Henry* in regard to the creation of the New York State Natural History Survey. Henry and Marcy corresponded during the 1840s and 1850s.

[2] Quite likely a reference to Sing Sing Prison whose site was originally the "Silver Mine Farm." In 1833 a legislative investigative commission reported on bad conditions at the prison. Walter David Lewis, *From Newgate to Dannemora: The Rise of the Penitentiary in New York, 1796–1848* (Ithaca, 1965), pp. 136, 141.

[3] Francis Bloodgood on January 1, 1833, gave an address on becoming Mayor of Albany. Munsell, *Ann. Alb.*, *9*:260–261.

Tuesday 6 o'clock. I did not finish my letter yesterday and will now add a few lines before sending it to the office. The Weather has changed much since Sunday. The thermometer to day has stood at 32°. The wind is from the north and we may now expect winter weather. The daily of last Friday was received to day. It contains however little but what we have seen before. I hope the change of weather will not affect mother for the worse. We expected a letter from you this morning but was disappointed. The mail from the north comes in every night at about 12 o'clock and we receive our letters the next morning. The paper we received to day contains an Eulogy on Wm. James by Mr. Baldwin of Syracuse.[4] It is well done but perhapse a little over coloured. I have heard nothing relative to the Will of Mr. James. It would afford me some gratification if you would inform me of any particulars in relation to it which you may have heard.[5] Has Mr Bullions called to see mother? When you see him give him my respets. Also remember me to Dr Ten Eyck, Mr McArthour, Mr Sammons, Dr Frank, Dr. Wing, Mr. Furguson, Mr Hammond, also to Mr Dean. Tell him I found the person to whom he gave me the letter of introduction a very agreeable gentleman

[4] Harvey Baldwin (1797–1863), an early settler in Onondaga County, New York, and first Mayor of Syracuse after its incorporation in 1848. Franklin B. Hough, *American Biographical Notes* (Albany, 1875), p. 14. William James of Albany was well known to Joseph Henry (see *Henry Papers, 1*:passim). He is better known to history as the father of Henry James (1811–1882; *DAB*) and grandfather of the novelist Henry and psychologist William than as a leading entrepreneur in upstate New York. The first William James had important investments in Syracuse; a leading street is named after him. We have not located a copy of the eulogy.

[5] Henry's query might be nothing more than curiosity over the estate of a very wealthy prominent acquaintance. It might arise from concern over the fate of his former student, Henry James, the elder, who did not get on well with his father. In the James Family Collection at Houghton Library, Harvard University, is a letter of November 12, 1829, from Archibald McIntyre (see *Henry Papers, 1*:10 and Henry to Harriet Henry, December 13, 1832, footnote 10) conveying the father's wish for his son to study law. On December 2, 1829, the elder William James was writing McIntyre expressing displeasure that his son was purchasing cigars and other objects and charging them to his father. In 1830 Henry James fled to Boston. He returned after a few months, however, graduated from Union College and was successively a lawyer and a bookkeeper before his father's death. Joseph Henry may have known of the uneasy relationship between father and son.

The will (in the Surrogate's Court, Albany County, New York) gave Henry James and his half-brother William only a small annuity. The founding father had tied up the bulk of the estate in a trust "to discourage prodigality and vice, and to furnish an incentive to economy and usefulness." The trustees (one being Gideon Hawley) had discretionary power to make the ultimate division "with a just regard to circumstances of . . . personal merits and demerits of each individual." That presumably meant not charging cigars to the estate. The sons, however, broke the will, and Henry James received an annuity of $10,000. Gay Wilson Allen, *William James, A Biography* (New York, 1967), p. 7.

Henry James attended Princeton Theological Seminary from 1835 to 1837 where he undoubtedly had contacts with his old teacher Joseph Henry (*Roberts*, p. 101). He left the Seminary without graduating and went to Europe. Henry James's contact with Joseph Henry in Europe in 1837 and later will be documented in volume three and subsequent volumes of *The Papers of Joseph Henry*.

and that I am much obliged to Mr D. for the pleasure of the acquaintance.[6] Have you received the money from Pruyn? Harriet has received a letter from the Misses Meads but not from Mrs Shankland. You must remind her of a promis she made to write. I suppose that Mr Gould and you have made an agreement relative to your continuing another year or longer.

Give Mother and Nancy our warmest love and assure them that they are not at any time long absent from my thoughts but that when not busily engaged in my duties my mind constantly reverts to them. I should however have been much more uneasy in refference to Mother had I not visited Albany as I did. The visit although in some respets painful was on the whole exceedingly gratifying to my feelings.

The mail closes in a few moments so I must stop.

From your Brother

[6] We do not know the person Amos Dean wrote introducing Henry.

FROM ISAAC W. JACKSON[1]

Henry Papers, Smithsonian Archives

Tuesday Mor., 8th Jany *1833*

My Dear Henry,

I send a couple of the Doctors pamphlets,[2] which you will be good enough to keep very close, as the exposure of them might injure him in several ways. His trial with Parker of Troy,[3] one of the invaders of his patent comes on before Judge Conkling[4] about the 17th of this month.[5] Were it possible for you to be present, it would benefit him to a very great

[1] Isaac W. Jackson (1805–1877), at this time Professor of Mathematics and Natural Philosophy at Union College. He had attended the Albany Academy with Henry prior to his graduation from Union in 1826 (*Henry Papers, 1*:254).

[2] Eliphalet Nott published several pamphlets concerning his stoves and the principles on which they were based. In Joseph Henry's Library is a bound volume of disparate material which includes two pamphlets, or fragments of pamphlets, evidently written by Nott and identified by Henry in his own index to the volume as "Dr Notts papers on stoves etc." Henry had the two pamphlets bound together with a printed list of Nott's patents which Jackson sent more than a year later (see below, Jackson to Henry, March 20, 1834). Neither of the pamphlets which Jackson is sending here bears a title. Henry's file note on this letter says only "From Prof Jackson with Dr Notts pamphlets." In any case, Henry was already familiar with Nott's work and had just spoken with him at length on the subject; see above, Joseph Henry to Harriet Henry, December 13, 1832.

[3] Sylvester Parker, who had a stove factory at 243 River Street in Troy. Troy City Directory, 1832–1833. *Burke's Index*, p. 144, lists him as receiving a patent for a cooking stove on January 16, 1835.

[4] Judge Alfred Conkling of the Northern District of New York.

extend. They deny all originality to the Doctors principles & mechanical contrivances, & he will be required to prove them. You must write me immediatly & let me know whether you can possibly come.[6] You will be able to select from the books I send you the principles, etc on which the stove is constructed, rejecting one or two, (that relative to the following—preventing the expansion of the gas for instance) which are not tenable.[7] I intended sending you the pamphlets before, but fifty things have prevented me.

I ask you not to delay a moment in letting me know whether you can possibly come.

You will not be surprized My Dear Henry when I tell you that Sundy, I connected myself with the Presbyterian Church in this place. I conceive it my duty to make a public profession of my faith in Jesus Christ & I have done it. God of his infinite mercy grant that I may not live unworthy of it. You can't conceive My Dear Friend how much it gratified me when you were here to perceive that your thoughts were employed on that infinitly important subject the Souls Salvation. I pray you cease not to make it the subject of more earnest inquiry than ever. You believe the bible to be the Word of God. Read it, My Dear Henry especially the New Testament, with an honest unprejudiced mind, determined to yield instantly & compleatly to all your convictions of duty. Read it with fervent prayer to our most gracious God that he would bless you in things spiritual as he has in

[5] In his affidavit filed in a suit which Nott had brought against him in the Southern District of New York late in 1832, Parker stated that he was defending four suits in the Northern District as well; perhaps Jackson is referring here to one of these. Parker also stated that Nott had nineteen suits against other individuals pending in the Northern District (Affidavit of Sylvester Parker, December 12, 1832, *Parker* v. *Nott*, United States Circuit Court, Southern District of New York, Equity Case File No. X–64, RG 21, National Archives). A brief discussion of Nott's legal attempts to protect his patents is in Codman Hislop, *Eliphalet Nott* (Middletown, Connecticut, 1971), pp. 268–269.

[6] We have no evidence that Henry testified for Nott or took any other part in the case, as the Northern District records for this period apparently have not survived. Nott evidently won the case; see below, Joseph Henry to James Henry, February 9, 1833. Just over a year later, however, it appears that Henry was involved in another of Nott's suits; see below, Jackson to Henry, March 20, 1834, and Joseph Henry to James Henry, April 25, 1834.

[7] Nott's stoves, which he began developing at Union College early in the century, were familiar household fixtures in pre-Civil War America. Joseph and Harriet Henry had just purchased one for their household in Princeton (see above, Joseph Henry to James Henry, November 24, 1832). Using anthracite coal, rather than soft bituminous coal or wood, they provided a much needed domestic market for the hard coal. Briefly, the Nott stove was a baseburner with a tall magazine into which the fuel was placed. The magazine cover was then closed; if it were left open by a forgetful user, the gas, which rose upward through the coal, would escape and, possibly, explode. (Nott ultimately made improvements in his first stoves in an attempt to solve this problem.) The all-important innovation of the Nott stove was the rotary grate, which enabled dead ashes to be dropped into an ashpit and thus allowed the coals to feed on an unimpeded draft. Hislop, *Eliphalet Nott*, pp. 255–271.

other matters, which concern only your temporal welfare, & you will sooner or latter receive a most merciful answer to all your petitions. He who has done so much for you, will in the kindest & most appropriate manner do much more, infinitly more. That it may thus be you have my fervent prayers.[8]

My family is well. My respets to your wife mother & brother. Believe me truly

far off friend
I.W.J.

Don't fail to act immediately. Reflect that your presence may save the Doct[or]s patent.[9]

[8] In this period of Henry's life we find only infrequent and indirect references to Henry's religious activities and beliefs. Possibly Jackson is referring in this passage to Henry's church attendance in Albany. Henry was baptised in Albany's First Presbyterian Church, where Eliphalet Nott served as pastor from 1798 to 1804 (*Henry Papers, 1*:3, 315n). Henry appears to have attended church there, perhaps with some regularity. When he visited Albany a month and a half after he moved to Princeton, Henry settled for his outstanding pew rent (Henry to Harriet Henry, December 15, 1832, Family Correspondence, Henry Papers, Smithsonian Archives). But neither Henry nor his wife ever became a member of that church. He eventually joined the First Presbyterian Church in Princeton in 1844 by examination, of which parish he later served as a trustee, 1846–1848 (William E. Schenck, *An Historical Account of the First Presbyterian Church of Princeton, N.J.* [Princeton, 1850], p. 77; "Minutes of the Proceedings of the Session of the Presbyterian Church at Princeton, 1822–1847," [Synod of New Jersey Collection, Speer Library, Princeton Theological Seminary], p. 411).

In contrast with Jackson, Henry's religious views would remain primarily a private matter. He appears never to have been as noticeably fervent as Jackson here; nor does he appear to have been either unconventional or innovative in his religious views.

[9] These lines were penned on the reverse of the letter. The words "In haste" appear below and to the left of the address.

MINUTES, FACULTY, COLLEGE OF NEW JERSEY[1]

Faculty Minutes, Volume 1820–1835, p. 267, Princeton University Archives

January 8th 1833

The Faculty met.

Present[2]
- Dr Carnahan
- Mr Maclean
- Mr Dod
- Mr Henry
- Mr Edwards
- Mr McDonald
- Mr Hart

[1] This is apparently the first faculty meeting which Joseph Henry attended at Princeton. The faculty met at regular intervals throughout the year: at the beginning of each

M[r] John M. Barclay, Sam[l] P. Richards, and Chas. S. Wayne,[3] were called before the Faculty to answer for the crime of having been intoxicated on the 3[d] inst., the day of their return to College. They were admonished of their fault, and compelled each to sign a confession of his error, and a pledge to abstain from all intoxicating liquors during his connection with the College.

---

term to record the opening of the college; shortly thereafter to define the duties of the professors and tutors; at examination times to note the beginning and ending of exams and to report the resulting student standings. They also met irregularly to consider action on student disciplinary problems as they arose. The minute printed here concerns this subject which shows up frequently in the faculty minutes of the period.

Henry was to attend many such meetings at Princeton. Despite his stern demeanor he gained the trust of the students in this unpleasant part of his college responsibilities. "Joseph Henry, more than any of the others, seems to have understood the undergraduates and to have commanded their respect. Whenever a fight with the village boys or some other serious riot was threatened, he would restore peace by convincing the students that he was on their side" (*Wertenbaker*, pp. 243–244).

[2] Those present at this faculty meeting include the President, the Vice President, two professors, and the three tutors. Carnahan seems to have abdicated many of his disciplinary functions to John Maclean, who became somewhat infamous in this regard for his inept and often ludicrous attempts at bringing the students into line. A. B. Dod, the Professor of Mathematics (see *Henry Papers, 1*:434n), and Henry were in attendance as the two top professors. The language professors, the Professor of Anatomy and Physiology, and John Torrey, who was not in Princeton for much of the school year, did not attend.

The somewhat disproportionate representation of the tutors at this faculty meeting is explained by their heavy involvement in student discipline. James Cooke Edwards (1807–1880, B.A. 1830), Samuel Higgins McDonald (1809–1895, B.A. 1828), and John Seely Hart (1810–1877, B.A. 1830) were fairly typical of Princeton tutors in this period. Recent graduates of Princeton, they were all students at the Princeton Theological Seminary. In frequent contact with students in their rooms, at meals, and during classes, the tutors, in addition to their teaching duties, had the unenviable responsibility of detecting and reporting disciplinary problems. "Selected for their piety and scholarly ability, egged on by the faculty and trustees, often inexperienced and tactless, they were resented and sometimes hated by the students" (*Wertenbaker*, p. 137). Having survived the ordeal, Edwards and McDonald went on to become ministers. Hart (for whom see below, Henry to Harriet Henry, March 24, [1834], footnote 13) became a teacher. *Roberts*, pp. 64–65, 69, 71.

[3] John Macgowen Barclay (d. 1887) and Samuel Potts Richards (d. 1900) were both seniors. They graduated with their class the following September. Charles S. Wayne was a freshman at the time. He disappears from the college records shortly after this disciplinary action. *Princeton Catalogue*, pp. 144, 145. *Princeton Annual Catalogue*, 1833, p. 9.

TO JAMES HENRY

Family Correspondence, Henry Papers, Smithsonian Archives

Princeton Jany. 15th 1833

Dear James

Your letter of the 5th inst was received the next morning after my last letter was sent off. We were all rejoiced to learn that Mother was so smart and also that Nancy had recovered her health. It is now ten days since the date of your last letter and I hope although with some fear of the contrary that Mother still continues better and that the sudden change of temperature has not had a bad effect. We have had quite cold weather since I last wrote. The thermometer on Friday was down to 5° and to day and yesterday has stood about freezing. Since I began to write (5 o'clock PM) it has commenced snowing and appearances bid fair for a snow storm. It appears from the act you mentioned which Mr Hammond[1] has been engaged in that his health is better than it has been for some years past. There are worse men in the world than Mr J. D. Hammond and I sincerely hope he may get smoothly through it with his new wife.[2]

I have nothing of interest to inform you. We are all well. The boy appears quite delighted with his new accomplishment of walking and sometimes exercises himself by *todling* from one side of the room to the other to and frow for more than half an houre together.

I perceiv by the Gazette that the executive committee of the N.Y. State Temperance society is about publishing an extra Temperance recorder intended as a New Year's offering to the common schools of the State.[3] As it will contain an article in which I am interested will you ask Arch[d] Campbell[4] or R. V. DeWitt[5] to send me a copy. You are acquainted with Mr Campbell are you not? If you be not introduce yourself as my Brother and he will give you one.

Inform me how you found Joseph Selkirk; from your account his course appears to be a short one.[6] I hope that he finds consolation in that which

[1] Jabez D. Hammond. *Henry Papers, 1*:98n.

[2] The *DAB* notes: "A contemporary reports Mrs. Laura Hammond as being exceptionally solicitous as to her husband's health and comfort, accompanying him during court term so as to take care of special foods, but in his portrait. . . , with its broad forehead, deep-set eyes, and kindly mouth, there is no suggestion of a self-centered or exacting man."

[3] *New Years Offering, From the New-York State Temperance Society, to the Common Schools of the State, Temperance Recorder, Extra,* published in Albany on January 1, 1833. The *Extra* featured a "Brief Account of the State of New York," containing state statistics, a political and historical survey, a geographical, geological, and industrial overview, ending with a plea for temperance. Henry may have had reason to expect that some of the statistics and measurements on topography and meteorology were based on some of the data he had collected for the State Road Survey (see *Henry Papers, 1*:97–105) or for the meteorological reports of the State Board of Regents (ibid., 400n). In fact, the section entitled "Face of the Country &c." was a condensed, edited version of his paper "Topographical Sketch of the State of New York . . ." which had appeared in the introduction to David H. Burr's *Atlas of the State of New York* (Albany, 1829) and in the *Transactions*, Albany Institute, 1830, *1*:87–112. (See *Henry Papers, 1*:232, 249, 250–251, 252.) The *Extra* cites the source for the entire article as the ninth volume of the *Encyclopedia Americana.*

[4] Archibald Campbell. See *Henry Papers, 1*:397–398n. Both Campbell and DeWitt (below) were on the executive committee of the New-York State Temperance Society. See above-cited *Extra*, p. 1.

[5] Richard Varick DeWitt. *Henry Papers, 1*:62n.

[6] Joseph Selkirk (*Henry Papers, 1*:452n) died on January 15, 1833.

alone can give comfort in a situation like his. Give my Love to Mother and Nancy. Tell them the boy has received the Kisses according to direction. Give my compliments to Mr McArthur, Mr Sammons & Dr. F. Stephen sends by the mail which closes in a few minutes a Catalogue of the Theological students in the seminary.

Your Brother

Harriet bids me add as a PS. that the boy put up his mouth very readily to receive the Kisses.

My[7] dear Grandmama & Aunty,

Don't you think I can walk alone. I go from one chair to the other. Sometimes I feel afraid, & then I fall down on my hands, and creep. I wish you could see me when I am on my feet. I feel so proud. Dear Gramma I do long to see you very much, but I don't know as I would know you.

Father has been giving me a ride on his back. I love to ride very much. I can't write yet. Mother says she hopes I will be able to write some time or other. She has put on my night gown & says I must go to bed but I would rather play. I wish I could give you a kiss for good night, wait till I come to Albany.

Your affectionate Nephew
and Grandson his
William Alexander X Henry
mark

[7] The rest of the letter is in Harriet Henry's hand.

TO JAMES HENRY

Family Correspondence, Henry Papers, Smithsonian Archives

Princeton Wednesday Jany
30th 1833[1]

Dear James

My time was so occupied last week that I neglected to write. I however sent you a Paper with a line on it informing you that we were all well. I expected a letter from you this morning but did not receive one. It will probably come tomorrow. I know that you have received my last letter for a copy

[1] The date given is 1832, an obvious slip of the pen from the context and also from James Henry's file notation on the reverse. A penciled correction of unknown origin appears after the date.

of the work I wished you to request Mr Campbell to send me came to hand this morning.[2] The family all continue in good health. The boy is constantly improving in the art of *Locomotion* but does not make any progress in talking. He can make himself very well understood by signs and will whistle tolerably well when you ask him, that is if he be in the humour. Harriet added a poscript to my last letter in the name of the young gentleman intended for Mother. I hope it gave her some little amusement. The weather has been very mild since I last wrote. The thermometer has been down to the freezing point in the day time only once in ten days past.

We saw an obituary notice of the death of Joseph Selkirk in the Gazette.[3] The text he chose for his funeral sermon was very appropriate and one which indicated that he had conquered the fear of death with the hopes of a happy futurity. Your sketch of the Politics of the "*Empire State*" was quite acceptable and I will be obliged if you will continue to give me any interesting news of the kind you may hear. I wish you would send me a copy of the report of the committee on State Prisons.[4] I wish it for Prof. Mclean[5] who is about writing something on the subject of prisons. Also when it comes out a copy of the Regants Report but it will not probably appear until late in the session.[6] I see by the Gazette that a new Medical School is about being established in Albany.[7]

[2] See above, Joseph Henry to James Henry, January 15, 1833.

[3] Joseph Selkirk, ill for some months (see above, Joseph Henry to James Henry, December 8, 1832), died of consumption on January 15, 1833. *Albany Daily Advertiser*, January 16, 1833, p. 2.

[4] In 1832 the New York State Assembly had voted to appoint a three-member committee to examine the state prisons at Mount Pleasant (Sing Sing) and Auburn and report to the next session (*New York Assembly Journal*, 55th Session, 1832, p. 514). The committee's findings were, in fact, transmitted to the Assembly on February 26, 1833, in a thirty-nine page summary (*New York Assembly Documents*, 56th Session, 1833, No. 199). The Senate had a standing committee on state prisons as well; one of its reports, concerning specifically the erection of a state women's prison (an issue which was being vigorously debated at the time), had been brought before the Senate on January 28, two days before Henry wrote this letter (*New York Senate Documents*, 56th Session, 1833, No. 32). It was very brief, however, and it seems more likely that Henry is referring here to the forthcoming report of the Assembly's special committee.

Both New York institutions discussed in this report were run on the Auburn or "congregate" system, whereby prisoners slept in individual cells at night but worked silently together in the daytime. This was in contrast to the Pennsylvania system, in which prisoners worked, as well as ate and slept, in isolated cells. The vigorous debate over the relative merits of the two systems during the early nineteenth century as well as other aspects of the penitentiary movement are discussed in David J. Rothman, *The Discovery of the Asylum: Social Order and Disorder in the New Republic* (Boston, 1971), pp. 79–108.

[5] John Maclean, Jr. (1800–1886), a Princeton faculty member and Vice President of the college, for whom see *Henry Papers, 1*:433.

[6] The *Annual Report of the Regents of the University of the State of New-York* (Albany, 1833) which contained, among other items, the yearly meteorological statistics, was transmitted to the legislature on February 28, 1833 (*New York Senate Documents*, 56th Session, 1833, No. 70).

[7] Although the Albany Medical College did not open until 1839, there had long been efforts on the part of many citizens and physicians, notably Dr. Alden March, to establish

Our ladies are beginning to become a little more acquainted with the people of Princeton. We find the President's family and also Mr Mclean's very pleasant and kind. The people generally however are not very easy to become acquainted with and in some degree justify the remark of Mr Caldwell[8] that we would have to eat a peck of salt before we knew them. Harriet says you must call on Mrs. Shankland and give her a severe scolding for neglecting to answer her letters and tell her if she will not write herself she must employ Mary Ann.[9]

I hope you have not omitted writing on account of not having received a letter from me last week as we are very anxious to hear from Mother. You say in your last that Mother had been attacked with a severe fit of coughing. I hope she has recovered and that she may meet with no sudden reverse as I have had strong hopes that she might yet live some time to be a comfort to her children. Assure her that I regret that I am not so situated as to be able to see her as often as I might desire and that I now regret that the time is past when I could be with her at any hour of the day.

Give my respects to All the Members of the family and my love to Nancy. Tell her Harriet the Boy and Myself will be in Albany if our lives be spared about the 10th of April next.

I Remain as ever
Your Brother

I feel half inclined to give you a scolding for not writing as usual. We expected a letter yesterday & to day again but have been twice disappointed. Do write as often as you can as we are very anxious to hear from you all.

Every thing goes on here as usual. We rise before we *take* our breakfast, but not before it is ready for us to take, and after it each one proceeds to his or her business.

Last evening Joseph & I attended a fair or sale of fancy articles. Such a squeeze I never have been in before, and was glad to escape with my life. Please give my love to Mother and Nancy. Tell them the boy improves, he

---

a medical school in Albany prior to that time. Dr. March had been offering lectures on anatomy and surgery since 1821, and an 1830 introduction to his anatomy course, for example, discussed the expediency of establishing a medical school in Albany (*Henry Papers, 1*:258). In January of 1833 the "Albany Medical School" issued a circular signed by twenty-one "patrons and supervisors" describing a course of lectures, beginning the following March, to be given by Dr. March and five other physicians. The fee was $50 for the three-month series, with a matriculation fee of $5.00. *Albany Daily Advertiser*, January 23, 1833, p. 3.

[8] Perhaps William Caldwell (1776–1848), an Albany businessman with interests in tobacco manufacturing and iron and grist mills, for whom see *Henry Papers, 1*:260.

[9] Mary Ann La Grange (1797–1848) was Susan Shankland's sister. She apparently lived with the Shanklands in Albany. Munsell, *Coll. Alb., 4*:115.

has been whistling and dancing for me this afternoon, does'nt talk yet, but Hub says I must stop so good night. Love to all.

Yours as ever
Harriet

FROM JAMES A. DE LA VERGNE[1]

Henry Papers, Smithsonian Archives

New Brunswick, Feby 2d, 1833.

Dear Sir

I have the honor to inform you that, at a late meeting of the Philoclean Society of Rutgers College,[2] you was unanimously elected as one of its Honary Members.

Permit me to add, that your acceptance will gratify our Society; that we profess to be only children sitting at the feet of Science; that we always receive with lively and grateful emotions the countenance of her Sons and Patriarchs.

Wishing you happiness and success in *all* your pursuits, the prosperity of the Institution with which you are connected,

I am, with sentiments of respect,
Your Obedient Serv^{nt},
James A. De La Vergne,
Pres^{nt} of Phi'^{n}. *Society.*

[1] James A. De La Vergne (d. 1899) was a member of the 1833 class at Rutgers, although he did not receive a degree. Later a Presbyterian clergyman, he was the first Superintendent of Public Schools, Clinton, Missouri (1867–1868). *Catalogue of the Officers and Alumni of Rutgers College in New Brunswick, N.J., 1766 to 1909* (Trenton, 1909), p. 57.

[2] Both of Rutgers's literary societies, the Philoclean and the Peithessophian (Philo and Peitho), were founded in 1825 shortly after the college reopened following a suspension of classes (1817–1825). Like their Princeton counterparts, the Whig and Cliosophic Societies (see below, Joseph Henry to James Henry, February 9, 1833, for a more extended discussion), Philo and Peitho met regularly for debates, oratory, and other literary activities, adding an important dimension to college life. Both made it a point to elect men prominent in literary, professional, and public endeavors as honorary members. William H. S. Demarest, *A History of Rutgers College, 1766–1924* (New Brunswick, 1924), pp. 298–299. Henry welcomed this recognition from Rutgers students, and he drafted a response on February 8, 1833, asking the President to inform the membership "that I accept with much pleasure this unexpected mark of their esteem" (Henry Papers, Smithsonian Archives).

In the Henry Library is a copy of *An Address, Delivered Before the Philoclean Society of Rutgers College, at Their Anniversary Meeting Held December 8, 1832*, by John D. Ogilby, Professor of Languages (New Brunswick, 1833). The inscription to Henry, dated February 26, 1833, reads "Please to accept this token of respect" and is signed by Henry Dusenbury, a graduate of the class of 1834 (A.M. 1837), who later became a lawyer. *Rutgers Catalogue, 1766–1909*, p. 58.

February 9, 1833

TO JAMES HENRY

Family Correspondence, Henry Papers, Smithsonian Archives

Princeton Feby 9th 1833
Saturday afternoon

Dear James

I wrote last week but by your letter of last Saturday it appears that you had not then received it. The letter was sent to the Office after the Mail closed and may therefore not have gone safely as it was put into the package as a way-letter.[1] We are all well and going on as usual without meeting with anything to change the monotany of a village residence except that the *expresses* employed by the Editors of New-York pass here on the run four times aday.[2] The weather has been quite cold this week and the thermometer down to 16, 18, 32 &c but the temperature of to day is quite high for this season. The thermometer stand now at 52°. You mention that the thermometer stood on saturday last at Albany at 8 degrees below *zero* on the same day it stood at this place at 13° in the morning, 22 noon. You have therefore much colder weather in Albany than we have here. I am pleased to see by the papers that Dr. Campbell has been chosen one of the Regents of the University. He will make an excellent member of that board.[3] I have heard that Dr. Nott[4] has gained a verdict against Parker of Troy[5] who has been Pirating on his patent for stoves. I am glad of this as I am convinced on examination of the subject that Dr Notts Stove is original in many particulars and that it is an admirable improvement. We have had a great deal of comfort with our stove on the Dr's plan and have burned only one tun of coal thus far during the winter.

We are much pleased to hear that mother still continues so smart. She has revived so much more than I ever expected to hear that I have now some hopes that she may recover from this attack if not to health at least to a

[1] A reference to the letter of January 30, 1833, above. A way-letter is one handed directly to the mail contractor or his agent (rather than deposited at a post office, for example). For this, the sender paid an extra fee, usually pocketed by the person carrying the mail between post offices. The contractor, in addition, received a fee from the Post Office Department. As the pouch containing the mail was closed, the way-letter was carried separately by the person transporting the mail from city to city, perhaps on his person. The way-letter might, as Henry fears in this case, get lost or delayed, instead of being placed in the pouch at the next office.

[2] The use of news expresses was a recent innovation for New York papers. Employing relays of horses, the *New York Journal of Commerce* led the race for news with an express from Philadelphia and later from Washington. See Allan R. Pred, *Urban Growth and the Circulation of Information: The United States System of Cities, 1790–1840* (Cambridge, Massachusetts, 1973), pp. 48–49.

[3] Dr. William Campbell. See *Henry Papers, 1*:100n.

[4] See footnote 7 of Henry's letter of November 24, 1832 and passim for Nott and his stove.

[5] See the footnotes to Jackson's letter to Henry, January 8, 1833, above, for these legal suits.

state of health similar to that which she enjoyed before she was sezed with this sickness. The boy is well and as troublesome as usual. He has given up all attemps at speaking but improves very much in understanding anything that is said to him.

I am sorry to learn that Old Mr Oakey[6] has lost his situation. It must be a very disagreable circumstance to him since he has held the place so long that the duties of it had become habitual and almost necessary to his happiness. I hope however that he has laid up sufficient money to render him and his wife comfortable for the remainder of their lives.

Give my respects to Dr Ten Eyck and tell him to keep the books for me until the river opens. Mr McCammon has received a letter from Enders[7] from which it appears that he has paid you a visit since I was in Albany.

Stephen has a recess in the Seminary at this time to continue two weeks. His studies occupy most of his time.

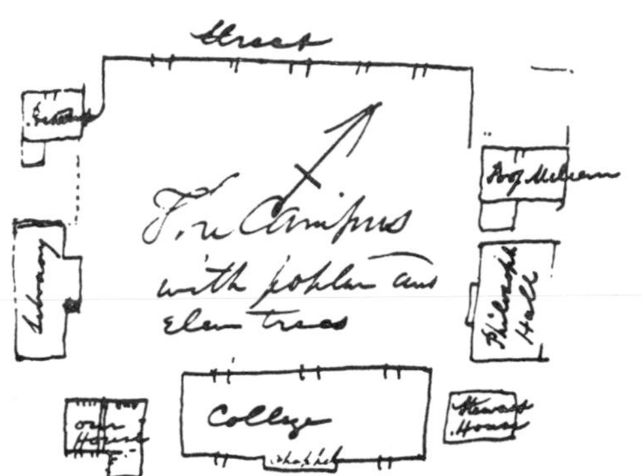

I do not reccollect of having given you a sketch of our situation. From the anexed diagram you will be able to come to our door when you visit Princeton without inquiring.[8] The ground floor of the Library is used for re[citation][9] rooms, the second or principal floor for the Library which contains several thousand volumes[10] and also a cabinet of

[6] In Henry's letter to his brother James of January 8, 1834, below, is a mention of the death of a Mr. Oakly in New York City. This is Abraham Oake or Oakey, formerly a clerk in the Treasurer's Office. His address, 27 Fayette, was close to Ann Henry's at 31 Fayette. *Daily Albany Argus*, December 9, 1833, p. 2 and Albany City Directory, 1832–1833.

[7] Perhaps Peter Enders (1812–?) who entered the Albany Academy, 1831–1832. He was originally from Montgomery County, New York. Hun, "Albany Academy."

[8] "College" in the diagram refers to Nassau Hall which was in use in 1756. In Joseph Henry's day the building was altered from its original state. After a fire in 1802 Benjamin Henry Latrobe (1764–1820, *DAB*) supervised the reconstruction. Latrobe's rendition of the structure was burned in 1855 and succeeded by still another architectural rendering by John Notman (1810–1865) in the then fashionable romantic style. A pair of towers added on at the ends of the building were subsequently removed.

"Our house" in the diagram is the first home of the Henry family in Princeton, and no longer stands. It is not the "Henry House," the second home of the family which survives but not in its original location. Outside of the occasional comments in letters in this volume, we know very little about the first house. Apparently, it was originally for the Professor of Languages. Henry's drawing is a very casual sketch; we cannot explain the lines and markings on his house. They do not match a surviving sketch of the campus made shortly before this date.

Of the three other residences, two were occupied by Carnahan ("President") and John Maclean, Jr. The house on the other side of Nassau Hall from the Henry residence was Henry Clow's, Princeton's Steward (see Henry

minerals.[11] The upper rooms are used by the two societies of the college viz the *Whig* Soc. and the Cliosophical Soc. All the students or nearly all belong to one or the other of these. All the proceedings of the two soc. are kept a profound secret and no person is permitted to enter the room who is not a member.[12] The President myself[13] and one of the Tutors belong to

to Torrey, April 2, 1835, footnote 4). Only the first still survives.

The Library building has been known as Stanhope Hall since 1915. Its mate across the campus, Philosophical Hall, was where Henry did his teaching and research. Later documents in this volume will treat the extension to this structure. Philosophical Hall was torn down after the Civil War upon construction of the library building used by Princeton until its replacement by the Firestone Library in this generation.

As a faculty member and later as a trustee, Joseph Henry was very much involved in the development of the Princeton campus; examples of this interest will occur subsequently.

Wertenbaker has many references to the development of the campus. Henry Lyttleton Savage, ed., *Nassau Hall* (Princeton, 1956). C. M. Greiff, M. W. Gibbons, and E. G. C. Menzies, *Princeton Architecture . . .* (Princeton, 1967).

[9] Part of the paper is missing here. This is a more likely reading than "study" rooms, the only other use we have found for these chambers in the last century.

[10] *Princeton Annual Catalogue*, 1833, p. 13, states that seven thousand volumes were in the college library. It was open twice a week for students who could borrow. Further discussion of students and college libraries occurs in footnote 12, below.

We cannot state precisely what was available to Henry in the college library at any given time. The surviving records simply do not permit that kind of discrimination. In this volume are a number of references to Joseph Henry using the libraries of the American Philosophical Society and of the U.S. Military Academy at West Point particularly for current scientific periodicals. We assume Henry moved to correct these deficiencies as funds permitted.

The Princeton University Archives contains an author catalog of the library prepared by John Maclean in 1843 in his capacity as librarian. It contains entries in another hand done perhaps as late as 1865. Taking into account entries of a later date in terms of the hand and time of publication, the overall impression is quite favorable. Although lacking leading scientific periodicals, the collection was quite varied. It was not overwhelmingly classical and theological as sometimes asserted of older college libraries, a point discussed in footnote 12. A compulsive reader like Joseph Henry would find much in the college library on science and many other areas.

[11] A gift of Dr. David Hosack. When the library was moved to Nassau Hall in 1860 the collection, now augmented, remained and the building was designated "Geological Hall" for a number of years. For Hosack, see C. C. Robbins, *David Hosack, Citizen of New York* (Philadelphia, 1964), Memoirs of the American Philosophical Society, vol. 62.

[12] Both societies originated in the previous century. By this date they loomed very large in the life of the College of New Jersey. In 1838 the two societies were moved into separate halls, a matter in which Joseph Henry was involved. Originally in stucco, these classic buildings were replicated in marble in 1893; they now stand as memorials to a defunct style of college life.

The literary societies at Princeton were part of a fairly extensive trend in American colleges in the past. The American Whig Society (to give its full name) and the Cliosophical Society were different from college fraternities and a later Princeton institution, the eating club. They were not exclusive nor did they provide meals. As Henry implies, a Princetonian of that era belonged to either one or the other.

In an era known for student turbulence, the societies were mechanisms for the self-policing of the students. Faculty were members, but student officers enforced both college and society regulations which, in fact, tended to be co-extensive. As the American Whig Society to which Henry belonged was organized on the model of the Presbyterian Church, the dictates of religion clearly reinforced the academic polity in prescribing student behavior.

Historians of the two societies see no real intellectual or ideological differences between them—despite their name, the Whigs honored Andrew Jackson. A sectional difference became troublesome as the Civil War ap-

the Whig society and the rest of the Faculty to the other. The President is not allowed to enter the room of the other society and consequently has never seen the Library or furniture of the Clios. as they are called. Stephen was elected last week a member of the Whig Soc. and has been inducted into its mysteries with all due cerimony.[14] On the ground floor of the Philosophical hall is the Kitchen and above this is the Dining room, the third story is the Museum and the chemical and Philosophical rooms in which most of my time is ocupied.[15] In the Chapel of the college which is a room in the rear of the building there is a very interesting old Picture of General Washington pain[te]d by *Peal the elder* for the college. It represents the general as he was at the time of the battle of Princeton. On one side of the picture General Mercer is seen wounded on the field and in the back

---

proached. Even before the Revolution, Whig tended to a greater southern coloration.

Rivalry between the two societies was principally in debates which were taken very seriously by all concerned. The rivalry extended further into the awards of academic honors at commencement. Feelings about honors ran high, and the faculty had to consider these emotions in their decisions on prizes.

A principal asset of the societies was their libraries which were cited in the college catalogs as assets of the institution. In 1833 the libraries of the two societies totaled 4,000 volumes. Many a student reminiscence at Princeton and elsewhere has fond words about the literary society libraries. They were freely open and liberal in circulation policies. They also were more likely to contain popular literary works than the college library. The college library catalog cited in footnote 10 discloses a collection quite varied in contents. Although belletristic works are only sparsely present, it is hardly accurate to characterize this library, at least, as being overly theological and classical. Not a library for entertaining browsing, the collection is more or less what the early nineteenth century expected of an intellectually serious institution.

After the Civil War the societies began a slow, steady decline. Beam, in the history of the American Whig Society, cites several causes. In 1872 the School of Science was opened bringing large numbers of nonhumanities students to Princeton. After the Civil War the increased enrollment necessarily meant that many students could not participate. In the same period the eating clubs emerged as centers of student life at Princeton. From 1889 to 1893 while the old wooden halls were being replaced by marble structures, the two societies languished. From 1928 through 1941 the two were progressively merged.

While generally agreeing with Beam, Wertenbaker places the decline in a different context by stressing the rise of college athletics as the focus of student life. The effect is rather striking. In the pre-Civil War years the modest but ambitious College of New Jersey has, according to its historian, a young, rather high-minded body of students. After the Civil War, as endowment, plant, and faculty increase, the student body becomes wealthier and more concerned with athletics rather than the intellectual topics of earlier classes of Princetonians.

Wertenbaker, pp. 201–208, 329–330, 354–356. Charles Richard Williams, *The Cliosophic Society, Princeton University* (Princeton, 1916). Jacob W. Beam, *The American Whig Society* (Princeton, 1937). Roscoe Rouse, "The Libraries of Nineteenth-Century College Societies," in David Kaser, ed., *Books in America's Past . . .* (Charlottesville, 1966), pp. 26–42.

[13] Henry was admitted as an honorary member of the Whig Society on November 11, 1832, presumably to balance the faculty division between the two societies. American Whig Society *Records*, volume 14, Princeton University Archives.

[14] Alexander is listed as becoming a member in 1832. *General Catalogue of the American Whig-Cliosophic Society of Princeton* (Princeton, 1956).

[15] The enlargement and extension of this building are referred to frequently in the correspondence between Torrey and Henry, below.

ground is a distant view of Princeton College. But the most interesting circumstance in refference to this picture [is] that the frame which is of carved work and gilded once contained a Portrait of George the Third but at the battel of Princeton a ball entred the Chapel and tore out the Portrait without injuring the frame. The trustees after the war requested General Washington to sit for his picture and thus procured a most appropriate substitute for the picture of the defeated Monarch.[16]

Give my love to Mother and Nancy and my compliments to Mr McArthur Mr Sammons and the Doctors.[17]

Harriet wishes me to tell Mother and Nancy that the boy has taken a great fancy to Mothers picture that he kissed it several times and shewed it all his play things.

[16] The painting by Charles Willson Peale is still at Princeton University. See Donald Drew Egbert, "General Mercer at the Battle of Princeton as Painted by James Peale, Charles Willson Peale, and William Mercer," *The Princeton University Library Chronicle*, 1952, *13*:171–194. The "Monarch" was actually George II, not George III as Henry states.

[17] Perhaps Dr. Francis N. Selkirk and Dr. Joel A. Wing.

FROM JOHN MILLINGTON

Henry Papers, Smithsonian Archives

207 Pine Street Philad[a] 22nd Feb[ry] 1833

Dear Sir

I duly received your favor of the 8th Inst.[1] and should have sent an earlier reply to it but have waited to give you a reply respecting the large Zinc Plates you stand in need of,[2] as I have nothing of the kind, all the plates I have on hand being small and my brass moulds for casting them being limited to 1 inch, 3 inches, 4 inches and 10 inches square. The only large Plates procurable in Philadelphia[3] are those used for covering roofs, and I quite agree with you, that on account of their thinness they are not worth the trouble of mounting in large apparatus. Having occasion for some large and stout Plates I had myself written to New England for them before I got your Letter, and delayed writing to you till I should procure an answer, which I this day got from the proprietor of the Rolling Mills, as he came in

[1] Not found.

[2] For the construction of a large battery to be used in electromagnetic researches discussed below.

[3] For the metal trade in Philadelphia, see Elva Tooker, *Nathan Trotter, Philadelphia Merchant, 1787–1853*, Harvard Studies in Business History, vol. 18 (Cambridge, Massachusetts, 1955).

person to me instead of writing. The Plates I required were much smaller than what you mention but even these I cannot get from him as he tells me he cannot roll plates more than 7 inches wide and 5 feet long provided they are 1/8th of an inch Thick as I required them to be, but he refers me to the Taunton Copper Compy Massachusetts,[4] where he informs me Zinc Plates may be had of any size and thickness to order, but adds that as Zinc will only bear rolling in a hot state, the Manufacture is only carried on in Summer and therefore unless they have the sizes required on hand, you will not be able to procure new plates for 2 or 3 months. He thinks J L James and Casswell[5] of New York are agents there for this concern. I intend writing to both the above, but to save time send you the above addresses that you may write to them yourself if you think proper, and am sorry I am unable to send you more satisfactory intelligence. But you have no idea how I am at times perplexed to find out where and how to procure many articles which I have occasion for, and wish to keep in my newly formed establishment.

As for the scale of chemical equivalents, I have been able to procure a few from Mr Durand,[6] and the other Drug stores which have answered my present demand, tho' they are not so full of names as the one Dr Green showed me.[7] They have however answered the purpose, and I shall not therefore engrave any scale, but shall wait the event of your hearing from Dr Beck, when I trust you will do me the favor to write me again upon that subject.

I cannot inform you of the price of the large Zinc plates, but I have lately paid 10 cents per lb for sheet zinc 6 inches wide & 1/8 inch thick, and this

[4] For Henry's large battery, if Millington's information is correct, there was only this one company capable of producing zinc sheets meeting Henry's requirements. Zinc was found in ores containing lead but the first notable mine in the United States was opened in 1838. The metal was used in making brass. The Taunton Copper Company probably produced the zinc sheets as a byproduct of the production of copper and lead alloys for which there were greater demands. The McLane report of 1833 is probably referring to this company when it reports a firm producing 300 tons of copper and 400 tons of sheet lead with 40 employees. As late as 1860, this company, according to Bishop, produced nearly $2,000,000 of copper, zinc, and muntz metal (a copper-zinc alloy). In 1833 and in 1860 these metals were utilized by the metal manufacturers in Taunton and elsewhere. Henry's needs for large sheets were quite uncommon for that day. The rolling mill proprietor is unidentified. U.S. Treasury Department, *Documents Relative to the Manufactures in the United States*, 2 vols. (New York, 1969), *1*:160–161, a reprint of the 1833 report prepared for Louis McLane, the Secretary of the Treasury. John Leander Bishop, *A History of American Manufactures . . .*, 3 vols. (New York, 1967), *3*:320, reprinting the 3d ed. of 1868. Walter Renton Ingalls, *Lead and Zinc in the United States* (New York, 1908).

[5] Josiah L. James and Nathan Caswell, merchants at 287 Pearl Street in New York City.

[6] Élie Magloire Durand. See *Henry Papers*, *1*:196.

[7] We know from Lewis C. Beck's autobiography that Henry and Beck published a second edition of their scale, since the first edition had been in such demand. In the second edition they included several additional substances (see *Henry Papers*, *1*:195). Durand's examples of the scale were of the first edition; Green's example was of the second.

may enable you to form some judgement of the Expense. 2 months ago I could have had the same thing for 8 cents, but zinc has lately risen in price as well as copper, tho' I know not the cause of the change.

I beg to assure you it will give me great pleasure to become personally acquainted with you whenever you may visit Philadelphia and remain

Dr Sir
yours very truly
John Millington

TO JAMES HENRY

Family Correspondence, Henry Papers, Smithsonian Archives

Princeton March 2nd 1833
Saturday afternoon

Dear James

I am very glad to learn from your last letter that mother is better again. I feared from the note on the paper you sent that your letter would bring intellegence of her being worse.

The receipt of her letter from Scotland must have given her great satisfaction and she was undoubtedly pleased to hear that her sister still remembered her youthful promise after the elapse of more than half a century.[1]

I cannot say if aunt[2] intends to go to Albany next summer or not. She will most probably visit the north in the fall (more correctly autumn). Motherinlaw will go to Albany after the return of Harriet and myself. We are pleased to hear that Catherine Alexander is pleased with her situation and that she can probably be happy with her old gentleman.

I saw Mr. Baldwin's's[3] marriage in the paper and noticed it on account of having once been introduced to Mr. B. at Wm. Jame's House.

We are all well except the boy is a little fretful on account of his teeth. He is about cutting one this afternoon.

This is the coldest day we have had this winter except one. The thermometer now stands at 7° in our yard. It has once before been as low as 6°,

[1] Two sisters, Margaret (b. 1755) and Jannat Alexander (b. 1753), remained in Scotland when other Alexanders emigrated to America in 1774. The exact nature of the promise is not evident. "Alexander Genealogy."

[2] Nancy Connor, sister of Maria Alexander, Harriet Henry's mother.

[3] Harvey Baldwin, for whom see above, Henry to James Henry, January 7, 1833, footnote 4.

in the morning early. There is about 8 inches of snow on the ground which fell yesterday and last night.

English William our Boy has learned to keep a regular record of the weather and records the degrees of the thermometer three times a day.

I have been lecturing this two weeks on Steam and the Steam engine. McCammon brough on a small working model and I had a number of drawings made of different engines so that we were able to give quite a treat on the subject to the students and other persons who attend the Lectures. They were all highly pleased with McCammons little engine which operates very prettily.

My time will be very much occupied for 12 weeks next summer as I will be required to attend to some extra duty but I will receive an addition to my salary which will be an equivolent.[4]

I see by the papers that the Chenango canal bill has passed and that a great supper was given on the occasion.[5]

Do you hear anything of Judge Trumpbour's claim[6] this winter. Is he in Albany attending the session?

There is a second cousin of Anthony Gould's in College in the Senior Class. His name is W. Dod.[7] He is one of the very first scholars in the Insti-

[4] Henry was asked to substitute for John Torrey in the summer chemistry course for juniors and seniors. On April 10, 1833, the Trustees resolved that "Professor Henry be requested to give instruction in Chemistry during the absence of Professor Torrey the next Summer, who it is expected will be absent in Europe during that time: and that $200. be appropriated as compensation for this Service. And that a sum not exceeding $100. be placed at the disposal of Professor Henry for the purpose of procuring a Chemical Assistant during the next session." (Minutes, Princeton Trustees, April 10, 1833, *1*:239.) For an assistant Henry chose George M. Maclean, for whom see below, Henry to George Maclean, October 9, 1833. John Maclean, *History of the College of New Jersey, 1746–1854*, 2 vols. in 1 (New York, 1969; reprint of 1877 Philadelphia edition), 2:291 (hereafter cited as *Maclean*).

[5] One of three major branches built southward from the Erie Canal, the Chenango Canal had been proposed as early as 1814. Repeated legislative defeats for the proposals served only to intensify the proponents' spirits. In February 1833, the Legislature approved the project. The *Albany Daily Advertiser* for February 23 (p. 2) noted that on the 21st a jubilant dinner for 200 was held at the Eagle Tavern in Albany. Even more jubilation was evident in the Chenango Valley (see "Chenango Canal Celebration," *Daily Albany Argus*, March 1, 1833, p. 2). But the canal, like the other southward branches, was a financial failure. See Noble E. Whitford, *History of the Canal System of the State of New York*, 2 vols. (Albany, 1906), *1*:672–695.

[6] Henry had previously encountered Jacob Trumpbour as a fellow surveyor and then later as an expert witness in Trumpbour's claim against Holmes Hutchinson (for these earlier contacts see the *Henry Papers*, *1*:99–113 passim, 428–432). On January 3, 1833, Trumpbour petitioned the Legislature for compensation after his premature dismissal from Hutchinson's canal survey. This petition, like several others of Trumpbour's throughout the 1830s, failed to win any compensation in addition to that granted in 1832. See *New York Assembly Journal*, 56th Session, 1833, pp. 84, 191, 701; also, *New York Assembly Documents*, 56th Session, 1833, No. 51 and *New York Assembly Documents*, 57th Session, 1834, No. 37.

[7] William Dod (1808–1883) graduated from Princeton in 1833. A clergyman, he taught languages and mathematics at various colleges

tution and although a modest man is much esteemed by all the Faculty. He formerly lived in Canada.

Give my love to Nancy and Mother. My respects to the rest of the Family.

As Ever Your
Brother

before taking charge of private schools in Ohio and New York. *Princeton Catalogue*, p. 145, and Allison Dodd and Joseph F. Folsom, *Genealogy and History of the Daniel Dod Family in America, 1646–1940* (Bloomfield, New Jersey, 1940), pp. 201, 205–206.

TO JAMES HENRY

Family Correspondence, Henry Papers, Smithsonian Archives

March 16th 1833

Dear James

Your two letters were received on the usual day of the week *viz* Wednesday. I was engaged on saturday last in the afternoon in preparing some articles of apparatus for my lectures and had only time to send you a paper informing you that we were all well.

We are hapy to hear that Mother is as well as she is and hope soon to give her the pleasure of seeing us with the Boy in Albany. Our term ends the 9th of April and we will start if nothing prevents as soon after that period as may be convenient. The Boy has been quite unwell this week on account of cutting one of his double teeth. He has however recovered and is to day apparently quite well. I fear that your many visitors will impose too heavy a task upon Nancy and that unless her health be very good she will be exhausted in attending to her guests and waiting on Mother at the same time.

We have had snow on the ground the whole time since I wrote last but it has nearly disappeared to day and this afternoon has the appearance of summer. The students are enjoying it as Saturday afternoon is a play spell to them. I am sorry to hear that John Wilson[1] is about finishing his course so soon but it is not surprising to me. Both he and Cushman[2] are melancholy examples of the baneful influence of the doctrines of Fany Wright.[3]

[1] According to Albany Academy records, John L. Wilson entered with the class of 1828–1829; John O. Wilson with that of 1829–1830. *Academy Seventy-fifth Anniversary*, pp. 87, 89.

[2] Several Cushmans studied at the Albany Academy. Robert S. Cushman and Thomas S. Cushman both entered with the class of 1829–1830, while Paul Cushman entered with that of 1831–1832. Ibid., pp. 88, 90.

[3] Frances Wright (1795–1852), the noted Scottish-born reformer who by 1833 had achieved a considerable reputation in the United States for her "radical" ideas and ex-

I am sory to learn by your letter before the last that Dr Beck[4] had some difficulty with his class. It is a circumstance which would have a tendency to give him great disquietud as he is peculiarly sensitive. It will not be proper for you to say anything about your surmise that the affair was instigated by persons in Albany. The acqusition has before been made that he is not a practicing phisician, but it is a rediculous one since the Dr. most industriously collects all the information published in nearly all the medical journals of the world and gives them to the class in a condensed and systimatic form. The students go to the Institution to learn the theory of medicine and not its practice as that can only be acquered in actual life. Dr. B. if he does not give the result of his own experience gives that of the most distinguished Physicians of the age. The mail closes in about 10 minuts. I can add no more.

Your Brother

P.S. Tell Mr McArthur that his old Teacher Mr Pryme has a son in the Theological Seminary. That he has been very sick and that nearly all of Mr Pryme's family have been in Princeton.[5] Mrs Pryme called at our house this afternoon. Her son is still unwell but is recovering.

My Love to Mother and Nancy
H

---

periments. These included the founding of the Nashoba settlement in western Tennessee, whose aim was to emancipate and then colonize slaves, and editing, with Robert Dale Owen, the *New Harmony Gazette*. Her attacks on religion from the lecture platform and her espousal of equal rights for women, with marriage based on moral rather than legal obligations, also went against established convention. *DAB*.

[4] Although Henry could be referring either to Lewis Caleb Beck (1798–1853), for whom see *Henry Papers, 1*:68–69, or to his brother Theodric Romeyn Beck (1781–1855), for whom see ibid., pp. 4–5, it seems more likely that he is here speaking of T. R. Beck. Both had practiced medicine before turning to teaching. Lewis Beck, however, lectured principally in the areas of botany, chemistry, and other allied subjects. T. R. Beck lectured primarily on medicine at the Western College of Physicians and Surgeons in Fairfield, Herkimer County, between 1815 and 1840 while serving as Principal of the Albany Academy (1817–1848). Both later taught at the Albany Medical College after its founding.

[5] Reverend Samuel McArthur (d. 1881), a tutor at the Albany Academy in 1831–1833 and 1834–1835 (*Academy Seventy-fifth Anniversary*, p. 70), is listed as a graduate of Union College with an A.B. degree in 1834, his residence at entrance being Cambridge, New York (*Union Catalog*, p. 45). Presumably he had attended the Cambridge Washington Academy in Washington County, New York, where Reverend Nathaniel S. Prime, for whom see *Henry Papers, 1*:320, was Principal in the 1820s before becoming Principal of the Mount Pleasant Academy, Westchester County, in 1830 (Franklin B. Hough, *Historical and Statistical Record of the University of the State of New York During the Century from 1784 to 1884* [Albany, 1885], pp. 593, 665). Prime's son, Samuel Irenaeus Prime (1812–1885), attended the Princeton Theological Seminary in 1832–1833. Ordained as a Presbyterian clergyman in 1835, he later went on to become a prolific author and editor for many years of the Presbyterian *New York Observer*. *Roberts*, p. 66 and *DAB*.

April 6, 1833

TO HARRIET HENRY

Family Correspondence, Henry Papers, Smithsonian Archives

Princeton Saturday 6 o'clock nearly
[April 6, 1833]

My Dear Hanky

I have just returned from evening prayers and although I feell some what fatigued will devote the time until the mail closes to you.[1] The examination commenced on monday last and will scarcely be finished before Tuesday next. We have had a very tedious time and this week and the latter part of the past have appeared of double the length of any equal space of time since I came to Princeton. What can be the reason? The weather has been charming. We have had company and all things have gone on prosperously with me. Still I have not been contented or hapy: perhaps you may guess the cause. I have found myself as it were involuntarily wandering from room to room as if in expectation of meeting with some person and been many times surprised on opening the door up stairs not to hear the exclamation "*dont wake* the baby". I have slept in the back room and your mother in our bead but the arrangement does not appear as yet quite natural & I have almost fancied myself in some strange house. I promised not to forget you and have kept my promise but am not intitled to much credit for doing so since I found it impossible to prevent the thoughts of you and our little boy from intruding themselves even when I should have been only occupied in attending to the recitations.

Stephen informed you how agreeably surprised we were in seeing Mrs. Meads[2] in Princeton. We had another visit to day equally unexpected, Mr & Mrs Morse[3] from Cherry Valley. They stoped but a short time and have gone to Burlington to spend the sabath and will return on monday when we expect they will dine or take tea with us. William and an old black man have been engaged several days in improving our court yard & have succeeded in making it quite respectable in appearance.

I have nothing new to tell you. Although the week has passed very heavily it has left nothing for rememberance. Mr. Jager[4] has called once and I

[1] Earlier correspondence, here omitted (Henry to James Henry, March 27, 1833, Family Correspondence, Henry Papers, Smithsonian Archives), shows that Henry sent his family ahead to Albany while delaying his own trip for the college examinations and his formal induction as Professor by the college Trustees. The dating of the present letter is easily ascertainable from the context of the surrounding letters.

[2] Louisa Meads, wife of John Meads.

[3] James O. Morse, identified in *Henry Papers, 1*:229n.

[4] Born in Vienna, the entomologist Benedict Jaeger (1789–1869) began his career as natural historian for the Czars of Russia, managing the natural history collections at the University of St. Petersburg and undertaking various

have spent one evening with Prof Dod[5] and last evening with Mr McLean. I must not forget to tell you that I employed a man this morning to tune your piano. He put in one new string. Mr Jager has promised to call this evening and try if it be well tuned. We accidentally heard from Webster[6] who was here last evening that Stephen gave his first address or sermon on Thursday evening last; he was so very shy about it that none of us suspected him of being engaged in preparing for it. Webster is about the same. The older Dod[7] and another student called last night with the hope of seeing Mrs. Henry. I was not at home.

If your next letter gives me no unfavourable intelligence concerning

---

expeditions in Russia and the West Indies. Accounts of his extensive entomological explorations through the Caucasus and the Crimea appeared in his *Reise von St. Petersburg in die Krim und die Länder des Kaukasus im Jahre 1825* (Leipzig, 1830).

Visiting the United States in 1831 and apparently introduced to Princeton through correspondence with John Torrey, Jaeger was hired by the college in 1832 to arrange its zoological collections, which led to subsequent appointments as Curator of the Museum, Lecturer on Natural History, and Professor of Modern Languages. In 1839 Jaeger arranged to exchange his personal natural history cabinet for a year's advance salary, a sign of the financial difficulties which may explain his abrupt departure from Princeton in 1841. According to Henry (see his letter to Snow, cited below), Jaeger hoped to recoup his losses through some manner of employment with the newly founded National Institute in Washington. He later resided in nearby Alexandria and in Providence, Rhode Island, and died in Brooklyn in 1869.

Jaeger's extensive writings include a manuscript catalog of the natural history collections at Princeton, a published lecture outline, *Analytical Table of a Systematical Course of Lectures on Zoology, Including Comparative Anatomy* (Princeton, 1835), and a text, *Class Book of Zoology* ... (New York, 1849). Jaeger's magnum opus was *The Life of North American Insects* (Providence, 1854), little more than a popular survey. According to Jaeger it was "a valuable ornament for the parlor table as well as an instructive and amusing companion" (as quoted in Weiss). Short on entomological fact and laced with personal and philosophical digressions, the work has been appraised as the "most worthless of all American insect books" (quoted in Weiss). But publication of three editions attested to its popularity among certain classes of readers. Harry B. Weiss, "Professor Benedict Jaeger, Early Entomologist of New Jersey," *Proceedings of the New Jersey Historical Society*, 1922, 7:196–207.

In a noncommittal response to an 1871 inquiry about Jaeger (Henry to [Edwin M. Snow], June 23, 1871, in volume labeled "Private Letters Written by Prof. Henry," Henry Papers, Smithsonian Archives), Henry confessed to knowing him intimately at Princeton, gave what he knew of his background, but deferred to Torrey for an appraisal of his scientific reputation. Henry certainly was familiar with Torrey's opinions from two 1835 letters (see Torrey's letters to Henry of January 16 and [March] 2, below). Having known Jaeger professionally and personally, Torrey confided that Jaeger was "only a clog to us" and prayed for his early departure from Princeton, hoping to replace him with his brilliant assistant, Asa Gray.

[5] Albert Baldwin Dod (1805–1845), Presbyterian clergyman and Professor of Mathematics at Princeton from 1830 until his death. See *Henry Papers, 1*:434n. A number of Dod's essays, devoted chiefly to theological and related subjects, were reprinted in the collection, *Essays, Theological and Miscellaneous, Reprinted from the Princeton Review* (New York and London, 1847).

[6] Richard Webster (1811–1856), a schoolmate of Stephen Alexander's at the Princeton Theological Seminary. *Henry Papers, 1*:73n.

[7] William Dod (1808–1883), for whom see above, Henry to James Henry, March 2, 1833, footnote 7. He was a classmate of his cousin Charles S. Dod (1814–1872) at Princeton. *Princeton Catalogue*, p. 145; Allison Dodd and Joseph F. Folsom, *Genealogy and History of the Daniel Dod Family in America, 1646–1940* (Bloomfield, New Jersey, 1940), pp. 201, 205–206.

mot[her] I will probably stop at West Point on my way up the river as I have some business there in regard to the N Philosophy they are about publishing.[8] I shall not be able to leave here until Wednesday and will probably not arrive in Albany until the last of the week.

Kiss the Boy for me. Give my love to Mother, Nancy & Aunt and for yourself be assured My Dear Wife I am more yours than ever.

J.H.

[8] E. H. Courtenay's *An Elementary Treatise on Mechanics* (New York, 1833). See above, Courtenay to Henry, January 3, 1833.

TO HARRIET HENRY

Family Correspondence, Henry Papers, Smithsonian Archives

Thursday evening [April 11, 1833][1]
Steamboat Constitution
¼ past 7 o'clock PM
about 25 miles above NY

My Dear Wife

I left Princeton yesterday morning and arrived at New York via Rail Road at 4 o'clock P.M. I left Mother and Stephen well and in very good spirits. The business of house cleaning was commenced the morning I started and it was with some difficulty, amid the taking up of carpets and the preparations for scouring and white washing, that I could make my escape. I was honoured by being the escort to N.Y. of Miss Provost the owner of the Parthenon villa near Jugtown.[2] She was very sociable and made the passage some what shorter by her chat &c.

[1] The original lacks the date. We have assigned this date based on our reconstructed itinerary of Henry's trip to West Point and Albany.

[2] Theodosia Ann Mary Prevost (1801–1864). A distant relative of Aaron Burr (her father, John Bartow Prevost, was a step-son of Burr), Miss Prevost never married and was a longtime prominent resident of Princeton who became legendary for her wealth and philanthropic activities. Bearing architect Charles Steadman's characteristic Greek Revival details, her home featured a six-pillared front portico which earned it the title "the Parthenon." The house was set back from Nassau Street, a few blocks east of central Princeton. That vicinity was called "Jugtown," a name derived from a pottery which prospered there from Revolutionary times until mid-nineteenth century. Evelyn Bartow, "The Provost Family in America," *The New York Genealogical and Biographical Record*, 1882, *13*:27–28. *Hageman*, *1*:268; V. Lansing Collins, *Princeton, Past and Present*, rev. ed. (Princeton, 1946), sections 143, 144; Constance M. Greiff, Mary W. Gibbons, and Elizabeth G. C. Menzies, *Princeton Architecture* (Princeton, 1967), pp. 89–94, and figure 62.

I called at Miss Van Antwerps[3] last evening and found Mrs King[4] and Miss Pegg both unwell with a cold. They were anxious to hear if you arrived safely in Albany. I promised to call again to day but did not find time to keep my promise. Mr Hart[5] came with me to New York also McCammon & Mr. Turner,[6] the person who loaned you the Dutchman's fire aid &c. Hart has gone to Hartford and Boston. McCammon to Long Island with a promise to be in Albany on Saturday. I informed you in my last that I would probably stop at West Point and intend doing so this evening. We will reach there in about two hours and a half from this time. Mr. Turner and two other students are on board and intend stoping with me at the Point.

I have been very busy to day in N.Y. in running about among the Literary Institutions. I called upon Prof. Renwick[7] and with him and his Lady visited the exhibition of the celebrated Ornithological drawings of Audubon.[8] Prof Renwick informed me that he was on the point of writing to me to come to New York a short time since inorder to meet Capt. Back who wished to see me in refference to my observations on magnetism and the aurora borealis[9] but the Capt* could not be detained in New York & I of course lost the oportunity of enjoying much pleasure from shuch an interview. The second object of Capt. Back's expedition is to descover the true position of the magnetic Poles of the earth. His instructions in refference to

* You will probably think this conversation was not very unpleasant to me.

[3] Margaret Van Antwerp, for whom see above, Henry to James Henry, November 7, 1832, footnote 3. In this same sentence Henry refers to her as "Miss Pegg."

[4] Sarah Van Antwerp King (1795–1867), wife of Jonathan O. King and sister of Margaret Van Antwerp. *New York Genealogical and Biographical Record*, April 1948, *79*:53; October 1948, *79*:220.

[5] Probably either John Seely Hart (for whom see below, Henry to Harriet Henry, March 24, 1834, footnote 13) or Alexander Chambers Hart. The latter was a Philadelphian in his senior year at Princeton in 1833. He received his M.D. degree from the University of Pennsylvania in 1836. He died in 1884. *Princeton Catalogue*, p. 145; *Princeton Annual Catalogue*, 1833.

[6] Fielding L. Turner was a senior at Princeton in 1833. His home was Natchez, Mississippi. We have found no further biographical information. *Princeton Catalogue*, p. 146; *Princeton Annual Catalogue*, 1833.

[7] James Renwick, Sr. (1792–1863). *DAB*. During his Albany years Henry had frequent contacts with Renwick on scientific matters, especially in terrestrial magnetism (see *Henry Papers*, *1*:passim). Renwick was Columbia's Professor of Natural Philosophy and Experimental Chemistry from 1820 until 1853. He was married to Margaret Ann Brevoort Renwick (1794–1868). Helen H. McIver, *Genealogy of the Renwick Family* (n.p., 1924), p. 3.

[8] John James Audubon (1785–1851), artist and naturalist, was first beginning to enjoy fame for his work on the *Birds of America* in the early 1830s. *DAB*.

[9] George Back (1796–1878), British Admiral and Arctic navigator. In February 1833 Back began a mission primarily to search for the missing Captain John Ross (1777–1856, *DNB*), but surveying the Arctic seacoast was an additional purpose. *DNB*. Henry had published his observations in *Silliman's Journal*, 1832, *22*:143–155, "On a Disturbance of the Earth's Magnetism, in Connexion with the Appearance of the Aurora Borealis, as Observed at Albany, April 19th, 1831." A related document is printed in *Henry Papers*, *1*:335–337.

his magnetic observations were drawn up by Prof. Christie[10] of Woolwich the person whom as you may recollect observed the deflection of the needle in England on the same evening that I did in America.

I also met with President Duer[11] of Columbia College. He was very polite. Said he was much pleased when he saw my appointment to Princeton and kindly invited me to visit him when I came to N.Y. It is not probable that I will be in Albany before Saturday evening as I have the old Hansteen Box of Needles with me and will make a set of observations with them at the Point. I had hopes of procuring from Col. Thayer the loan of the dipping needle belonging to the Point but unfortunatly the Col. is now in N.Y. and I was unable to find him.

Give my love to Mother and Nancy. Also to Aunt. Kiss the Boy for me (I am anxious to see how he will act when I present myself). I am very anxious to see you and several times to day have almost concluded to abandon my project of stopping at the Point but on reflection I think it important to spend some time in the Laboratory and Library of that Institution and shall not have an oportunity when I return.

Your Hubby

[10] Samuel Hunter Christie (1784–1865), mathematician and professor at Woolwich Military Academy from 1806 to 1854 (*DSB*, *DNB*). A well-known investigator of magnetism in that day, Christie published his observations, "On the Magnetic Influence Exhibited during an Aurora Borealis" in the *Journal of the Royal Institution of Great Britain*, 1831, 2:271–280. Christie later published an account of George Back's magnetic findings, "Discussion of the Magnetical Observations Made by Captain Back, R.N., During his Late Arctic Expedition," *Phil. Trans.*, 1836, part 2:377–415. The author's presentation copy survives in Henry's Library.

[11] William Alexander Duer (1780–1858), attorney, politician, and educator. As President of Columbia, 1829–1842, Duer's "attention was given particularly to certain curricular changes, notably the establishment of scientific courses in which Latin should not be required and the furthering of studies in the modern languages and in Hebrew." *DAB*. We know of no further contacts between Duer and Henry.

TO STEPHEN ALEXANDER[1]

Family Correspondence, Henry Papers, Smithsonian Archives

albany Tusday afternoon
April 16th 1833

Dear Stephen

Your letter reached Albany before me. It found all well excepting mother and she is about in the same state as when I last saw her in the winter.

[1] A file note by Henry indicates that he reacquired this letter at some later date.

The boy has been quite unwell since my arrival but is much better to day. He is broken out as before with a tooth rash and has suffered much in cutting a double tooth. Aunt has also been unwell with a very severe cold. She appears quite feeble and says she wishes she were at home again. We will probably go to Schenectady on Thursday. The ride will be of service to both Aunt and the Boy. You may be assured that we were all pleased with the communication of Dr Carnahan relative to the appointment or offer of appointment; to Harriet and Aunt it was quite unexpected. We hope you will not find it quite so disagreeable a post as the Dr represented it.[2] I called as I had intended, on my way up the river, at West Point and stoped there from Thursday evening 10 o'clock until saturday 11 AM. I arrived in albany at about 8 PM on the same day. My stay at the Point was of course very pleasant. The first morning was spent in the Library where I had an oportunity of seeing the latest No of the Annals of Chemestry and Physics.[3] The afternoon was occupied with drawing sparks from the large steel magnet which I touched when I was at the Point before. The next day, before my departure, from 7 until 11 o'clock I was engaged with Prof Courtnay[4] and his assistant Liut. Cam[5] in making the magnetic observations. I regretted to learn while at the Point that Col. Thayer had resigned his post as commandant of the military academy and that he leaves the Point the first of July. The cause of his resignation is that Pres. Jackson is a personal enemy and has reversed several orders of the Col.[6] The academic staff lament the circumstance of his leaving and have expressed their esteem for his character by requesting that he will sit for his Picture.

I forgot to mention that I procured from Prof. Renwick the Hansteen

[2] A reference to Alexander's appointment as a Tutor at Princeton with a salary of $300. College of New Jersey, Trustees' Minutes, April 10, 1833, Princeton University Archives.

[3] *Annales de chimie et de physique*. This leading French scientific periodical was not then in the Princeton college library.

[4] i.e., Edward H. Courtenay.

[5] Thomas Jefferson Cram (1803–1883), a West Point graduate (1826), then serving as Assistant Professor of Natural and Experimental Philosophy at the United States Military Academy. He resigned from this post and the Army in 1836. The *Royal Society Catalogue* lists him as the author of three articles from 1835–1837: one a mathematical description of the shape of the earth and two on the physical properties of materials. From 1836 to 1838 he worked as a private engineer on railroads in Pennsylvania and Maryland. In 1838 Cram became a Captain in the Topographical Engineers, reaching the rank of Major at the start of the Civil War and serving on various surveys and internal improvement projects. In 1865 Cram became a Colonel in the Corps of Engineers and for his services was brevetted as Brigadier and Major General, retiring in 1869. Despite this early instance of collaboration with Henry in electromagnetism and terrestrial magnetism, Cram does not loom large in Henry's later career. G. W. Cullum, *Biographical Register of the Officers and Graduates of the United States Military Academy at West Point, New York*, rev. ed., 2 vols. (New York, 1879; hereafter cited as *Cullum*).

[6] See Stephen E. Ambrose, *Duty, Honor, Country: A History of West Point* (Baltimore, 1966), pp. 106–124. Jackson did not relish the professional military spirit fostered so ably by Thayer (*DAB*).

needles and the observations I alluded to above were [made] with them and the splendid dipping needle of the Point. Col Thayer was absent when I arrived at the Point and did not return until the morning just before I left so that I had no oportunity of requesting him to loan me the Dipping needle to carry with me to Albany. Lieut Cam however has promised to come to albany some time during my stay and to bring the needle with him. Our observations at the Point were made in Military Stile under a large tent pitched for the purpose in the middle of the Campus.

I have made some inquire about the situation of the house in Schenectady and will endeavour to have the whole arranged.

Hugh Alexander of Galway was here this morning on his way from New York. He intended to stay some days in albany but was obliged to leave in the first car on account of hearing that his father, Uncle John,[7] had been struck with paralysis on Tuesday last. Hugh had heard no particulars but has promised to write immediatly on his return. Mother is very anxious to hear from Uncle John. This is the 2nd attack and little hopes can be entertained of his recovery.

Your Brother
Joseph

This letter has been accidentally delayed from not being sent to the Post Office. The delay however has furnished me with an oportunity of informing you that the two Miss Meads have concluded to accompany us on our return to Princeton. J.H.

[7] John Alexander, the twin brother of Henry's mother.

FROM T. J. CRAM

Henry Papers, Smithsonian Archives

West Point 16 April 1833.

Dear Sir,

The discordant results given by the observations we made on Saturday relative to the Dip determined Prof^r^ Courtenay & myself to take the observations anew. We did so on Monday (yesterday), with what success you will see from Table N° 2 relative to the Dip. The observations, or results in

Table No 1 are entitled to no, or very little weight. The errors, *probably*, are where pointed out in the column of remarks. The results however given in Table No 2, are entitled to be received with as much confidence as any Profr C. & myself are capable of obtaining.[1]

I extracted the article you wished from "Annals de Chimie"[2] rather than to attempt a translation which might have left some part imperfect. Any information I can render you in a similar, or any other, way, from our Library will most cheerfully be given, on an intimation from yourself to that effect.

I intend now to go to Albany next week, Thursday. Should any thing transpire to prevent you from being ready to take our observations on the following Friday & Saturday please let me know before by Thursday morning.

Have you a magnet in Albany to reverse the poles of our needles with?

Very respectfully
Yours sincerely T. J. Cram

[1] Perhaps Cram intended to bring the tables with him to Albany, as his letter, written on a small sheet of brown paper, would not seem to permit their enclosure. In any event, they have not been found. However, observations on the magnetic dip made at West Point on April 15 are included in a table in A. D. Bache and Edward H. Courtenay, "Observations to Determine the Magnetic Dip at Baltimore, Philadelphia, New York, West Point, Providence, Springfield and Albany," *Transactions of the American Philosophical Society*, 1837, n.s. 5:213. The observers are listed as Courtenay and Henry, but if the date is correct, the observers were Courtenay and Cram, as Cram notes; Henry left West Point on April 13 after he and Courtenay, assisted by Cram, had spent the morning making observations (see above, Joseph Henry to Stephen Alexander, April 16, 1833).

[2] Volume 51 of the *Annales de chimie et de physique*, the third for 1832 and the latest Henry could have seen at West Point, contains several articles that might have interested him. Included in this volume are: M. Hachette, "De l'Action chimique produite par l'induction électrique; décomposition de l'eau," pp. 72–76; M. Ampère, "Note de M. Ampère sur une expérience de M. Hippolyte Pixii, relative au courant produit par la rotation d'un aimant, à l'aide d'un appareil imaginé par M. Hippolyte Pixii," pp. 76–79; Étienne (Stefano) Marianini, "Mémoire sur les phénomènes que présente un arc métalique plongeant par des surfaces inégales à ses extrémités dans deux portions séparées d'un même fluide lors-qu'il sert à conduire l'électricité de l'une à l'autre," pp. 130–149; and "Lettre adressée à M. Gay-Lussac par M. Faraday, sur les phénomènes électro-magnétiques," pp. 404–434.

April 18, 1833

TO BENJAMIN SILLIMAN, SR.

Daniel C. Gilman Collection, Library, Johns Hopkins University

Albany April 18th 1833

Dear Sir

This will be given you by my Friend Dr Thomas Hun*[1] who is about visiting Europe for the purpose of improving himself in the Medical Profession. He expressed a desire to form an acquaintance with you before his departure and I take the liberty of giving him an introduction. He is a young Gentleman worthy of full confidence, is a member of one of the most respectable Dutch families of this city; a graduate of Union College and of the medical department of the University of Pennsylvania. I have been very intimate with Dr. H. for the last twelve years and know him to be a young Gentleman of fine talents although you will find him modest and unassuming. If on my recommendation you should think fit to give him letters to Persons in Europe I have no hesitation in saying that you will thus indirectly aid the cause of American Science as I am confident Dr Hun will profit by any opportunities he may have for acquiring scientific knowledge.

I am now on a visit to my Mother in Albany and have just finished my first term at Princeton. I am much pleased with my situation and thus far have no cause to regret my exchange. My duties are pleasant and congenial to my taste and I have so exerted myself as not entirely to disappoint the Trustees and Faculty of the college in the character you and some of my other friends were so kind as to give me. I have as yet however found no leisure for collateral studies as it is necessary to devote my undivided attention to the subjects I am called upon to teach at least until I have once gone over the course. Besides this I found the Philosophical apparatus in a very desarranged state and much of my time has been occupied in putting it in some what better order.

I have been much at a loss since my residence at Princeton in not being

* As I fear this letter will not wreach Dr Hun I have concluded to send it by mail. He will probably be in New Haven shortly after the receipt of this letter. J H

[1] Hun (1808–1896) was a contemporary of Henry's at the Albany Academy in the early 1820s. After attending Union (B.A. 1826) and the University of Pennsylvania (M.D. 1830), Hun practiced medicine in Albany and then studied abroad, 1833–1839. When Henry visited Paris in 1837, Hun acted as his interpreter (*Coulson*, p. 121). Hun returned to practice in Albany and distinguished himself as a leader in countless community affairs. For the last ten years of his life he served as President of the Board of Trustees of the Albany Academy. He published several medical lectures and a paper on agriculture, but he never published any contributions to science. W. L. L. Peltz, *The Top Flight at Number One La Fayette Street* (Albany, 1939), pp. 75–76.

able to see any of the Scientific Journals of the day. The college library although very valuable in some departments is defective in not having the Journals posted up to the present time.[2] Arrangements however on my suggestion have been made to remedy this.

I find several interesting papers on the subject of electro-magnetism in the last No of your Journal which have forcably recalled my attention to the subject.[3] The facts developed are all except one in accordance with my previous notions of the dynamic action of the electrical principle as exhibited in Magnetic and Galvanic <*action*> phenomina. The only one which appears surprising to me is that which you mention of a flash being observed between the lifter and the poles of the large Galvanic magnet. I am intirely at a loss to conceive how the magnetic action in that case could produce by induction an electrical current. The subject deserves investigation as it may lead to some new principle of electrical and magnetic action.[4]

On my passage up the Hudson I stoped at West Point and spent one day in the Library in posting up my knowledge of the sciences of magnetism and electricity: [5] before leaving Albany last fall I had an oportunity of studying Mr Farady's original papers in the last No of the Phil. Transactions[6] and

[2] Compare Henry's dissatisfaction with the Princeton library with the pride he took in the Albany Institute's library. See Henry to John Maclean, June 28, 1832, *Henry Papers*, *1*:435.

[3] The first number of volume 24 of *Silliman's Journal* contained John P. Emmet's "A New Mode of Developing Magnetic Galvanism, by Which May Be Obtained, Shocks, Vivid Sparks and Galvanic Currents from the Horse-shoe Magnet" (pp. 78–86), Oliver P. Hubbard's translation of Ampère's "Communication to the Academy of Sciences upon an Experiment of M. Pixii Relative to a Current Produced by Rotation of a Magnet with an Improved Apparatus, Oct. 29, 1832" (pp. 144–145; this is a translation of the article cited above, Cram to Henry, April 16, 1833, footnote 2), and Charles T. Jackson's "Notice of the Revolving Electric Magnet of M. Pixii, of Paris . . ." (pp. 146–149). Following Jackson's article are additional remarks by Silliman on experiments conducted at the Yale laboratory, described in the following footnote.

[4] Henry refers to the above-mentioned Silliman addendum, "Experiments in the Laboratory of Yale College.—Sparks and Shocks from the Magnet." In the first part of his remarks, Silliman obtained sparks between a permanent horseshoe magnet and its keeper using a setup like Emmet's, described in the same issue. A coil was wound around the keeper. One end of the coil was attached to the keeper itself and the other to the body of the magnet. These results apparently did not bother Henry.

In the second part, Silliman reports using Henry's Yale electromagnet and obtaining sparks between keeper and magnet when the electromagnet was energized and the keeper attracted up to it. There apparently was no coil around the keeper. The reason for Henry's puzzlement at this effect is discussed below in Silliman to Henry, April 23, 1833, footnote 4.

[5] At West Point a few days prior to this letter, Henry had been consulting the latest volume of the *Annales de chimie*. See above, T. J. Cram to Henry, April 16, 1833, footnote 2.

[6] Henry here refers to the First and Second Series of Michael Faraday's "Experimental Researches in Electricity." The First Series (1. On the induction of electric currents. 2. On the evolution of electricity from magnetism. 3. On a new electrical condition of matter. 4. On Arago's magnetic phenomena.) appeared in *Phil. Trans.*, 1832, pp. 125–163. In this article, Faraday announced his discovery of mutual electromagnetic induction, a discovery of paramount interest to Henry in Albany. The Series was noticed in *Silliman's Journal*, 1832, 22:386–387, 409–415, the latter

think I have now a clear and connected view of the whole subject as far as the facts have been published. The whole may be simply refered to the general laws of electro-magnetism as announced in the theory of Ampere with the exception of the fact you have noticed.[7]

The Senior Class of Princeton College are dismissed six weeks before the commencement and as I expect to be but little engaged during that period and will have finished my collegiate year I now propose to myself the pleasure of resuming my favourite pursuit at that time.

---

part being communicated by Alexander Dallas Bache. The Second Series (5. Terrestrial magneto-electric induction. 6. Force and direction of magneto-electric induction generally.) also appeared in the 1832 volume of the *Phil. Trans.*, pp. 163–194.

[7] Already an Ampèrian in Albany, Henry continued to frame his expanded electromagnetic researches at Princeton within the French physicist's electrodynamic theories. At this date, André-Marie Ampère was still the preeminent authority in the theory of electricity and magnetism. Although we know in retrospect that Michael Faraday would have resisted Henry's notion that his latest findings on induction fell totally within Ampère's compass, his publications reflected the extensive influence of the French theoretician. L. P. Williams maintains, however, that Faraday's First Series, despite its surface politeness to Ampère, marked a significant theoretical break from the Ampèrian framework. Relying on the Faraday laboratory *Diary* (Thomas Martin, ed., *Faraday's Diary*, 8 vols. [London, 1932]), Williams draws a distinction between Faraday's public politeness and tribute to Ampère and the strong private reservations that evidently guided him in the laboratory. *Michael Faraday* (New York, 1965), pp. 191–202, develops this interpretation. Yet we feel that Henry's perception of the basic agreement between Faraday and Ampère was not entirely mistaken and that their relationship was less antagonistic than Williams believes. Faraday's open enthusiasm for much of Ampère's work in the First Series may well have been more than politely superficial. In any case, evidence exists that the two physicists were eventually able to work out at least some of their theoretical differences. See Henry's "Record of Experiments," August 22, 1834, footnote 12.

Faraday's novel hypothesis of the electrotonic state, used in the First Series to explain the inductive effect, evidently failed to interest Henry. At least Henry makes no significant use of the concept for his own work. Nor does Henry specify how Faraday's discoveries were to be derived from Ampère's theories. His allegiance to Ampère, evident throughout his lecture notes and scientific papers, was more general than specific. His notes contain the repeated assertion that all electromagnetism depended on one Ampèrian fact and hypothesis: the fact of the mutual action of two currents and the hypothesis of the electrical basis of magnetism—the theory of the electrodynamic molecule. The latter was the one Ampèrian hypothesis that did find specific application throughout Henry's electrical research. For an extended discussion of Henry's use of the electrodynamic molecule see footnote 12 of the above-cited entry from the "Record of Experiments." By the middle of the 1830s Henry's devotion to Ampère was well known to his scientific colleagues. In "A Brief Account of the Theory of Ampère," an appendix to Robert Hare's *An Exposition of the Sciences of Galvanism and Electro-Magnetism, Abstracted from the Fifth Edition of Turner's Chemistry*, circa 1835, Hare pointed up Henry's debt to Ampère.

Henry's Library contains only two pamphlets by Ampère: "Mémoire sur une nouvelle expérience électro-dynamique, sur son application à la formule qui représente l'action mutuelle de deux élémens de deux conducteurs voltaïques, et sur de nouvelles conséquences déduites de cette formule," *Annales de chimie et de physique*, 1825, *29*:381–404; and *Exposé des nouvelles découvertes sur l'électricité et le magnétisme, de MM. Oersted, Arago, Ampère, H. Davy, Biot, Erman, Schweiger, De la Rive, etc.* (Paris, 1822). The latter is annotated. It appears, however, that Henry's knowledge of Ampère came principally not from the physicist's own writings but from authoritative secondary works by editors and translators like P. M. Roget and James Cumming, whose works are cited in the "Record of Experiments" entry referred to above.

I have not yet visited Philadelphia to avail myself of your kind introduction to Prof. Hare and Dr Morton but intend going there the last week of our pres[ent] vacation.[8]

I was much gratified to learn from a friend that Capt. Back had expressed a wish to have some conversation with the person who published a paper on the disturbance of the magnetic needle at the time of an Aurora, in the American Journal.[9]

Prof. Renwick has been so kind as again to intrust me with the Hansteen magnetic apparatus. I made a series of observations with the needles at West Point and in company with Prof. Courtnay accuratly determined the dip at that Place. I intend repeating during this visit my observations at Albany and expect a gentleman[10] from the Point with the dipping needle belonging to the military Academy. If he comes we will determine the dip and that will complete the series of observations necessary to a complete knowledge of the state of terrestrial magnetism at Albany.[11] I enclose $6 the ammount for the Journal fore one year. Please direct that my copy be sent either from New Haven or New York to Princeton by Mail. If you should happen to have any message to me please deliver the same to my Friend Dr. Hun. I am sir with sentiments of Gratitude and Esteem your Obt Serv

Joseph Henry

[8] Silliman wrote to Henry, October 11, 1832, informing him that he would write letters of introduction to Robert Hare and Samuel George Morton in Philadelphia. See *Henry Papers*, *1*:460–461.

[9] See above, Henry to Harriet Henry, [April 11, 1833], especially footnote 9.

[10] Lieutenant Cram. See above, Henry to Stephen Alexander, April 16, 1833, footnote 5.

[11] Henry's observations, completed during his April visit, were included in A. D. Bache and Edward H. Courtenay, "Observations to determine the Magnetic Dip at Baltimore, Philadelphia, New York, West Point, Providence, Springfield and Albany," (read November 7, 1834) *Transactions of the American Philosophical Society*, 1837, n.s. *5*:209–215. Henry's annotated reprint survives in the Henry Library.

FROM BENJAMIN SILLIMAN, SR.

Henry Papers, Smithsonian Archives

New Haven April 23 1833

Dear Sir

I annex a receipt for your remittance of $6. which will cover Volumes 24 & 25. I will send by Mr Hunn[1] Nos of Vol 24 presuming that you have not received your own copy altho you have seen the No.

[1] See Henry to Benjamin Silliman, Sr., April 18, 1833, footnote 1, above.

I am glad it interests you & I hope I shall hear from you again in due time respecting electro-magnetism which is becoming constantly more & more interesting. The spark seen between the keeper & the magnet when the keeper was lifted was reported to me by one of my pupils & was not seen by myself. He said it was very distinct & I have no reason to doubt that he actually saw it. Would it not be well to repeat this trial in a dark room in order that we may see whether it is a common occurrence. I presume that it would not be necessary to load the magnet & that a plunge of the battery & the lifting of the keeper would be all that is necessary. Probably it would be seen also as in the other magnet,[2] in sliding the keeper off from the poles, but with the great adhesion of your magnet it might not be easy to do that.

Why is it—a priori—improbable that your magnet should give a spark any more than that it should be given by the armed common magnet?[3] Is not the induced magnetism of yours a fair offset against the permanent magnetism of the other & thus both being magnets is not their relation to the circumscribing wire then the same & if the permanent magnet gives a spark, why should not the temporary magnet do the same.[4] But I submit this to your better judgment & I doubt not that you have taken a more enlarged & correct view of the electro-dynamic phenomena & theory than I have done.

The best way to receive your journal is by mail tho postage is the only

[2] The permanent magnets discussed in the first part of Silliman's article.

[3] i.e., a magnet fitted with a keeper, or armature.

[4] For Henry, the issue was not galvanic as opposed to permanent magnetism, for he knew that both types of magnet yielded induced currents and sparks under proper conditions. What he questioned was the ability of any magnet to induce a current in its armature rather than in the coil customarily wound around the armature. Silliman's meaning is unclear but it would seem that the two situations he described are not equivalent. In the case of the experiment with the permanent magnet, the coil around the keeper was connected directly to the magnet and the keeper itself, so that the induced current through the coil would flow through the magnet and armature. The coil of the galvanic magnet, on the other hand, was completely insulated from the magnet itself and any current in the magnetic core or armature must occur by induction, which Henry at this time thought unlikely. Henry later changed his opinion after investigating the effect of metal screens interposed between induction coils. In "Contributions III," (1838), Henry attributed the screening effect to neutralizing secondary currents induced in the interposed plates. He suggested that the same effect might interfere with the output of magnetoelectric machines. (See paragraphs 64–76.) In a note at the end of "Contributions III," Henry mentioned that the Viennese physicist Andreas Ritter von Ettingshausen recently sought to improve outputs of magnetoelectric machines by eliminating suspected secondary currents induced in the keeper of the machine. In this same period, the electrical experimentalist C. G. Page was pursuing a similar line of research, being especially interested in the technological possibilities of magnetoelectric machines. In 1842, Page announced his experimental confirmation of currents induced in the core of electromagnets. C. G. Page, "Magneto-Electric and Electro-Magnetic Apparatus and Experiments," *Silliman's Journal*, 1839, *35*:252–268, and "Notice of a Spiral Magnet, by Which Secondary Currents May Be Demonstrated in the Body of the Magnet," Franklin Institute *Journal*, 1842, 3d ser. *3*:166–167.

objection. There is an agent in Princeton but it may be 2 or 3 weeks before you get your N°. I could always send it promptly to my nephew, A. E. Silliman,[5] Merchants Bank, New York to await the call of any friend who may be going to New York. If I did not receive new directions I will continue to forward the N°. by mail.

I am pleased that you find your situation so agreeable in Princeton. It was indeed a very honorable & advantageous retirement from your severe labors & general treatment in Albany & if my opinion of you had any weight in deciding the matter I am much gratified.

I write in much haste having broken away from a college exhibition to give you this hurried scrawl by Dr Hunn for whom I will do every thing in my power.

Let me hear from you when convenient & believe me always very truly

your friend & servt
B. Silliman

Prof. Jos. Henry
Recd of Profr Joseph Henry Six Dollars in advance for Volumes twenty four & twenty five of the American Journal of Science & Arts.
New Haven April 23 1833

B. Silliman
Ed & Profr.

[5] Augustus Ely Silliman (1807–1884) was a New York banker, businessman, co-founder of the Mercantile Clearing House, and from 1857 to 1868 President of the Merchant's Bank. Silliman reportedly engaged in astronomical studies and literary pursuits, being the author of *A Gallop Among American Scenery* (New York, 1843). Harry R. Stiles, ed., *The Civil, Political, Professional and Ecclesiastical History and Commercial and Industrial Record of the County of Kings and the City of Brooklyn, N.Y., from 1683 to 1884* (New York, 1884); *Who Was Who in America: Historical Volume, 1607–1896*, rev. ed. (Chicago, 1967), p. 555.

TO HARRIET HENRY

Family Correspondence, Henry Papers, Smithsonian Archives

albany April 25th 1833

My Dear Hanky

You were informed by Judge Ryley[1] that Stephen arrived in albany on saturday last. I was much surprised to see the gentleman when I came home from Schenectady and was some what puzzled to make out the cause of a

[1] *Henry Papers, 1*:444, footnote 5.

strange appearance in the gentleman's figure. I however soon discovered that it was occasioned by his being incased in a frock coat of the Princeton cut. He left Princeton at 11 o'clock on Friday morning and arrived in albany at 5 o'clock the next morning, a passage somewhat shorter than your own. We expect Lieut. Cram from West Point to day and will be engaged with him in making observations tomorrow[2] so that you must not expect us before Saturday. Stephen thinks of going to Herkimer before his return to Princeton. As the canal is now open the jaunt will not be unpleasant or require a long time. Mother is about the same as when you left albany. She has asked me more than a doz of times if I have written to you and fears that you will be very anxious to hear from us. I arrived at home on Saturday evening about 9 o'clock. The ride was not very pleasant as we were delayed some time on account of one of the car's running off the road. Fortunatly no accident happened and the car was replaced on the rails by the united force of all the male passengers in the three cars.[3] The mail closes in a few minuts if it has not already closed so that I can only have time to assure you that I am as ever your most affectionate

To My Dear little Wiffe Husband

[2] Henry recorded the observations made on April 26, as well as those made the two previous days, in a small pocket notebook (no. [30031]; Henry Papers, Smithsonian Archives). He apparently used this and a similar notebook (no. [30032]) whenever he made observations on terrestrial magnetism in the field. Each entry (all between 1833 and 1835) consists largely of readings, headed by the date and place of observation, and sometimes the needle used. Henry occasionally gives a brief description of weather conditions and of unusual meteorological phenomena observed. Some of the notations appear to be by Stephen Alexander, who frequently observed with Henry.

[3] Henry was apparently traveling on the Mohawk and Hudson Railroad, which opened in 1831. The cars were pulled by a locomotive. Information from John H. White, Jr., of the National Museum of History and Technology.

TO JACOB GREEN

Private Collection, Albany, New York

Albany May 8th 1833

My Dear Sir

Permit me to introduce to your acquaintance My Friend Dr Thomas Hunn[1] of Albany. You are probably acquainted with some of his relatives in this city as he is of the Gansevoort family. Dr Hunn is about visiting

[1] Henry frequently misspells Hun, identified above, Henry to Silliman, April 18, 1833, footnote 1.

Europe for the purpose of increasing his stock of medical and general scientific knowledge and now goes to your city for the purpose principally of obtaining letters of introduction to some of the *Savants* of Germany France or England. If it be consistent with your custom in such cases you will confer a peculiar favour on me by furnishing him with letters to some of your scientific friends in Europe.

Dr Hunn is a graduate of Union College and also of the medical department of the University of Pennsylvania. I have been intimately acquainted with him since he was twelve years old and know him, although a modest unassuming person, to be a young gentleman of fine talents and for his years of extensive acquirements. He is worthy of any introduction you may be pleased to give him.

I intended to accompany Dr Hunn to Philadelphia but have been unexpect[edly] prevented by the sickness of my little boy. Our vacation at Princeton ends on the 16th inst and as I will not be able to leave albany before the 13th or 14th it will be impossible for me to visit you at this time.

I have spent part of the vacation at Albany in finishing a series of magnetic observations, which I commenced two years since,[2] on the variation of the needle, on the dip, and on the magnetic intensity. I beleave that albany is now the only place in the United States where all the observations have been made necessary to determine its actual magnetic state. There is a wide field in this country for the industrious observer in this department of Natural History[3] as it may properly be called.

I am Sir with the highest
Respect Yours sincerely
Joseph Henry

[2] In the fall of 1830. See *Henry Papers, 1*: 290n.

[3] In the sense of conducting a systematic inquiry into a "set of natural phenomena, as those connected with a country, some division of nature or group of natural objects, a species of animals or plants, etc." *Oxford English Dictionary*, 1961 ed., s.v. "History"; also "Natural History." This special usage of "history," which can be traced at least to Aristotle, did not involve a time dimension. Henry probably meant to distinguish a descriptive, classificatory activity from the more analytical or experimental parts of physical science. Natural history, which subsumed what are currently separate scientific specialties, now has a more popular, less scientific connotation than in Henry's day. It is now more familiarly applied to living things than to inanimate phenomena.

Henry's opinion here is supported by his advocacy of the inclusion of terrestrial magnetism observations in the New York State Natural History Survey (to be documented in volume three of *The Papers of Joseph Henry*).

May 17, 1833

TO JAMES HENRY

Family Correspondence, Henry Papers, Smithsonian Archives

Princeton May 17th 1833
Friday evening

Dear James

I sent word by Orlando Meads[1] that we had arrived safely at New York and that the boy was apparently no worse on account of the journey. He was very restless aboard the boat when awake but he slept tolerably well. We left New York at 6 o'clock on Wednesday morning and after a very plesent passage arrived at home a little after 12 O'clock at noon. The boy was much pleased with the ride until the last few miles when he began to be a little weary. The ride appeared on the whole to do him good and he has continued to get better and grow stronger almost every hour since our arrival. He attempted to walk a little to day but is still very weak although his appetite is most excellent. We found every thing in most excellent order at Princeton. Motherinlaw had exerted herself in having the house and garden perfectly arranged.

The College Campus or green has a most beautiful appearance and every thing about Princeton at this season is delightful.

We commenced our duties to day although the college was opened for the admission of the returning students yesterday at 2 o'clock.

Stephen has entered upon his new duties and will sleep in his room in college, for the first time to night. I would have written yesterday but was prevented by a meeting of the faculty until it was too late for the mail which now leaves here for Albany at 9 o'clock in the morning. The mail from New York and Albany arrives now at noon instead of the night as formerly, so that a letter from you will reach us several hours sooner than one before the new arrangement.

It commenced raining on Wednesday afternoon and continued to rain

[1] Orlando Meads (1806–1884) was a lifelong friend of Henry's. He attended the Albany Academy from 1815 to 1825 and was, therefore, a student with Henry. Meads graduated from Union in 1826 and was admitted to the bar in 1829. Active in local church and civic affairs, he also served as a Trustee of the Albany Academy from 1847 to 1884, and as President of the Board of Trustees from 1881 to 1884. Meads was an active member of the Albany Institute from its founding in 1824 until his death, serving the last four years as its President. W. L. L. Peltz, *The Top Flight at Number One LaFayette Street* (Albany, 1939), pp. 63–64.

Correspondence between the two men continued until Henry's death. Although some of the letters refer to financial matters which Meads was handling for Henry, much of the content is of a personal, philosophical nature. Henry was also acquainted with Orlando Meads's family, particularly with his father, John Meads, and two of his sisters, Charlotte and Louisa; in 1836 Louisa Meads married Stephen Alexander.

until to day when it cleared off about noon and the afternoon has been clear and very pleasant.

Mother has without doubt been very anxious to hear from the boy and will probably have come to the conclusion that he is worse on account of the journey. I hope however *she* has not become worse from apprehension and that this letter will satisfy her that we have all reached home in good health and spirits.

Write immediatly on the receipt of this and also let us hear from you as before once a week. Tell us if little Mary[2] has returned and if not whether there be any prospet of Nancy's getting another girl. It is too much for her to do the work of so large a family without some help.

Give my respects to Mr Bullions, Dr Ten Eyck, Mr. Dean, Mr. Newlands,[3] McArthur, Sammons, Dr Selkirk, Dr. Wing and all others whom I should remember.

Tell Mrs. Fisher or request Nancy to tell her that I regret that I could not find time to visit the Captain again,[4] but that I will pay my respects to him should we both live until next fall. Should you happen to see young Cushman[5] tell him that I have left his book at Mother's.

Harriet joins me in love to Mother and Nancy.

Your Brother
Joseph

Saturday morning
May 18th

All well. Stephen and myself were engaged last night in making observations, a most beautiful Aurora borealis which appeared in the form of an arch across the heavens. Enquire of Dr Ten Eyck if it was seen in albany and if it produced any effect on the needle. I have not finished the observation and therefore do not know as yet if the aurora disturbed the magnetism

[2] Unidentified.

[3] Luke F. Newland (ca. 1793–1855), an Albany resident who was a jeweler and then had a music store. He was a member of the Third Department (History and General Literature) of the Albany Institute, having joined in 1836. In 1851 Newland spoke on the philosophy of history before the Institute. Reynolds, *Alb. Chron.*, p. 587, refers to him as a man of "literary and social attainments." For his son, John Newland, see below, Henry to Harriet Henry, October 24, 1835, footnote 13.

[4] Mrs. Fisher is the person to whom Henry pays his pew rent (Joseph to Harriet Henry, December 15, 1832, Family Correspondence, Henry Papers, Smithsonian Archives). We have tentatively identified her as the Mary Fisher, wife of Dr. John Fisher, who died in 1840 (Munsell, *Ann. Alb.*, *10*:301). Munsell also notes the death of a Captain John Fisher in 1841 at age 81 (*Ann. Alb.*, 7:110). The city directories of this period do not list a physician of that name nor a person bearing that martial title. A John Fisher had a crockery store, 1830–1841, and other establishments earlier. We suspect that the crockery merchant, the captain, and the doctor are the same person—a John P. Fisher of N.Y. who was a Surgeon's Mate in the United States Navy, 1800–1803, the naval and medical titles being by courtesy, not by virtue of occupation.

[5] William M. Cushman. See *Henry Papers*, *1*:351.

of the earth or not. I will make an other observation to day and if the needle vibrates 300 times in precisely the same number of minutes and seconds that it did last night then the aurora had no effect but if the time be longer or shorter the magnetism of the earth was disturbed.[6]

[6] We do not know if Henry reached any firm conclusions from this comparison. Although Henry's rough data survives in a pocket notebook (no. [30031]) the readings are too sketchy for us to anticipate his conclusions.

TO JAMES HENRY

Family Correspondence, Henry Papers, Smithsonian Archives

Princeton [May] 25th [1833] Saturday[1]

Dear James

Your letter of the 18th was quite full of news. I am very sorry that mother was so much distressed on account of not hearing from us. I informed you in my last that Orlando Meads had promised to send word to Mother as soon as he reached home that he had seen us and that the boy was no worse from his journey. We are all well. The Boy continues to improve in health. He had however a slight attack of the relax[2] this week but is better again.

Motherinlaw with Dr Carnahan's lady[3] took an excursion of 5 miles into the country yesterday afternoon inorder to purchase a cow. They had a very pleasant ride and returned safely except that English William[4] who went as driver run the waggon against a post as he was entering the yard at home and broke off both shafts. He was much elated before the accident with his success in driving but was much mortified afterward and in a very manly way offered to pay the damages. We are to have a young cow and a calf for 24 dollars.

A small enclosure was made in the yard during our absence for the cow and the wood house and stable was repaired. The Death of Mr Packard and his son[5] was quite sudden and very unexpected. I walked up street from

[1] Joseph Henry had written "Princeton April 25th Saturday." The year 1833 was written in by someone else, and there is also a file note on the address side of the letter indicating the year. The reference to the floods, the mention of Meads, and a faint postmark indicate that the month was actually May rather than April.

[2] i.e., diarrhea.

[3] Mary Van Dyke (d. 1854) of Mapleton, New Jersey, married James Carnahan in 1803. She was the mother of two daughters. *Hageman*, 2:276; Donald Drew Egbert, *Princeton Portraits* (Princeton, 1947), p. 57. For her parents and sister, see note 3 of the letter of June 25, 1833, printed below.

[4] William Bannard (see note 8 of the letter of November 24, 1832, printed above).

[5] Benjamin D. Packard (1779–1833) was the

Littles[6] to the English church[7] with young Packard when I first went to Albany; he appeared feeble at that time but said that he was getting much better. It is a fortunate circumstance that the Misses Meads[8] did not come with us to Princeton.

I am very sorry to hear that Judge Conkling[9] is likely to get into difficulty and that he is loosing friends. He has allways been very kind and friendly toward me. I was first introduced to him by Mr. Gibson[10] at the time <*he*> (Mr Gibson) had the trial with Starbuck[11] on accont of his patent plough.[12] He afterwards attended Dr Beck's Lectures on chemestry when I was the assistant[13] and was a partener of Mr Hammond when I started on the Road survey.[14]

He has from the first uniformly treated me with attention and politeness

---

publisher of the *Albany Evening Journal*, an important Whig newspaper edited by Thurlow Weed. Packard's firm also printed and bound books. Benjamin Packard died on May 18; his son Charles (1816–1833) had died the day before. Munsell, *Ann. Alb.*, *4*:295 and *9*:265.

[6] Weare C. Little's bookstore (*Henry Papers*, *1*:318–319).

[7] Saint Peter's Episcopal Church (*Howell and Tenney*, p. 758). Saint Paul's would not be described as down the street from Little's (Albany City Directories).

[8] Charlotte and Louisa Meads (see note 10 of the letter of December 1, 1832, printed above).

[9] Alfred Conkling, Judge of the District Court for the northern part of New York state (*Henry Papers*, *1*:92–93). We have not discovered in what controversial trial he was involved during 1833 that prompted Henry's concern.

[10] John Gibson patented a plow on May 2, 1822, in Montgomery County, New York (*Burke's Index*, p. 16). We assume this is the same John Gibson with whom Henry corresponded in 1831 (*Henry Papers*, *1*:357–358, 361–362) in regard to steamboat construction. In the letter to James Henry of February 9, 1835 (printed below), Joseph Henry regrets to learn Gibson has "failed." Yet another mention of Gibson appears in a letter to James Henry of November 11, 1836 (Family Correspondence, Henry Papers, Smithsonian Archives), where Joseph Henry alludes to Gibson's failing health but says nothing of his business.

We now suspect John Gibson is the person of that name in Albany. He was born in Ireland in 1793 but had immigrated by July 7, 1822, when his son was born in Ogdensburg, New York. His Albany business of plane-making eventually grew to include a lumberyard and a planing mill. He died in Albany in 1870. Albany City Directories, 1833–1835; Hun, "Albany Academy."

[11] The only person of this name listed in *Burke's Index* (p. 137) is Benjamin Starbuck of Troy, an assignee for a stove patent issued in 1845. The city directory for Troy in 1833–1834 shows N. Starbuck and Sons as a firm of mechanics who manufactured steam engines and furnaces. Nathaniel Starbuck and Benjamin Starbuck are indicated as having separate dwellings in the town.

[12] During the period when Gibson took out his patent, inventors concentrated on replacing the old wooden parts of plows with standardized cast-iron shares, moldboards, and coulters that were easy to interchange if damaged in use. Cast iron resisted less in plowing through the soil and thus reduced the amount of animal power required in farming. In the next phase of plow improvement, circa 1835–1850, inventors were preoccupied with adoption of steel as a material and with questions of design. Clarence Danhof, *Change in Agriculture: The Northern United States, 1820–1870* (Cambridge, Massachusetts, 1969), pp. 187–199.

[13] For Henry's involvement with Theodric Romeyn Beck's public lectures on chemistry, see *Henry Papers*, *1*:107 and 113–114.

[14] For Jabez D. Hammond and Henry's work on the road survey of 1825, see *Henry Papers*, *1*:97–105.

and I sincerely hope that the affair may not be as bad as you think it is. Write me the particulars of the trial and what impression it has had on the public feeling in reference to the Judge.

Uncle James' Hugh has taken rather an unexpected start. I presume he is not well pleased with the return of James and his wife[15] into the family. It is rather unfortunate for Hugh[16] that he did not take a wife some years ago or started to seek a fortune earlier in life. He is rather old to learn the ways of the world and may meet with a *sharpe* in the course of his travels. Had he gone to Philidelphia he would most probably have stoped at Princeton. I would have been pleased to see him.

We have heard that the late freshet has done much damage to the Erie Canal as well as to the Merchants of Troy and Albany.[17] Our Friday paper has not yet arrived and we have therefore learned nothing beyond what was contained in your letter.

A P.S. in your letter informs us that you were to start on Monday for N.Y. but that you would not have time to visit us. Your business must have been very urgent indeed or you could have found leasure to come to Princeton as there are several lines of conveyance starting at different times of the day from N.Y. The fare to New Brunswick is only one shilling. As your jaunt to N.Y. this time must have been one of business we will expect you according to promise some time this summer. I have hopes that Mother will be well enough to come in the fall. Give my love to Mother and Nancy and remember me to the rest of the Family. If it would not be too much trouble I wish you would pack up a box of glass phials which I left in the garret or ask Mr Sammons[18] to pack them by rolling each phial in a piece of paper seperatly. Some of them contain acid. Let them be emptied before they are packed. They will be of great use to me in my experiments as I cannot get any nearer than N.Y. Direct the box to me "*care of A. Q. Thomp-*

[15] This may be a reference to an uncle and aunt on the Henry side of the family, but if not, Henry means James Alexander (1767–1850), a son of Henry's grandfather by his second marriage, and James's wife Janet Jolly (1767–1844). The "Alexander Genealogy" does not list any children by that marriage, but that source is admittedly incomplete.

[16] Not identified, but a likely name for an Alexander family member since it was Henry's grandfather's name.

[17] Rain had fallen steadily from Friday May 10 until Tuesday May 14. The merchants most seriously affected by the resulting floods were those along the piers and wharves of Albany, notably the lumber dealers. The gardens on the islands in the river were also destroyed. Poor people in the city, segregated into the low-lying sections of town, lost their few livestock as well as kitchen gardens. At first it was feared that the Erie Canal had been badly damaged, but the effect was less serious than supposed and the Canal was open to navigation by May 22. *Daily Albany Argus*, May 15–17 and 20–22, 1833.

[18] Stephen Sammons (see note 7 of the letter of November 13, 1832, printed above).

son[19] *on board the Steamboat New York Pier No. 2. foot of Morris Street N.Y.*" It will be best to Label the box "*glass with care.*"

Your Brother

PS Read My Letter to Mother your self and afterwards file it away. I make it a practice to file away every letter I get.[20]

[19] The New York City Directory for 1833 lists Aaron Q. Thompson as a mariner.

[20] Since Joseph Henry's letters to his brother are still extant, we assume that James Henry took his advice. Most of the letters in the other direction, however, are missing, leading us to believe that they were burned in the Smithsonian fire of 1865 or otherwise lost. In later volumes of *The Papers of Joseph Henry*, we will present evidence that Joseph Henry took pains to keep his correspondence files in order and reasonably complete.

TO JAMES HENRY

Family Correspondence, Henry Papers, Smithsonian Archives

Princeton June [1][1] 1833
Saturday Morning

Dear James

Your letter[2] was received two days since. We are very hapy to hear that Mother is so well that she is able to go to every part of the house. I hope she may continue to increase in strength and come with Nancy to Princeton in the Fall. It will be an excellent plan to shut up house and start at the beginning of the vacation and as Mr McArthour[3] does not return after the next vacation but goes to college there need be no hurry in opening the house again. During our stay in N.Y. Harriet was unable to leave the child scarcely an instant and every moment of my time was occupied from the moment of my arrival until I left in purchasing chemicals, and articles of Philosophical apparatus[4] so that I could find no time to call at Mr McMullens[5] although I had intended to do so.

Harriet has commenced in earnest to wean the Boy. He does very well during the day but was very troublesome night before last and bawlled most lustily. He has however become more recconciled to the deprivation and rested tolerably well last night. He is growing quite fleshy and appears now to be in good health.[6]

[1] Although Henry dated the letter June 2, a faint postmark reads June 1, which was a Saturday.

[2] Not found.

[3] Samuel McArthur. As a one-year student at Union, McArthur was to tutor at the Albany Academy before and after his senior year in Schenectady. He lived with the Henry family when in Albany. See *Henry Papers*, *1*:399.

[4] We have not discovered where Henry shopped in New York on this occasion nor what he bought.

[5] John McMullen; see letter to James Henry, November 13, 1832, footnote 1, above.

[6] Among the books in the Henry Library is

I would be very sorry if Jane McMullen should not be happy in her matrimonial connection. She is a good harted girl and deserves a better fate. I however saw nothing very much out of the way in the appearance of her husband and if he be a person that performs well his part his looks will be of little consequence. It might have been will for both you and Jane had you made a bargain but that is past.[7]

Aunt has recovered from her cold and now appears quite well. She is much obliged to Mr Sammons for the interest he takes in her plants. She thinks it an indication that the young Gentleman has a refinement of feeling and hopes he may live to get a wife capable [of] enjoying with him the pleasures of a rural life.

We are now in full operation in the college and have admitted betwen 15 and 20 new students so that there is no appearance of a falling off in numbers. Stephen appears well pleased with his employment and is indeed in his proper element when engaged in teaching. I received a News paper yesterday from S. Alexander[8] [of] Rochester containing a notice of the Aurora borealis. If you see any notices of its appearance at a distance in any of the papers I wish you would cut it out and save it for me as I am desirous of asert[ain]ing how extensively the phenominon was noticed in the U.S. and will afterwards acertain if it was seen in England or other parts of the world. I am obliged to go to the Philosophical hall[9] with some gentlemen and must therefore conclude with assuring you that I am still your

Brother.

P.S. Love to Mother & Nancy. Respects to Rest.

a copy of William Potts Dewees, *A Treatise on the Physical and Medical Treatment of Children* (Philadelphia, 1829), which has a section on weaning on pages 190–193. Dewees believed that the months of March to July and October and November were the optimal months to wean a child. He recommended that the process be undertaken when the child had enough teeth to manage foods other than milk, rather than being done when the child reached a certain age. Dewees remarked that most children were best weaned at age eight months to a year; William Alexander Henry (b. October 3, 1831) was older than Dewees recommended.

Dewees (1768–1841) received his medical degree from the University of Pennsylvania and taught there. He waged a battle against the prejudice, among both the medical profession and the population at large, that men should be excluded from the practice of obstetrics. *DAB*. Dewees was a member of the American Philosophical Society.

[7] James Henry was still a bachelor; he did not marry until April 9, 1835. We have not discovered the name of Jane McMullen's husband. She was probably an Albany resident and was possibly a sister of John McMullen of New York City.

[8] Alexander Stephenson Alexander (1800–1837), Joseph Henry's cousin, was an attorney in Rochester ("Alexander Genealogy"; Rochester City Directory, 1834). The *Rochester Daily Advertiser* for May 25, 1833, has an article on the aurora of May 17.

[9] This three-story stone structure was built in 1803 near Nassau Hall on the front campus to accommodate the mathematics and natural philosophy classes and to house the observatory. *Wertenbaker*, p. 131. Also see below, Henry to Torrey, April 23, 1835.

June 8, 1833

TO JAMES HENRY

Family Correspondence, Henry Papers, Smithsonian Archives

Princeton June
8th 1833 Saturday morning

Dear James

Your letter *via* steamboat of Tuesday came to hand yesterday at 12 o'clock. The box of glass came safley with only one of the vials broken and that only cracked in such a manner as to be readily converted into a little glass cup for chemical purposes. The whole accumulated charge from Albany to Princeton was one dollar. viz From albany to N Y .25. From steam boat to steamboat .25. From N Y to N Brunswick .25. From N B to Princeton 12½. Gave to the man who delivered it 12½ cents. Total 100 cents. The carriers and forwarders between this and N.B. are a great set of sharpers and may perhaps have charged the freight from Albany but I received a bill with the box signed by Q. A. Thompson[1] so that I am inclined to believe that the Steamboat down the Hudson recharged the ammount which you paid. You must therefore make the capt. or Steward refund, if not on account of the money at least on account of justice as the same thing is probably often done. When we came from N.Y. on our way from Albany we were obliged to leave two trunks in charge of the capt. of the Boat at N.B. They were sent to Princeton the same day and the carrier demanded and received two dollars for the transportation from Harriet because he said that he was obliged to pay one dollar to the boat. I had settled with the capt. for 25 cents and was of course indignant at the imposition and immediatly wrote to him stating the circumstances. He returned me next day a polite apology for what he said was a mistake on his part and inclosed a dollar.

We are all well. The Boy is weaned and appears quite healthy. He begins to show a great disposition to talk and can say some words quite plain.

Mr Sammons must have had fine sport in the fishing line. If he makes many more such hauls he will awake the jealousy of the Long Legged Van Wice family.[2]

Mother it appears has been dreaming about our cow and I suppose she will be pleased to hear that she is likely to be a profitable one. We have sold the calf and have now more milk than we can make use of in the family. Motherinlaw sels from 4 to 5 quarts every day to the steward of the college

[1] For Aaron Q. Thompson, see above, Henry to James Henry, [May] 25, [1833], footnote 19.

[2] We do not know what this refers to.

which amount to more than double the price of the pasture. The cow is a young one and has had only one calf.

The only news about this place is that the President is expected in Princeton on Tuesday or wednesday next. A committee of the citizens have been appointed to escort him from Philadelphia to this place and an old disbanded company of Light Horse have been rescusitated for the occasion. As he will probably visit the college we will have an oportunity of seeing the old man.[3]

I wish you would ask William McCammon[4] what bargain he made with his Washing Woman at Princeton as she has called on me and stated that he agreed to pay her 6 dollars for the session & that he left without paying her more than $4.75 leaving 1.25 cents due. If this be the case I will pay her. If not tell him to give you an account of the agreement. She sais that Mc left .75 cents with her sister which she received which makes up the 4.75.

My love to Mother and Nancy. Tell them we expect to see them in Princeton this summer or Autumn next.

Tell Nancy to give our respects to the Meads family. Tell them we much regret the circumstances which prevented our seeing them in Princeton. Respets to all Friends.

Your Brother
Joseph

[3] For Henry's description of President Andrew Jackson's visit to Princeton see below, Joseph Henry to James Henry, June 15, 1833.

[4] For McCammon see above, Joseph Henry to James Henry, November 13, 1832, footnote 9.

FROM WILLIAM BUELL SPRAGUE[1]

Henry Papers, Smithsonian Archives

Albany June 12. 1833.

My dear Sir,

I was disappointed in not seeing you before you left for Princeton, but as it turned out I was there before you. I made some inquiries of Prof^r Mc-

[1] Biographer and Presbyterian clergyman; see *Henry Papers, 1*:464n. This letter suggests Henry's involvement with the early discipline of history and with exchanges of all kinds of scholarly artifacts in addition to scientific instruments, specimens, and publications. We have not found additional letters about the particular matters discussed here, but Henry and Sprague remained correspondents throughout Henry's years at Princeton. Sprague sent Henry printed copies of funeral sermons and commencement addresses he had delivered, nine of which survive in the Henry Library.

Lean[2] about the old Ms. book of Dr Witherspoon,[3] but he knew nothing concerning it. As I am sure it would be a valuable addition to my collection of Antiquities, I shall feel greatly obliged to you, if you will secure it and send it to me, provided you do not want to retain it for yourself or any other friend. Mrs Hodge[4] has encouraged me to expect a small parcel of letters from the correspondence of her ancestors, and I have requested her to forward whatever she may have to send me through yourself, presuming that you may have frequent opportunities up the river. My enthusiasm in this matter I am aware must appear laughable to those who cannot sympathize in it; but I have reached that point that I am willing to be laughed at, provided only my laughing friends will give me their old letters.

I am, Dr Sir, very truly Y^r^ friend,
W B Sprague.

[2] John Maclean, Jr. *Henry Papers, 1*:433n.

[3] John Witherspoon (1723–1794) emigrated from Scotland in 1768 after a stormy career in ecclesiastical controversies. He assumed the presidency of the College of New Jersey (Princeton), vitalizing the school educationally and financially in the years before the American Revolution. Witherspoon served in Congress from 1776 until 1782, when he returned to Princeton to rebuild a college that had languished during the war. See *DAB*. Sprague was to write about Witherspoon as a Presbyterian minister and a patriot in *Annals of the American Pulpit,* 9 vols. (New York, 1857–1869), *3*:288–300.

[4] Sarah Hodge (?–1849) was the daughter of Dr. William Bache and Catherine Wistar of Philadelphia and great granddaughter of Benjamin Franklin. She married Charles Hodge in 1822 and had eight children. See *DAB* article on her husband, a professor at Princeton Theological Seminary who is further identified in footnote 1 of his letter of September 4, 1834, below. Sarah Hodge was also a first cousin of Henry's friend Alexander Dallas Bache (Leonard Labaree, ed., *The Papers of Benjamin Franklin* [New Haven, 1959], *1*:lxxvi).

AN OBSERVATION ON MERCURY AND AIR

Commonplace Book, Notebook [10615],[1] *Henry Papers, Smithsonian Archives*

Princeton, June 13, 1833.

Observed to day with W Dod[2] some what of a curious phenomenon.

In admitting a small quantity of air into a tube of mercury inclined to

[1] Henry's observation is recorded on a loose scrap of paper placed between the pages (pp. 394–395) of a large untitled commonplace book, Notebook [10615], preserved with his papers in the Smithsonian Archives. The book measures 12¼" x 8¼," considerably larger than the other notebooks containing Henry's reading notes and scientific thoughts. The content is also selected and organized more systematically than the rather eclectic material in the other reading notebooks. Typical of the genre, the commonplace book begins with a series of aphorisms and maxims, gleaned chiefly from the popular scientific and philosophical literature, about the proper conduct of scientific investigation and scien-

the horizon, the mercury desended, or the bubble of air appeared to asend up the tube with a wave like appearance on the surface of the mercury. The desending portion of mercury is waved from *a* to *b*; from *b* to *c* the mercury is quite smo[o]th. I cannot at present exp[l]ain the waved appearance.[3]

tific life. These were the kind of exhortatory quotations that Henry used repeatedly throughout his career to impress audiences and to advocate his idealistic visions of the scientific calling. Henry then broke down the commonplace book into sections devoted to various topics in natural philosophy: ordinary electricity, voltaic electricity, magnetism, electromagnetism, magnetoelectricity, thermoelectricity, mechanics, hydrostatics, hydraulics, pneumatics, heat, light, sound, and somatology. Only a fraction of the pages are filled. Ordinary and voltaic electricity contain by far the most matter, while the remaining topics received only a few pages each.

The text in the subject sections consists chiefly of extensive reading notes from an impressive range of scientific journals and monographs. Henry frequently interjected his own comments on the citations or on ideas or experiments suggested to him by the citations. We suspect that Henry kept his commonplace book primarily for research purposes, although he doubtless drew on it also for natural philosophy lectures. He may have also intended it as a place to organize material for a contemplated textbook in natural philosophy, to be discussed in a future volume of *The Papers of Joseph Henry*. Dated Henry comments place the bulk of the material in the early 1840s, when Henry's research began to branch out into the various areas covered by the notes. The present entry from 1833 probably did not originally belong in the commonplace book, but was filed there (by Henry or possibly Mary Henry) with related entries sometime later. (See footnote 3, below.)

[2] William Dod, a Princeton student. See above, Henry to James Henry, March 2, 1833, footnote 7.

[3] The circumstances in which Henry and his student encountered the phenomenon are unknown to us. Henry may have been instructing Dod or conducting a joint experiment with him, possibly on air, the barometer, or meteorology. The document was filed with the pneumatics section of Henry's commonplace book, suggesting gas experiments. But the observation on mercury's motion might bear a distant relation to Henry's later research on cohesion, capillarity, and surface tension. We have not discovered if Henry ever arrived at an adequate explanation of the effect. Nevertheless this brief record of a chance observation suggests that Henry's concentration on electricity and magnetism in his early Princeton years did not preclude interests in other physical phenomena. Henry's teaching ran the gamut of natural philosophy. He had always read widely and eclectically; his research interests would broaden significantly in the coming years.

TO JAMES HENRY

Mary Henry Copy, Memoir, Henry Papers, Smithsonian Archives

Princeton. June 15. 1833.[1]

Dear James. We had a very busy day in Princeton on Tuesday in preparing to meet Gen. Jackson. It was ordered by the corporation or rather the com-

[1] Easily ascertained from internal evidence, the year is erroneously given as 1883 by Mary Henry's transcribers.

mittee of arrangements that the faculty and students of the college should join the escort. Accordingly at five p.m. we assembled and walked in order about a mile out of the village where after waiting about three quarters of an hour the President's suite and an escort of Princeton Cavalry made their appearance. The President, Govs. Cass[2] and Livingston[3] and the Mayor of Trenton[4] were in an open carriage. The appearance of the President was venerable and dignified. He was conducted to the hotel almost directly opposite our house where he remained until eight o'clock and was then escorted to Capt. Stockton's[5] where a splendid supper had been prepared and all the ladies of [the] borough invited to meet him. The officers of the college called in a body at the hotel and were presented to the President by Dr. Carnahan.[6] The President was polite and very gentlemanly in his manners and made a very favorable impression. Dr. Carnahan gave him an invitation to visit the college. The General replied that he was an early man and that he would meet us at half past five the next morning. As that hour happened to be our prayer time it was agreed that the General should attend the morning prayers in the chapel and then be conducted through the several buildings of the Institution. Accordingly at half past five at the ringing of the college bell he and his Suite entered the chapel. After prayers the General's attention was directed to the picture of Washington[7] which hangs against the wall of the chapel and which once contained a portrait of George the Third which was torn from the frame by a cannon ball during the battle of Princeton. He afterwards visited the library, the museum and the philosophical hall. I was much interested in the appearance and conversation of Gen. Cass. He is undoubtedly a gentleman of talents and learning. The President appeared highly gratified with his reception in Princeton and on the whole left a favorable impression.

[2] General Lewis Cass (1782–1866), former Governor of Michigan Territory and Jackson's Secretary of War. *DAB*.

[3] Probably Edward Livingston (1764–1836), Jackson's aide-de-camp in 1814, his former Secretary of State, and his newly appointed Minister to France. *DAB*. Livingston was never a Governor; the designation may be Henry's error or one of transcription.

[4] Charles Burroughs (1788–1864) was Mayor from 1832 to 1847. Eli Field Cooley, *Genealogy of Early Settlers of Trenton and Ewing, N.J.* (Trenton, 1883), p. 19; Trenton Historical Society, *A History of Trenton, 1679–1929*, 2 vols. (Princeton, 1929), 2:1053.

[5] Probably Robert Field Stockton (1795–1866), one of Jackson's closest friends. On a ten-year leave of absence from the navy, Stockton lived at Princeton, engaging in various business pursuits. Stockton actually attained the rank of Captain upon returning to navy service in 1838. Stockton had an important role in the Mexican War. In 1843 his experimental ship, the *Princeton*, was the scene of an accidental cannon explosion wounding Stockton and killing the Secretaries of State and Navy. In a later volume we will discuss Henry's role as Chairman of a Franklin Institute committee investigating the disaster. *DAB*. Henry's Library contains a copy of S. J. Bayard, *A Sketch of the Life of Com. Robert F. Stockton* . . . (New York, 1856).

[6] President of Princeton.

[7] See above, Henry to James Henry, February 9, 1833, footnote 16.

June 25, 1833

TO JAMES HENRY

Family Correspondence, Henry Papers, Smithsonian Archives

Princeton June 25 1833
Tuesday

Dear James

I was so much engaged on saturday last that I could find no leasure to write and I must suppose that you also have been very busy as we have had no letter since a fortnight tomorrow. We are all well. The boy is getting quite fleshy and continues to feast daily on milk. Your last letter mentioned that Dr Frank[1] might perhapse give us a visit but we have seen nothing of him and conclude that he has returned to Albany. Tell Mother that Dr Neel[2] has been spending several days at Princeton. He is a Brothinlaw by his first wife of Dr Carnahan[3] the president of the College. When he learned that I was from Albany he made very particular inquires and appeared much pleased when I mentioned that Mother was one of his parisoners. He recollected her very well, & said he was much rejoiced to see me connected with Princeton College as he had himself been a tutor in the same Institution. We have also had Dr. Neels predecessor in Princeton Arthur J. Stansbury[4] but I did not see him. His daughter is married to a Mr Wines authour of "Two years in the Navy" who is proprietor of a large boarding school which he has lately purchased in Princeton.[5]

[1] Dr. Francis N. Selkirk, for whom see above, Joseph Henry to James Henry, November 13, 1832, footnote 6.

[2] William Neill (1778 or 1779–1860), for whom see *Henry Papers, 1*:11, was Pastor of the First Presbyterian Church in Albany from 1809 to 1816. An 1803 graduate of Princeton, he had served as a tutor from 1803 to 1805 and also was Clerk of Faculty, 1804–1805. *Princeton Catalogue*, p. 114.

[3] President Carnahan's wife was the former Mary Van Dyke, while Neill's first wife, to whom he was married in 1805, was Elizabeth Van Dyke (1782–1809). Both were daughters of Matthew Van Dyke (1752–1832) and his wife Lydia Longstreet Van Dyke. William B. Aitken, *Distinguished Families in America Descended from Wilhelmus Beekman and Jan Thomasse Van Dyke* (New York, 1912), p. 222.

[4] Arthur J. Stansbury (1781–1865, for whom see below, Stansbury to Henry, August 29, 1835, especially footnote 1) was Pastor of the First Presbyterian Church in Albany from 1817 to 1821. He thus was Neill's successor in the pulpit, not his predecessor.

[5] Arthur Stansbury's daughter Emma had married Enoch Cobb Wines (1806–1879) on June 14, 1832. Wines, a native of New Jersey, was graduated from Middlebury College in 1827. Two years later, after a brief experiment with a classical school in Washington, D.C., he became schoolmaster of midshipmen on the United States frigate *Constellation*, an experience that provided material for his two-volume work *Two Years and a Half in the Navy* (Philadelphia, 1832). In 1832 Wines bought Edgehill Seminary in Princeton, where he conducted a boys' school along the lines of a German gymnasium. Declining fortunes in 1839 led him to accept an appointment as an instructor at the People's College in Philadelphia, but in a few years he bought another classical school in Burlington, New Jersey, which likewise was not a financial success. In the late 1840s he turned to the study of theology and was licensed to preach by the Congregationalists, and he subsequently filled pulpits in Vermont, on Long Island, and in Pennsylvania. At age fifty-six he became secretary of the Prison Association of New York,

Will you call at Littles[6] for me and ask Charles[7] when my years subscription for the "Library of Useful Knowledge"[8] ends. I do not wish to subscribe for another year but if there be any Nos. due on the last subscription forward them to me by mail.

The present is one of the most rainy Seasons I have ever known. We have rain almost every day. I fear the summer crops will suffer by such continued wet weather. Are there any fears of the cholera in Albany? I saw a rumor in the paper some time since that it had again appeared in Montreall. The unusual dampness of the season I fear will form an exciting cause to the disease.

I received last week a letter from W. McCammon and will answer it if I can find time to day. The foundation for the new College building was laid last week and the work is going on with considerable expidition.[9] The fourth of July it appears is quite a day with the students at Princeton and according to an old custom the front of the college is illuminated in the evening and fire works desplayed in the campus. An Oration is given by a

---

thus beginning his major life work. His *Report on the Prisons and Reformatories of the United States and Canada* (1867), written after a tour with Theodore William Dwight, and his annual reports greatly stimulated the movement toward prison reform. *DAB*.

[6] The bookshop of Weare C. Little (1805–1885), for whom see *Henry Papers*, *1*:318–319.

[7] We are uncertain as to the identity of "Charles." The Albany City Directory for 1832–1833, however, does list a Charles A. Little, whom Munsell, *Ann. Alb.*, *10*:241, says "died at sea in 1835 at the age of 25."

[8] During the early part of the nineteenth century a number of publications were issued under the auspices of the Society for the Diffusion of Useful Knowledge in London, an organization which hoped to assure the progress of society by bringing information in such areas as scientific economic principles, natural science, and the lives of "useful" persons to a wide audience. Henry, Lord Brougham, one of the guiding lights of the society, began the Library of Useful Knowledge in 1827 with his "Preliminary Treatise—Discourse on the Objects, Advantages, and Pleasures of Science." The Library was to be a series of tracts, usually thirty-two pages in length (although some were much longer). Some later were bound into volumes; although the page numbers are the same as in the original tract, the volume dates do not always correspond to the publication dates of the individual components. For a discussion of the Society for the Diffusion of Useful Knowledge and some of its publications, with particular reference to science, see J. N. Hays, "Science and Brougham's Society," *Annals of Science*, 1964, *20*:227–241.

Joseph Henry's Library contains five bound volumes of the Library of Useful Knowledge, some of which he obviously acquired after the date of this letter. All published in London, these are: *Natural Philosophy, I* (1829), *Natural Philosophy, III* (1834), *Lives of Eminent Persons* (1833), *Mathematics, I* (1836), and *Mathematics, II* (1835). Because of the differences in dating noted above, we cannot be sure which (if any) Henry is referring to here. The Henry Library also has six volumes of the Society's weekly *Penny Magazine*, covering the years 1835 through 1840.

[9] In order to relieve the overcrowding of Nassau Hall, which had forced many students to find lodgings elsewhere, the Princeton Trustees had authorized construction of a new building in the spring of 1833. Facing the back campus southeast of Nassau Hall, it was to be four stories high and would contain eight rooms on each floor (Minutes, College of New Jersey Trustees, April 10, 1833). Construction proceeded rapidly on "East College," as it became known, and by January of 1834 some students already had moved in. It was fully occupied at the beginning of the 1834–1835 winter term, but by then the college had so many more students that West College, its opposite companion, was soon built. Logically enough, Nassau Hall was thereafter often

student from each of the two societies.[10] Harriet says if Mother is well enough she and Nancy must start for Princeton by the first oportunity. Harriet also bids me say that you are not a Brother Since you could come to N.Y. and not visit Princeton. I commenced this letter in the morning and left it unfinished until evening in hope of receiving a letter from you by the mail which arrives at 12 o'clock but I have been desappointed.

Give my respects to Mr [Bu]llions,[11] Dr Wing,[12] Dr Ten Eyck,[13] the Me[ads] family, Mr Dean.[14] Tell him that his friend Mr Adger[15] has been absent from Princeton ever since my return and thus I have not yet delivered the letter he gave me to Mr. Adger. My respects also to Mr McArthur, Sammons, Dr Frank. Love to Mother and Nancy.

Your Brother
Joseph

P.S. Tell Mr Dean that Adger has returned but that he has not yet called on me but will probably soon. If he does not I will carry the letter to him.

called "North College" by students and faculty. East College was torn down in 1897; West College, somewhat modified, still survives today. *Wertenbaker*, pp. 251, 351; Henry L. Savage, ed., *Nassau Hall, 1756–1956* (Princeton, 1956), pp. 44–45.

[10] That is, the Whig and Cliosophic societies. For Henry's description of the July 4 observances see below, Joseph Henry to Nancy Henry, July 6, 1833.

[11] Reverend Peter Bullions. Here and in the following reference to the Meads family, several letters have been obliterated by a hole in the paper.

[12] Dr. Joel A. Wing.

[13] Dr. Philip Ten Eyck.

[14] Amos Dean.

[15] We have not located "Mr. Adger." Perhaps Henry is referring here to a student, either James A. Edgar, who received a Princeton Bachelor of Arts degree in 1833, E. B. Edgar (B.A. 1835), or John M. Edgar (B.A. 1836). *Princeton Catalogue*, pp. 145, 148, 150.

TO NANCY HENRY

Family Correspondence, Henry Papers, Smithsonian Archives

Princeton Saturday July 6th 1833

Dear Nancy

We received James letter[1] of saturday last on Tuesday of this week. We were much surprised to learn that he had lost so much flesh: he must have been very sick and the attack a violent one. I hope he has not attempted to go to Utica before his entire recovery as exposure or unusual fatigue after an attack of the scarlet fever is said to be very dangerous.

We received a paper[2] from James to day with a line on it informing us that Mother is quite unwell and has been so for two days. This was quite unexpected as James mentioned in his last letter that she had been down-

[1] Not found. [2] Not found.

stairs at breakfast. I hope the attack is only a slight one and that she will speadily recover. We had anticipated the pleasure of seeing her in Princeton this fall as she appeared to be recruiting so fast and I still hope we may not be disappointed. We are all enjoying tolerable health except the boy who has been labouring for a few days past under an attack of the bowel complaint probably caused by the cutting of his eye teeth. Although he has lost considerable flesh he runns about as usual and has no feaver. We hope the disease will abate in a short time or as soon as the irritation caused by the teath is over.

The fourth of July was a great day among the students at Princeton.[3] In the morning a procession of the faculty and students was formed which marched to the church where two orations were delivered by two students of the senior class.

Also in the afternoon several orations were pronounced by students of the lower classes.

In the evening the college was illuminated according to an ancient custom which has been handed down from year to year since the Revolutionary war. In the yard before the college a great number of sky rockets and other fire works were set off. The superintendance of the fire works devolved on me and as they were attended with some danger of fire the eavening was rather an axsious one to me. Besides this there had very nearly been a very serious difficulty in the afternoon between the <*Soldiers*> members of a *Uniform Company* and the students on account of the soldiers first refusing to join in the procession and secondly on account of their disturbing the students by drumming &c. during the speeking in church. One of the students insulted the captain of the company for his improper conduct on which some of the members of the company seized hold of the student. His fellow students ran to his rescue and a general battle was about commencing when the parties were separated by the exersion of some of the sitizens and the officers of the college. Fortunatly no person was much hurt and the whole affair has apparently been settled and will rest unless some prosecutions be commenced by some who think themselves badly treated.[4]

Give my Respects to Mr Bullions[5] & Family and all inquiring friends. For Yourself and Mother receive my warmest love.

Your Brother
Joseph.

[3] According to *Wertenbaker* (p. 210), "Throughout the early decades of the century the Fourth of July celebration continued to be one of the bright spots in the college year, far more important than Christmas. . . . "

[4] Periodic student outbreaks, often bordering on riot, were by this time accepted facts of college life at Princeton. See Henry Lyttleton Savage, ed., *Nassau Hall, 1756–1956* (Princeton, 1956), pp. 124–138.

[5] Reverend Peter Bullions. See *Henry Papers, 1*:129, footnote 7.

FROM JAMES RENWICK, SR.

Gratz Collection, Historical Society of Pennsylvania

Washington 4th August 1833

Dear Sir,

Be so good as deliver to the order of Lt. Charles Wilkes Junr U.S. Navy,[1] the Magnetic apparatus of Hansteen[2] which is in your possession. As it is his intention to make a series of observations in this City, you will oblige me by furnishing him with any of your own needles that you may think will increase the probability of valuable results.

I am Dr Sr respectfully Yrs
Jas Renwick[3]

[1] At this date Wilkes (1798–1877, *DAB*) was the head of the Depot of Charts and Instruments in Washington, the Navy facility which became the Naval Observatory. Wilkes was the brother-in-law of James Renwick, Sr. Charles Wilkes was one of the Navy officers with a strong interest in science. His greatest contribution was as commander of the round-the-world expedition now commonly named after him. As the Wilkes Expedition (1838–1842) and its consequences are quite important in the development of science in ante-bellum America, Charles Wilkes will reappear in subsequent volumes of the *Henry Papers*.

[2] Originally given to Joseph Henry by Renwick, this was at least the second time Renwick directed that the apparatus be given to another. *Henry Papers, 1*:290–291, 335–337.

[3] Below the signature is another letter, Wilkes to Henry of October 2, 1833, printed below.

TO JAMES HENRY

Family Correspondence, Henry Papers, Smithsonian Archives

Philadelphia Aug
17th 1833

Dear James

Your letter of the 12th[1] came to hand on the 16th. The mails between albany and Princeton are very irregular. Mr Bullions and Orlando Meads arived nearly 2 days before your letter.

Miss Ryley[2] had not reached Princeton when we left home. My time for two months past has been much occupied. I have lectured 4 time[s] a week besides my ordinary recitations. My duties are now however ended for this term[3] and I will not be called on again until the beginning of the next ses-

[1] Not found.

[2] Jane Ryley of Schenectady.

[3] Senior examinations had concluded the previous Monday, August 12, and the seniors had been dismissed the next day. Henry had probably been particularly pressured with

sion which does not commence until the 10th of November nearly 3 months from this time. I have come on to Philadelphia inorder to spend a few days in Library of the Philosophical society and to see the different litterary and Scientific Institutions of the City.[4] Orlando Meads, his two sisters[5] and Harriet came on with me. They have staid one day in Philadelphia and are about to return this morning. I shall remain until the middle of next week.

I am very sorry to hear that mother is not as well as she has been and that there is some doubt as to the probability of your comming on to Princeton. I had concluded to go to Albany after the Commencement which takes place in about 6 weeks but s[h]ould mother be sufficiently strong to stand the fatigue of travelling I would go for her week after next. I wish you would get the opinion of Dr Wing[6] on the subject. I had made up my mind to start as soon as I could arraing my affairs but was rather discouraged by Mr Bullions account. He thought it would be hazardous for Mother to undertake the Journey in her present state. Write me in your next the opinion of Dr Wing. We are all well. The Misses Meads will call and give you all the news. They have enjoyed them selves very much at Princeton and are delighted with the Place and its Inhabitants.

Your Brother
Joseph

In haste

---

finishing his course and conducting examinations. In addition to his regular duties, in the summer of 1833 he taught John Torrey's course in chemistry. Although the session continued for the three lower classes, the dismissal of the senior class in effect released Henry from all teaching responsibility.

[4] This was apparently Henry's first visit to Philadelphia since moving to Princeton. Philadelphia was still the nation's leading scientific center in 1833, reason enough for Joseph Henry to want to travel southward. But his mother's illness and college duties undoubtedly delayed an earlier trip. On April 18, 1833, he wrote Silliman of his intention to see Robert Hare and S. G. Morton on the last week of the spring college vacation (see above). Silliman had previously written to them on Henry's behalf (*Henry Papers, 1*:460–461). On May 8 (above) Henry wrote Jacob Green that his son's illness prevented his going to Philadelphia.

In a letter to James Henry of August 27, 1833 (Family Correspondence, Henry Papers, Smithsonian Archives), Henry reports that he stayed in Philadelphia about a week and "was much gratified by my reception there from the Scientific Gentlemen." Henry does not specify here or elsewhere exactly whom he met. It is clear from his letter to his wife of November 1, 1833 (below), on his next trip to Philadelphia, that he had already met John Vaughan. It is unlikely that he met such important figures as Bache and Hare until the November visit. We have no further contemporary evidence on his first visit to Philadelphia. He may have visited Peale's Museum, as recounted later in life in an address on Charles Willson Peale (Undated lecture [ca. 1876], Henry Papers, Smithsonian Archives).

Henry was to visit Philadelphia many times both to catch up on the latest journals and to visit scientific institutions, notably the American Philosophical Society and the Franklin Institute. These trips became increasingly beneficial as he met and entered into close relationships with Philadelphia scientists.

[5] Charlotte and Louisa Meads, for whom see above, Henry to James Henry, December 1, 1832, footnote 10.

[6] Joel A. Wing, the Henry family's physician in Albany (*Henry Papers, 1*:50).

September 5, 1833

FROM PETER BULLIONS

Henry Papers, Smithsonian Archives

Albany Sept[r] 5th 1833

My Dear Sir

I have just returned from your Mother's. A letter from you arrived to day. James will probably write you tomorrow. Mother is tolerably well, all the rest well, and all enjoying in Anticipation your approaching visit.[1] We had a glorious Aurora this evening. About half past Eight a brillant luminous Arch spanned the heavens from west to east particularly bright at its western extremity somewhat faint at its eastern extremity. Its greatest Altitude in the centre seemed to be about 60°—when it rapidly disappeared. Its whole duration was not over 20 minutes. The Aurora however still continues to play but shews nothing remarkable.

I am afraid Margarets long visit may incommode you. Having so many visiters I beg that you will be at no trouble with her.[2] Will you have the goodness to get a pair of shoes for her and I will repay you when you come to Albany. Give my love to M[rs] Henry and all the Household. We have opened the Academy again with about 180 of which my quota is about 30 the smallest number I ever had.[3] M[r] Nathan Hawley[4] is my Assistant who gives half his time to D[r] Beck. Matters go on quietly. May every blessing and happiness attend you.

I am Dear Sir
Yours Sincerely
P Bullions

[1] Henry visited Albany in early October 1833. See below, Henry to James Henry, September 17, 1833, and Henry to Maclean, October 9, 1833. Originally he intended visiting in August to bring his ailing mother and other relatives to Princeton, but word reached Henry that her health was not good enough for the trip. He then postponed his trip until after the Princeton commencement. Henry to James Henry, August 27, 1833, Henry Papers, Smithsonian Archives.

[2] An Albany contingent had just spent time at the Henrys' home in Princeton. "We have had quite a representation from Albany at our house these few weeks past. The two Miss Meads Orlando Meads Mr Bullions & his daughter and Dr Ten Eyck." Ibid.

[3] Enrollment figures for the Albany Academy for the quarter beginning September 1833 indicate that a total of 250 students attended. But the order of magnitude is confirmed for Bullions' other assertion. The figures indicate that 37 scholars enrolled in classical studies for the quarter, indeed the smallest enrollment recorded in that department in the years 1825–1834. See *Henry Papers, 1*:238–239.

[4] Nathan Hawley (1816–1890) graduated from the Lancaster School in Albany, the Albany Academy, and finally Union College in 1833. As Bullions states, in that year Hawley became a tutor at the Academy. After assisting Bullions and T. R. Beck, Hawley practiced law in Albany until his death. *Academy Seventy-fifth Anniversary*, pp. 70, 85. Hun, "Albany Academy." *Union Catalog*, p. 43.

September 6, 1833

"GALVANIC EXPERIMENTS ON THE BODY OF THE MURDERER LE BLANC"[1]

Notebook [7171], pp. 23–27, Henry Papers, Smithsonian Archives[2]

Sept 6th 1833

Assisted on this day in performing a series of Galvanic experiments[3] on the

[1] The original is simply titled: "Galvanism." These words from the first sentence were substituted as being more enlightening.

[2] Three Mary Henry copies exist but contain nothing beyond the original. The notebook, No. [7171], has a number of dated Henry entries for 1833 plus other reading notes of literature appearing in that year. At the end are later entries. No other entries are physiological; the other entries indexed by Henry under "galvanism" are purely physical. Perhaps the notes most pertinent to this entry occur on pages 9–12 (dated August 1833) and on page 20 in a hand other than Joseph Henry's. This is Henry's abstract of Michael Faraday's paper on the identity of electricities (Third Series of the *Experimental Researches in Electricity, 1*:76–102). Henry's notes do not repeat Faraday on the physiological effects of the various electricities nor the section on animal electricity. Page 20 does copy Faraday's concluding paragraph (360), including the chart of the effects common to the various electricities. Although Faraday concluded that the preponderance of the evidence supported the hypothesis of identity, animal electricity at that date notably lacked experimental proof of production of sparks and heat. These gaps were filled later in the decade. Although the text is silent, we suspect Henry was alert to these possibilities in the experiments given below, even though circumstances prevented any pursuit of these points.

[3] What follows is unexpected in terms of Henry's historical identification as an experimental physicist, a calling not usually associated with physiological research. Finding Henry experimenting at an autopsy is certainly atypical of his research. But if unexpected and surprising, the application of galvanic currents to the body of an executed criminal had precedents in the science of that day and in various activities of Joseph Henry. The Morristown experiments were not anomalous but an instance in the later stages of a research tradition. Present in both Henry's published works and manuscript remains are two kinds of clues which should have prepared us for this document.

In Henry's own work, as in the investigations of Faraday and other contemporaries, are many instances of the use of humans for testing electromagnetic effects. Documents appearing later in this volume will show Henry reporting his own sensations. When he and Faraday do this, it is not simply because they lack proper physical instruments. They and their contemporaries were experimenting in accord with a specific, well-developed tradition. Galvani's work, after all, originated in physiological observations. It yielded a concept of animal electricity whose existence and relationships to other electricities were very much part of the reigning research tradition. Faraday investigated the gymnotus and the electric eel. There are instances in the literature where tissues from frogs are part of circuits in experiments which are not susceptible to a simple labeling as "biology" or "electricity." To use anachronistic terminology, Faraday and Henry were both practitioners of a combination of physiology and physics. Neither man in 1833 saw this intellectual mix as unusual; it was a convention about to split into separate specialties. The interaction of physics and physiology was increasingly less fruitful, particularly for physics. Possibilities existed elsewhere; the career of Helmholtz in optics and acoustics is the notable example but a rare one.

The second kind of clue is the presence of medical concerns exemplified in this volume by Henry's relation to Charles Hodge (see his letters to H. L. Hodge in the fall of 1834, printed below). In "Contributions III: Electro-Dynamic Induction" (1838), paragraph 52, Joseph Henry notes: "At the request of a medical friend, I have lately administered the induced current precisely in this way [using a helix to intensify inductive action at a distance], in a case of paralysis of a part of the nerves of the face." Surviving in Henry's Library are works on the medical applications of electricity. Henry had a wide-ranging interest in all the manners in which electricity and magnetism were or might be applied. Yet, very few applications of these elicited experiments from Henry. Nor was it fortuitous that his collaborators in Morristown were physicians and medical students. Given the interspersion of physics and physiology, galvanic experiments involving living matter promised both the advancement of knowledge and the staving off of pain and death.

Specifically Henry and his medical friends were in a research tradition going back to the dispute between Galvani and Volta over the latter's contact theory of current electricity. During the previous century serious investigators and not so serious showmen had applied static electricity to humans and to various animals. With Galvani's work, electrical currents were added to the repertoire. Humans, smaller animals, and even horses were attached to batteries, as were amputated limbs in hospitals and dismembered parts of cattle in slaughterhouses. Dismembered heads of oxen were particularly good targets to show rolling eyes upon discharge of current. Not everyone could emulate F. Rossi in Turin in 1803 who attached his battery to two guillotined heads.

In that year Giovanni Aldini (1762–1834, *DSB*) experimented on the body of a condemned criminal in London. Galvani's nephew, Aldini was the principal spokesman for his uncle's views about the existence of an animal electricity and against Volta's contact theory. The next experiment on an executed criminal known to us, Andrew Ure's in 1818, was specifically to test Aldini's work, the "only facts" contrary to the contact theory. It was a scientific spectacular often cited in later decades. Ure's description of his third experiment conveys the flavor of the event:

> The supra-orbital nerve was laid bare in the forehead, as it issues through the supraciliary *foramen*, in the eyebrow: the one conducting rod being applied to it, and the other to the heel, most extraordinary grimaces were exhibited every time that the electric discharges were made, by running the wire in my hand along the edges of the last trough, from the 220th to the 227th pair of plates; thus fifty shocks, each greater than the preceding one, were given in two seconds; every muscle in his countenance was simultaneously thrown into fearful action; rage, horror, despair, anguish, and ghastly smiles, united their hideous expression in the murderer's face, surpassing far the wildest representations of a Fuseli or a Kean. At this period several of the spectators were forced to leave the apartment from terror or sickness, and one gentleman fainted. [Ure, cited below, p. 290.]

In Albany in 1827 Joseph Henry had hoped to perform similar experiments (*Henry Papers, 1*:199). In 1839 Henry's friend, Robert Hare, also performed galvanic experiments on an executed criminal.

By 1833 the chemical theory was supplanting Volta's conception, largely through the efforts of Michael Faraday. But Volta had supporters, some of whom combined physics and physiology (to use convenient, if anachronistic terms). Near at hand was the elder Silliman. A few months before he published this example of use of humans to test electromagnetic effects (*Silliman's Journal*, 1833, *24*:148):

> Usually, the flash of light was not observed when the connection was made through the tongue only; with the stronger of these two magnets, however, this effect was observed; and when the wires of the weaker magnet were placed, one under the tongue and the other between the upper lip and gum, the flash was distinct; but it never failed with either, when one wire was laid on the tongue and the other made to touch the eye ball. As it was not quite convenient to move a wire around the eye, a small disk of copper (as large as a twelve and a half cent piece,) was soldered to the remote end of one of the connecting wires; when, to the moistened eye ball of the closed eye, this disk was applied and the other wire touched to the tongue, at the moment when the keeper was slid off, a flash was perceived as brilliant as lightning, and the whole of that side of the face received a convulsive twitch. All these effects, the spark, the shock and the flashes of light, were perceived, without apparent diminution, when the discharging wires were made to take a circuit of one hundred and fifty feet, and the poles for discharge were made to meet in the middle of this distance, that is, seventy five feet from the magnet—the shocks through the fingers were very strong. *It is a battery, always charged, and whose energy is independent of chemical agency.*—ED.

Other adherents of the contact theory were active at greater remove. Perhaps the most influential on Henry at this point was Stefano Giovanni Marianini (1790–1866, *Poggendorff*), at this date Professor of Experimental Physics at the University of Modena. In an article translated from the Italian in the *Annales de chimie et de physique*, 1829, *40*:225–256 (a

Body of the Murderer Le Blanc in the village of Morristown N.J.[4] For the purpose of these experiments Dr Howell[5] of Princeton myself and his three

journal read by Henry), Marianini reported experiments combining living tissues and electrical circuits from which he derived a theory explaining the physiological effects under study bearing distant resemblance to Henry's explanation of self-induction.

Henry never published an acount of these experiments on Le Blanc, perhaps for reasons mentioned below. But he did incorporate his concern for physiological effects into his lectures at Princeton without specifically mentioning Le Blanc. Among the Henry Papers in the Smithsonian Archives is an "Electricity" notebook (No. [23894]) with outlines and notes for class lectures. The notebook is undated. Although it contains datable additions and revisions as late as the early 1840s, there is every possibility the text was in use early in Henry's stay at Princeton—perhaps as early as 1833. At three points Joseph Henry considers such effects. The first (pp. 129–130) is on static electricity and culminates with a note to end the lecture by using a Leyden jar to give "a shock to the whole class; require each person to join hands with his neighbors." Next (pp. 148 and 150) is a discussion of animal electricity, part of the taxonomy of electricities whose identity was being proven by contemporary investigators. Here Henry raises the view that "the power of the will is transmitted along the nerves by a principal similar to or identical with electricity." A supposition of this nature was reason enough for experimentation on a corpse even though Henry later in the lecture speculates: "There is no electricity connected with the human subject under the influence of the will as in some of the lower animals."

The physiological effects of galvanic currents are finally considered on pages 187–188. The treatment is wholly conventional for the time, specifically citing such a common source as Roget at one point. Of particular relevance to the Morristown experiments are these lines: "Powerful contractions [of the muscles] are induced in large animals recently killed. *An entire sheep.*" There is also a reference to Nobili's article on the use of continuous currents to treat paralysis and interrupted currents for tetanus.

For Aldini, see *DSB* and his "Galvanische versuche, angestellt am Körper eines Gehängten zu London am 17ten Jan. 1803," *Annalen der Physik*, 1804, *18*:340–342. Francesco Rossi, "Rapport des expériences galvaniques faites sur des hommes et des animaux," *Journal de physique, de chimie, et d'histoire naturelle*, 1803, *57*:267–276. Andrew Ure, "An Account of Some Experiments Made on the Body of a Criminal Immediately after Execution, with Physiological and Practical Observations," *Quarterly Journal of Science*, 1819, *6*:283–294. L. Nobili, "Analyse expérimentale et théorique des effets électro-physiologiques de la grenouille, suivie d'un appendice sur la nature du tétanos et de la paralysie, et sur la manière de guérir ces deux maladies au moyen de l'électricité," *Bibliothèque Universelle . . .* , 1830, *44*:48–60, 165–182. Two good general contemporary surveys are Antoine-César Becquerel, *Traité expérimental de l'électricité et du magnetisme*, 1836, *4*:211–255 and A. De La Rive, *A Treatise on Electricity in Theory and Practice*, 3 vols. (London, 1853–1858), particularly extensive passages in volumes 2 and 3. Hare's brief reference to his galvanic experiments on a hanged murderer is on pp. 42–43 of his pamphlet, *Of Galvanism, or Voltaic Electricity*, a supplement to his *Compendium of the Course of Chemical Instruction . . .* (Philadelphia, 1840–1843).

[4] Antoine Le Blanc was a Frenchman or Swiss convicted of murdering Samuel Sayre, Sayre's wife, and their female black servant earlier that year. He was hired by Sayre as a farmhand not too long before. Apparently the motive for the triple killings was theft. The party in pursuit had no trouble following Le Blanc's trail as he continued to drop bits of the loot while fleeing toward New York City. Murders, trial, and execution were great sensations of that day in the region. Participants and onlookers recorded the events themselves or recalled them to later chroniclers. According to this local tradition, pocketbooks and other mementos were made from Le Blanc's skin.

We are indebted to the Morristown, New Jersey, Public Library for supplying us with references to this incident from various local history sources. A contemporary description is *The Trial, Sentence and Confession of Antoine Le Blanc, Who Was Executed at Morristown, N.J. on Friday the 6th Sept. 1833, for the Murder of Mr. Sayre and Family*, 2d ed. (Morriston [sic], New Jersey, 1833). See also Ambrose E. Vanderpool, ed., *Personal Memoirs of Edwin A. Ely* (New York, 1926), pp. 406–410.

[5] Samuel Ladd Howell (1787–1835), since September 1830 Professor of Anatomy and

puples[6] started on the eavning of the 5th and reached at about 11 o'clock the village of summerville[7] half the distance to Morristown. The night at first was quite dark but at about 15 minutes past 8 a faint light was observed in the north which soon afterwards expanded into a beautiful *aurora.* It gradually assumed the form of an arch extending around the north towards the east and west and embracing more than 70 degrees of the circle of the horizon. The apex of the arch was a little to the *east* of a verticle circle passing through the pole star. (Perhaps this was owing to the pole star's being in its greatest elongation west.) Beneath the arch of the aurora there was a dark cloud so near the horizon that it was at first taken for a mountain in the distance. The arch after a few minutes resolved itself into a number of beams which at first appeared to spring from the extrados[8] and to move laterally and with great velocity from the east to the west. The whole desappeared about nine not however before reappearing several times in the form [of] a number of faint short parallel beams forming as it were the rudiments of an arch.

We arrived at Morristown about 11½ o'clock the next day amid a great crowd of persons of all ages and both sexes who had assembled from all the adjacent country to witness the execution.[9] Preparations for the Galvanic experiments had been made in the court room of the court house a fine building which is also occupied in the lower story as a Jail. In the court room we found Dr Canfield of Morristown,[10] with Dr Rinlander,[11]

Physiology at Princeton. An abortive attempt at medical education at Princeton occurred in 1795. The attempt was revived in 1818, soon becoming linked with proposals for legal education. The first contemplated professor, John Vancleve, died in 1826, before the program started. Howell gave a required course for seniors in the winter. The course was open to Howell's private pupils who were permitted to use the library and to attend other lectures without payment of fees. During the summer Howell presented a private course, apparently aided to some degree by other instructors. His death ended a serious attempt to establish medical education at Princeton. *Maclean,* 2: 177, 256, 265, 284–286, 295–296, 300. *Hageman, 1*:261–262.

[6] Unidentified.

[7] i.e., Somerville, New Jersey.

[8] The exterior curve of an arch.

[9] The *Daily Albany Argus,* September 10, 1833, p. 2, quoting a New York City paper, reported 12,000 present at the execution which occurred at 12:30. Unlike Henry's statement, the account reported that women were a majority of the crowd.

[10] Isaac Washington Canfield (1793–1860). A Princeton graduate (B.A. 1816; A.M. 1827), Canfield graduated from the College of Physicians and Surgeons in New York City in 1819. He was a leading practitioner in the area and an officer in the local Morris District Medical Society at various times between 1835 and 1857. Frederick Alexander Canfield, comp., *A History of Thomas Canfield and of Matthew Canfield, with a Genealogy of Their Descendants in New Jersey* (New Haven, 1897), p. 63. Henry C. Pitney, Jr., ed., *A History of Morris County, New Jersey, Embracing Upwards of Two Centuries, 1710–1913,* 2 vols. (New York, 1914), *1*:108–109, 111.

[11] John Robert Rhinelander (1792–1857) was a graduate of Columbia (1811) and earned his M.D. from the College of Physicians and Surgeons (1824). He was a Demonstrator of Anatomy at the school (1826–1831) and Professor of Anatomy (1834–1839) as well as a Trustee (1840–1848). In 1833–1834 he delivered a series of lectures at the Medical College of South Carolina, Charleston. *Columbia Alumni,* pp. 24, 35, 37, 128, 201; Franklin B. Hough, *American Biographical Notes* (Albany, 1875), p. 339;

Dr Gale,[12] Dr ——,[13] and Mr James Chilton[14] of N Y. They had arrived the day previous with the large battery of the college of Physicians and surgeons consisting of 200 plates of 6 inches square.

Dr Gale requested me to make any alteration I chose in his arraingment which politeness I availed myself of by turning the battery into a more favorable position and making the connections between the different troughs more perfect. Still owing to the great hurry the preparations were far less perfect than I could have wished. We also joined the small apparatus which we brought with us from Princeton College.[15] This consisted of 116 plates of 4 inches square. In order to cause these to act with the battery of large plates the latter was not filled interely at first but when the action began to decline the smaler battery was detached and the larger troughs filled interely with fresh acid. The troughs were all filled by 4 assistants[16] each with a pitcher as soon as the body was laid upon the table. This was a great mistake as the battery should not have been filled until the dessection had been made for the operators owing to the accidental rupture of the carotid artery were from 10 to 15 minutes preparing the body for the first experiment; during this time the action of the battery was constantly diminishing in intensity[17] while the body on the other hand was loosing its susseptibility to the galvanic influence with the elapsing time.

The first experiment consisted in placing one of the poles at the neck and in contact with the nerve of respiration[18] and the other against the dia-

John R. Rhinelander, *An Address, Introductory to a Course of Lectures, Delivered in the Hall of the Medical College of South Carolina, Before the Trustees and Faculty, the Students of Medicine, and the Public Generally, at the Opening of the Session of 1833–4* (Charleston, 1834). See Torrey's letter to Henry of December 29, 1834, for a later reference to Rhinelander.

[12] Leonard Dunnell Gale (1800–1883) will play a very important role later in this series in connection with Joseph Henry's relations with S. F. B. Morse. He was a Union College graduate (1825) who received the M.D. from the College of Physicians and Surgeons in 1830. After serving as Professor of Geology and Mineralogy at New York University from 1835–1838, Gale was on the faculty of Jefferson Medical College, 1839–1841. During the years 1846–1857, Gale was a patent examiner and afterwards was a patent attorney. During 1847–1849, he was Associate Professor of Chemistry at the National Medical College in the District of Columbia. *Columbia Alumni*, p. 205. Sally G. Kohlstedt, "The Formation of the American Scientific Community: The American Association for the Advancement of Science, 1848–1860" (Ph.D. dissertation, University of Illinois at Urbana-Champaign, 1972), Appendix I—Biographical Directory of the AAAS, 1848–1860.

[13] Apparently Henry had not caught the name of this collaborator.

[14] See footnote 1 of Henry's "Note on Conversation with Chilton," of December 11, 1832, above.

[15] This description is not very helpful. We cannot state something as obvious as whether the circuit was in series or parallel.

[16] The three students and the unnamed physician?

[17] A problem of the state of the art. Batteries at that date did not deliver a steady current over appreciable time spans. Comments on this occur in this volume and will reappear in later volumes.

[18] Ure, op. cit., used the left phrenic nerve in the analogous experiment but suggested what was done in Morristown, using the vagus nerve.

phragm.[19] I soon discovered in applying the pole held by myself (the other being held by Dr Gale) that but little effect comparitively was produced by a continuous discharge or by what is usually denominated a galvanic current. A much more striking result was obtained by merely touching occasionally the pole to the orifice or even to the side of the body through the cuticle. From this it is evident that in experiments of this kind to produce the greatest effect the poles or rather the connecting wire should be held tightly against the body or connected with the nerve by passing a scewer through the nerve or what may perhaps be more convenient let the end of the rod be flattened and sharpened in the form [of] a scewer and thrust through the nerve. The rods should then be connected firmly with the battery by means of large plates or at least one should be so connected and the other attached by means of a cup of mercury to the last plate of the trough. The connection can then be broken and renewed at intervals.

Annother experiment was tried at my request which consisted in passing the galvanic current backwards and forward, first in the direction of the nerves and then immediatly in the oposite direction or from the branches to the trunk of the nerve. In this experiment a remarkable difference was observed in the intensity of the action when the direction of the current was changed: by far the greatest apparent effect was produced when the current passed in an oposite direction to the nerves or from the branches to the trunk.[20]

[19] This is a repetition of Ure's second experiment varied only by use of a different nerve. Henry does not describe the results. Ure, op. cit., p. 290, did:

> The success of it was truly wonderful. Full, nay, laborious breathing, instantly commenced. The chest heaved, and fell; the belly was protruded, and again collapsed, with the relaxing and retiring diaphragm. This process was continued, without interruption, as long as I continued the electric discharges.

The use of static electricity and galvanic currents to revive individuals was not new in 1818. For example Jacob Green and Ebenezer Hazzard wrote *An Epitome of Electricity and Galvanism* (Philadelphia, 1809), p. 157, describing the application of current and static electricity "to persons apparently dead." The electricity was applied on the body surface, not directly on a nerve as done by Henry and Ure. Green presented this work to Henry, and it survives in his library.

[20] The experimental conditions were not very satisfactory what with a severed carotid artery and weakening battery. The results now reported must have disconcerted Joseph Henry. Not only were they contrary to prior observations but he was frustrated, we suspect, in any efforts to carefully test the variables involved according to the latest theory of Marianini (see footnote 3).

Henry's lecture notes (see footnote 3 above) were clearly derived from P. M. Roget's *Treatises on Electricity, Galvanism, Magnetism and Electro-Magnetism* (London, 1832), from the Library of Useful Knowledge. Roget's text (pp. 17–19) of the section on galvanism has the shock acting on the nerve. "Convulsions" (i.e., contractions of muscles) occur when the circuit is made. When the current is running continuously, a smarting sensation is felt. When the circuit is broken, another shock occurs; Henry notes this "is a fact of some importance." That is, by analogy with static electricity, Henry perceived the possibility of self-induction, a theoretical matter to be discussed below.

Marianini observed stronger contractions

In making this experiment An instrument was used called the Basull.[21]

The connecting rods should be formed of Lead tube not less than ¼ of an inch in diameter or of copper wire 1/10 of an inch. They should be thekly covered with silk with corks at intervalls inorder to prevent a partial discharge from the rods striking some part of the body before coming in contact with the nerve. The two ends of the battery or poles should be placed as near the body as possible and inorder to effect this the battery several troughs of the battery should be placed at right angles to the body.

when the applied current went from the trunk to the limbs. To oversimplify, he postulated the existence of a steady current of animal electricity going from trunk to limb. When an external current was added in the same direction, the effect was additive. When an external current was applied in the opposite direction—from limb to trunk—the intensity of the contractions was diminished. Marianini carefully correlated the contractions with observations of contractions occurring when currents went in both directions, with the openings and closings of circuits, and with applications to nerves and to muscles. Henry was unable to repeat any of these refinements in the Morristown courtroom.

[21] i.e., bascule. So far, we have not located a contemporary description of this device. It occurs elsewhere in Henry's work. For example, the "Record of Experiments" entry of May 13, 1835, below, refers to a "*swiper* or Basule." In civil engineering, a bascule is a device counterweighted (in a seesaw manner) to produce oscillation. We assume the bascule was a device used for easily and quickly making and breaking contacts in Henry's circuits.

TO JAMES HENRY

Family Correspondence, Henry Papers, Smithsonian Archives

Princeton Sept 17th
1833 *Tuesday*

Dear James

Your letter of the 12th inst was received on Saturday last. We are very sorry to learn that Uncle James[1] is so unwell. He would be a great loss to his family and indeed to the country around him. I hope however that he will recover from the attack and that he may long be spaired in his usefulness.

I presume that Mother is very anxious to learn when we intend comming to Albany. You may tell her that we intend starting the latter part of next week but perhaps we will not be able to get off before the beginning of the week after. The commencement[2] is on Wednesday a week from tomorrow.

[1] James Alexander (1767–1850; "Alexander Genealogy").

[2] *Wertenbaker*, page 213, describes this major event in the Princeton academic year: "At the ringing of the bell the academic procession started from Nassau Hall to the Presbyterian Church, where the trustees, faculty, and distinguished guests took their seats on the rostrum and the students in the body of the building. The galleries were filled to over-

We may perhaps get ready to start on Friday morning but there are many circumstances which may prevent. You may also tell Nancy & Mother that we received a package of articles from the Misses Meads. Amoung other things it contained a little knife and fork for the Boy. He is delighted with them and eats at each meal at the table and handles his fork like an old man or at least so say the femamls of our family. The Aurora you mentioned in your letter was observed at this place by Stephen.[3] I had a very fine view of it on my passage to the Village of Morristown to which place I was going by invitation to assist in some galvanic experiments on the body of the murderer Le Blanc. I have also received an account of the same from Mr Bullions and by comparing his observation with mine I shall be able by a mathematical calculation to determine the absolute height of the meteor above the earth's surface.[4] Our examination commenced yesterday morning and will continue until saturday. This is the most tedious affair in the whole college course.[5]

We have prevailed on Jane Ryley[6] to stay with us until we go to Albany as her return will be much more pleasant if she accompany us.

I am indebted to David Kelly[7] for a letter[8] which I have not yet answered. It came to hand at a time when I was so much engaged that I could find no leasure. I will however indeavor to give the gentleman a reply.[9]

You must be quite lonesome at present without Mr McArthur. He will

---

flowing with gaily dressed women, alumni, and townspeople. The president opened the ceremonies with a prayer, after which came the Latin salutatory, followed by the English salutatory. While a band from Philadelphia provided music in the intervals between orations, one speaker after another rose and delivered the address which he had been practicing assiduously for weeks. In quick succession came eloquent harangues on moral science, belles-lettres, military characters, the character of a statesman, etc. . . . The exercises concluded with the conferring of degrees, the valedictory oration, prayer and the benediction." Clearly, not an occasion to be missed.

[3] i.e., Stephen Alexander at Princeton.

[4] For details on the problem of the height of the aurora, see footnote 3 of Henry's notebook entry for September 2, 1834, below.

[5] The students heartily agreed with Henry's judgment on examinations. The ordeal was held in the week before the September commencement, which forced students to study through the hot months of summer. Besides the comprehensive oral examination of the senior year, the students faced tests at the end of each earlier year to prove their worthiness to engage in the next level of courses. Professors, trustees, administrators, and even well-educated visitors might be among those quizzing the student on any subject he had supposedly covered in the year. The examiners had to sit through the whole course of questions rather than appear only for their topics, which made the occasion as boring for the professors at it was painful and anxiety-ridden for the student. *Wertenbaker*, pp. 101–102, 211, 237–238, and 249.

[6] Jane Ryley was the daughter of Judge James Ryley (*Henry Papers, 1*:444).

[7] David Kelly (1811–1880) was Joseph Henry's cousin once removed. See Mary Lydia Kelly, *Reminiscences* (Rock Island, Illinois, 1914). He received a degree from Union College, and then attended the Union Theological Seminary at Richmond, Virginia, before transferring to the Princeton Theological Seminary, where he finished his training for the ministry in 1838–1840. Kelly served as a substitute preacher for parishes in New York, Alabama, Iowa, and Illinois. *Roberts*, p. 104.

[8] Not found.

[9] Not found.

be a grand senior & doubtless will be much improved by his college course although it be somewhat short.[10] There are worse men however in the world than Mr Mc. notwithstanding he is somewhat queer in many particulars.

We have sold the House & Lot in Schenectady.[11] The purchaser must pay the Insurance. I will settle with you when I come to Albany for the ammount you paid. I paid the Insurance on Mother's property before I left Albany and I think I gave the receipt of the Insurance to Nancy. I do not find it amoung my papers[12]—perhaps I may yet find it.

Your Brother

[10] Samuel McArthur attended Union College. Henry was referring to the fact that McArthur spent only his senior year there.

[11] Probably a reference to Maria Alexander's home in Schenectady. We know very little about this real estate transaction. Henry, on behalf of his wife's family, attempted to sell the property during his first visit to Albany and Schenectady after his removal to Princeton. In a letter to Harriet of December 19, 1832 (Family Correspondence, Henry Papers, Smithsonian Archives), he reports being advised by friends to set the price at $2,500. Unable to complete a sale at that time, he left the unfinished business with an attorney. Both the actual selling price and the identity of the purchaser are unknown to us. Mentions of the money resulting from the sale of the property occur below in letters from Henry to James Henry of January 8 and February 12, 1834.

[12] Henry's editors haven't found it either.

NOTES ON THE AURORA BOREALIS BY JOHN TURNBULL[1]

Henry Papers, Smithsonian Archives

N. York
Sep. 30th 1833

On the 5th Sep. 1833 while travelling between Laprarie and St. John's Lower Canada,[2] between 7 & 9 in the evening, I saw the most brilliant exhibition of the Aurora Borealis[3] that ever came under my observation. The light

[1] Henry's file note identifies the author of this document as John Turnbull, a young Scottish acquaintance of Henry's (see *Henry Papers, 1*:355). Though not sent to Henry by mail, Turnbull's notes bear Henry's name and address on the reverse side.

[2] Laprairie, a St. Lawrence River town below Montreal, and nearby St. Johns.

[3] The brilliant aurora of September 5 aroused a flurry of scientific interest. Henry himself observed the phenomenon (see "Galvanic Experiments on the Body of the Murderer Le Blanc," September 6, 1833, printed above) and received numerous reports from others. In his letter to William Kelly of December 30, 1833, below, Henry acknowledged Turnbull's careful observations. Henry was especially interested in Canadian data, since comparison with more southerly results provided a means of determining the height of the auroral arch.

produced was equal to that of the moon in her first quarter, when she is covered by a thin veil of clouds. The light first appeared in the N.E. just after Sunset. Before 8 O'clock it had spread over the whole northern hemisphere, extending as high as the zenith. About 8 O'clock a *Bow* or Arch, of far more intense light than the milky-way, stretched across the heavens from N.W. to S.E. with the apex a little south of the zenith, say 5 degrees. It was a broad belt of pale silvery light, and continued about 10 minutes. The lights frequently disposed themselves into singular forms. One of the most remarkable of these, was several jets of light, from 10 to 15 in number, parallel to each other, and all arising from a line extending from S.E. to N.W. and sometimes from S.W. to N.E. shooting upwards to the zenith. Their length might vary from 5 to 8 degrees. The most distinct idea which I can give of them is by comparing them to jets of gas-light from small apertures in a straight tube. Those remarkable forms would continue from 5 to 10 minutes, then break up into parcels like fleecy clouds and move off with great rapidity to the N.W. and form again into new shapes. The movement of these cloud-like lights was greater than I ever saw clouds scud across the sky in a high wind. The whole body of light moved gently in the same direction, but the small clouds above alluded to passed swiftly over them, till they overtook others of a similar character with which they mingled and formed some new figure. During the whole of this time certain parts of the sky would seem to be covered with clouds resembling a dense fog. At 9 O'clock the whole sky was clear and only a glimmering light was perceived at the north. It may perhaps be worthy of <*research*> observation that the whole of the 4th was marked by an incessant and heavy rain. The 5th was clear and pleasant.

J.T.

FROM CHARLES WILKES[1]

Gratz Collection, Historical Society of Pennsylvania

Washing^{n} Octr 2^{d} 1833.

Sir,

Having been anxiously watching for an opportunity of sending this by a private conveyancer who might be returning through Princeton & have an opportunity of seeing you and getting the apparatus—but none likely to

[1] This letter occurs at the bottom of the sheet containing Renwick's letter of August 4, 1833, above, which Wilkes now is sending somehow to Joseph Henry.

happen so late in the season, the tide of traveling having set Southward, you would much oblige me by sending it by the first [trust?]ful person. Yours with respect

Charles Wilkes jr.

TO GEORGE M. MACLEAN[1]

John Maclean Papers, Princeton University Archives

Albany October 9th 1833

My Dear Sir

I am much indebted to you for your kind attention to my affairs in Princeton and for the trouble you have taken in calling at our house.

Your letter of the 3rd did not reach me until yesterday afternoon owing to the improved state of the mail under the reform administration.[2] I am happy to hear that the Gulick affair[3] has been amacably settled. We are all well and leave Albany for Schenectady tomorrow. I am much engaged in superintending the construction of the galvanic battery. It will be very powerful as it consists of 88 zinc plates surrounded with copper each 9 inches by 12 immersed in 8 troughs. The wood work will be made in Princeton but the copper part I will indeavour to have compleeted here.[4]

[1] George Macintosh Maclean (1806–1886), brother of John Maclean, was a physician and science teacher. He graduated from Princeton in 1824, received an M.A. in 1827 and, in 1829, an M.D. from the College of Physicians and Surgeons. In 1868 Princeton awarded him an honorary Ph.D. According to the *Princeton Annual Catalogue*, 1833, Maclean aided Henry when he taught the chemistry course during Torrey's absence (see also Henry to James Henry, March 2, 1833, footnote 4, above). Maclean practiced medicine in Princeton until 1840, was Professor of Chemistry and Natural History at South Hanover College, Indiana, from 1848 to 1849, and Professor of Chemistry at the Cincinnati College of Medicine and Surgery, 18[54?] to 1857. He apparently resided in Princeton in his final years. Maclean authored sundry minor medical and chemical articles for the *New York Journal of Medicine* and the *Reports* of the Indiana State Medical Society. A more dubious contribution was his *Elements of Somatology, A Treatise on the General Properties of Matter* (New York, 1859), Henry's copy of which contains the following penciled annotation: "This book is a gross plagiarism from my sylabus published in a pamphlet form and afterwards in the Report of the Smithsonian Institution. J H" *Princeton Catalogue*, p. 137; *Columbia Alumni*, p. 204; *Hageman*, 2:395; Alumni Biographical Files, Princeton University Archives.

[2] The letter has not been found. This is only one of Henry's frequent insinuations about the inefficiency of the mail system in a reform-minded era. For another, and a note of explanation, see below, Henry to James Henry, January 8, 1834, especially footnote 6.

[3] Not identified. Gulick may have been a student in the chemical course which Henry taught in Torrey's absence with Maclean's assistance. *Princeton Annual Catalogue*, 1833, lists a John Woodhull Gulick and a W. Armstead Gulick.

[4] For early stages of construction, see Millington to Henry, February 22, 1833, above.

I have explained my plan to Prof. Renwick & Dr Torrey.[5] The former thought it one of the most important improvements made in the galvanic apparatus in many years. The latter said it was new but expressed no opinion with regard to its operation.

Will you ask Dr Carnahan[6] if he wishes me to purchase in N.Y. *platina* points for the Lightning rods.[7] They will cost $5 apiece.

Will you also inform Mr Jäger that the Albany Institute has a small collection of Insects which requires Labelling. There [are] duplicates of most of the specimens & if he will give the names as far as they are known, the Institute will give him the duplicate specimens. This is a common way of doing business in this country but I know not if it will meet with the approbation of Mr Jager.[8]

The final product is described in Henry's "Contributions I: Battery." The paper was read before the American Philosophical Society in January 1835. For Henry, the chief innovation was the versatility of his battery. The large number of galvanic elements produced large effects of different kinds depending on how the elements were arrayed. The key feature of the apparatus was the mobility of the various components which were not permanently connected as in conventional batteries. Henry's article explains that the finished product comprised eight separate troughs, each partitioned into eleven cells. Each cell received a galvanic element or pair consisting of a plate of zinc in an insulated copper sleeve. The troughs were raised to the stationary galvanic plates by a windlass device and, by filling one or more troughs with electrolyte, Henry could vary the galvanic effect.

Added versatility was afforded by detachable connectors between the plates, allowing Henry to achieve the effects of both "quantity" and "intensity." Robert Hare's calorimotor and deflagrator provided the immediate models. A set of "homogeneous connectors" reproduced Hare's calorimotor in which all the copper elements are connected together, as are all the zinc, producing, in effect, one large copper and one large zinc plate. As Volta, Humphry Davy, J. G. Children, and Hare had shown earlier in the century, the "quantity" (amperage) of electricity increased with the size of the battery plates. On the other hand, small quantity and large "intensity" (voltage) could be obtained by reducing the size and increasing the number of battery plates, an effect which Henry reproduced with his "alternate or serial connector" which linked each zinc and copper plate. According to Henry, this configuration formed an eighty-eight element "deflagrator," another Hare invention which featured a suspension system allowing the simultaneous immersion of an extensive series of battery plates.

Unlike Hare, who explained the effects of his two batteries in terms of a linkage between caloric and electrical fluids, Henry was not concerned with the theory of the galvanic apparatus itself, but rather with its application to electromagnetic experiments. See Robert Hare, "A New Theory of Galvanism, Supported by Some Experiments and Observations Made by Means of the Calorimotor, a New Galvanic Instrument," *Silliman's Journal*, 1818, *1*:413–423, and "A Memoir on Some New Modifications of Galvanic Apparatus, with Observations in Support of His New Theory of Galvanism," *Silliman's Journal*, 1821, *3*:105–117. W. James King, "The Development of Electrical Technology in the 19th Century: 1. The Electrochemical Cell and the Electromagnet; 2. The Telegraph and the Telephone; 3. The Early Arc Light and Generator," *United States National Museum Bulletin No. 228* (Washington, D.C., 1962), pp. 234–240 (hereafter cited as *King*).

The galvanic battery, pictured on the frontispiece to this volume, was to be one of the most important scientific instruments in Henry's Princeton laboratory. Its completion was an essential first step for the resumption of his electrical research.

[5] We are unable to find any written communication between these scientists and Henry on this subject.

[6] *Henry Papers*, *1*:18n.

[7] To protect the tips from corrosion.

[8] Benedict Jaeger (identified above, Henry

Dr James McNaughton[9] sends his respects to your Brother the Professor. Give the Respects of Mrs H. and myself to your family and permit me to assure you that I am

Sincerely Yours
Jos. Henry

Excuse this paper.
P.S. I will if nothing unusual prevents be in Princeton the latter part of next week.[10]

to Harriet Henry, April 6, 1833, footnote 4) maintained a large entomological cabinet at Princeton. See *Princeton Annual Catalogue,* 1833, p. 13.

[9] *Henry Papers, 1*:452n.

[10] Making note of the appeals from James Renwick and Charles Wilkes which arrived during Henry's absence, Maclean listed the authors' names and the dates of the correspondence on the second page of this letter. Maclean mentions the matter in the second paragraph of his reply to Henry, immediately below. The Renwick item appears above, August 4, 1833, and the Wilkes note is also above, October 2, 1833.

FROM GEORGE M. MACLEAN

Henry Papers, Smithsonian Archives

Princeton October 12th 1833

Dear Sir

Your favour of the 9th inst came to hand this morning. Dr Carnahan is at the north. Mr Jaeger says that he would be pleased with the arrangement you propose respecting the insects. He wishes the duplicates sent to him numbered; those which are retained having corresponding numbers. As they are apt to be broken by transportation he wishes "2 or 3 specimens of each species" to be sent.

About a week ago Miss Conley[1] shew me a letter for you from Mr Ja^s Renwick requesting you to give up the apparatus of Hansteen to the order of Lt Chas Wilkes of the U.S. Navy. This letter was accompanied by one from Lt Wilkes desiring you to forward the apparatus to him at Washington City by the first safe opportunity. I did not think it necessary to take any step in this matter: & no opportunity has offered by which it could have been sent.[2]

[1] Perhaps a garbled reference to Nancy Connor, Harriet Henry's aunt residing with the family in Princeton.

[2] See footnote 10 of the letter of October 9, 1833. We have no further information about the possible loan of the needles to Wilkes. No Wilkes publications in terrestrial magnetism in these years are known to us.

I have some expectation of visiting Sing Sing next Tuesday: if I should I propose tarrying a few days in the city, where I should be pleased to meet you. If I visit the city, I will stop with Dr. Phillips[3] in Broome St at the corner of Grand.

My sisters join me in respects to Mrs Henry. My brothers are from home.

Sincerely yours
George M. Maclean

[3] The Reverend William Wirt Phillips (1796–1865) was a Trustee of Princeton from 1829 until his death. Phillips was also a Director of the Princeton Theological Seminary, 1825–1865. *Princeton Catalogue*, p. 20. A graduate of Union College (A.B. 1813), Phillips studied in the Associate Reformed Theological Seminary and in the Theological Seminary of the Reformed Dutch Church at New Brunswick, New Jersey. He became a Presbyterian and was ordained in New York City in 1818. He held pastorships in that city throughout his life. Alfred Nevin, ed., *Encyclopaedia of the Presbyterian Church in the United States of America* (Philadelphia, 1884), p. 619.

FROM EDWARD HENRY COURTENAY[1]

Henry Papers, Smithsonian Archives

U.S. Military Academy
West Point October 19th, 1833.

My dear Sir

Your letter of yesterday's date[2] is just received, and it affords me much pleasure to learn that you propose introducing the translation of Boucharlat's mechanics, at the ensuing term of the College of New Jersey.[3]

The publishers of the work are Messrs J & J Harper[4] 82 Cliff Street, New York, from whom it can, without doubt, be obtained on as reasonable terms as from any other Bookseller; and to promote your wishes in this particular, as far as is in my power, I will drop them a line by this evening's mail, informing them that such an order will probably be given.

I have made repeated attempts to find a private opportunity by which to forward a copy to you, but hitherto without success. Should you not stop

[1] The letter is addressed to Henry in Albany.

[2] Not found.

[3] *An Elementary Treatise on Mechanics* (New York, 1833). See above, Courtenay to Henry, January 3, 1833, footnotes 3 and 4.

[4] Founded in 1817 by John and James Harper, J. and J. Harper, later known as Harper and Brothers, became one of the best known houses in American publishing. Particularly strong in school and college textbooks, the firm published a number of early medical texts and, before Courtenay's translation, a series of mathematical and engineering texts by Charles Davies of West Point. See Eugene Exman's *The House of Harper* (New York, 1967), pp. 14, 163–165, and his *The Brothers Harper* (New York, 1965), p. 29.

at the Point on your passage down, you will oblige me by calling at the store of the Messrs Harpers who have been requested to deliver a copy to you.[5] I hope sincerely that the work may prove suitable to your wants at Princeton, as I am very confident that its introduction there will prove of great service in bringing it into notice elsewhere.[6] Should you think favourably of it, you would confer a favour by recommending it to the notice of such of your scientific friends as are engaged in giving instruction in this interesting subject.

We shall be much pleased to see you should you find it convenient to give us a call, either at this or any future time.

Respectfully Yours
Ed H Courtenay

[5] See above, Courtenay to Henry, January 3, 1833, footnote 3.

[6] Besides being used at Princeton, Courtenay's *Mechanics* by 1840 became a required text at Union College, Columbia, Wesleyan, and the University of Pennsylvania. By 1850, the text had gone through five more editions. Stanley M. Guralnick, "Science and the American College, 1828–1860" (Ph.D. dissertation, University of Pennsylvania, 1969), p. 114. L. C. Karpinski, *Bibliography of Mathematical Works Printed in America Through 1850* (Ann Arbor, 1940), p. 347.

HENRY NOTEBOOK ENTRY

Notebook [7171], pages 47–48, Henry Papers, Smithsonian Archives

Occt. 22nd 1833[1]

Mr Faraday[2] obtained an indication of magneto-electrical induction from the earth by means of a helix of wire first with a cylender of iron contained within it. The effect was produced by holding the cylender & coil in the direction of the dipping needle and afterwards suddenly inverting it. The same effect was produced but with less intensity when the helix was used in the same manner without the soft iron cylender. (The effect may be made more striking by using a large ring of copper ribbon. J-H)

[1] We have shifted the position of the date which originally appeared directly beneath Henry's first drawing, below.

[2] Henry is paraphrasing from Michael Faraday's "Experimental Researches in Electricity. 2nd Series. 5. Terrestrial Magneto-Electric Induction. 6. Force and Direction of Magneto-Electric Induction Generally," *Phil. Trans.*, 1832, pp. 163–194, sections 141, 148, 160, 162, in which Faraday extends the recently discovered principle of magnetoelectric induction to terrestrial magnetism. The natural magnetism of the earth, Faraday conjectured, offered the possibility of a new kind of electrical machine.

The same effect[3] may probably be produced by a large coil of copper ribbon made to revolve on an axis at right angles to the dip with two wires to the galvanometer proceeding one from each axis. Thus *a* & b are two smal copper discs revolving in two cups of mercury in order to form the communication. Try the experiment

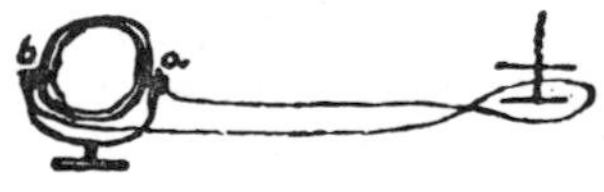

The effect will perhaps be farther increased by arranging several coils like the meridians of a globe and causing them all to revolve Thus Mr Faraday produced electrical action on a very delicate galvanometer by means of revolving a brass ball 4 inches in diameter. This experiment throws much light on the revolving ball of Mr Barlow.[4]

Mr Farady in his paper in the Transactions from which the foregoing have been extracted seems to think that the electricity produced from magnetic induction has but little intensity while my impression has been that the intensity is considerable.[5] J.H.

(Experiment on this point)

Make[6] a needle in the form of a tube, adjust glasses, suspend it by silk, and look through the glasses as a tellescope at a distant board placed at right angles to the magnetic meridian with divisions on it corresponding to the

[3] The next two paragraphs are Henry's own experimental suggestions, involving the application of his new ribbon coils, basic components of his forthcoming experiments on self-induction and mutual induction.

[4] In 1825, the British electrical physicist Peter Barlow was able to induce magnetism in thirteen- and eight-inch artillery shells by rotating them under the influence of the earth's magnetism. Barlow believed the experiment offered a model for explaining observed deviations in terrestrial magnetic force. The experiment was analogous to the induction of magnetism in iron by striking, drilling, and other mechanical means. Barlow, "On the Temporary Magnetic Effect Induced in Iron Bodies by Rotation," *Phil. Trans.*, 1825, pp. 317–327. Faraday and Henry explained the effect by postulating the induction of electric currents in the rotating iron ball.

[5] We infer that Henry is now referring to Faraday's First Series of Experimental Researches in Electricity: "1. On the Induction of Electric Currents . . . ," which immediately precedes Faraday's paper on "Terrestrial Magneto-Electric Induction" in *Phil. Trans.*, 1832, pp. 125–162. In section 57 of the article, Faraday points out that electricity produced from ordinary magnetism is feeble in intensity and small in quantity. We have no record of any experiments Henry may have conducted in this period on the specific problem of intensifying electric induction from ordinary magnets.

[6] At this point Henry shifts to a consideration of various ways of using telescopic devices to increase the precision of terrestrial magnetic readings. We suspect that the notes which follow were made at approximately the same time as the preceding excerpts from Faraday, since the theme of terrestrial magnetism continues. This dating is supported by a letter from Henry to William Kelly of December 30, 1833 (below), only two months later, in which Henry addresses himself to related terrestrial magnetic problems. At the end of 1833, Henry apparently is developing renewed interests in terrestrial magnetic measurements, specifically in the construction of large modified needles to achieve greater precision.

seconds and minutes of a degree.[7] And in this way notice the variations of the needle daily & hourly.

Another: suspend a tellescope under the needle (Like the magnetic Tellescope of Prony. See Humboldt vol 1st p 37 only noticed[8]).

Or Look through sight verges[9] on the needle.

Or Place a glass mirror on the needle and view with a tellescope placed at a distance. This method was sugested to me by Mr James Dean.[10]

[7] Observing the enlarged scale at a distance afforded more precise readings of the needle's variation. We have found no evidence that Henry actually constructed this modified needle or those that follow.

[8] Henry refers to Alexander von Humboldt and Aimé Bonpland's *Personal Narrative of Travels to the Equinoctial Regions of the New Continent, during the Years 1799–1804*, which appeared in numerous editions. Henry may have seen the third London edition of 1822, translated by Helen Maria Williams. On pages 34–40 of the first volume of that edition Humboldt listed the apparatus taken on his celebrated expedition. The list included a twelve-inch magnetic needle with sighting vanes suspended by an untwisted thread, an apparatus Humboldt likened to the "magnetic telescope" of the French mathematical engineer Riche de Prony (1755–1839).

Henry encountered Humboldt's work many times in his career, usually through indirect references such as this one. He gleaned useful facts from Humboldt on terrestrial magnetism, instrumentation, galvanism, meteorology, and geography. Most of these data stemmed originally from Humboldt's expedition to South America. Henry jotted down the information in scientific reading notebooks, particularly [6123], [7171], and [10615], and occasionally used it in lectures at Princeton, notably in those on geology. On occasion, Henry's investigations of specific physical phenomena such as auroras paralleled the work of Humboldt, but Henry did not explicitly acknowledge Humboldt as the inspiration or the model for these undertakings. No evidence remains that Henry was consciously influenced by Humboldt's general style as a scientist, a trait that sets Henry apart from those Americans who were enthusiastic Humboldtians. Henry's scientific papers, notebooks, and correspondence reflect no interest in Humboldt's major synthetic work, *Kosmos* (1845). Henry did own a used copy of J. F. W. Herschel's *Essays from the Edinburgh and Quarterly Reviews, with Other Addresses and Pieces* (London, 1857), which reprinted Herschel's long critique of *Kosmos* (pp. 257–364), but the marginal markings in that part of the book seem not to have been made by Henry. (William H. Goetzmann documents Humboldt's impact on American science in *Army Exploration in the American West, 1803–1863* [New Haven, 1959], and Walter Cannon amplifies that theme in "Humboldt or Baconianism? A Defense of American Science in the First Half of the 19th Century," paper read to the History of Science Society, December 1969).

[9] Henry probably meant to describe the vanes for sighting along the needle.

[10] A scientific friend often consulted by Henry; see below, Dean to Henry, November 27, 1833, footnote 1. The apparatus suggested by James Dean is remarkably similar to the apparatus only recently invented by the great Göttingen mathematician and physicist Carl Friedrich Gauss (1777–1855, *DSB*) for the absolute measurement of terrestrial magnetic intensity. Dean, in fact, may have seen an early report on the Gaussian apparatus given in the *Phil. Mag.*, 1833, 3d ser. 2:291–299 (*Phil. Mag.* will be used to designate the well-known London journal which began as *The Philosophical Magazine* in 1798 and appeared under various titles throughout Henry's life. See Henry Carrington Bolton, *A Catalogue of Scientific and Technical Periodicals, 1665–1895 . . .*, 2d ed. [Washington, D.C., 1897], pp. 445–446). There is no evidence that Henry already knew the article, although he was made aware of a later report on Gauss's magnetic apparatus in *Phil. Mag.*, 1834, 3d ser. 5:344–349. See John Vaughan to Henry, below, December 8, 1834.

Gauss's needles were large ones, about a foot in length, weighing about a pound. Later ones were about two feet long and nearly four pounds. The needles were suspended by silk threads and a plane mirror was fixed to the north or south end of the needle, perpendicular to the needle's axis. A theodolite was placed at a distance from the needle, and to the stand of the theodolite was attached a horizontal scale four feet in length. The experimenter measured the vibrations of the needle by observing through the telescope the image of the scale in the mirror at the end of the needle. The enlarged scale provided very precise readings of the needle's angle. Furthermore, remote viewing of the needle minimized any disturbances due to the body warmth of the observer or to any metal he might be carrying. The larger needles, Gauss believed, eliminated the disturbing influence of slight air currents. See *Phil. Mag.*, 1833, 3d ser. *2*:295–297. For Joseph Henry's use of giant magnetic needles, see his letter to Kelly below, December 30, 1833. In an undated note in notebook [7170], Henry described a similar method of observing the needle's variation proposed by the German Christian von Riese: "The author proposes to determine the variation by the distant azimuth of an object known in position with the direction of a small metalic mirror, vertical and parallel to the axes of the needle to which it is fixed." Then Henry added "N B This is a method very similar to one proposed by myself, the mirror was suggested by Mr Dean of Vert." The Riese article, which Henry read in translation, was "Bestimmung der Declination der Magnetnadel mittelst eines Spiegels," *Annalen der Physik und Chemie*, 1827, *9*:67–88.

TO HARRIET HENRY

Family Correspondence, Henry Papers, Smithsonian Archives

Philad. Nov. 1st 1833[1]

My Dear Wife

I have concluded to stop in Philadelphia until monday. I hope you will [be] recconciled to my long absence particularly when I inform you that I am spending my time here very profitably. Last evening after my letter to you[2] I called at Dr Hare's[3] but did not find him in. On my way however down Chestnut street I accidentally met with old Mr Vaun[4] who insisted

[1] This letter is in pencil, written late one evening, and probably carried back to Princeton by President Carnahan. The dating presents considerable problems when matched against later statements in the letter. An alternative date, November 2, assumes that Henry misdated the letter by one day. That dating also presents problems. Henry's account is unclear or inconsistent at several points. Keeping Henry's date, we will note these below in the context of Henry's account of his stay in Philadelphia.

Henry had visited Philadelphia once before since joining the Princeton faculty (see his letter to James Henry of August 17, 1833, above). It seems, however, that he did not meet such future colleagues as Bache and Hare until this November visit. Commenting on his August visit, Henry wrote, "I was obliged to defer several visits and did not deliver two letters of introduction which I took with me from Princeton" (Henry to James Henry, August 27, 1833, Family Correspondence, Henry Papers, Smithsonian Archives).

[2] Not found.

[3] For Robert Hare, see *DAB*, and *Henry Papers*, *1*:462.

[4] John Vaughan (1756–1841), an English-born Philadelphia merchant. Henry had probably first met Vaughan during his August 1833 trip to Philadelphia (see his letter of August 17), when he spent time in the Library of the American Philosophical Society. A dissenter, Vaughan matriculated at Edinburgh University, came to the United States with his father, Samuel Vaughan (1720–1802), merchant and West Indian planter, and with him helped form the First Unitarian Church of Philadelphia when Joseph Priestley came to this country.

John Vaughan became a member of the American Philosophical Society on January 16, 1784. He served as Secretary, 1789–1791; Treasurer, 1791–1841; and Librarian from

on my accompaning him to a party given by Mathew Carey[5] to Mr Lesley the painter on account of his return to America.[6] I was very politely received and introduced to most of the company which consisted of the principal & most celebrated *savants* of the city. Among the number were Dr Hare, Prof. Bache,[7] Dr Hase,[8] Dr. Chapman.[9] It consisted entirely of men and was one of the kind called "Whistar Parties."[10]

March 18, 1803, to his death. He was one of those unsung heroes, the devoted worker who undertook the many routine details required by the life of an active organization. A bachelor, Vaughan rented much of Philosophical Hall on Independence Square and ran his mercantile business from there. He was active in pursuing philanthropic and scientific affairs. (We are indebted to Mr. Murphy Smith of the American Philosophical Society Library for information on John Vaughan.)

Three of his brothers were well known in their day. William (1752–1850, *DNB*) was a London merchant noted for development of London port facilities. Joseph Henry met William and his nephew, Petty Vaughan, when visiting Britain in 1837. Petty's father, Benjamin Vaughan (1751–1835, *DNB, DAB*), was in retirement in Hallowell, Maine, by 1833, but remained active in promoting scientific and cultural pursuits. A friend of the Earl of Shelbourne and of Benjamin Franklin, Benjamin Vaughan edited the first edition of Franklin's *Autobiography*. An active supporter of the French Revolution, he fled Britain in 1794 to France and emigrated to the United States in 1796. Another brother, Charles (1759–1839, *DAB*), was a merchant and a developer of lands in Maine.

[5] Mathew Carey (1760–1839, *DAB*), publisher, bookseller, and economist. Born in Ireland, Carey was an ardent and controversial defender of his fellow Catholics. After coming to the United States in 1784, he published various periodicals before founding a very influential publishing house. Carey is best known as a proponent of protective tariffs for the encouragement of manufacturing. He also advocated internal improvements and universal education. His son, Henry C. Carey (1793–1879, *DAB*), continued in the family firm and was a very influential writer on political economy. Judging by the surviving correspondence, Joseph Henry had cordial but not particularly close relationships with the two Careys. See Earl L. Bradsher, *Mathew Carey: Editor, Author and Publisher* (New York, 1912).

[6] This return would be of short duration. After a few months of teaching drawing at West Point, Charles Robert Leslie (1794–1859, *DAB, DNB*) returned to England. Born in London to American parents, Leslie was brought back to Philadelphia as a child and later attended the University of Pennsylvania. In 1811 he went to London to study painting with such well-known artists as Fuseli, Benjamin West, and Washington Allston. For a time Leslie roomed with S. F. B. Morse. A successful artist best known for genre paintings, Leslie became Professor of Painting at the Royal Academy in 1847.

The party was a family affair, as well as a homecoming. Leslie's sister was the wife of Henry C. Carey. Another sister, Eliza (*DAB*), was a well-known popular writer of stories and essays. Charles Robert Leslie comments briefly on this visit to his old home in a posthumous autobiography: Tom Taylor, ed., *Autobiographical Recollections by the late Charles Robert Leslie, R.A. . . .* (Boston, 1860), pp. 83–85.

[7] Alexander Dallas Bache (1806–1867), at this date Professor of Natural Philosophy and Chemistry at the University of Pennsylvania. This is apparently the first meeting of Bache and Henry; no evidence survives to our knowledge of earlier contacts by correspondence. As the two men would become friends and collaborators in later years, future volumes of the *Henry Papers* will contain much on Bache's career.

A great-grandson of Benjamin Franklin, Bache was a graduate of West Point (1825) who resigned his commission in the Corps of Engineers after two years to accept a chair at the University of Pennsylvania. From 1836 to 1842 Bache was involved in the planning of Girard College. For two years (1836–1838) in this period he was overseas studying European education and produced an influential report on his observations. During part of 1837 Henry and Bache traveled together in Europe. After a brief return to the University of Pennsylvania, Bache succeeded F. R. Hassler as head of the Coast Survey. He was a notable

November 1, 1833

We adjurned at 11 o'clock, not however until I had received invitations to dinners & suppers sufficient to last me for several days should I stay so long in the city. I promised certainly to dine with Prof. Bache & to take tea with Dr Hare. Both these engagements I have kept to day.

---

administrator and an astute promoter of activities he favored. With Henry's arrival in Washington at the Smithsonian Institution, the two men became jointly involved on the national scene. In 1863 Bache became the first President of the National Academy of Sciences, a body he was instrumental in founding.

Bache graduated first in his class at West Point. He was well trained in mathematics and at home in the French literature on science. At Pennsylvania his interests encompassed chemical topics but more typical of his tastes were the investigations of terrestrial magnetism. At one point Henry and Bache contemplated collaborating on a textbook. In Washington Bache was concerned with geodesy, tidal studies, and seismology. Weights and measures were also in his official charge.

See *DSB*. Nathan Reingold, "Alexander Dallas Bache: Science and Technology in the American Idiom," *Technology and Culture*, 1970, *11*:163–177. As shall appear subsequently, Bache at this period was heavily involved in the work of the Franklin Institute in Philadelphia for which see Bruce Sinclair's *Early Research at the Franklin Institute, the Investigation into the Causes of Steam Boiler Explosions, 1830–1837* (Philadelphia, 1966) and his *Philadelphia's Philosopher Mechanics: A History of the Franklin Institute, 1824–1865* (Baltimore, 1974). The only full-length biography of Bache, M. M. Odgers's *Alexander Dallas Bache: Scientist and Educator, 1806–1867* (Philadelphia, 1947), is of limited usefulness.

[8] Probably Isaac Hays (1796–1879). Hays received a B.A. from the University of Pennsylvania in 1816 and then studied medicine with Nathaniel Chapman (see next footnote). He received the M.D. from Pennsylvania in 1820. Hays had a notable career as an ophthalmologist, being one of the first to detect astigmatism. With Henry he shared an interest in color blindness. Reprints of two of Hays's articles on his ophthalmic practice for 1839 and 1840 survive in Henry's Library.

In 1827 Hays succeeded Chapman as editor of the *Philadelphia Journal of the Medical and Physical Sciences* whose name he shortly changed to *American Journal of Medical Science*. Hays was its editor until his death. In addition, he was very active in medical journalism and in preparation of various works of medical reference. He was a founder of the American Medical Association.

In Philadelphia, Isaac Hays was clearly part of the circle of men with interests in the sciences. Like other physicians, he was an active naturalist. The 1828, three-volume edition of Alexander Wilson's *American Ornithology* was edited by him; from 1865 to 1869 Hays was President of the Academy of Natural Sciences of Philadelphia. An active member of the American Philosophical Society since 1830, Hays was also a founder of the Franklin Institute. *DAB*.

[9] Nathaniel Chapman (1780–1853), an eminent Philadelphia physician. Originally from Virginia, Chapman studied medicine with Benjamin Rush, receiving the M.D. from Pennsylvania in 1801. After a year of study at London and two years at Edinburgh, Chapman entered medical practice at Philadelphia. A successful and popular physician, Chapman became a leader of the city's medical community. In 1813 he became Professor of Materia Medica at Pennsylvania; in 1816 Chapman switched to the prestigious Chair of the Theory and Practice of Medicine, resigning in 1850. He was the founder in 1820 of the *Philadelphia Journal of the Medical and Physical Sciences*, published by Mathew Carey, and the first President of the American Medical Association (1847). An ornament of his profession, Chapman essentially retained theoretical and clinical views of the past century. Chapman was an active member of the American Philosophical Society. He joined in 1807, was Vice President from 1828 to 1846, and President from 1846 to 1849. Chapman was part of the well-meaning but intellectually and socially conservative gerontocracy in the APS during the period of its decline from primacy in the American scientific scene. A recent biography is Irwin Richman, *The Brightest Ornament: A Biography of Nathaniel Chapman, M.D.* (Bellefonte, Pennsylvania, 1967). *DAB*.

[10] Wistar Parties continue to this day in Philadelphia. They are named after Caspar Wistar (1761–1818, *DAB*), a Quaker physician and Professor of Anatomy at the University of Pennsylvania at the time of his death. Thomas

Nuttall named the wisteria after him. *DAB.*

Caspar Wistar succeeded Thomas Jefferson as President of the American Philosophical Society in 1815, a post retained until his death. On Sundays Wistar had soirées at his home notable for good conversation and good food. Members of the Society, other Philadelphians, and interesting visitors to the city were his guests. After his death John Vaughan took the lead in forming a Wistar Association of twelve members of the Society to perpetuate the agreeable practice. The members took turns in hosting the parties at their homes. Rules adopted during the last century specified the nature of the food and drink served to avoid any status contests among the Wistar Association members. The number of Philadelphians in attendance was limited, but Association members could freely invite notable strangers. By 1833 the parties occurred on the Saturday night following the weekly Friday meetings of the American Philosophical Society (a point to which we shall return). By mid-century according to W. J. Bell, Jr., of the American Philosophical Society (private communication) "the term 'Wistar Party' was almost generic in Philadelphia. Any evening conversazione, where gentlemen partook of good conversation and food, was apt to be called a Wistar Party."

Wistar Parties were suspended during the Civil War and not revived until 1886. A Fortnightly Club appeared in 1884, modeled on the Wistar Association. Surviving members of the Association revived the organization but modified the rules to absorb the new body, some of whose members were not in the APS. By 1898 the original requirement for Society membership was restored. The Association continues to the present with twenty-four members; the parties are now in clubs or elsewhere, not in private homes.

Henry may very well have used the term "Whistar Party" in a generic sense. November 1 of 1833 was a Friday. The party Henry attended would have taken place on Thursday, October 31, if we accept Henry's dating. The November 2 dating places the event on Friday, November 1, presumably after the American Philosophical Society's meeting. This may explain Henry's use of the term "Whistar Party," as well as the invitation by John Vaughan and the presence of so many APS notables.

The records of the Wistar Association in the Library of the American Philosophical Society are ambiguous on whether a party occurred on Saturday, November 2. One listing for the 1833–1834 season has a blank after that date. Another does list M. Carey as host but, we think, erroneously. Immediately after Carey's name is written "absent at Boston 25 Jan[y]." Entries for January 25 and February 18, 1834, indicate that another member was shifted to the January date because of Carey's absence. Our reconstruction of the events is that no Wistar Party, properly speaking, occurred on that weekend but that Mathew Carey did have a party for his son's brother-in-law on either October 31 or November 1.

The same year that Henry met Vaughan on Chestnut Street, an English traveler, Thomas Hamilton, published an account of his attendance at the APS and the Wistar Parties:

> I had the honour of being present at an annual celebration of the American Philosophical Society. About a hundred members sat down to a most excellent supper, and the wine and punch were equally unimpeachable. The President, Mr Du Ponceau, then made a speech, in which he gave a very interesting account of the rise and progress of the Society to its present flourishing condition. It was originally established by Franklin, and a few of his fellow-tradesmen, who met in some back-room of an obscure tavern, and having supped on bread and cheese, enjoyed the feast of reason over a pot of London Particular. The Society now includes in its members all that America can boast of eminence in literature or science.
>
> On the following evening, I passed an hour or two very agreeably at one of a series of meetings, which are called "Wistar Parties," from the name of the gentleman at whose house they were first held. Their effect and influence on society must be very salutary. These parties bring together men of different classes and pursuits, and promote the free interchange of opinion, always useful for the correction of prejudice. Such intercourse, too, prevents the narrowness of thought, and exaggerated estimate of the value of our own peculiar acquirements, which devotion to one exclusive object is apt to engender in those who do not mix freely with the world.
>
> These meetings are held by rotation at the houses of the different members. The conversation is generally literary or scientific, and as the party is usually very large, it can be varied at pleasure. Philosophers eat like other men, and the precaution of an excellent supper is by no means found to be superfluous. It acts too as a gentle emollient on the acrimony of debate. No man can say a harsh thing with his mouth

November 1, 1833

Early this morning after breakfast I called on Dr Green[11] and spent the time until 12 o'clock in his Lecture room making notes of apparatus & ex-

---

full of turkey, and disputants forget their differences in unity of enjoyment.

At these parties I met several ingenious men of a class something below that of the ordinary members. When an operative mechanic attracts notice by his zeal for improvement in any branch of science, he is almost uniformly invited to the Wistar meetings. The advantage of this policy is obviously very great. A modest and deserving man is brought into notice. His errors are corrected, his ardour is stimulated, his taste improved. A healthy connexion is kept up between the different classes of society, and the feeling of mutual sympathy is duly cherished. During my stay in Philadelphia I was present at several of these Wistar meetings, and always returned from them with increased conviction of their beneficial tendency.

Thomas Hamilton, *Men and Manners in America,* 2 vols. in one (1833; reprint ed., New York, 1968), *1*:340–343.

Whether or not Hamilton expressed the viewpoints of his Philadelphia hosts or a Joseph Henry is problematical. The evidence known to us is ambiguous. Certain points in his account are pertinent to a consideration of specialized professional communities. Note, first of all, his approval of the Wistar Party and its kind as a device for countering the "narrowness" of specialization. In histories of science the coming of specialization is usually taken for granted as part of the related development of professionalization and the increasing complexity and abstruseness of science. Among the British, it is assumed, there was a tradition of amateurism in the sciences long after its demise in Continental nations like France and Germany. Hamilton may reflect this supposed British tendency. His pronouncement may, on the other hand, reflect an older, widely diffused view of the need for well-rounded individuals in society to counter the excesses likely to emanate from narrow specialists—a reflection of the eighteenth-century distaste for "enthusiasm." Viewed broadly, "enthusiasm" contrasted to a concept of a balance and orderliness in nature and in human affairs. Although the conceptual framework has changed, the uneasiness about specialization persists. As in Henry's period, the very men who exemplified and promoted specialization still talk, almost ritualistically, of the desirability of "broad" knowledge.

And broad knowledge, in Hamilton's view, plays a role in the socialization of the lower classes. The "operative mechanic" is introduced to upper class society in the Wistar Party and exposed to polite learning, as a pleasant means of social control. A man who cannot say harsh words while mouthing turkey may say moderate phrases in other settings. At this point we might doubt if the Americans had quite the class-bound perspective of the English traveler.

Problems of class and social grouping will recur in subsequent documents in this and later volumes. These are difficult problems; issues are complex and the evidence is often sparse. But the problems are important as they relate to the place and role of scientists in American society. We interpret what was happening during this Philadelphia weekend as Henry's initiation into the leading American center of scientific research. He was a young man of promise and repute from a provincial setting. Not only does he meet scientific peers, but Henry goes to a social event of proper, intellectually inclined Philadelphia. (Clearly, he knows Wistar Parties count in some sense.) This is not a democratic assemblage in a representative sense, but a self-selected grouping, including leaders of the professions and business. (The banker Nicholas Biddle was a member of the Wistar Association.) Men interested in the sciences—at least some in Philadelphia—were part of the "establishment" or were decidedly in some upper stratum of the class structure. In this sense we can describe the emerging scientific community as part of an elite or as constituting an elite to which young scientists aspired. This is a theme to which *The Papers of Joseph Henry* will return in later volumes. The connotations and consequences are complex, important, and murky.

We are indebted for information furnished by W. J. Bell, Jr., and Murphy Smith of the American Philosophical Society Library, particularly copies of documents from the records of the Wistar Association. *History of the Wistar Association* (Philadelphia, 1945). Sir Archibald Geikie, *The Annals of the Royal Society Club* (London, 1917).

[11] Jacob Green.

periments. After this I went according to appointment to the University and there spent about 2 hours very profitably with Prof Bache in inspecting the apparatus and making additions to my stock of experimental science. From the University we adjurned to the Professors house where I was introduced to his mother[12] his sister[13] and to an interesting little Lady who assists him in all his magnetic observations and who of course must be his wife.[14] I suspet they have no children[15] since the lady has so much time for philosophical persuits. My next step was to Dr Hair's[16] whom I found in his laboratory busily engaged in preparing for his course of experiments.

He was very polite and devoted more than three hours to giving me an explanation of the various articles of chemical apparatus with which his extensive laboratory is furnished. He says that his lecture room is the best furnished of any in the world and that his experiments are made on a larger scale than they are in any other place.[17] I remarked to him that I feared he was giving me too much of his time and that I was encroaching on some of his engagements; his answer was that he had never exhibited his apparatus to one who more readily understood them & that he ment to make the most

[12] Sophia Burrell Dallas Bache (1785–1860). Leonard Labaree, ed., *The Papers of Benjamin Franklin* (New Haven, 1959), *1*:lxv.

[13] Six were alive in 1833; we cannot say which one was present during Henry's visit. Ibid.

[14] Nancy Clarke Fowler Bache (1803–1870) was the daughter of Christopher Fowler, a prominent citizen of Newport, Rhode Island. She married Bache in 1828. In the 1830s Nancy Bache assisted her husband by recording data on terrestrial magnetism in the small observatory shed behind their home in Philadelphia. She accompanied Bache on his European trip in 1836–1838, and Henry mentioned her frequently on those occasions when he met with them there. After Henry accepted the Secretaryship of the Smithsonian in 1846, he often visited Nancy and Alexander Bache in their Washington home. Nancy Bache served as a volunteer in the United States Sanitary Commission during the Civil War. Henry helped her administer the family finances during her husband's final illness, and after his death in 1867 they cooperated in securing his estate and creating a research fund in the National Academy of Sciences in his memory. According to the wife of Jefferson Davis, "Mrs. Dallas Bache was a petite and eccentric childless woman, with a great deal of character and much common sense, and she had not a little epigrammatic wit. Like Mrs. Gladstone, she had given up her life to her husband and was part of all his labors." Odgers, *Bache*, pp. 17, 20, 40, 115, 166, 174, 203 (quotation from Varina Howell Davis), and 214.

[15] Henry is correct. Having no direct heirs, Bache willed his estate to the National Academy of Sciences where it was an important source of research funds in the latter decades of the nineteenth century. The playful peculiarities in some of Bache's later correspondence sometimes cause the unwary to think Bache did have offspring. For example, he sometimes addressed his successor at Pennsylvania, J. F. Frazier, as "grandson." Bache also came from a large family and was related to an enormous number of people, or so it seems when leafing through genealogies, leading to another source of error about his "progeny." For example, even such a meticulous scholar as William H. Goetzmann incorrectly describes Bache as the father of Matilda Wilkins Bache, A. D. Bache's sister who married William H. Emory, an important member of the Corps of Topographical Engineers. Leonard Labaree, ed., *The Papers of Benjamin Franklin* (New Haven, 1959), *1*:lxv. W. H. Goetzmann, *Army Exploration in the American West, 1803–1863* (New Haven, 1959), pp. 129–130.

[16] i.e., Robert Hare.

[17] Perhaps true. Hare was known for the large scale of his experiments.

of me. To this compliment I could only say that I was very much interested in the subject & highly gratified by what I saw. I staid with the Dr from 4 o'clock until 9. I returned to my lodging. I found Dr Carnahan & his Lady making preparation for an early start in the morning. I had not been at the house since breakfast & had not seen the Dr or Mrs. C during the day. I intend leaving this house tomorrow morning and spending the sunday with Dr. Green.[18] I will return to Princeton on Monday or Tuesday. I am principally induced to stop until the begining of the week on account of an invitation from a committee of the Franklin Institute to assist tomorrow in making some experiments of a philosophical kind.[19] I have engaged to dine with one gentleman tomorrow and sup with another and have also promised to dine with a third on monday if I remain so long in the city so that I shall have very little eating to do at my lodging. I have thought it will be more pleasant for me to stop at Dr Greens over sunday than to remain here & they have given me a very pressing invitation. You will be convinced from this letter such as it is that I do not forget my little wife amidst all my engagements and flattering receptions. Do not let the Boy forget to say Papa.[20]

[18] If "tomorrow morning" is Saturday, November 2 (following the dating on the letter), then it is unclear where Henry stayed on Saturday night. A possible reading, supporting a November 2 dating of the letter, is that Henry left the lodging on Sunday, had the engagements mentioned later and stayed overnight with Jacob Green.

[19] Perhaps a reference to the experiments conducted on Smith's compass needle which Henry worked on according to the published report dated March 13, 1834. *Journal of the Franklin Institute*, 1834, *14*:318–320. This investigation originated with the Institute's Committee on Inventions in 1833. See the correspondence between Henry and Bache, July 13 and 15, 1834, below, for further details.

Again the dating is murky. "Beginning of the week" might mean experimenting on Sunday or, possibly, Monday if the date is really November 2. Otherwise, the experiments occurred on Saturday, November 2, when Henry tells Harriet he will dine and sup with two gentlemen.

[20] The letter is unsigned. Although addressed to Harriet Henry and folded as though for mailing, there are no postal markings. We assume Henry gave it to the Carnahans to deliver to his wife.

HENRY VETHAKE[1] TO JOHN MACLEAN

Maclean Papers, Princeton University Archives

New York, November 6th 1833.

My dear Friend,

I am much obliged to you for the names which you have furnished me for the review; and will be pleased if you shall succeed in obtaining an ad-

[1] Having left Princeton in 1832 and thereby providing the vacancy in Natural Philosophy which Joseph Henry filled, Henry Vethake (1792–1866, *DAB*) went to teach at the Univer-

ditional number. I am pledged to the obtaining of a certain number of subscribers—a number which with some exertion on the part of my friends I shall obtain. If I shall fail in doing so, I shall be obliged to pay the amount of the deficiency in money at the rate of one years subscription for each deficient subscriber. With the condition of which I speak, the contract has been concluded between myself and the publisher, and it is intended that the first number shall appear about the 20th of January. The prospectus will be out in a few days.[2]

Now I have a request to make. May I not expect occasional contributions from some of you at Princeton, say from yourself, Mr Dod, or Mr Henry?[3] I think Mr Dod will be inclined so to do. Ask him if he cannot prepare an article for the first number. It ought to be prepared by the middle of December at farthest. As to Mr Henry I would be disposed to ask him, whenever an opportunity should present itself by the publication of something new professedly on the subject, to prepare a *popular* view of the progress of late discovery in magnetism, electricity, and Electro-Magnetism; but this objection to asking him to do this occurs to me. I should wish honorable mention to be made of himself in the article.[4] Perhaps I may think of preparing some day such an article myself. When you write, which I wish you

---

sity of the City of New York (now New York University). After that "experiment" (see the third paragraph), Vethake served for a year and a half as President of Washington College (later Washington and Lee) in Lexington, Virginia. From 1836 he held teaching and administrative positions at the University of Pennsylvania and at the Polytechnic College in Philadelphia. Vethake appears in volume one of *The Papers of Joseph Henry* as a near-predecessor of Henry's at the Albany Academy (p. 17) and in connection with his resignation from Princeton (pp. 433–458, passim).

[2] Vethake's plan apparently did not succeed; we have searched in vain for even a first number of any such periodical edited by him. In this period New York City was a leading publishing center for periodicals. But many of the general, literary-review journals there were ephemeral at best. Frank Luther Mott, *A History of American Magazines, 1741–1850* (New York, 1930), pp. 375–380. A number of short-lived literary magazines, begun in the 1830s in New York, eluded Mott's survey and appear in the *National Union Catalog of Serials*.

[3] We have not found any evidence of the responses of Maclean, Albert B. Dod, or Joseph Henry, all of whom wrote for literary magazines sooner or later. All three, for instance, contributed articles to the *Biblical Repertory*. Known formally through most of its years as the *Biblical Repertory and Princeton Review*, this quarterly emphasized "Old School" Presbyterian theology but included articles on literature, science, and the arts. It was founded by Charles Hodge (for whom see below, Charles Hodge to Hugh L. Hodge, September 4, 1834, especially footnote 1) in 1825, who edited it for more than forty years. It ceased publication in 1888. See Frank Luther Mott, op. cit., pp. 529–535. Henry's three contributions came in 1841 and 1845 and will be discussed in subsequent volumes.

[4] Though Henry apparently never wrote for Vethake's intended "review," later he supplied articles on a range of topics for a volume which Vethake edited, *Encyclopaedia Americana: Supplementary Volume* [Volume XIV] (Philadelphia, 1847). Henry's annotation on the flyleaf of the Vethake volume in the Henry Library reads: "This volume contains a number of articles written by myself. J. H." Correspondence with Vethake in the Henry Papers, Smithsonian Archives, indicates that Henry contributed at least four, and possibly more, articles. They were "Magnetism," "Radiation," "Coast Survey," and "Steam Boilers (Explosion of)."

to do as soon as you shall have seen Mess Dod and Henry, tell me what I may expect from yourself.

The conduct of Dr Mathews[5] and his creatures, the majority of the Council of the University, has at length become intolerable, and Dr Torrey, Mr Mulligan,[6] and myself will very probably, nay almost certainly, resign our professorships in a very few days. I have not the least doubt that Mr Cleveland[7] would do the same, were he not just now very straightened as to pecuniary means. Though only a month with us he is altogether disgusted with the state of things. And so ends the University experiment (for the institution must go down) through the folly, vanity, ambition, and ignorance—not to say worse things—of one man. I must, of course, look out for another situation where I may rest myself for the remainder of my life, content with things as they go, without expecting to establish great institutions by the aid of instruments so frail and so hollow as Dr Mathews.

Do not omit to inform me in a day, or two at farthest what I may expect about subscribers, and more especially about contributions for the review. I must not forget to mention that the compensation to writers will be ordinarily at the rate of one dollar, and fifty cents per page, but for elaborate

[5] James M. Mathews (1785–1870), Chancellor of the University of the City of New York from 1831 to 1839. A graduate of Union College (B.A., 1803) and of the Theological Seminary of the Associated Reformed Church (1807), he taught at the latter from 1807 to 1817. He was Pastor of the South Dutch Reformed Church in New York City, 1812–1840, after which he peripatetically lectured on the relationship of the Bible to science and to civil government. As Chancellor of the University, Mathews attempted a program of rapid expansion of curriculum and facilities accompanied by a number of other extreme changes. His totalitarian administration and burdens on the school's finances as well as on the spirit of the faculty brought Mathews's "experiment" into difficulty. Vethake, John Torrey, and Mulligan resigned on November 9, 1833. *An Exposition of the Reasons for the Resignation of Some of the Professors in the University of the City of New York* (New York, 1833). Mathews continued to have difficulties with faculty members throughout the 1830s. See below, Torrey to Henry, February 4, 1834, especially footnote 3.

[6] Reverend John Mulligan (1793–1864). A native of Northern Ireland, Mulligan emigrated to America about 1825. He came to the University of the City of New York in 1832 as Professor of Latin and Greek. Mulligan played an active role as spokesman for the faculty's grievances. After resigning he became Principal of the Union Hall Academy in Jamaica, Long Island. [Henry M. Brown, ed.], *General Alumni Catalogue of New York University, 1833–1905* (New York, 1906), p. 169; Theodore F. Jones, ed., *New York University, 1832–1932* (New York, 1933), pp. 33, 38–41; S. Austin Allibone, *A Critical Dictionary of English Literature and British and American Authors*, 3 vols. (Philadelphia, 1859–1871), 2: 1386.

[7] Charles Dexter Cleveland (1802–1869). Born in Salem, Massachusetts, he studied at Dartmouth College (A.B., 1827). Cleveland served as Professor of Latin and Greek at Dickinson College in Carlisle, Pennsylvania, before coming to the University of the City of New York in 1833, where he was Professor of Latin. He departed from the University in 1834 and established the Young Ladies' School in Philadelphia, at which he was Principal for more than twenty-five years. He then served as U.S. Consul at Cardiff, Wales, 1861—1867. He was a prolific critic and editor of English, American, and Classical literature. Brown, op. cit., p. 169; Allibone, op. cit., *1*:396. *Herringshaw*, p. 226.

articles evincing extraordinary research and labour as much as two dollars. Walsh[8] now pays only $1.25, and the North American[9] has never paid more than $1.

I remain,
Yours sincerely,
Henry Vethake

[8] Robert Walsh (1784–1859) published the *American Quarterly Review* from 1827 to 1837. *DAB*. Frank Luther Mott, op. cit., pp. 272–276.

[9] The *North American Review*, begun as the *North-American Review and Miscellaneous Journal* in 1815, was active until 1940. About 1824 the *North American* fixed its payment at $1 per page. See Mott, op. cit., p. 197. See also Frank Luther Mott, *A History of American Magazines*, 3 vols. (Cambridge, Massachusetts, 1938), 2:220–261.

HENRY NOTEBOOK ENTRY

Notebook [7171], pages 75–78,[1] *Henry Papers, Smithsonian Archives*

[November 13–14, 1833][2]

Meterological Phenomina

On the morning of the 13th of Nov. 1833 I was called from bed by Mr W & W[3] of the Theological seminary to observe a remarkable appearance of the heavens. On looking out of the window I observed a shower of small meteors of the kind usually called shooting stars desending from near the zenith toward the horizon. When a position was taken in the open air so that nearly the whole heavens could be observed the meteors were seen desending in every direction in directions which if prolonged would intersect at the zenith. When first seen by me they were so numerous that 20 might be counted almost at the same instant desending towards the horizon in vertical circles of every azimuth or point of the compass. In one instance a meteor was seen approaching directly in the line of vision & consequently

[1] There is also a Mary Henry Copy of the entry, interesting only for its revelation of her transcribers' mistakes and "corrections" of the original text.

[2] We know Henry had the copy of the New York paper (see footnote 7, below) on November 14, because he mentioned it in his letter to James Henry of that date. It is possible, however, that Henry wrote up the notebook account on the evening of the 13th, if he got the paper that early.

[3] We have not identified Mr. W & W because there were more than two students whose last name began with that initial at the Princeton Theological Seminary in 1833. The Mary Henry Copy transcribes the observer(s) as WLW, but this reading disagrees with Henry's mention of two students later in the entry. Also, there was no WLW on the faculty or among the students of the seminary in 1833.

did not appear to change its position. Its projection on the horizontal plane (speaking in the language of descriptive geometry) was a point and it appeared and again disappeared in the same apparent place among the stars very near the zenith. The light in this case was at first faint and then became brilliant and appeared to explode with a slight noise.[4] Had this meteor desended it must have fallen near the spot on which I stood. This circumstance led me to reflect on the direction of the motion of the meteors in space in order to produce the regular and semetrical arrangment which they exhibited in their paths on the celestial vault. It was clear on a little reflection that they must have all fallen from a great height in the atmospher parallell to each other and at right angles to the surface of the earth. To make this

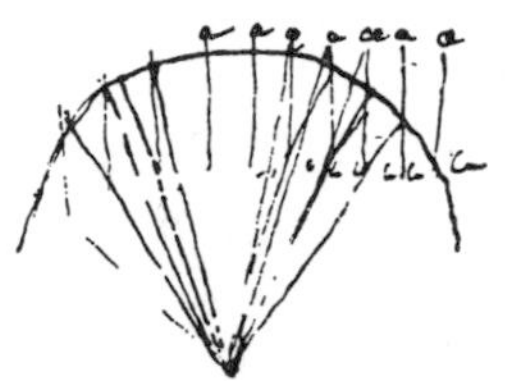

clear let *a a a* be the origin of the meteor and [*b b b*] the points of termination. Then although they were all parallel they appeared to diverge from the zenith as we viewed only their projection on the celestial vault.[5] It is evident from this view of the paths of the meteors that at Princeton we were in the midst of the shower and that had the meteors desended entirely to the earth they would have fallen around on every side like the flakes of snow in a calm day. I have heard no account of any falling so low as to be observed between any terrestrial object such as hills, treas, or buildings, and the observers. Some of them however descended within the influx of a <*strong*> west wind which was blowing at the time. One I observed in particular which desended leaving a very bright train behind it which remained several seconds and visible and was bent to the east by the wind.[6] They were very unequal in brilliancy, some faint other[s] as large as a common skye rocket.

The appearance of the meteor was that of the common shooting star as often seen in dry weather in the state of N.Y. The new york

[4] Denison Olmsted synthesized several American accounts (not including Henry's) in "Observations on the Meteors of November 13, 1833," *Silliman's Journal*, January 1834, 25: 363–411 and July 1834, *26*:132–174. Olmsted's theory that the meteors were dust particles from space required that they be silent, and he decided that the few observers who had reported sounds of explosion were overexcited amateurs who imagined things. Henry's remark on the noise could not have been so easily dismissed, had Olmsted seen Henry's account.

[5] Olmsted discussed the general problem of perspective, using a similar diagram, on page 148 of his article. Henry's sketch illustrates only the special situation where the radiant point is directly over the observer's head.

[6] Edward Hitchcock, who disagreed with Olmsted's theory that the meteoric material originated outside the earth's atmosphere, made much of the streamers' deflection by the wind (see his article "On the Meteors of November 13, 1833," *Silliman's Journal*, January 1834, 25:354–363). Henry's observations that the trails were blown out of line by the wind meant that the meteors fell within the earth's atmosphere for at least part of their paths, but did not imply that the meteors originated there.

papers[7] mention that the meteors commenced falling at 12 o'clock at this place. I am not aware of their having been seen until between ¼ past 4 and half past the same hour. Two young gentlement of the seminary went out of doors one at 4 and the other at 15 minutes past the same hour. They neather observed any of the meteors. The second person again went out at ½ past 4 and then saw the meteors shooting in every direction toward the earth. He at first attempted to count them and in the space of a few minuts says that he actually numbered 1500 when they became so numerous that he gave over the operation.

There is an account of a phenominon described in the Ballance[8] (a paper published in Hudson about 30 years ago) of which precisely agrees with what was observed here. This accont was taken from the Virginia Gazitt[9] of april 23 1803. The phenominon had occurred on the Wednesday preceding this dade which must have been therefore the 20th of April 1803 (See the Ballance vol 2—1803 p. 157 & 205). I am informed that there is also an account of the same appearance in Humboldt.[10]

There is also an account of two showers of stars mention in the chinese records copid from Dlambre[11] by Barlow in the Encycloped. article astronomy.[12]

The weather before the appear[ance] on the morning of the 12th was

[7] An article on the meteor shower appeared on November 13, 1833, in the *New York Commercial Advertiser*, an afternoon semiweekly newspaper. A clipping of this piece now is tipped in the notebook from which the entry is taken.

[8] The *Balance, and Columbian Repository*, 1803, 2:157–158 and 205.

[9] The *Virginia Gazette*, April 23, 1803, did have the article excerpted by the *Balance*. The observers stressed the numbers that fell, the variable brightness, and the seeming near approach to the earth. The apparent common point of radiation, explained by Henry in his notebook entry, was not a feature of the 1803 shower as reported in the *Gazette* or *Balance*.

[10] For Alexander von Humboldt and Aimé Bonpland's observations at Cumana, Venezuela on the shower of November 12, 1799, see their *Personal Narrative of Travels to the Equinoctial Regions of the New Continent, during the Years 1779–1804* (London, 1818), *3*:331–346. Like Henry, they found that exceptional dryness accompanied the meteor fall.

Such earlier accounts were important in determining whether meteor showers occurred erratically or at regular intervals. Astronomers of Henry's generation hypothesized that the shower of November 13, 1833, was a reappearance of the meteor swarm noticed thirty-four years earlier by Humboldt, and they accordingly predicted another shower in mid-November 1867, which indeed happened. Those meteors which fell in April 1803 were identified later in the nineteenth century as from a different swarm than the November group. Antonie Pannekoek, *A History of Astronomy* (New York, 1961), pp. 420–421.

[11] Jean Baptiste Joseph Delambre, *Histoire de l'astronomie ancienne* (Paris, 1817).

[12] Peter Barlow's article on astronomy in volume three of the *Encyclopaedia Metropolitana* fits this description. The title page for the completed series bears the date 1845, but the one volume with a title page of the partial set which survives in the Henry Library gives a date of 1830 (that set does not include the astronomy article). At least one article from volume five of the entire work was circulating by 1832 (see James Forbes's remark on George Harvey's meteorology article in Forbes's "Report upon the Recent Progress and Present State of Meteorology," British Association for the Advancement of Science, *Second Report*, 1832).

rainy cleared off about 10 oclock; the wind which had been south the afternoon before & in the morning changed to the west and became unusually dry. This fact was observed by Dr. Carnahan & the workmen employed in plastering the rooms of the new college.[13] The first coat of some of the rooms was put on in the morning of the 12th with the idea that they would be of the proper driness to put on the second coat the next day but when they were exhamined, they were found contrary to the usual experience of the workmen too dry for the operation & required wetting. The men said that they had never known wals dry so fast before.[14]

[13] i.e., the East College (see footnote 9 of the letter to James Henry, June 25, 1833).

[14] Henry's account of the meteor shower is interesting for what it omits as well as what it includes. He did not notice which stars were at the zenith when he first saw the meteors and he did not jot down the humidity and temperature readings at the time, both excusable slips when one recalls he had been awakened at four in the morning from sound sleep. What seems especially strange is that he did not record any fluctuations of the magnetic needle which coincided with the phenomenon. Some scientists, notably Hitchcock in his article for *Silliman's Journal* (see note 6 above), still advocated an electromagnetic theory to account for meteor falls.

TO JAMES HENRY

Family Correspondence, Henry Papers, Smithsonian Archives

Princeton Thursday Evening
Nov 14th 1833

Dear James

Your last letter came safely to hand but owing to the commencement of duties in college & other circumstances which I have forgotten I have been prevented from answering it. We are all well and have again commenced joging on in the old way. The college has opened with very flattering prospects. The number of new students is greater than any which has entered at one time for more than 15 years past.

I do not know the exact number of new students but it is between 60 and 70.[1] We find considerable difficulty in accomodating this accession at pres-

[1] Sixty-three new students were admitted at the beginning of the term on November 7, 1833; nine more were admitted after this date, making a total of seventy-two students for the winter term (Minutes of the Faculty of the College of New Jersey, 1820–1835, pp. 289–290, 292, 293, 297). By comparison, during the 1832–1833 winter term, forty-three new students had been admitted, twenty-two at the beginning of the session (ibid., pp. 257, 259, 260, 261, 266, 267, 272).

ent as the new college building is not yet finished but hope in the course of a month to be able to take possession.

We had a visitor from Albany yesterday Lawyer Davis the city attorney.[2] He came from N. York for the purpose of getting a release from Stephen & myself in behalf of Mr. Fassett[3] on account of the street which passes through the lot on which we have the mortgage in order that he might draw the money which was awarded him by the assessors. Davis informed me that it was very probable that he would loose his office as one of his party in politics had gone over to the other side and had signified his willingness to vote for Mr. Corning as Mayor.[4] I hope this change of affairs will not affect Peter Shankland's situation.[5]

Tell Mother the Boy is quite well at present, that he knew her picture, has not forgotten to smoke and spit like her and when asked where Grandmother Henry is he says "*Mome*" (home). He has learned several new words but does not attempt to put them together in a very grammatical manner as yet. He made way with a considerable portion of the cakes which were found in the drawer of the little table when it came from Albany to Princeton.

Stephen says if you find a good opportunity you may send his book.

Yesterday morning I was called up at a little before sun rise to see a very unusual phenominon which was probably noticed at Albany as I have seen an article describing it in Stone's paper of yesterday.[6] It consisted of a

[2] John Davis had been appointed attorney by the Albany Common Council, December 3, 1832 (Munsell, *Ann. Alb.*, *9*:259). He is probably the John Davis who later served as a trustee of the Albany Medical College and who died in 1847 at age forty (ibid., *2*:225; *10*: 379).

[3] Several Fassetts are listed in the Albany City Directory for 1833–1834: Timothy Fassett, of Fassett and Halenbake, builders; Benjamin Fassett, cartman; Asa Fassett, brigade inspector; and Amos Fassett, no occupation given. We do not know which Fassett Henry is referring to here.

[4] Erastus Corning (1794–1872) was elected Mayor on December 23 by the Common Council over his opponent, former Mayor Francis Bloodgood, for whom see *Henry Papers*, *1*:463. The vote was twelve (Democrat) to eight (Whig). Corning was elected to three subsequent terms as well, resigning in May 1837. A prominent Albany businessman, Corning was active in banking and iron manufacturing, President of the Utica and Schenectady Railroad (1833–1853), and first President of the New York Central Railroad (1854–1865). He also served as Regent and Vice-Chancellor of the University of the State of New York, State Senator, and was a Democratic Representative in the United States Congress. Reynolds, *Alb. Chron.*, opp. p. 509; Irene D. Neu, *Erastus Corning, Merchant and Financier, 1794–1872* (Ithaca, 1960); *DAB*. Corning evidently acted as Henry's banker in Albany; apparently there are no surviving financial records in the Corning Papers in the Albany Institute, but for descriptions of two transactions see below, Joseph Henry to James Henry, January 8, 1834 and February 12, 1834.

[5] Peter Shankland, for whom see *Henry Papers*, *1*:284, continued to be elected Chamberlain by the Common Council until his resignation in 1837. Munsell, *Ann. Alb.*, *10*: 247, 262, 273.

[6] The *New York Commercial Advertiser*, edited by William L. Stone (1792–1844, *DAB*), carried a story concerning the shooting stars on November 13. Stone published several books on New England history and culture as well as on Indian history. He is also remem-

shower of shooting stars falling apparently from a great height perpendicularly to the surface of the earth but although they fell nearly parallel like flakes of snow in a calm day yet they appeared to diverge from each other like the two branches of a rail road which appear at the most distant point to be near each other & to widen as they approach the observer.

They therefore appeared to diverge in all directions downwards from the Zenith along the heavens.

As I wish to collect every account which may appear concerning this meteor & if possible to determine its boundaries I wish you would cut from the papers all you may find. Recollect from which paper you cut the extract and if it be not too much trouble ask Robert Martin to make a collection for me of all that may be received in his Office.[7] I wish particularly to know at what places the meteors appeared in the south at what places in the north &c. and thus to determine over what extent of country the meteors were desending.

Frid. N B I neglected to send this in time to the post office this morning so that you will receive it several days after date.[8] Nothing new this morning except that we have just received a load of hay for the cow, have also a supply of coal & wood so that we are pretty well fixed for the winter. Coal is 8 dollars a tun when brought to the door Oakwood 3½ & 4 dollars hickory 5½.

Joseph has left for Philadelphia[9] to attend the funeral of one of the Senior Class who died of consequence [of] the Locked Jaw two or three weeks since he shot his hand very badly while out gunning. [He] refused to have it amputated. The Locked jaw was the consequence. It is a very melancholy death. He was a very promising young man considered by many the handsomest man in College, the oldest son of his Mother who was a widow.[10] Most of his class went on with Joseph. All well. In great haste

your Sister Harriet

P.S. If you see any of Mr Meads family please tell them I intend to write the beginning of the week. Love to all. H.

---

bered for his promotion of state archives and of the New York State Historical Agency (1838).

[7] Robert Martin (1798–1837) was one of the proprietors of the *Albany Daily Advertiser.* Albany City Directory, 1833–1834; Munsell, *Ann. Alb., 10*:273.

[8] The letter in fact bears a postmark of November 16.

[9] These lines are in Harriet's hand. A penciled note below them, apparently added later (by James?), reads: "The Miss Meads are very kind to Mother. They call often and are always bringing something for her."

[10] Alexander Henry Weir, son of the late Silas E. Weir, died at the age of nineteen in Philadelphia on November 14. The funeral was held the following Sunday. *American Sentinel* (Philadelphia), November 16, 1833, p. 2. Although the obituary does not state that Weir was a Princeton student, he was listed as a member of the junior class for the preceding year. *Princeton Annual Catalogue*, 1833.

FROM THOMAS COOPER[1]

Josiah C. Trent Collection, Library, Duke University Medical Center

College: Columbia S. Carolina
Nov. 16, 1833

Dear Sir

I observe by the Papers[2] that you have constructed a magnet that lifts 5000 lbs weight.[3] This so far surpasses any thing I have heard of before, that I have determined to intrude upon your politeness, by asking

[1] Thomas Cooper (1759–1839), known more for his political and theological agitation than for his scientific accomplishments, was nonetheless a respected chemist and professor in the early decades of the nineteenth century. In his classic biography, *The Public Life of Thomas Cooper* (New Haven, 1926), Dumas Malone emphasizes the political Thomas Cooper who campaigned endlessly and vigorously for human rights, states' rights, and free trade, among numerous other causes. Some of the formidable personal vigor with which Cooper tackled a wide range of intellectual problems is evident below in his letter to Benjamin Silliman, December 17, 1833. But Cooper was a physical scientist and professor by vocation, if not by reputation. "Perhaps no man of Cooper's generation did more than he to advance the cause of science and learning in America," Malone asserts (p. 399) without exploring Cooper's scientific endeavors. Certainly Henry knew of Cooper as a scientist (see his reply to this letter, dated November 26, 1833), even if the turmoil of Cooper's public life tended to overshadow that career.

Cooper was born and raised in England, where he read law and studied medicine. He was elected in 1785 to the Manchester Literary and Philosophical Society, but his outspoken sympathy with certain aspects of the French Revolution and friendship with Joseph Priestley occasioned his resignation there in 1791. By 1790 he had pioneered a chlorine bleaching process for which he claimed originality, but his business firm specializing in that process failed within three years. In 1793 Cooper emigrated to America, followed one year later by Priestley, both men settling in Northumberland, Pennsylvania. Cooper soon resumed his habitual political agitation, some of which won him a jail term. He became a friend of President Thomas Jefferson and a member of the American Philosophical Society.

The second decade of the century was Cooper's most productive. He read and published several original contributions in chemistry and geology. He conducted three volumes of his own journal, *The Emporium of Arts and Sciences.* He occupied the Chair of Chemistry at Dickinson College in Carlisle, Pennsylvania (1811–1815), and served as the University of Pennsylvania's Professor of Applied Chemistry and Mineralogy (1815–1819). He published a number of his course lectures on chemistry, mineralogy, and geology. He also produced his own editions of Friedrich Christian Accum's *System of Theoretical and Practical Chemistry* (Philadelphia, 1814) and Thomas Thomson's *System of Chemistry*, 4 vols. (Philadelphia, 1818).

At the South Carolina College Cooper was Professor of Chemistry (1819–1834) and President of the College (1821–1834). He was instrumental in establishing the state cabinet of mineralogy and in instituting the state geological survey. His years of retirement were spent mostly in political agitation and in compiling the statute laws for South Carolina. We have found no evidence that Cooper ever performed his intended magnetic experiments (as he outlined in his letter to Silliman, December 17, 1833, below). *DAB*, *DSB*, *National Union Catalog*, and *Royal Society Catalogue*.

[2] We cannot be certain which newspaper Cooper had read. The following article on Henry's large magnet appeared originally in the *New-York Standard*, October 1, 1833 (p. 2) and was reprinted widely in many other areas:

> PROFESSOR HENRY'S MAGNET.—An artificial magnet has recently been constructed by Professor Henry, of Princeton College, which far surpasses in power every thing of the kind. A number of interesting experiments on the subject of electro-

How far is this account correct?

Is it a Galvanic Magnet?

Will you favour me with a description of it, and directions to make one?[4]

As your magnificent Specimen cannot but be greatly interesting to men of Science, I have taken for granted that you will excuse the liberty I now take, and if your leisure will permit, send me the requested information.

Accept Sir my assurances of respect & good wishes.

Thomas Cooper MD
President of the South Carolina College

magnetism, were exhibited by means of this wonderful instrument, in the presence of the students, and a large number of gentlemen assembled to attend the late commencement.

Upon one trial of its strength, it was found to be capable of raising between three and four thousand pounds; and we learn that with some farther modifications of the apparatus, the magnet will probably be able to sustain *upwards* of four thousand pounds.

Professor Henry has also made important improvements in the construction of the Galvanic Battery, when it is to be applied to the production of a magnetic power. The particulars of his improvements we are unable to explain, but for the sake of science, we hope that this gentleman will soon give to the public a full account of these improvements, and of their important results.

[3] Note that the article reprinted above mentions only a potential lifting power of over 4000 pounds. Henry confirms that figure as a potential in his reply to Cooper of November 26, 1833, below. Despite a few scattered and indirect references to a two-ton demonstration, as in Hodge to Hodge, October 12, 1834, below, Henry himself did not claim to suspend more than 3600 pounds. Sometime in his early Princeton years Henry lectured to an unidentified audience on electromagnetism, saying,

> I regret that I cannot exhibit the power of one of these instruments.
>
> I find that the experiment is best shown by putting on a scale below the magnet several thousand lbs of iron raising this gradually to the magnet and showing the suspension.
>
> I have one at Princeton which readily supports 360[o] lbs with a small battery. [From an undated lecture on electromagnetism, in Henry's hand; folder 3A, box 19, Henry Papers, Smithsonian Archives.]

In a later unsigned article on "Magnetism" in Henry Vethake, ed., *Encyclopaedia Americana: Supplementary Volume* (Philadelphia, 1847), *14*:421, Henry seems to indicate a maximum lifting power of only 3500 pounds.

Henry never did pursue the development of a still stronger electromagnet. The magnet he constructed by this time was sufficiently powerful for both his classroom demonstrations and his research. For Henry, powerful electromagnets were important mainly as research instruments. "I expected no practical results from these magnets but I concluded that they would be the means of studying the subject of magnetism much more thoroughly than before and in this I have not been mistaken." (Quoted from the lecture cited above.) Further, designing a still more powerful magnet simply held no theoretical challenge for Henry. "By increasing the size of the iron, and the power of the battery, almost an indefinite amount of magnetic force may be developed." (From Vethake, op. cit., *14*:421.) The theoretical challenge of the electromagnets for Henry had been supplanted by his interest in new, versatile batteries for research on various electrical phenomena. A hint of Henry's battery work appears in the newspaper article in the preceding footnote; for more information on Henry's battery see above, Millington to Henry, February 22, 1833, and Henry to Maclean, October 9, 1833, especially footnote 4.

[4] See Henry's response of November 26, 1833, below.

November 22, 1833

FROM PHILIP TEN EYCK

Henry Papers, Smithsonian Archives

[ca. November 22, 1833][1]

Dear Sir,

I have made for you a *Kaleidorama* the invention of some German Professor whose name I do not recollect.[2]

You must make a wooden handle about a foot long and an inch thick  and bore a hole 3/4 of an inch from one end at an angle of 100° to receive the steel pin placing the small piece of iron in the wood for the plate of brass on the card to run against, and put the parts together thus

[1] The document is undated. A date of June 1, 1833, added at some later time, is clearly erroneous. We have assigned this approximate date based on the chronology made clear in several documents and other evidence. In a December 10, 1833, letter (Henry Papers, Smithsonian Archives), Henry told his brother James Henry that he had "received the German Toy from Dr. Ten Eyck. It has afforded amusement for all the knowing ones." So by December 10 Henry had received the instrument and assembled it. In Ten Eyck's letter here, he mentions that the instrument was received "at the Bazaar about a fortnight since." Advertisements for the "Bazaar" (for which see below, footnote 4), not evident in the Albany papers in the preceding months, appeared in the *Albany Daily Advertiser* from November 8, 1833, until at least the end of the year; the first ad, which was repeated daily for more than a month, boasted that "an extensive addition" had been received, including "many new styles, of French, German, English, India[n], Chinese and American articles. . . ." We presume that Ten Eyck sent the instrument to Henry around November 22, 1833, roughly two weeks after its introduction in Albany.

[2] Variously called "Kaleidorama," "Phantascope," or "Phenakistoscope," the instrument which Ten Eyck describes in this letter was a popular philosophical toy which also held considerable interest for scientists. It had its origins in the independent, nearly simultaneous inventions by the Austrian geologist and geometrician Simon Ritter von Stampfer (1792–1864, *Poggendorff*) and the Belgian mathematician and optician Joseph Antoine Ferdinand Plateau (1801–1833, *Poggendorff*). Appearing in late 1832 and early 1833, Plateau's phenakistoscope and Stampfer's stroboscopic disks both depended upon rotating disks with images and apertures to demonstrate effects of the persistence of the images on the retina of the human eye. These handheld devices quickly became popular toys and were produced in a variety of forms by different companies. The variant which Ten Eyck describes in this letter featured counter-rotating disks; with the images passing more rapidly before his view, the observer sensed greater continuity in the succession of motions. The kaleidorama, phenakistoscope, and phantascope, all names for the inventions from the same principle, were a significant development in the early history of the modern motion picture. Martin Quigley, Jr., *Magic Shadows, The Story of the Origins of Motion Pictures* (New York, 1960), pp. 85–97. Henry V. Hopwood, *Living Pictures: Their History, Photo-Production and Practical Working* (London, 1899), pp. 9–17.

Henry's interest in instruments for demonstrating the persistence of vision dates from as early as April of 1828, when he lectured to the Albany Institute on light and vision and showed experiments with the thaumatrope (see *Henry Papers, 1*:207). At Princeton Henry demonstrated both the thaumatrope and a "fantascope" to illustrate the persistence of images on the retina to his classes in natural philosophy (Henry's lecture on "Vision," as outlined in Weiner, "Joseph Henry's Lectures," p. 212). Henry's reading notes from his Princeton days clearly reveal his continuing interest in the persistence of vision. For instance, he read William George Horner, "On the Properties of the Daedaleum, a new Instrument of Optical Illusion," *Phil. Mag.*, 1834, 3d ser. *4*:36–41, a mathematical analysis of the workings of Horner's own invention (later called by its trade name "Zöetrope").

then slip one of the pictures on the brass tube & a small piece of blackened cord after it, keep it fast to the card. Whirl the card and look through the slits at the reflection from a looking glass after this fashion The cards require to be whirled in different directions.

I have seen no account of the instrument.[3] Groesbeck[4] has just recd it at the Bazaar about a fortnight since.

You will perceive that a great variety of motion can [be] imitated. If the slits are made larger the figures are seen in motion and are indistinct.

A beautifull variety is produced by whirling figures of stars & wheelwork upon a

---

The "Daedaleum" was a revolving cylindrical device with figures drawn on the inside and slits on the circumference; when viewed through the slits, the figures appeared animated. Henry's notes on the article are on page 56 of Notebook [6123], Henry Papers, Smithsonian Archives. Henry also took notes on the persistence of images on the retina from reading Charles Babbage's discussion of optical illusions in his *Reflections on the Decline of Science in England* (London, 1830), pp. 173–174, a book which has survived in Henry's Library. These undated jottings, with a brief note on an experiment to try, appear on page 94 of Notebook [7171] (Henry Papers, Smithsonian Archives) and were probably recorded during Henry's early years at Princeton.

Henry also used such devices for scientific experimentation. In 1834 he forwarded to Benjamin Silliman a translation of Adolphe Quetelet's report on the meeting of the British Association for the Advancement of Science (see below, Henry to Silliman, October 1, 1834). In that article Quetelet reports that Charles Wheatstone (for whom see below, Henry's Notes on a Trip to Philadelphia, December 5–7, 1834, footnote 14) demonstrated the instantaneous nature of a spark by rotating a black and white segmented disk in a darkened room and illuminating the disk with a spark nearby; the observation that the illuminated disk appeared to be stopped with its color divisions distinct, rather than blended or grayish, led Wheatstone to the conclusion that the spark had no appreciable duration. The Wheatstone experiment apparently fascinated Henry who first learned of it through Quetelet's report (the experiment was never published in that form). Based on information which we imagine Henry reported to Silliman when he forwarded the translation of Quetelet (that letter has not survived; see below, Henry to Silliman, October 1, 1834), the following footnote appeared below the mention of Wheatstone's experiment in the article:

> Prof. Joseph Henry, of Princeton, N.J., repeated the interesting experiment mentioned above, on the instantaneous illumination of an object by an electric spark. The effect is most easily shown by the common philosophical toy called the phenakistoscope. If one of the discs of this instrument be put in rapid motion, and then illuminated by a discharge from a Leyden jar, it will appear to be at rest with the picture on it distinctly visible. [*Silliman's Journal*, 1835, *28*:61.]

We have no clues that Henry persevered in this study. He did record in one of his notebooks a mention of "Wheatstones experiment Parabolic reflector with wheel before." (Notebook [23894], p. 119, Henry Papers, Smithsonian Archives.) Using the parabolic mirror to intensify the light appears to have been Henry's innovation in imitating the Wheatstone experiment.

While Wheatstone never published his experiment as described in Quetelet's report, he

seperate axis with different velocities and in an opposite direction.

Give my respects [to] Mrs H & the rest of the family

Yours in haste
Ph TenEyck

did go on to publish shortly afterward "An Account of Some Experiments to Measure the Velocity of Electricity and the Duration of Electric Light," *Phil. Trans.*, 1834, pp. 583–591, which contained experiments clearly derived from his earlier use of the phenakistoscope. Wheatstone presented a reprint of that article, originally inscribed by him for "M. Quetelet," to "Prof. Henry" at an undetermined date. It survives in the Henry Library. A discussion of that article and Henry's reaction to it appear below in an excerpt from a Henry notebook entry, [ca. 1835], following the documents of 1835.

[3] Stampfer's only published article relating to his stroboscopic disks was "Ueber die optischen Täuschungs-Phänomene, welche durch die stroboskopischen Scheiben (optischen Zauberscheiben) hervorgebracht werden," *Jahrbücher des kaiserlichen königlichen polytechnischen Institutes in Wien*, 1834, *18*:237–258. There he discusses the principles behind his development. Plateau, who had published a number of pieces on optical illusions, announced his invention in "Des illusions d'optique sur lesquelles se fond le petit appareil appelé récemment Phénakistiscope," *Annales de chimie et de physique*, 1833, *53*:304–308.

[4] William W. Groesbeeck (1783–1854), proprietor of an Albany variety store, the "Bazaar," an "Establishment of Fancy Goods and Household Articles, Wholesale and Retail." Groesbeeck advertised, "The vast collection of Foreign and Domestic Goods, Wares and Merchandize offered at this establishment is probably not equalled in this country." (Albany City Directory for 1834–1835, p. 47.) By 1845 Groesbeeck moved to New York City where he operated a fancy goods store. Munsell, *Ann. Alb.*, *6*:320. Albany City Directories, 1832–1837. New York City Directory, 1845–1846.

TO JAMES HENRY

Family Correspondence, Henry Papers, Smithsonian Archives

Princeton Nov 26th 1833
Tuesday Evening

Dear James

Your letter of the 19th inst[1] contained an unusual *quantum* of news. I am sorry to learn that Mother is not as smart as she has been. It appears that the cold weather affects her unfavourably. Does she still live in the room upstairs or has Nancy put up the little stove in the middle room as she thought of dooing?

We are all as well as usual. The Boy in particular is quite smart and is increasing every day in a knowledge of the use of the English Language. He has a very great taste for pictures and is particularly fond of a book of plates on the Steam Engine.[2] I put him in great extacy a few evenings since when his mother was out by shewing him the images made on the wall by

[1] Not found. [2] Unidentified.

a Magic Lantern belonging to the college. Nothing new in reference to the family unless it be that our Black woman has left us. We however get along very well without her as William and the Old Lady take charge of the cooking part of the concern. Our family is not large & we expect but few visitors this winter although we would be hapy to see them particularly Mr Sammons should he think fit to make us a visit. I am sorry to learn from your letter & the Public papers that some of the friends of temperance have been so indescreete as to have the Mayor of the city[3] indited on account of granting licences. It is not however unusual for Societies as well as individuals to be injured more by rash friends than avowed enemies. The course taken will I fear have a tendency to render the cause of temperance unpopular in Albany. It will certainly give those who are secretly unfriendly a handle by which to attempt its ruin. There is no objet of the day in which I feel so much interest as that of the temperance cause and there is none I am convinced which every good citizen is more bound to support. The temperance societies will do great good if they be properly conducted. But as in every objet of the kind it is very difficult to keep the proper course betwen cold indifference on the one hand and rash enthusiasm on the other: so it is to be feared, that by carring matters too far a reaction may be produced which will undoe all that has been done. But I hope there is good sense enough in albany not to condemn a good cause because some of its friends may have act[ed] indescretely. The temperance society appears to me to be founded on philosophical[4] principles. Its objet is not if I understand it right to reform those who have already contracted the habits of a drunkard but to protect the rising generation & those who have not yet acquired the habits. It indeavours to affect this object by rendering so unfashionable the custom of tippling & the common use of spiritous licquors as that no person except the most low and abandoned will be seen drinking in Public. In this country every reform must be affected by the force of public opinion & what is the public opinion but the opinion of each person taken in the agregate so that it is a duty of every man who wishes w[ell] to the cause of temperance to join the society not because he may be in any danger of becoming a drunkard himself but because his example counts one in making up the sum of public sentiment on the subjet.[5]

[3] Francis Bloodgood, the Mayor of Albany. See *Henry Papers, 1*:12, footnote 19.

[4] By this Henry means that the principles are sound because they are based on a correct general viewpoint. Later in the century Henry and others would use the word "scientific" to characterize something as being sound, good, proper, etc. Like the word "Baconian," which sometimes appears in similar contexts, "philosophical" and "scientific" are almost never defined in such usages, giving rise to odd problems for readers of a different era. For Henry and temperance, see *Henry Papers, 1*: 249, footnote 3.

[5] A democratic theory, not an elitist one. But what if public opinion did not aggregate

I cannot furnish you at this time with the exact number of students and it is not usual with us to publish the exact number until the next term or after the Spring vacation as we then generally receive nearly as great a number of new ones as in the Fall.[6]

I saw an account of Mr Clays reception in Albany and the presentation of the Cloak by Dea[n] in the journal & the Gazette.[7]

Your Brother

in accordance with philosophical principles? And what if nonscientists insisted on extending their count of one to scientific questions? Who decided what was philosophical? Here Henry makes a casual comment in the context of the temperance movement. In later volumes, the deeper issues underlying this comment will become explicit.

[6] 180 students as of June 16, 1834. *Princeton Annual Catalogue*, 1834, p. [2].

[7] We have not located issues of these Albany newspapers for the dates of Henry Clay's visit. Reynolds, *Alb. Chron.*, p. 505, notes his arrival on November 14, 1833. On the next day Amos Dean presented Clay with a cloak made in three hours by Relyea and Wright.

TO JOHN LEYBURN[1]

Gratz Collection, Historical Society of Pennsylvania

Princeton Nov 26th 1833

My Dear Sir

I am much indebted to you for your interesting account[2] of the Meteorological Phenominon observed on the morning of the 13th inst. I am anxious to collect all the information possible concerning its appearance at places distant from each other and have requested the students to give me every scrap they may find in the different papers which are received in College. Your communication was of course very acceptable. I was so fortunate as to

[1] John Leyburn (1814–1893), then attending Union Theological Seminary in Virginia, received a B.A. from Princeton in 1833 and an M.A. in 1836. Ordained a Presbyterian minister in 1838, he was prominent in church publishing activities. He later became a Trustee of Princeton (1875–1888) and of Hampden-Sidney College (1844–1850), from which he received a D.D. in 1849. Leyburn was elected to the American Philosophical Society in 1856 where he may have had further contact with Henry. Beyond the brief report which Henry here acknowledges, there is no evidence that Leyburn pursued scientific interests he might have acquired as a student of Henry's. Still, it is apparent from his warm reply to Leyburn that Henry made a sincere effort to arouse and sustain scientific concerns among his students. Since science was then not an obvious career alternative, it is not surprising that Leyburn, like almost all of Henry's other Princeton students, failed to engage in significant scientific activity after graduation. *Princeton Catalogue*, p. 145; Walter W. Moore and Tilden Scherer, eds., *Centennial General Catalogue of the Trustees, Officers, Professors and Alumni of Union Theological Seminary in Virginia, 1807–1907* (Richmond, 1907), p. 51.

[2] Not found.

witness the phenominon myself and observed precisely the same appearances you describe. The centre of apparent radiation was a little to the south east of the Zenith and retained its position relative to this point although the motion of the earth carried the stars more than 15 degrees to the west during the time of my observation.[3] The point of radiation also occupied the same position in refference to the Zenith at New Haven New York and Philadelphia. I was at first considerably puzzled to determine the true direction of the meteors and the cause of the apparent radiation but on a careful study of the phenominon I was convinced that the meteors were all descending nearly perpendicular to the surface of the earth and parallel to each other and that the radiating appearance was an optical illusion caused by the projection of the parallel paths of the meteors on the celestial vault.

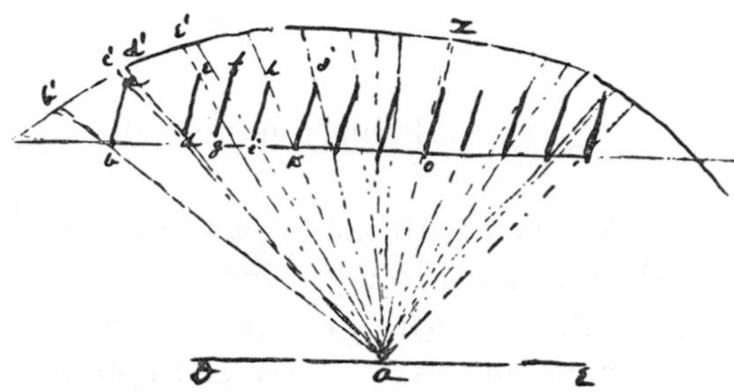

To make this plain Let *a* represent the place of the observer; *bc ed fg* &c represent the meteors falling parallel to each other and a little inclined to the surface of the earth *DE*. Then since all bodies at a small elevation appear projected on the celestial vault it is plain that the meteor cb or rather its path will appear projected onto the line c′b′ and would appear to move down the sky from c′ to b′. The same effect would be produced in the motion of all the others and the whole would consequently appear to radiate from a point at *Z* which in the Language of perspective is the 'vanishing point' of a system of parallel lines projected on a concave surface.

No approximation has yet been madc towards an explanation of the phenominon. All that can be done at present in reference to such appearances is carefully to collect all the facts observed in connexion with them and to leave to a future generation discovery of the laws of their formation.[4]

I regret that amid the bustle of commencement we neglected to make more observations on the magnetic intensity & that we did not determine

[3] Whether the center of apparent radiation followed the motion of the stars was to be a crucial theoretical point. Denison Olmsted rested his case for the superatmospheric origin of meteors on his observation—contrary to Henry's—that the radiation point shared the stellar motion and was therefore independent of the earth's rotation and atmosphere. Denison Olmsted, "Observations on the Meteors of November 13th, 1833," *Silliman's Journal*, 1834, *26*:140.

[4] The brilliant shower of November 1833 helped crystallize theoretical speculation on meteoric phenomena. See Henry's notes of November 13–14, 1833, above.

accuratly the rate of the needl which I gave you. If you find any difficulty in respect to any part of the observation drop me a line and I will give you the direction necessary. I shall always be happy to hear from you either in the way of Science or Friendship. We will see you I hope in Princeton during your next vacation.

Yours sincerely
Joseph Henry

TO [THOMAS COOPER][1]

Mary Henry Copy, Memoir, Henry Papers, Smithsonian Archives

Princeton Nov. 26. 1833.

Dear Sir,

Your favour of the tenth inst.[2] was received with much pleasure. I will cheerfully answer your inquiries and permit me to add, that I am happy thus to have an opportunity of communicating with one whose name has been familiar to me since the time my attention was first directed to physical science.[3]

The magnet you have seen noticed in the papers is an electro-magnetic magnet. I have not yet finished a battery of sufficient size to develope its full power and cannot therefore at present state its maximum. With a small battery belonging to the college it has supported 3300 lbs. With a proper sized battery it will probably sustain over 4000 lbs. The notice you saw was prematurely given to the public by someone slightly acquainted with the subject while I was on a visit to my friends in Albany. The story you will observe has lost nothing by travelling. I doubt not however from my

[1] Although Mary Henry omitted the name of the recipient in her copy of what apparently was a draft written by Henry, we are reasonably certain that the letter was intended for Thomas Cooper, for whom see above, Thomas Cooper to Joseph Henry, November 16, 1833, footnote 1. Cooper had inquired about Henry's magnet in this letter, and he mentions it again in a letter to Benjamin Silliman, December 17, 1833, below.

[2] Even though Henry refers here to "Your favour of the tenth inst." we presume that he means Cooper's November 16 letter and that the error in dating was introduced in the transcribing process.

[3] Thomas Cooper's edition of Thomas Thomson's *System of Chemistry*, 4 vols. (Philadelphia, 1818) may have been among the first of Henry's treasured texts in the sciences. A few scattered annotations in the volumes surviving today in the Henry Library suggest that Henry owned and read the work early in his Albany days. Henry used it extensively in preparing his address, "On the Chemical and Mechanical Effects of Steam," October 30, 1824 (see *Henry Papers, 1*:78–92).

<*other*> former experiments that when the instrument is in perfect order, the newspaper account will not be very wide of the truth.

The magnet is constructed on the general principles of the experiments made by me in Albany and which were published in the nineteenth volume of Silliman's Journal.[4] This as well as my subsequent papers,[5] you have probably seen as it excited considerable interest and was noticed in most of the foreign journals of science, although some of the statements by me were deemed incredible. They have since however been repeated by Faraday,[6] March, and Sturgeon[7] with perfect success although they have not as

[4] "On the Application of the Principle of the Galvanic Multiplier to Electro-Magnetic Apparatus, and Also to the Development of Great Magnetic Power in Soft Iron, with a Small Galvanic Element," *Silliman's Journal*, 1831, *19*:400–408.

[5] "An Account of a Large Electro-Magnet, Made for the Laboratory of Yale College" (with Philip Ten Eyck), *Silliman's Journal*, 1831, *20*:201–203; "On a Reciprocating Motion Produced by Magnetic Attraction and Repulsion," *Silliman's Journal*, 1831, *20*:340–343; and "On the Production of Currents and Sparks of Electricity from Magnetism," *Silliman's Journal*, 1832, *22*:403–408.

[6] Henry's claim here is slightly exaggerated. While being certain that Michael Faraday knew of his work, Henry could have only *assumed* that Faraday actually "repeated" his experiments.

As Henry has just claimed, his work in the development of an exceptionally powerful electromagnet and related experiments was noted in a number of the European scientific journals. More accurately, Henry's accomplishments were mentioned in several of the prominent journals, but certainly not "most of the foreign journals of science" (see *Henry Papers*, *1*:348, footnote 4). Faraday, among others, noticed Henry's work and undoubtedly was tempted to duplicate it. There were some researchers who aspired to possessing a magnet of comparable power (see the next footnote). The Dutch scientist Gerrit Moll (1785–1838), already known for his development of strong magnets, had consulted Faraday regarding his results in attempting to duplicate some of Henry's experiments (see *Henry Papers*, *1*:341–345). But Henry would not have become aware of Faraday's knowledge of his Albany work until sometime after Faraday published the complete version of his "Experimental Researches in Electricity. First Series," *Phil. Trans.*, 1832, pp. 125–162. In that article (pp. 138 and 154) Faraday mentions that his demonstrations would be considerably more emphatic if powerful electromagnets like Henry's were used. However, there is no evidence, explicit or implicit, that Faraday was "repeating" Henry's experiments or even used a magnet similar in design to Henry's.

Nonetheless, Henry's perception of Faraday's work is understandable in light of several factors. Both men were conducting experiments dealing with the phenomena of electrical intensity and quantity. Both too were concerned about the discovery of the induction of electricity from magnetism. In reading Faraday's article in the *Phil. Trans.*, Henry saw several close parallels to his own experiments, despite the fact that, in retrospect, each researcher was approaching the problem from different angles. Henry was surely gratified to have Faraday note his work on two occasions in the "First Series." Between the mentions of his electromagnet and the parallels to his own experiments, Henry obviously found it easy to believe that Faraday was "repeating" his Albany work. A more careful reading of Faraday's article makes such an extrapolation unwarranted.

For the background of this story, Henry's independent work on electromagnetic induction and his first awareness of Faraday's researches, see *Henry Papers*, *1*:375–376, 410, 435–439.

[7] James Marsh (1794–1846), an English chemist and experimenter whose work with rotating cylinders is briefly discussed in *Henry Papers*, *1*:317, and William Sturgeon (1783–1850), an English inventor for whom see *Henry Papers*, *1*:423, footnote 8. Sturgeon's and Marsh's attempts to duplicate Henry's design of an electromagnet are noted (pp. 199–201) in Sturgeon's article, "On Electro-Magnets," *Phil. Mag.*, March 1832, n.s. *11*:194–205.

yet as far as I have learned produced magnets on my plan, or any other which are as powerful as those which I have constructed. As it is possible that you may not have noticed the papers above referred to I have thought it proper to send with this a copy of each of the papers I happen to have now in my possession. I regret I cannot furnish you with a complete set. I intend however collecting all my experiments on the subject into one paper and addressing it to the Philosophical Society of Philadelphia[8] as soon as I shall have leasure to complete the investigations which occasionally have occupied the time I could spare from the duties in the college for some months past.

[8] Henry never prepared a paper summarizing his earlier work. Early in 1835 he commenced a new series of papers for the American Philosophical Society, beginning with "Contributions I: Battery" and "Contributions II: Spiral Conductor."

FROM JAMES DEAN[1]

Henry Papers, Smithsonian Archives

Burlington 27 November, 1833

Prof. Henry

Dear Sir,

I did not return quite so soon as I expected and since I have returned an accident together with a heavy cold have rendered me quite indisposed for the smallest action. I therefore took the liberty to persuade myself that the

[1] Educated at Dartmouth, James Dean (1776–1849) taught mathematics and natural philosophy at Dartmouth and the University of Vermont between 1807 and 1824. After resigning from Vermont in 1824, Dean continued his scientific work at Burlington, where he made money in real estate and lived off of other investments (information from the University of Vermont Archives). Described in Lindsay (cited below, p. 106) as "a gross fat man, so gross as to give the appearance of a diseased person, but there was nothing wrong with his head," Dean was reputed for his "mathematical attainments"—a reference in part to his interests in mathematical aspects of natural philosophy. A member of Boston's American Academy of Arts and Sciences, Dean produced a series of articles on computational astronomy for the Academy *Memoirs*, including: "On the Apparent Motion of the Earth Viewed from the Moon, Arising from the Moon's Vibration," 1809–1815, *3*, part 2:241–245; "Method of Displaying at One View All the Annual Cycles of the Equation of Time, in a Complete Revolution of the Sun's Apogee," ibid., pp. 329–332; "Description of a Cometarium," ibid., pp. 344–345. An 1823 contribution to *Silliman's Journal*, *6*:315–325, was his "Notice of Several Meteors," a subject which comes up in his present letter to Henry. In the same journal he published "Notice of an Aurora, in a Letter to the Editor," *Silliman's Journal*, 1838, *33*:212, and "Auroral Arch in Vermont. —Eclipse," *Silliman's Journal*, 1839, *35*:380. He was also author of *An Alphabetical Atlas, or, Gazetteer of Vermont* . . . (Montpelier, 1808). See Julian Ira Lindsay, *Tradition Looks Forward: The University of Vermont: A History, 1791–1904* (Burlington, 1954), pp. 105, 106, 108, 125, 191; *Appleton's*

memorandum I promised was not of immediate importance.[2] But at length here it is, "9h 15m eve 5 Sept. 1833: A luminous semicircle 2° to 4° broad. Arcturus and Vega on its N. edge, and Markab on its S. edge." This by the globe, (and the observation will by no means authorize any more accurate calculation,) calling the lat 44° 29′, makes the arch at the meridian about 10° S. of the zenith, and the horizon in the two points about 15° S of E and N. of W. I apprehend on reflection that I overrated the breadth. I suspect that it could no where have been 4°. There was at the same time a faint light low in the north.

I did not see the wonderful flashings which took place about a fortnight ago, but I hope you did; though I much fear that the phenomena were too numerous, too similar, too sudden, and too transient, to permit a hope of any one's being identified at two distant places, but if electricity or magnetism was disturbed at the time it would give us one point in the game. It ought to have occurred to us that by observing the variation in a mirror attached to the needle we should gain the further advantage of doubling the observed angle by reflection.

Yours with high respect,
James Dean.

P.S. Hope soon to hear of the success of your galvanic arrangement "contrived a double debt to pay."[3]

Cyclopaedia of American Biography; A. M. Hemenway, ed., *The Vermont Historical Gazetteer: A Magazine, Embracing a History of Each Town, Civil, Ecclesiastical, Biographical and Military* (Burlington, 1868), *1*:599–601. Marcus D. Gilman, *The Bibliography of Vermont* . . . (Burlington, 1897), p. 71.

We have not discovered the origins of his connections with Henry, who obviously valued his scientific opinion. One possible point of contact was Henry's June 1826 visit to West Point. Henry's journal for that date records the annual inspection of the Board of Visitors, of which Dean was a member. *Henry Papers*, *1*:160n. In any event, mutual scientific interests and the proximity of Albany and Burlington allowed ample opportunity for meeting. In 1835, Henry sent Dean reprints of his electromagnetic articles and received informed comments in return (see below, Dean to Henry, November 28, 1835). Experimental and reading notes dating from Henry's Princeton years and now in the Henry Papers, Smithsonian Archives, contain numerous references to Dean on subjects ranging from the aurora borealis to the physical characteristics of soap bubbles, part of Henry's research on molecular cohesion and strength of materials. See, for example, page 22 of notebook [7171] and the entries for April 22 and September 28, 1844, in Henry's "Record of Experiments." In addition, Henry's library contains a presentation copy of Dean's *A Course of Questions on Natural Philosophy* (Burlington, n.d.), an obscure college text (overlooked by even such specialized compendia as Marcus Gilman's *The Bibliography of Vermont*).

2 No earlier correspondence between Dean and Henry has been found. Dean may have encountered Henry and promised a report on the September 5 aurora during the latter's trip to Albany in October.

3 Quoting from Oliver Goldsmith's *The Deserted Village* (1. 227): "The chest contrived a double debt to pay,/ A bed by night, a chest of drawers by day," Dean may have had in mind the quantity and intensity outputs of Henry's new galvanic battery.

December 17, 1833

THOMAS COOPER[1] TO BENJAMIN SILLIMAN, SR.

Gratz Collection, Historical Society of Pennsylvania

Columbia S. Carolina Dec. 17. 1833

Dear Sir

I thank you for the pamphlet containing the present State of Yale College,[2] and I am truly glad to see it is in a condition so respectable.

I send you one of our papers, by which you will see, that I have resigned my Presidency of the South Carolina College, to enable me to comply with the request of many members of the Bar and of our legislature now in Session to deliver a course of Law Lectures, which may encrease but cannot diminish my present emoluments.

Notwithstanding my victory over the religionists who conducted the attack against me before the Board of Trustees,[3] I have not ceased to feel, that a suspicion exists even among those who agree with me in opinion, that many students are not sent here by religious parents on account of my known Infidelity as it is called: that is, my disbelief of facts related as of 2 and 3,000 years ago, written no one knows when, where, by whom, or in what language. For these positions respecting the old and the new testament, I know to be uncontrovertible by any man of competent learning. However, I acceded to the proposal of a Law Lectureship the more readily that the experiment might be fairly tried, whether my retreat from the supervision of this Institution, would encrease the number of Students. My Graduates at our recent Commencement were 37 Batchelors, and 3 M.A. I am persuaded we shall open in January 1834 with about half the number of Students that were here in January 1833. During the unremitting vio-

[1] For whom see above, Thomas Cooper to Joseph Henry, November 16, 1833, footnote 1.

[2] Perhaps Ebenezer Baldwin, *Annals of Yale College, in New Haven, Connecticut, from its foundation, to the year 1831 . . .* (New Haven, 1831).

[3] Cooper's troubles at South Carolina College were indirectly due to Silliman. In 1829 Silliman had published an American edition of Bakewell's *Introduction to Geology*, a text which Cooper had recommended to his students. Appended to the text was a syllabus of Silliman's geology lectures "founded on the Mosaic account of the formation of the earth and of the Deluge, as being delivered under the authority of Divine inspiration." Cooper used this edition because it was readily available to his students. However, he felt obligated to refute what he believed to be the false doctrines of Professor Silliman by personally presenting his own views to his students. His refutation of the Mosaic origin of the Pentateuch, and particularly of the book of Genesis, led to attacks upon him. At a trial held in December 1832 the Trustees dismissed the charge against him—that of perverting the religious views of the students. Cooper's case against Silliman and his defense before the Trustees of South Carolina College are printed in *The Connection Between Geology and the Pentateuch: In a letter to Professor Silliman, from Thomas Cooper, M.D., to Which is Added the Defence of Dr. Cooper before the Trustees of the South Carolina College* (Columbia, South Carolina, 1833).

Cooper's argument against Silliman's assertion of a Mosaic deluge was as follows: the only possible evidence for a universal deluge

lence of the attacks on me in 1831, the number of Students gradually encreased, and we opened in 1832 with 110, which is a fair proportion for a population of 250000 white people, *as times go in this Country.*

You have taken your side on the question of the Mosaic Deluge; which I greatly regret, because you must clearly see that the great preponderance of opinion among the able Geologists of Europe is <*greatly*> against it;[4] even of the Orthodox Class in England. I refer you to the Quarterly Review for Octr 27 Vol 36 p. 481 to 483 the review of Scrope's Geology of central France.[5] Also to the Quarterly Review of Lyell's 2nd Volume March 1832 page 129[6] and to Lyel's third Volume, in which he uses much the same explanation of the Mosaic Acc^{t} as I offered to you.[7]

---

is in the book of Genesis; having proven that there is no known authority for Genesis, that Genesis was not a product of divine inspiration through Moses, there is therefore no authority for the doctrine of a universal deluge. See Dumas Malone, *The Public Life of Thomas Cooper* (New Haven, 1926), especially chapter 11.

[4] A controversial point. At this date a considerable number of British scientists, undoubtedly adherents of (or influenced by) natural theology, were strongly disposed to believe geologic evidences presumably supporting the Biblical deluge. Others were openly hostile (like Cooper) or took an agnostic stance. Natural theology had fewer adherents on the Continent. What the majority opinion was cannot be simply determined, especially since many geologists were inclined to gloss over the points at issue by rereading the Bible to accord with the latest geological findings, particularly to muddy the issue by linkage to the discussion of the respective merits of catastrophism and uniformitarianism. A general study of the relationship of geology to religion, especially in Great Britain, is C. C. Gillispie, *Genesis and Geology* (Cambridge, Massachusetts, 1951).

[5] [Charles Lyell], "[Review of] *Memoir on the Geology of Central France; including the Volcanic Formations of Auvergne, the Velay, and the Vivarais, with a Volume of Maps and Plates.* By G. P. Scrope, F.R.S., F.G.S. London. 1827." *The Quarterly Review*, 1827, *36*: 437–483. Pages 474 to 483 are particularly relevant to Cooper's point.

Sir Charles Lyell (1797–1875), an Oxonian who studied with William Buckland. Perhaps the best-known geologist of the last century, his *Principles of Geology* (3 vols., London, 1830–1833) was extremely influential, particularly in its espousal of the uniformitarianism of James Hutton, that the forces presently discernible acting on the Earth are of the same kind and order as those operating in the past. *DNB*. See Leonard Wilson, *Charles Lyell, the Years to 1841: The Revolution in Geology* (New Haven, 1972).

G. J. P. Scrope (1797–1876, *DNB*), geologist and political economist. His study of the Auvergne, according to Wilson (p. 179), provided further evidences for Lyell's uniformitarianism. For a discussion of the issues, see W. F. Cannon, "The Uniformitarian-Catastrophist Debate," *Isis*, 1960, *51*:38–55.

[6] [William Whewell], "[Review of] *Principles of Geology, being an Attempt to Explain the Former Changes of the Earth's Surface by Reference to Causes now in Operation.* By Charles Lyell, Esq., F.R.S., Professor of Geology in King's College, London. Vol. II. London. 1832." *The Quarterly Review*, 1832, *47*: 103–132.

William Whewell (1794–1866), best known as a philosopher of science but also an important scientist in his own right. As will appear in later volumes, Henry was influenced by his philosophic views. *DNB*.

[7] In Lyell's review of Scrope (above, footnote 5), he states, p. 483, "Too much caution cannot be used against rash or premature attempts to identify questionable theories in physical science with particular interpretations of the sacred text." When reviewing Lyell's second volume (above, footnote 6), Whewell carefully exempts (p. 125) from the causative physical forces discussed by Lyell the successive creation of new species "which the Creator has confined the regulation and manifestation [of] to the depths of his own bosom." Whewell apparently inclines (p. 129) to Lyell's uniformitarianism because it "places geology in

As to your religious opinions, whether they are tenable or untenable I do not care one cent, but you have rendered us all too much service, not to care about your scientific character & opinions. You have not merely an American, but an European reputation, and the reputation of your own country is connected with yours. I do not believe there are half a dozen Geologists in Europe who would venture to coincide with your views. Lyell you know is lecturer in Geology in the *King's* University—the clerical Establishment in London in opposition to the *London* University, set up by Brougham and the Liberals.[8] Surely we ought to be permitted here, the same latitude they are allowed there.[9] However, you must take your own course. As to myself, I am fully persuaded that the Bible is in many respects a detestable, and in all respects an unauthenticated book: that religion is the great enemy of Science; and that I am not likely to die any thing else but what I have lived, since I enquired deeply & anxiously into the Subject,

---

contact with natural history and physiology, over a wide and almost indefinite extent." Lyell's position in the third volume of his *Principles of Geology . . .* (London, 1833), pp. 270–273, was to offer a diplomatic reading of the Biblical account of the deluge to cast doubt on its universality and on interpretations like William Buckland's (*DSB*) and Élie de Beaumont's (*DSB*) which stressed, among other features, the devastating effects of the inundating waves. The olive branch brought back by the dove was twice noted by Lyell "in hope of relieving the minds of some of our readers from groundless apprehensions."

[8] The London University (often called the University of London) came into existence in 1826 in large measure through the efforts of Henry Brougham (1778–1868). The ancient universities had a monopoly of higher education in England in the first quarter of the last century. Not only was there criticism of the nature of the education provided at these ancient foundations, but considerable resentment at the disabilities and exclusions they practiced against Dissenters, Catholics, and Jews. Many desirous of university education and degrees were forced to attend the Scottish universities.

Among the proponents of the university were Radicals similar in belief, no doubt, to Thomas Cooper, as well as representatives of various dissenting sects. Opposition from the established church to having different chairs of theology, as well as the inclinations of the Radicals and others, resulted in a purely secular establishment. This affronted both Anglicans and Evangelicals. The former reacted by establishing King's College in London. In 1836 King's and London University became part of a new body, the University of London. The old London University was known as University College in the new arrangement.

Henry Brougham had a very active career in politics and in numerous reform movements, as well as a strong interest in science. He was, for example, active in the Society for the Diffusion of Useful Knowledge. Several of its publications survive in Henry's Library.

Chester New, *Life of Henry Brougham to 1830* (Oxford, 1961). F. J. C. Hearnshaw, *The Centenary History of King's College, London* (London, 1929). Hugh H. Bellot, *University College, London, 1826–1926* (London, 1929). For Brougham's scientific impact, see Geoffrey N. Cantor, "Henry Brougham and the Scottish Methodological Traditions," *Studies in the History and Philosophy of Science*, 1971, *2*: 69–89. For Brougham as a popularizer, see J. N. Hays, "Science and Brougham's Society," *Annals of Science*, 1964 (pub. 1965), *20*: 227–241.

[9] In his review of Scrope (footnote 5, above), Lyell took what we can loosely characterize as an agnostic position on the question of the literal accuracy of the Mosaic deluge. He stressed both the complexity of the geological record and the divergencies of scriptural interpretations. In general, Lyell was careful to avoid extreme positions on this issue.

From 1831 to 1833 Lyell was Professor of Geology at King's College, London. According to his most recent biographer, Leonard Wilson, only Edward Copleston, Bishop of Llandaff and Dean of St. Paul, had reservations

a confirmed Infidel.[10] So much for heterodoxy, a subject I have been led into by my sincere respect for your public character as a man of Science, so honourably earned.

I find Mr Henry of Princetown New Jersey, is making a Galvanic Magnet that he expects to lift 4000 lbs. I am making a small one, that I want to use against:[11] the Tic Doloreaux,[12] and Rheumatic Affections. Might not Mr Henry's apparatus be applied somehow as a moving power? For if one magnet will lift 4000 lb, two or three of them connected as in common cases, might greatly increase the power? Your Journal reaches us here, very irregularly, which is a loss of pleasure & instruction.

Have you read the late Experiments on Animal Magnetism?[13] They are undoubtedly true in part, & incredible in part. Adieu Dear Sir, and believe me always with great respect.

Your friend & humble Servant
Thomas Cooper

---

about the appointment but voted for Lyell after an exchange of letters. Wilson is quite perturbed by the incident, stating Lyell had "compromised himself" and was "not quite candid." In his second lecture Lyell took an "agnostic" position "to remove from his uniformitarian doctrine the taint of . . . atheism." Wilson, op. cit., pages 308–313, 354–355.

To Cooper, Lyell was an exemplar. To Wilson from a twentieth-century vantage, Lyell was trimming.

[10] In his filing notation Silliman wrote "Dr Cooper a very improper letter not answered." Later Silliman elaborated: "In the last letter which I received from him he reviled the Scripture, especially of the Old Testament, pronouncing it in all respects an unsupported and in some respects a most detestable book. To this letter I made no reply feeling that it was such a violation of gentlemanly courtesy when writing to one whose sentiments he knew to be so opposed to his own, that I thought it better to drop the correspondence and I never heard from him again." John F. Fulton and Elizabeth Thomson, *Benjamin Silliman, 1779–1864: Pathfinder in American Science* (New York, 1947), p. 139.

The difference between Lyell and Cooper in this matter was not apparently visible to the latter. Benjamin Silliman, Sr., might very well have understood the difference. Cooper explicitly linked his geology with a denunciation of Christianity. Neither Whewell or Lyell were so obviously offensive to the religiously minded. Whewell carefully included a Supreme Being either as the initial Creator (in uniformitarianism) or as the successive Creator (under catastrophism). Lyell had serious reservations about natural theology, a widely pervasive viewpoint in his milieu, but he was not disposed to any actions against the existing order.

[11] Cooper had written directly to Henry concerning the magnet. See above, Cooper to Henry, November 16, 1833, and Henry's reply of November 26, 1833.

[12] Tic Douloureux is a very severe form of neuralgia affecting the trigeminal nerve of the face. *Black's Medical Dictionary*, 29th ed. (1971).

[13] Most likely a reference to *Report of the Experiments on Animal Magnetism, Made by a Committee of the Medical Section of the French Royal Academy of Sciences* [sic]*: Read at the Meetings of 21st and 28th of June, 1831, Translated . . . with an . . . Introduction . . . by J. C. Colquhoun.* (Edinburgh, 1833). This is a report of the Académie royale de médecine promoted by one P. Foissac and is a reinvestigation of Mesmerism in a medical context.

FROM PETER BULLIONS

Henry Papers, Smithsonian Archives

Albany Decr 19th 1833

Dear Sir

Yours of the 16th Inst is received and I am exceedingly gratified to hear from you again notwithstanding you begin with a business letter.[1] The name of the person who wrote the memoir on the Climate of Canada is William Kelly, MD. Surgeon RN.[2] I *guess* you intend to write him for an account of the meteor of 5th Septr last. Have you not been able to make anything of our blundering data. Next time I shall be more accurate.[3] I regret that I did not see the wonderful meteorological phenomenon of the 13th Ult[4]—it must have been a glorious sight. I am glad however that you had the opportunity of seeing it. What is your guess respecting the nature and cause of the phenomenon?

There is nothing now to be heard of but Kaleidoramas.[5] Half of the boys in the Academy are engaged in manufacturing them. Faraday's paper "On a peculiar class of optical deceptions" in the Journal of the Royal Institution

[1] Henry's letter of December 16, 1833, has not been found. The "business" referred to may have been either Henry's inquiry about the author of "the Climate of Canada" or Henry's request for a half dozen of Bullions's grammar texts, the subject of the fifth paragraph.

[2] William Kelly (1793–1862), a fellow of the Royal College of Surgeons of England and a surgeon in the Royal Navy, was active in the Literary and Historical Society of Quebec since its founding in 1824. He served as Chairman of the Class of Natural History in 1831, and as President, 1839–1840. A copy of the 1831 "Annual Report of the Literary and Historical Society of Quebec" was presented to "Professor Henry" and survives in the Henry Library; it was most likely presented by Kelly. Victor Gustave Plarr, *Plarr's Lives of the Fellows of the Royal College of Surgeons of England*, 2 vols. (London, 1930), *1*:652. *The Centenary Volume of the Literary and Historical Society of Quebec, 1824–1924* (Quebec, 1924), pp. 18, 96.

Kelly is credited with a dozen articles, mostly meteorological, in the *Royal Society Catalogue*. The "memoir" Bullions refers to is Kelly's "Abstract of the Meteorological Journal Kept at Cape Diamond, Quebec, from the 1st of January 1824 to the 31st December 1831, with Some Remarks on the Climate of Lower Canada," *Transactions of the Literary and Historical Society of Quebec*, 1837, *3*:46–71. Kelly's paper was printed in 1832 in the first part of volume 3.

Henry may have heard about the Kelly piece through Bullions, or have seen it at the Albany Institute in October 1833. Bullions was Henry's personal friend, former colleague at the Albany Academy, and successor to Henry's position as librarian of the Albany Institute. The Institute exchanged its *Transactions* with the Literary and Historical Society of Quebec, and Bullions had undoubtedly made a note of William Kelly's article when parts 1 and 2 of the Quebec *Transactions* volume 3 were received in the Institute library ("Albany Institute Catalogue of Properties, 1824–1838," entry for September 5, 1833, Library, Albany Institute of History and Art). Bullions had his own interests in observing the aurora borealis (see above, Bullions to Henry, September 5, 1833), and he was eager to help Henry in his more serious pursuit of observations.

[3] Probably a reference to the observations contained above in Bullions's letter to Henry, September 5, 1833.

[4] See the documents above, beginning with Henry's notes for November 13–14, 1833.

[5] For a description of the philosophical toy, the Kaleidorama, and of its interest for Henry

for Feby 1831 to which you refer exhibits the principle and the chief part of the results except the movements of different figures which is all that has been left for the German Professor to invent.[6] I have no doubt you have already thought of several improvements and modifications to produce still more surprising effects.

Of Burden's boat[7] I can give you but little intelligence and that mostly derived from an extract in the Evening Journal from the Troy press. It was the end of last month before he got his engine on board. Trial was made twice a short distance down the river and it was said that her performance equalled the expectations formed of her though from some defect in the engine only from 8 to 14 revolutions per Minute were obtained. The calculation is to make from 25 to 30. The number of revolutions per minute moreover gives the speed in miles per hour. She went to New York shortly before the river closed to be finished. If She does not perform the trip in six hours She is not to have the honour of carrying passengers but is to be employed in carrying lumber. I was told that a gentleman in Troy offered him 100,000 dollars for his boat and his right. If that is true he made one sad mistake that did not take the offer.

Mother is quite smart. I have been up twice since you left—night before last she was not quite so well having got a little cold. The Academy now numbers intoto 260.[8] Dr Beck[9] has gone to Fairfield. Mr Carpenter's

---

and other scientists, see above Ten Eyck to Henry, [ca. November 22, 1833], especially footnote 2.

[6] Both Stampfer (here referred to as "the German Professor") and Plateau, the independent inventors of these hand-held stroboscopes, cited the contribution of Michael Faraday, "On a Peculiar Class of Optical Deceptions," *Journal of the Royal Institution*, 1831, *1*:205–223. Stampfer's and Plateau's articles are noted above in Ten Eyck to Henry, [ca. November 22, 1833], footnote 3.

[7] Henry Burden (1791–1871), prolific inventor and ironmaster. Born in Scotland, Burden came to America in 1819 after having studied mathematics, drawing, and engineering at Edinburgh. He settled in Albany on the advice of Stephen Van Rensselaer, promptly establishing his inventive reputation by producing an improved design for a plow. Burden worked for the Troy Iron and Nail Factory, which company he eventually owned. He patented many inventions, including machines for making railroad spikes, horseshoes, and other special iron products. "He had early shown a deep interest in steam navigation, and in 1825 had made suggestions to the Troy Steamboat Association that later were largely adopted in the building of the *Hendrick Hudson*, which in 1845 made the trip from New York to Albany in seven and a half hours. . . . In 1833 he built for the Hudson traffic a passenger and freight boat of two cigar-shaped hulks, with a thirty foot paddle-wheel in the center. It was lost, however, in an accident in the following year." *DAB*. In February 1832 Burden was elected to membership in the First Department of the Albany Institute, where he and Henry undoubtedly became acquainted (Minutes of the Albany Institute, February 23, 1832, Library, Albany Institute of History and Art). The extent of their contact thereafter is not known, but Henry did note one of Burden's experiments on hydrostatics in a Princeton lecture notebook (Notebook [5908], "Hydrostatics," [p. 18], Henry Papers, Smithsonian Archives).

[8] Enrollment figures for the Albany Academy, 1825–1834, are reproduced in *Henry Papers*, *1*:238–239. Based on data from Academy Trustees' Minutes, 2:109–110, 143–144, Albany Academy Archives, total enrollment in December 1833 numbered 271.

[9] Theodric Romeyn Beck, principal of the

brother[10] superintends one room during his absence. We get along very smoothly. We have had two meetings of the Institute of late. The main project now on the wheels is an application to the Legislature to furnish the means of making a *State Collection* and hopes are entertained that it will be successful.[11] The Young men of the City to the number of nearly 300 have formed themselves into a Society for mutual improvement[12] and Mr Dean is elected President. They are taking measures to obtain a library, to keep a reading room and to have a Lecture or two every week. Age from 16 to 36.

I will write to Collins and Hannay to send on half a dozen of Grammars[13] to Princetown on Commission if you have any bookseller who would take care of them. The next edition will be reduced to about 300 pages and then it can be on a par with others in price. I would take it as a favour if any of your Professors would take the trouble to examine it and give such a recommendation as he thought it deserves.

Albany Academy who appears throughout volume one of the *Henry Papers*, gave medical lectures to the Western College of Physicians and Surgeons in Fairfield, Herkimer County, New York, from 1815 until 1840.

[10] The "Mr Carpenter" is George Washington Carpenter, a tutor at the Academy and surveyor in Albany (see *Henry Papers, 1*:299, footnote 14). His brother Henry Carpenter was officially instated as a tutor in the Fourth Department (Elementary School) of the Albany Academy in June 1834. He resigned in September 1835, and we have found no trace of his activities thereafter. Academy Trustees' Minutes, 2:122, 149, Albany Academy Archives.

[11] At a special meeting on December 11, 1833, the Albany Institute agreed on a course for "petitioning the Legislature for aid in forming a State Collection of the objects in Natural History found within its borders." (Albany Institute Minutes, Library, Albany Institute of History and Art.) This petition was not immediately successful. Repeated agitations of many of the Institute members, combined with formal petition of the American Institute of New York City, succeeded in gaining legislation which established the State Natural History Survey in 1836. The State Museum inevitably resulted from the survey's collecting activities. See Michele L. Aldrich, "New York Natural History Survey, 1836–1845" (Ph.D. dissertation, University of Texas, 1974). Documents from 1836 and later will demonstrate Henry's interest and involvements in getting the survey on what he thought was the proper scientific course.

[12] The Young Men's Association for Mutual Improvement enjoyed immense popularity in Albany and grew rapidly to include a membership exceeding 1,000. A self-help organization, receiving no government aid, the Young Men's Association succeeded in building a large library, acquiring philosophical apparatus, and drawing notable figures in science and learning for biweekly lectures. Amos Dean, the prolific writer on law, philosophy, history, and phrenology, served for many years as its leader (for Dean see above, Henry to James Henry, December 21, 1832, especially footnote 1). The Albany Young Men's Association was a model for similar organizations springing up in towns across the state. Wallace K. Schoenberg, "The Young Men's Association, 1833–1876: The History of a Social Cultural Organization" (Ph.D. dissertation, New York University, 1962).

[13] Bullions was editor and translator of James Moor's *Elements of the Greek Language* (Albany and New York, 1831). This first edition by Bullions was 408 pages. No second edition of this work by Bullions appears in the *National Union Catalog*; thus we have no evidence that Bullions succeeded in publishing a 300-page version. From 1840 until 1860, however, Bullions published no fewer than 42 editions of his own *Principles of Greek Grammar*, all of which were about 300 pages.

Comments regarding Bullions's 1831 grammar were long in coming from Princeton, but they were no less complimentary for their extended gestation. See below, Henry to Stephen Alexander, May 15, 1835.

Our family is pretty good health. Mrs B. however is laid up for a time with a sprained foot. Mrs B. & Meg join me in love to you all. Meg will write M^rs H during the Holidays. We have got Mrs Gyer to keep us out of the kitchen during the winter. Mrs B. bids me inform Mrs Alexander that she had the pleasure of seeing Adam and Eve[14] and was much pleased with the "dreadful pleasing" sight.

Your friends here I believe are all well. The Misses Meads called here yesterday. They are the same lively pleasing ladies as ever. I have no news of any consequence to communicate except the news of your Appointment to the Presidency of some College in the South.[15] Your Mother hopes you will not accept. You are far enough away already. I conclude from your saying nothing of it in your letter that you have not heard of it yourself or it must be some other Prof. Henry.[16] When do you appear again in Silliman?

Ever Yours
P. Bullions

[14] Advertised under the banner of "Adam and Eve," the show consisted of two large moral paintings by Claude Marie Dubufe (1790–1864), a French-trained genre painter who emigrated to America. Their titles were *The Temptation of Adam and Eve* and *The Expulsion from Paradise.* The paintings had a three-week showing in City Hall, from October 14 until November 2, during which they attracted 6,327 visitors who paid 25 cents apiece. The liberality of the proprietor permitted one day's income to go to charitable endeavors. *Daily Albany Argus,* October 14, 1833, p. 2, "Now Exhibiting At The City Hall" (advertisement); October 21, 1833, p. 2, "For the Benefit of the Poor"; October 25, 1833, p. 2, "The Paintings . . . "; November 5, 1833, p. 2, "A Card." Reynolds, *Alb. Chron.,* p. 504. G. C. Groce and D. H. Wallace, *The New-York Historical Society's Dictionary of Artists in America, 1564–1860* (New Haven, 1957), p. 191.

[15] The *Daily Albany Argus,* December 18, 1833, p. 2, reported: "Professor HENRY has been elected President of South Carolina College in the place of Dr. Cooper, resigned. Dr. C. still retains the situation of Professor of Chemistry."

[16] Bullions was right on both counts, judging by the comments in Henry's December 23 letter to James, immediately following. The "Prof. Henry" was not Joseph, but rather Robert Henry (1792–1856), the noted Presbyterian and Episcopal clergyman and educator. The latter Henry was appointed President *pro tempore* of South Carolina College, after the storm which resulted in Thomas Cooper's resignation in 1833 (for information on Cooper's resignation, see above, Cooper to Silliman, December 17, 1833). Not elected to the Presidency of the college because he allegedly shared Cooper's heretical views, Robert Henry departed from the school for a few years. He returned to teach metaphysics, logic, and belles-lettres in 1839, then served as President of the college from 1842 until 1845. Thereafter until his death he was Professor of Greek Literature. *DAB.*

TO JAMES HENRY

Mary Henry Copy, Memoir, Henry Papers, Smithsonian Archives

Dec. 23. 1833.

Dear James. I am somewhat surprised that any of my friends should think me the person alluded to in the Argus.[1] Such an appointment would not be congenial to my tastes, talents or acquirements. I made a resolve more than fifteen years ago to devote my life to the pursuit of science and no situation however lucrative or honorable could induce me to depart from my resolution. You can tell my acquaintances if any ask you I would as soon think of being appointed the Bishop of Calcutta or of receiving a Cardinal's hat as being made President of a college.

[1] See the preceding document. James's incoming letter does not survive.

TO WILLIAM KELLY[1]

Retained Copy,[2] Henry Papers, Smithsonian Archives

Princeton, College of New Jersey
Dec. 30th 1833

Respected Sir

From your reputation as a Gentleman of Science I am induced to believe that you will excuse the liberty a stranger thus takes in addressing you on a scientific subject.

I am much interested in some <*departments*> parts of your favourite science Meteorology particularly those which relate to the Aurora and the daily variations of the Magnetic needle. May I trespass so much on your politeness as to request that you will refer to your Meteorological register and inform me if an *aurora* was visible at your place on the evening of the 5th of Sept. last. Was there an arch formed? If so at what time did the arch appear? When disappear? What was the apparent altitude of the crown of the arch above the northern horizon in degrees? Or did it pass through your zenith. Was there more than one arch seen on the same evening and if so at what time did each of them appear and disappear?

[1] For Kelly, see above, Bullions to Henry, December 19, 1833, footnote 2.

[2] On the last page Henry noted: "Draft/Letter intended/to be sent to Kelly/Quebec." The language differs somewhat from Henry's usual file notation for a retained copy, raising the possibility that Henry did not send this letter to Kelly. The absence of a reply from Kelly is inconclusive; rarely do we have both sides of correspondence in this period.

I am most anxious to know if the meteor[3] passed through your zenith or south of it and at what time it was thus situated. If the meteor did not pass through the zenith perhaps you could furnish me with its apparent angular elevation from memory by recollecting its altitude in reference to the pole star or some other object.

My object in troubling you with these inquiries is to collect if possible data <*sufficient*> to determine the absolute elevation of the Meteor above the surface of the earth. I have already three observations which agree as to the time of the appearance of the arch; one made at this place (Princeton), one at Albany and the third at a point between Laprarie and St John's Lower Canada.[4] At these three places a bow was seen at the same time about 15 minutes past 8 o'clock P.M. This data would be abundantly sufficient to determine the absolute height of this <*arch of the*> aurora but a gentleman living at Burlington N.Y. writes me that the bow was seen by him at 15 minutes past *nine* o'clock.[5] It is possible that he has mistaken the hour. I wish therefore to gain further information.

The subject of the height of the aurora has you know created considerable discussion among the Meteorologists of Europe and has lately been reccommended to the particular attention of observers by a committee of the Great scientific meeting at Oxford England.[6]

It will afford me much pleasure to reciprocate the favour which [you] may do me on this occasion should an opportunity occur. I am giving considerable attention to the subject of terestrial magnetism and should you or any of the members of the Literary Society of Quebec be interested in the same persuit I would be glad to compare notes on our observations. I have lately discovered or devised a method by which a bar of steel 6 or 8 feet long can be instantaneously magnetized to saturation and am now about fitting up such a bar as a horizontal needle to observe the daily variations of the direction of the magnetic force.[7] If it will be acceptible and

[3] Used here in the sense of "a phenomenon or appearance in the atmosphere," not as one of the "particles of matter in the solar system observable directly only if it happens to fall into the earth's atmosphere. . . . " *Webster's Third New International Dictionary*.

[4] See above for the communications of Bullions (September 5, 1833) and Turnbull (September 30, 1833) to Henry and his own observations of September 6, 1833.

[5] This is a reference to James Dean of Burlington, *Vermont*, who does give the 9:15 P.M. time in his letter of November 27, 1833, above.

[6] A reference to the second meeting of the British Association for the Advancement of Science in 1832. The report on meteorology was prepared by James David Forbes, the Scottish scientist, who will appear below as a correspondent of Henry's. Henry was undoubtedly interested in the entire text of the report, a pamphlet copy of which survives in the Henry Library. The discussion of the aurora borealis (British Association for the Advancement of Science, *Report*, 1832, pp. 254–258) centered on the question of the height of the arch and on the connection with terrestrial magnetism. Henry must have been pleased with the laudatory reference (p. 217) to the meteorological data collected by the academies in the State of New York.

[7] Henry's interest in terrestrial magnetism is no surprise. What is astonishing is the state-

you can point out a method of conveyance I will send such a *bar* to your Society. If observations on the variations of the needle are not made in Canada it will be dooing an important service to the cause of science to institute a regular series.

It is possible that I am not entirely unknown to you by reputation as you may have seen an account of the powerful galvanic magnets made on a plan invented by me or may perhaps have seen my name in Sillimans Journal and the Transactions of the Albany Institute. I have lately been called

---

ment about the size of the needles and the existence of a method of magnetization. Henry may be referring to a plan for such needles in two documents below (see his "Notes on a Trip to Philadelphia," April 29–May 2, 1834, and his letter to Forbes, June 30, 1834); we have no evidence that the needle was ever completed. Henry never published any observations using steel bars 6 to 8 feet in length as needles to measure changes in declination. Nor have we found any references to such observations in his surviving manuscripts. The letter to Kelly antedates the set of experimental notebooks which starts in 1834. Neither his published works from this period nor the manuscript records (with one possible exception) disclose any new method for magnetization of steel. And a search of the later "Record of Experiments" did not yield attempts by any method to magnetize steel bars of such dimensions. Three questions arise: (1) Why did Henry abandon the use of large steel bars in terrestrial magnetism work? (2) What was the method of instantaneously magnetizing steel to saturation? (3) What can we infer from this letter about the direction of Henry's scientific work?

No published references in this period known to us mention magnets 6 feet to 8 feet in length. Earlier in the century Coulomb had prepared steel magnets 30 inches long. At the very time of the writing of this letter Gauss and Weber in Göttingen were developing their magnetic observatory whose instruments and system of taking observations would greatly affect all future work in terrestrial magnetism. To minimize accidental disturbances, they used needles far larger than those previously in use—26.4 inches, weighing about 25 pounds. In his *Magnetical Investigations* (London, 1843), p. 247, William Scoresby reported tests on 36-inch steel bars weighing nearly 99 pounds, from the context clearly a feat for the day. In the eighth edition of the *Britannica* (s.v. "Magnetism," pp. 76–77), Brewster reports a 96-pound magnet displayed at the 1851 Crystal Palace Exposition.

We have no idea of the weight of Henry's monstrous magnetic needle. Coulomb used a mechanical method for magnetizing his steel bars, as did Scoresby, and reported the production of multiple poles if the length/diameter ratio was greater than 30 to 1. A mechanically magnetized rod of Henry's would be more than 2 inches thick—and rather heavy. Although we have no data, we suspect that the same might be true of a steel bar magnetized by the electromagnetic devices of the day.

Being long and rather heavy, Henry's 6-foot to 8-foot magnetic needles would provide a serious problem to an investigator. While the movements and deviations would be readily discernible and measurable, merely mounting the needle would raise serious problems. Even Gauss's smaller magnet bars were eventually discarded; the length of time for a single vibration was too long for observations during periods of magnetic disturbances. Our assumption is that Joseph Henry found the long steel bars not practical for his proposed observations, even if the bars were hollowed, rather than solid.

Claiming a mechanical method of magnetizing steel appears unlikely. Placing magnets in contact with iron and steel and then stroking was well known to Henry from descriptions in the literature of techniques of the previous century. A natural supposition is to consider an electromagnetic application to this mechanical stroking technique. In a publication appearing between 1838 and 1840, Robert Hare credits Henry with a method "of charging Steel with Permanent Magnetism" by drawing a needle or bar over one and then the other pole of an electromagnet. As a friend and admirer of Henry's, Hare's word has some weight. Variants of this technique are discussed in other works of the period. One can describe it as an application of the great power

from Albany to the chair of Natural Philosophy in this Institution. These statements are made in order that you may identify the person who addresses you.

I regret that I did not sooner direct my attention to the subject of the height of the aurora as I might have collected data sufficient to solve the

---

developed by Henry's electromagnets. But Joseph Henry never claimed this method as his own.

In 1847 the supplementary volume of the *Encyclopaedia Americana* contained an article on "Magnetism" by Henry (*14*:412–426). Page 421 notes: "Professor Henry has found that bars of steel may also be magnetized by heating them to redness, and then plunging them into a cylindrical vessel of cold water, around which a current of galvanism is passing. The steel, cooled under the influence of the current, receives its maximum of magnetic development." No date is given but the context of the words in the encyclopedia article and the absence of any mention in the rather full "Record of Experiments" which starts in 1834 are circumstantial evidence that this is the method Henry devised in 1833. A third possibility is in the rough draft for the *Americana* article in the Henry Papers (Box 23, folder 1, item 10). Here, immediately before the words quoted above, Henry first wrote and then deleted mention of magnetizing steel in a coil through which a strong current was sent. By 1847 this was a well-known method which Henry could hardly have claimed then or even in 1833.

Magnetizing steel and iron was both an obvious and an intense concern of Henry's throughout his professional career. Direct and indirect references occur in both the published and unpublished sources. Given the profusion of references documenting this intellectual interest of Henry's combined with the lack of clear evidence on the method of magnetizing steel Henry had in mind when writing to Kelly, what follows is admittedly speculative. We assume that Henry's statement in the 1847 encyclopedia article is the technique. We further speculate on evidence to follow that Henry would not claim as original in 1833 either the method described by Hare or the use of a current-carrying coil around a steel bar. Nor do we think Henry would appropriate to himself another method he investigated about this time—the use of ordinary (i.e., static) electricity to produce magnetism.

In 1820 Arago showed that a galvanic current produces permanent magnetism in steel needles. Two years later Barlow reported extensive tests of the effects of heating to redness on magnetization. These were followed up by further experiments of S. Hunter Christie. By the time of this letter it was well known that heating reduces the magnetization as it softened steel; cooling hardened steel, fixing the magnetism induced in it. At this period Joseph Henry was very much aware of the article of Savary (*Annales de chimie et de physique*, 1827, *34*:5–57, 220–221). References to it occur elsewhere in this volume and will appear in other volumes of the *Henry Papers*. Savary instantly magnetized needles placed in a current-carrying wire partly wound in helices. By May 2, 1834 (see below) Henry noted reading a paper in *Phil. Trans.*, 1833 (pp. 333–342), by Francis Watkins that the best method of magnetizing a small round steel bar was by "placing it in a helix of copper wire and passing the galvanic charge." Volume three will contain experiments on developing permanent magnetism in steel using this method ("Record of Experiments" for March 19, 1836).

Unlike soft iron, steel was hard to magnetize; when magnetized, steel retained this condition far better than soft iron. It seems like a reasonable leap to combine the current-carrying coil with softening and hardening of steel by heat and cold, especially as a source familiar to Henry clearly suggests the process. Henry relied heavily on Roget's writings on natural philosophy in the Library of Useful Knowledge in developing his course in the early years at Princeton. The sections on electricity and magnetism were published in 1832. Henry's copy survives although rebound so that we cannot unequivocally state just when it was acquired. Pages 12–13 of the "Magnetism" section, bearing scorings in the margin, deal largely with heat effects. A penciled sentence, partially obliterated in the rebinding (p. 13), indicates Henry's intention to experiment on the decrease in magnetic intensity with increases in the temperature. On the previous page, Roget noted: "The greatest degree of magnetism is produced by heating the steel to redness, and, while it is under the influence of a strong magnet, quenching it suddenly with cold water." The

problem while in Albany since I had the direction in connection with Dr. T. R. Beck of the Meteorological Reports made by the several academies in the State of N.Y. to the Legislature. If a few observers situated to the north and south of each other would regularly note the angular elevation of the crown of each arch and the exact time of its appearance and disap-

---

only documentary evidence possibly linking the Roget text to Henry's claim in the *Americana* is a holograph fragment found in Mary Henry's Memoir (now in Box 50, Henry Papers, Smithsonian Archives). An undated mélange of notes on experiments and Henry's ruminations, its second paragraph reads:

> Steel bar quenched in water. Place the bar in the coil[;] raise the water. Try bar of hardened steel. Try superimposed magnetism. Try to what extent the magic circle will act. Use two coiles as a circle.

The first and a later paragraph refer to Barlow's work on the effects of heat on magnetism. Henry also notes his intention to redo Faraday's ring experiment which may indicate this is early in the Princeton period or even toward the end of the Albany period. Nowhere else, to our present knowledge, does Henry refer to a coil or coils as "the magic circle."

The previous paragraph in Roget discussed the transmission of electric discharge through a steel bar to produce permanent magnetism. The subsequent paragraph ascribes the permanence of magnetism in steel to how its structure obstructs disruptive forces. In his notes on Savary's work, Henry commented on the results of tempering the needles: "It appears that magnetization in the state of tempre is such a state of equilibrium between forces and resistances so great that an exterior cause alters it with more difficulty." The same notebook with references to Arago, Savary, and Watkins contains close to these pages an undated thought of James Dean: "May not the hardness of steel arise from the crystallization of the carbon similar to the crystallization of the same substance in the form of the Diamond" (Notebook [7171], p. 104).

Henry may not have published his method until writing the encyclopedia article because a very similar technique was described in print not long after the date of this letter by the French scientist Georges Aimé (1813–1846, *Poggendorff*). A red-hot bar of steel is wedged between the poles of a horseshoe shaped electromagnet. As the current flows from a battery, the entire assemblage—bar and horseshoe magnet—is tossed into a cold water bath. (*Annales de chimie et de physique*, 1834, 57:442–444.) Henry's technique was superior for large bars. Although we have not found this article cited in Henry's reading notes, the journal in which it appeared was regularly perused by Joseph Henry. Given the French publication, the words in Roget, and the abandonment of the giant needle observations, we assume Henry decided not to write up his method. Years later, when doing an unsigned article while quite self-conscious about unrecognized achievements, Joseph Henry carefully credited himself for this and for other research findings.

Perhaps even more important than the hypothetical priority anguish is the implication of this incident for Henry's future interests. The method of magnetizing steel was apparently important for possible use in terrestrial magnetism work. When that possibility somehow vanished, we speculate Henry did not think it worth publishing as such. Later in this volume will appear evidences of Joseph Henry's continuing concern with terrestrial magnetism, for example in correspondence with James David Forbes. Henry's friend, A. D. Bache, followed Gauss in having an iron-free house for magnetism observations. From Henry's letter to Bache of May 18, 1835, below, we know that he too built one at Princeton. Henry's interest in terrestrial magnetism and related geophysical topics continued through the rest of his life. Although Henry would continue to do research and to encourage others' work in geophysical topics, his own publications from now on were overwhelmingly concerned with topics in experimental physics. Priority conflict with Aimé over a matter of technique must have paled before Henry's increasing recognition of the formidable competition of Michael Faraday in the experiments in electricity and magnetism, a topic which will recur in documents to follow.

For examples of Henry's reading notes and other jottings, largely from the period prior to this letter, see Henry's notebooks [6123], pp. 40–45; [7170], pp. 9–11, 36, 67; [7171], pp. 66–71, 89–104. Notebooks [23894] and [23919] were started by Henry shortly after his arrival at

pearance the subject of the absolute elevation will soon be settled. All that is required to note at the moment is the several stars through which this bow appears to pass and the time of the observation. The altitude of these stars and consequently that of the bow can then be determined at any subsequent period.

Princeton and added to for many years. They are the notes on electricity and magnetism for his course.

Very useful for overviews of what was accepted, at least in the Anglo-American world, are certain semipopular texts and encyclopedia articles. They often have useful references. P. M. Roget, *Treatises on Electricity, Galvanism, Magnetism and Electro-Magnetism* (London, 1832) is a good example, besides being a work we know Henry read. Brewster's articles in the *Britannica* are very useful; we have used the eighth edition. William Scoresby's *Magnetical Investigations*, 2 parts (London, 1839) was given in 1844 to Henry by the author. Most of the pages are uncut. Snow Harris's *Rudimentary Magnetism* (London, 1850), another presentation copy, is a fine survey of the history of magnetism as seen by scientists of the day. Robert Hare's pamphlet referred to above survives in Henry's Library. *On Electro-Magnetism* is undated and probably designed for Hare's students. We think, with little evidence, it appeared in 1838 or 1839. The reference to Henry and steel magnetization is on pages 71–72. See also, Edward Walker, *Terrestrial and Cosmical Magnetism* (Cambridge, England, 1865), pp. 140–141.

HENRY NOTEBOOK ENTRY

Notebook [23915],[1] no pagination, Henry Papers, Smithsonian Archives

[1833][2]

Steam expansively

The cut off[3] is now used in all the steamboats on the Hudson and also on the Delaware.

[1] This is one of several notebooks in Box 16 of the Henry Papers from which Henry apparently lectured at Princeton. Each was devoted to a single topic, such as this one on steam. Henry drafted a basic text and then over the years spliced in notes updating or clarifying the material. He frequently included stage instructions to himself about items to show the class, experiments to demonstrate, and drawings or notes to put on the blackboard.

We shall print passages from these notebooks when they have more than routine interest. This page, for example, demonstrates Henry's continued concern with technical and scientific problems involving steamboats and also his interest in the development of railroad technology. The second point is further exemplified by Henry's visit to Matthias Baldwin's locomotive-building yards (see notes of his trip to Philadelphia, April 29–May 2, 1834, printed below). Henry had commented on locomotive design as early as 1831 (*Henry Papers, 1*:355–356).

[2] The dating is based on the fact that Robert Stevens's design for a cutoff was incorporated in Locomotive #6, constructed at the shops of the Camden and Amboy Railroad in 1833. John H. White, *American Locomotives: An Engineering History, 1830–1880* (Baltimore, 1968), p. 189.

[3] The first boat engines injected steam into the cylinder throughout the stroke. When they built the later high pressure engines, engineers modified valve gears to let steam in at the beginning of the stroke, and then to cut off the supply so that the expansion of the steam forced the piston to the end of the cycle. Full stroke operation was necessary only when the boat required maximum power, as in starting off; ordinary running would employ cutoffs to save fuel. Louis Hunter, ***Steamboats on the***

} Mr Stevens[4] informes me that he is about to apply it to the Locomotive car.

Show Drawing of cut off, *Renwick plate.*[5]

Cut off sometimes worked by the excentric.[6]

The work of an engine has been quadrupled by adopting this plan with the consumption of the same amount of fuel.[7]

When the steam is worked at 1½ atmosphers or ½ an atmos. above the pressure of the atmosphere it is the usual rule to cut off at half stroke.[8]

Western Rivers: An Economic and Technological History (Cambridge, Massachusetts, 1949), pp. 149–150.

[4] Robert Livingston Stevens (1787–1856), naval architect, had been privately educated on his family's estate in Hoboken, New Jersey. He assisted his father John Stevens in steamboat engineering starting in 1804; their collaboration continued for many years thereafter. Robert Stevens planned and supervised construction of over twenty steamboats, most of which included innovations in hull shape, engine design, or safety features. He became president and chief engineer of the Camden and Amboy Railroad in 1830. Stevens's railroad improvements included the T-rail, a double-slide cutoff for locomotives and better boilers. He also designed and built racing yachts and advanced ship armor and naval armaments. *DAB.*

[5] James Renwick, *Treatise on the Steam Engine* (New York, 1830) has a cross-section drawing of a cutoff valve, figure 6 of plate IV in the back of the book.

[6] This sentence and the next were written in pencil by Henry, probably inserted later into the lecture text than the rest of his notes on this page, which are in ink.

[7] Henry is stating an ideal case, as shown in the table in Renwick, p. 173. The temperature of the steam is assumed to stay the same despite expansion, the insulation is assumed perfect, and so on. The point about fuel consumption was important: as forests became depleted near factories, river banks, and railroad lines, American engine builders designed engines to cut down on amounts of wood required. They also experimented with coal-burning engines. White, *Locomotives*, pp. 83–90; Hunter, *Steamboats*, pp. 264–270.

[8] Almost a direct quotation from Renwick, p. 176: "Working with steam of the tension of 1½ atmospheres, it is customary to cut off the steam at half stroke." Hunter, *Steamboats*, p. 150, disputes this generalization: "With the less powerful engines of the early years [before 1840] the point of cutoff was fixed late in the stroke, usually at three-fourths or even seven-eighths."

1834

TO JAMES HENRY

Family Correspondence, Henry Papers, Smithsonian Archives

<*Albany*> Princeton Jany 8th 1834
8 o'clock in the evening

Dear James

Your last letter of Dec 27th was received the day before New Year's. The Telegraph[1] was also received. We have had nothing like sledding here until

---

[1] The Albany weekly *Journal* (1831–1899) was called the *Albany Journal and Telegraph* from 1831 to September 13, 1834. Winifred Gregory, ed., *American Newspapers, 1821–*

yesterday morning when the ground was covered with about 3 inches of snow. The weather was remarkable mild during the whole season until last Friday. Since then the thermometer has been pretty low not however as low as you have had it in Albany. It stood yesterday morning at +7° which is the lowest observed this winter. The coldest day as a whole which we have had this winter was on sunday last. The thermometer was at +14°, +21 & +15 at morning noon and evening. The students took possession of the New-College[2] on Friday last. Stephen[3] has also taken up his quarters in it and is the Police officer of the building. I am sorry to hear that Mother has been unwell. I regret that she was disappointed in not hearing from the boy in my last letter: He is quite smart and is constantly engaged from the time he rises in the morning until evening in play. I procured for him a number of smooth blocks of wood which have afforded him continual ammusement for several weeks.[4] He has become quite expert in building Cob-houses[5] with them and is engaged in this ammusement for several hours together. The Raritan is frozen & our mails arrive very irregularly. We often received papers & letters coming from Albany by the way of Philadelphia. So much for the Post Office reform.[6] Tell me where to direct my letter to Mr Sammons.[7] Is he at his Father's[8] in Montgomery Co? If so give me if you can his address. You mentioned the Death of Mr Oakly[9] and Mr Burhans[10] in one of your letters. I had observed in a New York paper the

---

1936: A Union List of Files Available in the United States and Canada (New York, 1937), p. 439.

[2] i.e., East College. See footnote 9, letter of June 25, 1833, above.

[3] Stephen Alexander.

[4] According to William P. Dewees, *A Treatise on the Physical and Medical Treatment of Children* (Philadelphia, 1829), a copy of which is in the Henry Library, "a quantity of regularly shaped pieces of wood, of various sizes, should also be given to them; these they will arrange, and that sometimes with great ingenuity, into houses, temples, churches, &c. . . ." (p. 108).

[5] Usually log cabins made of corncobs.

[6] By 1834, steamboat lines and stages had largely replaced horseback riders as carriers of mail, so that speed of delivery had increased. Henry was not referring to postal rates, which remained fixed from 1816 to 1845. George R. Taylor, *Transportation Revolution, 1815–1860* (New York, 1951), pp. 149–150. Unfortunately, William Barry, Postmaster General from 1829 to 1835, set records for incompetence and was the poorest cabinet selection Andrew Jackson had made. Congressional investigations in 1834 and 1835 revealed many abuses: poor methods of contracting, high costs, skipped deliveries, and bad accounting procedures. Amos Kendall replaced Barry in May 1835 and returned the post office to the high standards of Barry's predecessor, John McLean. Leonard White, *The Jacksonians: A Study in Administrative History, 1829–1861* (New York, 1954), pp. 251–269.

[7] Stephen Sammons; see above, the letter of November 13, 1832, especially footnote 7.

[8] Thomas Sammons (1762–1838) was a farmer, soldier, and Congressman at various times in his life. *Biographical Directory of the American Congress.*

[9] Abraham Oakey or Oake; see footnote 6 of February 9, 1833, above.

[10] William Burhans (1766–1833) had died at Bethlehem, New York on December 7, according to the *Daily Albany Argus* for December 9, 1833. This same issue of the *Argus* announced the death of Oake/Oakey on December 5 in New York City.

death of a person of the name of Oakly and conjectured that it was our old neighbour. The death of Mr Burhans was unexpected to me!

There is nothing very new in Princeton at this time. The Holidays are past and we are going on in the old way. About 1/3 of the students of college went home between New Years & Christmas or nearly all those whose parents reside in the State of New Jersey.

There is considerable excitement here on account of the money pressure. It is said that the commissioners of the New Jersey canal are unable at present to raise money to go on with their operations.[11] Their directors are warm Jackson men but are descidedly opposed to the removal of the deposits from the United States Bank.

Did you hear the address before the Young mens society[12] by Mr Barnard?[13] I see by the papers that the society have taken the rooms at the Knickerbocker Hall. The Albany Gazette of Friday last has just arrived. The mail comes in at present at about 6 o'clock in the evening. I see nothing of much importance or interest in it. The Legislature if I reccollect aright does not assemble until the first tuesday in Jan^{y}.[14] I noticed however the death of Jonathan Kidney's wife.[15]

Give our love to Mother and Nancy and respects to all the rest of the family. You mentioned in one of your letters sometime since that Jane Johnson[16] had a bad foot. Has she recovered?

[11] The Morris Canal, which eventually ran from New York Bay to the Delaware River, had been completed from Newark to Philipsburg in 1829 but was still being extended to Jersey City. Construction costs in hilly terrain had doubled the estimated price of building it. The company which ran the canal was especially sensitive to economic fluctuations because it simultaneously operated a bank and because New Jersey was parsimonious among the states in its direct aid to transportation projects. Although it stimulated the northern New Jersey iron industry, the canal itself was never a very profitable venture. Carter Goodrich, *Government Promotion of American Canals and Railroads, 1800–1890* (New York, 1960), pp. 125–126.

[12] On the association, see footnote 12 of December 19, 1833, above. A copy of Daniel Barnard, *An Introductory Address Delivered Before the Young Men's Association for Mutual Improvement, of the City of Albany, on the 7th* [*of*] *January, 1834* (Albany, 1834) is in the Henry Library.

[13] Daniel Dewey Barnard (1796–1861) graduated from Williams College in 1818 and then practiced law in Rochester, New York. He moved to Albany in 1832. Barnard served as Congressman from 1839 to 1845, when he returned to his law business in Albany, where he remained except during his work as minister to Prussia in 1850–1853. He wrote several short works on history and politics. *DAB.*

[14] Usually the State Legislature assembled in Albany to hear the Governor's Message and begin business on January 1 or soon thereafter. The Albany newspapers tended to be dull reading in the period between the elections in November and the opening of the Legislature. Henry was correct about the delay in the session: the 1834 legislature began on Tuesday, January 7. *New York Assembly Journal,* 57th Session, 1834, p. 3.

[15] Hannah Kidney (b. 1764), wife of the blacksmith Jonathan Kidney (1760–1849), died on December 30, 1833. Albany City Directories; *Proceedings of the Common Council and the Various Religious Organizations of the City of Albany Relative to the State Street Burial Grounds* (Albany, 1867), p. 17.

[16] Jane Alexander (1797–1840), a distant relation of Henry's, had married Michael Johnston, an accountant, in 1817. Albany City Directories; "Alexander Genealogy."

N.B. Before I left Albany when [about] to remove for Princeton I gave my note to Robey of the Firm of Benedict & Robey[17] for about 30 dollars for articles which we purchased from him when we took Seymours[18] house. This note he agreed to present to Erastus Corning[19] on the first of Jany 1834 who promised to take it up for me when presented as he has money in his hand due on the above date for interest to our family.[20] I promised to jog Roby's memory in reference to the transaction as he said he would forget it in the multitude of his transactions. Will you call and request him to present the note to Corning according to agreement for if he does not present it the money in Corning's hands will be lying idle while Roby's note will be drawing interest against us. I also gave an order of 50 dollars to Dun[21] which Corning likwise promised to accept. If you see Angelo Ames[22] you may ask him if he presented the order according to agreement on the 1st of Jany inst. Write me the particulars.

Your Brother[23]

Bub has not forgotten how "damda eny" smokes, he says she is "ome" & shows us how uncle Jimjy gives him a dozen. He grows fast & is very fleshy, tries to say a great many words, calls butter bumpo & his pantalets pampos, & amuses us very much by his efforts to talk.

P.S. Please tell the Misses Meads that I intend to write soon, [but] have been very much occupied. Happy New Year to all our friends. I think Mary Ann or Susan[24] might drop us a line. Love to all.

Yours H.

[17] A hardware business of this name was conducted in Albany by Joseph Roby, Jr., and Lewis Benedict. Albany City Directories.

[18] On Timothy and William Seymour, see footnote 2 of Henry to James Henry, November 8, 1832, above.

[19] Identified above, in footnote 4 of November 14, 1833.

[20] Henry apparently arranged for Corning to hold the money for the family, pending further transactions. The money resulted from selling some Alexander family property in Schenectady (see above, Henry to James Henry, September 17, 1833, and below, Henry to James Henry, February 12, 1834). For a mention of another real estate transaction, see below, Henry to Harriet Henry, March 24, 1834.

[21] Presumably, one of three Albany merchants, Richard Dunn, his son Edward Dunn, or Thomas Dunn. Albany City Directories.

[22] Angelo Ames (1802–1886), the son of the portraitist Ezra Ames, attended the Albany Academy in 1818–1819. According to Hun, "Albany Academy," Ames lived out the rest of his life in Albany as a philanthropist. A book in the Henry Library titled *The Philosophical Poetry of the Bible of Nature and the Substance of Virtue* (Albany, 1845) has on the flyleaf this inscription by Henry: "The compilation of Angelo Ames of Albany N.Y a man of warm heart and good intentions whos life has been thrown away by attempts to reform mankind by insufficient and unphilosophical means." Ames corresponded with Joseph Henry in the 1870s about disposing of Ezra Ames's paintings still in Angelo Ames's possession.

[23] Harriet Henry wrote the rest of this letter.

[24] Mary Ann LaGrange, for whom see above, Henry to James Henry, January 30, 1833, footnote 9, and her sister Susannah Shankland (1802–1838), for whom see *Henry Papers, 1*:284.

TO JAMES HENRY

Family Correspondence, Henry Papers, Smithsonian Archives

Princeton Jany 27th 1834

My Dear James

Your letter[1] was received more than a week since but owing to the press of business during our quarterly examination which took place last week I was unable to find time to answer it.

I am very glad to learn that mother is as well as she is. We hope she will be able to come to Princeton next spring and spen the summer with us.

We are all well. The Boy is more healthy at present than he has ever been before. He improves but slowly in speeking but understands the art of making himself understood in all his wants as well as of keeping his mother's room in confusion with his play things. I am pleased to learn that the young men's association is getting on so well. I saw by the Paper that The Chevalier Huygens[2] has presented 100 for the purchase of Book &c. You must endeavour to attend all the Lectures. I think Anthony[3] has very narrow views if he opposes such an institution or throws any obstacle in the way of your attendance on the Lectures. The weather has been very cold for several days past. The thermometer was down to 6 degrees on Saturday last in the morning which is the greatest degree of cold we have had in Princeton this winter. My time thus far in the term has been very much occupied as I lecture 3 times each week and hear as many recitations in a new work on Mechanics[4] which I have never before read and which requires considerable research among other works on the same subject in order to a full understanding. I will however have considerable leisure towards the close of the session as I then do not hear the class recite. Give my respects to Mr Bullions. Tell him we have seen nothing of the copies of his book which were to be sent to the book seller at Princeton.[5] Give my respects

[1] Not found.

[2] Rutger Bangeman Huygens (1805–1885) was called "The Chevalier Huygens" in recognition of his Dutch and Danish nobility, conferred by the kings of the two countries. He was the son of C. D. E. J. Bangeman Huygens, Dutch minister to the United States from 1824 until 1832. He served under his father in the Dutch embassy in Washington from 1825, becoming acting minister before the arrival of his father's replacement in late 1833. In 1826 he accompanied Dutch Army General Bernhard von Sachsen-Weimar on a tour through the southern United States and later wrote a report on southern arts and sciences. Upon his return to the Netherlands he held various diplomatic and military posts. He died in England. Information from the General State Archives, The Hague. The report is in the Archives.

[3] Anthony Gould (1801 or 1802–1858) who operated, along with his uncle William Gould, a law bookstore in Albany at which James Henry was employed. Munsell, *Ann. Alb.*, *10*: 417.

[4] Edward H. Courtenay's translation of Boucharlat's *Mechanics*. See above, Courtenay to Henry, October 19, 1833.

[5] Bullions promised to send a half dozen of his grammar texts by way of the New York

also to Dr Ten Eyck, Mr Sammons, Dr Frank. Tell the last mentioned gentleman that I saw a toast of his in the Gazette—which appeared like a change of party in Medicine if not in Politics.[6]

Give my love to Mother & Nancy and assure them I often wish that I could just pop in one of these cold days and see how they are coming on this winter.[7]

Joseph was obliged to stop abruptly by a call from one of the Professors last evening. Since then he has been much occupied in preparing for this morning's lecture. He has now gone & left me to finish his letter. I believe Joseph has told you all the news. We are very anxious to hear from Albany. The mails have been so irregular this winter that our papers come few & far between. We have all enjoyed good health this winter. Joseph is rather fleshier than when he was at Albany last & then you know he was in very good condition. Stephen has taken up his quarters in the new College.[8] Little Bub has been our principle source of amusement this winter. He is now seated by me with a piece of paper and a 'penby' as he calls a pencil to write to "damda heny." He tries to imitate all he sees done—just now dipped his pencil into the inksteand, bedaubed all his fi[ngers] to his no small annoyance for he can not bea[r] soiled fingers. He still remembers that Uncle jimy gave him a dozen at Albany. I often wish he could go and see [Nancy?] but am afraid he would require an interpreter to be understood. He speaks so crooked.

Please give our love to all. Tell Susan & Mary Ann[9] I think they might write us a few lines & tell them they must not forget their promise to visit us next summer.

I have been so much occupied that I could not possibly find time to write the Misses Meads yet—please tell them so. They must not be particular but write to me as often as they can & I will pay them with interest as soon as I have leisure. I never found so much to do as I have this winter. Last sum-

publisher. See above, Bullions to Henry, December 19, 1833.

[6] As printed several days later (January 31, 1834) in the *Daily Albany Argus*, p. 2,"Medical Society," Francis N. Selkirk's volunteered toast was:

> Dr. Alden March, Ex-President—He has *spiked* the guns of prejudice by his benificence—*reduced* opposition by skill and perseverance; and *cut* his way, through jealousy to imperishable fame.

For Selkirk, commonly referred to by Henry and others as "Dr. Frank," see above, Henry to James Henry, November 13, 1832, especially footnote 6. For Dr. Alden March, a key figure in medical education in Albany, see *Henry Papers, 1*:258. We do not pretend to have full awareness of the implications, medical or political, of Selkirk's toast.

[7] At this point in the letter Henry's handwriting stops. The remaining gossip is Harriet's.

[8] That is, the newly completed "East College," for which see Henry to James Henry, June 25, 1833, especially footnote 9.

[9] Susan Shankland and Mary Ann LaGrange.

mer was one of confusion—with the sickness of the baby and in visiting to & from Albany. I was obliged to neglect my sewing & in consequence find very much of it to be done. Tell the girls Mr Jaeger[10] was married to Miss Sansbury last week has been out of town since. Write soon and often as you can. Joseph has so much to attend to he cannot be as regular in his correspondence as he would wish.

I don't believe you, any of you, wish to see and hear from us as often as *we* do from *you*. I wish Mr Burden[11] had tried to invent a flying machine —we would often alight upon you unexpectedly. Love to all. Tell the girls they must write as often as they can & I will answer as soon as possible. Mother & Aunt wish to be remembered to all friends. If I write unintelligibly charge it to Bub for he can not sit still. Believe me yours as ever

Harriet

[10] Benedict Jaeger, for whom see above, Henry to Harriet Henry, April 6, 1833, especially footnote 4. We have found no information on his bride.

[11] The prolific inventor Henry Burden, whose steamboat had recently made its debut on the Hudson River near Albany. See above, Bullions to Henry, December 19, 1833, especially footnote 7.

FROM JOHN TORREY

Henry Papers, Smithsonian Archives

New York, Feby 4th 1834.

My Dear Sir

More than a month has elapsed since I had the pleasure of spending a little time with you, and promised to write immediately on returning home. I fear you think I have either forgotten or neglected you. Neither is the case. I have had my hands so full of business that I was obliged to give up writing letters for two or three weeks.

I have seen my clock maker & he thinks that he can, for a moderate sum, probably not exceeding thirty or forty dollars, put the college clock in *fair time keeping* order. The man's name is A. Hotchkiss[1] & his shop is in Hudson St. corner of Hamersley St. If you will pack up the clock & send it to the above address it will be taken in hands at once.

[1] The clockmaker Alva Hotchkiss is listed in Brooks Palmer, *The Book of American Clocks* (New York, 1950) as being in Poughkeepsie, 1825–1835, and New York City, 1835–1845. The earlier location is probably in error. He appears in the New York City Directories as "Albert" in the 1826–1827 issue, residing there until 1845–1846 when he moved to Brooklyn.

February 4, 1834

I wish you would take the trouble to enquire a little more respecting a boarding house for me. I should like to be a little out of the town, or at least not on the main street. I should like accommodations for myself, wife, three small children, & a nurse. We should need one comfortable room as to size, & two smaller ones. The lady who formerly lived in Mr. Alden's house has been highly recommended. We do not care about *style,* but should like to have everything comfortable & neat. It is very desirable to have a place where the children can play—otherwise I may as well keep them in the city. The terms for the whole family per week I should be glad to know.[2] I am giving you much trouble, but I know of no other way of accomplishing my object for poor Maclean has his hands so full that it would be unjust to put more upon him.

I am anticipating much pleasure from our joint labours next Summer, & I hope we shall not be disappointed in the calculation we have both made.

You have doubtless heard that Dr Lewis Beck has been appointed in my place in the University. He is not to do any duty there till next year, that is till next October. It is *very doubful whether he will ever lecture in that Institution,* for I do not think it will exist another year. The chancellor is nearly wound up.[3]

Our Med. college term will close in a little more than three weeks & then I shall (D.V.[4]) have a little rest. But I cannot be idle long. I must labour hard at Botany till I go to Princeton.[5] Early in the Spring I shall probably pass through Princeton again, when I hope to make you another visit.

Your truly
John Torrey

[2] Apparently the quest was unsuccessful. According to Torrey's biographer, he lived at a tavern which "degenerated from a 'Temperance House to a rum shop.' " In the following year the Torrey family stayed on a farm about two miles from Princeton. We have not identified "the lady" and Mr. Alden. Andrew Denny Rodgers, *John Torrey, A Story of North American Botany* (Princeton, 1942), pp. 114–115.

[3] Torrey is referring to difficulties in the young New York University. See Vethake's letter of November 6, 1833, above. Interference by the Chancellor, James M. Mathews, in what the faculty considered to be their province, resulted in strained relations between the faculty and Mathews. With David B. Douglass's resignation in June 1833, followed by those of Reverend John Mulligan, Henry Vethake, and Torrey in November 1833, only one faculty member remained. Lewis C. Beck was one of those recruited for the second faculty. As early as 1835, the new faculty expressed their discontent with the Chancellor, largely because their salaries had been suspended due to debts accrued by Mathews in financing construction. Beck and the second faculty, with one exception, were discharged in September 1838. In February 1839, Mathews resigned under pressure from the Council. Theodore Francis Jones, ed., *New York University, 1832–1932* (New York, 1933), pp. 38–52.

[4] Deo Volente—God being willing.

[5] Since 1827, Torrey had the chair of botany and chemistry at the College of Physicians and Surgeons in New York City. His chemistry lectures were usually through in March; by mid-May or June 1, Torrey was in Princeton. Rodgers, op. cit., p. 110.

February 12, 1834

TO JAMES HENRY

Family Correspondence, Henry Papers, Smithsonian Archives[1]

Princeton Feby Wednesday 12th 1834

Dear James

Your paper and introduction to Mary's[2] letter were received the latter yesterday and the former this day. The paragraph which you marked in the paper gave me some uneasiness as you know that Mr Corning[3] has a part of the money received for the sale of Property belonging to the estate of the Family.[4]

But should he fail I think that he would consider that in our case the debt is a confidential one. Your letter of yesterday releived me of the anxiety by assuring me that he is safe.

I am very much engaged at this time & have scarcely a moment to spare from Monday morning until Saturday night. The cause of this is that Dr Torrey comes to Princeton to Lecture on chemistry next summer & I wish to get as far through with the class as possible this term so that we may not interfere with each other. Dr Torrey's comming will make my duties light next session. Your account of Mother is very discouraging but I still hope that she will survive this turn and be able to visit us in the summer. The variable weather is much against her. Harriet will inform you concerning the reception of the letter. I am some what surprised to learn that the two Banks could not support (or would not) Mr Knower. I am informed that his failure in Albany has caused several houses in Philadelphia to stop payment. Those that sow must expect to reap accordingly. Knower however has bolted I believe from the strict Regency course once or twice.[5]

[1] On the first page of this letter is the following note, apparently penciled at a later date by Robert Proudfit, Union College Professor of Greek and Latin (*Union Catalog*, p. xii):

> Miss Jane Riley called today (Tuesday). She has been expecting a letter for one or two days. She thought Harriet was the last person who would forget her old friends so soon. Miss Riley is a nurse for Mrs. Ludlow. They are all well and send their Love to all.
> Proudfit

James evidently sent the letter to Proudfit, who presumably read it and then returned it to James with the message concerning Miss Ryley, for whom see *Henry Papers, 1*:444–445, and Mrs. Ludlow, wife of Reverend John R. Ludlow (*Henry Papers, 1*:106).

[2] Perhaps a reference to Mary Morrow, the daughter of James Henry's future wife, Caroline. William H. Eldridge, *Henry Genealogy: The Descendants of Samuel Henry . . . and Lurana (Cady) Henry* . . . (Boston, 1915), p. 128.

[3] Erastus Corning (1794–1872), for whom see above, Joseph Henry to James Henry, November 14, 1833, footnote 4, was at this time Vice-President of the New York State Bank in Albany. When the Albany City Bank was incorporated in April 1834, Corning resigned this office to become President of the new institution, a position he held until his death. *Howell and Tenney*, pp. 531, 538.

[4] Apparently a reference to the financial transaction Henry described in his letter of January 8, 1834, to James Henry, printed above.

[5] Benjamin Knower (1775–1839) had long

Last Saturday was not by many degrees the coldest day we have had at Princeton. The thermometer one day last month was down as low as +6° but on Saturday in the morning stood at +14°. Give my love to Mother and Nancy. I will leave the remainder of the letter for Harriet as I have an engagement at this hour.

N B Do not mention what I have told you concerning Corning. Inform me if Samuel Pruyn is still solvent as he has a small sum of my money in his possession.[6] He is a very prudent man & I have little fears of him.

Little Willy[7] was very much pleased with Mary's letter and listened to it very attentively. I think he would recognise Mary. In the afternoon as I was putting on his hat previous to his taking a ride in his little waggon he looked at me and said "damda heny!" I believe he thought he was going to pay her a visit. I wish he could for he is more interesting & playful than ever & enlivens us all. Ellen's favorite song is the Campbells are coming &c.[8] When we ask him what she sings he says 'the damdas tum, the damdas tum.' I am delighted with the improvement Mary has made in writing. It certainly is unusually plain & prity for a girl of her age. Tell her she must write to William again & that he will answer her as soon as he is able.

Rachel[9] must be quite fleshy this winter an[d] outweigh Nancy. I am afraid *she* does not take time to grow [fleshy]. I have thought of her very

been an influential member of the Albany Regency, the Democratic leadership that dominated New York politics during the 1820s and 1830s. A hatter by profession, he became involved in numerous speculative enterprises, particularly following his resignation in 1824 after three years' service as New York State Treasurer. In 1811 he had been instrumental in the organization of the Albany Mechanics' and Farmers' Bank and had been its President since 1817. Knower was closely allied with New York Governor William Marcy (1786–1857), his daughter Cornelia having married Marcy in 1824. Marcy, in fact, became involved in his father-in-law's activities to some degree, and early in 1834, when Knower was experiencing financial difficulties, Marcy endorsed some notes for him which were then sent to the Bank of the United States for discount. As an opponent of the bank, Marcy was displeased when this fact came to his attention, and he asked that the endorsements be canceled (see his letter to Nicholas Biddle, January 30, 1834, in the Historical Society of Pennsylvania, quoted in Ivor D. Spencer, "William L. Marcy Goes Conservative," *Mississippi Valley Historical Review*, 1944, *31*:212). Shortly thereafter on February 3, 1834, Knower had to resign the bank presidency. While Knower was not ruined completely, Marcy had to spend a great deal of time straightening out his business dealings, drawing some criticism from those who felt that his banking policies were being influenced by his father-in-law's needs. For a good discussion of the Knower-Marcy relationship, see Spencer, "William L. Marcy Goes Conservative," pp. 209–213. See also Munsell, *Ann. Alb.*, *10*:295; *Howell and Tenney*, p. 529; Edgar A. Werner, *Civil List and Constitutional History of the Colony and State of New York* (Albany, 1889), p. 175.

[6] A reference to Pruyn's still outstanding debt to Henry, for which see above, Joseph Henry to James Henry, December 21, 1832; January 1, 1833; and January 7, 1833.

[7] The following lines are in Harriet's hand.

[8] We have not identified Ellen. "The Campbells are Comin," a popular Scottish tune, is sometimes given as "Hob Nob, or the Campbells are Comin."

[9] Probably Rachel Alexander (1804–?), a cousin of Harriet and Joseph Henry. "Alexander Genealogy."

frequently this winter. I hope your next letter will give us more favorable accounts of Mother's health. We will still hope to see her next Summer.

Little plague has given me no peace untill I have taken him on my lap & he is now engaged in making "tatows" as he calls scarecrows on my paper with a dry pen so that the scratches you may observe are chargeable to him. I know that what I write of him will interest Mother and Nancy. Your amusement yonder is not taken into the account. We are well except Mother who has been complaining of sick head ache for several days. Every thing goes on as usual. Joseph and Stephen constantly occupied. Please give our love to all our friends & write as often as you can. You don't know what pleasure your letters afford. They are always hailed with delight by the whole family. Joseph has not had time to answer Mr Sammons letter[10] yet I believe I have heard him speak of it several times. He has three or four lectures to prepare every week & several recitations to hear besides numerous other calls upon his time, but it all appears to agree with him. He has grown very fleshy and looks uncommonly well, at least so I think. But the mail I fear will be closed. Love to all. Believe me yours truly

Harriet

[10] Not found.

FROM JACOB GREEN

Henry Papers, Smithsonian Archives

Philad[a] Feb. 13th 1834

My dear Sir

Mr Lukens[1] has just finished 6 of Mr Saxtons Electro Magnetic Machins,[2] for sparks, shocks &[c]. Bache, Hare, Gummery,[3] Banker,[4] & myself have

[1] Isaiah Lukens (1779–1846), from a mechanically gifted Pennsylvania family, moved to Philadelphia in 1811 to pursue a career in invention, clockmaking, and the manufacture of medical instruments. An ingenious method to expose the defect in a perpetual motion machine under investigation by the State legislature gave Lukens an early national reputation. After abortive attempts to market his improved instruments in Europe, Lukens manufactured public clocks for the city of Philadelphia and eventually assumed the responsibility for the astronomical observations necessary for keeping city time. Among the best known products of Lukens's shop was a new clock, constructed in collaboration with his partner Joseph Saxton, for the Independence Hall steeple.

A frequent visitor in Lukens's establishment, George Escol Sellers described him as "one of the greatest of our pioneer mechanics" and "a bachelor, of rather eccentric habits. He lived in his shop, sleeping in an adjoining room. . . . He called his shop his wife, and he really loved it." His versatile shop engaged in a variety of inventive and mechanical activities, including the production of the Saxton machines discussed in this letter.

each taken one. They are 30 dollars each. I promised Lukens to write to know if you wanted the remaining one, as he says he will make no more at that price. So if you want it you can just drop a line.

Lukens, along with others mentioned in Green's letter, formed the core of a well-known and tightly knit community of inventors in Philadelphia. A notable feature of this community was its interaction and overlap with the scientists. It was not unusual that Lukens, a founder and Vice-President of the Franklin Institute (1824 until his death), was also a long-standing member of the American Philosophical Society and the Academy of Natural Sciences of Philadelphia. Lukens's necrologist in the Franklin Institute *Journal* stressed that his subject's acquirements extended beyond "mechanical science" to a "taste for the study of mineralogy and other departments of natural science." Collaborations between scientist and inventor were not unusual. Although Henry and others perceived distinctions between the inventors and the scientists, in practice barriers to social and intellectual fraternization were far less formidable in that period than today. The distinctions perceived by Henry are viewed in a different framework by contemporary observers, not to mention historians of science and technology. Eugene S. Ferguson, ed., *Early Engineering Reminiscences [1815–1840] of George Escol Sellers* (Washington, D.C., 1965), p. 55. Sellers gives a colorful picture of Philadelphia's mechanical community. Arthur H. Frazier, "Joseph Saxton's First Sojourn at Philadelphia, 1818–1831, and His Contributions to the Independence Hall Clock," *Smithsonian Journal of History*, 1968, *3*:45–76. "Obituary Notice of the Late Isaiah Lukens," *Journal of the Franklin Institute*, 1846, *12*:423–425.

[2] Joseph Saxton (1799–1873), one of Philadelphia's premier inventors. After minimal formal schooling, Saxton followed an inventor's typical apprenticeship route from nail manufacturing, watchmaking, and engraving to working in the shop of Isaiah Lukens, an association marking the start of a brilliant inventive career. After work on the Independence Hall clock, he pursued his fortunes in London (in late 1831 or early 1832) at the Adelaide Gallery for the Illustration and Encouragement of Practical Science. Through engineering colleagues at the Adelaide he met Michael Faraday, whose recent discovery of electromagnetic induction fired Saxton's imagination. Originally responsible for constructing a large compound magnet, Saxton, upon hearing of Faraday's work, fitted his magnet with current- and spark-inducing attachments. The apparatus was featured at the Gallery's formal opening in June 1832. Saxton claimed no scientific novelty; his main concern according to a later account by Henry ("Memoir," cited below, p. 296) was to render Faraday's discoveries "palpable." To enhance the spark effects, Saxton improved his "magneto-electric machine" with a rotational design and a primitive commutator to maximize and give continuous form to Faraday's transient inductive effects. The result was a brilliant spark and "the prototype of electrical generators" (Eugene S. Ferguson, ed., *Early Engineering Reminiscences [1815–1840] of George Escol Sellers* [Washington, D.C., 1965], p. 131). Saxton described his apparatus in an August 1833 letter to Isaiah Lukens, parts of which were published by A. D. Bache in "Description of a Revolving Keeper Magnet, for Producing Electrical Currents," *Journal of the Franklin Institute*, 1834, *13*:155–156. Bache notes that Lukens constructed several models to Saxton's specifications. These were undoubtedly the reconstructions that Green was offering to Henry. In the following number of the *Journal*, Green published "An Account of Some Experiments Made with Mr. Jos. Saxton's Electromagnetic Machine" (1834, *13*:219–222), in which he used one of Lukens's machines to produce various sparks and shock effects. According to W. James King, Saxton's magneto, as such devices were called, became popular for laboratory demonstrations and medical experiments. *King*, p. 346. One of Lukens's reproductions is presently on exhibit at the Franklin Institute. See Arthur H. Frazier, "Joseph Saxton at London and His Magneto-Electric Devices," unpublished xerox copy in Joseph Henry Papers files, p. 18, which also traces the evolution of Saxton's machine and the details of his London experience. A replica of one of Saxton's original machines is in the collections of the National Museum of History and Technology in Washington, D.C. Good technical accounts of the devices appear in the above articles by Bache and Frazier and in a Joseph Henry necrology, "Memoir of Joseph Saxton, 1799–1873," *Biographical Memoirs, National*

Academy of Sciences, 1877, *1*:297–299.

Saxton left London in 1837 to become curator of measuring and weighing apparatus at the United States Mint and, in 1843, Bache hired him at the Coast Survey to superintend the Office of Weights and Measures, the forerunner of the National Bureau of Standards. Throughout his career Saxton sustained a remarkable rate of inventive activity. Our biographical account has been drawn from Frazier's above-cited article and especially Henry's "Memoir," still the best Saxton biography (another study is currently underway by Frazier). Henry based his biography on reminiscences and Saxton diaries, now in the Smithsonian Archives.

Henry was to meet Saxton in London in 1837 and, by the date of his "Memoir," considered the inventor both a respected colleague and good friend. As depicted by Henry, Saxton's career exemplifies the ambiguities of the relationship between scientist and inventor in nineteenth-century America. Henry was obviously fascinated and inspired by Saxton's inventions. Future volumes will document Henry's esteem for the inventor's work as well as frequent instances of their collaboration and mutual influence. Henry's eulogy—"A labor of love" in his words—was in part a tribute to Saxton's scientific contributions, a prerequisite, Henry explains, to membership in the National Academy of Sciences, of which Saxton was one of the fifty original members. Saxton also belonged to the Franklin Institute and American Philosophical Society. Despite Saxton's mechanical preoccupation, his work often impinged upon Henry's scientific investigations. In many cases, they used and developed similar instruments. Yet there were also notable differences in attitude and accomplishment. Upon completion of his inducing magnet, Saxton's inclination was only to display his device at the Adelaide, not to publish; a scientist's instincts would be otherwise. Only the rival claims of the inventor E. M. Clarke induced him to rush into print himself (see p. 299 of "Memoir"). Henry's eulogy implied important distinctions. Saxton emerges from Henry's "Memoir" not as a fellow scientist but, significantly, as Henry's conception of the ideal practitioner of the useful arts. Henry concludes that "Mr. Saxton was at no period of his life a profound student of science. He possessed more wisdom than learning . . . ," but:

> Mr. Saxton was not a mere practical man in the ordinary sense of the term—that is, one who by repetition and empirical imitation, becomes expert in the performance of operations devised by others, and has no knowledge of principles. On the contrary, he had clear and definite conceptions of the scientific elements of physical energy in its multiform manifestations, and, with an ever-teeming imagination applied them with success. [p. 314]

Henry's sensitivities to these subtleties became manifest many years later in an episode involving an artistic tribute to America's greatest inventors. An 1861 painting, entitled *Men of Progress* (now in the National Portrait Gallery of the Smithsonian Institution), includes a portrait of Henry with those of eighteen inventors. The painter was Christian Schussele. In a December 6, 1859, letter to John Skirving, Henry politely resisted the honor of his inclusion, pointing out that "although a number of my discoveries have been found useful in the arts, the application in most cases has been made by other persons. . . . I would however suggest that the portrait of Mr. Joseph Saxton of the Coast Survey, be substituted for that of myself." Both Saxton and Henry appear in the finished group portrait. Before acquisition by the National Portrait Gallery, *Men of Progress* hung on the wall in the White House Press Room with no visible consequences for either public policy or American journalism.

[3] This is undoubtedly John Gummere (1784–1845), for whom see *Henry Papers, 1*:59. The terminal "e" in Gummere was evidently pronounced so that the name could be easily misspelled "Gummery." See Arthur H. Frazier, "Joseph Saxton's First Sojourn at Philadelphia," p. 61.

Gummere's interest in apparatus probably arose from his duties as teacher of mathematics at the newly founded Haverford School. He also served as superintendent during part of his service with the school. Before 1833, he had operated his own boarding school in Burlington, New Jersey, where "he introduced chemistry and 'natural philosophy' into the curriculum, sending to London at considerable expense for apparatus and supplies." *DAB*.

[4] Charles Nicoll Bancker (1778?–1869), importer and insurance executive. A member of the American Philosophical Society (elected in 1825) and "a man of general scientific tastes and attainments," Bancker amassed a large collection of philosophical apparatus. The sale catalog of the collection survives: *Administrators Sale. Extensive Rare and Beautiful Cabinet of Science . . . Catalogue of Valuable Philosophical Apparatus Being a Collection Made by the Late Charles N. Bancker*

I have been looking for the apparatus you promised me when here—your sheeps tails[5] so send me one by wednesday next if pos[sible]—as I expect then to talk about Electro mag- to a *popular* audience.[6] Some one coming from Princeton could bring it, if put up in a small box. We are all well & do well. Resp[ts] to Mrs H. & other friends.

Yours in haste
Jacob Green

(Philadelphia, 1869).
Surviving correspondence with Henry shows that Bancker may have aided Henry in procuring philosophical apparatus as well as loaned him instruments from his own collection. Bancker's eulogist states that "public lecturers on natural philosophy and on experimental chemistry, had always the free use of his apparatus." "Obituary Notice of Mr. Bancker by Judge Cadwalader," *Proceedings of the American Philosophical Society*, 1869, *11*:85–91. For a consideration of Bancker as a representative of a special kind of amateur contributor to America's early scientific community, see Nathan Reingold, "Definitions and Speculations: The Professionalization of Science in America in the Nineteenth Century," forthcoming in the Proceedings of the Colloquium on the Early History of Societies for Promoting Knowledge in the United States, American Academy of Arts and Sciences, held in June 1973.

[5] i.e., the rocking arm of Henry's reciprocating electrical motor. See Henry's "On a Reciprocating Motion Produced by Magnetic Attraction and Repulsion," *Silliman's Journal*, 1831, *20*:340–343.

[6] See Henry's reply below of February 17, footnote 3.

TO JACOB GREEN

Joseph Henry Collection, Firestone Library, Princeton University

Princeton Feby 17th 1834

My Dear Sir

Your letter of the 13th inst came to hand on saturday and agreeable to your request I have sent off a box containing my *"sheeps tail."* Your Brother[1] took charge of it this morning and promised to forward it from Trenton by Tomorrows boat. I hope it will arrive in time for the lecture. I regret that my college duties this winter have left me no leisure for completing the one which I have commenced for you. The magnets are finished and also the stand. The batteries which I have sent are those I had constructed when last in Albany for you.[2] They are sufficiently large for exhibiting the princi-

[1] James Sproat Green. *Henry Papers, 1*:440n.

[2] For Henry's original motor, the batteries consisted of a plate of zinc surrounded with copper, while, according to this letter, Green's batteries utilized zinc and copper cylinders, a galvanic arrangement Henry normally used for his large electromagnets. See Henry's "On a Reciprocating Motion Produced by Magnetic Attraction and Repulsion," *Silliman's Journal*, 1831, *20*:342.

pal elec-mag. phenomina, can be used separately or combined and will be found a very convenient table apparatus. I am fitting up the article for you on a some what different plan.[3] The magnets are of this form curved so that both poles may act on the galvanic magnet instead of one. By this improvement I anticipate a moving force double of that in the other plan with the same ammount of galvanic & magnetic power. Many different forms of the instrument have suggested themselves to my mind and it would require but little ingenuity to vary the appearance of the machine by the addition of wheels &c. so as to make it appear like a new article. I believe that Mr Richee has lately reinvented my machine in this way and described it before the Royal Society. Perhaps I do him injustice.[4]

[3] Although Henry seems to be on the verge of completing the modification of his reciprocating electric motor for Green, it is unclear whether he actually achieved a finished product. We have been unable to locate either any later references to the modified motor or any example of the device itself. Whether completed or not, Henry's machine on a "different plan" deserves a place in the history of electrical technology. The episode also shows Henry seriously reevaluating the potential capacity and perhaps practical application of an invention which he had earlier described as a philosophical toy.

It is not surprising that Henry showed the improvements to Green as Green had witnessed the first demonstrations of Henry's original motor and had suggested modifications which included replacing the permanent magnets with electromagnets. Green later demonstrated the advantages of this substitution at a meeting of the Franklin Institute on May 22, 1834. See "Monthly Conversation Meetings," *Journal of the Franklin Institute*, 1834, *14*:5.

[4] A Scottish physicist who had abandoned a church career for teaching and science, William Ritchie (1790–1837; *DNB*) was a well-known experimentalist. He held concurrent professorships of Natural Philosophy at the Royal Institution (from 1829) and the University of London (from 1832). A prolific scientific publisher, his contributions included "On a New Photometer...," *Phil. Trans.*, 1825, pp. 141–146; "On a New Form of the Differential Thermometer with Some of its Applications," *Phil. Trans.*, 1827, pp. 129–131; and "On the Reduction of Mr. Faraday's Discoveries in Magneto-Electric Induction to a General Law," *Phil. Mag.*, 1834, 3d ser. *4*:11–13. Electromagnetic research, much of it built upon the work of his colleague Faraday, accounted for the bulk of his published work.

At this date Henry may have received only a verbal report of Ritchie's presentation of a rotating electromagnetic motor, which was described in the final pages of Ritchie's "Experimental Researches in Electro-Magnetism and Magneto-Electricity," *Phil. Trans.*, 1833, pp. 313–321. We know that Henry saw the printed account at least by May 2, 1834 (see the entry for that date of Henry's Notes on a Trip to Philadelphia, April 29–May 2, 1834, below). There Ritchie noted that a series of experiments on reversing the poles of an electromagnet afforded a "most beautiful result:" an electromagnet which, through interaction with an arrangement of permanent magnets, achieved "rapid rotation... about its center" (p. 319). (At the end of the same article, Ritchie was able to obtain the reverse effect with a similar revolving apparatus producing "an almost continuous current of electricity.") One modification of his electric motor, Ritchie claimed, could lift a weight of several ounces. The basic principle involved was clearly identical with that of Henry's motor. There was no acknowledgment of Henry's prior invention, only an oblique reference to Henry in a discussion of "an electromagnet according to the American method" (p. 317), a passage which Henry carefully quoted in one of his Princeton notebooks (No. [7171], pp. 86–87) along with a general consideration of Ritchie's publication.

Henry's imputation reflected several enduring concerns: a growing awareness of his priorities, a sensitivity to plagiarism, a sense of frustration at the apparent neglect of his work among his European peers, and, more fundamentally, long-standing convictions about the crucial elements of technological innovation. Henry's annoyance with Ritchie's claims was an intermittent concern for over two decades. Although notes from Henry's 1837 European trip show he was impressed with the "rapidity and force" of a rotary motor Ritchie demonstrated at the Royal Institution (European Diary, Henry Papers, Smithsonian Archives, entry for April 27), his continued irritation surfaced several years later in letters to his friend the Swiss scientist and editor A. A. De La Rive. In a letter of November 24, 1841 (De La Rive Papers, Bibliothèque Publique et Universitaire, Geneva), Henry asked De La Rive to retract a passage in a recent article attributing the first electromagnetic machine to Ritchie ("Coup d'oeil sur l'état actuel de nos connaissances," in A. A. De La Rive, ed., *Archives de l'électricité*, 1841, *1*:27–28). De La Rive claimed to have seen Ritchie demonstrate the machine in London in 1828. While Ritchie may well have missed Henry's article on the motor in *Silliman's Journal* and any reports that might have appeared in the European literature, Henry's letter pointed out that Faraday demonstrated a reproduction of the machine at the Royal Institution as soon as his article reached England. A May 8, 1846, letter to De La Rive in the Henry Papers, Smithsonian Archives, complained politely of the same misattribution, adding that in the 1837 Royal Institution lecture which he attended, Ritchie claimed no novelty but presented his invention as a modification of Henry's. Henry simply wanted recognition in the published record. The Henry Library contains further evidences of the apparently one-sided priority debate in Henry's copy of the English edition of De La Rive's *A Treatise on Electricity in Theory and Practice*, 3 vols. (London, 1853–1858), where Ritchie's machine again received precedence (*1*:293). In his annotations to this passage, Henry reasserted his claims and noted further that Ritchie witnessed Faraday's early demonstration of his reciprocating motor. While plagiarism was doubtless on Henry's mind, his letter to De La Rive blamed the neglect of his contribution on slow transatlantic communication as a general obstacle to the recognition of American priorities abroad.

Fundamental to Henry's reaction was a personal interpretation of technology that emerged early in his scientific career. According to Henry, scientific discovery was the moving force of technology. Whatever the technological virtues of Ritchie's particular design, it was typical of Henry to emphasize underlying scientific principles and to downgrade the effect of empirical modifications. The language of his attack on Ritchie—particularly the lack of "ingenuity" he perceived in Ritchie's variation—echoed earlier attacks on American inventors. Similar language will appear below in his letter of September 10, 1835, to Benjamin Silliman. While Ritchie was far more sophisticated theoretically than the inventors and mechanics Henry condemned so vehemently, his reputation for great experimental and technical ingenuity suggests a view of technology less theoretical than Henry's. Without commenting on the propriety of Ritchie's omission of Henry's name, we suspect that Ritchie viewed his rotary design and the production of a continuous motion as an important innovation, not a mere reinvention.

King credits Ritchie with the invention of the first electric motor with a rotating electromagnet, in retrospect a technological development of first consequence. Although contemporaries such as William Sturgeon saw practical possibilities in Henry's reciprocating design, the thrust of electric motor technology followed the lines of Ritchie's approach. See *King*, p. 261; William Sturgeon, "Historical Sketch of the Rise and Progress of Electromagnetic Engines for Propelling Machinery," *The Annals of Electricity, Magnetism, and Chemistry...*, 1839, *3*:432. At this time, Henry saw few technological possibilities in electric motors of any design (see especially the above-cited letter to Silliman) and certainly no particular advantage in the addition of a few wheels for rotary motion. Any significant practical development, in Henry's view, would necessarily combine the fruit of new scientific discovery with his own innovation: the novel application of electromagnetic attraction and repulsion to a mechanical device, "a power ... never before applied in mechanics," according to Henry's 1831 article (p. 340). Henry's definition of natural "powers" and his understanding of the proprietary rights of those who first apply these powers to practice were ambiguous but crucial aspects of his technological views, which are discussed at length in terms of the patent law in *Henry Papers*, *1*:424–425. While Ritchie claimed a scientific basis for his invention in his experiments on reversing electromagnetic polarity in soft iron, Henry could point to numerous earlier experiments of his own on the same phenomenon; see, for example, *Henry Papers*, *1*:424–425.

The upright magnets[5] are too soft & do not well retain their magnetism. I retouched them this morning and they will probably answer the purpose of exhibition several times. By closely inspecting the brass bands which bind the magnets into bundles you will find on the edge of two of them markes with a file corresponding with similar markes on the edge of the brass sockets on the mahogany stand. Put each marked end of the magnets into the corresponding marked socket and the magnets will be properly placed for the motion.

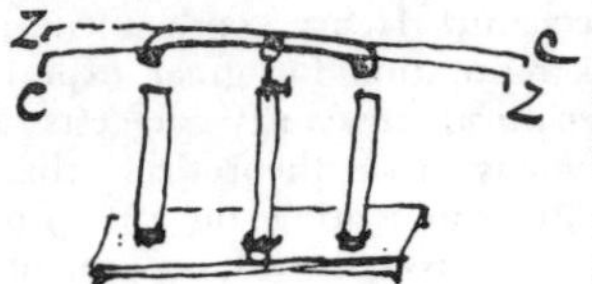

In arranging the battery be careful to note that if one of the ends of the lateral conducting wire dip into a cup from the copper the other must dip into one from the Zinc as shewn in the Fig. You will find in the same paper with the "*tail piece*" a magnetic needle with a ball of pith on each end. This you may reccollect adds considerably to the effect of the exhibition by its constant motion.[6] You may contrive to place it directly above the tail piece supported on the point of a needle attached to a stand of cro[oked] wire thus I found it impossib[le to] put the battery into perfect order on so short a notice. I called at the Turners immediately after the reception of your note to get two wooden rings turned to attach to the bottoms of the zinc cylenders but will not get them done in several days. You will find one ring in the box which I happened to have on hand. You can probably make them (the batteries) answer equally well by cementing some bits of cork to the bottoms of the zinc cylenders.

N.B. Do not forget to amalgamate the ends of the conducting wires and also the new brass thimbles with a solution of nitrate of mercury.[7] If I reccollect aright I informed you that I performed Faraday's primary experiment with a battery of the kind I send you. Two wires may be made to revolve one around each of the <*two*> poles of a horse shoe magnet. Thus *a b* are two large phials cut off at the middle and semented on the ends of the magnet. In this exp both batteries must be used. If you have a good sized magnet the exp can be made on a large scale.[8] Give my respects to my Friend Lukens & tell him if I can raise money from

[5] This paragraph follows a space in the original text where Henry started to add a bit more on the Ritchie episode but changed his mind and crossed it out; he now returns to Green's device.

[6] The revolving magnetic needle would show different patterns of interaction of the electromagnetic forces. An elaborate array of these needles can be seen in Francis Watkins's modified copy of one of Joseph Saxton's electric motors, pictured in Arthur H. Frazier's unpublished article "Joseph Saxton at London and his Magneto-Electric Devices," p. 22d, in the files of the Joseph Henry Papers.

the trustees at their next meeting for an increase of the apparatus I will purchase the remaining machine[9] but do not let him loose an oportunity of selling it on my account.

My time has been constantly occupied this winter in my college duties. It is settled that Dr Torrey returns to Princeton next summer and will continue during the whole term. I am therefore obliged to hurry my course in order that I may not interfere with his course next session as we both lecture to the same class. My battery[10] is still unfinished although I have expended about ½ a day's labour on it every week since I saw you last.

Your Friend
Jos Henry

[P.S.] Give my Respects to our friend Prof Millington[11] also to Prof Bache.

The original illustration appeared in the July-December 1835 issue of *The London and Edinburgh Philosophical Magazine and Journal of Science.*

[7] The wood was used to separate the zinc and copper, while the amalgamation improved electrical contacts. *Henry Papers, 1*:422; Henry's copy of Jacob Green's *Electro-Magnetism* (Philadelphia, 1827) describes the amalgamation techniques, pp. 173–174.

[8] We cannot specify the immediate reason for Henry's repetition of Faraday's seminal discovery in 1821 of the phenomenon of electromagnetic rotations, considered in L. Pearce Williams, *Michael Faraday* (New York, 1965), pp. 151–168. Classroom demonstration is the best possibility. The phenomenon was normally introduced as the "fourth fact" of electricity in Henry's physics lectures at Princeton. See the natural philosophy lecture notes of his student W. M. Whitehead, Lecture 47, January 19, 1837 (Rare Book and Manuscript Library, Princeton University); also Henry's 1836 "Lecture on Electromagnetism prepared for Dr Torrey," Henry Papers, Smithsonian Archives, Box 19, in folder "Electricity and Magnetism Notes." An apparent reference to the effect also occurs in an undated Albany lecture, printed in *Henry Papers, 1*:469.

Though ascribing fundamental significance to Faraday's discovery, Henry's lecture notes adduce no particular theoretical conclusions from electromagnetic rotations, beyond interpreting it as an important consequence of Ampère's electrodynamic theory. In his lectures Henry makes no reference to the initial theoretical controversy surrounding electromagnetic rotations, which opposed Faraday's circular construction of electromagnetic forces to Ampère's linear, action-at-a-distance interpretation. An avowed Ampèrian, Henry probably took Ampère's theoretical resolution of the problem for granted and considered the matter generally settled. In any event, Henry's handling of the effect was altogether typical. His first inclination, as with the electromagnet, was to conduct new experiments on the largest possible scale.

Though obviously struck by surface similarities between Faraday's revolving wires and his own electromagnetic motor, Henry drew no theoretical connection between the devices. Ampère offered a unifying theoretical framework, but Henry seemed unaware of the continuous line of development seen by modern historians from electromagnetic rotations to the electric motor (see Williams, *Faraday*, p. 156; *King*, p. 260).

[9] There is no record of such a purchase in the Trustees' minutes nor does a Saxton machine appear in Henry's accounts of apparatus purchased for Princeton (see "J. Henry's a/c with Philosophical Hall previous to 1837" in the Princeton University Archives). The latter does list a similar magnetoelectric machine by Saxton's rival Edward M. Clarke of London. See also Allen G. Shenstone, "Joseph Henry's Bills...," *The Princeton University Library Chronicle*, 1967, *28*:150–155. Nevertheless, Henry later experimented extensively with one of Saxton's devices, whether his own or borrowed. See the May 14, 1840, entry in Henry's "Record of Experiments" (in the Smithsonian Archives), to appear in a future volume of *The Papers of Joseph Henry.*

[10] See above, Henry to George Maclean, October 9, 1833.

[11] See Millington to Henry, December 31, 1832, footnote 1.

I finish my course of lectures on electricity tomorrow. It occupies in all 12 lectures. I have been deeply engaged for some weeks past studying the x + y of electricity.[12]
[P.P.S.] You have probably seen by the papers that Mr *Benedict* Jaëger[13] has become a married man.

[12] Henry may refer to the basics of electricity covered in his lectures or, perhaps, to the use of algebra in the electrical course, mentioned by Henry in his letter to Rogers of March 9, 1835, below, footnote 7.

[13] See above, Henry to Harriet Henry, April 6, 1833, footnote 4. Henry underlined Jaeger's first name because of its meaning from Shakespeare's *Much Ado About Nothing*, an old bachelor, now newly married.

FROM PARKER CLEAVELAND[1]

Henry Papers, Smithsonian Archives

Brunswick March 3, 1834.

My dear Sir,

Day after day for nearly a year I have been intending to write you, to thank you for your friendly attention in helping me to an electro magnet, and to trouble you with a few queries.

I was not able to put it in operation until last May,[2] when its performance gave great satisfaction to the class. I put on about 1500 lbs (all I could conveniently obtain), which remained suspended, until I had withdrawn more than half the Battery.

[1] Parker Cleaveland (1780–1858, *DAB* and *Henry Papers, 1*:373), scientist, author, and educator at Bowdoin College, Brunswick, Maine. This is the first letter to pass between Cleaveland and Henry since Cleaveland's of June 18, 1832, in which he reimbursed Henry for expenses in constructing a magnet for Bowdoin. (See *Henry Papers, 1*:420–426 for Henry's description of the electromagnetic apparatus and some experimental procedures.)

As he revealed in the text of this letter, Cleaveland was previously unaware that Henry had moved to Princeton, although he apparently suspected that Henry no longer lived in Albany. Addressing the letter to Henry in Albany, Cleaveland wrote on the cover, "If Prof. H. has left Albany, this P[ost] M[aster] will please forward this to him." In turn the cover sheet was stamped "FORWARDED" and "ALBANY MAR 10." Determining the date of Henry's receipt of the letter is problematical. In a letter to James Henry of February 9, 1835, below, nearly a year later, Henry thanked his brother for forwarding Professor Cleaveland's letter on magnetism which had been sent to Albany. Could this forwarded letter have been mislaid in the mails for eleven months? Or might there have been a second Cleaveland letter, also sent to Albany, now not found? Surviving Cleaveland-Henry correspondence is certainly fragmentary, but it may not have been voluminous to begin with. No Henry response to this letter has been located.

[2] Cleaveland informed Henry in June of 1832 that other business would prevent his assembling the apparatus until autumn. See *Henry Papers, 1*:432–433.

1. You mention in your letter,[3] that Mr. Sturgeon recommends water 1 part, nitric acid 8 pts. Have you employed this? Do you find it superior to a mixture of Sulph. & muriatic acids?

2. I saw in the newspapers a *very short* notice of a magnet of uncommon power by Prof. Henry of Princeton.[4] Are you *the man*? Does the great power of this magnet depend on size &c, or is there any new principle concerned, or new manipulation?[5]

3. Does the *lifting power* of the Battery suffer any change from year to year, provided its poles &c are kept in good order?

4. I believe you do not mention in your letter the design in soldering two *wires* to the strips of copper which terminate the two poles.

I did not find so much magnetism retained, on account of the hardness of the iron, as I had anticipated. I have so connected my battery, that the whole is almost instantaneously immersed by turning a winch once round.

If your engagements will permit a short reply to my queries in the course of a few days, it will much oblige

Yrs with much esteem
P. Cleaveland

[3] The reference is to Henry's letter to Cleaveland of May 8, 1832, where Henry discussed the conditions which must be met to gain maximum strength from the electromagnet. See *Henry Papers, 1*:422–423. As far as we know Henry left no record of any systematic investigations of his battery solutions. The solutions he applied in his electromagnetic and induction experiments seem to be derived from standard electrical and chemical reference books. For example, in notebook [23894], Henry took extensive notes on the relative effects of different types and dilutions of acid solutions given by Benjamin Silliman in his *Elements of Chemistry* (New Haven, 1831), 2:656. Other Henry notebooks also contain sporadic jottings on these topics.

[4] At least two Boston papers printed verbatim the article originating in the *New-York Standard,* reprinted above, Cooper to Henry, November 16, 1833, footnote 2. The article appeared in the *Boston Daily Advertiser & Patriot,* October 5, 1833, p. 1, and the *Boston Weekly Messenger,* October 17, 1833, p. 1.

[5] Such questions as these are asked and answered above in Cooper to Henry, November 16, 1833, and Henry's response to Cooper, November 26, 1833.

TO JAMES HENRY

Family Correspondence, Henry Papers, Smithsonian Archives

Princeton Monday
March 10th 1834

Dear James

We have been expecting a letter from you for 4 or 5 days past but as yet have been disappointed. Mother I suppose is anxious to hear from us but my time has been so much occupied for a week or two past that I found it inconvenient to write. Harriet is quite smart although she has not yet been down stairs. She sits up and is well with the exception of being very weak. The Boy is quite harty, still sleaps with me and is not in the least jealous of the attention which his little sister[1] receives from his mother.

Nothing new with us. The weather has been quite summer like for a few days past. We have commenced operations in our garden. English William planted peas on Saturday.

There has been a great meeting of the inhabitants of Princeton to petition Congress to return the deposits.[2] The chairman was a prominent Jackson man lately reformed. The Administration party also got up an oposition meeting but it was very thinly attended. They are said however to have made up in noise what they wanted in numbers. Harriet has received a very kind letter from Jane Ryley. She has expected one from her friends the Misses Meads, but they have not as yet found leasure to write although Harriet thinks they might find leasure were they so disposed.

I[3] will find fault with *you too*. We have been expecting a letter from you for several days but in vain. I am quite out of humour with you all.

We all get along smoothly here. Bub is very much pleased with the babe & she grows finely—has been very healthy & good thus far.

Joseph is as usual much occupied in preparing for the class. I have not been down stairs yet but hope to go this week. The naming of Puss has been given to Mother. She proposes calling it Mary Anna after herself and Mammy. Please give our united love to Mother, Nancy & all friends. We wish frequently for them all. Tell the Misses Mead we expect to hear from them soon & look forward to visit from their Mother this month. Excuse this scrawl as I have a miserable pen and eyes are so weak I dare not write more. Do write [and] let us hear from Susan, Mary Ann & all our friends.

Love to all. Yours as ever
Harriet

PS. Sis weighed lb 6 two weeks ago but has gained I expect a pound or more since then. She looks like Aunt.

[1] Henry's second child, Mary Anna Henry (1834–1903), future champion of his scientific reputation. Mary Henry diaries for the years 1858–1868 and for European trips survive in the Henry Papers, Smithsonian Archives, as well as scattered letters. To this project, her work on the surviving records of her father looms above all else. Like some other unmarried daughters, she is historically defined, as it were, by the relationship with her father. Yet she was clearly the strongest personality of the Henry children, and her diary entries for the Civil War years are interesting in their own right. For Mary Henry's relationship to this edition, see the Notes on Style in this volume.

[2] See above, Henry to James Henry, January 8, 1834.

[3] Harriet wrote the remainder of the letter.

March 20, 1834

FROM [ISAAC W. JACKSON][1]

Henry Papers, Smithsonian Archives

March 20th *1834*

Dear Henry,

I write you in much haste to inform you that the Doctors reference, (the referees being Judges Woodworth & Spencer—Platt is recently dead) comes in N. York on the 10th of April.[2] The Doctor will be there a week before that time, & if it be possible for you to meet him there five or six days before the trial commences, he will be under great obligations to you. You will learn where to find him by calling at the store of Howard Nott & Company.[3] I hope you will be able to arrange your concerns so as to comply with the Doctor's wishes, as he depends greatly upon you. The old gentleman has obtained some highly interesting results, which he will give you, from the heating of the air for the cupola, by means of the steam after it has performed its office in the Engine—the saving of fuel is so great, under the circumstances of the experiment, that if made with accuracy, it can I think be accounted for only by supposing that the amo[un]t of heat afforded by a given quant of fuel increases with the temperature.

The Doctor's furnace presents I presume a more philosophical mode of operating with heat, than can any where else be found—thus a quant of that

[1] From the handwriting, subject matter, and a Mary Henry notation, this is clearly a letter of Isaac Jackson's. The surviving manuscript is incomplete. The last paragraph given below appears in the margin of the first page. The paragraph immediately before breaks off. The remainder of the letter, including the signature, apparently no longer survives.

[2] Apparently a reference to one of the numerous court actions initiated by Union College President Eliphalet Nott to protect the patents for his well-known "Nott Stove." Henry had been asked to testify in one of Nott's earlier suits (see above, Isaac Jackson to Joseph Henry, January 8, 1833), but we have no evidence that he did so. Here, however, we can assume that he played some active role in the case. In a letter to his wife dated December 13, 1832, printed above, Henry mentioned a conversation with Nott and stated that he had a high opinion of his work. This being so, it seems logical that he might have testified in Nott's behalf. The case file for *Eliphalet Nott* v. *James Wilson* is with the records of the U.S. District Court for the Southern District of New York in the National Archives Federal Records Center in Suitland, Maryland, but the file gives no indication if Henry did or did not appear on Nott's behalf.

On October 14, 1833, the parties to the suit agreed to submit to the arbitration of a panel composed of former justices of the New York State Supreme Court. Jonas Platt (1769–1834), James Kent (1763–1847, *DAB*), along with Ambrose Spencer (1765–1848, *DAB*) and John Woodworth (1768–1858) were named to the original panel. With the death of Platt and the withdrawal of Kent, it was necessary to add Joseph Curtis to the panel. Joseph Henry was presumably to testify before these referees. A copy of their award in the library of Union College has no reference to Henry. They found in favor of Nott on the question of infringement.

[3] Howard Nott was President Nott's son. As he was under twenty at the time the firm was founded, Hislop, op. cit., pp. 265–266, implies strongly that he and his brothers were fronting for their father in his inventing and entrepreneurial ventures.

element or property leaving the furnace gives elasticity to the Steam by which thro' the Engine the condensed air is furnished for the fire, & then enters into this very air & reappears in the furnace, thus performing a circuit, with greater or less loss according to the greater or less perfection of the mechanical arrangements & structures.[4]

Do you *hear* any thing about hard times, for we salaried men like the office holders are not obnoxious to *feeling* them. The "pressure" & embarrassments are very great here—the mechanics intend to indicate their sense of it by wearing crape at a meeting to be held next week in the Old College Yard. We have certainly fallen upon evil times just now, but I confidently look for better, as I believe the Jackson & Van Buren party has run its course. Tis said Van Buren begins to lose somewhat of his . . .

I send you a copy of the Doctors patents etc.[5] Conversation with him previous to the trial will be the best preparation for it. I wish you would write me *immediately* that I may inform the Doctor when you will meet him in N. York. He will I presume leave here Thursday for Albany as the term closes & I may not see him again.

[4] Like Jackson, Henry had a high regard for the Nott stove. Jackson credits the recycling of heat—whether an element or a property—for the great success of the stove, rather than the rotary grate removing the ashes from the anthracite coal. The referees in the award cited in footnote 2 were also taken with the arrangements for heating and circulating air within the stove.

[5] A reference to an undated, five-page printed list of thirty-six of Nott's patent specifications and a summary of their improvements over previous heating techniques. The patents listed date from March 1826 through June 1833. Henry retained the list, having it bound into a volume for his library along with related pamphlets which Jackson sent previously (see Jackson to Henry, January 8, 1833).

TO HARRIET HENRY

Family Correspondence, Henry Papers, Smithsonian Archives

Albany Monday
one o'clock [March] 24th [1834][1]
at Shanklands

My Dear Wife

I arrived safely at New York on Friday but as I was obliged to see Dr Torrey I found it impossible to leave for Albany until saturday evening. I stoped at the American but spent Friday evening and also the night at Dr Torrey's.

[1] The letter is postmarked March 24, which fell on a Monday in 1834.

I was pleased with Mrs. Torrey.[2] She is quite a good looking Lady and very candid in expressing her opinions. The Dr and she will probably accompany me to Princeton on My return inorder to make arrangements for their sojourn during the comming summer.[3] I did not find it convenient to call at Miss Van Antwerps but will endeavour to do so on my return.[4] I arrived at Albany about 8 o'clock on Sunday morning. We had a pleasant passage up the river. I found on board the boat Prof Davies[5] of West Point, Mr Gilchest[6] of Albany and also Mr Clark[7] the engraver—with such company of course the evening would not appear teadious. I found Mother about in the same state we left her last fall. She has been very feeble but the Dr has given her a new medicine which has revived her considerably. Last night she had a very bad paroxism of coughing which continued more than two hours. She however slept will afterward. I have not yet seen her to day. She was much pleased to see me asked many questions about the *children* and said she was not as much disappointed in seeing me at this time without you and the children as she would have been had I waited until May. Nancy and James are will. Nancy has had 7 men in her family all winter. One has left. Orlando Meads called this morning before I was dressed. He is busily engaged in preparing his address which is to be delivered in about 2 weeks from this time.[8] I called at Mrs. Beck's[9] about 10 o'clock. The old Lady ap-

[2] This is apparently the first time Henry met Eliza Torrey (d. 1855). The daughter of William and Eliza Robertson Shaw of New York City, Eliza Robertson Shaw married John Torrey in 1824. We know little about her. Torrey's biographer merely records that she was "many years an invalid suffering from pleurisy, rheumatism, and other ailments." A. Hunter Dupree, however, seeing her through the adoring eyes of Asa Gray, comments on "her strong and scholarly mind, her radiant piety, and her angelic presence." Apparently able to read Latin and Greek, Eliza Torrey is evaluated by Dupree as "such an extraordinary woman that her personality and intellect rose above the limitations of ill health and the ornamental position of her sex." Andrew Denny Rodgers, *John Torrey: A Story of North American Botany* (Princeton, 1942), pp. 69, 198, 245. A. Hunter Dupree, *Asa Gray, 1810–1888* (Cambridge, Massachusetts, 1959), pp. 38, 175.

[3] Torrey usually went to Princeton in mid-May or the first of June to lecture through July. Rodgers, *John Torrey*, pp. 110, 111.

[4] This sentence is in the margin of the first page of the manuscript.

[5] Charles Davies (see *Henry Papers, 1*:280n) was Professor of Mathematics at West Point.

[6] Henry may be referring to Robert Gilchrist, an Albany merchant, or to Edward R. Gilchrist or John T. Gilchrist, all involved in the firm of Robert Gilchrist and Company. Albany City Directories, 1832–1836.

[7] Asahel Clark, for whom see *Henry Papers, 1*:251n.

[8] Orlando Meads delivered the annual address to the Albany Institute on April 17, 1834. See below, Henry to James Henry, April 25, 1834, footnote 4.

[9] Probably Catherine Theresa Romeyn Beck (1769?–1854?), the mother of T. R., Nicholas F., John B., Abram, and L. C. Beck. She became a widow in 1798 upon the death of her husband Caleb Beck. According to her granddaughter, "she determined that no exertion should be spared on her part to give her five sons a liberal education, her ardent desire being that each of them should embrace a profession, a desire encouraged by her father and in furtherance of which she had his advice and assistance while he lived." Her father was the Reverend Derick (Theodoric) Romeyn (1744–1804, *Herringshaw*), a founder of the academy which later became Union College. Sylvester D. Willard, *Annals of the Medical*

pears just as she used to do. Time stands still with her. Helen[10] has grown astonishingly. She is almost as tall as her sister.[11] Mrs B says that Dr Lewis[12] will probably remove to New Brunswick next summer with his family. Mrs B. also informed me that Mrs Bullions gave birth to a daughter yester day morning. I have not yet called on Mr Bullions as he is ingaged in the School and Mrs Bullions cannot see me. Mrs Beck thinks she will visit Princeton the coming summer, *ie* if she goes to New York. My next visit was to Meade's. The Old Lady had gone to church (this is Passion week). Charlotte was just going out of the door. She however turned back and stoped until she had read your little letter and asked me an hundred questions. I was next questioned by Luiza for more than half an hour about the baby, its Mother, the Boy, your Mother, Aunt, Stephen, Hart, Wilson[13] & so on. She informed me that they had learned that Dr Mclean was to marry the elder Miss Wilson so that the coast is clear for the Old Batcheldor should he think fit to make an assault on the fortress.[14]

Society of the County of Albany, 1806–1851. With Biographical Sketches of Deceased Members (Albany, 1864), p. 293.

[10] Helen Louisa Beck (1821–1863) was the younger daughter of T. R. Beck. Educated at the Albany Female Academy, she began contributing to the periodical press at the age of fourteen. Specializing in poetry, she also wrote on the early history of New York. In 1848 she married William Parmalee, Mayor of Albany from 1846 to 1848 and from 1854 to 1856. Information from *In Memoriam: Helen Louisa Parmalee* (Albany, 1864), presented to Henry by her sister, and now in the Henry Library.

[11] T. R. Beck's older daughter was Catherine Beck, later Mrs. Pierre Van Cortlandt of Croton, New York. She authored the biographical sketches of her father and of her uncle L. C. Beck, in Sylvester D. Willard, *Annals of the Medical Society of the County of Albany* . . . (Albany, 1864), pp. 258–270, 292–302.

[12] Lewis Caleb Beck. See *Henry Papers*, *1*:69n. Beck had become Professor of Chemistry and Natural History at Rutgers in 1830.

[13] Stephen Alexander, John Seely Hart, and Hugh Nesbitt Wilson were at this time tutors at Princeton and students at the Princeton Theological Seminary. From this juncture in their careers, each was to pursue a different occupation.

Stephen Alexander remained at Princeton for the rest of his life, holding the Professorships of Mathematics, Astronomy, and Natural Philosophy at various times.

John Seely Hart (1810–1877) became an educator, author, and editor. A graduate of Princeton (1830) and of the Theological Seminary (1834), Hart was licensed to preach in 1835, but turned to a career in education. He was teacher and principal at various schools in Princeton, Philadelphia, and in New Jersey. From 1842 until 1859, Hart was Principal of Central High School of Philadelphia and, therefore, a successor to Henry's friend, A. D. Bache. In 1872 he returned to Princeton as Professor of Belles-Lettres, English Language and Literature, resigning in 1874. Hart was always a prolific contributor to the periodical press, specializing in education, literature, and religion. He was also involved in the editing of numerous journals. Hart evidently became a friend of Joseph Henry's. Later correspondence, often concerning recommendations, exists between the two. One of Hart's pamphlets, *Some of the Mistakes of Educated Men* . . . (Philadelphia, 1861), exists in Henry's Library. *DAB; Princeton Catalogue*, p. 142; *The Biographical Encyclopaedia of New Jersey of the Nineteenth Century* (Philadelphia, 1877), pp. 425–427.

In contrast to Stephen Alexander and John Seely Hart, Hugh Nesbitt Wilson (1813–1878) actively entered the ministry after graduating from Princeton Theological Seminary in 1834. Ordained in 1835, Wilson spent his career attached to various churches in New York and New Jersey. *Roberts*, p. 75.

[14] Neither Dr. George Maclean nor Dr. John

My next visit was to the *Dominie's*[15] and before I had time to enter the room my attention was arrested by the voice of the young gentleman whom you intend as a beau to your little daughter. I was first welcomed by old Aunty. She appears about as well as usual. Next Jane[16] came bounding into the room with such haste that I was almost affraid that she was going to take me round the neck but she did not and of course my fears soon subsided. She was much pleased to see me and made a thousand inquiries about all in Princeton. She next brought down the Young Dominie. He is a very large child and I think resembles Mr Ludlow, a noble looking little fellow not handsom has a good eye and strongly marked features. Next came Mrs Ludlow. She looks uncommonly will and says she enjoyes good health. Jane says that Anna and herself have been seperated all winter, one or the other being continually at Albany.

She also stated that it is probable that Ellen Proudfit[17] will return with me. I gave your letter to Jane and also suffered her to read the one you sent to Miss Proudfit. Jane took the liberty of inserting the words *"or Hubby"* after the letter *m* which occurs in your communication. I had almost forgotten to mention that Mr Meads starts for Washington this afternoon as one of the committee to present the memorial to Congress and the President from the Great Meeting at Albany.[18] Perhaps Mrs Meads will accompany me to Princeton on my return and remain with us until Mr M returns from Washington.

Maclean married the elder Miss Wilson; John Maclean never married. The "Old Batchel-dor" undoubtedly refers to Louisa Meads's brother, Orlando Meads, who married Elizabeth Wilson in 1834. W. L. L. Peltz, *The Top Flight at Number One LaFayette Street* (Albany, 1935), p. 64.

[15] i.e., the family of the Reverend John R. Ludlow.

[16] Probably Jane Ryley, the sister of Mrs. Ludlow.

[17] One of the daughters of Robert Proudfit (*Henry Papers, 1*:444).

[18] The "Great Meeting" took place on March 18, 1834, at the height of the panic over the removal of deposits from the Second Bank of the United States. Sponsored by the anti-administration, pro-Bank forces, the meeting appointed a committee of seventeen, composed largely of local businessmen, including John Meads, to personally deliver a memorial to Congress and the President. The committee undoubtedly met with a cool reception by Jackson. "When deputations of distinguished citizens came to Washington to see the President personally and beg him to restore the deposits, he was contemptuous." However, their memorial was presented to a sympathetic Senate by Daniel Webster. The *Albany Argus*, mouthpiece of the anti-Bank Regency, reported on the committee's activities and Webster's presentation of the memorial with contempt: "The Bank ... got up a panic meeting in the good city of Albany, where, as in duty bound, it was resolved, that the Bank was great—the distress great—and that there was a great need of sending a distress committee to Washington, to hold up the hands of the Bank attorneys." Of Webster's speech, "there was never palmed off upon this community, (save perhaps the Senate of the United States,) such a series of Munchausen stories." On April 4, 1834, the House passed resolutions which essentially killed the Bank. The *Argus* commented on April 8th, that "the game was up before [the committee] reached the capitol." Robert V. Remini, *Andrew Jackson and the Bank War* (New York, 1967), p. 149; *Daily Albany Argus*, March 27, 1834, p. 2, April 8, 1834, p. 2, April 9, 1834, p. 2.

According to the doctrine of probabilities you may therefore infer that some person will accompany me on my return.

I next called at the tailors and bespoke a coat. I am not altogether pleased with the appearance of my costume and must indeavour for the sake of appearances to improve it. I have taken dinner at Shanklands and find them all well. Susan looks unusually healthy. Shankland is in good condition. Mary Ann has been a little troubled with the dispeptia. I have delivered Aunts injunction that Mary Ann should come to Princeton. She says that she will visit us as soon as she can but neither her nor Susan will set the time at Present.

Mary Ann sends her best love to Aunt and would have been very hapy to have seen her with me. The family send their love to all. The Young ladies who were at Shanklands have returned home. I have nothing more at this time. All have been very kind in the receptions and have made many inquiries respecting your Mother and the whole family.

I remain My Dear Wife
Your own Hubby

I have done nothing as yet in reference to the Land but shall commence operations this afternoon.[19]

[19] In the margin of the third page of the original. Documents to be printed in the next volume will elucidate Henry's subsequent real estate transactions in Schoharie County, New York.

EXCERPT,[1] MINUTES, TRUSTEES, COLLEGE OF NEW JERSEY[2]

Trustees' Minutes, 3:260–268, Princeton University Archives

April 9th 1834 9 o'clock A.M.

The Board met according to adjournment.

Present as before.

The minutes of yesterday were read.

[1] We have omitted routine matters unrelated to Henry's activities at Princeton.

[2] The formal title of the College will be used in designating administrative sources such as the Minutes of the Trustees. "Princeton" will usually be used in reference to the College of New Jersey, as was often done during this period. The present name was adopted in 1896 when the College formally assumed university status. See *Wertenbaker*, p. 373.

The committee of Audits *Reported,* that they had examined the accounts[3] of Professor Henry, respecting the Philosophical Hall, and found them correct, leaving a balance in favor of Professor Henry of twenty three Dollars & forty-nine cents 1/4.

James S. Green[4] }
Roswell L. Colt[5] } Com.

Dated April 9. 1834...

The Committee appointed at the last meeting of the Board, to select, instruct and appoint, a suitable agent or agents for the purpose of soliciting donations, for the support & improvement of the College.[6]

Reported, That immediately after the adjournment of the Board, they attended to the object of their appointment. They unanimously agreed upon an Agent of whose acceptance and successful services they had sanguine hopes. He took the appointment into consideration, and gave the com-

[3] Henry's accounts had been submitted to the Committee during the Trustees' meeting on the previous day. The original accounts which Henry maintained for auditing purposes have not been found. Only a chronological summary listing of Henry's acquisitions of philosophical apparatus, from 1832 until 1837, survives. "J Henry's a/c with Philosophical Hall previous to 1837," Princeton University Archives.

[4] James Sproat Green, for whom see *Henry Papers, 1*:440, footnote 3.

[5] Roswell Lyman Colt (1786–1856) was a Trustee of Princeton from 1833 until his death. A highly successful member of a family known for its cotton mills in northern New Jersey, Roswell Colt was a generous benefactor for the College. He became legendary in Paterson, New Jersey, when, upon looking in vain for a hill on which to build a residence, he hired teams of workers to create a hill which he then topped with an elaborate home and gardens. L. R. Trumbull, *A History of Industrial Paterson* (Paterson, 1882), pp. 46–49; *Maclean,* 2:287, 298, 305, 334, 341, 438. *Princeton Catalogue,* p. 20.

[6] Princeton had been experiencing a period of marked stagnation and declining fortunes in the early decades of the nineteenth century. Financial instability, deteriorating teaching by an overworked faculty, and student rebelliousness contributed to the College's desperate condition. Princeton was among the many American colleges that suffered stagnation during the 1820s and early 1830s because of rigid and increasingly irrelevant, outmoded classical curricula (Stanley M. Guralnick, "Science and the American College, 1828–1860," Ph.D. dissertation, University of Pennsylvania, 1969, pp. 30–81). Retaining newly recruited and talented faculty members, like Torrey, Henry, and Stephen Alexander, and attracting good students required an outstanding fund-raising effort.

The Alumni Association of Nassau Hall, organized in 1826, took the initiative in trying to rescue the Alma Mater. Encouraged by the success of a loosely organized fund drive in 1830 which netted $10,200, the Association at the 1833 commencement launched an effort to collect $100,000 for the extension and improvement of the College. Their earlier efforts had suffered from lack of coordination between several part-time solicitors. In 1833 their primary innovation was the appointment of a single, full-time, paid campaign agent, the Reverend Daniel Newell (for whom see footnote 9). But by 1837 the campaign was recognized as only a partial success, perhaps mostly due to the financial problems of the country in the days of Andrew Jackson's second presidency. Additional problems were presented by Newell's ill-health and resignation in 1835 (*Maclean* mistakenly dates it 1836). Of the money that had been collected, however, some $500 was allocated for Henry's philosophical apparatus, $420 for a new telescope, and $4000 for the college endowment. See *Wertenbaker,* pp. 215–219; *Maclean,* 2:360–363. For evidence of Joseph Henry's willingness to help, see below, Henry to Van Rensselaer, October 23, 1834.

mittee reason to hope that in the course of the Autumn & Winter he would be able to devote a considerable portion, if not the whole of his time, to this important object. In this expectation however the committee were disappointed. The circumstances of the Agent did not admit of his giving more than a very small portion of his time to the service for which he was chosen, and the derangement of the currency, & credit of the country,[7] which commenced in a few days after the adjournment of the Board rendered it very doubtful in the estimation of those who were the most competent to judge in the case, whether any attempt to raise money by solicitation in the present state of things would not injure rather than promote the interests of the College.

Another obstacle occurred in the prosecution of the business entrusted to the committee, which they knew not how entirely to surmount. The *Alumni* Association impelled by a laudable desire to promote on a large scale the extension & improvement of the College; and having resolved to raise for that purpose if practicable the sum of $100,000, very soon after the adjournment of the Board in September last took measures by their committee to appoint one or more agents for the immediate prosecution of their plan. It soon became apparent that these two appointments would perplex the public mind, and materially interfere with one another. The same places would of course be visited, and the same individuals applied to, by both classes of Agents.

On a deliberate view of these circumstances, the committee would respectfully recommend to the Board, the adoption of the following resolutions viz *Resolved*

I. That in present circumstances it is expedient that all further proceedings on the part of this Board, in soliciting donations to the College be suspended until the aspect of things shall be more favorable to such an enterprize and until the plan of the *Alumni* shall disclose its probable results.

II. *Resolved.* The forgoing resolution is adopted in the full hope & confidence that if the *Alumni* Association shall succeed in its laudable plan, a portion of its avails will be applied at as early a period as possible to liquidate a part, or the whole of the debt incurred by the erection of the new edifice,[8] now nearly compleated.

III. *Resolved.* That this Board cordially approve the enterprise of the *Alumni* Association, and recommend it to the patronage of all the Guard-

[7] The reference is to the uncertainties following President Andrew Jackson's transfer of federal funds from the Second Bank of the United States to the state-chartered "pet banks."

[8] A reference to the "East College." See above, Henry to James Henry, June 25, 1833, especially footnote 9.

ians, Officers, Alumni and friends of the College as promising if carried into execution, great advantage to the College.

And as the Revd Mr. Newell[9] has been appointed an Agent for the purpose above referred to by the committee of the *Alumni* Association, the Board would earnestly recommend Mr. Newell to the confidence and patronage of every friend to the extension & improvement of the College.

The above report was adopted . . .

The Board proceeded to consider the motions made yesterday for raising the salaries of Professors Henry & Alexander.[10]

Whereupon, it was *Resolved*, That the salary of Professor Henry be and it hereby is raised to the sum of $1200. per annum.[11]

Resolved, also, that the salary of Professor Alexander be $1000. per annum.

[9] The Reverend Daniel Newell (d. ca. 1848) was an apparently peripatetic Presbyterian clergyman who held no pastorships for any appreciable time. He was ordained in New York City in 1827. According to *Maclean*, 2:361, Newell "had been quite successful in a somewhat similar enterprise for an institution in Western New York." From 1838 until his death he resided in New York City. He was the editor of *The Christian Family Magazine*, 1842–1844. Information from the Presbyterian Historical Society, Philadelphia, Pennsylvania.

[10] James Waddel Alexander (1804–1859), Presbyterian clergyman and educator, was the son of Archibald Alexander, a founder of the Princeton Theological Seminary. A graduate of both Princeton (B.A. 1820) and the Theological Seminary (1824), he tutored mathematics and classical studies at Princeton (1824 and 1825) before leaving for various clerical posts. In 1833 he returned to Princeton as Professor of Rhetoric, Latin, and Literature. He then left for pastorships in New York City. He was a frequent contributor throughout his lifetime to the *Biblical Repertory*, and he remained interested for many years in chemistry, physiology, mineralogy, and geology. He died in Virginia. *Roberts*, p. 21; *Princeton Catalogue*, p. 132; *The Biblical Repertory and Princeton Review: Index Volume from 1825 to 1868* (Philadelphia, 1871), pp. 67–82.

[11] This was Henry's first raise from his starting salary of $1000. According to *Maclean*, 2:295, $1200 was "the highest salary then paid to a Professor" at Princeton. His salary was raised again to $1500 at the Trustees' meeting of September 30, 1835 (below), when an addition to his house was also authorized. The circumstances for his second raise are depicted in documents below for the summer of 1835.

FROM LEWIS GAYLORD CLARK[1]

Henry Papers,[2] Smithsonian Archives

April [15], 1834

be of a very superior character. The *materiel* and execution will be of the best kind which can be commanded.

[1] In May 1834, Lewis Gaylord Clark (1808–1873) officially became editor and, with Clement M. Edson (see below, Clark and Edson to Henry, May 27, 1834), publisher of the

I come now to the request, which I would prefer of you, and in granting which, you will confer a distinguished favor. Will you furnish us a paper of interest, upon any subject of solid interest, which will form six, eight or ten pages of the number for May? And will you become an occasional contributor, for a reasonable remuneration,[3] hereafter? Will you have the goodness to inform me, also, whether or no [there] be not some others connected as officers with [the] institution in your delightful town, who would not, upon similar terms, occasionally favor us with brief articles of merit?

Will you please answer this, as soon as agreeable, care of Rawdon, Wright, Hatch, & Co.[4] 35, Merchant's Exchange? In the interim, I remain, Dear Sir,

Yours Very Respectfully
Lewis Gaylord Clark

P.S. An article for the May number should be received by the 15th instant. If you have any prepared, upon any subject, its early transmission would insure the insertion of a more *solid* article for the first paper, than any we have on hand.

Knickerbocker Magazine, a new literary venture which under Clark's guidance attained some popularity and prestige. Reared in upstate New York, Clark moved to New York City in the early thirties after deciding on a literary career. Clark and Edson bought the *Knickerbocker* from Peabody and Co. in 1834 and promptly rescued the magazine from inauspicious financial beginnings. Editor from 1834 to 1860 and briefly at the end of 1863, Clark saw the magazine through its most successful years, assembling a distinguished list of contributors, including his twin brother, the poet Willis Gaylord Clark, Washington Irving (in whose honor the magazine was named), Longfellow, Hawthorne, and Whittier. A popular figure in New York literary circles, Clark was especially noted for the reviews, gossip, and humor of the "Editor's Table," regarded as the highpoint of the magazine.

Humor was always an important element of the magazine, whose contents have been described as "an engaging fare which was never too heavy and seldom inane or pointless." Notes on drama and music, travel articles, and book reviews were typical monthly offerings of the "Old *Knick*." One of Clark's specific aims was the encouragement of an American literature. There was a modicum of scientific discussion in the thirties, especially on geology and religion. Though Clark wanted nothing "too heavy" for an educated but unspecialized audience, his request for articles of "solid interest" from Henry suggests at least a serious initial concern with scientific "materiel," as Clark liked to put it. We have no record of Henry's reply to this solicitation nor to the May 27, 1834, letter of Clark and Edson, printed below. No contributions by Henry appeared in the magazine. In any event, the mix that Clark sought of science and other cultural topics was of a familiar nineteenth-century genre.

While the *Knickerbocker Magazine* survived under various titles, editors, and owners from January 1833 to October 1865, it was never secure financially. Clark's brief return to the editorship in 1863 could not prevent its demise. *DAB*; Frank Luther Mott, *A History of American Magazines, 1741–1850* (New York, 1930), pp. 449–450, 606–614.

[2] Only this last portion of Clark's letter survives. "April 1834" and the title of Clark's magazine appear in file notes at various points on the fragment. We have placed the letter at April 15, on the basis of Clark's postscript, although it must have been written before that date.

[3] In his May 27 letter, Edson offered two dollars per page.

[4] A banknote engraving firm. G. C. Groce and D. H. Wallace, *The New-York Historical Society's Dictionary of Artists in America, 1564–1860* (New Haven, 1957), p. 525.

April 25, 1834

TO JAMES HENRY

Family Correspondence, Henry Papers, Smithsonian Archives

Princeton April 25th 1834

Dear James

You have not heard from us for several weeks and Mother is proably beginning to be uneasy about us. I was detained 8 or 9 days in New York with Dr Notts Stove Suit.[1] Since my return I have been very busily engaged in completing my battery which will be ready for operation in a day or two.[2] All the family are well. The Boy is improving very rapidly in talking, attemps to say every thing and succeeds tolerably well. He is however somewhat puzzled with some words which Stephen requests him to repeat such as Meteorology.

The girl growes very rapidly. She weighed last Monday 11 ½ lbs and probably has increased a half lb since. Motherinlaw and Stephen accompanied me to New York but returned before me. I called at Mr McMullen's,[3] took tea there, saw all the family. Jane & her husband still reside at her fathers. I did not learn what business he is engaged in.

Princeton is quit[e] plesant at this time. The trease are in full foleage and the campus covered with a beautiful carpet of short grass. The making of our garden was finished to day.

I see by the papers that Orlando Meads has delivered his Oration before the Institute.[4] Did it take well with the audiance? I was in N.Y. during the last two days of the election but did not see much of the shameful proceedings which took place.[5] The Albany Regency are certainly rejoicing like the man of Whose when his horses ran off and killed his [?children] ex-

[1] See above, [Isaac W. Jackson] to Henry, March 20, 1834.

[2] See above, Henry to George Maclean, October 9, 1833.

[3] John McMullen, for whom see above, Joseph Henry to James Henry, November 13, 1832, footnote 1.

[4] Orlando Meads, for whom see above, Henry to James Henry, May 17, 1833, footnote 1, delivered the annual address to the Albany Institute on April 17. Meads's subject was "the relation and mutual dependence of all the departments of science as contributing to its permanent advancement," reported the *Daily Albany Argus* on April 18 (p. 2).

[5] The New York City elections of April 8–10, 1834, were marked by numerous disorders, particularly in the Sixth Ward. Party feelings ran high among the voters, and rallies, parades, and other demonstrations sometimes degenerated into mob violence. Joel Tyler Headley, *The Great Riots of New York, 1712–1873* (1873; reprint ed., New York, 1970), pp. 66–78. When the smoke cleared, Cornelius Lawrence (1791–1861), the Jacksonian candidate, had been elected Mayor. Lawrence, who had served briefly in the United States House of Representatives (*Biographical Directory of the American Congress*), defeated his Whig opponent, Gulian Verplanck (1786–1870; *DAB*), by a narrow margin. The Whigs, however, gained a majority on the Common Council.

clamed I am thankful it is no worse.[6] I have not yet seen the late message of the President. It is said to be a very plausible paper.[7]

Richard Webster[8] returns to Albany from the Theological seminary next week. He will call to see Mother while in the city and will give her all the minutia of information which she may require from Princeton.

Inform me in your next what you did in reference to the land. Has Mr. Sammons heard anything more definite from Washington? Do you think of visiting Princeton this summer?

Joseph[9] has gone to the Philosophical Hall and as usual left his letter unfinished. We received your last in Jos absence. Bub was delighted with the large Cake damda Heny sent him. They all came safely. We have been cleaning part of our house but [. . .][10] was obliged to stop by cold & rainy weather. Aren't you coming to see us? [I] don't know how you can conscientiously [stay][11] away. Please give our love to M & [. . .]. Tell them we will hope to see them here.

Sis is bawling lustily. She has good lungs. Love to all

Yours in haste
Harriet

[6] Perhaps a garbled reference to Job, from the land of Uz, although this particular story does not appear in the Book of Job.

[7] Henry is probably referring here to Andrew Jackson's protest against the passage, on March 28, of Senate resolutions which charged that his policies and actions with regard to the Bank of the United States were unconstitutional. The President, in a message dated April 15 and communicated to the Senate April 17, denied the charges. He also asked that his reply be inserted into the Senate journal, but the request was denied. The House subsequently refused to concur with the Senate resolutions, and there the matter rested. The full text of Jackson's protest can be found in James D. Richardson, comp., *A Compilation of the Messages and Papers of the Presidents, 1789–1897*, 10 vols. (Washington, 1896–1899), *3*:69–93. A summary of the events is in Glyndon G. Van Deusen, *The Jacksonian Era, 1828–1848* (New York, 1959), pp. 87–89.

[8] Richard Webster (1811–1856), for whom see *Henry Papers, 1*:73, graduated from the Princeton Theological Seminary in 1834 (*Roberts*, p. 69).

[9] The following lines were added by Harriet.

[10] One illegible word.

[11] Here, a hole in the letter, caused by the seal being broken, has obliterated several words.

April 29, 1834

HENRY'S NOTES ON A TRIP TO PHILADELPHIA, APRIL 29–MAY 2, 1834

Mary Henry Copy (in part),[1] *Henry Papers, Smithsonian Archives*

April 29, 1834

Arrived in Philadelphia at about five P.M. Stopped at the North American Hotel.[2] Visited the mechanical exhibition[3] in Chestnut Street. It is a model of the machinery for manufacturing cotton. The whole is put in motion by the power of four dogs working on a movable inclined platform, they are not attached; employ their force by constantly walking up the inclined plane which as constantly recedes beneath their feet. I was most interested in a contrivance for drawing out the thread: the cotton in this case is drawn out between two revolvers and to prevent the untwisted string from breaking it receives a twist by passing through a tube which revolves with great velocity. The same tube untwists the string by merely passing the thread out at a hole in the side and then again through another hole into the axis of the tube when it passes onto the spool without being twisted.

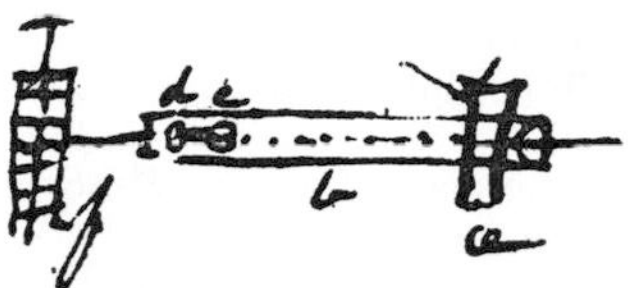

b the tube with the thread represented by the · · · · ; *a* small pulley on the tube to receive the motion from a strap; *c d* the holes; the thread passes out at *c* is returned through d and then passes on to the spool *f* without twist.

At about eight o'clock visited the museum,[4] found it crowded about the door with persons waiting to catch a sight of David Crocket whose visit to the museum this evening has been announced. The colonel arrived with a great mob about him a few minutes after eight o'clock. He is a tall man, with somewhat the appearance of a Methodist clergyman; has long hair

[1] This item is in Box 50, folder 1. The first seven paragraphs of the notes as printed are based on a Mary Henry Copy. Her text, apparently corresponding to the first eight pages of Henry's notes, is the sole surviving copy. She transcribed the notes in her own hand, and cut out the drawings from the original sheets and pasted them to hers. For the first sketch Miss Henry included her father's original description, which we have printed at the right of the drawing. Henry's fragmented writing on the back of that snippet confirms Mary Henry's transcription from the middle of the third sentence of the first paragraph to the words "thread: the cotton . . ." in the fifth sentence. The rest of Henry's notes, consisting of sheets folded into a booklet form measuring 4″ x 7″, have survived in the original.

[2] The North American Hotel was on Chestnut Street, between 6th and 7th Streets, one block east of the State House (Independence Hall). Philadelphia City Directory, 1837.

[3] Apparently the same "Hall of Industry" which Henry visited in his December 1834 trip to Philadelphia. We have found evidence of no other such exhibition, but an 1835 opening date makes this identification tentative. See below, Henry to Harriet Henry, December 5, 1834, and footnote 3 thereunder. See also Henry's Notes on a Trip to Philadelphia for December 5, 1834. We have not identified the inventor of the contrivance which fascinated Henry.

wears a white hat, is between forty five and fifty; is rather a good-looking man with a good-natured expression.[5]

Observed among the philosophical apparatus in the museum, a jar with

[4] Charles Willson Peale's Philadelphia Museum, known more commonly simply as Peale's Museum. Peale (1741–1827) began his museum as an art gallery, a commercial extension of his own prolific career as an accomplished portraitist. He found that displays of natural history specimens and, later, philosophical apparatus, attracted more visitors than his art. His exhibits grew rapidly in number and forced Peale to move the museum from its original quarters to the hall of the American Philosophical Society, then to the second floor of the State House (Independence Hall), and to its final resting place, the Arcade (for which see below, Henry to James Henry, May 7, 1834, footnotes 7 and 8). Peale lobbied incessantly, and in vain, to establish municipal ownership for his museum which he hoped would eventually become a national museum. Yet it would remain for a later time, during Joseph Henry's Secretaryship of the Smithsonian, that the United States National Museum was established under the direction of that Institution in 1857.

What distinguished Peale's Museum from others in Philadelphia and elsewhere was Peale's determination that the museum should offer an educational experience open to all the public. The museum became a significant educational institution in its day, an age not known for its instruction of the general populace, young and old, especially in the sciences. Exhibits of natural history specimens were arranged according to the Linnaean system. Where possible, specimens were presented in ecological settings. Exhibits of curiosities in the physical sciences often consisted of the newest advances. For instance, Henry almost invariably found items of interest there; see the next paragraph in the text or see below, Henry to Harriet Henry, May 4, 1835. In addition, Peale's Museum offered frequent series of lectures, again open to the public, on topics germane to the exhibits and to science.

Upon the death of the elder Peale in 1827, the museum continued to be operated by his sons. Under their management, the museum began to drift away from its educational ideal toward achieving a more popular appeal, in part a response to increased competition from several strictly commercial museum ventures in Philadelphia which aimed at sheer entertainment value. In this 1834 visit Henry was not seeing Peale's original conception of the museum. Nonetheless, Henry—who was especially critical of attempts at mere amusement in museums—still marveled at a number of the exhibits.

This was not Henry's first visit to Peale's Museum, according to documentary evidence. He toured its New York City branch in June 1826 (*Henry Papers, 1*:160–161). Earlier, as a youngster Henry knew the Philadelphia Museum by reputation; as he recalled many years later, Peale's Museum was the main attraction for him in Philadelphia. "The impression which the sight of this interesting collection made upon [my] youthful mind is still retained with a vividness which will be among the last to be obliterated by advancing years . . ." (Joseph Henry undated lecture, [ca. 1876,] Henry Papers, Smithsonian Archives).

The history of Peale's Museum is given in Charles Coleman Sellers, *Charles Willson Peale*, 2 vols. (Philadelphia, 1947), 2: passim. See also Richard P. Ellis, "The Founding, History, and Significance of Peale's Museum in Philadelphia, 1785–1841," *Curator*, 1966, *9*:235–258; Irwin Richman, "Charles Willson Peale and the Philadelphia Museum," *Pennsylvania History*, 1962, *29*:257–277; Whitfield J. Bell, "Charles Willson Peale," *DSB*.

[5] David Crockett (1786–1836) of Tennessee who was serving his third term in the United States House of Representatives. He consistently opposed Jacksonian legislation there. In April and May of 1834 Crockett conducted his "tour of the north," stopping at Baltimore, Philadelphia, New York, and Boston before returning to Washington and then to his home constituency to campaign in vain for reelection in the fall. He subsequently took up the cause of Texas independence and died defending the Alamo in February 1836. *DAB*.

Crockett attracted massive crowds at all of his public appearances in Philadelphia. Newspaper accounts varied according to their political orientation. Philadelphia *Pennsylvanian*, April 29, 1834, "Crockett Still Flourishes." By now almost a mythological figure, Davy Crockett is seen by us as rugged, unschooled, and a frontier warrior. To Henry, his contemporary, he resembled a Methodist clergyman.

several strips of tin foil pasted on it for electrical light. The jar is of the same shape and size as the one in the Hall, containing the pile of DeLuc.[6]

April 30. This morning visited Dr. Hare; had a long discussion with him on the subject of electricity and magnetism. Inspected his new battery; it consists of thirty zinc plates arranged in six elements, each plate 24 inches by 14. I think this is the size. It is immersed by raising the acid in the manner described by the Doctor in the Journal of the Franklin Institute. Instead of ropes the acid box is suspended by chains.[7] When the acid was first put on, no action took place because the plates had been dried after being dipped and an oxide had thus been formed which prevented action until it was slowly removed by the action of the weak acid. The Doctor says his rule is in such cases to let the action continue until the plates begin to hiss; then if they be removed from the acid and suffered to rest a short time, on a second immersion they will act powerfully.[8] The Doctor's battery will ignite a piece of cut iron, a little longer and about the thickness of a tenpenny cut nail.

I was also shown by the Doctor Saxtons magneto-electric machine.[9] It gave sparks rapidly on being turned. Also visited Mr. Lukens. Was shown by this ingenious mechanic a new artificial horizon. It consists of a circular piece of plate glass placed as the cover of a brass box, about the size of a common snuff box. It is adjusted by screwing it into a block or bench and

[6] While the particular configuration of the apparatus for demonstrating electric light may have been new to Henry, he was aware of the principles and the type of equipment used in such demonstrations. In a notebook ([23894], pp. 119–120, Henry Papers, Smithsonian Archives) Henry made numerous drawings and took extensive notes on various apparatus for electrical light, all of which operated on common principles. Static electricity was passed through a gapped series of tin foil strips or plastered iron filings, resulting in multiple sparks and a good deal of light. The long and narrow jar, similar to that of a DeLuc column, merely provided a convenient and spectacular medium of display; its size and shape had no bearing on the principle involved. For a discussion of DeLuc's column, see below in this document, under May 1, Henry's evening conversation with Walter Johnson and footnotes 30 and 31. For another effective display of electric light from the same principle, see Henry's description of Walter Johnson's arrangement in the last paragraph of this document.

[7] Robert Hare, "Description of a Process and an Apparatus for Blasting Rocks, by Means of Galvanic Ignition," *Journal of the Franklin Institute*, 1833, *12*:221–226. The battery which Hare described consisted of sixteen zinc and twenty copper plates, each 12″ x 7″, arranged in four elements. The acid reservoir was raised to the plates by means of ropes attached to the rims of two large-diameter wheels. The wheels were rotated, drawing the ropes upward, by depressing a lever mounted perpendicularly to the middle of the axle which was fixed to the wheels. Simple and compact, this was a contrivance for quickly lifting an acid tray of a small, portable battery for field use.

[8] Conducting experiments with his own battery on September 7, 1834 (below), Henry noted that he too had a problem with oxidation of the plates. Hare's plan was an effective way to de-oxidize the plates, which began to "hiss" when clean.

[9] For which see above, Green to Henry, February 13, 1834, footnote 2.

then rendered level by means of three screws. It is ascertained to be level by a bubble of alcohol under the glass. When this is concentric with the circumference of the instrument the adjustment is complete.[10]

I was also shown by Mr. Lukens another contrivance, a substitute for a transit instrument. It consists of an axis on two supports Ys, with a plate of black glass pasted on one side thus which throws a shadow, or image [of] the sun on the distant wall. By making a meridian mark on the wall or several parallel lines on each side of a point directly north of the meridian,[11] the meridian transit will be obtained with considerable exactitude.

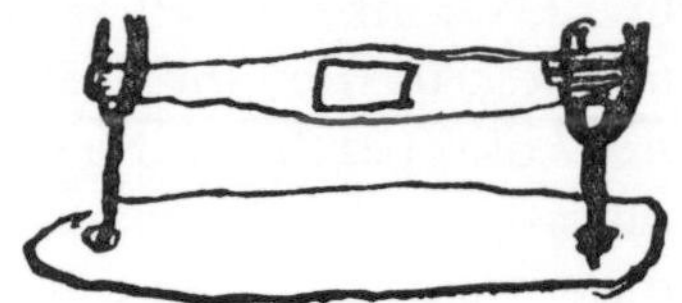

At five P.M. accompanied Mr. Lukens, agreeable to appointment, in his gig to the foundery[12] in Kensington on the west side of the city of Philadelphia. From the Foundery we went to the glass house where we witnessed the process of making glass lamps also the process of annealing the glass. The articles in this process pass through the annealing furnace which is an arch of masonry forty or fifty feet long.

Before starting with Mr Lukens I called on Mr Baldwin,[13] saw the process of boring the air piece of a small steam engine. The cutter for cast iron is used without water, for wrought iron with water. The workman[14] informed me that there is a proper motion for boring [and] turning cast iron; if the velosity be too great the tool will be destroyed, if too slow the work will not advance sufficiently rapid.

[10] The advantage of Lukens's device was that it could find an accurate level in all directions at once, obviating the need, for instance, of leveling in a north-south direction, and then moving the instrument to an east-west one.

[11] Mary Henry inserted a question mark above this word, indicating that she was uncertain of either her reading of the word or her understanding of what may have been Henry's own expression. In any event, it is possible that Henry originally wrote or intended "instrument" instead of meridian. In either case, Henry is describing a relatively inexpensive and reasonably accurate instrument for determining time by observing the transit of the sun through the meridian, the common way of determining astronomical time. Lacking such an instrument or other more sophisticated astronomical devices, Henry would have difficulty in resetting the astronomical clock in Philosophical Hall (see below, Henry to Torrey, November 18, 1834).

[12] Henry went to the iron foundry to order a wheel and pinion which he needed for his battery. See below in this document (the next day) and footnote 22.

[13] Matthias William Baldwin (1795–1866) became an important locomotive manufacturer after dabbling successfully in a number of enterprises, including the manufacturing of engravers' tools, hydraulic presses, and printers' equipment. By 1834 Baldwin's shop, located between 7th and 8th Streets south of Market Street, became well established as a leader in manufacturing stationary steam engines and locomotives. Baldwin turned out 1500 locomotives by his death. He was active among the founders of the Franklin Institute, and he was elected to the American Philosophical Society in 1833. He engaged in many civic duties and philanthropies, and was a devout Presbyterian. "His speech was shrewd and concise, his views decided and positive. Doubt was foreign to his nature." *DAB.*

[14] Not identified.

The fact of the tool's being destroyed is analogous to the effect produced by the exp. of cutting steel with a wheel of soft iron.

May 1st Agreably to appointment I breakfas[te]d with Mr. Vaughan.[15] The old gentleman takes breakfast every morning in summer about 7. At nine leaves his rooms for his daily occupation and doesn't return until towards evening.

He was an inmate of Dr Franklins family when in France and was presented by the Dr to the Royal Family as one of the Dr's family.

Nine o'clock visited Mr Millington[16] found him at breakfast.

Agreed on a plan for needle &c. Was shown the method used by the Prof. in working an electrical machine. The rubber is faced with the silk which is kept clean, the amalgam is applied by being spread on a plaster of buckskin. First the cylender is greased with a tallow candle. This is rubbed off and the amalgam put on by holding the plaster under the cylender when in motion.[17] The Prof. gave me an important fact that is when the amalgam becomes hard it may be [softened][18] by warming and should always be heated slightly before being used.

Was shown Prof. M's drawings for the illustration of astronomy.[19] They are beautifully executed.

Called on Mr Lea.[20] Found in his study a copy of Mrs Summerville's

[15] John Vaughan, for whom see above, Henry to Harriet Henry, November 1, 1833, especially footnote 4.

[16] For John Millington see above, Millington to Henry, December 31, 1832, footnote 1. The needle plan Henry and Millington agreed to may pertain to the large declination needle Henry mentions both in his letter to Kelly (above, December 30, 1833) and later in his letter to Forbes (below, June 30, 1834).

[17] An excellent contemporary description of such a cylindrical static electric machine is George John Singer, *Elements of Electricity and Electro-Chemistry* (London, 1814), pp. 48–52. Singer's account served as the authoritative source for such later accounts as P. M. Roget's treatment in *Treatises on Electricity, Galvanism, Magnetism, and Electro-Magnetism* (London, 1832), pp. 14–17 and David Brewster's article, "Electricity," in the *Encyclopaedia Britannica*, 8th ed., p. 536. Singer suggested constituting the amalgam by melting together one ounce of tin and two ounces of zinc to which six ounces of mercury should be added. Cooled and reduced to a powder, the ingredients were mixed with hogs' lard to constitute a paste. The paste was then applied to the cylinder as Millington demonstrated. The "rubber" was the rubbing mechanism of the machine.

[18] Henry wrote "hardened" here, but as this must be a slip of the pen, we have substituted this word. As Henry noted in notebook [23894], p. 19 (Henry Papers, Smithsonian Archives), "Amal. may be made soft by heating after being made."

[19] Astronomy was among the departments for which Millington's shop sold "instruments, apparatus and materials." From the prospectus of Millington's store, as quoted in George F. Holmes, "Professor John Millington, M.D.," *William and Mary College Quarterly*, 1923, 2d ser. *3*:28.

[20] Isaac Lea (1792–1886, *DAB*, *DSB*), an eminent Philadelphia malacologist. He was born in Wilmington, Delaware, moved to Philadelphia in 1807, and subsequently (1821) married into the family of Mathew Carey, thereby entering the prominent publishing firm. Although connected with the firm for the next thirty years, Lea used his evenings to become an extremely prolific and highly respected investigator of mollusks. Whitfield J. Bell, Jr., terms him "a striking example of

connection of sciences. Was pleased to find she made mention of my experiments in magnetism.[21]

---

the self-taught amateur who by single-minded attention to a limited subject makes a comprehensive, basic, and lasting contribution to knowledge" (*DSB*). He gathered a collection of more than 10,000 shells, minerals, and other specimens which he bequeathed to the United States National Museum, then under the Secretaryship of Henry's successor, Spencer F. Baird.

Henry probably first met Lea during his November 1833 trip to Philadelphia. As reported in a letter to his wife of November 1, 1833, above, Henry attended a party at Mathew Carey's, a family affair which Lea would likely have attended. Although we are aware of very little correspondence between Henry and Lea, particularly during Henry's years at Princeton, there was ample opportunity for contact between the two. Lea was active in the American Philosophical Society from his election in 1828, serving on the Committee of Publications for many years. Lea was also active in the Academy of Natural Sciences of Philadelphia. In 1860 he served as President of the American Association for the Advancement of Science.

[21] A native of Scotland, Mary Somerville (1780–1872, *DNB*) suffered from considerable restrictions on her intellectual inclinations toward science during her childhood and first marriage. Widowed and financially independent in 1807, she associated herself with a number of young scholars at Edinburgh who encouraged her and guided her in the study of mathematics and the physical sciences. Her second husband, William Somerville (1771–1860, *DNB*, a cousin whom she married in 1812), likewise fostered her scientific inclinations. She soon became especially proficient in mathematics and astronomy but also dabbled in botany and geology. Although in her early work she was barred, as a woman, from research facilities and scientific meetings, she was aided by notable and willing male intermediaries who provided research materials and presented her work. Later, by the late 1820s, she and her husband moved freely in the circles of London scientists.

Mary Somerville's first book, *The Mechanism of the Heavens* (London, 1831), an English rendition of Laplace's *Mécanique céleste*, drew immediate praise and established her reputation as a scientific writer. Joseph Henry, whose library contains a copy of the first edition, read and annotated this primarily mathematical treatise in his Albany days. Somerville's next book, *On the Connexion of the Physical Sciences* (London, 1834) was a synthesis of a wide range of scientific topics and reflected the latest findings of a host of well-known physical scientists. It drew greater acclaim than her first book and went through ten editions in forty years, always keeping up to date as a result of Somerville's vigilance. Henry owned the fifth London edition, dated 1840. In a discussion of electromagnetic induction (p. 329 of the first edition), Somerville mentions the extraordinary power of the electromagnets Henry built in Albany: "a temporary magnet of this kind made by Professor Henry of the Albany Academy, in the United States, sustained nearly a ton weight." That reference persists, verbatim, in subsequent editions.

By the time Mary Somerville composed her *Connexion*, Henry's Albany work on magnets was well-known in the British scientific journals (see above, Henry to [Cooper], November 26, 1833, especially footnotes 6 and 7). Somerville certainly kept current in reading those journals, but recent scholarship suggests that the importance of Henry's work could have been made clear to her by another source. Elizabeth C. Patterson, "Mary Somerville," *The British Journal for the History of Science*, 1969, *4*:311–339, discovered that Somerville also kept up with the latest findings and views of notable physical scientists by maintaining frequent contacts with those researchers, mainly through correspondence. She frequently sent drafts of sections of the book to her contacts for revisions and suggestions. Her correspondence reveals that in the preparation of her *Connexion* she received considerable help from Michael Faraday, both in substantive matters and in details of style. We can confidently conclude that Faraday was aware of Somerville's citation of Henry's work; it is even possible that Faraday, perhaps Somerville's most active collaborator, suggested including Henry's work in the first place.

Henry read Somerville's publications with interest. He recorded his reaction to a section in her *Connexion* on "accidental colours" in a notebook ([10615], p. 509, Henry Papers, Smithsonian Archives) and he later paraphrased that discussion in opening his article,

In the afternoon accompanied Mr Lukens to the glass house & foundry. Got my wheel & pinion[22] which were ordered yesterday. Paid 150 cts. Castings 5 cts per lb when paterns are already made in the shop.

On our way to the glass house passed the monument erected by the Pennsyvania historical society on the site of the elm tree under which the celebrated treaty of Penn with the Indians was made. The monument is of white marble about 5 feet high of a prismatic form in the plan & a pyramidal termination. Thus It is in an obscure corner hid by a pile of boards from every eye but one acquainted with its locality.[23]

I forgot to mention that Mr Lea introduced me to Dr Griffin[24] the editor of the Journal of Pharmacy.[25] He is a man of about 30 agreeable and obliging.

"On Color-Blindness," *Princeton Review*, 1845, *17*:483–489. And in the same notebook (p. 103) he criticized her first published piece, "On the Magnetizing Power of the More Refrangible Solar Rays," *Phil. Trans.*, 1826, pp. 132–139, a copy of which he kept in his library.

On April 19, 1837, accompanied by Mrs. Michael Faraday, Henry visited Mary Somerville in England and found her impressively erudite and "unassuming." (Henry's 1837 European Diary, Henry Papers, Smithsonian Archives.) This meeting will be documented in the next volume of *The Papers of Joseph Henry*. Other than their meetings during the European trip, we know of no other contacts between Henry and Somerville, either through correspondence or personal encounter.

[22] In constructing his versatile battery, Henry attached the large, cogged wheel to the end of the windlass roller; it was driven by the pinion, a smaller gear, to which a hand crank was fixed. This mechanism is clearly depicted in the plate accompanying Henry's "Contributions I: Battery," pictured on the frontispiece to this volume. Henry regarded the wheel and pinion arrangement as compact, convenient, and inexpensive. See below, Henry to Silliman, August 29, 1835.

[23] Henry's account is confirmed by other historical accounts of the monument, with one exception. The monument was erected in 1827 not by the Historical Society of Pennsylvania, but by the Penn Society, a local association dedicated to commemorating historical sites and subjects. The original elm stood in the midst of what is now called Penn Treaty Park, which served as a lumber yard in the 1820s and 1830s. The proprietor of that yard refused to give up space in the middle, thus forcing the Penn Society to place their marker at the northeast corner of his lot. Hence, it is not surprising that Henry observed a pile of boards obscuring a small monument in an unlikely setting. The Society fully expected to replace this modest monument with a more elaborate one, but to this day the original one has survived as the sole commemorative marker. Information from George Baker, Folcroft, Pennsylvania, and J. Thomas Scharf and Thompson Westcott, *History of Philadelphia, 1609–1884*, 3 vols. (Philadelphia, 1884), *3*:1873. The monument is pictured in David B. Tyler, *The Bay & River Delaware: A Pictorial History* (Cambridge, Maryland, 1955), p. 224.

[24] Robert E. Griffith (1798–1850) received his M.D. degree from the University of Pennsylvania in 1820. He taught at the Philadelphia College of Pharmacy and edited its journal (for which see the next footnote), 1831–1836, in which he published fourteen of his pharmaceutical contributions. In 1836 he went to Baltimore to teach materia medica, therapeutics, hygiene, and medical jurisprudence at the University of Maryland medical school. In 1838 he joined the medical faculty of the University of Virginia, but he resigned one year later due to ill health and returned to Philadelphia.

Griffith was a member of the Philadelphia Board of Health in the 1830s and he was also a member of the Board of Managers of the Franklin Institute. Yet he was far more active in both the Academy of Natural Sciences of Philadelphia and the American Philosophical Society. A member of the former from 1815, he served on many committees and was Vice President at the time of his death. A curator of the APS, to which he was elected in 1828, he was active on several committees, includ-

In the evening visited Mr Johnson[26]—had a long discourse with him on science generally.

He informed me that he was engaged in experimenting on the conduction of vapour in a transparent and in a clouded state. In the former it is

ing the Committee on Publications, 1828–1836. He became a member of the American Association for the Advancement of Science at its founding in 1848. The editor and translator of several works on medical jurisprudence and physiology, he authored two books on pharmacy and published two of his lectures on anatomy and pathology. He also published articles on botany and conchology. *Herringshaw*, p. 425; Frank Luther Mott, *A History of American Magazines, 1741–1850* (New York, 1930), p. 539; Venia T. and Maurice E. Phillips, *Guide to the Manuscript Collections in the Academy of Natural Sciences of Philadelphia* (Ann Arbor, 1963), p. 103; Rossiter Johnson, ed., *The Twentieth Century Biographical Dictionary of Notable Americans*, 10 vols. (Boston, 1904), *4*:no pagination; James Grant Wilson and John Fiske, *Appleton's Cyclopaedia of American Biography*, 7 vols. (New York, 1896), 2:765.

[25] Griffith was the third editor of the *Journal of the Philadelphia College of Pharmacy*, a quarterly during his tenure. Founded in 1825, it claims to be "the oldest pharmaceutical journal in the English language." It traditionally emphasized scientific, not commercial, aspects of pharmacy. In 1835, under Griffith's editorship, its name was changed to *The American Journal of Pharmacy*, which name it continues to bear. Mott, op. cit., pp. 539–540.

[26] Walter Rogers Johnson (1794–1852) became a close friend of Henry's from their frequent Philadelphia contacts and their shared interests in the physical sciences. Born in Leominster, Massachusetts, Johnson graduated from Harvard in 1819. He taught school in Massachusetts before becoming Principal of the Germantown Academy in Philadelphia, 1821–1826. During these years Johnson was particularly concerned with new approaches in education and was active in the Pennsylvania Society for the Promotion of Public Schools.

In 1826 the Franklin Institute established its high school to provide science-oriented technical education for aspiring mechanics' apprentices. Johnson was named its Principal and one of its five teachers. In the first year enrollment reached 300, but three years later the Institute abandoned the school in a disagreement with Johnson over financial matters. Johnson continued to operate the school on his own, at first using the same rooms of the Institute building on South Seventh Street; but in 1832 he moved the school to other quarters on St. James Street, near Seventh. By 1835, when Johnson's high school closed, he relied upon Henry and other scientific comrades in his search for a new job (see below, Henry's Recommendation for Walter R. Johnson, July 1835).

Meanwhile Johnson continued to be active as the Franklin Institute's Professor of Mechanics and Natural Philosophy, in which capacity he delivered seasonal lecture series. He served on the Institute's Committee on the Explosions of Steam-boilers and headed its Sub-committee on the Strength of Materials. Johnson was also active in the Academy of Natural Sciences of Philadelphia, holding many official positions including that of Corresponding Secretary, 1841–1848. He was Chairman of the Academy's Committee on Physics, mentioned below in Bache to Henry, February 15, [1835], footnote 6.

After a brief service in the United States Exploring Expedition, Johnson returned to Philadelphia to teach chemistry and natural philosophy at the Pennsylvania Medical College (1839–1843). Aterwards he conducted special scientific investigations for the Navy Department and for the United States Congress. In connection with the latter he affiliated with the newly founded Smithsonian Institution under its Secretary, Joseph Henry. Johnson became a specialist in the availability and uses of anthracite coal, publishing several works on that topic. He was among the founders of the Association of American Geologists and he served as the first Corresponding Secretary (1848–1849) of its successor, the American Association for the Advancement of Science.

Johnson and Henry remained close, personally and professionally. Their interactions will show up regularly in this and subsequent volumes of *The Papers of Joseph Henry*. Johnson was a prolific writer, whose many publications ranged from poetry to essays on education, a text on Greek literature, and original contributions in the physical sciences.

a non-conductor.[27] He is now giving a course of Lectures on electricity;[28] Drys the air by means of basins of sulphuric acid. Found in one case that the acid absorbed 2½ lbs of water in the course of a day. Informed me of a curious fact in galvanism from Berzelius viz if a battery be connected at one end with a bar of [soap][29] that end will be discharged but if the other end be connected with the ground by the same article it will not cease to affect the electrometer. Prof J. also gave me a method of restoring a DeLucs column by simply taking apart the column & rebuilding it with the precaution of not placing the same discs in contact. In this way new surfaces are brought in contact which before on account of the inequalities did not touch.[30]

Henry's Library contains one of Johnson's books and a dozen of his articles, some of which were presented by the author. A full bibliography of Johnson's publications, liberally construed, appears in George E. Pettengill, "Walter Rogers Johnson," *Journal of the Franklin Institute*, 1950, *250*:93–113, which is also the most complete biographical sketch available. The Franklin Institute High School is treated there and in Bruce Sinclair, "The Promise of the Future: Technical Education," in George H. Daniels, ed., *Nineteenth-Century American Science: A Reappraisal* (Evanston, Illinois, 1972), pp. 249–272.

[27] By this time Johnson had done static electrical experiments in conditions of varying moisture. He reported his findings in the January 1834 number of *Silliman's Journal* ("Observations on Some Experiments in Electricity," *25*:57–68). There he made no mention of his experiments on the conductivity of vapors (which experiments were clearly an extension of the ones he reported), but he did deal with topics closely relating to points which Henry noted in their evening of scientific conversation. For instance, in the article Johnson discussed factors which artificially affected the relative humidity inside the lecture hall; and Johnson told Henry about his effective use of sulfuric acid to absorb moisture from the indoor air. Later in their talk Johnson touched upon the effects of moisture on a DeLuc pile (see below, and footnotes 30 and 31). The final point noted by Henry that evening, on the significance of the difference between the temperature and dew point at a magnetic north pole (see footnote 32), is also in Johnson's article. There he asserts that static electrical experiments produce demonstrably longer sparks under conditions where the temperature and dew point differences are the greatest. Neither Henry nor Johnson traveled to Siberia to test the climatic effects on their experiments. In his career at the Smithsonian Institution, however, Joseph Henry promoted efforts to gather physical data and perform experiments at many points on the earth's surface.

[28] Henry refers to Johnson's lectures on electricity in the last two paragraphs of this document.

[29] In moving from the bottom of one sheet to the top of its verso, Henry omitted this word. We are certain that "soap" is the proper substance in this experiment. Johnson picked up this information from J. J. Berzelius, *Traité de chimie*, 8 vols. (Paris, 1829–1833), *1*:160–161, where Berzelius discusses the phenomenon of unipolar conductors. Soap, he found, can discharge a battery from its positive pole, but not from its negative one. Conversely, phosphorous discharges only the negative pole.

Jöns Jacob Berzelius (1779–1848, *DSB*), the Swedish chemist, was trained to be a physician. As a chemist he was largely self-taught. In formulating his chemical theories, he posited that electricity was elemental to chemical processes. The first volume of his *Traité de chimie* (which Henry had in his library) contains a sizable section on electricity. Henry read that volume avidly (in French) and recorded numerous references to it in two of his notebooks ([10615] and [23894], Henry Papers, Smithsonian Archives). Though Henry introduced himself to Berzelius by sending him several of his reprints in 1841, there is no evidence of active exchanges between the two men.

[30] The 1810 invention of Jean André DeLuc (1727–1817, *DSB*), DeLuc's electric column or pile was a modification of the voltaic pile.

The same state of the atmosphere which affects ordinary electrical exp. influences the action of the pendulum of the pile.[31]

Also stated that it had been discovered that at the magnetic or cold Siberian pole[32] of the earth the difference of the temperature of the air and the

---

DeLuc pressed together in a glass tube discs of zinc, silver, and paper, connecting a wire from the silver disc of one end to the zinc at the other. As in the voltaic pile, current was observed to pass through the wire, but in DeLuc's pile the current was longer lasting and of greater intensity but lower in quantity. The main difference in their construction was that DeLuc's used dry paper discs, whereas voltaic piles used paper moistened with salt water or other solutions. DeLuc's was often referred to as the "dry pile." The construction and performance of DeLuc's pile and later modifications are aptly described in Robert Hare, *A Compendium of the Course of Chemical Instruction in the Medical Department of the University of Pennsylvania*, 4th ed. (Philadelphia, 1840–1843), supplement "Of Galvanism or Voltaic Electricity," pp. 23–27.

When Alessandro Volta announced his voltaic pile in 1800, he asserted that current was produced by means of the contacts between different metals. Almost immediately a differing theory emerged, as William Nicholson and Anthony Carlisle found that current from the voltaic pile decomposed water; they concluded, then, that electrical current was the product of chemical activity within the pile. DeLuc attempted to demonstrate that current could still be obtained from what he believed to be an absolutely dry (free of any chemicals) pile, thereby substantiating Volta's theory of the contact origins of electricity. (See L. Pearce Williams, *Michael Faraday* [New York, 1965], pp. 56–59; Edmund Whittaker, *A History of the Theories of Aether and Electricity*, rev. ed., 2 vols. [New York, 1973], *1*:69–78; *DSB*, s.v. DeLuc, Jean André.)

The chemical and contact theories of electricity carried well into the first half of the nineteenth century and in his readings Henry encountered explanations and experiments supporting both theories. Examples of such contemporary treatments which Henry digested are George John Singer, *Elements of Electricity and Electro-Chemistry* (London, 1814), pp. 425–463 and P. M. Roget, *Treatises on Electricity, Galvanism, Magnetism, and Electro-Magnetism* (London, 1832), "Galvanism," pp. 1–32. Henry in turn passed on both theories to his Princeton students, judging by a surviving lecture notebook ([23894], pp. 160–172, Henry Papers, Smithsonian Archives). In his lectures Henry demonstrated, at great length, both the chemical theory, which he ascribed to the English writers, and the contact theory ascribed to the French writers. Like Singer, especially, and other observers of his period, Henry was careful not to favor any single theory: "We will adopt an intermediate view and consider the action of the galvanic apparatus to be due to both contact & chemical action at least in some cases" (Notebook [23894], p. 162). After demonstrating the dry pile, with many experiments taken directly from Singer, Henry hinted at why he and others felt that both contact and chemical processes could be operating at once: "We have exhibited the dry pile as an example of a battery made to act by contact. Some however contend that it is caused to operate by the moisture imbibed by the paper" (p. 170). In other words there was really no such thing as an ideally dry pile which could still produce current. The next paragraph in the text, and the following footnote, bear on the effects of atmospheric moisture on the performance of DeLuc's dry pile.

31 With his "aerial electroscope," developed in 1813, DeLuc attempted to aid the study of meteorology with an application of his dry pile. The principle involved was that varying humidities affected the levels of current, which could be observed to change by various forms of pendant apparatus (such as a pith ball on a string) in proximity to the pile. Many researchers developed their own modifications on this principle and noticed that the motion of the pendulum, though seemingly perpetual since the dry piles produced uninterrupted current for several years, was irregular from day to day. The pendulum apparatus and observations on the irregularity of its motion are given in Singer, op. cit., pp. 453–463. Humidity levels would have related effects on experiments with ordinary, or static, electricity. This observation served as another factor in Henry's and others' attempts to determine the identity of all electricities.

32 The reference is made not to our known magnetic north pole, but rather to a second magnetic north pole which was supposed to

dew point was 50°. This is probably the dryest point on the surface of the earth[33] as no heat is given off by the condensation of vapour.

May 2nd 1834 Breakfasted this morning with Mr Vaughan. Met at his table Mr Dunbar the son of the author of an article of great merit on the Topography of the Missisipie river.[34] This gentleman is a graduate of Princeton and is a soninlaw of Mrs Field[35] of our village.

Mr Vaughan showed us several curiosities. Among the rest some large casts in painted plaster of the organic remains of the gigantic reptiles. Also several models of machines deposited in the Society and described in its transactions. Amoung them was a pump for a ship worked by a wheel over the side of the vessel. Thus The wheel turns by the progressive motion of the ship. In large vessels this wheel would be very large unless its axis is to pass through a port hole near the bottom.[36]

exist. Christopher Hansteen (like others before him) hypothesized, on the basis of observations of magnetic deviations, that the earth had two magnetic norths of unequal size and strength. One was in the Hudson's Bay area and the other in Siberia. This theory remained generally accepted until 1839 but was never substantiated by mathematical explanations which Hansteen and others attempted. In that year Carl Friedrich Gauss announced a mathematical explanation for a single magnetic north pole. See *DSB*, s.v. "Hansteen," "Gauss"; P. M. Roget, *Treatises on Electricity, Galvanism, Magnetism, and Electro-Magnetism* (London, 1832), "Magnetism," p. 29.

[33] Johnson's statement, as recorded by Henry, is partially substantiated by modern climatology, at least to the point that weather in the southern highlands of the Indigirka River in Eastern Siberia is extraordinarily cold and dry. It may rank as one of the driest (in terms of relative humidity) regions, but not the driest. Richard Perry, *The Polar Worlds* (New York, 1973), p. 138; W. G. Kendrew, *The Climates of the Continents*, 5th ed. (Oxford, 1961), pp. 263–283.

[34] The father is William Dunbar (1749–1810, *DAB*). Born and educated in Scotland, with advanced training in mathematics and astronomy in London, Dunbar emigrated to American soil in 1771, eventually settling near Natchez. He depended primarily upon agriculture for his support, but he successfully pursued such studies as astronomy, meteorology, archeology, and natural history and became perhaps the "foremost scientist of the Southwest." Through correspondence he became friendly with Thomas Jefferson, and soon thereafter he was elected to the American Philosophical Society. The paper to which Henry refers is "Description of the River Mississippi and Its Delta, with That of the Adjacent Parts of Louisiana," American Philosophical Society *Transactions*, 1809, *6*:169–187.

William Dunbar's oldest son and namesake was born in Natchez in 1793. Seventeen at the time of his father's death and intending to follow his father in science, he relied upon the advice of John Vaughan in educational and other matters. He graduated from Princeton in 1813, then took his M.D. degree (1818) from the University of Pennsylvania. Thereafter Dunbar devoted himself to managing "The Forest," his father's plantation, which became known for its hospitable, religious, and intellectual atmosphere. He died in 1847. Mrs. Dunbar Rowland [Eron Opha (Moore) Rowland], *The Life, Letters, and Papers of William Dunbar, 1749–1810* (Jackson, Mississippi, 1930), pp. 391–394. Alfred Nevin, *Encyclopaedia of the Presbyterian Church in the United States of America* (Philadelphia, 1884), p. 201.

[35] Abigail Stockton Field (Mrs. Robert C. Field) was widowed in 1810; she was a daughter of Richard Stockton (1730–1781, *DAB*, a signer of the Declaration of Independence). She was the mother of Richard Stockton Field (for whom see below, Henry to Rogers, March 9, 1835, footnote 2) and two daughters, both of whom married William Dunbar. She died in 1853. *Hageman, 1*:88, 345, 350.

[36] Richard Wells, the inventor of this contrivance, intended it for emergency use in

From Mr Vauns called on Mr Lea, was requested to call at his hous in the afternoon and see the last number of the Phil Transactions.[37]

From Leas to Millingtons and from Millingtons to the university in order to meet Prof Bache[38] according to appointment.

While the Prof was engaged in some duties of the board[39] I examined the articles of aparatus in the Chemical laboratory.

On inspecting one of Dr Hares[40] deflagrators I was struck with the idea that the instrument could be insulated in each plate by inserting between each plate a partition which should be watertight. The acid could in this arrangement be poured on and off as before.[41]

---

small sailing vessels. "In the course of the immense trade now pursued on the ocean, vessels are continually subject to leaks, which too often prove fatal to the crews, who, wearied out with incessant pumping, are obliged, at last, to submit to their unhappy fate, and desponding sink into their watery graves." "Account of a Machine for Pumping Vessels at Sea, Without the Labour of Men," *Transactions of the American Philosophical Society*, 1789, *1* (2d ed.):353–357 (quote is from p. 353). The apparatus was kept simple to facilitate its assembly under adverse circumstances.

Wells was a Philadelphia merchant and, as of 1794, cashier of the Bank of North America. Elected to the American Philosophical Society in 1768, he served as Secretary, 1774–1776. Apparently his only other presentation before the Society came in 1774, on "raising water in wells without the help of pumps or other machines." It was not published. *Early Proceedings of the American Philosophical Society . . . from 1774 to 1838* (Philadelphia, 1884), pp. 85, 90, 95, 98 (this appears as part of volume 22, 1885, of the *Proceedings* of the Society and is a "condensed copy" of the manuscript minutes, prepared by the geologist J. P. Lesley, then Librarian of the American Philosophical Society. The volume ends with the entries for 1837; later *Proceedings* were in print already). Charles E. Peterson, "Library Hall: Home of the Library Company of Philadelphia, 1790–1880," *Transactions of the American Philosophical Society*, 1953, n.s. *43*:131n.

[37] Henry fulfilled that invitation. See below in the text.

[38] Alexander Dallas Bache, for whom see above, Henry to Harriet Henry, November 1, 1833, footnote 7.

[39] We are not certain which board Bache was serving on that day, but presumably Henry is referring to the Girard College Board of Trustees. That Board was scheduled to meet the following day. Bache was one of fifteen Trustees elected in February 1833 to set up a school for orphans, according to the will of Stephen Girard. By July 1836 Bache was named President of the College. At the urging of Francis Lieber, another Trustee, the Board sent Bache abroad to study various European educational systems, a trip lasting from September 1836 to October 1838. During several months of 1837 Joseph Henry traveled to Europe, where he met up with Bache and his wife and toured with them. Henry's 1837 trip to Europe, and his contacts with Bache there, will be extensively documented in volume 3 of *The Papers of Joseph Henry*. Merle M. Odgers, *Alexander Dallas Bache, Scientist and Educator, 1806–1867* (Philadelphia, 1947), pp. 27–89.

[40] Robert Hare, whose deflagrator battery design Henry used in his Albany days (see *Henry Papers, 1*).

[41] This is perhaps the first instance of Henry's curiosity about the different effects that would be produced in these distinct arrangements. That is, in what respects would the results differ when the plates are separated into individual elements or all immersed in a common reservoir? He explored this question in his "Contributions I: Battery," pp. 221–222. In constructing his battery, Henry chose to immerse the plates in individual, insulated cells.

Amoung other articles was a tortion galvanometer on Mr Ritches plan[42] made by Prof. Bache. The article is simple and of great exactness. It rest on [the] hypothesis of the force being as the tangent of the < [i.e., angle] of declination.

As the Prof. still continued engaged I walked down to Mr Baldwin's where I had an interesting conversation on the subject of steam, power &c. Mr B. informed me that if a number of holes be bored into a thick iron ladle, the article heated and water poured in while the whole is very hot the water will not pass through the holes. The exp. will probably succeed much better if the water be previously heated to the boiling point.[43]

Mr B. also informed me that the locomotive engines were made much liter now than formerly and in order to increase the adhesion when the machine is going up hill a part of the weight of the tender is thrown on the hind wheels by means of a lever.[44]

Returned to Prof. B[ache]'s Laboratory and accompanied the gentleman to his house where we inspected his needles. The long declination needle is contained in a box covered with paist board with only a small slit for viewing the end of the needle which carries a mirror. The slit is covered

[42] William Ritchie, "Description and Application of a Torsion Galvanometer," *Journal of the Royal Institution*, 1831, *1*:29–38. For Ritchie, see above, Henry to Green, February 17, 1834, footnote 4; also see below in the text of this document and footnote 48. In his oversimplified drawing nearby, Henry captured the essential components. The center vertical line represents the glass thread which is hung from the top cross-member (supported by the uprights to either side) and which suspends a needle at its bottom; the needle is centered in an upright insulated rectangular coil through which the electrical current is passed. Ritchie suggested that the instrument could be made still more sensitive if a single fiber of silk is substituted for the glass thread.

This was not Henry's first exposure to Ritchie's galvanometer. In his "On the Application of the Principle of the Galvanic Multiplier to Electro-Magnetic Apparatus . . . ," *Silliman's Journal*, 1831, *19*:400–408, Henry found that the tangents of the angles of deflection varied proportionally with the length of the wires he used in separate experiments (p. 402). His results, he claimed, agreed with "the law discovered by Mr. Ritchie..." (p. 403). The "law" was Ritchie's finding that "the degrees of torsion [measured on his torsion galvanometer] will be found to be proportional to the surface of the plates immersed" (Ritchie, op. cit., p. 33). Consequently, on seeing Ritchie's apparatus for the first time, Henry was quick to cite, from his own perspective, the principle which he had found and which he knew served as the basis for the instrument's accuracy.

[43] The water would not pass through the holes for two reasons. First, its rapid vaporization created a slight back-pressure at the holes. Secondly, any water beginning a descent through the thick ladle would have been vaporized by the hot metal. As Henry emphasized, both the ladle and the water must be "very hot." Henry's surviving lecture notes do not indicate that he ever demonstrated this heat transfer experiment to his Princeton classes.

[44] Baldwin's representation of this development was accurate. The lever device was patented by Ezra L. Miller in June 1834 and many of Baldwin's locomotives used it. John H. White, Jr., *American Locomotives: An Engineering History* (Baltimore, 1968), pp. 34, 269–270.

with a small piece of glass. The past board cover was substituted for the one of glass on account of the electrical excitation.

The aparatus is inclosed in a small frame house the sides of which are formed of cotton duck.[45]

Met at dinner the two older Rodgers.[46] The oldest is about starting on a tour to Virginia to recruite his health and to examine the mineral springs of the western part of the state which are very numerous. He informs me that Prof Daubeny[47] is very anxious to obtain the analysis of the waters of springs particularly of those which are thermal.

From Prof. Bache's I went to Mr Lea's to see the last No of the Phil. Transactions.

[45] As early as May 1833, Bache kept his magnetic instruments in an outbuilding. Bache used wood and cotton duck in an attempt to construct an iron-free surrounding for his terrestrial magnetism experiments. A. D. Bache, "Note of the Effect upon the Magnetic Needle, of the Aurora Borealis, Visible at Philadelphia, on the 17th of May, 1833," Franklin Institute *Journal*, 1833, *12*:5–9. In 1835 Henry constructed his own iron-free house for his terrestrial magnetic work (see below, Henry to Bache, May 18, 1835).

[46] The oldest of the two was James Blythe Rogers (1802–1852, *DAB*), first born of the sons of Hannah (Blythe) and Patrick Kerr Rogers, all four of whom became distinguished scientists. James was educated in Baltimore and at the College of William and Mary (1820–1821), where his father was Professor of Natural Philosophy and Chemistry. James then took an M.D. degree at the University of Maryland (1822). After practicing medicine for a brief period, he turned to teaching chemistry at the Washington Medical College in Baltimore, then at the medical department of Cincinnati College. He joined his brother William on the Virginia State Geological Survey in 1837 and later (1840) assisted his brother Henry in the Pennsylvania survey. He held several teaching positions in Philadelphia in the 1840s, culminating in his appointment in 1847 to succeed Robert Hare as Professor of Chemistry at the University of Pennsylvania, a position which Joseph Henry was invited to fill.

William Barton Rogers (1804–1882) was the second oldest of the Rogers brothers. Like James, he was educated in Baltimore schools and at William and Mary. He taught school briefly and lectured at the Maryland Institute. In 1828 he assumed his deceased father's Chair of Natural Philosophy at his alma mater. Seven years later he accepted a professorship at the University of Virginia which Joseph Henry had been offered (see below, documents in July and August 1835). Concurrently, from 1835 to 1842, he directed the Virginia State Geological Survey. In 1853 he moved to Boston, where he advocated and eventually set up (1861) the Massachusetts Institute of Technology. He presided over M.I.T. for the remaining years of his life, except a number of years due to ill health. Rogers had served as Chairman of the Association of American Geologists and Naturalists (1845–1847) and later as Corresponding Secretary of the American Academy of Arts and Sciences. A charter member of the National Academy of Sciences, he succeeded to its presidency in 1878, upon the death of its second President, Joseph Henry.

William Barton Rogers is most noted for his work on the geological structure of the Appalachian Mountains. But, like Joseph Henry, he had a wide range of interests in the physical sciences and was a prolific experimentalist. As documents in this and subsequent volumes will show, Henry's contacts with William Barton Rogers remained infrequent nearly until the 1850s when they increased significantly. A helpful source book on Rogers is Emma Savage Rogers, *The Life and Letters of William Barton Rogers*, 2 vols. (Boston, 1896).

[47] Charles Giles Bridle Daubeny (1795–1867, *DSB*), an English physician who abandoned his practice in the course of teaching chemistry and botany at Oxford. His most significant research centered on his chemical theory of volcanic activity, in which he attempted to prove, with elaborate evidence, that volcanoes result from water penetrating to the free alkali and alkaline earth metals supposedly under the earth's crust. (*Description of Active and Extinct Volcanoes* [Lon-

Read two papers one by Mr Richee the other by Mr Watkins.[48] Mr R. says that all that is necessary in order to make a powerful galvanic magnet is to wind a ribbon of copper around the keeper and use the horse shoe for a keeper. This is not true. Mr Watkins in his paper shows that a piece of soft iron may be made to retain its magnetism by merely keeping the lifter in contact.

He touched several horse shoe magnets of soft iron by the ordinary method of touching which retained the magnetism as long as the keeper was attached.

Also interposed several strata of paper & mica between the poles and the lifter.

Leaving Mr Lea I called at Mr Johnson's lecture room. Mr J is now engaged in giving a course of Lectures on Elect. He has a most splendid apparatus for which he paid according to Mr Espe[49] $3000. Mr J. says it is worth 5000.[50]

---

don, 1826].) Later, Daubeny applied his knowledge of chemistry to the study of botany. He was a fellow of the Royal Society (elected in 1822) and was among the founders of the British Association for the Advancement of Science in 1831, which he served in various official capacities.

Daubeny prepared several articles on thermal springs, one of which relates to Henry's mention of Daubeny in the context of the Rogers brothers. In his "Notice of the Thermal Springs of North America," *Silliman's Journal*, 1839, *36*:88–93, Daubeny explicitly makes use of observations on the Virginia thermal springs sent to him by William Barton Rogers, who was then head of the Virginia geological survey.

[48] William Ritchie, "Experimental Researches in Electro-magnetism and Magneto-electricity," *Phil. Trans.*, 1833, pp. 313–321, and Francis Watkins, "On the Magnetic Powers of Soft Iron," ibid., pp. 333–342. Henry recorded extensive notes on both articles in a notebook ([7171], pp. 85–93, Henry Papers, Smithsonian Archives), perhaps at this time. His notes comprise little more than an outline of the major facts elucidated in the articles. With regard to the Ritchie piece Henry was particularly indignant, as his challenge to the author in this paragraph suggests. He resented both Ritchie's apparent reinvention of the elementary reciprocating electrical motor which Henry first developed and Ritchie's use of Henry's design of an electromagnet without specific mention of Henry, only of the "American plan" (see above, Henry to Green, February 17, 1834, especially footnote 4). In his notebook Henry voiced no such objections to the Watkins article, although he did record Isaiah Lukens's claim that Watkins obtained his method of magnetizing soft iron and failed to cite him. Henry noted a few of Watkins's experiments which he intended to try. Also, Henry saw that one of Watkins's experiments involving shielding might shed light on his own experiments with the hollow tube (mentioned below in his "Record of Experiments" beginning August 19, 1834).

[49] James Pollard Espy (1785–1860, *DAB*, *DSB*) was first an educator and later a meteorologist. Born in Pennsylvania, he was raised in Kentucky and graduated from Transylvania University (1808). After studying law and teaching school in Xenia, Ohio, he became Principal of an academy in Cumberland, Maryland (1812–1817). Thereafter he taught mathematics and the classics in Philadelphia, during which time, about 1825, he began studying meteorology.

Espy was elected to the American Philosophical Society in January 1835, at the same time as Joseph Henry (for which see documents below in late 1834 and early 1835). But Espy's most active institutional affiliation was with the Franklin Institute, where he joined with A. D. Bache, Walter R. Johnson, Sears C. Walker, Isaiah Lukens, and Samuel V. Merrick to form an enthusiastic coterie bent on raising the level of scientific activity at the Institute (Bruce Sinclair, *Philadelphia's Philosopher Mechanics: A History of the*

Mr J. exhibits a very imposing experiment which consists in transmitting a char[g]e from his lecture room in a retired lane through several hundred feet of copper wire to a board in a public street on which the word Electricity is written in large letters with interspersed tin foil. The ligh[t]ing flashing over the word with the noise of a small pistol. He also passes it through a zig zag course on a board, repres[ent]ing the path of a stroke of lightning.[51]

Franklin Institute, 1824–1865 (Baltimore, 1974), pp. 151–153. Espy was also a member of "the club," an informal association of scientists which is alluded to in documents below, and discussed in footnote 13 of Henry's Notes on a Trip to Philadelphia, December 5–7, 1834.

In 1835 Espy began his full-time devotion to the study of meteorology. He developed a theory of storms which, though proving only partially correct, placed him in the center of meteorological debate for many years. Drawing upon his own experiments to form physical concepts of the weather, Espy erroneously described the mechanism of storms. His convectional theory, however, correctly described precipitation as the result of the upward movement, expansion, and cooling of moist air. Espy's staunch defense of his theory, on both sides of the Atlantic, drew still more attention to his innovative concepts.

Espy's other major contribution to meteorology resulted from his tireless efforts to develop a national system of standardized weather observations. As the state meteorologist, beginning in 1836, he set up such a system for Pennsylvania. In 1842 Espy went on to establish a national meteorological system, for which Congress made small appropriations to various federal agencies. When Joseph Henry, as Secretary of the Smithsonian, established a network of weather observers linked by telegraph, Espy's work was incorporated into it; this first formal national weather service was a forerunner, through several administrative changes, of our present United States Weather Bureau.

Henry's Library contains five reprints of Espy's articles on meteorology, dating between 1836 and 1841. In addition, Espy's best-known work, *The Philosophy of Storms* (Boston, 1841), has survived in the Henry Library, bearing Henry's extensive annotations. Espy and Henry developed a warm personal and close professional relationship. Their correspondence, which will appear in subsequent volumes of *The Papers of Joseph Henry*, sheds considerable light on Espy's manifold impact on the rapidly professionalizing world of meteorology, a subject which was of great interest to Henry. For some background material on Espy and his relationship to fellow meteorologists, see the documents and commentary in Nathan Reingold, ed., *Science in Nineteenth-Century America* (New York, 1964), pp. 92–107, 128–134.

[50] Whether of $3000 or $5000 in value, even by today's standards Johnson's apparatus must have been extraordinarily elaborate. We have not determined what piece of electrical equipment would have carried such a high value.

[51] These spectacular exhibitions of electric light were of the same principle as that mentioned above in the text and discussed in footnote 6. The tin foil strips could be arranged in practically any configuration on a nonconducting surface (wood and glass were most commonly used). For instance, Robert Hare, *A Compendium of the Course of Chemical Instruction in the Medical Department of the University of Pennsylvania*, 4th ed. (Philadelphia, 1840–1843), supplement "Electricity," pp. 36–44, explains a number of the principal demonstrations of electrical light. Joseph Henry's notes for his Princeton classes (Notebook [23894], pp. 119–120) indicate that Henry incorporated many of these displays into his lectures on electrical light. Illuminating the word "electricity" at a great distance may have been "imposing," especially as an advertisement in a public street for Walter Johnson's school. But Johnson was certainly not the first to demonstrate words illuminated in this manner. George John Singer, *Elements of Electricity and Electro-Chemistry* (London, 1814), pp. 92–94 and plate 11, discusses the manner of constructing such displays and suggests (p. 93) illuminating "words, flowers, and other complicated forms." From undated lecture notes (Henry's lecture on electricity, [5929], p. [9], Henry Papers, Smithsonian Archives) we know Henry exhibited a "luminous word" for his Princeton students.

May 7, 1834

TO JAMES HENRY

Family Correspondence, Henry Papers, Smithsonian Archives

Princeton May 7th 1834

Dear James

Last week I spent in Phil[a] when I met Dr Beck.[1] He promised to call and see Mother as soon as he returned. Dr Ten Eyck[2] passed through while I was in the city but we did not meet. We are all well, the children quite healthy. The boy is very fond of being in the garden and works very industriously with his little wheel barrow in wheeling chips and stones to different parts of the yard. The girl continues to grow and now weighs more than 12 lbs.

I hope Mother will be better when the weather becomes more settled. The spring is the most trying part of the year and this one has been unusually changable. Harriet has surmized that your business will lead you to N.Y. and that you intend to surprise us with a visit. We have seen nothing of Fuller[3] as yet. Dr. Beck told me something in reference to his coming on but I did not distinctly understand him. I passed a very [pleasant] week in Phil[a] I left home on Tuesday and returned on Saturday. I did not call at Mr Harpers[4] as he is in Washington. I saw two persons from Albany Archibald Robison[5] formerly cleark in the State house and C. M. Moor[6] the auctoneer. The latter has a fine store in the Arcade[7] under the Museum.[8] Amoung the curiosities I had a peek at Col. Crocket, and was some-

[1] Both Lewis Caleb Beck (*Henry Papers, 1*: 69) and Theodric Romeyn Beck (*Henry Papers, 1*:4–5) were living in Albany at this time, and either one might have been in Philadelphia on scientific business.

[2] Philip Ten Eyck (*Henry Papers, 1*:214).

[3] Not identified.

[4] James Harper (1780–1873) emigrated from Ireland in 1791. From 1820 to 1830 he was a wholesaler specializing in grains and groceries. He served in Congress from 1832 to 1836. A member of the Franklin Institute, Harper experimented in the manufacture of bricks by machine, which led angry persons presumably fearing unemployment to destroy his plant in 1844. Harper also worked with associations dedicated to prison reform and to alleviation of poverty. *Biographical Directory of the American Congress; Proceedings of the Right Worshipful Grand Lodge of Pennsylvania . . . in Reference to the Death of Past Grand Master Brother James Harper* (Philadelphia, 1873); Franklin Institute, *Charter of Incorporation, Constitution and By-Laws* (Philadelphia, 1824).

[5] The Philadelphia City Directories for 1833–1836 list an Archibald Robinson as lottery broker but give no information on a Robison.

[6] C. M. Moore is listed as a dry goods merchant located at the Arcade in the Philadelphia Directories for 1833–1836.

[7] The Philadelphia Arcade, designed by John Haviland and constructed of white marble in 1826, stood on Chestnut Street between Fifth and Sixth Streets. It was patterned on the Burlington Arcade in London. Restaurants took up the cellar level, shops occupied the first floor, and offices were on the second floor. Philadelphia City Directory, 1834, p. 14; and Charles Coleman Sellers, *Charles Willson Peale: Later Life, 1790–1827* (Philadelphia, 1947), p. 395 (figure 45 is an undated lithograph showing the exterior of the building).

[8] Peale's Museum moved to the third floor

what disappointed in his appearance. He reminded me of a Methodist Minister, is a tall man with long black hair, wears a white hat with a tolerably wide rim. He is younger than I had supposed and does not appear more than 45 and on the whole is a pretty good looking chap.

We have had a short visit from the Misses Meads. They return to Albany from N.Y. the Last of this week. They came on a visit to Elizabethtown. You will receive from them a particular account of all the affairs in the Jerseys. They had rather an unpleasant time in regard to the weather but according to your account they would not have found the weather more pleasant at Albany. We had feared that the frost which we had on Saturday week would have destroyed the fruit but it has not.

Your Brother

Give all the family our Respects. My love to Mother and Nancy.

---

of the Arcade in 1827 and remained there until its collections were auctioned off in 1845. Sellers, *Peale*, pp. 380–381, 396, and 407. For Joseph Henry's association with this important scientific and cultural institution, see his Notes on a Trip to Philadelphia, April 29–May 2, 1834, footnote 4.

FROM WILLIAM HAMILTON[1]

Henry Papers, Smithsonian Archives

Hall of the Franklin Institute
Philad[a] May 21/34

Dear Sir

Agreeably to my promise I take the liberty to inform you that the conversation meeting of the Franklin Institute will take place tomorrow evening 22nd inst at 8 oclk. Prof[r] Green has just informed me that he will exhibit your magnet.[2] If it would suit your convenience we should be much gratified with your attendance.[3]

Yours respectfully
Will[m] Hamilton
actuary

---

[1] William Hamilton served as actuary of the Franklin Institute from 1828 until his death in 1871. As such, he managed the Institute's business affairs. W. H. Wahl, *The Franklin Institute of the State of Pennsylvania* (Philadelphia, 1895), p. 8.

[2] Jacob Green's exhibition of Henry's magnet is noticed in the *Journal of the Franklin Institute*, 1834, *14*:5. The Institute very soon became more than a place for the uplift of artisans under the leadership of men like Alexander Dallas Bache, who successfully advocated a more scientific orientation. See *Henry Papers*, *1*:394, footnote 28.

[3] This letter arrived too late for Henry to participate. See his comment in the letter to Bache of July 15, 1834, below.

May 27, 1834

FROM CLEMENT M. EDSON[1]

Henry Papers, Smithsonian Archives

New York, May 27, 1834.

Dear Sir,

We took the liberty a short time since of sending you the May No of the Knickerbocker Magazine[2] which we hope has been received. We have indulged the hope that you would honor us with a communication for the magazine of a scientific character. We are desirous of enlisting the best talents of the country in favor of the publication, and of inserting some articles calculated to instruct, as well as to entertain, for which we are willing to make a fair compensation, viz: two dollars per page. Our prospects as regards increase of subscribers are quite cheering at present,[3] and the work has been very favorably spoken of by the public. It must be made, however, intrinsically valuable in order to secure patronage and have it take the lead of other publications of the day. May we expect to hear from you sir, and to receive an article for the "Knickerbocker"? Assistance at this time will enable us to move onward with increased confidence in ultimately placing the Magazine upon a sound foundation.

You will particularly oblige us by favoring us with an answer to this immediately, that we may complete our arrangements for the next volume.

With sentiments of esteem, we are sir
Very Respectfully, Your Obt Servants,
Clark & Edson.

by Clement M. Edson

[1] This is a follow-up to the letter of Lewis Gaylord Clark, of April [15], 1834, above, the co-proprietor with Edson of the *Knickerbocker Magazine*. Edson (1811–1853) was with the periodical for five years and sold his interest in 1839 after a quarrel with Clark. He afterwards practiced law. See footnote 1 of the April [15], 1834 letter and *Knickerbocker Magazine*, 1853, *41*:476.

[2] For a sketch of the *Knickerbocker Magazine*, see L. G. Clark to Henry of April [15], 1834, footnote 1.

[3] Clark and Edson had reason to be concerned about the number of subscribers. In selling the magazine to them, Peabody & Co. had claimed 1,000 subscribers—the number was actually less than 500. However, in three years Clark and Edson had increased the number of subscribers to over 5,000. Frank Luther Mott, *A History of American Magazines, 1741–1850* (New York, 1930), p. 607.

May 30, 1834

TO JAMES HENRY

Family Correspondence, Henry Papers, Smithsonian Archives

Princeton May [30,] 1834[1]
Friday morning

Dear James

Our term has fairly commenced and I am again engaged in the duties of the college. Owing to the money pressure we have not received as many new students as was anticipated from the great number which joined college last Fall. Our Catalogue will be out in a short time when I will forward you a copy. After I get fairly under way in the course I hope to be more punctual in writing as I know that Mother is very anxious to hear as often as possible—and indeed nothing gives our family more pleasure or nothing is more anxiously expected than a letter from Albany.

We are all well although Harriet is getting very thin with nursing the little girl. The Daughter however appears to gain as much as the mother looses.

The Boy is well but not as fleshy as he was during the winter. He takes a great deal of exercise and is growing in height. The fruit around here has [not] apparently suffered much by the frost although some of the garden plants have been killed. Yesterday (Thursday) was a cold rainy day. The rain commenced Wednesday. Friday is still cold and cloudy. The students have been watching in the woods for the appearance of the Locust which have been predicted to make their appearance about this time after an absence of 17 years. They are to be seen in considerable numbers but are not as abundant as was expected. They are perhaps waiting for better weather.

Amoung the *Blacks* of this place the story is that these insects are hatched in China and eat their way through the earth to us in the course of 17 years. Not so bad an explanation! The celebrity of these animals illustrate the influence of name. They are not the same animal which is found in Africa & the East and which devour every vegetable in the course. The eastern Locust is a large kind of grasshopper which has a mouth and eats the leaves and bark of the trees. Our insect (improperly called insect[2]) has no mouth and receives its nourishment through a small tube or sucker. It deposits its eggs in the extreme and tender branches of trees. These soon drop off & the egg falls into the ground where it remains several years in

[1] Henry actually dated this May 28. But the context indicates that Friday is correct, which was May 30, a dating confirmed by the postmark.

[2] Henry probably meant to write locust, not insect. The Princeton insects are actually cicadas, although the term locust is commonly applied.

some cases before it is hatched. The regular period of 17 years is probably fabulous and has its origin in the general love of the marvelous.[3] Give my respects to Mr Gould[4] and inform him that I have not been able to see Mr Harlow[5] since receiving your letter. He does not board in college. I will see him to day if possible and write his answer in [my] next. I have had my battery [in] operation and find that it succeeds most admirably. Harriet will finish.

Stephen has seen Mr Harlowe who says he has written to Mr Gould. Our little ones grow sweeter every day. Bub insists upon going to Albany with Uncle Jimmy. He asked for you several times after you left. Sis grows enormously fleshy, but continues very good.

Please give our love to Mother & all. Tell the Misses Mead we are much indebted to them for their long letter of last week. Write again soon & as often as possible.

Joseph will be more punctual after all things are well arranged about College. There is always a great deal to be done at the commencement of the term. We have had [a] fire for the last two days. This morning is cold and cheerless. Tell the girls Mr Hart[6] is still confined [?with] his eyes.

Yours in haste. *The mail will close* in a few moments

Harriet

[3] Henry's physical descriptions of the insects are accurate, but not his account of the life-cycle of the cicada. The eggs drop to the ground, hatching in one or two weeks. The larvae burrow and live in the ground for seventeen years, accounting for the regular periods of infestation. A thirteen-year variety exists in the southern United States, overlapping with the seventeen-year cicada as far as southern Pennsylvania, probably not reaching Princeton. (Information from R. C. Froeschner, Department of Entomology, National Museum of Natural History, Smithsonian Institution.) Especially among farmers there was an active popular tradition and literature on the periodic cicada; Henry was habitually suspicious of such traditions. Yet there was also a scientific literature confirming the regularity of the insect swarms. For example, in "Notices and Observations on the American Cicada or Locust," *Silliman's Journal*, 1830, *18*:47–50, S. P. Hildreth estimated that the eggs hatched within sixty days and concluded that "these insects are tenants of the ground for seventeen years and until He who created them again calls them forth to propagate their kind, to fulfill their destiny, and die" (p. 50).

[4] Either Anthony or his uncle William Gould (*Henry Papers, 1*:446).

[5] Perhaps James M. Harlow (1808–1894), B.A. Princeton, 1835; he boarded at Mrs. Gastons. He attended Princeton Theological Seminary, 1836–1839, and was ordained in 1839. He was Pastor and Stated Supply at numerous churches in the northeastern states until his death. *Princeton Annual Catalogue*, 1835; *Princeton Catalogue*, p. 148; *Roberts*, p. 101.

[6] Harriet Henry's words are cryptic to us. Perhaps John Seely Hart; see above, Henry to Harriet Henry, March 24, 1834, footnote 13.

June 23, 1834

HENRY NOTEBOOK ENTRY

Notebook [7169], pp. 222–224,[1] *Henry Papers, Smithsonian Archives*

June 23[d] 1834[2]

In exhibiting the compound blow pipe <*use*> force into the tubes a quantity of brass wire so as to nearly fill the whole caliber. Otherwise there is some danger of an explosion. This was verified in the lecture room this morning. Dr T. had been exhibiting the blow pipe[3] before the class and after the lecture was exhibiting some further experiments to some gentlemen who remained. They were all standing around the table when an explosion[4] suddenly took place in the vessel containing the hydrogen. The pressure had been suffered to go down & as the compound orifice had several times been closed by the melted substances during the experiments, the gas had passed from the oxygen to the hydrogen & produced an explosive mixture.

In exhibiting the blow pipe show its effects 1st on iron wire size of a nitting needle. 2 on copper on a coal. The copper made to boil a piece as big as a large [bean?]. 3. Show the effect on zinc foil or wire. 4 on platina melt smal wire. 5 on cast iron makes a most brilliant display of compound cintillations. 6 on asbestos. 7 on a plate of mica, cuts it in two by passing the plate under the flame like a knife. 8 on watch spring. 9th on lime a piece of crayon held in the fingers.

As platina may be fused into maleable lump by means of the blow pipe this instrument may be used in the artes for obtaining a quantity of the

[1] From page 193 to the end, this notebook contains Henry jottings on chemistry clearly intended for guidance in preparing lectures on that subject. Other chemical information appears elsewhere in the notebook, such as pages 162–166 dealing with metals. These notes are in no clearly discernible order; some are dated as late as 1837. Most entries are undated but we assume from the datings present and internal evidence that the notebook was started early in Henry's stay at Princeton.

Just prior to this entry, page 221, are notes on the use of electricity to cause an explosion of hydrogen and oxygen to form water. Immediately following this entry are notes on the decomposition of water. This brief notebook entry is an example of how Henry worked as a teacher. Readings, conversations or observations (as in this case) were noted for possible future use in preparing lectures to his classes. On page 222, just above the item printed here, under the heading "Light," Henry has a description of the use of the blowpipe in the Drummond light for lighthouses.

[2] In the original the date appears in parentheses and underlined immediately following the words "this morning."

[3] Robert Hare devised a means of feeding oxygen and hydrogen gases by hydrostatic pressure to produce an intense directed flame. Blowpipes using the human mouth or a bellows for impelling the flame were known earlier and used in the arts and industry. Hare's device, like others, was also used for chemical and mineralogical analysis. Benjamin Silliman, Sr., worked with Hare on the development and use of the blowpipe; an early description by him is in Nathan Reingold, ed., *Science in Nineteenth-Century America* (New York, 1964), pp. 8–9. See *Encyclopaedia Britannica*, 8th ed., s.v. "Blow-pipe."

metal in a maleable state. It[5] may be purchased from the gun smiths for about $2 per oz. When rendered maleable it is worth $8.

Mention that the flame of the compound blow pipe is solid throughout where as the common flame is hollow.

[4] Apparently Humphry Davy was the first to note that a small orifice prevented the explosions which had plagued Hare. In the compound blowpipe the oxygen and hydrogen were kept separately within the device and fed out to a common vent where ignition occurred. If the opening was too large, the flame would ignite the mixture of gases within the blowpipe. *Encyclopaedia Britannica,* 8th ed., s.v. "Blow-pipe."

[5] i.e., platina.

TO JAMES D. FORBES[1]

Forbes Papers, Library, St. Andrews University, Scotland

Princeton, College of New Jersey
June 30th 1834

Dear Sir

From a knowledge of your zeal in the cause of science I am induced to take the liberty of transmitting to you by My Friend Mr John Turnbull[2] a magnetic needle on the plan of Hansteen.[3] My object is to effect if possible an interchange of observations on the intensity of terrestrial magnetism and thus to determine a standard of comparison between this country and your city.

May I ask sir that you will make such a disposition of the needle as will best further the object. Either return it by Mr Turnbull after having determined its rate in your city or send me in exchange another which has been rated and is perminent in its magnetism.[4] I would prefer the latter plan and should you think fit to adopt it I will vibrate your needle in some of the principal cities in this country and transmit the results to you when I return the article.

Mr Turnbull has given me so short a notice of his intention to visit Scotland that I have had no oportunity of making any experiments on the variation of the intensity of the needle by a change of temperature. It was

[1] Forbes (1809–1868) was Professor of Natural Philosophy at the University of Edinburgh (*Henry Papers, 1*:355 and 437–438). *DSB*; *DNB*.

[2] Turnbull is identified in *Henry Papers, 1*:355.

[3] For Christopher Hansteen and his system of rendering needles useful for observations on terrestrial magnetism, see *Henry Papers, 1*:198 and 290–291.

[4] Forbes was to do both. See his reply to Henry of September 21, 1834, printed below.

magnetized about 3 years since and first vibrated in Albany in August 1831.[5] Since then it has changed its rate but little and has I think now become stationary in its magnetic intensity. I send you a copy of four observations made with this needle on the 27th and 28th inst.[6] The time was noted by a watch which indicates quarter seconds and as 1/4th of this division was noted the register is given in seconds and 1/16^{ths} of seconds. In determining the mean time of 300 vibrations I have simply taken the mean of ten vibrations from the arithmetical mean of the whole set given in the last column and afterwards multiplied by 30. The observations are not as numerous as I could wish but they will serve when compared with those made at Edinburgh to give a first approximation of the relative intensities.

It is not necessary to detail my method of observation as it is the same as that of Hansteen with the exception that a piece of soft iron is used to give motion to the needle when suspended in its box instead of a magnet. The iron is repeatedly approached and the proper amplitude of vibration obtained very gradually so as to produce motion only in one plane.[7] I regret that I am not able at this time to send you the dip and declination of the needle at Princeton. I have however the promise of the use of an excellent instrument belonging to the government[8] and will determine with it the dip during the course of the present summer and also the declination with an instrument which I am now fitting up.[9]

Accompanying the needle I send four Nos of the Meteorological observations made by the different academies in the state of N.Y. Before leaving Albany I had the charge, in connection with Dr. T R Beck, of making the abstract of returns of observations to the Regents of the University. The No for 1832 contains a paper on a disturbance of the magnetic needle by an aurora observed by me in 1831.[10] This country affords a fine field for studying the laws of terrestrial magnetism but very little has as yet been done in the way of accurate observation. The Regents of the University of

[5] Renwick's Hansteen needle had been magnetized long before August 1831, so we suspect that Henry is forwarding Forbes a needle he had prepared himself, rather than the one he had received from Renwick.

[6] Henry enclosed with this letter lists of the observations and times of duration, copied in another hand (by Harriet Henry?) from one of his pocket notebooks ([30031], pages [63–72]). We have omitted these.

[7] See *Henry Papers, 1*:335–337, for Henry's directions on how to make observations on terrestrial magnetism.

[8] Henry may have hoped to borrow the needle of the United States Military Academy from Edward Courtenay. Henry had used the West Point needle to determine the dip at Albany (see the last paragraph of the letter of Henry to Silliman, April 18, 1833, printed above).

[9] Possibly the six-foot-long needle Henry mentioned in his letter to William Kelly, December 30, 1833, printed above.

[10] "On a Disturbance of the Earth's Magnetism, in Connection with the Appearance of an Aurora Borealis, as Observed at Albany, April 19, 1831," Regents of the University of the State of New York, *Annual Report* (Albany, 1832), pp. 107–119.

the State of N.Y. contemplate establishing magnetic observator[i]es at several academies under their direction provided funds can be obtained for the object from the next legislature.[11]

Your Report on the recent progress and present state of Meteorology[12] has been read with much interest in this country and will do much towards advancing this interesting department of science.

I am sir with the highest respect
Your most obedient servt.
Joseph Henry
Prof. Nat Phil.
College N.J.

N.B Princeton is mid way between the cities of New York & Philadelphia.

[11] Beginning in 1832, the Regents had tried to persuade colleges and academies to measure the magnetic meridian at their locations, and thereafter once a year to measure the deviation from the original figure. Simeon DeWitt, Chancellor of the Regents, supported this project vigorously, but the Regents lacked the authority to compel the schools to cooperate. By 1835, only Geneva College and eight academies (of which Albany was one) had sent in data. Regents of the University of the State of New York, *Annual Report* (Albany, 1833), pp. 25–33; (Albany, 1834), pp. 9–10; and (Albany, 1835), pp. 11 and 178. After Simeon DeWitt died in December 1834, the Regents' enthusiasm for the project seemed to wane; no attempt was made to seek legislative funding or authority for the program. However, Joseph Henry did try to add the study of terrestrial magnetism to the state natural history survey in 1836, as shall be documented in volume three of the *Henry Papers*.

[12] James D. Forbes, "Report upon the Recent Progress and Present State of Meteorology," British Association for the Advancement of Science, *Report of the First and Second Meetings* (London, 1833), pp. 196–258. This volume, as well as a pamphlet of Forbes' "Report," is in the Henry Library.

TO NANCY HENRY

Family Correspondence, Henry Papers, Smithsonian Archives

Princeton July 12th 1834

My Dear Sister

James has probably gone to Utica and I therefore address this letter to you. I would have written sooner but have been unusually ingaged for a week or more past. One of our Officers[1] was absent from College and I was ingaged in his duties.

Annother reason for not writing is that Aunt[2] is in Albany and has given you all the information you could desire. We are all well. The little girl

[1] We do not know which Princeton colleague is being referred to at this point.

[2] Nancy Connor.

in particular is growing finely. She was taken to church last Saturday and there received the name of Mary Anna. She behaved very well except when we first went in; the black girl who carried her accidentally scratched her arm with a breast pin when the young lady made the whole church ring with her cries. She was however soon pacified and said not a word when the clergyman put the water on her face.[3]

The weather has been very warm this week. The thermometer on Wednesday & Thursday read at 95° in the shade in our yard. The temperature however of today & yesterday is very plesant. We heard through the letter of the Misses Wilson[4] that Aunt had arrived safely at Albany; when she left we were a little apprehensive that she would not get farther than New York as she was unwell and appeared quite feeble. She has given you all the News. Nothing unusual has happened since she left. Our house has been rather lonely. We have had no visitors except on the evening of the 4th of July when several Ladies came to our gate to see the display of fire works in the college campus. The celebration of the *Day* whent off among the students quite pleasurably. We had two orations and fire works consisting of a great number of rockets stars &c and after these the fire balls. Fire Balls are made every 4th of July by the students. They purchase nearly a barrel of the Spirits of turpentine and steep with it balls of cotton wick until they are perfectly saturated. On the evening of the 4th they all assemble in the campus or green before the college, set fire to the balls and then throw them from one to the other. The appearance is most beautiful; sometimes nearly a hundred balls are seen in motion at the same instant and in every direction. The blazing balls are thrown by the hand, (some times) covered with a glove. The Boy was so much pleased with the Lights, that he could not be pervailed to go into the house until 10 o'clock when the whole ended.

We are very happy to hear that Mother is quite smart and were much surprised to learn that you had caught her up stairs attempting to make a bed. The Albany paper for Friday has just arrived. This is the first we have received this week. James must write as soon as he returns & I will answer his letter as soon as convenient.

Love from All to All. The family charges Aunt to be careful of her health.

Your Brother
Joseph

[3] An auspicious public debut for Joseph Henry's oldest daughter.

[4] Probably the sisters of Hugh Nesbitt Wilson for whom see footnote 13 of Henry's letter to his wife of March 24, 1834, above.

July 13, 1834

FROM ALEXANDER DALLAS BACHE

Henry Papers, Smithsonian Archives

Philad. July 13th. 1834

My dear Sir,

Will you have the goodness to let me know where to find the *antique* corresponding to Smith's needle?[1]

[1] Bache's interest in Moses Smith's improved compass needle stems from its examination by the Franklin Institute's Committee on Science and the Arts which was concluded March 13, 1834, and printed in the *Journal of the Franklin Institute*, November 1834, *14*:318–320. Bache was chairman of that Committee. Moreover, he was instrumental in its founding (February 1834), having served earlier on the predecessor Committee on Inventions and having reshaped that arm of the Institute into a scientific council to review improvements in the useful arts. Spearheaded by Bache and encouraged by such fellow committee members as Isaiah Lukens and Samuel V. Merrick (1801–1870, engine manufacturer and railroad executive, a founder of the Franklin Institute and its President, 1842–1854, *DAB*), this movement represented a transformation of the Institute in the 1830s from a mechanics' society to an institute for science. The investigation of Smith's needle neatly reflects the direction in which Bache and his coterie were steering not just the committee but also the Institute. As Bruce Sinclair has written (*Philadelphia's Philosopher Mechanics: A History of the Franklin Institute, 1824–1865* [Baltimore, 1974], p. 151), "The Committee on Science and the Arts still retained the responsibility for the examination of new inventions; but it was also made the society's scientific arm, with power to initiate whatever investigations it chose, and was charged in its efforts to sustain 'the scientific character of the Institute.'"

Moses Smith had patented his improvement in the mariner's and surveyor's needle in 1830. The editor of the Franklin Institute *Journal*, a journal "devoted to the Mechanic Arts, Manufactures, General Science, and the Recording of American and other Patented Inventions," Thomas P. Jones (1774–1848, *DAB*) printed the specifications of Moses Smith's patent in October 1830, *6*:238–240, appending to the description his own reaction that Smith's claims were lacking in any scientific merit:

> Whilst those who are acquainted with all the known facts are unable to explain and connect them, it so happens in this, as in similar cases, that there are bold spirits who, although they have acquired but half an idea respecting a single fact, are able by the aid of 'the stuff which dreams are made of' to draw the inferences, and arrive at conclusions, which are far in advance of those who think it necessary to 'render a reason'.... To anyone acquainted with electricity the absurdity [of Smith's claims] . . . will be at once manifest; we are of opinion that the whole is in good keeping in this particular, and that the only advantage resulting from the patent will be to the treasury of the United States.

As Superintendent of the Patent Office, his opinion was influential, even though the law at that time did not give him authority to block issuance of the patent.

Smith was understandably dismayed. Portraying himself as "a mere practical man . . . in the eve of my life," Smith implored Jones not "to prejudice the minds of most of your readers against the needle itself. . . . Leaving, therefore, the discussion of the theories to others, and abandoning every thing in my specification which is merely theoretical, I will merely ask you to state to the public the facts which I have recently exhibited to you, as I think by so doing you may do an essential service to society, and perhaps benefit an humble individual." *Journal of the Franklin Institute*, February 1831, 7:95. Annexed to Smith's plea, Jones's response indicated that he conceded that the invention did work and did indeed have important practical applications. Ibid., p. 96. At about this point, apparently, Jones referred the invention and claims to the Committee on Inventions (records of which have not survived).

Smith's invention was intended to nullify the deflection of a surveyor's or mariner's compass needle caused by its magnetic attraction to large or nearby masses of metal. Compass deflection was prevalent aboard ships of the day carrying massive cannons and other bulky iron equipment. The problem was well known and studied long before Smith's patented improvement. For instance, Peter Barlow, *An Essay on Magnetic Attractions* (London, 1820; Henry had the second edition, London, 1824) offered a system for determining the amount and nature of the deflection by means of a movable metallic disk and for calculating the true compass reading. Peter Lecount, *A Description of the Changeable Magnetic Properties Possessed by All Iron Bodies* (London, 1820), used a similar approach, claiming that his work was independent of Barlow's. Both books survive in the Henry Library, and annotations indicate that Henry had read them carefully in his Albany days.

Smith's invention aimed not at correcting deflected needle readings but at avoiding them in the first place. He proposed placing metallic caps, or "feeders," over the ends of the needle, thus effectively de-sensitizing the magnetic needle to a point where it would not be attracted to the nearby iron; the earth's magnetism would therefore have overriding influence on the compass. He also patented his system of restoring magnetism to the needle in the event that its magnetism was deranged by the firing of cannons or other violent disturbances. He called for tapping the needle with an "electric rod," a long thin brass rod. Producing magnetism by percussion was by no means new, and that aspect of Smith's patent, while practicable, was a case in point for Thomas P. Jones's critical remarks.

On the other hand, Smith's use of caps, or "feeders," on the needle was of considerable interest to Bache and his colleagues at the Institute. Their investigation was one of six which were begun by the Committee on Inventions and later completed by the Committee on Science and the Arts. Joseph Henry was invited to join the Committee in its experiments when he was visiting in Philadelphia in the fall of 1833 (see above, Henry to Harriet Henry, November 1, 1833). The findings of the Committee were reported in March 1834. The draft of the report, surviving in the Franklin Institute Archives, is in Bache's hand and was signed by Bache and Lukens.

Significantly, the report filed by the Committee in March 1834 (*Journal of the Franklin Institute, 14*:318–320) treated both the practicability of Smith's "feeders" and their scientific principle. The Committee conceded "that the needle is less deflected with the 'feeders' on, than when they are off. . . ," but they asserted that Smith's invention held nothing new for science. Henry's contribution bears on that conclusion. In the final paragraph of their report the Committee added not only that the principle was not new, but also that the invention had essentially been made some forty-six years earlier. Their report states that Captain O'Brien Drury in the *Transactions* of the Irish Academy for 1788 had employed the same kind of device for the same effect. The Committee concluded, "Capt. O'Brien Drury . . . modestly submits his invention to the judgment of those who are qualified to appreciate its merits, and we conceive that this judgment may be considered to have been formed by the neglect of the invention during the forty-six years which have elapsed since its publication." Ibid., p. 320.

Helping with the experiments in the fall of 1833, Henry may have mentioned seeing some such "feeder" device in the existing literature. We do know that Henry read avidly in this field of study. So when Bache, in this particular letter, asks for "the *antique* corresponding to Smith's needle," Henry readily supplied him with the citation (see below, Henry to Bache, July 15, 1834). The final paragraph of the draft of the Committee's report, containing that citation, was clearly added by Bache at a later but unspecified time. The date of the entire report remained unchanged in the printed version (March 13, 1834); this concluding paragraph was simply added, undoubtedly after Bache had examined the Drury article (see below, Bache to Henry, July 25, 1834), in time for inclusion in the November 1834 number of the *Journal*.

This was Henry's first documented experience at sitting on a council of scientists to review inventions and patents (an earlier such appointment for which there is no supportive evidence appears in *Henry Papers, 1*:210). In subsequent years he would serve in that capacity many times. Because scientists often apply different standards arising from a frame of reference alien to the inventors' world, scientific councils' judgements on inventions frequently disquiet the inventors, as in this case with Smith's needle. This area of conflict between such scientific committees and inventors will present itself many times in Henry's later activities. Henry's continued interest in the problem of the deflection of shipboard compass needles will reappear later in a similar context. See Nathan Reingold, "Science in the Civil War: The Permanent Commission of the Navy Department," *Isis*, 1958, *49*:307–318.

We shall have one more coadjutor in this quarter, in our friend Courtenay.[2] I expect to see him here in a week or ten days.

Have you ever worked for the diurnal changes of intensity.[3] On the fourth, 5th and 6th, I had leisure to do so & with good results.

Very truly Yours
A D Bache

When was the needle wh. you gave me magnetized? It is a most lively little gentleman.

[2] Edward C. Courtenay (for whom see above, Courtenay to Henry, January 3, 1833, footnote 1) served as Professor of Mathematics at the University of Pennsylvania from 1834 to 1836.

[3] At this time Bache was working with Courtenay to compare the magnetic intensity at Philadelphia with that of New York and, later, other locations in the Northeast. Determining a corrective for the diurnal variation (which they conceived of as a cyclical change within each day) was an important step in standardizing intensity readings taken at different times of the day. But, applying additional corrections for arc and temperature, they still encountered gross variations for which they sought Joseph Henry's advice. See below, Bache to Henry, September 17, 1834.

For Henry's reply to Bache's question, and the others in this letter, see the next document.

TO ALEXANDER DALLAS BACHE

Bache Papers, Smithsonian Archives[1]

Princeton July 15th 1834

My Dear Sir

Permit me to congratulate you on the election of your friend Prof. Courtney to the chair of Mathematics in your Institution. To me the event was entirely unexpected as the rumour with us was that either Prof. Vethake[2] or Davies[3] was to be the person.

My object in writing at this time is to inquire if you think the degree of *A M* would now be acceptable to Prof. C— from Princeton. I mentioned to Prof. Mclean the vice Pres. of our College about six months ago the propriety of conferring on Courtney the degree of *A M.* He requested me to bear the subject in mind until the next meeting of the board of trustees when it should be attende[d] to. The thought now strikes me that perhaps Prof. C. or his friends may have some objections to his receiving *A M* from

[1] The document bears several of Mary Henry's editorial marks, indicating she had copies made. One copy survives.

[2] Henry Vethake, identified in *Henry Papers, 1*:17; in 1834, he was Professor of Mathematics, Astronomy, and Natural Philosophy at New York University.

[3] Charles Davies, Professor of Mathematics at West Point; *Henry Papers, 1*:280.

Princeton or any other Institution since he has become one of the faculty of the University of Pennsylvania. I presume however that there is no necessity, of the fact of his receiving the degree being made public and he may thus have the advantage of the *letters* without attracting any attention in receiving them.

I have had no communication with Prof. C. on this subject, but took it for granted that while at West Point a degree would not be unacceptable and intended that he should be agreeably surprised by receiving a mark of respect which he so eminently deserves.[4]

I am at present so much engaged in my course that I can find no leisure for any thoughts but those which relate to my college duties. The senior class however leave college in about 4 weeks from this when I hope to be able to complete some investigations which have been laying on hand for months.

We will be very happy to see Mrs B. and yourself in Princeton at any time you can make it convenient but particularly in the month of August after the first week as I shall then be a free man. Do not forget that you have promised me a visit.

Mr. Hamilton of the Institute was so good as to send me a notice of the meeting of the Institute[5] but owing to the reform mail system the letter did not reach Princeton until the day after the event.

Yours in haste
Jos Henry

PS Write me in reference to Courtney

July 15th 10'oclock PM

I wrote this letter in the morning, sent it to the office & supposed it was in Phila^d^. This evening I accidentally called at the office a few minutes since, found your favor of July 13th and learned that my letter [had] arrived to late for the mail.

The paper I mentioned describing a feeder similar to Smith's may be found in the Transactions of the Royal Irish Academy for 1788.[6]

I find the following short account of it in a work entitled Memoirs of Science and the Arts or an abridgement of the transactions of the Learned Societies in Europe and America vol 1 part 1st p. 426—

[4] Courtenay received an A.M. from Princeton in 1834. Henry's quandary is understandable in view of the persistent ambiguities about the significance and roles of higher academic degrees, particularly the Masters, in the United States. See below, Bache to Henry, July 25, 1834, footnote 3.

[5] See above, Hamilton to Henry, May 21, 1834.

[6] "Observations on the Magnetic Fluid," pp. 119–120.

"Observations on the Magnetic fluid. By Capt. O'Brien Drury, of the Royal Navy"

"The subject of this very short paper is an experimental observation, that by casing the needle of the compass with thin polished soft iron, or arming it with the same at its poles, it preserves its magnetism much more perfectly than without those precautions."[7]

The casing with thin soft iron appears to me to be identical with the plan of Smith;[8] by referring however to the original paper more may be learned on the subject.

I have never made a series of observations to determine the daily variation in intensity but have observed differences in my observations made at different times of the day which I ascribed to the daily variation.[9] The needle was magnetized about april 1831—or more than 3 years since.[10]

J.H.

[7] Henry's account is complete. The full title of the journal, published in London, was *Memoirs of the Sciences and the Arts, or an Abridgement of the Transactions Published by the Principal Learned and Oeconomical Societies Established in Europe, Asia, and America*. Volume one, part one, appeared in 1793.

[8] It was not; see Bache's reply of July 25, below, footnote 4.

[9] See, for example, *Henry Papers, 1*:336n.

[10] A response to Bache's final question in his foregoing letter to Henry, July 13, 1834. Bache and Courtenay used Henry's horizontal vibrating needle in their observations, "On the Relative Horizontal Intensities of Terrestrial Magnetism. . . ," for which see below, Bache to Henry, September 17, 1834, especially footnote 4.

FROM EBENEZER EMMONS[1]

Henry Papers, Smithsonian Archives

Williams College July 15 1834[2]

Dear Sir,

My Object in addressing you at this time is to make inquiry in relation to the place where the best *magnetic* & *electro magnetic* instruments may be purchased. Whether magnetic instruments of the best kind may be procured in this country & if so where?[3] Or to put the question in another

[1] Ebenezer Emmons (1790–1863), for whom see *Henry Papers, 1*:347. He started at Williams as a lecturer in chemistry; by this date he was Professor of Natural History.

[2] The year is entered in a hand other than Emmons's, perhaps in Mary Henry's day.

[3] Henry's reply has not been found. His file note on this letter indicates the response was dated August 15, 1834. Henry undoubtedly mentioned the shop of James R. Chilton in New York City. At Princeton Henry had frequent contact with Chilton, who not only carried a regular line of electromagnetic apparatus but also constructed special equipment for others, sometimes to Henry's specifications (see below, Chilton to Henry, December 29,

shape in case one of our Prof is going out to Europe to purchase apparatus will it be better to purchase instruments of the above mentioned kind abroad or at home.[4] If Sir, you will favor me with an early answer to these questions you will

Oblige yours
Truly
E Emmons

Mr Hopkins[5] Prof. of Math etc in this institution goes out to Europe early next fall for the purpose of procuring apparatus both Philosophical & Chemical.

1834). Henry found electrical and magnetic equipment at the shop of Isaiah Lukens in Philadelphia (for whom see above, Green to Henry, February 13, 1834, footnote 1). Henry also had dealings for apparatus with John Millington in Philadelphia (see above, Millington and Green to Henry, December 31, 1832), as well as a number of lesser known individual instrument makers mentioned in "J Henry's a/c with Philosophical Hall previous to 1837," Princeton University Archives.

[4] Despite commendable American efforts, European instrument makers still represented the highest standard for philosophical apparatus in general. Many of their American counterparts, like Chilton, marketed both imported and domestic products. But for magnetic and electromagnetic apparatus specifically a European trip would probably not have been justified. Nonetheless, many college presidents and professors (including Joseph Henry in 1837) preferred a European junket, and many did just that in this period. They were enticed to Europe by the ready availability of a general line of philosophical apparatus, as well as books. Stanley M. Guralnick, "Science and the American College, 1828–1860" (Ph.D. dissertation, University of Pennsylvania, 1969), pp. 121–123.

[5] Albert Hopkins (1807–1872), a graduate of Williams (B.A. 1826), was Professor of Mathematics and Natural Philosophy at Williams, 1829–1838. Thereafter he was Professor of Natural Philosophy there until his death. He did indeed travel to Europe in 1834 for the purpose of acquiring philosophical apparatus for the College. Bringing back "sidereal clocks, Troughton and Simms transit instruments, and a Herschelean reflector of ten feet focus," Hopkins launched a campaign to build an observatory at Williams. Largely through his efforts the Williams observatory was completed in 1838. In use today, it is "probably the first observatory of true permanence" in the United States. Ibid., pp. 276–277; quotes are from p. 146.

FROM ALEXANDER DALLAS BACHE

Henry Papers, Smithsonian Archives

University
Phila[d] July 25. 1834

My dear Sir

Excuse me that in the midst of a press of college business I have not hitherto been able to reply to your letter[1] and now have but a few lines of answer written in the examination room.

[1] Above, July 15, 1834.

Courtenay could not be otherwise than gratified by a degree from your institution whatever situation he may occupy; he was recommended by our Faculty for the degree of A.M. before there was any notion that Dr Adrain would find it expedient to resign,[2] and degrees from different quarters are perhaps now a days the only mode of testifying respect for a man's character since a degree from *some where* is obtainable so readily.[3]

I thank you for your reference to O'Brien Drury, or some name of that sort; his paper is not much longer than the extract, occupying but a page if laterally compressed. Very truly Yours

A D. Bache

I am not quite satisfied that the armature which he proposes is intended to be like Smith's and the casing is total; this by the bye would "serve (still better) to collect the scattered particles of magnetism." I quote.[4] Yours.

[2] Robert Adrain (1775–1843), previously of Rutgers and Columbia, taught mathematics from 1827 to 1834 at the University of Pennsylvania, where he was also vice-provost. Administrative failures and unpopularity with students reportedly led to his resignation, after which he turned to grammar school teaching. *DAB*; *DSB*; S. M. Guralnick, "Science and the American College, 1828–1860" (Ph.D. dissertation, University of Pennsylvania, 1969), pp. 234–236.

[3] The Master of Arts at American colleges in this period could be either an honorary or semiautomatic degree. As an honorary award, it was analogous to the higher status Doctor of Divinity or Laws. It was a common practice for a college graduate to obtain an M.A. in course. That is, three years after graduation, a B.A. recipient could receive a virtually automatic M.A. by returning to his college just before commencement, showing that he was "worthy thereof," and paying a modest degree fee. In 1840, Columbia College required eight dollars and usually some trivial scholarly exercise. Of nineteenth-century Harvard, it was said that "All a Harvard man had to do for his Master's degree was to pay five dollars and stay out of jail." (Morison, cited below, pp. 34–35). Automatic conferral generally faded out with the advent of the graduate school in the second half of the century.

Even "degrees from different quarters" did not necessarily signify accomplishment, since a B.A. or M.A. holder from one American college could obtain the same degree "*ad eundem gradum*" from another college upon request and payment of degree fees. Milton Halsey Thomas, Introduction to *Columbia University Officers and Alumni, 1754–1857, Compiled for the Committee on General Catalogue* (New York, 1936), p. xiii; Samuel Eliot Morison, *Three Centuries of Harvard, 1636–1936* (Cambridge, Massachusetts, 1936), pp. 26, 34–35; Harvard University, *Quinquennial Catalogue of the Officers and Graduates, 1636–1920* (Cambridge, Massachusetts, 1920), p. 928.

[4] We cannot identify the source of this quotation. It does not appear in the full or excerpted Drury article, nor in Smith's patent specifications. A prevalent theory was that the magnetization of iron depended on the alignment of constituent magnetic particles. The purpose of Drury's casing or armature (a bit of soft iron connecting the poles) was the preservation of the needle's power, while Smith's feeder was designed to minimize local magnetic disturbances from iron masses on land or shipboard.

July 26, 1834

TO STEPHEN BELKNAP[1]

Retained Copy,[2] Henry Papers, Smithsonian Archives

Princeton July 26th 1834

Mr Stephen Belknap

Sir

In answer to your inquiries respecting the application of a great magnetic power to a common compass needle I must inform you that the thing is utterly impossible.

A small piece of iron or Steel is capable of receiving only a small magnetic power.[3] If you wish to construct a powerful magnet you must use a large piece of metal for the instrument itself and when you wish to test its power it must be applied to a large piece of iron. There are many visionary projects afloat among ingenious mechanics in respet to the application of magnetism to some purpose in the arts but from the present state of

[1] With the aid of a fragmentary document found among Henry's Papers in the Smithsonian Archives, we have tentatively identified Henry's correspondent as one Stephen Belknap (1766–1848) from Newburgh, New York. We strongly suspect that the fragment is a portion of Belknap's incoming letter which elicited this response from Henry. Another vexing piece of Mary Henry's legacy, the document consists of an edited portion of an original letter inserted in Mary Henry's manuscript draft of the biography of her father. Dated "Newburgh, July 14o, 1834," the letter begins "D Sir, A few days ago I noticed in a N York paper the subject [which] is as follows." Editing out this sentence, Mary Henry retained only the newspaper quotation that followed. The quotation corresponds verbatim with the first two paragraphs of the report on Henry's magnet in the *New-York Standard* of October 1, 1833, a widely reprinted article that we have given in full above, Cooper to Henry, November 16, 1833, footnote 2. Mary Henry excised all but a few traces of the remainder of the letter, leaving no signature or indication as to why the letter was written. Similarity of subject matter and the proximity of the dates of the fragment and Henry's letter suggest Belknap as the victim of Mary Henry's editing. Our suspicions are reinforced by the fact that Belknap was a familiar and prominent name in early nineteenth-century Newburgh, although Stephen Belknap himself left no identifiable mark on local history. So far as we know, Stephen Belknap appears only as a name in local genealogies and as an inscription in a Newburgh cemetery. Edward M. Ruttenber, *History of the County of Orange with a History of the Town and City of Newburgh* (Newburgh, New York, 1875), pp. 358–359, 361. Rufus Emery, *A Record of the Inscriptions in the Old Town Burial Ground of Newburgh, New York* (Newburgh, New York, 1898), p. 42. The substance of Henry's letter vaguely hints at some industrial or commercial connection for Belknap. See footnote 4, below.

[2] Henry's letter bears no signature, address, or postmark. The words "not sent" occur at the bottom of the document, and a file note reads "Answer to Belknap Lette[r] not sent 1834." We have no evidence that any other reply was drafted. Henry may indeed have reconsidered and sent a more sympathetic reply than this one or simply have declined to respond out of his evident exasperation with Belknap's inquiry.

[3] Henry and Ten Eyck had carefully investigated the limits of magnetization in a small quantity of soft iron in Henry's early article "On the Application of the Principle of the Galvanic Multiplier to Electro-Magnetic Apparatus, and Also to the Development of Great Magnetic Power in Soft Iron, with a Small Galvanic Element," *Silliman's Journal*, 1831, *19*:400–408, especially p. 407.

knowledge on the subject these projects must be pronounced intirely unphilosophical.[4]

[4] The only possible clue we have to Belknap's mechanical ingenuity are three patents assigned to Stephen Belknap for various tool designs in 1809, 1811, and 1814. For the first patent, Belknap is listed as being in New York, probably the City. For the last two, he is in the Washington, D.C. area. Henry's outburst against Belknap's "unphilosophical" (i.e., unscientific) ingenuity was by now habitual rhetoric. See his response to a similar solicitation in *Henry Papers, 1*:349. *Burke's Index*, pp. 54, 219, 275.

"RECORD OF EXPERIMENTS"

Henry Papers, Smithsonian Archives

August 15, 1834

With the following entry from Henry's "Record of Experiments" we introduce an extensive, important series of documentation that will run through the next several volumes of *The Papers of Joseph Henry*. The entries, drawn from three large manuscript books preserved among Henry's papers in the Smithsonian Archives, begin in 1834 with the document printed below and continue through 1863. The title, Record of Experiments, appears on the spine of one of the volumes. In modern terminology, these are Henry's laboratory notebooks—the principal and most consistent record of his activities as a working experimental physicist at Princeton and, later, at the Smithsonian Institution.

Although a broad range of subject areas are represented in the Record, the majority of entries deal with experiments in electricity and magnetism, chiefly from Henry's highly productive Princeton years. In the pages of the Record are the theories, suppositions, and results underlying Henry's scientific publications, as well as copious experiments on topics never treated directly by Henry in print. The experimental notes both enhance and go far beyond the published record, mapping out the full dimensions of Henry's scientific life.

Almost all of the entries in the Record of Experiments will be printed in these volumes. Even the sketchiest entries represent stages in the research process, if only to depict temporary confusion, a wrong turn, or inconclusive results. But it is the cumulative effect of the entries that makes the Record such a valuable source for understanding Henry's scientific development. Collectively, the entries from the laboratory notebooks provide a relatively continuous framework for tracing the direction and scope of Henry's experimental activity. Almost as important, they enable us to pull together the scientific references scattered in other Henry manuscripts—in his correspondence, reading notes, lecture materials, and in other notebooks of the period. The experimental notebooks are the only surviving Henry documents that provide this kind of unifying structure.

Out of Henry's carefully maintained laboratory record emerges not only the content of research but the tempo of a scientific life—the creative episodes, the stagnant interludes, the interruptions of classroom responsibility, the heightened activity inspired by a recent article or conversation with a colleague. Far more than a mere catalog of experimental data, the notebooks also functioned as a kind of scientific journal for Henry, depicting not only the progress of experiments but aspects of Henry's nonlaboratory activities as well, especially as they impinged on the pace of his experimental work. Thus, after a significant gap in his research schedule, Henry mentions overriding obligations like classroom lectures or responsibilities in another city, often with a suggestion of frustration: "Since the last date," he noted on March 24, 1840, "I have been constantly engaged with college duties and consequently my investigations of the experimental kind have been at a stand." In a one-man laboratory like Henry's, the arrival or departure of a laboratory assistant could also have a significant impact on his progress—another fact Henry notes in the Record.

Whatever the obstacles, Michael Faraday was always a strong incentive for renewed attention to experimental activity. At one point, after a six-month interregnum in his experiments, Henry resumes the record with the note, "I have lately received Dr Faradays 14th Series, and find that he has crossed the track of my last paper . . . commenced to day some experiments to determine the cause of Dr F's not getting the same results" (entry of May 13, 1839). There are also long-term patterns discernible in the development of the record. The entries are rather sparse in the beginning but begin to assume substance as the Princeton years progress. Certain years, like 1838 and 1840, were particularly productive, at least as measured by the number of entries. Understandably, there are visible increases in activity during the spring and fall vacation periods at Princeton and even more pronounced surges during the weeks preceding a major publication. There is a rather sudden diminution of activity reflected in the record as Henry approached the administrative responsibilities of the Smithsonian years, and entries become sporadic afterwards.

The Record of Experiments may be seen as performing a dual function in Henry's work. While they are personal, working documents, they also served as a rather formal record of Henry's experimental accomplishments. We will first consider them in their more formal aspect.

Assuming that the Record represents the only systematic long-term record of research kept by Henry, the question arises as to why Henry started making these notes in 1834. The most obvious explanation is that Henry had reached a stage of professional maturity at which keeping an experimental record was a proper thing to do and necessary in view of projected researches. Soon after coming to Princeton, Henry embarked on an extensive research program in electricity and magnetism, the results of which would be communicated to the American Philosophical Society in a series of major papers. The experimental notebooks mark the beginning of that program, delayed for a time by the need to adjust to the new environment, by teaching responsibilities, and by the necessity of preparing new research apparatus, especially the galvanic battery.

The Record may have had a further, equally important purpose for Henry, related to his continuing concern for establishing the priority of his discoveries in electricity and magnetism. His published claims to discovery having been undermined more than once, Henry recognized the importance of documenting his actual progress in the laboratory. For instance, finding his 1832 paper on electromagnetic induction overshadowed by the prior publications of Faraday on the same subject, Henry maintained that his results had been achieved over a long period independently of Faraday,[1] but apparently could offer no systematic documentation in support of his claims. A carefully dated laboratory account would provide at least some evidence for similar claims in the future, if such were necessary.

Henry indeed intended the laboratory record for other eyes as well as his own, judging by important, unexpected evidences found in the pages of the Record itself. At several points in the volumes are insertions in what appears to be an official secretarial hand witnessing Henry's periodic submission of the original records to a committee of the American Philosophical Society for which most of his published results were destined. According to these brief notations, the laboratory records were submitted on four different occasions: November 2, 1838; June 19, 1840; June 17, 1842; and November 3, 1843. These dates correspond precisely with Henry's submission to the Society of Contributions III, IV, V, and a fourth communication in 1843.[2] With one minor discrepancy, the committee of the Society to which the record books were referred is the same committee which refereed the publications submitted by Henry on the same date. Although the committee members (such as Bache, Patterson, and Hare) did not sign the Record themselves but left the duty to a secretary, the notebooks were clearly turned over to the Society in the interests of priority. Henry says as much in a June 24, 1842, letter to A. D. Bache (Mary Henry Copy, Henry Papers, Smithsonian Archives), "I gave a verbal account of my last series of experiments to the Society on Friday night and presented my record of the same for reference to a committee of which you were chosen chairman. . . . The book contained a record of all the experiments placed under their proper dates. I wish these inspected by the committee as my vouches for the time these were submitted to the society." Bache, deeply concerned with Henry's problems of priority, may in fact have urged Henry to follow this strategy. The notebooks

[1] "On the Production of Currents and Sparks of Electricity from Magnetism," *Silliman's Journal*, 1832, 22:403–404.

[2] This last submission date presents something of a mystery. According to the *Proceedings of the American Philosophical Society* for November 3, 1843 (*4*:22–23), in addition to an oral presentation on diverse electrical topics, Henry submitted a communication "in continuation of his researches on electro-dynamic induction," which was referred to a committee of Bache, Patterson, and Lukens. As yet, we are unable to locate any published result of this communication. A fragment in the Henry Papers suggests it may have been intended as another "Contribution" and dealt with the topic of magnetic distribution (see Box 23, folder 2, "Electricity and Magnetism Notes Etc."). The fate of Henry's paper may be disclosed in our researches for a later volume of *The Papers of Joseph Henry*.

were apparently only briefly in the hands of the committee, for, in most cases, Henry's record resumes shortly after the dates of presentation. We would guess that the committee's examination of the documents was no more than a formal gesture verifying their submission. Henry's practice of presenting his original data to an examining committee was apparently highly unorthodox. So far as we can judge from the Society's records, scientists were not expected to submit their original notes along with their publications, nor did any make it a practice to do so.

Despite this intended public function of the notebooks, the Record of Experiments is at the same time a collection of highly personal documents that reveal a side of science rarely seen or documented so fully. They constitute an invaluable resource for understanding how a very competent physical scientist of the nineteenth century actually worked. In October 1843, Henry paused to observe in his laboratory notebook, "These experiments exhibit the difficulty of passing from the known to the unknown, and by what almost insensible gradations, the truth is presented to the mind" (a marginal comment to the entry of September 25, 1840). More than any other documentary source left to us by Henry, the Record of Experiments bears out the truth of this maxim. In these laboratory records are not the clear experimental progressions displayed in published articles but a complex evolution of results and ideas, proceeding on several levels and in several directions. Rather than a succession of discoveries, one discerns tendencies and possibilities as Henry proceeds on the basis of working hypotheses and tentative, often tenuous, analogies, which he refines and reinterprets as his research develops. The notebook entries also yield subtle insights into Henry's working habits in the laboratory—his pace of research, how he organized experiments, how he dealt with the notorious unreliability of contemporary electrical instruments, or how he managed the ambiguities of the data.

We emphasize that the notebooks are very much a working record. Many of the entries are ambiguous and frustratingly sketchy; some were entered in haste; others appear on the basis of an uncrystallized idea; and still others were written in the midst of confusion and bafflement. There are also the inevitable inscrutabilities arising from Henry's frequent but understandable neglect at spelling out procedures or techniques obvious to him and to his contemporaries but cryptic to us today. Precisely how and when Henry entered his results in the Record is open to question. The relative neatness and clarity of the majority of entries, coupled with the absence of acid stains, damaged pages, and other signs of an active laboratory milieu, suggest the possibility that the notebooks were not literally at Henry's side during the actual performance of an experiment. Odd scraps of paper containing bits of experimental data scattered among Henry's papers may well have served this immediate purpose. Yet, Henry's notes are rough enough and display an air of immediacy casting doubt on the notion that they represent but a smoothed-over version of his experimental findings composed at some later time. In most cases, Henry apparently first compiled working data, then entered his results promptly into the Record—after each trial or perhaps after the completion of a short experimental series.

The Record soon became an invaluable aid to research, not only in the preparation of publications but in providing perspective on long-term progress. The documents show a pattern of careful editing and reediting by Henry himself, in at least two different kinds of ink. It is clear from this and other evidence that Henry regularly scrutinized his entire record to detect patterns of data, to draw together ideas, to cross-reference similar experiments and results, and to clear up problems in early experiments with more definite results reached, in some cases, years later. For instance, beside an experiment recorded on August 22, 1834, Henry noted at some later time, "I have found this really to be the case, see exp april 1840." In order to present Henry's entry as it was originally written, we have omitted such later commentary from our edited version of his text. We will discuss Henry's remarks and cross-references in our annotations. In most cases, any later results or experiments referred to by Henry will appear under an entry in a later installment of our series.

The Record of Experiments also conveys other subtleties of Henry's scientific personality and research style. For example, early entries in the notebooks tend to be rather terse statements of intentions and results. As Henry's research develops over the years, however, one has the impression of a fuller, more literary record. Entries expand in interpretation and commentary. In its later stages, Henry's record attains a rich narrative style such as one finds, for example, throughout the laboratory *Diary* of Michael Faraday.

Other experimental records survive among Henry's papers, but none approach the fullness or completeness of the Record of Experiments. They tend to be sporadic and to deal with specialized topics. Other laboratory notebooks of a more systematic and general character may have once existed (especially for the Albany period), but, to our knowledge, none has survived. For the Princeton period and after, all evidence points to the Record of Experiments as the most faithful reflection of Henry's ongoing research activities and interests.

Physically, the three volumes of the Record of Experiments are large in format, measuring approximately 13 inches by 8 inches. Like some other notebooks kept by Henry, they show evidence of other uses before his. The first volume, for example, contains what appear to be accounts in an unknown, neatly clerical hand. For reasons obscure to us, Henry's notes commence (with the item printed below) at the middle of the first volume, carry through to the end, and then resume at the beginning of the volume. Notes in the subsequent volumes follow a more conventional pattern. The first volume of the Record spans researches conducted through September 1839. The second volume carries the record forward into 1842; the third concludes in 1863, ending with some undated remarks and a brief index. Most of the entries follow a chronological sequence, each entry corresponding to a single day's efforts; items out of chronological order or undated will be footnoted by the editors.

In our editing, we have preserved the style of Henry's notes as far as possible within the limits of clarity. The format of the entries has been standardized somewhat in the interests of readability. We have moved Henry's experiment numbers to the left margin and italicized them. We have shifted Henry's marginal comments—usually very brief evaluations like "good experiment"—to our footnotes, and removed the lines Henry often used to separate experiments. At the same time, to preserve the spontaneity of the documents, we have been more liberal than usual in retaining idiosyncracies of spelling and punctuation. The documents show evidence of careful scrutiny by Mary Henry's editorial corps. Fortunately, it appears their notations are consistently in pencil, contrasting with the ink used by Henry. We are, as usual, systematically omitting Mary Henry's markings from the text.

Exp on the spark from long & short wire with circular battery.[3]

[3] This entry is the first clear evidence that Henry has resumed the experimental researches on electromagnetic induction that occupied his last months in Albany and would become the foundation of his scientific reputation. During his first year and a half at Princeton, Henry was busy with setting up his laboratory at Philosophical Hall and constructing needed apparatus. In the meantime, he pursued nonlaboratory observations of terrestrial magnetism, auroras, and meteor showers. When he resumed laboratory research, he began with an extension of the self-induction experiments discussed briefly and hurriedly at the end of his article "On the Production of Currents and Sparks of Electricity from Magnetism," *Silliman's Journal*, 1832, 22:408. While Michael Faraday, working independently, had preceded Henry into print on the discovery of mutual induction, Henry believed that the self-inductive discovery was uniquely his. As Henry described the effect in 1832, he was able to convert a low intensity output from a small galvanic battery into high intensity by connecting long wires and various coils across the electrodes. When the circuit was interrupted, the heightened intensity was evidenced by vivid sparks at the point of disjunction. By analogy with mutual induction, Henry believed that the intense spark was produced by the inductive reaction of the current upon itself. At the time, he concluded that the effects were only "somewhat increased" by the substitution of coils for straight conductors. Although Henry's experiments on self-induction in 1832 were hasty and inconclusive, he obviously thought the subject eminently worthy of future investigation.

Documentary background is scarce for Henry's early work on the phenomenon in Albany. The entry now under consideration seems to take up the subject esentially where Henry left it with the 1832 publication. Henry was virtually the only worker in that area. Michael Faraday, in his first article on electromagnetic induction in 1831, had predicted a self-inductive effect theoretically, but apparently had dropped the subject for the time being. (See Section 74 of his "First Series" of Experimental Researches in Electricity.) In a later article, he pointed out that electrical investigators had long known of sparks produced when the coil surrounding an electromagnet was interrupted (Section 1050 of his Ninth Series). But Henry was evidently the only major physicist to subject the phenomenon to extensive systematic investigation. Future documents in this volume will show that Faraday was soon close on Henry's heels, working independently, publishing quickly, and, once again, arousing Henry's fears about scientific priority. (According to Faraday's laboratory *Diary* [London, 1932], 2:330, Faraday began his experiments on self-induction in October 1834.)

Henry presented the results of his renewed investigations orally to the American Philosophical Society early in 1835 and published them later in the year in the Society's *Transactions* as "Contributions to Electricity and Magnetism. No. II. On the Influence of a Spiral Conductor in Increasing the Intensity of Electricity from a Galvanic Arrangement of a Single Pair, Etc.," 1837, n.s. 5:223–231. As the title indicates, Henry had taken a heightened interest in the effect of coils in intensifying currents inductively. Henry's growing recognition of the remarkable effects of coils is already evident in this initial notebook entry. Far less evident is the role of any theories

Exp 1st Battery feebly excited with piece of bell wire[4] 5 inches long *no* spark

2nd With same sized wire 20 feet long, feeble spark

3 With larger wire 1/10 inch, spark rather brighter

4 With coil about 40 feet long, wire same as 1st & 2nd bright spark with snap—

5 With coil of copper ribbon[5]—60 feet long 1 inch wide, thin as paper—loud snap more intense than with the coil of small wire

6 With the copper ribbon of same length as last but con[tain]ing about 1/10th matter, no spark when straight, when coiled a bright spark. When straight again no spark—spark the same from coiled wire:

7 Exp 6 repeated with the same result

8 The batteries were both used and arranged for intensity;[6] when the poles were united by two copper ribbons, each about 2 feet long. The spark given was then feeble but there appeared to be a slight deflagration[7] of the copper when the two were rubbed together—

9 Instead of the ribbons in the last exp two coils of ribbons one 60 feet & the other 30 were used, the result was a brilliant spark and vivid deflagration of the metals

---

Henry might have already had in conducting his experiments on this subject. Later notebook entries are equally wanting in theoretical content. Nevertheless, in the published results, Henry unhesitatingly discusses the various hypotheses "which have served as the basis of my investigations. . . . " In his correspondence, Henry also occasionally refers to unspecified theoretical explanations. We have reserved our reconstruction of Henry's theory of self-induction for one of these later mentions; see below, Henry to Bache, January 12, 1835, footnote 5.

[4] Henry elsewhere specified bell wire as being .045 of an inch in diameter. "On the Application of the Galvanic Multiplier to Electro-Magnetic Apparatus, and Also to the Development of Great Magnetic Power in Soft Iron, with a Small Galvanic Element," *Silliman's Journal*, 1831, *19*:402.

[5] The introduction of insulated coils of flat copper ribbon was one of Henry's major innovations in this period. Not evident in his Albany researches, the coils were apparently devised soon after his coming to Princeton. The first known occurrence of the coils in Henry's manuscripts is in a notebook entry from October 22, 1833, printed above. Henry soon discovered that, with suitable power sources, ribbon coils gave the maximum intensification of inductive effects. The coils became the mainstays of his subsequent electromagnetic researches, especially in self- and mutual induction. The unique coils became widely known through Henry's publications. In November 1839 Michael Faraday noted that five of Henry's induction coils were in use in Britain (Thomas Martin, ed., *Faraday's Diary*, 8 vols. [London, 1932–1936], *4*:14). Several examples of the ribbon coils survive among the Henry apparatus at Princeton University (see the illustrations to this volume).

[6] We assume that Henry has introduced another circular battery, connected in series with the first one.

[7] For the deflagration effect, see below, Sept 25, 26th [1834], footnote 2.

Exp 10 When the batteries were arranged for quantity[8] all else as before the spark was about the same & the same difference as before with the short ribbons.

Ex 11 Gold leaf between the coils on the surface of mercury,[9] no increased effect over the short ribbons or at least the difference was not very perceptable

12 Long th[in] wire used 300 feet in a coil, very feeble spark

13 Small wire between the poles of the large coils: action on iron filings about the same when passed through whole length or merely through the wire which was about 5 inches long

14 With the square battery when the action is somewhat intense a short ribbon will deflagrate the mercury, when a long coil of copper ribbon only causes a succession of snaps[10]

[8] Connected in parallel.

[9] Henry generally made his connections by immersing the ends of the wires in cups of mercury.

[10] Following this entry on the same page is a related observation dated September 18, printed below.

FROM JOHN TORREY

Henry Papers, Smithsonian Archives

New York, August 18th 1834

My dear friend

I am ashamed that I have so long delayed writing to you. My time has been very much occupied since I returned to the city. Still I might have found time to have prepared at least a short letter for you. You must not suppose that this is another examplification of the adage "out of sight, out of mind". Not so my friend. I think of you very often, & long to see you again. Your good wife has doubtless given you an account of our pleasant journey here from Princeton. I should certainly [have] taken her, & *suite* to our house, had not your friend[1] been waiting for [them] on the dock. If *you* dare pass through New York without stopping at my house—take care—but I won't threaten.

I called on James Chilton[2] the day after I returned & he said that you

[1] Not identified.

should have the wire. Has it been sent? Perhaps he is waiting for a private opportunity to forward it.

We are doing but little here in the way of science, for most of our naturalists & chemists are out of town. The attention of the people is a good deal taken up with the Cholera, which seems to be making slow advances among us. There is no panic, however, nor even any general alarm. You would not suppose, from walking the streets, that anything was amiss, but in private circles you are sure to hear frequent remarks on the health of the city. The epidemic does not appear to have reached Princeton, nor has it shown itself in the towns nearer New York, but it will probably spread, though it is to be hoped that its ravages will not equal those of the year 1832.[3]

My time since I returned has been a good deal occupied in botanical pursuits. Tell Mr. Dod,[4] I hope he will work at the map of Princeton, for I wish to have it lithographed at West-Point. It should be on a scale sufficiently large to indicate the principal localities where the rarer plants are found.

If you wish me to send out for an Electrical Machine for Princeton College, let me know as soon as possible. Can you do nothing with Kean[5] or Sprigg?[6] I have not seen Fyler[7] since he left us at Princeton. If I can catch

[2] For James Chilton, see above, Henry's notes of December 11, 1832, footnote 1.

[3] The cholera outbreak in 1834 was to be far less serious than that of 1832. The disease then disappeared from America until 1848. The favorite preventive measure for those people who could afford the expense was to leave the cities (physicians had theorized that cholera was caused by atmospheric contaminants or imbalances of atmospheric gases; the country air was presumed less dangerous). Consequently, most of the fatalities occurred among immigrants and poor black people. Charles E. Rosenberg, *The Cholera Years: The United States in 1832, 1849, and 1866* (Chicago, 1962), pp. 37, 39, 57, 75, 98, and 101.

[4] Albert Baldwin Dod, Professor of Mathematics at Princeton (see *Henry Papers, 1*:434). We have not found a copy of the map Torrey mentions.

[5] Torrey may be referring here to two persons he had in mind to build an electrical machine, but we have found no information on artisans named Kean and Sprigg. On the other hand, he may be mentioning two men associated with Princeton who were potential sources of funds. John Kean (1814–1895) graduated from Princeton in 1834. Three years earlier he had already inherited the estate of his uncle William Livingston (1723–1790) through the will of his paternal grandmother. John Kean's mother, Sarah Sabina Morris Kean (b. 1788), was a daughter of General Jacob Morris (1755–1844), an heir to the Morris fortune of New York. John Kean himself went on to great wealth as a railroad entrepreneur after graduation. Francis B. Lee, *Genealogical and Memorial History of the State of New Jersey* (New York, 1910), *4*:1532–1539.

[6] On the assumption that Torrey meant a donor of funds to build the machine, he may be referring to Samuel Sprigg (1782 or 1783–1855), who graduated from Princeton in 1806. Sprigg was Governor of Maryland from 1819 to 1822; during his administration, issues arose of popular election of the governor, proportional representation in the legislature, and the need for a rational transportation system. A landowner in Prince Georges County, Sprigg was active in the internal improvements movement of the state after leaving the governorship. Heinrich Buchholz, *Governors of Maryland from the Revolution to the Year 1908* (Baltimore, 1908), pp. 91–94. His son Osborn Sprigg also attended Princeton, and graduated in 1834. *Princeton Catalogue*, p. 147. Since Osborn and John Kean were classmates, there is a slight possibility that Torrey's remark about being able to do nothing

him on his way from the north, I shall exert myself to lighten his purse exactly \$100![8] Then you shall see what a pneumatic trough[9] I can make. Stop—"first *catch* a turbot."[10]

Do let me know what you are doing, & how I can serve you. After neglecting you so much about the promised *wire*, you will not feel disposed to favor me with any new commissions, but I will amend & endeavour to break up this wicked habit of *procrastination*, & the *irregularity* of action that so greatly injures my usefulness.[11]

The iron tube I will have prepared for you as soon as I have a little leisure. Did I understand you that one as large as a gunbarrel would answer, & that the length must be about 18 inches?[12]

with them refers to a discipline problem. We have found no evidence to support this hypothesis.

[7] Reverend Jared D. Fyler (d. 1853) graduated from Princeton in 1810 and then taught at the Princeton Academy until 1814 or shortly thereafter, when he moved to Charleston, South Carolina, to run a preparatory school there. He came back to Trenton, New Jersey, in the 1820s and began another academy, during which time he was nominated for the vice presidency of Princeton College. Fyler never held that post because the incumbent decided not to resign. In September 1833, Fyler was a member of the committee of alumni that set out to raise \$100,000 for the college endowment. He moved to Natchez, Mississippi, around 1837 and apparently lived in comfort there until his death. *Hageman*, 2:220; *Maclean*, 2:113, 246, and 360; and *Princeton Whig*, November 10, 1837.

[8] On April 8, 1834, the Princeton Trustees "On motion *Resolved*. That \$100. be appropriated for the use of the Philosophical Department." (Trustees' Minutes, *3*:259, Princeton University Archives.) There was nothing recorded in the minutes about Fyler being designated to transmit the funds, however. He was not a member of the Board of Trustees. As shown in letters printed below, Torrey believed that the alumni fund-raising committee might begin to dispense money before the entire sum was gathered. He was incorrect in this notion, but it would explain why he thought \$100 could be obtained from Fyler as a member of that committee.

[9] A device for collecting and holding gases over liquids. For a detailed description of the trough Torrey had in mind, see his letter to Henry below, December 29, 1834.

[10] This saying is probably a popular version of the line from Samuel Butler, *Hudibras* (1664–1668), part ii, canto iii, line 921:

> Make fools believe in their foreseeing
> Of things before they are in being
> To swallow gudgeons ere they're catch'd
> And count their chickens ere they're hatch'd.

William S. Walsh, *International Encyclopedia of Prose and Poetical Quotations* (Philadelphia, 1908), p. 287. Gudgeons and turbots are fish of no particular resemblance to each other.

[11] Torrey was being too modest here. One of the most valuable functions he served in the American scientific community in this period was to supply fellow practitioners with high quality instruments and books and to facilitate exchanges of botanical specimens among naturalists. The Torrey Papers at the New York Botanical Garden reflect this aspect of his career. His efforts were enhanced by his part-time residency in New York, with its many book and instrument dealers, and by his trip to Europe in the winter and spring of 1833, when he caught up with innovations in instrumentation there and met important foreign botanists eager for exchanges of plants with American colleagues. Andrew Denny Rodgers, *John Torrey: A Story of North American Botany* (Princeton, 1942), pp. 99–114. Joseph Henry's trip to Europe in 1837, to be documented in volume three of *The Papers of Joseph Henry*, was equally vital for his work as a physicist.

[12] We do not know precisely what Henry proposed to do with this simple piece of equipment. In his experiments at the Albany Academy, he used a gunbarrel to demonstrate that magnetism concentrated at the surface of iron rather than pervading the metal ("On the Application of the Principle of the Gal-

Has that sleepy bookseller[13] attended to my directions about the books?[14] If he has collected the money & will send it to R. Lockwood,[15] with the unsold volumes, I shall feel relieved—for I am responsible for the whole number of copies. Please tell Mr Maclean about this business.

Remember me to Mr. Alexander & all our Princeton friends.

Your truly
John Torrey

vanic Multiplier to Electro-Magnetic Apparatus, and Also to the Development of Great Magnetic Power in Soft Iron, with a Small Galvanic Element," *Silliman's Journal*, January 1831, *19*:406–407). His notes on electromagnetic experiments for August 23, 1834, printed below, indicate Henry used an iron tube to test shielding effects, probably with a larger diameter than a gunbarrel.

[13] Moore Baker (fl. 1830s) ran a Princeton bookstore which sold stationery, college texts, and books on theology and the classics. He experimented with a bindery and a circulating library as part of the business. Baker was also partner in a short-lived Princeton publishing firm that printed a novel and E. C. Wines's unsuccessful *Monthly Journal of Education* (1835). *Hageman*, 2:59; *Princeton Whig*, August 29, 1834; and Varnum Lansing Collins, *Early Princeton Printing* (Princeton, 1911), pp. 26–27.

[14] Torrey used Edward Turner, *Elements of Chemistry* (London, 1827), which was reprinted in several editions. The Henry Library, for example, contains the fifth American edition (Philadelphia, 1835, prepared from the fifth London edition, with notes and emendations by Franklin Bache). According to Stanley Guralnick, "During the period 1825–1835 when chemistry made its most dramatic gains in the college, a new class of young men was teaching the subject. . . . They quickly extended the scope of recitation and introduced laboratory experiences; and virtually all of them adopted Turner's *Chemistry* . . . until about 1850 when kinetic-molecular concepts appeared in newer textbooks." "Science and the American College, 1828–1860" (Ph. D. dissertation, University of Pennsylvania, 1969), pp. 172–173.

For details on the transaction involving Baker, the book, and Torrey and Henry, see the letter of Henry to Torrey of November 18, 1834, printed below.

[15] Roe Lockwood was a bookseller in New York, according to the City Directory for 1833–1834.

"RECORD OF EXPERIMENTS"

Henry Papers, Smithsonian Archives

Aug 19th 1834[1]

1 Exp Suspended needle in a large coil of ribbon conductor [and] noted the effect when the current was stoped & transmitted— sudden start of the needle. The magnetism always in the same direction.[2]

[1] On this date, Henry began a series of experiments on shielding that continued through the end of August. He interposed a variety of substances between sources of magnetism and pieces of iron (filings, needles, and rods). The work had theoretical relevance for Henry, the nature of which is discussed in note 12 to the entry of August 22, 1834, printed below. Yet Henry published only the briefest mention of one of the experiments in this series (see note

2 Exp Tried several effects of a coil of 30 feet inch ribbon internal diameter 3½ or 4 inches. When iron put in became strongly magnetized. Always tended to the side of the coil except when a little without at either side.

In the position a or b the point of equilibrium was in the centre of the ring

3 Exp With the same ring a needle floated by a cork was used [and] in this way the exp. was more satisfactory. In every case there appeared to be a repulsion betwen the edge of the ring and the end of the magnet when the magnet or needle was without the plan[e] of the ring.

4 Exp. A glass tube with water was introduced into a hollow tube of iron held perpendicular to the horizon and this into the coil of the last exp. The needle when thrown into the water immediatly jumped out so that its lower extremity was on the upper edge of the tube.

5 Exp When a coil, was introduced, (of thick wire) into the interior of an iron tube no magnetism was produced.[3]

6th Placed a piece of cylindrical soft iron in a coil of copper ribbon. Introduced a bar of round iron. When the round iron projected it was magnetic but within the tube showed no signs of magnetism. It was tested by small pieces of soft iron.

Thinking that the single coile with its spires in the same plane might have some effect in this exp. the next was instituted.

7th The cylinder of iron inserted in the last was wound with a ribbon of copper[4] & then submitted to the galvanic action and in order to test the magnetism of the interior a smal piece of soft iron was fastened to a fibre of silk from the cocoon. The bit of iron being suspended in the middle of the axis of the tube was not in the least affected by transmitting the current. When however it was gradually drawn up to the end of the tube it was suddenly thrown out and adhered to the out side. This curious phenomenon

4 of his letter to Harriet Henry of May 1, 1835, below). He studied shielding effects again in 1838, while preparing to publish "Contributions III: Electro-Dynamic Induction," but at that time he was concerned with screening induced electrical currents rather than magnetism. Henry returned to the subject of shielding in 1840; his laboratory notebook entries on those experiments will appear in a later volume of *The Papers of Joseph Henry*.

[2] Presumably the north polarity was at the same end of the needle each time.

[3] Henry probably sent a current through the wire on the inside of the tube and then tested for magnetism on the outside of the tube. He tried the experiment again the next day, possibly with slightly different equipment, and found another result.

[4] That is, Henry wound a piece of insulated copper ribbon like a helix down the length of the tube and then ran a current through the ribbon. In the sixth and ninth experiments, by contrast, he used the same iron tube in conjunction with a flat coil.

was produced when a shingle nail was thrown in to the top of the tube. The lower end came up last as if the inner part of the tube was differently magnetized. This effect is the same as that of No 4

8 A plan[e] coil (ie one with the spire in the same plan[e]) was placed around a cylindrical piece of thick brass. The magnetic effect within the cylinder the same as with in the coil alone.

9th To render the results more certain the plan[e] coil was placd around the *middle* of the tube[5] and a piece of iron let down into the tube opposite the coil. When transmitting the galvanic current the bit of iron was not effected until drawn up to the edge of the tube when it instanly adhered.

10 Exp In order to determine the thickness of the magnetic stratum[6] a hollow cylinder of tinned iron was placed in the plan[e] coil as in the last exp. This tube under these same circumstances as in the last expt showed magnetism throughout on the inside.

12th Exp[7] An interesting method of showing the jumping up of the needle is by means of a glass tube with water in which a needle is floated. When the glass tube is forced down into the iron tube the needle always stops at the upper edge of the iron tube. Or when the needle is forcibly thrown into the water it returns and stops with its lower end at the upper edge of the iron tube

[5] No doubt an iron tube as in the fifth, sixth, and seventh experiments rather than the brass tube used in the eighth one.

[6] That is, how deep the magnetism extended past the surface of the iron.

[7] Henry skipped eleven in his numbering.

"RECORD OF EXPERIMENTS"

Henry Papers, Smithsonian Archives

Aug 20th [1834]

13 Placed a spiral of thick wire within a tube of common tinned iron. The tube showed polarity without—and of an oposite kind from that of the helix which was left projecting at one end.[1] The polarity was tested with a compass needle.

[1] This experiment is similar to the fifth experiment Henry did on August 19, in which he passed a current through a wire spiral that was placed inside a tube, but from which he

14 When a quantity of iron filings were put into the mouth of the tube an[d] the whole gently tapped with the finger while the current was passing through the coil, the filings flew out of the mouth of the tube and arranged themselves around the edge.[2] This exp was made with the iron tube and the coil on the out side

found no magnetism on the outside. In repeating the experiment, he may have chosen a thinner tube or used a more sensitive detector of magnetism. It is also possible that by inserting the wire helix only part way, Henry allowed the end which remained outside to magnetize the exterior of the tube. On August 22, Henry again tried the experiment and recorded magnetism on the outside of polarity opposite from that of the wire. There he offered an explanation for the results (see the experiment numbered twenty-one among the entries for August 22, 1834, printed below).

[2] This experiment is a variant of the fourth, seventh, and twelfth experiments of August 19, with iron shavings substituted for a needle or a single piece of iron. The results are consistent with the earlier findings.

"RECORD OF EXPERIMENTS"

Henry Papers, Smithsonian Archives

Aug. 22nd [1834]

Exp 15 Arranged 4 flat magnets in the form of a hollow parallelopiped put a small cylinder of soft iron within. The tendency to fly out appeared the same as in the experiments with the tube but the attraction within was the same as with a common magnet. When repeated the tendency to fly out was not observed[1]

Exp 16 Repeated the exp of No 6 & 7[2] with a piece of soft iron suspended to a silk thread. At first there appeared to be some attraction but this was found to be owing to the magnetism of the iron wire[3] itself. Another piece was taken which shewed no magnetism when dipped into iron filings. In

[1] For comparative purposes, Henry is evidently attempting to approximate the shape of a helical coil with four magnets. Inserting an iron cylinder in the parallelopiped, he then repeats some of the experiments he ran with the coils. Apparently the iron needle or bar adhered to the side of the cylinder showing the absence of shielding with ordinary magnets.

A possible inspiration to these experiments on magnetic shielding was Francis Watkins's article "On the Magnetic Powers of Soft Iron," *Phil. Trans.*, 1833, pp. 333–342. Henry notebook [7171] contains extensive reading notes on the article, especially on the effect of interposing a thin sheet of mica between the poles of an electromagnet and the keeper. At one point, Henry interjects "May this not throw some light on the exp of hollow tubes," a possible reference to the current series of experiments.

[2] Above, August 19, 1834.

[3] That is, the small iron probe.

this case not the least sign of magnetism could be observed until the wire was drawn up to near the surface of the circular end of the ring when it as usual instantly sprang out.

Exp 17 A quantity of filings were put into the tube and a cylinder of iron run in so as to project a little beyond the tube. The end within attracted filings & the intensity became stronger the farther the tube was drawn out. When the cylinder was pushed in so far that the end was within the tube it exhibited scarcely any signes of magnetism.[4] A slight effect was produced when the connection of the coil with the battery was broken. The filings appeared to start a little, this was probably owing to the induction from without*

Exp 18 A bar 1 inch wide 12 long of hardened steel[6] was put into the tube so that its end was even with the end of the tube. When the latter was excited the steel did not become permanently magnetized

19 The same bar of steel was put into the tube in part or so that one half of it projected. The tube was then magnetized and the bar in this case was found to be magnetic. The end which projected was the stronger. Care was taken to interrupt the current before the bar was withdrawn, as otherwise the bar would have been magnetized by contact or by the influence of the external part of the tube.

18[7] A small compass needle was put in the tube and exhibited a slight magnetic action

19 A bundle of magnets being put into the iron tube used in the other exp., the tube showed polarity without and of the same kind as that of the magnets[8]—or in other words the appearance was as if the magnetism acted

**17* The same effect was produced when a short cylinder of iron was used; at each solution[5] and connection of the coil with the battery the filings were moved

[4] Shielded from the inductive force when entirely within the tube, the iron core only became magnetic when its unshielded projecting end was magnetized by forces outside the tube.

[5] The word is used in the unfamiliar sense of an interruption of continuity. Henry's explanation is unclear to us. Evidently he felt that the shielding effect remained and that the magnetic induction still came from outside the tube even with the shorter cylinder inserted. Perhaps Henry believed that breaking the circuit intensified the coil's magnetic effect through self-induction.

[6] In the next two experiments Henry finds that steel is shielded in the same way as soft iron.

[7] Henry either misnumbered this and the next experiment or meant to indicate that the same tubes were being used as in the previous two experiments.

[8] Henry does not indicate if the bundle of magnets projected from the ends of the iron case. We assume not. Compare this result with experiments 5 and 13 on interior coils above. A completely encased coil produced no exterior magnetism. When one end of the coil projected outside the iron case, the latter received

directly through the tube. The polarity was changed by chang[ing] the position of the interior magnets

Perhaps this effect was produced by magnetizing the tube in putting the magnets in

20 The last suggestion was proved not to be correct by putting a rod of iron within the tube and magnetizing it by means of a coil around it after it was put in; the same polarity appeared on the outside as in the iron within as was shown by testing the magnetism of the rod. When the current was reversed the polarity was also changed. The exterior magnetism was however very feeble, when compared with the magnetism of the bar without the iron tube, acting as a screen or case[9]

N.B. If a plate of iron be interposed between a magnet and a needl, will not the needle be affected; does not a row of particles become magnetic directly through the plate or tube

21 The thin tin case[10] was tried again with the coil inside. The reverse polarity was produced by the coil. Is not the difference of effect produced by the coil and the iron due to the superior action of the iron magnet or in other words does not the coil produce a contrary magnetism by induction while the iron magnet acts directly through the sides of the tube.[11]

If this be the case it would favor the hypothesis of Ampere in reference to the constitution of magnets. The currents on the inside of the tube will

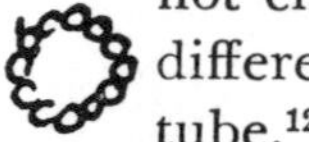

not circulate in the same direction as those on the outside, hence different states of polarity in the helix and the external part of the tube.[12]

a reverse polarity. A coil within a thin case is tested below, experiment 21.

[9] The exterior magnetism may have been weakened by the countervailing effect of the coil. See experiment 21, following.

[10] Probably the thin tinned iron case used above in experiment 10 of this series.

[11] Henry's reference to the "superior action" of the permanent magnets on iron is obscure, but part of his general concern for the comparative magnetizing powers of coils, electromagnets, and permanent magnets. See, for instance, his Fragment on Magnetic Induction [ca. February 1, 1835]. His theoretical distinction between the direct magnetizing effect of the magnet and the inductive effect of the coil is unclear and not explained further. By the direct effect, he probably meant the usual result of touching soft iron to a magnetic pole. The induction by the coil is discussed in the next footnote.

[12] In the 1830s the French physicist Ampère was still one of the leading authorities in electrical theory. It is by now clear that Ampère provided general theoretical justification as well as inspiration for much of Joseph Henry's electromagnetic work. In this passage, Henry makes one of his most specific and important applications of Ampèrian electrodynamic theory to his experimental researches.

The Ampèrian hypothesis to which Henry refers is the famous and highly complicated electrodynamic molecule. Believing that electricity underlies all magnetic forces, Ampère posited a system of positive and negative electrical fluids circulating through the molecules of all bodies. In iron (and other magnetizable substances) these molecular currents were capable of being aligned. The alignment of the currents, by a permanent magnet or an electric current, magnetized the iron. According to Ampère's highly obscure description of the electrodynamic molecule, positive and negative fluids emerged from one end of the molecule and reentered it at the other end, forming a shell of continuously circulating fluids. Since the effects of the negative fluid were just the reverse of the positive, the net effect was of a single fluid flowing around the molecule.

Although Michael Faraday remained skeptical of Ampère's molecule, Henry, with his general admiration for Ampère, made frequent use of the model in his lectures at Princeton, though always aware of the model's peculiar difficulties. In one of his lecture outlines Henry wrote:

> It may be urged as an objection to this theory that the assumption on which it is founded of the circulation of the currents that it is hypothetical in the extreme and violates every analogy and semblance of probability. But to this it may be answered that the facts to be explained are themselves at variance with all the other operations of nature and consequently require a peculiar cause. [Henry notebook No. 23919.]

It is doubtful that Henry obtained his knowledge of the model directly from Ampère's writings. Rather, his custom was to rely on good English language secondary accounts such as P. M. Roget's *Treatises on Electricity, Galvanism, Magnetism, and Electro-Magnetism* (London, 1832) and James Cumming's translated edition of J. F. Demonferrand's *A Manual of Electro Dynamics* (Cambridge, England, 1827). Demonferrand was an especially important source for Ampère's theory for both English and Continental physicists. Both books are found in Henry's Library and show evidence of his scrutiny of various Ampèrian points. Certain peculiarities in Henry's use of the Ampèrian model, to be discussed below, also suggest his reliance on these volumes.

Both sources illustrate in detail how, in the process of magnetization, the circular electrodynamic molecules align themselves in a system of cylindrical electrodynamic "filaments" running parallel to the axis of the magnet. Henry's diagram gives a cross-sectional view of the cylinders formed along the length of the magnetized iron tube. A diagram similar to Henry's can be seen in Cumming's edition, plate 3, figure 56, and in Roget's section on "Electro-Magnetism," p. 83. Pages 96–171 of Cumming contain Demonferrand's principal discussion of Ampère's theory. Roget, who probably relied extensively on Demonferrand, gives his interpretation under the heading "Electro-Magnetism," pp. 81–92.

Henry envisions the electrodynamic cylinders as all rotating in the same direction, giving a resultant electrodynamic force in one direction around the outside of the magnetized tube. The inside of the tube, under the influence of the opposite sides of the molecules, showed a net circular force in the reverse direction. Although Ampère evidently believed that magnetism resulted from the orientation of pre-existing molecular currents in the iron, Roget and Demonferrand left open the possibility that the currents were not pre-existing but were excited by the applied electromagnetic forces (see, e.g., Roget, p. 88 and Cumming, pp. 146–147). Henry's reference to the coil's production of a "contrary magnetism by induction" suggests the latter approach—the excitation of new molecular currents by the coil.

Ampère never clearly explained how his electrodynamic molecules became aligned or how they behaved in general. The confusion of his commentators is perfectly understandable. Henry's application of Ampère's theory presents special problems. Henry's diagram is crude and perhaps meant to be merely suggestive of the basic principles. Or it may be that he paid little attention to the niceties of the model. Nevertheless, the following discussion takes Henry's diagram literally and deals with its specific implications in order to show contemporary difficulties in applying Ampère. According to Henry's account in this note, the induction of molecular currents by the interior coil produced opposite polarities at the end of the helix and at the outside end of the iron tube. The opposing polarities resulted from the fact that "the currents on the inside of the tube will not circulate in the same direction as those on the outside. . . ." Henry refers to the opposing current flows on opposite sides of each electrodynamic molecule or cylinder. (Note that Henry's schematic diagram assumes a single molecular layer in the tube. The same effect would result from an odd number of layers.) Henry's account presupposes that the current flow in the helix will induce a current in the *same* direction in the nearest part of each electrodynamic molecule. That is, if the helix current is clockwise, each molecule will flow counterclockwise. Both Cumming and Roget give the same induction patterns. See especially Roget, pp. 88–89 and figure 164.

The problem is that Faraday's theory of "volta-electric" induction, announced in his First Series of Experimental Researches and well-known to Henry, held that a beginning current induced a current in the opposite direction in a neighboring circuit (see Section 26.) Significantly, Faraday himself had great difficulty reconciling his own findings with what he saw as Ampère's early suggestion of electromagnetic induction. In his First Series, Section 78, Faraday wrote, "But all my results tend to invert the sense of the proposition stated by M. Ampère, 'that a current of electricity tends to put the electricity of conductors near which it passes in motion in the same direction,' for they indicate an opposite direction for the produced current. . . . "

Faraday was even moved to write Ampère about the apparent discrepancy, as he points out in a note dated April 29, 1833, in his collected *Experimental Researches in Electricity*, 3 vols. (London, 1839–1855), *1*:108. The French physicist's reply convinced Faraday that he had misinterpreted Ampère, who took a typically positivist position: "M. Ampère tells me in a letter which I have just received from him, that he carefully avoided, when describing the experiment, any reference to the direction of the induced current. . . . " Even more important for understanding Henry's view of Ampère, Faraday admitted that one source of his error was that he, like Henry, relied on Demonferrand's presentation of Ampère's theory. Given Ampère's obscurities, it is no surprise that Faraday shared Henry's preference for good secondary accounts of the French physicist's theories.

Despite the ambiguities, Ampère's electrodynamic molecule becomes one of the most important theoretical models for Joseph Henry's future electromagnetic researches, giving concrete significance to his repeated statements of allegiance to Ampèrian electrodynamics. The model will appear time and again in his "Record of Experiments" as a guide to research and a powerful explanatory tool.

The best guide to Ampère's models is L. Pearce Williams's "Ampère's Electrodynamic Molecular Model," *Contemporary Physics*, 1962, *4*:113–123. Faraday's attitudes toward the model are in *Michael Faraday* (New York, 1965), pp. 146–151, by the same author. Also recommended is Williams's "Ampère" in *DSB*.

At the end of this entry Henry noted at some unspecified later time that "I have found this really to be the case, see exp April 1840." The reference is to the April 23, 1840, entry, containing a similar, though clearer, diagram using Ampère's electrodynamic molecules. There, Henry confirms to his satisfaction that the effects that occur within a magnetized iron tube are due to the behavior of molecular currents. The entry will be treated in a forthcoming volume of *The Papers of Joseph Henry*.

"RECORD OF EXPERIMENTS"

Henry Papers, Smithsonian Archives

Aug 23 [1834]

22 Placed a small compass needle within the tube which[1] and applied a magnetic bar along the out side. The i[n]fluence of the bar passed apparently through the sides of the tube and affected the needle in the same manner as if the tube did not intervene except that the action was very feeble.[2]

23 Placed the tube within the coil, inserted a small needle which entered with the north end foremost by[3] after being put in about 2 inches turned

[1] A slip of the pen that Henry apparently forgot to scratch out.

[2] Henry did this experiment to answer the question he posed after experiment 20 on August 22, 1834 (see entry printed above).

[3] Henry probably meant to write "but" instead.

round and pointed in the opposite direction.[4] The iron tube was then withdrawn from the coil which remained in the same connection with the battery. The needle was then gently passed along the axis of the coil but did not turn round as before.

24 When the same exp was retried with a thin tube the effect was the same as with the coil alone.

[4] In view of the results earlier in the series of experiments that began August 19, which showed no magnetic forces in the interior shielded area, Henry may have found this phenomenon puzzling, unless he supposed that the magnetsim at the mouth of the tube had affected the needle. The rest of experiment 23 rules out the possibility of anomalies in the coil.

"RECORD OF EXPERIMENTS"

Henry Papers, Smithsonian Archives

Aug [24–31, 1834][1]

Exp with a compass needle to determine more accurately if there is a difference of intensity with in a hollow bar of iron under the same circumstances when a piece of iron rod is put in the hollow or when the same is empty. For this purpose the hollow tube mentioned in the former exp was used & inorder to obviate the action of the exterior magnetism[2] an iron stoppel was put into each end of the tube. The compass was placed at about 2 feet distance and in such a position that the direction of the tube was about a tangent to the circumference of the compass and when the magnetic action was suspended the needle stood at right angles to the same direction.[3]

The iron plug being in the ends of the tube & a piece of round iron in the hollow the needle was deflected.

1st set	2nd set	3rd	4th
In[4] 22°	Iron out 20½	out 16½	In 17
The iron out 21½	in 18½	In 17	out 17½
In 22	out 17½	out 17	In 16½[5]

[1] This entry appears after the one for August 23, but Henry has abandoned the system of numbering his experiments, suggesting that a time had elapsed since the earlier entries. The work of this partially dated entry is still related to screening effects.

[2] Henry means the magnetism around the mouth of the tube, which might affect the results if the iron rod were long enough to be close to the entrance and if the external magnetism was intense.

[3] We assume Henry put a coil on the outside of the tube, although the coil is not sketched in on the diagram or mentioned in the text.

[4] That is, the iron rod is in or out. Henry tests the effect of the plug being in or out a few lines later in this same entry.

[5] The slight effect of the presence of an iron rod is not especially surprising if one believes

The iron was next drawn out in part from the farther end of the tube, the needle remaining as in the last exp ie at 16 ½, when ½ out needle stood 19°. When entirely out but the ends touching[6] needle stood at 20°.[7]

Series 2nd A quantity of fresh acid being thrown into the battery, a new series was commenced similar to the 1st series.

1st set	2nd set	3rd set
Iron in 34	Iron out 30½	Iron
— out 32	— in 30	
— in 30	— out 29½[8]	

To determine the effect of the iron stoppel the following were made

Stoppel in 38	Stoppel out 33
—— out 38	in 35°
—— in 36½	out 33
	in 34
	out 32½
	in 33½

magnetism resides principally at the surface of the tube. Henry mentioned the concentration of magnetism on surfaces in one of his earliest scientific papers, "On the Application of the Principle of the Galvanic Multiplier to Electro-Magnetic Apparatus, and Also to the Development of Great Magnetic Power in Soft Iron, with a Small Galvanic Element," *Silliman's Journal*, 1831, *19*:407.

[6] i.e., the end of the iron rod was in contact with the mouth of the tube.

[7] The magnetism seems to increase as the unshielded surface area increases.

[8] The results for the second series suggest that the decline in readings from set 1 to set 4 in the first series may be accounted for by the increasing polarization of the battery.

TO HARRIET HENRY

Mary Henry Copy, Memoir, Henry Papers, Smithsonian Archives

Princeton Aug 27, 1834

To my dear little wife. Your letter was not in the box this morning with the other articles received at that time. I accidentally called at the office at eleven as I often find myself doing since your departure and seized on it as an unexpected prize.[1] I hardly regret that mine to you was too late for the mail; it was written in rather a gloomy state of mind and would not have given my dear wife that pleasure I hope my letters may always afford her. . . . I have become somewhat habituated to our lonely life yet I am as anxious for

[1] The letter does not survive.

your return as you can be to leave Albany. I will come for you whenever you wish but I can remain away only a few days as I am obliged to give some lectures to the junior class and must be here during the general examination previous to the vacation .

I have confined myself to my little study and to my pursuits in the Hall[2] but have promised to visit Professor Dod this evening. I have been much interested in some of my late results but meet with constant retardation in my experiments from a want of ready access to materials and from the tardiness as well as want of skill of the mechanics of the place.[3] Sometimes I fear my devotion to the Hall and to my study may seem to interfere with my duty to my wife, but I do not believe that such pursuits can ever be incompatible with the warmest feelings towards my family. We should not perhaps forget that I have now the responsible duties and the dignity of a somewhat public character to support and you those of a wife and a mother. You are no longer a girl: when of one mind and one interest, the labour of each serves only to heighten the love and esteem of the other. If I may have lost in the eyes of my wife some attractions as a ladies man, may I not think I have gained on the other hand in respect since I am endeavoring in the constant exercise of my official duties and with every honorable means in my power to extend the field of my usefulness and to establish for myself and to deserve the reputation of a scientific man. Never has my wife been more to me than now. By my removal to Princeton I have been separated from all my early associates—from the friends interested in my welfare because they have witnessed my early struggles and the many dangers a Divine Providence has enabled me to escape. Here the friendships we have formed are as yet but new, not long tried. I have been more than ever impressed of late with the fact that here at least I stand alone; that I must rise or fall by my own exertions and in this state of mind even when I am actively engaged in my pursuits I would draw my wife even more closely to me and have her yet more intimately a part of myself.

Stephen has been much engaged in making paper geometrical figures for his class, also in establishing in its place in the Hall the transit instrument. His class has just commenced nautical astronomy. On that account there has been something of a bustle, cleaning of old globes, quadrants &c. He is in fine spirits. Now that the transit instrument is in place I hope that the Post Office will be more regular in the time of closing the mail. Probably you will recommend that our letters be sent a little before the time in future; the advice is good.

[2] Philosophical Hall.

[3] A constant problem forcing Henry to rely on artisans in Philadelphia and New York, as well as his own efforts.

I think I can find time to receive a message of love from my wife. I wish she were here so that I might press her to my heart and make her feel how she reigns there. If you are good I will send you two letters a week until I see you.

"QUERIES IN REFERENCE TO THE SPARK FROM LONG & SHORT COIL"

Henry Papers,[1] *Smithsonian Archives*

[August 1834][2]

1 How is it modified in reference to the length of the coil. Is there a length with respet to the quantity of galvanism which produces a maximum effect.

2 Does a coiled or straight wire or ribbon produce greater effects?

3. How does it vary with the intensity of Electricity—does greater intensity require a longer coil?

4 How does the effect vary with reference to the quantity of metal in the coil and the quantity of galvanism.

5 Will the effect be produced when a large quantity of acid[ulated] water forms part of the circuit.[3]

6 If a pile of Ritter[4] be introduced will there be an increase or will the effect be produced.

7 Determine the direction of the current by a needle placed a little to the right of the wire & fasened there so as to be capable of motion only in one

[1] The manuscript is located with other undated notes on electricity and magnetism in folder one of box twenty-three of the Henry Papers.

[2] Our assigned dating is tentative. With this undated list of queries and suggestions for experiments on self-induction in coils and long conductors Henry appears to be laying the groundwork for the experiments on these topics recorded in his "Record of Experiments." Our dating was designed to juxtapose this document with the commencement of those experiments on August 15, 1834. Because of Henry's continuing interest and work in these topics, it is conceivable that the manuscript was written as late as mid-1835, when Henry's articles on self-induction were coming into print. Many of the questions Henry raises in this manuscript will be answered, or at least considered, in forthcoming entries from his "Record of Experiments" printed below.

[3] We have discovered no record of an experiment designed by Henry to answer this question.

[4] Ritter's secondary pile is described below in Henry's Notes on a Trip to Philadelphia, December [5–7,] 1834, footnote 30. Again we know of no actual experiment by Henry along these lines.

direction. Then if the current is reversed by the disruption the needle will be deflected in the adverse direction.

8 Is not this phenominon connected with the one mentioned by Nobily that an electric discharge sent through a coil of silkened wire gives a brilliant cintilation. Try this exp.[5]

9 Try how far the spark may be heard from a plate of zinc one inch square excited by a strong solution of nitric acid.

In these experiments let the battery preserve its power by immersing it gradually. The power should be tested after each experiment by a galvanometer properly placed.

10 Determine if the wire or coil preserves any of its electricity so as to affect a galvanometer. Make the communication with the galvanometer without touching the copper of the coil so as to discharge the electricity.

11 Note if there be any difference in the spark produced from the negative or positive pole.

12 Note if a point or ball gives any difference in the spark. This may be done by cups of mercury & wires. (*12 bis*) Fire ox & hydrogen by the spark.

13. Notice the effect on a sewing needle; first put it on the coil see if be magnetized—in a certain direction when it is put in the coil & then with drawn—afterwards note the kind of magnetism when the circuit has been suddenly broken.

14 Suspend the article for shewing the repulsion of Ampere; break the circuit, see if any sudden start takes place. In this exp put one wire in front and the other in the rear so as to make a rotatory motion around the thread of suspension.[6]

[5] The Italian physicist Leopoldo Nobili published these results in "Sur la lumière des auroras boréales, imitée par une expérience électro-magnétique," *Bibliothèque Universelle, Sciences et Arts*, 1824, *25*:38–42. The results were reported in *The Quarterly Journal of Science, Literature, and the Arts*, 1824, *17*:162–163. Nobili's insulated wire was closely wound into a flat spiral of up to twenty-four turns. When Nobili sent a static charge from a Leyden jar through the coil, he noted that "a vivid light, something resembling that of an artificial fire-work, will occur, originating from the center of the spires." Nobili attributed the effect to the electromagnetic state of the spiral, suggesting further that the aurora depended similarly on the earth's magnetism. In the final paragraphs of his "Contributions II: Spiral Conductor" Henry again suggested a theoretical relationship between Nobili's effect and his own experiments with self-inductive sparks. The relationship between static and voltaic self-induction through long conductors and coils became the subject of Henry's upcoming electrical researches, culminating in "Contributions III: Electro-Dynamic Induction."

[6] Henry no doubt envisioned an Ampèrian experiment showing the repulsion between two current-carrying wires. His sketch of the

15 Fire a mixture of oxy[g]en and Hydrogen. It will not fire powder of eather.[7]

16 Try the deflagration of gold leaf. Place the leaf so that the discharge will take place through it when the circuit is broken.

---

apparatus is obviously incomplete. We are unable to reproduce his experimental set-up.

[7] This is a cryptic statement. We assume Henry meant "either," but we make no sense out of "powder" of oxygen or hydrogen. We can only assume that Henry intended to complete the sentence with the names of some known inflammable compounds.

HENRY NOTEBOOK ENTRY

Notebook [7171], page 124, Henry Papers, Smithsonian Archives

Sept 1st 1834[1]

Would it not be worth the labour to repete the experiment made by exciting an electrical machine in different gases. May this not lead to some new and interesting results.[2] The gases should be well dried and admitted in[t]o

---

[1] We have shifted the date from its original position above Henry's initials at the middle of the entry.

[2] Henry is concerned with the role of ambient gases in the excitation of static electricity by friction electrical machines. According to his description in the paragraph following, Henry intended to enclose a modified cylindrical electrical machine in a glass jar designed to receive different gases. He could then investigate the possible effect of the different gases on the exciting power of the enclosed machine. As Henry gives no source as the inspiration for this entry, it is unclear whether he wants to explore the phenomenon in general or whether he has seen a particular account of it that he wants to repeat. In any event, experiments of this nature date back to the beginnings of electrical science, providing early investigators with important insights into the basic nature of electrical forces. Joseph Priestley records, for example, how the early English electrician Francis Hauksbee (1666–1713, *DSB*) investigated the electroluminescence produced in whirling glass cylinders, either full of air or exhausted, by rubbing them in vacuo. Joseph Priestley, *The History and Present State of Electricity*, 3d ed., 2 vols. (London, 1775), *1*:24–25 (Joseph Henry acquired this edition in London in 1837).

We have discovered a possible immediate inspiration for Henry's proposed experiments in another notebook, containing his notes for class lectures on electricity (no. [23894]) as well as scientific thoughts and gleanings from various readings. The pertinent entry occurs in a section dealing with various modes of producing static electricity (p. 25). The entry is undated but is strikingly similar to the dated one now under consideration, suggesting that Henry may have simply transferred the text from one notebook to the other. After proposing the repetition of an experiment by Joseph Priestley showing that a "tube into which the air was condensed lost its power of exciting," but "regained it by letting the air escape," Henry continued with a paraphrase from one of his most frequently used electrical sources, P. M. Roget's *Treatises on Electricity, Galvanism, Magnetism, and Electro-Magnetism* (London, 1832). Roget points out in the section on "Electricity," p. 58, that the chemist Wollaston, in asserting the chemical origins of electricity, introduced different gases into a vessel containing a conventional electrical machine. To show oxidation as the true source of electricity, Wollaston demonstrated that a machine capable of being excited in air failed to function in an atmosphere of carbonic acid. Henry further noted Roget's statement that Humphry Davy repeated the experiment with contrary results, attributing

a prepared vessel from a receiver over mercury by means of the air pump.

The electrical apparatus may be on a very small scale and consist of a tube placed upright on a transferring plate (of glass) and excited by a rubber passing through an air tight collar. The gas can be dried by passing it through a bottle of glass moistened with strong sulphuric acid. J.H.

Or perhaps the same experiments may be tried by means of a tube electrical machine described in Sillimans journal of the present year.[3]

---

any differences in excitation to gas density rather than composition. The oxidation theory of static electricity was also denied by experiments in vacuo and in carbonic acid by Stephen Gray and Gay-Lussac; see *Encyclopaedia Britannica*, 8th ed., s.v. "Electricity," p. 539.

We know that a few months later Henry and Torrey proposed collaborating on such experiments, along with others on various modes of producing static electricity (see the letters of March 2 and March 7, 1835, below). We have no further evidence on the proposed collaboration or any results with different gases that Henry might have achieved on his own. Any theoretical purposes Henry might have had in conducting the experiments are unknown. Henry's view of the basic nature of static electricity, as far as he articulated it, was the conventional Franklinian hypothesis of a single "subtle imponderable elastic fluid which pervades the earth and all material objects" (Henry notebook [23894], p. [54]). Henry's preference for the one fluid theory is discussed below in an excerpt from a notebook entry, [1835], the final document in this volume.

[3] By the electrical inventor and experimenter and Henry's future correspondent, Charles G. Page, "Notice of Some New Electrical Experiments," *Silliman's Journal*, 1834, *26*:110–112. Page's "electric syringe" was a portable static electric machine consisting of a small glass tube with a piston to develop the charge, which was collected on a brass cap at the bottom of the tube.

Below this entry Henry later inserted the following addendum, dated November 1837: "In the museum of the Royal Institution a small electrical machine in a jar is preserved, made by Sir H Davey for experiments of the above kind," something Henry doubtless observed on his recently completed trip to Europe.

HENRY NOTEBOOK ENTRY

Notebook [7171], page 22, Henry Papers, Smithsonian Archives

[September 2, 1834][1]

Mr James Dean[2] of Burlington Vermont communicated to me the following observed auroras 1834.

7 Feby 1834 10h PM Aurora bright tranquil 8° high.
31 Aug from 9 to 10 do do do from 12° to 14 high.
2 Sept " 8 to 9 do Do active about 45° high.[3]

[1] Since we do not know when Dean gave Henry these data, we have assigned the date from the last observation mentioned in the document.

[2] See footnote 1 of the letter of November 27, 1833, above.

[3] On this same page of notebook [7171],

Henry jotted three lines above the text printed here:

For a paper on the height of the aurora see annals of Philos vol 4 N.S. 418 By Mr Dalton.

An Aurora was observed at Albany by Mr Bullions on Wednesday evening the 16th of Oct. [1833.]

I observed an aurora at Schenectady on Sunday evening 13th Occt. [1833.]

These lines were presumably composed sometime in late October 1833.

There are two theories to account for the appearance of the Dean figures and the earlier lines on the same page. First, Henry may have simply wanted miscellaneous jottings on auroras in the same place for easy reference when composing publications and the like. Or, second, it could be argued that everything on this page is connected logically, despite having been recorded a year apart and despite being a mélange of bibliographical citation, recollection, and excerpt.

The contents of John Dalton's paper ("On the Height of the Aurora Borealis above the Surface of the Earth; Particularly One Seen on the 29th of March, 1826," *Phil. Mag.*, 1828, n.s. *4*:418–428) provides the connection between the observations by Bullions, Henry and Dean. Dalton calculated the height from measurements of the angle from the horizon to the aurora, the datum Dean supplied for Burlington in 1833, 1834, and 1835. Dalton used figures from cities a goodly distance apart but roughly on the same magnetic line north-south. Henry could therefore not calculate the height from observations in Albany and Schenectady, which were too close and east-west of each other. However, he could perform the operation from Dean's figures if he also received simultaneous observations from either Albany or Schenectady, which are many miles south of Burlington.

Other scientists challenged Dalton's conclusion that the aurora was about 100 miles high. Henry read one of these later pieces, Samuel Hunter Christie's "On the Height above the Surface of the Earth of a Luminous Arch of the Aurora Borealis, on the 7th of January, 1831," Royal Institution of Great Britain (London), *Journal*, May 1831, *1*:525–531 and took notes on the article on pages 57–59 and 62 of Notebook [7171]. Christie decided that most auroras occurred five to fifteen miles high, although exceptional ones might reach the height Dalton had given. He warned that one must note whether the aurora moved about while one took the reading, and it is thus no surprize to see Dean reporting whether the aurora was tranquil or active. As it turned out, Henry did not get the data required to check the accuracy of Christie and Dalton, because his correspondents in different cities never happened to record measurements on the same day. The general problem of assembling simultaneous atmospheric data was one that Henry dealt with as Secretary of the Smithsonian Institution.

CHARLES HODGE[1] TO HUGH L. HODGE[2]

Charles Hodge Papers, Firestone Library, Princeton University

Princeton Sepr 4 1834

My dear Brother,

I have written to you several times of late hurried letters on the spur of a moment as an oportunity offered. And now Mr Allen[3] goes early in the

[1] Charles Hodge by this time was emerging as a powerful theologian in the Presbyterian church. Born in Philadelphia in 1797, one and a half years after his brother Hugh L. Hodge, Charles graduated from both Princeton (A.B., 1815) and the Princeton Theological Seminary (1819). In 1820 he began a lifelong teaching assignment at that Seminary, except for only two years of European study. In his theology he was a spokesman for conservative Presbyterianism, known as the "Old School" Presbyterianism after the 1837 split in the church.

morning instead of at noon, & it is after bed time. I have been very busy lately writting for the Repertory & writting my *Book*.

I think my self worse—my limb is certainly more painful & susceptible than it has been for 6 or 8 months.[4] I wish to try the galvanism. Prof Henry of the college has a small *battery* which he is to bring me. He is very kind & offers to do any thing to arrange it &c.[5]

When does the election[6] in the University come on?

Active in church business, founder of, editor of, and contributor to the *Biblical Repertory and Princeton Review* (to which he alludes in the first paragraph), and prolific author of books on religious topics, Hodge gained a commanding position in the Presbyterian church. His first book, *A Commentary on the Epistle to the Romans* (Philadelphia, 1835), to which he also alludes, went through nineteen editions by 1880. He died in 1878. *DAB*.

[2] Hugh Lenox Hodge (1796–1873) was a notable Philadelphia obstetrician. After graduating from Princeton (A.B., 1814), he studied medicine under Caspar Wistar and received his M.D. degree from the University of Pennsylvania in 1818. Spending intervening years practicing medicine and lecturing in Philadelphia, Hugh Hodge was appointed in 1835 to the chair of obstetrics at the University of Pennsylvania, which position he resigned in 1863 due to failing eyesight. Books he wrote were influential in the development of gynecological and obstetrical thought and practice. *DAB*.

[3] Possibly John Newton Allen (1808–1835), a student at the Theological Seminary graduating about this time.

[4] Diagnoses at a historical distance are often risky. Hodge's condition would persist. According to his other letters (of September 8, quoted in footnote 5, and of October 12, 1834, below), Hodge's pain was concentrated in the groin area (Hodge said Poupart's ligament was affected) and in the upper thigh.

[5] In a September 8, 1834, letter to his brother Hugh Hodge (Charles Hodge Papers, Firestone Library, Princeton University), Charles Hodge wrote: "I have tried two or three times a galvanic battery of 25 plates—of course of but little power for a battery—but much greater than that of the apparatus usually applied to the person. I do not know whether it has produced any effect. I thought it lessened the pain, but I am doubtful about it. I should like to know how you would advise its use. When I said I thought myself worse, I meant in comparison to my state a few months since. I have much more pain on exercise, or lifting the limb, by its own muscles. It is altogether much more tender, & sensitive. The swellings are as they were." From this description we assume that the battery was Henry's "Shaker" battery (for which see below, "Record of Experiments" for May 12, 1835, especially footnote 2). See the October 12 letter for more on Hodge's condition and experimental electrotherapy.

The earliest applications of electricity to medical therapy used static charges. But well before the 1830s voltaic batteries provided electrical current of lower intensity for electrotherapy. Hodge's use of Henry's battery was not innovative.

As far as we know, Henry did not participate in the experiments. Hodge implies here and in his letter below that Henry simply volunteered to loan and set up the battery. That Henry had an interest in related electrical experiments we know from his work in animal electricity (see above, "Galvanic Experiments on the Body of the Murderer Le Blanc," September 6, 1833) and in the physiological effects of electricity (see below, "Record of Experiments," May 13, 1835). But none of Henry's laboratory or reading notes, nor the surviving Henry Library, indicate that by this time he had an active interest in electrotherapy. Henry's first mention of such experimentation comes offhandedly in 1838 in connection with his experiments on induction at a distance, in the course of which he used induced current to treat facial paralysis (see above, "Galvanic Experiments . . ." of September 6, 1833, footnote 3). Sidney Licht, "History of Electrotherapy," in Sidney Licht, ed., *Therapeutic Electricity and Ultraviolet Radiation*, 2d ed. (New Haven, 1967), provides an extensive bibliography.

[6] At the October 7, 1834, meeting of the Trustees of the University of Pennsylvania, William P. Dewees (for whom see above, Henry to James Henry, June 2, 1833, footnote 6) was elected Professor of Midwifery and of the Diseases of Women and Children (Phila-

Sarah[7] wishes Margaret[8] to get her a fawn coloured silk dress. The price she cannot tell. I inclose $10. But this may not be enough.

Good night.

Won't cousin Sally come up with James & his bride.[9]

your Brother—C. Hodge

delphia *National Gazette*, October 10, 1834, p. 2). Hugh L. Hodge was clearly interested in filling that position, but Dewees's election was a certainty since he had served for nine years as the University's Adjunct Professor of Obstetrics. When Dewees resigned one year later, Hodge secured that chair, having succeeded in strenuous competition with Charles D. Meigs (for whom see below, Nomination for Membership in American Philosophical Society, November 7, 1834, especially footnote 2). *DAB*.

[7] Sarah Bache Hodge, Charles Hodge's wife, for whom see above, Sprague to Henry, June 12, 1833, especially footnote 4.

[8] Margaret Aspinwall Hodge, to whom Hugh L. Hodge was married in 1828. She was the daughter of John Aspinwall, a New York City merchant. She died in 1866. Francis B. Lee, ed., *Genealogical and Personal Memorial of Mercer County, New Jersey*, 2 vols. (New York, 1907), 2:460–461.

[9] These relatives we have not identified.

"RECORD OF EXPERIMENTS"

Henry Papers, Smithsonian Archives

Sept. 7th 1834

Exp to determine the force of different batteries on the magnet.[1] The plates of the battery have been standing for 5 days, so that they are now covered with an oxide which prevents their full action.[2]

Exp 1st with the compass needle instead of the torsion balance[3] which is found rather inconvenient

[1] By "different batteries," Henry meant the various arrangements of troughs and plates in his convertible galvanic battery. The following experimental series seems to meet two purposes: to test further the diverse capabilities and outputs of the new battery; to continue the previous month's investigations of electromagnetism, this time varying the power of the electrical input. Henry fails to specify his experimental arrangement, except that a compass needle was used to measure the induced magnetism. It appears that Henry connected the large battery to a coil around some kind of small iron core. The compass needle may have been positioned as in the diagram in the entry of August 24–31, above. Several years earlier, using small batteries, Henry investigated the dependence of electromagnetic induction in soft iron on the quantity and intensity of the inducing current. See "On the Application of the Principle of the Galvanic Multiplier to Electro-Magnetic Apparatus, and Also to the Development of Great Magnetic Power in Soft Iron, with a Small Galvanic Element," *Silliman's Journal*, 1831, *19*:400–408.

[2] Henry had evidently left the plates standing in air, perhaps since the time of their use in his last experiments. See the following footnote.

[3] Immediately preceding this experimental series is a very brief undated set of experiments using a torsion balance, which was evidently yielding inconclusive results. The

Battery arranged as 8 [pairs][4] of plates. Plates diped to the *stop*[5]
Angle 47°

Exp 2ᵈ Battery arranged as 8 elements united into 4, or a double battery, each member of 4 elements[6]—
Angle 61°

Exp 3ʳᵈ The battery was arranged as a single battery of 4 elements
Angle 62°

When one of the wires was lifted from the mercury cup in the last experiment (the communication was formed by means of two thick wires 4 feet long) the needle moved about a degree, showing that a little more electricity was transmitted with the thicker conductor.[7]

Exp 4. Whole Battery arranged as two elements
Angle 67°

Exp 5 Whole Battery arranged as one element
Angle 64°

Repeated the above
Angle 62°

Exp 6 Battery arranged as 4 batteries, each a single element operating together,[8]
Angle 67½

---

undated experiments were probably recorded sometime after the last dated series, August 23, and before the present series.

[4] Originally "plates," clearly a slip of the pen.

[5] It will be recalled that Henry's battery consisted of eight separate troughs, each partitioned into eleven insulated cells, designed to receive the galvanic plates suspended above. To arrange the battery as "eight pairs," Henry applied the "homogeneous connectors" to the plates so that within each of the eight troughs all of the zinc plates were connected together and all of the copper. This gave the equivalent of one large element, or galvanic pair, for each trough, which were then connected in series to produce an eight-element battery. For Henry's technique of rearranging the plates see "Contributions I: Battery."

Throughout this experimental series, the battery functions as a "calorimotor," yielding, in Henry's terms, low intensity, high quantity currents. Successive rearrangements increase the quantity of electricity applied to the magnet. However, the incompleteness and ambiguity of Henry's notes make it difficult to be certain of the precise galvanic arrangements employed. Even allowing for ambiguities in the circuitry, some of Henry's results are problematical. It should be borne in mind that batteries of the period produced very unstable currents; losses due to local action and polarization, for example, could cause enormous variations in power even within the duration of a short experiment. More importantly, many of Henry's results proved meaningless because the magnet was energized beyond saturation (see Henry's comments after experiment 2 of the September 8 entry, below).

Dipping the plates to the "stop" probably meant maximum immersion, that is, until the troughs could be cranked no higher. The battery plates were nine inches wide and twelve inches long.

[6] The two four-element batteries were probably connected to each other in parallel.

[7] Experiments on the "modulus of conduction" follow on September 9 and 10, below.

[8] We assume that Henry is now using only four of the eight troughs, probably connected in parallel.

Exp 7th Battery separated into 4 parts,

1st part alone

Angle 50°—2nd 42°

2nd part

Angle 52½°—2nd 52½

3rd part

Angle 40°

4th part

Angle 45°

Exp 8th After standing 1 ½ hours,

2nd part of battery as above

Angle 64°

1 pt

Angle 64°

3 pt

Angle 57°

4th pt

Angle 58°

Exp 7 & 8 shew the influence of time on the plates. Possibly they have been somewhat more soaked by standing which may have influenced the result.

Exp 9 With 2 parts 3 & 4th

Angle 61°

With 3 parts 2nd, 3rd & 4th

Angle 65°

With the whole battery

Angle 65°

Exp 10 All the parts attached

Angle 65°

1st part thrown off—

Angle 64°

2nd part thrown off

Angle 60

3rd part thrown [off]

Angle 55°

Exp 11 Battery arranged as 2 elements

Angle 67°

Exp 12 Battery arranged as 2 batteries each of two elements

Angle 70°

Arranged as 4 plates[9]
67°

[9] Henry presumably meant pairs of plates.

"RECORD OF EXPERIMENTS"

Henry Papers, Smithsonian Archives

Sept 8th 1834

Exp 1 After standing over night, the same arrangement (ie as 4 elements)[1] gave

Angle 70°

When the plates were 8 inches diped

Angle 71°

N B The compass needle stood precisely at zero <*as it had been arranged at first*> before the dip but afterwards stood at about 10°; it however gradually returns to the zero point showing that time is required to discharge the magnetizm

{N.B.[2] This effect was afterwards found due to the current from the wooden wedges between the plates

Exp 2 Battery arranged half as a battery of 4 elements other half as a battery of a single element.

When the single element was connected

Angle 65

When the part of 4 elements

Angle 66½

The magnet after this exp, seemed to retain a greater magnetic power than usual, as after the acid was withdrawn the needle lowered to about 30°. This effect was found to be produced by the current which is generated from the moistened wood between the copper & zinc

When the one element part of the battery was connected and out of the acid, the

Angle 11°

When the equal surface of 4 elements was connected

Angle 1°

[1] A continuation of the experiments of September 7. From the context, we infer that Henry is utilizing all eight battery troughs.

[2] Possibly added at some later date.

When all the parts were together as one element

Angle 30° under same circumstances.

From the foregoing experiment[3] it would appear that the Battery is more powerful than is necessary to charge the magnet and that for this purpose two boxes are nerely sufficient, although a greater effect is produced by using the whole battery as 4 elements.

Or in other words, although an increase of zinc surface after two boxes does not increase the effect, yet by increasing the intensity of the current,[4] a greater effect is produced.

Exp 3 To observe if any increased effect be produced by a sudden change of polarity, the magnet was galvanized,[5] the needle stood at

Angle 59°

The poles were reversed and rereversed,

Angle 58° about

From this it appears that no increased effect is produced by changing the poles.

The exp was repeated with smaller dip

Angle 45

Poles reversed &c

Angle 42

Exp 4 Miscellaneous

Placed a piece of iron red hot in a coil transmitted the current. The rod was still powerfully magnetic.[6]

Ex 5 Placed a cup of mercury in a coil with one end of the coil in the mercury, the other attached to the battery; also a wire was placed between the mercury & the battery, a rapid rotation took place around each pole.[7]

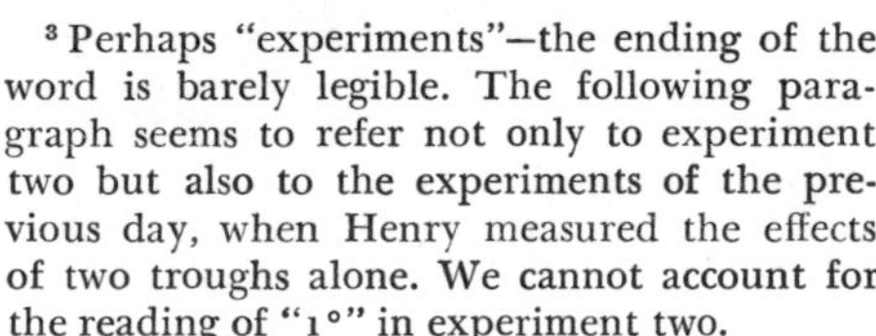

[3] Perhaps "experiments"—the ending of the word is barely legible. The following paragraph seems to refer not only to experiment two but also to the experiments of the previous day, when Henry measured the effects of two troughs alone. We cannot account for the reading of "1°" in experiment two.

[4] By increasing the number of separate plates.

[5] i.e., current was introduced.

[6] This possibly relates to Henry's technique for magnetizing steel bars; see above, Henry to Kelly, December 30, 1833, footnote 7.

[7] Another method for illustrating electromagnetic interactions, the rotation of the energized mercury within the current-carrying coils was a variation on known principles. The effect was essentially an extension of Faraday's classic demonstration in 1821 of "electromagnetic rotations," where a current-bearing wire rotated around a permanent magnet placed upright in a cup of mercury. Inspired by Faraday, Humphry Davy was the first to alter the apparatus to allow the rotation of the mercury conductor. An undated entry in one of Henry's reading notebooks ([6123], p. 47) shows that Henry had read Davy's "On a New Phenomenon of Electromagnetism," *Annals of Philosophy*, 1824, n.s. 7:22–25, an article taken from the 1823 *Phil. Trans.* Davy first achieved the rotary effect by immersing two conducting wires in a cup of mercury. The conductors

were connected to the immense plates of the Royal Institution battery. When the pole of a powerful permanent magnet was held above or below the wires, the mercury began to rotate about the wires as an axis. Henry simply substituted his large induction coils for the permanent magnets used by Davy. While both Davy and Faraday used the new effects as an occasion for speculating about the basic nature of electrical forces (on Faraday, see L. P. Williams, *Michael Faraday* [New York, 1965], pp. 156–157), Henry evinced no special theoretical interest in the phenomenon. Henry seems to have used the effect primarily to demonstrate the powers of his battery and induction coils. Once perfected, the experiment became one of the showpieces of Henry's classroom electrical demonstrations. See below, Henry to Silliman, September 10, 1835. Henry's interest in the motions of mercury will surface now and again in future documentation. See, for instance, "Record of Experiments," October 8, 1839 (Henry Papers, Smithsonian Archives).

"RECORD OF EXPERIMENTS"

Henry Papers, Smithsonian Archives

Sept 9th 1834

Exp to determine the modulus of conduction.[1]

For this purpose a wire[2] of an inch of copper was coiled into a galvanometer of one spire in the form of a rectangle. Six inches of wire formed the rectangle and five inch were left projecting from each end. By the side of this was placed another rectangle con-

[1] By the modulus of conduction, Henry apparently meant something like coefficients of conductivity of wires of varying lengths. Henry compared the conducting powers of long and short wires, using different battery arrangements and outputs. We believe his interest in the topic may have been inspired by reading William Ritchie, "Experimental Researches in Electro-Magnetism and Magneto-Electricity," *Phil. Trans.*, 1833, pp. 313–321, on which Henry took notes in Notebook [7171], pages 85–88. Ritchie asked his scientific colleagues to "examine the law, if any exists, which connects the conducting powers of wires with . . . the diameter of the wire, its length, the size of the battery, and the strength of the battery" (p. 315) because he found previous formulations of the relationships contradictory. Henry varied the last three items mentioned by Ritchie in the experiments of September 9 and 10. Such studies pointed towards the concepts embodied in Ohm's Law (for Henry's knowledge of Ohm, see note 8 to the letter of December 17, 1834, below).

Henry did not publish these experiments on the modulus of conduction. However, there is an undated fragment of a rough draft in Box 23 of the Henry Papers, Smithsonian Archives, which suggests Henry might have thought of reading a report on the topic to a learned society or of submitting the results to a journal. The apparatus and the numbers in the draft vary slightly from those of the "Record of Experiments" account of his work, so the document may have been written from other laboratory notes we have not found.

[2] There is a blank in the manuscript at this point, suggesting that Henry meant to write in a fraction later and forgot to do so. In the rough draft mentioned in note one, Henry specified that the galvanometer be constructed of bell wire, which was usually .045 inches in diameter.

sisting of two turns of wire.[3] The ends were placed in an opposite direction & one of them was 5 inches: the other was left indefinetly long.[4]

Exp 1st A plate from the battery was placed in well water after having been dipped into a solution of acid. A slight galvanic action was thus produced. The action of this through the short galvanometer turned the needle to the right through the double to the left.[5]

When both acted together so as to produce an equilibrium of the needle the length of wire attached to the double galvanometer was 24 + the length of the coil; the other was only the length of the coil.[6]

Exp 2 Acid was added 1/64th[7]
Length of wire 17 inches + coil
other as before
Remarkable result[8]

Exp 3 When two plates were used so as to form a compound battery the lengths were about the same. These effects are different from what I expected. The greater the intensity the greater should be the unit of conduction.[9]

[3] In his unpublished draft on the modulus experiments, cited above, Henry mentioned that the wire for the second galvanometer was taken from the same bundle as that for the single spire, in order to minimize differences in the composition of the two instruments.

[4] That is, the two ends of the single-spire galvanometer came off to one side, and the two ends of the longer galvanometer came off to the other. He drew a diagram suggesting this interpretation of "opposite direction" to accompany experiment four of the entry for September 10, printed below. By arranging the apparatus in this way, Henry may have tried to avoid a tangle of four ends that interfered with changing the length of wire, or he may have sought to minimize inductive effects from too many wires in a small space.

[5] Given these results, Henry must have connected the second galvanometer backward relative to the way he connected the first one. If both had been connected to the battery the same way, the needle would have been deflected in the same direction but more intensely by the second arrangement.

[6] The two coils were connected in parallel, and the needle was deflected. To make the needle stationary, Henry added twenty-four more inches of wire to the galvanometer with two turns.

[7] We are unsure what Henry meant by this ratio. He may have increased the strength of the solution up to one part of acid for sixty-four parts of water.

[8] According to Ritchie (see footnote one), the long wire should draw relatively more power than the short one when the acid was increased (p. 315). Thus, Henry would have predicted that he needed to lengthen the long wire in order to balance the needle between the coils.

[9] Henry connected the two plates in series, which increased the intensity of the battery. In an early paper ("On the Application of the Principle of the Galvanic Multiplier to Electro-Magnetic Apparatus, and Also to the Development of Great Magnetic Power in Soft Iron, with a Small Galvanic Element," *Silliman's Journal*, 1831, *19*:403), Henry endorsed Robert Hare's belief that one could lessen the effect of resistance in long wires by using a current of sufficient "projectile force" or intensity. Puzzled at not having to lengthen the wire, Henry changed the battery arrangements in these experiments on September 10 and finally achieved the desired results (see next document).

The Princeton campus. Anonymous pen-and-ink drawing, circa 1804–1833, in the Princeton University Library. Courtesy of the A. C. Smith estate.

James Carnahan (1775–1859), 1850,
by Edward Ludlow Mooney (1813–1887).
Courtesy of the Princeton University Archives.

John Maclean (1800–1886), n.d.,
engraving by T. B. Welch from
daguerreotype by M. P. Simons.
Courtesy of the Princeton University Archives.

Charles Hodge (1797–1878), n.d., engraving by H. G. Wagner from daguerreotype by M. P. Simons. Courtesy of the Princeton University Archives.

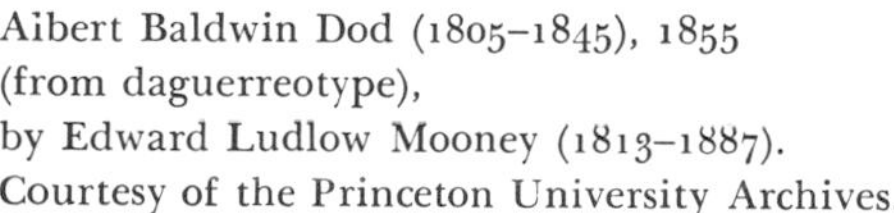

Aibert Baldwin Dod (1805–1845), 1855 (from daguerreotype), by Edward Ludlow Mooney (1813–1887). Courtesy of the Princeton University Archives.

33

May 10 1835 — Princeton

Exp 1 wound 60 feet of copper wire covered with cotton thread around one leg of a horseshoe magnet then connected the ends with a galvanometer — a current was formed through the galvanometer by merely putting on drawing off the keeper —

Magnet of small power

May 11 Exp 1 Two batteries arranged as on the coil with 60 feet copper ribbon inch & 1/2 wide gave great snap. When hands were placed to connect the extremities of coil no shock. When iron vice was brought to the side of the copper of the battery & connected with the end of the coil, brilliant scintillations

Exp 2 The current passed through a galvanic magnet, no increased effect perceived in the shock — current passed in the opposite direction no increased effect.

Exp 3 Passed the current through the large magnet, and afterwards around it, so as to magnetize the iron at the instant of making the contact, or demagnetize it at the instant of breaking the circuit — Small shock Experiment not satisfactory, must be tried again

Entries of May 10, 11, and 12, 1835, from Henry's "Record of Experiments."
Courtesy of the Smithsonian Archives.

34

May 12th 1835

mistake

Exp 1 Passed currents of about the same intensity through parallel ribbons — a continued current accelerated an instantaneous current — when the current was passed through one a spark was produced by the other when in the same direction. Good Exp.

Exp 2nd

A current from a small battery (Shaker) passed through coil parallel with current from single circular battery; the current from single pair appeared in every case to be decreased in intensity by the passage of the other in either direction. Try this on large scale.

N.B.

Exp 3rd Passed the current through a hollow electro magnet filled with mercury — observed no increase of intensity

Ex 4 The two wires from the large magnet were connected with the galvanometer and the keeper suddenly separated the needle made a complete revolution

Exp 5 Repeated Exp 1st, but with a very different result; the intensity was lessened & no increase action could be obtained — Repeat these on a larger scale tomorrow

One of Henry's induction coils. Courtesy of the Physics Department, Princeton University.

Alexander Dallas Bache (1806–1867), 1854,
by James Reid Lambdin (1807–1889).
Courtesy of the
University of Pennsylvania Archives.

John Vaughan (1756–1841), 1823,
by Thomas Sully (1783–1872).
Courtesy of the
American Philosophical Society.

John Torrey (1796–1873), circa 1836.
Anonymous miniature.
Courtesy of the Smithsonian Archives.

Benjamin Silliman (1779–1864), 1825,
by Samuel F. B. Morse (1791–1872).
Courtesy of the Yale University
Art Gallery (gift of Bartlett Arkell).

September 10, 1834

"RECORD OF EXPERIMENTS"

Henry Papers, Smithsonian Archives

Sept 10th [1834]

On reflection it occured to me that this effect so different from what I had expected might be produced by using the same battery for both currents.[1] In order to test this two different plates were used.

Exp 4 When two plates were used in order to equalize the action of each a differential galvanometer was used consisting of two equal wires about 15 inches long [which] were bent into a rectangle & applied in contrary directions to each other with a needle within. This instrument was proved before being used by being placed on the same cup. The ends were then cut off until the needle remained at rest.[2]

When two plates (batteries) were use[d] and the action equalized by pouring acid into one or the other until the equalizing galvanometer showed an equal action. In this exp the plates were dipped about 8 inches in weak acid. The modulus was 94 feet!!![3]

Modulus in another exp 86 feet![4]

Exp 5 Four plates were now used and arranged so as to form two batteries of two elements. The modulus in this case was much increased[5]

[1] Henry thought this was the most important point of his modulus experiments, according to the unpublished rough draft he prepared (cited in note 1 of the previous document): "In the case when it is required to transmit two currents through different parts of an apparatus I find that a great difference is produced in the effect when the two currents are from the same battery or the two halves of the battery. [I] discovered in the first case if there be any difference in the conductability of the two routs required to be passed by the fluid the better rout conducts an undue quantity [of] the fluid. The better conductor almost intirely discharges the battery." Henry also reported this finding to Bache in his letter of December 17, 1834, printed below.

[2] Small differences in the material of each length of wire required that one be trimmed slightly shorter than the other in order to carry the same amount of current. By "same cup" Henry probably meant that he connected the wire loops to the same two-plate battery cell.

[3] After insuring that the amount of current from each trough of two plates was the same, Henry disengaged the equalizing galvanometer and connected the single-spire coil of September 9 to one battery and the double-spire coil to the other. He mentioned this step in his unpublished draft although he omits it here. He then added ninety-six feet of loose wire to the double coil in order to balance the apparatus.

[4] We are not sure what was varied in the second attempt.

[5] This result is what Henry predicted should happen in his work on September 9—increased intensity should lead to greater conductivity. He did no further experiments on the modulus of conduction to our knowledge; the closest he came to returning to this work was his investigation of certain aspects of Ohm's Law in 1838, a report of which appeared in "Contributions III."

September 16, 1834

TO JAMES HENRY

Family Correspondence, Henry Papers, Smithsonian Archives

Princeton Tuesday
Morning Sept [16][1] 1834

Dear James

We arrived safely at home yesterday afternoon at about 4 o'clock. Our passage down the river on Saturday was very plesant although the boats raced all the way and were within a short distance of each other during the whole passage. We reached N.Y. at about 5 o'clock and as we landed saw the smoke of the Wall Street church.[2]

The children were well during the day but on saturday night the boy was seized with the diarrhea and Harriet was up with him several times in the night. We gave him a dose of castor oil on Sunday which appeared to check the disease. He was well yesterday although some what fretful and appears to have entirely recovered to day. We had a very plesant journey yesterday from N.Y. Started about 10 and came by the way of the rail road. The only circumstance of regret was that we lost the Boys little waggon on the boat. We were very kindly intertained by Mr & Mrs Ireland[3] at whose house we stopped while in the city. Tell Misses Meads that I called on their Mother the evening I arrived in N.Y. She had not yet made her visit to Elizabeth Town but leaves New York for there to day with Mr Meads and has promised if a good oportunity offers to visit us the last of this week. We have learned since our return that She will have an opportunity as Mr Wilson[4] somewhat expects his sisters the latter part of this week; he has engaged board for them at Mrs. Morford's.[5]

All things have gone on as usual about the college since our absence. The

[1] Henry mentions below that Princeton's commencement will occur "on Wednesday a week from tomorrow." Commencement took place on September 24, giving us the date for this letter. Henry had just returned from a short trip to Albany to pick up his family.

[2] The New York *Times* of September 16, 1834, reported that the Wall Street Church burnt to the ground on the afternoon of the 13th. "The scene, though melancholy, was grand in the extreme—the tottering and final fall of the spire, with its gilded ball and vane, after they had been for some time encircled by flame—the falling of the burning posts of the steeple—and the vast sheet of fire in which the building was wrapped—presented a painful but interesting scene." Arson was suspected.

[3] A later family letter gives Mr. Ireland's address in New York City as 3 Jay Street. A William H. Ireland lived at this address. Franklin B. Hough, *American Biographical Notes* (Albany, 1875), p. 222, states that William H. Ireland, a prominent politician, died in New York in August 1849. The *New York Weekly Evening Post*, August 30, 1849, p. 4, gives his age as eighty-one at time of death. We have no further information on Henry's friend.

[4] Probably Hugh Nesbitt Wilson; see Henry's letter to Harriet, above, [March] 24, [1834], footnote 13.

[5] Mrs. Morford is listed in *Princeton Annual Catalogue*, 1834, as boarding a number of Princeton students.

examination commenced yesterday & will continue during the present week. The commencement is on Wednesday a week from tomorrow. Stephen will leave for albany in about a week after. We could not prevail on Mr or Mrs Ireland to accompany us to Princeton. Mr & Mrs Meads called on us on sunday evening.

Give our love to Mother, Nancy, the Meads family & all others to whom we are indebted for a like favour. To Eliza Selkirk[6] and Mr McArthour. The examination has commenced for this morning and therefore I must be off.

Your Brother

[6] Elizabeth Selkirk. See *Henry Papers, 1*:xviiin, 452n.

FROM ALEXANDER DALLAS BACHE

Henry Papers, Smithsonian Archives

Philad. Sept. 17. 1834

My dear Sir,

In comparing with our friend Courtenay the different observations for magnetic intensity which compose parts of the series undertaken to connect West Pt. & Philad., we have found in the different results variations which have disappointed us not a little. Similar differences exist in the observations of Parry[1] & Foster,[2] Fox[3] & others. Having reviewed our methods &c

[1] William Edward Parry (1790–1855), a British naval officer best known for his Arctic explorations. *DNB* and Ann Parry, *Parry of the Arctic* (London, 1963). He made three attempts to find the northwest passage (1819–1820, 1821–1823, and 1824–1825) and one attempt to reach the North Pole over the ice in 1827. Parry attained the rank of Rear Admiral in the Royal Navy. Henry had a copy of Parry's *Journal of a Second Voyage for the Discovery of a North-West Passage . . .* (New York, 1824), perhaps acquired in Albany. This is the voyage prior to the one producing the data Bache refers to.

[2] Henry Foster (1796–1831), another scientifically-inclined British naval officer. *DNB* and *DSB*. Foster was a geophysicist. His first notable work was with Basil Hall on the acceleration of gravity. In the 1824–1825 Parry expedition, Foster did observations on terrestrial magnetism, the velocity of sound, the acceleration of gravity, and refraction of the atmosphere. These investigations brought him the Copley Medal of the Royal Society and an assignment to do similar work in the South Seas. He was drowned on an expedition to determine the difference of longitude across the Isthmus of Panama by rockets.

Bache is referring here to the results reported by Parry and Foster jointly and Foster alone which appear in *Phil. Trans.*, 1826 (part IV), pp. 71–187. The most important finding according to Foster was that the temperature had no effects on his observations of the daily variation of horizontal intensity (p. 182f). If true, this had considerable theoretical significance as many contemporaries assumed causal relationships between terrestrial magnetism and atmospheric phenomena (including the aurora). Foster explained his findings by postulating that the sun produced a "small variation in the position of the magnetic axis." Although Foster does not say so specifically, the presumption is that the exposure to sunlight produces thermoelectric effects which, in turn, yield the diurnal and annual vari-

we cannot think that the differences are chargeable to them or to want of care; in the smallest needles, particularly the rapidly vibrating one which you were kind enough to give me, there is abundant evidence of the influence of the air which in the case alluded to obliterated every mark of a proper correction for temperature. You have had great experience in this matter & before positively determining to present the results, which we are inclined to do with the irregularities brought out into high relief, I should like to have the benefit of knowing the results of your own observation on this branch. After the corrections for arc & temperature have been applied what differences from observations on different days are apparent in the magnetism at the same place.[4] I need hardly say that I do not allude to any differences which a permanent loss of magnetism in the needles would produce.

Have you seen Mr Christies paper on the improvement of the means in use for obtaining magnetic obs^ns? As far as I have examined it seems to me to [be] a step en arrière.[5]

Let me hear from you in answer as soon as you can.

Very truly Yours
A. D. Bache

ations, a well-known hypothesis at the time of publication. Foster's contribution is the hypothesis of the changes in the magnetic axis.

[3] Robert Were Fox (1789–1877). *DNB*. His report of irregularities appears in the *Proceedings of the Royal Society*, 1832, *3*:123–125 and the *Phil. Mag.*, 1832, 3d ser. *1*:310–314. Fox was interested in such topics as the internal temperature of the earth as part of a concern for relating geological structure to physical and chemical factors. In this article Fox was testing the irregularities in observations of diurnal variations produced by currents of air, particularly due to solar heat. He then speculates about how the chemical and physical nature of some geological strata would produce observed geomagnetic effects. In a footnote Fox notes William Snow Harris's apparatus for vibrating magnetic needles in vacuo in the *Phil. Trans.*, 1831. Years later Henry and Fox corresponded.

[4] In the paper which Bache and Courtenay read before the American Philosophical Society, May 6, 1836 ("On the Relative Horizontal Intensities of Terrestrial Magnetism at Several Places in the United States, with the Investigation of Corrections for Temperature, and Comparisons of the Methods of Oscillation in Full and Rarefied Air," APS *Transactions*, 1837, n.s. *5*:427–457), the authors systematically checked the accuracy of their chronometers and allowed corrections for temperature (in which they included corrections for diurnal variation) and arc. They still observed wild variations in vibrating the needles. In effect, their corrections served to bring seeming "irregularities . . . into high relief," as Bache tells Henry. Bache and Courtenay solved the problem by using apparatus which suspended the needle in rarefied air, a solution for which they credited Snow Harris.

The earliest surviving exchange between Bache and Henry (July 13 and July 15, 1834, above) concerned, among other things, their work in terrestrial magnetism. Though we have not found Henry's reply to this letter (if one were sent), other letters below indicate that Henry continued to work with Bache in these investigations. See the letters to Bache of December 17, 1834, and, particularly, May 18, 1835.

[5] Bache is probably referring to Samuel Hunter Christie, "On the Improvements in the Instruments and Methods Employed in Determining the Direction and Intensity of the Terrestrial Magnetic Force," *Phil. Trans.*, 1833, pp. 343–358. For Christie, see above, Henry to Harriet Henry, April 11, 1833, footnote 10.

September 18, 1834

"RECORD OF EXPERIMENTS"

Henry Papers, Smithsonian Archives

Sept 18th [1834][1]

Observed to day that when the copper and zinc of two different pairs of elements of the large battery are connected by a long ribbon of copper a spark is produced at the moment of separation. I have not tried if the same effect will be produced if the elements be perfectly insulated

[1] In Henry's notebook this item appears out of order, directly following related experiments of August 15, 1834. Possibly Henry meant to date this August 18.

TO JOHN TORREY

Torrey Papers, Library, New York Botanical Garden

Princeton Sept 20th 1834[1]

My Dear Friend,

Can you forgive me for so long delaying to answer your kind letter of Aug. 18th.[2] It came to hand at a time when I was much engaged in some experiments and when I expected to see you in New York in a few days. I have however passed twice through your city to and from albany without being able to call at your house. Do not condemn me unheard—I will indeavour to plead my cause when you come to Princeton.

I returned from albany with my family the beginning of this week and on account of my being obliged to attend the examination &c I have only to day (saturday) and monday left to make some hurried preparations in the way of experiments with my battery which as you may reccollect is to be exhibited on tuseday at 4 o'clock and to be followed in the evening with your desplay of fire-works. Do not fail to come. The class expects to see you & will be disappointed if the fire works be not exhibited. There are no speakers prepared to address the societies or the alumni. The persons chosen in both cases have failed. Mr Mclean has indeavoured to get Mr Biddle of the Bank but owing to the invitation being so late he was unable to accept.[3]

[1] In the upper left-hand corner Torrey noted the receipt of this letter on September 22 and that it was answered verbally.

[2] See above.

[3] Nicholas Biddle would deliver the 1835 commencement address. As these were usually printed, the absence of any 1834 address may indicate that no outside speakers were present this year. Biddle (1786–1844, *DAB*), an alumnus of Princeton (A.B., 1801), was a notable

Your Books have all been paid for but 4. The persons owing for these will be here at commencement & I will see them at that time.

In great haste from
your sincere friend
Jos Henry

P.S. Do not forget to bring Mrs Torrey and the chickens[4] with you to commencement. It will be a pleasant jaunt for them as the temperature is now most agreeable for travelling. J.H.

---

scholar as well as President of the second Bank of the United States (1823–1839). Elected to membership in 1813, Biddle held elected offices in the American Philosophical Society, 1831–1839. Throughout the 1830s Biddle was an active participant in the cultural circles where he and Henry met on several occasions to be documented in this and following volumes.

[4] Presumably, the Torrey children.

FROM JAMES DAVID FORBES

Henry Papers, Smithsonian Archives

Edinburgh 21st Septr 1834

My Dear Sir

I was much obliged by your communication[1] accompanied by the magnetic needles, and I assure you it gives me great pleasure to be of any use in promoting so interesting an object as the comparison of European & American Magnetic Intensities.

When I received your letter I was overwhelmed with the duties of Secretary to the British Association,[2] the meeting of which at Edinburgh is just past, & I have seized the earliest possible opportunity of cooperating as far as I could with your undertaking. You will find I hope satisfactory observations annexed,[3] with your No 1., made yesterday—both with 300 & 100 vibrations; the observations I am in the habit of making being chiefly of 100. The mode of registering you will easily comprehend—the seconds of real time being alone noted. As to the corrections, I leave you to determine that for Temperature[4] for your No 1. I have applied an approximate cor-

[1] For which see above, June 30, 1834.

[2] Forbes served as the Junior Secretary for the Edinburgh meeting (September 8–13, 1834) of the British Association for the Advancement of Science, which he helped found in 1831. Among other duties Forbes was responsible for delivering a report on the general progress of the Association. He sent a copy of his address to Henry; see the following document.

[3] Forbes enclosed five sheets of recordings of his observations which we have omitted.

[4] Henry demonstrated his knowledge of Christopher Hansteen's formula for correcting observations for temperature in his 1832 article, "On a Disturbance of the Earth's Magnetism, in Connexion with the Appearance of an Aurora Borealis, as Observed at Albany, April 19th, 1831," *Silliman's Journal*, 1832, 22:143–155. See especially p. 147.

rection for the Temperature of Needle A which I send you; this is a reduction to the freezing point derived from a single observation, which therefore requires verification—which indeed is a very troublesome matter. This Needle A is by no means steady in its magnetism, but by swinging it in the United States & returning it quickly & again swinging it here we may make it available for comparison.

	s[econds]
8th Sept 1829. 4 PM Needle A made 300 vib. at Greenhill in	910.84
9th Feb. 1832. 3 PM	949.66
2nd June 1832 11 AM	946.37
19th Sept. 1834 5 PM	973.71

All corrected.[5]

The corrections for arc in the accompanying observations are derived from the following tables, the mode of calculating which & making other corrections I shall explain in a paper I am about to communicate to the Royal Society of London on Intensities in the Alps.[6]

Number of vibrations required to reduce the amplitude to ½ the commencing arc.	Log. Correction, the Initial Arc being 10° (on each side) & the time of 100 vib. determined	Log. correction, the initial arc being 20° (on each side) & the time of 300 vibrations determined
70	9.99978	9.99967
80	75	60
90	72	53
100	70	46
110	67	40
120	65	33
130	62	27

[5] Forbes corrected his enclosed observations with his needle A not only for temperature but also for the rate of gain or loss of his chronometer, and for deviations in time inherent in large oscillations of the needle ("corrections for arc").

[6] Forbes's article, read before the Royal Society December 19, 1836, was entitled "Account of Some Experiments Made in Different Parts of Europe, on Terrestrial Magnetic Intensity, Particularly with Reference to the Effect of Height," *Phil. Mag.*, 1837, 3d ser. *11*:58–66, 166–174, 254–260, 363–375. Forbes improved upon Hansteen's earlier attempts to establish tables of corrections for needle vibrations by including tables for 100 vibrations starting from a 10° semi-arc and for 300 vibrations from a 20° semi-arc. Hansteen used only the latter, and Forbes recognized the necessity of using both 100- and 300-vibration observation for comparisons. The method was logarithmic: that is, the "log. correction" was added to the logarithm of the observed time (the appropriate "log. correction" corresponding in the table to the number of vibrations required to reach half the initial arc), and the result being a log from which the corrected time could be calculated. Forbes included this table in his article. The "other corrections" he systematized similarly in the article were those for the

I should farther observe, that the Hansteen Instrument I have admits of less than 5 inches of suspending silk which is probably shorter than you employ, & is too short with such strong silk as that used for your N° 1. I have however employed it. The suspension which I used for Needle A is attached to it, & it is desirable that it should not be changed.

In packing the two needles I shall take care to place them with their opposite poles nearest, in which way they suffer I believe less alteration than when packed single, avoiding of course all contact.[7]

The dip here determined approximately in 1832: it is about 72°30′.

We have great want of accurate tables of hourly & monthly changes of Intensity without which observations on different days & at different hours cannot be accurately compared. Would anyone in America undertake this investigation?[8] The effect of Temperature requires accurate experiment. I have found most perplexing anomalies.

I have given Mr Turnbull some papers for you, & I shall be very glad to hear of the arrival of the needles & your progress in this investigation.[9]

I am my Dear Sir
Yours very faithfully
James D. Forbes

rate of the chronometer, temperature, and variations in the needles' magnetism. We know of no instances in which Henry applied such sophisticated analysis to his raw observations, with the exception of temperature standardization cited in footnote 4.

[7] The package was delayed, and the needles were noticeably weakened in their magnetism. It is possible that this letter was in the package and was not received by Henry until the spring of 1835. For a description of the delay in the delivery of the package, see below, Henry to Torrey, February 23, 1835, especially footnote 8.

[8] Alexander Dallas Bache raised a related question in his letter to Henry to July 13, 1834. Hourly and daily observations of the changes in the earth's magnetic intensity were considered important. But until these became routine at observatories and, later, were done by automatic registering devices, it was a rare, devoted investigator who would and could make such observations around the clock over extended periods of time.

[9] Henry enclosed a copy of Forbes's letter in a May 18, 1835, letter to A. D. Bache, printed below.

FROM JOHN TURNBULL[1]

Henry Papers, Smithsonian Archives

Edinburgh Sep. 23 1834

My Dear Sir

I have received the accompanying parcel at too late an hour to write you as I wished but I will do so in about a fortnight. I received from Prof. Forbes

[1] See *Henry Papers, 1*:355n.

several pamphlets to yourself and other individuals, but they are at my lodgings 1½ miles from this & the Bearer, Mr R. Murray[2] goes in so short a time that I cannot get them. But I will send by first opportunity. It contains his address[3] at the opening of the British Association.

I attended a number of the meetings and saw several of the most eminent Scientific men in Europe & heard many of them speak; such as Sir David Brewster,[4] Sir Charles Bell,[5] Dr Lardner,[6] Prof. Buckland,[7] Prof. Sedgwick,[8] M. Arago,[9] Secretary of the French Institute, Dr Dalton,[10] Manchester, Lord Greenock,[11] an eminent geologist &c. Dont you wish you had been in my place?

Please to swing the needle and send it back immediately addressed to Prof. Forbes or me care of Andrew Taylor & Co. Liverpool. I will see that it reaches its destination.[12] If you send it to N. York to the care of my friend

[2] Not identified.

[3] Forbes's address was printed in *Report of the Fourth Meeting of the British Association for the Advancement of Science, Held at Edinburgh in 1834* (London, 1835), pp. xi–xii. This volume, though not the original pamphlet sent by Forbes, is contained in the Henry Library.

[4] Brewster (1781–1868), the Scottish physicist, was a Vice President of the Edinburgh meetings. *DSB*. Brewster's contributions to the meetings included a report to the Section on Chemistry and Mineralogy on the optical qualities of various minerals. See the above-cited *Report*, p. 575.

[5] Anatomist and pioneer in correlating anatomical differences in the nervous system with functional differences (discoveries which influenced the neural theories of Johannes Müller), Bell (1774–1842) gave "Observations on the Proper Method of Studying the Nervous System," *Report*, pp. 667–670. *DSB*.

[6] Dionysius Lardner (1793–1859), scientist and encyclopedist, edited the extremely popular 133-volume Cabinet Cyclopaedia, several volumes of which are found in the Henry Library. Henry, who found Lardner's popular and semipopular writings useful in his own research (see e.g., *Henry Papers, 1*:80n), had an angry confrontation with the erudite encyclopedist over capabilities of American steamboats at the 1837 meeting of the British Association. Their confrontation, to be documented in a future volume of *The Papers of Joseph Henry*, is mentioned in Henry's 1838 letter to Bache, in Nathan Reingold, ed., *Science in Nineteenth-Century America* (New York, 1964), p. 85.

[7] The geologist William Buckland (1784–1856; *Henry Papers, 1*:124n) presented communications on fossil plants and animals to evening meetings of the Association. *Report*, p. xliv.

[8] Adam Sedgwick (1785–1873), President of the preceding year's meetings, assessed the progress of the British Association and delivered geological communications. *Report*, pp. ix–xi, xlvii. *DNB*.

[9] Officers of the 1834 meetings conferred with the eminent French astronomer and physicist D. F. J. Arago (1786–1853), the Perpetual Secretary of the French Institute, on possibilities of cooperation between the French society and the British Association. Elected a corresponding member of the BAAS, Arago gave communications on magnetism and optics. *Report*, pp. xxvii, xxx, xxxi, xliii. Aside from his work in optics and astronomy, Arago had physical and geophysical concerns of special interest to scientists like Henry and A. D. Bache. Henry's early notebooks show him consulting Arago's work on terrestrial magnetism (see *Henry Papers, 1*:336n). For overlaps with Bache, see Nathan Reingold, "Alexander Dallas Bache: Science and Technology in the American Idiom," *Technology and Culture*, 1970, *11*:170. *DSB*.

[10] John Dalton (1766–1844; *DSB*) reported on the progress of research in determining specific gravities of oxygen, hydrogen, and carbonic acid. *Report*, p. xlii.

[11] Charles Murray Cathcart (1783–1859), Lord Greenock, second Earl Cathcart (in 1843), was an Edinburgh native, more eminent as a British general than as a geologist. Discoverer of the mineral Greenockite in 1841, Cathcart reported to the 1834 BAAS meetings on mineral formations in Scotland. *Report*, pp. xlv, 639–642. *DNB*.

Mr George Hart[13] 41 South St. he will forward it by the packet or otherwise.

My best regards to Mrs. Henry and the other members of your family. I remain

My Dear Sir
very truly yours
J. Turnbull

[12] The scientific exchange encountered a delay, for which see below, Henry to Torrey, February 23, 1835, footnote 8. It is possible that this letter, like the Forbes letter immediately above, was enclosed in the package and did not reach Henry until the spring of 1835.

[13] A frequent emissary for Turnbull, Hart remains unidentified. Perhaps the merchant George Hart, listed in the 1839–1840 New York City Directory.

"RECORD OF EXPERIMENTS"

Henry Papers, Smithsonian Archives

Sept 25, 26th [1834][1]

Exp. with the large battery

Battery charged with a mixture of sulphuric & nitric acids, 4 pints of the former, & one of the latter, to a barrel of water.

Battery as a Deflagrator[2]

[1] This experimental series is a continuation of the experiments begun on August 15, 1834, and resumed on September 18 (see above). In the "Record of Experiments" it appears out of order before the entry of September 7, 1834.

[2] In this experimental series, Henry focuses on various heat, light, and burning effects generated in conductors by his battery, arranged alternately for intensity and quantity. Comparison of effects obtained directly from the battery with those from induction coils and ribbons connected to the poles of the battery provided another measure of self-induction. Some of his results were published in "Contributions II: Spiral Conductor."

Ever since the invention of the voltaic pile, electrical physicists had taken a lively interest in the heat and light (as well as chemical) effects accompanying the passage or discharge of an electric current. Observations of sparks, incandescence, heat, fusion, and burning afforded insight into the nature of voltaic electricity, comparisons with static electricity, and gauges of the power of batteries. Henry's experiments were routine, modeled upon the work of electrochemists like Humphry Davy, J. G. Children, William Wollaston, and, in America, Robert Hare. (For a later overview of the subject, see *Encyclopaedia Britannica*, 8th ed., s.v. "Voltaic Electricity," pp. 626–628.)

Electrical investigators distinguished two primary effects: "ignition" and "deflagration." According to Robert Hare, ignition occurred when a continuous current flowed through a conductor placed between the battery electrodes. Heated to incandescence, the conductor often fused or burned. The more brilliant phenomenon of deflagration took place when the contact between the conductor and electrodes was interrupted by the effects of the current itself or by the experimenter, producing scintillations, burning, snapping, and even small explosions. See Hare's "Of Galvan-

Exp 1 15 inches of platina wire $1/50$ inch diameter, heated to white heat—suddenly cooled by lifting up one of the connections. This exp was performed with battery as a caloromoter.

Exp 2 The vises by which the articles were fastened to the poles burned.

Exp 3 The points of two steel knitting needles burned with intense light.

Exp 4 Two copper points burned with greenish light—very beautiful

---

ism, or Voltaic Electricity," supplement to his *Compendium of the Course of Chemical Instruction in the Medical Department of the University of Pennsylvania*, 4th ed. (Philadelphia, 1840–1843), pp. 45–48. Not so careful as Hare in maintaining the distinction, Henry often used the terms interchangeably to indicate any brilliant manifestation of electrical energy.

Of special concern to electrical physicists were the variations in the intensity of the ignitions and deflagrations produced by manipulating the form and output of the battery. The intensities of heat and light also depended on the size and nature of the conductors. The interrelations were still unclear in Henry's day, due in part to continuing confusion about the properties of quantity and intensity currents and an inadequate understanding of electrical resistance. One of the most comprehensive theoretical explanations, and probably the one most familiar to Henry, was that of Robert Hare, the inventor of the calorimotor and deflagrator, whose effects Henry reproduced with his convertible battery. Hare theorized that the galvanic current was actually a fusion of heat and electrical fluids—electrocaloric. (Later he introduced light as a third constituent.) Hare's various batteries, introduced in the decade before Henry's present experiments, were designed to bring out the individual manifestations of each constituent, as predicted by his theory. In general Hare held that a small number of large plates augmented the volume of caloric—hence the calorimotor—while an extensive series of small plates accentuated the electrical effects at the expense of heat. Each array had specific properties regarding the production of sparks, shocks, the heating of metals, incandescence, and burning. Though not entirely clear, Hare apparently conceived of his deflagrator, consisting of a long series (80 pairs) of large plates, as an instrument of intermediate design, but one that seemed capable of the most dramatic effects, due to a peculiar reinforcement of the caloric by the high intensity electricity. Somehow the electrical power imparted sufficient "projectile force" to the caloric to produce the most brilliant deflagrations. See the following series of articles by Hare in *Silliman's Journal*: "A New Theory of Galvanism, Supported by Some Experiments and Observations Made by Means of the Calorimotor, a New Galvanic Instrument," 1818, *1*:413–423. "A Memoir on Some New Modifications of Galvanic Apparatus, with Observations in Support of His New Theory of Galvanism," 1821, *3*:105–117 (introducing the deflagrator). "Notice of the Galvanic Deflagrator of Professor Robert Hare . . . in a Letter to That Gentleman from the Editor," 1822, *4*:200–204. "Correspondence Between Robert Hare . . . and the Editor, on the Subject of Dr. Hare's Calorimotor and Deflagrator, and the Phenomena Produced by Them," 1822, *5*: 94–112. See also Silliman's *Elements of Chemistry*, 2 vols. (New Haven, 1831), 2:648–655, which gives Hare's ideas as well as the state of the art.

In this experimental series, Henry duplicates many of Hare's procedures and results, with the idea of intensifying the deflagration effects by self-induction (see experiment 10). Among Henry's reading notes are extensive excerpts from Hare's above-cited "A Memoir on Some New Modifications of Galvanic Apparatus, with Observations in Support of His New Theory of Galvanism" (Notebook [7171], pp. 45–46). Hare describes his deflagrator, details his experimental procedures for eliciting various heat and light effects, and speculates further on his electrocaloric theory of galvanism. Typically, Henry carefully notes the specifications for Hare's apparatus, the experimental techniques, and the results, but records nothing of Hare's speculations on the nature of electricity. For the purposes of Henry's research, heat, ignition, and deflagration were simply measures of electrical power and clues to self-induction.

Exp 5 Mercury deflagrated very brilliant

Exp 6 A piece of charcoal from the forge was placed on the metallic cup attached to one pole for the purpose of deflagrating mercury and a small quantity of mercury thrown into the dish and [the charcoal] pressed down so as to be surrounded by the fluid metal. When the other pole, a thick copper wire was brought near the coal, a most vivid and intense ignition took place. This is by far the best method of deflagrating charcoal which I have ever known. The mercury gives a good metallic contact, and coal can be ignited <*fussed*> with a smaller number of plates than by any other process.

The battery <*fu*> ignits the coal when arranged so as to form but 8 plates of zinc & 8 copper.

exp 7 The battery was changed to a caloromoter of 8 pairs of plates. The scintillations from the vises was more in quantity, not as brilliant as when the instrument acted as a deflagrator.

Exp 8 Deflagration of mercury not as brilliant as before

Exp 9 The heating power of the battery much increased as shewn by the platina wire.

Ex 10 A very beautiful effect was produced when one pole was connected with the end of a coil [of] copper ribbon,[3] and the other end of the coil drawn along the edge or back of one of the copper connections. A series of loud and rapid explosions or snaps were produced with a vivid scintillation of the end of the copper ribbon

Ex 11 Fine brass wire placed between the poles instantaneously melted.

Ex 12 Platina wire placed between the poles becomes white hot; lift up one of the connecting rods, & the heat suddently falls; put down the connector, the heat again rises

Ex 13 A wire happened to be on a balance on a curved part between the poles, both ends dipping into the mercury cups. As soon as the acid was applied to the plates, the wire commenced vibrating with a series of brilliant deflagrations. This exp might be shown on a large scale by poising a wire thus[4]

[3] This experiment is apparently the only one of the current series using the ribbon coils.

[4] Experiment thirteen is followed by a note in Henry's hand, added at a later date: "Made a machine to move by this action. See Exp april 1840." The pertinent entries are those of April 9 and 13, in the second volume of his "Record of Experiments," to be published in a future installment of *The Papers of Joseph Henry*. A notice of Henry's demonstration of the apparatus appeared in *Proceedings of the American Philosophical Society*, 1838–1840, *1*: 301.

September 26, 1834

TO JOHN VAUGHAN

Miscellaneous Manuscripts Collection, Library, American Philosophical Society

Princeton College
Sept 26th 1834

Dear Sir

Permit me to introduce to your acquaintance my friend Prof. Jager of our College. He occupies the chair of Natural History in the Institution & will be much interested in viewing the collection of specimens etc belonging to your society.

With the highest respect
I am your most obdt.
Serv
Joseph Henry

TO BENJAMIN SILLIMAN, SR.

Daniel C. Gilman Collection, Library, Johns Hopkins University[1]

Princeton Oct 1st 1834

My Dear Sir

About the beginning of Sept. I sent by mail a package for the Journal containing a Translation of M Quetelet's[2] Tour in England and also a let-

[1] Henry retained the draft of this letter and preserved it in his papers, now in the Smithsonian Archives. Henry's outgoing letter has a number of minor stylistic changes from the draft but no substantive changes, except as mentioned in footnote 4, below.

[2] Adolphe Quetelet (1796–1874), a Belgian astronomer, mathematician, and statistician with geophysical interests quite compatible with those of such Americans as Alexander Dallas Bache and Joseph Henry. Born in Ghent, Quetelet studied at the Paris Observatory and under Pierre Simon Laplace. In 1828 he founded and became the head of the Brussels Observatory. Like Henry and Bache, his wide-ranging interests in the physical sciences led him into studies of meteorology, terrestrial magnetism, and geodesy. Quetelet actively pursued the development of systems for gathering simultaneous observations of astronomical, meteorological, and geodetic phenomena throughout Europe. His ambition was to derive general mathematical laws from the study of the statistics of the natural phenomena of man's environment, including the social and biological aspects of man himself. To some extent Quetelet's objectives served as a model for some of Henry's aspirations when he became Secretary of the Smithsonian Institution in 1846. *Encyclopaedia Britannica*, 1970 edition, *18*:960, s.v. "Quetelet." David Landau and Paul F. Lazarsfeld, "Adolphe Quetelet," *International Encyclopedia of the Social Sciences*, 17 vols. (New York, 1968), *13*: 247–257. Nathan Reingold, "Alexander Dallas Bache: Science and Technology in the Ameri-

ter to you.[3] In my letter which was written on the last pages of the communication I stated that I had procured two subscribers for the Journal, Mr Wines[4] of Princeton and Dr William Dunbar of Natchez Mississippi.[5] As my copy of the Journal for Oct has arrived unaccompanied by the copy for Mr Wines I must conclude that the package did not reach New Haven or that it has been mislaid.

Enclosed are ten dollars six of which are for Dr Dunbars subscription for one year and the other four are to placed to my credit.

Since my last I have tried my battery[6] in all its forms. The results fully answer my expectations. I beleave a greater variety of experiments can be exhibited with it than by any other battery ever before constructed. I mentioned in my letter that I was not anxious for the publication of the Translation of Quetelet's Tour but that perhaps some interesting extracts could be made from it.[7]

Our commencement is just over and I am now preparing to spend the greater part of our vacation of six weeks in making experiments. My Battery is now intirely finished. It has cost me nearly all my leisure time for a

---

can Idiom," *Technology and Culture*, 1970, *11*:163–174, especially pp. 168–169. Liliane Wellens-de Donder, *Inventaire de la correspondance d'Adolphe Quetelet* (Brussels, 1966).

There is a remote possibility that Quetelet sent a reprint of an article to Henry as early as 1834 (see the next footnote), but Henry and Quetelet appear not to have met until 1870. Quetelet was out of town at the time of Henry's visit to Brussels in July 1837. Nonetheless, they exchanged numerous letters; surviving in Henry's Library is one book by Quetelet and seven reprints, two of which bear the author's inscriptions.

[3] Henry's letter has not been found but the translation of Quetelet's account of a tour in England appears as "Notes Extracted from a Tour in England, During the Months of June and July, 1833; by Mr. QUETELET, of Brussels. Translated for this Journal, by a pupil of Prof. Jos. Henry, of the College of Nassau Hall, Princeton, New Jersey, and communicated by that gentleman," *Silliman's Journal*, 1835, *28*:55–68. The notes appeared as part one of "Notice of the Meetings of the British Association for the Advancement of Science, in 1833, at Cambridge, and in 1834 at Edinburgh; in Two Parts." We have not identified which student of Henry's did the translation. The article originally appeared in Quetelet's journal as "Notes extraites d'un voyage en Angleterre aux mois de juin et de juillet 1833: Réunion générale des savans Anglais à Cambridge," *Correspondance mathématique et physique*, 1834, *8*:1–18. A reprint of the French piece survives in the Henry Library; numerous ink smears and linear annotations suggest that this was the copy from which the translation was prepared. As there is no evidence that the reprint was presented to Henry by the author, we have no way of determining how Henry acquired it. One demonstration reported by Quetelet, namely Charles Wheatstone's illustration of the instantaneous nature of an electric spark, was repeated by Henry and so noted in Silliman's reprinted version, p. 61. See above, Ten Eyck to Henry, [ca. November 22, 1833], footnote 2.

[4] Enoch Cobb Wines, for whom see above, Henry to James Henry, June 25, 1833, footnote 5. Henry originally drafted the letter to say, "Mr. Wines of Princeton, Author of two years in the Navy and Principal of the Edge Hill Seminary."

[5] For identification of William Dunbar, M.D., see above, Henry's Notes on a Trip to Philadelphia, April 29–May 2, 1834, footnote 34.

[6] Henry commenced testing his new versatile battery on September 7, 1834. For a description of the battery see above, Henry to Maclean, October 9, 1833, footnote 4.

[7] Silliman ignored Henry's suggestion, choosing instead to print the complete translation of Quetelet's "Notes extraites. . . ."

year past. As there are no mechanics who work in metal to be procured in this place all the soldering has been done by myself and an assistant.[8] This has been a very unprofitable waste of the little time my college duties have left unoccupied.

I would be pleased to find leisure to make a hurried visit to New Haven during the present vacation but I fear that I shall have to defer it until next spring.[9]

I am sir with the highest
Respect
Yours sincerely
Joseph Henry

[8] Henry's assistant remains unidentified. In Princeton Henry laments the dearth of "mechanics who work in metal," just as in 1832 he complained, "I can get nothing made in Albany in the philosophical line except I stand continually over the workman during the operation or unless, which is most often the case, I do the work intirely myself. . . ." *Henry Papers, 1*:420.

[9] Henry's plans for a spring trip to New Haven went unfulfilled, perhaps due to the activity resulting from the death of his mother and several trips to Philadelphia. His next journey to New Haven, more than a year from the date of this letter, is described below in letters to his wife on October 24 and October 28, 1835.

FROM BENJAMIN SILLIMAN, SR.

Henry Papers, Smithsonian Archives

New Haven Octob[er] 9, 1834

My Dear Sir

My absence in the remotest part of Maine from Sept[r] 27 to Octob 2 will explain my silence for neither of your letters had arrived previous to my departure.[1] On my return so many duties pressed upon me that I was not able instantly to meet them: I have however dispatched the three last N[os] of the Journal as desired to your friends M[r] Dunbar & M[r] Wines & have credited the money you have remitted, viz $6. to M[r] Dunbar & $4. to yourself. I thank you for this kind effort on your part. I am gratified to hear of your new battery which I believe is quite original & must be I think both convenient & economical. When your paper is printed I trust you will send me a copy.[2]

[1] A reference to Henry's letter of October 1, 1834, above, and the letter in early September which Henry enclosed in a package containing the Quetelet translation.

[2] This is the first explicit reference to Henry's "Contributions I: Battery," the first of a series of papers to be published in the *Transactions of the American Philosophical*

The enclosed you can use in any way you think proper or put it into the fire as you choose.[3]

If you write to Mr Dunbar please say that I know nothing of the effort to obtain subscribers in Natchez—neither names nor money have been ever transmitted to me from that place. There was indeed a house named to me there as agents—I should think 10 or 12 years ago—& I sent on a package of Journals, I think a dozen copies of special nos. but no returns were ever made & the name (now out of my recollection) was not the one you mention.

I thank you & your pupil[4] for the interesting translations from the French pamphlet. I last evening received the new Vol giving the papers of that meeting, but I think I shall still wish to make use of your communication in whole or in part as you kindly permit me to do.

I remain Dr Sir
Yours very truly
B Silliman

Society. Henry may have mentioned the paper in his letter to Silliman of early September, which no longer survives. In mentioning it, he must have indicated that the paper was not intended for *Silliman's Journal*. For the first evidence of Henry's contacts with John Vaughan and the American Philosophical Society concerning this paper, see below, Vaughan to Henry, November 8, 1834.

[3] We have no idea what this refers to.

[4] Unidentified.

BENJAMIN SILLIMAN, SR. TO JOHN VAUGHAN

Archives, American Philosophical Society

Yale College Octob^er^ 9, 1834

Dear Sir

I do not recollect what rules are prescribed for the election of members of the philosophical society: I presume however that the opinions of actual members & especially of the senior fellows will never be regarded as underserving of attention. In this view I take the liberty to ask your influence & that of some of my other friends in the society in favor of Prof^r^ Joseph Henry of Princeton College, Nassau Hall, Prof of Nat Phil.

Mr Henry is one of the most promising of our younger natural philosophers & is already distinguished for some very fine advances in Science as may be seen in the American Journal, in the Transactions of the Albany Institute, in the Annual Reports of the Regents of the University of the

State of New York &c.[1] Prof^r Henry['s] great galvanic magnets have far surpassed any done elsewhere. One made by him & which is now in my possession has lifted over 2000 lbs & this power has been nearly doubled by him since.[2] I understand he has recently constructed a galvanic battery combining in one instrument all the principal forms heretofore invented.[3]

Although Mr Henry excells in practical philosophy[4] he is not less distinguished for fertility of invention & superior powers of intellectual analysis both mathematical & physical.

His private character is also excellent & I am sure the society does not possess a member of his age of greater merit nor any member of more promise.

I should therefore be much gratified if you in your wisdom & perfect knowledge of the proper modes of proceeding will so manage as to have Mr Henry elected.

I am sure my friends Mr Duponceau,[5] Dr Hare, Mr Lea,[6] Prof^r Bache, Dr Morton,[7] Dr Harlan[8] & others will pay respect to my opinion & as far as you see occasion I will thank you to shew them this letter, which I ought to add is written entirely of my own motion & without Mr Henry's knowledge: *I* have not leisure to write to others.[9]

I continue to receive occasionally letters from your brother Mr B. Vaughan & now & then one from Mr Wm Vaughan[10] of London, who are always like yourself public spirited & personally kind.

I remain dear sir as ever
yours very truly
B Silliman

[1] For examples of Henry's contributions to the Albany literature, see *Henry Papers, 1*: 104n, 107n.

[2] See Henry's "An Account of a Large Electro-Magnet, Made for the Laboratory of Yale College," *Silliman's Journal*, 1831, *20*:201–203, where he reported surpassing 2000 pounds. For a discussion of the more powerful magnet, see above, Cooper to Henry, November 16, 1833.

[3] See above, Henry to Silliman, October 1, 1834.

[4] Silliman means experimental research, not applied science.

[5] Pierre Étienne (known as Peter Steven) Du Ponceau (1760–1844), prominent lawyer and author best known for historical and linguistic studies, especially of the languages of the American Indian. President of the APS since 1828. *DAB*.

[6] Isaac Lea; see Henry's notes on his Philadelphia trip, April 29–May 2, 1834, footnote 20, above.

[7] Samuel George Morton. See *Henry Papers, 1*:461.

[8] Richard Harlan (1796–1843), Philadelphia physician and naturalist, interested in comparative anatomy; pioneer in the study of vertebrate paleontology in the United States. Despite some conspicuous deficiencies, his *Fauna Americana* (1825) was the first systematic study of North American zoology. *DAB*. *DSB*.

[9] For a comment by Vaughan on the influence of this letter, see below, Vaughan to Henry, January 3, 1835.

[10] For the Vaughan brothers, see above, Henry to Harriet Henry, November 1, 1833, footnote 4.

October 12, 1834

CHARLES HODGE TO HUGH L. HODGE

Charles Hodge Papers, Firestone Library, Princeton University

Princeton oct 12 1834

My dear Brother

I write you although Sarah[1] is with you because I wish to talk to you. I wish to say

1st I think it outrageous that you did not answer my letter about Sarah's coming & the cholera, and that I am still left in ignorance of the result of the University election on Tuesday last.

2d I want Professor Henry elected a member of your philosophical society. He is one of the first men in the country, so say Profs Silliman & Renwick & so thinks every body here. His discoveries in Electro-magnetism have attracted attention in Europe. He has made I believe the largest magnet in the world—one capable of lifting fr. 4 to 5 thousand pounds & he has made a great improvement in the Galvanic battery. I state most of these things on the say so of others. I think him myself a genius, who would do honour to the Royal Society of London, or any other body of the kind. He goes now to the city to spend a week in your Philosophical-Society Library. He has a brother in law, a much younger man one of our students last year, but now an Associate Professor in College who also bids fair greatly to distinguish himself.[2] He is going in a few days to the Arkansa Territory—or some place down there—to make observations on the eclipse of the Sun which is to occur towards the close of November & which will there be total. This is a good proof of zeal. Such men ought to be encouraged.

3d I have been trying a powerful galvanic trough—so strong that the effect is like a thousand Red hot needles running into you. I have tried it three times, nearly an hour at a time, i.e. applying & reapplying it every minute or two for that time. The effect I cannot determine.

4th I am in general more discouraged about myself than I have been. I can rarely maintain an erect position for five minutes without bringing on pain that may be called severe, principally about Poupar[t's] ligament[3] & the upper part of the thigh. I cannot believe that exercise & an erect position should be so decidedly unfavourable, if there was not something wrong there. How much worse am I now than when at the cape I used to walk 50 or 100 yards repeatedly without trouble![4]

[1] Sarah Bache Hodge, Charles's wife (see footnote 4 of Sprague to Henry, June 12, 1833).

[2] i.e., Stephen Alexander.

[3] A band of tissue in the region of the hip, named after the French anatomist François Poupart (1661–1709).

[4] Hodge still suffered from pain later in the year, according to a letter he wrote Hugh on

Sarah's letter of the 9th was not received until the 11th. The Post mark was the 9th as well as the date. This has happened repeatedly before.

Love to sister M.[5] &c. Your brother
C. Hodge

Prof Henry takes with him his Mother-in-Law who is to spend the week at Dr Cuyler's.[6]

5th I forgot my 5th & main item. Mr Dod[7] has had a cough for 4, 5, or 6 weeks which he has been trifling with. His friends & myself among the number, as winter is coming on begin to be uneasy about him, & think it high time he should take it seriously in hand. He has been urged to go & consult Dr Jackson, who has the character of being a "lung Doctor."[8] He said he would go & consult you & if you sent him to Jackson well & good. Yet he keeps putting off his visit to the city. I hope he will go in a day or two. I think he looks better, but is far from being well.

December 3, 1834 (Charles Hodge Papers, Firestone Library, Princeton University). He continued to use crutches and to wear a splint.

[5] Margaret Aspinwall Hodge, Hugh Lenox Hodge's wife (see note 8 of the Hodge letter of September 4, 1834, above).

[6] Cornelius C. Cuyler (1783–1850) graduated from Union College in 1806, superintended a girls' school in Albany for two years, and then was licenced to preach in Schenectady. From 1809 to 1834 he was pastor of the Reformed Dutch Church in Poughkeepsie, New York. In 1834 he became pastor of the Second Presbyterian Church of Philadelphia, at which post he remained until his death. Sprague, *Annals*, *4*:432–434.

[7] Albert Baldwin Dod, Professor of Mathematics at Princeton (identified in *Henry Papers*, *1*:434), was distantly related by marriage to Charles and Hugh Lenox Hodge. Francis B. Lee, ed., *Genealogical and Personal Memorial of Mercer County, New Jersey*, 2 vols. (New York, 1907), 2:460.

[8] Samuel Jackson (1787–1872) gained his reputation in the 1820s for diagnosing respiratory problems by listening to breathing sounds of patients in the Philadelphia Almshouse and then verifying his diagnosis by dissection after their deaths. Jackson had received his degree from the University of Pennsylvania and had initially worked in materia medica (pharmacy). From 1827 to 1863 he taught physiology at the University. *DAB*. In 1856, Henry was to ask Jackson to evaluate a manuscript on physiology submitted for publication to the Smithsonian.

TO HARRIET HENRY

Mary Henry Copy, Memoir, Henry Papers, Smithsonian Archives

Philadelphia [October 15,][1] 1834

My dear Wife. We arrived safely about six o'clock last evening but found great difficulty in finding Dr. Cuyler's house. . . . I go this evening to see

[1] The Mary Henry Copy gives a date of September 14, 1834. However, the Philadelphia elections took place on October 14, 1834, and the text indicates Henry is writing the day after the election.

Professor Bache. The most interesting piece of information I can communicate is that Dr. Ludlow[2] has been unanimously elected to the Provostship of the University[3]. . . .

There was great excitement last night in the suburbs although in the city proper the election went off very peaceably, considering the state of public feeling. . . . Throughout the county the Jackson party have gained the day. Last night about one o'clock six houses were destroyed by a mob and report says that many persons were wounded and several killed.[4] The opinion among the intelligent I have met here is that the government is rotten to the core and that any form would be better than the present. Keep cool. Do not make yourself unhappy by imaginary difficulties and believe that you are never forgotten by your devoted J.H.

[2] John R. Ludlow (1793–1857); see *Henry Papers, 1*:106n.

[3] Ludlow was the Trustees' second choice, after they had been turned down by Francis Wayland of Brown (Edward Cheyney, *History of the University of Pennsylvania, 1740–1940* [Philadelphia, 1940], p. 227). According to the *National Cyclopedia of American Biography, 1*:343, Ludlow was to be a popular lecturer at the school; as an administrator, he is credited with reviving the University's law school.

[4] The riots took place at Moyamensing. After the balloting closed, crowds assembled at the polling place to hear the election results, with some shoving and pulling between Whigs and Democrats for good spots to stand. Upon learning their victory, the Jacksonians cheered and yelled, probably mixing in a few jeers at their defeated opponents. The Whigs then swung around the corner to Democratic headquarters where they tore down the tent, beat up the Democratic campaign manager and his wife, and burned down the symbolic Hickory Tree. The infuriated Jacksonians, now apparently drunk and armed with clubs and augmented in numbers from nearby towns, stormed Whig headquarters, where they were met by gunfire from the house. Between fourteen and twenty persons were wounded, one fatally. The Democrats tore off the exterior woodwork, fired the house, and used the trim to burn the Whigs' Liberty Pole. Firemen arrived but the Democrats held them off until the pole had burned. The blazing timber fell on a nearby house, which set off a chain fire that destroyed five three-story buildings belonging to James Robb, a Whig and a former postmaster in the area. Crowd estimates varied from two to five thousand people.

Newspaper accounts varied with the politics of the editor. The Democrats' Philadelphia *Pennsylvanian* for October 15, 1834, asserted that the Whigs started the fray, that the Jacksonians were unarmed, and that the Democrats helped put out fires once the pole had burned. The Whig *National Gazette* of Philadelphia for October 15 claimed that the Jacksonians attacked Whig headquarters with no provocation and that the Democrats carried clubs and even firearms. They did not mention the early Whig actions, although they did admit and deplore the shooting from Whig headquarters. On October 16 the *Gazette* printed an account from the *American Sentinel* which detailed the situation before the Democratic assault on Whig headquarters.

HENRY'S NOTES ON A TRIP TO PHILADELPHIA

Henry Papers,[1] *Smithsonian Archives*

Phil. Oct. 20th 1834

In conversation with Mr Mason Mathematical instrument maker[2] he informed me that he could make any glass cylender a good electric by well washing the interior with oil. After wards pour in some ammonia or caustic potash so as to form a soap. Wash this out with water &c.
He also uses a single slip for a rubber.[3]

Mr. Lukins shewed me a hollow needle which he made for Prof. Patterson.[4] He spoke to me of the plan when I first went to the city on Wednesday.[5] I recommend the plan so highly to him that he made it forthwith.

At Mr Lukins I saw a new Lathe with two treadles and an indian rubber

[1] These notes were entered in the booklet which is mainly devoted to an account of Henry's visit of April 29–May 2, 1834 (see note 1 of the diary of that visit, printed above). Some blank pages follow the entry for October 20, after which Henry jotted an undated reminder to test whether reversing the polarity in a piece of soft iron affected its subsequent ability to acquire magnetism.

[2] Henry thought he had designated precisely which one of the several Masons he had met. Unfortunately, at the distance of a century and a half, we find at least three Masons who might fit the description. Biographical details even among these three are mixed up: authorities differ, for example, on whether William Mason or David Hastings Mason was Matthias Baldwin's business partner. William Mason, identified in note 1 of the letter to Harriet Henry of December 5, 1834, printed below, was listed as an instrument maker in Philadelphia City Directories in the 1820s. David Hastings Mason (1784–1848), a founding member of the Franklin Institute active in its investigations of steam boiler explosions, was variously described as a machinist, engineer, and "gentleman" in the directories for the 1830s. He received patents for inventions in a number of fields. He moved to Georgia in 1837 and was chief coiner of the United States Mint there from 1837 until his death. Sometime late in life he was also ordained as a Presbyterian minister. Alva Mason, whose profession was given as engraver and philosophical instrument maker in the directories for 1817 to 1859, seems the most likely of the three to be Henry's Mason. In the 1833 Franklin Institute exhibit, Alva Mason won commendation for his manufacture of an air-pump, eudiometer, pyrometer, blowpipe, and static electricity machine (Franklin Institute *Journal*, 1834, *13*:91). For information on all three Masons, see G. C. Groce and D. H. Wallace, *The New-York Historical Society's Dictionary of Artists in America, 1564–1860* (New Haven, 1957), pp. 427–429. Data on David Hastings Mason are available in *National Cyclopedia of American Biography*, *10*:228; Bruce Sinclair, *Philadelphia's Philosopher Mechanics: A History of the Franklin Institute, 1824–1865* (Baltimore, 1974), pp. 31, 55, 73, 177, 293; and *Burke's Index*. On William Mason's technological career, see Eugene Ferguson, ed., *Early Engineering Reminiscences (1815–1840) of George Escol Sellers* (Washington, D.C., 1965), pp. xv–xvi, 15, 40, 54–55, 77, and 84.

[3] Henry is describing a static electricity machine. The surface of the glass cylinder had to be free of dust and film, which explains Mason's choice of strong cleaning solutions. The "rubber" was so called because it rubbed against the glass cylinder or plate; it was a hair-stuffed tube of leather coated with silk or a metallic amalgam. P. M. Roget, *Treatises on Electricity, Galvanism, Magnetism, and Electro-Magnetism* (London, 1832), "Electricity," pp. 14–16.

[4] Isaiah Lukens devised the apparatus for Robert Maskell Patterson, Professor of Natural Philosophy at the University of Virginia (identified in note 3 of the letter from John Provost, June 12, 1835, below). Large needles used in terrestrial magnetism observations were hard to work with unless their weight were reduced by hollowing them.

cloth band. Mr L informed me that Mr Gummery had attempted to fix a needle with a looking glass on the side so as to reflect the sun.[6]

Prof. Franklin Bache[7] informed me that he had published in the Portfolio an article on galvanism which may be found by reference to the last edition of Turners chemestry.[8]

He also reccommended exp. to be made on the difference of galvanic effect of thick and thin plates of zinc.[9]

[5] That is, October 15.

[6] John Gummere (*Henry Papers, 1*:59 and note 3 of the letter from Jacob Green, February 13, 1834, above). The mirror made the needle easier to orient with respect to the sun during observations.

[7] Franklin Bache (1792–1864), a first cousin of Alexander Dallas Bache (Leonard Labaree, ed., *The Papers of Benjamin Franklin* [New Haven, 1959], *1*:lxiii and lxv), received a Bachelor's degree from the University of Pennsylvania in 1810 and an M.D. from the same school four years later. He served as a surgeon during the War of 1812. From 1816 to 1826 he presumably combined private practice with editing British chemistry textbooks for the American market. During 1826–1831 Bache was in charge of the *North American Medical and Surgical Journal*; he also taught chemistry at the Franklin Institute in those years. He then became Professor of Chemistry at the Philadelphia College of Pharmacy for ten years and changed in 1841 to the same post at Jefferson Medical College, where he taught until his death. He wrote an important series of pharmacy handbooks but published few original scientific papers. Bache was an active member of the American Philosophical Society, serving successively as Secretary, Vice-President, and President. *DAB*. In the 1820s, Bache experimented with locally inserted needles to relieve severe pain (James Cassedy, "Early Uses of Acupuncture in the United States, with an Addendum [1826] by Franklin Bache, M.D.," New York Academy of Medicine *Bulletin*, 1974, 2d ser. *50*:892–906).

[8] Franklin Bache prepared several editions of Edward Turner's *Elements of Chemistry* for publication in America. This is a reference to the fourth American edition (Philadelphia, 1832) from the third London edition. The article on galvanism, mentioned on page 94 of the text, is "Dr. Hare's Improved Galvanic Deflagrators," *Port Folio*, April 1824, *17*:323–324. Bache explained a seemingly anomalous polarity in Hare's apparatus as caused by a peculiar method of linking the copper and zinc plates. *Port Folio* was a popular and important literary magazine in early Philadelphia; it was published from 1801 to 1827 under a distinguished series of editors. Frank Luther Mott, *A History of American Magazines, 1741–1850* (New York, 1930), pp. 223–246.

[9] Presumably a suggestion on how to improve the output of batteries which used zinc plates. We find no evidence that Henry tried the experiment.

TO STEPHEN VAN RENSSELAER[1]

Gratz Collection, Historical Society of Pennsylvania

Princeton Oct. 23[d] 1834

My Dear Sir

You have probably heard that the alumni association of Princeton College have resolved to raise if possible one hundred thousand dollars for

[1] See *Henry Papers, 1*:8n.

increasing the facilities of education and for establishing a fund for the more permenent support of the Institution. In persuance of this object they have appointed the Rev. Mr Newell their agent[2] and as he intends visiting the north I have been requested to furnish him with a letter to yourself on the subject. I comply with the request reluctantly knowing that the public have scarcely any farther claims on you in reference to the support of the cause of Religion or Education. Yet I am induced to appeal to you in behalf of our college from the consideration that your acts of benevolence will only cease with your life and that Nassau Hall has peculiar claims on your kind regard. You have been one of her pupils[3] and know that she has educated a large proportion of the men who have directed the affairs of the general government[4] since its first establishment and that from the first she has been the steady friend of true Religion and has furnished the church in this country with a long list of eminent Divines[5] who have earned for her the appellation of "the school of the Prophets."

I am Sir with the highest Respect
your hum. servt
Joseph Henry

[2] On Newell and the fund-raising effort, see above, excerpt of April 9, 1834, Minutes, Trustees, College of New Jersey.

[3] Although Stephen Van Rensselaer graduated from Harvard (1782), he attended Princeton briefly in 1779–1780. Despite the war, President John Witherspoon was attempting to revive the college. He personally escorted Van Rensselaer to Princeton. In 1780, however, Van Rensselaer was removed to the safety of Cambridge. Munsell, *Ann. Alb.*, *3*:213–214, and information from Dr. Edith Blendon, Princeton University Archives.

Van Rensselaer responded to this solicitation with a pledge of $500. See listings in "Subscriptions Nassau Hall, 1834–35," Alumni Association of Nassau Hall, John Maclean Papers, Princeton University Archives.

[4] Princeton was extremely proud of its famous alumni in civic life, such as James Madison. Witherspoon's administration (1768–1794) was particularly fruitful in this regard. See the listings of graduates in *Maclean*, *1*:357–363 and *Wertenbaker*, p. 115.

[5] Presbyterian Divines of the New Light variety spawned by the Great Awakening. After an initial thrust into New England, Princeton ministers were in particular demand among pious Scotch-Irish immigrants in the South. The South in turn provided numerous candidates for the ministry at Princeton. *Wertenbaker*, pp. 19, 112–115.

TO JAMES HENRY

Family Correspondence, Henry Papers, Smithsonian Archives

Princeton Oct 27th 1834

Dear James

Your last letter containing a variety of items of information came to hand while Mother and myself were in Philadelphia. It served to cheer the loneliness of Harriet. We left home on Tuesday and did not return until the following Wednesday. Our visit was prolonged one day on account of being left by the steam-boat; we arrived 4 minutes too late. Aunt & Stephen arrived on Friday or rather Aunt as Stephen was left at the Rail road with a large box containing a Tellescope which he borrowed in New York for his southern eclipse expidition. He came home on saturday so that we are again all assembled after a separation of four months. Give my thanks to James Eights[1] for the Medalion in Plaster of the Sweedish chemist Berzelius.[2]

Our visit to Phil[a] was a very plesant one. My time was principally occupied with study in the Library of the Philosophical Society. I find it necessary to go to Phil[a] one or twice a year to post up my knowledge of the current discoveries in Science during the year &c. Motherinlaw has a cousin there I know not how many times removed The Rev Dr Cuyler formerly of Poughkeepsie. The family received her very cordially and rendered our stay very agreeable. The Rev Mr Ludlow came on friday and stayed at the same house with us until wednesday following. He appeared highly pleased with his appointment as Provost of the University of Pennsylvania and will I think have a very plesant situation. He has not been used very well by the Dutch in Albany in reference to the affair of Gates.[3] I intended to call on Mr Harper[4] but the first days of our arrival were at the time of the election and consequently was an improper time to call. Afterwards my time was so much ingaged that I found no leisure. You have probably heard the result of the New Jersey election—our county (Middlesex) has given a Whig majority, but not so the whole state.

It is rumoured that our neighbour Mr James Green[5] (brother of Jacob Green[6] formerly a book seller in Albany known to W[m] Gould)[7] is to be the

[1] James Eights (1798–1882), the Albany physician, naturalist, and artist, is identified in *Henry Papers, 1*:69.

[2] For a brief note on this important scientist, see footnote 29 of Henry's Notes on a Trip to Philadelphia, April 29–May 2, 1834, above.

[3] Gerrit Gates (1784–1862) was a merchant and local politician active in the affairs of the Reformed Dutch Protestant Church, of which Ludlow was Pastor from 1823 to 1834 (Munsell, *Ann. Alb.*, *9*:167, 174, 217, 232, 239, and 247; Munsell, *Coll. Alb.*, *2*:113). We have not discovered the cause of his quarrel with Ludlow.

[4] James Harper, the Democratic Congressman (see footnote 4 of the letter of May 7, 1834, above).

[5] Peter Vroom was undecided whether to run for United States Senator or to seek reelection as Governor. By October 30, he had spoken for the governorship and other Democrats stood aside (*Newark Daily Advertiser*, October 30, 1834). James Sproat Green (*Henry Papers, 1*:440) was the unsuccessful Democratic nominee in 1837 (*Biographical Encyclopedia of New Jersey of the Nineteenth Century* [Philadelphia, 1877], pp. 30 and 34) but we have been unable to verify the rumor of his candidacy in 1834.

[6] On Jacob Green (1790–1841), see *Henry Papers, 1*:322–323.

[7] William Gould, an Albany bookseller (see footnote 11 of the letter of December 21, 1832, above).

next Governor of the State. I hope he may succeede as he is a very clever gentlemanly man.

Harriet bids me tell you that her children are very much pleased with their Pitchers. Harriet herself would like to be a child again in order that she might play with them. The Girl has interely recovered from the effects of the vaccination and is as pleasant tempered as formerly. The Boy has grown quite fleshy since his return from Albany—performs considerable labour in the eating way. Harriet is quite thin and complains much of the teeth ache. She must teach her Daughter to eat more from the spoon and depend less upon her for nourishment. The college commences on the 6th of next month. We have a fair prospect of a good class in place of the one which graduated.

Stephen requests me to ask you to tell Dr Ten Eyck[8] that he succeeded in getting the Fraunhoffer Telescope[9] of which he spoke when in albany. It belongs to Werkmeister[10] the German Toy seller corner of Broad way & Liberty street N.Y. We are about making preparations for winter in the way of stores &c. The canal has lowered the price of coal so that this fuel is cheaper than wood. Last year coal was from 8 to 9 dollars per tun. This season it is 5½ delivered.

The intelligence in this letter relative to the Girl & Boy is intended for Mother & Nancy. Mother will I hope be easy in reference to the children. Aunt says he has greaved much about them because they were not well

[8] Philip Ten Eyck (1802–1892), identified in *Henry Papers, 1*:214, Henry's successor at the Albany Academy.

[9] Joseph Fraunhofer (1787–1826), the son of a German glazier, worked in the optical shop of Joseph von Utzschneider and Pierre Louis Guinard as a young man. He learned the science of optics as part of his trade, and took active part in the scientific life of Munich. Fraunhofer made theoretical studies and practical applications of the phenomena connected with flame and solar spectra and with diffraction of light by gratings. He used a wave theory of light to explain the results of his experiments. Fraunhofer died young from tuberculosis, but the firm continued to build telescopes of his design. (*DSB*.)

Reflecting and refracting telescopes constructed in the eighteenth century were relatively small in aperture, up to five inches. Early in the nineteenth century, reflectors built by William Herschel and others surpassed this size and revealed astronomical details hitherto undisclosed. At first refractors could not compete. Then Guinard began to make large pieces of flint glass and Fraunhofer applied his scientific studies to the creation of reliable indices and tests for optical constants. Their shop succeeded in making large lenses virtually free of flaws and of chromatic and spherical aberration. The Dorpat telescope, completed in 1834, had a nine and one half inch lens and featured an equatorial mounting that Fraunhofer had designed for these bigger instruments. Henry King, *History of the Telescope* (London, 1955), pp. 180–186; information from Deborah Warner, National Museum of History and Technology. Stephen Alexander used one of the smaller Fraunhofers (see below, footnote 4 of the letter of Henry to Alexander, November 29, 1834).

[10] Michael Werckmeister (1766–1844) emigrated in 1801 from Tyrol to New York City, where he started in business as a wallpaper manufacturer and later became a merchant (Gertrude Barber, *Deaths Taken from the New York Evening Post* [New York, 1940], *20*:57; New York City Directories for 1803–1804 and 1844–1845; and information supplied by the Local History and Genealogy Division of the New York Public Library).

when they left Albany. I will indeavour to be more punctual in writing after we are settled for the winter. You have heard so often from us through Stephen the Meads &c that we did not think it necessary to write as often as usual. Give our Love to Mother and Nancy. Respects to Mr McArthur,[11] Dr Frank,[12] [and] Mr Bullions.[13] Stephen left a Book at Mother's—Key to Algebra[14]—intended for William Bullions.[15] Will you do it up in a piece of paper put his name on it and send or give it to him. He will not wish probably that the other boys know that he has received it. I send it for him to use in reviewing his algebray by himself.

Your Brother

[11] Samuel McArthur (see *Henry Papers, 1*:399).

[12] Francis N. Selkirk, identified above, footnote 6 of the letter of November 13, 1832.

[13] Peter Bullions (*Henry Papers, 1*:129).

[14] A copy of William Davis, ed., *Key to Bonnycastle's Algebra*, 2d ed. (London, 1810) is in the Henry Library. "Albany Academy *Joseph Henry* 1827" is inscribed on the title page. Davis worked through the problems in the text by Bonnycastle, presenting all the steps and supplying the answers.

[15] William G. Bullions (1818–1887) was a son of Peter Bullions. He graduated from Albany Academy in 1827 and in 1834 was an aide there for Philip Ten Eyck. Bullions assisted Joseph Henry in scientific work at Princeton from December 1835 to June 1836, when he left briefly to work as an assistant engineer on a northern New Jersey railroad. He returned to help Henry in November 1836 and was also at work in the laboratory in February 1838. Bullions was employed on the Rochester and Auburn Railroad in 1840, and after joining the gold rush to California in 1849, spent the rest of his life as an engineer. Hun, "Albany Academy" and letter of December 25, 1835, below. See also Joseph Henry to James Henry, June 6, 1836, Family Correspondence; Joseph Henry to Harriet Henry, September 23, 1836, Family Correspondence; Joseph Henry to James Henry, November 28, 1836, Family Correspondence; entry for February 1838, Record of Experiments; M. G. Bullions to Harriet Henry, November 14, 1840, Family Correspondence; and Peter Bullions to Joseph Henry, January 20, 1849, all in Henry Papers, Smithsonian Archives.

FROM PETER BULLIONS

Henry Papers, Smithsonian Archives

Albany. Nov[r] 1st 1834

My Dear Sir

Last evening by M[r] Newlands[1] and this morning by M[r] O Meads we heard that you had had a pretty serious and rather singular attack of sickness, but that you had recovered so far as to walk out.[2] I hope by this time

[1] See above, Henry to James Henry, May 17, 1833, footnote 3.

[2] Henry suffered only a "slight attack of fever," but was later startled to find that many of his out-of-town friends thought the illness far more serious. See below, Henry to Harriet Henry, December 5, 1834, and Henry to James Henry, December 22, 1834.

you are entirely recovered. M[r] Newlands who you know knows a great deal of every thing says if you do not take a great deal more exercise and avoid *reclining when you read* or study you will be in danger of another attack. I hope therefore that let fame go as it may you will be careful of your health. You must remember that your life is of much more consequence now than when we in former days footed it through Albany on New Years day. There is no news but what you will have by the papers as early as they can arrive. The bearer of this is a M[r] Schenck[3] I believe from Johnstown. He was a student three months here last summer and proposes to enter your Sophomore [class]. You will find him a very fine fellow and I recommend him to your friendship and advice. M[rs] B. and Margaret and William join in love to you all. Bill appears to be doing pretty well in his studies and is getting to be D[r] Ten Eycks right hand man. Let me hear from you soon. Is anything said of the Grammars?[4] I am Dear Sir

Ever Yours
P Bullions

[3] Edward T. Schenck (1815–1902) attended the Albany Academy in 1833–1834 and entered Princeton in 1834 as a sophomore, graduating in 1837. Hun, "Albany Academy"; *Princeton Catalogue*, p. 152; *Princeton Annual Catalogue*, 1835. T. R. Beck also wrote Henry a letter of introduction for Schenck on this date (in the Henry Papers, Smithsonian Archives).

[4] Bullions had sent Henry a half dozen of his Greek grammars and was anxious to have comments on the edition from Princeton faculty members. See above, Bullions to Henry, December 19, 1833.

TO JAMES HENRY

Family Correspondence, Henry Papers, Smithsonian Archives

New York Nov 6th 1834

Dear James

Your letter by the hand of English William arrived in Princeton on Wednesday. He reached home safely leaving however his charge of butter at the Rail road house. I am now in New-York with Stephen who is on his way to South Carolina or Georgia to observe the great Eclipse of the 30th of this month. He leaves heare tomorrow in the Steam Packet for Charleston. The college commenced its session yesterday with very flattering prospects. There was an unusually punctual attendance of the old students and a much larger number of new ones than had been anticipated. We were sorry to hear by your letter that mother was not as well as she had been. We hope that her attack was only produced by some change of weather and that she will soon recover her former state. We are all well. The Boy continues to grow and is at present in a better state of health than he has been in for more than a year past. The Girl has got one tooth which event took place without apparently giving her much uneasiness. She does not however sleep quite as soundly as she did.

New York Saturday [November 8, 1834]

Stephen and myself have been much ingaged this morning in procuring the necessary instruments for his tour; he is now about ready and will start at 4 o'clock.

I met Mr Little[1] in the Street and he said that he wished to get you as a clerk. I would be very much rejoiced could you get into a better situation than the one you now occupy. At Littles you would have a better chance of making yourself known as a correct business man and you only require to be known to be highly estimated. Perhaps Gould[2] would well object to your leaving. If you stay to oblige him of course it should be in consideration of receiving a larger salary. Write me if there be any thing that I can do for you in the way of assistance &c.[3]

I forgot to inform you in my last letter that the book you mentioned I loaned several years since to young Bacon[4] while he was a student in College. I asked him for [it] about 3 years ago. He then said that not supposing that I wanted it he had loaned it to a poor student in one of the lower classes. Will you get the book[5] and keep it for me.

The college graduates are attempting as you have heard to raise 100 thousand dollars. If they succeed the Institution will be among the first in the country and that they will succed I think that there is very little doubt since the agent[6] has already since the commencement obtained 20 thousand. I have given him letters to several Gentlemen in Albany and amoung others one to the Patroon.[7] I wish you would settle the affair with Little as soon as possible in order that should you leave Gould I may write to some of my acquaintances in reference to you.

Mr Schenck has entered Princeton College. In haste

Your Brother

My Love to Mother and Nancy.

[1] Weare C. Little (*Henry Papers, 1*:318–319).

[2] William or Anthony Gould.

[3] For the resolution of the situation, see the letters of December 22, 1834, and January 13, 1835, below.

[4] Of the five former students of the Albany Academy with this last name, the only one residing in Albany at the time of this letter was Marshall J. Bacon, the son of John F. Bacon. Marshall Bacon attended the Academy in 1819–1820 and later became a lawyer; his father had been clerk of the State Senate. Albany City Directories; Hun, "Albany Academy."

[5] Not identified.

[6] i.e., Daniel Newell. See notes for the Trustees' Minutes of April 9, 1834, above.

[7] Stephen Van Rensselaer (1764–1839). The letter appears above, October 23, 1834.

NOMINATION FOR MEMBERSHIP IN AMERICAN PHILOSOPHICAL SOCIETY

Archives, American Philosophical Society

Hall of Am. Philos. Society
November 7th. 1834.

The undersigned members of the Society beg leave to present as a candidate for membership Joseph Henry Professor of Natural Philosophy in the College at Princeton & lately Professor in the Albany Academy. Prof. Henry is well known both at home & abroad by his discoveries in Magnetism & Electro-Magnetism, & Galvanism, and is in every respect most worthy of the honour proposed for him.

Hugh L. Hodge[1]	Jn Vaughan
A. D. Bache	Ch. D Meigs[2]
Franklin Bache	R. Harlan

To the Pres^t^ of the
Am. Philos. Soc^y^[3]

1835
D^r^[4] Joseph Henry
Elected 2 Jan^y^

[1] For whom see above, Charles Hodge to Hugh L. Hodge, September 4, 1834, footnote 2.

[2] Charles Delucena Meigs (1792–1869), a physician known in his day for his specialization in obstetrics and gynecology. A son of Josiah Meigs (*DAB*), C. D. Meigs graduated from the University of Georgia in 1809; his father was then President of the institution. In 1817 he received his M.D. from the University of Pennsylvania; a few years later, C. D. Meigs started practicing in Philadelphia. He engaged in medical journalism, translated French texts, and wrote several works in his field. From 1841 to 1861 C. D. Meigs was Professor of Obstetrics and the Diseases of Women at Jefferson Medical College (*DAB*). His son, M. C. Meigs (*DAB*), was a close friend of Henry's in Washington.

[3] Peter Stephen Du Ponceau. This appears in the original to the left of the signatures of the nominators, perhaps in the hand of A. D. Bache as APS Secretary. Letters which may have prompted this nomination are printed above, Silliman to Vaughan, October 9, 1834, and Hodge to Hodge, October 12, 1834.

[4] A title given in error.

FROM JOHN VAUGHAN

Henry Papers, Smithsonian Archives

Philad^a^ 8 Nov. 1834

D Sir

You will excuse me if I express a wish that you could have your *memoir* or *memoirs* if possible by the first fryday in December, certainly *one by the first fryday or at the latest,* by the 3[d] Fryday in December, any other may follow after as speedily as you can as we are in press.[1] Whenever your plate is ready also I would wish it—as it will take some time to engrave. Favor me with advice on reply. Prof. Bache urges your attention to my application. Remember, my room & any assistance I can give will be Chearfully at your service.

Yrs
Jn Vaughan

[1] Presumably during his last Philadelphia trip (see above, Henry to Harriet Henry, October 15, 1834, and Henry to James Henry, October 27, 1834) Henry and Vaughan discussed the possibility of including one or more of Henry's papers in the American Philosophical Society's *Transactions.* Vaughan was not a member of the Committee on Publication at this time. However, as Librarian and Treasurer of the Society Vaughan informally took responsibility for APS publications. Henry's reply to Vaughan, November 17, 1834, is printed below.

Vaughan's expression, "*memoir* or *memoirs,*" suggests that Henry indicated he had papers on more than one topic in preparation for the APS *Transactions.* Documents to follow show that by the time Henry submitted his first paper ("Contributions I: Battery") to the Society he was able to give a substantial abstract of his second ("Contributions II: Spiral Conductor"). Writing to Benjamin Silliman on November 4, 1839 (Daniel C. Gilman Collection, Library, Johns Hopkins University) Henry emphasized the integral nature of the papers in his series.

Up to this point Henry's important papers on electricity and magnetism had been published in *Silliman's Journal* where they had received probably the widest possible exposure. Why was Henry making this shift to the APS *Transactions* for his contributions? Perhaps sufficient explanation is embodied in Henry's own recollection in the above-cited letter to Silliman: "I regretted at the time that it ["Contributions II: Spiral Conductor"] was not published in your journal since it would then have been much more widely known. But I was anxious to do something in connection with Dr. Hare, Bache and a few other working men to resusitate the Phil Society and without much egotism I think considerable has been done within the last two or three years." Henry's remark reflects his attitude toward revitalizing the American Philosophical Society as evidenced in several letters below; see, for example, Henry to Torrey, December 20, 1834, especially footnote 6.

FROM AMOS DEAN[1]

Henry Papers, Smithsonian Archives

Albany November 12, 1834

Dear Sir

In part to bring myself within the pale of your remembrances, as also to acquaint you with a valued friend of mine, I take this opportunity of writing you a single line. The Bearer of this is Mr. B. Goodrich[2] a former

[1] For whom see above, Henry to James Henry, December 21, 1832, footnote 1.

[2] Butler Goodrich (1809–1836) graduated from Union College in 1832. He attended Princeton Theological Seminary from 1834–1836, presumably until his death. *Roberts,* p. 89.

graduate of Union College whose intentions are to enter the Princeton Seminary. You are, or by this time should be, a sufficient Judge of Developements to know that nothing is ever lost even to an adept in Electro Magnetism, in the formation & continuance of an acquaintanceship with an intellectual and moral nature as is indicated by his cerebral organisation.[3] I shall look to a good account of Both—The one of the other, and upon the coming in of the Reports shall be the better Judge of my own infallibility as to estimate of character.

Yours as ever truly
Amos Dean

[3] Phrenological rhetoric?

TO JOHN VAUGHAN

Archives, American Philosophical Society

Princeton Nov 17th 1834

My Dear Sir

An absence, of several days, from home will account for my not sooner answering your kind letter of the 8th.[1] I have been spending a few days in the city of New York in assisting my Brotherinlaw Mr Alexander to procure the necessary instruments for observing the great eclipse of the 30th.

He has left Princeton for the purpose of going to Georgia with the intention of stationing himself as near the middle of the track of the total shadow as possible and will probably make his observations at a place called Ebineezer near the city of Savannah. He was so fortunate as to procure an excellent Telescope, made by the celebrated Fraunhofer, and a good chronometer. The result of his observations should the day prove clear will be given to the American Phil Society.[2]

With regard to my papers I will endeavour to furnish the first, a de-

[1] Printed above.

[2] For an account of the trip to New York, see above, Henry to James Henry, November 6, 1834. Dealings regarding the telescope are described below in Henry to Stephen Alexander, November 29, 1834, and in Henry to Harriet Henry, October 24, 1835. Stephen Alexander apparently never published his observations on the eclipse; nor have we found any evidence that he presented them orally to the American Philosophical Society. See below, Vaughan to Henry, December 8, 1834, especially footnote 5. Henry discusses Alexander's observations in his letter to Bache of December 17, 1834, below, and in two succeeding documents.

scription of my battery, by the time you mention & will be in your city probably next week with my drawing.[3] Give my respects to my friend Prof. Bach.[4]

I am Sir with the highest
Respect Yours sincerely
Joseph Henry

[3] Henry's trip to Philadelphia appears in the documents below of December 5, 1834 and in Henry's letter to Bache, December 17, 1834.

[4] Alexander Dallas Bache.

TO JOHN TORREY

Torrey Papers, Library, New York Botanical Garden

Princeton Tuesday Morning
Nov 18th 1834

My Dear Dr.

I have closed your book a/c with Mr Baker[1] and given the copies unsold to Prof. Maclean. I intended to forward the ammount due by him but arrived this morning at his house just in time to see the stage convey him around the corner. Below I give you Baker's statement of the account and enclose an order on the Bank of New-York for the Balance.

I have commenced my course & intend to get through this session so as to leave the field enterely to your culture.[2] The class thus far have been very attentive and nearly fill the seats in the lecture room. My time will be very much occupied this session so that you need not expect to hear from me unless it be to trouble you in purchasing some articles in the Philos. line. We are all well—nothing new—have had a letter[3] from Mr Alexander dated "off Cape Hatteras," sent by the steamer Packet David Brown. By my stay in New-York on monday I have lost the *rate* of the astronomical clock in the Hall.[4] It run down on tuesday at 12 o'clock. I did not reach home until

[1] Moore Baker, for whom see above, Torrey to Henry, August 18, 1834, footnote 13.

[2] Henry's course on natural philosophy normally began in early November and ran beyond the end of the winter session (mid-April) into the summer session. Torrey taught chemistry in the summer session only. Both courses were for Seniors. *Princeton Annual Catalogue*, 1835, p. 13.

[3] Stephen Alexander was on an expedition to make observations of a solar eclipse. His letter has not been found.

[4] We cannot be certain exactly which clock would have been in Philosophical Hall at this time. A later inventory of apparatus for the Hall lists an astronomical clock by Edward Nairne (1726–1806, British instrument maker, *DNB*), which would have been a first-rate and expensive clock dating from the late eighteenth century. We suspect, but cannot prove, that the Nairne clock was in the Hall at the time of this letter. "Inventory of All Observatory Equipment," 1906, Princeton University Observatory.

about one. Too late! I will indeavour to regain the time but have no very good instruments.[5] Mr. Alexander has taken his sextant with him. I was anxious to observe if nothing else the exact duration of the eclipse at Princeton as this is an element of some importance to the Astronomer—however insignificant to the Chemist or Natural Philosopher. Give my Respects to Mrs Torrey & Dr Gray.[6]

In Haste your
Friend
Jos. Henry

Prof^{r} J Torrey

To Moore Baker Dr

1832 May 25th To Turners Chemestry $2.00

1834 Novbr By Cash received for

17 Turners Chemestry 1.37½ 23.37½

$21.37½

[5] Resetting an astronomical clock could not be done reliably from ordinary chronometers, the accuracy of which was greatly inferior. In fact, most other clocks were set in accordance with the time on the astronomical clock. So Henry would have to use a sextant or other astronomers' observational equipment to regain accurate astronomical time.

[6] Asa Gray (1810–1888), who became a leading American researcher and teacher of botany, also became one of Joseph Henry's closest advisers and confidants. A. Hunter Dupree, *Asa Gray, 1810–1888* (Cambridge, Massachusetts, 1959), is a thorough, scholarly, and readable biography. See also Dupree's "Asa Gray" in the *DSB*.

Henry and Gray first met in 1830. Gray was nearing completion of his M.D. studies at the College of Physicians and Surgeons of the Western District (in Fairfield, New York). Passing through Albany, he called upon botanist Lewis C. Beck at the Albany Academy, where he also met "a grave-looking man who I was told was Professor Henry, who had just been making a wonderful electro-magnet" (Gray, as quoted in Dupree's *Asa Gray*, p. 17). Direct contact between Henry and Gray remained sporadic for the next several years.

Throughout his medical training, and few years of medical practice and school teaching, Gray's main interest was botany. He gravitated toward John Torrey, perhaps the most active and prominent American botanist at the time. In the early 1830s he established an acquaintance with Torrey through correspondence which led to Torrey's hiring Gray as an assistant for his botanical research and writing. While working for Torrey, Gray lived with the Torreys in New York City and became a close family friend. Ibid., pp. 17–42.

Torrey was impressed with Gray's scientific abilities and attempted, unsuccessfully, to find full-time employment for him (for instance, see below, Torrey to Henry, January 16, 1835). Eventually Gray won an appointment to the Wilkes Expedition in 1836, but withdrew two years later, before the mission began, to join the faculty at the University of Michigan. In 1842 he was appointed a Professor at Harvard, where he taught botany and developed the botanical garden without interruption (except for several European trips) until his retirement in 1873. Gray's publications total more than 780 titles.

Gray first met Charles Darwin in 1851. By 1855 Darwin and Gray corresponded on botanical findings which contributed to Darwin's *On the Origin of Species* (1859). Gray became an outspoken defender of Darwin in America in the ensuing controversy. Gray, a "New School" Presbyterian since living with the Torreys in 1833, also defended Darwinism against both its religious opponents and those who associated it with agnosticism. In these controversies, Gray's intellectual conviction brought him into conflict with scientists (i.e., Louis Agassiz and Benjamin Peirce) with whom he already disagreed on educational and scientific policies. Until the publication of the Dupree biography, there was a relative downgrading of Gray's impact in these disputes.

Gray held many positions of national importance, including charter membership in the National Academy of Sciences, President of the American Association for the Advancement of Science, and Regent of the Smithsonian Institution.

Gray and Henry, naturalist and physicist, developed a close personal and professional relationship. Selections from their life-long, steady correspondence, to appear in subsequent volumes of the *Henry Papers*, are rich in observations on the developments in science and the scientific community in mid-nineteenth-century America.

TO JAMES HENRY

Family Correspondence, Henry Papers, Smithsonian Archives

Princeton [November][1] 24th 1834 Monday

Dear James

We have heard nothing from Albany except by way of the papers since your letter of the 4th inst. I have commenced my lectures and am therefore very much ingaged.

We are all well. The Boy grows rapidly. The Girl has cut two of her under teeth. Stephen sailed on the 8th for Charleston in the steam Packet. We have had two letters[2] from him, one from on board the packet off Cape Hatteras, the other from the city of Charleston. He intends making his observations near Savannah, is in good spirits and appears thus far much pleased with his jaunt. The college is quite full—about 200 students perhaps one or two more or less.[3] Nothing new. Now that election is over all is quiet. I spent a part of Friday evening with Mr Southard.[4] He thinks there will be something of a stormy session. He starts for Washington today. Aunt is not very well. She has a bad cold or the influenza which is prevailing at this time in Princeton.

Harriet says that you must tell the Misses Meads that she will write to them in a few days. We saw an article in the paper which was a piece of

[1] We have determined the month from the context of the document.

[2] Neither letter has been found.

[3] The *Princeton Annual Catalogue*, 1835, reports 211 students as of June 15, 1835.

[4] Samuel Lewis Southard (1787–1842, *DAB*) was a prominent New Jersey judge and politician. He held many important posts in both the New Jersey and national government, serving as Senator from New Jersey from 1821 to 1823 and from 1833 to 1842, as Governor of New Jersey from 1832 to 1833, and as Secretary of the Navy from 1823 to 1829. As Secretary of the Navy, he advocated reforms including a comprehensive charting of the coast, and the establishment of naval hospitals and a naval academy.

Southard was also active in Princeton affairs. An 1804 graduate of Princeton, he was a Trustee from 1822 to 1842, serving during this same period as a Trustee of the Princeton Theological Seminary.

Five pamphlets of Southard's addresses survive in the Henry Library. He was a member of the American Philosophical Society.

news to us, the marriage of Dr Frank.[5] Harriet says that the Dr must bring his lady to Princeton and give us an introduction. When at New-York last time I stoped one night at Mr McMullens.[6] Lucinda has gone to Philadelphia with Mr Harper.[7] The family are all well. John McMullen shewed me a box which James Selkirk[8] had painted for Lucinda. I was much surprised at the beauty of the execution and [could] scarcely believe that it was his production. He appears to have quite a taste for painting and may I think excel in the art by industry well directed. Love from all to all. Mother and Nancy must be anxious to hear from us. We have concluded that you are sick since we have not heard from you in so long a time.

Love to Mother and Nancy
Your
Brother

[5] Dr. Francis N. Selkirk married Helen Winne on November 8, 1834. *Daily Albany Argus*, November 11, 1834, p. 2.

[6] For John and Lucinda McMullen, see above, Henry to James Henry, November 13, 1832, footnote 1.

[7] Perhaps James Harper of Philadelphia. See above, Henry to James Henry, May 7, 1834, footnote 4.

[8] Unidentified; perhaps a brother of Francis N. Selkirk.

TO STEPHEN ALEXANDER

Mary Henry Copy, Family Correspondence, Henry Papers, Smithsonian Archives

Nov. 29, 1834.

My dear Stephen: We have received your letter[1] and are rejoiced to hear that you reached Charlestown in safety and have so far been much favored by circumstance. . . . The sky to-day is covered with clouds, we are all very anxious, particularly on your account, that it may be clear to-morrow. I intend to observe the duration and the time of a magnetic needle.[2] The Princeton papers announced in a short paragraph your departure for the South with a Fraunhofer Telescope. It has been copied into almost every paper of the North,[3] and may have found its way into some of the southern

[1] Not found.

[2] We have no evidence that Henry actually made his observations.

[3] We have been unable to locate any surviving Princeton newspapers for November 1834. The following account appeared in the *Trenton Emporium and True American* for November 29, 1834:

> The Great Eclipse will occur on Sunday, 30th inst. and will be total in the southern part of the Union. Already several scientific

prints. It would be well for you to bring back the telescope with you to Princeton; it has become something of a favorite with some of the Professors, and if the one hundred dollars can be raised it may become the property of Nassau Hall.[4] I wish I could make some experiments on polarization,[5] etc. but have nothing prepared. I hope you will write us immediately after the eclipse a full account, while all the circumstances are fresh, and while you are under the influence of the feelings produced by the appearance. As this letter will be of some importance to yourself, you need not trust it to the mail but deliver it personally.[6]

---

gentlemen are on their way south, to make observations on this rare and interesting phenomenon.

Professor Alexander, of Princeton, has gone to Effingham county, in Georgia, where the darkness will be total.

[4] Alexander's biographer C. A. Young states that the college did acquire the 3½-inch telescope, "the little Fraunhofer" which Alexander treasured until the end of his life. *Biographical Memoirs of the National Academy of Sciences*, 1886, *2*:253–254. One hundred dollars may have been the going price for the used instrument in 1834, though we cannot vouch for the accuracy of Mary Henry's transcription of that figure. We have found a reference in 1836 to $320 for a new imported Fraunhofer of unspecified aperture from Werckmeister's shop (see Henry to Titus Powers, January 14, 1836, to appear in the next volume of *The Papers of Joseph Henry*). Minutes of the meetings of the Princeton Trustees (September 29, 1835, Princeton University Archives) record that the college's Alumni Association raised $420 for a "new telescope." On October 24, 1835, Henry and Alexander paid Werckmeister for the item (see Henry's letter to Harriet of that date, below). The funds may have been for Stephen's "little Fraunhofer" (suggesting that the price indicated in the present letter is incorrect) or for another refractor.

[5] For earlier conjectures by Henry on the possible polarization of light during an eclipse, see *Henry Papers*, *1*:379.

[6] Alexander's impressions, if any were written, have not been found.

TO HARRIET HENRY

Family Correspondence, Henry Papers, Smithsonian Archives

Philadelphia Dec 5th 1834
9 o'clock PM at the
Drawing room of Mr Mason[1]

My Dear Wife

We arrived safely in the city yesterday at about 4 oclock in the afternoon. I le[f]t the two ladies[2] at a house in Walnut Street and then made my way

---

[1] In Philadelphia to have the illustrations drawn up for his forthcoming "Contributions I: Battery," Henry took the opportunity to visit friends and colleagues. A detailed account of the trip from Henry's diary follows this letter.

Mr. Mason is probably William Mason, the well-known Philadelphia engraver, landscape

to the N American Hotel. After tea as I had nothing particularly urgent to engage my attention I went to the exhibition called the Hall of Industry[3] where there is a working set of models of the different pieces of machenery employed in the manufactory of cotton. There was also an exhibition of automata, a writting Lady of wood besides several desplays of Legerdeman &c &c. I was considerably ammused but not much edified.[4] Often thought of Dad as there was a little fellow on the seat before me who appeared to enjoy the scene very much although he was not much larger than our little gentleman.

After reading the papers I went to bed about 11 oclock and slept very soundly until breakfast time this morning.

My first business this morning was to deliver the package of letters I carried with me from Princeton. Amoung others was one from Mr Mclean to one of the clerks of the U S Bank on delivering which I saw the director of the Monster, Nick Biddle. Another letter was from Mr Imbrie[5] of the college to his brother.[6] I was rece[ived] very politely by the gentleman who was requested by his Brother to send by me some books.

When I returned to the Hotell at dinner time found a little note from Mr Imbrie stating that he would be pleased to see Prof Henry at No 192 south 9th st &c. I also called at Carys Bookstore,[7] at Dobsons[8] and at the work shop of my friend Lukens. At 12 o'clock I called at the Laboratory of Dr Hare & found him just preparing to commence his lecture.

---

and still-life painter, and drawing teacher, who was active from 1808 to 1844. Mason commenced his Philadelphia engraving businesses in 1810, but gave up the art around 1830 to become a drawing master. Henry may have met Mason through the Franklin Institute, which had secured Mason's services in 1834 for a Drawing School, where he instructed in architectural and other renderings. G. C. Groce and D. H. Wallace, *The New-York Historical Society's Dictionary of Artists in America, 1564–1860* (New Haven, 1957). *Journal of the Franklin Institute*, 1834, *14*:381.

[2] We cannot identify Henry's companions.

[3] The exhibition, which had apparently just opened, stood in Fotterall's Hall at Fifth and Chestnut Streets. Later known as the American Museum, under the management of J. H. Myers, the establishment burned down in 1854. J. Thomas Scharf and Thompson Westcott, *History of Philadelphia, 1609–1884*, 3 vols. (Philadelphia, 1884), 2:979. This source places the opening in 1835, perhaps the date of the formal opening of the Hall.

[4] A perennial complaint of Henry's about popular museums.

[5] Charles Kisselman Imbrie (1814–1891) graduated from Princeton in 1835, then attended the Princeton Theological Seminary, 1836–1840, meanwhile tutoring at Princeton. Ordained in 1841, he was a pastor in New Jersey. He served as a Princeton Trustee from 1861 to 1891. *Princeton Catalogue*, p. 148; *Roberts*, p. 103.

[6] Not identified.

[7] Started in 1829 by Edward L. Carey and Abram Hart, the firm was a successor to Mathew Carey's immensely successful publishing and distributing firm. Mathew Carey broke his formal connections with the house in 1824 but continued to exert influence through his sons. Earl L. Bradsher, *Mathew Carey: Editor, Author and Publisher* (New York, 1912), pp. vii–viii.

[8] Judah Dobson's bookstore. Princeton later purchased textbooks from the firm. See John Maclean's accounts for 1836 in "Librarian's Reports, 1832/33 to 1847," Princeton University Archives.

He received me very warmely. I stoped to hear the lecture and was much pleased with the Drs Experiments. His laboratory is said to be the most extensive of any in the world and his illustrations on the largest scale.[9] After the lecture the Dr said that he had want to see me when he was writing his new text book particularly on the subjects of which I have the reputation of knowing something. He presented me with a copy of the several parts which are published. He has made a very favourable notice of me in the work[10] and spoke in high terms of my experiments in his course. There are

[9] Robert Hare's laboratory at the University of Pennsylvania Medical School, reputedly the best equipped laboratory in the United States at that time, was widely known for its ingenious apparatus, much of it devised by Hare himself. According to Silliman, Hare's huge classes at the Medical School required large-scale demonstrations and experiments. *DSB*; and Benjamin Silliman's necrology in *Silliman's Journal*, 1858, 2d ser. *26*:100–105. The frontispiece of Hare's *A Compendium of the Course of Chemical Instruction in the Medical Department of the University of Pennsylvania* (Henry owned the 4th edition, Philadelphia, 1840–1843) depicts Hare's famous laboratory and lecture room. Individual pieces of apparatus are pictured throughout the text. Hare prepared a guide to the apparatus for his students: *Engravings, and Descriptions, of a Great Part of the Apparatus used in the Chemical Course of the University of Pennsylvania with Appropriate Theoretical Explanations*, 2 vols. (Philadelphia, 1826).

A long-time admirer of Hare's experimental genius, Henry would later acquire his laboratory apparatus for the Smithsonian Institution, not only for experimental illustration but for original research—a matter to be treated in a future volume.

[10] Henry's reference is difficult to pinpoint. Hare published many books and pamphlets designed for student use in his chemical course, issuing new editions periodically to reflect the latest advances in the fields covered in his course. Many of the pamphlet editions, often bearing no date or place of publication and distributed only to students, have proved ephemeral, eluding both rare book collections and standard bibliographies.

Although we have been unable to locate Henry's reference, we conjecture that Hare was preparing a new edition of the electrical supplements to his principal chemical text, *A Compendium of the Course of Chemical Instruction in the Medical Department of the University of Pennsylvania*, published in several editions in Philadelphia beginning in the 1820s. Considering electricity and chemistry intimately related, Hare regularly included electrical topics in his chemical lectures, usually treated under three rubrics: mechanical (static) electricity; galvanism or voltaic electricity; electromagnetism. Organized under these headings, the supplementary tri-partite electrical lectures, appearing in print as early as 1824, evolved into a major adjunct to the fourth edition of 1840–1843 of Hare's chemical *Compendium*, which Joseph Henry owned. Henry's Library also contains a separately bound edition of the electrical pamphlets, which bears no date but seems to be a slightly earlier and briefer version of the one attached to the *Compendium*. The third segment, on "Electro-Magnetism," in both of these later editions paid numerous compliments to Henry's work on electromagnets, electric motors, and induction coils (see, e.g., pp. 108, 118–120 of the fourth edition of the *Compendium*).

Our problem has been in locating a possible earlier edition of the electrical pamphlets underway during Henry's 1834 visit. Although the 1836 (third) edition of the *Compendium* lacks supplements on galvanism, voltaic electricity, and electromagnetism, there may have been a recent revised edition of the electrical supplements. The preface to another undated Hare text, *An Exposition of the Sciences of Galvanism and Electro-Magnetism, Abstracted from the Fifth Edition of Turner's Chemistry*, apparently published sometime in 1835 or 1836, refers students to copies of his "lectures on galvanism and electro-magnetism, *as they appeared last year* . . ." (italics ours). Conceivably, the "lectures" were the regular electrical supplements, undergoing revision during Henry's visit.

We have dwelt on these bibliographic problems because these favorable notices of Henry in the mid-1830s signaled the beginning of Robert Hare's increasing appreciation of

8 or 9 students from Princeton who w[ere] well pleased to hear my name mentioned or at least so they appeared to be.

This afternoon I called on Dr Ludlow, found the gentleman & his lady at home but just prepared to walk. I sat some time while Mrs Ludlow was in the same room with her hat and tipet on as I though[t] just returned from a walk but when I rose to go she then informed me that they were just starting for a walk. The Dr has not yet commenced his duties in the College[11] and may perhaps pay a visit to Princeton before the beginning of the next term which is in Jany. He did not promise but spoke as if a little [wo]uld induce him. I will try to per[suade] the Dr and Mrs to promis us a visit.

I next called on Bache at the University. Several persons in this city have asked me if I had been sick as the news was that I had been attacked with a fit of the apoplexy. Dr Ludlow I believe brought the intelligence from albany. I called this morning on Mr Mason with my drawings but he is so much ingaged that nothing could be done until 6 o'clock this evening. I am now with him & his son. The young man is engaged on the drawing[12] while I am scribbling this letter with a steel pen which gives me so much trouble that I fear I will not be able to send you a letter quite as well spelled as might be inorder. I cannot possibly return until monday as my drawings will not be finished before that time. I am engaged to take tea at Dr Ludlows tomorrow evening and to go with Dr Hare to the Whistar party[13] in the evening.

As ever your
H[ubby]

Joseph Henry's research. Clearly, Hare came to rely on Henry for keeping his electrical lectures up to date, especially on electromagnetic topics; in turn, he publicized Henry's discoveries, paying particular attention to his scientific priorities.

[11] Ludlow was Provost of the University of Pennsylvania.

[12] S. Rufus Mason is the name on the engraving printed in APS *Transactions*, 1837, n.s. 5:plate 22 (see the frontispiece of this volume). We have not been able to identify him nor to confirm that William Mason was his father.

[13] See Henry to Harriet Henry, November 1, 1833, footnote 10.

HENRY'S NOTES ON A TRIP TO PHILADELPHIA, DECEMBER 5–7, 1834[1]

Henry Papers,[2] Smithsonian Archives

Friday Dec. 5th 1834

Arrived in Phila about 4 oclock P.M. Took Lodgings at the N. American. Not knowing what to do during the [evening] concluded to visit the mechanical Hall in chestnut street.

Was on the whole much diverted with the performance but not much edifyed. The exhibition consisted of the desplay of the writing Lady, Autometa &c &c.

The autometa were very ingeniously contrived and well desplayed.

The most singular feat performed consisted of a man's placing himself on his back and in this position ballancing a long heavy pole on both his feet causing it to spin round like the arm of a windlass. A fine illustration of the power of habit in controoling the action of the muscles.

Friday morning at 8 oclock took breakfast after which went in serch of Mr Mason the Draftsman with the plates of my battery. Found his son; agreed to meet the father at 5 o'clock.

Delivered my letters, one at the U S Bank the others to Mr Dobson, Mr Imbrie &c. Called at Carey & Harts Book store, purchased the vol of Lardners Library on the Arts of the Greeks and Romans.[3] Also called on my friend Lukens—made but a short stop, promised to call again.

At 12 o'clock went to the Lecture room of Prof Hare. Found him just preparing for the commencement of his lecture. Gave me very cordial welcome. Was much pleased with the lecture and favourably so as the Dr gave a very interesting discourse illustrated with splendid experiments.

The Lecture was on heat—the means of producing it and also of diminishing the same principle by means of solutions and evaporization. In freezing water by evaporization the eather was thrown in considerably quantity on the water and a cake of ice formed of about 6 inches in diameter and of the thickness of a dollar.[4]

[1] The original is dated December 5 when Henry started this record. Events of Saturday, December 6, appear also, from which we infer the Sunday date. In a later footnote, we will discuss the possibility that part of the text was written after the return to Princeton.

[2] This small bookletlike item is located in folder 1 of Box 50.

[3] Volume one of Dionysius Lardner's *A Treatise on the Arts, Manufactures, Manners, and Institutions of the Greeks and Romans* (London, 1833) survives in Henry's Library. This was volume 47 of the Cabinet Cyclopaedia which Henry may have confused with the Library of Useful Knowledge; both series are represented in Henry's holdings of books.

[4] By the fourth edition Hare's text, *A Compendium of the Course of Chemical Instruction*

The method of keeping <*water*> ice solid by means of sulphuric acid was shown and a cake of ice exhibited which had been kept in that state for 24 hours.[5]

The Dr presented me with a copy of his work and made me promis to call at 8 o'clock at his house tomorrow evening and attend with him the Whistar party at Mr Stricklands.[6]

I forgot to mention that before attending the Lecture of Dr Hare I called on Mason the Math. Instrument maker. Was shewn a small glass bell with two long tubes intended to illustrate the principles of the diving bell. On the top of one tube was placed a small syringe for condensing the air and another pipe for permitting the air to pass out. A candle with two little images may be placed on the shelf at the bottom and the candle or taper kept burning although the article be sunk a foot or more beneath the surface of water in a deep glass jar.[7]

Also I noticed a number of lead weights covered with red varnish. These may be made in any number with little trouble. Also two little reaction wheels for moving either by water or air on the air pump.[8]

Mr. Lukens supposes that Iron may be made brittle by sulphuric acid in the way of absorption of the sulphur. He found that when Iron tubes were cleaned by means of sul. acid that they became brittle but when muriatic acid was used for the same purpose the tubes retained their tenacity.[9]

Mr. Baldwins engines or the one on the Trenton and Phil. rail way weighs about 6 tuns without water. The water weighs 1½ tuns.

The passenger cars weigh when filled about 4 tuns. It is more difficult

---

in the Medical Department of the University of Pennsylvania (Philadelphia, 1840–1843), pp. 68–70, had a more elegant experimental technique for producing "cold by vaporization" than throwing the ether on water.

[5] Hare describes the process in "Apparatus for Freezing Water by the Aid of Sulphuric Acid," *Phil. Mag.*, 1834, 3d ser. *5*:377–379.

[6] William Strickland (1787–1854, *DAB*), an engineer and architect. For Wistar Parties, see Henry's letter of November 1, 1833, above, footnote 10. Henry and Strickland were not close, so far as we can judge from the surviving evidence.

[7] This pre-noon visit to Mason, the instrument maker, is not mentioned in Henry's letter to his wife which was written in the evening of the same day. For Mason, see footnote 2 of Henry's Notes on a Trip to Philadelphia of October 20, 1834, above.

Diving bells were well known by this date. Jacob Bigelow's *Elements of Technology . . .* (Boston, 1829), which Henry had at Princeton, dates their invention in the sixteenth century and describes a recent example fundamentally similar to Mason's device.

[8] A variant of Barker's mill (see *Henry Papers, 1*:308) using air as well as water.

[9] The effect of sulphur on the brittleness of iron was well known by this date. The process of puddling, among other things, reduced the percentage of this impurity.

to cause an engine to move slowley when moving with a light load than with a heavy one.[10]

Mr Espy thinks that the fixed point of ice is about the zero of Fahrenheit. To determine this however he proposes to take two thermometers, coat one with ice. If it does not fall, the one which is coated, it will give the fixed point of ice.[11]

Mr Rodgers[12] informes the club[13] that he saw Mr. Wheats[t]on[e][14] make

[10] We assume this is a continuation of Henry's conversation with Lukens on the morning of December 5. According to John H. White, Jr., of the Smithsonian Institution, the weights given are reasonable. The water weight is for both locomotive and tender. The concluding sentence is puzzling; we doubt that it is true.

[11] This is a confusing note about a topic of great interest to both James P. Espy and Joseph Henry. The fixed points are the melting and boiling temperatures of water. Espy and Henry use "zero" here in a generic sense as 32° is the fixed point in the Fahrenheit scale. We think this is a reference to the realization that the zero in many thermometers in time deviated slightly from the melting point. J. F. Daniell discussed the problem in his *Meteorological Essays and Observations*, 2d ed. (London, 1827), pp. 368–369, a work probably familiar to both men. Like some investigators on the continent, Daniell ascribed the phenomenon to changes in the "form and capacity" of the glass after calibration due to atmospheric pressure on the vacuum, an explanation Middleton points out was untenable on the evidence at the time. To evade this source of error, some investigators favored waiting a time period—a year, let us say—before calibrating a thermometer. By the end of the century, changes in the composition of the glass minimized this problem. Middleton notes that careful observers in the last century checked the zero points before and after important experiments. We assume this is what is being discussed here. Literally coating with ice rather than using melting ice seems strange. The role of the second thermometer is obscure unless, as we might speculate, the thermometer immersed in ice somehow acted as a standard for the calibration of the other. Standardizing meteorological instruments was a matter of great concern to both men in their promotion of networks of meteorological observers. For Epsy see *DSB* and footnote 49 of Henry's Notes on a Trip to Philadelphia, April 29–May 2, 1834, above. W. E. Knowles Middleton, *A History of the Thermometer and Its Use in Meteorology* (Baltimore, 1966), pp. 142–147.

[12] Henry Darwin Rogers (1808–1866, *DAB*), the geologist, will reappear in this and later volumes of *The Papers of Joseph Henry*. He and his three brothers were important figures in the ante-bellum American scientific community. A Philadelphian, Rogers briefly taught in Dickinson College (1830). In 1832 he accompanied Robert Dale Owen to England where he became much interested in geology. In 1833 Henry Darwin Rogers became a volunteer lecturer at the Franklin Institute, which meant that he received no salary but depended on the admission fees for income. In 1835 he attained the chair of geology and mineralogy at the University of Pennsylvania from which he resigned in 1846.

In 1835 H. D. Rogers also became head of the New Jersey Geological Survey with Henry's assistance, a matter treated in several documents below. The Pennsylvania Survey was entrusted to him in the following year. After its completion in 1842, Rogers continued to work on the report which is important for its description of the Appalachian Mountains and for the suggested explanation of their formation. He collaborated on the mountain-building theory with his brother W. B. Rogers. In 1855 Henry Darwin Rogers became Regius Professor of Natural History at the University of Glasgow, serving until his death. Several of his publications, some presentation copies, survive in Joseph Henry's Library.

[13] This first reference to "the club" is elaborated on in Henry's letter to Torrey of December 20, 1834, below. Writing to Henry on February 15, 1835 (below), Bache asserted the idea originated with John Torrey. Henry is here describing the first meeting, perhaps on Saturday afternoon, December 6, 1834.

Besides Henry, Bache, Rogers, and Torrey, the original members included James P. Espy, Stephen Alexander, and Edward Courtenay. A distinguished group, all except Espy were then or later connected with higher edu-

experiments with the revolving mirror on the brush of light from the electrical machine. It is composed of an infinite number of minute sparkes which are separated from each other by the action of the revolving mirror.[15]

cation. Except for Courtenay, they were to have notable careers as scientists. All were engaged in full-time professional activities, even by the standards of our day. Membership was not closed; in his necrology of Espy, Bache lists the astronomer Sears C. Walker as one of the club. Further research may disclose other members. According to the letter to Torrey, it was to meet three or four times a year "for mutual support and instruction. . . . It has no name and must be kept secret so as to excite no jealousy &c." We will simply refer to it as "the club." Comments about activities of the club will appear subsequently in this and later volumes. As yet, we cannot state when this informal body went out of existence.

Without claiming undue significance for the club, in retrospect it represented a stage in the development of the community of professional scientists. Like the early Royal Society, the American Philosophical Society was composed of devotees of the sciences, both casual friends and enthusiastic practitioners. At a later stage more specialized organizations appeared like the Academy of Natural Sciences of Philadelphia. Professionals and amateurs, active practitioners and passive onlookers were in its ranks. Groups at the analogous stage in Britain are referred to by a recent study as "study associations." Some of these in Britain became true professional scientific societies. Analogous bodies in the United States were less specialized; none evolved into professional societies.

What seems to have occurred in some situations in the United States is that the active scientists followed a dual strategy. On the one hand, they attempted to take over and reform the existing bodies. Dislodging or converting amateurs and lay friends of science was not always easy; founding purely professional bodies was rather a risky proposition at this date in America. The club provided a counterweight to the American Philosophical Society just as the later Lazzaroni headed by Bache did for the American Association for the Advancement of Science. The informal groups acted as nuclei to influence, directly and indirectly, larger formal bodies and programs.

Small, informal groups with social aspects were obviously not unique to America. The Lunar Society of Birmingham is a fine example from the British scientific scene of the eighteenth century. Nor are such groups limited to the sciences. Before the Civil War, Joseph Henry in Washington joined a club with general interests which functioned for many years. Perhaps this proliferation of organizations related to the supposed tendency of Americans to be "joiners." Some circles in Philadelphia, at least, were prone to forming organizations. The Wistar Party and the club were not unique. After a while one ceases to be surprised on encountering a necrology with a mention of Bache belonging to a dining club, The Six. Good food, good drink, and good conversation were excuses to form groups; why not good science also, even to performing work together?

For all the eminence of the members of the club and, later, the Lazzaroni, their existence did not denote elite power but backwardness in scientific development. Were the community of scientists stronger, they would have undoubtedly emulated the British by forming specialized societies. Even the one group that had the strength, the geologists, eventually merged their Association of American Geologists into the nonexclusive American Association for the Advancement of Science. Between the Civil War and World War I, American scientists formed many specialized professional societies.

See N. Reingold, "Definitions and Speculations: The Professionalization of Science in America in the Nineteenth Century," to appear in the proceedings of the American Academy of Arts and Sciences' Conference on the Early History of Learned Societies in America. Sally Kohlstedt, "The Formation of the American Scientific Community: The American Association for the Advancement of Science, 1848–1860" (Ph.D. dissertation, University of Illinois, Urbana, 1972). Geoffrey Millerson, *The Qualifying Associations: A Study in Professionalization* (London, 1964). The necrology which mentions The Six is in the American Philosophical Society *Proceedings*, 1854, *6*:60–64. Bache's necrology of Espy is in the Smithsonian Institution *Annual Report*, 1859, pp. 108–111.

[14] Sir Charles Wheatstone (1802–1875, *DNB*) started his career as a musical instrument maker before turning to research in acoustics and in electricity and magnetism, as well as other areas of physical science. He was also

The condensation of air in the path of a spark cannot be the cause of the light of the spark since in the exp. of the French Philos. no light is given by the condensation of any gas which does not support combustion. The light in the condensing machine is due to the burning of the oil.[16]

Mr Rodgers sais that Mr W's revolving mirror is not at right angles to the action of the motion.[17]

On Saturday evening attended the Lecture of Mr Rodgers on Geology.[18] He stated the 3 Theorys of the formation of the earth.

1st Theory that of Werner of the aqueous state of the earth[19]—fishures ca[u]sed by the drying and the shrinking of the crusts.

---

a notable inventor. In 1834 Wheatstone became Professor of Experimental Physics in King's College, London. Several copies of Henry letters to him survive (but no examples of his correspondence to Henry), as well as two copies of articles presented by him to Henry. Although not close, their relationship was long standing and cordial. Years later, in 1870, Henry noted in Robert Smith's *A Compleat System of Opticks . . .* (Cambridge, England, 1738) that Wheatstone had bought the books for him at the sale of the library of Sir James South. References to Wheatstone occur in many documents to appear subsequently in *The Papers of Joseph Henry*.

15 Presumably Rogers witnessed the Wheatstone experiment on his British visit of 1832. This is the series of experiments discussed in footnote 2 of Ten Eyck's letter of [ca. November 22, 1833], above, resulting in an 1834 publication surviving as a presentation copy in Henry's Library.

16 From Henry's notes it seems the club extended its discussion of the Wheatstone experiment on velocity of electricity and duration of electric light to consider the nature of the spark produced in the air.

Henry is here discussing an interpretation of the light produced by discharges of static electricity. Roget, relying on Biot, ascribed the light produced in air on violent compression to the resistance of the medium; by analogy the electric light was a manifestation of resistance of the air to the passage of the electric fluid. This position was taken to deny that the spark was the fluid itself.

At this time, as will appear in a subsequent footnote, Joseph Henry was reading the French translation of volume one of J. J. Berzelius's chemical text, *Traité de chimie* (Paris, 1829) where the question is discussed in the broader reference of whether electricity could pass through a vacuum. In a notebook ([23894], p. 33) used around this time in preparing class lectures, Henry notes from page 114 of this source: "The passage of electricity through a vacuum is a very important fact that should be established with great care. It has an important bearing on our opinion of the nature of electricity for if it can only be transmitted by or through matter then it may be considered as a property of matter." The alternative was to consider electricity as a separate kind of matter.

Berzelius cited Davy's work showing the sparks were due to the ignition or combustion of minute particles from the bodies from which sparks originated. In this same notebook (p. 115) Henry cites the later work of the Italian scientist Ambrogio Fusinieri (1773–1853, *Poggendorff*) which he encountered in the *Britannica*. Henry here treats the spark as a combustion effect exclusively but Brewster, the author of the encyclopedia article, (s.v. "Electricity") clearly refers to luminous effects arising from causes other than combustion.

Just above the note on Fusinieri, Henry notes, without attribution, that the light produced by an air condenser "is due to the burning of the oil & leather of the piston in the syringe," a position quite in conformity with Davy's earlier findings. The nature of the electrical spark was an important question to investigators like Faraday and Henry. As will appear in later volumes, the relation of electromagnetic effects to vacuums had important theoretical implications for Joseph Henry.

17 "Action of the motion" is ambiguous. We think it refers to the path of the spark.

18 Probably part of the series given by Rogers at the Franklin Institute.

19 A reference to Abraham Gottlob Werner's "Neptunian" theory with its assumption of a

2nd The Theory of Hutton on the Igneous formation of the earth—all in solution by fire.[20]

3rd The theory of central heat with that of solution of the water on the surface. The contortions of the surface accounted for on this Theory by the shrinking of the surface. It is caused to occupy a smaller space.[21]

Mr R. mentioned the fact that it has lately been discovered that very hot water under pressure has the property of desolving glass—but not quartz cristals. Dr. Wollaston discovered that his thermometer in the steam was corroded.[22]

Air will pass along the surface of glass down this cup and up the barometer tube.[23]

In[24] looking over the Chemestry of Berzelius,[25] I find that he state[d] that

---

primeval ocean from which the geological strata were precipitated. See *Henry Papers, 1*: 138.

[20] The Scottish geologist James Hutton (1726–1797, *DNB*), principal propounder of the "Plutonian" theory of the earth's origins. As it stressed the role of heat, it was the principal rival to Werner's views. Perhaps of greater importance in the long run was Hutton's belief that contemporary observable processes were also responsible for past changes in the earth's structure and that past and present rates of those processes were the same.

[21] Perhaps a reference to the theories of Pierre-Louis-Antoine Cordier (1777–1861, *DSB*) and Jean-Baptiste-Armand-Louis-Léonce Élie de Beaumont (1798–1874, *DSB*). For an earlier comment by Henry on the idea of a central heat, see *Henry Papers, 1*:171, especially the discussion in footnote 29.

[22] The Wollaston referred to here is Francis John Hyde Wollaston, a brother of the better known William Hyde Wollaston. Rogers is referring, incorrectly, to "Description of a Thermometrical Barometer for Measuring Altitudes," *Phil. Trans.*, 1817, pp. 183–196 in which thermometers were exposed to boiling water. No corrosion of the glass was reported. Henry had referred to this article in his 1824 lecture on steam, *Henry Papers, 1*:82. The dissolution of glass under superheated steam was reported by the French scientist Cagniard de La Tour. The abstract of the original from the *Annales de chimie et de physique*, 1822, *21*:127–132, is in the *Phil. Mag.*, 1823, *61*:58–61 with a confirming editorial note that the glass bulbs became "opake" before fracturing. Perhaps this is what Rogers had in mind.

The reference to quartz crystals is cryptic. Given high enough temperature and pressure, they will dissolve. We are uncertain as to what work Rogers is referring to here. By this date, it was well known that quartz crystals were impervious to all acids save hydrofluoric.

[23] This solitary sentence is unclear to us.

[24] In the manuscript this text occurs on separate pages after the discussion of the Baldwin locomotive and passenger cars and before the paragraph on Espy. The writing instrument is different from the other passages in ink, but we are unable to state unequivocally if these passages were made with the same steel pen Joseph Henry had so much trouble with when writing to Harriet on the evening of December 5 at Mason's. If written that evening, this assumes that Henry acquired volume one of Berzelius's *Traité de chimie* at Dobson's or Carey and Hart's bookstore; borrowed Hare's copy which survives in the library of the Smithsonian's National Museum of History and Technology; or sat down to read Mason's copy. In any event, we think Henry would have noted receiving or seeing a work of such great professional importance. What follows has all the earmarks of Henry's penchant for compulsive note taking, using whatever paper was convenient. Presumably, these jottings were done shortly after returning to Princeton.

[25] Henry's Library contains Berzelius's *Traité de chimie. . .*, 8 vols. (Paris, 1829–1833). We have, as yet, no idea when Henry acquired this French translation of this influential work. Volume one contains the sections on electricity, magnetism, light, heat—all topics of great interest to Joseph Henry. Except for a few blurred words in ink on the front flyleaf, the volumes apparently are unmarked. This is quite unlike Henry's normal penchant for marking interesting passages. We suspect

a pile may be made of perfect non conductors interposed between perfect conductors.[26]

In shewing the action of zinc & copper on the toung solder two pieces of silver to two long wires and a plate of copper and zinc to the other ends. Put a piece of paper between them moistened by acid. Bring them in contact while the toung of one of the audience is between the plates of silver.[27] J H

Berzelius mentions that when a person has 50 pairs of plates the best method of operating with them is to form the pile as the increased energy will repay for the increased labour of piling them &c.[28] He also mentions the exp of Hare and Silliman[29] on the incompatibility of different batteries.[30, 31]

Henry purchased the volumes years later, perhaps in Paris in 1837, and found the work no longer interesting.

[26] Apparently a reference to Berzelius, *1*: 126–127. This occurs in the course of the treatment of the excitation "par le contact mutuel de corps heterogènes." Berzelius next considers the action of semiconductors placed in the voltaic pile, and then liquid conductors,

[27] This is a variation of an experiment described by Berzelius in his *Traité*, *1*:131 and plate 1, figure 11. The effect was observed in the eighteenth century before the work of Galvani and Volta by Johann Georg Sulzer (1720–1779, *Poggendorff*). The phenomenon is also noted in another work familiar to Henry, Farrar's English version of Biot, *Elements of Electricity, Magnetism, and Electro-Magnetism* . . . (Cambridge, Massachusetts, 1826), p. 129.

[28] The nearest thing to this statement by Henry in Berzelius's *Traité* occurs on pp. 143–144, in the discussion of the differences in effects of batteries and of piles in terms of the surface area of metals involved. In the former the effect is proportional to the total area exposed to the liquid; in the latter, the effect is proportional to the number of pairs. Henry's statement about efficiency is his own conclusion and is not in Berzelius.

[29] Berzelius, *Traité*, *1*:150. In Hare's copy this is annotated with the words: "The only foreign author who has noticed this incongruity." See *Silliman's Journal*, 1822, *4*:201–204 and *5*:94–108.

[30] Immediately below this passage occurs a penciled reference to an article of Stefano Giovanni Marianini (1790–1866, *Poggendorff*), "Sur les piles secondaires de Ritter," *Annales de chimie et de physique*, 1828, *38*:5–40. We do not know when Henry jotted down his penciled bibliographic note.

Johann Wilhelm Ritter (1776–1810, *Poggendorff*) constructed a pile composed of alternating pieces of a metal and pieces of moistened paper. When placed in a circuit with a voltaic pile, this secondary pile became weakly charged. Ritter ascribed the effect to the difficulty the alternating moist and metallic conductors presented to the passage of the electricity. Consequently, part of the current was retained in the secondary pile. Marianini, an adherent of the contact theory, in this article demonstrated (to his satisfaction at least) that the effect arose from the alterations produced by the voltaic current of the electrical state of the surfaces of the metal in contact with the moistened papers. Berzelius discusses this, *1*:158. The effect is described in electrostatic terms analogous to the Leyden jar. See A. A. Cazin, *Traité théorique et pratique des piles électriques* . . . (Paris, 1881), pp. 262–268. Joseph Henry probably knew previously of Marianini's work on the secondary piles from James Cumming's translation of J. F. Demonferrand's *A Manual of Electro Dynamics* . . . (Cambridge, England, 1827), pp. 272–275.

[31] On the facing page is a text we cannot completely decipher and cannot, therefore, fully explain:

> When the − p[ole] of the battery dips into a strong solution [three words unclear] a small platina wire at the + pole will be def[lected] but when the arrangement is reversed no effect.

This is related to the other passages bearing on the properties of conductors and nonconductors. We have not found it in Berzelius. The effect described is apparently electrostatic.

On the last sheet of the booklet Henry wrote

in pencil—now blurred and faded—two statements of Mason, the instrument maker. Typical of Henry, they record curious facts. The first is barely decipherable:

> The mechanics of Philad[elphia] have noticed that a nail cannot be [drawn? driven?] as fast by an [one unclear word] rod as when the [two unclear words] Mr Mason

The second is legible:

> It is impossible to cut into a bag of cotton lightly stuffed. Mr Mason
> This is a trick among clearks.

FROM JOHN VAUGHAN

Henry Papers, Smithsonian Archives

Phil. 8 Dec 1834

D Sir

On the 19th Inst. our last meeting for the Year will be held & I am very anxious your communication to our Society should be introduced at that meeting;[1] should you afterward want to retouch or alter, no difficulty will arise. We are also ready to go on with a 2nd N° of Vol V—so thus no danger of delay in publication. Let me have the pleasure of hearing from you. Remember I am not alone in this application.

Do you receive the Philos. Mag of London? I have this day recd the Nov number. There are in it two articles interesting to you. 1. Account of the new observatory for magnetic observations at Gotingen.[2] 2. Account of Magneto-Electrical Expts made with the large Magnet at the Exhibition room at Adelaide Mus London by Mr Sturgeon.[3]

If you do not receive it, I will send it to you but it must be immediately returned to me by mail as a periodical. Let me know immediately as if *known* to be here, I could not send it & I must have it back by Fryday.[4]

ys Jn Vaughan

I suppose no good observation was had of the Eclipse as Mr Alexander was absent. When he returns we should [be] much pleased to have *his observation* for our Society.

[1] As will come out in documents below, Henry's paper describing his new galvanic battery was read to the Society on January 16, 1835.

[2] A description of the observatory of Gauss and Weber taken from the *Göttingische gelehrte Anzeigen*, August 1834. *Phil. Mag.*, 1834, 3d ser. 5:344–349. The observatory housed the apparatus which for the first time permitted absolute determinations of the intensity of terrestrial magnetism.

[3] Ibid., pp. 376–377. Vaughan was apparently less impressed with the two pieces by Faraday and W. H. F. Talbot on optical experiments in the same issue. For Sturgeon, see *Henry Papers, 1*:423n and *DNB*.

[4] Henry apparently accepted Vaughan's offer. He reports on his reading of the November *Phil. Mag.* in his letter to Bache of December 17, 1834, below.

We had 6 obs. here one from Balti[more], one from Charlottesville & expect further ones. They are to be arranged by the Committee with a view to publication.[5]

[5] On March 6, 1835, the committee (A. D. Bache, Joseph Roberts, Jr., and Isaiah Lukens) presented its collection of observations of the solar eclipse of November 30, 1834, to the Society. American Philosophical Society, *Transactions*, 1837, n.s. 5:233–248. Alexander did not contribute to this publication.

FROM JAMES R. CHILTON

Henry Papers, Smithsonian Archives[1]

New York Dec 13. 1834

Dear Sir

I have received an order from West Point Phil. Departm[t] for a sett of Electro Dynamic apparatus, and being a little at a loss to know what constitutes a complete sett, I take the liberty of asking your opinion on the subject and must also trouble you to sketch on a sheet of paper, the forms which you approve of.

Prof[r] Cram[2] who gave me the order for the above has also ordered one of your large Electro magnets. He wishes to have it constructed according to your directions, and if possible to obtain your certificate as to the correctness of its performance, when finished. I told him I would write to you and take advantage of any improvement which you might suggest. Have the goodness to mention the length of wire you think advisable to wind on it, (the manner of winding it I understand) and also the size and form of the galvanic part.[3] I am anxious for your sake to make it a superiour one.

By complying with the above request you will much oblige yrs Truly

J. R. Chilton

[1] Henry's response, noted below in Chilton to Henry, December 29, 1834, has not been found. This letter by Chilton, like the later letter, shows evidence of Mary Henry's handling.

[2] Thomas Jefferson Cram, for whom see above, Henry to Stephen Alexander, April 16, 1833, footnote 5.

[3] We have no evidence that Henry ever certified the apparatus made by Chilton. Nor had Henry attempted any improvements on the large electromagnet which he demonstrated first in September 1833. Chilton ended up experimenting with various sources of power, so Henry may have given him several choices on "the size and form of the galvanic part." See Chilton's letter below, December 29, 1834.

December 17, 1834

TO ALEXANDER DALLAS BACHE

Bache Papers, Smithsonian Archives

Princeton Wednesday evening
Dec 17th 1834

My Dear Sir

I send you this evening my drawings[1] & hope they will reach you in time for the Friday evening meeting of the Phil Society.[2]

I would apologize for my thus occupying so much of your time but you know that I shall always be willing if able to discharge the debt. The following is the title of my paper which you can alter in any way to suit your more refined taste in such matters.

Description of a galvanic battery intended to produce intensity or quantity with some observations on the peculiar effect of a long conductor in producing sparks in a galvanic circuit. By Joseph Henry Prof. of Natural Philosophy in the College of New Jersey, Princeton, (Late of the Albany Academy) Member of the Royal Physical Society of Edinburgh &c.[3]

This title will need a little explanation. I have been induced to add the second part "Some observations &c" on account of a paper by Mr Faraday in the last (Nov) Num of the London & Edinburgh Magazine, p 349.[4]

By a reference to this paper you will see that Mr Faraday has come across my fact of the production of a spark by means of a long wire. I am now anxious to publish my observations on this point as soon as possible and

[1] Presumably the ones, as amended, which appear as Plate 22 (facing p. 218) in the fifth volume (n.s.) of the *Transactions* of the American Philosophical Society illustrating Henry's "Contributions I: Battery." See the frontispiece to this volume.

[2] December 19, 1834. The subsequent history of these drawings and Henry's text will appear in later documents.

Apparently the drawings reached Bache in time. The printed proceedings of the American Philosophical Society for that date state:

> Dr. Bache, on the part of Prof. Bache, explained some modifications of the galvanic battery made by Prof. Henry of Princeton, which, with the peculiar effect of a Long Conductor in producing Sparks in a Galvanic circuit, will be the subject of a communication to be made at a Subsequent Meeting.

"Dr. Bache" is Franklin Bache. *Early Proceedings of the American Philosophical Society . . .* (Philadelphia, 1884), p. 662.

[3] As will come out subsequently in this volume, Henry's work ultimately appeared as two separate pieces published back-to-back, the first on the new galvanic battery, the second on the influence of the spiral conductor on increasing the intensity of electricity. The latter, responding to Faraday's work, is dealt with extensively in documents below.

[4] "On the Magneto-electric Spark and Shock, and on a Peculiar Condition of Electric and Magneto-electric Induction," *Phil. Mag.*, 1834, 3d ser. 5:349–354. This is a letter to the editor, Richard Phillips, and is dated October 17, 1834. The December issue, pp. 444–445, has a later letter (November 20, 1834) containing corrections. Although these were reprinted in Faraday's *Experimental Researches in Electricity*, 2:204–211 (London, 1844), they were not part of Faraday's series of experimental researches in electricity, parts of which were appearing simultaneously in *Phil. Mag.*

do not know a more ready method than to append them or to incorporate them with my description of the battery. Fortunately I published a notice of the fact soon after I discovered it in the same No of Sillimans journal which contains your paper on the magneto electric spark sometime in 1832. It is however so long since I have seen the article that I know not what I have said on the subject. Since then I have made a number of additional observations in reference to this subject which are at variance with the views of Mr Faraday. These I will carefully repeat.[5] Mr F has probably not seen my paper or has forgotten the fact.[6]

The same journal contains a remark which perfectly agrees with my opinion in regard to the magnetometer formed of a long wire, p 349. It is stated that a pair of plates one inch in diam will produce with the applica-

[5] Henry's paper, "On the Production of Currents and Sparks of Electricity from Magnetism," appeared in the July 1832 number of *Silliman's Journal* (22:403–408). The passage in question is the last paragraph of the article:

> I have made several other experiments in relation to the same subject, but which more important duties will not permit me to verify in time for this paper. I may however mention one fact which I have not seen noticed in any work and which appears to me to belong to the same class of phaenomena as those before described: it is this; when a small battery is moderately excited by diluted acid and its poles, which must be terminated by cups of mercury, are connected by a copper wire not more than a foot in length, no spark is perceived when the connection is either formed or broken: but if a wire thirty or forty feet long be used, instead of the short wire, though no spark will be perceptible when the connection is made, yet when it is broken by drawing one end of the wire from its cup of mercury a vivid spark is produced. If the action of the battery be very intense, a spark will be given by the short wire; in this case it is only necessary to wait a few minutes until the action partially subsides and until no more sparks are given from the short wire; if the long wire be now substituted a spark will again be obtained. The effect appears somewhat increased by coiling the wire into a helix; it seems also to depend in some measure on the length and thickness of the wire; I can account for these phaenomena only by supposing the long wire to become charged with electricity which by its reaction on itself projects a spark when the connection is broken.

Faraday and Henry elaborated their experimental findings and explanations—Faraday in his Ninth Series and Henry in "Contributions II: Spiral Conductor." The parallelisms between the two investigators are striking, giving rise to a particularly tangled priority question. Questions of scientific content and of the very real psychological crisis facing Henry are dealt with in documents appearing subsequently. At this point all Henry knows is that Faraday has published findings in an area which Henry "had not seen noticed in any work," jeopardizing his claim to original discovery.

The "Bache paper" is actually extracts of two letters from Joseph Saxton, "Notice of Electro-Magnetic Experiments" (*Silliman's Journal*, 1832, 22:409–415) sent by Bache to Silliman in advance of publication by the Franklin Institute's *Journal*, a precedent, as it were, for what will occur to Joseph Henry in this priority race with Faraday.

[6] Henry's 1832 article was in the appendix of the July 1832 issue; the relevant passage was the very last paragraph. Henry is probably correct in his inferences; it could have been missed or the last paragraph forgotten in the intervening time period. When the Smithsonian Institution published its two-volume edition of Joseph Henry's *Scientific Writings* (Washington, 1886), the reprinted text of the July 1832 article had a heading added before the final paragraph, "*Electrical self-induction in a long helical wire*" to call attention to the basis for the priority claim. What Faraday did or did not know about Henry's work will be elaborated below in footnote 2 of John Vaughan's letter of August 5, 1835.

tion of mere spring water an effect not much less than that produced by a very large pair of plates with the application of strong acid &&c. Read the paper as I know you will.[7]

Can you give me any information about the *"beautiful theory established by Ohm"*? Where is it to be found? I am anxious to see his papers. See the same page of the journal.[8]

[7] Henry knew Bache would read the article as it was the description of Gauss's magnetic observatory at Göttingen. At the very end of the article, just above the start of Faraday's letter to Richard Phillips, is a concluding paragraph describing electromagnetic apparatus devised by Wilhelm Eduard Weber (1804–1891, *Poggendorff*). Henry is referring to Gauss's account of Weber's running of wires, "nearly 6000 feet" between the astronomic observatory and the cabinet of natural philosophy, one end being attached to the magnetic intensity apparatus. At the other end, Weber produced currents by batteries: "It is wonderful how a single pair of plates placed at the other extremity immediately impart to the magnetic rod a motion equal to considerably more than a thousand divisions of the scale." Henry's sentence about the plates one inch in diameter is a paraphrase of the text. These results are in accordance with Henry's work, as in the modulus of conduction experiments of September 9, 1834, above.

[8] This occurs on p. 349 in the account by Gauss of the apparatus at his magnetic observatory immediately after the report of experiments with the pair of plates of one-inch diameter. The full sentence reads: "This circumstance, however, is after all not surprising, as it only tends to confirm the beautiful theory first established by Ohm." This is the first time Henry ever heard of the work of Georg Simon Ohm (1789–1854), the German mathematical physicist best remembered for the law bearing his name. Henry's knowledge and use of the work of his German contemporary is important in its own right; such knowledge and use has bearing on historiographic questions arising from the literature on the reception of Ohm's work.

Clearly, neither Henry nor Bache (see his reply of January 3, 1835, below) had heard of Ohm. We assume Henry's eagerness to learn of the theory but have no evidence of Henry's concrete knowledge of Ohm's Law until 1837 during the course of Henry's European trip. Volume three will treat this incident in which Charles Wheatstone gave Henry a copy of an article in French dealing with Ohm written by M. H. von Jacobi. Ohm's work afterwards is assimilated into Henry's without any difficulties discernible to us. In later volumes we will discuss instances in which Ohm's Law surfaces in Henry's experimental work and in print. The natural philosophy lectures to his students incorporated Ohm's work; a few unpublished fragments refer to Ohm—for example, in connection with unipolar conductors. Henry's Library contains a copy of the French translation (Paris, 1860) of Ohm's 1827 monograph, *Die Galvanische Kette, mathematisch bearbeitet.*

A small but important body of secondary literature exists on how Ohm's contemporaries received his contributions. Ohm's Law is now seen as the product of the interaction of experiment and mathematics regarded by many as exemplifying the best of modern physics. Its reception is viewed almost as a litmus test. Henry's case has relevance to this literature. In "The Reception of Ohm's Electrical Researches by his Contemporaries" (*Phil. Mag.*, 1944, 7th ser. *35*:371–386), H. J. J. Winter notes that Faraday's and Henry's researches were made without knowledge of Ohm's Law. Relying upon a garbled passage in an article by Mary Henry, Winter cites Henry's query to Bache in this letter, giving her incorrect date, December 17, *1833*. (Mary Henry, "America's Part in the Discovery of Magneto-Electricity—A Study of the Work of Faraday and Henry —1," *The Electrical Engineer*, 1892, *13*:27–30, especially p. 30. On the same page she cites another letter without date or addressee, asking about Ohm and his theory. Such a document has not turned up.) Henry's query to Bache appears in Winter, we feel, because of the date. The implication is that the reception and acceptance came towards the end of the decade, being signaled by Ohm's Copley Medal in 1841 and the appearance of his work in translation in the same year in Taylor's *Scientific Memoirs* (2:401–506). Given the laudatory reference by Gauss and the existence of other favorable notices in German by 1834, there is every probability that active investigators of

I recollect that in my paper mentioned above there are some typographical blunders which render parts unintelligable I believe but they do not affect the point in question.[9]

---

electromagnetism would behave like Henry—be curious and try to find out the new law. Hegelians impeded Ohm's reception in Germany according to Winter. Given the strong and prompt support Ohm received from many eminent German scientists, this seems dubious. That reason is certainly not applicable to Great Britain and the United States.

A later article by Morton L. Schagrin, "Resistance to Ohm's Law," *American Journal of Physics*, 1963, *31*:536–547, continues to be cited although little evidence is offered for its thesis. In Schagrin's view, Ohm inevitably encountered resistance because his contribution was a conceptual innovation. To support this, Schagrin treats one of the men discussed by Winter, G. F. Pohl, and has a misleading footnote to another German scientist, P. Erman (1764–1851). Winter cites a few other instances, such as Berzelius's opposition to Ohm's views on unipolar conductors. One could just as easily list an equal number of eminent scientists backing Ohm. The "proof" of the resistance apparently rests on the time required for Ohm to get a full professorship in a German university and that hinges, in all probability, on the general state of the German universities and on academic politics. Ohm was not unique in not receiving quickly a chair upon publication of a notable research finding.

The articles in question assume resistance because they assume Ohm's Law, now taken for granted, must have been viewed as a revolutionary innovation by contemporary scientists. A contrary case is possible, that prior work had paved the way for Ohm's acceptance. In an 1823 article by Oersted and Fourier ("Sur quelques nouvelles expériences thermoélectriques," *Annales de chimie et de physique*, 1823, 2d ser. 22:375–389) occur these words:

> . . . it is evident that, in the case where a current A of an intensity equal to that of another current B, but of a larger quantity, is presented to a conductor which is sufficient only to transmit the quantity of B, this conductor ought to be capable of transmitting a part of the current A equal to current B; and if we suppose A to have an intensity stronger than that of B, the transmission of A will be yet more abundant. [p. 384; translation from Pierson, see below]

L. Pearce Williams has shown how close Faraday came to discovering the law (*Michael Faraday* [New York, 1965], pp. 210–211). One could argue that the sense of the law was implicit in the researches of Faraday, Henry, and others. Certainly the subject area was actively under investigation as evidenced by, for example, the "Record of Experiments" entries of September 9 and 10, 1834, above, on the modulus of conduction.

We suspect many contemporaries regarded Ohm's work as interesting and useful but not an overwhelming conceptual innovation. The Law was usable in a narrow positivistic sense without inhibiting the development of various causal explanations. Among these scientists (Henry being one example) there was not resistance but recognition of a convenient advance. Ohm is explicitly absent from the indexes to Faraday's work even though the simple equation was within his competence. Faraday's conceptual concerns were elsewhere. References to Ohm are fairly scarce in Henry's publications and personal papers. Henry did send Ohm a copy of "Contributions II: Spiral Conductor" addressed to Berlin rather than Nuremberg. Winter (p. 380) quotes an 1842 letter of Ohm listing "Henry in England" as one of the investigators favoring his theory. There is evidence of closer connections of Henry with Lenz and Jacobi in distant Russia. The conceptual innovations animating Henry were those of Ampère and Faraday, not Ohm.

In addition to Winter and Schagrin, we are indebted to an unpublished paper by Stuart Pierson, "Is Ohm's Law Ohm's Law?" and to Kenneth L. Caneva for an advance copy of his *DSB* article on Ohm, particularly the comprehensive bibliography. Henry's Address Book in the Smithsonian Archives has the note about the reprint sent to Berlin.

[9] None are obvious to us in Henry's paper, *Silliman's Journal*, 1832, 22:403–408. He may be referring to omitted punctuation which creates awkward run-on sentences on pages 405 and 407. As Henry wrote to Bache, the meaning is clear in the text on self-induction. Henry was probably mistakenly thinking of the typographical errors which occurred on pages 404 and 407 of an earlier article of his,

Young Mason[10] has promised to superintend the engraving of my drawing should the Society agree to publish it. I wish him to attend to the following corrections. 1st The wheel is too wide in the direction of its axis *ie* the teeth are too long. In the machine they are not more than an inch whereas in the drawing they appear comparatively about 2 inches long. 2nd In the plan the plates are a little too thin, or the spaces between the several elements are a little too great.

3. There is a small mistake in the arrangement of the conductors which I have corrected in the rough drawing which I send with the others.

4. The cups should be shown at the sides of the straight conductors on the lower half of the plan since they are wider than the connectors. This is also shown on the plan drawing which I have made. Mr Mason will understand these corrections and they can be made by the engraver.[11]

Almost every moment of my time has been occupied by my college duties since my return from Phild I wish to finish my course of lectures entirely in the Winter session so that I may have some leisure for experiment &c in the Summer.

I regret that I did not see my very kind old friend Mr Vaughan when last in your city. I called at his rooms but did not find him in. Will you give him many thanks for his kind offer of the use of the library &c.[12] I hope to meet with him at the Whister Party on Saturday evening but was disappointed.[13] I am now in the humor for working and will give you my paper before New Year. Give my respects to Courtnay[14] [and] Dr Ludlow[15] —tell him he is expected at Princeton before he commences his duties in the university—and also to Mrs. Bache.

I find that I shall have to use a wrapper so I may as well fill my sheet.[16] Mr Alexander returned today from his southern expedition. On the whole had an interesting tour and is well satisfied with his observations. Spent

---

"On the Application of the Principle of the Galvanic Multiplier to Electro-Magnetic Apparatus . . . ," *Silliman's Journal*, 1831, *19*:400–408.

[10] S. Rufus Mason.

[11] From Plate 22 of APS *Transactions*, n.s. *5* (see the frontispiece to this volume), this is Joseph Yeager (ca. 1792–1859), active in Philadelphia from 1809 to circa 1845. Yeager mostly etched portraits and engraved views of scenery and buildings; he was also a print seller and publisher of children's books. In 1848 Yeager became President of the Harrisburg and Lancaster Railroad, later part of the Pennsylvania system. *DAB*.

[12] A reference to John Vaughan's letter of December 8, 1834, above.

[13] We assume Henry was at the Wistar Party of December 13, 1834, and at that date discussed his paper, perhaps even the priority conflict with Faraday.

[14] E. H. Courtenay.

[15] Reverend John R. Ludlow.

[16] We assume Henry had to have an additional sheet as a wrapper because the drawings referred to at the start of the letter were enclosed. Consequently, this sheet could be used for further writing because space for the address was not needed. Frugally, Henry was using up the inner sheet. Prior to the postal reform of 1845, mail rates were determined by the number of sheets, not by weight as at present.

some days with Paine[17] in Charleston. Mr A. says that the shooting stars were not more numerous on the evening of the 13th & 14th than usual. He saw it stated in the papers that Mr Paine was on shipboard and requested the watch to keep a sharp look out. A greater number than usual was not seen. Mr Alexander has received 22 letters from different Post masters along the line of the total Eclipse in answer to a circular addressed to them. Shooting stars were seen in two places during the total darkness. Paine does not believe in Olmsteads Theory, neither does Bowditch.[18] A comet under the circumstances supposed could not revolve twice in the same orbit on account of the great perturbations from the earth & moon.[19]

You will probably read with much interest the article in the Edinburgh & London Mag. which I have alluded to on the Magnetic Observatory. The instrument with a long wire is I suppose intended to indicate the changes of atmospheric electricity by the use of a galvanometer made with a very long wire coiled many times around the needle box.[20]

[17] Robert Treat Paine (1803–1885), a member of a distinguished Boston family, graduated from Harvard in 1822. An active astronomer until his death, Paine was a practicing attorney of independent means. He helped establish the *American Almanac* and contributed the astronomical content from 1830 to 1842. During his active lifetime he observed four total and five annular eclipses. For nearly sixty years Paine maintained a continuous meteorological record. Alexander was presumably with Paine at Beaufort Arsenal, South Carolina, to observe the total solar eclipse of November 30, 1834. American Academy of Arts and Sciences, *Proceedings*, 1886, *21*:532–535. Clark A. Elliott, "The American Scientist, 1800–1863: His Origins, Career, and Interests" (Ph.D. dissertation, 1970, Case Western Reserve University), p. 321.

[18] Nathaniel Bowditch. Denison Olmsted's theory of the annual recurrence of the meteor shower was being tested by attempting to count shooting stars to see if they were more or less numerous at the time of Olmsted's prediction of their return.

[19] Olmsted's explanation of the meteor swarms of November 12–13, 1833, was that they were from the tail of a comet. From contemporary observations and from past descriptions of showers of shooting stars in the literature, Olmsted postulated a "cloud of small bodies" in an orbit of a half a year around the sun which met the earth each year at about the same time. Henry here expresses doubt that such a small body could continue in such an orbit in view of the perturbations to which it was subject.

Olmsted's theory was not clearly disproved until 1867 by John Couch Adams. This partiular meteor swarm was named the Leonids because the apparent radiation point was from the head of Lion constellation. After 1834 the Leonids displays became scarce and a thirty-three year orbit was proposed. Adam's calculations confirmed the latter, as did later observations. When the 1899 Leonids failed to appear, further calculations disclosed that the orbit was displaced by the gravitation of the larger planets, now passing twice the prior distance from the earth.

For Olmsted, see his "Observations on the Meteors of November 13th, 1833," *Silliman's Journal*, 1834, *26*:132–174 and A. Pannekoek, *A History of Astronomy* (New York, 1961), pp. 419–422.

[20] Henry here misinterprets Gauss's intentions, which were not to measure changes in atmospheric electricity. The description here (pp. 348–349) does not give a full picture of what Gauss and Weber were doing. Henry, a man greatly interested in problems involving atmospheric electricity, erroneously concluded that the large-scale, sensitive, galvanometer was to detect charges in the air. In an earlier description, Gauss stressed that his "stout, heavy needles . . . were the most sensible and convenient galvanometers both for the strongest and weakest energies of the galvanic current." A simple wire sufficed for the former; "for very weak energies a multiplier is wound

My page is full and the slowly moving finger of time "points to the west of the key stone of nights black arch."[21]

Your Friend J.H.

Please reccollect that my battery consists of 88 plates or elements similar to those now in your possession, that I can change it from a [calorimotor][22] of one element to a battery of two &c up to one of 88 elements. One trough can be used or even one element separately. Different parts of the battery can be used at the same time producing electricity of different intensity (See next margin).[23] Thus while one half of the battery is arranged as a deflagrator the other may be acting as a calorimotor and the combined effects of these instruments determined. A series of experiments have been made in reference to insulation and non insulation.[24]

---

round the box containing the needle." Using the observational method Gauss devised, "the measurement of galvanic forces may be conducted with a degree of ease and precision unattainable by the hitherto employed laborious modes by means of observed times of vibration; and it is literally true that by it we are enabled to follow from second to second the gradual increase of the intensity of a galvanic current. . . ." This possibility of precision measurement, as in astronomy, is not as clear in the November 1834 article in the *Phil. Mag.* Instead, there is the reference to Ohm (cryptic to Henry) and the account of transmission of current from the cabinet of curiosities to the magnetic observatory in Göttingen followed by a prediction about telegraphy. Gauss, we infer, links Ohm's Law to this possibility of precision measurement. The setup for terrestrial magnetism, by the coiling of wire around the needle box, is adapted to measurement of even minute flows of galvanic current.

The quotations are from *Abstracts of the Papers Printed in the Philosophical Transactions . . . ,* 1837, *3*:173.

[21] "That hour, o'night's black arch the keystane." Robert Burns, *Tam o'Shanter*, stanza 7.

[22] In a slip of the pen, Henry originally wrote "magnetometer," clearly an error. In his published description of the battery (p. 219), the point in the letter is made using the correct term, as he does later in this paragraph.

[23] The text immediately preceding is in the margin of the first page of the original. From "Thus while one half . . ." to "and non insulation," the text is in the margin of the second page. The remainder, to the postscript, is in the third-page margin. Having given his initials at the very bottom of the page, Henry scribbled on in the margins in this sequence. The postscript, on the last page, we assume was added after these words about the battery.

[24] These experiments are described by Henry on p. 221 of "Contributions I: Battery":

> This apparatus readily furnishes the means of making comparative experiments on the difference produced by partial and perfect insulation. When no higher degree of intensity is required than that afforded by eight pairs of plates, perfect insulation is obtained by the eight separate troughs. In higher degrees of intensity the partitions in the troughs furnish the means of perfectly insulating forty-eight of the elements: this is effected by simply charging with acid every other cell in each of the troughs, and connecting the corresponding element by conductors, which pass over the intermediate elements without touching them: with this arrangement we have six cells in each trough separated from one another by a cell without acid, or in effect by a stratum of air. For comparison with these a set of troughs has been constructed without partitions.
>
> The want of perfect insulation is not very perceptible in the common experiments of the deflagration of large and perfect conductors; but where the decomposition of a liquid is attempted, or the battery required to act on a small or imperfect conductor, the loss of power is very great, the apparatus partially discharging itself through its own liquid, and the intensity at the poles does not increase with a short interruption of the current.
>
> There is also considerable loss on account

I find that it is very important in an electro magnetic experiment where two currents are required to act simultaneously not to draw them both from the same battery but in all cases to use two unconnected batteries even should one battery be equal in power to the two.[25]
P.S. You will find a drawing of the US for $5, enclosed Much obliged—a friend in need &c.[26]

---

of imperfect insulation even in the case of low intensity, and when the poles are connected by a perfect conductor. In one experiment with an arrangement of five pairs, and the poles united by a conductor composed of thirty strands of copper bell wire, each forty feet long, the loss was found to be at least one seventh, as measured by the quantity of zinc surface required to be immersed in order to produce the same magnetic effect.

[25] Henry reached this conclusion as a result of his experiments of September 9 and 10, 1834 (printed above as the "Record" entries for those dates). In attempting to determine the modulus of conduction, he discovered that the better conductor of two drew a disproportionate amount of current from a single battery, to the point of virtually discharging it. When he used two batteries, one for each conductor whose properties he was testing, Henry obviated this effect.

[26] We do not know what this transaction is all about.

TO JOHN TORREY

Torrey Papers, Library, New York Botanical Garden

Princeton Saturday
Morning Dec. 20th 1834

My Dear Sir

Since my receipt of your kind letter of the 13th[1] I have been unusually busy. Do not smile at the old excuse. I have been in Phila and of cours was obliged to do double duty on my return.

Besides this Prof. James Alexander[2] had the misfortune to lose his younger little son. The child died on monday after an illness of a few hours from a sudden attack of croup. The family are much grieved with the loss as the little fellow was a universal favourite—the name sake of his grandfather[3] and of the most interesting age of about 2 years and a half.

Owing to this melancholy event I have heard Prof. Alexanders recitations as well as my own.

[1] Not found. Torrey noted on the first sheet of this letter "Recd 25th. Ansd Dec. 29th." His reply of the 29th is printed below.

[2] James Waddel Alexander, for whom see above, Trustees' Minutes, April 9, 1834, footnote 10.

[3] Archibald Alexander, for whom see below, Henry's "List of Persons . . ." [ca. August 21,] 1835, footnote 40.

The present senior class I think a very interesting one and contains many fine fellows who will entre on the study of your department with zeal. I am driving them very steadily in Natural Phil and wish if possible to finish my intire course before your arrival.[4] I have given thus far in the session 3 lectures a week with one examination or review lecture. These with my recitations keep me well employed. I am besides just now engaged in preparing a paper for the Phil. Society of Phil[a] which I think will be published imediatly as the committee[5] inform me they have put to press every paper on hand and are now waiting for more matter.

The Society appears to be awaking from its slumbers and now contains a number of young men who are ardent and industrious & will not I hope be quite as exclusive as their predecessors.[6] I visited Phil[a] about 10 days since inorder to have the drawings of my machine corrected & put in proper form for publication. While in the city a meeting of the *club* was held and an informal organization effected. It is to consist of a few Individuals associated for mutual support and instruction. The members are Bache, Courtenay, Espy (the Meteorologist), Rodgers, Yourself, Myself and Mr Alexander. The meetings to be held 3 or 4 times a year at such times and places as may be convenient. It has no name and must be kept secret so as to excite no jealousy &c.

Mr Alexander has returned and was on the whole much gratified with the result of his tour. He addressed a great number of circulars to the sev-

[4] Henry made a similar comment to Torrey about one month earlier. See above, the letter of November 18, 1834, and footnote 2 of that letter.

[5] The Committee on Publication consisted of Franklin Bache, Isaac Lea, and Robert E. Griffith. They had been annually elected and reelected from 1829 through 1834. *Early Proceedings of the American Philosophical Society . . . 1744 to 1838* (Philadelphia, 1884), pp. 588, 599, 613, 623, 630, 646.

[6] It is difficult to know exactly which members Henry was labeling "ardent and industrious." Such men as A. D. Bache, Franklin Bache, Isaac Lea, Charles N. Bancker, Charles D. Meigs, Isaiah Lukens, John Vaughan, and Robert Hare attended meetings regularly, took active roles in the Society, and shared interests with Henry in the physical sciences. Henry hoped that intellectual vigor, not social distinction, would be the main criterion for election; he may have known at this time that he and certain of his friends had been proposed for membership (see above, Nomination for Membership . . . , November 7, 1834, and below, Bache to Henry, January 3, 1835, especially footnote 10).

Henry's optimisim for increasingly scientific activity at the American Philosophical Society was to be proved correct. For the next ten years or so the Society flourished, mainly through the efforts of these men and their interests in terrestrial magnetism and related geophysical sciences. Walter E. Gross, "The American Philosophical Society and the Growth of Science in the United States, 1835–1850" (Ph.D. dissertation, University of Pennsylvania, 1970), argues that the Society declined in the mid and late 1840s because its work in geophysics, although of high quality, resulted in vast projects beyond its scope. Yet this decline was symptomatic of the weakened position of virtually every American local scientific society in the face of the increasing roles of the government, of national societies, of universities, and of other research institutions in the support of scientific projects.

eral Post masters along each side of the path of the dark shadow of the eclipse in order to determine the effect of the obscuration on the course of the wind and other meteorological phenomena. Betwen 20 and 30 answers have been received containing matter which he considers interesting.

With regard to your Pneumatic Trough I think there can be no hazard in commencing with it immediately. In reference to the medical school you must ask information of Prof Maclean. I think however you have nothing to fear on account of its operations.[7] I hope you are getting on pleasantly at your Institution and that it will not suffer as much as was anticipated by the appointment of the new Prof.[8] There is quite a blow up in Philadelpha University—on account of the unpopularity of Dr Cox[9]—300 students had entered into a covenant not to attend his course. This was about two weeks since. You have seen in the papers that a duel has grown out of the affair, between two medical students*. With regard to Dr. Rhinelander from his & your relation to the village of Princeton[11] would it not be well on your part to make the best of the circumstance and give him no

* The student who lost his finger in the duel is a graduate of Princeton by the name of Wideman.[10] I believe on second thought that he did not graduate but left the college about the time of Prof Vethakes resignation. The Prof. was his guardian.

[7] Money was donated to Princeton to prevent the development of a full-fledged medical school from the early professorship of anatomy and physiology. See below, Torrey to Henry, December 29, 1834, especially footnotes 7 and 8. Torrey preferred expanding the College of Physicians and Surgeons, where he hoped to find full-time employment so that he would no longer have to move his family back and forth between Princeton and New York each year. See his letters below of January 16 and February 18, 1835.

[8] A reference to the 1834 appointment of John R. Rhinelander (for whom see above, "Galvanic Experiments on the Body of the Murderer Le Blanc," September 6, 1833, footnote 11) as Professor of Anatomy at the College of Physicians and Surgeons, a position he held until 1839. See Torrey's response of the 29th, below.

[9] John Redman Coxe (1773–1864, *DAB*) was Professor of Materia Medica and Pharmacy at the University of Pennsylvania. He came to that position in 1819, after serving for ten years as Professor of Chemistry there. Although an early advocate of vaccination, "he was possessed of considerable classical attainments, and was well versed in the ancient literature of Medicine. The doctrines and opinions of the earlier fathers of Physic had so superior a value in his estimation as to lead to too exclusive an exposition of them in his lectures. This was more particularly the case when occupying the Chair of Materia Medica and Pharmacy. . . ," which he relinquished in 1835 by resolution of the Trustees. Joseph Carson, *A History of the Medical Department of the University of Pennsylvania* (Philadelphia, 1869), pp. 157–160. The quotation is from p. 160.

[10] John Weidman, of Lebanon, Pennsylvania, attended Princeton for his sophomore and junior years, 1830–1832. The duel took place on December 9. Since by this time dueling was taboo in the North, the opponents, accompanied by their seconds, a surgeon, and a few friends, crossed the Mason-Dixon line into Delaware. The only injury was to Weidman's trigger finger. Philadelphia newspapers, including the *National Gazette*, the *Pennsylvanian*, and the *American Sentinel*, published notably short stories on the duel in the next day or two. As the *American Sentinel* explained on December 11, 1834 (p. 2), "We have heard all the particulars, the names, distance, &c. &c. but it is scarcely worth while to give them to the public. Dueling is at best a censurable practice."

cause of complaint. Opposition will only strengthen him and should he suceed his triumph would be the more complete. These remarkes are made in confidence & friendship and will be received by you without offence. In reference to your battery[12] I think the troughs on the plan you propose will be excellent. I know not if you intend to introduce the principle of moveable connections.[13] I would not advise this for the whole series as where there are many plates it will be inconvenient but I would divide the battery into sections say of 10 plates each and arrange them so with moveable connections as to produce intensity or quantity. Give me a further detail of your plan.

Your Friend
Jos. Henry

Your intelligence of the appointment of Prof Vethake[14] gave great pleasure to his friends in Princeton.

I have no intention as yet to turn authour even with the prospect before me of falling into the back ground. I know "that it is plesant to see ones name in Print/ A Book's a Book athough theres nothing in't."[15]

[11] We know nothing about Rhinelander's relation to Princeton.

[12] This appears to be a battery which Torrey is building for demonstrations in his chemical lectures. Presumably Torrey first mentioned the device in his missing letter to Henry of the 13th of December.

[13] Moveable connections, or "moveable connectors" as Henry termed them in print, were basic to his versatile battery. By shifting from a "homogeneous connector" (a parallel connector) to an "alternate or serial connector" (a series connector), Henry could change his battery from a "calorimotor" to a "deflagrator." "Contributions I: Battery."

[14] Henry Vethake was appointed President of Washington College (later Washington and Lee) in Lexington, Virginia. He held the position for a year and a half.

[15] More accurately,

'Tis pleasant, sure, to see one's name in print,
A book's a book, although there's nothing in't.

George Noel Gordon, Lord Byron, *English Bards and Scotch Reviewers*, line 51. We do not know what Henry refers to.

TO JAMES HENRY

Family Correspondence, Henry Papers, Smithsonian Archives

Monday morning Dec 22nd
1834

My Dear James

Want of leisure must be my only excuse for not answering your letter sooner. We are all tolerably well. Harriet and the Boy have been under the Drs[1] care but are both much better. The Boy had the influenza and his

[1] Samuel Ladd Howell; see footnote 5, "Galvanic Experiments on the Body of the Murderer Le Blanc," September 6, 1833, printed above.

mother complains of weakness arrising no doubt from nursing the little girl. They are better and the Dr has discontinued his visits.

I was much surprised on my visit a few days since to Phil[a] to be asked by allmost all my acquaintance there if I had not been dangerously ill since my last visit. I answered in all cases no. At length it came out that I had been attacked with a fit of apoplexy. The intelligence came from albany and schenectady. We had a letter[2] from Mrs Van Slyck[3] only a few days since which also regretted to learn that I had been dangerously ill. All this probably arose from my slight attack of fever during the last vacation.

Thirty or forty persons in the village and neighbourhood were attaced in precisely the same manner. I have since questioned Dr Howell our Physician to know if he had given currency to the report but he informed that there was nothing like appoplexy in my case and that he had never dreamed of such a thing during my illness.

I have received a letter[4] from Little requesting some information from me, if I know any [reason] why you will not accept his offer.[5] He says that he has gone as high as $800 which is as much as he can afford. You of course will do what you think best but I would not stay with Gould[6] for the present salary and you should receive at least $500.

Whatever may be the character of Little amoung the trade he has been of service to you in this affair although for his own interest and of course you will treat him politely and honourably. Also Mr Gould I think should have the first offer and be delt with openly and fairly but while you owe this much to him you owe more to your own well fair—and are free to act as Mr Gould would do were he in your circumstances. I will inform Little that I know not what arrangement you have made with Gould & that I can do nothing in the way of advising you to accept his offer. It will probably be as well that you do not mention the fact of his having written to me on the subject unless he mention it to you.

Stephen has returned and is much pleased with the result of his tour. He has become a gentleman of very extensive correspondance. Having addressed circulars to all most all the Postmasters along the edge of each side of the dark shadow of the eclipse in order to learn what effect the phenomi-

[2] Not found.

[3] Mrs. Van Slyck (whose first name we have not discovered) was the wife of Anthony Van Slyck and the mother of Harman Van Slyck, who attended Albany Academy from October 1831 to June 1833. She lived in Rotterdam, New York. When Joseph Henry went to Europe in 1837, Harriet Henry boarded with Mrs. Van Slyck. Joseph Henry to James Henry, February 8, 1837, Family Correspondence, Henry Papers, Smithsonian Archives; Hun, "Albany Academy."

[4] Not found.

[5] See above, November 6, 1834, for Weare C. Little's offer and below, January 13, 1835, for James Henry's decision and his reason for it.

[6] James Henry's employer, the Albany bookseller Anthony Gould (see *Henry Papers, 1*: 446).

non had on the wind & other circumstances which might be observed he has received nearly 30 letters in answer which contain some interesting information.

Stephen was 8 days on the water and amoung these was the cold sunday and monday of last week. He was quite satisfied with the experiment of a sail and does not appear to be very anxious to try that mode of travelling very soon.

I received a circular from Ithaca[7] containing resolutions in reference to [the] death of Mr DeWitt. I regret much to hear of the unfortunate condition of the affairs of his son.[8] The old gentleman allways treated me with kindness and attention and I feel much greaved that I had not written to him as I intended to do during his illness. I always feared that the Ithaca rail road[9] would involve Richard in dificulty. It is to be regretted that a gentleman of his amiable qualities should have involved himself in such a project. Love to Mother and Nancy.

Your Brother

We are glad to learn that Aunt Betsy[10] is doing so well in the way of Boarders.

[7] Henry is probably referring to a one page broadside, published as an extra of the *Ithaca Journal*, "Tribute of Respect to the Memory of Simeon DeWitt, Surveyor-General of the State, Who Died at his Residence in Ithaca, Wednesday Night, Dec. 3d, 1834." A copy is in the New York State Library. The resolutions were also printed in the *Ithaca Chronicle* for December 10, 1834.

[8] Richard Varick DeWitt (1800–1868), financially committed to the Ithaca and Owego Railroad (see next note for the railroad; R. V. DeWitt is identified in *Henry Papers, 1*:62).

[9] This line was designed to connect Cayuga Lake and the Susquehanna River watershed, and thus to serve as part of a transportation system between the Great Lakes and Chesapeake Bay via the Erie Canal. The citizens of Ithaca and Owego had built a turnpike between their towns in 1811, but found it too slow for rapid export of lumber, flour, cloth, gypsum, and other local products. The townspeople petitioned the state legislature successfully in 1828 for a railroad charter. Simeon DeWitt and Richard DeWitt had subscribed for about $150,000 of the company's stock by the 1840s.

Construction began in 1832 and was completed in 1834. Originally, bridges were to carry the line across the steep ravines between the two towns, but for safety's sake, the engineer had substituted cuts and embankments, which raised the building costs substantially above the first estimates. Furthermore, the day-to-day operations of the road were poorly managed: toll collection, for example, tended to be erratic. Most seriously, the links east-west with the New York and Erie Railroad and south to Pennsylvania via the North Branch Canal were slow to materialize. The company mortgaged itself to New York State in 1838 for a loan. The state foreclosed in 1841 and auctioned off the roadbed and equipment for $17,500, causing Richard DeWitt to lose nearly all of his investment in the project. Rechartered under new ownership as the Cayuga and Susquehanna Railroad, the firm became profitable only after the connection with the Pennsylvania railroad system in the 1850s. James Hijiya, "Making a Railroad: The Political Economy of the Ithaca and Owego, 1828–1842," *New York History*, 1973, *54*:145–173.

[10] Presumably Elizabeth Selkirk (see *Henry Papers, 1*:xviii and 452).

December 22, 1834

FROM RICHARD VARICK DEWITT

Henry Papers, Smithsonian Archives

Albany Dec 22 1834

Dear Sir,

My Father, before his death expressed a wish that my brother Linn[1] should, if he wished to pursue mathematical studies this winter, preparatory to devoting himself to Engineering as a profession, be placed under your instruction.[2] Linn is desirous himself of pursuing mathematical studies under your care, & in pursuance of this plan my object is to ask you whether your arrangements would allow of your taking him as a private pupil, & whether it would further be possible for you to take him as an inmate of your family. This would in many respects be desireable to him & to me as his guardian. I am very solicitous that he should be able to avail himself of the best opportunities to prosecute mathematical studies till May. He declines entering into a College course, & is now too old to continue at the Academy. We, my fathers family & my own, shall probably spend much of our future years at Ithaca, & now I must see that my brother prepares himself for some profession. Engineering would suit his taste, but he wants habits of *method*, application & industry. I am satisfied that you could make a great deal of him, whilst every moment spent here is literally lost to him. It would be therefore particularly gratifying to our whole family especially to me to see him placed under the care of one who in addition to peculiar fitness to communicate the instruction desired, would feel an interest in our brother.

Believe me ever your friend
Rich Varick DeWitt

[1] William Linn DeWitt (1817–1903) was the son of Simeon DeWitt and his third wife, Susan Linn, daughter of the Reverend William Linn (1752–1808, *Herringshaw*, p. 589). Richard Varick DeWitt, author of this letter and son of Simeon DeWitt and his second wife, Jane Varick Hardenberg, was seventeen years older than his half-brother Linn. Simeon DeWitt had died December 3, 1834.

Linn studied at the Albany Academy from 1830 until 1834. After studying with Henry at Princeton during the winter and spring of 1835 (see below, Henry's letters to James Henry, January 13 and 23, and February 9, 1835), Linn resided in Ithaca, New York, of which town his father had been a major proprietor. Linn had earlier assisted his father in surveying Ithaca properties, but after his father's death Linn studied and practiced law there. He became in part responsible for the financial mismanagement of his father's estate, which originally consisted of vast land holdings in the Ithaca area, including the present site of Cornell University. Linn left Ithaca in 1850, residing in Wisconsin, California, and Nevada until his return in 1873 to more modest circumstances in Ithaca, where he remained until his death. "Ithaca's Founder of Holland Stock," *Ithaca Journal*, October 14, 1903, p. 1. Hun, "Albany Academy."

[2] Simeon DeWitt's recommendation that Linn prepare for an engineering career by studying mathematics under Henry is especially interesting in light of what the career of Simeon DeWitt meant for Henry. The model of Simeon DeWitt the "mathematical practitioner" is outlined in the *Henry Papers, 1*:xxv–xxvi.

December 29, 1834

FROM JOHN TORREY

Henry Papers, Smithsonian Archives

New York, December 29th 1834

My dear "*Sir,*"

I have had your last letter on hand for more than a week,[1] & being comparatively at leisure these holiday times I take the opportunity of answering it, though I have nothing of especial interest to communicate. It grieves me to hear of the several affliction of our friend Alexander. I do not see how a parent of keen sensibility can be supported in so dreadful a trial except by the consolations of religion. The sympathies of friends will do much in assuaging sorrow, (& he has my warm sympathy & prayers) but He alone, who inflicted the wound can apply the true healing balm.

Did you attend to the request that I made of you in behalf of young Chilton[2]—to make out a list of electromagnetic apparatus, that he might supply an order from West Point? He has now set up a fine large magnet for that Institution, *wound* according to your plan. It works well, but he has not tried its full powers. Do you know that *Mr. Bartlett*[3] (who graduated

[1] This is a reply to Henry's letter of December 20, above. Despite Torrey's words, his notation on the manuscript indicates the letter was received on December 25.

[2] James R. Chilton, the New York instrumentmaker.

[3] William H. C. Bartlett (1804–1893) was appointed Acting Professor of Natural and Experimental Philosophy in November 1834 and was named to the full professorship in April 1836, a position occupied until retirement in February 1871. He was a West Pointer (first in the Class of 1826) who had previously served on the teaching staff at the U.S. Military Academy, 1827–1829, and in various capacities in the Corps of Engineers. After retirement and until 1889, Bartlett was actuary of the Mutual Life Insurance Company of New York. He was one of the original members of the National Academy of Sciences. Among his honorary degrees is one relevant to this document, an A.M. (1837) from the College of New Jersey in Princeton. Although little known today, Bartlett's career is instructive about certain conditions or forces acting upon the American scientific community in the last century. After describing Bartlett's professional work, this footnote will consider the relationship between Henry and Bartlett and conclude with comments on some interpretive points made by Edward S. Holden in the Bartlett biographical memoir published by the National Academy of Sciences.

Although not extensive, Bartlett's research output was distinguished. In 1840 Bartlett made an inspection tour of European observatories for the benefit of the proposed West Point Observatory which opened in 1843. Although West Point's is rightly regarded in retrospect as a teaching observatory, Bartlett and his assistants did make observations, which were never reduced and published. A paper appeared on the use of lunar culminations for longitude determinations (1845). In 1843 Bartlett published observations of the comet of that year; a mathematical analysis of the comae and tails of comets was printed in *Silliman's Journal* in 1859. In 1854 Bartlett photographed the partial solar eclipse, quite likely the first such use of photography in America. These photographs were then used to determine the distance between cusps. Modest by later standards, this was the first time photographs were used for astronomical measurements.

But observational or experimental work was not typical of Bartlett's intellectual bent. An 1860 paper on molecular motions in plane polarized light was representative of what his memorialist later characterized as the "purely mathematical point of view," as is Bartlett's study of rifled guns (1866) in the first volume of the National Academy of Sciences' memoir series and the actuarial work at the end of his career.

Bartlett spent most of his professional life as a teacher. What he taught had impact beyond West Point as he authored a number of textbooks widely used in American institutions. A course in optics appeared in 1839. In 1850 Bartlett published a two volume *Elements of Natural Philosophy* (in Henry's Library). The first volume, mechanics, appeared simultaneously with the nearly identical *Elements of Synthetic Mechanics,* of which at least six editions existed by 1871. The second volume of the *Elements of Natural Philosophy* covered acoustics and optics; five editions were published by 1873. A fourth section on spherical astronomy was issued as a separate in 1855; four later editions appeared, the last in 1877. Another work, *Elements of Analytical Mechanics,* had nine editions from 1853 to 1875, and a twelfth edition of unknown date exists. Except for this last title, these Bartlett works are systematic expositions with a minimum of mathematics. The *Elements of Analytical Mechanics,* in contrast, makes no concession to the uninitiated; in 1860 Bartlett described mathematics as "the language in which alone natural philosophy can be read with any permanent benefit." Judging from the number of editions and printings, for roughly a quarter of a century Bartlett's texts were widely used in American collegiate institutions.

The *Analytical Mechanics* was clearly *the* great work of Bartlett's career. It replaced Courtenay's translation of Boucharlat's *Mechanics* in the West Point curriculum in 1853. In the first edition preface Bartlett wrote (pp. iii–iv):

> Mechanics has for its object to investigate the action of forces upon the various forms of bodies. All physical phenomena are but the necessary results of a perpetual conflict of equal and opposing forces, and the mathematical formula expressive of the laws of this conflict must involve the whole doctrine of Mechanics. The study of Mechanics should, therefore, be made to consist simply in the discussion of this formula, and in it should be sought the explanation of all effects that arise from the action of forces.

From the Newtonian idea of action and reaction, expressed in mathematical terms, Bartlett deduced the mechanics of solids and fluids, giving at the conclusion examples of applications to various mechanical devices.

Mechanics dealt with the properties of inanimate bodies acting under external forces. Forms of bodies were derived from molecular forces which were, in turn, subject to analysis by the mathematical mechanician. For the behavior of atoms, Bartlett wrote approvingly of the point-atomic hypothesis of Boscovich. Bartlett even suggested that Boscovich's hypothesis provided an explanation for light and heat. By 1860 he was writing how the "imponderables"—light, heat, and electricity—could be treated in terms of the mechanics of molecules. Near the close of his career, the 1874 edition identified his action and reaction formula with the law of the conservation of energy "which has since [1853] revolutionized physical science in nearly all its branches. . . ."

The *Synthetic Mechanics* modestly acknowledged indebtedness to the writings of the Frenchman, Jean Victor Poncelet (1788–1867), and the German, Karl Friedrich Peschel (1793–1852). Works of both men are in Henry's Library. No such attribution appears in the *Analytical Mechanics.* In 1874 Bartlett claimed: "It is believed that this not only was the first, but that it even still is the only treatise on analytical mechanics in which all the phenomena are presented as mere consequences of that single law."

Whatever the merits of that claim, the subject matter was certainly familiar to Joseph Henry whose library contains a number of works of this nature by other authors. The first and second editions of the *Analytical Mechanics* survive among Henry's books, the latter a presentation copy. We know Joseph Henry examined this copy as he corrected two minor errors in equations.

Evidence exists of a closer connection between Henry and Bartlett in the form of correspondence in the Henry Papers in the Smithsonian Archives. On February 24, 1844, Henry asked Bartlett to become a candidate to succeed A. D. Bache in the chair of natural philosophy at the University of Pennsylvania. Henry wanted Bartlett in Philadelphia to continue the kind of close relationship he had with Bache. Bartlett on March 1 declined, citing the obligation of completing the revision of the system of instruction in his care—that is, the *Elements of Natural Philosophy* and the *Elements of Analytical Mechanics.* He went on to ask Henry to write a text bringing electricity, galvanism, and magnetism "within a reasonable compass by subjecting them to a single rational theory." Henry's negative reply of March 11 has not turned up; later volumes will say something about abortive Henry plans of producing monographs and text books. To this missing letter Bartlett replied on March 16:

> Your general views of the mode of conducting enquiry are similar to my own, and your fondness for just generalization would aid & encourage my efforts to simplify and reduce to theoretical subordination the almost countless facts in the various & now arbitrary divisions of physical science.

Present-day historians would stress the differences between Henry the experimentalist and Bartlett the applied mathematician. They saw themselves in juxtaposition, even in fulfilling identical roles. Henry was both familiar with and sympathetic to the West Point orientation derived from the École Polytechnique. Both Henry and Bartlett were friends of Charles Davies. Despite Bartlett's appointment, the tradition he and Davies represented was to be short-lived.

Some measure of the change is apparent in Edward S. Holden's (1846–1914, *DAB*) biographical memoir presented to the National Academy of Sciences in 1911. A former student of Bartlett's at the Point (class of 1870) and a distinguished civilian astronomer, Holden was sympathetic and appreciative in most respects. Yet, Holden was really from the succeeding tradition and had reservations about Bartlett. The memoir presented Holden with a real problem. Not only was Bartlett's memory dim, but Holden's version of the Point's tradition might have less appeal to most research-minded scientists of the twentieth century.

Many of the factual details in the memoir derived from an earlier necrology by Peter S. Michie (1839–1901, *DAB*), Bartlett's successor at West Point. Holden starts by citing the large number of Bartlett's contemporaries who had distinguished careers, paying particular attention to those involved in railroads and canals and in explorations and surveys. After easily detailing Bartlett's work as a practical astronomer, Holden displays a slight uneasiness about Bartlett "as a pure mathematician."

This theme reappears in the section on Bartlett's teaching. From Michie we learn that the earlier *Synthetic Mechanics* was opposed as too elementary for students already possessing the calculus. Holden thinks the introduction of the *Analytical Mechanics* in consequence was most unfortunate. Pronouncing the former as an excellent text, Holden feels the cadets needed a more practical course. The "upper men" destined for the technical arms of the service might profit from the advanced treatment of the *Analytical Mechanics.*

> The ideal of the mathematical studies at the academy is to create *power* by means of *useful* knowledge. There is no science or art so practical as war, and all our training must be directed toward giving, *first*, power —mental and moral—and toward giving it, *second*, th[o]rough, useful, available, practical knowledge . . .
>
> Perhaps this is an appropriate place to point out that the U.S. Military Academy is not, and never has been, a school of pure science. It is a technical school for war. Pure science is taught as a means of mental discipline, but still more as a basis for the application of science to the military art. This is a fact, and it ought always to be so. [p. 185.]

Holden must have realized his audience represented a research ethos not likely to find a recital of names of railroad engineers and surveyors very exciting. He had to explain Bartlett's modest research output, particularly as both he and the audience were aware of the tradition of the École Polytechnique which initially influenced West Point. Not surrounded by a great intellectual center like Paris, Holden asserted that the faculty at West Point lacked intellectual stimulation and concentrated on teaching rather than advancing science.

Bartlett saw the matter differently. In an 1860 deposition in an investigation of the Academy, he condemned the basic scheme in effect even at that date: "The tendency of the present system is to break down a scientific academy, and to erect upon its ruins a school of practice; to make the institution more attractive to pleasure-seekers than useful to science and the Army. There is too little of repose, and too much of parade and show" (p. 189). Bartlett's main heritage would not be a scientifically oriented officer corps but what his texts contributed to the growth of a sophisticated engineering profession and of a small body of practicing physical scientists.

The Holden memoir appears in the *Biographical Memoirs* of the National Academy of Sciences, 1913, 7:173–193. Michie's necrology is in the Association of the Graduates of the United States Military Academy, *Annual Reunion* (1893), pp. 105–112. Bartlett's 1860 deposition is on pages 185–189 of the report of the investigating commission (*Senate Misc. Doc.* No. 3, 36th Congress, 2nd Session). Henry's copy of the report was given to him by Capt. A. A. Humphreys who notes that he prepared the greater part of the text. *DAB.*

the 2nd year of my service at W. Point) has succeded Courtenay?[4] Poor Cram[5] is sadly disappointed, but Bartlett is much his superior in every way. It is very doubtful, however, whether any of the officers of the Academy will hold their places long. The General's government have doomed it![6]

I saw Dr Kearney Rogers[7] on Saturday. He says that he subscribed $1000 to the College upon condition of their not establishing a medical school in the Institution—or at least of not conferring degrees.[8]

You seem to have your hands full of business, & to be laying out plenty of work for me also. I hope you will not be disappointed in your expectations of what I shall be able to accomplish.

Our Medical College has been a poor Concern this winter. I have only about 96 in my class, & nearly one third of these are 3rd courses & or on credit—which means given away. I receive less this year than I did two years ago by nearly one thousand dollars.[9] Still I don't despair, if we can only have a new building next year, & this I am determined to have if exertions on my part will obtain it. Rhinelander & I get along well enough. We meet pretty often & exchange our views respecting the College. A principal cause of the thinness of our ranks this season is the resolution of many of our city students, taken last autumn, to attend some other Instn in the event of Rhinelander's appointment. R. is tolerably popular & he might succeed if he would adopt the right policy & listen to advice. I think he takes some heed to what I say, but he is headstrong & has a very good opinion of himself.[10]

[4] For Courtenay, see his letter to Henry, January 3, 1833, footnote 1, above.

[5] For Cram, see Henry to Stephen Alexander, April 16, 1833, footnote 5, above.

[6] The administration of Andrew Jackson, a reference undoubtedly to the forcing out of Thayer. See the earlier mention of this in Henry's letter of April 16, 1833.

[7] John Kearney Rodgers (1793–1851), a Princeton graduate (1811) who graduated from the College of Physicians and Surgeons in 1816. An anatomist and surgeon, Rodgers became much interested in ophthalmological surgery following studies in London. From 1827 to 1851, Rodgers was a Trustee of the College of Physicians and Surgeons. *Columbia Alumni*, p. 195 and Howard A. Kelly, *Cyclopedia of American Medical Biography* (Philadelphia, 1912), p. 990. Rodgers's opposition to Princeton's opening a medical school was probably related to the opposition that year to the proposal for a medical faculty in Columbia College. The College of Physicians and Surgeons was then independent of Columbia.

[8] Such a donation is listed in the John Maclean Papers, Princeton University Archives, but neither this source nor the Trustees' Minutes and the Treasurer's Accounts give any mention of a condition attached to the gift. *Wertenbaker*, p. 229, regards Samuel Ladd Howell's chair in anatomy and physiology as an "embryo medical school." For Princeton's attempts to provide medical education, which ended with Howell's death in 1835, see above, "Galvanic Experiments on the Body of the Murderer Le Blanc," September 6, 1833, footnote 5.

[9] It was customary in American medical schools—as in many European ones—for the professors' incomes to depend on student fees; "3rd courses" probably referred to advanced courses not required for degrees.

[10] We do not know why Rhinelander was unpopular with the students. In addition to his personal attributes, he might have ruffled his colleagues by reducing his course fee to a nominal sum. Thomas Gallagher, *The Doctors' Story* (New York, 1967), p. 194.

When will you finish your paper for the Philad. Trans.? How long will it be? Have you seen what Faraday has been doing of late? As I glanced over a late number of the Lond Sc. Mag. I saw a paper of his on Elect^{y}. The Philad. Soc^{y} will prosper if they will not let the old Knickerboker[s] have all to say.[11] They should adopt a liberal policy, & then they may claim the right of using the title which they have assumed.

I hope the *Club* will be able to accomplish something. I fear that I shall be of little use or credit to the association— at least for a year or two to come —for much of the time that I can spare from teaching must be given to finish two or three botanical works that I have long had in hand.

I have had the pneumatic trough made for Princeton. You will say it is the handsomest & best that you ever saw. I intend to have *glass* air holders, made of very large Carboys.[12] They *will never leak*—at least any where but about the mouth, & they will cost only 2/5th of copper ones. Should one break, it can be replaced for one or two dollars, as all the metallic appendages belonging to it will answer for another vessel. By the way, why can't you use demijohns, cut off a little above the middle for your acid holders in your galvanic battery? The oval ones would answer very well, & they can be purchased without the wicker, for 60 cents each.

If you think I can get $150 appropriated at the Spring meeting of the Trustees, I will have a trough constructed according to the plan that I proposed.[13] The principal peculiarity in it, will be the glass cells—the plates, arranged like a *couronne des tasses*[14] will be lowered into the liquor by a simple contrivance. It will only be intended for *intensity*, & therefore there will be no need of the shifting connectors, or of having the plates more than three inches square.

Yours very truly
John Torrey

[11] A reflection of the hopes of the younger men like Torrey, Bache, and Henry that the American Philosophical Society would not remain dominated by the old guard.

[12] A cylindrical container, cushioned in an outer box, jacket, or drum.

[13] See Trustees' Minutes, April 15, 1835, printed below.

[14] A reference to the battery of Volta in which cups containing a saline solution had a pair of differing metals in each. When one electrode was joined to its opposite in the next cup and this continued to produce a circuit, the result was a crownlike appearance. *King*, pp. 235–236. Torrey is suggesting an improvement to Henry's galvanic battery based on his experience with a device in pneumatic chemistry.

December 29, 1834

FROM JAMES R. CHILTON

Henry Papers, Smithsonian Archives

New York Dec 29. 1834

Dear Sir

A few days after writing to you respecting the Electro Magnet, and before I had received your answer,[1] I commenced winding the wire on the Horse Shoe. I thought I understood perfectly the manner of putting it on. I divided my wire into pieces of 60 feet in length, and had 14 of them. After coating the Iron first with a thick coat of Shellac varnish, and then with a layer of Silk, I wrapped one length of wire on, commencing at the extremity of one leg, and continued it as far as it would go. The next length I wrapped in the contrary direction. The next in the same direction as the first, and so on until I had got about half finished, at which time I rec[d] your Letter. By refering to your marginal figure (which I suppose you sketched rather hastily) I felt persuaded that I had been winding the wires right, and so I continued with them till they were all on, interposing layers of Silk between each layer of coils.

After the whole was finished I tried it, and found to my surprise that any one sett of wires made the magnet lift almost as much as when the whole was connected, the greatest weight it would support being about 60 or 70 lbs. After striving for some time to ascertain the cause of its not acting properly, I found that I had made a great mistake in arranging the extremities of the wires, for I always commenced the winding on the same side of the Magnet the consequence of which was that I had currents running in contrary directions. This error I could not easily correct, for I had omitted marking and numbering the ends, and so I had the vexatious job of taking the whole off, and commencing anew.[2] But I have been amply repaid for the trouble, in finding that it now works well.

The Zink cylinder of the galvanic Element is 5½ inches diameter and 9 inches high. The connection between the poles and the extremities of the wire is made by means of two little copper troughs filled with mercury and soldered on the poles. This mercurial contact I find to be better than soldering the wires fast.

The frame is made of Mahogany and altogether it is a fine affair. I tried it on Saturday before a number of persons, and this afternoon the Store was filled with Literary and Scientific Gentlemen who had come to see it.[3]

[1] Chilton's letter appears above, December 13, 1834. Henry's letter was not found.

[2] On Henry's technique of marking the ends of his parallel windings and of preventing the current from moving in opposite directions in the wires, see *Henry Papers, 1*:401–402, 421.

[3] Filed near Chilton's letter in the Henry correspondence is an undated, unidentified

We gave it another trial; after putting it into action we placed on the scale 56 pound Weights, and others, to the amount of 1100 lbs. We then attached a small caloromoter to it, which caused it to support about 1300 lbs. I then thought I would try a very small galvanic apparatus. I made use of a circular piece of copper, and another of Zinc, the size of a *shilling piece*; the weight supported in this case was 33 lbs.

Tomorrow morning I intend to try it again for the purpose of letting Dr Torrey see it, and then I will put it on board the boat.

The reason why I have had to hurry it so much, is the fear that the river may close.

Prof^r Cram was in the City on Christmas day at which time the magnet was not completed. I enquired about the other Electro Mag. Apparatus and find he wants the ordinary ones such as we have made up before.[4] I have set our man to work, and expect to have them finished soon.

Accept my thanks for the kind offer you have made to assist me, and believe me yours Truly

Ja^s R. Chilton

---

newspaper clipping, probably from a New York paper, giving an account of Chilton's demonstration. The reporter remarks at the rapidity with which the apparatus is magnetized and demagnetized—"the Giant shrinks again into an inert lump of iron."

[4] In his letter to Chilton, Henry may have suggested additional electromagnetic apparatus that a good teaching laboratory could use. The Henry electromagnet soon became a routine item in Chilton's shop, relieving Henry of the considerable burden of personally meeting the wide demand for his apparatus.

"RECORD OF EXPERIMENTS"

Henry Papers, Smithsonian Archives

Dec 31st 1834

Exp 1 One of the small circular batteries was charged with dilute sulphuric acid, the connection was formed by a wire of 4 inches long, no spark on breaking contact. With a thick wire 1/10 of an inch in diameter, coiled into a spiral, spark on breaking contact. Iron cylender inserted, no increased effect.

Exp 2nd Copper ribbon formed of thin copper plate 1½ inches diameter,[1] 60 feet long, rolled around a short cylender of iron, spark on breaking con-

[1] Presumably Henry refers to sheet copper and meant 1 ½ inches in width, not diameter.

tact. Iron withdrawn, spark on breaking contact. Iron inserted, spark on breaking contact. The difference in the two cases not perceptable. The wire was then suddenly unrolled from the coil, in this case no spark from the broken contact.

The form of the spiral not favourable to the production of mag effects[2]

[2] This statement appears in the margin, referring to experiment 2. Henry's remark about the effect of iron cores becomes clearer in light of his published statements:

> A number of experiments were made to determine the effect of introducing a cylinder of soft iron into the axis of the flat spiral, in reference to the shock, the spark, &c.; but no difference could be observed with the large spiral conductor; the effect of the iron was merged in that of the spiral. When however one of the smaller ribbons was formed into a hollow cylindrical helix of about nine inches long, and a cylinder of soft iron an inch and a half in diameter was inserted, the spark appeared a little more intense than without the iron. The obliquity of the spires in this case was unfavorable to their mutual action, while the magnetism was greater than with the flat spiral, since the conductor closely surrounded the whole length of the cylinder.
>
> I would infer from these experiments, that some effects heretofore attributed to magneto-electric action are chiefly due to the re-action on each other of the several spires of the coil which surround the magnet.

"Contributions II: Spiral Conductor," pp. 227–228, experiment 12. Henry's inferences about the effect of inserting the iron core followed from his general assumptions about electromagnetism and induction, as outlined below in Henry to Bache, January 12, 1835, footnote 5. He construed induction as an essentially electrical phenomenon, and, according to his Ampèrian views, believed magnetized iron introduced inductive effects by virtue of its inherent molecular currents ("Record of Experiments," August 22, 1834). That is, magnetoelectricity was not the conversion of a distinct magnetic force into electricity, but only the interaction of electrical forces. The large, highly inductive flat spirals submerged the electrical induction from the weakly magnetized core, while the small, helical coils permitted the effect of the soft iron to emerge. In "Exp 2nd" of the current series the long copper ribbon and short core meant a relatively flat spiral "not favourable to the production of mag effects." In experiment 1, Henry evidently hoped to intensify the effect of the core by a helical winding of shorter wire, a result he achieved in the next day's experiments (see below) and reported in his publication. On the possible influence of Hare's theory on Henry's method of winding the magnetic core with tight helices to maximize surface contact, see L. Pearce Williams, "The Simultaneous Discovery of Electro-Magnetic Induction by Michael Faraday and Joseph Henry," *Bullétin de la société des amis d'André-Marie Ampère*, 1965, no. 22:18.

In contrast to Henry, Michael Faraday ascribed far more importance to iron cores in self-induction as well as mutual induction. By this date, Henry had evidently seen only Faraday's preliminary announcement of self-induction in "On the Magneto-electric Spark and Shock, and on a Peculiar Condition of Electric and Magneto-electric Induction," *Phil. Mag.*, November 1834, 3d ser. 5:349–354, a prelude to his Ninth Series of Experimental Researches in Electricity. Using a set-up basically like Henry's, Faraday was able to intensify shocks and sparks markedly by inserting iron cores into the helices connected to the battery: "Every experimenter on electro-magnetism is aware, that when the current from a single pair of plates is passed through a helix surrounding a piece of soft iron (to produce an electro-magnet) the spark, upon breaking contact, is much brighter than if the soft iron were away" (pp. 351–352). Henry's reprint copy of Faraday's article bears no annotations, but Faraday's positive results with iron cores perhaps prompted his experiments of this date.

Faraday's brief announcement began with a statement of the theoretical importance of his self-induction experiments. The essence of magnetoelectric induction was the conversion of the magnetism of the soft iron core into electricity. In his mutual induction experiments, involving two coils around a primary and secondary iron core, the conversion processes were obscure. Self-induction allowed him to dispense with the secondary core and thus brought him "one step nearer" to the electricity of the "exciting magnet" (p. 350).

In his *Phil. Mag.* announcement, Faraday considered self-induction to be the explanation for the shocks but not the sparks produced upon interrupting the circuit (see below, Henry to Alexander, May 15, 1835, footnote 7). Later, in his Ninth Series, he demonstrated conclusively that the sparks were also inductive. In both articles, the iron cores played an integral theoretical role. Faraday emphasized the magnetic forces emanating from the energized iron core which put the surrounding helix under an intense state of strain. Henry, too, postulated a state of strain, but minimized the magnet's role. In his Ninth Series (*Phil. Trans.*, 1835, p. 55) Faraday theorized that some as yet unknown interconversion of magnetic and electrical forces accounted for the strain and release of strain in self-induction. Henry's annotated copy of the Ninth Series affords no particular evidence of Henry's interest in Faraday's concepts.

"RECORD OF EXPERIMENTS"

Henry Papers, Smithsonian Archives

[December 1834][1]

When two very long coiles were arranged so as to transmitt the current through both the spark  was very intense. This was compaired with a <*thick wire*> the spark from two short thick wires. The difference was very perceptable[2]

[1] This undated entry appears above that of December 31, 1834. Its content would also justify placing it in the first half of 1835.

[2] We assume Henry connected the coils in series. A roughly similar setup appears below in the "Record of Experiments," May 14, 1835.

A few years later Henry wrote below this entry: "This was fully developed in the exp of 1838." The October 24, 1838, entry, to be printed in a forthcoming volume, seems to be a related one from that year. There Henry puts thick wires between the coils in order to enhance the inductive effect. This may have been Henry's procedure in the current entry.

HENRY NOTEBOOK ENTRY

Notebook [7171], page 43, Henry Papers, Smithsonian Archives

[1833–1834][1]

Suppose a small quantity of some kind of salt which readily christalizes[2] were put into the focus of the solar microscope[3] as in the common experi-

[1] Unfortunately, nothing on page 43 indicates when Henry wrote this note. The evidence on which we base the date is circumstantial: the entries on pages 1–123 of notebook [7171] which are dated by Henry are marked as 1833 or 1834 (one is dated earlier). On pages 124–147, at the back of the book, Henry datelined several jottings from 1835 to 1838.

[2] Notice that Henry did not restrict the dissolved salt to compounds of iron or to other

ment of showing the christalizing of salt with the microscope and while the crystals were forming submit the mass to the action of a magnet or to the action of a galvanic current or to a magnet instan[tan]eously produced by a galvanic current. The apparatus might be so arranged that a piece of soft iron surrounded with a coil of wire might be placed very near the saline solution on a plate of glass and at the moment when the crystals were observed to shoot on the screen the magnetism of the iron should be developed by transmitting a current of galvanism; what would be the effect?[4] Try the experiment.[5]

J.H.

materials which might be expected *a priori* to exhibit polarity. Rather, he seems interested in the general effect of magnetism upon patterns of crystallization.

[3] A projecting microscope whose source of illumination was sunlight rather than a flame. Princeton had acquired one by 1801 (Trustees' Minutes, 2:50–52, Princeton University Archives).

[4] Michael Faraday was to report on a similar experiment in his Twenty-Second Series of Experimental Researches (1848). He melted bismuth and allowed the metal to cool and crystallize slowly in the presence of a magnetic force; the crystals showed no alignment. This was an offshoot of his investigation of what he called the magnecrystalline effect, an inquiry which was mainly devoted to the phenomenon of magnetic polarity in minerals.

[5] If Henry ever attempted it, he did not record the results in any of his surviving notebooks.

HENRY NOTEBOOK ENTRY

Notebook [7171], pages 30–31, Henry Papers, Smithsonian Archives

[1834][1]

Mr Savary[2] has made some interesting experiments on the "magnetization" by electric Sparks and currents. These are described in Brands Jour. vol 22 for 1827, p 383.[3]

[1] Henry's mention of the ribbon coil and of powerful currents suggests he took these notes after he had equipped his Princeton laboratory for original research. He wrote them before "Contributions II: Spiral Conductor" was read to the American Philosophical Society on February 6, 1835.

[2] Félix Savary (1797–1841) was Professor of Astronomy and Geodesy at the École Polytechnique of Paris. *Poggendorff.*

[3] "New Facts in Electro-Magnetism," *Quarterly Journal of Science*, December 1826, 22: 383–384. The editor, William Brande, suggested that the discoveries were of especial interest to all physicists working on electricity. In his paraphrase of these facts in "Contributions II: Spiral Conductor," pp. 230–231, Henry cited "Cumming's Demonferrand, page 247; also Edinburgh Journal of Science, October, 1826." The Henry Library copy of James Cumming, *A Manual of Electro Dynamics, Chiefly Translated from the Manuel D'Électricité Dynamique, or Treatise on the Mutual Action of Electric Conductors and Magnets, of J. F. Demonferrand. With Notes and Additions, Comprehending the Latest Discoveries and Improvements* (Cambridge, England, 1827) has a penciled line in the margin of page 247 next to Cumming's paraphrase of the Savary experiments. Henry probably copied the brief citation in "Contributions II" to "On the Magnetising of Needles by Currents and Elec-

The direction of the polarity of a "very" small needle submitted to the action of a straight current[4] varies according to the distance of the current. At a certain distance if it be +, remove it a little farther. It becomes 0, then –.

The distances required for the changes vary with the length of the wire, its diameter, and the intensity of the discharge.

A modifyied effect is produced when a helix is used.

The saturation of a needle only takes place when a certain ratio exists between the length of the wire, its thickness, & the intensity of the discharge.

Repeat the exp. of Savary with a powerful current and Small bars of soft iron placed at different distances from a ribbon of copper.[5] Is not the effect produced by the action of the current on the air and the sudden production of an instantaneous current in an opposite direction as in the exp. of Mr Farady with two parallel wires.[6] J.H.

tric Sparks," *Edinburgh Journal of Science*, April–October 1826, 5:369 from Cumming rather than looking at it himself.

The brief accounts of Savary's discoveries, published in the above journals and elsewhere, appeared in print months before Savary published the full formal report, "Mémoire sur l'Aimantation," *Annales de chimie et de physique*, 1827, *34*:5–57 and 220–221. Henry took notes on the *Annales* version on pages 95–99 of notebook [7171] and on the early pages of notebook [7170]. Savary's work influenced Henry's subsequent research. In "Contributions V," 1842, for example, he reported further experiments on the 1826 findings.

4 Meaning a current going through a straight wire rather than through a helix.

5 If Henry ever tried this, he failed to write the results in his "Record of Experiments."

6 Henry refers here to "volta electric induction," about which Faraday wrote in the First Series (November 1831) of Experimental Researches in Electricity and on which Henry commented in "Contributions II," p. 229. For a discussion of Faraday's experiment, see note 5 to the letter of Henry to Bache, January 12, 1835, below. Henry described Faraday's and Savary's discoveries and his own observations on spiral conductors as separate manifestations of the same phenomenon, "precisely what would take place if we suppose that the principal current induces a secondary one in an opposite direction in the air surrounding the conductor, and this again another in an opposite direction at a great distance, and so on." ("Contributions II," p. 231.)

1835

"RECORD OF EXPERIMENTS"

Henry Papers, Smithsonian Archives

Jany. 1st 1835

Exp 1 Two ribbons of copper plate well covered with silk through[ou]t the length, each 28½ [feet] long, 13/16 of an inch wide, amalgamated at the ends, and being from the same sheet of coper were every way similar,[1] <*They were first made straight then co[iled]*> were used to form the <*contact*> connection in <*between*> the poles of a battery of a single element (one of the cylindrical batteries). They each gave a faint spark when not coild and the intensity of the spark in both was the same, no spark was produced by a <*plate*> ribbon of the same 7½ inches long.

Exp 2nd The two strands of ribbons above mentioned were coiled into two seperate spirals, with all the spires in the same plane, one however was first doubled so that the electricity in each spire should be moving in an opposite direction to that in the one contiguous. In this case the single coil gave a spark which could be heard in an adjoining room with the door closed, while the other under the same circumstances gave no spark. This establishes the effects of coiling.[2]

[1] Compare with the coils used in experiments 5 and 6 of Henry's "Contributions II: Spiral Conductor."

[2] Henry announced the discovery of noninductive coils in paragraph 6 (pp. 225–226) of his publication, noting that "the result was in accordance with the anticipation." Henry's theoretical explanation of the "effects of coiling" is quoted below, Henry to Bache, January 12, 1835, footnote 5. The action of the doubled spiral conductor was a corollary to this theory: "In the case of the double spiral conductor, in experiment sixth, the fluid is passing in an opposite direction [i.e., in neighboring spires]; and according to the same views, a retardation or decrease of intensity should take place" (p. 230). Allowing for ambiguities in Henry's wording, the crux of his explanation was Faraday's volta-electric induction: when current first flows into a coil, the current in each spire induces a current of opposite direction in each succeeding spire. A state of tension and equilibrium follows, when the coil simply transmits the fluid from the voltaic source. When the circuit is interrupted, the spires lose their induced tensions and return to their natural equilibriums, either reinforcing the original current in ordinary coiling or retarding that current in doubled coiling.

Again, Faraday followed Henry on a parallel path. Coulson notes that Faraday hit upon a similar effect with mutual induction as early as 1832, in his Second Series of Experimental Researches (paragraphs 194–195). *Coulson*, p. 111. In his Ninth Series "On the Influence by Induction of an Electric Current on Itself:—and on the Inductive Action of Electric Currents Generally," *Phil. Trans.*, 1835, pp. 50–51, Faraday reported getting the same effect as Henry, and attributed it to similar causes:

> By applying the laws of the induction of electric currents formerly developed (6. &c.), various new conditions of the experiments could be devised, which by their results should serve as tests of the accuracy of the view just given. Thus, if a long wire be doubled, so that the current in the two halves shall have opposite actions, it ought not to give a sensible spark at the moment of disjunction: and this proved to be the case, for a wire forty feet long, covered with silk, being doubled and tied closely together to within four inches of the extremities, when used in that state, gave scarcely a perceptible spark; but being opened out and the parts separated, it gave a very good one. The two helices i and ii being joined at their similar ends, and then used at their other extremities to connect the plates of the electromotor, thus constituted one long helix, of which one half was opposed in direction to the other half: under these circumstances it gave scarcely a sensible spark, even when the soft iron core was within, although containing nearly two hundred feet of wire. When it was made into one consistent helix of the same length of wire it gave a very bright spark.

In Henry's reprint of this article this section is bracketed and starred. Henry had not known of Faraday's work with noninductive coils at the date of the current experiments.

Exp 3 A cylinder of soft iron was introduced into the centre of the coil. The effect was not sensibly increased although the exp was repeated many times with either coil.[3]

Exp 4 The double coil was unwound and laid at length. In this case there was no spark visible, while a brilliant deflagration of the mercury took place with the other strand in the form of a coil.

Exp 5th With a ribbon 25 feet long 1½ inches wide, rolled oblique around a cylinder of iron, spark appeared more brilliant when the cylen[der] was in the axes of the coil than when out.

Exp 6[4] Several coils were used of the same length but of different quantities of metal. There appeared to be a thickness of ribbon beyond which the effects are not increased or but slightly decreased with a moderate length of wire. The maximum was attained in this experiment by the coil mentioned before 28½ feet long.

Exp 7 The battery appeared to produce the greatest spark when the action was feeble and constant. A rapid evolution of hydrogen is unfavourable to the effect. The greatest effect[5] was produced from a small plate by a solution of about ⅓ nitric acid in water. (Doubtful)[6]

Exp 8 A large trough of mercury was placed in the circuit between two coils but no increased effect. Three coils* were then connected by cups of mercury into one circuit. A spark was produced at any one of the junctions but was not apparently more intense with all the coils than with the one of 60 feet.

* 3 coils, one of 60 feet, 25 feet, 95 feet[7]

[3] See Henry's experiments of the previous day, footnote 2.

[4] The rest of the document was first put down in pencil, then retraced in ink.

[5] Polarization, which results from gaseous or solid formations at an electrode, hindering the action between the acid solution and battery plates, was a principal cause of declining and irregular currents in early batteries. In 1836, J. F. Daniell succeeded in stabilizing the output with his nonpolarizable "Constant Battery," described in *Phil. Trans.*, 1836, pp. 107–124, 125–130; 1837, pp. 141–160. See *King*, pp. 241–242. Another advantage of the cell's efficiency was the possibility of substituting cheaper electrolytes for expensive ones like nitric acid. See *Encyclopaedia Britannica*, 8th ed., s.v. "Voltaic Electricity," p. 614, where the action of the cell is given in detail. For "Contributions IV: Electro-Dynamic Induction," Henry used a battery on Daniell's design.

[6] Possibly a later annotation. At one point, Henry's publication noted the use of dilute sulphuric acid.

[7] Compare this experiment to experiment 10 of Henry's published account. The largest single coil used for Henry's publication was ninety-six feet long, an inch and a half wide, and fifteen pounds (p. 226).

FROM JOHN VAUGHAN

Henry Papers, Smithsonian Archives

Phil. Jan 3d [1835][1]

D Sir

You will receive thru' the Secretary A D Bache a formal notice of your election as a member of the Am Philos Socy[2], but as it may be delayed I cannot deny myself the pleasure of making the Communication & request you will transfer the information to Professor Silliman whose letter[3] I used on the occasion in addition to our own recommendation. Our [next] meeting 16 Jany. As soon as I can get the Certificate[4] prepared & signed it shall be sent. Would you wish it folded, or left uncreased, it is a large sheet.

Ys

Jn Vaughan

The sooner the Communication[5] comes the better.

[1] The letter is actually dated 1834, but the 1835 date given in Henry's file note on the verso accords with internal evidence.

[2] Henry's election to America's oldest continuously existing scientific body was formal recognition of his achievements as well as his already close association with key figures in the Society. Henry accepted this honor in person. See his letter to Torrey of February 23, 1835, especially footnote 7.

[3] Above, Silliman to Vaughan, October 9, 1834. Although we have not found a letter from Henry to Silliman containing this information, Silliman acknowledges Henry's election in his letter of May 27, 1835, below.

[4] The original certificate is lacking in the collection of such items preserved at the Smithsonian Institution.

[5] Given in the original as "Comn" This may refer either to correspondence concerning Henry's membership or, more likely, to the paper in preparation which Henry had promised by this time (see above, Henry to Bache, December 17, 1834).

FROM A. D. BACHE

Henry Papers, Smithsonian Archives

Jany 3rd. 1835.

My dear friend

Your memoir did not come to hand before the New Year,[1] from press of other matters I suppose. The inclosed official note[2] I need hardly say gives me great pleasure to communicate. Send me your paper as soon as you can.

[1] As Henry promised it would in his letter to Bache of December 17, 1834 (printed above), to which this is a reply.

[2] The American Philosophical Society's official notification of Henry's election to membership. It has not survived as an enclosure to this letter and has not been found elsewhere.

I was confined to my room at the last meeting of our Society & substituted Doct. Bache for myself in the explanation of your battery so far as to have the fact of the construction & the fact relating to the long conductor referred to on our minutes.[3] Has Mr Alexander determined how to dispose of his Southern observations? We should be very glad to have them at the Philos. Soc. A Com. has been appointed to collect obs[ervatio]ns[4] and I would have written to him on their part had I not supposed from the announcement in the Nat. Gaz. that his results were intended to be communicated to us & would be forthcoming without a formal request.[5] Let me know how this matter stands.[6]

Mr Olm I do not know, nor his beautiful theory. One Olm-sted I know but he cannot stand in the stead of Olm:[7] he is probably one of those outlandish men who write in the unknown tongue—German.[8] Gauss' memoir[9]

[3] As Henry requested in his letter of December 17, this was a move to make it a matter of record that Henry had a report on his experiments with a long conductor in preparation. The paper on the battery was delivered at the American Philosophical Society's meeting of January 16, 1835. Henry at the same time made a brief verbal communication on deriving a spark from a long conductor. These remarks were copied into the APS *Proceedings* and were hastily printed in the *Journal of the Franklin Institute* (1835, *15*:169–170) in essentially the same form to protect Henry's priority claims. Dr. Bache is Franklin Bache.

[4] At their December 5, 1834, meeting, the American Philosophical Society appointed Bache, Isaiah Lukens, and Joseph Roberts, Jr., a "Committee to collect observations upon the Eclipse of 1834." *Early Proceedings of the American Philosophical Society . . . 1744 to 1838* (Philadelphia, 1884), p. 661.

[5] The article in the Philadelphia *National Gazette and Literary Register* (November 22, 1834, p. 2) is given here in its entirety:

> Extract from a letter from Princeton:—Fifty new students have been admitted to the College, and there is an uncommonly large accession to the Seminary. Professor Stephen Alexander has gone to Ebenezer, Georgia, with a splendid telescope, (made by Utzschneider & Fraunhofer, at Munich,) to observe the central solar eclipse on the 30th instant. This eclipse is quite an American affair, and the European savans will look to us for the elements of astronomical correction, &c. Alexander is equal to Payne himself as an observer. The results will be given to your Philosophical Society. This young, diffident man, is a prodigy in the exact sciences."

"Payne" is a misspelling of Robert Treat Paine, the eminent American astronomer mentioned above in Henry to Bache, December 17, 1834, especially footnote 17.

[6] Henry did not respond to this, at least not in his reply of January 12, below. Perhaps he opted for Bache's suggestion in the last line of this letter. Stephen Alexander's observations would not be forthcoming; see above, Henry to Vaughan, November 17, 1834, especially footnote 2.

[7] Bache's puns are in reply to Henry's query in his letter of December 17, 1834, above. Henry asked about the German physicist Georg Simon Ohm's "beautiful theory;" the American Denison Olmsted (1791–1859) was better known to both Henry and Bache. Henry met Olmsted at Yale in 1830, at which time (and at the time of this letter) Olmsted was Professor of Mathematics and Natural Philosophy. *Henry Papers, 1*:274–276, 279–280, and *DAB*.

[8] Keeping informed of the achievements of German scientists was particularly vexing for English-speaking scientists. Bache's problems with the German language, apparently shared by Henry, were akin to the handicaps of many scientific colleagues on both sides of the Atlantic. As Michael Faraday wrote to Otto Ernst Julius Seyffer of Stuttgart (April 19, 1848): "I had the honor a few days ago to receive the copy of your work on *Galvanism* and beg to assure you how much I am moved by this mark of your attention and approbation. The only regret it excites is that through ignorance of the German language I cannot

on the means of determining terres. mag. intensity has just reached me, written as it ought to be when a man writes in Germany or Sweden—in Latin. How long shall we for want of early or present study remain ignorant of what is doing in one of the most active portions of the Continent. You who were brought up north of Gotham perhaps have the advantage of the illiterate to the South of that reverend locale. Courtenay was elected with you last night.[10] Your friends here are well.

Do not fail to let me hear with your *usual punctuality*; viva voce answers if you like.

Yours truly
A.D. Bache

profit by it . . . . Often do I grieve for this deficiency for it shuts me out from the wonderful stores of knowledge not only physical but universal which are from day to day treasured up in that language." Heineman Collection, Pierpont Morgan Library.

[9] Carl Friedrich Gauss's "Intensitas vis magneticae terrestris ad mensuram absolutam revocata," appeared first in 1833 in *Commentationes recentiores Societatis Regiae Scientiarum Göttingensis*, 1832–1837, *8*:3–44. Widely reprinted in other European journals, in various forms, the paper was important for its introduction of absolute units of distance, mass, and time into magnetic phenomena and its descriptions of particularly accurate magnetic needles.

We have seen that on several occasions Henry's activities in terrestrial magnetism paralleled Gauss's. See above, Henry's notes of October 22, 1833; his letter to Kelly of December 30 of the same year; and his letter to Bache of May 18, 1835, below. Despite the language barrier, Henry probably acquired at least a passing acquaintance with Gauss's work through abstracts published in the British journals, for example the *Phil. Mag.*, 1833, 3d ser. 2:291–299 and 1834, 3d ser. *5*:344–349. The latter on Gauss's "magnetic observatory" seems to have been of particular interest to Henry. However, Gauss's influence on Henry's terrestrial magnetic interests seems to have been meager. Some of the communications problems would later be alleviated by publications like Richard Taylor's *Scientific Memoirs*, beginning in 1837, which stressed the translation of German articles.

[10] Edward H. Courtenay was among several new American Philosophical Society inductees of special interest to Henry. Henry Darwin Rogers, James P. Espy, and John Torrey were also elected at the January 2, 1835, meeting. *Early Proceedings of the American Philosophical Society . . . 1744 to 1838* (Philadelphia, 1884), pp. 663–664.

"RECORD OF EXPERIMENTS"

Henry Papers, Smithsonian Archives

Jany 6th 1835

To determine the difference in effect try a change in the quantity of the wire or ribbon.[1]

[1] A continuation of experiments begun on January 1, 1835, above.

9 A long wire was arranged with loops to dip into the mercury in the cups of one of the cylendrical batteries. A length of 10 feet gave no spark 15 feet very feeble spark 30 feet, 45 feet and so on up to 120 feet; after this the effect did not appear to be increased, and a wire of 300 feet appeared to produce <*the same*> a rather smaller spark.[2]

10 The coil 28½ feet long was then applied; vivid spark. Also coil of 60 feet spark more intense (containing 4 [times] as much copper)[3]

11 Coil with 95 feet containing nearly <7> ten times the quantity of copper spark about the same as the last

12 Small coil 28½ feet compared with electro-magnet[4] which will support 700 lbs, spark much brighter & louder from coil.

13 Small coil compared with large electro-magnet—scarcely any spark from magnet, vivid one from coil. It appears that the difference in the effects of different coils is greater the lower the intensity of the battery

NB The loudest sparkes appear on the side of the thimble. To compare the intensity they should be drawn from the middle of the surface of mercury in the cups

[2] The results of this arrangement were presented in experiment 2 of Henry's "Contributions II: Spiral Conductor." There Henry reported that the spark intensified constantly up to 120 feet of wire, noting that the maximum effective length of conductor depended on the intensity and size of the battery. Beyond 120 feet the increasing resistance of the wire accounted for the diminished spark. At this time, Henry apparently made no systematic attempt to correlate battery strengths with the intensifications due to the long and spiral conductors.

[3] Henry used thicker ribbon. He noted in experiment 3 of his publication that the increased electrical intensity due to thickness also appeared to depend on the size of the battery.

[4] We have no specifics on Henry's arrangement of the electromagnet, although we would guess the setup was that of his first electromagnetic induction experiments described in "On the Production of Currents and Sparks of Electricity From Magnetism," *Silliman's Journal*, 1832, 22:403–408. That is, the sparks were drawn from a coil around the electromagnet's armature as the battery was connected and disconnected. It should be noted that on May 12, 1835, below, Henry's "Record of Experiments" shows that he also induced currents in the windings around the horseshoe core of the magnet. See experiment 4 of that entry.

"RECORD OF EXPERIMENTS"

Henry Papers, Smithsonian Archives

Jany 7th 1835

13[1] It occurred to me this morning before rising from bed that if I could solder two copper handles to the coil used in the foregoing exps a shock might be obtained.

Accordingly two thick pieces of copper plate were soldered one to each end of the coil. When these were grasped in the hand & the circuit formed a shock [is] given with the small cylindrical Battery which may be felt to the shoulders.[2]

(Good Experiment)

14 The effect was then tried with one of the plates of the large battery. This gives a very vivid spark but the shock did not appear to be more intense than in the former exp. The sparks however in this exp. fired at two different times the hydrogen which was evolved from the action of the acid on the zinc plate

15 The contact was broken in a vessel containing a mixture of oxygen & hydrogen. A[n] explosion of the gas was produced.[3]

N.B. After operating with the battery this evening noticed that my hands very very moist, probably produced by the action of the acid. After a short time they became dry and spots form—this circumstance uncomfortable <*To determine the direction of the collateral current which produces the shock*>[4]

[1] Henry accidentally began with the number of his last experiment on January 6.

[2] Henry published an account of this experiment in "Facts in Reference to the Spark, &c. from a Long Conductor Uniting the Poles of a Galvanic Battery," Franklin Institute *Journal*, March 1835, *15*:170, which had been read to the American Philosophical Society on January 16, and in "Contributions II," page 226, which was read February 6. In the arrangement of the articles, these are experiments number seven and eight respectively. The copper handles used for testing shocks from coils became a standard piece of equipment in Henry's laboratory, and appear henceforth throughout the "Record of Experiments."

[3] This experiment is also reported in the two papers cited in note 2 as experiments number ten and eleven respectively.

[4] Henry remarked in "Contributions II," page 226 that "This shock is rather a singular phenomenon, since it appears to be produced by a lateral discharge, and it is therefore important to determine its direction in reference to the primary current." He contrasted it to the less intense effect obtained "when the copper of the battery is grasped by one hand, and the handle attached to the copper pole of the ribbon with the other. This may be called the direct shock, since it is produced by a part of the direct current." Henry's next entry in the "Record of Experiments" (January 26, 1835, printed below), shows him pursuing investigations other than the direction of the lateral current, but these concerns do reappear in Henry's work on lateral discharge in 1836, 1837, and 1838.

January 12, 1835

TO ALEXANDER DALLAS BACHE

Bache Papers, Smithsonian Archives

Princeton Jany 12th
Monday morning 1835

My Dear Friend

With my *usual punctuality* I have risen at a very *unusual* hour to answer your interesting communication of the 3rd inst.[1]

The intelligence of my election as you may suppose was very acceptable, not that I value the honor so much although I am not entirely insensible to such affairs[2] but because it will give me a better opportunity of doing something with you and Courtenay in the way of science.

I acknowledge that I am a sad fellow in not being more punctual in reference to my paper but I have been so unfortunate as to be obliged to do double duty all the time since my return from Phila, except last week, on account of the illness of Prof James Alexander.[3]

I have been much engaged in repeating my experiments on the long and short conductors and in arranging them for publication. While thus engaged many new suggestions were tested and the result is that the subject has grown much more interesting. Some new facts have been developed which conclusively prove that the phenomenon (as I suggested in my article in Silliman[4]) is intimately connected with magneto-electricity.[5] The influence of coiling the conductor I have clearly made out and can produce with a lar[g]e coil and one plate of my battery shocks which may be felt at the elbows. The presence of soft iron has little effect in producing the *spark* or at least far less than the coiling of the conductor.

[1] See above, January 3, 1835.

[2] Henry displayed a different sensibility to his brother several days later. See his letter of January 23, 1835, below.

[3] See above, Trustees' Minutes, April 9, 1834, footnote 10.

[4] "On the Production of Currents and Sparks of Electricity from Magnetism," *Silliman's Journal*, 1832, 22:408, Henry's first announcement of self-induction.

[5] This is the first explicit dated manuscript reference we have found to Henry's theory of self-induction, a theory that he sketchily developed in his publication on the spiral conductor that he is about to submit to Bache. On the basis of this article and various undated notes from the period, we have attempted to reconstruct some of Henry's thoughts on the subject as of this date. A rather proper statement of the hypothetico-deductive method at the end of Henry's article indicates the importance he ascribed to these theoretical ideas:

> The foregoing views are not presumed to be given as exhibiting the actual operation of nature in producing the phenomena described, but rather as the hypotheses which have served as the basis of my investigations, and which may further serve as formulae from which to deduce new consequences to be established or disproved by experiment.

"Contributions II: Spiral Conductor," p. 231. We give these ideas not as a definitive statement of Henry's views, but as a description of ideas in flux that will be modified by further thought and experimental research.

By magnetoelectricity, Henry referred to the

production of electric sparks from the coils of electromagnets—the principle of mutual induction. Relating self-inductive sparks to magnetoelectricity was clearly part of Henry's general strategy of uniting the various forces of electricity and magnetism, a goal widely shared by contemporary electrical physicists. Several Henry articles begin with a statement of this suspected unity. Among his papers is a set of extensive reading notes, dated August 1833 (Notebook [7171], pp. 9–12, 20), on Faraday's Third Series of Experimental Researches in Electricity on the identity of electricities from different sources (*Phil. Trans.*, 1833, pp. 23–54).

The origins of Henry's discovery of self-induction in 1832 remain obscure. But a key discovery by Faraday was a major influence on Henry's theory correlating magnetoelectricity and sparks from spiral conductors. In his article on the latter effect, Henry invoked Faraday's discovery of "volta-electric induction," announced in Faraday's First Series of Experimental Researches. Faraday showed that, upon receiving a current from a battery, a wire could generate an opposing instantaneous current in a neighboring wire. Henry had not seen the account until after his own initial discovery of mutual and self-induction, but the facts seemed to accord with his general assumptions about the nature of induction. That is, all induction resulted from the mutual action of electric currents. Thus, as seen above, the operative agent in magnetoelectric induction from his large electromagnet was not the iron core but its internal system of Ampèrian molecular currents. Henry called Faraday's volta-electric induction a "fundamental fact in Magneto-Electricity" [p. 229].

Although experiments on the long spiral conductor involved only one circuit, not two, the basic inductive principle was the same for Henry: through induction, the numerous spires of the coil reinforced the currents in one another (see the quotation below). Curiously, volta-electric induction seems to have played a less prominent role in Faraday's conception of electromagnetic induction than in Henry's. At least, this is the impression given in *Michael Faraday* (New York, 1965), by L. Pearce Williams (see chapter 4).

The presence of sparks upon breaking circuits of spiral conductors immediately suggested to Henry a more basic mechanism: static electric induction. Dealing with self-induction in 1832, Henry made an apparent reference to the static origins: "I can account for these phenomena only by supposing the long wire to become charged with electricity, which by its re-action on itself projects a spark when the connection is broken." "On the Production of Currents and Sparks of Electricity from Magnetism," p. 408. (For the possible influence of Robert Hare's theory in this connection, see L. Pearce Williams, "The Simultaneous Discovery of Electro-Magnetic Induction by Michael Faraday and Joseph Henry," *Bullétin de la société des amis d'André-Marie Ampère*, 1965, no. 22:12–21.) By the time of Henry's paper on the spiral conductor, the static electric explanation became explicit, further evidence of the identity of all electricities. Henry's explanation amounted to treating the electric current as a "dynamic" condition of static electricity, for which the inductive effects were well known. Henry's description bears full quotation:

> The above fundamental fact in Magneto-electricity appears to me to be a direct consequence of the statical principles of "Electrical *Induction*" as mathematically investigated by Cavendish, Poisson, and others. When the two wires *A* and *B* are in their natural state, an equilibrium is sustained by the attractions and repulsions of the two fluids in each wire; or, according to the theory of Franklin and Cavendish, by the attractions and repulsions of the one fluid, and the matter of the two wires. If a current of free electricity be passed through *A*, the natural equilibrium of *B* will be disturbed for an instant, in a similar manner to the disturbance of the equilibrium in an insulated conductor, by the sudden addition of fluid to a contiguous conductor. On account of the repulsive action of the fluid, the current in *B* will have an opposite direction to that in *A*; and if the intensity of action remains constant, a new state of equilibrium will be assumed. The second state of *B* however may perhaps be regarded as one of tension, and as soon as the extra action ceases in it, the fluid in *B* will resume its natural state of distribution, and thus a returning current for an instant be produced.
>
> The action of the spiral conductor in producing sparks, is but another case of the same action; for since action and reaction are equal and in contrary directions, if a current established in *A* produces a current in an opposite direction in *B*, then a current transmitted through *B* should accelerate or increase the intensity of a current already existing in the same direction in *A*. In this way the current in the several successive spires of the coil may be conceived to accel-

The subject opens to me a wide field of experiment which I intend to cultivate. I have concluded however to publish first what I have done and then follow with a second memoir.[6]

I intend if nothing unusual happens to be with you on friday next and to present to you my papers for the society.[7] With regard to my experiments on the coil please not to mention it. I will explain more fully when we meet.

I have accidentally heard that Rodgers[8] has lately been appointed one of your faculty. I hope the news is correct.

Please tell him that I will make it one of my errands to Phi[d] to see him and that if I should be prevented from coming I will write to him.

My respects to Your *Best Half* and to Courtenay. I have written to Mr Vaughan.

There is a package for me at New York from a friend who has been in Edinburgh during the late scientific meeting.[9] I hope it will arrive before my jaunt to Phil[d]

Sincerely Yours
Joseph Henry

> erate, or to tend to accelerate each other; and when the contact is broken, the fluid of the first spire is projected from it with intensity by the repulsive action of the fluid in all the succeeding spires. [pp. 229–230.]

Ampère, Henry's constant inspiration, drew a sharp theoretical distinction between electrodynamics—or current effects—and static-electric effects (see Theodore M. Brown, "The Electric Current in Early Nineteenth-Century French Physics," *Historical Studies in the Physical Sciences*, 1969, *1*:85–89). But Henry, drawing eclectically upon a wide variety of sources, either missed Ampère's distinction or decided to modify it. In his view, there was but one form of electricity. Some light is shed on this topic by two notebooks on "electricity" found in the Henry Papers ([23894] and [23919]). The undated notes appear to be for lectures at Princeton. After an extended discussion of electrostatics, Henry introduces a new topic "Elect in motion or *The Electro Dynamics of Ordinary Elect*," which he interprets as the transfer of the "electric principle" through bodies. He begins with this statement: "The term electro-dynamics has of late years been applied to the phenomina of electro-magnetism. This is to[o] restricted." The actual subject, he believed, is the motion of static electricity and the velocity of the static discharge. The implication is that static and current effects were thoroughly equivalent. Showing similarities between electricities from static and voltaic sources became the direction of Henry's future research for the American Philosophical Society.

To Henry, self-induction was perhaps even more fundamental theoretically than mutual induction. The effects from long conductors and coils revealed electrical induction in its basic form as the interaction of neighboring currents. In attempting to explain Henry's priority over Faraday in the discovery of self-induction, Williams notes that while the effect fell clearly within Henry's theoretical presuppositions it had "no obvious interpretation" in Faraday's scheme. "The Simultaneous Discovery of Electromagnetic Induction," p. 20. For other theoretical differences between Henry and Faraday on self-induction, see above, "Record of Experiments," December 31, 1834, footnote 2.

[6] There was no immediate sequel.

[7] At the January 16 meeting, Henry presented not the full account of the spiral conductor work but a shortened verbal communication on the subject along with his paper on the galvanic battery.

[8] Henry Darwin Rogers (see above, Henry's Notes on a Trip to Philadelphia, December [5–7], 1834, footnote 12) was appointed Professor of Geology and Mineralogy at the University of Pennsylvania.

[9] See below, Henry to Torrey, February 23, 1835.

TO JOHN VAUGHAN

Archives, American Philosophical Society

Princeton Jan[y] [12][1] 1835

My Dear Sir

I embrace almost the very first moment of my leisure since the receipt of your *very interesting* and kind communication to acknowledge the many obligations you have placed me under and particularly in reference to the warm part you have taken in my election. It shall be my constant endeavour as far as mere labour in the cause of science can effect it to prove to the society that you have not imposed on it a member entirely unworthy [of] the honor it has bestowed.

Unfortunately I have been obliged to do double duty for three weeks past on account of the illness of one of our Professors. Every moment has been engaged and what little time I could spare from my college duties has been devoted to the repetition of the experiments for my paper. I hope to be able to communicate some results at the next meeting and will if nothing unusual happens be with you on friday next.

With regard to the diploma keep it until I come to the city.

With the highest respect I am
sir your obliged & humble
serv
Joseph Henry

[1] Determined by the postmark.

FROM ROBERT G. RANKIN[1]

Henry Papers, Smithsonian Archives

New York Jan[y]. 12th [1835][2]

Sir

I am instructed by the Board of Directors of the New York City Lyceum[3] —"respectfully to request that you will deliver a Lecture before the Lyceum on the subject of Galvanism."[4]

[1] Robert Gosman Rankin (1806–1878), a native of New York City, graduated from Yale College in 1826 and studied at the Litchfield Law School. By 1829 Rankin began practicing law in New York City. He ultimately pursued careers in manufacturing of both iron and cotton textiles, as well as in developing railroads and acting as a consulting engineer. In 1847 he was appointed a member of the New York Board of Regents, which position he held until his death. In the 1850s he became a member of the American Association for the Advance-

The Lyceum was organized in Nov 1834 and has already opened a Reading Room of a useful & popular character. The general objects of the Lyceum you will learn by the 2nd article of the Constitution herewith enclosed.[5]

The Lectures take place on Thursday evening of each week, and should your inclination & duties allow you to comply with our request it will be esteemed a high favor conferred upon the Lyceum and the citizens residing in the upper part of the City. May I request an early answer to this Letter, and, as to the time it will suit your convenience to Lecture, and where the Executive Comee of the Lyceum may wait upon you on your arrival in town.

Very Respectfully
Your obnt sevt
Robt G Rankin 27 Wall St

ment of Science. Rankin also published *The Economic Value of the Semi-Bituminous Coal of the Cumberland Coal Basin* (New York, 1855). He met with repeated financial reverses in his peripatetic career and spent the last fifteen years of his life in Newburgh, New York, where he founded and directed a religious school. Rankin was corresponding secretary of the New York City Lyceum from its founding until 1838. Selden Haines, comp., *A Biographical Sketch of the Class of 1826 [of] Yale College* (Utica, New York, 1866), pp. 76–79. John J. Nutt, comp., *Newburgh: Her Institutions, Industries and Leading Citizens* (Newburgh, 1891), p. 119.

[2] The original is mistakenly dated 1834. Internal evidence and the history of the society clearly indicate 1835.

[3] The New York City Lyceum was founded in 1834; by 1837, when it sought incorporation, the society changed its name to the Stuyvesant Institute upon the New York Lyceum of Natural History's complaints that their names were too alike. Neither should be confused with still another institution in this period, the New York Lyceum which was founded in 1838 as an extension of the Young Men's Associations movement (for which see above, Bullions to Henry, December 19, 1833, footnote 12).

The New York City Lyceum completed its home at 659 Broadway by 1837, which building it shared at later times with both the New-York Historical Society and the Lyceum of Natural History. As the Stuyvesant Institute it survived at least nominally into the 1870s. Its main purpose, especially in its early years, was the edification of its membership through a well-stocked library of newspapers and journals and an active schedule of popular lectures. Some records of the society are preserved in the New-York Historical Society.

[4] Henry's name was among the list of eleven prominent invitees. Other notable lecturers named were (all in *DAB*): William Beach Lawrence, Ralph Waldo Emerson, John McVickar, Francis Lieber, Denison Olmsted, Chester Dewey, and John Breckinridge. Minutes of the Board of Directors of the New York City Lyceum, January 2, 1835, New-York Historical Society. Henry's reply to this invitation has not been found, but we assume, circumstantially, that he declined. The Henry documentation does not suggest that he had appreciable interest in giving popular science lectures in this period.

[5] The enclosure has not survived either in Henry's papers or in his library. Its second article reads: "Objects: Its object is the diffusion of useful knowledge by POPULAR LECTURES; the establishment of a READING ROOM, LIBRARY, a MUSEUM or CABINET OF NATURAL HISTORY, and by such other means as the Board of Directors may judge expedient." *Constitution of the New-York City Lyceum* (New York, 1834).

TO JAMES HENRY

Family Correspondence, Henry Papers, Smithsonian Archives

Princeton Jany 13th 183[5][1]

Dear James

I have been unusually engaged for several weeks past on account of the illness of Prof. James Alexander and did not find leisure to write to you until saturday night when I penned a long letter but on coming to fold it on monday morning I found that I had written on all the sides of sheet and left not place for the direction.[2]

The last week has been a very cold one in Princeton and the temperature similar to that which we formerly experienced in albany. The most intense cold was on Sunday week wen the thermometer stood at eleven below zero. I see by the papers that it has been very low in Albany 32° below. We received your paper containing the Governors message some days since but I have had no time but merely to glance at it. I perceive that he mentions the death of the old surveyor general. This is propper.[3] Richard V DeWitt a few days since addressed me a letter requesting that I would take his Brother into our family for the remainder of the winter as it was the request of his Father that Linn should be placed under my care for some time. I know not whether he intends to send him or not this [?winter] but since the navigation has close[d] I rather think that he will not come at this time. We are all well now although Harriet has had quite a severe attack of the desentary but she is now much better and is about again. The children have also had the influenza but are also much better at present.

The Boy often talks of Albany and Mother. Last evening he gave a very particular account of a little fire engine which he saw at Schanklands. The Girl is improving very rapidly and can almost talk. She has four teeth can perform several little tricks and is in the opinion of her Mother quite a prodigy. Aunt has to mourn the loss of some of her best Plants destroyed by the intensity of the cold. It is perhaps quite as well that you did not

1 Given as "1834" in a common error in letters so soon after the New Year. From the content this is clearly 1835.

2 That is, Henry had to rewrite the letter. Envelopes came into general use somewhat later. The folded sheet had to have a blank space for the address.

3 Governor William L. Marcy noticed the death of Simeon DeWitt, Henry's friend from Albany (see *Henry Papers, 1*:passim), on January 6:

> . . . A life thus commenced by services and sacrifices in the cause of civil liberty, and well sustained to its end by unremitting labors directed with singleness of purpose to the public good, should be held in just remembrance by those among whom it was spent, and presented as an encouraging example to posterity.

New York Senate Journal, 58th Session, January 1835, p. 24.

engage with Little[4] since from your letter it is evident that he wished to get you for the purpose of becoming acquainted with the law business. We have nothing new about Princeton. The cold weather has engrossed all the conversation for some time past. The Holidays have passed over quite peacibly and the college is going on smoothly and prosperously. I saw by one of the papers that an alarm of fire had been in Washington Street. I hope it did not much alarm Mother. She is however a much better soldier when danger really comes than a person would imagine from her usual timidity. How does the very cold weather affect her? Has Nancy re[covered] from her cold? How is Mr McA[rthur] get on. I hope he is still with you.

Wen last in Philad[a] I delivered the package of papers which Mrs Fisher[5] sent but did not see the Lady to whom it was addressed. She was not in the city at the time. I will however visit Phil[a] very often if my life be spared and will call at some time. Love to Mother & Nancy. Respects to Shankland, McArthur, Prof Bullions, Ten Eyck, Wing, Dean,[6] Meads, Frank and all others to whom I should be remembered.

Your Brother
Joseph

Do write soon. A Happy new Year to you all.

H[arriet]

[4] Apparently Weare C. Little, the Albany bookseller, *Henry Papers*, *1*:318–319, footnote 3.

[5] For whom see Joseph Henry's letter to James Henry, May 17, 1833, footnote 4, above.

[6] Amos Dean of Albany.

FROM JOHN TORREY

Historic Letter File,[1] Gray Herbarium Library, Harvard University

New York, Jan[y] 16th 1835

My dear friend

I wrote you about a fortnight since but there was nothing special in my letter[2] that required an answer. I am as *busy* as a bee, but I am not as successful in treasuring up any thing useful. How I should like to have looked

[1] This file is one of several important manuscript collections at the Gray Herbarium Library. The bulk of the Historic Letter File consists of the personal and professional correspondence of Asa Gray. However, items not to or from Gray, such as this letter of Torrey to Henry, also appear in the collection, a fact to which researchers in the history of nineteenth-century science should be alert.

Parts of this letter were printed in Andrew Denny Rodgers, *John Torrey: A Story of North American Botany* (Princeton, 1942), pp. 112–113 and 114; and in A. Hunter Dupree, *Asa Gray, 1810–1888* (Cambridge, Massachu-

in upon you last New Years! Are your spirits good? Will Newall[3] certainly succeed? And are we to wait till the whole proposed sum is subscribed before any thing is done for our departments? I long to fit up a new laboratory for Princeton & I think we shall have one yet. Our good friends there need a little *pushing* on the subject.

The pneumatic trough that I wrote to you about has been sent to New Orleans. A friend of mine[4] there wrote to me to have him one sent on without delay & I let him have what I had made for Princeton. I was glad that this request came, for I saw that several improvements could be made in the apparatus. Another is far advanced, & will be finished next week. It will be just the thing & will be a credit to Princeton. Pray have the old rickety concern be sent to Botany Bay or where I will never see it again. I should like to spend about $100 on the Trough & its appendages. Let me know soon what I may expect to expend on the Chem! Dept next spring.[5] What do you think I have engaged for you? A grand pair of large tinman's shears. This is an article that you have long needed greatly. You *must* also have a good grindstone & a turning lathe.

Does Jäger talk any more of leaving Princeton?[6] I wish he would go, for he is only a clog to us. Gray (my assistant) would be a great acquisition in Jäger's place. He is a *first rate* fellow & is good both in Chemistry & Natural History. He would do great credit to the college, for he must make a noise in the world, & he will be continually publishing. He has just prepared for publication in the Annals of the Lyceum, two capital botanical papers.[7] He is a good scientific & practical mineralogist. Keep your eye upon him. I

---

setts, 1959), pp. 43–44.

[2] i.e., the letter printed above of December 29, 1834.

[3] Daniel Newell and the fund drive are discussed above in the Trustees' Minutes for April 9, 1834.

[4] Not identified.

[5] An appropriation of $150 for the Chemical Department was authorized on April 15, 1835. See the Trustees' Minutes of that date, printed below.

[6] He did not leave until 1841.

[7] Gray read two papers to the New York Lyceum of Natural History in December 1834, "A Monograph of the North American Species of Rhynchospora" and "A Notice of Some New, Rare, and Otherwise Interesting Plants from the Northern and Western Portions of the State of New York." They were published in the Lyceum *Annals*, 1828–1836, *3*:191–220, and 221–238. Dupree, *Asa Gray*, p. 42, points out that these plants were poorly classified as of the time Gray undertook publication, and that by unsnarling their taxonomy, Gray won attention as a young botanist of considerable promise.

The New York Lyceum of Natural History was founded in 1817 to promote research in geology, botany, and zoology. The Lyceum assembled a useful museum of plant, animal, and mineral specimens (including fossils) and had a decent library of scientific monographs and journals. The organization published mainly taxonomic and descriptive papers in its *Annals*. The 1830s were especially productive years for the Lyceum; monetary troubles and problems of organization led to a decline thereafter, reversed in the 1870s when prominent scientists of the city metamorphosed the Lyceum into the New York Academy of Sciences. Herman L. Fairchild, *History of the New York Academy of Sciences* (New York, 1887).

should be very sorry to have him leave me, but he will have to be in some public institution[8] one of these days.

Have you been dubbed with a diploma from the—I must *now* say—*AMERICAN* philosophical Society?[9] They have had the penetration to discover my modest merits, & as you so greatly resemble me (I mean in *modesty*) I suppose you have likewise had this blushing honor put upon you!

We had a meeting of the Trustees & Professors of our Medical College night before last, & we feel pretty confident of obtaining a new building[10]—one that will be worthy of New York, & of the Medical Profession.

Remember me to the Macleans,[11] Dod,[12] Mr[13] & Prof. Alexander[14] & all our friends & associates. Present my kind regards to Mrs H, & believe me very truly, yours,

John Torrey

[8] Gray was appointed librarian and curator at the New York Lyceum of Natural History in February or March 1836, according to Dupree, *Asa Gray*, p. 56.

[9] Scientists such as Torrey and Henry who did not live in Philadelphia complained of the arrogance of the organization calling itself American rather than Pennsylvanian or even Philadelphian. The Society had "an obvious tendency of appealing to Philadelphia people, rather than scientists from the country as a whole" in its programs. Furthermore, "in 1834, . . . 110 of the 203 American members of the Society lived within ten miles of the Hall." Walter Elliot Gross, "The American Philosophical Society and the Growth of Science in the United States: 1835–1850" (Ph.D. dissertation, University of Pennsylvania, 1970), pp. 369 and 304–305.

[10] Land was purchased in May 1835 in the upper part of the city which was then being built up. By November 1837 the school began to move into new quarters. James J. Walsh, *History of Medicine in New York: Three Centuries of Medical Progress*, 5 vols. (New York, 1919), 2:424.

[11] John and George Maclean.

[12] Albert Baldwin Dod, Professor of Mathematics at Princeton (*Henry Papers, 1*:434).

[13] Stephen Alexander.

[14] James Waddel Alexander, Professor of Rhetoric, Latin, and Literature at Princeton (see note 10 of Trustees' Minutes for April 9, 1834, above).

TO JAMES HENRY

Family Correspondence, Henry Papers, Smithsonian Archives

Princeton Jany 23rd 1835

Dear James

Your letter[1] was received yesterday. We are sorry to learn that Mother is so feeble. I was afraid that the very severe weather would affect her seriously but I hope she will get better as the weather becomes warmer or more

[1] Not found.

settled. We are all well. Harriet has recovered from her indisposition. The children are now free from the colds which afflicted them for several weeks.

I visited Philadelphia last week on Friday and returned on Monday of the present. I saw Dr Ludlow. He has just commenced his duties in the University and appears much pleased with his situation.[2] His oldest son has entered the Freshmen class and his younger has joined the academy or grammar school connected with the college.[3] The communication from Princeton to Philadelphia will be next summer very easy since the rail road from Trenton to the city is completed. I came from Phil. to Trenton in about an hour and a half and from Trenton to Princeton in about the same time. R. V. DeWitt was at our house last Wednesday. He came from New-York with his Brother Linn who has taken up his quarters with us for the remainder of the winter. I am very glad to learn that there is a prospect of our friend Dr Campbells being elected or appointed to the office of Surveyor General.[4] He is a very worthy man and would fill the office with profit to the state. I saw it mentioned in one of the papers that Mr Broadhead of Utica[5] was a candidate but Linn DeWitt says that he will not accept should he receive the appointment. I wish that you would ask B Van Rensselaer[6]

[2] John R. Ludlow (1793–1857), an acquaintance of Henry's from Albany, was inaugurated Provost of the University of Pennsylvania on December 22, 1834. *Henry Papers, 1*:106n. Ludlow's address on that occasion is in Henry's Library.

[3] John Livingston Ludlow (1819–1888) was the eldest son of John R. Ludlow, graduated with high honors from the University of Pennsylvania in 1838 and received a degree from its medical school in 1841. He practiced in Philadelphia and wrote many articles in his field. Ludlow authored *A Manual of Examinations upon Anatomy and Physiology, Surgery, Practice of Medicine, Chemistry, Materia Medica, Obstetrics, Pharmacy, Therapeutics*; a presentation copy of the second edition (Philadelphia, 1844) is in Henry's Library. From surviving letters to Joseph Henry and Harriet Henry, John Livingston Ludlow was a good friend of theirs. He may be the "Livingston Ludlow" referred to in *Henry Papers, 1*:454. John L. Ludlow attended the Albany Academy.

The youngest son of John R. Ludlow, Richard, may have died in infancy. At least we find no dates for him. This reference is probably to James R. Ludlow (1825–1886), the second son. A Pennsylvania graduate (1843), he practiced law in Philadelphia (1846–1857) before election to the Court of Common Pleas. William Seton Gordon, *Gabriel Ludlow (1663–1736) and his Descendants* (New York, 1919), pp. 28–29. (Reprint from *New York Genealogical and Biographical Record.*) *The National Cyclopedia of American Biography, 3*: 499–500. Alfred Nevin, ed., *Encyclopedia of the Presbyterian Church in the United States of America* (Philadelphia, 1884), pp. 455–456.

[4] William Campbell (*Henry Papers, 1*:100–101) did succeed Simeon DeWitt as Surveyor-General of New York State.

[5] Charles C. Brodhead (1772–1852). Commissioned Sheriff of Oneida County, New York, in 1800, Brodhead's main occupation was surveying. He served in the Surveyor-General's office and in 1816 was in charge of the preliminary surveys for the eastern section (Albany to Rome) of the Erie Canal. In 1817 he was one of the commissioners involved in determining the boundaries of the town of Utica. Retiring to private life, he became a corresponding member of the First and Second Departments of the Albany Institute. Noble E. Whitford, *History of the Canal System of the State of New York . . .*, 2 vols. (Albany, 1906), 2:1151. Isaac P. Bielby, *Sheriffs of Oneida County* (Utica, 1890), p. 5. Daniel E. Wager, ed., *Our County and its People: A Descriptive Work on Oneida County, New York* (Boston, 1896), part 1, p. 284. *Transactions*, Albany Institute, 1830, *1*, part 2:Appendix, pp. 66, 70.

[6] Bernard S. Van Rensselaer, *Henry Papers, 1*:250–251.

to send me one of the Reports of the superintendent of common schools.[7] Something is attempting in reference to the subject of schools in the state of New Jersey and all the information which can be collected on the subject is desirable.[8] Has Dr Frank commenced house keeping or does he live with his motherinlaw?[9] I think with you that the visits of a certain person to a certain house which contains a young and beautiful lady is rather a dangerous custom to indulge in.[10] I have nothing new to communicate unless it be that I have lately been elected a member of the American Philosophical society and visited Phila[d] last week for the purpose of attending one of the meetings and also to submit a paper on some experiments which I have made together with a description of my battery &c. These are to be published in the cours of a few weeks. I felt it something of an era in my life to join a society formed by the immortal Franklin and to subscribe my name in the same list with those of Jefferson, Rittenhouse[11] and many others of the same class.

The President of the society (Mr DuPonceau) sits in the same chair which Franklin once occupied. The society is important to me on account of its library which [contains] upwards of 9000 vols. of Book[s] on [the] subject of science and those of the most rare and choice kind. During the summer season I can leave Princeton at 2 or 3 o'clock and arive in Phil[a] in time for the meeting in the evening. I hope if my life and health be spared to do something in the way of science and to prove myself no insignificant member of the society. Perhaps it will be as well not to say much about this as it may awaken some little feelings of envy among my former associates and I wish to get on smoothly.

Saturday Morning

Hubby has gone to the Hall & left me to close this poor torn sheet for him.[12] I wish you could see Sis. She said Papa very plainly this morning, creeps all over & is altogether very very sweet. Bub is as noisy as ever, grows large & fat—talks every thing—has got two cents with which he is going to the Baker's to buy cake.

[7] At this date, the duties of the Superintendent of Common Schools were exercised by the Secretary of State of New York, John A. Dix (1798–1879, *DAB*).

[8] In 1834 individuals at Princeton formed a New Jersey Lyceum to fight for development of common schools in the state. Both before and after that date individuals in the Princeton community were active in this cause, including John Maclean, A. B. Dod, and E. C. Wines. See Nelson R. Burr, *Education in New Jersey* (Princeton, 1942), chapters 18 and 19.

[9] Francis N. Selkirk's mother-in-law was Alida Winne (d. 1836), widow of Daniel I. Winne. Munsell, *Ann. Alb.*, *10*:265.

[10] Henry's coy remark is impenetrable, at least to us.

[11] David Rittenhouse (1732–1796), an American astronomer. See Brooke Hindle, *David Rittenhouse* (Princeton, 1964).

[12] Literally true. Both Joseph and Harriet Henry carefully wrote around a missing piece of the sheet.

Tell the girls I received their nice, kind letter last week—thank them for me. I hear sad accounts of you through them. I shall have to take you in hand when I see you. Love to Mother Nancy & all. I wish I could see you all—wish I could fly.

Yours as ever
Harriet

"RECORD OF EXPERIMENTS"

Henry Papers, Smithsonian Archives

Jany 26th 1835

A pair of cruckshank troughs were charged with diluted acid, a mixture of sul[phuric] and murieatic, with a quantity of common salt. The effect of the coil appeared to be little or nothing; there was a deflagration of the mercury when the contact was formed but no snap when broken. With the coil there was a shock when the contact was formed and also a slighter one when broken.[1]

The effect was greater with the coil than with out it. There is a current apparently in an adverse direction when the contact is broken in a battery of a hundred pairs.

In this exp. the coil was placed at one [of the] extremites of the two troughs and the hands at the other. A shock was felt when the contact was made and broken. The same effect was produced with a short wire. The battery therefore produces in itself an effect similar to the coil. The coil appeared in some cases to increase the effect, in others not to produce the effect.[2] The subject requires further investigation—make exp. on the same point with the large battery.

Apparent result of this exp

[1] As reported in "Contributions II: Spiral Conductor," each trough contained fifty-six four-inch plates, yielding high intensity and relatively low quantity. The troughs were wired for intensity, i.e., in series. In "Contributions II," p. 228, Henry concluded that the spiral conductor has virtually no effect on high intensity currents, but speculated that increasing the length of coil in proportion to the battery's intensity might produce a perceptible effect. Henry subsequently attained some positive results. In his later "Appendix" on these subjects published in *Silliman's Journal*, July 1835, *28*:330–331, Henry experimented with a hundred-plate intensity battery (also mentioned in the next paragraph of this entry). Producing no increased effects with a sixty- to one-hundred-foot coil, Henry did perceive an increased action with a wire coil of five or six hundred feet. "The length of the coil," he explained, "must be in some ratio to the projectile force of the electricity. . . ."

[2] Henry distinguished these experiments on the "direct shock" from the "lateral shock" experiments, where the body formed a parallel branch of the circuit. See above, "Record of Experiments," January 7, 1835, and "Contributions II: Spiral Conductor," p. 226.

Henry then omitted the coil and still re-

1st battery gives a shock when the current is broken with or without a coil—
2nd Electricity of high intensity appears not be affected by the coil
3[3] ,,

Try the effect of heating the coil or spiral conductor[4]

Try to charge a Lyden jar by means of the coil[5]

See copy of Galvanism for notes on experiments to be made[6]

Experiment on the alternative current on Large animal[7]

Is the intensity of Electro-magnets as great as that of steel *No* Will a steel magnet be changed in polarity as quick when brought near an Electro magnet as when near a steel one of the same strength.

Exp on this point[8]

Also the relative lifting power of one or two poles

Magnetize Chiltons magnet then wind it with ribbon, magnetize it in contrary direction; Try effect

Borrow strong steel magnet from Lukens[9]

May not the experiment of Ampere be correct which is given in Demon-

---

ceived pronounced inductive shocks when the circuit was made and broken. (He experienced little or no effect while the current flowed.) To explain this, Henry wrote: "The phenomenon of the secondary shock with the battery, appears to me to be a consequence of the law of Mr. Faraday. The parts of the human body contiguous to those through which the principal current is passing, may be considered as in the state of the second wire B [in which Faraday induced a current by passing a current through a neighboring wire A]; when the principal current ceases, a shock is produced by the returning current of the natural electricity of the body." "Contributions II: Spiral Conductor," p. 230. Henry later ascribed the battery-induced shocks to the "induction of a secondary current in the battery itself. . . ." "Contributions IV: Electro-Dynamic Induction," pp. 10–11. Henry considered the inductive effect of the battery alone a novel discovery. See p. 229 of "Contributions II" and, below, Henry to Bache, February 9, 1835, footnote 8.

[3] The original has nothing but a ditto mark for this third result. We cannot say why Henry repeated his second conclusion.

[4] No further record of this experiment is known to us.

[5] His results are unknown. This is the reverse of the experiment by Nobili cited by Henry, in which a charge from a Leyden jar is sent through a coil. See above, "Queries in Reference to the Spark from Long & Short Coil," [August 1834], footnote 5.

[6] We are uncertain of Henry's reference. Although we know he relied heavily on Roget's *Treatises on Electricity, Galvanism, Magnetism, and Electro-Magnetism* (London, 1832), two copies of which survive in his library, the sections on "Galvanism" bear no notes or annotations of apparent relevance to self-induction. Nor do other volumes of similar title offer hints on possible experiments.

[7] The "alternative current" probably referred to inductive shocks produced in bodies arranged in parallel with the primary galvanic circuit. The phenomenon was alternatively referred to by Henry as the "lateral" or "collateral" shock. See footnote 2, above. Again, we have no further account of the experiment.

For one of his lecture-demonstrations at Princeton, Henry even proposed applying electricity to a horse and "an entire sheep." Henry notebook [23894].

[8] For some of Henry's results in this experiment and the one that follows on the relative strength of one and two poles, see the next document, "Fragment on Magnetic Induction." For Henry's possible plans for these experiments, see the "Fragment" and his letter to Harriet Henry, [May 1, 1835], footnote 4, below.

[9] Isaiah Lukens, identified in Green to Henry, February 13, 1834, footnote 1, above. Henry evidently intended first to magnetize the iron core of Chilton's magnet by touching it with Lukens's steel magnet. Then, to com-

ferrand relative to the current in a ring of copper. May there not be a current in the direction of the coil and also another in an opposite direction for an instant.[10]

Is the inductive action of magnets on currents greater or less than the induction of currents on currents. Try— It should be less since a current produces a greater effect on a magnet than on another current.[11]

---

pare the magnetizing power of the steel and galvanism, Henry would apply power through the ribbon windings.

[10] The relevant experiment seems to be from James Cumming's translation and edition of J. F. Demonferrand, *A Manual of Electro Dynamics, Chiefly Translated from the Manuel D'Électricité Dynamique* . . . (Cambridge, England, 1827). The fourth part deals with the interaction of conductors and Ampère's magnetic theory. To demonstrate that a current-carrying conductor induces magnetism in a neighboring conductor, Ampère, according to Demonferrand (pp. 147–148), suspended a circle of copper wire within a spiral conductor. When a current was sent through the spiral and a magnet presented to the movable copper ring, the ring oriented itself as "if it had been traversed by a current, passing in the same direction as that in the spiral." In his copy of the book Henry marked the passage stating Ampère's conclusion that ". . . *an electric current tends to induce magnetism in conductors in its vicinity, and that the induced electricity moves in the same direction as the current.*" The author was uncertain whether Ampèrian molecular currents allegedly in the copper ring were actually induced by the current in the spiral or were preexisting and simply reoriented in the act of magnetizing. This was a clear foreshadowing of volta-electric induction discovered by Faraday. Knowing of Faraday's demonstration that the induced currents were only instantaneous, Henry suggests that Ampère actually induced an instantaneous current when the spiral was connected with the battery and another (in the opposite direction) when disconnected.

Note also that the direction Ampère ascribed to the induced current was opposite to that reported by Faraday in his theory of "volta-electric induction." This apparent contradiction is discussed above in Henry's "Record of Experiments," August 22, 1834, footnote 12.

[11] From Henry's sketchy comments, we can only conjecture that his experiment involves some kind of qualitative comparison between electrical induction in a wire produced by approaching a magnet to the wire (magnetoelectric induction) and by transmitting current through a neighboring wire (volta-electric induction). Although his second statement would seem to involve some kind of reciprocal situation allowing him to argue from the apparent symmetry of the two effects, his statements are too ambiguous for precise interpretation. The action of currents on magnets may refer to galvanic currents reversing the poles of a steel magnet.

FRAGMENT ON MAGNETIC INDUCTION[1]

Henry Papers, Smithsonian Archives

[ca. February 1, 1835]

In my first paper on magnetic induction by galvanism I stated that there was a remarkable difference in the lifting power of one and two poles.[2]

[1] The precise nature of this manuscript fragment is unknown. It was originally found among Henry's miscellaneous notes on electricity and magnetism; surrounding notes provide no clues about its origins. There are signs that it might have once been part of a letter. The document, now filed among Henry's undated personal correspondence, consists of a single page, torn and apparently a quarter of a larger sheet. Henry wrote on the front and

This undoubtedly arises from the reaction between the magnet and the soft iron when the circuit is complete. The magnetic intensity is much increased on account of the ease of inductive action between the iron and Iron magnet. When a galvanic magnet is applied to steel moderatly hard the adhesion is not as great as between it and soft iron. The difference is astonishing as is shown in passing round a  circuit of two horseshoe bars a voltaic magnet where near the hardened poles the adheasion is scarcely nothing where in the middle the adhesion is very great. It would appear that although the intensity and the quanity of magnetism is very great it is easily moved.[3]

A strong steel magnet and a galvanic one do not act as two steel magnets or as two galvanic ones. The steel magnet will have its poles much sooner reversed by another steel magnet than by a galvanic one of much greater attractive power. I also believe that galvanic magnets do not act as powerfully on galvanic currents as steel magnets in proportion to the power.[4] A galvanic magnet is the stronger the shorter . . .[5]

---

back; at the bottom of the back is the following passage upside down:

> summer when I hope to visit the city as often as once a month.
>
> I have seen nothing of the pamphlets which you promised to send. The mail arrangements are in bad condition. It is probable that they have miscarried.

We do not know the intended recipient, but the words are reminiscent of other Henry letters talking about shuttling between Princeton and Philadelphia. Possibly he intended to send these thoughts to a Philadelphia friend; or he may simply have written down a draft of his ideas on a convenient scrap of paper that happened to have a draft of part of a letter.

Our conjectural dating of the document is based upon its apparent relationship to three queries posed at the end of Henry's "Record of Experiments," January 26, 1835, above. There, Henry asked questions about changes of polarity involving electromagnets and steel magnets; about the relative lifting powers of one and two poles of a magnet; and about the inductive actions of magnets and currents—precisely the array of questions Henry attempts to answer in this fragment. Since it appears that Henry already has experimental results to support the ideas in this document, we have placed it after the above notebook entry, arbitrarily at February 1.

We speculate that Henry was assembling some thoughts for a future publication, probably for the American Philosophical Society, although, to our knowledge, this particular array of ideas was never printed. Yet, there is clearly some relationship between the topics in this fragment and Henry's projected, but never realized, publication for the American Philosophical Society, discussed below in Henry's letter to his wife of May 1, 1835, footnote 4.

2 See Henry's "On the Application of the Principle of the Galvanic Multiplier to Electro-Magnetic Apparatus, and Also to the Development of Great Magnetic Power in Soft Iron, with a Small Galvanic Element," *Silliman's Journal*, 1831, *19*:406. There Henry was surprised to find that when both poles of his magnet could together lift 700 pounds, one pole alone supported no more than five or six pounds. In 1830 Henry had received a puzzled query about the phenomenon from Isaac Jackson. See *Henry Papers*, *1*:313–315.

3 Henry is apparently comparing the attraction at the two areas where the hardened poles meet with that at the apex of each horseshoe magnet. Presumably, the hardened poles interfered with the "ease of inductive action" between the soft iron of each magnet, resulting in a shift of the magnetic force away from the poles.

4 Henry had an abiding theoretical interest in the similarities and differences between different kinds of magnets, especially between electromagnets and others.

5 The fragment simply ends, and we cannot state just what Henry intended beyond this point.

February 7, 1835

COMMITTEE REPORT OF THE AMERICAN PHILOSOPHICAL SOCIETY

Archives, American Philosophical Society

February 7th. 1835.[1]

The Com. appointed on a paper by Prof. Henry entitled "Contributions to Electricity & Magnetism, Article First. Description of a Galvanic Battery for producing electricity of different intensities"[2] report that they consider the method employed by the author for combining in one instrument the means of obtaining the different effects of the Galvanic Battery to be ingenious & satisfactory, & they recommend the description for publication in the Transactions of the Society.

Respectfully Submitted
A. D. Bache
Robt Hare[3]

[1] According to APS minutes, the committee actually read its report at the Society's February 6 meeting. American Philosophical Society, *Early Proceedings of the American Philosophical Society . . . From the Manuscript Minutes of its Meetings From 1744 to 1838* (Philadelphia, 1884), pp. 665–666. We cannot say whether this document was simply misdated or written after the fact.

[2] Published in the APS *Transactions*, 1837, n.s. *5*:217–222. The paper was read before the Society on January 16, 1835. American Philosophical Society, *Early Proceedings* . . . , p. 664. The article was reprinted in Richard Taylor, ed., *Scientific Memoirs*, 1837, *1*:540–547, an influential British reprint journal, noted for translations of foreign articles, especially from the German.

[3] According to American Philosophical Society, *Early Proceedings* . . . , p. 664, Franklin Bache was also a referee.

TO JAMES HENRY

Family Correspondence, Henry Papers, Smithsonian Archives

Princeton Feby 9th 1835

My Dear James

Your letter and paper came to hand some days since but as usual my engagements have prevented my writing soonner. I fear Mother will be worrying again about us but she may be assured that I would write if any thing important should occur in our family. We are all well. The children in particular are enjoying very fine health. The girl can almost walk alone and manages very finely to cross the floor by pushing a chair before her. Her Mother bids me tell you that she is quite a prodigy, can say *papa, take care, See there* very plainly. The boy has lately acquired some enlarged views on the subject of commerce. He has become possessed of a sum of ready money equal in ammount to two cents and with these he has offered to purchase a coat for Papa a gown for Mamma and several other articles for the other members of the family. He can point out the place on a map of albany where grandmother Henry lives. Yesterday was another cold Sunday. The thermometer stood in the morning at −3 and at 12 oclock at +8. This day is somewhat warm. The mercury was at zero at sunrise and now (12 oclock) is at 19°. We had an alarm of fire on Sunday morning almost the first since our removal to Princeton. It occurred in Jolines Tavern[1] nearly opposite the college. Little damage was done and it was well that the fire was discovered before it got fairly under way or with the high wind and the inexperience and ineficiency of the fire men[2] of the place much damage would have been done. All was confusion and the engines unmanagable and each person vying with the other in crying fire fire without making any attemp of consequence to stop the flames. Nothing new to break the monotony of a Princeton winter except what we learn from the Papers and the letters from our friends.

I received the letter from Maine from Prof Cleaveland which you directed to be forwarded to me from Albany.[3] It is on the old subject of magnetism &c. Linn DeWitt is an inmate of our house and studies with me in the Philosophical Hall. He is doing very well and appears well pleased with his situation. I am sorry to learn that his brother Richard is likely to loose by DeWitt Bloodgood.[4] I see by the Albany paper that a lecture before the Young Mens Society[5] was postponed on account of the absence from the city of Orlando Meads Esq. The gentleman was at the time in New-Jersey *attending to some court business.*[6]

[1] Better known as the Nassau Inn. This structure, undergoing many changes, was operated as a hotel from 1769 to 1937, when it was razed to make room for Palmer Square and a modern Nassau Inn. The Inn was the site of many gala college functions and local celebrations. John Joline, "most popular of all the keepers of this famous inn," was the proprietor from about 1812 to 1835 or 1836. Varnum Lansing Collins, *Princeton, Past and Present,* 2d rev. ed. (Princeton, 1946), pp. xvi–xviii (quote from p. xviii). *Hageman,* 2:42–43.

[2] At this time, there were two private fire companies chartered in Princeton: the Princeton Fire Company and the Resolution Fire Company, incorporated in 1825 and 1833, respectively. *Hageman,* 2:21.

[3] Perhaps Cleaveland's letter of March 3, 1834, above. See footnote 1 to that document for speculation about the delay in Henry's receiving the letter.

[4] Richard Varick DeWitt and, perhaps, Simeon DeWitt Bloodgood (1799–1866), lawyer, author, merchant. *Herringshaw;* Munsell, *Ann. Alb.,* 8:105. We cannot identify the event Henry refers to. Since both Bloodgood and DeWitt were lawyers, Henry could refer to litigation, or even a minor local election. The event was not recorded in the Albany newspapers, nor in local histories. Probably R. V. DeWitt informed Henry of the matter on his recent visit at the Henry home. See above, Henry to James Henry, January 23, 1835.

[5] See above, Bullions to Henry, December 19, 1833, footnote 12.

[6] We cannot account for Henry's emphasis.

Harriet says that Nancy Mammy and yourself must shut up house and come to see us as soon as the river opens.

Dr Wing is a very clever man but has little concience in the way of charging. We find a great difference in the way of Drs bills between Princeton and Albany. Our whole bill for two and a quarter years attendance is about twenty dollars.[7] I am sorry to learn that our old friend Gibson[8] has failed.

Charlot Meads complains that there is much mischief between you and Louisa and that Harriet must [write?] you a lecture on the subject or something to that effect.

Your Brother
Joseph

Love from all to Mother & Nancy. Respects Mr Mc[Arthur] and the Meads family.

[7] Joel Wing (*Henry Papers, 1*:50n) was reportedly kinder to the poor, to whom "he was kind and liberal, bestowing upon them his best services without expectation or hope of reward." Munsell, *Ann. Alb., 9*:104.

[8] John Gibson. See above, Henry to James Henry, May 25, 1833, especially footnote 10.

TO ALEXANDER DALLAS BACHE[1]

Bache Papers, Smithsonian Archives

Princeton Feby 9th 1835

My Dear Sir

I wish to introduce your work on optics[2] as a class book in our college and now write to request that you will direct your publisher to send me as soon as possible 50 copies. Let them be delivered to the agent of the rail way at the Robi[n]son Crusoe Hotel in 3rd Street directed to me and entered on the waybill. It is desirable that I should deliver them to the class at as cheap a rate as possible and since 50 copies are ordered it is expected that the bookseller will give them at the trade price not however if your pecuniary interest is connected with the sale of the book.

[1] The document bears editorial notations by Mary Henry. Her partial transcription of the letter exists in the Henry Papers.

[2] In 1833 Bache published the first American edition of Sir David Brewster's *Treatise on Optics*. Bache's text was the first printed introduction of the undulatory theory of light into American colleges. His revision of Brewster included almost ninety pages of mathematical techniques for the analysis of refraction and reflection. The text was quickly and well received, going through several editions. (Henry may have ordered the new 1835 edition.) Two copies of the 1833 edition survive in the Henry Library. Stanley M. Guralnick, "Science and the American College, 1828–1860" (Ph.D. dissertation, University of Pennsylvania, 1969), p. 116.

What are you about in the way of science: as much engaged as ever? Have you made any further experiments on the production of electricity from a Nott's stove by means of a poplin and a silk shirt? In sober earnest I think that you could make a very interesting paper from the facts you mentioned together with some others which might be collected of the same class.[3] I neglected to mention while this subject was under discussion that Dr Torrey had communicated to me a fact of the same kind. He was called by a grocer in the upper part of the city of New York into his shop to see a new kind of an electrical machine which consisted of a common coffee mill. When this was turned a few times and the finger applied to the desending coffee or to a vessel underneath a shock was received. The electricity was probably produced by the friction of the coffee on itself or the sides of the vessel beneath.[4] A number of facts of the kind you described will serve to show the importance of guarding against many errors in delicate experiments in electricity. I believe that in some cases the mere working of a *condenser* is sufficient to generate electricity enough to charge the instrument.[5] In this point of view the publication would be useful.

Was my paper received in time for the meeting of the society. What disposition was made of it? Cannot both papers be published within a few weeks and thus save the necessity of an abstract? Do with it however what you think proper. Are my allusions to Mr Faraday in good taste and proper? I regret that my communication to the society produced other feelings in

[3] Bache published nothing on the subject, nor do his written replies to Henry shed light on his experiments. Apparently Bache attempted to draw sparks from the body of the stove. From published reports of an APS meeting several years later devoted to this and related subjects, we know that Bache was simply verifying someone else's experiments with the stove. Bache was inclined to discount the results, tracing the electricity to the shirt of the experimenter. Despite Bache, Henry later took the phenomena seriously. See APS *Proceedings*, 1838–1840, *1*:320–325, the minutes of the December 18, 1840, meeting.

At the time of this letter, Henry was chiefly interested in the effect as yielding possible clues to sources of error in delicate static electrical measurements. But he soon developed a serious theoretical interest in the subject as well. See the above-cited APS *Proceedings*, where Henry related the Nott stove to electricity generated from the formation of water vapor and from changes of state in general. See also Henry's letter to Torrey of March 7, 1835, below, where he proposes a set of experiments on similar effects. Henry's developing interest in these topics will emerge in future volumes of the *Henry Papers*.

[4] See also Henry's letter to Bache, May 18, 1835, below, for a further mention of the coffee mill.

[5] The purpose of the condenser, invented by Volta, was to collect weak electricity dispersed on a large body into a smaller body, where it could be concentrated, measured, and examined. See P. M. Roget, *Treatises on Electricity, Galvanism, Magnetism, and Electro-Magnetism* (London, 1832), sections 193–194 of the discussion "Electricity." The reference is in Henry's Library. The instrument was based on the static inductive action between two parallel metallic plates, one grounded and the other in contact with the body whose electricity is to be measured. One version of the instrument involved a nonconducting varnish coating to keep the plates apart. Electricity contracted by the varnish frequently interfered with the accuracy of the instrument.

reference to the announcement of my fact by Mr Faraday than I intended.[6]

I have lost the memorandum of the interesting fact you mentioned in reference to the effect produced by plunging one pole of a battery into a solution of some salt as discovered by Dr. Hare. If it be not too much trouble will you state it to me in writing.[7] Did you examine my 16th experiment or that which relates to the secondary shock from a galvanic battery of many pairs. Is this a new fact or has it been published before?[8] I would be pleased to [have] some criticism from the club on the speculations at the end of my paper.[9] I will expect the members to examine it and make such alterations as they may think proper.

You will I fear begin to think or rather I should say have cause to think that the club is of more cost than profit since I have made so many claims on your time in reference to my affairs and have done so little in the way of reciprocating the favours.

My Respects to Rogers, Espy and our friend Courtenay. I hope that he has recovered from his indisposition. You must not let him work too hard. Science has many claims on him which bad health must not be permitted to disappoint. If he will permit me to prescribe for the next attack I will order a trip to Princeton. My Respects to Mrs Bache.

Your Friend
Jos Henry

Yesterday (Sunday) was another day [well] suited in regard to temperature for Mr Espy's experiments on the dew point.[10] The thermometer at sunrise with us was −3, at 2 o'clock +8, and at 6 PM +7. This morning it stood at zero and now (12 oclock) 19°.

[6] Bache was not likely to think that Henry had been too strong on Faraday. If anything, he was more aggressive than Henry on the latter's priorities. Henry continued to be uneasy, especially after the inclusion of Bache's prefatory remarks. See his letter to Bache below, May 18, 1835.

[7] Bache apparently failed to answer Henry in writing and the contents of the memorandum, whether Bache's or Henry's, are unknown to us. Contemporary articles by Hare do not clarify this allusion.

[8] Henry's reference is at first puzzling. His "Contributions II: Spiral Conductor," to which he refers, lists only fifteen experiments. None of the enumerated experiments evidently utilized a battery of "many pairs," including no. 8 on the secondary shock. The unnumbered paragraph which follows the fifteenth, however, seems to be the one referred to by Henry. Perhaps this paragraph had been numbered as the sixteenth in Henry's original manuscript, the numbering having been dropped in the published version. The paragraph deals with what Henry considered a new effect—the production of self-inductive shocks without the use of the induction coils but with the battery alone. See "Contributions II: Spiral Conductor," pp. 228–229. For the experiment and Henry's tentative explanation of it, see above, "Record of Experiments," January 26, 1835, footnote 2. Bache apparently did not question the novelty of Henry's results. There appear to be no comparable experiments in the Faraday article Henry had recently seen.

[9] The final paragraphs of Henry's paper contain several speculations on the origins of the sparks and shocks from spiral conductors. These speculations, centering on Faraday's law of volta-electric induction and comparisons with static electricity, are discussed above, Henry to Bache, January 12, 1835, footnote 5.

[10] In the original, this appears in the margin

of the first page. Espy, a member of the "club," may have been preparing his article on the "Theory of Hail," *Journal of the Franklin Institute*, 1836, *17*:240–246. Here, in a number of places, Espy relates a general theory of storms, which he is developing, to dew point data.

FROM ALEXANDER DALLAS BACHE

Henry Papers, Smithsonian Archives

Sunday ev^{g} Feb^{r} 15. [1835][1]

My dear friend.

I have ordered the books as requested & the book seller promised to forward them on Saturday at furthest. I shall however send to him to-morrow morning & ascertain if he has fulfilled his word & if not urge him to send them at once. I ordered them from Carey & Hart, and have no pecuniary concern in the matter.[2]

Up to the eyes in work as usual, & this evening which is not a lawful working night a West Point friend[3] makes it out of the question for me even to wag a finger seriously for your service.

Your paper came in good time, viz. a week before a stated meeting of the Society. It will be reported upon next Friday & I am urgent with the Com. of Pub^{n} to dispose of the first which has been ordered for publication.[4] Dr Bache my stand-by has resigned from the Com.[5] but I will endeavour strenuously that your interests shall not suffer. The abstract was directed to be made & is already in type in the Journal of Institute, from whence I shall send you a slip in a few days; it is to go to Silliman & to the Advocate of Science published here.[6] The club have not met since you were with

[1] The document bears an identical date written in during Mary Henry's period, in our opinion. We have shifted the date given at the end of the letter to this position, adding the year given by Henry in his file notation. This is clearly a reply to Henry's letter of February 9, 1835, above.

[2] Apparently Bache was not getting royalties on sales from the publishing house of Carey and Hart.

[3] Unidentified.

[4] See the Committee Report of February 7, 1835, above, for the first, and the Report of February 20, 1835, below, for the second contribution.

[5] Franklin Bache was on the committee, an ad hoc body, considering Henry's two papers. On January 16, 1835, the Society appointed Isaac Lea, Isaac Hays, and Robert E. Griffith, Jr., to the Committee on Publication, a standing body. *Early Proceedings of the American Philosophical Society . . .* (Philadelphia, 1884), p. 665.

[6] Although the abstract appeared in *Silliman's Journal* (July 1835, *28*:327–329), Bache was not successful in getting it into the *Advocate of Science*. This journal was started in 1833 by William P. Gibbons (1812–1897). In August 1834 the title was enlarged to *The Advocate of Science and Annals of Natural History*. The last number appeared in April 1835. Under the motto, "Knowledge is power, happiness, virtue," Gibbons aimed at younger readers. He wrote in the first issue in 1833:

them. What means Doct. Torrey, he has not answered his letter of admission,[7] to make acknowledgment? Urge him in regard to the club which certainly originated in idea with him. All well.

Yours truly
A. D Bache

"To enlarge the boundaries of science by brilliant discoveries in any of its branches is not within our expectations. . . . What is the exclusive possession of scientific men, we shall strive to put in the possession of the unscientific. . . ." Given the audience, this stated goal, and the strong (but not exclusive) natural history inclination, Bache's choice might seem odd. True, Henry's friend Jacob Green contributed two essays in natural history and an article was reprinted at the suggestion of John Torrey. Henry himself had no direct contacts to our knowledge with the journal or its editor.

In issues of the *Advocate* in 1834 and 1835 are printed minutes of the proceedings of the Academy of Natural Sciences of Philadelphia. Bache appears in these reading his own and others' papers on topics far removed from natural history. He discussed Olmsted on meteor showers and read John William Draper on light and magnetism. Bache in this period apparently saw the Academy of Natural Sciences as a possibility for his kind of research. The printed minutes disclose the formation in the Academy of a Committee on Physics chaired by W. R. Johnson with Bache in its ranks. The Academy did not move in that direction. Bache, we assume, was mistakenly confident in his ability to get Gibbons to deviate from his editorial practice. The journal has interesting statements on the state of science in America. See also, George W. White, "The History of Geology and Mineralogy as Seen by American Writers, 1803–1835: A Bibliographic Essay," *Isis*, 1973, *64*:197–214, which discusses the *Advocate of Science* on pp. 209–211.

[7] i.e., to the American Philosophical Society. Henry apprised Torrey of Bache's annoyance in his letter of February 23, 1835, below.

FROM JOHN TORREY

Historic Letter File, Gray Herbarium Library, Harvard University

New York, Feby 18th 1835

My dear friend.

I wrote you a letter on the 29th of December last,[1] but no answer [to it] has yet been received. Perhaps it miscarried. I hope it did, for then you have a good excuse for not writing.

My course in the Medical College[2] is nearly completed for this season. It terminates on the 28th of the month. There are pretty good prospects of our obtaining a new building[3] in time for our next session. Our professors &

[1] Printed above. Parts of Torrey's letter of February 18 were published in A. Hunter Dupree, *Asa Gray, 1810–1888* (Cambridge, Massachusetts, 1959), p. 44 and in Andrew Denny Rodgers, *John Torrey: A Story of North American Botany* (Princeton, 1942), p. 113.

[2] The College of Physicians and Surgeons of New York, where Torrey taught chemistry and botany.

[3] See note 10 of Torrey's letter of January 16, 1835, above.

Trustees are to have a joint meeting this evening, & I hope we shall be able to make definite arrangements on the subject. If the college is not built next summer, I have some idea of renting my house for a year & hiring one at Princeton. Can one be obtained that would suit me—not *in* the Village? I would like to live in the "West End"—not because it is stylish, but because it is a pleasanter, & I think, a healthier situation than towards N. Brunswick.[4]

I informed you that I had a new pneumatic trough for the College under consideration. It is now completed, & will, I think, please you. The glass air holders perform admirably. The whole will cost not much short of $100, but it will last as long as the College stands.

I wished to be informed whether there is any prospect of Jaeger leaving the Institution. I wish we could find a place for my friend Dr Gray in the College. He is an uncommonly fine fellow & will make a great noise in the scientific world one of these days. It is good policy for the College to secure the services & affections of young men of talent, & let them *grow up* with the Institution. How would it do for Gray to be a Tutor or assistant in Chemistry? Dr Maclean[5] cannot have any desire now to be an assistant. It would injure him as a practitioner very much, & prevent him from taking a high stand in his profession. Besides he is not exactly calculated for the situation. If the College prospers & the classes increase, an assistant will be needed in my department & it appears to me that he might also be a Tutor.[6] Gray has a capital Herbarium & collection of minerals. He un[der]stands most of the branches of Natural History well, & in Botany he has few Superiors. You know that he is my ass^t in Chem^y, but I cannot afford to retain him with my present income.

I had a letter from Johnny Vaughn yesterday. The old man[7] wishes me to make some remarks on Nuttall's[8] botanical paper[9] for Dr Short of Kentucky,[10] one of the subscribers to the Phil. Trans.[11]

[4] John Torrey ended up renting a house in the country near New Brunswick after all, according to his letter to Henry of June 22, 1835, Henry Papers, Smithsonian Archives.

[5] George Maclean had assisted Henry in giving the chemistry classes in 1833 while Torrey was in Europe, and then went on to build up a medical practice in Princeton. See note 1 of October 9, 1833, above.

[6] Gray was not appointed at Princeton. See note 6 of Henry's letter to Torrey, November 18, 1834, for the course of his career.

[7] John Vaughan was seventy-nine years old at this time. Although his titles at the American Philosophical Society were Librarian and Treasurer, he functioned in fact as general manager for the organization. See note 4 of November 1, 1833, above.

[8] Thomas Nuttall (1786–1859) was apprenticed as a youth to a printer in Liverpool, England, and received a scanty formal education. He immigrated to Philadelphia in 1808 and studied botany there with Benjamin Smith Barton. Nuttall explored the American South for new plants, and in 1818–1820 headed west to the Arkansas territory to gather specimens. He was curator of the Harvard Botanical Garden from 1822 to 1834, and was also an active member of the Academy of Natural Sciences of Philadelphia. He published *A*

February 18, 1835

I purpose making a visit to Princeton shortly so you must brush up your jimcracks & prepare for an inspection. Why have none of the Princetonians been here this winter? Will you not come soon?

I have no time to write more, 'though I have much to say. Write soon & believe me yours truly

John Torrey

Prof. Jos. Henry. F.A.P.S.?[12]

Manual of Ornithology of the United States and Canada in 1832, a book popular for its clarity, cheapness, and portability relative to the lush, cumbrous, and expensive works of John James Audubon and Alexander Wilson. Nuttall also wrote several papers on mineralogy, one of which included an early correlation (1820) of rock formations by means of fossils. Nuttall accompanied the Wyeth expedition from St. Louis to Oregon in 1834–1835, and then explored the Pacific Coast for plants, returning via Hawaii and Cape Horn. In 1842 he returned to England and devoted the rest of his life to growing rare plants on an estate he had inherited. *DAB.*

[9] Nuttall had read "Collections Towards a Flora of the Territory of Arkansas" to the American Philosophical Society on April 4, 1834; the monograph appeared in the Society's *Transactions*, 1837, n.s. 5:139–203. This paper, which presented the botanical findings of Nuttall's explorations in 1818–1820, had been promised to the Society since 1821. Scientists such as Short and Torrey also had collections of plants sent in by explorers from the Arkansas region, and were anxious to see what Nuttall would come up with for new species. Jeannette Graustein, *Thomas Nuttall, Naturalist: Explorations in America, 1808–1841* (Cambridge, Massachusetts, 1967), pp. 157, 285, 288, 290, and 292.

[10] Charles Wilkins Short (1794–1863) graduated from Transylvania University in Lexington, Kentucky in 1810. He received an M.D. from the University of Pennsylvania in 1815 after completing a dissertation on a botanical subject. Short taught medical botany and served as dean of the faculty at Transylvania from 1825 to 1837, and was a professor at the Medical Institute in Louisville from 1838 to 1848. He then retired to a plantation to work on botany, continuing to publish catalogs and taxonomic papers on trans-Allegheny species and to exchange and grow plants. He willed his personal collection of over 15,000 specimens to the Academy of Natural Sciences of Philadelphia. During the years of 1830 to 1835 alone, Short estimated that he and two other Kentucky botanists distributed over 25,000 plants to American and European collectors. (*DAB.*) Other botanists such as Torrey and later George Engelmann of St. Louis also served as exchange agents, and found much of their time taken up in the process. Joseph Henry rationalized and streamlined these operations by setting up an international network through the Smithsonian Institution, freeing scientists to research rather than to function as mailmen.

[11] The *Transactions* of the American Philosophical Society, not the British *Philosophical Transactions.*

[12] Fellow American Philosophical Society. As with "Phil. Trans." Torrey is mocking the Society's admiration of overseas scientific institutions.

February 20, 1835

COMMITTEE REPORT OF THE AMERICAN PHILOSOPHICAL SOCIETY

Archives, American Philosophical Society

Friday Febr^{y} 20th. 1835.[1]

The Com. on Prof. Henry's paper in relation to the effect of the interposition of a long conductor between the poles of a galvanic battery, on the production of the spark, shock &^{c} report that the subject and the experimental investigation of it now presented are worthy of the attention of the Society, and recommend the paper of Prof. Henry for publication in the Transactions of the Society.[2]

A. D. Bache
Robt Hare
Franklin Bache

[1] This date occurs at the lower left-hand corner of the original manuscript.

[2] This report concerns "On the Influence of a Spiral Conductor in Increasing the Intensity of Electricity from a Galvanic Arrangement of a Single Pair, Etc.," APS *Transactions*, 1837, n.s. 5:223–231 ("Contributions II: Spiral Conductor"), the second of a series of papers on electricity and magnetism which Henry presented to the American Philosophical Society. At the January 16, 1835, meeting of the Society, Henry read "Contributions I: Battery" and made a "verbal communication" of this paper, supplemented by experimental production of sparks. At the February 6, 1835, session which approved the report of the committee on the battery paper, A. D. Bache read the full paper which was referred to the same committee (A. D. Bache, Franklin Bache, Robert Hare). For some reason, this report was not presented at the February 20, 1835, meeting but on March 6. *Early Proceedings of the American Philosophical Society* . . . (Philadelphia, 1884), pp. 664–668.

TO JAMES HENRY

Family Correspondence, Henry Papers, Smithsonian Archives

Princeton Fe^{by} 23rd 1835

Dear James

We are all well nothing new amoung us. All things go on as usual. Your letters were received. We have had another cold time but have managed to keep quite comfortable with our Notts stove. The weather has been very fine for my experiments on electricity. I am now on that part of my course.[1]

[1] According to a complete set of student notes taken in 1846–1847, Henry broke his physics course at Princeton into nine sections, of which electricity and magnetism comprised the sixth or seventh, depending on whether he covered sound before or after those topics. He gave seventy-five lectures in the course, eighteen of which were on electricity and magnetism. We assume the early course followed a similar pattern. Weiner, "Joseph Henry's Lectures," pp. 70–73 and 148–206.

To day we have the renewed appearance of winter and the ground is again covered with snow.

I suppose the most prominent topic of discourse about these days with you as with us is the prospect of the French War. It does not however appear to me that we will have a War in earnest.[2] I believe & hope it will blow over. I am some what interested in the affair since there is a prospect of an addition to our Phil. apparatus which I wish purchased in France and which could not be procured in case of a War. I wish you would procure a copy of the Annual report of the Regents of the University as soon as it is published.[3] I received a few days since the Report of the committee of the Trustees of Union College relative to the affair of Dr Nott. The committee exhonorate the Dr from all blame and say that he has acted with sagasity and an eye to the wellfare of the Institution over which he presides.[4] The affair has thus far turned out as I expected. The Dr will not readily be found tripping. The children are quite well. The Girl has been somewhat restless for some nights past on account of cutting her teeth. The Dr[5] lanced her gums this morning and since then she has been more quiet. She can almost talk and is quite dexterous in the use of her limbs in the way of creeping &c.

The boy says that he intends to buy Mother a box for her smoking[6] and

[2] Napoleon had seized and destroyed American ships for several years after 1805. After long negotiations, the French agreed in 1831 to pay damages of 25,000,000 francs in six installments. However, the Chamber of Deputies refused to appropriate funds for the first installment in April 1834, and Andrew Jackson suggested in December that French property in America be seized in retaliation. He also asked Congress for authority and funds to build up the navy and coastal fortifications preparatory to war, a measure successfully disputed by his Whig opponents. The matter died down in December 1835 after Jackson offered an explanation which the French accepted as an apology and after the Chamber voted funds to pay the claims. Thomas Bailey, *A Diplomatic History of the American People*, 8th ed. (New York, 1969), pp. 195–198.

[3] The Regents submitted their report to the legislature on February 27. It was published as *New York Senate Documents*, 57th Session, 1834, No. 70. As usual, the report contained meteorological data of interest to Henry as well as summaries of the activities of state-supported colleges and academies.

[4] Henry refers here to the interminable dispute between Eliphalet Nott and the businessmen who conducted the state-sanctioned lottery on which Union depended for revenue. John B. Yates, Archibald McIntyre, and the other lottery managers sued Nott and the College in 1834 for interference with contract specifications. Codman Hislop, *Eliphalet Nott* (Middletown, Connecticut, 1971) treats the controversy in exhaustive detail.

William L. Marcy, Silas Wright, Jr., and John P. Cushman comprised the special committee of the Trustees. On November 22, 1834, they told the Trustees that "the course of the President . . . has been marked by fairness and liberality toward the contractors, and by firmness, sagacity, and disinterested zeal for the interests of the College . . . the full powers with which he was invested by the trustees, have been exercised with wisdom and restraint. . . ." *Report of a Select Committee of the Trustees of Union College, in Relation to the Pending Controversy with Yates and McIntyre* [Schenectady, 1834], p. 8.

[5] Probably Samuel Ladd Howell, the physician who treated the Henry family in Princeton.

[6] Rachel Jackson, wife of the President, had smoked a pipe, but arbiters of Washington society ridiculed her for it. Pipe smoking was

that he will put it down on the hearth beside her when he goes to Albany. He has had some queer speculations lately on the groth of trees and is very anxious to know who made them and how they are made. The rain a few days since covered all objects with so thick a coating of ice that the limbs of many of the trees in the campus were broken by the weight. The Boy after asking his Mother where the being lived who made the trees said very seriously then He will have to come from Heaven to mend the trees broken by the ice in the campus.

Mother must have been much delighted to see old Uncle John.[7] We are happy to learn that he is quite smart. Has he completed the bargain with regard to the selling of [the] farm. I was much pleased to learn that our old Friend Dr Campbell has received the appointment of Surveyor General.[8] I presume he will live in Albany at least a part of his time & I hope to have the pleasure of meeting with him sometimes. I see by a Schenectady paper published by G. Yates[9] and sent to Stephen that Dean is giving a course of lectures on Phrenology[10] in that city and that his lectures are attracting much attention.

I have communicated two papers of a series to the American Philosophical Society which have been well received and ordered printed in their transactions.

John Turnbull left here for Edinburgh last Autum and I sent with him a package to some scientific gentlemen of that city. About 3 months since I received a letter from a person in New York by the name of Hart sta[ting] that he had a package from Turnbull for me th[at] he would send by any person I might direct. I wrote requesting him either to leave it at Jacksons the bookseller Maiden Lane or to send it by the Post Office. I have heard nothing [so] far from him and have been so unfortunate as to loose his address. I am some what anxious to know what the package contains.

Linn DeWitt is well and is kept pretty closely to his books. You may men-

---

not uncommon among women in the 1830s and earlier, especially on the frontier. John S. Bassett, *The Life of Andrew Jackson*, 2 vols. (Garden City, New York, 1911), 2:461.

[7] John Alexander (1760–1841) of Galway, the twin brother of Joseph's mother Ann Henry. "Alexander Genealogy."

[8] William Campbell (1767 or 1768–1844), whom Henry knew from his work on the road survey (*Henry Papers, 1*:100).

[9] Giles F. Yates bought the defunct Schenectady County *Whig* and used its fonts and presses to begin the *Reflector and Schenectady Democrat* in December 1834. Under Yates's aegis as publisher, the weekly included news and feature pieces on the history and daily life of the town and its environs. He sold the paper in 1838 and it continued to thrive in other hands. George R. Howell and John H. Munsell, eds., *History of the County of Schenectady, N.Y., from 1662 to 1886* (New York, 1886), p. 138.

[10] Amos Dean, the Albany lawyer, had a special interest in medical topics (see note 1 of the letter of December 21, 1832, above). A copy of Dean's *Lectures on Phrenology Delivered Before the Young Men's Association for Mutual Improvement of the City of Albany* (Albany, 1834) is in the Henry Library.

tion this to his Brother[11] should you see him. I have urged him to write but he does not seam much disposed to inform his relatives concerning his situation. Give our love to Mother and Nancy.

Your Brother
Joseph

Motherinlaw, Aunt Nancy and the rest send their love to Mother and Nancy and wish to be rem[em]bered to the Meads family.

[11] Richard Varick DeWitt (*Henry Papers, 1*:62).

TO JOHN TORREY

Torrey Papers, Library, New York Botanical Garden

Princeton Feby 23[rd] 1835

My Dear Friend

Your letters[1] have been received and I have not the excuse you were so kind as to hope for me. I will not attempt an apology for my procrastination but merely state that the present session has been one of the most laborious periods of my life. You know that I am pressing on with my course so as to leave the field entirely to you during the next summer.

I have been twice at Phil[a] and on my return have been obliged to do double duty inorder not to fall behind in the prescribed course of lectures & recitations. Besides this I have submitted two papers to the Phil Society of which we were at the same time made members. The First paper is a description of my battery described as an instrument of research and to be refered to in my suceeding articles. My second paper is the second of a series which I intend to communicate under the head of Contributions to Elect. and Magnetism; it is an account of my experiments on the spark &c produced by connecting the poles of a battery of a single pair of plates. I announced the first fact of this phenominon in Sillimans journal for 1832 and in the Nov number of the Annals of Philos. Mr Farraday mentions the same fact without however noticing my publication. This induced me to arrange my experiments for publication and in so doing many new suggestions were presented to my mind which required imediate testing by direct experiment. The result was that the subject grew very rapidly under

[1] Torrey's letters of December 29, 1834, January 16, 1835, and February 18, 1835, printed above, which Henry had not had time to answer prior to this letter.

my investigations and has opened quite a field of research. I have given to the society all my labours up to this time and must dismiss the subject from my thoughts until the next vacation when if it please Providence I intend resuming my experiments. You will see by the above that my procrastination in your case has not been from want of inclination but from the belief that I would have more leisure in a few days.

With regard to Mr Jager[2] I have heard nothing about his leaving Princeton. He is now married and I think has learned something of the value of the situation which he occupies and will not be quick to leave; he appears to me to be more prudent than formerly and has need to be so since he has lost his situation at Lawrenceville[3] which lessens his income by the sum of 400 dollars. I have no doubt that Dr Gray would be an acquisition to the college and from my intercourse with him at your house I have formed a high opinion of his mind and acquirements and would do all in my power consistant with what I might deem my duty to others, to forward his interest but at present I see no indication of a change in our arrangements for the present year. All our Tutors will remain and no new post will probably be created at the next meeting of the Trustees. They will do nothing in anticipation of the success of the 100,000 dol. subscription as that is an affair of the Alumni Assosciation.[4] We will confer on this subject when you come to Princeton.

I am anxious to see your *ne plus ultra* of a pneumatic Trough—some arrangement must be made to pay for it. The appropriation must come directly from the Trustees as an extra to the chemical department.[5] My family as well as myself will be much rejoiced if you will make arrangements to remove to Princeton. Mr Mclean says that there is a house to let near the Seminary. Several new buildings have been erected during the last Autumn and I hope you will be able to procure one to answer your purpose.

I received a letter a few days since from Bache who wishes me to hint to you that a letter of acceptance to the Society would be in order.[6] I gave mine in person at the time of making my communication.[7]

As I hope soon to see you in Princeton I will defer other communications until we meet. I must however trouble you with a commission for me which I fear will give you some labour in executing.

About two or three months since I received a letter from a person in New

[2] For Benedict Jaeger, see above, Henry to Harriet Henry, April 6, 1833, footnote 4. Torrey had been suggesting that it would be nice if Jaeger were to leave Princeton and make room for Asa Gray.

[3] The Lawrenceville School, founded in 1810 and still in existence. Roland J. Mulford, *History of the Lawrenceville School, 1810–1935* (Princeton, 1935).

[4] For the fund-raising drive, see the Trustees' Minutes of April 9, 1834, especially footnote 6, printed above.

[5] See the Trustees' Minutes of April 15, 1835, printed below, for the appropriation.

York named *Hart* stating that he had received a package[8] for me from our mutual Friend *John Turnbull* from Edinburgh, that he did not like to send the package by the ordinary conveyance and that he would retain it until I sent for it or would dispose of it as I should direct. I first sent to the No directed, by one of the students who found the house of a Mr Hart as directed in south street but could learn nothing of a package for me. He did not however *mention* the name of John Turnbull.

I next wrote to Mr Hart requesting him to leave it at Jacksons bookstore Maiden Lane[9] and then sent to Jacksons by Prof Dod[10] and gave him Harts letter. The package had not been received at Jacksons & unfortunately Prof Dod gave me the letter in a moment of hurry at the rail road just as I was starting in an oposite direction to him for Phil[a]. I lost the letter & do not reccollect the address of Hart and am unacquainted with his person. He says in his letter that he had an introduction to me some time since but that I probably do not recollect him. Were I in New York I think I could find Mr Hart by calling on some of the friends of Turnbull or at his late boarding house.

Turnbull is a young Scotchman who resided some time in Albany and afterwards kept a lottery office in New-York. He sailed last summer for Edinburgh and took a package for me to Prof. Forbes.[11] He is intimate at Rawdon Wright &c engravers in the Exchange building[12] and it is probable that some one in their establishment can tell where Mr Hart is to be found. The student with whom I first sent states that the house he called at was a

[6] In his letter to Henry of February 15, 1835, Bache had expressed annoyance that Torrey had not acknowledged his election to the American Philosophical Society.

[7] Henry had attended the January 16, 1835, meeting of the American Philosophical Society to present his "Contributions I" and give an abstract of "Contributions II." The proceedings note that he was introduced as a new member at this time. *Early Proceedings of the American Philosophical Society . . . From 1744 to 1838* (Philadelphia, 1884), p. 664.

[8] Forbes sent this package to Henry on September 21, 1834, by way of John Turnbull (for whom see *Henry Papers, 1*:355n). Its contents, as described in Forbes's letter to Henry of May 26, 1835, included the needle Henry had sent to Forbes on June 30, 1834, Forbes's observations with Henry's needle, a needle Forbes was sending Henry, and some pamphlets. In this letter, and in a letter to his brother James of the same date, Henry describes the causes for the delay in receiving the package. George Hart, mentioned by Turnbull in his letter to Henry of September 23, 1834, seems to have been the culprit. His correspondence with Henry does not survive. By March 2, 1835, Torrey had the package and on April 2, 1835, Henry wrote Torrey that he had finally received it. Although Forbes wrote Henry on May 26, 1835, to inquire whether the package had arrived, Henry did not reply until June 7, 1836, when he apologized for the delay and explained the reasons.

[9] William Jackson is listed as a bookseller at 71 Maiden Lane in the New York City Directory for 1834–1835. His letterhead describes him as a publisher, an importer of English books, and "Agent for all the Publications of the Society for the Diffusion of Useful Knowledge." Receipt of September 11, 1835, in Librarian's Reports, 1832/33–1847, Princeton University Archives.

[10] Albert Baldwin Dod.

[11] See Henry's letter to Forbes of June 30, 1834, printed above.

[12] See above, Clark to Henry, April [15], 1834, footnote 4.

grocery in south street not a very respectable looking place & on that account he did not make as many inquiries as he might have done. He did not ask for a package from John Turnbull but merely for one for Prof Henry.

I am somewhat vexed to have a package laying for 3 months in a city so near without being able to get it. I have lately sent by Mr Philips[13] but he returned to Lawrencevill without giving me any information relative to his researches. If it be not asking too much will you make some inquiries of Rawdon & endeavour to find the said Hart. I wrote for him to send it by mail. Perhaps it may have been left at Jacksons. Should you be so fortunate as to find the article bring it with you when you come to Princeton. P.S. I will send this letter by the bookseller Mr D'Hart.[14] If you can make a search for the package he will take charge of it. I will make some inquiries respecting a house. Mrs Solimans[15] is about to remove to the Pavillion near Jugtown, the house which you & Mrs. T. inspected last summer.

The House which she leaves will probably be vacant. You would not perhaps be pleased with that location although I think it a pleasant one. Dr Carnahan has purchased the farm on which you lived last summer. He will rent you the house and garden for 130 dollars a year. Also I am informed that the house occupied by Canves White[16] will be to let in a few weeks. I will [make] further inquiry.

Your Friend
Jos. Henry

I forgot to state as an item of intelligence that we have an extra servent about college. He is a carpenter and has been of great assistance in my lectures in making wood articles; he works better than any carpenter in the village. We will keep him if possible for your use the next summer.

If I do not write often I give good measure when I do write as you will allow before you have decyphered the whole of this scrall.

What is the *use* of a friend unless you can *use* him says an old proverb.

[13] Alexander Hamilton Phillips (1804–1880) was Principal of the Lawrenceville School at this time. He graduated from Union College in 1825, attended the Princeton Theological Seminary from 1826 to 1829, and became Co-principal of Lawrenceville in 1832, buying the school two years later. In 1837 he sold the school and moved to Victoria, Texas, where he became a prominent lawyer. Roland J. Mulford, *History of the Lawrenceville School, 1810–1935* (Princeton, 1935), pp. 25, 28, 35–36.

[14] William D'Hart had a stationery and book store in Princeton and was also involved in publishing. Varnum Lansing Collins regrets "the absolute silence of local history as to the personalities of [D'Hart and others.]" *Early Princeton Printing* (Princeton, 1911), pp. 23–24.

[15] Perhaps Mrs. Susan Salomans. See above, Henry to Harriet Henry, December 13, 1832, footnote 5.

[16] Canvass White (1790–1834) had died in December 1834. At the time of his death he was chief engineer of the Delaware and Raritan Canal and was considered to be "in the first rank of American civil engineers of his day." He had worked for nine years on the Erie Canal as the assistant of Benjamin Wright. Thereafter until his death, he held various important engineering posts. *DAB.*

I have given you a commission which I fear will afford you much trouble yet my wife wishes me to make a farther draught on your kindness & to request that you will bring for her a few quarts of the dried cherries which we had last summer from your city.

FROM JOHN TORREY

Historic Letter File, Gray Herbarium Library, Harvard University

College of Phys & Surgs, New York. [March][1] 2nd 1835

My dear friend

Seated at the table in our Examination Hall, I feel that I cannot wile away the time more agreeably than in writing you a few lines. Your letter of the 23rd ult came to hand on Saturday & this morning Mr. Hart (as I suppose) came into my laboratory to tell me that he had a parcel for you, enquiring whether I expected to have an opportunity of sending it to Princeton shortly. I sent for it at once, & it is now lying on the table at my side. I know not where to find your Mr D'Hart, or I would send it by him. He dropped your letter to me into the post office. Dr Rhinelander says that he will send to Princeton on Wednesday, & perhaps I will entrust the parcel to him.

So you mean that I shall not be idle next summer! You must not expect me to lecture much oftener than I did last summer—not that I wish to be idle—but the young men must have time to study the subject, & to attend recitations. Pray let us have the text books[2] in readiness this year. I will ascertain in time, whether there will be a new edition of Turner out before the course commences.

I wrote to Bache last week, & returned thanks for my election. It is not probable that I shall send them a paper very soon for I have work on my hands that is hardly the thing they want, & besides, my botanical memoirs are pledged for the Lyceum.[3]

[1] Torrey mistakenly dated this letter "Feby." This communication is practically a point-by-point response to Henry's letter to Torrey of February 23, 1835, printed above. Henry's response to Torrey is below, March 7, 1835. This letter is printed, with minor variations, in Nathan Reingold, ed., *Science in Nineteenth-Century America* (New York, 1964), pp. 49–51, using Torrey's mistaken date.

[2] Torrey used Edward Turner's *Elements of Chemistry*. Franklin Bache brought out the fifth American from the fifth London edition in 1835, a copy of which Henry added to his library in 1837. But Torrey was compelled to use remainders of a previous edition for his 1835 course. See below, Torrey to Henry, April [23–24], 1835.

[3] Torrey at this time was serving as second vice president of the Lyceum of Natural History of New York. He had already published

I should like to work with you on Electricity.[4] When will you conclude your experiments? Do post up all your discoveries & secure them in the *Phil Trans*, & then begin a fresh score. Has Farady anticipated any more of your results?

Really I am sorry that Gray cannot obtain a place in Princeton, for I *know* he would be a great acquisition. He has no superior in Botany—considering his age—& any subject that he takes up he handles in a masterly manner. He will stay with me till I go to Princeton, & then I know not what arrangements to make with him. Surely Jaeger cannot live in Princeton on his present salery, if he was sore pinched when he had two situations! I would not on any account drive him away, though I think he is of very little use to us, but if he *should* take it into his head to leave us, why I should like to see a very good man in his place.

Cherries! Cherries! Cherries! You shall have some if they are to be got—I mean Mrs. Henry shall—for I would not hunt them up for you, as much as I care for you. I have several times looked for some for myself, but I could find none that pleased me. There are some to be had with the *stones* in them, but they are not so good as the others. Tomorrow, or the next day, I will make a fresh search for some.

The pneumatic trough is in my laboratory. I think it best not to have it varnished till it reaches Princeton, for it may get bruised in the transportation. You must not expect to see anything *very grand*, or you will be disappointed. It is a good article, however, & will not disgrace the college, as the old one did. I shall have [it] packed shortly, & take it on with me, for I must visit Princeton when our examination is over. *Then* I hope to make arrangements for the accomodation of my family during our residence there.

It was a good thought to hire a tinker for a servant. Pray hold on to him till I come, & then the fellow can't go if he will. He shall have his hands full. I would rather have a worker in metals than in wood. You don't say whether you will take the large shears.[5] I can get an excellent pair—quite large—for $6!

It is time for me to stop, as it is nearly my turn to examine. Present my regards to Mrs Henry, & remember me to all our friends in Princeton.

Yours very truly,
John Torrey

---

five articles on botany and mineralogy in the *Annals* of the Lyceum, the earliest appearing in 1824. Three additional articles of his appeared in the *Annals* subsequently.

[4] Henry was anxious to collaborate with Torrey. See below, Henry's reply of March 7, 1835.

[5] A reference to Torrey's offer to buy tin shears in his letter to Henry of January 16 1835, printed above.

March 2, 1835

FROM ROBERT HARE

Henry Papers, Smithsonian Archives

Wistar Party[1]

Dr Hare requests the pleasure of Professor Henry's company on Saturday evng. next.

Philad[a] March 2nd [1835][2]

[1] See Henry's letter to his wife of November 1, 1833, above, footnote 10, for Wistar Parties.

[2] From Henry's file notation on verso.

TO JOHN TORREY

Torrey Papers, Library, New York Botanical Garden

Princeton March 7th 1835

Dear Friend

Your letter[1] was received on Wednesday last. We expet to see you next week and I will then manage to have some leisure to talk with you on all the affairs of the college &c &c. I now write to request that you will call at Jacksons Maiden lane and bring with you a package of books which is there waiting for an opportunity. I am much in want of them. I have not received the *package* and therefore conclude that you will bring it with you.[2]

I would like very much to commence a series of experiments on electricity with you particularly on electricity developed by pressure *freezing, contact, animal action, atmospheric electricity &c* &c. Also the subject of excitement in different gases.[3] For these experiments we could easily fit up

[1] Torrey's letter of March 2, 1835, is printed above.

[2] Jackson is identified in note 9 of Henry's letter to Torrey, February 23, 1835, printed above. We do not know what books Henry had ordered. "The *package*" contained data and instruments for terrestrial magnetism sent by James David Forbes from Scotland.

[3] We find no evidence that Henry and Torrey collaborated on these experiments. They did share laboratory results from work each had done alone; many of Henry's scientific notebook entries include ideas on improving apparatus and experiments which he had learned from Torrey. Torrey did not publish any articles on static electricity.

Henry had an abiding interest in some of the subjects he listed here. In other letters (especially to Bache and Torrey), he mentioned static electricity generated from clothing, laboratory equipment, and household items such as coffee mills. Henry and Bache discussed sparks drawn from coal-burning stoves at a meeting of the American Philosophical Society on December 18, 1840 (APS *Proceedings*, 1838–1840, *1*:320–325). By the time of this letter to Torrey, Henry had already speculated on the variability of elec-

a room and dry it perfectly by strong sulphuric acid or some other absorbent of vapour.

I have been studying with some success the art of manipulating in delicate experiments of the kind in my present course on electricity.[4] We could soon cut out the labour of years.

There is some prospet of having an addition to the rear of the Phil. Hall in the way of a prop. Some rooms might be made which would be admirable for exp. & study. Come on and urge the importance of the project and help to plan for the improvement of the whole affair.[5]

Nothing very lately has been heard from Newell. He received a subscription of about 3 thousand dollars in Washington. He is now in Phil^a^.[6]

Mr Maclean intended to go to N.Y. this week but has been prevented by a swollen face—he suffers much with bad teeth. You do not say anything about the Dr's House. He has not let it yet and wishes to know what your intention is in reference to it.[7]

I have a class to meet in a few minutes and must therefore be very brief.

Yours Sincerely
Jos. Henry

P.S. You will not be expected to lecture more often than before. I wish to complete my course so that we may have no double lecturing at or towards the close of the session as in the case of last year. J H.

---

tricity generated in the presence of different gases (see the notebook entry for September 1, 1834, printed above). Throughout Henry's Albany and Princeton notebooks, especially [6123] and [7171], are reading notes and ideas for experiments on the topics which Henry suggested to Torrey. These subjects also appear in Henry's classroom lectures and demonstrations, and constitute a frequent theme in correspondence with scientific colleagues. Eventually, physical scientists of Henry's era hoped to find enough analogies and identities among forms of electricity to make possible a grand synthesis of how such forces operated in nature and in the laboratory.

4 Although Henry jotted down experiments used to illustrate his lectures on electricity in notebook [23894], we have found no evidence of what improvements he might have made at this time in "manipulating" in experimental demonstrations.

5 The renovation and additions to Philosophical Hall would become a preoccupation for Henry in the months ahead. Torrey served as a sounding board for his colleague's ideas and frustrations throughout the process of change.

6 On Daniel Newell and the attempt to increase the Princeton endowment, see notes 6 and 9 to the Trustees' Minutes, April 9, 1834, printed above.

7 Henry mentioned in his letter of February 23 that James Carnahan, President of Princeton, had bought the house which Torrey had rented the year before and was willing to lease it. Torrey had not indicated any interest in the place in his response to Henry of March 2. Eventually, Torrey stayed at another house (see note 4 of Torrey's letter of February 18, 1835, above).

March 9, 1835

TO HENRY DARWIN ROGERS

William Barton Rogers Papers, Archives, Massachusetts Institute of Technology

Princeton March 9th 1835

My Dear Sir

I know that you must be very anxious to learn something relative to the Geological survey[1] and I am sorry that I can give you no definite information with regard to the final result. Mr Field[2] was not in town until the last of last week. He informed me that the bill provides 1000 dollars for the first years work and gives the power of appointment to the Governor.[3] No person had been appointed on Friday last although some names had been mentioned. Mr F. has reccommended you strongly to the Governor and has placed in his hands your paper on the survey of the state together with a letter from me stating your qualifications[4] &c.

The probability is strongly in favor of your being appointed although I do not wish you to be too confident as I know not what influences may operate in the State of New Jersey to influence the Governors choice. Be assured that you have my warmest wishes for your success and that My Friend Mr Field has done all he could to promote your interest. Mr Field is not on the same side in Politics with the Governor although I do not think that will have much influence yet it might perhaps be well for you to get a letter from some Scientific gentleman of Philadelphia addressed to the

[1] On February 26, 1835, the New Jersey Legislature passed a bill authorizing a geological and mineralogical survey of the state. The principal source for information about this first New Jersey survey is George P. Merrill, ed., *Contributions to a History of American State Geological and Natural History Surveys* (United States National Museum Bulletin 109, Washington, 1920), pp. 307–309.

[2] Richard Stockton Field (1803–1870, *DAB*). A graduate of the College (1821) and a resident of Princeton, Field pursued law and politics. He served in the New Jersey Assembly, 1833–1838, then as Attorney-General of the State, 1838–1841. Subsequently he worked in Stockton family businesses (the Camden and Amboy Railroad and the Delaware and Raritan Canal Company), served in the State Constitutional Convention of 1844, and became professor of law at the College. From 1855 to 1870 he was the first President of the product of his longtime advocacy, the State Normal School. He also served briefly in the United States Senate (1862–1863) and as a United States District Court Judge, 1863 until his death.

At the time of this letter Field was active on the legislative committee responsible for the survey bill (see the next document, Henry to Green, March 16, 1835). A few surviving letters and a copy of an 1853 Field address in the Henry Library are fragmentary evidence of Henry's and Field's cordial and enduring relationship.

[3] Peter Dumont Vroom (1791–1873, *DAB*), Jacksonian Governor of New Jersey, then in his second term, 1833–1836.

[4] Searches through the printed New Jersey legislative documents, the New Jersey Archives, and the three known repositories of Governor Vroom's papers (Columbia University, New Jersey Historical Society, and Rutgers University) have failed to turn up either Henry's recommendation or Rogers's unpublished prospectus on the survey.

Governor. I have stated in my letter that your design is purely scientific. Let this be distinctly expressed in the letter you may send.[5]

Mr Field is at present out of town but will probably return this week on Friday or Saturday. I will confer with him again as soon as possible and should he give me any information of importance I will immediatly communicate it to you.

The roll of black paper[6] came safely and has been covered with algebraic characters to illustrate the mathematical theory of electricity.[7] The senior class of Nassau Hall are much indebted to you for the promptness with which you executed the commission and yet they are so ungenerous as not to esteem the black paper or its contents a very interesting article. Do not forget that I am your debtor for the ammount of the paper.

I am much engaged in my course of lectures and will not be able to visit you until after the 15th of April at which time our term closes. I hope dur-

[5] Rogers was selected to head New Jersey's first geological survey. In three years he completed the field work for the survey, working with little or no assistance. He published three reports on the progress of the survey (1836, 1837, and 1839) and a final report in 1840; copies of the first and the final reports, presented to Henry by the author, have survived in the Henry Library. The first, Henry Darwin Rogers, *Report on the Geological Survey of the State of New Jersey* (Philadelphia, 1836), bears Henry's annotations and a list of basic geological terms in Henry's hand in the endpapers. Henry used both Rogers's reports and his own list of geological terms in teaching geology at Princeton, which course he first offered in the 1838–1839 academic year. ([G. M. Giger,] "Notes on a Series of Lectures on Geology by Proff Joseph Henry at Nassau Hall," August 1841, Presbyterian Historical Society.) Henry had printed, apparently for pedagogical purposes only, a "Glossary of Geological Terms, Selected from Lyell, Mantell, and Others" (Princeton, 1841), two copies of which survive in the Henry Papers, Smithsonian Archives; included in the "Glossary" are practically verbatim all the items and definitions listed by Henry in the back of Rogers's 1836 *Report*.

[6] Presumably Henry used the black paper to supplement limited blackboard surface in Philosophical Hall. He could record symbols or other references on the paper and hang the paper on the wall, leaving the blackboard free for more frequently changing illustrations.

[7] This instance of Henry's use of "algebraic characters to illustrate the mathematical theory of electricity" is an unusual teaching practice for Henry in this period, at least judging by his own lecture notes and surviving student notebooks. Throughout the 1830s Henry used practically no mathematics in his electricity lectures; the main exception is his use of elementary mathematics for determining static electrical forces of attraction and repulsion of bodies (Joseph Henry's lecture notes, notebook [23894], Henry Papers, Smithsonian Archives). Student notes in the 1830s confirm that Henry used mathematics only sparingly, and even then only in discussions of static electricity (see, for instance, John Miller's notes [1835–1836], Princeton University Library). In the 1840s the student notes reflect Henry's increased use of algebra to derive electrical forces between bodies (William Gibson's notes, August 1842–November 1843, pp. 123, 127, Princeton University Library). But in no recorded instance did Henry use algebra in lecturing about current electricity or electromagnetism.

Henry's course on natural philosophy was required of all Princeton seniors, the vast majority of whom were not aspiring practitioners of science. Many of the students would not have enough background to understand sophisticated mathematical explanations of the phenomena Henry demonstrated. His course is best described, in modern terms, as a general physics course for nonphysics majors. It is understandable that most of Henry's students did not have high regard for his algebraic characters illustrating the mathematical theory of electricity.

ing the next summer to make up for my absences from the meetings of the club. Do not dispose of all the business before I come. Tell Mr Espy that I saw a fine display of the Aurora at this place on Sunday ev[ening] a week ago. It consisted of a well defined arch at about 9 oclock but was most brilliant at about ½ past 8 at which time it was seen by Mrs H. but not by myself. The elevation at 9 oclock was about 18 degrees.[8]

The pamphlets you promised me have not been received. I have also been expecting a copy of the abstract of my paper which Bache mentioned in his last letter. The mail is in a sad condition.

My respects to the club jointly and singly

Your Friend
Jos Henry

My respects to Mr Vaughn.

[8] Other evidence of Henry's interest in the height of the aurora is found above in Henry's Notebook Entry, September 2, 1834, and passim.

TO JACOB GREEN

Joseph Henry Collection, Firestone Library, Princeton University

Princeton March 16th[1] 1835

My Dear Sir

You have probably seen by the papers that the State has ordered a Geological survey. There are several candidates for the office of surveyor and among others Mr Rogers of your city. I have reccommended him to the Governor. He furnished through me a paper to the Committee of the Legislature, on the importance and nature of a survey of the kind and also a plan of one suitable for the state of New Jersey—stating how the Survey should be conducted, what points should receive particular attention &c.

These papers together with my letter has been given to the governor by Mr Field one of the committee. No appointment has yet been made. The governor is probably waiting until other applications are made. Since acting in favour of Rogers I have heard that your name was mentioned at Trenton as a candidate. I called on your Brother[2] inorder to know the truth of the statement and to inform him that I had reccommended Mr Rogers not knowing of your design. He informed me that he had not mentioned your name & that no communication between you & himself in reference to the survey had taken place.

[1] The date is not completely legible; it may be March 11.

[2] James Sproat Green. *Henry Papers, 1*:440n.

He advised me to write to you on the subject that there might be no misunderstanding. I have reccommended Rogers warmly because I considered him well qualified for the business and because I am anxious for the good of science that a proper person may be appointed. I have heard no person except yourself & Rogers mentioned as candidates who can know any thing of Geology. I need not assure you that if I have acted in this affair contrary to your interest it will give me very unplesant feelings. Although your Brother has great influence with the Governor he is somewhat delicately situated in reference to bringing you forward as a candidate. If you wish the appointment I presume your influence in the state will be sufficient to secure it.[3]

If you be not a candidate will you do so much for the good of the cause of science as to mention to your Brother your opinion of the qualifications of Rogers.

Nothing new except that Dr Torrey thinks of removing his family to Princeton for the next year. I expect him with us the present or next week. You have finished your course & [?haven't] recently come to Princeton. The Phil Hall has now a stove in it and I will endeavour to make you more comfortable than at your last visit. I hope you have intirely recovered; you looked very much like a *spook* when I last visited Phil:

In great Haste
Your Friend
Jos. Henry

[3] We can provide no further information on Green's rumored candidacy.

TO JAMES HENRY

Family Correspondence, Henry Papers, Smithsonian Archives

Princeton March 17th 1835

Dear James

Your letter of the 6th inst[1] was received the first of last week but my college duties now occupy so much of my time that I have scarcely leisure for anything else. The most important part of your letter required an immediate reply and I regret the delay. I know not what to advise with regard to the removal of the Family to Kanes Walk.[2] I do not wish to interfere with

[1] Not found.

[2] Kane's Walk, an area then just outside of central Albany, at the intersection of Westerlo and Broadway (Market Street). Kane's Walk was once the site of prosperous James Kane's (1771–1851) mansion, ornamental gardens, and

your arrangements and yet I am very anxious that Mother and Nancy should be hapy in the change. Their comfort and wishes must be consulted. I will be in favour of any change which will relieve Nancy from the drudgery to which she is now subjected. She would have enough to do were it only to take charge of Mother. If you are to be married this spring and do not intend to take your Wife into Mothers family I would not advise that Nancy should keep house alone. The sum paid for the house rent with a small addition would be sufficient to pay the boarding of Mother and Nancy. Besides this should Mother's health permit it will be the wish of Harriet and myself that she and Nancy come to Princeton in the summer. She can stay as long as she is contented and then return. The presence of the children will recconsile her to this place.

You are about to assume a responsible charge and I sincerely hope that you may be enabled to discharge all its duties with pleasure and profit to your self and those with whom you are to be connected. Your Intended[3] is an agreable and active person & I have no doubt that she will make you a wife who will do all in her power to render you hapy. The circumstance of her having two children is not quite as plesant as otherwise but there is no connection of the kind but what has something which might be better. I shall always feel the deep interest of a Brother in your welfare and will be hapy in extending the warmest and kindest feelings to your wife. I know that Harriet will join me in wishing you every happiness the married state is susseptable of and that she will cordially receive your wife as a sister.

What ever arrangements you may make with regard to Mother & Nancy you may calculate on my continuing to contribute as much as I have done towards their support and should my circumstances permit I will do more.

I leave the remainder of this letter to be filled by Harriet. She will give you the intelligence respecting the children &c.[4]

There is only time for me to add a few words. Little ones are quite well & grow finely. Bub talks [about] every thing & can ask more questions than I am able to answer. Sis can almost walk alone, is very playful and appears to understand all that is said to her. She climbed up the two steps that lead

promenades. As Kane fell into less fortunate times, the area was parcelled up for residences and churches, but "Kane's Walk" remained for many years a quiet and beautiful neighborhood away from the downtown bustle. Gorham A. Worth, *Random Recollections of Albany*, 3d ed. (Albany, 1866), pp. 52–53; this volume was presented to Henry by the publisher, Joel Munsell, and survives in Henry's Library.

[3] James Henry married Caroline Morrow (1806–1884), widow of William Morrow (d. 1827), on the night of April 9, 1835. *Daily Albany Argus*, April 10, 1835, "Married," p. 3. Albany City Directories, 1832–1835. Munsell, *Ann. Alb.*, *9*:145. Hun, "Albany Academy," under John P. Henry.

[4] Harriet Henry does indeed write the following concluding paragraphs.

from my room—quite alone & appeared to be quite delighted with the feat. Somtimes stand alone & feels so proud of it calls see there.

We expect Orlando Meads next week.

All well here. This has been a very quiet winter with us. Weather so cold it would have done credit to the polar regions. This week have had a few mild days which have carried off our snow. The river will soon be open I suppose.

I should like much to visit you all before the old home is broken up. Please give my warmest love to Mother & Nancy. I will hope to see them here. I think Mother would suffer comparitively little more fatigue now that the canal[5] is navigable, in coming here than she would in going down Kanes' walk. We have a nice comfortable, quiet room for her and our happiness would be very much increased by having Mother with us.

Yours in great haste
Harriet

[5] A reference to the newly completed (1834) Delaware and Raritan Canal, the southernmost of three canals built across New Jersey and New York to connect Delaware and Hudson River commerce. The canal passed alongside Princeton, skirting present-day Lake Carnegie. Robert F. Stockton, who owned a sizable land tract in the path of the waterway, headed the canal interests; he and other businessmen optimistically foresaw a boon to the local economy. "Princeton Basin," at the base of Alexander Street (then called Canal Street), handled brisk commerce for only a few years but witnessed a steady flow of traffic passing by. Despite mismanagement, this well-constructed canal "became one of the most important transportation routes in the country in the period before the Civil War. For a few years the Delaware and Raritan actually carried a greater tonnage than did the Erie." George Rogers Taylor, *The Transportation Revolution, 1815–1860* (Harper Torchbook edition, New York, 1968), pp. 40–41. V. Lansing Collins, *Princeton, Past and Present,* rev. ed. (Princeton, 1946), section 151. Constance M. Greiff, Mary W. Gibbons, and Elizabeth G. C. Menzies, *Princeton Architecture* (Princeton, 1967), p. 89 and figures 74, 75.

"RECORD OF EXPERIMENTS"

Henry Papers, Smithsonian Archives

March 19th 1835

Transmitted a current through a thick wire from the small circular battery, lifted small quantity of filings.

Transmitted same current through thin wire, quantity much greater. Does not this principle operate in electromagnetic magnets—may we not in some cases have too many wires?[1]

[1] In his electromagnets, as originally designed, Henry attempted to maximize the induced magnetism by multiplying the number of separate wires coiled in parallel around the magnet's core. See his "On the Application of the Principle of the Galvanic Multi-

plier to Electro-Magnetic Apparatus, and Also to the Development of Great Magnetic Power in Soft Iron, with a Small Galvanic Element," *Silliman's Journal*, 1831, *19*:402. Henry believed then that numerous small wires in parallel provided more "conducting power" than a single large wire of equivalent cross-sectional area and that the induced magnetism increased with the conducting power. His latest experiments evidently led him to question the strict dependence of the magnetic induction on the cross-sectional area and conducting power of the inducing wires.

HENRY NOTEBOOK ENTRY

Notebook [23894],[1] page [163], Henry Papers, Smithsonian Archives

23 March 1835

Make a pile with cups of copper, zinc soldered on the bottom, with acid in cups.[2] J H

[1] This lecture notebook is devoted to electricity; Henry noted in it experiments used to illustrate his lectures and occasionally included a research idea he had while preparing to teach. For a description of similar notebooks on other topics, see note 1 of the entry for [1833], printed above. The entry appears on a page facing the beginning of Henry's classroom discussion of the voltaic pile.

[2] Henry is proposing a variation of the common voltaic pile, a piece of equipment used for generating electricity in the early years of the nineteenth century. The first versions consisted of pairs of silver and zinc disks separated by paper which had been saturated with a salt solution. The replacement of silver by copper and the saline solution by acid probably came about from analogy with the materials used in trough batteries. *King*, pp. 234–236.

We find no evidence that Henry built the pile described here, but Kenneth T. Kemp (1806–1843, *Poggendorff*) reported constructing a somewhat similar one in 1828. Kemp's article on the subject ("Description of a New Kind of Galvanic Pile, and Also of Another Galvanic Apparatus in the Form of a Trough," *Edinburgh New Philosophical Journal*, October–December 1828, *6*:70–77) suggests some of the difficulties Henry might have encountered had he tried it. First, the zinc became rapidly oxidized by the acid and had to be renewed. Kemp circumvented this problem by rearranging the elements and employing a zinc-mercury amalgam. Second, provision had to be made for the escape of the hydrogen thrown off when the zinc was immersed in the acid. To acomplish this without splashing the acid out, Kemp made the zinc plate convex and also put a rim around the cup above the level of the acid (*King*, p. 237, illustrates Kemp's voltaic pile).

TO JOHN TORREY

Retained Copy, Henry Papers, Smithsonian Archives

Princeton April 2nd 1835

My Dear Doctor

I have expected you with every stage arrival this week but since the time has arrived at Thursday night and you have not yet made your appearance I now conclude that we will not see you in Princeton this week.

I now write principally to say to you not however in anger that since you have delayed your comming so long I hope you will not think of visiting Princeton for 10 or 12 days to come.

Our cession closes next Tuesday when Mr Maclean[1] immediatly leaves Town. I am suddenly called to albany on account of the sickness of my Mother. She is quite feeble and requests to see me as soon as possible. I leave here with Mrs Henry on saturday. I shall not have time to call on you on our way to albany but hope to see you when I return. I intend if possible to be in Princeton on the 14th of the present month at which time the board of Trustees of the College meet. I wish to push a project of improving the Phil. Hall and would be much gratified if you could be at Princeton at the same time to give it the weight of your influence. Mclean says little about it. The Dr[2] I think is in favour of it. The plan is as follows. The back wall of the building on account of the lateral pressure of the arches in the dining room has bulged out the back wall of the building. The trustees ordered at the last meeting a new roof to the building[3] but Dr Carnahan thinks that it would be improper to put it on while the back wall is in its present state. It must be supported or proped in some way. I propose to erect a building against the wall similar to one we spoke of last summer and which I believe you proposed to consist of three stories or as high as the present building and to form three rooms communicating with the three floors of the present edifice.

The lowest room to be a kitchen for Mr Clow[4] and the present kitchen to be transformed into the dining room. The second room to be a work laboratory and the large (now dining) room to be seated for another lecture room with cases along the wall to contain the articles of the museum. The present museum to be used as a room for the best articles of apparatus and the third room in the abutment or that off the present Philosophical Hall

[1] John Maclean, Jr., Vice President of Princeton.

[2] James Carnahan, President of Princeton.

[3] On September 24, 1834, the Trustees "*Resolved* that the Building Committee be authorised to put a new Roof on the old Refectory: *Provided*, they think it necessary." Trustees' Minutes, *3*:280, Princeton University Archives.

[4] Henry Clow (d. 1867) emigrated from Scotland in 1804 and set up as a baker in Princeton. From 1816 to 1845, he was steward of Princeton College, "the most popular of all stewards with the students. His breakfast rolls were celebrated [throughout the town.]" (*Hageman, 1*:341.) Clow was active in Democratic politics in Princeton, serving at various times on the common council and as Mayor and Recorder. He also wrote and published poetry. *Maclean*, 2:313; *Hageman, 1*:209, and *Princeton Catalogue*, p. 81. Clow was later a modest contributor to electrical science. According to Henry's laboratory notes, he attempted to test the electrical screening effects of cast iron with "Mr Clows griddle for buckwheat cakes." Entries for April 22 and June 4, 1840, "Record of Experiments," Henry Papers, Smithsonian Archives.

to be a work shop and private Laboratory for the Phil. Department.

This plan will render the building one of the most convenient and plesant edifices for Philosophical purposes in the country and can be carried into effect at an expense not greater than 2 thousand dollars. To get the same additional room in any other way would require an expenditure of more than four times as much money with less conveniences. The present Kitchen is a disgrace to the Institution & by converting it into a dining room not only will so much additional space be gained but an absolute nuisance removed. By removing all the lumber partitions &c and putting in a new floor it will form a very plesant room.

I wish the plan had been started by Maclean as I am sure it would then have been carried into immediate execution but he has at present fish of a larger size to fry & cannot attend much to this affair.[5] If you could make it convenient just to happen to come to Princeton at the meeting of the Trustees I think we would have little difficulty in convincing the gentlemen of the importance of the improvement and also of the necesity of a better collection of apparatus. If the plan should be adopted it must be commenced immediately so as to be finished if possible by the commencement of the next term or during the summer.

The professorship of chemistry and Mineralogy in the university of south carolina is vacant as well as several other professorships. The salary is $2000 and a good brick house. A circular has been addressed to Dr Carnahan requesting him to give in names of candidates. The professors are chosen by ballot by the Trustees in June next.[6]

Both the packages came safely. The one was received just one month after it was put up and the other after a delay of more than 5 months.[7]

[5] Besides the problem of repairing college buildings, Maclean and the Trustees had to worry about the fund raising underway by the Alumni Association, to find a new Clerk for their meetings, to consider whether instruction in law should be added to the curriculum, and to decide how to use properties recently willed to the College. *Maclean*, 2:297–298.

[6] Thomas Cooper (see note 1 of the letter of November 16, 1833, above) had held the chair of chemistry and mineralogy at South Carolina College from 1819 to December 1834, when he resigned from the college along with several other professors. Over thirty applications were received for his job. In June 1835, the trustees selected William H. Ellet (*Henry Papers, 1*:337), who held the post until 1848. Ellet had an excellent reputation as a teacher and popularizer of chemistry, although he had no special interest or competence in mineralogy. His high salary was offset by a lack of laboratory facilities relative to northern schools, a deprivation which did not prevent him from doing research. Daniel W. Hollis, *University of South Carolina: South Carolina College* (Columbia, South Carolina, 1951), *1*:75, 116, 123, and 128.

[7] For the matter of the package, see the letter of Joseph Henry to John Torrey, February 23, 1835.

TO STEPHEN ALEXANDER

Mary Henry Copy, Memoir, Henry Papers, Smithsonian Archives

Albany April 6th 1835

My dear Stephen. You have probably received James's letter giving the intelligence of my mother's death. She died on Saturday[1] morning about ten o'clock. . . . The event was a great shock to me. I have come to Albany several times with much anxiety but had become accustomed to find her better, and in this case was not in the least prepared for the circumstance of her departure. She expressed great anxiety to see Harriet, the Boy and myself. On Thursday she said to Nancy that she knew that on that day Harriet was making preparations to come with the Boy. The Boy does not seem to have any definite idea of the death of his grandmother Henry. He asked me why she was put in that box and said she would be cold there. Mother died with scarcely a struggle and her last prayers were for her children and grandchildren.

[1] April 4.

FROM HENRY D. ROGERS

Henry Papers, Smithsonian Archives

Philadelphia April 11 [1835]

My Dear Friend,

I sympathise sincerely, in your late afflicting loss, knowing but too well myself that the world has no solace that can console us for the destitution of heart caused by the death of a Parent.[1]

Hoping that this may find you returned to Princeton upon Monday I am desirous of making known to you the state of things in regard to my prospects of the survey. I have since your absence seen the Governor & procured to be placed in his hands a number of letters with the Journal of Science all as vouchers of my competency.[2] In a former interview with the Governor at Somerville I had a good deal of conversation from the *general tenor* of which I was induced to be sanguine of my success. I find that after-

[1] Henry's mother died on April 4, 1835.

[2] Perhaps a reference to letters from the elder Silliman and reprints of articles in *Silliman's Journal.*

wards some other names were brought before his notice and backed I presume with a good amount of weight in their favour. This he told me made his pause in his decision longer than he had led me to anticipate and has influenced him to call in the assistance of his constitution[al] advisers the *Council,* four of whom I believe are requisite to constitute a legal council with him. I do not on the whole feel by any means as much in glee with my prospects as I was and what further to do of an efficient kind to promote my chances I hardly know.

It has occurred to me that an interview on your part if I can ask you to attempt so unpleasant a task, with the Governor and any of his council who are to be consulted & whom you know or can see would be perhaps the most useful thing remaining to be done.[3]

The decision will probably be made in a day or two after your reaching Princeton, and I hardly know if it takes place so early whether you will have time for such exertions in my behalf.

I wish you in conversation on the subject to dwell with stress on the necessity there is that the executor of the survey be a *Chemist,* for the analysis of the *soils* & many mineral products is to be one half of the useful portion of the plan. Now most of my competitors are not chemists.

The Geologist again ought to be a To[po]grapher which I do not think one of them is. I mean he ought to be familiar from practice with field research of a scientific kind such as I have witnessed with De la Beche[4] in Eng. so that when necessary he can *amend* or *resurvey* his *map.* Clemson[5] is neither Geol[ogist], topographer nor Naturalist, knowing nothing of *fossils* so essential to all accuracy in the science.

Mr Pierce[6] of Conn, was spoken of by the Governor as an ardent cultivator of the subject. True he did some years ago call attention to the Marl in Monmouth Co. & the state is grateful to him, but this does not make him the fitter man for the survey. By the geologists in the county he is *not known* & has in his few writings done absolutely nothing to prove him a man of *any* science. Tho Clemson understands a little mineralogy & chemistry, [of] geology he is grossly ignorant in all its improvements as you may

[3] We do not know if Henry spoke to the Governor.

[4] Henry Thomas De la Beche (1796–1855, *DSB*), was the first head of the Geological Survey in Great Britain (1851). From 1832 to 1835 he conducted a geological survey of Devonshire under the auspices of the Ordnance Survey.

[5] Thomas Green Clemson (1807–1888) was a native of Philadelphia with a taste for mineralogy. While in Europe, Clemson had attended lectures of European chemists (Thenard, Gay-Lussac, Dulong, Robiquet). He moved to Washington where he married John C. Calhoun's daughter. From 1832 to 1839 Clemson was a consulting mining engineer. From 1844 to 1850, Clemson was Minister to Belgium. He inherited Calhoun's homestead which was given to South Carolina to found a college which now bears his name. *DAB.*

[6] For James Pierce, see *Henry Papers, 1*:137, footnote 2.

readily see by reading his pamphlet on York County Pa.[7] Come to Phila & you will learn the true position here of this very specious intriguer.

The circumstance that my brother Wm. has received the appointment to the survey in Va. which will be something superior is certainly a reason why I could perform that of Jersey better [than] any other person. For all discoveries made in the *same formations* I could have knowledge of long before they could reach anyone else in print & thus I should work with greatly improved light.[8] If a chance occurs dwell on these points & pray let me hear from you as soon as you have anything to communicate.

Your ever grateful friend.

Henry D. Rogers

I treated myself to a sight of your mammoth battery at Princeton.

[7] "Observations on the Geology of York County, Pennsylvania," was read before the Geological Society of Pennsylvania in October 1834 and appears in its *Transactions*, vol. 1, pt. 1, Appendix.

[8] After having defined the post of state geologist to place his rivals at a disadvantage, Henry Darwin Rogers introduces this new argument, one of scientific nepotism. Pierce and Clemson could, no doubt, counter the previous arguments; this was unanswerable. What weight it had, we cannot say.

EXCERPT,[1] MINUTES, TRUSTEES, COLLEGE OF NEW JERSEY

Trustees' Minutes, 3:292–294, Princeton University Archives

April 15, 1835

The Committee appointed on the Refectory building and College[2]

Reported I. That an addition be made to said Refectory building in the rear thereof, of the length of not more than thirty-five feet, and of the depth of not more than 25 feet and of the hight of said building.

II. That the said addition be made of stone, covered with tin or slate, and divided into such apartments as may be determined by the building Committee, under whose direction the same Shall be done.[3]

III. That said committee make such repairs to the Refectory building, as may in their judgment be necessary . . .

All which is respectfully submitted.

[1] We have not included several resolutions dealing with the improvement of Nassau Hall and other matters not germane to Henry.

[2] By "refectory" the clerk of the Trustees meant Philosophical Hall, the building which housed Henry's classes and his laboratory. "College" refers to Nassau Hall.

[3] These vague guidelines left Henry and Maclean free to rearrange and substantially increase the science facilities of Princeton.

The above report was accepted.

Resolved. That an appropriation be made to cover the expenses, which shall be incurred in making the above repairs &c. And that warrants be issued by the President to the building committee for the same.

Resolved. That one hundred and fifty Dollars be appropriated to the Chemical Department: and one hundred Dollars to the Philosophical Department under the direction of Professor Henry . . .

Resolved. That Mr. Brown,[4] Mr. Green[5] Mr. Comfort[6] and Dr. Carnahan, be the building committee;[7] and that in erecting the building and making the repairs in the Refectory & College as agreed by this Board, they be empowered to employ an agent to attend to the business.

[4] Isaac Vanarsdale Brown (1784–1861) graduated from Princeton in 1802 and served as a Tutor there in 1805–1806. He studied theology and was ordained as a Presbyterian minister in 1807. In 1810 Brown established a boarding school in nearby Lawrenceville, known as the Lawrenceville School, which he headed until 1833, when he moved to Mount Holly, New Jersey, to organize its Presbyterian church. He held several other pastorships in New Jersey later in life. Brown was a Trustee of Princeton from 1816 until his death. He was also active in the American Colonization Society and the American Bible Society. *Princeton Catalogue*, pp. 113–114; Alfred Nevins, ed., *Encyclopaedia of the Presbyterian Church of the United States of America . . .* (Philadelphia, 1884), p. 105. Roland J. Mulford, *History of the Lawrenceville School, 1810–1935* (Princeton, 1935).

[5] James Sproat Green (see *Henry Papers, 1*:440).

[6] David Comfort (d. 1853) graduated from Princeton in 1795. He was a Trustee of Princeton from 1816 until 1853 and was also on the Board of Directors (1814–1831) and a Trustee (1822–1853) of the Theological Seminary. *Princeton Catalogue*, p. 109. *Maclean*, 2:340 lists Comfort as a clergyman of Kingston, New Jersey and gives his death date as 1854.

[7] Other than their decree that the outside dimensions should not exceed 30 feet by 25 feet (see below, Henry to Torrey, April 27, 1835), the building committee had little to do with the changes in Philosophical Hall. The addition and other renovations were directed by Henry and Maclean in consultation with Torrey and Carnahan.

TO JOHN TORREY

Torrey Papers, Library, New York Botanical Garden

Princeton April 23rd 1835

My Dear Dr.

The Trustees have passed a law authorising the building of the projection to the Phil. soph Hall[1] and operations are to commence as soon as the materials can be procured which will be I suppose about the commence-

[1] See above, Excerpt, Trustees' Minutes, April 15, 1835.

ment of the next session or college or about the time when you will begin your lectures.[2]

It is necessary however before the stone & wood be purchased that the dimentions and general plan of the structure should be settled.

There are several plans proposed and I wish you were here to give in your views with those which have been offered. Mr Jager has gone to Cannonsburgh[3] so that the planning now devolves on Mr McLean and the Dr.[4] and myself. There are principally two plans for the arrangement of the 2nd and 3rd stories which are as follows:

1st

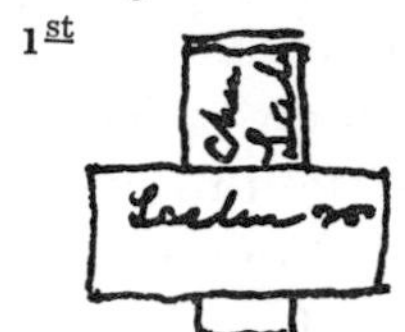

To convert the projection on the 2nd floor into a laboratory with cases for chemicals &c and to use the large room (now dining room) as a lecture room with the cases for the museum of animals, minerals &c around the walls. The seats to be placed circular before the large door leading to the laboratory.

Thus

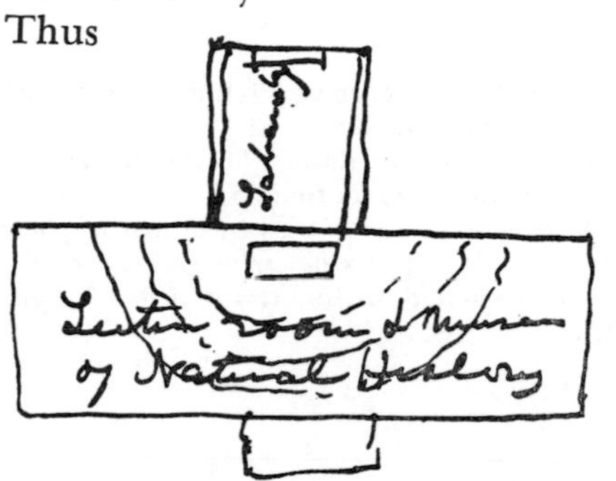

The upper story devoted entirely to Natural Phil and a work shop for the carpenter or other mechanic. The other plan is to use the large room entirely for a museum with cases around the wall and flat cases in the centre. It is supposed that nearly the whole room may be thus occupied as the minerals from the other building[5] will be brought over and also one person[6] has subscribed to the Alumni fund $500 worth of minerals. Besides this Mr

[2] The winter session had ended April 15th. After a five-week break, the summer session, during which Torrey gave his chemistry course, would begin May 20th. *Princeton Annual Catalogue*, 1835, p. 16.

[3] Canonsburg, Pennsylvania was the home of Jefferson College. Although we are not aware of any connection between Jaeger and the college, he may have had an interest in its mineral cabinet (see below, Ramsey to Henry, May 29, 1835).

[4] Dr. James Carnahan, the College's President.

[5] Some minerals were kept on the second floor (main floor) of the Library. See above, Henry to James Henry, February 9, 1833.

[6] Samuel Fowler. In 1835 Fowler subscribed $500 to the Alumni Fund, a pledge he fulfilled in 1837 when he gave nearly 600 mineralogical specimens to the College. John Maclean Papers, 2:Alumni Association of Nassau Hall, Subscription Books, 1834–1836, Princeton University Archives; John Maclean to James Carnahan, April 11, 1837, Maclean Papers, 1:Letters, Princeton University Archives; *Princeton Annual Catalogue*, 1837, p. 16.

Born in 1779, Fowler received medical training at the Pennsylvania Medical College and practiced medicine in northern New Jersey, where he owned zinc mines and an iron works. He published two articles, on mineralogy in New York and New Jersey, in *Silliman's Journal* (1825 and 1832), and was the discoverer of Fowlerite, a mineral named for him. He served as a U.S. Representative, 1833–1837; he died in 1844. *Biographical Directory of the American Congress.*

Van Doren[7] of this place has lately become possessed of the cabinet formerly owned by Nuttal[8] which he will sell very cheaply, & which Mr Maclean intends to have purchased. According to this plan the upper story will be used for N P and Chemistry. The projection for a laboratory & work shop and the now museum for a Phil cabinet. In this arrangement the two departments will not be entirely seperated and as long as *we two* are in the chairs all things I trust will go on plesantly but it might be otherwise should any change occur.[9]

I am anxious that such an arrangement should be made as will be bes[t,] all things considered, for the interests of the college. If you cannot come to Princeton before the plan is decided on give us your opinion by letter. I wish to go to Philadelphia the beginning of next week. Write this week.

Your Friend
Jos. Henry

[7] John Van Doren (1804–1892) was Treasurer of the College, 1829–1839. A merchant who turned to farming later in life, Van Doren served briefly in the New Jersey Assembly and was active in the First Presbyterian Church of Princeton. *Princeton Catalogue*, p. 27; *Hageman*, 2:175, 177–179, 186; Abraham Van Doren Honeyman, *The Van Doorn Family in Holland and America, 1088–1908* (Plainfield, New Jersey, 1909), pp. 367–368.

[8] For whom see above, Torrey to Henry, February 18, 1835, footnote 8.

[9] Henry drew a revision of the first of these two plans. It appears below at the end of the documents dated within the month of April 1835.

TO JAMES HENRY

Mary Henry Copy, Memoir, Henry Papers, Smithsonian Archives

Princeton April 23, 1835[1]

Dear James,

We arrived in Princeton safely on Tuesday afternoon in time for the Trustees. Found all well. . . .

I have become so accustomed in writing to you to fill the greater part of my letter with accounts of little Will to please Mother that I have gone on in the same way without reflecting that she who would take most interest in these accounts now requires no information in regard to the affairs of this world. I hope that you have become settled by this time and that you are

[1] Mary Henry had written 1853 by mistake. The ellipses indicate her omissions.

becoming accustomed to your new relations.[2] That you may succeed in life, in becoming useful to yourself, your family and your fellow men is the most earnest wish of your Brother. The death of our Mother has severed one of the principal ties which connected me with Albany but it should have the effect to draw us closer if possible to each other and to Nancy. I hope she is somewhat reconciled by this time to the loss which she even more particularly has sustained in the death of our dear Mother.

The Trustees have passed an order for erecting an addition to the Philosophical Hall, the one which I proposed and on account of which I was so anxious to be in Princeton at the meeting of the Board. It will be of great convenience to me and will much improve facilities in the chemical and Natural History departments of the college.

Your Brother

[2] That is, James's wife Caroline Morrow and her two children by a previous marriage. See the text and note 3 of the letter to James Henry, March 17, 1835, above.

FROM JOHN TORREY

Henry Papers, Smithsonian Archives

New York, April [23–24],[1] 1835

My dear friend

I am disappointed in my plan of visiting Princeton. Last week I lost several days, & some money too, in attending the trial of Matthias,[2] & now my wife is sick, so that I do not like to leave her alone. You have doubtless determined the matter respecting the addition to the refectory. If the Trustees have agreed to the plan, do drive matters that we may have all

[1] Although dated April 23, this is clearly a reply to Henry's letter of April 23. On that document, Torrey notes its receipt and answer on April 24. From the text it is possible Torrey wrote the first three paragraphs on the day before receipt of Henry's letter.

[2] Identified variously as Mathies or Robert Matthews. He was on trial for murder in Westchester County, New York. Claiming either divine inspiration or divinity, Matthias convinced a small number of individuals who provided him with funds and a residence. He originally came from Washington County, New York, to Albany where he attempted to join E. N. Kirk's Fourth Presbyterian Church. (For Kirk, a Henry acquaintance, see the letter of December 1, 1832, footnote 3.) When one of his supporters withdrew from Matthias and then died under suspicious circumstances, poisoning was suspected. The corpse of the supposed victim was disinterred, and the stomach and its contents sent to Torrey for analysis. He reported no traces of poison, undoubtedly contributing to the prophet's acquittal on the murder charge. William L. Stone, *Matthias and His Impostures, or the Progress of Fanaticism . . .* (New York, 1835). Stone links Matthias to the perfectionism of men like Kirk and the religious excitements in upstate New York. See also, W. E. Drake, *The Prophet . . .* (New York, 1834).

the details settled before I leave Princeton. I will take either apartment—just as you please. The upper one will accommodate me very well, should the Museum be allowed to remain where it is—but I am not *anxious* to have it.

Did you get an appropriation for the pneumatic trough? If you did not, please let me know, for I will send it, in that case, to Chilton's to be sold. I have paid all the bills for it except one, & the mechanic wants his money for that. I advanced also for another trough, just like this, but the person has not repaid me, though I sent him the apparatus months ago! It is rather too much to take so much trouble & then bear the expense too. I don't speak now with regard to Princeton, but of the person at the south to whom I sent the trough.[3] If the College will take this I will have it boxed up & sent on without delay.

In order that there may be no difficulty respecting class books in Chemistry,[4] I wish you would speak to the bookseller at Princeton[5] to have the requisite number provided. The ballance of the copies that I got of Lockwood[6] are still on hand. I could not send them back after they were detained so long, & I have to settle for them myself. These I should like to have sold the present season.

I have just received your letter of yesterday. I am glad you are really in earnest about enlarging the philosoph. & chem! Depts. Still, I say, make whatever arrangements you think best, but I would *rather* have the bugs & alligators in a close room by themselves. If old Jäeger thinks he can fill the present eating Hall & the Trustees say *aye*, I say ditto. We can agree very well upstairs, but, as you say, my successor may not be such a pattern of amiableness as *I* am & you must look to the future. How *deep* do they intend making the *projection*? Ask for enough while you are about it. Perhaps we can make room enough for the *working* part of the laboratory, & a *shop*, on the same floor! Many tools will answer for both of us. It would be a pity to have a *double* set. You cannot live without a *shop*, & a *shop* is almost as indispensable to me.

I shall have my hands full of *planning*, this season. You have been told that we have purchased the High School in Crosby St. for our Medical College. If we can get an old lady (who holds a lease of it for two years) to let us come in, we shall soon commence enlarging & ornamenting the building & I shall have a new laboratory. If you don't have something particularly nice in Princeton we shall *take the shine* from you.

[3] The person at the south is unknown to us.

[4] Torrey used Turner's *Elements of Chemistry* (see above, Torrey to Henry, August 18, 1834, footnote 14).

[5] Moore Baker.

[6] Roe Lockwood, a bookseller at 415 Broadway from 1832 to 1836, New York City Directories.

Remember me to Maclean, the Dr,[7] & all our good friends at P.—not by any means neglecting Mrs. Henry.

Your very truly
John Torrey

[7] James Carnahan.

TO JOHN TORREY

Torrey Papers, Library, New York Botanical Garden

Princeton Monday 10 oclock
AM. April [27] 1835

My Dear Dr

I am just about to start for Philadelphia this morning and having received your letter[1] send the following as a hasty answer. The Trustees passed an order for the payment of your trough with the usual appropriation, in the whole $150.

The committee on the new building met on saturday last and decreed that the projection should be 30 feet long and 25 wide on the outside, the internal arrangements to be settled hereafter. Mr Maclean however is much in favour of seating the present eating room as a lecture room with the museum cases around the walls. Let the arrangements be what they may, we will all be much better accomodated than at present and the appearance of things about the establishment much improved. There is a very fair prospect at present of a good addition to our number of students at the begining of the next term.[2] I know not what to answer with regard to the class book.[3] Our bookseller[4] in this respect is a great trouble. I was obliged to purchase a set of Brewster's optics[5] for the class just before the end of the term and was not able to collect more than 2/3 of the purchase money; the remainder will be paid, I hope at the beginning of the next term.

I regret to hear that Mrs Torrey is unwell. I hope a residence in the country during the summer will be favourable to her health.

[1] Torrey's letter to Henry of April 23–24, 1835, immediately preceding.

[2] The number of students in the academic year 1834–1835 was 206; in 1835–1836, the number rose to 239. *Maclean*, 2:296 and 299.

[3] Torrey used Turner's textbook in teaching chemistry at Princeton. See note 14 of the letter of Torrey to Henry, August 18, 1834, above.

[4] Probably Moore Baker.

[5] On this book and Henry's decision to use it in his Princeton course, see note 2 of the letter of Henry to Bache of February 9, 1835, above.

Mr Blackwell[6] has given up his house to a person from Trenton, I believe, who is said to keep a good table and to manage the establishment very well. The barkeeper informed me this morning that yourself and Family can be accomodated with boarding at a moderate rate but could not give me the price per week. The proprietor is not at present at home. I intend stopping in Philadelphia about a week in order to post up the contents of the journals &c. Give my respects to Mrs. Torrey and Dr Gray. Mrs Henry wishes to be remembered to Mrs Torrey the little girls & yourself.

From your Friend
Joseph Henry

[6] Probably Elijah Blackwell, an innkeeper who was preparing to build Mansion House (adjoining the Nassau Hotel). His new building functioned as a public house from 1836 to 1875, but we do not know where his previous establishment was in Princeton, nor to whom he sold it. Blackwell prospered at his trade and died a wealthy man. *Hageman*, 2:47 and 184.

HENRY'S DRAWING OF PHILOSOPHICAL HALL

Henry Papers, Smithsonian Archives

[April 1835]

Henry apparently sketched this set of floor plans for Philosophical Hall during the time of its renovation. He had already demonstrated an interest in problems of laboratory design during his trips to West Point in 1826 and Yale in 1830,[1] and had learned enough about architecture to teach short courses on the subject at Princeton and the Albany Academy. We are printing the item below because it shows the physical environment in which Henry did his scientific experiments for the next several years. Henry was to devote much of his time to stocking his laboratory with apparatus, particularly during his visit to Europe in 1837, and he also superintended additional structural changes to Philosophical Hall in 1840. Looking back in 1844, he reflected that "After 11 years labour I have succeeded in getting the apparatus, the lecture room and the laboratory all arranged to my satisfaction and completely fitted for both my labours in the line of instruction and in that of research."[2]

The sketch printed below fits Henry's description in the letter to Torrey of April 2, 1835, but supplies more detail.[3] Three other undated items in the Smithsonian Archives provide additional information about the improvements

[1] *Henry Papers*, *1*:157–158 and 274–277.

[2] Draft, Henry to [Robley Dunglison], February 10, 1844, Henry Papers, Smithsonian Archives.

[3] In the upper corner Henry noted the dimensions for the bakery and for the new part: "32 feet or 40 feet" and below that "35." The figures for the new part, presumably referring to length, are basically in accordance with the "not more than thirty-five feet" stipulation of the April 15 Trustees' meeting but they exceed the 30 feet agreed upon at the committee meeting of April 25 (see Henry's letter to Torrey of April 27, 1835, above).

in the Hall. A positive photographic print of a lost original drawing shows that six semicircular rows of seats were to be arranged around the demonstration table, which backed on the new wing. This floor plan had "Plan Adopted" written on it by Henry and gives the correct dimensions for the wing. A second drawing, marked by Henry "1st floor," provides more detail on Henry Clow's kitchen arrangement. The third sketch is of the same outline of walls and windows as the kitchen plan, but is filled in for the top floor, which was to be set aside for Henry's classes and laboratory. This item duplicates the wording for the third floor in the drawing below except that it adds the fact that a forge would be on one side of the galvanic battery and the large magnet on the other.[4]

Henry's science facilities at Princeton, if small by twentieth-century standards, were about on the same scale as those available to his contemporaries. Michael Faraday's arrangements in the Royal Institution were nearly as modest as those at Princeton. Faraday had a chemical laboratory similar in size to Torrey's on the second floor of Philosophical Hall. The dimensions of the natural philosophy section of the Royal Institution seem about the same as the physics laboratory at Princeton, but Faraday's room was in the basement and must have been gloomier than Henry's due to the lack of windows. The lecture room at the Institution held more rows of seats than the Princeton hall, and the rows were graduated in tiers to give all parts of the audience a good view of demonstrations.[5] Faraday had a separate study in the Institution building which was part of his living quarters and which was functionally equivalent to the library at Henry's house but which was much better provided with books.[6] The Faradays were childless, so their library did not have to double as a nursery.[7]

Comparing science buildings at Princeton to those at other American colleges of the period is difficult for two reasons. First, other schools surpassed Princeton in providing for some disciplines, while lagging in certain branches. Yale, for example, had virtually no space or collections to use in teaching botany and zoology. Yale's provision for physics was only slightly more generous than Princeton's, the difference amounting to a few small storage rooms for large pieces of equipment in addition to the lecture room and laboratory. However, Yale devoted a whole building to chemistry, dwarfing the arrangements for Torrey at Princeton.[8] The second factor which complicates comparisons is the indifference of antebellum scientists to the building itself relative to their fas-

[4] The drawing we have printed is in Box 30 of the Henry Papers, in a folder marked "Henry Illustrative Material." The sketch of the first floor is also in that folder. The plan for the third floor appears with the letter from John Torrey of December 15, 1835 (see note 3 of that letter, printed below). The photograph of the lecture room and wing drawing is in folder 10 of Box 13 of the Photographs Collection in the Smithsonian Archives.

[5] Robert Hare arranged his lecture room at the University of Pennsylvania like that of the Royal Institution. Hare's laboratory apparatus probably matched Faraday's in completeness and quality, and surpassed Princeton's. For details, see note 9 of the letter to Harriet Henry for December 5, 1834, above.

[6] Alan Jeffreys supplies illustrations of Faraday's scene at the Royal Institution in Plates 4, 5, and 6 of *Michael Faraday: A List of His Lectures and Published Writings* (London, 1960).

[7] Henry's apparently did. See below, Henry to Stephen Alexander, May 15, 1835.

[8] On science at Yale, consult Ebenezer Baldwin, *Annals of Yale College, from Its Founda-*

cination with problems of equipping it.[9] Once Henry had secured the large room on the third floor of the new wing of Philosophical Hall—an inexpensive project of no special architectural merit—he became preoccupied with instruments to put in it.

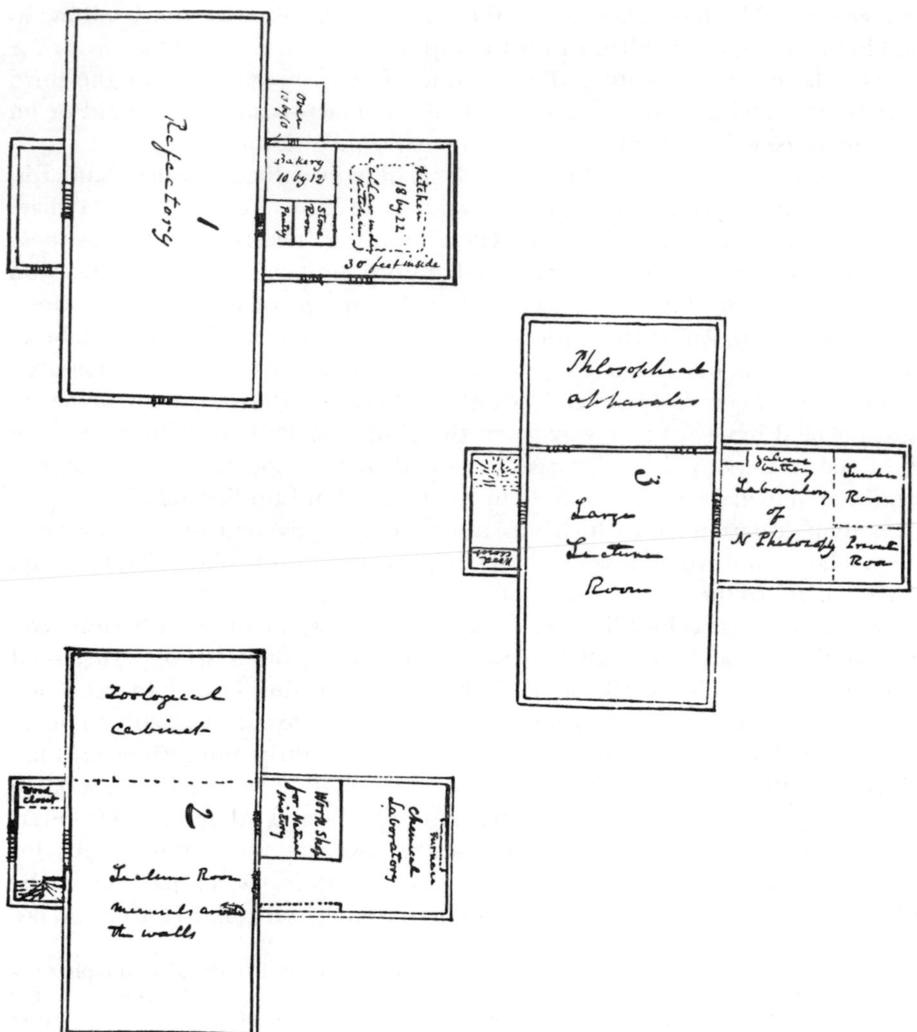

tion, to the Year 1831. To Which is Added, an Appendix, Bringing It Down to 1838 (New Haven, 1838), pp. 236–242, 252–253, and 260–264.

[9] John White Webster at Harvard (see *Henry Papers, 1*:330) was an exception to this indifference. His elaborate series of chemical furnaces were built into the laboratory, with flues running under the floor of the room. Webster's design must have presented structural challenges to the builder, but the size of the work area and lecture room was no larger than Torrey's at Princeton. Webster's laboratory is illustrated in plate 8 of his *A Manual of Chemistry* (Boston, 1826).

TO HARRIET HENRY

Mary Henry Copy, Memoir, Henry Papers, Smithsonian Archives

Philadelphia, room of American Phil[l] Soc.
Friday [May 1, 1835][1] 3 o'clock

My dear Wifey. I have been many times to the post office with the expectation of receiving an answer to my letter of Tuesday,[2] but have been disappointed. My letter may have miscarried. I sent it to the office by a little negro boy, who on being questioned did not give me a very satisfactory account of the delivery of it . . .

I have been very much engaged in study and in making an analysis and abstract of all the articles I could find on the subjects of magnetism, electricity, galvanism, heat &c. in the Library of the Philosophical Society. Old Mr. Vaughan has as usual been very kind—he had a lock put on the drawer of a table for my especial use this morning. I paid the locksmith but was obliged to receive the money back again or offend the old gentleman. I breakfast with him and have been up and at work before six o'clock but have not gone to bed except the first night much before twelve.

Prof. Bache, Green and Rodgers[3] were all out of town when I arrived. Bache has returned. I took tea with him last evening. Mrs. Bache says she intends to visit Princeton the beginning of the next vacation which is in August.

There is to be a meeting of the Society this evening at which I intend to give an abstract of the principal facts which are to form the subjects of the two next articles of my series of papers.[4] The two papers[5] are printed but

[1] We have arrived at this date from references to the Philadelphia trip in surrounding letters and from Henry's mention at the end of the letter of presenting an abstract to a meeting of the American Philosophical Society.

[2] Not found.

[3] Probably Henry Darwin Rogers.

[4] This reference to subjects Henry intended to pursue in forthcoming articles for the American Philosophical Society raises questions about the course of Henry's researches in this period. Henry did in fact deliver an oral communication to the Society that evening. His presentation is summarized as follows in the Society's minutes:

> Prof. Henry made a verbal com. referring to certain facts which he intended to present to the Society at a future time:
>
> 1. That a hollow Cylinder of Steel, one-tenth of an inch in thickness, may be magnetised on the Surface without exhibiting Signs of free magnetism in the interior, and vice-versa, and showing that a body is susceptible of different magnetic Strata.
>
> A future confirmation of this point he stated to have been furnished by a Steel magnet of the horse shoe form, which had acquired a permanent polarity in one direction, so strongly that the effect of reversing the Poles by a galvanic current, was only transient, the magnet returning to its original polarity on the cessation of the current.
>
> 2. The magnetism of Steel and Soft Iron differ in many particulars; a small steel magnet capable of lifting 10 lbs. was able to confer a more powerful change upon Steel than an electro-magnet which could support 100.

the plate is not finished. I will be obliged to remain until Monday. I hope to return in a proper state of mind and body to resume the duties of *my life.* I hope all are well. There is a very pretty little girl nine years old standing at the opposite side of the table waiting for this letter. She says I need not hurry. She thinks I write too fast and says that her schoolmistress does not allow her to write so fast and that she is required to take more pains . . .

The transient effect of a galvanic current on a Steel magnet and on a soft-iron electromagnet is different.

3. That he had investigated the best mode of making Electro-Magnets.

Early Proceedings of the American Philosophical Society . . . 1744 to 1838 (Philadelphia, 1884), pp. 670–671. These experiments on the magnetization of steel and on the comparison of galvanic and steel magnets were obviously intended for "Contributions III" and "Contributions IV." As events turned out, neither publication dealt with the topics addressed by Henry at the May 1, 1835, meeting of the Society, but instead carried forward his work on electrical induction. One or two major articles on steel magnets and electromagnetism may have been in preparation in spring 1835, but there clearly was an interruption in Henry's publication schedule and a shift in the direction of his research. "Contributions III," his next major publication for the American Philosophical Society, did not appear until 1838.

Perhaps the experiments discussed in Henry's May 1835 abstract had proved inconclusive or inadequate for an extended publication. More likely, other research interests took precedence—his investigations of the lateral discharge and his further work in electrical induction. In his introduction to "Contributions III," Henry traced these latter interests to the spring of 1836.

Before Henry's oral presentation to the American Philosophical Society in May 1835, there were few signs that he was contemplating major publications on the magnetization of steel. Still, his interest in the problem can be traced at least as far back as 1833 when he claimed a new galvanic technique for magnetizing steel bars for use in studying terrestrial magnetism (see his letter to Kelly of December 30, 1833, footnote 7). These investigations can also be seen as an outgrowth of general experiments on electromagnetic induction that run sporadically as a subtheme through Henry's early Princeton researches. In Henry's "Record of Experiments" for August 1834 (printed above) there is a systematic investigation of electrically induced magnetism, chiefly in soft iron but with occasional comparisons with steel. Comparisons of permanent steel magnets with electromagnets are touched upon in the entry of January 26, 1835, above, and, again, in the undated fragment on magnetic induction, which we have assigned to February 1, 1835, above. More systematic experiments on these topics crop up in Henry's "Record of Experiments" in 1836 (see his entries of March 19, May 3 and 5), which will be discussed in the next volume of the *Henry Papers.*

[5] "Contributions I" and "Contributions II."

TO HARRIET HENRY

Mary Henry Copy, Memoir, Henry Papers, Smithsonian Archives

Philadelphia, Monday May 4, 1835.

My dear Wifey. I have been every day at the Post Office since my arrival in Phil. except yesterday (Sunday) and have only this moment received your letter of the first written in the spirit I love.[1] I need not tell you it gave me great pleasure.

[1] Not found. Very few of Harriet's letters to her husband survive.

After writing to you on Friday I called at Mr. Lukens'[2] shop with the intention of going with him to see the Balloon ascension, but he had gone before I arrived. I was not very anxious to witness the exhibition as from the many accounts we had had, I had lost in a measure my curiosity on the subject. I accordingly made my way to the university but had not walked more than a square when I was overtaken by Mr. Lukens in his gig, bound for the balloon. I was of course soon by his side and in a few minutes came in sight of the yard, containing a huge bag of varnished linen, which towered as high as the adjoining house, and by its incessant motion as it was agitated by the wind, appeared like some monster impatient to escape into the realms of air. Mr. Lukens had furnished the aeronaut[3] with a barometer and as we belonged to the philosophical corps, we were admitted without pay. The houses and streets around were crowded with thousands of spectators but the yard exhibited "a beggarly array of empty boxes,"[4] not more than two or three hundred persons. It was the first ascension, and as the sovereign people had shortly before been gulled, it was generally thought that this would be a hoax. I was admitted within the operating ring so as to have a close inspection of the whole process. The arrangement was very simple and on the plan described in most books on the art. My attention was most arrested by the appearance of the aeronaut who was standing on his basket surrounded by about twelve men who were holding the balloon and tying the basket to a hoop attached to the balloon by a netting thrown over the top.[5] His face exhibited feelings of the most intense anxiety. It was his first experiment; the balloon cost $1000; the ascension had been once postponed. A mob of many thousands stood without ready in a moment should he not succeed to demolish the balloon and perhaps endanger his life. When all was ready, he said in a tone of desperation: *Let me go! Let me go!* The rope was loosened, he began to ascend, his face immediately assumed the most joyful expression, which was however of a most transient duration for the balloon after ascending about 40 feet descended. He threw out his

[2] Isaiah Lukens.

[3] John Wise (1809–1879, *DAB*), a pioneer American balloonist. As Henry says later in the letter, this was Wise's first flight. His interest went back to his adolescence. Wise is credited with the invention of the rip panel. In 1859 he set a distance record of 804 miles which stood until 1900. As he studied storms and general meteorological conditions to improve the performance of his balloons, Wise and Henry crossed paths a few times subsequently. In 1879 Wise was drowned in a ballooning accident.

[4] Henry's version of Shakespeare's line "A beggarly account of empty boxes." *Romeo and Juliet*, act 5, sc. 1, line 45.

[5] The drawing reproduced here is in the Mary Henry Copy. In other documents, we can state that drawings in a Mary Henry Copy are tracings of the original. In this case we cannot determine whether this is a tracing or a transcriber's rendering. More likely the latter.

ballast, again ascended and passed over a four story house, again sunk, when the mob commenced a movement towards the balloon. He then threw out his instruments, his coat, hat, and every article and, just as his balloon appeared on the point of destruction, began to ascend and continued to ascend to the north west until at an elevation of perhaps a mile he met the upper current and he remained directly over the city at an elevation of about ¾ of a mile. The feelings of the mob of course were changed, and he was greeted with repeated cheers. I followed him by the aid of a telescope until he was lost by the hills of New Jersey.[6] The whole exhibition was to me one of the most exciting I have ever witnessed, more however in reference to the moral than the physical effect.

I have dwelt so long on the balloon that I have little time for my own movements. After our return from the balloon Mr. Lukens took me to Peale's museum to see and feel the effects of a magnet which he had fitted up for giving shocks and producing sparks. I was surprised beyond description by the great effect produced with an arrangement discovered accidentally by Prof. Emet . . .[7]

[6] Henry's account is substantially in agreement with a contemporary newspaper story:

> Mr. Wise made quite a successful balloon ascension yesterday afternoon. He started from a lot at the corner of Ninth and Green Streets, cheered on by the shouts of a vast multitude. About five hundred persons entered the vast enclosure, and eight or ten thousand men, women and children, occupied the streets and house tops of the surrounding neighborhood. He attempted to start exactly at four o'clock, but unable to proceed, he was compelled to throw out several bags of ballast—and still unable to ascend, he took off his coat, hat and shoes, threw them to the ground, and passed upwards with considerable celerity. The balloon for the first half hour was borne to the south west, when passing into another current of air, its direction was changed, and the aeronaut passed over the city, at the distance of about a mile, and in the view of thousands, of all ages, and both sexes. We learn that Mr. Wise returned to the city, with his balloon, last evening, between 8 and 9 o'clock, having landed in New Jersey, seven or eight miles from Camden.

Philadelphia *National Gazette,* May 2, 1835, p. 2.

[7] The Mary Henry Copy ends here with this reference to John Patton Emmet (1796–1842), Professor of Chemistry at the University of Virginia. Irish-born, Emmet came to the United States in 1804. He entered West Point in 1814 and taught there until 1817. In 1822 Emmet received his medical degree from the College of Physicians and Surgeons in New York City. After practicing his profession and lecturing on chemistry for a few years in South Carolina, Emmet became one of the original faculty at Virginia where he remained the rest of his life. In addition to chemistry, he also delivered lectures on materia medica.

In a previous letter to Benjamin Silliman, Sr., April 18, 1833, Henry had expressed surprise at Emmet's reported results in "A New Mode of Developing Magnetic Galvanism . . . ," *Silliman's Journal,* 1833, *24*:78–86. Emmet wound a coil of insulated wire around the keeper of a horseshoe magnet. One end of the wire is then connected with the keeper, the other with the magnet. Another pair of wires lead off from the keeper and magnet "serving as conductors of the galvanic fluid. . . ." Otherwise, Emmet assumed that the induced galvanic current circulated through the magnet which acted as conductor.

This is apparently the first time Henry had seen Emmet's experimental arrangement; on May 9, 1835 (see below), he reported experimenting to test Emmet's results, using Peale's magnet, assisted by Lukens. Emmet's name occurs only one other time in Henry's "Record of Experiments." In a subsequent volume, Henry will appear in the role of a referee of an Emmet article. Henry displayed no interest discernible to us in Emmet's theoretical views (*Silliman's Journal*, 1834, 25:269–281 and 1835, *26*:26–44).

Paul Brandon Barringer, James Mercer Garnett, and Rosewell Page, eds., *University of Virginia, Its History, Influence, Equipment and Characteristics with Biographical Sketches and Portraits of Founders, Benefactors, Officers and Alumni*, 2 vols. (New York, 1904), *1*:345–346.

HENRY NOTEBOOK ENTRY

Notebook [7171], pages 139–140, Henry Papers, Smithsonian Archives

May 5th 1835.[1]

Exps suggested by reading Mr Faradays paper Phil Trans 1832 p 127.[2]

The current produced by induction in a conductor contiguous partakes more of the nature of an electrical wave.[3]

1. N.B. Try the instantaneous action of a current suddenly stoped or set in motion on a parallel current. Try this by the galvanometer.[4]

[1] Henry wrote the date after the third sentence; he was probably reading journals in the library of the American Philosophical Society at the time. The notes exemplify Henry's habits in handling material published on scientific topics of interest to him. He jotted down a brief summary of an author's results, and also proposed experiments to test or amplify each point when he returned to the laboratory. Many years later, he reviewed the reading notes and recorded experiments he had done along the lines suggested by his study of the literature.

[2] Henry was rereading section one of Faraday's first paper in the series entitled "Experimental Researches in Electricity," *Phil. Trans.*, 1832, pp. 125–162. He had quoted the paper in "Contributions II," presented to the American Philosophical Society on February 6, 1835, and was familiar with its conclusions some years before.

[3] A paraphrase of Faraday's remark on p. 127 that "The results which I had by this time obtained with magnets led me to believe that the battery current through one wire, did, in reality, induce a similar current through the other wire, but that it continued for an instant only, and partook more of the nature of the electrical wave passed through from the shock of a common Leyden jar than of that from a voltaic battery, and therefore might magnetise a steel needle, although it scarcely affected the galvanometer."

[4] Several years later, Henry wrote after this sentence "Tried this Feby 1838 also in March & April with astonishing effect. See other book." He made no notes in March 1838; of the many items recorded for April, the ones for April 12, 13, and 21 seem more germane. Since these entries will appear in a later volume of *The Papers of Joseph Henry*, a summary will suffice here. Henry noticed that discharges from a Leyden jar had destroyed the ability of one of his coils to give shocks (February entry). He also tested its weakened properties with a galvanometer connected to a helix that had been placed in the center of the coil (April 12). He decided that the intense charge from the jar had ruined the insulation of the coil, allowing the electricity to pass virtually at the same time through each of the concentric spires, analogously to currents along two parallel wires (April 13). He then devised and tried several other experiments to supply additional details on the analogy between galvanic charges from the jar and electrical currents from the battery (April 21).

This difficult paragraph in the May 5 entry is subject to another reading. Henry may have been referring in the "Tried this" sentence to other experiments in 1838 for which we have not found documentation, a missing "other book" that recorded work which directly tested Faraday's statements.

2. Try also the effect of suddenly approaching two currents.[5]

Mr Faraday has tried the above experiments and states that there is an instan[tan]eous effect but that it lasts only for a moment and that collateral currents either in the same or oposite directions, exert no perminent inducing power on each other affecting their quantity or tension.[6]

26 The action of common electricity cannot be determined as the effect of the jar discharge is so instantaneous.[7]

Try the conducting power of a magnetic bar before & after magnetization. See Phil. Mag. 1827 april p. 266.[8]

Try if spongy platina evolves with hydrogen any electricity. See Bulletin 1827 p. 370.[9]

[5] On page 129 of the article Henry was reading, Faraday reported inducing a current in a wire by moving a second, current-carrying wire close to it. Faraday also tried the effect of running currents first in the opposite and then in the same direction through two stationary wires close by each other. We assume Henry intended to combine these two experiments by swiftly moving two current-carrying wires close to each other, but we find no report of precisely such an attempt in his laboratory notebook.

[6] Faraday stated on page 129 that "collateral currents, either in the same or opposite directions, exert no permanent inducing power on each other, affecting their quantity or tension."

[7] Henry has simplified Faraday's remark in paragraph 25 (not paragraph 26, as Henry said) on page 130: "it appears impossible to separate the effects produced at the moment when the discharge begins to pass from the equal and contrary effects produced when it ceases to pass . . . , inasmuch as with ordinary electricity these periods are simultaneous, so there can be scarcely any hope that in this form of the experiment they can be perceived."

Some years later, possibly in 1838 when he was reviewing his own work on the discharge of Leyden jars, Henry wrote "not correct" after his paraphrase of Faraday.

[8] The article on which Henry took notes is J. H. Abraham, "New Phenomena Caused by the Effect of Magnetic and Electric Influence, and Suggestions for Ascertaining the Extent of the Terrestrial Magnetic Atmosphere," *Phil. Mag.*, 1827, 2d ser. *1*:265–271. Abraham asserted that magnetized lightning rods would protect buildings much better than unmagnetized ones.

On returning to his reading notes years later, Henry added "Have tried this and found no results see exp book April 1838." The entry in the "Record of Experiments" for April 7, 1838, gave the results of two tests which led Henry to conclude "that the assertion [of Abraham] was not well founded."

[9] Giovanni Giobert and Vittorio Michelotti published an article in the Turin Academy of Sciences *Memoirs*, 1826, *30*:189–194, which reported that electricity could be generated when hydrogen was burned in the presence of platinum. An abstract of their piece appeared in *Bulletin des sciences mathématiques, physiques et chimiques*, June 1827, 7:370. For bibliographical details on the *Bulletin*, see *Henry Papers*, *1*:209–210. We have found no evidence that Henry repeated their experiment.

May 9, 1835

"RECORD OF EXPERIMENTS"

Henry Papers, Smithsonian Archives

May 9 1835[1]

Exp in Philadelphia with the large magnet[2] of Mr Peal.[3]

[1] According to his published account ("Appendix to the Above—On the Action of a Spiral Conductor, &c.," *Silliman's Journal*, July 1835, *28*:331), Henry experimented with Peale's magnet on May 1 or May 2. He said in his letter to Harriet Henry of May 4 that he did the work on May 1. We believe Henry wrote this entry as a reminder of this recent experimental work.

[2] Henry described Peale's magnet as 53 pounds and capable of lifting 310 pounds. Henry's own magnet at Albany weighed only 21 pounds but could lift 750, a capacity Henry compared to Peale's in "On the Application of the Principle of the Galvanic Multiplier to Electro-Magnetic Apparatus, and Also to the Development of Great Magnetic Power in Soft Iron, with a Small Galvanic Element," *Silliman's Journal*, 1831, *19*:405.

Henry reported the results of his May 1835 experiments on Peale's magnet in the article cited in note 1. He found that "the intensity of the shock will be astonishingly increased" if a current passed through a wire wound around the keeper of a magnet and continued through a wire coiled around the magnet as well. The brightest spark appeared when the experimenter broke the circuit at the same time that the keeper was detached from the magnet. Henry also remarked that a current circulated around one magnet could be intensified by running it through a wire around a second magnet. Finally, he said that he had improved Emmet's method of increasing current by running it through the magnet itself (see note 7 of the letter to Harriet Henry of May 4, above) but he did not supply details.

[3] Titian Ramsay Peale (1799–1885), a son of the museum's founder, managed Peale's Museum in Philadelphia from 1833 until 1838 and again in 1843–1845. In the interim he was on the Wilkes Expedition to the Pacific. Charles C. Sellers, *Charles Willson Peale*, 2 vols. (Philadelphia, 1947), 2:380–381.

Peale had attended anatomy lectures at the University of Pennsylvania. He was an artist on the Long Expedition to the Rocky Mountains in 1820 and also did scientific illustrations for Thomas Say and Charles Lucien Bonaparte. A naturalist himself, Peale specialized in entomology, making the Academy of Natural Sciences of Philadelphia the base of his scientific work. Peale did scenic drawings for the Wilkes Expedition and prepared a volume on the vertebrates collected during its explorations. From 1849 until 1872 he was an examiner for the United States Patent Office. *DAB*, *DSB*.

"RECORD OF EXPERIMENTS"

Henry Papers, Smithsonian Archives

May 10 1835 Princeton

Exp 1 Wound 60 feet of copper wire covered with cotton thread around one leg of a horseshoe magnet. Then connected the ends with a galvanometer

—a current was formed through the galvanometer by merely putting or drawing off the keeper.[1]

Magnet of small power

[1] From Faraday's work and his own earliest experiments on the induction of electricity, Henry knew that instantaneous currents accompanied any change in the magnetic intensity of the iron about which the helix was wound. Experiment also indicated that merely linking the poles of a magnet with iron increased the magnetic intensity, explaining the inductive action of the keeper as it was placed on or drawn off the horseshoe magnet. In his first paper on magnetoelectric induction, Henry reported results from a similar experiment. The horseshoe electromagnet used in the experiments was disconnected from the battery, leaving the core with a residual magnetism. Detaching the keeper from the magnet caused the galvanometer to deflect. "On the Production of Currents and Sparks of Electricity from Magnetism," *Silliman's Journal*, 1832, 22:405–406; and see Henry's notes on magnetic induction, above, [ca. February 1, 1835].

"RECORD OF EXPERIMENTS"

Henry Papers, Smithsonian Archives

May 11 [1835]

Exp 1 Two batteries arranged as one. The coil with 60 feet copper ribbon inch & ½ wide gave greatest snap.[1] When hands were placed to connect the extremities of coil no shock. When iron vice was brough[t] to the side of the copper of the battery & connected with the end of the coil brilliant scintilations[2]

Exp 2 The current passed through a galvanic magnet no increased effect perceived in the spark—current passed in the opposite direction no increased effect.

Exp 3 Passed the current through the large magnet and afterwards around it so as to magnetize the iron at the <*same*> instant of making the contact or demagnetize it at the instant of breaking the circuit. Small spark. Experiment not satisfactory must be tried again[3]

[1] Henry apparently tried several of his ribbon coils and found this one to produce the best effect. He used it throughout most of the series of experiments that begins here and ends on May 18.

[2] Henry improved this test slightly and used it again in experiment seven of the entry for May 13, printed below.

[3] The wire may not have been long enough, or the difference in the spark may have been too small to perceive visually. See experiment two of the entry for May 14–15, printed below.

May 12, 1835

"RECORD OF EXPERIMENTS"

Henry Papers, Smithsonian Archives

May 12th 1835

Exp 1 Passed currents of about the same intensity through parallel ribbons—a continued current accelerated an instantaneous current.[1] When the current was passed through one a spark was produced by the other when in the same direction.

Good Exp

Exp 2nd A current from a small battery (Shaker)[2] passed through coil, parallel with current from single circular battery; the current from a single pair appeared in every case to be decreased in intensity by the passage of the other in either direction. Try this on large scale.[3]

[1] From Henry's cryptic account of this first experiment, we speculate that he first passed two currents through parallel wires, then interrupted one of the circuits to produce a self-inductive "instantaneous current," manifested by the spark. Henry probably sought to reinforce a self-inductive force in one wire by the juxtaposition of a current-carrying wire with additional inductive force. Henry first thought he detected a positive result, but later labeled the result a mistake in the margin after repeating the procedure in experiment number 5, below. To prove a theoretical point, Michael Faraday proposed a similar experiment in "On the Magneto-electric Spark and Shock, and on a Peculiar Condition of Electric and Magneto-electric Induction," *Phil. Mag.*, November 1834, 3d ser. 5:354.

[2] According to Henry's later description ("Record of Experiments," May 18, 1835), this instrument was a small trough battery of twenty-five pairs of plates, yielding moderate intensity and low quantity currents. A device of this general description is preserved along with other Henry apparatus in the collections of the Division of Electricity of the Smithsonian's National Museum of History and Technology. The Smithsonian instrument, traced to Henry's Albany period, is approximately eight inches long with plates about two inches square.

We cannot account for the origins of the "Shaker" designation. The name may have been the manufacturer's. Or possibly the battery was a product of one of America's Shaker religious communities, known for their inventiveness and craft industries. Two such communities flourished near Henry's Albany. At New Lebanon, New York (in the vicinity of Albany) and elsewhere, the Shakers were known to apply electrostatic machines of their own design to electrotherapy. The Shaker static machines were prevalent in the 1820s, if not earlier. The Shakers may have applied small galvanic batteries to the same purpose, but we have been unable to trace the use of such batteries to any of the Shaker communities. Edward D. Andrews, *The Community Industries of the Shakers* (Albany, New York, 1933), pp. 16, 110. Nevertheless, it is noteworthy that what appears to be Henry's Shaker battery was being used for therapeutic purposes at Princeton several months earlier. See the letter of Charles Hodge to Hugh Hodge, above, September 4, 1834.

We assume that Henry's small battery was of conventional design, with no unusual features. We have found no mention of a Shaker battery in standard histories of the galvanic battery. We have consulted, among other sources, A. A. Cazin, *Traité théorique et pratique des piles électriques* (Paris, 1881), and Donato Tommasi, *Traité des piles électriques* (Paris, 1889).

[3] We have found no evidence of this experiment being conducted on a larger scale. Yet, Henry obviously considered the experiment an important one, since he wrote "*NB*" by it in the margin.

Exp 3rd  Passed the current through a hollow electro-magnet filled with mercury—observed no increase of intensity[4]

Ex 4 The two wires from the large magnet were connected with the galvanometer and the keeper suddenly seperated. The needle made a complete revolution[5]

Exp 5 Repeated Exp 1st, but with a very different result; the intensity was lessened & no increase[d] action could be obtained. Repeat this on a larger scale tomorrow[6]

[4] A variation on experiments two and three of the previous day, above.

[5] This is related to the experiment of May 10, above.

[6] No further record of this experiment has been found.

"RECORD OF EXPERIMENTS"

Henry Papers, Smithsonian Archives

May 13th [1835]

Ex 1 Charged one of the troughs of the large Battery with mixture of nitric & sul. acid. 1st arranged as deflagrator 11 elements spark sharp, with coil 60 feet. With this same as calorimotor[1] of one element the spark about the same, a little more obtuse.

Exp 2nd Charged a second box with pure water, transferred the battery from the strong acid to the water, some acid remained on the plates.[2] The spark was as vivid as when in the strong acid—*ie* with arrangement of one plate. When the battery was converted into a deflagrator of 11 plates, then the spark was scarcely perceptible—

From this exp it is clear that to produce the greatest effect with a coil it

[1] The distinction between the two ways of arranging a battery is explained in note 4 of Henry's letter to George Maclean, October 9, 1833, above. Here, Henry connected the pairs of one trough in series (the deflagrator arrangement) and then in parallel (as a calorimotor). He had thought of doing these experiments using the large battery in conjunction with a ribbon coil on January 26, 1835 (see "Record of Experiments" entry of that date, above) and had published some preliminary results in "Contributions II" on February 6, but apparently college business had delayed further work on the problem until May 13.

[2] Henry wrote in the margin of this page "In these exp. Battery No 11 was used." This instrument had been built by Henry in 1833 and was described in "Contributions I." Henry now demonstrated another aspect of its versatility—he did not have to drain the trough each time he tested a new solution, as was required with a simpler battery.

is only necessary to use a battery of large dimentions charged with water or very weak acid

One plate of the battery gave a feeble spark, hence quantity and low intensity is required.[3]

Exp 3 The battery was put into the acid & the coil prepared for shocking by soldering two copper cylenders, one on each end, by a small wire. The shock was felt in the arms as high [as] the elbow in the muscles of the fore arm. On Dr White[4] the effect was to act on the *pronator* teres or twisting muscle of the arm.

The most severe shock was experienced when the end of the coil was drawn along the necks of the cups forming the communication. A continued series of shocks was thus obtained.

The sensation on myself was a peculiar thrilling in both arms. When one cylender was put into the mouth a shock was felt in the other arm and in the teeth

When Dr W. put one cylender into the mouth, the other being held in the hand, a shock was only felt in the arm grasping the cylender none in the mouth and the only muscle apparently affected was in both cases the same as mentioned above. When a cylender was grasped by each ha[n]d the sensation was similar to that experienced when the ulnar nerve is struck or the sensation vulgarly called a limb asleep[5]

Exp 4 After the plates had remained about 25 minutes in the water the spark appeared not quite as vivid. This may have happened by the acid being desolved off the plates, or in other words, the concentrated acid solution became distributed through the whole mass of water.

When the ends of the cylenders were rubbed together sparks were produced between them.

[3] Henry published an account of this experiment in "Appendix to the Above—On the Action of a Spiral Conductor, &c.," *Silliman's Journal*, July 1835, *28*:330. He mentioned the practical consequences of the discovery in his letter of May 18, 1835, to A. D. Bache, below.

[4] Henry might have known any one of the physicians by this name in Albany, Philadelphia and New York City. Possibly he meant James Hamilton White, a New Jersey resident who had just received an M.D. from the University of Pennsylvania a few months before and who had graduated from Princeton in 1831. *Princeton Catalogue*, p. 144. The following occurs in a small booklet of miscellaneous undated jottings by Henry, found amidst Mary Henry's memoir of her father and now housed in the Smithsonian Archives: "Mr Hamilton White for his own improvement has assisted me at intervals for two years past as [sentence ends here.]"

[5] An account of this experiment, shorn of the physiological detail lovingly dwelt upon here, appears on p. 330 of Henry's "Appendix" of July 1835. The work is similar to that recorded in the "Record of Experiments" entries for January 7 and January 26, 1835, printed above; in the parlance of those earlier experiments, Henry has rigged the apparatus to give "lateral" rather than "direct" shocks.

Exp 5 When the plates are in the acid and arranged as a deflagrator the shock is full as intense as with the arrangement of a single pair

Exp 6 Tried the shock with the use of the *swiper* or Basule.[6] The effect was greater with the basule than with the simple breaking of contact but not as great as when the end of the coil was rubbed along the necks of the cups.

Exp 7 Screwed a nail into the jaws of a small vice with the end of the copper ribbon. When the point of this was drawn over the copper conductor a brilliant deflagration of the metal was produced[7] although the plates were in pure water or water containing only the acid which adhered to the plates.

The conductor is coated with sealing wax which appears to increase the effect. When two boxes of plates are used and connected by a coil the effect appears but little increased. In these exp no effect of the kind is produced by a straight copper ribbon 2 feet long.

The battery appeared to be more active after remaining in the air about 2½ hours.

The above exp (5, 6, 7) when attempted with a short wire and the plates in acid completely failed. Pure water gives spark and deflagration with the coil. When the same plates in acid and a short ribbon was used, gave no spark with the nail.

NB in these exp. either the coil of 60 or the one before described of 90 feet was used. The one of 90 feet in all cases for the shock

Soldered two wires to two zinc cylenders

Exp 9[8] When the two zinc cylenders were united to the two boxes arranged as a calorimoter of two pairs slight burning was produced on the surface of the zinc when the two were rubbed together. When the two boxes were united by one of the coils, zinc to copper, & the extremities connected temporarily by the wires from the zinc cylender & when one of these was grasped by each hand & the edge of one rubbed against the side of the other a singular thrilling sensation was experienced accompanied by a vivid light between the cylenders.

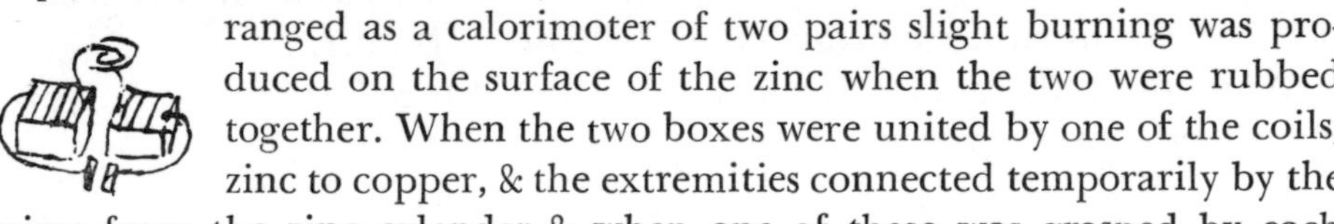

This is a new way to get the shock

[6] Our guess at the nature of this device is outlined in note 21 of "Galvanic Experiments on the Body of the Murderer Le Blanc," September 6, 1833.

[7] A standard test in Henry's laboratory repertoire, inspired by the pyrotechnics of Robert Hare. For typical examples of its previous use, see Henry's "Record of Experiments" entries for September 25, 1834, and May 11, 1835, printed above.

[8] Henry skipped eight in his numbering. A summary of this experiment appears on p. 330 in the July "Appendix."

When a short connecting wire was put into the same place a slight deflagration of the metal took place but much inferior to that from the coil. The battery was arranged in this exp. as two pairs of plates

"RECORD OF EXPERIMENTS"

Henry Papers, Smithsonian Archives

May 14th 1835

Commenced making a wide coil of thin copper 45½ feet long 3¼ wide and of the thinnest sheathing copper.

The current does not appear to be much increased in intensity by passing through a succession of currents[1] introduced into different parts of the galvanic circuit. Is this not caused by the first coil accelerating the current and the next becomes inactive in the same way that the current is not affected by coil when it is produced by a trough.[2] *Exp. on this point*[3]

[1] From the sentence that follows, we have to conclude that Henry meant to write "coils," not currents. Henry has evidently connected several coils in series with a battery.

[2] i.e., a high intensity trough battery. In "Contributions II: Spiral Conductor" where Henry intensifies currents with long wires and coils, he notes that the spiral conductor had little or no effect on an already high intensity current from two Cruikshank troughs. He conjectured, but did not attempt to prove, that longer coils might yield some intensification (p. 228).

[3] For the next two years at least, there is no indication that Henry pursued this line of research.

"RECORD OF EXPERIMENTS"

Henry Papers, Smithsonian Archives

May 14th May 15th 1835

The plates used in the last experiments after standing 24 hours in the open air gave the spark when immersed in the water. Water used yesterday.[1] *Exp 1st* Charged Shaker battery, tried to produce a spark with tin foil ribbon, did not succeed. Next with long wire around armature of 2nd magnet. The effect not increased. Next used the very long wire around the magnet and also in a coil

[1] The water still contained acid washed off the battery plates during Henry's experiments on May 13.

m magnet *a* coil *b* battery with this arrangement the spark was quite vivid. The effect due either to the action of the magnet or the long wire.[2]

Exp 2nd The same trough used in the last was charged. It gave a spark with the long copper wire 210 feet around the armature; also a slight spark with small ribbon 60 feet long but none with large ribbon of the same length. The spark was the same with the wire whether the armature was applied to the magnet or otherwise or when the keeper was reversed on the magnet

It would appear from this exp. that an increased effect may be produced from a battery by using a very long wire coiled into a helix or flat spiral.[3]

Make a long helix of small wire. Try the effect[4] with the Mercer battery[5]

May 15th 1835

Invented this afternoon a method of making coils of fine wire without silk covering. Fig. is A, spool of wood with a piece of thick sheet lead nailed on each end for the sides of the spool; a coating of silk was first put on the wood, after this a layer of fine wire, the several spires of which did not touch but were about 1/30 or 1/40 of an inch apart. They were evenly and rapidly wound on by means of the crank and causing the wire to pass on the spool through a loop of thick paper or paste board, this causes all the spires to be at the same distance from each other. But the most important part of the method consists in brushing over the wires a coating of hot electrical cement which almost

[2] In these first experiments, Henry replaced the battery of large plate size but low acid solution, used in his May 13 experiments, with the smaller Shaker battery. The tin foil ribbon and the long wire around the magnet yielded no results when hooked to that battery, but a very long wire wound around the magnet and into a coil created a spark.

[3] Henry recharged the Shaker battery presumably to eliminate the effects of polarization within it. He then ran a second series of experiments to determine what arrangements and lengths of ribbon coil and wire gave the greatest results.

[4] On this page of the "Record of Experiments" Henry later jotted the note "This was done. See April 1838." Among the entries for April 21, 1838 is the following, number three among the eight experiments of that day:

> While the battery was in operation last night for the exp on the charcoal points, repeated the exp. with the long and short coil. Also with the shock on breaking contact. The short coil did not increase the effect. With the long helix the effect was very intense both in burning and the shock.
>
> The <*latter also*> shock on breaking contact was also quite perceptible and was thought to be produced by the action of the fluid in the battery on itself, as well as the fluid in the body. It was found to increase on increasing the length of the circuit.

[5] This is probably the Cruikshank trough on display at Jadwin Hall at Princeton University and marked "Made in London and Presented by Charles F. Mercer 1809."

Charles Fenton Mercer (1778–1858) graduated at the head of his class at Princeton in 1797. He became a lawyer and was elected as a Congressman from Virginia in 1817–1839. Mercer supported public education and better transportation facilities in the new nation. He worked to end the slave trade. Mercer also advocated colonizing freed black Americans in Africa. *DAB*.

immediatly hardens[6] and thus fixes the spires in their places and insulates them at the same time.[7]

When the spool is filled with wire, the ends may be knocked off & the wood bored out. The form for holding the spool is made of two pieces of upright boards with a cross piece at the bottom

[6] Henry copied three recipes for electrical cement in an undated entry on page 175 of notebook [23894]. They required various proportions of wax or linseed oil, ochre or brickdust, and rosin. Henry gave his source as Benjamin Silliman, *Elements of Chemistry, in the Order of the Lectures Given in Yale College,* 2 vols. (New Haven, 1831), 2:645. Silliman, in turn, was paraphrasing George Singer, *Elements of Electricity and Electro-Chemistry* (London, 1814), p. 472. Both books are in the Henry Library.

[7] Winding the insulating material around the wire to be used in electrical experiments was a slow, tedious process that Henry tried to shortcut here. Automating the manufacture of equipment was one answer to this absorption of scientists' time; another solution was recruiting assistants to undertake such chores. Henry tried both methods but still spent hours perfecting and refining apparatus.

TO BENJAMIN SILLIMAN, SR.

Daniel C. Gilman Collection, Library, Johns Hopkins University

Princeton May 15th 1835

My Dear Sir

Prof. Bache has forwarded a copy of an abstract of a communication made by me to the Phil. Society for insertion in your journal.[1] If you have not given the article into the hand of the printer will you delay doing so until I can request Prof. Bache to furnish another abstract as the one given does not answer the purpose intended. It does not give the date of my communication[2] which is of some importance since Mr Faraday has given the same facts to the Royal Society. See Lond. and Edingburgh Magazine for April under the head of Proceedings of the Royal Society.[3]

[1] The abstract had appeared in the Franklin Institute *Journal,* March 1835, *15*:169–170 ("Facts in Reference to the Spark, &c. from a Long Conductor Uniting the Poles of a Galvanic Battery"). Silliman had trouble finding his copy (see his letter to Henry of May 27, 1835, printed below) but finally did reprint the abstract in the July 1835 issue of his *Journal* (*28*:327–329).

[2] To his mortification, Henry discovered he was incorrect on this point (see his letter to Bache of May 18, 1835, printed below). Bache had supplied the date of January 16, 1835, in his cover letter which was printed with the abstract in the Franklin Institute *Journal,* and had repeated it in the subtitle to Henry's text which appeared after the cover letter ("Extract from the Proceedings of the Stated Meeting of the American Philosophical Society, January 16, 1835"). Silliman reprinted both Bache's cover letter and the subtitle with the text of the abstract.

[3] "Proceedings of Learned Societies. Royal Society," *Phil. Mag.,* April 1835, 3d ser. *6*:301–

My paper developes some principles not noticed by Mr Faraday, and I have since applied the same to magneto electricity with much success.[4]

In haste yours truly
Joseph Henry

302. This paper is an abstract of Faraday's Ninth Series of "Experimental Researches in Electricity."

The "same facts" are that a long wire supplies a much more intense shock than a short one, and that a wire wound into a helix provides a more intense effect than a straight wire of the same length. Henry and Faraday disagreed on the effect of inserting a soft iron core into the helix or coil, Henry contending that the increase in intensity was negligible and Faraday reporting that it was appreciable.

[4] Henry had found that the flat ribbon coils created an even more intense shock than a cylindrical wire helix. One of the applications of this discovery consisted of connecting a ribbon coil to a battery in order to produce powerful effects, such as deflagration of metals, with little expenditure of the acid and zinc in the battery. In this arrangement, Henry dipped the plates briefly in acid, then removed them to pure water, where the residual acid clinging to the plates was sufficient to do impressive experiments when the battery was used in conjunction with a coil. He provided details in a letter to Bache of May 18, 1835, printed below. Henry published these conclusions in an addendum to the *Silliman's Journal* version of the Franklin Institute abstract, "Appendix to the Above—On the Action of a Spiral Conductor, &c.," July 1835, *28*:329–331. The addendum showed how much farther Henry had carried his work since "Contributions II" and thus implied that he had also progressed beyond the experimentation reported in Faraday's Ninth Series.

TO STEPHEN ALEXANDER[1]

Family Correspondence, Henry Papers, Smithsonian Archives

Princeton Friday evening
May 15th 1835.

My Dear Stephen

Harriet is ingaged in copying Prof. Forbes letter[2] for Prof. Bache who expressed a wish to see it and I have commenced at the same time this scrawl to you. We are now in the library <*nursery room*> I at the desk and H is attempting to make a table of the leaf of the rocking chair. Aunt has gone to sleep <*with your Intended Miss Lydia*>.[3] Your Mother is sitting with

[1] The letter is addressed to Alexander at Schenectady.

Several penciled changes and remarks are made on the first page, probably by Mary Henry or one of her collaborators. The phrase "Copied" is in the left margin and "To be preserved on account of mention of experiments in it" is written across the top.

[2] The letter to Henry of September 21, 1834, printed above.

[3] Stephen Alexander was to marry Louisa Meads within a year of the date of this letter, so Henry is probably teasing here. We have been unable to identify "Miss Lydia" other than to eliminate the possibility that she was Stephen and Henry's cousin Lydia Alexander (1802–1894), who had married Stephen Hays (d. 1862) in 1824 and who was already the mother of two sons by 1835 (information from Margaret Lydia Hays, Saratoga Springs, New York).

folded arms on the opposite side of the fire place in which a very cheerful fire is now burning and Mother has just said it is quite comfortable here. So much for us as we are now. (I should have mentioned that the youngsters are asleep & English William and the other auxiliaries of our establishment are discussing some point of culinary philosophy in the room below). All things have gone on about as usual in the Borrough since your departure but in our house I should be very sorry to say that we have been as usual since the house has been turned completely *topsey turvey* to use an expressive *classical* term. We have had no fewer than *three* Blacks scrubbing at one time in as many different rooms. The weather too has been most shiveringly cold so that the *toute ensamble* has made the most unplesant times we have experienced since the grand packing period in albany in 1832. I have taken refuge in the Hall and have been much ingaged with the assistance of Caspar[4] in working out some new facts relative to the acceleration of currents &c.[5] The april No of the Annals of Phil. came on Wednesday. It contains an abstract of Mr Faraday's ninth paper on Electricity. This paper was read before the Royal Society on the 5th of Febry.[6] and contains an exposition of the phenomina of a spark from a long & short wire. You may be sure that I read the abstract with much interest and was not much displeased to find that the gentleman had only traveled over a part of the road previously gone over by myself in my communications to the Phil. Society. There is however a wonderful coincidence in the results of the exper[imen]ts and also in the deductions from them. Mr F appears by the abstract to refer this class of phenomina to the same cause which I have suggested in my paper.[7] My communication to the Phil Society of which an

[4] Not identified. He may be the unnamed workman mentioned in Henry's letter to Torrey of February 23, 1835, printed above.

[5] i.e., intensification due to self-induction.

[6] According to the abstract Henry was using, Faraday began reading the paper on January 29 and completed it on February 5. The full version of the paper, published in *Phil. Trans.*, 1835, pp. 41–56, gives the date of reading only as January 29. Henry mentions seeing the unabridged edition in a letter to James David Forbes, June 7, 1836, Forbes Papers, Library, St. Andrews University, Scotland. There Henry again states that the paper was read February 5, 1835. A presentation copy of the full paper survives in the Henry Library and has lines inked in the margins next to points of interest to Henry. For the date and means by which Henry received his copy of the paper, see footnote 2 of John Vaughan's letter of August 5, 1835, printed below.

[7] That is, to induction. In his first brief paper on some of the phenomena described in his Ninth Series, Faraday had attributed the spark-producing current to electrotonic effects rather than to induction ("On the Magneto-electric Spark and Shock, and on a Peculiar Condition of Electric and Magneto-electric Induction," *Phil. Mag.*, November 1834, 3d ser. 5:349–354). According to Faraday, an induced current should move in a direction opposite to the primary current from the battery. At first, he erroneously believed that the spark-inducing current moved in the same direction as the primary. After a month of additional experiments, he changed his mind and ascribed the current to induction after all ("Additional Observations Respecting the Magneto-electric Spark and Shock," *Phil. Mag.*, December 1834, 3d ser. 5:444–445). In the abstract Henry was reading in the April 1835 *Phil. Mag.*, Faraday repeated his endorsement of induction as the explanation.

abstract was published in the Franklin Journal was made on the 16th of Janry—so that I am before Mr Faraday in respect to time of publishing as well as in the descovery. My paper however was not read until Feby 6 one day after the date of Mr Faradays.[8] It was however two weeks before that time in the hands of the Secretary.[9]

I have since your departure made some very interesting additions to the facts on the same subject which have an important bearing on the method of using galvanic batteries &c.[10]

Saturday Morning [May 16, 1835] A plesant morning some what cold at least in the house. Mr Maclean has gone to Philadela. The Dr.[11] is not expected home until after the commencement of the session. We yesterday received the Schenectady paper givin[g] an account of the death of Mrs Vanantwerp.[12] The ladies send several commissions for your trouble: 1st Get a tin baker an article which you must ask Miss Luisa Meads about. 2nd Get a pair of half boots for William at Orsler's.[13] 3 If you have money will you pay Garner[14] in New York 6 dollars & some cents ballance due on stove. 4 Webb[15] of albany advertizes tea very low. Get.

Give my respects to Mr Bullions. Refer him to the remarkes on his Grammers in the Repertory.[16]

[8] The sequence of readings and publications is as follows. Henry read "Contributions I" and an abstract of the experiments from "Contributions II" on January 16. Faraday read his Ninth Series on January 29 (and finished it February 5). Henry presented the full text of "Contributions II" on February 6. The abstract of experiments from "Contributions II" was published in the March Franklin Institute *Journal*, while Faraday's abstract appeared in the April issue of the *Phil. Mag.*

[9] Alexander Dallas Bache, one of four APS secretaries for 1835, informed Henry that he had received "Contributions II" one week before the February 6 meeting, that is, the day after Faraday started reading his article to the Royal Society. See his letter of February 15, 1835, above.

[10] See the entries from the "Record of Experiments" for May 13–15, 1835, printed above, and the letter to Bache of May 18, 1835, printed below.

[11] James Carnahan, President of Princeton.

[12] Deborah (or Debora) Wemple Van Antwerp (b. 1788) died on May 3, 1835. She was born in Schoharie County, married Philip Van Antwerp in 1810 in Albany, and was the mother of four sons. Her death was reported both in the *Schenectady Cabinet* (May 6, 1835) and in the Schenectady *Reflector* (May 12, 1835). Information from the New-York Historical Society and the Schenectady County Historical Society.

[13] The Albany City Directory for 1835–1836 lists John Orsler as a bootmaker.

[14] Thomas Garner (1805–1867), who worked as a youth in the coal mines, emigrated from England in 1832 and became a merchant in New York City. He purchased the Harmony Mills fabric factory in 1850 but was content with absentee ownership of that prosperous enterprise rather than taking active part in its management. New York City Directory for 1834–1835; *Howell and Tenney*, pp. 952 and 954–955.

[15] Henry Y. Webb, Jr., is listed as a victualler in the Albany City Directory for 1834–1835.

[16] Henry is referring to an anonymous critical review of "*A Grammar of the New Testament Dialect.* By M. Stuart, Professor of Sacred Literature in the Theological Seminary, Andover, 8vo. pp. 256. Andover, 1834," *Biblical Repertory and Theological Review*, April 1835, 7:233–239. The reviewer compared Stuart's book to Peter Bullions, ed., *Elements of the Greek Language, Exhibited, for the Most Part, in New Rules, Made Easy to the Memory by Their Brevity: Being a Translation of Dr.*

You forgot to leave a statement relative to the performance of the telescopes.[17]

Love from all to all. Fetch all the Ladies. Give our love particularly to James Nancy & Mrs *James.*

[*James*] *Moor's Celebrated Greek Grammar* (Albany, 1831) and found Bullions's to be much the better textbook.

[17] Henry and Alexander had run tests for the Franklin Institute comparing the magnifying powers of the refracting Fraunhofer telescope at Princeton to Amasa Holcomb's reflector. See note 6 of the letter to Bache, May 18, 1835, printed below.

"RECORD OF EXPERIMENTS"

Henry Papers, Smithsonian Archives

May 18th [1835][1]

Finished long coil described on May 15th. With the little shaker battery with 25 plates, the coil magnetized strongly a cylinder of soft iron. The same battery had no effect on the little red magnet.[2] With one of the circular batteries the magnetic effect with the small coil was very little[3]

[1] Henry continued to do scientific work after these experiments, but wrote about it in documents other than his laboratory notebook. The next entry in the "Record of Experiments" is dated March 16, 1836.

[2] Henry may have tried to reverse the magnet's polarity.

[3] Henry seemed to be testing the properties of pieces of equipment rather than raising scientific questions in his work on May 18. He did not publish an account of these experiments.

TO ALEXANDER DALLAS BACHE

Bache Papers,[1] Smithsonian Archives

Princeton May 18th 1835

My Dear Bache

With this I send a copy of Prof. Forbes' letter[2] which my good wife has

[1] There is also a Mary Henry extract of this letter in the Smithsonian Archives. The first five paragraphs are omitted in her version, and several other changes occur in the text. This letter is printed with a few minor differences in text in Nathan Reingold, ed., *Science in Nineteenth-Century America* (New York, 1964), pp. 73–75.

[2] The Forbes letter to Henry, dated September 21, 1834 and printed above, was delayed in transit and did not come to Henry until a month or so before his early May visit to Philadelphia. It was of interest to Bache for its explanation of how to calculate arc corrections in magnetic intensity readings.

transcribed after putting her chickens to roost. I have engaged the carpenter[3] to make the magnetic house[4] & hope to be ready in a few days to commence operations.

The first work will be to determine the rate of the needles sent by Prof. Forbes[5] and next to establish approximately a meridian line; these I hope to accomplish by the aid of Mr Alexander.

The comparison of the telescopes was made on the evening after my return. The night was pretty good and we had some most splendid views of the moon &c. Mr Alexander promised to furnish a statement of the result which your committee could use at discretion; he has however gone to Albany for a few days and in the hurry of departure forgot his promise. We expect him to return tomorrow or next day when he will probably give the required statement. The reflector stood the test very well, had more light but less defining power than the refractor.[6]

You have probably received the last No of the Annals of Philosophy & have read Mr Faraday's abstract. The facts given are almost identical with those communicated by me.[7] I think it probable that he has given a more definite & analytical exposition of the subject than I have. He does not appear to have used the flat spiral ribbon and consequently has not produced results as striking as those which I can now exhibit. I have devoted three or four days to experiment since my visit to Philadelphia and have succeeded in deducing some new phenomena relative to the action of the coil.[8]

[3] The unnamed individual also mentioned in the letter to Torrey of February 23, 1835, printed above.

[4] Henry visited A. D. Bache's magnetic house during his trip to Philadelphia, for which see his "Notes . . ." of April 29–May 2, 1834, printed above. Another inspiration for Henry's construction project was probably John Vaughan's letter of December 8, 1834, where he suggested Henry read the "Account of the New Observatory for Magnetic Observations at Göttingen," *Phil. Mag.*, November 1834, 3d ser. *5*:344–349. The Göttingen structure is described there as a rectangular one-story wooden building about sixteen by thirty-four feet in size. Copper replaced iron wherever metal was required in the construction. The building sheltered instruments from drafts and temperature fluctuations, without introducing the influence of iron in nails, hinges, and locks. The house itself may not have been prepossessing; rather, what distinguished Göttingen was the amount and quality of its equipment.

[5] Henry did not get around to this until the autumn vacation at Princeton (September 30 until November 12 in 1835), according to his letter to James David Forbes of June 7, 1836, Forbes Papers, Library, St. Andrews University, Scotland.

[6] The Committee on Science and the Arts of the Franklin Institute had tested Amasa Holcomb's reflecting telescopes on May 4. Apparently, Bache (who headed the Committee) felt the need of comparative data, and asked Henry to assess the powers of the reflectors relative to those of the Fraunhofer refracting telescope borrowed by Stephen Alexander to study the eclipse of November 1834. However, the Committee drafted its report on May 14, so the delay caused by Alexander's absence forced Henry to miss the deadline. "Report on Holcomb's Reflecting Telescopes," Franklin Institute *Journal*, July 1835, *16*:11–13. For Holcomb, see note 1 of his letter to Henry of May 26, below.

[7] The citation to this article and a summary of the same facts are provided in note 3 of the letter to Silliman for May 15, 1835, above.

[8] See note 4 of the letter to Silliman of May

When I charge my large battery with pump water or with pump water and the acid which adheres to the plates by one immersion into a strong solution of acid in order to disolve the oxide, the coil produces loud snaps, deflagrates the metals and gives shocks for many hours and even days by only immersing in the water. This fact furnishes a very cheap method of showing many experiments in galvanism and may give the means of producing for a long time a continued stream of electricity of considerable intensity.[9]

Owing to the circumstance of my being disappointed in procuring a strong magnet from Mr Lukins[10] I have not been able to do much in the way of magneto-electricity and shall be obliged to make a magnet for myself before going on with the subject.[11] The magnet loaned me by Mr L. does not hold its power.

I have read with much pleasure the description of your contrivances for shewing the radiation, absorption &c of heat[12] and intend to direct the attention of Dr Torrey to the paper that he may introduce them before his class. The Dr. will commence in Princeton in about a week from this time. If you wish any information relative to the *coffee* experiment I will give it in my next. Perhaps it would be well for you to make some experiments on the electricity evolved by the agitation of coffee and other similar substances.[13] I forgot to look over your account of the facts which I communicated to the society on the evening I spent at your house as I intended; there was a mistake in one part which I do not reccollect but which I wished to alter. I suppose that I can make the correction when I next attend the society.[14]

Do not forget that you are to furnish me with a formula of observation

15, 1835, and the entries for May 10–15 inclusive and May 18 from the "Record of Experiments," printed above.

[9] Henry printed a passage very similar to this in "Appendix to the Above—On the Action of a Spiral Conductor, &c," *Silliman's Journal*, July 1835, *28*:330.

[10] For Isaiah Lukens and Henry's use of his contrivances, see notes 1 and 2 of the letter from Jacob Green, February 13, 1834, printed above.

[11] Henry resumed experiments on electromagnetism in March 1836. He had been deterred from scientific work by the repairs to Philosophical Hall.

[12] "Experimental Illustrations of the Radiating and Absorbing Powers of Surfaces for Heat, of the Effects of Transparent Screens, of the Conducting Power of Solids, &c," Franklin Institute *Journal*, May 1835, *15*:303–309. Bache reported several simple but dramatic classroom demonstrations he had used successfully to illustrate phenomena of heat.

[13] Henry gave more detail on the point in his letter to Bache of February 9, 1835, printed above. Henry's later interest in similar manifestations of static electricity is discussed in footnote 3 of that letter.

[14] Henry is referring to his communication of May 1, quoted above in note 3 of his letter to Harriet Henry of that date. He did go to Philadelphia again sometime after May 18 and before July 4, according to his letter to James Henry of July 9 (printed below). He may have corrected the error then. There is no handwritten correction on the formal manuscript minutes of the Society, but Henry may have made the change on Bache's rough notes before the scribe copied them into the minute book. The error is unknown to us.

relative to the magnetic intensity[15] and also to order an exhausting syringe. I think that instead of a wooden bottom to the cylender, or glass receiver, a flat plate of metal with a stop-cock soldered to the lower surface will be better. The cement can be placed on this & the whole warmed until the cement melts by a spirit lamp placed under. In this way the adjustment of the bar-magnet will be less liable to be disturbed in cementing down the glass.[16]

I will magnetize a steel bar according to promise for you as soon as I put my battery in full operation with acid.[17]

I most sincerely hope both for your own sake and the advance of science that you may fully make out the disturbance of the needle on account of the eclipse.[18] I know no fact more important or interesting in Terrestrial Physics if it can be established than the Thermo-electrical origin of the magnetism of the earth.[19] During the next eclipse should we live to see it we must all be active in watching the needle for you.[20]

[15] The last item in notebook [7171], after the numbered pages with Henry's notes, is a three-page undated document in Bache's handwriting entitled "Directions for observing the magnetic intensity with the horizontal needles." The instructions outline the best way to take readings and the corrections necessary for temperature and other factors. Virtually the same instructions appear in Henry's handwriting in notebook [6123], where Henry says they originated in a communication from Edward Sabine to James Renwick (see *Henry Papers, 1*:336). We cannot be sure if these "Directions . . ." were the set Henry would have requested at this time. When Bache and Courtenay used the apparatus which suspended the needle in vacuo, they modified their procedures from those in the "Directions . . ." (see their article, cited in the next footnote).

[16] We assume Henry suspended the bar magnet inside a glass cylinder which was closed at the top. Since the delicate suspension could be easily upset during the process of attaching the bottom of the cylinder to a base, Henry proposed melting the sealing compound with heat applied under a metal plate. A wooden base, which normally might have been used, would have transferred the heat much too slowly and might have burned during Henry's version of the sealing process. When he wanted to make observations on the magnet in a vacuum, Henry attached the exhausting syringe to the stopcock in the base and removed the air from the cylinder. Bache and Courtenay described a similar contrivance in a paper, "On the Relative Horizontal Intensities of Terrestrial Magnetism at Several Places in the United States, with the Investigation of Corrections for Temperature, and Comparisons of the Methods of Oscillation in Full and in Rarefied Air," American Philosophical Society *Transactions*, 1837, n.s. *5*:432.

[17] On Henry's involvement with problems of magnetizing steel, see note 7 of his letter to William Kelly, December 30, 1833.

[18] Bache had told the American Philosophical Society on March 6, 1835, that he would present information on the correlation between magnetic variation and the eclipse of November 30, 1834 (American Philosophical Society *Transactions*, 1837, n.s., *5*:238). So far as we know, he never published such a paper.

[19] Henry's scientific contemporaries had proposed many ingenious theories to account for the earth's magnetism. Among these was the idea that the sun's rays had generated electricity in the earth's surface or in the atmosphere. The electricity then induced the magnetism. If this were true, the intensity of terrestrial magnetism should fluctuate during a solar eclipse. A more direct way to test the theory was to determine whether the sun's rays actually did create electricity; the inability of careful experimenters such as Faraday to show such a conversion led eventually to the disfavor of the theory. See David Brewster's articles on electricity and on magnetism in the eighth edition of the *Encyclopaedia Britannica*.

[20] The next eclipse was May 15, 1836. Henry promised on May 10, 1836, to observe it at Princeton and forward the results to Bache (letter in the Bache Papers, Smithsonian Ar-

I committed a most ridiculous blunder in writing to Prof. Silliman a few days since which if you have not sent the copy of the abstract I wish you would correct. It may however have the effect of preventing the appearance of the abstract in the next N° of the journal. When I received the copy of the Annals of Philosophy and read Mr Faradays abstract I saw that his paper was read on the 5th of Feby. I imediatly turned to a copy of my paper and found it dated Feby 6th or one day later.[21] At the same time I had the impression that your abstract of my communication to the Society did not give the date of the communication but only stated "at the last meeting" and under this false impression I wrote to Prof Silliman requesting him not to give the article into the hands of the Printer until I could have time to request you to make some additions and give the date. I have since refered to the article and much to my chagrin have found that you give the date (16th of Jany) twice. I committed this mistak by writing in a great hurry while the mail was closing for the east.

Does not the latter part of your heading place me in rather a pugilistic position with regard to Mr Faraday and would not it be as well in the republication in Silliman to strike out the passage "*Mr Faraday having recently entered upon a similar train of observations, the immediate publication of the accompanying is important, that the prior claims of our fellow countryman may* not be overlooked"—Perhaps I am over squeamish on this point and have been rendered somewhat more so by a remark of Prof Green[22] which amounted to this that there was 'much cry and little wool.'[23] On shewing the passage to wife she says it ought to stand as it is. I will leave you to decide. I do not wish to make more of the affair than it is really worth. Please write me immediatly on the receipt of this and inform me if you have sent the article to Prof Silliman.[24] I am very sorry to give you as much trouble as I have done in reference to my affairs. You must put more duties on me in retaliation. I will send the bars of antimony

chives), but Bache did not include any information from Henry in his brief report on the subject ("Observations of the Solar Eclipse of May 15th, 1836," Franklin Institute *Journal*, August 1836, *18*:100).

[21] On the dates of Henry's paper relative to that of Faraday, see note 8 of the letter to Stephen Alexander of May 15, 1835, printed above. Henry's letter to Silliman of May 15 did not delay the reprinting of the abstract; the article appeared in the July issue of *Silliman's Journal*.

[22] Jacob Green (*Henry Papers, 1*:322–323). Henry respected Green's opinions and was likely to weigh objections from him heavily.

[23] Samuel Butler describes pigs as creatures producing "all cry and no wool" (*Hudibras*, Part I, Canto 1, Line 852). Miguel de Cervantes used a similar phrase in *Don Quixote*; the term goes back at least to John Fortescue (1395–1476).

[24] The next surviving letter of Bache to Henry is dated January 1836, but they were certainly in touch before then. Silliman did include the sentences about priority in his July reprinting of Henry's abstract. This was not the first occasion on which Henry expressed sensitivity about asserting his claims (see the letter to Bache of February 9, 1835, above).

and zinc by the first oportunity. I find that they can be sawed and this will probably be the best method of constructing the small bars for our Thermoscope.[25]

Give my respects to Mrs Bache. Mrs Henry will be very happy to see her in Princeton as soon as Mrs B can find it convenient to come.[26] A jaunt at this time would be found very plesant. Princeton is now dressed in its most pleasing garb. The college campus is extremely beautiful at this season of the year.

I am with the highest respect
Your Friend
Joseph Henry

[25] Henry and Bache were evidently building a thermoelectric pile which, with a measuring device, would be a thermoscope. The optimum metals would have been antimony and bismuth, but zinc would have been a suitable substitute for bismuth. In his European diary entry for April 22, 1837, Henry comments that two years earlier he had tried to get a spark from thermoelectricity but that he lacked a pile of thirty or forty elements. He says also that he had sent metal to Isaiah Lukens for the construction of a larger pile which, however, was not completed. Henry's interest in thermoelectric piles will be discussed in the above-cited diary entry and related documents to appear in the third volume of *The Papers of Joseph Henry*.

[26] So far as we know, Nancy Bache did not visit Princeton in 1835 despite the Henrys's invitation. She had hoped to do so in August, according to Henry (see his letter to Harriet Henry of May 1, 1835, printed above).

FROM AMASA HOLCOMB[1]

Gratz Collection, Historical Society of Pennsylvania

Southwick May 26th 1835

Dear Sir

I have repaired the Telescope belonging to your College,[2] so far as was

[1] Amasa Holcomb (1787–1875) learned science and mathematics by reading in the library of an uncle. He then taught school and began to make instruments to use in teaching science in his classroom. Holcomb also compiled and published almanacs as a young man. After 1825 he concentrated on building telescopes, and later in life experimented with daguerreotypy. He served at various times as selectman, representative to the General Court, and Justice of the Peace for Southwick, Massachusetts. *DAB*.

Holcomb constructed his most important telescopes in the 1830s. He built refractors on occasion, but preferred to specialize in reflector models patterned after the designs of William Herschel (1738–1822; see *DSB*), in which the light is reflected only once before reaching the observer. The object under study is thus really behind the observer, and the telescope maker must compensate for the viewer's head blocking the light, a problem Holcomb struggled with in his instruments. The Herschel style allowed Holcomb to achieve a larger visual field than possible with a refractor. He could also increase the light reaching the observer since the light did not have to be reflected twice, as in the pre-Herschel reflectors.

expected of me. I have succeeded quite as well as I expected. I wish you would send in your letter[3] the distance at which you can distinctly read common print with your Fraunhofer telescope.[4] Please to state the size of the print as well as the distance. It may perhaps be convenient for you to use the sheet that contains an account of your late experiments,[5] as I have that; I can use the same, and thus have a comparative test. You will please to inform me the name and number (if convenient) in New York where you wish me to send your telescope. On the receipt of your letter I shall forward it immediately.

Yours Respectfully
Amasa Holcomb

Holcomb built telescopes of about six to ten foot focal length; Herschel reached forty feet in one bizarre and nearly unusable instrument but his most successful telescope had a twenty-foot length. Henry King, *History of the Telescope* (London, 1955), pp. 120–135; Franklin Institute *Journal*, September 1834, *14*:169–172; July 1835, *16*:11–13; August 1836, *18*:109–110; and November 1836, *18*:312; and *Silliman's Journal*, January 1833, *23*:403 and January 1835, *27*:185–186.

[2] On the address side of the letter, Joseph Henry wrote "Holcomb on repair of large reflector for the College of NJ." Princeton had acquired a four-foot reflector from London in 1801, according to *Wertenbaker*, p. 125. The repair might have been to the base of the telescope—Holcomb's schemes for the mounting of his instruments were especially commended by the Franklin Institute in the citations given in note 1—or it might have been a repolishing of the mirror surface. The repairs cost $45.00 (receipt dated August 28, 1835, listed in "J. Henry's a/c with Philosophical Hall previous to 1837," Princeton University Archives).

[3] Not found.

[4] This would be the instrument Stephen Alexander used to observe the eclipse of 1834 (see the text and note 9 of the letter of October 27, 1834, above) and which he persuaded Princeton to buy (see note 4 of the letter of November 29, 1834, above). Holcomb could use this datum on the Fraunhofer for comparing his own telescopes to a product of one of the great European shops.

[5] Henry published "Facts in Reference to the Spark, &c. from a Long Conductor Uniting the Poles of a Galvanic Battery" in Franklin Institute *Journal*, March 1835, *15*:169–170.

FROM JAMES DAVID FORBES

Henry Papers, Smithsonian Archives

London 26th May 1835

My Dear Sir

I have long intended to write by Post to enquire whether my magnetic dispatch reached you safely last autumn which was forwarded as you desired by Mr Turnbull I think about the middle or end of September.[1] It

[1] Forbes is following up his letter of September 21, 1834, above. Henry's letter to Torrey of April 2, 1835, announces that he had finally received the long-awaited shipment. Henry did not respond to Forbes's letter until June 7, 1836, when he explained that the

consisted of your needle returned, with the observations which I had made & another needle which I had also observed (marked (A)) which I sent for you to observe & return in like manner. I also sent some copies of papers of mine. I should be very glad to know that the packet reached you safely.

I am My Dear Sir faithfully Yours
James D. Forbes

P.S. Please address to me at Edinburgh.

---

packet had been misplaced in New York for over six months and that one of the magnetic needles had apparently been disturbed in transit, something Henry wanted to check thoroughly before replying. Apologizing for his delayed response, Henry renewed scientific contact with reports on experiments with the magnetic needles and a packet which included two of his recent articles on electricity and magnetism. Henry's reply, to appear in volume three of the *Henry Papers*, is in the Forbes Papers, St. Andrews University Library.

FROM BENJAMIN SILLIMAN, SR.

Henry Papers, Smithsonian Archives

New Haven May 27, 1835[1]

My dear sir

My absence prevented me from the pleasure of seeing your friend Mr Wines[2] & of shewing him kindness. I thank you for the papers forwarded by him, which, having just returned from a long absence I have not had time to peruse.

I am much gratified that you have been elected to the Philos. Soc^y^ & introduced to its library & to Dr Hare & other highly cultivated men.

I regret that your valuable labors should slumber so long in waiting for the Philos. Trans:[3] & I should regret still more if I have overlooked anything of yours which ought to have appeared but my absence since Feby except a few days will account for it. Perhaps you can send me that paper as at this moment I know not where to lay my hand upon the Franklin Journal. I should wish very much to become acquainted with the construction of your battery especially as I am to deliver some chemical &

[1] This letter does not seem to be a response to Henry's letter of May 15, above. Although we have found no intervening correspondence from Henry to Silliman, Wines may have delivered a letter which raised the questions answered here.

[2] E. C. Wines.

[3] The *Transactions* of the American Philosophical Society were so denoted in imitation of the Royal Society's famous scientific publication. Here Silliman is indicating one ground for the superiority of his *Journal*: rapid publication.

physico-chemical lectures in Boston next March[4] & might wish to avail myself of your improvements, especially as I may lecture to many of their most intelligent people & I should like also to exhibit one of your magnets in its most improved forms, especially if it could be fitted with a lever (steel yard fashion) so that the application of a great weight might be proved without the inconvenient piling of so much iron upon the scale. What would your most improved galvanic battery cost delivered in Boston? I mean one that will demonstrate the galvanic phenomena on a wide range & also a powerful galvanic magnet; it would not be important that either instrument should be *the greatest of its kind,* but that it should be sufficient to show the effects to 1000 people if so many should attend. I should like to announce your name & discoveries to a community of very high intelligence, to which you may have heard I have already lectured.[5]

I should be glad to receive your paper provided the society cannot publish it promptly.[6]

On the annexed page you will find a memorandum of the dues of Mr Wines, & of Mr Olmsted[7] & I should be obliged to you to obtain & forward the money from those gentlemen & to transmit it in future; the societies must I think be supplied by some of the agents as I do not recollect any transactions with them.[8]

Please give me Mr Olmsteds Christian name. I have this day forwarded his Journals by steam boat in a strong bundle.

I remain my dear sir as ever
yours very truly
B Silliman

Mr Wines owes for Volumes 26, 27 & 28 of the American Journal @ \$3=\$9. If convenient to remit \$10 it will make but one postage & will go \$1. towards Vol 29.

Mr Olmsted will owe for Vol^s^ 23, 24, 25, 26, 27 & 28 (No 2 of the latter to follow by mail next month) 6 volumes @ \$3.=18\$. If convenient to remit \$20, it will save postage & leave \$2. in advance towards Vol 29.

A gentleman named C. G. Olmsted[9] of Franklin Tennessee (Williamson

[4] This is the start of intermittent correspondence on Silliman's lectures. He was a highly successful popular lecturer, an activity of little interest to Joseph Henry.

[5] For Henry's reply to this letter, see his of August 29, 1835, below. Since the point of the powerful electromagnet was its great lifting power, using a mechanical aid blunted the visual effect.

[6] Another instance of Silliman's helping Henry. As is customary among many journals even today, Silliman would not simply reprint a current article in a competing journal.

[7] See Henry's reply of August 29, 1835, below.

[8] Silliman owned the *Journal* and carried out its editorial and business affairs largely on his own in this period.

[9] Unidentified.

County) formerly remitted $5. for the Journal & had sent him volumes 19, 20, 21, 22, 23, 24 & 25. I suppose this is not the same person. I should be glad to receive any information of Mr C. G. O.

BS.

FROM WILLIAM RAMSEY[1]

Henry Papers, Smithsonian Archives

Cabinet Room May 29^h^ 1835.

Respected Sir.

From a deep sence of your character as a scholar and from the interest you evince in the cause of Science in general the Lyceum of Natural Science of Jefferson College has enrolled your name on the catalogue of her honorary members.[2]

Yours Respectfully,
Wm Ramsey Secretary

[1] A William Ramsey, otherwise unknown, is listed as an 1836 graduate of Jefferson College, a Presbyterian institution in Canonsburg, Pennsylvania. A native of Canonsburg, Ramsey later became a lawyer. *General Catalogue of Jefferson College, Canonsburg, Pa. From the Time it was Chartered in 1802 to 1856* (Pittsburgh, 1857), p. 17 and *Catalogue of the Officers and Students of Jefferson College, Canonsburg* (Pittsburgh, 1835), p. 7.

The Lyceum of Natural Science, which Ramsey is representing, was primarily a student facility, which had a "respectable Cabinet of Minerals, and numerous collections in Natural History and Indian Antiquities." (1835 Jefferson *Catalogue*, p. 15.) The recommendation for Henry's honorary membership probably came from Jacob Green, Professor of Chemistry, Mineralogy, and Natural History at the College, and Professor of Chemistry at the school's Medical Department in Philadelphia. The latter was his principal position. Although Jefferson Medical College functioned largely independently of the parent institution, Green delivered lectures on chemistry and mineralogy at Canonsburg during the summer session. See the above-cited catalogs. Joseph Smith, *History of Jefferson College* (Pittsburgh, 1857), pp. 113–115, discusses Green's role in founding the Medical School, the best known department of the college. Henry's Library contains a copy of the 1836 Jefferson College *Catalogue*, presented by W. D. V. Downing, listed in 1836 as a student in the College's "Preparatory School."

[2] An undated retained copy of Henry's letter of acceptance survives among his papers in the Smithsonian Archives. The draft appears to have been written sometime in late summer 1835. Along with his acceptance Henry sent Ramsey reprints of "Contributions I" and "Contributions II."

June 12, 1835

FROM JOHN PROVOST[1]

Henry Papers, Smithsonian Archives

Castlehill June 12th 1835

Prof Henry
Respected & dear sir

I take the liberty of addressing you on a subject you may not think unworthy of consideration. The professorship of Natural Philosophy in the University of Virginia is at present vacant.[2] Professor Patterson with whom you may be acquainted, has recently resigned and is going I believe to Philadelphia.[3] Several gentlemen, to supply the vacancy, have been recommended to the notice of the visitors (or trustees of whom there are some six or eight,) viz yourself, Rogers of Williamsburg[4] Va, Vethake of Lexington,[5] do, Renwick of NY[6] & Olmsted of N. Haven.[7] The Hon. W. C. Rives[8] in whose family I am living is one of the visitors. He expresses himself highly pleased with the information he has had respect-

[1] John Provost came from Bloomfield, New Jersey, to Princeton. He received the B.A. in 1833 and the A.M. in 1836. His death occurred in 1864. Provost has eluded us beyond this. His presence with the Rives family might indicate that he was a tutor there. *Princeton Catalogue*, p. 145.

[2] This is an informal query followed on July 8 by a formal communication from John H. Cocke of the University's Board of Visitors, below. On the verso Henry wrote "Letters to be answered." We do not have a reply, assuming one was written, and cannot state what encouragement Henry did or did not give. A letter of Charles Bonnycastle, July 9, 1835, may indicate another contact in Charlottesville before the formal offer. These informal contacts may explain the point made in footnote 2 of the letter of Cocke.

[3] Robert Maskell Patterson (1787–1854) was Professor of Natural Philosophy at Virginia from 1828 to 1835. He returned to his native city to become Director of the United States Mint, serving there until 1851. His father, Robert Patterson (1743–1824; *DAB*), had previously served as Director of the Mint. Robert Maskell Patterson's appointment followed the precedent set in Great Britain with Sir Isaac Newton as Master of the Mint. At the start of the Republic, David Rittenhouse became head of the Mint. The elder Patterson served for many years as Professor of Natural Philosophy and, briefly, as Vice-Provost of the University of Pennsylvania. Here, also, the son followed in the father's steps.

After receiving the bachelor's degree from Pennsylvania in 1804, Robert Maskell Patterson studied medicine, graduating in 1808. While spending several years studying in Paris, his interests turned toward the physical sciences. In 1811–1812 Patterson studied with Sir Humphry Davy. Shortly after his return to Philadelphia, he received two appointments at Pennsylvania: Professor of Natural Philosophy in the medical school and Professor of Natural Philosophy, Chemistry, and Mathematics in the College. The Vice-Provostship came in 1814.

Like his father, Robert Maskell Patterson became President of the American Philosophical Society (1849–1854). He was a considerable personage in the small American ante-bellum scientific community but published little. Henry corresponded with him; examples will appear in later volumes. American Philosophical Society, *Proceedings*, 1854, *6*:60–64.

[4] William Barton Rogers. See footnote 46 of Henry's Notes on a Trip to Philadelphia, April 29–May 2, 1834.

[5] Henry Vethake, *DAB*, had just been chosen President of Washington College, now Washington and Lee University.

[6] James Renwick, Sr., of Columbia.

[7] Denison Olmsted of Yale.

[8] William Cabell Rives, 1793–1868, *DAB*. An important Virginia political figure of the day. Originally a Jackson supporter, Rives eventually became a Whig. He was in the House of Representatives (1823–1829) and the Sen-

ing you as a gentleman, instructor and a man of science. Now, sir, if you are disposed to consider the matter and will signify to me your willingness to accept an appointment of this kind I will signify it to some of the visitors. Such information respecting the candidates will doubtless be acceptable to them before they proceed in their election to supply the vacancy. You would not fail, I think sir, to find the place agreeable. The University is situated near Charlottesville in the midst of one of [the] finest countries in the State. The town is about the size of Princeton and similar to it in some other respects, particularly in its healthy and airy situation. The manners and character of the Virginians I think will also please you. I have found them uniformly kind-hearted, generous and hospitable. The compensation of the Professor, Mr Rives informs me, will be between 3 and 4 thousand dollars. Mr Patterson the late occupant of the chair recieved a fixed salary of 1500 dollars, besides 25 dollars, tuition fee, from every student who attended his recitations or lectures. The advantages the University will afford for prosecuting your scientific researches are at least equal, and I presume, superior to those of Nassau Hall. There is an Observatory[9] upon a lofty eminence near the University which will doubtless be of great service to you; also, I believe, an excellent and complete philosophical apparatus belonging to the institution. A meeting of the visitors will take place on the 1st of July. If therefore you should think proper to make any communication on this subject and will address me at "Lindsay's Store Albemarle C^o^ Va" I will attend to it with great pleasure.

Should you not think the subject worthy of attention, yet it would be very gratifying to me indeed kind sir to hear from yourself and family if you can without inconvenience redeem a few moments from your busy pursuits to favour me with a few lines. I love to hear from Princeton and especially from my "Alma mater" who is still dear to me from a thousand pleasing reccollections. In her welfare I shall ever feel deeply interested and am pained at the remotest idea of your dissolving with her a connection of which she cannot but be proud. Yet, however dear to me, I could by no means wish an individual to make great personal sacrifices to her prosperity. Please give my best respects to Mrs Henry and accept the same yourself and believe me to be with abiding sentiments of esteem and affection

Your quondam pupil
John Provost

ate (1832–1834; 1836–1839; 1841–1845). Rives served as Minister to France, 1829–1832 and 1849–1853.

[9] "A small structure was erected on the reservoir mountain about March 1828; but it appears to have served no practical purpose owing to the lack of proper fitting out, and in 1859, it was pulled down. . . ." Philip Alexander Bruce, *History of the University of Virginia, 1819–1919*, 5 vols. (New York, 1920–1922), *1*:271–272.

P.S. There is also an excellent house & garden that will be at your service. Mr Rives for one is very anxious that you should signify your willingness to accept and will use his best endeavours with the rest of the visitors to have you appointed. Mr Rives is strongly opposed to their going abroad for a professor of which there has been some talk. He greatly prefers some eminent countryman of his own in order to encourage the cultivation of literature & science in our own country. JP[10]

[10] Faintly in pencil near the address are these words, possibly by Provost: "Please send me the publication containing *the* discoveries and improvements you have made in your department."

HENRY NOTEBOOK ENTRY[1]

Notebook [6123], page 90, Henry Papers, Smithsonian Archives

June 14th 1835.

Make exp. on sound[2] by *stopping* one ear and taking the direction of a bell with an instrument for measuring angles. Also with the ears open compare the results.[3] See Manchester Mem vol 5[4]

[1] These lines appear on a page headed "*Sound*" just below an undated jotting by Henry on a query from James Dean (for whom see note 1 of the letter of November 27, 1833, above). Dean asked why a violin and a flute of the same pitch, when played at the same loudness, sounded different to an audience. Henry explained this difference when he defined the quality of timbre in his lectures on sound in the physics course at Princeton.

[2] As a physicist, Henry was to have a persisting interest in questions of sound. His Princeton lectures on natural philosophy included a section on sound, and when he lectured to the Mercantile Library Association in January 1839, Henry chose to devote two of the six sessions to the subject. He jotted down other reading notes and experiments on sound, dated June 1836 to November 1840 but not chronologically organized, on pages 572–574 of notebook [10615], which is further described in note 1 of the entry of June 13, 1833, printed above. His published papers on the topic included "On Acoustics Applied to Public Buildings," American Association for the Advancement of Science *Proceedings*, 1856, *10*: 119–135 and a long series of "Researches in Sound, in Relation to Fog-Signalling," in the United States Department of the Treasury, Light House Board *Reports* for 1874–1877. His investigations for the Light House Board, which began in 1865, had theoretical as well as practical consequences.

[3] Henry did not record the results of these experiments in his notebooks, but he may have used them as classroom demonstrations in his Princeton lectures. Notebook [23920] in Box 16 of the Henry Papers at the Smithsonian Archives, a book from which Henry lectured on the topics of light and sound, has the following in it: "Sound not of same intensity in all directions. Firing of a cannon—ringing of a bell—bell glass—speaking trumpet."

[4] Henry is probably referring to John Gough, "An Investigation of the Method Whereby Men Judge, by the Ear, of the Position of Sonorous Bodies Relative to Their Own Persons," Manchester Literary and Philosophical Society *Memoirs*, 1802, *5*:622–652. He took notes on this article on page 150 of notebook [7169]. Gough (1757–1825), the author of this essay, was an able botanist and teacher of mathematics despite blindness incurred from a childhood bout with smallpox (*DNB*).

June 29, 1835

FROM STEPHEN VAN RENSSELAER

Henry Papers, Smithsonian Archives

Albany June 29th 1835

Dear Sir

Mr Devenport[1] of Vermont has exhibited in my Office a machine which evinces great ingenuity. He visits Princeton to submit to your inspection its operation and to obtain your opinion on the practicability of applying it to useful purposes. I beg leave to introduce him to your notice. He is an intelligent unassuming Mechanic. He is destitute of Funds to make experiments on a large scale. I think he merits encouragement.

Yours respectfully
[in] haste
S V Rensselaer

[1] Thomas Davenport (1802–1851, *DAB*), who started his career as an inventor in 1833 at Brandon, Vermont, where he was a blacksmith. C. W. Mittman's account in the *DAB* dates his interest in electromagnetism from 1831 but this is contradicted by Davenport's manuscript autobiography in the Vermont Historical Society. 1833 is also consistent with later events recounted by Davenport.

He was from a poor family and had a very modest education, being apprenticed at an early age. In the summer of 1833 Davenport learned of a powerful "galvanic battery" in Crown Point, New York, at the Penfield and Taft plant. Henry had built an electromagnetic iron ore separator for the firm. (See *Henry Papers, 1*:340–341; 346; 364–372, for Henry's involvements with iron ore separators.) Up to that point, Davenport had never heard of galvanism nor of any of the investigators in the field. On learning of Henry's role in the construction of the device, Davenport went to Albany to see Henry who was not there, having moved to Princeton in November of the previous year. Davenport had not yet seen a demonstration of "an anvil being suspended between the heavens and the earth by magnetic power," the feat which had first attracted him to Crown Point. This was demonstrated in December 1833, moving Davenport to buy one of the devices and devote the remainder of his life to developing electromagnetic motors.

In his autobiography Davenport reports his neighbors talked about his work as development of perpetual motion—which he indignantly denied. By July 1834, Davenport had a device with rotary motion; the costs involved, however, were too great for practical application. Persisting in his work, in December 1834 Davenport turned, not without trepidation, for advice to the professoriate, first consulting Edward Turner (1779–1838), Professor of Mathematics and Natural Philosophy at Middlebury College. Turner encouraged him, as did other Vermonters of prominence. Perhaps through Turner's agency, Davenport had his first glimpse of literature on electricity and magnetism. Up to this point Davenport had proceeded meticulously and laboriously by trial and error. In January 1835, Davenport looked into the elder Silliman's *Elements of Chemistry* . . . (1831) "which contained some of Prof. Henrys experiments in electromagnetism, by which I learned for the first time the true names of the instruments and materials which I was using." The contrast between the working methods of the "Brandon Blacksmith" and Joseph Henry was clearly delineated by those words written around 1851. Henry, laboriously and methodically, had mastered the available literature and continued to do so as his research broadened. Henry belonged to a research tradition and to a research community. Davenport was essentially alone except for the intermittent collaboration of other ingenious mechanics. A community of electrical technologists did not exist at that date. Had he worked with steam rather than electricity and magnetism as sources for motive power, Davenport's situation would have been quite different. Henry's research was primarily directed toward theoretical understanding of his experiments; Davenport's research was primarily directed to contriving a working device. Henry was both conscious and proud of his tradition and community.

Nothing survives from the years 1833–1835 from which we can gain insight into Davenport's viewpoint. In retrospect, at least, when writing the autobiography, he was conscious of the worth of his calling as inventor:

> I hope the reader does not believe that inventions are "lucky hits," and are struck out by a single thought of the inventor. No! it requires profound study, and the most intense application of the mind. To invent is to read nature's laws.

In early June 1835, Davenport determined to go to Washington to obtain a patent. First, he presented a letter of introduction from Turner to Amos Eaton asking the latter to interest Stephen Van Rensselaer in the device. Eaton, in turn, gave Davenport a letter to the Patroon stating:

> I told Mr. Davenport that no one could consistently aid him without Professor Henry's consent. I advised him to exhibit his machine to Mr H after you had seen it. This, he will do. Prof. Henry suggested the practicability of applying his great power to machinery, but I did not from him understand that any plan was fixed on. Mr. Davenport's is a simple and efficient plan. A line from yourself to Mr. Henry would of course draw from him all you would wish after he has inspected Mr D's machine, nearly the whole subject is absolutely and fully illustrated. It appears to me that Mr Henry would be greatly delighted with such a satisfactory exemplification of a principle which has extended his name to the ends of the earth.

This is Van Rensselaer's letter of introduction, presumably presented to Henry in Princeton early in July. For the outcome of his meeting, see Henry's letter to Benjamin Silliman, Sr., of September 10, 1835, below.

The quotations are from Davenport's autobiography. We are indebted to Robert Post of the Smithsonian's National Museum of History and Technology for providing a transcription of the manuscript in the Vermont Historical Society. Walter Rice Davenport, a descendant, authored a *Biography of Thomas Davenport, The "Brandon Blacksmith"* . . . (Montpelier, 1929), containing complete and partial texts of Thomas Davenport's papers now apparently lost. See also, *King*, pp. 260–271.

RECOMMENDATION[1] FOR WILLIAM BARTON ROGERS

Rogers Papers, Archives, Massachusetts Institute of Technology

Nassau Hall
July 6th 1835

Mr William Rogers of Virginia is well known as an ardent and successful cultivator of science. I am personally acquainted with him and have a very

[1] Emma Rogers printed this letter, with some slight differences in the transcription of the text, in her *Life and Letters of William Barton Rogers* (Boston and New York, 1896), *1*:126. We decided to publish the letter again because of Henry's interesting comment about American scientists who made careers of disseminating ideas from overseas.

We believe that Henry composed this letter for general use by Rogers rather than for a specific purpose. The format is similar to Henry's letter of July 1835 for Walter R. Johnson, printed below. Johnson decided to use his letter for obtaining a job on the Wilkes expedition, but to our knowledge, Rogers never expressed an interest in joining that expedition. Henry was not among the nine men who recommended Rogers for membership in the American Philosophical Society, to which Rogers was elected on July 17, 1835. Rogers did not intend visiting Europe in 1835, so the letter was not to introduce him to sci-

high opinion of his talents and acquirements. He is one of those who, not content with retailing the untested opinions and discoveries of European Philosophers, endeavor to enlarge the boundaries of useful knowledge by experiments and observations of their own.

Should Mr. Rogers' life and health be spared[2] I am confident he will do much towards elevating the scientific character of our country.

Joseph Henry
Prof. Nat. Phil
College of N. Jersey
Princeton

entists overseas (the sentiment in the letter was hardly tactful, if this was its function). He had already been appointed state geologist of Virginia by July. We doubt Henry intended the recommendation for Rogers's use in winning the University of Virginia professorship, since Henry himself was a nominee for that post.

The address side of the letter is not helpful: it says "William Rogers Esq Care Professor Bache University of Penna Philadelphia." A file note on the letter is too faint to elucidate its purpose.

[2] Rogers had suffered intermittently from health problems since 1825. In the spring of 1834 he was struck by an ailment that racked him alternately with fever and chills. Nevertheless, he was well enough by summer 1834 to spend that season doing geological field work. Rogers, *Life and Letters, 1*:31 and 109–110.

FROM JOHN H. COCKE[1]

Henry Papers, Smithsonian Archives

University of Virginia July 8. 1835

Dear Sir,

I am instructed by the Board of Visitors of the University of Virginia to inform you, that you have been appointed to the professorship of Natural philosophy in this Institution.[2] The Salary is a thousand Dollars with the

[1] John Hartwell Cocke (1780–1866) graduated from William and Mary (B.A.) in 1798. He was a tireless temperance worker and an original member of the Board of Visitors of the University of Virginia, serving from 1819 until 1852. Paul Brandon Barringer, James Mercer Garnett, and Rosewell Page, eds., *University of Virginia: Its History, Influence, Equipment and Characteristics with Biographical Sketches and Portraits of Founders, Benefactors, Officers and Alumni*, 2 vols. (New York, 1904), *1*:328–329.

[2] The Board of Visitors was not expecting Henry to accept the appointment. "He is said to be a very able man, but it is doubtful he will accept," wrote Gessner Harrison (1807–1862, *DAB*) to Henry Tutwiler (1807–1884, *DAB*), July 8, 1835, University of Virginia Library. Even Henry knew somehow that he was not expected to accept (see below, Henry to James Henry, August 2, 1835). Henry declined in his letter to Cocke, July 24, 1835, printed below. But the Board had resolved on July 8, "That Professor Henry of Princeton, be appointed Professor of Natural Philosophy in this Institution; and if he shall decline

further compensation from the fees, which in this school the last Session amounted to $2090. In addition to the above, a tenement sufficient for the accommodation of a family is furnished to the Professor rent free.[3] The Salary to commence from the date of your acceptance.

It is desirable to know your determination as soon as possible. I have therefore to request you will address me Winnsville post office, Fluvanna Co. V[a] and send a duplicate to John A. G. Davis[4] Chairman of the Faculty of the University of Virg[a]

I send you herewith a copy of the enactments from which you will be enabled to judge of the organization of the University & the duties of the particular department which you have been invited to occupy by a unanimous vote of the Board.[5]

Yours with high respect
John H. Cocke Rector pro. tem:

the appointment, in that case Professor Rogers of W[ms] Burgh be, and is hereby appointed to that professorship." (Typescript of the Board of Visitors' Minutes, July 8, 1835, University of Virginia Library.) William Barton Rogers (1804–1882, *DAB*) was appointed and served from 1835 until 1853.

[3] The salary which Cocke outlined here was, in Henry's words, "the largest in the United States" (see below, Henry to James Henry, August 2, 1835). In his letter of July 9, 1835, below, Charles Bonnycastle outlined Henry's salary, benefits and duties. More than simply a compliment to Henry, the tendered appointment brought improvements in Henry's position at Princeton. See the letters below in July and early August.

[4] John A. G. Davis (1802–1840). Educated at William and Mary College and the University of Virginia, Davis served as Professor of Law at the University from 1830 until his death. He was a prolific writer on legal topics. As Chairman of the Faculty, he was attempting to disperse a rebellious student assemblage when he was fatally shot by one of the rioters. Barringer, Garnett, and Page, op. cit., p. 351. We have not located any duplicate response sent to Davis.

[5] No such enclosure has survived either in Henry's Library or in his personal papers.

FROM CHARLES BONNYCASTLE[1]

Henry Papers, Smithsonian Archives

University of Virginia
July 9th 1835

Dear Sir

Our Board of Visitors yesterday appointed you Professor of Natural Philosophy in this Institution, the situation having become vacant by the

[1] Charles Bonnycastle (1792–1840), son of the more famous English mathematician John Bonnycastle (1750?–1821, *DNB*). After helping his father in the writing of several mathematical textbooks, Bonnycastle came to Virginia in 1825 to accept the University's Chair of Na-

resignation of D^r R: Patterson,[2] who, with the view of returning to his friends, has accepted the situation of Director of the Mint.

The income produced by the several professorships of our University varies with circumstances: Dr Patterson's during the past session stood as follows

	$
Salary....................................	1000
D° for care of Observatory...	500
Fees of 84 students	2100
	3600

to which compensation must be added a handsome house.

The Professor of Chemistry,[3] whose school sometimes exceeds, sometimes falls short of that to which you have been appointed, received this year $4075; whilst in another school the compensation was $4500, and with the addition of an office shared biennually among us, $5000.

The earliest appointed Professors receive a salary of $1500 in lieu of $1000,[4] but with the latter you will observe that, supposing us to remain stationary, your income would vary from 3 to $4000; and with the rapid increase which we have every right to anticipate, will probably amount to, or exceed, the latter sum.[5]

The labour required of you is three lectures a week, each of two hours; and even adding a few hours spent in every month in examining candidates for degrees, time will still be allowed for prosecuting your experiments & studies.

tural Philosophy. From 1827 until his death he was Professor of Mathematics there. He authored several articles in the physical sciences as well as three books in mathematics. Paul Brandon Barringer, James Mercer Garnett, and Rosewell Page, eds., *University of Virginia, Its History, Influence, Equipment and Characteristics with Biographical Sketches and Portraits of Founders, Benefactors, Officers and Alumni*, 2 vols. (New York, 1904), *1*:346–347.

[2] Robert M. Patterson, for whom see above, Provost to Henry, June 12, 1835, especially footnote 3.

[3] John Patton Emmet was Professor of Chemistry at Virginia from 1825 until 1842. See above, Henry to Harriet Henry, May 4, 1835, especially footnote 7.

[4] That is, original faculty members and those starting in the first few years of the college received $1500, while those entering more recently received only $1000. See Philip A. Bruce, *History of the University of Virginia, 1819–1919*, 5 vols. (New York, 1920), *2*:180–182.

[5] According to gleanings from the archives and printed histories of Virginia and some comparable colleges in the mid-1830s, the pay for professorships in mathematics, natural philosophy, and chemistry was on a par with or was higher than the pay for other academic disciplines. But faculty salaries at Virginia exceeded those of the other American colleges. Such schools as Brown, Harvard, Williams, Union, Amherst, Dartmouth, and Yale offered salaries ranging between $700 and $1500, all emoluments included. Columbia had a nearly competitive salary scale, from $2200 to $2800, including a housing allowance. Henry's salary at Princeton, starting at $1000 and a house in 1832 and reaching $1500 and a house by 1835, placed him among the most highly paid of American science educators.

The short time that we passed together at Philadelphia made me anxious to have you for a colleague, and I feel that in pressing your appointment upon the Board I have done a duty to the Institution.

The official notice was yesterday sent to you by the Secretary of the Board,[6] & *if you accept* it would be proper to communicate the fact immediately to Professor Davis,[7] who succeeds me as Chairman. If you do not accept, or are not decided I will suggest the following course—

At the particular request of Mr W: C: Reeves[8] I have written to you by return of post, but at the same time I have expressed to that gentleman my intention of visiting Princeton in about 10 days, when further explanations can be given to you: let me suggest therefore that [if] any doubts exist with respect to your acceptance, you should write immediately to me at "Locust Hill—Leesburg, Loudon Va"—when I will hasten my visit.

My own wishes in regard to your appointment I have already mentioned, and I understand from some of the Board that Dr Patterson named you among those whom he thought qualified to promote the rising importance which our Institution is attaining in the South.[9]

With hopes of seeing you among us
I remain
Yours truly
C: Bonnycastle

[6] John Hartwell Cocke. See Cocke to Henry, immediately above.

[7] John A. G. Davis, for whom see ibid.

[8] William C. Rives, for whom see above, Provost to Henry, June 12, 1835, especially footnote 8.

[9] A letter from Gessner Harrison to Henry Tutwiler of July 8, 1835 (University of Virginia Library), confirms Patterson's support of Henry. Harrison, thinking he had secured Patterson's support for Tutwiler, reports his surprise: "Since the election took place I have, to my utter amazement, understood on unquestionable authority, that Mr. Henry was strongly recommended by Dr P.!!"

TO JAMES HENRY

Family Correspondence, Henry Papers, Smithsonian Archives

Princeton July 9th 1835

Dear James

Since the receipt of your last letter[1] I have been at Philadelphia and the 4th of July has intervened which will account for my long silence. Nancy

[1] Not found.

is well and in good spirits. She cannot tell at what time she will return. Harriet says she cannot leave until after commencement, and that she will go up with Motherinlaw.

The 4th of July went off quite peaceably with the usual accompaniments of orations fire works & fire Balls. On Monday after noon the Presbyterian Church was discovered to be on fire and although it apparently could have been put out with little exertion yet it was entirely consumed except the brick walls.[2] A Fire in this place is much more to be dreaded than in the city on account of the want of experience and the bad state of the engines. Both Harriet and the children have been unwell with the summer complaint.[3] I have also had touch of the same. We are however somewhat better. We have had quite a number of visitors this summer almost [in] succession. Miss Ryley and her Father[4] were here a week or two since. We have now Miss Cuyler[5] from Philad[a] and Miss Outhout[6] from Schenectady. Nancy is pleased with Princeton and has been much engaged in visiting &c. She wishes you to tell her all the news. Has Mr. Campbell[7] returned? How is Caroline? Have you heard any thing more about Mr. Webster?[8]

Give our love to Caroline and Aunty Platt[9] Your Brother

[2] "The conflagration was supposed to have been caused by the stick of sky-rocket fired on the evening of the 4th of July, two days before, which had entered an attic window, and there smouldered until the fire burst out. The burning of the church affected the Commencements and some other exercises of our whole College course." William Edward Schenck, *Biography of the Class of 1838 of the College of New Jersey, at Princeton, N. J.* (Philadelphia, 1889), p. 12. A new church was built by November 1836. Designed by Charles Steadman, a prominent Princeton architect of the period, the new edifice was the third Presbyterian church to occupy the site. With modifications, it survives today. Constance M. Grieff, Mary W. Gibbons, and Elizabeth G. C. Menzies, *Princeton Architecture* (Princeton, 1967), p. 94 and figure 123.

[3] A form of diarrhea associated with the hot weather and thought to be mainly a children's affliction. "During our summers, the action of heat is both uniform and excessive; the liver feels its influence, and is forced to an inordinate secretion of bile, which being suddenly and rapidly poured into the bowels, stimulates them to excessive action, either by quantity or quality, or both, and thus the 'bilious diarrhoea' is produced." William P. Dewees, *A Treatise on the Physical and Medical Treatment of Children* (Philadelphia, 1829), p. 362; *The Journal of Health*, 1830, *1*:22–24. Both volumes survive in the Henry Library.

[4] Jane Ryley and James Van Slyck Ryley (1761–1848), for whom see *Henry Papers, 1*:444, footnote 5.

[5] Probably Jane Cuyler (1810–1865), eldest daughter of Cornelius C. Cuyler, for whom see above, Charles Hodge to Hugh Hodge, October 12, 1834, footnote 6. In March of 1837 she married Joseph Patterson (1808–1887), a Philadelphia merchant and banker who became a life-long friend and admirer of Joseph Henry. See *Coulson*, p. 296. *Appleton's Cyclopaedia of American Biography*, 7 vols. (New York, 1894), *4*:672. Maud Churchill Nicoll, *The Earliest Cuylers in Holland and America* (New York, 1912), p. 44.

[6] Not identified. The Outhout family was large and prominent through several generations in Albany and Schenectady.

[7] Archibald Campbell, for whom see *Henry Papers, 1*:397.

[8] Probably a reference to the declining fortunes of Matthew Henry Webster (for whom see *Henry Papers, 1*:62). Since the death of his wealthy father, Charles R. Webster (for whom see ibid., p. 27) in July 1834, Henry Webster watched his reputedly enormous inheritance dissipate in the hands of numerous of his father's creditors. Much of the estate became subjected to public auction, and Henry Webster was unfairly labeled the squanderer. Munsell, *Ann. Alb.*, *5*:240.

[9] Probably a relative of Caroline Henry's.

July 20, 1835

FROM HENRY VETHAKE[1]

Henry Papers, Smithsonian Archives

New York, July 20th, 1835.

My dear Sir,

I have had an interview with Mr Lenox,[2] and conversed with him concerning your affair,—of course concealing from him that I had called upon him expressly to do so. I am well satisfied that his remark to you concerning your and Mr Maclean's families should be construed *most* favorably. He seemd to me to have a due appreciation of your value to the institution at Princeton, and of the magnitude of the temptation offered you to quit it; and said that *the* difficulty in the way of any member of the board of trustees undertaking to promise that what you desire should be complied with was the responsibility which he would thereby incur. To conclude, I would not let any incidental remark of Mr L's operate upon your mind to induce you to *leave* Princeton; but act entirely without reference to your conversation with that gentleman.[3]

Yours Sir
in haste,
Henry Vethake

[1] Henry Vethake had been Professor of Mathematics, Astronomy and Natural Philosophy at New York University since 1832. He was about to assume his duties as President of Washington College. *Princeton Catalogue*, pp. 408–409.

[2] James Lenox (1800–1880), well known New York City real estate investor, merchant, bibliophile, and philanthropist; graduated Columbia 1818. Lenox owned superb collections of fifteenth-century imprints and pioneered in the collection of Americana; founded the Lenox Library, now part of New York Public Library. A Trustee of Princeton Theological Seminary, 1831–1879, and of Princeton, 1833–1857, Lenox was an important benefactor of the College. *DAB*.

[3] We have no clues to Lenox's real or imagined slight, evidently concerning Henry's bargaining with the Princeton Trustees over his Virginia offer. Was Lenox possibly struck by the fact that Henry and John Maclean each had a relative associated with the Princeton faculty? In any event, later correspondence of Henry and Lenox shows the two as being on good terms.

July 22, 1835

JOHN SNOWDEN HENRY[1] TO JOHN MACLEAN

Maclean Papers, Princeton University Archives

Philad[a] 22 July 1835.

My dear Sir,

I have called a meeting of the Comm[ee] on the Law-School for the 30th inst at 5 oclock P.M. in the College Library. I do hope in the meantime to hear from Mr Southard.[2]

As respects Mr Henry we must not lose him for the paltry consideration of $300 or for any other sum. He is entirely right according to my code of ethics to better his condition by a removal, if the Trustees do not make him comfortable in his present situation. But they will never refuse I am sure to do what is right in the premises. I have seen Dr. McDowell[3] who authorises me to say that he is in favour of acceding to the wishes of Professor Henry.

I hear friend Newell has given up his agency.[4] This matter should be

[1] John Snowden Henry (1795–1835), A.B. Princeton 1813, was a Trustee of the College from 1833 until his death. A successful Philadelphia merchant, he was a Director of the Bank of the United States there and a founder of several local institutions. He was the father of a future Philadelphia mayor, Alexander Henry, who served from 1860 to 1866. They were not related to Joseph Henry. Townsend Ward, "The Germantown Road and its Associations," *Pennsylvania Magazine of History and Biography*, 1881, 5:252–253. *Princeton Catalogue*, p. 125.

[2] Trustee Samuel L. Southard. The meeting concerned an attempt to establish a law school at Princeton. In 1835, a committee, consisting of Colt, Miller, Lenox, and Shippen, was appointed to prepare for a course of lectures on law, provided extra funds could be raised. Assured of funds, the committee recommended the establishment of a law faculty. Samuel Southard was one of the three Professors of Law elected by the committee. When all three turned down the position, the law school effort failed. The action by the three professors may have been linked to the effort to keep Henry at Princeton. See Charles Hodge's letter to Henry of July 29, 1835, below.

This was the second attempt to found a Princeton law school. The first effort aborted in 1828. The proposal was briefly revived in 1847 and again in 1890, but ultimately failed. *Wertenbaker*, pp. 229–230, 232, 377–378; *Maclean*, 2:265, 298, 299.

[3] John McDowell (1780–1863), leading Presbyterian clergyman, was a Princeton Trustee, 1814–1863, a Director (1812–1863) and Trustee (1822–1863) of the Princeton Theological Seminary. Ordained in 1804 McDowell was in charge of the Presbyterian church in Elizabethtown, New Jersey, until called to the Central Presbyterian Church of Philadelphia in 1833. He was a prolific writer and strong supporter of education. *DAB*; *Princeton Catalogue*, p. 113.

Over a number of years, McDowell, along with Samuel Southard, Maclean, and others, was actively engaged in fund-raising efforts to upgrade the Princeton faculty and to revive the fortunes of the College. Recruiting and keeping Joseph Henry at Princeton was part of this effort. In 1830, McDowell, Southard, and Maclean, sought to raise $20,000 for the endowment of a professorship—a difficult and frustrating endeavor which prompted McDowell to vow he would never again participate "in begging with anybody in Princeton." Quoted in *Wertenbaker*, p. 217.

[4] For Newell and the fund-raising program, see above, Trustees' Minutes of April 9, 1834, footnotes 6 and 9.

attended to at once, & I hope the Comm^ee^ who have charge of the business will employ a suitable agent to take his place at once,

I remain dear Sir
very truly
yours,
Jn° S. Henry

TO JOHN H. COCKE

Alderman Library, University of Virginia

Princeton July 24th 1835

Dear Sir

Your letter of the 8th inst. informing me of my appointement to the Chair of Natural Philosophy in the University of Virginia was received about ten days since. I regret that the delay in arranging some affairs which would influence my decision has prevented an earlier answer to the highly flattering proposition of the Board of Visitors of the University. I regret this the more since I have concluded to decline the appointement.

Permit me sir through you to assure the Board that this determination has not been formed without a due appreciation of the high honor and great advantages I would enjoy by a connection of the kind with the University of Virginia. Did no other considerations influence me than those of personal aggrandizement I would not hesitate a moment to accept the appointement but I feel myself under some obligations and am much attached to the Institution with which I am now connected. It is only a short time since I was called from an academy at Albany to Princeton. I have since been treated with the greatest kindness and every disposition manifested by the Board of Trustees and the Members of the Faculty to render my situation pleasant.

A new Building is now erecting principally for my accomodation and on the occasion of the present appointement I have been assured that my salary will be immediatly increased as much as the present promising condition of the College will warrent.

Besides I had before expressed a determination not to leave the Institution while I receive a competent support and am kindly treated. Under the influence of these considerations I decline the appointement and I much mistake the character of your Board as Virginians if they do not properly appreciate my motives whatever they may think of the inducements which would prompt the opposite course.

With sentiments of the highest regard for your Institution and a deep interest in its continued prosperity I am with much Respect

Yours &c
Joseph Henry

FROM CHARLES HODGE

Henry Papers, Smithsonian Archives

July 29 1835.

My dear Sir,

I have received a most satisfactory letter[1] from Mr J. S. Henry.[2] He says repeatedly & strongly "we cannot afford to lose Prof. Henry."[3] "That there cannot be a doubt that the Trustees will grant the moderate compensation which he asks."[4] "That he would rather abandon the law school than not furnish the necessary support to Prof. Henry." "That with a view principally to this matter he has called the committee (on the law-school) to meet in Princeton on the 30th"[5] &c &c.

I trust my dear Sir you will find the friends of the college appreciate your talents & excellence too highly to allow you to be taken from Princeton as long as you are willing to remain, and they are at all able to retain you.

With affection & respect
your friend
C. Hodge

[1] Not found. But see J. S. Henry's letter to John Maclean, July 22, 1835, above.

[2] John Snowden Henry, the Princeton Trustee (see note 1 of the letter of July 22, 1835, above).

[3] Joseph Henry wrote a file note on the address side of this letter: "Prof Hodge relative to my going to Virg July 1835."

[4] For the salary raise of $300, see the Trustees' Minutes for September 30, 1835, printed below.

[5] When the committee reported to the Trustees in September 1835, they stated that the funds for the law professors' salaries would come from tuition of the students in the law school. *Maclean*, 2:299. This source of funds would not conflict with the allocation of higher salaries for Joseph Henry and other College professors.

July 1835

RECOMMENDATION FOR WALTER R. JOHNSON[1]

Letters Received by the Secretary of the Navy Relative to the U.S. Exploring Expedition, 1836–1842, RG 45, National Archives[2]

Nassau Hall
July 1835

Professor Walter R. Johnson of Philadelphia is well known to the Philosophical world as one of the most industrious & successful experimental Philosophers of our country.

His scientific character is fully established by his several papers on Mechanics, Physics, Chemistry &c published in Silliman's journal, the transactions of the Academy of Natural Sciences, the Franklin Journal &c &c. These papers are all highly interesting & in my opinion important contributions to the science of the age.

I am intimately acquainted with Mr. Johnson & have the highest respect for his character as a gentleman as well as a scholar.

(Signed) Joseph Henry
Prof Nat. Philosophy, College of
New Jersey, Princeton

[1] Biographical information for Walter Rogers Johnson is given above in Henry's Notes on a Trip to Philadelphia, April 29–May 2, 1834, footnote 26. Henry named no recipient for this letter. Evidence cited in the next footnote indicates that Henry handed this testimonial directly to Johnson for use as the latter saw fit. In the next month, Henry wrote to Silliman (below, August 29, 1835), asking Silliman's aid in recommending Johnson, and Silliman replied approvingly (below, September 19, 1835).

[2] The original of this letter has not been found; this copy is written in Johnson's hand. As Johnson explained in his letter of application of October 26, 1836, he was forwarding to the Secretary of the Navy, Mahlon Dickerson, letters in his behalf "furnished about a year since in expectation of being used at a distance from this city [Philadelphia], but as the occasion for their employment has not occurred the originals were left in the hands of a friend to be returned on a convenient occasion & are too remote to be obtained in season for this application." (Letters Received by the Secretary of the Navy Relative to the U.S. Exploring Expedition, 1836–1842, RG 45, National Archives.) We have not determined to which position Johnson expected to apply a year earlier or who the friend was who retained the originals. Henry's recommendation of Johnson was accompanied by copies, in Johnson's hand, of similar statements from John Farrar, Benjamin Silliman, and John Kearsley Mitchell (1793–1858, Philadelphia physician, chemist, *DAB*). These recommendations were also dated in July 1835. Silliman's was dated July 24, 1835. We cannot explain why Silliman would have enthusiastically endorsed Henry's request on September 19, 1835, if he had already written the recommendation for Johnson in July. This anomaly could arise from a variety of causes, ranging from either Silliman's absentmindedness, his extreme politeness toward Henry, or to a transcribing error of Johnson.

These recommendations were accompanied by others sent to the Secretary of the Navy, and Johnson was appointed to the Wilkes Expedition with responsibilities for magnetism, electricity, and astronomy. Like Asa Gray and others he resigned from his position before the long-delayed expedition left port. He returned to Philadelphia in 1839 to become Professor of Chemistry and Natural Philosophy at the newly founded Pennsylvania Medical College. George E. Pettengill, "Walter Rogers Johnson," *Journal of the Franklin Institute*, 1950, 250:93–113.

TO JAMES HENRY

Family Correspondence, Henry Papers, Smithsonian Archives

Princeton Monday
August [3] 1835[1]

Dear James

You must be anxious to hear my determination relative to my call from the south concerning which you were informed by Mr Fasset[2] whom I met in New York a few days since. The call was from the University of Virginia at Charlottsville, the Institution founded by Mr Jeferson and liberally endowed by the state. You will see a drawing of the establishment on the Large map of Virginia which hangs in the Governor's room in the capital. The call was a very flattering one since they elected me without asking if I would except and even although they had some doubts that I would accept. The salary is the largest in the United States and if the Institution continues flourishing will probably be 4000 dollars. It was last year 3600 and a house. The situation was occupied by Mr. Patterson of Philadelphia who has resigned for the office of director of the United States Mint. After all this I have declined accepting the appointement and my reasons are these. I have been at Princeton but a short time and have assured the Trustees that I did not accept their call for the purpose of making Princeton a stepping stone but that I intended to stop with them if they gave me a good support and treated me kindly. At the last meeting of the board of Trustees they ordered a new building to be put up at an expense of 3 or 4 thousand dollars for my special accomodations. This building is now almost completed and will be of great conveniance to me. From these circumstances and in consideration that I am well situated here, have been kindly treated, have the full confidence of the Trustees, I was induced to say that if they would immediately give me a new house and raise my salary I would stay. This all the trustees have at once agreed to do so that I must now settle down in my old track. The affair has much perplexed me and caused me considerable trouble on account of getting an assurance from the Trustees that they would do as I desired before I sent my answer to Virginia.

Had I been longer at Princeton and did I not conceive that I was under some obligations to the Institution I would not have hesitated to accept the call from Virginia. I do not much like the idea of living in a slave state or

[1] Henry dated this letter August 2, which was a Sunday. His reference to lecturing makes Monday, August 3, a more likely dating.

[2] Unidentified. See footnote 3 of the letter of November 14, 1833, above.

going much farther to the south. Still these considerations would not alone have weighed against the salary and other advantages of the place.

Nancy has gone to Philadelphia and has been there a week past on Friday. We expect her to-day or to-morrow. She went with Miss Outhout from Schenectady and will stop at Dr Cuylers (a distant relative of Motherinlaw) and at Dr Ludlow's.

The little girl has been quite unwell with the summer complaint and is still quite feeble. My time has been so much occupied with my college duties and the Virginian affair that my letters are all behind hand. Love from all to all. I am in great haste and am obliged to give a lecture of an hour this morning.

Your Brother

Write immediately

FROM JOHN VAUGHAN

Henry Papers, Smithsonian Archives

Phil. 5 Aug 1835

D Sir,

I send by mail a publication of M Faraday which I this day rec^d & in my nephews[1] letter he remarks "Had Dr Faraday known that Professor Henry had been making the experiments published by your Soc. in the Franklin Journal he would have noticed them in his last essay. He considers them as Very Interesting."[2]

Y^s

Jn Vaughan

[1] Petty Vaughn (1788–1854) was the son of John Vaughan's eldest brother Benjamin Vaughan (1751–1835, *DAB*, *DNB*). Benjamin had immigrated to America in 1796. Petty was subsequently sent back to London to live with his uncle William (1752–1850, *DNB*), with whom he later entered into business. In 1842 Petty was elected to the American Philosophical Society.

Petty Vaughan apparently acted as an intermediary between the Franklin Institute and the American Philosophical Society in Philadelphia and scientific societies in London. In this exchange, he may be passing on information which he received directly from Faraday or he may be merely acting as his elderly uncle's agent. John H. Sheppard, *Reminiscences of the Vaughan Family . . .* (Boston, 1865), pp. 13, 26–27. APS *Proceedings*, 1841–1843, 2:205. Bruce Sinclair, *Philadelphia's Philosopher Mechanics: A History of the Franklin Institute, 1824-1865* (Baltimore, 1974), p. 30.

[2] Although Vaughan does not say which Faraday article was accompanying his letter, a June 7, 1836, letter from Henry to J. D. Forbes (to appear in volume three of *The Papers of Joseph Henry*) points to Faraday's Ninth Series of Experimental Researches. This was apparently the first time that Henry had

I will with pleasure forward any reply.[3]

seen the unabridged version of the Faraday paper on self-induction. In the same letter to Forbes, Henry noted that Faraday had "politely sent me a copy of his paper and stated to a friend that he had not seen my publication on the subject or he would have given me credit." We infer that the Vaughans were merely forwarding Faraday's presentation copy, which survives in Henry's Library. Significantly, Faraday's presentation of the Ninth Series marks the first known direct contact between Michael Faraday and Joseph Henry.

It is not surprising that Faraday had missed Henry's first announcement of self-induction in 1832. Henry's account of the effect was rather inconspicuously appended to his paper on mutual induction in *Silliman's Journal*, 22:408. Faraday eventually brought himself up to date on Henry's self-induction researches. His interleaved and annotated copy of his *Experimental Researches*, preserved in the Library of the Royal Institution, contains an undated listing of references in Faraday's hand alongside the Ninth Series of researches. Among the list are Henry's 1832 paper announcing self-induction, "Contributions II," and the abstract in the Franklin Institute *Journal*.

[3] We have found no reply.

TO JAMES HENRY

Family Correspondence, Henry Papers, Smithsonian Archives

Princeton Aug. 21st 1835

Dear James

Your last letter was well filled with news and was received with much pleasure. Harriet on the suggestion which it contained has written to the Meades and asked forgiveness for her seaming neglect.

Nancy has returned from Philadelphia after a visit of nearly two weeks. She was much pleased with the jaunt but suffered considerably from the heat. Stephenson Alexander[1] from Rochester arrived day before yesterday at our house and leaves this morning. He goes from here to Boston by the way of New York and the Sound. He will return to albany in about a week. We have not as yet heard anything of Mr. Bullions[2]. Perhaps he will be here before the close of his vacation.

Nancy will probably stay in Princeton until after commencement when Motherinlaw and she will go to the north together. If you intend giving yourself a week's vacation come on with Caroline[3] to Princeton. Our senior examination has just finished and the class have gone home so that I have

[1] Alexander Stephenson Alexander; see footnote 8 of the letter of June 2, 1833, above.

[2] Peter Bullions.

[3] Caroline Morrow Henry, James Henry's wife (see footnote 3 of the letter of March 17, 1835, above).

some leisure at this time. Do you know a man by the name of DeWitt?[4] a brother of the late Andrew DeWitt.[5] I believe he is a lumber merchant. He purchased at the sale of DeWitt Clinton's Library a large book on Architecture called the *Ruins of Pestum*.[6] He once offered to sell it to me for 8 dollars I think. I now wish to purchase it for the College Library and will give him 10 dollars for it but no more.[7] If he will sell it for that price I will send a draft on one of the banks in my next letter for the ammount. If it can be purchased I wish to procure it as soon as possible that I may make use of it in my lectures on Architecture which I intend to deliver in a week or two to the Junior class.[8] Nothing new in Princeton. Aunt has had a very poor turn somewhat similar to the attack she had in Albany at Mr Meads'.

Nancy says that when Stevenson Alexander returns to Albany he must go to your house and take possession of her room.

Nancy is much pleased to learn that Mary Ann[9] has not forgotten her. I send you a copy of my communications to the American Phil. Society and

[4] William H. DeWitt began his career as a dealer in barrel staves and lumber in the 1830s. He was variously Vice-President and a Director of the Mechanics and Farmers Bank in Albany during the 1840s and 1850s. DeWitt acquired enough wealth by the mid-1860s to purchase the land and erect the building and school for Holy Innocents Episcopal Church in the city. Albany City Directories; *Howell and Tenney*, pp. 529 and 761; and Munsell, *Coll. Alb.*, *3*:280.

[5] Andrew H. DeWitt (1794–1832) was an inspector of lumber. Albany City Directory, 1832–1833; Munsell, *Ann. Alb.*, *9*:254.

[6] Thomas Major, *The Ruins of Paestum, Otherwise Posidonia, in Magna Graecia* (London, 1768). Paestum, located on the Gulf of Salerno, is the site of important Doric ruins.

[7] Henry eventually sold "*Ruins of Pestum*" to the Princeton Library for ten dollars (Receipt of February 13, 1837, Librarian's Reports, 1832/33–1847, Princeton University Archives), so we may presume he did get the book.

[8] Henry gave a class on architecture in 1831 at the Albany Academy (*Henry Papers*, *1*:190). He taught a short course of six to ten lectures on the subject at Princeton from 1833 to 1837–1838. Thereafter, Albert Dod took over the responsibility for instruction in architecture, and Henry began teaching a brief course on geology (*Princeton Annual Catalogues*).

Three student notebooks from the architecture course, now in the Princeton University Archives, indicate Henry's approach to the subject. Aaron B. Belknap's notes are dated September 1835, and those of John Miller, class of 1836, seem to have been taken at the same time. The notebook of Benjamin H. Williams apparently dates from 1836. Williams records ten lectures and Belknap and Miller, six. In both cases, Henry confined his discussion to civil architecture, especially churches and public buildings constructed by the ancient Greeks or of the Greek Revival style. In 1835 and 1836, Henry began with a description of the materials used in building, and then devoted the next two lectures to the parts of buildings, from the foundation to the roof, with special attention to arches, vaults, domes, and columns. The last three lectures in 1835 were devoted to Greek and Roman styles of architecture. In 1836, Henry expanded that section to five lectures, and added two on the Gothic style.

Three of Henry's own lecture notebooks for the architecture course are in Box 16 of the Henry Papers at the Smithsonian Archives. Apparently two of them hold the notes for the longer course and one for the short version, but none of the three are dated. Henry wrote the basic lecture on right hand pages and entered new material from his reading on the left pages. These additions show that he consulted encyclopedias, standard textbooks on architecture, and books on mechanics with sections on building problems.

[9] Mary Ann LaGrange (see footnote 9 of the letter of January 30, 1833, above).

will also send some copies to some of my friends in albany.[10] I am pleased to hear that Mr Carpenter gets so good a salary but I fear that his place cannot easily be supplied in the albany academy.[11]

James Boyd the clergyman will, I presume, get a situation in the Academy.[12] Does Dr Wing intend visiting Princeton this summer? Have you and the Dr with Frank made a final settlement yet. Cannot a turn be made so that Franks debt may be secured. If it is not got in this way he will never pay. Dr Wing should make a deduction. He has rendered his charging price and not his taking one.[13]

Your Brother

Nancy bids me say that her face is better than when she left albany. Also write in your next how Aunty Selkirk[14] is. Rachel Selkirk[15] is I believe in Albany & Nancy wishes to hear from her. Stephenson A. did not hear of your marriage intil he came to P[rinceton].

[10] The next document in this volume lists the recipients.

[11] George Washington Carpenter had resigned as Tutor at the Academy and had begun his career as City Surveyor for Albany (*Henry Papers, 1*:299).

[12] James Robert Boyd (1804–1890) had recently arrived in Albany to be editor of the *Telegraph*. Boyd graduated from Union College in 1822, attended Princeton Theological Seminary until 1826, and then served in various clerical posts. After his editing stint in 1835–1836, Boyd became an educational administrator for institutes in New York and Massachusetts. *Roberts*, p. 29. He is not listed in histories of the Albany Academy as a Trustee, administrator, or teacher at that school.

[13] We assume this problem between Joel Wing and Francis Selkirk, both physicians, arose over a matter of high fees, about which Joseph Henry complained in regard to Wing in his letter to James Henry of February 9, 1835, printed above.

[14] Elizabeth Selkirk, a relative of Joseph Henry probably on the Henry side of the family.

[15] Not identified.

"LIST OF PERSONS TO WHOM COPIES OF MY PAPER HAVE BEEN SENT"

Henry Papers, Smithsonian Archives[1]

[ca. August 21,] 1835[2]

In the following document Joseph Henry lists the names of recipients of reprints of his first two articles for the American Philosophical Society. Although

[1] The item is presently located in Box 28: "Papers: Research & Lectures; Notes & Other Material." It is with miscellaneous material in the last folder bearing the label "*Notes* by M. A. Henry on Jos. Henry's Association with the Albany Academy."

[2] Henry's file note supplies only the year. Although Henry's title implies the list follows the sending of reprints, we have arbitrarily given it the same date as Henry's first mention of sending reprints (in the letter to his brother James immediately above). Henry apparently did not send the reprints out all at once, judging from the surviving acknowledgments which range over a period of several months.

Henry's caption indicates only one paper sent, later correspondence will show that Henry was distributing reprints of "Contributions I: Battery" and "Contributions II: Spiral Conductor," both of which had apparently just appeared in print, after having been accepted for publication in February and March. Henry probably indicated only a single paper because the offprints were issued together as a small booklet, a proof copy of which survives in Henry's papers in the Smithsonian Archives. The papers eventually appeared back-to-back in part 2, n.s. 5 of the APS *Transactions,* which, due to the slow publication schedule of the Society, did not appear in print until the end of the year.

Although sketchy and incomplete, this distribution list is important for what it reveals about the range of Henry's scientific and intellectual associations as of 1835. The document gives us some measure of Henry's professional growth during his first years at Princeton and an idea of whom Henry considered his professional peers as of this date.

The names listed fall under three broad categories. The first column consists of science professors at various American schools and liberal arts colleges, organized roughly by institution and region. The second column lists personal friends and acquaintances, mainly from Albany. Finally Henry listed three Princeton Trustees, none of them scientists.

We know the listing is incomplete, since there are letters acknowledging the reprints from people who are not listed, such as Henry's friend Titus W. Powers (his letter of March 13, 1836, is in the Henry Papers, Smithsonian Archives). Other significant omissions from the list will be discussed below.

For assessing Henry's growing scientific role and associations, the most interesting group are the science professors listed in the first column. Some were friends or colleagues from the Albany days. Others were more recent acquaintances or men whom Henry knew only indirectly or by reputation. For a few on the list, there is no known contact with Henry beyond their inclusion on this list.

Most of the professors listed had an active professional interest in Henry's electromagnetic research. The majority were physical scientists, many holding professorships of mathematics and natural philosophy. The medical men or natural historians on Henry's list—such as Edward Hitchcock—had generally evinced some prior interest in Henry's electromagnetic work for their own research or teaching. A few of the recipients, like James Dean of Vermont, responded in detail to various points in Henry's publications (see Dean's letter of November 28, 1835, below).

Despite the apparent brevity of Henry's professorial list, it appears that his reprints reached a good proportion of his fellow physical scientists in America. The number of active practitioners of physical science in America during this period was very small. Through his extensive contacts with the college professors Henry knew the core of the community. A recent study of American scientists in the first six decades of the nineteenth century has pointed up the importance of college teaching as a scientific occupation. Physical scientists were particularly apt to be professors. Using a sampling of scientists who published three or more papers, this study concludes that "Professor of science was the leading occupational category of mathematical, physical, and geophysical scientists." (Clark A. Elliott, "The American Scientist, 1800–1863: His Origins, Career, and Interests," [Ph.D. dissertation, Case Western Reserve University, 1970], pp. 203–204.) Henry's reprint list shows that he had extensive contacts within this very small but active and influential community of teaching scientists.

There are two groups of scientists notably missing from Henry's distribution list. None of the Philadelphia group appears, even though Philadelphia was already clearly the center of Henry's research activity, and scientists like Bache and Hare were becoming Henry's closest colleagues and collaborators. The obvious explanation is that most were American Philosophical Society members who had already heard the oral presentation of the articles and would receive the printed papers in due course from the Society. Or, rather than sending the reprints, Henry may have distributed them personally at one of the Society's meetings.

The other major omission was the European physical scientists whom Henry surely wanted to impress and whose publications figured so importantly in his own electrical research. Despite his hope for European recognition, Henry perhaps felt it immodest and presumptuous to approach his famous European colleagues at this early stage of his career. By this date, Henry had only one European correspondent—James David Forbes of Edinburgh. Henry eventually sent Forbes the papers, but not until June 7, 1836 (see above, Forbes to Henry, May 26, 1835 for the reasons for the delay). The most notable omission is Michael Faraday, whose line of electrical research in this period coincided so closely with Joseph Henry's. Even receiving a reprint of Faraday's Ninth Series (see above, Vaughan to Henry, August 5, 1835) apparently did not induce Henry to reciprocate. Modesty combined with a certain amount of trepidation at challenging Faraday's priority on self-induction may have restrained Henry from contacting him.

In the next few years, Henry's relationship with the European scientists would change dramatically. His 1837 European visit noticeably bolstered his self-confidence. Correspondence and reprints would soon flow freely between Henry and his European colleagues, including Michael Faraday. An address book for Henry's 1837 trip (Henry Papers, Smithsonian Archives), containing later notes and additions, illustrates the dramatic broadening of Henry's scientific associations over the next several years. Interspersed with the addresses of European scientists are several distribution lists like the one below for reprints of various Henry articles and reports. The list of recipients of Henry's next major effort for the APS, "Contributions III: Electro-Dynamic Induction," shows not only a significant increase in the names of American scientists but an impressive list of important Europeans, including Jacobi, Lenz, and De La Rive. The address book also shows that Henry, to make up for his earlier omission, later sent copies of Contributions I and II to scientists abroad like Savary, Melloni, Gay-Lussac,

Arago, Ohm, Poggendorff, and several other leading figures. By the 1840s it is clear that Henry was confident in his European reputation and exchanging research information freely with his counterparts abroad. At the same time, the appearance of more American scientists on Henry's later distribution lists reflected both the growth of the American physical science community and Henry's gravitation to the center of that group.

Prof Bonnycastle[3]
Emmet[4]
Renwick[5]
Dewey[6]
Cleavland[7]
L C Beck[8]
Eaton[9]
James Dean[10]
Hitchcock[11]
Ten Eyck[12]
Webster[13] } Boston
Farrar[14] } Boston
Dod[15]
Olmsted[16]
Silliman[17]
Young[18]
Totten[19]
Joslin[20]
Jackson[21]
Strong[22]
Torrey[23]
Gale[24]

R Yates[25]
Brother[26]
Judge Conkling[27]
Dr Hawley[28]
O Meads[29]
Dr Campbell[30]
Rev Dr Campbell[31]
Dr McNaughton[32]
Mr McIntyre[33]
James Chilton[34]
Mr Newland[35]
Hon S Van Renselaer[36]
Leibre[37]
Dr Mclean[38]
Mr Stansbury[39]

Trustees
Dr Alexander[40]
Mr Cooley[41]
Dr Miller[42]

[3] Charles Bonnycastle, Professor of Mathematics at the University of Virginia. Identified in his letter to Henry, above, July 9, 1835, footnote 1.

[4] John Patton Emmet was the University of Virginia's Professor of Chemistry. Henry knew Emmet's work but had little personal contact with him. See above, Henry to Harriet Henry, May 4, 1835, footnote 7.

[5] James Renwick, Sr., of Columbia, Professor of Natural Philosophy and Experimental Chemistry, *Henry Papers, 1*:59n.

[6] Chester Dewey, chemist and naturalist, formerly a Professor at Williams College, was at this time Principal of the Berkshire Gymnasium in Pittsfield, Massachusetts. In 1836, he began teaching science in Rochester, New York, becoming, in 1850, the first Professor of Chemistry and Natural Philosophy at the University of Rochester. Dewey published extensively in natural history and had a lifelong interest in meteorology. While there is no evidence of contact between Henry and Dewey before the date of this document, the two later corresponded on meteorological subjects. *DAB*; *Henry Papers, 1*:124n.

[7] Henry's long-time scientific correspondent Parker Cleveland taught mathematics and natural philosophy at Bowdoin College, Maine. *Henry Papers, 1*:373n.

[8] Henry's old friend Lewis C. Beck was at this date Professor of Chemistry and Natural History at Rutgers. *Henry Papers, 1*:69n.

[9] Amos Eaton, one of Henry's first teachers,

was lecturing at Rensselaer Polytechnic Institute. *Henry Papers, 1*:124n.

[10] James Dean, formerly a science professor at Dartmouth and the University of Vermont, still did scientific work in Burlington, Vermont. See above, Dean to Henry, November 27, 1833. Henry consulted him frequently on scientific matters. Dean thanked Henry for the reprints in his letter of November 28, 1835, below, and was one of the few of Henry's colleagues to respond to the theoretical assertions in Henry's reprints, so far as we can tell from the surviving manuscripts.

[11] Edward Hitchcock, Professor of Chemistry and Natural History at Amherst College (*Henry Papers, 1*:142n), had a few years earlier constructed an electromagnet for his college on Henry's Albany prototype.

[12] Philip Ten Eyck, Henry's early scientific collaborator, succeeded him as Professor of Mathematics and Natural Philosophy at the Albany Academy. *Henry Papers, 1*:214n.

[13] Probably John White Webster, physician and chemist, teacher of chemistry at Harvard, who had evinced an early interest in Henry's research in an article in *Silliman's Journal*, 1831, *20*:143–144. There was apparently no prior personal contact with Henry. *Henry Papers, 1*:330n.

[14] John Farrar, also of Harvard, was Hollis Professor of Mathematics and Natural Philosophy. *Henry Papers, 1*:227n. Although Henry apparently did not know Farrar personally, he had used Farrar's texts in his teaching. Farrar acknowledged receipt of the papers in a letter of November 19, 1835, below. He was particularly interested in Henry's battery. See also his letter to Josiah Quincy of October 7, 1835, below.

[15] Henry's Princeton colleague Albert Baldwin Dod, Professor of Mathematics. *Henry Papers, 1*:434n.

[16] Denison Olmsted, Professor of Mathematics and Natural Philosophy at Yale, had known Henry from the Albany days. *Henry Papers, 1*:274n.

[17] Benjamin Silliman, Sr., was particularly interested in Henry's latest articles in view of the public lectures he planned to deliver in Boston. Henry's researches were always a source for interesting experimental demonstrations. See his acknowledgment of Henry's articles below, September 19, 1835.

[18] Perhaps Ira Young (1801–1858), Professor of Mathematics and Natural Philosophy at Dartmouth from 1833 to 1838, when he became Professor of Astronomy and Natural Philosophy. Though a lifelong student of science and known for his erudition, Young never published any research. He was considered an excellent scientific administrator and organizer at Dartmouth, being credited with raising the funds for the Dartmouth Observatory. Stanley M. Guralnick, "Science and the American College, 1828–1860" (Ph.D. dissertation, University of Pennsylvania, 1969), pp. 320–321. We have no evidence of any prior or later contact between Henry and Young. Henry may have known him by reputation or through his friend James Dean (see footnote 10 above), a former Dartmouth professor. Young's son, Charles Augustus Young (1834–1908), became Professor of Astronomy at Princeton in 1877 while Henry was a Trustee of the College of New Jersey.

[19] Perhaps Silas Totten (1804–1873), an ordained Episcopal minister, Professor of Mathematics and Natural Philosophy at Trinity College, Hartford, Connecticut, from 1833 to 1837, when he assumed the presidency of the College. In 1848 Totten became Professor of Belles-Lettres at William and Mary College, Virginia. We have found no correspondence between Totten and Henry, but Henry may have met Totten through faculty acquaintances at Union College where Totten went to school (class of 1830) and tutored for two years (1831–1832). Two Union faculty members who were friends of Henry's follow Totten's name on the list. Totten wrote *A New Introduction to the Science of Algebra* (Hartford, 1836). *Herringshaw*. Union College, *A Record of the Commemoration of the Hundredth Anniversary of the Founding of Union College Including a Sketch of Its History* (New York, 1897), p. 381.

[20] Professor of Mathematics and Natural Philosophy at Union College, Benjamin Franklin Joslin had numerous scientific contacts with Henry in Albany. *Henry Papers, 1*:256n.

[21] Another long-time acquaintance of Henry's, Isaac Wilber Jackson also taught mathematics and natural philosophy at Union. *Henry Papers, 1*:254n.

[22] Theodore Strong (1790–1869), a mathematician, was Professor of Mathematics and Natural Philosophy at Rutgers. An 1812 Yale graduate, Strong taught at Hamilton College before going to Rutgers, where he was Vice President from 1839 to 1863. A proficient though unoriginal mathematician, he was the author of two books and numerous papers on mathematics. Losing interest in mathematical research, Strong proved more successful and influential in applying his knowledge of mathematics to celestial mechanics. His three long astronomical papers evidenced a high technical competence in celestial mechanics,

unusual among American astronomers of the day. Through forceful teaching, Strong became the central figure in a small but influential group of American mathematical astronomers. He became a member of the American Philosophical Society in 1844 and, in 1863, an incorporator of the National Academy of Sciences. *DAB.* Marc Rothenberg, "The Educational and Intellectual Background of American Astronomers, 1825–1875" (Ph.D. dissertation, Bryn Mawr College, 1974), pp. 72–73, 173–178.

[23] John Torrey, who divided his teaching between Princeton and the College of Physicians and Surgeons.

[24] Leonard D. Gale, Professor of Geology and Mineralogy at New York University, would later become involved in the telegraph controversy between Henry and S. F. B. Morse. See above, "Galvanic Experiments on the Body of the Murderer Le Blanc," September 6, 1833, footnote 12.

[25] Having completed the list of his scientific colleagues, Henry now lists relatives, personal friends, and acquaintances, mainly from Albany. Richard Yates is identified in Henry to James Henry, December 1, 1832, footnote 8, above.

[26] James Henry.

[27] Alfred Conkling (*Henry Papers, 1*:92n–93n) was a member of the Albany Institute and a Trustee of the Albany Academy.

[28] Gideon Hawley, Albany Academy Trustee and a prominent figure in the educational life of Albany, had participated in ceremonies marking Henry's professional maturity: Henry's inauguration as Professor of Mathematics and Natural Philosophy at the Albany Academy. *Henry Papers, 1*:50n, 162, 163.

[29] Henry's good friend Orlando Meads. See Henry to James Henry, May 17, 1833, footnote 1.

[30] Dr. William Campbell, a politician, physician, and surveyor who met Henry through the New York State Road Survey in 1825, was both a friend and scientific correspondent of Joseph Henry's. *Henry Papers, 1*:100n.

[31] Possibly the clergyman William Henry Campbell (1808–1890), although we have no evidence of any prior connections with Henry. Campbell attended Dickinson College, 1824–1828, and Princeton Theological Seminary until 1829. He was licensed to preach in 1831, then became co-pastor at Chittenango, New York, 1831–1833. Henry may have known Campbell through Stephen Alexander's connections with Yates Polytechny in the same town. From 1833 to 1839 Campbell was Principal of Erasmus Hall in Flatbush, Long Island. He was Principal of the Albany Academy from 1848 to 1851. President of Rutgers from 1863 until 1882, Campbell is credited with the resuscitation of the college during his tenure. *DAB.*

[32] The Albany physician James McNaughton. *Henry Papers, 1*:452n.

[33] Archibald McIntyre was a Trustee of the Albany Academy. *Henry Papers, 1*:10n.

[34] The philosophical instrument maker James R. Chilton of New York City. See Henry's notes of December 11, 1832, above, footnote 1.

[35] Luke F. Newland, an Albany friend. See above, Henry to James Henry, May 17, 1833, footnote 3.

[36] Stephen Van Rensselaer, outstanding patron of Albany cultural life. *Henry Papers, 1*: 8n.

[37] Our reading of this name is conjectural. Our best guess is the German-born political scientist and educator Francis Lieber (1800–1872; *DAB*). After a turbulent youth in German political causes, Lieber emigrated to Boston in 1827 and to Philadelphia in 1834, where he drafted the constitution and regulations of Girard College. In 1835, he was elected to the chair of history and political economy at South Carolina College, succeeding Thomas Cooper in the latter subject. During his twenty-one-year tenure at the school, he published the political science works that made his reputation. Although the first known correspondence between Joseph Henry and Lieber does not occur until 1847, the two could have easily met through Henry's Philadelphia connections, such as A. D. Bache, soon to be associated with Girard College. Lieber and Henry eventually had extensive correspondence on science and other matters. Lieber took a chair at Columbia in 1857 and in 1865 moved to the Columbia Law School.

[38] Henry's colleague and Princeton Vice President John Maclean, Jr., *Henry Papers, 1*: 433n.

[39] Arthur J. Stansbury, former pastor of the Henry family church in Albany and a personal friend of Henry's. His letter acknowledging Henry's reprint appears below, August 29, 1835.

[40] Archibald Alexander (1772–1851) was a Trustee of Princeton from 1824 to 1851. A Presbyterian clergyman noted for his devotion to evangelical religion, Alexander was President of Hampden-Sidney College, 1796–1801, 1802–1807, after which he became pastor of the well-known Pine Street Church in Philadelphia. From that pulpit, he helped initiate the movement for a Presbyterian Theological

Seminary, which was founded in Princeton in 1812. Alexander became the first professor at Princeton Theological Seminary, organized the courses, and put a lasting stamp on the future development of the Seminary. He taught theology and church government at the Seminary until 1851. *DAB. Roberts*, p. xx. *Princeton Catalogue*, p. 20.

[41] Eli Field Cooley (?–1860) graduated from Princeton in 1806 and served as Trustee from 1828 to 1860. He was also a Trustee of the Princeton Theological Seminary from 1830 to 1860 and, in 1856, received a D.D. from Rutgers. *Princeton Catalogue*, p. 118.

[42] Samuel Miller (1769–1850), Presbyterian clergyman, educator, and author, was a founder of the Princeton Theological Seminary, where he taught church history and government. A prolific scholar, Miller was a Princeton Trustee from 1807 until his death. He was the father of John Miller (1819–1895), a student of Joseph Henry's (B.A. 1836). *DAB. Princeton Catalogue*, p. 19.

TO JOHN TORREY

Torrey Papers, Library, New York Botanical Garden

Princeton Aug. 26th 1835

My Dear Friend

Your kind letter[1] came to hand the day before yesterday. The senior examination closed on the Monday after your departure. The next day the grades were read out and the class dismissed. The first man on the list was McClune[2] the 2nd Janvier[3] & the 3rd Wilson[4] who was appointed to deliver the valedictory.[5]

Mrs Henry and myself talk of visiting your city in a few weeks but when I cannot precisely tell. We will certainly make your hospitable mansion our home. Mrs H will not however take her chickens with her.

[1] Not found.

[2] James McClune (d. 1890) delivered the English Salutatory. He became Professor of Higher Mathematics and Astronomy at Philadelphia High School, 1855–1877, and an Examiner at the United States Mint. He received honorary degrees from Princeton in 1839 and 1874 and was a member of the American Philosophical Society. *Princeton Catalogue*, p. 148. John Rogers Williams, ed., *Academic Honors in Princeton University, 1748–1902* (Princeton, 1902), p. 38.

[3] Levi Janvier (1816–1864) gave the Latin Salutatory. He went on to Princeton Theological Seminary, 1837–1839, and was ordained in 1840. He was a missionary in India from 1841 to 1864, where he died. *Roberts*, p. 106. Williams, op. cit., p. 38.

[4] William Sidney Wilson (d. 1862) of Maryland was to deliver the Valedictory but was "excused" and replaced by another honor student, J. C. Moffat. Wilson was a Lieutenant Colonel in the Confederate Army, 1861–1862, and a member of the Provisional Confederate Congress in 1861. *Princeton Catalogue*, p. 149, and Williams, op. cit., p. 39.

[5] The Valedictory address, the English Salutatory and the Latin Salutatory were the three major undergraduate prizes, hotly contended for by Princeton's student societies. According to *Wertenbaker*, "when one society won a decided victory by carrying off most of the honors, the members of the other often charged the faculty with partiality and threatened to withdraw from participation in the commencement exercises . . . a source of serious worry to the faculty . . ." (p. 207).

I have done nothing scarcely since you left but attend to some account business and read miscellaneous works.

The Phil. Hall remains in the same state in which you left it. With the usual promptness of action in Princeton the carpenters have been obliged to wait for more than 3 weeks for lumber. They had ceased work except one man some time before you left & have not again commenced. I am informed however that operations will begin again as soon as the present rain stops. I have spoken to Dr Carnahan relative to your proposition of an iron bar in the upper room of the *nose*.[6] He appears to agree to the plan and says that it can be secured in that way without much difficulty. I will speak to the carpenter so that the thing may be done as it should be.

Send on the chemical bills. I will draw the money & send you a draft. The Trustees at their last meeting as you probably reccollect appropriated $150 to the chemical department. You can therefore draw at anytime to that ammount.

I am happy to learn that Chilton has returned and that he has enjoyed good health during his Tour.[7] I am anxious to have a long crack[8] with him as the Scotch men say. Do you know that I have your copy of Thompson's journal[9] and also that you left your best specimen of Iceland spar in the drawer of the table in the Hall. Have you procured the book from Hopkins[10] which you mentioned to me sometime since. I would like to look at it for a short time when I come to the city.

That principle of amalgamated Zinc is one of great practical importance. I intend to use it in some experiments relative to the size of wire required to transmit all the electricity which can be generated by a given quantity of zinc & copper. For this purpose a number of zinc & copper plates of the same size but united by wires of different thickness may be plunged into the same solution of acid. If the zinc be amalgamated the whole action will alone be due to the conduction of the wire which unites the zinc with the copper. By weighing the different plates we can determine how much zinc

[6] "*Nose*" probably refers to the addition to the Hall. We do not know the purpose of the iron bar.

[7] For health and professional reasons, George Chilton (see *Henry Papers, 1*:295), father of James R. Chilton, visited Europe from July 1834 to August 1835. He was well received by the European savants and reportedly prepared remarks for the British Association meeting at Edinburgh. *Silliman's Journal*, 1837, *31*:423.

[8] Talk, chat, gossip.

[9] The *Records of General Science*, edited by Robert D. Thomson with the assistance of Thomas Thomson. Published in London, the journal apparently came out in only three volumes in 1835 and 1836. It was devoted principally to chemistry, applied chemistry, geology, medicine and natural history but also contained a few articles on physics. Volume one had several reports on the latest electrical work of Faraday. See below, footnote 11.

[10] Unidentified. There are two Hopkins listed as printers at the time in the New York City Directory. The book is unknown to us.

has been dissolved in a given time & thus estimate the ammount of galvanic action.[11]

With the highest
esteem
Yours sincerely
Jos. Henry

[11] The effect of amalgamating the zinc electrode of a galvanic battery—coating it with mercury—was a relatively recent discovery of great importance for the development of efficient batteries. The amalgamation technique minimized waste from what we now know as local action. In 1830 Auguste De La Rive showed that local action resulted from metallic impurities in commercial zinc which formed galvanic combinations with the zinc of the electrode, detracting significantly from the energy output of the battery (*King*, p. 240, notes that with the zinc commercially available in Henry's day as much as three-quarters of the energy could be lost). Although De La Rive demonstrated that a pure zinc electrode would not suffer such losses, the pure metal was too expensive for ordinary use. Around the same time, it was discovered that amalgamated zinc plates acted like pure zinc electrodes. The amalgamation method somehow prevented the impurities from acting without interfering with the interaction of the zinc and the electrolyte. Davy hinted at the effect in 1826 (Humphry Davy, "On the Relations of Electrical and Chemical Changes," *Phil. Trans.*, 1826, pp. 383–422). K. T. Kemp and William Sturgeon developed the principles and were the first to apply amalgamated plates in their experimental work. The theoretical reasons for the amalgamation effect remained unclear. Auguste De La Rive, "Note relative à l'action qu'exerce sur le zinc l'acide sulfurique étendu d'eau," *Bibliothèque universelle, sciences et arts*, 1830, *43*:391–411. K. T. Kemp, "Description of a New Kind of Galvanic Pile, and Also of Another Galvanic Apparatus in the Form of a Trough," *Edinburgh New Philosophical Journal*, 1828, *6*:70–77. William Sturgeon, *Recent Experimental Researches in Electro-Magnetism and Galvanism* (London, 1830), pp. 41, 42, 74, a pamphlet owned by Henry. Sturgeon reprints key papers on the subject of amalgamated zinc in his *Annals of Electricity, Magnetism, and Chemistry*, 1837, *1*:81–102. *King*, pp. 240–241, gives a good overview of developments.

The immediate spur to Joseph Henry's new interest in amalgamated plates may well have been Michael Faraday, whose recent researches on the subject were excerpted (pp. 232–236) in the above-cited journal of Thomson (footnote 9). Faraday, in his Eighth Series of Experimental Researches (*Phil. Trans.*, 1834, pp. 425–470), relied upon the efficiency of amalgamated plates in establishing his electrochemical laws, specifically the precise and constant relationship between the amount of chemical decomposition and the quantity of electricity involved in electrochemical reactions (Sections 916, 946, 947, 960, 996). Faraday's tentative explanation for the effect of amalgamation was that the fluid mercury created a uniform surface on the electrode, eliminating the point-by-point differences on the zinc plates which seemed to foster local action (Section 1000). Note that Henry assumed Faraday's proportionality between decomposition and electrical action in his own use of an amalgamated electrode, since he intended to measure the galvanic action by the amount of zinc dissolved. The next volume of *The Papers of Joseph Henry* will document further experiments by Henry on the effects of amalgamated zinc.

TO BENJAMIN SILLIMAN, SR.

Daniel C. Gilman Collection, Library, Johns Hopkins University

Princeton August 29th 1835

My Dear Sir

I received some months since a letter[1] from you relative to some accounts to be settled for the journal also making inquires relative to a magnet and a galvanic battery which you wished constructed for the purpose of exhibition at Boston. I have delayed answering the letter from time to time with the hope of making a remittance in favor of the Journal but have not found it possible to collect anything until this time.

Enclosed you will find a draft on the Bank of New York for 25 dollars; 20 of which is from Mr George D. Olmsted and the remaining 5 you will please to place to the cr. side of my account. In your letter you charged Mr Olmsted with more numbers of the journal than he had received or were sufficient to make up his set. I afterwards received a package from New York containing the numbers mentioned in the letter. Mr Olmsted received the proper number of parts to complete his set from the 25½ vol to the present time from *Mrs* Silliman by the hands of a young gentleman who came from New-Haven to be a teacher in Mr Wines' school. Mr Olmsteds account therefore commences with you at the 52nd number instead of the 46th. The remainder of the 20 dollars after paying for the numbers he has received is to be placed to his credit for the suceeding numbers. Mr Olmsteds christian name is George. He is a distant relative of the person of the same name in Ohio.[2]

I sent the second package to you by a Lad from Mr Wine's school. Please mention in your next if you have received it.

Mr Wines has promised to forward the amount of his debt for the journal by letter. The last person who acted as agent for the Journal in Princeton was Mr D'Hart.[3] He has just returned to this Place after an absence of two years and informs me that he has in possession about 15 back numbers of the journal which he will deliver to me on your order. If you will send me an order and a statement of the account with him I will attend to it and make what settlement I can. I believe he failed before leaving this place & therefore but little can be hoped from him. If your agents have not been

[1] May 27, 1835, above.

[2] These last two sentences originally appeared in the margin. George D. Olmsted may actually be the George T. Olmsted who appears variously in *Hageman*. He was a prominent resident of Princeton who later served as president of a local bank and mayor of the borough. He was the brother-in-law of Henry's friend, Richard S. Field. The Ohio Olmsted is unknown to us.

[3] See above, Henry to Torrey, February 23, 1835, footnote 14.

more faithful in other places than in this I do not wonder that the Journal should want <*patronage*> for support.

In reference to the Magnet & Battery, I have instructed James Chilton of New York in all the minutia of making magnets on my plan and he has succeeded in constructing one for West Point of great power.[4] You can procure one by applying to him on a notice of a few weeks which will answer your purpose. It can be easily so adjusted as to act by means of a lever or steelyard without using a large number of weights.

The effect however of this method of operation is far less striking to the class than by using a heavy weight. Perhaps you might have a smal "*truck*" with low but stout wheels loaded with heavy stone wheeled for the time under the magnet and the whole raised to the proper height by levers placed under each side.

I sent you by mail a few days since a copy of my paper containing a drawing of my battery by which you will readily understand the general arrangement of the parts. The instrument was constructed as I have stated principally for original research. I have found it very convenient and admirably adapted to my purpose yet in other hands and for occasional exhibition in a chemical course I fear it would not be found very managable particularly with as many seperate parts as are exhibited in the drawing above mentioned.

An apparatus consisting [of] about 8 alternations of zinc and copper so arranged as to be immersed into 8 seperate troughs well insulated and united by moveable conductors such as I have described so as to form one pair or any intermediate number of pairs up to 8 will be found most convenient for ordinary magnetic & calorific experiments.

There is a great loss when imperfect conductors are used even with Dr Hare's Calorimotor of two pairs in the same fluid. I have been able with my battery when arranged as a single pair to produce some of the most astonishing magnetic effects ever witnessed. I can reccommend the mechanical arrangement of the wheel and pinion for raising the troughs to the proper level as very compact and convenient. Besides it does not cost much since the wheel & pinion given in the drawing were purchased in Phil[a] for 1½ dollars.

You may perhaps have heard that I was lately appointed to the chair of Natural Philosophy in the University of Virginia and that I have declined the appointment. The inducement in the way of salary was very great and but that I considered myself under some obligations to this Institution I would not have hesitated to accept. The salary is in part contingent and

[4] See above, Torrey to Henry, December 29, 1834.

has varied from 3000 to 3600 for a year or two past. The chair of chemistry yielded last year $4025, of mathematics $4500. These are very tempting salaries but there may be many things in the situation &c not quite as pleasant as the remuneration. Mr Rogers[5] of Virginia has since received the appointment.

With the highest Respect
Yours sincerely
Joseph Henry

[P.S.] My Friend Mr W. R. Johnson is at present unengaged except as a lecturer in the Franklin Institute. He would accept a situation as Prof. of Chemistry or Natural Philosophy in any respectable Institution. He has had some thoughts of turning to the law and of abandoning Science since his labours do not yield him a support. Should any situation of the kind mentioned come within your knowledge you will do a favour to Mr Johnson and advance the cause of science in this country by recommending him as a candidate. I think there are few men in this country who are capable of doing more in the way of exact experimental enquiry than Mr Johnson. The papers which he has published in the Journal are all of the first order.[6] J.H.

There were a few errors in my paper published in the last No of the Journal which probably originated in copying my <*paper*> manuscript. If it be necsary I will send an erata for the next No.[7]

[5] William Barton Rogers.

[6] Johnson's numerous contributions to *Silliman's Journal* by this date included papers on mechanics, electricity, and steam.

[7] See above, Henry to Silliman, May 15, 1835. No errata appeared in subsequent numbers of *Silliman's Journal*, nor do any draft manuscripts of the article survive for comparison. The portion of the article originally published in the Franklin Institute *Journal* varies only slightly from corresponding passages in Silliman's reprint.

FROM ARTHUR J. STANSBURY[1]

Henry Papers, Smithsonian Archives

Washington August 29. 1835

Dear Sir

With sincere pleasure, and many thanks, I have to acknowledge the re-

[1] Arthur Joseph Stansbury (1781–1865), son of Joseph Stansbury (1742–1809, Loyalist, writer and lyricist, *DAB*) and father of Howard Stansbury (1806–1863, soldier, topographical engineer, and explorer, *DAB*). Arthur J. Stansbury not only had been pastor of the Henry family's Presbyterian Church in Albany and a Trustee of the Albany Academy

ceipt of your "Contributions to Electricity and Galvanism," which you were so kind as to send me. The facts detailed are of the most interesting kind, and cannot fail of being duly acknowledged as important additions to the stock of general knowledge on the subjects to which they pertain. I am happy to find that the tribute so justly due to your enterprise and industry in this field of Science is readily accorded, on both sides of the Atlantic. Our country owes much to those who thus advance her reputation: while the world at large is debtor to labourers who increase its light and promote its improvement.

The drawing of your very ingenious Galvanic apparatus is well made, and presents a very clear intelligible view of its construction and advantages. I hope you will follow up the course of investigation you have thus far so successfully prosecuted, and that the results may do more for Science, and for you, than your modesty will allow you now to anticipate.

With sincere respect & regard
I am, dear Sir,
Your obed^t Servt
Arthur Jo: Stansbury

(concurrently, 1817–1821), but also was a personal friend of Henry's with some scientific interests. Before graduating from Columbia (B.A., 1799), he studied medicine in the College of Physicians and Surgeons, 1795–1796. Henry included Stansbury's name among those receiving reprints of his scientific papers (see above, "List of Persons . . . ," [ca. August 21,] 1835); Stansbury's name is also mentioned above in Henry's letter to James Henry, June 25, 1833 (see especially footnotes 4 and 5). By 1827 he had moved to Washington where he apparently abandoned his clerical career, becoming first a stenographer, then a Congressional reporter. Soon afterward he authored a school textbook on the Constitution of the United States and a report on the impeachment proceedings against Judge James H. Peck (*DAB*). By 1850 he held positions in the Treasury Department and later in the General Land Office. A number of biographical sketches of Stansbury (including *Henry Papers, 1*:40) err in listing his death date as circa 1845. See *Columbia Catalogue*, pp. 118, 182. *Academy Seventy-fifth Anniversary*, p. 65. *Herringshaw*. Washington, D.C., City Directories, 1827–1860. F. H. Wines, comp., *Descendants of John Stansbury of Leominster* (Springfield, Illinois, 1895), p. 10.

FROM BENJAMIN SILLIMAN, SR.

Mary Henry Copy, Memoir, Henry Papers, Smithsonian Archives

Nantucket[1] Sep. 4. 1835.

Dear Sir. The newspapers announce the application of your electro-motive

[1] In September 1835, Silliman gave a course of lectures in Nantucket, Massachusetts. John F. Fulton and Elizabeth H. Thomson, *Benjamin Silliman, 1779–1864: Pathfinder in American Science* (New York, 1947), p. 179.

magnetic apparatus to mechanics. . . .[2] Will you be so good as to communicate to me *here* the truth. If there is anything in it I must try to find room for you in the October no. if possible although it is chiefly pledged to Ohio coal.[3]

Another matter. I am to give a popular course of chemistry in Boston next March and April[4] & I wish to do justice to your discoveries. I shall have a calorimotor there of considerable power. I wish to know whether the poles of this could be conveniently adapted to your galvanic magnet, so as to supersede the necessity of having a distinct battery appended. . . . I would take care to do justice to your discovery that a small battery will answer the purpose. . . . Are there any improvements in winding the wire? I shall wish to give minute directions to a practical man in Boston that I may have everything ready early in season. An immediate answer will oblige me as I am to leave this for Boston on the morning of the 23. inst. & I wish to give the directions there in person. I remain dear Sir Yours very truly

B. Silliman

[2] A report on the electromagnetic machine of Thomas Davenport. See Henry's response, below, of September 10, 1835.

[3] See Ten Eyck's letter to Henry of December 7, 1835, footnote 4, printed below.

[4] See above, Silliman to Henry, May 27, 1835.

TO BENJAMIN SILLIMAN, SR.

Daniel C. Gilman Collection, Library, Johns Hopkins University

Princeton Sept 10th 1835

My Dear Sir

Your letter of the 4th inst came to hand this morning and I answer it by the return post. The great importance of the invention of the Brandon blacksmith exists principally in the fertile immagination of Professor Eaton who is said to be the writer of the article you have seen and who probably intends to edify the public with an account of the wonder. I was somewhat displeased with the article and think it calculated to injure the inventor of the machine who appears to be a modest unassuming and ingenious young man. He came to Princeton about a month since with a letter to me from the Patroon (Mr Van Renssaler) of albany with a request that I would give an opinion on the merits of the article. I stated in a certificat that as the production of a person but little acquainted with the subject of electromagnetism the machine evinced much ingenuity but that I did not believe that electro magnetic power would be found sufficiently cheap for mechanical purposes.[1]

I felt considerably interested in the welfare of the Inventor and with friendly motives advised him to abandon the invention as I was fully convinced that he never could do anything with it except in the way of exhibition as a curiosity. I gave him a letter to Mr Peale of the Museum of Philadelphia that he might make something by exhibiting it for money and thus indemnify himself for the time he had expended in the construction.

The truth is that there is nothing new in the whole affair. Every <*principle*> part of the machine has been invented before and in fact it differs nothing in principle from the first one of the kind which I described in the Journal, as you will reccollect, about 1831.[2] I have been pestered with let-

[1] At this point we pick up the account of Thomas Davenport, the Brandon, Vermont, blacksmith, who invented an electromagnetic motor (see footnote 1 of Van Rensselaer's letter to Henry of June 29, 1835, above, for the sources of this note). In this letter Henry gives the only report by him known to us about what transpired in Princeton in early July of 1835. It differs in certain respects from the two versions deriving from Davenport, his autobiography and the biography by his descendent, Walter Rice Davenport.

In the former, A. D. Bache is at Princeton; in the latter Davenport meets Bache later in Philadelphia. Henry's "certificat" does not survive. The two Davenport accounts do not give Henry's rather patronizing evaluation of the invention, mentioning only Henry's praise of the originality of the device. The autobiography—the obvious source of the later account—quotes Henry's advice to build on a small scale to minimize the public reaction in case of failure. Neither account mentions Peale's Museum (see below). Instead, Bache has Davenport exhibit the invention at the Franklin Institute. On July 15 Bache gives the Brandon blacksmith a warmer certificate than Henry's—the text is given in the Davenport autobiography—which suggests continuing the work on a full-size model. Davenport then continues to Washington but, owing to the 1836 fire in the Patent Office, only receives his patent in 1837. After returning home in 1835, a newspaper story by Amos Eaton praised the invention. News of this had apparently reached Silliman. Henry was not impressed by Eaton's prose.

[2] Henry's sensitivity on this particular priority problem is apparent in his reaction to William Ritchie which is given in his letter to Jacob Green of February 17, 1834 (and especially footnote 4), above. During his lifetime, Henry's achievement was recognized by at least some of his peers. In 1839 Sturgeon noted that ". . . it is to the ingenious American philosopher, above named [Henry], that we are indebted for the first form of a working model of an engine upon the principle of reciprocating polarity of soft iron by electrodynamic agency." In Hare's *Compendium*, the section on Electro-Magnetism, Hare gives Henry credit for "more fully" presenting the "susceptibility of opposite magnetization," while giving Ritchie credit for the first rotary motion (pp. 120–122 in "Of Galvanism, or Voltaic Electricity," supplement to *A Compendium of the Course of Chemical Instruction. . .*, 4th ed. [Philadelphia, 1840–1843]). In Brewster's article in the *Britannica* on "Voltaic Electricity" (8th ed., p. 641) Henry's reciprocating apparatus is cited as the source of Davenport's invention. While balming his pride, these references did not compensate for the neglect of his work by others. Sturgeon's remarks are in "Historical Sketch of the Rise and Progress of Electro-magnetic Engines for Propelling Machinery," Sturgeon's *Annals of Electricity, Magnetism, and Chemistry*, 1839, *3*:429–479. The quotation is from page 429. Sturgeon himself claimed to have made a motor in 1832 and demonstrated it in the following year.

A recent work (*King*, pp. 260–261) states "Henry's apparatus was the first clear-cut instance of a motor capable of further mechanical development. It had the essentials of a modern DC motor: a magnet to provide the field, an electromagnet as armature, and a commutator to apply the mechanical forces at the right time. . . ."

ters from almost every state in the Union since my first paper on Electro magnetism appeared in the Journal, containing discriptions and plans of machines to be moved by the magnetic power. I have uniformly referred them to the description of my little machine in the Journal and stated that I freely renounced all right to the invention as I consider the machine in the present state of the science only a philosophical toy.[3] It is surprising how many times this machine has been reinvented and described with slight modifications since my first description of it. One invention of this kind was made in Germany[4] another in France[5] and in the last No of the

[3] See, for example, the fragment of Henry's reply to S. Belknap, July 26, 1834, above. As in similar instances in volume one, we lack the letters Henry received from inventors. From his replies, we know some conceived of electromagnetism as a source of perpetual motion. Others, such as Davenport, did not have that aim, being sincerely interested in developing a new motive power. In this period —let us say, 1832–1835—a number of men in Europe and America began seeking ways of practical application of electromagnetism. In contrast, having demonstrated a particular scientific effect in his reciprocating motor, Joseph Henry turned to other scientific problems in electromagnetism.

[4] Most likely a reference to Moritz Hermann von Jacobi, *DSB* (1801–1874), brother of the eminent mathematician C. G. J. Jacobi (1804–1851). Originally an architect, M. H. von Jacobi had constructed an electromagnetic motor in May 1834. In 1834 Jacobi was at Königsberg practicing his profession. Jacobi submitted a report to the French Academy and the first publication of his work known to us appeared in France in that year in *L'Institut, journal général des sociétés et travaux scientifiques*, December 2, 1834, 2:394–395. As we shall see in footnote 6, word of Jacobi's device was out, in print or otherwise, before this publication. In 1835 he became a Professor of Civil Engineering at Dorpat in the Russian Empire. In 1837 he became associated with the Imperial Academy of Sciences at St. Petersburg. After 1840 he was solely at the Academy. With the support of the Russian government, Jacobi in 1838 constructed and ran a motor-propelled boat. He was an active investigator in both the theory and the application of electromagnetism.

After his removal to Russia, Jacobi's work, including his first full description of the motor, appeared often under the auspices of the Imperial Academy. A partial English translation appeared in 1837 in Sturgeon's *Annals* (*1*:408–415, 419–444). By that date Jacobi was aware of competing claims for priority by Italian investigators (but not by Joseph Henry) which he dismissed (p. 409):

> A discussion of priority has only a historical interest. It is not surprising that men between whom there is scarcely any communication, should study the same subject nearly at the same time. But we ought not to deceive ourselves that after the great discovery of M. Oersted, and the essays of Mr. Sturgeon . . . it was not difficult to conceive the idea that some motion or some mechanical work might be produced by the electromagnetic excitation of soft iron.

One experiment Jacobi reports is footnoted by Sturgeon (p. 440) as having been originally done by Henry.

In the same piece, he displayed an attitude towards applications and pure science quite different from Henry's:

> I was first struck with these considerations when the means of putting them into execution were yet unknown, but I always had their practical application in view, and the object appeared to me of too great importance, to exhaust my powers in the construction of playthings which could only claim the honour of being put in the rank of electric chimes in relation to their effect, and still more with regard to the noise with which they are accompanied.

Another but less likely possibility is that Henry has heard of the Swiss-German Rudolph Schulthess (1802–1833?, *Poggendorff*). He had suggested the idea of an electromagnetic motor in a December 10, 1832, lecture to the Zurich Philosophical Society. At the start of the next year, he heard of the Italian Dal Negro's work which he criticized in a February 18, 1833, talk before the Society. This

Edinburgh Journal (Jameson's) but one, a detailed account is given of one by a person in Milan almost precisely the same as mine except, that it vibrates like a pendulum instead of moving like the working beam of a steam engine.[6] The plan of the Brandon Blacksmith, is however the best although not the most simple which I have seen. It is still however nothing more than a philosophical toy—a new power cannot be introduced as a moving principle in mechanics unless it be cheaper in its production, or more convenient in some respect than steam.[7]

In answer to the inquiries relative to the calorimotor &c &c, there is no

---

lecture described his own device. (See Taylor's *Scientific Memoirs*, 1837, *1*:534–540.) Although Henry was not named, Schulthess was aware of Henry's work on the great lifting magnet.

[5] Unknown to us unless this is a confusion with Jacobi because of the French publication.

[6] G. M. Botto's "On the Application of Electro-Magnetic Power to Mechanics" is in the *Edinburgh New Philosophical Journal*, 1834–1835, *18*:151–154. Botto published this article after reading a reference to Jacobi's work. Botto (1791–1865, *Poggendorff*) was on the faculty at Turin and not from Milan. Two other Italian scientists producing motors (loosely speaking) in this period, Salvatore Dal Negro (1768–1839, *Poggendorff*) and Giuseppi Zamboni (1776–1846, *Poggendorff*) are from Padua and Verona, respectively. We are uncertain if Henry simply confused Turin and Milan or if he had heard of still another Italian working on electromagnetic motors.

[7] Discoveries in electromagnetism stimulated interest in applications among both scientists and inventors. Accompanying this interest in many instances were optimistic expectations, sometimes verging on technological hubris. Henry was a hardheaded dissenter, stressing very real practical difficulties. Although inventors and ingenious mechanics aroused his ire, fellow scientists were not immune to a facile optimism disregarding legitimate objections.

Consider the matter of perpetual motion. The translation of the Botto article in the *Edinburgh New Philosophical Journal* (see footnote 6) has Botto responding to word of Jacobi's development of perpetual motion. The original of Botto's article in the *Bibliothèque universelle, sciences et arts*, 1834, n.s. 2:312, says Jacobi obtained "un phenomène de mouvement continu," a far different matter, which the editor of a leading scientific journal apparently did not notice. Jacobi himself, in the 1834 article in *L'Institut* (see footnote 4), asserts, "Dans la machine électrique, la vitesse ne coûte pas d'argent." Henry's ire against inventors and untutored mechanics might equally apply to a number of very eminent fellow scientists.

Henry's cool reaction came down ultimately to the recognition that coal and water were cheaper than metals and acids, a fact recognized by many of his contemporaries. *King*, pp. 269–271, in his discussion of this point, also notes that the absence of a means of distributing electricity over long distances was a handicap. Even Jacobi's initial optimism waned. Brewster, reporting a conversation with Bassel, states that Jacobi abandoned his efforts because of induced "counter-currents generated by the very motion of the machine." More typical were investigations comparing the work performed by electric and steam power. As late as 1876 Henry was repeating these arguments. And Theodore du Moncel's *Exposé des applications de l'électricité* (3d ed., Paris, 1878) continued in this vein at the point where the recent invention of the dynamo would change the situation drastically.

Reading the arguments for and against electrical power in the first three quarters of the last century is reminiscent of the contemporary experience with atomic energy. Sanguine hopes for the new source of power were not immediately borne out. Not only were scientific and technological problems involved in the new technology underrated but so also was the competitive resiliency of the older power technologies.

Brewster's comments are in the *Britannica*, "Voltaic Electricity," 8th ed., pp. 645–646. Henry's late views are in the Smithsonian Institution, *Annual Report*, 1876, p. 39.

difficulty in attaching temporarily the terminations of the wires[8] which envelope the magnet to the poles of an ordinary calorimotor. This may either be done by cups of mercury or by means of the two vises usually attached to the instrument. If you are about constructing a new calorimotor I would advise that all the plates be well soldered to broad slips of thick copper instead of the lead bars described by Dr Hare. Much of the power of this apparatus depends on the perfect conduction of the "*connectors*" of the several parts. The only precautions in making the electro-magnetic magnet is that all the wires should be of the same length and that they do not touch either in the different spires of the same wire or in the spires of different wires. If the spires of the same wire touch each other the effect produced is the same as that of shortening the strand of wire so touching this causes it to conduct more than its share of the galvanism. If the spires of different wires touch the galvanism may pass from one to the other and not circulate around the magnet. The strands should be about 50 feet long and well covered with silk. Another very important precaution is that the electricity pass in the same direction through each wire or that no two wires neutralize each other by transmitting adverse currents. To guard against this it will be proper before soldering all the projecting ends together that each be tried by a small battery the poles of which are furnished with cups of mercury. If each wire gives the same polarity to the same leg of the magnet (which may be tried with a [common?] compass needle) then they must be all soldered together in the order in which they have been tested; if not then the one which is found to give a contrary polarity must have its ends reversed in reference to the terminations of the other wires.

I have shown to my class with my large battery some of the most magnificent experiments on electromagnets which I believe have ever been exhibited. I form a hoop of copper ribbon of about the size of the small wheel of a waggon by rolling on its self in the same plane about 100 feet of copper ribbon one inch wide well covered with silk. When this circle of copper ribbon is supported horizontally about 8 or 9 inches from the lecture table and a large apparatus like Amperes revolving cylender[9] is placed in the centre the cylender begins to move as if by magic when the current is passed through the copper ribbon. If a large plate filled with mercury be placed on a short cylender of iron & these placed in the middle of the coil the

[8] This account by Joseph Henry is essentially similar to those appearing in *Henry Papers, 1*: 400–402, 420–425. As we shall see below, this account did not answer all the questions in Silliman's mind.

[9] Although Henry had reason to believe Silliman was familiar with this piece of apparatus, Silliman claimed he was "not acquainted" with it in his reply of September 19, 1835, below. See especially footnote 9.

mercury commences a gyratory motion; and in this way a variety of experiments of the most surprising kind are shown. The most astonishing exhibition however of the power of galvanism [in] developing magnetism in soft iron is made by placing the large coil before mentioned perpendicularly to the horizon and holding in its centre the lifter of my large magnet (which, the lifter, weighs 25 lbs.) and when the galvanic current is passed through the coil the iron in its center becomes so powerfully magnetic as to support itself and three or 4 times its own weight from the ends of a piece of bar iron bent thus  or like a *U* with two long legs which pass over the coil and reach down as far as the centre of the coil on each side. These experiments belong to a series which I have intended to publish as a continuation of my papers in the Phil. Transactions.[10] I would be pleased that you should exhibit this and will give you any information necessary for that purpose. I owe you many thanks for the favour you have done me in making my experiments known; that my labours are appreciated and commended by those who are capable of judging in such matters is very greateful to my feelings but I must confess that I have become somewhat too fastidious to relish the newspaper puffing which has become so common and disgusting in this country.[11]

I wrote you a letter some weeks since about the accounts of the Journal, also informing you that I had been elected to the Chair of N. Philos in the University of Virginia but had declined the appointment. I also stated that James Chilton of New York had succeeded in making a powerful magnet on my plan for West Point and that he will furnish them of any power at a short notice.[12]

The Trustees of the College at the last meeting ordered the erection of

[10] "Contributions III: Electro-Dynamic Induction" does not specifically go into these experiments. The closest to these topics are paragraphs 50 and 51 which appear almost as asides to the main argument. In the latter, Henry notes that induction at a distance provides "astonishing experiments, in the line of *physique amusante*." Experiments with hoops of copper ribbon were a common part of Henry's laboratory work; a variation of the experiment on the gyration of mercury is dealt with in experiment 5 of the "Record of Experiments" for September 8, 1834, above. In an extended letter of March 2, 1836, to appear in volume three, Henry goes into considerable detail on the experimental setups and on his explanations of the effects.

Another possibility is that Henry is referring to the proposed, but never realized, publication discussed in his letter to Harriet Henry of May 1, 1835, above. See especially footnote 4.

[11] Perhaps a reference again to the newspaper publicity for Davenport. This theme will recur in the *Henry Papers* (for an earlier comment, see Henry's letter to Cooper of November 26, 1833, above). Joseph Henry felt strongly that new discoveries and scientific controversies were matters for consideration first within learned organizations and scientific journals, not in the popular press. Subsequent dissemination of scientific findings in the popular press was unobjectionable; Henry himself wrote some such articles for newspapers.

[12] See Henry's letter to Silliman of August 29, 1835, above.

an addition to the Philosophical Hall. This has interrupted all my researches for 4 months past & I fear I will loose nearly the whole semester.[13]

Yours sincerely
Joseph Henry

[13] In his March 2, 1836, letter Henry explains he had not had time to develop the experiments in this letter. Between May 1835 and March 1836 the reconstruction of Philosophical Hall effectively stopped Henry's experimentation. The March 2, 1836, letter signals the return to the laboratory. In the "Record of Experiments" he magnetizes a soft iron cylinder by a coil (March 18, 1836) and the next day magnetizes steel by electricity. From this point Joseph Henry goes into the work forming the bulk of "Contributions III."

FROM BENJAMIN SILLIMAN, SR.

Henry Papers, Smithsonian Archives

Nantucket Sept[r] 19, 1835

My dear Sir

After I wrote to you from this place I received from N Hav[en] your obliging letter of Aug 29[1] & yesterday I received that of Sept[r] 10[2] for both of which I render you my best thanks. I duly received the Journals that were returned—also the money from M[r] Wines & M[rs] Silliman received your draft $25, $20 for M[r] G. D. Olmsted & 5$ for yourself: when I return I will see all these things correctly entered. I had supposed that M[r] G D. O. might be the same gentleman who used to write to me from Tennessee which was the cause of sending more n[os] than were wanted & the sending them twice was my own blunder. As to M[r] D'Hart he may as well send back the N[os] in his hands. I could never obtain from him any satisfactory returns & rarely any returns at all. When I get home I will see if I can make any statement that is exact. I know in general that several copies—three I believe—were sent to him year after year for subscribers & I think I received only one small remittance. I suppose of course that the rest must be lost. It will give me much pleasure to aid *your* I may say *our* friend M[r] Johnson should it be in my power & I will keep him in view for that purpose. I have the same opinion of him which you express & have placed a high value on his communications. It would be a great pity should he be lost to science. You will be the best judge of the importance of the errata in your late notices in the Journal;[3] I will insert them in the ensuing N[o] should you desire it & I think

[1] See above. [2] See above. [3] See Henry's August 29, 1835 letter, above.

I can find room for any original notices or others which you may send provided I receive them soon after my return. I expect to be at home on the 28 or 29. I am much gratified to learn that Chilton is instructed how to construct your apparatus, a fact which was confirmed by a note from James last evening & I shall probably avail myself of his services. I want now particularly the rotating magnet to produce sparks & decompositions.[4] I shall on going home examine with attention your printed communication, with drawings[5] for which I thank you & will make up my mind what I will do. In the mean time as I do not go to Boston till the first week in March and in the mean time shall be entirely engaged in chemistry at N Haven, there will be time for you to make any communication as to any point in your discoveries which you would wish particularly illustrated for I have great pleasure in giving due prominence & effect to your very successful labors. They are a part of the reputation of the country & both in the Journal & otherwise I shall always be happy to advance your reputation. I was not aware that the chairs in the University of Virginia are so lucrative & I regret (other things being equal) that you could not avail yourself of a situation which would have placed you so much at ease in a pecuniary view & if there would not have been too great an absorption of time might have enabled you to advance in science still more rapidly. Referring now to yours of the 10th I thank you for the explanation relative to the new invented (so called) application of your electro magnetic power. It turns out much as I expected. Would it not be well for you to send me a short notice of the real state of facts that the public may not be misled; & from the Journal it would be copied into the newspapers which might save you from some of those troublesome importunities to which you allude.[6]

I thank you for your directions relative to the construction of the electro-

[4] A reference to the magnetoelectric generators developed by Joseph Saxton and others (see above, Green to Henry, February 13, 1834). Though James Chilton probably mentioned the new apparatus to Silliman, Chilton evidently did not yet manufacture or stock the apparatus. Isaiah Lukens was still the principal manufacturer of Saxton's machines. A later letter from Henry (March 2, 1836) shows that Silliman had to borrow a machine in the absence of Lukens.

[5] Henry's "Contributions I: Battery."

[6] No such notice appeared in *Silliman's Journal* nor, to our knowledge, in the newspapers. Silliman's opinions apparently changed, for, after examining two examples of Davenport's machine in 1837, he wrote a highly laudatory report on it: "Notice of the Electro-Magnetic Machine of Mr. Thomas Davenport, of Brandon, near Rutland, Vermont," *Silliman's Journal*, 1837, *32* (No. 1):Appendix. Silliman not only pointed up the unique aspects of Davenport's contribution, but, contrary to Henry, emphasized its technological prospects, calling for further application of funds, scientific knowledge, and mechanical skill, so that "science and art, the handmaids of discovery, will both receive from this interesting research a liberal reward." Without mentioning Ritchie's device (or other ones in Henry's letter), Silliman considered Davenport "to have been strictly the inventor of a method of applying galvanism to produce rotary motion." Moreover, contrary to Henry's skepticism, he saw no reason why the power of the machine could not be indefinitely increased.

magnet: they are precise—intelligible & altogether philosophical & reasonable. I shall be very happy to see your additional researches & am much struck with those which you have stated. I got one of your copper coils made in Boston: it was copper ribbon 1 inch wide & about 75 long covered with silk & coiled in the same plane. On attaching a wire connected with one end to one side of the calorimotor & bringing a wire from the other into contact with its termination there was a small but vivid spark & a distinct report or snap—a little like that of the remaining charge in a Leyden Jar after it has been discharged & then the discharging rod is applied again. It was not sufficiently vivid to make it worth while to shew it to my popular audience here & therefore I did not mention it.[7] As this coil of 75 feet did not make a wheel of more than 5 inches diameter I do not understand how yours of 100 feet should make one as large as a waggon wheel, unless inde[e]d you separated the strands by some interposed substance to keep them more effectually apart.[8] What you say of the magnetic powers of this coil interests me very much indeed & I shall be very desirous to exhibit it both at Y[ale] C[ollege] & in Boston. I am not acquainted with Ampere's revolving cylinder[9] & do not either precisely understand how you can attach the lifter of your great magnet in the centre of the coil when placed perpendicularly, unless you run an axis through it & support that axis at the two ends so as to enable it to sustain the weight of the lifter & of the attached weight. How are your engagements say from Jan. 8 to the 16 or thereabouts—say not earlier than the 6 nor later than the 20th within which time I might perhaps

[7] Attempting to reproduce results in Henry's "Contributions II: Spiral Conductor," Silliman apparently looked for self-inductive sparks at the moment of completing the galvanic circuit. Henry, by contrast, produced visible sparks only when breaking the circuit. Noting that induced secondary currents move in contrary directions at the start and end of the primary current, Michael Faraday ascribed the feeble effect on making the circuit to the retarding force of the secondary current. When the circuit was broken, the secondary current accelerated the primary. Ninth Series of Experimental Researches, paragraphs 1101 and 1102. The same explanation is later implied in Joseph Henry's "Contributions IV: Electro-Dynamic Induction," paragraph 19.

[8] Nothing was interposed. It was simply that Silliman had made tight windings while Henry, according to his September 10 letter, fashioned a "hoop" in order to demonstrate different phenomena which required a hole in the middle of the induction spiral. For the particular spark effects Silliman wanted, Henry used a tightly wound spiral, as can be seen in a March 2, 1836, letter to Silliman, where Henry carefully details his various demonstration techniques. According to that letter, to appear in Volume 3 of *The Papers of Joseph Henry*, a tightly wound coil of from one to two hundred feet had a diameter of from twelve to twenty-four inches.

[9] Silliman apparently forgot Henry's illustrated description of the apparatus in a December 28, 1830, letter to Silliman (*Henry Papers, 1*:317) and a footnote on it in Henry's "On the Application of the Principle of the Galvanic Multiplier to Electro-Magnetic Apparatus, and Also to the Development of Great Magnetic Power in Soft Iron, with a Small Galvanic Element," *Silliman's Journal*, 1831, *19*:408. It is apparent from these and other slips that Silliman, while spreading word of Henry's work, was less than perceptive in understanding the details and principles of his experimental achievements. For the proper demonstration of Henry's results, Silliman clearly needed the closest guidance.

find it possible to give you a call at Princeton & see your apparatus & the mode of using it; then I should fully understand it & could give the necessary directions for construction. Will you at the time named be sufficiently at liberty to shew me the experiments that I may [run?] no hazard especially in Boston for you or myself. At the time I have named we have a vacation of 2 weeks & this is the only time I could command.[10]

I agree with you as to the newspaper puffs but I do not know how they are to be prevented.

I remain my dear Sir with the greatest respect & regard

yours very truly
B Silliman

[10] We know of no such Princeton meeting, but Henry doubtless gave some directions on his trip to New Haven on October 26 and 27, 1835. In any case Henry gave Silliman a full account of his demonstration apparatus in the aforementioned letter of March 2, 1836.

FROM MECHANICS INSTITUTE[1]

Henry Papers, Smithsonian Archives

New-York, 21st September, 1835.

SIR,

We beg leave to solicit your assistance as Judge[2] of Models of Machinery

[1] This letter is a printed form with only the names of the four "Coadjutors" and the phrase "Models of Machinery & Philosophical Apparatus" written in by hand.

The Mechanics Institute of New York City, founded in 1830 and chartered in 1833, patterned itself mainly on the Franklin Institute of Philadelphia (for which see *Henry Papers, 1*:394). The membership grew quite large—from 45 at its beginning to 700 in July 1835 and 1400 in 1840—because the organization offered many services while keeping dues at only $2 a year. The Institute had a library and a reading room, plus a museum of machines, scientific equipment, and minerals. The Institute held very popular fairs, sponsored weekly lectures during the winter, and lobbied for public schools. "Fair of the Mechanics Institute of the City of New-York," *Mechanics Magazine*, August 1835, *6*:71–72; "Proceedings of the Mechanics Institute of the City of New York," *American Repertory of Arts, Sciences, and Manufactures*, 1840, *1*:34–35; and Brooke Hindle, "The Underside of the Learned Societies in New York, 1754–1854," draft of a paper for the Colloquium on the Early History of Societies for Promoting Knowledge in the United States, sponsored by the American Academy of Arts and Sciences, June 1973, pp. 33–34.

[2] So far as we know, Joseph Henry was not among the judges. The accounts of the fair in newspapers and journals do not list the names of any of the judges, but in late September, Henry was apt to be involved in final examinations and commencement preparation at Princeton. He had no aversion to such appointments, having served a similar function on occasion for the Albany Institute (see *Henry Papers, 1*:210) and for the Franklin Institute (see note 19 of the letter of November 1, 1833, and the letter of July 13, 1834, both printed above).

& Philosophical Apparatus at the approaching Fair[3] of the Mechanics Institute of the City of New-York, to be held at Castle Garden.[4]

The Exhibition will commence on the 29th instant, and continue four days: the morning of each day, until fifteen minutes before 10 o'clock, will be appropriated to the Judges.

With great respect,
Your Obedient Servants,

GEORGE BRUCE,[5]
HENRY CUNNINGHAM,[6]
WILLIAM PARTRIDGE,[7]
HENRY DURELL,[8]
JOHN M. DODD,[9]
ADAM HALL,[10]
JOHN BELL,[11]
W. H. HALE,[12]
J. S. REDFIELD,[13]

Committee on Premiums.

Your Coadjutors are Prof Steele[14]
Messrs. Adam Hall
W. C. Redfield[15]
George N Miner[16]

[3] The fair, which was open from September 29 to October 3, seemed to be very successful. Over 40,000 people attended, and the receipts of $2,188 more than paid for expenses. The Institute recruited 300 additional members as a direct result of the undertaking. The entries were a glorious mélange of American invention and taste—"porcelain pitchers of mammouth size, splendid trumpets and bugles, iron and copper wire, mantel lamps of superb finish, splendid pianos, hearth rugs, matrasses [flasks] of ground cork, barometers, anthracite ornaments, fire proof safes, dorick fireplaces, printing presses" were all there, according to the *New York Evening Post* for October 2, 1835. Joseph Henry would have been especially interested in the dipping needles, magnets, and electromagnetic apparatus (not further described) among the scientific displays. "First Annual Fair of the Mechanics Institute," *Mechanics Magazine*, November 1835, *6*:249–253; Hindle, "Underside," p. 34. Joseph Henry did visit the fair of 1836 and remarked on "the great variety and beauty of the articles" (letter to Harriet Henry, September 11, 1836, Family Correspondence, Smithsonian Archives).

[4] This structure was used as a fort until 1823, when the United States government leased it to the city for a public recreation spot. An awning and walkway over the top of the walls permitted strollers to admire the views of the harbor and cityscape. The space within the walls was large enough to accommodate 10,000 people at a time for concerts, firework displays, and other occasions. New York City Directory for 1835.

[5] George Bruce (1781–1866) was born in Scotland and educated in public schools there. He immigrated to Philadelphia in about 1796 and was apprenticed to first a bookbinder and then a printer. Bruce worked in Albany for a while around the turn of the century before joining the *Daily Advertiser* staff in New York City, for which he became printer and publisher in 1804. In 1806 he began his own printing firm, and introduced stereotyping from England in the firm's operations in 1812. He improved the process by several innovations himself. Bruce began typefounding in 1816; a typecasting machine he invented was used well into the twentieth century. Bruce was associated with several mechanics' institutes in New York City. *DAB*.

[6] Henry Cunningham is listed as an accountant in the New York City Directory for 1832–

1833. He does not appear in the compilations for 1834–1835 or 1835–1836, but his widow is listed in the directory for 1836–1837.

[7] William Partridge was in the dyestuffs business, according to the New York City Directory for 1835–1836. His profession is given as chemist in "Proceedings of the Mechanics Institute for April 1836," *Mechanics Magazine*, 1836, 7:267.

[8] The New York City Directory for 1835–1836 gives Henry Durell's occupation as paper-stainer.

[9] John M. Dodd is listed as a mason in the New York City Directory for 1835–1836.

[10] Adam Hall is described as a machinist in the "Proceedings . . . April 1836" and as an engineer in the New York City Directory for 1835–1836.

[11] Not identified. No John Bell is given in "Proceedings . . . April 1836" while the New York City Directory for 1835–1836 shows that nine men by that name lived in the city those years.

[12] William H. Hale seems to have been involved in a variety of businesses. The New York City Directories for 1834–1835 and 1835–1836 list him as a marblecutter, but that for 1831–1832 gives his interest as silver pencils. "Proceedings . . . April 1836" describes Hale as a pencil-case maker.

[13] After attending school in New Hampshire, Justus Starr Redfield (1810–1888) went to Boston and then New York to train as a printer. From 1834 to 1841, he published the popular *Family Magazine*. Redfield ran a successful bookstore-publishing house from 1841 to 1860. The firm was noted for its important early edition (1850–1856) of the works of Edgar Allan Poe. Redfield was a United States Consul in Italy from 1861 to 1866, returning thereafter to edit and translate various European literary works. *DAB*.

[14] The Mechanics Institute grew out of John Steele's chemistry lecture series in 1830–1831. Steele was metallurgical consultant for Archibald McIntyre's iron mines in the Adirondacks in 1831 and again from 1837 to 1843. He was superintendent of the works there from 1832 to 1836, during which time he apparently also lectured in New York on scientific topics. Hindle, "Underside," p. 33; New York City Directories; Arthur H. Masten, *The Story of Adirondac* (Syracuse, 1968), pp. 43, 47–48, 52–54, 81, and 88.

[15] William C. Redfield (1789–1857) became an important scientific associate of Joseph Henry. They shared an interest in meteorology and in the cause of steamboat boiler explosions. He will appear frequently in subsequent volumes of the *Henry Papers*.

Redfield grew up in Cromwell, Connecticut, where he educated himself by reading in the scientific library of Dr. William Tully (see *Henry Papers, 1*:279). He worked at first as a saddle and harness maker, but about 1820 became interested in steamboat technology. In 1826 he founded the Steam Navigation Company, a successful business in which he was involved for the rest of his life. His company devised a system of freight barges towed at a safe distance by steamboats which were prone to accidents. Redfield's business concerns led him to develop safer steam boilers and to gather statistics on accidents, which prodded the transportation industry into other reforms. He was also an early advocate (1829) of a cross-Appalachian railroad to link the Hudson and Mississippi Rivers.

Redfield's interest in meteorology dated from September 1821, when he noticed the pattern in which the great storm of that month had felled trees in New England. He described the gale from this datum as a giant cyclone of winds whirling rapidly around an axis, the center of which moved slowly over the landscape. In 1831, he chanced to meet Denison Olmsted (*Henry Papers, 1*:274), who urged him to publish his ideas in *Silliman's Journal* for that year. Redfield worked steadily on meteorology thereafter. For his major papers, he gathered data from all ocean vessels caught in the same storm and then plotted the information on maps to show patterns in the natural history of the gale or hurricane. He discovered that the winds always moved in the same direction around the axis of storms. He also found that the paths of storms within a given region—say, the North Atlantic—paralleled each other. Redfield advocated a theory that storms were caused by the daily and yearly revolutions of the earth, an idea that conflicted with the beliefs of his contemporaries that atmospheric heat or electricity accounted for weather patterns.

Redfield also published several papers on American geology, mostly on fossil fish and on the tracks of extinct animals. He was an early member of the Association of American Geologists, and when that organization became the American Association for the Advancement of Science in 1848, he was its first president.

DAB; Denison Olmsted, "Biographical Memoir of William C. Redfield," *Silliman's Journal*, November 1857, 2d ser. *24*:355–373.

[16] The New York City Directory for 1834–1835 and "Proceedings . . . April 1836" describe George N. Miner as a machinist.

September 23, 1835

FROM JOHN PAGE[1]

Henry Papers, Smithsonian Archives

Williamsburg Septr 23rd 1835

Sir

You may have heard that Mr Rogers our Professor of Chemistry and Natural Philosophy has accepted the Professorship at the University which was offered to you.[2] Many of the Visitors & Governors, and other friends of William & Mary College are anxious that you should succeed him. They have had, however, but little hope that you would accept the appointment, and this has prevented an application being made to you by some other friend of the College. But the account which I have received of your devotion to Science, and of your general character, determines me to make the effort at least, to obtain your aid in upholding the character, and rising prospects of our venerable Institution. It is true, the pecuniary emoluments of the situation can present no temptation, but to one, who *values his independence,* and who *desires literary leisure,* no institution in the United States can offer stronger inducements. You will be in every respect on a perfect equality with the President[3] and other Professors. The President is the mere chairman of the Faculty, and in no respect whatever the superior of the other Professors. He is an amiable and learned man, in whose family, I doubt not, you will soon find yourself at home, as you will also, in almost every family in town. The other Professors are agreeable gentlemen & men of ability. With the reputation of Professors Dew[4] &

[1] John Page (ca. 1800–1838) was a member of the prominent Page family of Virginia. A lawyer, he served in the Virginia House of Delegates (1825–1826) and Senate (1832–1836). He became a Visitor of the College of William and Mary in 1827. R. C. M. Page, *Genealogy of the Page Family in Virginia* (New York, 1893), pp. 78–80; *The History of the College of William and Mary* (Baltimore, 1870), p. 68.

[2] William Barton Rogers (for whom see above, Henry's Notes on a Trip to Philadelphia, April 29–May 2, 1834, footnote 46) taught at William and Mary, his alma mater, from 1828 to 1835. Letters relating to the University of Virginia's attempt to hire Joseph Henry appear above in the summer of 1835.

[3] Reverend Adam Empie (1785–1860). Born in Schenectady, New York, Empie graduated from Union College (A.B. 1807) and became an Episcopal minister. He held numerous pastorships, including that of West Point (1813–1817) where he served as Acting Professor of Ethics, Geography, and History. He was elected President of William and Mary in 1827. Resigning that office in July 1836, Empie resumed his clerical life in Richmond, Virginia. "Under Dr. Empie the college began rapidly to revive from long continued depression. The old jealousies had fallen into the background, and the sale of its formerly unproductive lands in different parts of the state had realized a considerable endowment fund." *National Cyclopedia of American Biography, 3*:235. The foregoing account lends credence to Page's view of the "rising prospects of our venerable Institution." *Union Catalog,* p. 5. Charles K. Gardner, *A Dictionary of . . . the Army of the United States,* 2d ed. (New York, 1860), p. 165.

[4] Thomas Roderick Dew (1802–1846). A graduate of William and Mary (B.A., 1820), Dew traveled in Europe before becoming Professor of Political Law at his alma mater in 1827. As an economist he wrote and lectured

Tucker[5] you are probably acquainted, but from all you will meet with a kind and cordial welcome. The duties of the Professorship are light. You will be required to be with your Classes, in Lecturing & examining them, only one hour each day during the Session of eight months. So that you will have the whole of the Twenty four hours of the day, with the exception of the one hour above mentioned to prepare your lectures; and will have Four entire months in the year viz. from the 4th of July to the last monday in October, at your absolute disposal, either to devote to your favourite science, or to your friends & pleasure, and no one to question the manner in which it is spent. I regret to add that a prudent regard for your health may require that you should be absent from town six or eight weeks of this time; but no place can be more healthy than this, during the whole of the Collegiate term of eight months. The emolument, though at present small, is amply sufficient to support a family here, and will no doubt increase. There is a fixt salary of One Thousand Dollars paid on the 1st of January & July, and a fee of Twenty Dollars from each student in each class on matriculating. The funds of our College have been badly managed for several years past, so that the salary has not been regularly paid, but both the Faculty and Visitors of late have paid more attention to the fiscal concerns of the College, and we (the Visitors) hope, not only to free the funds from debt, but also to be able to increase the salaries of the Professors. As you will have two classes (a chemical & a Nat. Philosophical Class, to each of which you will lecture three times a week) you may expect to have in both classes, at least three fourths of the whole number of the students who may attend the College. Your class, and of course your emoluments will depend upon the prosperity of the College, which has been growing in public favor for two or three years past. I think you may reasonably expect to receive at least Fifteen hundred dollars, and this for only eight months service. It is confidently believed, that, but for the resignation of Mr Rogers and a false & unfounded rumor of the resignation of two other Professors, there would be not less than one hundred students during the approaching session, in which case, the tuition fees alone would amount to above Fifteen Hundred dollars and the entire receipts of the Professor to at least Two thousand five hundred dollars, and this I think you may expect to receive once in

---

in favor of free trade policies. His pro-slavery writing became immensely popular in the South. He was installed as President of the College in 1836 and accelerated the College's rejuvenation. He died in Paris during his honeymoon. *DAB.*

[5] Nathaniel Beverley Tucker (1784–1851), law professor, author, and advocate of Southern rights. He became Professor of Law at William and Mary in 1834, and thereafter his writings reflected many of Dew's opinions. *DAB.*

two or three years. If you should come, you will be received cordially by the Professors and citizens of the town, and you will have every right to expect indulgence & favor from the Visitors at whose solicitation you will have come. Let no fears with regard to the Natural Philosophical Chair deter you—neither Dr Jones,[6] nor Dr Hare[7] delivered lectures on Nat. Philosophy the first course, and indeed I do not doubt the Visitors will sanction any course you may pursue, or approve of any you may recommend.

In a pecuniary point of view, a Professorship in W^m^ & Mary can *bear no comparison* with one in the University*; but in every other respect a Chair in this College is preferable to one in that institution. There the Professors are under the supervision and control of the Visitors, and both Visitors & Professors are the servants of the Legislature and of the people. Here they are responsible only to the Visitors, who are themselves influenced by none but the Professors and a sense of duty to the interest of the College, which must ever be the interest of the Professors. There the Professors are occupied with their classes not less than two hours a day for ten months in the year, and are obliged to reside in a particular house or spot assigned to them. Here they live where they please and as they please, and during four months in the year may go where they please. With regard to pride of feeling & patriotic associations—If the University be the offspring of Mr Jefferson's old age, this is his alma mater. Here he laid the broad foundation of his fame, as did most of the Illustrious men of our Commonwealth. I beg you sir to permit me to say to the Visitors & Governors of the College, that if elected you will accept the appointment. I write without any special authority, but I feel authorised, from my knowledge of my associate Visitors & Governors of the College, to state, that any reasonable indulgence will be accorded to you, either as to the time of your coming, or as to the mode of your lecturing, though it would be desirable that you should be here on

* This is too strongly expressed. With 80 or 100 students here, which we may calculate on (under favourable circumstances) the difference would be very inconsiderable.

[6] Despite published William and Mary catalogs which list a Thomas L. Jones on the faculty, the records of the College indicate that Thomas P. Jones (for whom see above, Bache to Henry, July 13, 1834, footnote 1) served as Professor of Chemistry and Natural Philosophy, 1814–1817. Further confirmation of Thomas P. Jones's appointment at William and Mary is difficult. For Jones's early life see Bruce Sinclair, *Philadelphia's Philosopher Mechanics: A History of the Franklin Institute, 1824–1865* (Baltimore, 1974). Jones's predecessor in that chair was John Maclean (1771–1814, *DAB*), whose son and namesake was Henry's contemporary at Princeton.

[7] Robert Hare succeeded Jones in the Chair of Chemistry and Natural Philosophy at William and Mary in 1818 but stayed for less than one year. *The History of the College of William and Mary* (Baltimore, 1870), p. 68.

the 1st of November or the 1st of January at the latest. The Visitors will meet on the 7th of Octr by which time I hope to receive an answer.[8]

I am
Very respectfully
your Obt Sert
J Page

P.S. We have several candidates who come highly recommended, but although their testimonials are of a high character, and as satisfactory as testimony of that kind can be, yet I have more confidence in private & unsolicited communications and indeed if I am not misinformed you would suit us better than any other man in the United States. Please direct to John Page Rector of Wm & Mary College Williamsburg Virga JP.

[8] Henry's refusal has not been found. His friend John Millington (for whom see above, Millington and Green to Henry, December 31, 1832, footnote 1) filled the vacancy and served until 1849. Ibid.

EXCERPT,[1] MINUTES, TRUSTEES, COLLEGE OF NEW JERSEY

Trustees' Minutes, 3:302, 303–304, Princeton University Archives

[September 30, 1835][2]

The committee appointed to enquire and report whether any, and, if any, what increase of salary should be made to the Professors; *Recommended*, that three hundred dollars be added to the salaries of Professors McLean, Dod, Henry[3] and J. W. Alexander.

John S. Henry
John McDowell[4]
Samuel Miller[5]
Wm Shippen[6]
Wm W. Phillips . . .[7]

This report was *adopted*.

[1] We have omitted less relevant proceedings of the Trustees.

[2] This was the second day of Trustees' meetings at the time of commencement. The fortunes of the College had begun to recover from their previous slump (see above, Minutes of the Trustees, April 9, 1834, footnote 6). According to *Maclean*, 2:298, the alumni's fund raising drive:

added several thousand dollars to [Princeton's] funds, and had no little influence in increasing the number of students, and in stimulating afresh the ardor of the graduates and other friends of the College in its behalf. . . . [At this meeting in September], of the twenty-three Trustees, including the Governor of the State and the President of the College, twenty-one were present,—a

The committee appointed to take into consideration the propriety of erecting a new College Edefice; and also, of building a house for Professor Henry, *Reported*, that after maturely deliberating on the subject referred to them, they recommended the adoption of the following resolutions, viz,

Ist *Resolved*, that measures be taken with all convenient expedition for erecting an additional College Edefice, exactly opposite the North East College, of the same materials and dimensions with that building, and in all respects on the same model.[8]

II^{d} *Resolved*, that the necessary funds, for carrying on and completing said Edefice, be borrowed from the Bank in this place, or elsewhere, from time to time, as they may be wanted, on the draught of the Treasurer of the College, countersigned by the chairman of the committee entrusted with the execution of this resolution.

III^{d} *Resolved*, that an addition be made to the house of Professor Henry, by erecting a wing on the south west end of the house,[9] which shall contain four comfortable rooms, of such materials, and on such plan, as the building committee may judge proper, and that the funds necessary, for com-

---

fact indicative of the increasing interest which the Trustees were beginning to manifest in the welfare of the institution.

[3] For Joseph Henry this was the second raise since his arrival in Princeton. The timing was particularly important. Not only was Princeton in a better position to pay more to Henry and other senior professors, but Henry was being wooed by other institutions. Scattered documents, printed above, in the months prior to this meeting, depict how the generous offers made to Henry effectively improved his lot at Princeton.

[4] For whom see above, John S. Henry to Maclean, July 22, 1835, especially footnote 3.

[5] For whom see above, Henry's "List of Persons. . . ," [ca. August 21,] 1835, footnote 42.

[6] William Shippen (1791 or 1792–1867) was a Trustee of the College (1824–1865) and of the Theological Seminary (1846–1865). A member of the notable Philadelphia Shippen family which was active in Princeton affairs, he was a physician and lecturer on anatomy at the University of Pennsylvania, his alma mater (A.B. 1810, A.M. 1813, M.D. 1814). *Princeton Catalogue*, p. 20; *Roberts*, p. xvii.

[7] For whom see above, George Maclean to Henry, October 12, 1833, footnote 3.

[8] Built opposite East College (for a description of which see above, Henry to James Henry, June 25, 1833, especially footnote 9), West College, here proposed, added symmetry to the grounds behind Nassau Hall, which came to be called North College. Construction began just after the finishing touches had been made to East College. Completed in late 1836, West College survives today with some slight modifications. See *Maclean*, 2:299, 303; *Wertenbaker*, pp. 251–252; Henry Lyttleton Savage, *Nassau Hall, 1756–1956* (Princeton, 1956), pp. 44–45.

[9] Faced with the University of Virginia's most lucrative appointment, Henry requested of Princeton's Trustees not only a salary increase but also a new house. His request was informally agreed to (see above, Henry to James Henry, August 2, 1835), but here the compromising Trustees formally authorize only a commodious addition to the existing Henry house. The addition was to be movable, so that it could form part of a new house at a later date; this arrangement was a disappointment to Henry (see below, his letter to James Henry, October 19, 1835). Ironically, due to the severity of the winter and the lack of carpenters and masons, the addition was never built and within a year the Trustees resolved to build an entirely new house for the Henrys. Trustees' Minutes, *3*:314, Princeton University Archives.

pleting this addition be procured in the same manner, as prescribed in the second resolution.

The above report was *adopted*. Robert Lenox[10] on behalf of the Com^{ee}

Resolved that Dr Carnahan Mr Green[11] and Mr Cooley[12] be a committee to carry the above resolution into effect....

[10] Robert Lenox (1759–1839) emigrated from Scotland to New York City at the age of 20. According to F. B. Hough, *American Biographical Notes* (Albany, 1875), p. 254, Lenox was "one of the most enterprising and wealthy of the merchants of that city." A general merchant and real estate investor, he became President of the New York Chamber of Commerce, 1827–1839. He was a Trustee of the College, 1813 until his death, and was a Director and Trustee of the Theological Seminary between 1813 and 1830. His only son and principal heir was James Lenox (see above, Vethake to Henry, July 20, 1835, footnote 2). *Princeton Catalogue*, p. 19. *National Cyclopaedia*, *1*:498.

[11] James Sproat Green.

[12] Eli F. Cooley, for whom see above, Henry's "List of Persons . . . ," [ca. August 21,] 1835, footnote 41.

JOHN FARRAR[1] TO JOSIAH QUINCY[2]

Harvard College Papers (Second Series, Vol. VII), Harvard University Archives

Cambridge Oct. 7th 1835

Dear Sir,

The apparatus to illustrate the new branch of science, called by Mr Faraday *magneto-electricity*, is so matured & so exceedingly curious that it may be considered as constituting an important part of a Philosophical Apparatus. I have not yet met with any account of the instrument in question in the Instrument Maker's Catalogues, & am unable therefore to say what the expense will be. I should think it need not cost more than about $50, when provided with a Galvanometer which ought to accompany it.[3] We are also in want of a new Voltaic apparatus which may cost perhaps double the above sum, or even more. The apparatus for Voltaic Electricity which seems to me the best adapted to a course of lectures of the most con-

[1] John Farrar (1779–1853; *Henry Papers*, *1*:277n; *DSB*) was Hollis Professor of Mathematics and Natural Philosophy at Harvard.

[2] Josiah Quincy (1772–1864), politician, city reformer, and educator, was President of Harvard from 1829 to 1845. Addressed to Quincy, Farrar's letter, according to a note on the verso, was also referred to Boston's outstanding mathematical astronomer, Nathaniel Bowditch (*DAB*; *DSB*), who was then a Harvard Fellow—an influential member of the Harvard Corporation, the governing body of the college.

[3] Joseph Saxton's variation on Faraday's magnetoelectric induction apparatus was a current favorite for laboratory demonstration. In 1834 such a machine, without galvanometer, sold for about thirty dollars. See above, Jacob Green to Henry, February 13, 1834. *King*, p. 346.

venient & the most comprehensive, is that of Professor Henry, of Princeton, New Jersey, described in the Transactions of the American Philosophical Society. There is no mention made of the cost of the Instrument. I could make inquiry of Professor Henry on this point and ascertain also whether I could obtain a similar instrument from the maker of his.[4] Professor Henry claims to have anticipated Mr Faraday in some of his most brilliant discoveries.

Respectfully yours
J. Farrar

[4] Farrar had apparently seen an advance copy of Henry's "Contributions I: Battery." See his letter to Henry below of November 19, 1835. Although Henry enlisted the aid of instrument makers in the construction of his battery (see the letter from Millington of February 22, 1833, above), the design of the instrument was sufficiently unconventional to require that he do most of the construction himself, as he noted in his October 1, 1834, letter to Silliman, above. Henry's battery was not a standard item like his electromagnet, which by this time was being constructed and sold by James Chilton (see Henry to Silliman, August 29, 1835).

TO JAMES HENRY

Mary Henry Copy,[1] Memoir, Henry Papers, Smithsonian Archives

Monday morning Princeton Oct. 19. 1835

My dear James.... You have probably seen an account of our commencement, it was one of the most interesting ever held at this place. Mr. Gaston[2] of the South and Mr. Biddle ("Old Nick" of the Bank) gave each a very excellent oration. It is thirty-nine years since Mr. Gaston graduated and thirty-four since Mr. Biddle left the walls of the college. They are both quite young looking men. Biddle appears about forty-five, he must in reality be considerably over fifty.[3]

[1] Two copies exist, one written and the other typed. This text is based on the first which has somewhat more words and seems closer to the style of Henry's original letters of the day.

[2] William Gaston (1778–1844) was a North Carolinian who received the B.A. from Princeton in 1796 and the A.M. in 1799. An attorney, he served in the Senate and Assembly (Speaker 1808) of his state legislature and two terms (1813–1817) in the House of Representatives. From 1834 until his death, Gaston was a Judge of the Supreme Court of North Carolina. His speech, *An Address Delivered Before the American Whig and Cliosophic Societies of the College of New-Jersey, September 29, 1835*, was issued in two editions in 1835. *Princeton Catalogue*, p. 110. *Biographical Directory of the American Congress.*

He was a member of the American Philosophical Society and received the LL.D. from Pennsylvania, Harvard, New York University, Columbia, and Princeton, the last at this commencement.

[3] Biddle was forty-nine.

October 19, 1835

The Trustees at the last meeting of the Board, held at the time of the Commencement, raised my salary according to agreement and also ordered an addition to the house. They could not agree in reference to repairing the present or building another and so ordered a movable part, that may form the kitchen of a new house. I do not like this arrangement and will endeavour to have the plan altered at the next meeting of the board. . . .[4]

The comet has been a very important object of interest to Stephen; he has been making many observations on its place in the heavens in order to mark its path &c. You have probably learned by the newspaper accounts that this comet returns only at intervals of about seventy-five years and that its return the time before this was first predicted by Edmund Halley, an English astronomer, a contemporary of Newton. There are only two others whose return in the present state of science can be predicted viz Biela's, which has a period of return of 6¾ years and Encke's which returns every 3⅓ years. These are both very small and cannot be seen unless under very favorable circumstances with the naked eye. So that Halley's comet is the most interesting of all that have ever appeared . . .[5]

[4] Henry's views prevailed at the next meeting of the Trustees on April 12, 1836, with the passage of a resolution empowering a committee to "make such arrangement for the accomodation of Professor Henry with a house, as they shall think expedient." Trustees' Minutes, *3*:314, Princeton University Archives. See also the Trustees' Minutes of September 30, 1835, printed above, especially footnote 9.

[5] Our copy gives "3½" years as the period for Encke's Comet. This we believe was a transcribing error. In all probability Henry's source for this data was J. F. W. Herschel, *Astronomy* (London, 1833), a volume in the Cabinet Cyclopaedia edited by Dionysius Lardner. Henry's copy is heavily annotated throughout. Chapter 10, "Of Comets," has the predicted return of Halley's Comet (at the perihelion on November 7, 1835) marked in the margin by a line and three exclamation points. Henry's statement that only these three comets had predictable returns is not quite true. By that date Gauss's work on orbits provided a good method of calculating the paths of comets, in particular elliptical orbits of short period. These three were the ones whose predictions were verified by observations by this date. Encke's and Biela's Comets had short periods, making verification simple. A. Pannekoek, *A History of Astronomy* (New York, 1961), pp. 351–352, 357–359.

Alexander did not publish any results of his observations at this period. Later in his career, Alexander wrote a number of articles on comets.

October 22, 1835

TO BENJAMIN SILLIMAN, SR.

Daniel C. Gilman Collection, Library, Johns Hopkins University

Princeton Oct 22nd 1835

My Dear Sir

My Friend Mr Nyce[1] leaves the Theological seminary of this place and goes to New Haven on account principally of the Lectures in your Institution.

Permit me to introduce him to your notice as an intelligent young gentleman who takes much interest in the study of Physical Science[2] and who will assiduously avail himself of the advantages your extended courses furnish for improvement in this department of knowledge.

Mr Nyce is a graduate of a college in Pennsylvania, was occupied about two years in teaching in the Deaf and Dumb Asylum of Philadelphia[3] and has spent the last two years in the study of Theology at Princeton.

With the highest Respect
Sincerely
Yours
Joseph Henry

S.P. Professor Torrey & myself purpose visiting your city; probably next week. J.H.

[1] Benjamin Markley Nyce (1809–1866), born in Pennsylvania, graduated from Dickinson College in 1829, attended Princeton Theological Seminary, 1834–1835, and then Yale Divinity School. Ordained in 1839, Nyce served in various clerical and teaching capacities in numerous cities, dying in Cleveland, Ohio. He was also described as an inventor although no patents are attributed to him. *Roberts*, p. 84.

[2] In a May 10, 1836, entry on lightning rods in his laboratory notebook, Henry took note of an observation by Nyce that lightning had been seen to travel along a railroad track for at least a mile.

[3] The Pennsylvania Institution for the Deaf and Dumb, incorporated in 1821. *Picture of Philadelphia, or, A Brief Account of the Various Institutions and Public Objects in this Metropolis* . . . (Philadelphia, 1835), pp. 62–63.

October 24, 1835

TO HARRIET HENRY

Family Correspondence, Henry Papers, Smithsonian Archives

Saturday Evening Oct 24th 1835
Dr Torrey's study ½ past 9P

My Dear Hanky

We[1] arrived safely in this city at about three o'clock. We were detained on account of the wind which was against us. Our company to Height's Town was very plesant. It consisted of Dr Miller,[2] Mr Nyce,[3] and a gentleman from Phila a lawer very intelligent and communicative. On board the steam boat I met with an old school mate who formerly lived on the corner below Mother's old house in Pearl street. His name is Malary.[4] He has become a man of considerable welth and consequence in the city of Troy. Was much pleased to see me said he often heard my name mentioned with respect &c and that it gave him much pleasure to call me [h]is acquaintance, &c &c. The time between Amboy & New York was principally spent in reviving old impressions &c &c. When we arrived in the city we had our trunk carried to Chiltons and then left while we made an excursion to a refectory where two plates of rost beef were ordered and pretty nearly dispatched in a reasonable time. Also two small peach pies as an accompanyment. We were tolerably sharp set as our dining took place about 4 oclock.

After the operation of eating (for which we paid 2/- apiece[5]) we called on Mr Blunt[6] who made many inquiries relative to the commet and its two tails. After this we called at a hat store for the purpose of purchasing a "*Golgotha*"[7] for Stephen's use. After some picking and choosing the gentleman was at length fitted with an article which I with a voice and tone of one who knows what's what in such matters pronounced very good.

[1] From the context of the letter, the group traveling to New York City consisted of Joseph Henry and Stephen Alexander.

[2] Samuel Miller, for whom see above, Henry's "List of Persons . . . ," [ca. August 21,] 1835, footnote 42.

[3] For whom see the foregoing document.

[4] Not identified. There were several men by the name Mallary or Mallory who were notable citizens of Troy, but none whose "welth and consequence" has rated biographical treatment in Rensselaer County and Troy histories. A Mallory and a Mallary resided at Pearl Street in Albany, both merchants. Albany City Directories, 1813–1819. None attended the Albany Academy. This "Malary" may have attended school with Henry before his apprenticeship.

[5] Two shillings.

[6] Either Edmund March Blunt (1770–1862) or his son George William Blunt (1802–1878). *DAB*. Both hydrographers, they operated a printing house in New York City which specialized in navigational publications. The younger Blunt began to work for the Coast Survey in 1833, through which position he had dealings with Henry in later years. Harold L. Burstyn, *At the Sign of the Quadrant* (Mystic, Connecticut, 1957).

[7] A hat. This slang expression became obsolete in the early twentieth century. Eric Partridge, *A Dictionary of Slang and Unconventional English*, 6th ed. (New York, 1967), p. 340.

We next made our *way* to Broad*way* (no pun) and after many stops at book stors, print shop wind[ow]s &c &c we arrived at Mr Workmasters[8] (I may not have given the gentlemans name correctly in the way of orthography but you know whom I intend to designate). The old gentleman appeared much pleased to see us and quite as much to receive his money for the telescope.[9] He said that he was very glad to see us in New-York and would always be happy to see us at his store when we came to the city &c &c. We next returned to Chiltons—not however before stopping in at a book store—where we met an old acquaintance of Stephen's a Mr Richards[10] a former student of Chittenango.

From Chiltons we started for Dr Torreys having sent our trunk by a cartman. We arrived at the Dr about 7 o'clock while the family (viz Dr & Mrs T., Dr Gray,[11] Miss Shaw[12] and a Lady whoes name I have forgotten) were at tea. We were received very kindly and many inquiries made about Mrs H and the little ones, Aunt &c. After tea Dr T. informed me that a Gentleman was waiting for me in the study. I was not at a loss to conjecture who this was since we had met with Mr Bullions on our first arrival in the city and made an appointement to meet with him at Dr Torrey's in the evening.

He says that Mrs B is not very smart but is in better health than she was. Margaret is quite unwell. The Dr thinks her disorder is the change of constitution induced by the age of puberty. He thinks that when the change has become complete she will again be restored to health. Mr B also informed me that Mr Newland had written to Princeton agreeing to the proposition relative to John.[13] His letter was probably in the office this morning when we left. Mother is now in Albany expecting [the] arrival of Stephen. Orlandow Meads has just commenced house keeping and is much annoyed with procuring the small articles of a house establishment. I ac-

[8] Michael Werckmeister, for whom see above, Henry to James Henry, October 27, 1834, especially footnote 10.

[9] The telescope is discussed above in Henry to Stephen Alexander, November 29, 1834, especially footnote 4.

[10] Not identified. Alexander taught at the Yates Polytechny in Chittenango, New York, before 1831. See *Henry Papers, 1*:115–117, 257, 315.

[11] Asa Gray.

[12] Most likely a relative of Mrs. Eliza Robertson (Shaw) Torrey's. See above, Henry to Harriet Henry, [March] 24, [1834], footnote 2.

[13] John Newland (1820–1880) was the son of Luke F. Newland (see above, Henry to James Henry, May 17, 1833, footnote 3). John Newland was born in Scotland. Attending the Albany Academy during Joseph Henry's teaching years there, Newland graduated in 1835. He won awards for his scholarship in mathematics, geography, chemistry, and optics, as well as French and penmanship. He was given advanced standing at Princeton, graduating in 1837. Returning to Albany, he became an attorney and maintained his interest in learning. He was active in the Albany Institute, serving as Recording Secretary of the Third Department (of History and General Literature). He joined the American Association for the Advancement of Science in 1853. *Princeton Catalogue*, p. 152. Hun, "Albany Academy."

companied Mr Bullions a part of the way to his lodgings. He is to preach tomorrow in one of the Scotch churches.

Dr Torrey will accompany us to New Haven on Monday; we start at 7 o'clock A.M. I have now my Dear Wife given you an account of the events of the day. They are but the merest trifles immaginable but I know they will be prise by you since they relate to two persons in whom you are much interested. (Dr interrupts me by saying it is time to go to bed).[14]

[14] The letter is unsigned. Its postmark, "New York, October 27," suggests that Henry handed the letter to someone to mail. By the 27th Henry was in New Haven.

TO HARRIET HENRY

Family Correspondence, Henry Papers, Smithsonian Archives

Wednesday Oct 28th 1835

My Dear H.

We are now on our way to N.Y. from New Haven on board a little steamboat in the sound. The boat is a slow one and we have little prospect of getting to N.Y. before 3 o'clock although we started at 7 this morning.

Our visit to New Haven was a very plesant one and has been repetedly declared so by each member of the party. Dr Torrey according to agreement accompanied us. We started at 7 on Monday morning and arrived at about one o'clock. We dined and then made our way to the college and first stoped at the door of the Laboratory, were very politely received by a young Gentleman who happened to be present. He gave a very particular account of all the articles of apparatus and among other curiosities pointed out the wonderful magnet of Prof Henry. He commenced some explanations &c which would have placed me in rather a disagreeable position. I therefore hastily withdrew into another room as if attracted by some new object.[1] This young gentleman we afterwards learned is Mr Hubbard[2] the

[1] Whether out of modesty or discomfort at an inaccurate explanation we cannot say.

[2] Oliver Payson Hubbard (1809–1900), B.A. Yale, 1828, M.D. South Carolina Medical College, 1837, was Benjamin Silliman's chemical assistant from 1831 to 1836. He married Silliman's daughter Faith in 1837. In 1836 Hubbard became Professor of Chemistry, Mineralogy, and Geology at Dartmouth. In 1866 he became a lecturer at the College and, from 1871 to 1883, Professor of Chemistry and Pharmacy. Hubbard was an Overseer of the Thayer School of Engineering, and a member of various natural history societies as well as the American Association for the Advancement of Science. His publications were in geology, mineralogy, and natural history. *Obituary Record of Graduates of Yale University, Deceased from June, 1890, to June, 1900* (New Haven, 1900), pp. 659–660. Stanley M. Guralnick, "Science and the American College, 1828–1860" (Ph.D. dissertation, University of Pennsylvania, 1969), pp. 277–278.

reputed suitor of Miss Faith. We left our card for Prof Silliman & then called at Prof Olmsteds room. The Prof. did not recognise me with my additional load of *adipose matter* accumulated since I was last at New Haven and a sad evidence of the effects of Matrimony on a sensitive man. Grief puffs one up sadly according to the *Fat* Knight.[3]

Many inquiries were made by the Prof for Mrs Henry and the little Henry's. He was very attentive to Mr Alexander and commenced a discussion on the nature and appearance of the comet which continued until Prof Silliman made his appearance. He had been expecting our arrival and had made arrangements to be disengaged from college duties on the days of our stay. He arranged our occupation for the evening by requesting that we would attend a party at Prof. Kinsleys.[4] This we found a very plesant assembly consisting principally of the Professors & Tutors of College, and the "*ladies of the Institution.*" Mrs Silliman looked very well, made many inquiries about Mrs Henry. Miss Faith was also there, looked very pretty, said she was not in good health however. I was introduced among many other persons to Mrs Olmsted. She is rather a good looking Lady, not very young, has 3 children.

Next morning after the party we repaired to the Laboratory immediatly after breakfast, there found Prof. Silliman & his assistant Mr Hubbard waiting for us. Prof Olmsted soon after arrived according to agreement. After some very plesant conversation with Prof Olmsted & the other gentlemen we all went to a public square about ¼ of a mile from the College to make our magnetic observations & in these we were engaged until near dinner time. In the afternoon we visited the Philosoph[ical] apparatus, the Trumbull Galery of pictures[5] (which has been added since we were to-

[3] According to Sir John Falstaff: "A plague of sighing and grief! It blows a man up like a bladder." *Henry IV*, part 1, act 2, sc. 4, lines 365–366.

[4] James Luce Kingsley (1778–1852) was the first Professor of Languages at Yale (1805–1851). Noted as a Latin scholar, he also taught Greek and Hebrew. Kingsley wrote extensively on Connecticut and New England history, but displayed a breadth of interest typical of many learned men of the period. He was interested in science and mathematics, especially in astronomical calculations. *DAB*. In 1808, he and Benjamin Silliman wrote "Account of a Remarkable Fall of Meteoric Stones in Connecticut," *The Philadelphia Medical and Physical Journal*, *3*:39–57, an account and chemical examination of the results of a spectacular meteor shower over Weston, Connecticut, in 1807. The paper attracted wide scientific interest in the United States, and was known for having elicited a celebrated comment from Thomas Jefferson, who questioned the alleged extra-terrestrial origin of the phenomena: "it is easier to believe that two Yankee professors could lie than to admit that stones could fall from heaven." John F. Fulton and Elizabeth H. Thomson, *Benjamin Silliman, 1779–1864: Pathfinder in American Science* (New York, 1947), pp. 76–78. Nathaniel Bowditch reacted differently than Jefferson in an 1811 article in *Nicholson's Journal.*

[5] The Trumbull Art Gallery, later the Yale University Art Gallery, opened in October 1832. Silliman, the first curator of the gallery, was instrumental in its founding. Silliman was a long-time friend of the Revolutionary portraitist Colonel John Trumbull (1756–1843,

gether in New Haven). Also the refectory and the kitchen. Every thing about the eating establishment is neat clean and well arranged. I wished for Mr Colow[6] that he might take a lesson of good order from the Yankey cooks. In the early part of the evening we went according to promis to Prof Silliman's to take tea; here we met several of the college officers and other gentlemen invited on our account. We however concluded not to spend the whole evening with Mrs Silliman but, that we might make the most of our time, we adjourned with Professor S. to the house of President Day to attend a meeting of the Connecticut Academy of Sciences[7] which held one of its stated meetings that evening. This meeting was somewhat interesting. Several discussions were held on the subjects of mineralogy, Geology, magnetism, the comet &c. In these the Princeton Gentlemen took a part. Before going to the meeting I should have stated that we were taken to the observatory and shown the great telescope[8] of the College.

We promised Mrs Silliman to return to her house after the adjournment of the meeting but this happened at so late an hour that we concluded it would not be propper although the Professor urged us to do so. We went to our lodging, paid our passage for the mornings start, unanimously declared that we had been very politely treated and had made a very plesant visit. Stephen in particular was unusually warm &c.[9] in expressing his gratifica-

---

DAB), the uncle of Silliman's wife. In 1830, Silliman sought to obtain Trumbull's art collection for Yale. It was agreed that the artist, lacking means of support in his later years, would donate his art collection, in return for a thousand-dollar lifetime annuity. Admission fees to the collection, consisting mainly of Trumbull's own work, were to provide scholarships for poor students. After securing funds for the annuity, Silliman obtained money from the State Legislature for a building to house Trumbull's paintings. The gallery, one of the first to be attached to an American college, opened the way for the founding of the Yale School of the Fine Arts (1866), another pioneering addition to the college curriculum in America. Fulton and Thomson, *Benjamin Silliman*, pp. 164–172.

[6] Henry Clow, one of Princeton's stewards (see above, Henry to Torrey, April 2, 1835, footnote 4).

[7] The Connecticut Academy of Arts and Sciences (see *Henry Papers, 1*:209n) held six meetings a year, on the fourth Tuesday of every other month, beginning in February. Until 1862 the meetings were held at the private residences of the members. Yale President Jeremiah Day (1773–1867, *DAB*), known for his texts on algebra, geometry, trigonometry, and applied mathematics, was President of the Academy from 1817 to 1836, when he was succeeded by Silliman. The Academy published no transactions at this time; the usual vehicle for their scientific publications was *Silliman's Journal*. Elias Loomis, "Connecticut Academy of Arts and Sciences," in William Kingsley, ed., *Yale College: A Sketch of its History*, 2 vols. (New York, 1879), *1*:329–337.

[8] The Yale telescope, a benefaction in 1828 of Sheldon Clark, was a five-inch Dolland refractor, the most powerful telescope in America in that period. Just two months previously, Olmsted made a public demonstration of the power of the instrument in observations of Halley's comet. Under Olmsted, the Yale observatory, housed in the Athenaeum, became the best in America and nurtured a generation of astronomers. Though declining in importance after the 1830s, the observatory helped launch America's intense interest in astronomy in the ensuing decades. David F. Musto, "Yale Astronomy in the Nineteenth Century," *Ventures Magazine*, 1968, *8*:7–18.

[9] The remainder of the letter was written in the margins.

tion. This morning just as we were about to start and at ½ past six o'clock Prof Silliman called at the Hotel to give us a parting visit. He promised to visit Princeton about New Years. Professor Silliman has been engaged to lecture to the Library association in N.Y. and for a short course is to be paid 100 dollars a lecture pretty good pay.[10] It appears a long time since we left home. We intend going up the N[orth][11] river in the evening boat and will probably reach West Point about 10 o'clock. We will stop at the Point until the next evening Boat, making our observations in the mean time and then proceed to Albany without stopping at Athens.

I propose stopping in Albany long enough to vibrate the needles[12] and then leave for N.Y. with your Mother. Stephen will stop at Athens to transact the business[13] so that you may expect us the beginning of next week *ie* Mother & myself. Our new arrangements about albany &c were made last evening at New Haven. I hope you will think them the best.[14]

[10] The Mercantile Library Association, a typical self-improvement society, was founded in 1820 for the intellectual betterment of the "merchants' clerks" in New York City. The prime goal was the establishment of a library and reading room. The Association, after feeble beginnings, began a vigorous expansion in 1826. By the end of 1835, they owned a new building, Clinton Hall, and a library of over 11,000 volumes. The public lecture program began as an ad hoc venture but proved increasingly successful. The lectureships were first supported by admission fees (one dollar for twenty-four lectures, delivered by several speakers), but later enjoyed the security of a permanent lecture fund. The success of the activity induced the Directors of the Association to upgrade the program. They called for a "liberal remuneration" in order to attract the most talented speakers available. In early 1839, Joseph Henry lectured before the Association, an activity to be documented in later volumes. Benson J. Lossing, *History of New York City* (New York, 1884), pp. 167–168. *Annual Reports of the Board of Directors of the Mercantile Library Association of the City of New York, From 1821 to 1838* (New York, Reprinted for the Association, 1868), Reports of 1821, 1826, 1831, 1834, 1836.

[11] i.e., the Hudson.

[12] Henry recorded the data from the observations in Albany, West Point, and New Haven in two of his pocket notebooks ([30031] and [30032], in the Henry Papers, Smithsonian Archives). The data appear under the dates October 27, 29, and 31, 1835.

[13] i.e., matters bearing upon the family estate.

[14] Above the address Henry wrote "To be read first," that is, before the letter immediately following.

TO HARRIET HENRY

Family Correspondence, Henry Papers, Smithsonian Archives

New York Wednesday
Evening [October 28, 1835][1] at Dr Torreys

My Dear Wife

The enclosed letter was written on board the steam boat with the intention of being droped into the Post office on our way to the North river boat but we were disappointed in getting off this evening on account of our trunk's not arriving at the warf in time for the starting of the boat. We had left it at Dr Torreys and before the boy could get it dow[n] the last bell had rung. After repairing to the eating establishment which we have so often patronized we made our way to Dr T's where I was very happy to find a letter[2] from My Dear Dear little wife and still more pleased to learn that you are all well. I regret to learn that Dr Howell is not yet well and that he has been so very ill.[3] I am glad that you have called in Dr Maclean[4] in reference to Mitty's[5] face. I hope the dear little one will have intirely recovered before the beginning of next week. I know that you must be very lonely and I am "home sick" with the thoughts of the litle and very dear family I have left behind. You will see by the other letter that I have concluded to go with Stephen to albany and return immediatly with your mother leaving Stephen at Athens to transact the business. I go to albany to vibrate the Scotch needle.

We will probably leave this [city] tomorrow morning in the 7 o'clock boat, reach West Point about 12, make our observations in the afternoon and then purpose taking the evening boat so as to reach Albany on Friday morning. I then intend to make the observations this A.M. and to leave as soon as your mother is ready to start. Two gentlemen have just called who are going to Princeton tomorrow. One of them has promised to hand this to you the same evening and is now waiting while I make the scrall.[6]

[1] This letter was composed the same day as the previous document. Henry had written above "My Dear Wife" the phrase "Read the other letter first." October 28, 1835, was a Wednesday. The texts clearly relate to the same trip.

[2] Not found.

[3] Samuel Ladd Howell died November 1, 1835. His son William Meade Howell had died October 4, 1835. James W. Alexander mentioned that Howell's wife, two of his daughters, and another son survived the disease, which Alexander identified as typhus. *Hageman, 1*:262.

[4] The Princeton physician George Maclean (see footnote 1 of the letter of October 9, 1833, printed above).

[5] Henry's nickname for his daughter Mary.

[6] The address side of the letter indicates that "Mr. Scudder" took the letter to Harriet. We do not know which of the many persons by that name associated with the town and college of Princeton did this favor.

I am very much fatigued with the long walkes we have taken to the steam boat, the Refectory &c.

I believe I gave you all the incidents of our tour to New Haven. I might have mentioned that Miss Faith made some inquiries about Mr Winkoop.[7] She wished to know if he was wealthy talented &c &c. She did not speak very highly of the intellect of the Lady[8] but was not severe or incharitable in her remarkes.

I did not meet with Dr Tully;[9] he was out of the city. I received a card from our old acquaintance Mr. Baldwin[10] the Albany gentleman who was so polite to us when we were together at N.H. I passed the house where *we* put up, the stage house, you reccollect it. The sight brought some peculiar feelings into action. I could not but think to myself a visit now with my wife would be better enjoyed than the one I formerly had with my bride young, fresh, & novel as she was then to me. I did not then think that she loved me very much nor were my own feelings to her of precisely the same kind that they now are.[11] But I am detaining the gentlemen too long & must close with assuring you that nothing since my departure from home has given me more pleasure than the receipt of your letter. You have been a dear good wife and I will give you many many kisses for it when I return. Kiss the children for me. Love to Aunt. Stephen is with Mrs Torrey & some other Ladies in the Parlor. I am writing in the study. From your

own
Hubby

[7] Stephen Rose Wynkoop (1806–1876) graduated from Union College in 1829, taught at the Albany Female Academy, and was a missionary agent to Africa in 1830–1831. He attended the Princeton Theological Seminary from 1834 to 1837, and renewed his acquaintance with the Henry family at that time. After two minor ecclesiastical posts, Wynkoop held the pastorship of the First Presbyterian Church in Wilmington, Delaware from 1839 until 1858 when ill health forced him into early retirement. *Roberts*, p. 92; Joseph Henry to James Henry, January 22, 1836, Family Correspondence, Henry Papers, Smithsonian Archives.

[8] Not identified.

[9] William Tully was Professor of Materia Medica and Therapeutics at Yale (*Henry Papers, 1*:279).

[10] Simeon Baldwin (*Henry Papers, 1*:276).

[11] Henry is reminiscing here with Harriet about their honeymoon trip to New Haven and New York in May 1830 (*Henry Papers, 1*:274–282).

FROM BENJAMIN SILLIMAN, SR.

Henry Papers, Smithsonian Archives

New Haven Octob[r] 31, 1835

My Dear Sir

I was much impressed by your statement relative to the induced magnetism by the coil[1] & feel very desirous to exhibit the fact in my lectures. I should be very sorry to give you any extra trouble but wishing your reputation to be safe in my hands I would enquire whether you will construct for me or cause to be constructed under your direction a powerful apparatus for that purpose the expense of which I shall most cheerfully pay with many thanks. If you have not given the directions with sufficient precision to Chilton perhaps you will do it.[2] I should like to shew the fact in New York in January & in Boston in March and if there is any thing in the way of directions as to making the experiments, more than is contained in your printed memoir & in your letters you would greatly oblige me by making a memorandum of the facts & forwarding them to me. An early reply will oblige me much.[3]

I reflect with much pleasure on your late visit & hope you found your family well on your return. Our kind regards to M[rs] Henry & Prof[r] Alexander.

very truly your friend
B Silliman

[1] A reference, apparently, to something said by Joseph Henry on his October 26–27 visit at New Haven.

[2] Silliman's reluctance to deal directly with Chilton may reflect nothing more than a continuing uneasiness with this new area of electricity and magnetism.

[3] We know Henry did not reply to this letter until March 2, 1836, because of illness. On January 4, 1836, Silliman again renewed his request for assistance. Both letters will appear in volume three of the *Henry Papers*.

FROM JOHN FARRAR

Henry Papers, Smithsonian Archives

Cambridge Nov. 19th 1835

Dear Sir,

I am much obliged to you for the copy you were so kind as to send me of your communications to the Philosophical Society.[1] I have taken great

[1] Farrar is included as a recipient of Henry's "Contributions I" and "Contributions II" on the list printed above, [ca. August 21,] 1835.

interest in the new & striking experiments you have given to the scientific world. I had already made myself acquainted with the contents of the papers now received,[2] & had proposed to obtain a voltaic apparatus upon your plan, & the principal object of my now writing to you is to learn from you the expense of such an apparatus & also whether I could obtain one from the person who made yours.[3] If you will have the goodness to inform me upon these particulars[4] you will greatly oblige, dear Sir,

Yours very respect[y]
J. Farrar

[2] The section of the APS *Transactions* containing Henry's communications was not yet in print. Farrar may have seen someone else's presentation copy before his arrived. John White Webster of Harvard, who was also on Henry's list, is a likely possibility.

[3] See above, Farrar to Josiah Quincy, October 7, 1835, for Farrar's proposal to acquire the apparatus for Harvard.

[4] We do not have Henry's response to Farrar, nor do we know of any other correspondence between the two men. There is no evidence that Harvard acquired Henry's apparatus. Farrar retired from Harvard shortly after this letter, in 1836.

FROM LEWIS W. WASHINGTON[1]

Henry Papers, Smithsonian Archives[2]

Baltimore Nov 22nd 1835

Mr Henry
D[r] Sir,

I recollect on a former occasion in conversation with you, relative to a machine invented by you for the purpose of separating iron dust from the earthy matter, you stated (if I mistake not) that it had succeeded, and the person had applied in Washington for a patent right for the same, which he was not entitled to.[3] In conversation to day with some of my friends in

[1] A former student of Joseph Henry's, Washington (1812–1871) entered Princeton as a sophomore in 1831, graduated in 1833, and received his A.M. in 1837. Washington, the great-grandson of George Washington's half-brother Augustine, was born in Georgetown, D.C., lived for some time in Baltimore, and moved to Jefferson County, West Virginia, where he maintained *Beall Air*, a family estate. Washington was a hostage in John Brown's raid on Harper's Ferry. *Princeton Catalogue*, p. 146. *Princeton Annual Catalogues*, 1831–1833. Albert Welles, *The Pedigree and History of the Washington Family* (New York, 1879), pp. 218–219. Millard K. Bushong, *Historic Jefferson County* (Boyce, Virginia, 1972), pp. 39, 175, 180, 184–185. We know of no further contact between Henry and Washington.

[2] Mary Henry notations at the top of the original document indicate her use of this item.

[3] We presume this is a reference to two patents for "magnetic cylinders," originally obtained in 1814 by Samuel Browning and revived in 1831 by a special act of Congress.

this city (the Messrs Ellicott[4]) who are largely engaged in the manufacture of Iron they stated that they had applied for this same apparatus and the sum of $20,000 was required for it. I mentioned, as well as my memory served me from our conversation, that you would have the *exclusive* or *principal* right to the invention.[5] They therefore requested me to address you on the subject and request the necessary information and by this compliance through a letter[6] addressed to me in George Town, DC, will place me under many obligations.

I remain Dr Sir Respfy yr quondam pupil
Lewis. W. Washington

The possible holder of the revived patent was James Creighton Odiorne of Boston. See *Henry Papers, 1*:340–341, for an extended discussion of these patents and Henry's involvement with iron ore separation. The patented separators apparently employed permanent magnets, not the electromagnets that interested Henry. According to Henry's view of the patent law, the Browning patent was invalid because its underlying principle, the action of magnets on iron, was an old one and public knowledge. We know that Henry's friend and colleague Lewis C. Beck, in an Albany lecture, expressed similar views, specifically about the Browning patent. See ibid., pp. 368n, 370n.

[4] The Ellicotts were a prominent Maryland Quaker family involved in manufacturing and iron making. We cannot specify which of the Ellicotts were friends of Lewis Washington. Several Ellicotts had iron furnaces in Maryland, some near Baltimore, in the nineteenth century. One possibility was the furnace at Elkridge in Howard County, established in 1826 by Andrew Ellicott, Jr., and brothers. Still operating in 1835, the establishment was rebuilt in 1854. Another was E. T. Ellicott and Co. who erected the Patapsco Furnaces in Baltimore in 1835. For family background and their extensive role in the Maryland iron industry, see *DAB*; Joseph J. Singewald, Jr., *Report on the Iron Ores of Maryland with an Account of the Iron Industry* (Baltimore, 1911), pp. 159–160, 168, 173, 270; J. P. Lesley, *The Iron Manufacturer's Guide to the Furnaces, Forges, and Rolling Mills of the United States . . .* (New York, 1859), pp. 48, 49, 85; Martha E. Tyson, *A Brief Account of the Settlement of Ellicott's Mills* (Baltimore, 1865), pp. 40–46.

[5] The Ellicotts obviously hoped to circumvent the $20,000 fee for the separating machine; however, Henry never obtained a patent of any kind. What Henry may have told Washington was that the patent rights for electromagnetic ore separation were deservedly, if not legally, his. We know that in the 1830s there were several magnetic or electromagnetic ore separators in use in the Adirondack mining region. At least one, and possibly another, was constructed using one of Henry's powerful electromagnets. See *Henry Papers, 1*:340–341, 346, 365. For Henry, the Browning patent, involving ordinary permanent magnets, was void and, in any case, different from his own pioneering applications of electromagnetism to ore separation. There is evidence that, after the Browning patent was revived in 1831, the Adirondack iron men had planned to join together to fight any infringement suit. At least in that mining region, the owner of the revived patent—perhaps Odiorne—never pressed his claims. Ibid., p. 367n. Evidently, he hoped for greater success in pressing his monopoly rights in Maryland. The extravagant fee being demanded of the Ellicotts must have reinforced Henry's already considerable frustration with the patent law.

[6] Not found.

November 23, 1835

TO ALEXANDER DALLAS BACHE

Bache Papers, Smithsonian Archives

Princeton Monday morning
Nov 23[d] 1835

My Dear Bache

The sky has been cloudy every night at 11 o'clock at this place since my return from Philadelphia so that no reccord of meteors has been made. We will watch the first clear night this week. On Tuesday night we had a fine display of the aurora. I noted with some precision the position of an arch which remained stationary for nearly an hour.[1] Also made observations on the intensity of magnetism during the appearance of the aurora and corresponding ones the next morning.[2]

In haste
Yours sincerely
Jos. Henry

I will send the account of the shooting stars seen on the night of the 13th as soon as my duties will permit.[3]

[1] Henry recorded this datum in order to calculate the height of the aurora above the surface of the earth. See footnote 3 of Henry's notebook entry for September 2, 1834, above.

[2] Henry used one of the needles loaned by James David Forbes and recorded observations at about 7:30 on the evening of November 17 and again at about eleven on the morning of November 18. The data appear in a pocket notebook in the Henry Papers, Smithsonian Archives ([30032], pp. [26–33]). Henry's early interest in the connection between auroras and magnetism has been documented in volume one of *The Papers of Joseph Henry*. Bache also studied the problem ("Note of the Effect upon the Magnetic Needle, of the Aurora Borealis, Visible at Philadelphia, on the 17th of May, 1833," Franklin Institute *Journal*, July 1833, *12*:5–9, and "Observations on the Disturbance in the Direction of the Horizontal Needle, During the Occurrence of the Aurora of July 10th, 1833," Franklin Institute *Journal*, January 1834, *13*:1–9). Bache would naturally be interested in Henry's continued observations on the topic.

[3] Bache had entered into a controversy with Denison Olmsted about the relation between the meteor shower of November 1833 and that of November 1834. Olmsted asserted that the 1834 phenomenon was another manifestation of the one a year earlier; he had predicted its reoccurrence as a test of his theory that the shower resulted from extra-terrestrial dust particles. Bache contended that the size of the shower in 1834 was not in excess of the numbers of meteors usually counted on fall evenings. Bache, "Replies to a Circular in Relation to the Occurrence of an Unusual Meteoric Display on the 13th of November, 1834, Addressed by the Secretary of War to the Military Posts of the United States, with Other Facts Relating to the Same Question," and "Meteoric Observations Made on and About the 13th of November, 1834," Franklin Institute *Journal*, September and December 1835, *16*:149–153 and 369–372. Olmsted, "Facts Respecting the Meteoric Phenomena of November 13th, 1834," Franklin Institute *Journal*, December 1835, *16*:367–369. Olmsted, "Zodiacal Light," *Silliman's Journal*, 1835, 27:416–419. Bache, "Observations upon the Facts Recently Presented by Professor Olmsted, in Relation to Meteors Seen on the 13th of November, 1834," Franklin Institute *Journal*, January 1836, *17*:33–36.

The disputants both called upon their friends in the scientific community to report details of the 1834 shower. Henry had taken notes on the shower of 1833 (see his notebook entry for November 13–14, 1833, printed above) but had apparently been too absorbed in November 1834 with other business to record the shower of that year. However, in November 1835, Henry kept a special watch to count the meteors of that month. The data are reported in the next document.

TO ALEXANDER BACHE

Bache Papers,[1] *Smithsonian Archives*

Princeton Nov 25th 1835

Dear Sir,

Agreeably to your request that a look-out might be kept at this place about the 13th of Nov. for the appearance of shooting stars, in connection with Messrs Alexander and Miller[2] of Princeton College I instituted a watch on the night of the 13th but by reference since made to the accounts of the meteors of 1833 I find that the 14th was the night on which the display was expected to take place. I was led into the mistake by a hasty perusal of your letter.[3]

[1] The document is a composite of two letters. The first letter, dated November 25, 1835, in Henry's hand, was originally composed by Henry on that date and transcribed in the neater hand of Harriet Henry at a later time. Harriet presumably finished transcribing more than a month later, when Joseph Henry dated the letter, made minor editorial corrections, canceled one sentence, and appended the second letter, his personal note dated "30 minutes before 1836." The first part of this document is Henry's effort to supply Bache with observations of the November shooting stars.

[2] John Miller (1819–1895, *DAB*), was in his senior year at Princeton (B.A., 1836). Miller served as Henry's assistant during that year in preparation for his becoming a professor of natural philosophy. He was shaken from that determination by a religious revival (and undoubtedly some encouragement from his father, the Reverend Samuel Miller, for whom see above, Henry's List of Persons, [ca. August 21,] 1835, footnote 42), and he entered the Princeton Theological Seminary in 1838. Later he held pastorships in Philadelphia and Virginia, served as a chaplain in the Confederate Army, and returned to Princeton in 1871. He split from the Presbyterian Church in 1877 on doctrinal issues and in 1880 organized an independent congregation in Princeton, for which he was pastor until his death. John Miller will appear in subsequent volumes of *The Papers of Joseph Henry*, both as Henry's student and assistant and later as a correspondent.

[3] Bache's letter has not been found. Nor have we found any "accounts of the meteors of 1833" which suggest that the night of November 14th was the night to make observations. Further, Bache never published any account of the 1835 meteors, which would have stated the night for which observations were compiled. In the absence of better evidence, we conjecture that Harriet or Joseph Henry erred in writing the "14th was the night . . ." and that they should have said "12th was the night on which the display was expected to take place." As Henry states in his opening sentence, Bache requested observations from "about the 13th of Nov." In Henry's "hasty perusal" of Bache's request, his mistaken conclusion to watch on the night of the 13th is understandable. Apparently Henry should have been instructed to watch on the night of the 12th and the morning of the 13th; that is when Denison Olmsted made his observations in November 1835 ("Zodiacal Light," *Silliman's Journal*, 1835, 27:416–419).

Despite the fact that Henry's observations were made on the wrong night, they still should have been helpful to Bache in his

The following is however the result of our observations which you are at liberty to use as you may think fit.

1. The whole number of meteors noticed during the night, one of us watching at a time, was 103.

Of this number before 12 Oclock			7	were seen
from	12 "	to 1 Oclock	6	" "
"	1 "	to 2 "	3	" "
"	2 "	to 3 "	4	" "
"	3 "	to 4 "	16	" "
"	4 "	to 5 "	41	" "
"	5 "	to 6 "	26	" "

<*The whole number noted in the last hour was probably less than* [. . .] *on account of the morning dawn.*> The watch was strictly kept after 12. O Clock, not so before that hour. From the above however it evidently appears that the number greatly increased towards morning.[4]

2. The greater number appeared very small and much less brilliant than those which occasionally attract the attention of the casual observer. I think a greater part seen by myself would not have been noticed but by a person purposely watching for appearances of the kind.[5]

3. In many cases several meteors were observed to shoot in succession from near the same point, and to follow nearly the same path. This was noticed so frequently, that at length when one was seen to start from any

continuing debate with Olmsted. Olmsted was arguing that on the mornings of November 13, in both 1833 and 1834, there were "unusual" occurrences of meteor showers. Bache countered that only the 1833 occurrence was extraordinary; the 1834 meteors, he wrote, "were similar both in degree and kind to ordinary meteors." (Bache, "Meteoric Observations Made On and About the 13th of November, 1834," *Journal of the Franklin Institute*, 1835, *16*:371). If Henry could observe a large number of meteors on a night for which Olmsted would not have predicted them, then Bache would have additional evidence that the meteors of November 13, 1834 and 1835, were not unusual.

[4] Most observers noted the frequency of the meteors throughout the night. Henry's observations, showing a peak of activity around 4 and 5 A.M., generally conform with the findings of observers on both sides of the Bache-Olmsted debate.

[5] Throughout the Bache-Olmsted debate, the single-mindedness of the observers was a continuing point of disagreement. After their initial conflicting observations on the 1834 meteoric showers were printed in *Silliman's Journal* (Bache, 1835, 27:335–338; Olmsted, ibid., 416–420), Bache and Olmsted questioned each other's use of uncritical observers. For instance, Olmsted attacked Bache's systematic use of Army sentinels as observers, claiming that sailors are better observers of celestial phenomena than soldiers (Olmsted, Franklin Institute *Journal*, 1835, *16*:369). Olmsted felt that Bache's observers missed the meteoric display because they were not looking for it. Bache countered that Olmsted had overlooked corroborating observations from serious scientists who had made intensive watches and faulted Olmsted for accepting imprecise accounts from "a member of the Theological Seminary at Andover, an anonymous writer in the St. Louis Observer, and a female servant at Zanesville . . ." (Bache, Franklin Institute *Journal*, 1836, *17*:35–36; quote is from page 35).

Henry's point is to underscore the necessity of correlating observations of people comparable in their purposeful watching of the meteoric phenomena.

point, it was considered as a signal that several others would soon appear at the same place. Thus out of the whole number 3 were seen to start in rapid succession from a point in Cassiopeia and to descend north westerly towards the horizon—3 from near *Algol* and pass towards the west—3 from a point near *Sirius* and descend to the South—6 started within a few minutes of each other from near *Capella* and passed towards the north west, and 8 were observed to shoot from about the middle of *Orion* towards the south. But the greatest number seen to start from any one point was about 40 from near the Moon in *Leo*, and these passed nearly all in one direction towards a point midway between *Betelguese* in *Orion* and *Sirius* in Canis Major.[6]

4. The course of the greater number was westerly or in opposition to that of a gentle breeze which continued from the west during the whole night. The temperature during the night varied from 24 to 28 Fah. The wind for several days about the 13th was from the W. or N.W.[7]

I regret that it is not in my power to offer you any thing more important, on this very interesting department of Meteorology;[8] It is certainly worthy of all the attention which for many years it has received but will require much additional observation before any thing definitely can be known

[6] Olmsted claimed that the 1834 meteoric showers exhibited a similarity in direction and a common "radiant" (the point from which the meteors radiated) which proved their identity with the 1833 phenomena (Olmsted, *Silliman's Journal*, 1835, *27*:418). Bache countered that there was a lack of a common radiant in 1834 which supported his position that the meteors were not like those of 1833 (Bache, Franklin Institute *Journal*, 1836, *17*: 33). Henry's observation that the greatest number of the meteors emanated from Leo correlates with Olmsted's idea of the location of the common "radiant."

[7] Olmsted's observers noted on the night of November 12–13, 1833, an uncommonly drastic drop in temperature and humidity throughout the entire region where the meteors had been observed; he associated these weather conditions with the meteor showers. Bache and his observers recorded weather conditions as a matter of course in subsequent years' meteoric displays and found that the weather conditions of 1833 were not approximated in 1834 and 1835, either locally or throughout larger regions.

[8] At this time scientists did not always make fine distinctions between meteorology and astronomy, at least for purposes of classifying the meteor showers. In fact, as noted in the preceding paragraph and footnote, Olmsted and others were convinced that there was some relationship between atmospheric conditions and the meteoric displays. The problem was to determine whether the meteors caused the weather change, or vice versa, or both were effects of some "common and remote cause" still undetermined. Olmsted, *Silliman's Journal*, 1834, *25*:402. Olmsted opted for the first explanation in subsequently formulating his hypothesis about the origin, height, direction, and other characteristics of the meteors. Olmsted, "Observations on the Meteors of November 13th, 1833," *Silliman's Journal*, 1834, *26*:132–174. James P. Espy, who worked closely with Bache in these scientific inquiries, was the first to counter Olmsted's elaborate hypothesis with an equally elaborate rebuttal ("Remarks on Professor Olmsted's Theory of the Meteoric Phenomenon of November 12th, 1833, Denominated Shooting Stars, with Some Queries Towards Forming a Just Theory," Franklin Institute *Journal*, 1835, *15*:9–19, 85–92, 158–165, 234–238). Espy was primarily a weather scientist. Skepticism of Olmsted's theory also came from such astronomers as Robert Treat Paine and Nathaniel Bowditch; see above, Henry to Bache, December 17, 1834, footnote 19, for an outline of Olmsted's theory, its significance, and its opposition.

respecting it. I do not subscribe to any hypothesis which has yet been advanced in reference to the nature of the meteors, nor do I believe that a sufficient number of well attested facts have yet been collected for the deduction of even an approximation to a rational theory of their origin.[9] It is however not impossible that some hypotheses may be invented even with the little light which we now possess which if properly used may serve to direct attention to certain points of observation and thus become important aids in the accumulation of facts—but these should be used with great caution and by no means insisted on as being either absolutely or even partially true.

With much respect. Yours &c.
Joseph Henry

Princeton 30 minutes
before 1836

My Dear Bache

On the opposite pages you have a letter which my Better-half has transcribed for your use. I hope it will answer your purpose.[10] If you would like any thing added in the way of opinion or [fact] write me and I will make any correction or addition consistent with the nature of the case.

My college duties have since the commencement of the term occupied my whole ti[me from] 8 in the morning until 10 at night.

I proposed to watch for meteors e[ver]y Friday night during the winter[11] but since my last letter to you there has not been one unclouded friday at Princeton.

I start tomorrow morning for Philadelphia[12] and should the night[13] be

[9] At the heart of Bache's attack on Olmsted was Bache's disapproval of Olmsted's use of the hypothesis about meteor showers which was based on observations of only the 1833 event. Bache implied that Olmsted saw fit to use 1834 observations "verifying a prediction made by him as a consequence of his peculiar theory." (Bache, Franklin Institute *Journal*, 1836, *17*:33.) Undoubtedly Bache was more emphatic in his personal conversation with Henry and others in his circle. This statement by Henry supports Bache's position by implying that neither Olmsted, nor anyone else, has amassed enough data for a reliable explanation. But Henry goes on in the next sentence to caution Bache that not all uses of hypotheses are improper in the line of scientific inquiry, adding a final caveat which, again by implication, characterizes Olmsted's sins of commission.

[10] Presumably Bache intended to assemble and publish another batch of observations for 1835, as he had done for 1834 (Bache, Franklin Institute *Journal*, 1835, *16*:149–153). But Bache never put Henry's carefully transcribed remarks, or anyone else's, into print; he never published any article on the 1835 meteor showers.

[11] Henry's proposed vigil would be kept to help Bache determine the normal levels of meteoric displays on dates other than November 12–13.

[12] In his letter to Bache, January 18, 1836, Henry confesses that he erred in saying "Philadelphia." He meant to say he was going to New York.

[13] Friday night, January 1.

clear Mr Alexander will watch for shooting stars alone and direct his attention to those which may appear on each side of the line joining Princeton & Philadelphia. My respects to Mrs. B. and Courteny.

Yours Sincerely
Joseph Henry

FROM JAMES DEAN

Henry Papers, Smithsonian Archives

Burlington; 28 November, 1835.

Dear Sir,

Many thanks to you for the Articles from the Am. Phil. Trans. containing your Contributions to Elec. & Gal.[1] With the powerful and flexible instrument which you have devised for operating on those subjects, and with your industry and sagacity your contributions must be numerous and valuable. But the explanation of the action of the spiral conductor on p 230 does not appear to me satisfactory. It seems to me that the current in B which would accelerate the current in A must be in that direction which the current in A would tend to produce, or in that direction which would produce a current in A in the same direction with that which it is supposed to accelerate; unless the current in A is retarded by producing the counter current in B, which is directly opposite to my notions of electrical induction.[2]

[1] Dean appears on Henry's distribution list for "Contributions I:Battery" and "Contributions II:Spiral Conductor," [ca. August 21,] 1835, above.

[2] Henry's words are:

> If a current of free electricity be passed through A, the natural equilibrium of B will be disturbed for an instant, in a similar manner to the disturbance of the equilibrium in an insulated conductor, by the sudden addition of fluid to a contiguous conductor. On account of the repulsive action of the fluid, the current in B will have an opposite direction to that in A; and if the intensity of action remains constant, a new state of equilibrium will be assumed. The second state, however, of B may perhaps be regarded as one of tension, and as soon as the extra action ceases in it, the fluid in B will resume its natural state of distribution, and thus a returning current for an instant be produced.

APS *Transactions*, 1837, n.s. 5:230.

Dean's views are not far from Henry's views; he does not fully grasp Henry's point. In the first state an equilibrium is established which Henry on the previous page explicitly identifies with the accepted principles of static electrical induction. When the new state of equilibrium is ended by breaking the circuit, "a returning current [will] for an instant be produced." Applying this to the spiral conductor, Henry then says, "when the contact is broken, the fluid of the first spire is projected from it with intensity by the repulsive action of the fluid in all the succeeding spires."

Henry has explained phenomena in galvanic electricity by accepted concepts in static electricity. Each spire is assumed to act similarly to a separate wire. The observed accelerated current from the first spire restores the initial equilibrium. It is the result of currents generated in the other spires upon the removal of the cause of the disturbance.

The Aur. Bo. have not been very active for the year past. I have noted "27 & 28 Feb. 10 P.M. A.B. 7° or 8° high, bright but tranquil."

"1st March, 10 to 20m after nine, two large masses of light in the east—one just S of Arcturus commencing 12° or 15° from the horizon, inclining northwardly, and fading away in Ursa major, 10° or 12° broad at the broadest and brightest part, which was about 20° high and bore S. 84° E. The other mass was narrower but longer lying along the northern edge of the zodiac." They disappeared in about 10m after I first saw them.

The appearances here on the 17th inst. were much as described throughout the country. The most uncommon one was the complexion, which, especially in the western portion and till near 8 oclock, was far and wide, that of the brightest red ever painted on the clouds by the horizontal sun. The only feature which I saw sufficiently definite and durable to be identified by distant observers was a strong red column 5° or 6° broad and from 40° to 60° or 70° high, bearing about N. 55° W. It stood without any apparent change of place from about half after five till after seven.

About 10 P.M. of the next Friday a most violent gale commenced very suddenly, wind varying from S.W. to N.W. and continued several hours. It has been very cold ever since. Early the next Monday morning it began to snow and continued thru the day, and we now have tolerable sleighing.

I was at considerable expense and pains to ascertain the exact time for the purpose of fixing our longitude from the late transit, but was not much disappointed in being totally defeated, for "*Tum* mihi caeruleus supra caput astitit imber."[3]

What do you think of Wheatstone's estimate of the velocity and duration of the electric spark? I was much pleased with it at first, but subsequent reflexion has very much shaken my faith in its sufficiency.[4]

I fear you have not seen the circumstance of thick masses of ice melting slowly which I described to you.[5]

[3] "At that moment a dark raincloud came to rest above my head." *Aeneid*, Book III, line 194.

[4] See footnote 2 of Ten Eyck's letter of [ca. November 22, 1833], above, for a discussion of this experiment and its relation to Henry's work. Henry's reading notes on Wheatstone's article appear below, [ca. 1835]. We have no further information on Dean's doubts.

[5] A response, apparently, to a letter of Henry's no longer surviving. In a notebook ([10615], p. 431), Henry has an undated entry quoting Dean on an aspect of the melting of ice:

> Professor Dean of Burlington informes me that in the melting of ice, the mass disolves into crystals having their axes at right angles to the surface of freezing. They are not hexigons as far as he has had opportunity of observing the appearance. Are the optical properties of ice well made out.
>
> This is a general fact in regard to the cooling of all bodies which tend to crystalize. Cast a cylender of zinc in a cold mold, the rod will sometimes be hollow as if regularly bored through the axis, and all the crys[t]als will be arranged in radii at right angles to the axis and to the surface of the cylender.

While this notebook entry may be contemporary with this letter, there is other evidence

Be pleased to present my respectful good wishes to [Mrs. Henry][6] and accept for yourself the sincere assurances

of the highest regard from
JAMES DEAN.

of Henry keeping Dean's words in mind in later years. Notebook [23907] dates from the late years of Henry's Princeton tenure. Facing page 22 of his printed course syllabus (1844) is the following note in Henry's hand, a comment on his observation of the parallelism between electromagnetic polarity and crystallization:

Prof Dean informs me that when Ice melts it is resolved into prisms the axes of which are perpendicular to the surface. The cracking of ice on ponds takes place when the temperature increases (Look at this).

[6] Although a hole occurs in the manuscript at this point, we suppose that Harriet Henry was meant to be the recipient of Dean's greeting.

TO ALEXANDER DALLAS BACHE

Bache Papers, Smithsonian Archives

Princeton Tuesday [December 1, 1835][1]

My Dear Bache

We watched for meteors on Tuesday night and succeded in registering eleven.[2] Since then we have not watched although there has been two clear nights. We find the process attended with considerable difficulty on account of having no movable time keeper. The observations were made in the Philosophical Hall with two assistants[3] who alternated with each other in calling at the top of the voice the seconds of the clock. The observations were painful as we were obliged to reach out of the window during the whole time. We have made arrangements to get access to the roof of the building, and propose if you dare again to trust us, to look out every clear Friday night, if that time will be convenient to you.

The next evening Wednesday was clear but I caught a very severe cold on Tuesday night and was disturbed in my rest by sickness in our family.

[1] The letter is postmarked December 1; a perpetual calendar yields 1835 for Tuesday December 1. The mention of measles and of writing to Albany about meteors verifies the year 1835.

A note by Mary Henry appears on the left margin of the first page of this letter: "This is an interesting letter referring to the observations made of shooting stars—see the other matter about it."

[2] Henry and other friends of Bache needed data on normal numbers of meteors that fell on winter evenings in order to refute Olmsted's contention that the extraordinary showers of mid-November 1833 had reappeared in 1834 and 1835. See note 3 of the letter of Henry to Bache for November 25, 1835, printed above.

[3] Probably Stephen Alexander and John Miller.

Our little boy has had the measles but is now convalescent. I have been much troubled with the idea of causing Mr Espy[4] and yourself to watch without corresponding diligence on our part. If you agree to the proposition of watching on Friday night drop us a line on the recept of this.

I have written to albany asking the questions proposed by Mr Espy and also concerning the meteors.[5] I will incorporate what information I receive in my letter to you for publication.[6]

Below is a list of the times of observation.[7]

The mail has closed. I send this by a passenger[8] & have not my notes by me.

Jos Henry

[4] For Espy's involvement with the meteor controversy, see note 8 of the November 25, 1835, letter to Bache.

[5] Henry had written Philip Ten Eyck on November 29; his letter has not been found, but see Ten Eyck's reply of December 7, 1835, printed below.

[6] Henry's formal report to Bache of November 25 was not actually sent until December 31.

[7] Between this sentence and the next, there is a blank space in the letter. The next sentence looks like a hasty scrawl compared to the leisurely handwriting of the first part of the text.

Although Henry apparently did not send the data to Bache at this time, Henry and Alexander's observations were eventually employed by another researcher for a different purpose. On December 20, 1839, the astronomer Sears Walker reported the information in a paper on calculating longitudes. Walker had received notes on the Princeton observations from Stephen Alexander (American Philosophical Society *Proceedings*, 1838–1840, *1*:161–162).

[8] Not identified. The letter has a Philadelphia postmark, but Henry forgot to write who carried it from Princeton to that city.

FROM PHILIP TEN EYCK

Henry Papers, Smithsonian Archives

Albany Dec[r] 7 1835

My Dear Sir

I have delayed answering yours of the 29[h] last in expectation of learning something more precise concerning the rain of the 11th Nov. but have not been successful. All I get from D[r] Beck's journal[1] is Nov. 11th wind (South A.M.), West P.M. rain 0,25. The evenings from the 11th to the 17 were either cloudy or hazy and did [not] give me any inducement to set up later than 11 OClock. The night of the 17 commenced very clear. At 5h 20m I saw a bright crimson light near the horizon North of East which in a few

[1] Probably a reference to T. Romeyn Beck's meteorological notes which he maintained at the Albany Academy. In his Albany days Joseph Henry collaborated with Beck in recording weather phenomena and reporting annual compilations to the State Board of Regents. See *Henry Papers, 1*:passim.

minutes extended across the heavens in the form of an arch terminating in the horizon north of west the highest part about five degrees below the pole star. This arch whose edges were not as well defined as I have seen remained in the same position the greater part of the evening. Its colour at first crimson. About 5h 30. . the eastern portion changed to a yellowish white. At the same time something resembling a white cloud formed near horizon south of east. This was presently included in a pale white arch which rapidly shot across the heavens apparently parallel to the red arch. This did not last longer than five minutes. Its vertex was higher than the pole star. A third arch whose vertex was below the first red arch but appeared to spring from the same points in the horizon with the first.

Stanwix Hall & the 2^{d} Presb^{n} church obstructed my view of the horizon. Below the third arch the dark cloud which accompanies the aurora [and] numerous streamers of red & blue & pale green moving gradually towards west. The appearance was grand but I could not trace any order untill about 11h 45m when an irregular crimson belt south of zenith and apparently terminating about the East & West points and streamers of various colours from every part of the horizon all terminating in a point marked by a star west of the Pleiades which at the time I thought I could not forget. I think it was star 41 Æ 2h 40m Dec^{n} 26[2] on map published by Socy for Diff^{n} Usefull Knowdge.[3] Clouds now became so dense as to obscure the stars. No stars shoots this night. On the 18th a low arch and [?strewments] pointing toward the same point but did not extend 45° above Horizon. Saw several small meteors and about 10h 41m as well as I could ascertain by the light of the sky a large meteor fell from near the zenith towards the south west. I wish I was so situated that I could observe with you the shooting stars. I can only see from my room from the west to the north, and as to time may be astray 5 or more seconds. If however you think it would be an object I will look out one night a week, any one you wish. My transit instrument gets along by degrees. I have finished the axis and turned the bell metal ends to my satisfaction. The glasses of the telescope though not quite achromatic give a tolerably well defined image of a star. Nothing new here. Saw your brother to day said all well. Jim Eights has just returned from the Pennsylvania coal mines and threatens to blow up Silliman & the fellow who filled up his

[2] The star is known today as "41 Arietis."

[3] London's Society for the Diffusion of Useful Knowledge was organized in 1826. See above, Henry to James Henry, June 25, 1833, especially footnote 8. The Society's *Six Maps of Stars* (London, 1833) were good star charts of great popularity to laymen and astronomers on both sides of the Atlantic. They were reprinted several times.

last journal.[4] Mr Ferguson[5] left here this day for Maryland to look for points for his triangles while the trees are bare. M Bullions sends his respects. Remember me to Stephen, Mrs H, Mrs Alexander and all friends.

yours sincerely
Ph Ten Eyck

[4] Benjamin Silliman alluded to the Ohio coal piece in his letter to Henry, September 4, 1835, above. But Henry undoubtedly noticed Silliman's statement in the prefatory pages to his July 1835 number (*Silliman's Journal*, July 1835, *28*, Number 2:8): "the next number of this work will be devoted *chiefly*, to an elaborate account of the great formation in the valley of the Ohio, and in the valleys of the confluent rivers. This memoir has been, at the Editor's request, prepared with great labor and considerable expence, by Dr. Hildreth, of Marietta, Ohio. . . ." Samuel Prescott Hildreth (1783–1863, *DAB*) was a practicing physician who wrote prolifically on geology, meteorology, and other topics relating to the natural history of the Ohio River Valley. His "Observations on the Bituminous Coal Deposits of the Valley of the Ohio, and Accompanying Rock Strata" (*Silliman's Journal*, 1836, *29*:1–154), along with sixteen pages of "Miscellanies," comprised the entire number of the *Journal*. James Eights (1798–1882, for whom see *Henry Papers*, *1*:69) led a life of inconsistencies. He does not appear to have followed up his threat against Silliman and Hildreth in print. We can therefore only speculate that his objections stemmed either from honest disagreement on the geological content of the article or from jealousy and frustration from being preempted in an area where both he and Hildreth had studied. In any event, Eights never published any article on the geology or natural history of either Pennsylvania or Ohio.

[5] James Ferguson of the Coast Survey, for whom see above, Henry to James Henry, December 1, 1832, footnote 12.

FROM JOHN TORREY

Henry Papers, Smithsonian Archives

New York, Dec[r] 15th 1835

My dear friend

I was agreeably surprized by a visit from D[r] Maclean, last evening. Understanding that he leaves town for Princeton tomorrow morning, I cannot let the opportunity pass of send[ing] you a few lines, though you hardly deserve any thing but a good scolding. Why did you not write by the Doctor?

Silliman will be along in a few weeks & you must get ready your notes & apparatus for Electro-magnetism.[1] Now make up your mind to talk to my class yourself. I told them perhaps you would, & there was quite a cheering. I shall expect you to oblige me in this.[2]

[1] See above, Silliman to Henry, October 31, 1835.

[2] Henry was in New York from the first to the fifth of January, saw Torrey, but declined to lecture to his class. See Henry's letter to Bache, January 18, 1836, to appear in volume three of *The Papers of Joseph Henry*.

Bring along with you the plan[3] (according to scale) of the lecture room & laboratory that we may settle every thing relating to shelving &c. If, however, the large brick pillars are not taken out of the old refectory, Mr. Cooley[4] & the Doctor[5] may have every thing their own way. I shall not trouble myself in the matter. If they will do as *we* think right I will exert myself to get up for Princeton the best Laboratory in the country. Do press this business & tell Maclean what ought to be done.

I am now on *Sulphur* (following Turner[6]) in my course. My Class is a small one. Politics have killed the College—or at least paralysed it. Jacob Green says they have 360 *bona fide* pupils in Jefferson Coll. & he has rec[d] in Cash between 4000 & 5000 dollars.

I have no time to write more. Remember me very kindly to Mrs Henry, Mr. Alexander, Mrs Alexander[7] & all my good friends in P.

I send you the proceedings of the Dublin meeting.[8] Please return the book when you come here *to lecture.*

Truly yours
John Torrey

[3] Filed with this letter is a plan for the renovation of the third story of Philosophical Hall. We cannot say if this is the plan referred to or who drew it up. We suspect it was filed with Torrey's letter at a later time, probably not by Henry. For a discussion of the various plans for the new addition, see above, Henry's Drawing of Philosophical Hall, April 1835.

[4] See above, Henry's List of Recipients, [ca. August 21,] 1835, footnote 41.

[5] Probably John Maclean.

[6] Edward Turner, *Elements of Chemistry* (London, 1827). Henry owned the 1835 Philadelphia edition, which he apparently acquired in 1837.

[7] Probably Stephen Alexander and his mother.

[8] The 1835 meeting of the British Association for the Advancement of Science.

TO JAMES HENRY

Family Correspondence, Henry Papers, Smithsonian Archives

Princeton Dec. [25] 1835[1]

Dear James

I take advantage of a holy day to answer your last letter which was received some weeks since. We are all well. The children have recovered from the measles. The little Girl was attacked shortly after the recovery of the Boy. She was much more troublesome than he, but has endeavoured to

[1] The letter originally lacked a day of the month. At some unknown later time, an unidentified hand suggested the 26th, based on the postmark of that day. We are supplying the date as the 25th, based on Henry's reference to the "holy day" in the first line.

make amends by being pretty good natured since. We were sorry to hear that Caroline was unwell and hope that she has recovered before this time. I regret that Nancy should be influenced by remarks of the kind you mention. Mr. Newland[2] was with us last saturday a week. He stopped from Saturday until monday, brought Stephens umbrella, and some other articles from the Mead's family. There is certainly a very striking likeness in the general features of the countenance between Henry Clay and Joseph T. Rice.[3] The likeness however is confined entirely to external appearances. Henry Clay is a highly polished gentleman very intelligent on almost every subject. He has twice visited Princeton within a year so that we have had some opportunity of forming an acquaintance with him. He has a son and two grandsons at Mr Wine's school at this place—the son will enter college next spring.[4] You had a fine display of the Aurora about the time your last letter was written. It has been described to me by Dr TenEyck[5] in a letter and also by Mr Newland. Henry Clay described the same Aurora as seen by himself in Kentucky on the same evening.

This fact confirms a position which I advanced in one of my papers that the Aurora when it appears with splendor at any one place is seen at the same time over a large portion of the northern hemisphere.[6]

We are much obliged to you for the trouble you have taken in reference to the money affair between Yates & Fassett.

I conclude that Frank[7] has rather too much of a good thing. Butter is

[2] Luke F. Newland, for whom see above, Henry to James Henry, May 17, 1833, footnote 3. He is the father of John Newland, mentioned above in Henry to Harriet Henry, October 24, 1835, especially footnote 13.

[3] Joseph Taft Rice (1787–1854), an Albany silversmith and jeweler. His son, Joseph Taft Rice, Jr. (1822–1890), attended the Albany Academy, 1830–1837, and may have known Henry as a teacher there. Hun, "Albany Academy."

[4] Clay visited Princeton late in November 1834 and again about December 1, 1835. His son John M. Clay (1821–1887) attended Enoch Wines's Edgehill Seminary from 1834 to 1836, after which he attended Princeton. He entered as a Sophomore in 1837 but completed only two years there. He became known nationally for his race horses and breeding stable. Henry Clay's grandsons were Martin Duralde (1823–1846) and Henry Clay Duralde (1824–before 1850), the children of Susan Hart Clay and Martin Duralde, Jr. After their mother died in 1825, they were reared with John M. Clay and attended the Edgehill Seminary from 1835 to 1836. They died young, both unmarried. Information from Mary W. M. Hargreaves of the Papers of Henry Clay, University of Kentucky. Also, *Princeton Annual Catalogues*, 1837–1839.

[5] See above, Ten Eyck to Henry, December 7, 1835.

[6] Henry concluded that the "simultaneous appearances" of the aurora in Europe and America meant that "the aurora borealis cannot be classed among the ordinary local meteorological phenomena, but that it must be referred to some cause connected with the general physical principles of the globe; and that the more energetic actions of this cause, whatever it may be, affects simultaneously a great portion of the northern hemisphere." "On a Disturbance of the Earth's Magnetism, in Connection with the Appearance of an Aurora Borealis, as Observed at Albany, April 19th, 1831," *Silliman's Journal*, 1832, 22:143–155. Quotes are from the conclusion on page 155.

[7] Probably a reference to Dr. Francis Selkirk.

very high with us—22 & 23 cts per lb. The sudden closeing of the canal has also increased the price of coal. We contracted for our winter supply at $5 per tun but the merchant is not able to furnish us with a sufficient quantity and the article is now up to 7 dollars.

The Albany papers are filled with accounts of the great fire in New York.[8] It was distinctly visible at Princeton during the whole of the night of the principal conflagration. As many as 6 or 7 of the parents of students in the College are sufferers by the calamity.

Stephen sent you a copy of Biddles address[9] which you have probably received. The Globe has made an attack[10] on the college in consequence of the address. This is unjust as the college is of no party and the speaker was selected not by the officers of the college but by the members of the Alumni or graduate Society. There are two persons chosen annually to deliver addresses at the commencement one by the Alumni Association and the other by one of the two literary societies of College. In both cases a graduate of the college is chosen and one that is distinguished if possible in Public life. The administration party will have no cause to complain of the selection for next year since the American Whig Society has chosen for its orator, Mr Livingston[11] late Minister to France who is a graduate of the college and

[8] The fire broke out on December 16, 1835, in lower Manhattan. Fanned by near gale-force winds, it raged uncontrollably for twenty-four hours and continued to burn and smolder for several days. Temperatures below zero seriously hampered fire-fighting efforts. Despite the contributions of fire-fighting teams from neighboring cities, including even Philadelphia, the fire devasted some 674 buildings, causing unemployment for upwards of 5,000 workers and damages totaling $26 million. Lowell M. Limpus, *History of the New York Fire Department* (New York, 1940), pp. 150–158. C. Foster, *An Account of the Conflagration of the Principal Part of the First Ward of the City of New York* (New York, [1835?]). The *Daily Albany Argus* printed extensive stories on the catastrophe on December 21 and 22, 1835.

[9] Henry retained two copies in his library of Nicholas Biddle's *An Address Delivered Before the Alumni Association of Nassau-Hall on the Day of the Annual Commencement of the College, September 30, 1835* (Princeton, 1835). As an alumnus of Princeton, Biddle urged the graduates to enter public life, for which their Princeton education had made them particularly fit. As the embittered Director of the Second Bank of the United States, recently deflated by President Andrew Jackson's popularity and policies, Biddle characterized the Jacksonians as demagogues and predicted, "these banditti will be scourged back to their caverns."

[10] Biddle's address was not published until late November. On December 5, 1835, the Washington *Globe*, p. 2, "Nicholas Biddle, The Stock Jobber," complained that, "after thus being convicted in the eyes of the whole Republic, of the prostitution of the means of the Bank . . . he should undertake to preach political morals to the Princeton pupils." Henry exaggerates in citing the article as "an attack on the college." The *Globe* merely concluded by saying, "we trust the Republican party will bear in mind that Mr. Biddle's speech was well received by the Faculty of Princeton." Henry's reaction might appear to be indicative of some Whiggish leanings, but his personal friendship with Biddle and his escalating pride for Princeton may have been stronger motives.

[11] Edward Livingston died before the following commencement. Henry mentions that event in a letter to James Henry, June 6, 1836, Family Correspondence, Henry Papers, Smithsonian Archives. The Whig Society substituted John Morin Scott (1789–1858), Princeton A.B.

a member of the society. It is said that he has sent a letter of acceptance. This has not yet been made public by the Society so that I do not as yet wish it to be announced in the p[apers].

William Bullions is with me in the Phi[losophical] Hall. He renders himself very useful and I hope will improve by his sojourn with us. We have had pretty cold weather this season the lowest point of the thermometer is 3° above zero. We have no sleighing.

James Ferguson[12] spent two or three days in the vicinity of Princeton in searching for high points on which to place his signals for the coast survey. He will establish a point somewhere near this and will probably remove his family to Princeton or Mount Holley a place about 20 miles nearer Philadelphia. He left this [place] for Washington & will not return here until next March although [he] will be in Albany some time during the winter.

Your Brother

(1805), soldier, lawyer, Philadelphia Mayor (1841–1844) and Trustee of the University of Pennsylvania (1834–1856). *Herringshaw*, p. 826. *Princeton Catalogue*, p. 117. Scott's address survives in the Henry Library.

[12] For whom see above, Henry to James Henry, December 1, 1832, especially footnote 12.

EXCERPT, HENRY NOTEBOOK ENTRY

Notebook [7170], no pagination, Henry Papers, Smithsonian Archives

[ca. 1835]

Documentary evidence suggests that Joseph Henry was first exposed to Charles Wheatstone's experiments to determine the velocity of electricity when Henry Darwin Rogers gave a personal account of them at a meeting of "the club" on December 5, 1834.[1] Apparently soon afterward Henry read Wheatstone's article, "An Account of Some Experiments to Measure the Velocity of Electricity and the Duration of Electric Light" (*Phil. Trans.*, 1834, pp. 583–591), a presentation copy of which survives in the Henry Library.[2] Henry took extensive notes which follow Wheatstone's experiments step by step. In general, such reading notes do not merit publication in this letterpress series, as they are normally merely outlines or nearly verbatim extracts of published works. In the instance of Wheatstone's article, however, Henry took important exception to one of the

[1] For which see above, Henry's Notes on a Trip to Philadelphia, December 5–7, 1834.

[2] For an earlier mention of this article, in the context of Henry's interest in the persistence of vision phenomenon, see above, Ten Eyck to Henry, [ca. November 22, 1833], especially footnote 2.

author's conclusions, thereby making the following excerpt of Henry's reading notes a significant holograph probably dating from sometime in 1835.

Wheatstone attempted to determine the velocity of electricity by observing sparks at the beginning, middle, and end of a half-mile wire circuit. By measuring the timing of the appearance of each spark, he could calculate how fast the current would pass over a mile. Three spark gaps from the beginning, middle, and end of the wire were set on a single board, a "spark board," which was placed opposite (ten feet away) a revolving mirror. The mirror turned on a horizontal, hand-cranked axis, which also carried a contact point mounted to complete the circuit whenever the mirror was positioned at forty-five degrees. Turning the axis rapidly and stroboscopically viewing the elongated images of the three sparks as presented by the mirror, Wheatstone measured the velocity of the axis and calculated that the speed of electricity was 288,000 miles per second.[3] In his notes Henry did not object to Wheatstone's methods, his calculations, or his results, save one conclusion.

Wheatstone noted that the sparks at the beginning and end of the wire occurred virtually simultaneously, whereas the spark in the middle lagged behind. From that observation he concluded that two distinct electrical fluids[4] proceeded simultaneously through the wire in opposite directions, beginning at the opposite ends. A single fluid of electricity proceeding from the positive center of the Leyden jar, Wheatstone asserted, would have caused the sparks to occur sequentially through the three spark gaps; his experiment, then, tends to discount the single fluid theory of electricity. In the following excerpt, Henry objected to that assertion.

I do not think this exp at all conclusive on the theory of one or two fluids since the outside of the jar is negative while the inside is positive, and the negative electricity or rather the negative state[5] is preserved by the

[3] Wheatstone's figure is high, Whittaker alleges, because he arranged his wire circuit in a coil of twenty straight windings. His calculations would have produced a more accurate velocity had he used a straight half-mile wire. Edmund Whittaker, *A History of the Theories of Aether and Electricity*, rev. ed., 2 vols. (New York, 1973), *1*:227–228.

We are not certain if Henry ever duplicated Wheatstone's experiment. In his "Record of Experiments," Henry noted on June 24, 1842, his intention to try a modification of the experiment: "Repeat Wheatstones exp with the revolving mirror, instead of long wire, use tubes filled with water." No evidence has yet surfaced either to confirm that Henry followed up his own suggestion or to clarify exactly what Henry wished to prove.

[4] The two fluid theory of electricity, positing that there are two distinct electrical fluids ("vitreous" and "resinous" electricity), was first advanced by Charles-François de Cisternai Dufay (1698–1739, *DSB*). Dufay wished to formulate a theoretical explanation for the observed powers of electrical attraction and repulsion. Benjamin Franklin (for whose theories see *DSB*) countered that there is only one electrical fluid, one which could exhibit both a positive and negative state. George John Singer, *Elements of Electricity and Electro-Chemistry* (London, 1814), pp. 5–19, which Henry read and kept in his library, gives a contemporary view of the development of both theories.

[5] Note that Henry is quick to correct his own statement. "Negative electricity" is semantically unclear; it could imply either the resinous electrical fluid of the two fluid theory

inductive action of the + elect through the glass. Take one spark from the inside and a spark will be liberated on the outside by lessening to that degree the tension.[6]

J H.

or the negative state of the single electrical fluid. Henry's clarification, "or rather the negative state," unequivocally substitutes a Franklinian concept.

[6] While Henry's terminology is hazy, his essential point, that the Franklinian theory is entirely consistent with Wheatstone's findings, is sound. That is, a spark-producing current is drawn from the end of the wire toward the outside of the Leyden jar at the same time as positive electricity is discharged from the inside of the jar.

This is one of the rare documented instances in the mid-1830s where Henry concerned himself with such theoretical issues, and it is interesting to note his acute defense of Franklin's theory. Certainly in this period such issues did not bear directly on his own research. Even in his 1842 jotting (mentioned in footnote 3), where Henry intended to try a modification of Wheatstone's experiment, Henry does not indicate any theoretical quibbling. Throughout the 1830s Henry explained both the one and two fluid theories to his Princeton students, stating only the slightest preference for the one fluid theory. He emphasized that the two theories were mathematically equivalent. But in the 1840s he shifted toward stating a clear preference for the one fluid theory with his own modification. See Weiner, "Joseph Henry's Lectures," pp. 170–178.

INDEX

Under a name, "letter from" signifies a letter from that person to Henry, while "letter to" indicates a letter from Henry to that person. When Henry is neither sender nor recipient, the names of both parties are given. In the case of Henry, "letters from," followed by a list of names, indicates letters to Henry; "letters to," Henry's letters to various recipients. Subentries are so arranged that letters and documents precede the customary alphabetical listing.

Index

Warren Buckland

Dedication

This book is dedicated to the memory of my father.

ACKNOWLEDGEMENTS

Most of this book has grown out of lectures that have been 'tested out' in the UK on undergraduate students at both the University of East Anglia and John Moores University. The need to present points that are obvious to the lecturer/writer (points that have, in fact, only been acquired over years of study) but which are new to the listener and reader requires a determined effort to be concise and informative at the same time. I hope I have gone some way to achieving these qualities in this book. This book, therefore, owes a great deal to the students who sat through the original lectures. Their reactions helped me to transform my notes into the following chapters.

On a more personal note, many friends and colleagues have read individual chapters, and have offered critical and creative suggestions for revision. I would, therefore, like to thank Glen Creeber, Sean Cubitt, Kevin Donnelly, Thomas Elsaesser, Sibel Karabina, Peter Krämer, Steve Marchant and Lydia Papadimitriou for their comments and suggestions. I would also like to thank Philip French and *The Observer* for allowing me to reproduce Philip French's review of *The English Patient*.

The author and publisher would like to thank the following for permission to reproduce film stills: BFI Stills, Posters and Designs (Figures 1, 3, 4, 5, 6); The Kobal Collection (Figures 2, 7); The Ronald Grant Archive (Figures 8, 9); Universal Pictures (Figure 10).

CONTENTS

INTRODUCTION

To study the cinema: what an absurd idea!
Christian Metz

In this book I hope to show you that studying the cinema is not an absurd idea (Metz, the French film scholar, made his living out of studying the cinema, so of course he didn't think it was an absurd idea either). To study film should not be thought of as an activity inferior to studying other arts such as theatre, painting or opera, for two reasons. Firstly, film occupies a dominant place in society and because film is a popular medium, it should be studied seriously. Secondly, if the film student adopts a serious, responsible and critical approach to film, then film studies becomes as important as any other type of study. I use the term 'film student' in the broadest sense – that is, anyone who wants to develop an interest in analysing, comprehending and evaluating films; the term does not just refer to those who study in higher education. Ultimately, it is the student's attitude that justifies the study of film, not the nature or popularity of film. If the student takes his or her task seriously, then studying Steven Spielberg's film *The Lost World: Jurassic Park* becomes as important and legitimate as studying Shakespeare's play *Hamlet*, Hans Holbein's painting *The Ambassadors* or Mozart's opera *The Magic Flute*.

Metz also wrote that 'The cinema is difficult to explain because it is easy to understand'. In this book I also hope to show you that the cinema is not so difficult to explain, once you become familiar with the main critical tools film scholars use to analyse films. As a secondary aim, we shall look at films that are not easy to understand and we shall see what makes them difficult. By analysing the complex nature of difficult films we should be able to appreciate them more.

The starting point for studying a film is to analyse the way it has been constructed. This involves looking at the various technical, stylistic and narrative options available to a film maker and the choices that he or she makes in putting together a film or sequence of film. To emphasise a film's construction combines the study of film practice and film aesthetics. This is because we consider both the practical choices that are made when a film is constructed and the aesthetic effects these choices have on the film spectator.

For example, what is the difference between shooting a scene in one continuous take, where the camera is left rolling while the whole of the action takes place, and shooting the same scene in several shots? The first option involves the film maker filming the action as it unfolds, uninterrupted. The second option involves breaking the action down into individual shots. Each new shot will include a change in camera position, camera angle, shot scale (the distance between the camera and the action) and so on. Film makers have to weigh up the advantages and disadvantages of choosing one technique over another for each scene, since the choice of technique will influence the way spectators respond to the film. This is just one of the questions we shall be looking at in this book.

However, you may think that analysing a film in this way destroys the pleasurable experiences we get when we go to the cinema. My response to this point is to argue that film studies does not destroy our experiences of films but *transforms* them. In his poem 'The Dry Salvages', T.S. Eliot wrote that:

> *We had the experience but missed the meaning*
> *And approach to the meaning restores the experience*
> *In a different form ....*

The opposition Eliot sets up between experience and meaning is useful in explaining the relation between watching a film and analysing it. Our aim in this book is to employ critical tools to analyse a film's meanings, which involves the spectator taking a step back from his or her experience of the film. Yet, as Eliot makes clear in his poem, the analysis of meaning will restore the experience in a different form. So my main point is that critical analysis does not destroy the spectator's pleasurable experience of a film, but transforms it. This transformed experience primarily involves developing a critical understanding of how films are made and what effects they have on you.

This leads me to one of my main arguments about the aim of film studies. Film studies is not simply about accumulating more and more information about films, film makers and the film industry. This is a passive form of learning. In this book I do not present you with pages and pages of facts on the cinema. Instead, you will find an emphasis on an active form of learning in which you develop critical and analytical skills – skills that can be applied to any film. I want to discourage you from merely talking about your personal impressions of a film and simply passing judgement on it ('I liked this film' or 'I didn't like this film'). This is a very superficial way to talk about films and I hope this book will enable you to go beyond this impressionistic type of criticism and become an expert critic.

Film studies consists of a huge amount of histories, theories, critical tools and discussions of individual films. Due to the overwhelming amount of information available, I have decided to be very selective in the topics I write about. One of the questions I asked myself when selecting topics is the following: What works in film studies? A great many of the issues and problems that film scholars decide to write about are badly chosen and ill-formed. Because they don't always work in particular instances (they are not general enough), the theories and critical tools that some film scholars use are irrelevant and misguided.

Furthermore, I have divided up the topics in this book into those that develop an internal perspective on film, and those that develop an external perspective. An internal perspective develops an intrinsic approach to film and studies a film's inner workings. That is, an internal perspective studies the film itself, in isolation from any historical, moral or social context. This approach is often referred to as poetic. Chapters 1 to 3 outline those approaches that develop a poetic perspective on film. Chapter 1 scrutinises the work of the formalist film scholars (such as Rudolf Arnheim and Sergei Eisenstein) and the realist film scholars (such as André Bazin) and looks at the particular filmic techniques they promote in their cause to define film as an art. The formalists promoted editing, montage, low and high camera angles and so on, while the realists promoted the long take and deep focus photography. This chapter also offers a brief survey of the techniques of continuity editing and film sound. Films discussed include: *The Magnificent Ambersons* (Orson Welles), *Secrets and Lies* (Mike Leigh), *Notorious* (Alfred Hitchcock), and *Jurassic Park* (Spielberg). Chapter 2 investigates the structures of narrative and narration at work in the cinema, including narrative structures such as cause-effect logic, character motivation, transformation, linear and non-linear chronology, together with restricted and omniscient narration. Films discussed include: *Psycho* (Hitchcock), *North by Northwest* (Hitchcock), *Taxi Driver* (Martin Scorsese), *Magnificent*

Obsession (Douglas Sirk) and *Pulp Fiction* (Quentin Tarantino). Chapter 3 explores the concept of the director as *auteur* (author), charting the history of this approach to films from the 1950s up to the present day. The chapter looks at the stylistic and thematic approaches to auterism and investigates the careers of two directors: Hitchcock and Wim Wenders. It can be argued that auterism is an external approach to the cinema. However, I have emphasised that auterism looks for stylistic and thematic patterns in a group of films, which therefore defines it as an internal approach.

Chapters 4 to 6 outline those approaches that develop an external perspective on film. An external perspective studies the relation between the film and particular aspects of reality outside it. This type of criticism places a film within its historical and social context. For this reason, external approaches are often called contextual criticism. Chapter 4 examines the problematic area of film genres. Genre study is both internal and external: it is internal to the extent that it attempts to identify the common intrinsic attributes of a group of films and external to the extent that it attempts to relate a film to its historical and social context, arguing that genre films manifest the basic anxieties and values of a society. This chapter examines the following genres: the melodrama (and analyses films such as Josef von Sternberg's *Blonde Venus*, John Stahl's *Only Yesterday*), the *film noir* (in particular the neo-*films noirs* of John Dahl), and the 1950s science fiction film (such as *Them!* and *Invasion of the Body Snatchers*). Chapter 5 looks at the way documentary film makers organise and structure reality. Prominence is given to the five types of documentary format: expository (in films such as *Coalface*), observational (*High School*), interactive (*Roger and Me*), reflexive (*Man With a Movie Camera*) and performative (*The Thin Blue Line*). Finally, in Chapter 6, the activity of film reviewing comes under scrutiny. Here I expose the conventions film reviewers adopt in writing about and evaluating films. As examples, reviews of *The English Patient* and *The Lost World: Jurassic Park* are closely examined.

Following each chapter you will find a list of books that have been quoted in the chapter and recommendations for further reading. This book is intended to function only as the first step in the long and enjoyable path called film studies.

Further reading

Corrigan, Timothy, *A Short Guide to Writing About Film*, Second Edition (New York: HarperCollins, 1994)
A concise and practical guide for students on how to write about films, from taking notes during screenings, to the style and structure of essay writing.

Hayward, Susan, *Key Concepts in Cinema Studies* (London and New York: Routledge, 1996)
More than a glossary, this invaluable reference book includes both shorter entries and mini-essays on the industrial, technical and theoretical concepts that currently dominate film studies.

1 FILM AESTHETICS: FORMALISM AND REALISM

> *... film had to legitimize its place in our culture. And the way that it initially set about getting itself taken seriously was to prove that it was an art – an art on a par with its seven predecessors.*
>
> **Noël Carroll**

Once we have accepted the notion that studying the cinema isn't an absurd idea, the question arises: How do we study the cinema? The cinema has been studied from a multitude of approaches. Following, and modifying, a list put together by Charles Altman, we can identify ten approaches to the cinema (the list is not exhaustive):

1. A technological history which may emphasise pioneers, such as the Lumière brothers or Edison, and/or technological innovations such as the coming of sound, the development of colour, etc.
2. A study of techniques: either historically, which asks questions such as: When was the first close-up used? or – as in this book – critically and analytically: What technical choices are available to film makers?
3. A study of personalities (studio moguls, stars, etc.).
4. Study of the relation between film and other arts, usually theatre or the novel; this type of approach was one way in which university departments of English justified their study of film in the 1960s and early 1970s.
5. A chronological history of classical or important films. Such histories canonised a small group of films (the most unusual, such as *Citizen Kane*, Orson Welles, 1941) and marginalised the majority of films from study (usually the typical or ordinary film).
6. Film in relation to society. Film can be studied in relation to important social events such as the Second World War.

7 History of Hollywood studios (including economic histories).

8 Study of directors (see Chapter 3).

9 Study of genres – either formally or as a social ritual (see Chapter 4).

10 Regulation of the film industry by means of censorship and anti-trust (or monopoly) laws; censorship is briefly discussed in Chapter 4.

This chapter focuses on point 2, a critical and analytical discussion of the technical choices available to film makers. In the first part of this chapter, we shall examine three technical choices film makes have to make. The first concerns set design, or *mise-en-scène*. The second concerns *mise-en-shot* – the way the *mise-en-scène* is filmed. Here we shall look at the long take, which is sometimes combined with deep focus photography. Finally, we shall look at editing and montage. In the second half of this chapter, we shall see how realist and formalist film scholars concentrated on these, and other, filmic techniques in their attempts to defend film as an art.

As I pointed out in the introduction, my aim here is to enable you to go beyond the informal practice of merely verbalising your personal impressions of a film. The starting point for rejecting this impressionistic talk about films is to study the basic components of the medium of film and the way these components are organised in a particular film. In the following three chapters we shall explore the stylistic and narrative dimensions of various cinemas – Hollywood studio films, independently produced American films and European cinema.

The critical and analytical study of films therefore begins with the way a film is constructed. This emphasis on a film's construction combines film practice and film aesthetics, because it analyses the choices that are made when a film is constructed, and the effects these choices have on film spectators. The aim of the first section of this book is therefore to enable you to study in an exact and orderly fashion the basic choices available to film makers, the effect making a choice has on a film's meaning and effect.

Mise-en-scène

One of the most frequently used terms in film analysis is *mise-en-scène*, which literally translates as 'putting on stage', or 'staging'. The term originates from the theatre, where it designates everything that appears on stage – set design, lighting and character movement. In film studies, *mise-en-scène* often has a vague meaning: it is either used in a very broad way to mean the filmed events together with the way those events are filmed, or it is used in a narrower sense (closer to its original theatrical meaning), to designate the filmed events. In this book the term *mise-en-scène* will be used in its narrower sense to mean what appears in front of the camera – set design, lighting and character movement. Another term will be used to name the way the filmed events, *mise-en-scène*, are filmed – namely, *mise-en-shot*, which literally means 'putting into shots' or simply 'shooting (a film)'.

Set design

If you read film credits, you may notice the category Art Director. Art directors are people who design or select the sets and decor of a film. Initially, their job was simply to create a background in which the action of the film was to unfold. In the heyday of the Hollywood studios (from the 1920s to the end of the 1950s), art directors built entire worlds inside movie studios. More recently, some art directors have become production designers, whose job is to coordinate the look of an entire film. They develop a visual concept around which sets, props, lighting and costumes are designed to work together. This is particularly important in contemporary science fiction films, in which the production designer creates a total concept and image of the future. The director Ridley Scott takes set design so seriously that he almost takes over the job of art director on some of his films (he trained as an art director). On his film *Blade Runner* (1982), for instance, he worked closely with the art department in conceiving and designing sets. Michael Deely, the film's producer, goes so far as to argue that the futuristic ambience and look of the film was essentially designed by Ridley Scott.

The production designer begins by making sketches and by building miniature sets in order to determine the best way to construct and film the actual sets. This is particularly important from a financial point of view because a film may need several – even dozens – of sets, all of which require an army of carpenters, prop buyers and so on, to construct and take down again. This is in opposition to the theatre, where only a few sets are constructed. Because of the expense, many film sets are only partly constructed. In other words, only those parts of the set that appear in the film need to be constructed.

We shall now consider the stylistic options available to art directors/set designers and the choices that two Hollywood studios made in the 1930s. These choices strongly determined the look of the films; in fact they determined the identity of the studio.

Set design in 1930s Warner Bros. films

In the 1930s, Warner Bros. produced low-budget films, many of which had a contemporary theme, since their stories were in large part inspired by newspaper stories. One of the themes that dominated American society in the 1930s was gangsterism, so it was little wonder that Warner Bros. made a number of gangster films – the most notable being *Little Caesar* (Mervyn Le Roy, 1932) and *The Public Enemy* (William Wellman, 1931). Due to Warner Bros.' policy of low-budget films, little was spent on set design. Many Warner Bros. films of the 1930s have simple, bare sets – shabby, dank rooms and bare streets (Figure 1). This economic factor largely determined the visual style of Warner Bros. films in the 1930s. But like all artists, Warner Bros. film makers made the most of this limitation and even used it to their own advantage. Directors were frequently forced to use medium shots (shots of the actors from waist to the top of their head) or close-ups (a shot of an actor's head and shoulders) so that the actors would take up most of the frame. Low-key lighting (in which only part of the set is lit) was also used in order to partly conceal the cheapness of the set and their small size. Much of the set was shrouded in darkness. Further, Warner Bros. was one of the first studios to use fog generating machines, which also served to hide the set.

Yet, these sets are consistent with the stories and the circumstances that the characters find themselves in. Many of the gangster films are about the impoverished backgrounds of the gangsters. The sets and lighting therefore add to the story's meaning – they complement the story. Although the stylistic options available to Warner Bros. film makers at this time were severely limited, they used this economic limitation to their own advantage.

MGM set design

In complete contrast to Warner Bros., MGM spent a great deal of money on sets and lighting. In fact, MGM had the biggest costume, property and art departments in Hollywood. MGM art directors created large elaborate sets, which were lit using full, high-key lighting, creating a very bright image with little or no shadows. In MGM colour films, the colours are usually saturated. MGM's philosophy was to create clear, clean images.

One problem was that the set occasionally dominated the action and the stars – think of the sets of two very famous MGM films – *The Wizard of Oz* (Victor Fleming, 1939) and *Gone With the Wind* (1939). The director Vincent Minnelli made musicals for MGM, including *Meet Me in St Louis*, which opens with a long, elaborate shot of the set of St Louis built on the MGM backlot (Figure 2). It seems imperative that, if the studio was to spend a great deal of money on the sets, then they should be lit properly and should be 'showed off' on screen, which frequently meant that the director used long shots (showing the whole actor in his or her surroundings) or very long shots (in which the actor appears small within the frame).

Mise-en-shot

Above I made the distinction between *mise-en-scène* (staging) and *mise-en-shot* (shooting, or filming). *Mise-en-scène* (in the narrow definition adopted in this book) designates the filmed events – set design, lighting, and the movement of the actors. In this sense, *mise-en-scène* refers to a stage of film production that exits prior to filming. In this narrow definition, we can clearly distinguish the filmed events from the way they are filmed. The process of filming, of translating *mise-en-scène* into film, is called *mise-en-shot*.

A major part of the art of film making involves the interaction between the filmed events (*mise-en-scène*) and the way they are filmed (*mise-en-shot*). To make a successful film, film makers need to establish a productive relation between *mise-en-scène* and *mise-en-shot*.

The main parameters of *mise-en-shot* include:

- camera position
- camera movement
- shot scale
- the duration of the single shot
- the pace of editing.

In the following pages we shall look at three options directors have in rendering a scene on film. The three options are:

- using a long take
- using deep focus photography
- using editing.

The long take

A long take is the name given to a shot of long duration. In itself, this definition is not very informative, because we have no background information with which to define 'long duration'. Fortunately, the work of the film analyst Barry Salt can help us establish this background information. Salt has calculated the average length of shots in Hollywood films across the decades. The work he carried out is extensive and detailed, and the results reveal the most common shot lengths for each decade. For example, Salt has calculated that the most common shot length in 1940s Hollywood films is 9 seconds. This means that, in a Hollywood film of the 1940s there is, on average, a change in shot every 9 seconds. What this average can define are the deviations from the norm, such as the long take. A long take refers to a shot that is significantly longer than the norm. Any shot in a Hollywood film of the 1940s that lasts significantly longer than 9 seconds is therefore a long take.

Deep focus photography

Deep focus photography keeps several planes of the shot in focus at the same time (foreground, medium ground, background), allowing several actions to be filmed at the same time. This decreases the need for editing to present these actions in separate shots.

The long take and deep focus photography are usually combined. Orson Welles was one of the most celebrated directors in 1940s Hollywood who consistently used the long take with deep focus photography. Several scenes in Welles' films *Citizen Kane* (1941) and *The Magnificent Ambersons* (1942) were filmed using the long take with deep focus. The long take plus deep focus is therefore one of the stylistic choices made by Welles.

Why did Welles make this stylistic choice? We can approach this question by considering one of the most celebrated long takes in *The Magnificent Ambersons*. Welles uses a long take with deep focus to film the parlour scene. George is seated in the left foreground of the shot while his aunt Fanny (Agnes Moorehead) feeds him huge quantities of strawberry shortcake (Figure 3). The tension of the scene is created by the fact that they are talking about Eugene, with whom aunt Fanny is in love. George's uncle Jack enters into the scene and, indirectly, makes fun of aunt Fanny's love for Eugene. Aunt Fanny runs out of the scene, crying hysterically. While all of these events are taking place, the camera remains in its same location throughout the whole scene, with only slight camera movement for reframing.

The way Welles shot this scene suggests that he was unwilling or refused to interrupt the events as they unfolded and developed. In other words, the translation of *mise-en-scène* into *mise-en-shot* is kept to a minimum. The film critic André Bazin wrote the following about this shot:

> *The refusal to move the camera throughout the scene's duration, particularly when Agnes Moorehead has her emotional crisis and rushes away (the camera keeping its nose obstinately glued to the strawberry shortcake), is tantamount to making us witness the event in the position of a man helplessly strapped to an armchair.*
>
> **André Bazin, *Orson Welles*, p. 74**

What Bazin suggests is that the static nature of the camera for a long period of time limits the spectator's involvement with the events and characters. In summary, the long take distances the spectator from the events and characters. It is as if the scene never gets beyond its establishing shot. The long take eliminates editing that would place the spectator within the action. Below we shall see how editing involves the spectator in the action.

So far, we have described the deep focus shot in predominantly negative terms. Yet there are many positive aspects to Welles' stylistic choice. Firstly, the space and time of the scene remain whole and continuous. The scene is not fragmented into several shots (that is, into several fragments of space and time). In other words, the long take observes the dramatic unities of space and time.

One of the consequences of observing the dramatic unities of space and time is that it emphasises the actor's performance. Rather than cutting a performance up into many shots, it is realised on screen uninterrupted. If the actor's performance is particularly important in a scene, the director may decide to use the long take so as not to interrupt the actor's performance as it develops.

This principle does not only hold for Hollywood films of the 1940s. Contemporary directors occasionally use the long take when they want to maintain the dramatic unities of space and time or to emphasise the actor's performance. Two recent examples: *Secrets and Lies* (Mike Leigh, 1996) and *Before Sunrise* (Richard Linklater, 1994). *Secrets and Lies* focuses on two characters: Hortense (Marianne Jean-Baptiste), as she searches for the mother she has never met, and Cynthia (Brenda Blethyn), an unhappy, working mother preoccupied and distracted with the mundane problems of everyday life. In one scene Cynthia talks to her brother Maurice on one of his infrequent visits to her. After talking about mundane matters, Cynthia is suddenly overcome by emotion and hugs her brother. They hug each other for over two minutes, which Leigh films in one take, with little camera movement (except a very slow zoom in). Leigh does not interrupt or distract from this sudden expression of repressed emotion with any marked camerawork or editing. He allows the emotion to express itself uninterrupted.

Leigh's use of the long take is more pronounced later in the film when Hortense has telephoned Cynthia, informing her that she is Cynthia's daughter and they meet in a café; Leigh films the scene in one take lasting 7 minutes 40 seconds (and, this time, with no camera movement). The drama of this scene is created by Cynthia's gradual realisation that Hortense, who is black, is her daughter (Cynthia is white). The long take then shows the desperate attempts of the two women to communicate with one another. Leigh allows these dramatic and emotional events to unfold uninterrupted; indeed, the shot is relentless and unyielding in its depiction of the two women trying to communicate with each other.

Richard Linklater employs a long take in *Before Sunrise*. An American student, Jesse, meets a French student, Celine, on a train going from Budapest to Vienna. Jesse persuades Celine to tour Vienna with him. The film charts their growing relationship during their 14 hours in Vienna. In an early scene, Linklater decides to film the two of them on a tram as they begin to get to know one another. Linklater films the scene using a long take lasting 6 minutes. The long take shows the characters' interaction as it unfolds and blossoms into friendship.

Continuity editing

In this section we shall briefly look at the techniques of continuity editing. Continuity editing refers to a series of techniques that attempt to imitate, in the cinema, the space of Renaissance painting and the proscenium space of nineteenth-century theatre. These techniques are necessary because, unlike the long take and deep focus photography, editing breaks down a scene into a multitude of shots (fragments of space and time). The techniques of continuity editing function to create a synthetic unity of space and time from these fragments. Below we shall address the reason why a film maker may want to use editing rather than the long take. But first, we shall seek an answer to the question: What are the major techniques of continuity editing and how do they work?

Continuity editing is all about coherence and orientation. If a film maker randomly stuck together a series of shots, the spectator would soon become disoriented. The separate spaces in each shot would not add up because the spectator would not be able to relate them to one another. The way shots are edited together must therefore be controlled and regulated by a series of techniques that permit the spectator to fit them together like the pieces of a puzzle. Once all the pieces of the puzzle have been fitted together, the whole picture becomes clear. When we watch a film that is made up of numerous shots, we piece the shots together in our mind to create a coherent picture. The techniques of continuity editing enable the spectator to create a coherent picture from the shots presented on screen.

I noted above that continuity editing attempts to imitate the space of Renaissance painting and the proscenium space of nineteenth-century theatre. Both of these arts attempt to create coherence and orientation, and achieve this by adopting a strategy that may sound rather obvious, but is fundamental and shouldn't be taken for granted. That is, in Renaissance painting and nineteenth-century theatre, the spectator is positioned on the same side of the scene or action. In the theatre, for example, the action takes place within a scenic space consisting of three walls, and the audience always occupy the space of the invisible fourth wall. The techniques of continuity editing create a coherent scenic space and orient the spectator so that he occupies the position of the invisible fourth wall.

In more technical terms, each film creates coherence and orients the spectator by means of the 180 degree axis of action line. David Bordwell writes that:

> *The assumption is that shots will be filmed and cut together so as to position the spectator always on the same side of the story action. Bazin suggests that the 'objective' reality of the action independent of the act of filming is analogous so that stable space of proscenium theatrical representation, in which the spectator is always positioned beyond the fourth wall. The axis of action (or center) line becomes the imaginary vector of movements, character positions, and glances in the scene, and ideally the camera should not stray over the axis.*
>
> **David Bordwell, in *The Classical Hollywood Cinema*, p. 56**

A change in shot always involves a shift in vantage point but if the axis of action line is obeyed, then screen direction will be maintained when there is a cut from one shot to another.

Other techniques that create coherence and orient the spectator include:

- the eyeline match
- point-of-view cutting
- the match on action cut, and
- directional continuity.

In the eyeline match, a character in one shot glances at something off-screen (out of the frame) and a cut reveals the object the character is looking at. The line of the character's glance has therefore matched the two shots together, creating coherence and spatial orientation.

Point of view cutting is a variant of the eyeline match. The structure is the same: a character looks off-screen – cut to – the object the character is looking at. However, what distinguishes point of view cutting is that the object is shown from the character's optical vantage point. In other words, the object is seen through the character's eyes.

Point-of-view shots are usually marked to indicate that they represent the character's optical vantage point. In a scene in *The Maltese Falcon* (John Huston, 1941), Marlowe is drugged. As he becomes dizzy, the camera takes his exact optical vantage point. The camera moves from side to side, goes out of focus and eventually fades to black. All of these filmic devices are used to represent Marlowe's (loss of) vision and consciousness.

Similarly, in *The Birds* (Hitchcock, 1963), Mitch Brenner spies Melanic Daniels in a small boat on the water of Bodega bay. He runs into his house, gets a pair of binoculars, and directs them at Melanie. As he does so, the camera cuts to a close-up of Melanie in the boat. The edge of the image is blacked out by a mask, a cinematic convention signifying a point of view shot of a character looking through binoculars.

In the match on action cut, the cut from one shot to another occurs when an action is being performed, in which the action is continued from one shot to the next. It is the continuity of the same action across the cut that creates coherence and orientation.

A related technique is that of directional continuity. If a character exits the shot from the right of the screen, he should enter the next shot from the left of the screen. In addition to creating continuity across the cut, directional continuity also maintains screen direction.

All of these techniques create an impression of a coherent scenic space, and they position the spectator on the same side of the action, creating orientation. But these techniques are popular for financial as well as aesthetic reasons. The cameras, crew and technicians remain relatively fixed on the side of the invisible fourth wall and only three walls of the set need to be built.

Editing versus the long take

In contrast to the long take and deep focus photography, editing breaks down a scene into a multitude of shots. But why would a director go to all the trouble of shifting vantage point on the event and actors and risk disorienting the spectator? One answer is that editing gives the director almost complete control over the events and actors, since the scene only comes together when the shots are edited together. One director who is particularly notable for insisting on complete control over events and actors is Alfred Hitchcock. In 1938 Hitchcock wrote:

> *... if I have to shoot a long scene continuously I always feel I am losing grip on it, from a cinematic point of view. The camera, I feel, is simply standing there,* hoping *to catch something with a visual point to it ... The screen ought to speak its own language, freshly coined, and it can't do that unless it treats an acted scene as a piece of raw material which must be broken up, taken to bits, before it can be woven into an expressive visual pattern.*
>
> ***Hitchcock on Hitchcock*, pp. 255–6**

The advantage of editing over the long take and deep focus is that, through the changes in viewpoint implied by the change of shot, the director can fully involve the spectator in the action. We can see this happen in the last scene of Hitchcock's 1946 film *Notorious*. Devlin (Cary Grant) rescues the undercover spy Alicia (Ingrid Bergman) from the house of the Nazi Alex Sebastian (Claude Rains). Alex has finally discovered that Alicia, his fiancée, is really a spy. Alicia is upstairs in her bedroom, suffering from poisoning. Devlin rescues her while Alex is in a meeting with other Nazis. Alex leaves the meeting and discovers Devlin and Alicia walking down the stairs, but he avoids intervening because otherwise Devlin will inform the other Nazis that Alicia is a spy, and that would get Alex into trouble. So Alex has to allow Devlin to take Alicia out of the house.

The action in this scene is therefore very simple: Devlin guides Alicia down the stairs and out the front door, under the gaze of the other Nazis and Alex's mother. So why does Hitchcock decide to use 57 shots in only 2 minutes 5 seconds in filming this action (from Devlin and Alicia exiting the bedroom door to them exiting the front door)? Throughout the action, Hitchcock cuts rapidly between five set-ups: Devlin and Alicia occupying the frame alone (15 shots), Alex occupying the frame alone (17 shots), Alex's mother (5 shots), Devlin, Alicia, Alex and his mother together (5 shots), and the Nazis downstairs (9 shots).

The rapid cutting swiftly moves between the five points of action, giving the spectator optimal access to the events, as well as the reaction of each character to those events as they unfold second by second.

Surprisingly, the rapid cutting does not speed up the action; instead, it emphasises the slowness of Devlin and Alicia as they descend the stairs. The rapid cutting helps to prolong the suspense (will Devlin and Alicia escape or not?). Furthermore, Devlin and Alicia are in love with one another, but they have been kept apart because of Alicia's undercover job. If they escape from Alex's house, they will be free to express their love. A lot is at stake in this scene and Hitchcock expertly uses rapid editing to emphasise the gravity of the situation.

As a footnote, it is worth mentioning that, although Hitchcock is famous for his skilful deployment of editing, he experimented with the long take in the late 1940s, in his films *Rope* (1948) and *Under Capricorn* (1949). However, during the 1950s he returned to editing as his preferred way of filming a scene. In Chapter 3 we shall discuss Hitchcock's work in much more detail.

Editing in *Jurassic Park*

As a contemporary example of editing, we shall briefly look at the opening scene of Steven Spielberg's *Jurassic Park* (1993). The main action consists of a number of park wardens releasing a dinosaur into the park. But the dinosaur manages to drag one of the wardens into its crate and kill him. This scene lasts 2 minutes 30 seconds and contains 43 shots, making an average shot length of 3 seconds (or, on average, a change in shot every 3 seconds). The function of this rapid change in shots is to involve the spectator in the two main points of action – the wardens attempting to release the dinosaur into the park and the dinosaur in the crate. In the second half of the scene, in particular, Spielberg cuts rapidly between the two points of action – that is, from both inside and outside the crate.

The first thing that the opening of *Jurassic Park* tells us is that Spielberg, like Hitchcock, relies on editing in his film-making process. This is because Spielberg's first concern is to involve the film spectator in the action, rather than focus on character psychology and the actor's performance. Spielberg stresses the importance of action and spectator involvement with that action by storyboarding his films – that is, by breaking the final shooting script down into detailed pictures representing the frames of a particular scene. These storyboards usually contain information about camera angles, camera movement, the placement of characters in the frame and so on.

Spielberg storyboards most of his films, particularly the action sequences, although he did not use story boards for *Schindler's List* (1993) for the film is (unusually for Spielberg) based on character psychology, not action sequences. Some critics argue that storyboarding stifles creativity and spontaneity, for the film's look and structure is determined in advance of the shooting. The process of making the film (*mise-en-shot*) is, according to these critics, simply a technical and mechanical exercise for Spielberg, because he has worked out everything in advance.

Summary

- *Mise-en-scène* designates what appears in front of the camera – set design, lighting and character movement.
- *Mise-en-shot* means 'putting into shots' or simply 'shooting (a film)'.
- The long take and deep focus emphasise the drama as it unfolds within the shot. These techniques create a fusion between actors and settings, allow the actor's performance to shine through, and have the potential to sustain a mood or emotion over a long period of time; however, they distance the spectator from the unfolding action.
- Editing, which consists of breaking down a scene into a multitude of shots, allows the director to fully involve the spectator in the action at the expense of breaking the film's actual spatial and temporal unity; however, a synthetic unity is restored by means of the techniques of continuity editing (which include: the axis of action line, the eyeline match, point-of-view cutting, the match on action cut and directional continuity).

Film sound

Before we leave behind this technical discussion of film aesthetics and move on to a more theoretical discussion, we can briefly review another important set of stylistic options and choices made by film makers – those concerning film sound.

The options available to film makers in the construction of sound are as rich as the options available in the construction of the image track. Here we shall look at only one – but nonetheless essential – question concerning the soundtrack: What is the source or origin of the sound? The following section will simply offer a classification of sound in the cinema; the basis for this classification is determined by the origin of the sound.

A crucial term that needs to be introduced in the discussion of sound is diegesis, which in film studies simply means the story (or narrative) world of the film.

The first term of classification is the most obvious: diegetic sound, which refers to sound whose origin is to be located in the story world. Diegetic sound includes the voice of the characters and the sound of objects that exist in the story world. This includes music made by instruments that form part of the story world (for convenience, we can refer to this type of music as screen music).

We need to distinguish external diegetic sound from internal diegetic sound. External diegetic sound has a physical origin in the story world. The examples I gave are examples of external diegetic sound. By contrast, internal diegetic sound has its origin inside a character's mind. In other words, internal diegetic sound refers to subjective sounds – either the rendition of a character's thoughts or imagined sounds. These sounds are still diegetic because they derive from the story world, but they are internal because they cannot be heard by other characters. The ending of *Psycho* (Hitchcock, 1960) is very instructive from this perspective. (*Psycho* will be analysed in some detail in Chapter 2.) Norman Bates has been arrested for killing his mother, her lover, Marion, and the detective Arbogast. Bates has now become totally psychotic, as he has taken on his mother's identity. In the police cell, we see him looking passive and hear him thinking to himself – but he is thinking to himself in his mother's voice, and talking as if he were his mother. Although spectators comprehend the technique of rendering thoughts (internal diegetic sound) as a voiceover, nonetheless, in the case of *Psycho* the spectator needs to have listened to the psychiatrist's speech in the previous scene in order to comprehend this unusual relation between image and sound, in which Norman is thinking to himself in his mother's voice.

A comical play with internal diegetic sound is to be found in the film *Dead Men Don't Wear Plaid* (Carl Reiner, 1982). The film is a spoof on *films noirs* of the 1940s (*films noirs* will be discussed in Chapter 4). The first time we see the hero, private detective Rigby Reardon (Steve Martin), he is sitting in his office. Juliet Forrest (Rachel Ward) visits and hires him to find the killer of her father. As the film progresses, Rigby falls in love with Juliet. In one scene in his office, he begins to express his love for her in voiceover (internal diegetic sound representing his thoughts). His voiceover ends: '… but how can I explain that a man in my business can't take on a wife, have a bunch of kinds', to which Rachel responds: 'We wouldn't have to have kids'. Clearly, the film is challenging – for comic effect – the convention of internal diegetic sound by suggesting that it could be external. Only the spectator should be able to share the internal thoughts of the character.

The final category of sound I shall introduce is that of non-diegetic sound, in which the origin of the sound derives from outside the story world. The music soundtrack of films is, of course, non-diegetic. In documentary films, the voice-of-God commentary (to be discussed in Chapter 5) is also non-diegetic, since the narrator does not appear in the film's story world.

Theoretical analysis of film aesthetics

In the first half of this century, film theorists attempted to justify the serious study of the cinema by arguing that it is a legitimate form of art. They set about achieving this aim by trying to identify the specific property that defines film as film – that is, that distinguishes film from the other arts.

The first school of thought to defend film as art were the formalists, such as Rudolf Arnheim and the film maker Sergei Eisenstein. For the formalists, film's specific property is its inability to perfectly imitate normal visual experience of reality. It may at first sound odd that the formalists concentrated on the limitations of film to define it as an art. But they argued that these limitations define the expressive potential of film. The limitations of film offer the film maker the opportunity to manipulate and distort our everyday experience of reality for artistic ends.

Filmic techniques such as editing, montage, fast and slow motion, the use of low and high camera angles, together with film's transformation of a three-dimensional world on to a two-dimensional surface and so on, prevent film from imitating our normal visual experience. By exploiting these limitations film makers can present a unique – a specifically filmic – vision of the world. It is this unique vision of the world, made possible by film's specific properties (editing, etc.), that distinguishes film from the others arts and define film as an art. For the formalists, film is an art because its specific properties, which prevent it from imitating reality, can be exploited by directors to express their vision. In Chapter 3 we shall see that directors who exploit the specific limitations of film for expressive purposes are conferred the prestigious title of *auteurs*.

In opposition to the formalists, the realists, such as André Bazin, Siegfried Kracauer and, more recently, Stanley Cavell, reject montage and expression in favour of film's recording capacity. They begin by arguing that, by means of its automatic mechanical recording of events, film does perfectly imitate our normal visual experience of reality. Furthermore, they argue that film's ability to imitate reality is what defines film as an art. The realists therefore identified film's specific property in its photographic representation of reality. Furthermore, they identified the long take and deep focus shots as the elements of film style that realise film's specific property. Deep focus allows for a number of actions to be composed in the same shot. By contrast, editing would present these actions one after another in separate shots. Deep focus therefore supports the use of long takes by reducing the need for editing, thereby maintaining the spatial and temporal unity of the scene.

Bazin emphasises the unrealistic nature of editing in a long footnote to his essay, 'The Virtues and Limitations of Montage' (*What is Cinema?*, vol. 1, pp. 41–52). He refers to a scene from the film *Where No Vultures Fly*. The film is about a young family who set up a game reserve in South Africa. In the scene that Bazin discusses, the young son of the family picks up a lion cub in the bush and takes it home. The lioness detects the child's scent and begins to follow him. The lioness and the child with the cub are filmed separately and the shots are simply edited together. But as the child reaches home, 'the director', write Bazin, 'abandons his montage of separate shots that has kept the protagonists apart and gives us instead parents, child and lioness all in the same full shot. The single frame in which trickery is out of the question gives immediate and retroactive authenticity to the very banal montage that preceded it'. In this particular example, the realism of the shot for Bazin is a matter of spatial unity – the fact that the child appears in the same shot as the lioness. Indeed, Bazin concludes his footnote by writing that: 'Realism here resides in the homogeneity of space'.

Film's capacity to record reality in all its movement was severely criticised by the formalists, who regarded mechanical recording to be a hindrance to film's attempt to be defined as an art. This is because, for the formalists, mechanical recording limits film to the (imperfect) imitation of reality, not to the expression of a new and unique vision of reality.

In realist aesthetics, Bazin understood that the filmed event (whether staged or not) dominates, as is evident in the use of the long take to allow the event to unfold uninterrupted. Eisenstein instead emphasised the film-making process rather than the filmed event and developed – in both theory and in his film-making practice – a tendency towards editing, or more accurately, montage. Whereas editing simply refers to the joining together of shots, montage refers to the expressive use of editing to confer symbolic and metaphorical meanings onto the filmed events. For Eisenstein, shots simply constitute the raw material of film making. From the raw material of the shots meanings are created that do not exist in the raw material.

Montage

Earlier in the chapter we discussed continuity editing, which attempts to create a coherent scenic space by means of a number of techniques: axis of action line, the eyeline match, the point-of-view shot, the match on action cut and directional continuity. In relation to montage, continuity editing is simply sequential cutting. This is because montage does not attempt to construct a coherent scenic space, but attempts to create symbolic meanings. It achieves this primarily by juxtaposing shots together, with little regard for coherent scenic space.

Eisenstein called the symbolic meanings created by montage 'associations'. Montage creates associations (symbolic meanings) that are greater than the sum of their parts. In other words, from the montage of two shots is created a chain of associations that do not exist in any of the shots.

Eisenstein explained how montage works by referring to Egyptian hieroglyphs:

> *The point is that the combination of two hieroglyphs of the simplest series is regarded not as the sum total but as their product, i.e. as*

> *a value of another dimension, another degree: each taken separately corresponds to an object but their combination corresponds to a concept. The combination of two representable objects achieves the representation of something that cannot be graphically represented.*
>
> *For example: the representation of water and of an eye signifies 'to weep'. But – this is montage!!*
>
> **Sergei Eisenstein, *Writings 1922–1934***

The crucial passage here is: 'each taken separately corresponds to an object but their combination corresponds to a concept. The combination of two representable objects achieves the representation of something that cannot be graphically represented'. Hieroglyphs and montage create abstract and symbolic meanings by juxtaposing concrete objects.

As an example, we shall look at a celebrated scene in Eisenstein's film *Battleship Potemkin* (1925). After the cossacks have massacred the people, the famous Odessa steps sequence, the Potemkin battleship fires on the headquarters of the military. This is followed by three shots of stone lions at the Alupka Palace in the Crimea. The first shot depicts a lion lying down, the second depicts a lion seated, and the third a lion standing up. (The lion is therefore used by both the realists and the formalists to put across!)

of the lions create a montage unit. In terms of the content image, we simply have: a stone lion sleeping, a stone lion tone lion standing up. Three concrete objects juxtaposed hat does it mean, and what effect does it create?

he framing of the three separate lions, Eisenstein creates the t *the same* stone lion has moved from its sleeping position up. In terms of these three shots by themselves, Eisenstein has d an abstract meaning that does not exist in each individual s of the stone lions (the raw material), when taken in isolation, representation of each lion. No shot shows a stone lion going notions of standing up. Such an action is impossible anyway. ng of the shots together creates the impression or the illusion of eing woken up. Eisenstein creates this impression purely and rough the juxtaposition of the shots – montage.

o further and consider abstract and symbolic meanings these relation to the scene that these shots interrupt. Why would

Eisenstein insert three shots in this sequence to give the impression that a stone lion is rising up? There are at least three possible answers:

- to suggest that even a stone lion would be shocked by the massacre on the Odessa steps;
- the lion could represent the Russian people who have finally risen against their oppressors;
- a clever film critic may say that the shots are modernist – they draw attention to the cinema's creation of movement from the rapid projection of still images.

This is another point about montage: the montage sequences do not contribute to the creation of a unified story world. They interrupt the story world created by continuity editing.

We can also see the principle of montage at work in the shower scene murder in Hitchcock's film *Psycho*. The scene continually cuts from Marion Crane in the shower to Norman's 'mother' wielding a knife. The shots (the raw material) do not contain images of Marion being cut or stabbed by the knife. Nonetheless, the rhythm of the cutting creates a meaning that goes beyond the literal content of the images – Marion's murder. This scene therefore illustrates Eisenstein's argument that the arrangement of shots into a rhythmic pattern is more important that the single shot just as, in music, the arrangement of notes is more important that the single note.

But the realists stressed the importance of the single shot because it maintains film's recording capacity, which is interrupted by the cut, or the transition to another shot. The realists argued that the formalists are denying film's unique capacity of mechanical recording. For the realists, the exploitation of the recording capacity of film by means of the techniques of the long take and deep focus fulfils, for the first time in the history of art, the aim of art – a life-like representation of reality.

In general terms, the formalists developed their arguments within a modernist framework (a concern with the internal structure of a medium). For the realists, the function of art is to imitate nature.

Filmic examples of these two theoretical positions have already been discussed in the first part of this chapter. But now, hopefully, the significance of the filmic techniques championed by each side – deep focus and the long take in the case of the realists, editing, montage, etc. in the case of the formalists – are more apparent. Furthermore, I have no intention of favouring either the formalists or the realists. Both have put forward strong and cogent arguments and the reader may wish to read the original books, that present each side of the argument, to get a more informed view. However, it may be worthwhile mentioning that both sides have decided to argue that film has only one function and both have emphasised that this function can be achieved only through a limited number of filmic techniques. By considering both arguments, we can see that film performs both functions. A film can be made using the unified, unedited space of the long take, or with the synthetic, constructed space of montage. Film records as well as distorts.

Summary

- The formalists, such as Rudolf Arnheim and the film maker Sergei Eisenstein, defended film as art; they argued that the limitations of the filmic medium enabled film makers to manipulate and distort everyday experience of reality for artistic ends.
- By contrast, the realists, such as André Bazin, Siegfried Kracauer and Stanley Cavell, promote film's recording capacity; they argue that, by means of its automatic mechanical recording of events, film does perfectly imitate our normal visual experience of reality and it is this unique quality of film that makes it an art.
- The formalists favour filmic techniques such as editing, montage, fast and slow motion, and the use of low and high camera angles.
- The realists favour filmic techniques such as the long take and deep focus photography.

Further reading

Altman, Charles, 'Towards a Historiography of American Film', *Cinema Journal*, 16, 2 (1977), pp.1–25
An invaluable outline of various approaches that have been adopted in film studies (I have modified Altman's list in the opening of this chapter).

Andrew, Dudley, *The Major Film Theories* (New York: Oxford University Press, 1976)
This book is still the most accessible introduction to the work of the formalists (Hugo Münsterberg, Rudolf Arnheim, Sergei Eisenstein, Bela Balazs), the realists (Siegfried Kracauer, André Bazin) as well as the film theories of Jean Mitry, Christian Metz, Amédée Ayfre and Henri Agel.

Arnheim, Rudolf, *Film as Art* (London: Faber and Faber, 1958)
Arnheim's formalist statement on film art.

Bazin, André, *What is Cinema?*, 2 volumes (Berkeley: University of California Press, 1967, 1971)
Bazin's seminal collection of essays that defend a realist film aesthetic.

Bazin, André, *Orson Welles: A Critical View* (California: Acrobat Books, 1991)
A concise and lucid analysis of Welles' early films. For me, this book contains Bazin's clearest defence of the techniques of the long take and deep focus.

Bordwell, David, Janet Staiger and Kristin Thompson, *The Classical Hollywood Cinema: Film Style and Mode of Production to 1960* (London: Routledge, 1985)
The undisputed, authoritative heavy weight study of classical Hollywood cinema, covering the history of film style, technology and mode of production.

Eisenstein, Sergei, *Writings, volume 1: 1922–1934* ed. and trans. Richard Taylor (London: British Film Institute, 1988)
The first of three authoritative volumes of Eisenstein's collected essays.

Salt, Barry, *Film Style and Technology: History and Analysis*, 2nd edition (London: Starword, 1992)
The research carried out for this book is phenomenal and simply overwhelming. Salt has analysed literally thousands of films shot by shot from each decade of the cinema, noting the stylistic parameters of each shot and scene and representing this information statistically (including bar charts of shot scales of individual films). The book is also packed with information on the history of film technology.

2 FILM STRUCTURE: NARRATIVE AND NARRATION

... narrative is a way of organizing spatial and temporal data into a cause-effect chain of events with a beginning, middle, and end that embodies a judgement about the nature of the events.
Edward Branigan, *Narrative Comprehension and Film*, p. 3

The filmic techniques studied in Chapter 1 make up the micro (or small scale) properties of a film's structure. In this chapter we shall examine the macro (or large scale) properties of a film's structure. These macro structures fall into two main categories – narrative and narration. These structures will be defined and illustrated in relation to both classical and contemporary Hollywood films. Finally, the chapter will end with an analysis of the unusual narrative structure of *Pulp Fiction* (Quentin Tarantino, 1994).

The concept of 'narrative' refers to what happens or what is depicted in films (as well as novels), and 'narration' refers to how that narrative is presented to the film spectator (or reader of a novel). So 'narrative' refers to actions, events and characters, whereas 'narration' describes a mechanism that controls how the spectator gains information about those actions, events and characters. Below we shall look at narration. But first, a description of what is meant by narrative.

Narrative structure

A narrative does not consist of a random series of events, but a series of events related to one another in terms of cause and effect. If a film is based on narrative logic, an event on screen will be caused by a previous event: event B happens *because of* event A.

For example: A man in shot A points a gun in an off-screen direction and fires. In shot B another man is shown collapsing to the ground. Because of the way the shots are edited together (shot B immediately following shot A), the spectator reads the event in shot A as the cause of the event in shot B.

The causal link between the two shots can be illustrated by reversing their order: shot B, of the man collapsing, followed by shot A, of another man firing a gun. The logic of the two shots is incomprehensible to the extent that the spectator cannot understand the event of the man collapsing as being caused by the event of the man shooting the gun.

Scenes as well as shots are also linked together by a cause-effect narrative logic. We can see this by looking at the first three scenes of Alfred Hitchcock's film *Psycho* (1960). First, a partial synopsis of the film. *Psycho* begins by narrating the story of Marion Crane (Janet Leigh). She is first shown in a seedy hotel room with her lover, Sam. They talk about getting married, but Sam has no money. Sam goes to the airport and Marion returns to her workplace (a real estate office), where she works as a secretary. Her boss asks her to deposit $40,000 into the bank. She leaves the office and then goes home, where she packs and drives out of town. One night she stops to rest at the Bates' motel....

> **Scene 1**. The first scene, Marion and Sam in a seedy hotel room during lunch break, establishes a problem: Marion and Sam cannot be married because he has no money (he is not financially independent and so cannot support a wife).
>
> **Scene 2**. The second scene, of Marion returning to work, develops the theme of marriage further. The spectator learns that Marion's boss, George Lowery (who deals in real estate) is lunching with a wealthy man, Tom Cassidy. Cassidy's daughter is to be married the following day, so he visits the office to buy a property as a wedding gift for his daughter. Cassidy hands over $40,000 in cash and Lowery asks Marion to take it to the bank. She asks Lowery if she can go home afterwards, since she has a headache and wants to sleep it off.
>
> **Scene 3**. The third scene opens with Marion in her apartment. When she turns her back to the camera, the camera dollies in to an envelope on the bed and the spectator sees that it contains the $40,000. The camera then pans right to show a suitcase, which Marion is in the process of packing. In a matter of seconds, this scene (within the context of scenes 1 and 2), establishes Marion's motives: she is going to steal the money and leave town (Figure 4).

The cause-effect logic in these three scenes is very tightly constructed. One of the most fruitful ways to analyse cause-effect logic in narrative film is to imagine the scenes in a different order. For example, if *Psycho* began with scene 3, a sense of mystery would be created, because we would not have sufficient information to understand Marion's motives. Beginning the film with scene 3 is certainly plausible, but would it be logical? It would certainly raise many questions in the spectator's mind: for example, whose money is this and what is this woman going to do with it? However, in the actual film, scene 3 is an *effect* of the previous two scenes (just as shot B in the hypothetical example above is an effect of shot A).

A lack is established in scene 1 – Sam's and Marion's lack of money; a surplus is established in scene 2 – Cassidy hands over $40,000 in cash. Its surplus status is emphasised throughout the scene: Cassidy stresses that he only carries as much money as he can afford to lose, and that he is rich because he doesn't pay taxes. Scene 3 then neatly ties up the lack and surplus – Marion steals the money.

The film only presents information relevant to is cause-effect logic. After all, is it a coincidence that the $40,000 is presented in the scene immediately after Sam and Marion talk about their inability to get married because of their lack of money? Is it a coincidence that Cassidy pays cash? And is it a coincidence that the money just happens to be for a wedding present? We can also ask other questions, such as: Is it a coincidence that the first three scenes directly follow on from one another? Why don't we see Sam leaving the hotel room and going to the airport? And why don't we see Lowery and Cassidy eating lunch?

By asking these questions, we begin to make explicit the film's cause-effect logic. The last two events just mentioned are left out because they are not relevant to the film's cause-effect logic, since they would not cause any effects in subsequent parts of the film. At the end of scene 1 we see Marion closing the door of the hotel room. Scene 2 begins with her entering the office. All extraneous information is simply eliminated (although we see the director, Hitchcock, standing on the sidewalk just outside the office – how relevant is this to the film's cause-effect logic?!).

As with the transition from scene 1 to scene 2, Marion's journey from the office to her apartment (via the bank?) is eliminated between scenes 2 and 3. In scene 2 Marion claims that she will go to the bank and then go home. Because, in scene 3, we see her at home, we initially assume that she has already gone to the bank. However, we soon have to revise our assumption, since the camera then shows the money on Marion's bed. Here the ellipsis between scenes 2 and 3 is significant to the cause-effect logic of the film, whereas the ellipsis between scenes 1 and 2 is insignificant.

Not all shots and scenes in narrative films are linked by causal logic. We can imagine a shot of a man walking a dog followed by a close-up shot of the dog. If the shots are reversed, the meaning is still the same, since there is no causal logic linking these two shots. Such shots can be characterised as being descriptive, rather than narrative. It is common for most narrative films to contain moments of description. Indeed, the opening of *Psycho* contains several shots of the skyline of Phoenix, Arizona, which are descriptive because they simply aim to describe the space in which the narrative events are to unfold. However, the dominant structure that holds a narrative film together (including *Psycho*) is still causal logic.

In summary, for a film to appear coherent and meaningful, the relations between its actions and events need to be motivated. In narrative films, this motivation is supplied by the cause-effect logic.

But we need to go further than discussing narrative films in terms of cause and effect. Narrative development is dependent on the way in which the cause-effect logic is worked out in relation to the film's character (or characters), who motivates that cause-effect logic. This point can be made by referring to Hitchcock's 1959 film *North by Northwest* (which will also be discussed in my analysis of narration). First, I shall simply outline the rather complicated series of events contained in the film.

After a hard day's work, Roger Thornhill (played by Cary Grant), a Madison Avenue advertising man, goes to the bar of the Plaza Hotel to meet a couple of friends. He decides to send a telegram to his mother to cancel their night out at the theatre. But, as he calls the bell boy, he is mistaken by spies for the CIA agent George Kaplan. The spies kidnap Thornhill and take him to the head of the spy-ring, Vandamm (played by James Mason). Thornhill manages to escape from Vandamm and begins searching the Plaza Hotel for George Kaplan. But Thornhill, pursued by the spies, is implicated in the murder of a UN delegate (who was in fact murdered by the spy-ring). Wanted by both spies and police, Thornhill catches a train to Chicago. On the train he is assisted in his escape by a stranger on the train, Eve Kendall (Eve Marie-Saint), who hides Thornhill in her bathroom when the porter arrives, and in the top bunk of her sleeping compartment when the police search the train. But the film spectator discovers that Eve is Vandamm's mistress and, once the train arrives at Chicago, she sends Thornhill into a trap – the famous 'crop-duster' sequence. Eve has supposedly contacted Kaplan and has sent Thornhill to meet him in desolate farm country. But, once Thornhill has reached the arranged location, he is pursued by a crop-dusting plane which almost kills him. He manages to escape and tracks down Eve at the Ambassador Hotel. After confronting Eve, Thornhill follows her to an auction room, where he finds her with Vandamm. Vandamm's men attempt to seize Thornhill but he saves himself by creating a disturbance at the auction and getting himself arrested by the police. It is at this point in the film that the CIA 'Professor' who created the decoy agent intervenes. At Chicago airport he informs Thornhill that Eve is the real CIA agent and that Kaplan is a non-existent decoy. Because Eve is in danger, Thornhill continues playing Kaplan in order to divert suspicion from Eve. The film then shifts to Mount Rushmore, where the caféteria becomes the stage of a mock killing, in which Eve 'shoots' Thornhill in order to regain Vandamm's trust. Eve then flees from the police and Thornhill is driven away in an ambulance. In a nearby wood, Eve and Thornhill meet up briefly and declare their love for one another. (It is only at this point in the film that Thornhill meets the 'real' Eve.) Eve then returns to Vandamm, who later discovers her real identity. She is rescued by Thornhill and they escape across the stone faces of the presidents on Mount Rushmore. They are finally reconciled as a married couple after Vandamm is defeated.

Thornhill motivates the film's cause-effect logic, since he must prove his innocence by finding George Kaplan. The forward momentum of the film is therefore driven by the needs and wishes of Thornhill. The resolution of these needs and wishes give the film a strong sense of closure, for Thornhill not only proves that he is the wrong man, but he also manages to expose Vandamm's spy ring and find a wife at the same time!

As this description of *North by Northwest* implies, narrative does not simply consist of a series of events linked together in a causal chain motivated by characters. Narratives are also structured into three stages: a beginning (Thornhill meeting his friends in the bar of the Plaza Hotel), a middle (mistaken for Kaplan leads to Thornhill's kidnapping and to his subsequent adventures) and an end (Thornhill's successful attempt to prove his innocence, expose Vandamm and marry Eve).

The narrative theorist Tzvetan Todorov also describes narratives in terms of three stages:

- a state of equilibrium
- the disruption of this equilibrium by an event
- the successful attempt to restore the equilibrium.

Here narrative is not defined as a linear structure, but as circular. An initial state of affairs is introduced and is then disrupted. The narrative is then driven by attempts to restore the equilibrium, which is finally achieved at the end. However, the equilibrium achieved at the end is not identical to the initial equilibrium. As Todorov argues, narrative involves a transformation. In *North by Northwest*, it is primarily Thornhill who goes through a transformation. At the beginning of the film he is an unmarried advertising man planning to go to the theatre with his mother. But by the end of the film he is a married advertising man. This transformation is brought about by his temporary loss of identity (he is mistaken for a CIA agent and taken out of his everyday lifestyle by kidnappers). The middle part of the narrative has therefore caused Thornhill's transformation.

We can characterise the middle part of the narrative as the narrative's liminal (or transitional) period, which means that it takes place outside of established (or 'normal') social events. The liminal period of a narrative therefore depicts transgressive events, events that exist outside of normal social events, whereas the initial and final equilibrium stages of the narrative represent social normality.

The concept of liminality can clearly be applied to *North by Northwest*. The film begins with the everyday routines of Roger Thornhill. He is then literally taken out of his everyday routines by the kidnappers, whereby he loses his identity (the kidnapping therefore signals the beginning of the film's liminal period). It is only when Vandamm is arrested that Thornhill can regain his true identity and return to his original routines – but with a new wife.

David Lynch's independently produced American film *Blue Velvet* (1986) parodies this three-fold narrative structure. It begins with an excessively picturesque series of shots of small town America; a simplistic, naive and innocent environment. However, underneath this chocolate box image, there is a terrifying world of horror, violence and evil. The film depicts the journey of Jeffrey Beaumont (played by Kyle MacLachlan) from this picturesque environment to the underworld, and back again. In the liminal space of the film's underworld, Jeffrey confronts Frank Booth (played by Dennis Hopper), the incarnation of evil, whom Jeffrey has to confront and defeat in order to return to the light of day. With the help of Sandy (Laura Dern), Jeffrey manages to defeat Frank, which then enables Jeffrey to return to the world of innocence. As with the opening scene, this world is presented in an excessively idealistic way, a parodic image of normality (or established social events). As with Roger Thornhill in *North by Northwest*, Jeffrey has been transformed, for he has found himself a partner, Sandy, as a 'reward' for his journey into, and successful emergence from, the underworld.

Psycho is notable for not conforming to this three-fold narrative structure because the main character, Marion, is killed a third of the way through the film. (She therefore goes through a radical transformation.) However, her act of stealing the money marks the beginning of the film's liminal period. After Marion is murdered, Norman Bates then becomes the film's dominant character. The film's liminal period comes to an end when he is arrested for the murder of Marion (as well as his mother).

Finally, a few words about the actual arrangement of the narrative events. Most narratives are linear and chronological, because they present events in the order in which they happen. This applies equally to the two Hitchcock films discussed above – *Psycho* and *North by Northwest*. However, a film that, for instance, contains a flashback does not have a chronological narrative, because the narrative events are not presented in a linear order. By rearranging the narrative events in a non-linear order, flashbacks upset a film's cause-effect logic. Flashbacks are evident in *films noirs* (such as *Mildred Pierce* and *Double Indemnity*) and are one of the main devices that create the complex and convoluted narratives that are typical of *film noir*. (*Film noir* will be discussed in Chapter 4). If we return to the discussion of *Psycho*, where I talked about beginning the film with scene 3, it is possible to imagine that, when Marion drives out of town with the money, scenes 1 and 2 could appear on screen in the form of flashbacks. These two scenes would then supply the cause of Marion's actions. At the end of this chapter we shall look at the complex and convoluted narrative structure of *Pulp Fiction*.

Summary

So far we have established that:

- A narrative is a series of events related to one another in terms of a cause-effect logic.
- The cause-effect narrative logic is motivated by the needs and wishes of characters.
- Narratives are structured in terms of a beginning (the initial state of equilibrium), a middle (disruption of the equilibrium) and an end (restoration of equilibrium).

- The progression from initial equilibrium to the restoration of equilibrium always involves a transformation (usually of the film's main character).
- The middle period of a narrative can be called liminal because it depicts actions that transgress everyday habits and routines.
- Narrative events are not necessarily presented in a linear, chronological order.

We shall now move on to discuss how narratives are conveyed to the spectator.

Restricted and omniscient narration

The term 'narration' refers to a mechanism that determines how narrative information is conveyed to the film spectator. Here I shall discuss how narrative information is conveyed to the spectator by means of two modes of filmic narration – omniscient narration and restricted narration.

Restricted narration ties the representation of film narrative to one particular character only. The spectator only experiences those parts of the narrative that this one particular character experiences. We can therefore think of restricted narration as a 'filter' or barrier that only allows the spectator limited access to the narrative events. This type of narration is typical in detective films such as *The Big Sleep* (discussed below), in which the camera is tied to the detective throughout the whole film. In omniscient narration, on the other hand, the camera is more free to jump from one character to another so that the spectator can gain more information than any one character. Omniscient narration is therefore more like the view from a large window, which allows the spectator a panoramic view of the narrative events. Omniscient narration is typical in melodramas. However, many films (such as *North by Northwest*) combine restricted and omniscient narration.

Furthermore, these types of narration produce a particular response in the spectator. In restricted narration, the spectator only knows as much as one character, resulting in mystery. In omniscient narration, the spectator knows more than the characters, resulting in suspense.

A good illustration of these different spectator responses can be found in an example given by Hitchcock in his famous interview with François Truffaut

(*Hitchcock* by François Truffaut, p. 52). In this interview Hitchcock gave the example of a bomb placed in a briefcase under a table. If the spectator knows about the bomb and the characters around the table do not, then the spectator, placed in an omniscient position in relation to those characters, will feel suspense as he or she anxiously waits for the bomb to explode or to be discovered. But if the spectator is not privileged over the characters' knowledge, then the spectator, like the characters, is in for a shock. In this second example, the scene is governed by restricted narration.

In omniscient narration, the spectator is implicated in a fantasy of 'all-seeingness', where he or she can imagine seeing everything of importance in the narrative. At certain moments in the film, the camera disengages itself from one character and begins to follow another character, which means that the spectator gains more information about the narrative than any of the characters. This results in suspense because it manipulates the spectator's expectations as to how a character will react to a particular piece of information that the spectator already knows about, but which the character does not yet know about.

Restricted narration involves the spectator in the narrative in a different way. Because the camera is usually linked to a single character, then we only know as much as that character. This results in mystery because the spectator, like the character we are following, does not know what will happen next. In detective films, in which the camera follows the detective around the narrative world attempting to uncover the motives of a crime, these motives are hidden equally from the spectator and character by the restricted narration.

We shall now see how restricted narration structures Howard Hawks' 1946 film *The Big Sleep*, Martin Scorsese's 1976 film *Taxi Driver*, see how *North by Northwest* mixes restricted and omniscient narration and, finally, see how omniscient narration predominates in Douglas Sirk's melodrama *Magnificent Obsession* (1955).

Restricted narration in *The Big Sleep*

In *The Big Sleep*, Marlowe (Humphrey Bogart) is hired by General Sternwood to follow a man called Geiger because he is blackmailing Sternwood's younger daughter, Carmen. Marlowe follows Geiger to his home but remains outside in his car. As he waits, another car pulls up and the driver goes into Geiger's house. Marlowe looks in the car and finds out that it belongs to Carmen. Nothing much happens afterwards, so Marlowe rests. Then he hears a scream and sees a flash of light coming from Geiger's house. As he approaches Geiger's house, Marlowe hears gunshots, footsteps as someone exits the house via the back door, and sees two cars pull away. Marlowe enters Geiger's house and finds Geiger dead on the floor and Carmen drunk. He also finds an empty camera and a book written in code. Marlowe takes Carmen home....

What is significant about *The Big Sleep* in terms of narration is that it strictly adheres to restricted narration – that is, the camera is always tied to Marlowe, so the spectator only finds out what happens in the narrative when Marlowe does. For example, while waiting outside Geiger's house, Marlowe sees a car pull up outside. He hides in his car so as not to be seen. Interestingly, the camera remains outside the car and shows a figure get out of the other car and enter Geiger's house. Yet, the figure remains in shadow. So, even though the camera does not directly imitate Marlowe's point of view as he hides in the car, it does not privilege the spectator either. The spectator does not know who got out of the car and neither does Marlowe. It is only when Marlowe goes to inspect the car that he and the spectator find out at the same time that the car belongs to Carmen.

The spectator hears the scream and sees the flash of light at the same time as Marlowe does. We are not privileged into knowing who screamed (although both we and Marlowe can guess that it was Carmen) and we don't know what the flash of light represents. As Marlowe approaches Geiger's house, he hears someone leaving via the back door. He does not see who it is, so neither do we. However, we do see a shot of the feet of the person leaving. This is an aural point of view shot. It would have been easy for the director to have shown the whole figure (we later find out that it was Sternwood's chauffeur, Owen Taylor; he was followed by Joe Brody in the second car). But if the film had revealed the identify of Owen Taylor (and Joe Brody), this would have violated the film's adherence to restricted narration.

Inside Geiger's house Marlowe attempts to find out what happened. Again, the spectator closely shadows him, and discovers what happens only when Marlowe does. This analysis of a segment from *The Big Sleep* therefore illustrates the film's strict adherence to restricted narration.

Restricted narration in *Taxi Driver*

Taxi Driver narrates the story of Travis Bickle (played by Robert de Niro). An ex-marine, he is unable to sleep at nights, so he gets a job as a night time taxi driver. He begins to date Betsy (Cybill Shepherd), who works in the presidential campaign office of Charles Pallatine. But after Travis takes Betsy to a porn film, they split up. Travis's increasing paranoia (brought on by a multitude of causes) leads him to buy an arsenal of weapons. He meets a young prostitute, Iris (Jodie Foster), and decides that his mission in life is to save her. At first, Travis decides to assassinate Charles Pallantine, but his attempt is thwarted. The climax of the film consists of Travis shooting and killing Iris's pimp, Matthew (Harvey Keitel), and several other men associated with him. Travis is himself wounded in this massacre, attempts to shoot himself but runs out of bullets. The end of the film shows that the media has treated Travis as a hero, because he saved Iris and returned her to her parents. In the last scene, Travis picks up Betsy in his cab but they fail to communicate with one another. Travis drops off Betsy at her destination and drives off alone.

A few words about the narrative structure of *Taxi Driver* before proceeding to analyse its narration. The narrative is motivated by Travis's attempts to find meaning in his life. This attempt leads him briefly to Betsy, but when their relationship breaks up, Travis quickly descends into paranoia and the underworld of New York city (the transition from initial equilibrium to disequilibrium is not clearly marked, but takes place very gradually). The shootout marks the violent end to the disequilibrium period of the narrative, leading to a new equilibrium, marked by the transformation of Iris. However, Travis is not transformed by his journey into paranoia and into New York's underworld. He remains the same insomniac unable to communicate with people.

Taxi Driver is based almost exclusively on restricted narration. This means that the flow of narrative information is filtered through a single character. Travis Bickle acts as the film's dominant character, the narrative agent who determines the flow of narrative information to the spectator.

The almost obsessive attachment of the camera to Travis means that spectators gain a very limited perspective on the narrative world. This attachment of the camera to Travis is clearly signified in the film's credit sequence, in which three shots of New York city as seen through a car windscreen are framed by two close-up shots of two eyes (presumably Travis's) looking off-screen.

Furthermore, this positioning of Travis as dominant character is strengthened in the first three scenes of the film. Scene 1 opens with a shot of a glass office door with the words **DEPENDABLE TAXI SERVICE** printed on it, through which we see a man sitting behind a desk. Within a second of this shot appearing on screen, a man enters screen right and physically dominates the frame, even though he has his back to the camera. On his back is written the name 'Bickle. T'. As he walks through the door, the camera moves with him. In other words, the camera has attached itself to Travis's movement. The camera then moves round to focus on Travis's face, thus linking name and face in the same shot. This opening shot also links together the words 'Bickle' and 'dependable', an ironic commentary when we realise how highly unstable and unbalanced Travis is.

In this opening shot, it is as if the camera is 'waiting' for someone (anyone) to approach and enter this door; whoever does so becomes the film's dominant character. This process of looking for a dominant character is common to the opening of most narrative films, but the seeming randomness of this process was turned into an art form by Hitchcock. In the opening of *North by Northwest*, for example, the camera wanders through a busy rush-hour crowd before finally attaching itself to Roger Thornhill. And, in the opening of *Psycho*, the camera pans across the skyline of Phoenix and gradually moves towards a hotel; it seems to randomly pick one hotel room window, penetrate it and find its dominant character in the form of Marion Crane.

But back to *Taxi Driver*. The first three scenes are based on concentrated exposition, which is to say that their function is to provide in condensed form background information about the film's dominant character. The man behind the desk interviews Travis for the job of a taxi driver. From his questions the spectator comes to understand Travis's motivation for wanting to work nights as a cab driver, about his honourable discharge from the marines, his age, lack of education and so on.

The final three shots of this scene consist of Travis walking out of the office, through the cab station and into the street. None of these shots provides additional narrative information about Travis; instead, their aim is indirect, to provide atmosphere, and to set the scene in which the film is to unfold. Furthermore, this gives Scorsese the opportunity to play with film style. As Travis walks out of the office, he looks towards the taxis and then walks off-screen right. The camera then pans left across the garage and stops at the entrance, by which time Travis has re-entered screen space, this time from the left. In other words, he has walked behind the camera.

This use of the space behind the camera is an unusual practice because, as we saw in Chapter 1, narrative film attempts to imitate the space of Renaissance painting and the proscenium space of nineteenth-century theatre. The rules of continuity editing aim to position the spectator in the cinema in a similar way in which the spectator is positioned in theatre – on the side of the invisible fourth wall.

However, in the shot under discussion, Scorsese breaks this rule by allowing Travis to briefly occupy the imaginary space occupied by spectators. This stylistic trick (which is also evident in the films of Ernst Lubitsch and Carl Dreyer) is repeated again, when Travis returns his taxi to the garage after his first night. The taxi is driven behind the camera, rather than in front, as would be usual in order to maintain the proscenium space of theatre and Renaissance painting.

The second scene of *Taxi Driver*, depicting Travis in his apartment, consists of one shot – a slow panning shot which functions to describe his domestic space (hence the shot is expositional). Furthermore, this shot is accompanied by Travis's voiceover, which serves to strengthen his role as dominant character. As we shall see in more detail below, this shot is repeated in the film's penultimate scene. This time it pans across the wall of Travis's apartment, upon which is pinned a series of newspaper articles defining him as a hero and a letter from Iris's parents, thanking him for returning their daughter. Travis's voiceover in scene 2 is now replaced by the voice of the father. Like Rupert Pupkin in Scorsese's *The King of Comedy*, Travis has attained recognition through controversial means.

The third scene then re-establishes one of the film's internal norms – point of view shots of New York at night from the perspective of Travis in his taxi. These shots, as with the last three shots of scene 1, serve to set the scene in which the narrative is to be played out and are immediately given meaning by the continuation of Travis's voiceover offering a negative evaluation of what is shown on screen. This serves further to define Travis's contradictory character – contradictory because he is at once fascinated and reviled by the low life on New York's streets.

The windscreen of Travis's taxi, the use of camera movement and placement, together with Travis's voiceover, mark the narration as restricted. It could be argued that some scenes are not focused around Travis (in other words, that the film does rely on moments of omniscient narration after all). The first scene that may conform to this reading occurs in Charles Pallantine's campaign office, which consists of Betsy talking to a fellow worker, Tom. However, as the scene begins to draw to a close, Betsy notices Travis sitting in his cab staring at her. We then retrospectively read this scene as being focused around Travis. Travis may not be able to hear what Tom and Betsy are talking about, but the scene is nonetheless based on his visual experience.

Another scene in *Taxi Driver* that could more legitimately be defined as beyond Travis's awareness is the scene in Matthew's apartment, where he attempts to convince Iris that he loves her. However, this scene begins with Travis outside the apartment sitting in his cab, looking off-screen. The implication here is that Travis is well aware of the events going on in the apartment.

Another shot we need to consider in terms of restricted narration is the penultimate scene of the film, already mentioned above. Here, the camera pans across the wall of Travis's apartment, showing the newspaper clippings and a letter from Iris's parents. Travis is not present in the apartment, so the camera movement is not determined by his awareness at this moment in time. The shot is therefore not focused around Travis, although it doesn't offer the spectator any information Travis is not already aware of. Instead, it functions as a new expositional scene, informing the spectator (with some surprise) what happened to Travis after the shoot out. The film reached its climax with the shoot out so we have now reached a new equilibrium.

However, in the shoot out, there are a few seconds of omniscient narration, as a man is seen coming out of Iris's room. The spectator sees him come out of the room and shoot Travis in the shoulder. Furthermore, once the massacre is over, the camera pans over the scene of the carnage. With the exception of these few shots, it is possible to argue that the rest of *Taxi Driver* is structured on restricted narration.

As this analysis of *Taxi Driver* shows, it is very difficult for any film to rigidly adhere to restricted narration, that is, tie itself exclusively to the experiences of the dominant character. However, in *Lady in the Lake* (Robert Montgomery, 1946), virtually the whole film's narrative is constructed around the point of view (POV) of the detective:

Edward Branigan has described the effects this has on the film:

> *For most of the 103 minutes,* [Lady in the Lake] *appears to be an elaborate POV shot from the private eye of detective Phillip Marlowe (played by Robert Montgomery). Characters look*

directly into the camera when speaking to Marlowe. At various times we see Marlowe's arms and feet at the edges of the frame; we see his shadow, smoke from his cigarette, his image in mirrors; we see extreme close-ups of a telephone receiver as he talks, lips approaching for a kiss, an on-rushing fist approaching for a knock-out blow. The camera sways as Marlowe walks, shakes when he is slapped, loses focus when liquor is splashed in his eyes, and black out when his eyes close for a kiss and when he's knocked out.

Edward Branigan, *Narrative Comprehension and Film*, p. 142

These shots are only interrupted by shots of Marlowe sitting at a desk and speaking directly to the camera about the events being shown. The overall effect is one of artificiality and claustrophobia.

Restricted and omniscient narration in *North by Northwest*

We shall now see how *North by Northwest* uses omniscient narration at strategic points in order to manipulate the spectator's engagement with the narrative. At specific moments in the film, the camera disengages itself from its dominant character, Roger Thornhill, in order to give the spectator some additional information about the narrative that Thornhill does not possess.

Narration does not become omniscient in haphazard fashion; rather, it does so only at specific moments in the narrative. There are several significant moments when the narration becomes omniscient in *North by Northwest*. (Remember that omniscient moments are those which lie outside Thornhill's span of awareness; sometimes it may be a single shot, sometimes an entire scene).

- The first omniscient moment is in the bar of the Plaza Hotel, when Thornhill attracts the attention of the page boy who is paging George Kaplan. The camera quite suddenly and dramatically disengages itself from Thornhill and the group of men he is drinking with to show the two kidnappers. The spectator then sees, from the kidnapper's point of view, the page boy walk up to Thornhill. The kidnappers then wrongly infer that Thornhill is Kaplan.
- The second moment is when Thornhill, his mother and the police go to the house where Thornhill said he was taken, to

check up on his story about the kidnapping. As this group drive away from the house, the camera remains behind and pans left to reveal a gardener, who is in fact one of the kidnappers.

- The third moment is in the public lounge in the UN building, when the camera cuts from Thornhill to the same kidnapper.
- So far, these examples refer to single shots which are inserted into scenes constructed around restricted narration. But the fourth example of omniscient narration refers to an entire scene, in which the CIA professor explains to his colleagues that Kaplan is a non-existent decoy agent (although he is in fact indirectly explaining to the spectator who Kaplan is). This scene comes between the shot of Thornhill escaping from the UN and his arrival at New York Central Station. In other words, the scene 'interrupts' Thornhill's escape, for we can easily imagine the scene at the train station directly following on from his escape from the UN.
- The fifth major moment of omniscient narration is when a cashier at the train station looks at a news photo of Thornhill and then telephones the police. But in this instance, Thornhill has guessed the additional information that the spectator is privileged to see, for Thornhill turns away from the window before the cashier returns.
- The next moment occurs on the train, when Thornhill meets Eve. In Eve's compartment, Thornhill hides in the washroom while the porter makes up the bed. The camera remains with Thornhill in the washroom. But afterwards, we see the porter carrying a message to Vandamm. Here, the narration has become omniscient, for the camera has disengaged from Thornhill in order to provide the spectator with additional information – namely, that Eve is working with Vandamm. Yet the narration is not being completely omniscient – at this stage in the film, it does not reveal the true identity of Eve (a CIA agent).

There are a few other moments of omniscient narration – when Eve telephones Leonard (Vandamm's right-hand man) at Chicago train station when Thornhill is, again, in the washroom having a shave; there are two shots of the professor at the auction and, finally, the shots of Eve and Vandamm walking towards the plane near the end of the film while Thornhill is still in the house.

These are the major moments in the film when omniscient narration dominates. Their primary aim is to create suspense; they create suspense because the spectator knows more than Thornhill, and is anticipating how Thornhill will react to this situation.

Omniscient narration in *Magnificent Obsession*

In opposition to restricted narration, a film based predominantly on omniscient narration presents the spectator with a wide breadth of narrative information. This is achieved by the narration shifting from one character to another, so that narrative information is conveyed to the spectator from many sources. This type of narration is commonly used in melodramas and television soap operas, in order to create a discrepancy in knowledge between the spectator and characters.

Like the moments of omniscient narration in *North by Northwest*, the spectator of melodrama is presented with more narrative information than any one character can possibly know. However, unlike melodrama, *North by Northwest* is not based on the systematic use of omniscient narration. The purpose of systematically employing omniscient narration in melodrama and television soap operas is to create a plethora of dramatic scenes where characters find out what the spectator already knows.

To illustrate how omniscient narration is systematically used in melodramas, I shall analyse Douglas Sirk's film *Magnificent Obsession*. As with most melodramas, *Magnificent Obsession* narrates the story of more than one character. The film begins with Bob Merrick (Rock Hudson), a rich playboy testing his speed boat on a lake. The boat crashes and he has to be revived with the help of a neighbour's resuscitator. However, while the resuscitator is being used on Merrick, its owner Dr Wayne Phillips, has a heart attack and dies. Merrick is admitted to the hospital run by the late Dr Phillips. Merrick discharges himself from the hospital and tries to walk home. He is given a lift by Helen (Jane Wyman), the widow of Dr Phillips. At first, the two do not recognise one another. But Merrick soon discovers who Helen is. He collapses and Helen takes him back to the hospital. It is only then that she finds out who he is. The rest of the film narrates the interrelation between Bob Merrick and Helen Phillips and the transformations they undergo. Helen, at first, hates Bob because he indirectly killed her husband but Bob has fallen in love with Helen. In a scene where he attempts to express his love to her, she is run down by a car and blinded (remember this is a melodrama!). Doctors proclaim that she will never see again. On a trip to Europe, Helen decides to disappear (aided by her best friend, Joyce). Meanwhile Bob, a former medical student, gives up his playboy lifestyle and returns to medical school, eventually setting up his own hospital. Finally, Joyce telephones Bob to tell him that Helen is living in New Mexico and is extremely ill. Bob visits her, and performs an operation on her eyes. When she awakes, she regains her sight. They are then united as a couple.

We shall look at how omniscient narration structures the first 15 minutes of the film. Once Bob Merrick is revived after his accident, the police take the resuscitator back to Dr Phillips. The film then follows the trauma of the Phillips family as they discover that Dr Phillips has died while his resuscitator was being used by Bob Merrick. The film is therefore shifted from one story (that of Bob Merrick) to another (the Phillips family).

The following scene takes place in the hospital, where Bob is recovering. A discrepancy of knowledge exists in this scene because, unlike the spectator and the other characters, Bob does not know that Dr Phillips has died, nor does he know he was the cause of his death. In the middle of the scene his is eventually told about Dr Phillip's death, thus reducing some of the discrepancy in knowledge. But crucially, he does not know how Dr Phillips died.

Bob leaves the hospital and begins to walk home. He is picked up by Helen as she drives from the hospital. The discrepancy in knowledge at work in this scene is more pronounced than in the scene in the hospital. At first, Helen and Bob do not know one another, whereas the spectator knows both of them. As soon as she tells him who she is and how her husband died, we see Bob in a close-up shot, as he reacts to what the spectator already knows. The discrepancy of knowledge between Bob and the spectator is overcome as he now shares the same amount of narrative information as the spectator.

However, Helen still does not know the identity of the man she has picked up. After he collapses, she takes him back to the hospital, where she is told that he is Bob Merrick. The discrepancy in knowledge between Helen and the spectator is finally overcome.

The scenes in the hospital and in the car (as well as many subsequent scenes in the film) are based on omniscient narration. The scene in the car creates dramatic suspense as the spectator waits to see how the characters will react to one another once they discover each other's identity. Bob collapses when he finds out Helen's identity and, later, Helen is shocked when she finally discovers that she drove Bob Merrick to the hospital. Later in the film, after Helen is blinded, this discrepancy in knowledge is revived when Bob visits Helen but pretends to be someone else. The spectator, of course, knows his real identity, whereas Helen does not initially know who he is, thus leading to additional scenes of dramatic suspense.

Summary

- Narration refers to a mechanism that determines how narrative information is conveyed to the film spectator.
- There are two dominant modes of filmic narration – omniscient narration and restricted narration.
- Restricted narration conveys the narrative to the spectator via one particular character (thus aligning the spectator to that character), leading to a sense of mystery.
- Omniscient narration shifts from one character to another, conveying narrative information to the spectator from many sources. This creates a discrepancy in knowledge between the spectator and characters, for the spectator knows more narrative information than any one character, creating scenes of dramatic suspense.

Narrative chronology in *Pulp Fiction*

One of the dominant characteristics of *Pulp Fiction* in terms of narrative is the non-linear ordering of its events. In this respect it is similar to Stanley Kubrick's *The Killing* (1956) and, more recently, David Lynch's *Lost Highway* (1997) in the way it radically alters the sequence in which the events are presented. In the following analysis we shall attempt to discern the exact chronology of the film's events.

Firstly, the events rendered chronologically (*not* how they appear in the film):

1 Captain Koons (Christopher Walken) presents a gold watch to the young Butch Coolidge; the watch is a gift from Butch's father, who died in a prisoner-of-war camp. This

sequence, coded as Butch's memory, occurs about 20 years prior to all the other events that take place in the film.

2 **a**) Vincent Vega (John Travolta) and Jules Winnfield (Samuel L. Jackson), two hit men, carry out a job for mobster Marsellus Wallace (Ving Rhames). They retrieve a valuable case from four 'business partners' who tried to double cross Marsellus. Two of the partners are shot. **b**) After shooting the two partners, Vincent and Jules escape injury when another one of the partners rushes into the room and shoots at them. Vincent and Jules shoot him and take the fourth partner (Marvin) with them.

3 In the car, Vincent accidentally shoots Marvin and both Vincent and Jules have to clean up both the car and themselves.

4 **a**) In a restaurant, Honey Bunny (Amanda Plummer) and Pumpkin (Tim Roth) talk about their previous heist jobs. They decide to hold up the restaurant they are occupying. **b**) Vincent and Jules enter the restaurant, before it is held up, and Jules talks about quitting his job. As Honey Bunny and Pumpkin rob the restaurant, there is a stand off between them and Vincent and Jules. Vincent and Jules convince Honey Bunny and Pumpkin to leave the restaurant. Vincent and Jules then leave the restaurant with the case.

5 The boxer Butch Coolidge (Bruce Willis) is seen talking to Marsellus in Marsellus's bar. Marsellus pays Butch to throw a boxing match. Vincent and Jules enter the bar with the case. Vincent buys some drugs, then takes out Marsellus's wife Mia (Uma Thurman) for the evening (at Marsellus's request). She takes Vincent's drugs and becomes ill. Vincent is able to revive her.

6 Butch in his dressing room, thinking about his father's watch (scene 1). He decides not the throw the fight and, after winning, escapes from the city. However, he has to return to his apartment the next day to retrieve his watch. Vincent is waiting inside but Butch kills him. Butch then, literally, runs into Marsellus. After a chase, both are trapped in a basement by two homosexuals. Butch manages to escape, sets Marsellus free and therefore cancels their debt.

These events are presented in *Pulp Fiction* in the following order:

4 a) (the pre-credit sequence where Honey Bunny and Pumpkin talk about their previous heist jobs; the scene ends with both of them pulling out their guns in preparation to rob the restaurant) credit sequence

2 a) (Vincent and Jules go to retrieve the case for Marsellus)

5 (Butch and Marsellus; Vincent and Jules enter)

1 (Butch receiving his father's watch)

6 (Butch winning the fight, killing Vincent, gets even with Marsellus)

2 b) (the end of segment 2, of Vincent and Jules retrieving the case)

3 (Vincent kills Marvin)

4 b) (Vincent and Jules in the restaurant held up by Honey Bunny and Pumpkin).

The causal relation between the pre-credit sequence and 2a) remains unexplained up until the end of the film. Furthermore, the spectator doesn't realise that the film has moved backward in time from the pre-credit sequence to 2a) (because, in the pre-credit sequence, Vincent and Jules are also in the restaurant after retrieving the case, although we don't see them in the restaurant until the end of the film).

There doesn't seem to be a major ellipsis between 2a) and 5. The only sign that suggests that Vincent and Jules haven't come directly from the apartment is their change of clothes. This remains unexplained but doesn't appear to be significant. Segment 5 begins with Butch (talking to Marsellus) and so do segments 1 and 6. Segment 1 is retrospectively coded as Butch's memory, as he prepares (beginning of Segment 6) for the fight that Marsellus has paid him to throw. After Butch has escaped from the basement, it is not evident that this is the last action that takes place in the film's chronology.

When the film returns to the apartment where Vincent and Jules retrieve the case, the transition is quite marked, not least because we saw Butch kill Vincent in the previous segment, and we thought that the events in the apartment had been resolved. But instead, we come to realise that the path from Vincent and Jules retrieving the case to them returning it to Marsellus was far from straight. The intervening events explain both the change in clothes and link up the Honey Bunny and Pumpkin story with the Vincent and Jules story, therefore finally placing the pre-credit sequence within the film's cause-effect logic. We also come to realise that the pre-credit sequence and the sequence with Vincent and Jules in the restaurant talking to one another take place at the same time, even though they are shown at different times in the film.

Furthermore, there is a systematic structure to the film's non-linearity. The film begins with events in segment 4; it jumps back to segment 2; jumps forward again to 5; it then jumps right back to 1 before jumping to the end, events in 6. Finally, it jumps back to events in segment 2, picks up where it left off and then progresses chronologically to segment 4, where it began.

The film's chronology therefore begins and ends with events that take place in the middle (segment 4). It then jumps backwards and forwards, in wider and wider arcs until it returns to 2 and moves along to the events it began with. What I mean when I say that the film jumps backwards and forwards in wider and wider arcs can be illustrated with a series of diagrams:

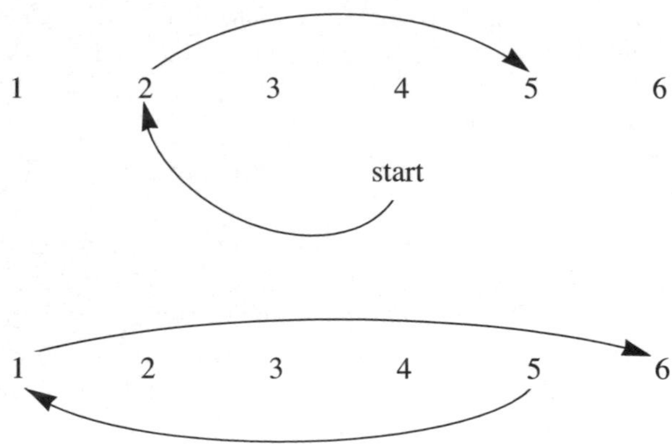

As you can see from these two diagrams, the movement from one segment to another is equal, but the movement in the second diagram is more encompassing. From 2 to 5, the film then moves back to the events before 2 and then moves forward to the events after 5 (1 and 6). From 6, the film then returns to 2 and ends where it began, at 4.

Although the chronology of *Pulp Fiction* is an extreme example, its complexity evidently did not detract from the film's huge popularity. However, whatever we make of *Pulp Fiction*, I hope to have shown that it is not structured randomly, but according to a definite pattern. By concentrating on the chronology and cause-and-effect logic of *Pulp Fiction*, we can begin to understand that films do not need to represent the cause-and-effect logic of a film in chronological order. Returning to *Psycho*, it would after all have been perfectly logical for Marion to steal the $40,000 first before any causes were given.

Further reading

Bordwell, David, *Narration in the Fiction Film* (London: Routledge, 1985)
A long and wide ranging book that discusses both how spectators comprehend narrative films, and various historical modes of narration (Hollywood cinema, Art cinema, Soviet cinema, the films of Jean-Luc Godard).

Branigan, Edward, *Narrative Comprehension and Film* (London: Routledge, 1992)
This book is similar in some respects to Bordwell's *Narration in the Fiction Film*, in that it discusses how narrative is comprehended by film spectators. However, Branigan's book focuses on more specific issues (such as 'levels of narration' and 'focalization') and discusses them in great dctail; it is a very erudite, sophisticated and complex book.

Truffaut, François, *Hitchcock* (Simon and Schuster, 1967)
The most famous book on Hitchcock, based on more than 50 hours of interviews between Truffaut and Hitchcock.

3 FILM AUTHORSHIP: THE DIRECTOR AS *AUTEUR*

The director is both the least necessary and most important component of film-making. He is the most modern and most decadent of all artists in his relative passivity toward everything that passes before him. He would not be worth bothering with if he were not capable now and then of sublimity of expression almost miraculously extracted from his money-oriented environment.

Andrew Sarris, *The American Cinema*, p. 37

One aim of Chapter 1 was to introduce the ideas of *mise-en-scène* and *mise-en-shot*. These ideas are important for this chapter, so I shall briefly summarise them here:

- *Mise-en-scène* as it is used in this book refers to filmed events, what appears in front of the camera – set design, lighting, and character movement.
- *Mise-en-shot* designates the way the filmed events, the *mise-en-scène*, are translated into film images.

Most critics do not distinguish *mise-en-scène* from *mise-en-shot*, but are content to absorb *mise-en-shot* into *mise-en-scène*. However, this distinction is crucial when discussing the director as *auteur*, as this chapter will attempt to show.

Chapter 2 outlined the key structures of narrative and narration. It concentrated on the narrative's cause-effect logic and the difference between restricted narration (narration tied to one character only) and omniscient narration (narration that jumps from character to character, or which shows the spectator information that no character knows about).

In this chapter we shall see how individual directors use *mise-en-scène*, *mise-en-shot*, and strategies of narrative and narration. In particular, we shall look at the rise of the critical approach to film known as the *auteur* policy (or *la politique des auteurs*, to use its original French name). The aim of the *auteur* policy is to assign to certain directors the title of artists, rather than thinking of them as mere technicians. *Auteur* critics study the style and themes (or subject matter) of a director's films and assign to them the title of art if they show a consistency of style and theme.

Directors whose films show a consistency of style and theme are called *auteurs*. By contrast, directors who show no consistency of style and theme in their work are called *metteurs-en-scène*, and are relegated to the status of mere technicians rather than artists. According to *auteur* critics, the difference between an *auteur* and a *metteur-en-scène* is that, whereas an *auteur* can transform a mediocre script into a great film, a *metteur-en-scène* can only make a mediocre film out of a mediocre script. *Auteur* critics made the evaluative distinction between an *auteur* and a *metteur-en-scène* because an *auteur* is able to maintain a consistency of style and theme by working against the constraints of the Hollywood mode of production. In other words, an *auteur* is able to transcend the restrictions imposed upon him or her by the Hollywood studio system.

But more central than the distinction between an *auteur* and a *metteur-en-scène* is the question: Is it legitimate to concentrate on the director as the primary creator of a film? *Auteur* critics acknowledge that the cinema is, of course, a collective activity involving many people at various stages of pre-production, production and post-production. Nevertheless, the *auteur* critics argue, it is the director who makes the choices concerning framing, camera position, the duration of the shot, and so on – those aspects of *mise-en-shot* that determine the way everything is visualised on screen. And it is precisely *mise-en-shot* that *auteur* critics focus on, because this is what makes film unique, what distinguishes film from other arts.

The first half of this chapter will look at the origin of the *auteur* policy, which initially concentrated exclusively on the stylistic consistencies of a director's work. Other *auteur* critics expanded the scope of the *auteur* policy by looking at an equally important consistency – the thematic consistency in a director's work, the uniformity and coherence of subject matter across a director's films. The auteurist's emphasis on the consistency of style and theme is expressed in the statement that *auteurs* are always attempting to make the same film. The second half of this chapter will consider the dominant styles and themes in the films of Alfred Hitchcock and Wim Wenders.

François Truffaut and *Cahiers du Cinéma*

The auteur policy emerges from the film criticism of the French journal *Cahiers du Cinéma* in the 1950s. This policy was put into practice by a number of critics who became well-known film makers of the French New Wave of the 1960s, including Jean-Luc Godard, François Truffaut, Jacques Rivette, Eric Rohner and Claude Chabrol. The manifesto of the *Cahiers du Cinéma* critics is Truffaut's 1954 essay 'A Certain Tendency of the French Cinema' whereas the manifesto of the New Wave film makers is Jean-Luc Godard's 1960 film *A bout de souffle* (*Breathless*). I shall look at each in turn.

In 'A Certain Tendency of the French Cinema', Truffaut criticises the dominant tendency in French cinema during the 1940s and 1950s – which he calls the tradition of quality. This cinema is a contrived and wooden cinema that projects a bourgeois image of good taste and high culture. In Ginette Vincendeau's definition, the tradition of quality

> *... refers to a loose industry category, actively promoted (by financial aid and prizes) to project a 'quality' image of French film: expertly crafted pictures with high production values and often derived from literary sources. Psychological and/or costume dramas such as Jean Delannoy's* La Symphonie pastorale *(1946), Claude Autant-Lara's* Douce *(1943), Rene Clement's* Jeux interdits/Forbidden Games *(1952), Max Ophuls'* La Ronde *(1950), Jacques Audry's* Minne, L'ingénue Libertine/Minne *(1950), Jean Renoir's* French Cancan *(1955), Rene Clair's* Les Grandes manoeuvres *(1955), all projected an image of Frenchness tied to good taste and high culture.*
>
> **Ginette Vincendeau, in *Encyclopedia of European Cinema*, pp. 426–27**

These values were achieved by the following means:

- high production values
- reliance on stars
- genre conventions
- privileging the script.

For Truffaut, the tradition of quality offers little more than the practice of filming scripts, of mechanically transferring scripts to the screen. As Truffaut emphasises, the success or failure of these films depends entirely on the quality of their scripts. Truffaut's attack is focused primarily on two script writers – Jean Aurenche and Pierre Bost. Truffaut writes:

> *Aurenche and Bost are essentially literary men and I reproach them here for being contemptuous of the cinema by under estimating it.*
>
> **'A Certain Tendency of the French Cinema', p. 229**

These literary men write script writers' films, in which the film is seen to be completed when the script has been written. Incidentally, the French director Bertrand Tavernier returned to the tradition of quality film making in the 1970s. He opposes himself to the New Wave, which was clearly signified when he asked Aurenche and Bost to script his first film *The Watchmaker of Saint Paul* (1974).

The privileging of the script in the tradition of quality deflected attention away from both the film making process and the director. The *Cahiers du Cinéma* critics and the New Wave film makers defined themselves against literature, against the literary script, and against the tradition of quality, and instead promoted 'the cinema' as such. Whereas the tradition of quality advocated a conservative style of film making, in which the best technique is one that is not seen, the style of the French New Wave films is similar to the decorative arts, where style draws attention to itself. In the tradition of quality, film style is a means to an end, a means of conveying story content to the spectator. But in the New Wave films, style becomes independent of the story. New Wave films dazzle the spectator with style rather than story content. The *auteur* policy therefore embodies Marshall McLuhan's idea that 'the medium is the message'.

The critics of *Cahiers du Cinéma* respected the work of Hollywood film makers, such as Alfred Hitchcock, Howard Hawks, Orson Welles, Fritz Lang, John Ford, Douglas Sirk, Sam Fuller and Nicholas Ray, all of whom worked against the scripts imposed upon them by the studios. In the following extract, Jacques Rivette attempts to explain why Fritz Lang is an *auteur*, while Vincente Minnelli is only a *metteur-en-scène*:

> *When you talk about Minnelli the first thing you do is talk about the screenplay, because he always subordinates his talent to something else. Whereas when you talk about Fritz Lang, the first thing is to talk about Fritz Lang, then about the screenplay.*
>
> **Jacques Rivette, quoted in Jim Hillier, ed., *Cahiers du Cinéma: the 1960s*, p. 3**

An *auteur* in the Hollywood studio system is a director who transcends the script by imposing on it his or her own style and vision. An *auteur* film involves subjective and personalised film making, rather than the mechanical transposition of a script on to film. The script is the mere pretext for the activity of film making, and an *auteur* film is about the film making practices involved in filming a script, rather than being about the script itself. But how does a Hollywood director impose his own vision on a studio film? Primarily through his manipulation of *mise-en-scène* – or, more accurately, *mise-en-shot* (as I pointed out in Chapter 1 and at the beginning of this chapter, most critics do not distinguish *mise-en-scène* from *mise-en-shot*). In the following quotation, we see John Caughie linking the *auteur* policy to what he calls *mise-en-scène* (although it is evident from the quotation that he means *mise-en-shot*):

> *It is with the* mise-en-scène *that the* auteur *transforms the material which has been given to him; so it is in the* mise-en-scène *– in the disposition of the scene, in the camera movement, in the camera placement, in the movement from shot to shot – that the auteur writes his individuality into the film.*
>
> **John Caughie, *Theories of Authorship*, pp. 12–13**

Mise-en-shot names those techniques through which everything is expressed on screen. An *auteur* works out his or her own vision by establishing a consistent style of *mise-en-shot,* a style that usually works in opposition to the demands of the script.

For the French New Wave film makers, the script merely served as the pretext to the activity of filming. Indeed, for *auteur* critics, there was no point in talking about the film script at all, for an *auteur* film is one that does not represent a pre-existing story, but is one that represents the often spontaneous events that took place in front of the camera.

The French New Wave can be seen as a film-making practice that rejects classical Hollywood cinema's dominance by producers (in which the producer acts as the central manager controlling the work of the technicians), in favour of a more 'archaic' mode of production that favours the director. Consequently, the New Wave directors strongly supported the idea of filming unimportant stories, which then allows the director great freedom to impose his own aesthetic vision on the material. This is one reason Truffaut chose to film Henri Pierre Roche's novel *Jules and Jim* in 1961.

Movie magazine

Before moving on to the New Wave film makers I shall mention, in passing, how the *auteur* policy was taken up in Britain and North America. The *auteur* policy was adopted by the British film critics Ian Cameron, Mark Shivas, Paul Mayersberg and Victor Perkins in the magazine *Movie*, first published in May 1962. Like the critics of *Cahiers du Cinéma*, the *Movie* critics sought *auteurs* within the Hollywood studio system. Similarly, *Movie* critics also defined the *auteur* in terms of self-expression, as manifest in the stylistic and thematic consistency across a director's work. However, *Movie* was more flexible than *Cahiers du Cinéma*. The *Cahiers* critics were notoriously well known for preferring the worst films of an *auteur* to the best films of a *metteur-en-scène*. For example, *Cahiers* critics regarded Nicholas Ray to be the ultimate *auteur*. For this reason, in 1961 they hailed *Party Girl* to be a masterpiece, Ray's best film to date (above his other films such as *They Live by Night* and *Rebel Without a Cause*). However, *Party Girl* is generally considered a routine and hack piece of work – even Ray himself called it 'a bread-and-butter job'.

In contrast to the judgements of *Cahiers du Cinéma*, *Movie* critics were more moderate. They recognised that even *auteurs* can make bad films and that the *metteur-en-scène* can, occasionally at least, make a good film. The prime example of the latter is Michael Curtiz, who is regarded by *auteur* critics to have directed only one film of lasting value in the history of the cinema – *Casablanca* (1943).

For such an avowedly evaluative mode of criticism as the *auteur* policy, it is inevitable that the critics of *Cahiers du Cinéma* and *Movie* would differ about the directors they identified as *auteurs*. For example, whereas *Cahiers* classified Minnelli as a *metteur-en-scène* (as we saw above in the quotation from Jacques Rivette), *Movie* defined him as an undisputed *auteur* and discussed him in three issues of *Movie*, including the first issue which consisted of an interview with Minnelli together with an article called 'Minnelli's Method' by Mark Shivas. In this article, Shivas argues that the consistency of Minnelli's film style is sufficient to define him as an *auteur*, since Minnelli's style transcends the film script – a defining characteristic of an *auteur*. Shivas argues for the superiority of style over script in relation to two of Minnelli's films, *The Reluctant Debutante* and *The Four Horsemen of the Apocalypse*:

> *Minnelli's way with William Douglas Home's rather dreary play* [The Reluctant Debutante] *is to emphasise the falseness and untrammeled idiocy of the Season by insisting that the adults behave like children and the children like adults, reinforcing the less than witty lines primarily in its visual treatment. ... As a result of Minnelli's visual style, a mediocre story becomes as sophisticated as* The Philadelphia Story *is verbally witty.*
>
> *With* The Four Horsemen, *Minnelli was once more landed with a turkey, an old one, too, of which only a primitive like King Vidor (*Duel in the Sun*) could have made a meal. ...* The Four Horsemen *is not, except from the point of view of decoration, roses all the way, but at its best it transcends its story by the brilliance of its* mise-en-scène.
>
> **Mark Shivas, 'Minnelli's Method',** ***Movie*****, 1, 1962, p. 18**

For Shivas, Minnelli is an *auteur* because his films go beyond the mediocre scripts handed to him by the studio. A *metteur-en-scène*, by contrast, would have simply made two mediocre films from these mediocre scripts.

Andrew Sarris

During the early 1960s, Andrew Sarris introduced the *auteur* policy into North American film criticism via his essay 'Notes on the Auteur Theory in 1962' in the journal *Film Culture* (No. 27, Winter 1962–63). Sarris translated the term *la politique des auteurs* into the term *auteur* theory, giving it the prestige that goes with the word 'theory'. Furthermore, he argued that the *auteur* theory is primarily a history of American cinema, since it develops a historical awareness of what individual directors have achieved in the past. This is in contrast to Hollywood practice where, according to studio executives, a director is only as good as the last film he or she made. Finally, an auteurist history of the cinema needed to be evaluative, according to Sarris, if it was not to become a hobby like stamp collecting or trainspotting. The criteria for evaluation were the same for Sarris as for other *auteur* critics – consistency in style and theme across a director's films. Sarris published an evaluative history of American *auteurs* in 1968 in the form of his comprehensive book *The American Cinema: Directors and Directions, 1929–1968*, which became the bible of *auteur* critics.

A bout de souffle/Breathless

So far we have surveyed the work of the *Cahiers du Cinéma* critics and New Wave film makers in an attempt to explain the motivations for their privileging of the director as *auteur*. We then saw how the idea of the director as *auteur* entered British and North American film criticism. We shall now turn to Godard's film *A bout de souffle/Breathless* to look at the aesthetics of the French New Wave at work.

The French New Wave is one of the major movements of European Art Cinema. Ginette Vincendeau (in the *Encyclopedia of European Cinema*, p. xiv) defines European Art Cinema as sharing the following aesthetic features:

- a slower editing and narrative pace than Hollywood cinema
- a strong 'authorial voice'
- an investment in realism and ambiguity
- the desire to provoke thought and sometimes shock
- a taste for unhappy endings.

In *A bout de souffle* (1960), we see Godard creating most of these aesthetic features by using the following production techniques, all of which were innovative when Godard made the film:

- location shooting (rather than the studio, as in the tradition of quality)
- a hand-held camera (made possible by the invention of lightweight cameras)
- natural lighting (rather than artificial studio lighting)
- casual acting
- subversion of the rules of classical editing.

All these techniques, none of which are to be found in the tradition of quality, turn the films into spontaneous and improvised performances, rather than being the mere representation of the script, which exists before the film-making process begins.

A bout de souffle begins with Michel Poiccard (played by Jean-Paul Belmondo) stealing a car to drive to Paris. However, two policemen on motorcycles chase him. He turns off the road, but is followed by one of the policemen. Michel shoots the policeman and runs off. What makes this part of the film unusual and innovative is the way it is filmed.

I shall describe the shots beginning with Michel being chased by the police to the moment when Michel shoots one of the policemen. I shall then begin to discuss the production techniques used in this sequence of shots:

Shot number

1 The camera is inside Michel's car. He overtakes a lorry and is spotted by two policemen.

2 The camera, outside the car, shows Michel overtaking the lorry. The car is shown travelling from screen right to screen left.

3 The camera, inside the car, quickly pans from the windscreen of the car to the back window, where the police can be seen chasing Michel.

4 Cut to a slightly different shot of the police chasing Michel. The camera then pans to inside the car (that is, it reverses the pan of shot 3).

5 The camera, outside the car, shows it moving from screen left to screen right.

6 Shot of the policemen on their motorcycles. They are shown travelling from screen right to screen left.

7 Michel pulls off the road. He looks off screen left, and sees …

8 One of the police motorcycles racing by.

9 Michel opens the bonnet of the car to try to get it started again. He looks off screen left and sees …

10 The second police motorcycle racing by.

11 Cut back to Michel attempting to repair the jump lead that will start the car again. Michel looks up and sees …

12 The second motorcyclist heading towards him.

13 Shot of Michel reaching into the car.

14 Close-up of Michel's head in profile, facing screen right. He says 'Stop, or I'll kill you'.

15 Close-up of Michel's hand holding a gun.

16 Close-up of the gun as Michel gets ready to fire.

17 The cut to shot 17 occurs as the sound of the gun going off is heard. Shot 17 consists of the policeman falling down.

18 In this shot, Michel is shown running across open fields.

This description cannot capture the frenetic nature of this series of shots. The first 17 shots last just 44 seconds, which makes on average a change of shot every 2.6 seconds. (The final shot lasts 14 seconds.) All the innovative production techniques mentioned above are apparent in this series of shots. The scene is shot on location, on the highway. The rest of the film is also shot on location, particularly on the streets of Paris. The camera is very mobile and shaky. The pans in shots 3 and 4 are very quick, creating blurred images. The lighting is natural. In shot 7, the sun shines directly into the lens, creating a bloomer. Belmondo is renowned (and often imitated) for his casual acting style in this film. He seems to improvise most of the time. Finally, this series of shots subverts the rules of continuity editing. The cut from shot 3 to shot 4 is less then 30 degrees and, therefore, creates a jump cut. In shot 5, Michel's car is travelling from screen left to screen right. But in shot 6, the police are shown travelling in the opposite direction, from screen right to screen left. The cameraman has crossed the road after filming the car to film the motorcycles. Such a change of direction creates a confusion of screen space. Similarly, when Michel stops the car, he looks screen left at the police passing by. But after he has picked up the gun, he looks screen right at the policeman, rather than screen left, as we would expect. Finally, the cut from 15 to 16, the shot of Michel's hand to the shot of the gun, creates another jump, because there is very little difference between the two shots.

The use of a shaky, hand-held camera, together with the use of location shooting and natural lighting, jump cuts and discontinuous editing, do not aim to show the action clearly; instead, it offers a fragmentary and partial vision of the scene. These 'imperfect' techniques represent the *auteur*'s presence and serve as clear marks of the way he or she writes his or her individual vision into the film.

The effect these production techniques create is one of spontaneity and improvisation. However, what interests me in the use of these techniques is that they give the film a documentary feel. The blurred pans, the shaky camera movements and abrupt editing testify to the difficulty the cameraman has filming in the conditions he found himself in, and to his physical interaction with the event.

It is important to point out that the stylistic choices made by the French New Wave directors were not simply determined by aesthetic considerations, but also by economics. The French New Wave is a low-budget film-making practice. Filming on location with natural lighting decreases production costs, just as the emphasis on spontaneity defrays pre-production costs such as script writing. Nevertheless, far from being despondent by the lack of money, the French New Wave directors identified low production costs with artistic freedom. They saw an inverse relationship between the size of the budget and artistic freedom: the higher the budget, the lower the artistic freedom. They even saw economic failure at the box office as a sign of artistic independence.

These economic considerations also fed into the judgements the New Wave directors made when they were *auteur* critics. When assessing the films of American directors, *auteur* critics defined an *auteur* as a director who transcended the high production values of the Hollywood studios. In other words, an *auteur* managed to stamp his or her personality on a high-budget film, whereas a *metteur-en-scène* was swamped by high production values and became an anonymous technician.

Consequently, a Hollywood *auteur* film is one that contains a tension between the demands of the studio system and the director's self-expressiveness. As John Caughie explains.

> *... the struggle between the desire for self-expression and the constraints of the industry could produce a tension in the films of the commercial cinema ..., encouraging the* auteurist *critics to valorize Hollywood cinema above all else, finding there a treasure-trove of buried personalities, and, in the process, scandalizing established criticism. Uniqueness of personality, brash individuality, persistence of obsession and originality were given an evaluative power above that of stylistic smoothness or social seriousness.*
>
> *The business of the critic was to discover the director within the given framework, to find the traces of the submerged personality, to find the ways in which the* auteur *had transformed the material so that the explicit subject matter was no longer what the film was really about ...*
>
> **John Caughie, *Theories of Authorship*, pp. 11–12**

As a final point, we need to consider the implicit criticism of the *auteur* policy that Caughie refers to the first quotation above, when he writes that 'Uniqueness of personality, brash individuality, persistence of obsession and originality were given an evaluative power above that of stylistic smoothness or *social seriousness*' (emphasis added). Both the *auteur* critics and the New Wave directors have been criticised for their lack of social commitment. However, the *auteur* policy offers a defence against standardised film making practices in favour of an alternative – a more expressive and personalised – cinema. The New Wave, while concerned primarily with the personal lives of the young French middle class, put into practice this alternative style of film making. Moreover, after 1967, Godard's film making practice entered a second phase by becoming strongly politicised, in which he experimented with video, different forms of film distribution and feminism. In his third phase, in the 1980s, he returned to narrative cinema.

Summary of the *auteur* policy

- The aim of the *auteur* policy is to distinguish between directors as artists (*auteurs*) and directors as mere technicians (*metteurs-en-scène*).
- An *auteur* is a director who manifests a consistency of style and theme across his or her films.
- The director is privileged by *auteur* critics because he or she is the one who visualises the script on screen.
- The *auteur* policy was formulated by François Truffaut in his essay 'A Certain Tendency of the French Cinema', in which he attacks the French 'tradition of quality' school of film making, particularly for its over reliance on scripts.
- *Auteur* critics privilege the work of Hollywood directors (including Hitchcock, Hawks, Welles, Lang, Ford, Sirk, Fuller and Ray) whose visual style transcends the scripts imposed on them by the studios.
- Many of the *auteur* critics associated with *Cahiers du Cinéma* in the 1950s (Truffaut, Godard, Chabrol, Rohmer, Rivette) started to make their own *auteur* films in the 1960s; they abandoned the script in favour of improvisation and spontaneity.
- The *auteur* policy was developed in Britain in the magazine *Movie* and in North America by Andrew Sarris.

Style and themes in Alfred Hitchcock's films

Alfred Hitchcock is an undisputed *auteur* for all the *auteur* critics mentioned above – *Cahiers du Cinéma*, the *Movie* critics and Andrew Sarris. I shall briefly review the ways in which these three schools of *auteur* criticism discussed Hitchcock before listing the stylistic and thematic elements that unify his films. *Cahiers* published a special issue on Hitchcock in 1954 (no. 39), which comprises of two interviews with Hitchcock, one by André Bazin, the other by Claude Chabrol. In 1957, the *Cahiers* critics Eric Rohmer and Claude Chabrol published the first book-length study of Hitchcock, simply entitled *Hitchcock* and translated into English as *Hitchcock: The First Forty-Four Films* (New York: Ungar, 1979). Rohmer and Chabrol develop a thematic and stylistic analysis of Hitchcock's films. They identified the following themes:

- the influence of Catholicism
- the theme of shared guilt
- homophobia and misogyny.

In terms of form and style, they noted at the end of the book that:

> *Hitchcock is one of the greatest* inventors of form *in the entire history of cinema. Perhaps only Murnau and Eisenstein can sustain comparison with him when it comes to form. Our effort will not have been in vain if we have been able to demonstrate how an entire moral universe has been elaborated on the basis of this form and by its very rigor. In Hitchcock's work, form does not embellish content, it creates it.*
>
> **Rohmer and Chabrol, *Hitchcock: the First Forty-Four Films*, p. 152**

Rohmer and Chabrol's book was followed by a book by another *Cahiers* critic, Jean Douchet, whose *Alfred Hitchcock* was published in 1967. Douchet identifies three worlds operating in Hitchcock's films:

- the world of the mundane (of everyday events)
- the world of subjective desire
- the intellectual world.

For example, *Psycho* (1960) begins with the mundane. The camera pans across the skyline of Phoenix, Arizona and we are supplied with mundane information: the name of the city, the date and the time. We see and hear about the mundane lives of Sam and Marion and see the mundane office job that Marion has. The film then moves on to the world of subjective desire – in this instance, Marion's, as she steals the $40,000 to fulfil her love with Sam. But after Marion is murdered, the film moves into the intellectual world as several characters try to work out what happened to her.

Douchet was one of the first critics to draw the (by now familiar) analogy between Jeff (James Stewart) in *Rear Window* (1954) and the film spectator. Jeff is a photographer who is confined to a wheelchair after breaking a leg. He spends his days spying on his neighbours across the courtyard. For Douchet, Jeff replicates the film spectator – the spectator confined to a chair observing a spectacle at a distance. In *Rear Window* the windows of the apartments across the courtyard replicate the cinema screen.

The most famous book on Hitchcock was published in 1967 – François Truffaut's *Hitchcock*, which was based on more than 50 hours of interviews in which Truffaut and Hitchcock talk about Hitchcock's films in chronological order, covering such issues as the inception of each film, the preparation of screenplays, directorial problems and Hitchcock's evaluation of each film.

The *Movie* critics also interviewed Hitchcock and wrote several essays on mechanisms of suspense in his films. Robin Wood, who wrote regularly for *Movie*, published a book on Hitchcock, simply called *Hitchcock's Films* (1965) (which has been revised and updated several times), which is almost as famous as Truffaut's book. Wood argues that we should take Hitchcock seriously because of his thematic and formal unity, and because his films have a thematic depth similar to Shakespeare's plays.

Finally, in *The American Cinema*, Sarris defined Hitchcock as a pantheon director, the highest and most prestigious category in his evaluative history. Pantheon directors, according to Sarris

> *are the directors who have transcended their technical problems with a personal vision of the world. To speak any of their names is to evoke a self-contained world with its own laws and landscapes.*
>
> **Sarris, *The American Cinema*, p. 39**

Stylistic unity in Hitchcock's films

1 Emphasis on editing and montage

Early in his career, Hitchcock was influenced by German Expressionism and Soviet theories of montage. The first two films he completed as director – *The Pleasure Garden* (1926) and *The Mountain Eagle* (1926) were made in German studios. Examples of Hitchcock's reliance upon editing are numerous, but one can do no better than look closely at the end of *Notorious*, already analysed at the end of Chapter 1. Hitchcock's reliance in editing is also illustrated in the famous shower scene murder in *Psycho*, in which 34 shots appear on screen in a matter of 25 seconds. The style and themes of this scene were analysed in detail by the *Movie* critic Victor Perkins in his book *Film as Film* (Penguin Books, 1972).

2 High number of point-of-view (POV) shots

Hitchcock has a tendency to use shots that represent a character's look. It is common to find that about 25 per cent of all shots in Hitchcock's films are POV shots, which critics interpret as Hitchcock's fascination with voyeurism. The clearest examples are *Rear Window* (the shots of Jeff looking out of his window at his neighbours) and *Vertigo* (1957), in which the private detective, Scottie (James Stewart), is hired to follow Madeleine (Kim Novak).

3 Shooting in a confined space

In the 1940s and early 1950s, Hitchcock imposed upon himself a technical constraint – he made a number of films in confined spaces. In films such as *Lifeboat* (1944), *Rope* (1948), *Dial M for Murder* (1954) and *Rear Window* (1954), most of the action takes place in the same space (a lifeboat in the film of the same name, the Manhattan penthouse of Brandon Shaw in *Rope*; Tony Wendice's apartment in *Dial M for Murder*, and Jeff's apartment in *Rear Window*). This self-imposed constraint limited the stylistic choices that Hitchcock could make and offered him a challenge on how to construct the film.

Considering *Rope* would be useful, because it marks a deviation in Hitchcock's film making. In the late 1940s Hitchcock temporarily abandoned his emphasis on editing and experimented with the long take (plus camera movement). *Rope* takes the long take to its logical conclusion, because the film consists of only 11 takes, two of which last 10 minutes, which is the maximum length of the reel of film that fits into the camera. Yet, despite the limitations Hitchcock imposed on himself – limitations of space and a severe limitation on cutting from one shot to another – the camera moves almost continuously around the apartment, in the hallway and in the kitchen, demonstrating Hitchcock's skill in translating *mise-en-scène* into *mise-en-shot*.

Moreover, the effect of these long takes, as I pointed out in Chapter 1, is to emphasise the actor's performance, which is not cut up into many shots. This is because the long take maintains the dramatic unities of space and time. In *Rope*, the events in Brandon's penthouse take place in one evening; in fact, the skyline outside Brandon's penthouse slowly changes from daylight to evening twilight as the film progresses. Hitchcock combined editing and long takes in his film *Under Capricorn* (1949) and returned to editing from *Stage Fright* (1950) onwards.

Themes in Hitchcock's films

Narrative structure

We can identify two basic narrative structures in Hitchcock's films. These two narrative structures are related in that both involve investigations – usually the investigation of a murder. These narratives are distinguishable by whether the main protagonist is the one who carries out the investigation, or whether the main protagonist is the one who is under investigation.

In the first narrative structure, the film focuses on the protagonist as he carries out an investigation. Furthermore, he is usually set up with a mistaken identity. The solving of the crime occurs simultaneously with the unmasking of the mistaken identity (I shall discuss this point below).

In the second narrative structure, the protagonist comes under investigation – that is, the film focuses on the protagonist who is being investigated. For example, Marnie in the film of the same name, Tony Wendice in *Dial M for Murder*, Manny Balestrero in *The Wrong Man* (1956), Marion and Norman in *Psycho*. *Psycho*, for example, begins with a crime (Marion stealing $40,000), which is then investigated – by Arbogast, Lila and Sam. But as the investigation continues, it soon becomes evident that it is not only Marion's theft that is being investigated, but also the murders committed by Norman.

This discussion of murder and their investigation lead to the other themes in Hitchcock's films, which are:

- **Confession and guilt**, as Rohmer and Chabrol point out in their book. Marion in *Psycho* realises her guilt in stealing the $40,000; Marnie is plagued by guilt concerning a childhood experience – she murders a man who attacked her mother; in *I Confess* (1953), Otto Keller confesses a murder to Father Michael Logan (Montgomery Clift), who is then bound to silence.
- **Suspense** (Hitchcock as the 'master of suspense'). This applies to most of Hitchcock's films, but is epitomised in *North by Northwest* (1959), analysed in Chapter 2.
- **The perfect murder**. A single character or group of characters devise complex and unusual methods of committing the perfect murder; however, the investigator always finds a clue overlooked by the murderers. In *Rope*, there is no motive for Brandon and Phillip to kill David Kentley; they are simply acting out the existential theory of their former teacher Rupert Cadell. After killing Kentley and hiding his body in the apartment, Brandon and Phillip hold a party at the scene of the crime and invite Rupert as one of the guests. However, upon leaving the party, Rupert is mistakenly given Kentley's hat; this is the clue that leads to his solving of the crime. In *Rear Window*, Thorwald cuts up his wife's body; but Jeff and Lisa find her wedding ring, disconfirming the claim that she has simply left town. One more example: in *Strangers on a Train* (1951) Bruno Anthony meets by chance Guy Haines, a famous tennis player, on a train. Bruno knows that Guy wants to divorce his wife Miriam and marry his girlfriend Anne Morton. As the two of them get talking, Bruno mentions that he wants to kill his own father. He suggests to Guy that they swap murders – Bruno would murder Guy's wife Miriam and Guy could murder Bruno's father, making two perfect (that is, motiveless) crimes. Guy does not take Bruno seriously, but simply humours him. Nevertheless, Bruno carries out the murder of Miriam at a fairground. However, he is spotted by an attendant in charge of one of the rides, who

later confirms that it was Bruno, not Guy, who was at the scene of the crime at the time of Miriam's murder.

- **The wrong man**. As is apparent from the discussion of narrative structures, one of the dominant themes of Hitchcock's films is the wrong man. In *The 39 Steps* (1935), Richard Hannay (Robert Donat) is falsely accused of the murder of the spy Anabella Smith. In *To Catch a Thief* (1955), Cary Grant plays John Robie, a retired cat thief who is accused of carrying out new thefts. In *The Wrong Man* (1956), Manny Balestrero (Henry Fonda) is falsely accused of robbing an insurance office. In *North by Northwest*, Thornhill is mistaken for the nonexistent decoy agent George Kaplan. Finally, in *I Confess*, Father Michael Logan, who hears Otto Keller confess to murdering Mr Villette, is mistakenly suspected of committing the murder.

The cinema of Wim Wenders

Wim Wenders is one of the dominant figures in the New German Cinema which, like the French New Wave, is a dominant school of European Art cinema. In the *Encyclopedia of European Cinema* (pp. 304–5), Thomas Elsaesser and Joseph Garncarz identify the following characteristics of New German Cinema:

- It is a German art movement that was dominant from 1965 to 1982.
- It rejected the work of post Second World War German commercial directors, who had begun their careers during the Third Reich.
- It rejected established German film genres and stars.
- It was indirectly influenced by American cinema, rather than by German cinema (with the exception of the films of Fritz Lang and F.W. Murnau).
- It dispensed with the producer and scriptwriter, as the directors of the New German Cinema (such as Werner Herzog, Alexander Kluge, Rainer Werner Fassbinder, as well as Wim Wenders) took on theses roles.

We shall go through a number of these points in more detail by considering the work of Wim Wenders.

Thematic analysis of the films of Wim Wenders

The influence of American culture

It is significant to note that Wim Wenders was born in 1945, a few months after the end of the Second World War. He grew up in a Germany dominated by the American occupying forces. Germany after the Second World War was based on a collective amnesia, an unwillingness to speak about the Nazi regime. Those who grew up in the post-war period therefore had little or no access to recent German history or culture. Instead, their sense of culture was dominated by American culture and this domination is reflected in many of the films of Wenders, as well as other directors of what came to be known as New German Cinema.

What characterises New German Cinema is its representation of 'the German situation' – of a nation self-exiled from its own past and its own culture. In its place, the Germans found American culture. It should not be surprising, therefore, that American culture plays a prominent role in New German Cinema (as well as post-war German literature). Indeed, a number of German writers travelled through America and wrote about their experiences, which were made up of a combination of familiarity and estrangement.

One of the most prominent writers in German to tackle the German situation is Peter Handke. He travelled across America in 1971 and wrote a book called *Short Letter, Long Farewell*. In an interview, Handke explains:

> *America is for the story only a pretext, the attempt to find a distanced world in which I can be direct and personal. For if I imagine writing the same adventure in Europe, I can't think of a place where the objects, the outer world, would constitute a similar challenge, and at the same time, there is no other place except America which provokes in me such depersonalisation and estrangement. I tried to represent the inner world of my characters as exactly as possible. But I also tried to depict the outer world as a fiction. So that everything that the protagonist sees becomes a sign for him of what he has experienced, or what he would like to do. America is an environment which is known to me in advance by its signs.*
>
> **Peter Handke, quoted in Thomas Elsaesser, 'Germany's Imaginary America: Wim Wenders and Peter Handke', pp. 7–8**

America is also known to Wenders in advance by its signs and images, and these signs and images constantly recur in his films. Wenders collaborated with Handke on three films – *The Goalkeeper's Fear of the Penalty* (1971), which is based on a novel by Handke, *Wrong Move* (1975) and *Wings of Desire* (1987).

Road movies

It is this experience of travelling – of travelling through a land that both constitutes one's identity and at the same time alienates oneself – that becomes one of the dominant themes in Wenders' films. Most of his films can be defined as road movies – particularly *Alice in the Cities* (1974), *Kings of the Road* (1976), *The American Friend* (1977), *Paris, Texas* (1984), culminating in the ultimate road movie, Wenders' *Until the End of the World* (1991), in which the characters literally travel around the entire world and then travel into their inner selves (as I shall point out below).

The first ten minutes of *Alice in the Cities* consists of the main protagonist, a German writer called Philip, travelling across America in an attempt to write a story about American culture. But he ends up taking Polaroid photographs of typical signs and images of American culture. The whole film is a record of Philip's journey. Moreover, his journey is presented as a series of returns: the film begins with Philip in California as he prepares to return to New York. From New York, he flies back to Europe (landing in Amsterdam) and then finally on to Germany, where he drives around various cities looking for childhood homes – first the home of a lost ten-year-old girl, Alice, who is travelling with him, but also his own childhood home.

The journey in *Alice in the Cities*, and Wenders' films in general, depicts a search for one's identity, which involves a return to origins. The link between journey and identity is made explicit in *Alice in the Cities*, when Philip's former girlfriend tells him that he takes Polaroid photographs of what he sees in order to prove that he exists.

Wenders goes one step further than the Polaroid in *Until the End of the World*. After the main characters have travelled around the world, they employ computer technology to record their own dreams – which are predominately childhood images. This is simply an advancement of the use of Polaroids in *Alice in the Cities*. In *Until the End of the World*, the journey around the world leads to a journey into the inner self in search of one's origin and identity.

From male bonding to male–female relationships

Probably Wenders' most well-known road movie is *Paris, Texas* (1984). This film charts the journey of Travis (Harry Dean Stanton) as he walks out of the desert in search of his wife, Jane (Nastassja Kinski) and son, Hunter. But he is also searching for the place where he thinks he was conceived – a place called Paris, Texas. The link between journey and identity is therefore explicit in this film. Travis is aided in his journey by his brother, Walt (Dean Stockwell), who, along with his wife, is looking after Travis's son, Hunter. Travis and Hunter eventually find Jane working in a seedy peep-show joint. Travis realises that they cannot return to being a couple, although he does reunite Jane with Hunter.

The introduction of the brother into the journey charted in *Paris, Texas*, also introduces another dominant theme in Wenders' films – male bonding. The following Wenders' films involve the bonding between two male characters on the move – *Kings of the Road*, *The American Friend*, *Paris, Texas*, and *Wings of Desire*. By contrast, *Alice in the Cities* involves a journey taken by Philip and a ten-year-old girl.

The themes of these films point towards Wenders' relation to women. In fact, we can chart a progression in his films. In early films such as *Kings of the Road* and *The American Friend*, women are almost nonexistent. And when they are introduced in his early films, it is for pure innocence, as with the ten-year-old Alice in *Alice in the Cities*. However, in *Wings of Desire*, we see a strong female character, Marion, dominating the narrative. The male bonding between two angels, Damiel and Cassiel, is gradually broken up by Marion, with whom Damiel falls in love. He even forfeits his eternal angelic existence and becomes human in order to experience that love with her. Furthermore, *Until the End of the World* is a road movie featuring a journey taken by a woman in search of her identity. We can therefore discern a progression in Wenders' films when it comes to his depiction of women – from nonexistent (*Kings of the Road*) to the innocent ten-year-old Alice in *Alice in the Cities*, to Jane, the fallen woman in *Paris, Texas*, Marion in *Wings of Desire*, and finally Claire in *Until the End of the World*.

Does this gradual introduction and dominance of women in Wenders' films mean that he offers a veritable image of male–female relationships? Far from it! The way in which Travis and Jane are brought together in

Figure 1 Set design in Warner Bros' *Public Enemy*

Figure 2 Set design in MGM's *Meet Me in St Louis*

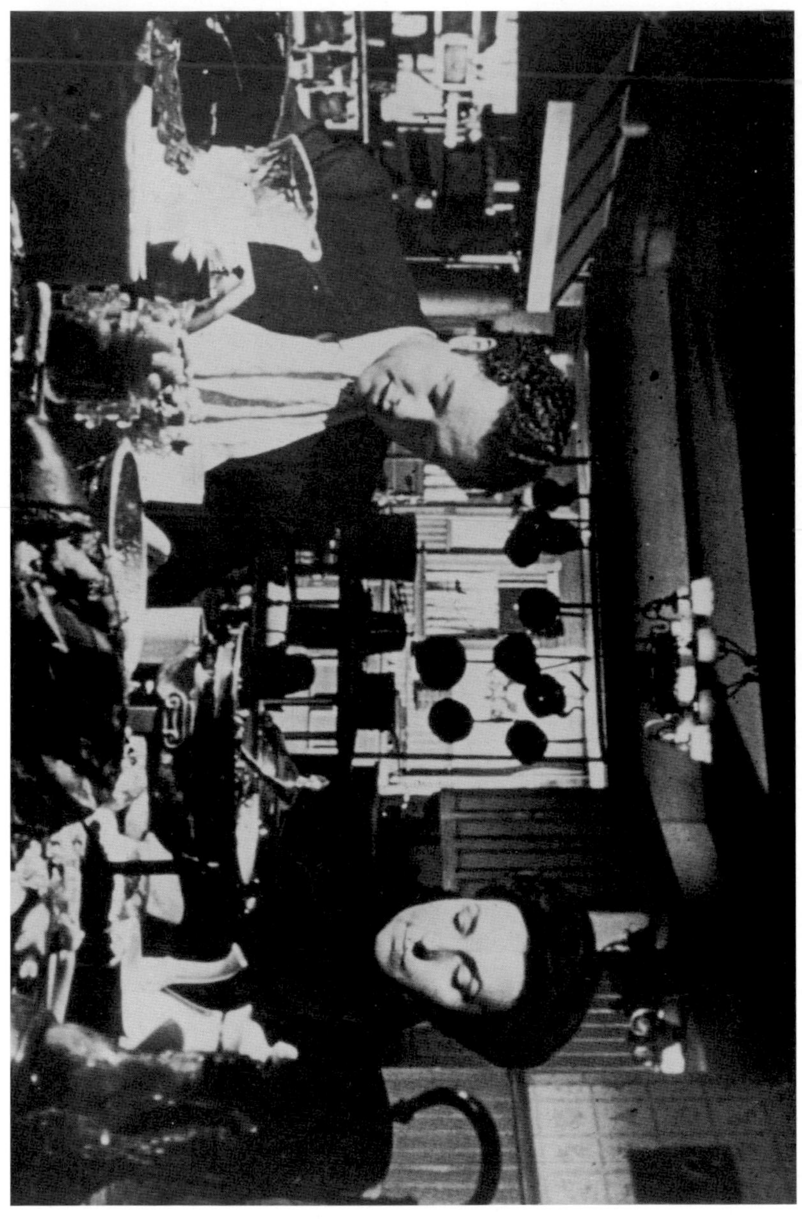

Figure 3 Deep-focus photography in *The Magnificent Ambersons*

Figure 4 Marion stealing the money in *Psycho*

Figure 5 Marion and Damiel in *Wings of Desire*

Paris, Texas shows the unbridgeable gap between the sexes. Travis finds his wife in a seedy peep-show joint, consisting of booths in which the customers can talk to the women through a two-way mirror, where the men can see the women, but not vice versa. When Travis finds Jane in one of these booths, he tells her about the relationship between two people he knows. He tells her how the couple fell in love, how the man gradually became obsessed and jealous of the woman, and how that eventually led to the breakdown of their relationship. Jane gradually realises that the story is about her and Travis, and that Travis is narrating it to her. But the couple are not brought together again. Travis tells Jane where to find Hunter and then he drives off.

The scene in the booth consists almost entirely of a monologue delivered by Travis about the disintegration of a relationship. The visual nature of the image, with the couple divided by a two-way mirror, sums up Wenders' philosophy about male–female relationships (or the impossibility of such relationships). *Wings of Desire* seems to transcend the problems of male–female relationships, as Damiel is able to break through the seemingly impossible barrier between angels and humans in order to express his love of Marion (Figure 5). Furthermore, the penultimate scene consists of a monologue delivered by Marion about male–female relationships, in which she expresses her belief that she can, for the first time, become seriously involved in a relationship. To some extent, then, *Wings of Desire* transcends the two-way mirror of *Paris, Texas* by giving the woman a voice to express her desire. Nonetheless, Marion expresses her desire in hopelessly idealistic terms, which brings into doubt the idea that her relationship with Damiel can be long term. Even the relationship in the more optimistic *Until the End of the World*, between Claire and Eugene, breaks down by the end of the film.

Formal elements in Wenders

In recent debates in film studies, the auteurists' opposition between *mise-en-shot/mise-en-scène* versus the script has been redefined as an opposition between image and narrative. This is important to keep in mind here because Wenders talks about his own film in these terms.

In the majority of narrative films, the elements of the film image (camera movement, camera angle, cutting, etc.) are completely motivated by the script's narrative logic. What this means is that camera movements, cutting, and so on simply serve the function of presenting the actions and events of the narrative to the film spectators. But in European Art cinema, there is a more ambiguous relation between the film image and the script's narrative. Another way of saying this is that the image is not completely subordinated to the narrative, but is largely separate from the narrative.

Wenders' films show this ambiguous relationship between the image and narrative. Yet, his films do not simply eliminate narrative logic either. However, their images are not completely subordinated to the narrative logic. Wenders describes his films as consisting of carefully composed and framed images:

> Summer in the City *[1970] had been done with a two- or three-page exposé. The shorts, too, were done without any script; there were only a few sketches of images. I came to filmmaking through images and as a painter. The concept of story was foreign to me, it was new territory. In those days, it was a process of gradually feeling out the filmmaking process, and for me the script was the strangest part of it.*
>
> **Wim Wenders, interviewed by Jochen Brunow, in *The Cinema of Wim Wenders*, ed. Roger Cook and Gerd Gemünden, 1997, p. 65**

Wenders' films avoid action and drama in favour of observation – the camera simply observes and shows events from a detached viewpoint. In temporal terms, these moments are called dead time.

Only a cinema of the image and dead time can reply to the hectic pace of Hollywood action films – its explosions, car chases and gun battles. Wenders' cinema challenges the supremacy of narrative causality by foregrounding the space and time of the image. This is particularly evident in *Alice in the Cities* and *Wings of Desire*. In *Alice in the Cities*, Alice and Philip search for the home of Alice's grandmother. The grandmother's home could have been found almost immediately. A narrative event would then have been completed, leading to another event. Instead, the grandmother is never found. The process of searching becomes the main focus of the film. What we see is a catalogue of events loosely linked together by the search for Alice's grandmother. Part of the search consists of the following actions:

- Alice and Philip have breakfast (14 shots).
- They drive to Essen (9 shots).

- They stop to ask a couple sitting on a bench if they recognise the grandmother's house from a photo that Alice has (6 shots).
- Alice and Philip drive through an area of town full of empty houses (6 shots).
- One shot of the industrial landscape.
- Alice and Philip stop to ask some children and a cab driver if they recognise the photo of the grandmother's house (14 shots).
- Alice's views of the passing townscapes (5 shots).
- Alice and Philip in a photo booth having their photographs taken (1 shot).
- Alice and Philip in a car park doing warm-up exercises for swimming (1 shot).
- One shot of the industrial landscape.
- Alice and Philip drive around Gelsenkirchen and find the grandmother's house. But Alice's grandmother no longer lives there. They decide to go swimming (25 shots).

Most of the events in this segment are unimportant to the narrative – for example, the shots of the empty houses, the shot of Alice and Philip doing the warm-up exercises and the shot of the two of them in the photo booth. Furthermore, the order of the events is not important. We can change around many of these events without creating confusion. Is it important that the shot of Alice and Philip doing the warm-up exercises comes before or after the shot of the two of them in the photo booth? Unlike the opening three scenes of *Psycho*, analysed in Chapter 2, the events in *Alice in the Cities* are not linked together by a strong cause-effect logic. We can say that *Alice in the Cities* has an episodic structure, because each scene consists of an autonomous episode.

Yet, this is not to suggest that the actions are totally arbitrary. Many scenes described above do have a symbolic meaning. To give just two examples: the empty houses symbolise the loss of stability that both Philip the German writer and Alice the temporarily abandoned girl feel as they drive around Germany. And in the shot of the warm-up exercises, Alice closely mimics Philip's actions, symbolising both the child's innocence, but also her total dependency on the adult.

Summary of Hitchcock and Wenders

- Hitchcock is identified by all *auteur* critics as an undisputed *auteur* because of his consistency in style and themes.
- Hitchcock's style consists of: 1) an emphasis on editing and montage; 2) a high number of point-of-view shots; and 3) filming in confined spaces, which provided Hitchcock with challenges on how to construct scenes.
- Hitchcock's themes include: 1) a narrative involving an investigation (usually of a murder), in which the film's protagonist is either the investigator or the one who is investigated; 2) confession and guilt; 3) suspense; 4) the perfect murder; and 5) the wrong man.
- Wenders is an *auteur* of the New German Cinema.
- The main themes in Wenders' films include: 1) the influence of North American culture; 2) road movies; 3) male bonding; and 4) the impossibility of male–female relationships.
- The main stylistic elements in Wenders' films include: 1) an emphasis on the image, rather than narrative; and 2) an emphasis on dead time.

The contemporary *auteur*

The *auteur* is no longer just a critical category, but also an industry category. In contemporary Hollywood, this is due to new production practices. Instead of the assembly-line production of the old Hollywood system, where stars, directors and technicians were tied to long-term contracts, in contemporary Hollywood talent is hired on a film-by-film basis. Rather than a few directors being defined as *auteurs*, every director has to set him- or herself up as an *auteur* in order to get work. Directors must establish for themselves a distinct visual style so they can be considered for a particular project:

> *By treating film-makers as independent contractors, the new production system places particular emphasis on the development of*

> *an idiosyncratic style which helps to increase the market value of individual directors rather than treating them as interchangeable parts. Directors such as Steven Spielberg, David Lynch, Brian DePalma and David Cronenberg develop distinctive ways of structuring narratives, moving their camera, or cutting scenes which become known to film-goers and studio executives alike. The emergence of the auteur theory in the 1960s provided these directors with a way of articulating and defending these stylistic tendencies as uniquely valuable.*
>
> **Henry Jenkins, 'Historical Poetics', p. 115**

One can go further and argue that contemporary Hollywood directors are marketed as *auteurs*, with their own brand image. The director's name is used to achieve pre-production deals (as a director's name can guarantee to the studio executives a certain style of film making) and particularly in the distribution and marketing of films (*Batman and Robin* is identified in its trailer as 'A Joel Schumacher Film', *The Lost World* is clearly identified as 'A Steven Spielberg Film', and so on).

Further reading

Caughie, John (ed.), *Theories of Authorship* (London: British Film Institute, 1981)
A representative sample of essays on the various schools of auteurism, although Caughie has taken the liberty of shortening a number of the papers, in some cases quite drastically.

Cook, Roger and Gerd Gemünden (eds), *The Cinema of Wim Wenders: Image, Narrative, and the Postmodern Condition* (Michigan: Wayne State University Press, 1997)
A wide ranging collection of essays that serves both as an introduction to Wenders' cinema as well as detailed discussion of specific films (including *Until the End of the World* and *Wings of Desire*).

Hillier, Jim (ed.), *Cahiers du Cinéma, The 1950s: Neo-Realism, Hollywood, New Wave* (Cambridge, Mass.: Harvard University Press, 1985); *The 1960s: New Wave, New Cinema, Reevaluating Hollywood* (1986)
The first two volumes in a three-volume series publishing representative essays from *Cahiers du Cinéma*. An indispensable collection.

Jenkins, Henry, 'Historical Poetics' in *Approaches to Popular Film*, ed. Joanne Hollows and Mark Jancovich (Manchester: Manchester University Press, 1995), pp. 99–122
Jenkins offers an overview to the internal (or poetic) approach to the cinema. A useful supplement to the first part of this book.

Rohmer, Eric and Claude Chabrol, *Hitchcock: The First Forty-Four Films* (New York: Ungar, 1979)
The first book-length study of Hitchcock's films, first published in French in 1957 by two prominent writers for *Cahiers du Cinéma*.

Sarris, Andrew, *The American Cinema: Directors and Directions: 1929–1968* (New York: Da Capo Press, 1996)
First published in 1968 and fortunately republished by Da Capo Press, this is the bible of *auteur* studies. The eleven categories in which Sarris places various directors ('Less than meets the eye', 'Make way for the clowns!') may be a little quirky, but the dictionary length and mini-essays on, predominately, American directors are invaluable.

Vincendeau, Ginette (ed.), *Encyclopedia of European Cinema* (London: Cassel, 1995)
A comprehensive and informative reference book with a slight bias towards French cinema. The longer entries are particularly valuable.

4 FILM GENRES: DEFINING THE TYPICAL FILM

Genre movies have comprised the bulk of film practice, the iceberg of film history beneath the visible tip that in the past has commonly been understood as film art.

Barry Keith Grant, Introduction to *Film Genre Reader*, p. xi

What the film critic, who sits blindly through films week after week, could be expected to do is to contribute to an aesthetic of the typical film.

Lawrence Alloway

The genre film is the mass-produced product of the Hollywood film industry. Whereas the *auteur* approach to Hollywood cinema, discussed in the previous chapter, privileges invention and personal creation, the study of genre privileges convention and collective meaning. Auteurism therefore emphasises the uniqueness of a film, whereas genre study emphasises the similarities that exist between a group of films. Genre study privileges a film's conformity to a pre-existing set of conventions.

More accurately, auteurism identifies the common attributes that make an individual director's films unique, whereas genre study identifies the common attributes that define a particular group of films. Auteurism groups together a small body of films according to their specific stylistic attributes, which are equated with the director's authorial signature. Genre study groups together a large body of films according to the common attributes that make that film a typical example of its type.

The contrast between auteurism and genre study can be spelt out in the following terms:

- genre study privileges what is general, standard, ordinary, typical, familiar, conventional, average and accepted in a group of films
- auteurism privileges what is specific, unique, unusual, inventive, exceptional and challenging in a group of films.

The same film, of course, can be analysed from the perspective of genre study or auteurism. Each perspective will simply privilege different aspects of the film. For example, *Blonde Venus* has been studied both as a genre film – a melodrama – and as an auteurist film – a film by the well-known auteurist Josef von Sternberg, containing the typical attributes of his *mise-en-scène*, such as shallow depth, created by lace or netting occupying the foreground and covering the entire image, which obscures the story and characters in favour of reducing story space to an abstraction, emphasising pattern, texture and rhythm (indeed, Sternberg downplayed story and character to such an extent that he wanted his films to be projected upside down!). Below I shall discuss *Blonde Venus* as a melodrama.

There are two main approaches to genre: a descriptive approach and a functional approach. A descriptive approach divides up the Hollywood cake into genre slices and defines each genre according to its properties, or common attributes. But it is not sufficient merely to describe the common attributes of each genre. This descriptive approach needs to be supplemented by an approach that defines the function of genre films. Below we shall see how the notion of genre enables us to determine the relation between a film and the society in which it is produced and consumed. This involves defining the genre film as a cultural ritual, or a myth. In the second part of this chapter we shall see how genre critics have attempted to describe and define the function of three film genres: the melodrama, the *film noir*, and the 1950s science fiction film.

Problems in the study of genres

The word 'genre' means 'type' or 'category'. To study a film as a genre involves treating it, not as a unique entity, but as a member of a general category, as a certain type of film. In the descriptive approach, a film is subsumed under a particular genre category if it possesses the necessary properties or attributes of that genre. The aim of the descriptive approach to genre is therefore to classify, or organise, a large number of films into a small number of groups. Yet, in film studies at least, this process of classification does not systematically organise films into genres. This is because the boundaries between film genres are fuzzy, rather than clearly delineated. Moreover, genres are not static, but evolve. Therefore, their common attributes change over time. Most films are hybrid genres, since they possess the common attributes of more than one genre. A typical example is the singing cowboy film, which possesses the attributes of both the musical and the Western.

Further problems arise in the descriptive approach. For example, how do we define genres? Do we rely on categories identified by the film industry, or categories defined by film critics? And how do we identify the common attributes of genres? If we start by grouping films together and then identifying their common attributes, we must ask ourselves: Why did we group these particular films together? If you answer that it is because of their common attributes, then you have pre-empted the descriptive aim of genre study, which is precisely to identify those common attributes.

The descriptive approach to genre is therefore fraught with difficulties. At the end of this chapter we shall see that the functional approach also raises difficulties. But despite these difficulties, I shall still endeavour, in this chapter, to see what results both the descriptive and functional approaches to film genre have so far achieved.

Genre film as social ritual

Genre films create expectations that condition our responses. The familiarity of the genre film enables each spectator to anticipate and predict what will appear in them. The genre film sets up hopes and promises and brings pleasure if these hopes and promises are fulfilled. In studying genre films, we first need to isolate the patterns and themes that appear repeatedly in them. For genre critics, these recurring patterns are not merely formal patterns; instead, they reflect the basic questions, problems, anxieties, difficulties, worries and, more generally, the values of a society and the way members of that society attempt to tackle those basic questions and problems. A genre film is satisfying, then, if it addresses those questions and problems that spectators expect them to address. The genre film is a form of collective expression, a mirror held up to society that embodies and reflects the shared problems and values of that society.

The genre film also offers solutions to those problems, and reinforces social values. Of course, a genre film cannot offer real solutions to real questions and problems; its solutions are imaginary and idealistic. But this may explain one of the attractions of the cinema, and the genre film in particular: it offers imaginary answers to real problems, although during the film, these answers seem to be more than mere fantasy. It is only upon leaving the movie theatre, as we try to get home, or after we switch off the television, that the real problems begin to emerge again.

From this discussion of the function of genre films, we can argue that watching them is a form of cultural ritual. To study genre films is one way of studying the culture that produces and consumes them. Barry Keith Grant argues that:

> *Surely one of our basic ways of understanding film genres, and of explaining their evolution and changing fortunes of popularity and production, is as collective expressions of contemporary life that strike a particularly resonant chord with audiences. It is virtually a given in genre criticism that, for example, the thirties musicals are on one level 'explained' as an escapist Depression fantasy; that* film noir *in the forties expressed first the social and sexual dislocations brought about by World War II and then the disillusionment when it ended; and that the innumerable science fiction films of the fifties embodied cold war tensions and nuclear anxiety new to that decade.*
>
> **Barry Keith Grant, 'Experience and Meaning in Genre Films', pp. 116–17**

The genre film offers a lesson in how to act within society and how to deal with current problems and anxieties. But it does not offer neutral ways of dealing with social problems; instead, it prescribes a preferred set of values: those of capitalist ideology, with its emphasis on the individual – the individual's right of ownership, private enterprise and personal wealth; the nuclear family with the wife staying at home and the husband working, the necessity of conforming to moral and social laws, and so on.

New studies of melodrama

In the following pages we shall review the common attributes of film melodrama and then look at recent studies that have divided up the genre of melodrama into thinner slices. The genre of melodrama has been exhaustively studied: see, for example, the books by Barbara Klinger, Christine Gledhill and Jackie Byars (see Further reading). Rather than attempt to summarise this enormous body of work and repeat its conclusions, it is more beneficial to concentrate on the more recent and narrowly focused studies. But first, a few general remarks.

Historically, melodrama has replaced religion as a way of thinking through moral issues and conflicts. As with religion, the function of melodrama is to clarify ethical choices that we have to make in our lives. This is why the conflict between good and evil is central to melodrama. But rather than focusing on the sacred, as religion does, melodrama focuses on moral issues and conflicts as experienced by ordinary people on a personal, everyday basis.

The genre of the film melodrama is frequently defined as a woman's genre, because it represents the questions, problems, anxieties, difficulties and worries of women living in a male-dominated, or patriarchal, society. The first and most prevalent property, or common attribute, of melodrama is that it is dominated by an active female character. Below I have attempted to list the melodrama's primary attributes.

- A woman often dominates the narrative of the melodrama.
- Melodrama narrates the perspective of the victim; in conjunction with the above attribute, melodrama can be said to turn its female character into a victim.
- Melodrama makes moral conflict its main theme or subject matter, particularly the moral conflicts experienced by women within patriarchal society.
- Melodrama is usually based on an omniscient form of narration; Chapter 2 illustrated omniscient narration by means of Douglas Sirk's melodrama *Magnificent Obsession*.
- The plot of melodrama consists of unexpected twists and sharp reversals in the story line.
- The plot of melodrama also consists of chance events and encounters.
- Secrets also dominate the melodrama plot.
- Finally, the melodrama contains dramatic knots, which complicate the plot and which create the moral conflicts.

Almost all melodramas contain some or all of these attributes, although not all are dominated by women. A number of Douglas Sirk's films (such as *Written on the Wind* and *Tarnished Angels*) are called male melodramas because their narratives are dominated by men, who are set up as victims, and who experience moral conflicts because they cannot live up to the roles carved out for them by patriarchal society.

We shall now look at the more narrowly focused and recent studies of melodrama. We shall first consider what Lea Jacobs calls the fallen woman film and then analyse *Blonde Venus* (Josef von Sternberg, 1932) as a fallen woman film. I shall then discuss what Stanley Cavell, the philosopher, calls the melodrama of the unknown woman and then analyse *Only Yesterday* (John Stahl, 1933) as a melodrama of the unknown woman. Finally, I shall examine what Mary Ann Doane calls the paranoid woman's film and briefly discuss several films that belong to this subgenre.

The fallen woman film

Although the term 'fallen woman film' has been used for some time, it has now been immortalised in a book by Lea Jacobs, called *The Wages of Sin: Censorship and the Fallen Woman Film, 1928–1942*. A representative sample of fallen woman films includes: *Anna Karenina* (Clarence Brown, 1935), *Ann Vickers* (John Cromwell, 1933), *Baby Face* (Alfred Green, 1933), *Bachelor Mother* (Garson Kanin, 1939), *Back Street* (Robert Stevenson, 1941) *Blonde Venus* (Sternberg, 1932), *Camille* (George Cukor, 1937), and *Marked Woman* (Lloyd Bacon, 1937).

Jacobs defines this group of films in the following way:

> *These films concern a woman who commits a sexual transgression such as adultery or premarital sex. In traditional versions of the plot, she is expelled from the domestic space of the family and undergoes a protracted decline.*
>
> ***The Wages of Sin*, p. x**

Because of the transgressive nature of their subject matter, these films were strongly censored. Lea Jacobs attempts to demonstrate how censorship shaped and defined the fallen woman's film – or, more specifically, how censorship imposed certain narrative conventions on studios which made fallen woman films. The influence of censorship can therefore be found in the way it affected a film's cause-effect logic.

As we saw in Chapter 2, classical narrative films are governed by a cause-effect logic, which means that one action or event is perceived by the spectator to be caused by another action or event. These actions and events are normally carried out by a single character, or small group of characters, who thereby initiate, motivate, and link together in a cause-effect logic the film's actions and events across the entire film. However, some actions and events were deemed offensive by film censors. In the early 1930s, due to public pressure (notably by the Legion of Decency, which had 11 million members, and which recommended to all its members that they boycott offensive films), the Hollywood film industry established a form of self-regulated censorship, in which all film scripts had to be sent to the Studio Relations Committee before shooting began. The film studios then attempted to incorporate the censors' suggestions into the script before shooting (so scripts were primarily censored in Hollywood, not final films). The censors' recommendations usually meant that the film's cause-effect logic had to be distorted, for censorship did not so much affect what was to be depicted in films, but how it was to be depicted.

Jacobs points out that, at the level of the whole film, censorship clearly sought to encourage unambiguous forms of representation (that is, films with a unified moral message). But at the level of the shot and the scene, censors recommended that film makers represent potentially offensive events in an indirect way. Such a strategy resulted in ambiguous forms of representation.

Jacobs analyses in detail how censorship affected *Blonde Venus*. Before reviewing Jacobs' analysis, I shall sum up the film's plot. The film centres around a former cabaret performer Helen Faraday (played by Marlene Dietrich), her chemist husband Ned Faraday (Herbert Marshall) and their son Johnny. Ned develops chemical poisoning which can only be cured in Europe. In order to pay for his journey and his treatment, Helen returns to the stage. While Ned is in Europe being cured, Helen develops an affair with a rich politician called Nick Townsend (Cary Grant). On his return, Ned discovers that Helen is having an affair and tries to take custody of Johnny. Helen goes on the run with Johnny. She falls into destitution and becomes a prostitute. She is found by an undercover cop hired by her husband and gives up her son. She eventually picks herself up and becomes a famous cabaret star in Europe. In Europe, Helen meets Nick and they return to America to enable Helen to see her son again. But, during the visit, Helen decides to remain with Ned and Johnny.

Blonde Venus is clearly a melodrama, for the following reasons:

It is dominated by a woman, Helen Faraday, who is also a victim. She is confronted with moral conflicts throughout the film: she has to give up her successful career for a domestic life; she sleeps with Nick in order to obtain the money to cure her husband; she leaves home with her child when her husband finds out that she is having an affair; she gives up her child and eventually returns home again. These are not straightforward choices that Helen makes; each requires a sacrifice and creates a moral dilemma. Moreover, many of these dilemmas are shared by most women living in a patriarchal society. There are several unexpected twists and sharp reversals in the plot: Ned returns early from Europe, which is how he finds out about his wife's affair (the main secret in the film), and Helen very quickly pulls herself out of destitution and becomes a cabaret star in Europe. Ned and Helen first meet each other by chance while Ned is on a walking tour in Germany and Helen and Nick meet by chance in Europe at the time that she has become a famous cabaret star (Figure 6).

According to the censors, there were three basic problems with *Blonde Venus*: 1) the affair between Helen Faraday and Nick Townsend; 2) scenes of Helen soliciting; and 3) the film's ending. The film's director, Josef von Sternberg, incorporated or avoided the censors' criticisms of the script through the manipulation of the film's causal logic.

The script of *Blonde Venus* indicates that, after singing one evening in a club, Helen must sleep with Nick in order to obtain $300 to pay for her husband's treatment in Europe. The depiction of Nick sleeping with Helen was obviously objectionable to the censors, but Sternberg filmed it in such a way as to make it acceptable (but at the cost of making the scene ambiguous). First, we see Helen and Nick in Helen's dressing room. This scene is followed by an insert of Nick writing a cheque for $300 to Helen; and finally, we see a shot of Helen being driven home.

We do not see Helen go to Nick's apartment to sleep with him. Yet it is precisely this event which motivates (which is the primary cause of) the action of Nick giving the cheque to Helen. All we see is Nick writing out a cheque. The reasons why he does this are not explicitly stated in the film itself. The spectator has to supply the repressed part of the narrative – namely that, after Nick and Helen met in Helen's dressing room, Helen returned to Nick's apartment and slept with him for $300. So the spectator has to infer the cause of Nick's action of writing the cheque.

Later in the film, Nick offers Helen an apartment while her husband is in Europe. But we do not directly see or hear Helen agree with Nick's proposal. We only know that she has taken up Nick's offer when she returns to her own empty apartment to pick up the mail. As with the scene just described, this is an indirect representation of events that the censors found objectionable (namely, a married woman living with another man).

This part of the film is indirectly stating that Helen is living with Nick in his apartment. But because we do not see on the screen Helen cohabiting with Nick, the censors cannot object. With only a small amount of information, the spectator can infer the cause of Helen's return to her own apartment to pick up the mail – namely, that she took up Nick's offer to live in his apartment. Rather than happening on screen, the film prompts the spectator to infer the objectionable material.

During her fall – that is, when she runs away, taking her son Johnny, Helen resorts to prostitution. The censors objected to a number of scenes in the script where Helen walks the streets and solicits men, is arrested by an undercover cop and is then charged in court with soliciting. In the actual film, the scene of Helen walking the streets and soliciting has been removed. Nonetheless, she still appears in court (although she is arrested for vagrancy, not soliciting). Helen therefore appears in court without motivation – she is not shown being arrested or causing a nuisance. In one scene we see her and Johnny take a ride on a hay cart. Cut to a shot of a card from the bureau of missing persons which indicates that Helen has been sighted. Cut again to Helen being led into court on the charge of vagrancy.

An event consisting of what censors regarded to be objectionable material but which is crucial to the cause-effect logic of the film is eliminated, resulting in an ambiguous, elliptical sequence. Later in the film, we do see Helen soliciting (she picks up the undercover cop) but this scene is not motivated in order for Helen to gain money from sex; rather, it is motivated so that Helen can humiliate the undercover cop (obviously acceptable to the censors!).

Finally, we need to say something about the ending of *Blonde Venus*. In one version of the script, Helen's husband Ned is reported to have had an affair with the housekeeper. This would then have given Helen sufficient reason to keep her son and to marry Nick Townsend. In this version of the ending, Helen retains her successful career in show business, keeps her son and marries the romantic lead. But the censors objected that this ending violated what they called the rule of compensating moral values, which states that all immoral actions must be compensated for in the film by means of the punishment of the immoral character or through the redemption of her immoral ways. But in this unfilmed ending of *Blonde Venus*, Helen's immorality (living with Nick, soliciting, etc.) is not compensated for; it is merely paired off with an immoral action performed by her husband. Sternberg's decision in the final script to end the actual film by pairing off husband Ned to his wife Helen was acceptable to the censors because it meant that Helen gives up Nick Townsend and her successful show business career in order to return to a domestic life for the sake of her son. Thus, Helen's illicit love affair and soliciting are compensated for at the end of the film by her maternal affections and her conformity to patriarchal values.

The melodrama of the unknown woman

For Stanley Cavell, 'failure' is the defining characteristic of the melodrama of the unknown woman. This failure is an inability to recognise – the male character's failure to recognise a woman from the past with whom he had a brief love affair. But it is also a matter of the female character's failure to prove her existence to a man – that is, her failure to be recognised by a man with whom she had a brief love affair. The female character is in control of all the relevant information, whereas the male character is distinguished by his ignorance. The moral conflict, the secret and the dramatic knot of the melodrama of the unknown woman are generated by the male character's lack of recognition of the female character. The moral conflict in the melodrama of the unknown woman can be summed up by the following question: How should the unknown woman make her presence known to the man she once loved? Furthermore, does she reveal to him the secret that only she remembers? The dramatic knot of these films is represented as a struggle: 'The woman's struggle is to understand why recognition by the man has not happened or has been denied or has become irrelevant' (Stanley Cavell, *Contesting Tears*, p. 30). Perhaps it would have been more accurate if Cavell called this subgenre the melodrama of the forgotten woman, because it clearly involves a loss of memory.

Stanley Cavell takes *Gaslight* (George Cukor, 1944), *Letter From an Unknown Woman* (Max Ophuls, 1948), *Now, Voyager* (Irving Rapper, 1942), and *Stella Dallas* (King Vidor, 1937) to be the quintessential melodramas of the unknown woman. But, as my own following analysis will attempt to demonstrate, *Only Yesterday* (John Stahl, 1933) is also a melodrama of the unknown woman, a film Cavell doesn't mention at all.

Only Yesterday opens on the day of the Wall Street crash. Jim Emerson (John Boles) loses all his, and his friend's, money. He goes into his study to commit suicide, but finds a long letter on his desk. The film then returns to the past to follow the story narrated in the letter. The letter begins with Jim, in uniform, meeting Mary Lane (Margaret Sullavan) at a party for soldiers. They leave the party together to walk by a lake. When they return to the party, they discover that everyone has left. Jim walks Mary home. Jim leaves

Figure 6 Helen and Nick in *Blonde Venus*

Figure 7 Mr Carroll admiring his portrait of his first wife in *The Two Mrs Carrolls*

Figure 8 Re-enactment of a murder in *The Thin Blue Line*

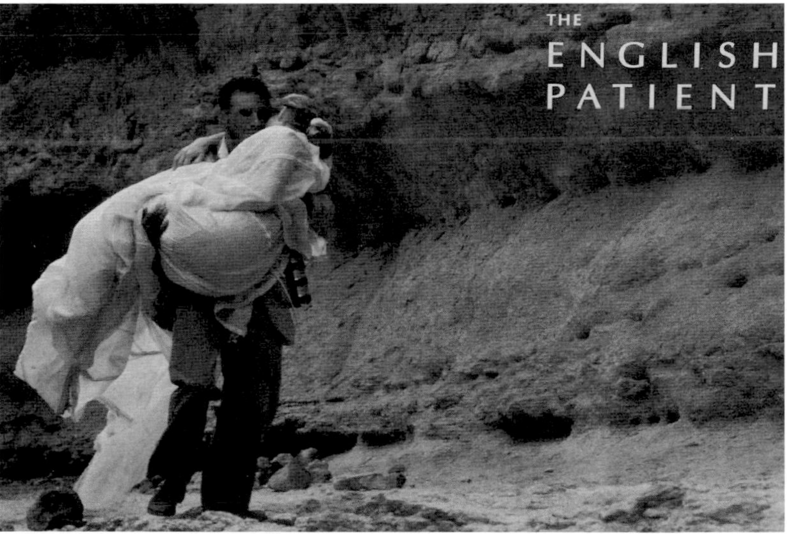

Figure 9 Almásy carrying the crippled Katherine along a cliff ledge in *The English Patient*

Figure 10 *The Lost World: Jurassic Park*

to fight in the war without saying goodbye to Mary. Later, Mary talks to her mother, who is saddened and ashamed by the news that Mary tells her (we only find out later what the news is: that Mary is pregnant). Mary goes to New York to stay with her aunt Julia. Mary has a baby boy and, later, goes to greet Jim as he returns from the war. But Jim fails to recognise Mary. Mary, who continues to live with aunt Julia, brings up her son on her own, and also works successfully as a fashion designer. Several years later, Mary meets Jim again at a new year's party. Jim still does not recognise her. Soon afterwards, Mary falls ill and decides to write the letter to Jim. She finishes just before she dies. We then return to Jim reading the letter. He rushes to Mary's home, but is too late, as Mary has died. However, Jim introduces himself to his son.

What defines *Only Yesterday* as a melodrama of the unknown woman is Jim Emerson's inability to recognise Mary as he returns from war (or, from the opposite point of view, Mary's failure to get herself recognised by Jim). This structure of unknownness is made more dramatic by the fact that Jim just happens to be the father of Mary's illegitimate child.

Mary's misfortune in becoming pregnant out of wedlock is therefore compounded by Jim's failure to recognise her. Mary could have become a fallen woman as well as an unknown woman if it wasn't for her broad-minded aunt Julia in New York. Julia remarks that 'this type of thing isn't even good melodrama' – by which she presumably means nineteenth-century literary and theatrical melodrama, in which the sexually transgressive woman automatically becomes a fallen woman and an outcast from society. Aunt Julia prevents Mary from becoming a fallen woman, but she cannot prevent her from becoming an unknown woman.

There are a few seconds of dramatic tension during Jim's return from the war, as we see Mary's face in extreme close-up as she finally realises that Jim does not recognise her, which become the crucial moment in the film's definition as a melodrama of the unknown woman. This crucial moment consists of a brutal discrepancy of knowledge between Jim and Mary – and, correspondingly, between Jim and the spectator, for the film is, of course, taking the point of view of the female victim. This discrepancy of knowledge is created by means of omniscient narration, a defining characteristic of melodrama. The whole of the film's narrative is then focused around the resolving of this discrepancy. However, this resolution is retarded through Mary's self-sacrifice (and later, through her realisation that Jim has married another woman). The discrepancy is overcome only after Mary writes a letter to Jim on her death bed.

Furthermore, we must remember that the discrepancy of knowledge in the film is overlaid by an illicit sexual relationship that resulted in a pregnancy. Such a transgression must be punished, according to the censor's logic of compensating moral values. Punishment is realised in the melodrama of the unknown woman in the woman's death and/or in the death of the illicit child. Here we can note a fundamental difference between Max Ophuls' film *Letter From an Unknown Woman* and *Only Yesterday* (films which are otherwise quite similar to one another). In Max Ophuls' film both the unknown woman and her illegitimate child die, whereas in *Only Yesterday*, the child lives but the mother dies.

This difference between the two films is crucial for understanding the role of the father in the melodrama of the unknown woman. Because both the illegitimate child and the unknown woman die in *Letter From an Unknown Woman*, these two deaths can only be compensated for through the father's death and *Letter From an Unknown Woman* ends with the father preparing to fight a duel he will surely lose. In *Only Yesterday*, however, the illegitimate child lives, permitting the father to redeem himself by looking after the child, since the mother has recently died (as is common in melodramas, the father has arrived 'too late'). Mary's death at the end of *Only Yesterday* is a compensation for her illicit sexual transgression (as well as her success as a business woman). At the beginning of *Letter From an Unknown Woman*, we see the father, Stefan, preparing to leave Vienna, after being challenged to a duel. But after reading the letter from Lisa, the unknown woman, Stefan changes his mind and decides to fight the duel which will lead to his death. But the opposite happens in *Only Yesterday*. Jim is just about to commit suicide after losing all his money (and all the money of his friends) during the Wall Street crash. But after reading Mary's letter, Jim finds new hope and rushes off to see his son. The letter in both films therefore dramatically changes the course of events for the male character. This is all the more noticeable in *Only Yesterday*, because it takes over 16 minutes of screen time before Mary's letter is discovered. The film has taken over a quarter of an hour to introduce a number of characters who have been affected by the Wall Street crash, which leads us to believe that the rest of the film will be concerned with the aftermath of the Wall Street crash and its effects on these characters. But then Mary's letter dramatically changes the course of the film by introducing a long flashback.

We need to return to the moment when the film communicates Mary's pregnancy to the spectator. The illicit affair and subsequent pregnancy is represented in an indirect manner, as is the potentially offensive material in *Blonde Venus*. But unlike *Blonde Venus*, *Only Yesterday* contains moments that are simultaneously under-represented and over-represented. The illicit love affair and Mary's pregnancy is under-represented in the sense that it is never explicitly stated in the film that Mary is pregnant. The film openly acknowledges Mary's condition only when the baby is born. Nonetheless, Mary's condition is over-represented in the sense that, throughout several scenes, the film continually hints at Mary's illicit love affair and pregnancy. Firstly, as Mary and Jim walk towards the lake in the moonlight, there is a several second fade out. After the fade in, Jim and Mary are seen hurriedly walking away from the lake. They pause while Jim reties Mary's sash; the camera then cuts to a medium close-up of Mary's face, emphasising her guilty expression. In effect, this part of the film – or, more precisely, the fade and Jim's action of retying Mary's sash – is indirectly saying that Mary and Jim have just had sexual intercourse.

After the scene in which Mary learns that Jim has gone to war, we cut to a scene in which Mary argues with her mother as her mother talks about the family being disgraced. Mary decides to stay with her broad-minded aunt Julia in New York, who talks about 'it' being just another one of those biological events. In total, Mary talks about her pregnancy with her mother and aunt Julia for over three and a half minutes of screen time, without actually mentioning the word 'pregnant'. Compare this long-winded form of indirect representation with the extremely short, elliptical narrative elisions in Sternberg's *Blonde Venus*. Furthermore, like *Blonde Venus*, *Only Yesterday* is representing the problems and difficulties that women experience in patriarchal society, but in the case of *Only Yesterday*, the difficulties involve pregnancy out of wedlock.

The paranoid woman's film

In the paranoid woman's film, a subgenre identified by Mary Ann Doane in her book *The Desire to Desire*, the active female character is inflicted with mental states such as paranoia. In addition to possessing some or all of the attributes of the melodrama, the paranoid woman's film also contains one or more of the following three attributes:

- it is based on a wife's fear that her husband is planning to murder her (the institution of marriage is haunted by murder)
- the husband has usually been married before, and his previous wife died under mysterious circumstances

- it contains a space in the home not accessible to the female character.

The narrative structure of the paranoid woman's film derives from the gothic novel – from Ann Radcliffe to Daphne du Maurier and beyond. Indeed, the first paranoid woman's film, Hitchcock's *Rebecca* of 1940, is based on du Maurier's novel of the same title. Other films belonging to the genre include *Gaslight* (George Cukor, 1944), *Jane Eyre* (Robert Stevenson, 1944), *The Spiral Staircase* (Robert Siodmak, 1946), *The Two Mrs Carrolls* (Peter Godfrey, 1947) and *Secret Beyond the Door* (Fritz Lang, 1947).

In terms of the first attribute, how does the wife begin to fear that her husband is planning to murder her? It is precisely from the other two attributes of the paranoid woman's film – the death of the first wife and the secret that the husband keeps locked behind closed doors (both attributes refer to the Bluebeard folk tale). In Hitchcock's film *Rebecca*, Rebecca was the first wife of the male lead Max de Winter. Like the first wife of the male leads in most paranoid woman's films, Rebecca died under mysterious circumstances. In *Secret Beyond the Door*, the first wife of Mark Lamphere, called Eleanor, also died under mysterious circumstances. In *The Two Mrs Carrolls*, the first Mrs Carroll suddenly dies when Mr Carroll (played by Humphrey Bogart) decides to marry Sally (played by Barbara Stanwyck) (Figure 7). But after one and a half years of marriage, Sally falls ill and at the same time discovers that Mr Carroll has fallen in love with another woman. After he husband tells her a number of lies, Sally finally figures out that Mr Carroll is planning to murder her.

The secret kept behind a locked door is the second attribute that leads to the woman's paranoia. In *Jane Eyre* there is, of course, the secret locked in the tower room, which is concealed from Jane. In *Gaslight*, the locked room is the attic where the husband searches for his dead aunt's jewels. It is precisely the husband's searching, which creates strange sounds and which dims the gaslight in the wife's room, that help drive her paranoid. In *Rebecca*, both the boat house cottage and Rebecca's bedroom are barred to the new Mrs de Winter. And in *The Two Mrs Carrolls*, it is the husband's painting studio that is kept locked. In the studio, Mr Carroll has painted a portrait of Sally, which he keeps out of Sally's view (for it is the custom of Mr Carroll to paint a 'death' portrait of his wife after he has decided to murder her). Mr Carroll inadvertently leaves the key to the studio with his daughter (the daughter of the first Mrs Carroll) and so Sally and the daughter (called Bea) decide to enter the studio when Mr Carroll is in London. It is by entering the forbidden room in order to satisfy her curiosity that drives Sally paranoid, for she is confronted with her husband's unflattering 'death' image of her.

The main motivation that drives the narrative in the paranoid woman's film is for the second wife (the second Mrs Carroll, the second Mrs de Winter in *Rebecca*, Celia Lamphere, the second wife of Mark Lamphere in *Secret Beyond the Door*) to distinguish herself from the first wife in order to gain her own identity and avoid suffering the same fate as the first wife. Many commentators have noted that the gothic narrative emphasises the closeness of mother and daughter and, also, emphasises the daughter's fear of being like her mother. This is therefore one of the fears thc paranoid woman's film represents. Perhaps we could argue that the function of the paranoid woman's film is very specific: to represent a woman's fear of being like her mother. And because the narratives of the paranoid woman's film is motivated by the second wife's attempts to distinguish herself from the first wife, we can argue that the function of the paranoid woman's film, as with gothic narratives in general, is to convince women that they are not their mothers. Mary Ann Doane therefore defines the paranoid woman's film, not only in terms of its common attributes, but also according to its function – the way it addresses the fears and anxieties of the female audience.

Film noir

For many film critics *film noir* does not refer to a genre, but to a style within the thriller or gangster film. However, I think that *film noir* does have a sufficient number of attributes and a cultural function that can identify it as a legitimate genre. Here we shall review the common stylistic and narrative attributes of *film noir* and then, briefly, look at its social function.

In terms of *mise-en-scène* and *mise-en-shot* (the traditional way of identifying *film noir*), the *film noir* has the following attributes:

- expressionist devices such as chiaroscuro lighting and skewed framing, creating a high contrast image made up of dense shadows, silhouettes, oblique lines and unbalanced compositions
- subjective techniques such as voiceovers and flashbacks
- equal emphasis given to actors and setting.

The *film noir* style uses the formalist techniques of image distortion discussed in Chapter 1. The *film noir*'s use of these techniques is usually attributed to the influence of German expressionist films (such as *The Cabinet of Dr Caligari*) and partly to the fact that many *films noirs* were directed by European expatriate directors such as Edward Dmytryk, Fritz Lang, Robert Siodmak and Billy Wilder.

In terms of narrative and themes, the *film noir* has the following attributes:

- in terms of major characters, a *femme fatale* and an alienated hero, who is usually a private detective living on the edge of the law
- a network of minor characters (who nonetheless play a prominent role), most of whom are morally ambivalent and somehow interrelated
- convoluted and incoherent narratives, created by ambiguous character motivation, the detective following false leads and sudden reversals of action
- the foregrounding of a narrator or a commentator, motivating the use of voiceover and flashbacks
- the representation of crime and its investigation
- an emphasis on realistic urban settings (which give some *films noirs* a semi-documentary look)
- the loss of hope, leading to despair, isolation and paranoia.

The *femme fatale* is the dominant attribute of the *film noir*. She is presented as a desirable but dangerous woman, who challenges patriarchal values and the authority of male characters. In fact, the *film noir* can be described as a struggle between the transgressive *femme fatale* and the alienated hero. Sometimes the hero is destroyed but, more often, he overcomes the desirability of the *femme fatale* and destroys her.

The alienated hero is usually a detective. *Films noirs* are based on the detective fiction of writers such as Dashiell Hammett, Raymond Chandler, Cornell Woolrich and James M. Cain. What is significant about the *film noir* detective is that he is sharply distinguished from both the gentleman mastermind, such as Sherlock Holmes, and the compliant detective working for the professional police force. The private detective is a lone individual who embodies his own moral law. The emphasis in the *film noir* is on the independent male fighting the criminals, the *femmes fatales*, as well as the inefficient, corrupt and inhuman government organisations.

These two figures, the *femme fatale* and the alienated detective hero, are a symptom of the upheavals witnessed during the 1940s in North American society. Feminist film critics point out that the *femme fatale* is a 'masculine construct', since she reflects male concern and insecurity over women's changing roles during the Second World War – particularly women's entry into the traditionally male workplace. This signifies women's economic independence, the fact that many women no longer believed that setting up a family to be their top priority and that there were fewer jobs available to the men who returned from war.

But the *film noir* is not simply a reaction to its immediate historical context. It is traditionally thought to reign from 1941 (beginning with John Huston's *The Maltese Falcon*) to 1957 (Orson Welles's *Touch of Evil*). Yet the *film noir* emerged again in contemporary Hollywood, with films such as *The Long Goodbye* (Robert Altman, 1973), *Chinatown* (Roman Polanski, 1974), *Body Heat* (Lawrence Kasdan, 1981), *Blood Simple* (Coen Brothers, 1985), *The Grifters* (Stephen Frears, 1990), *Pulp Fiction* (Tarantino, 1994), *L.A. Confidential* (Curtis Hanson, 1997), *Lost Highway* (David Lynch, 1997), and the films of John Dahl – including *Kill Me Again* (1989), *Red Rock West* (1993) and *The Last Seduction* (1994). To end this section on *film noir*, we shall look at the way John Dahl's neo-*noir* films develop and transform traditional attributes of *film noir*.

The neo-*films noirs* of John Dahl

In Dahl's debut film *Kill Me Again*, Fay Forrester (Joanne Whalley-Kilmer) and Vince Miller (Michael Madsen) steal money from the Mafia. Fay double crosses Vince and steals the money from him. To escape from both the Mafia and Vince, Fay hires a private detective, Jack Andrews (Val Kilmer), to pretend to kill her so that she can have a new identity. Jack is down on his luck and owes money to loan sharks. Yet he is shown to have an honest and integral character. Due to his debts, Jack takes the job, places himself on the margins of the law and becomes caught up in the web of evil spun by Fay, the *femme fatale*. Fay pays Jack \$5,000 before faking her murder and will pay him another \$5,000 afterwards (she says to Jack: 'I'll pay you \$10,000, half now and the other half after I'm dead', which echoes a similar line uttered in Orson Welles's *film noir The Lady From Shanghai*).

After the fake murder, Fay escapes from Jack without paying him the second instalment. He eventually tracks her down in Vegas and they become romantically involved. They decide to run away together, so they plan to fake their own deaths (Fay asks Jack to 'kill me again'), which involves drowning in a lake. Jack hides the money near the lake, to be retrieved in their getaway. But upon retrieving the money, Fay double-crosses Jack, shoots him and takes the bag of money. She escapes – with Vince, who has caught up with her. However, Vince and Fay are killed in a car crash. Jack survives the shooting and we see him carrying a different bag, which contains the money. He had obviously learnt not to trust Fay completely, so he switched the money to another bag. The film ends with him driving off with the money.

Kill Me Again contrasts the clear, bright, wide open spaces of the desert with the hazy, dark claustrophobic interiors. Unlike traditional *films noirs*, Dahl's neo-*noirs* are set away from the city in small towns, a location which irritates the *femmes fatales*, who want to live in the city. The film's credit sequence consists entirely of shots of the open desert landscape, an unconventional way to begin a *film noir*.

Fay is the typical *femme fatale* – she is desirable but dangerous and leads the luckless hero, the private detective Jack, into trouble. She clearly identifies his weaknesses and uses her knowledge of these weaknesses to manipulate him. Fay is relentless in her pursuit of money, doing almost anything to obtain it – switching her allegiance from Vince to Jack and back again when it suits her. She is even willing to shoot Jack when he has served his function.

Finally, it may be worthwhile noting that Dahl makes brief references to the work of Hitchcock throughout his films. In *Kill Me Again*, Jack stages the fake murder of Fay in a motel that looks remarkably like the Bates' motel in *Psycho*. Furthermore, when Jack dumps the car in a lake, it only sinks halfway. The scene is staged in the same way in *Psycho* when Norman sinks Marion's car in the swamp.

Like *Kill Me Again*, Dahl's second film, *Red Rock West*, focuses on the lone male – in this instance an injured war veteran Michael Williams (Nicholas Cage). The film begins in the same way as *Kill Me Again* – in a bright, clear, wide open landscape. Michael applies for a job with an oil drilling team, but his leg injury makes him unemployable. The fact that he refused to lie about his injury shows that, like Jack in *Kill Me Again*, he has an honest and integral character. But also like Jack, he gets himself into trouble. Out of work and with no money, Michael ends up in a bar in the small town of Red Rock. Here he is mistaken by the bar's owner, Wayne

(J.T. Walsh) for Lyle, a hired killer. Wayne has hired Lyle to kill his wife, Suzanne (Lara Flynn Boyle) for $10,000 ($5,000 before and $5,000 after the murder). Due to his circumstances, Michael takes the money.

When he meets Suzanne, Michael warns her of her husband's plan. She offers Michael double the money to kill her husband. As the plot becomes increasingly complicated, Lyle, the real hired killer (played by Dennis Hopper) turns up and Michael discovers that Wayne and Suzanne stole $2 million and are being sought by the FBI. But by this time, Michael has become romantically involved with Suzanne. At first, she is presented as the victim, but once Michael finds out about the money, he realises that she is duplicitous.

The film comes to an end with Michael, Suzanne, Wayne and Lyle in a graveyard at night, where the money is hidden. When the money is dug up, Wayne is fatally injured and Suzanne shoots Lyle. Suzanne and Michael escape on a goods train with the money, but Suzanne turns her gun on Michael. Luckily for Michael, it is empty. The film ends with Michael throwing both Suzanne and the money off the train; police cars are shown heading towards Suzanne.

In terms of visual motifs, *Red Rock West* is similar to *Kill Me Again*. It contrasts the wide open landscapes and small town community with the city. Furthermore, when it is not focusing on the landscape, most of *Red Rock West* takes place at night in dark, claustrophobic rooms. In terms of narrative, *Red Rock West* is almost identical to *Kill Me Again*. Fay is transformed into Suzanne, Vince into Wayne and Jack into Michael. The films mainly focus on the couple (Fay and Vince, Suzanne and Wayne) stealing money and then double-crossing one another. The honest hero (Jack/Michael), down on luck and money, momentarily transgresses and becomes involved in the couple's conflict – or more accurately, becomes romantically involved with the *femme fatale*, who eventually double-crosses him once she has used him. But like most *femmes fatales*, she is punished in the end (in *Kill Me Again*, Fay dies in a car crash, and in *Red Rock West* Suzanne is arrested). In both films, the hero escapes. But in *Kill Me Again*, Jack gets to keep all the money, whereas in *Red Rock West* the money is lost (except for one batch of notes, which Michael keeps).

Finally, there are a few Hitchcockian moments in *Red Rock West*. Firstly, Michael is set up as 'the wrong man' and, secondly, in a scene on the road, Michael is almost run over, which is filmed in the same way that Roger Thornhill is almost run over in *North by Northwest* (after he escapes from the crop-dusting plane).

The Last Seduction, Dahl's third film, contains many of the *noir* attributes found in his first two films, but this time there is a change in the film's narrative focus, since *The Last Seduction* follows the *femme fatale*. The *femme fatale* is Bridget Gregory (Linda Fiorentino), who persuades her husband Clay, a doctor (played by Bill Pullman), to sell medicinal cocaine to a drugs gang for $700,000. In characteristic Dahl style, Bridget double-crosses Clay and leaves the big city with the money for the small town – in this instance, Beston. Here she is picked up in a bar by Mike (Peter Berg), the naive, weak and luckless hero. She decides to become romantically involved with Mike in order to hide from Clay. She also gets a job in Beston together with a new identity (shades of *Kill Me Again*). But Clay, who owes money to loan sharks (more references to *Kill Me Again*), hires a private detective to track down Bridget. She manages to kill the detective and make it look like an accident. She then manipulates Mike in a plan to kill Clay in his apartment (and she achieves this not just by means of her desirability, but also by knowing Mike's weaknesses, particularly about his previous marriage). Just as Michael is unwilling to kill Suzanne in her home in *Red Rock West*, Mike is unwilling to kill Clay. However, Bridget murders Clay and double-crosses Mike by framing him for the murder. The film ends with Mike in jail and Bridget escaping with the money.

The differences between *The Last Seduction* and Dahl's previous two films are just as important as their similarities. *The Last Seduction* opens on the New York skyline, rather than the small town or countryside. Nonetheless, the small town plays a prominent role later in the film. As well as focusing on the *femme fatale*, *The Last Seduction* also shows her succeeding, for this time there is no attempt to make the film conform to the prescriptive system of compensating moral values. Bridget is not punished for stealing the $700,000, for killing her husband, or for framing Mike.

There is a Hitchcockian moment near the beginning of the film. Bridget escapes with the money while Clay is having a shower. She leaves him a note, which she writes backwards, in mirror writing. This echoes a scene in *North by Northwest*, when Eve Kendall 'escapes' from Thornhill. As he pretends to take a shower, Eve takes a telephone call, makes a note of an address and leaves. Thornhill then reads the imprint of the note on the writing pad and follows Eve to the address.

The continuity of style and themes across John Dahl's first three films clearly identifies him as an *auteur* – but one who is making (or reinventing) the genre of the *film noir*. Dahl makes smart, understated and unpretentious independently produced films. They are modestly made, but are technically superb and, unlike most films today, they are based on strong scripts. *Kill Me Again* was written by John Dahl and David Warfield, *Red Rock West* was written by John Dahl and his brother Rick Dahl and *The Last Seduction* was written by Steve Baranick. However, Dahl's latest film, *Unforgettable* (1997), has moved into new directions and was produced by a major studio. The film suffers as a result.

I hope this short study of Dahl's first three films show that auteurism and genre study can be reconciled. There is no absolute opposition between auteurism and genre study, since they occupy different positions along a continuum. The more we study subgenres within genres, the more we narrow down the films we group together, until we reach very special subgenres (as do Stanley Cavell and Mary Anne Doane, for example), or the work of a particular director.

1950s science fiction

The science fiction film of the 1950s shares some of the paranoia and insecurities of the *film noir*. Indeed one film, *Kiss Me Deadly* (Robert Aldrich, 1955) combines attributes from both genres. It contains the attributes of *film noir* – from its expressionistic lighting to the conflict between a detective and a *femme fatale*. *Kiss Me Deadly* is dominated by a search for a mysterious glowing box which, by the end of the film, the *femme fatale* opens to deadly consequences. The box evidently contains nuclear material that, in the wrong hands, unleashes havoc on the world.

The 1950s science fiction film is a favourite of genre critics who undertake the task of interpreting the function of genre films. Before we discuss the function of this genre, we shall briefly have a look at some of its common attributes. It usually consists of:

- a meditation on the implications and consequences of scientific and technological advances
- space travel and/or contact with aliens
- a setting in the distant future.

These three attributes are obviously linked, since the genre considers how science and technology in the future can take humanity into the distant realms of the universe and possibly come into contact with other life forms. This then leads to a number of science fiction films taking on some of the attributes of the horror film as the aliens, codified as monsters, become a 'supernatural' threat to humanity.

However, the science fiction films of the 1950s are not usually set in the future, but in the present, since they meditate on the implications and consequences of scientific and technological advances in the newly created nuclear power. The implications and consequences are usually (but not always) coded as negative. In *Them!* (Gordon Douglas, 1954) for example, a race of giant ants is found to be living in the desert of the American Southwest. The cause of these giant ants, which threaten humankind's existence, is identified as nuclear fallout from atomic tests. Similarly, in *When Worlds Collide* (Rudolph Maté, 1951), Earth is threatened and, in the end, destroyed by a runaway star. The star can be read as an allegory of an approaching nuclear war and the destruction of the Earth is the inevitable consequence. In these, and many other science fiction films of the 1950s, humanity is indirectly identified as the ultimate cause of the threat unleashed upon it. Humans are their own worst enemy. The fear manifest in 1950s science fiction films is a fear that, for the first time in history, mankind is able to destroy itself, by means of its own science and technology. Humanity has become decentred and vulnerable to extinction. Such films can therefore be read as reflecting the anxieties of the American public in the 1950s.

However, the threat is not always read by genre critics as a threat from 'humankind', but as a threat from a part of it – namely, communists. The science fiction films can therefore be understood as allegories of the Cold War. Ants are an appropriate metaphor for communists in *Them!* because ants are a warlike mass of undifferentiated, regimented soldiers, who are depicted in the film as threatening the lives of the American public. Such was the ideological image of communists perpetuated in America during the Cold War.

But the most celebrated film to be read as an allegory of the Cold War is *Invasion of the Body Snatchers* (Don Siegel, 1956). The film depicts the inhabitants of a small town in California being gradually replaced by pod people, who grow out of pods and look exactly like the people they replace, but with one crucial difference: they lack emotions and feelings. One message this film seems to perpetuate is that communists may look just like us, but they lack a crucial human trait. The film indirectly represents the result of a communist invasion and take over of American minds by means of communist ideology. In effect, the film is depicting the result of communist brainwashing: one will become an emotionless robot passively conforming to the totalitarian state.

This, at least, is the standard way to read *Invasion of the Body Snatchers*. But is it the only way? It is certainly possible to give the film an almost opposite reading: it can be read as a criticism of placid conformity to American Cold War ideology. The ideology perpetuated by the American government about the threat of communism to the American way of life instilled fear in the American public. The American government's ideology (as with all ideology) imposed a restriction on the way the public thought about and lived their everyday lives. This ideology established hysteria about an imminent invasion of America by Soviet communists, who would be aided by members of the communist party in America. This ideology encouraged the American public to root out the communists (the aliens) living amongst them, because they posed a threat to national security. Each individual's allegiance to the American way of life had to be affirmed and demonstrated, otherwise you were considered to be a traitor to the American way of life, for which you must be marginalised and punished.

For an ideological position to be successful, it must appear to be natural. During the 1950s, the 'Red Scare', as it came to be known, was very pervasive, which allowed the American government to justify its 'witch hunt' for communists, as well as its stockpiling and testing of nuclear weapons.

But not everyone bought into this ideology. Both Don Siegel, the director of *Invasion of the Body Snatchers* and the scriptwriter, Daniel Mainwaring, were highly critical of the process of 'podlike' social conformity, the repression of free speech and the loss of individuality that American Cold War ideology produced. Mainwaring was associated with communism in the 1930s, while Siegel's films of the 1950s depict a recurrent theme: the lone individual's defiance towards conformity, which shows Siegel to be a director with a liberal social conscience. From this perspective, the pods in *Invasion of the Body Snatchers* can be read as representing the American public's complacent conformity to their government's Cold War ideology, not as a threat of communist ideology to the American way of life. However, both Siegel and Mainwaring couldn't risk openly opposing the Cold War ideology, so they disguised their opposition in an allegorical science fiction story. Allegorical stories flourish in a time of censorship and repression.

The fact that the same film can be read from two completely different political perspectives raises problems about genre study, which I shall briefly discuss after a summary of this chapter.

Summary

- Genre studies is divided up into a descriptive approach and a functional approach.
- The descriptive approach classifies films within a particular genre according to the common attributes they possess.
- The functional approach attempts to relate a film to its historical and social context and argues that genre films embody the basic anxieties and values of a society.
- The film melodrama is frequently defined as a woman's genre, because it represents the anxieties women experience living in a patriarchal society.
- Recent studies of melodrama have identified the following subgenres: the fallen woman film, the melodrama of the unknown woman, and the paranoid woman's film.
- The *film noir* is dominated by a *femme fatale* and an alienated detective hero; both are symptoms of the upheavals witnessed during the 1940s in North American society.
- The science fiction films of the 1950s meditate on the implications and consequences of scientific and technological advances in the newly created nuclear power and on the 'threat' of communism to the American way of life.

One of the biggest problems with the external approach to film studies, of which genre studies is the representative example, is being able to establish a causal link between a film and its social and historical context. As we saw with *Invasion of the Body Snatchers*, the same film can be given an opposite meaning when related to its context (in this example, American society of the 1950s). *Invasion of the Body Snatchers* can be read as either supporting or opposing American Cold War ideology. What role does the film's historical and social context play? Does the film's context constitute evidence that supports an argument?

The purpose of the functional approach to genre studies is to bring a film back into the realm of the everyday; or, more accurately, to relate a fiction film to its nonfictional context. Genre critics do this in order to answer the question: how do films speak to us? What events in our everyday lives are they indirectly representing? These questions are necessary because they explain why millions of people go to the cinema every week. The answer genre critics give to these questions are plausible but not conclusive. Additional work needs to be carried out into the cultural meanings of the cinema.

Further reading

Byars, Jackie, *All That Hollywood Allows: Re-Reading Gender in 1950s Melodrama* (London: Routledge, 1991)
A feminist reading of popular melodrama from the 1950s, especially Douglas Sirk's *Magnificent Obsession*, *All That Heaven Allows*, *Written on the Wind* and *Imitation of Life*, as well as the male melodramas of James Dean: *Rebel Without a Cause*, *East of Eden*, and *Giant*.

Cavell, Stanley, *Contesting Tears: The Hollywood Melodrama of the Unknown Woman* (Chicago: University of Chicago Press, 1996)
Cavell's idiosyncratic (and rather unevenly written) study of a genre he has christened – the melodrama of the unknown woman.

Copjec, Joan (ed.), *Shades of Noir* (London: Verso, 1993)
This theoretically informed anthology reassesses the status of *film noir* as a genre, and argues that such a reassessment is necessary for two reasons: the re-emergence of *film noir* in contemporary Hollywood and due to the uneasy sense that *film noir* was never adequately discussed in the first place.

Doane, Mary Anne, *The Desire to Desire: The Woman's Film of the 1940s* (London: Macmillan, 1988)
Doane's book is a sophisticated and lucid study of four types of 1940s women's films – films dominated by medical themes, the maternal melodrama, the classic love story and the paranoid woman's film.

Gledhill, Christine (ed.), *Home is Where the Heart is: Studies in Melodrama and the Woman's Film* (London: British Film Institute, 1987)
A seminal collection of (occasionally difficult) essays on the melodrama, including Thomas Elsaesser's foundational essay 'Tales of Sound and Fury: Observations on the Family Melodrama'.

Grant, Barry Keith (ed.), *Film Genre Reader* (Texas: University of Texas Press, 1986)

A comprehensive anthology of 24 essays, divided evenly into theoretical approaches and studies of individual genres.

Jacobs, Lea, *The Wages of Sin: Censorship and the Fallen Woman Film: 1928–1942* (Wisconsin: University of Wisconsin Press, 1991)

An articulate and well-researched study of the representation of fallen women in the 1930s melodrama, demonstrating how censorship has influenced the genre.

Kaplan, E. Ann (ed.), *Women in Film Noir* (London: British Film Institute, 1980)

This is *the* authoritative guide to the way women are represented in *film noir*. It is concise, lucid and accessible. Essential reading.

Klinger, Barbara, *Melodrama and Meaning: History, Culture, and the Films of Douglas Sirk* (Bloomington: Indiana University Press, 1994)

Barbara Klinger looks at the way Sirk's films have been promoted and discussed in reviews, by fans and by academics, and studies in detail Rock Hudson's star image.

Neale, Steve, 'Melodrama and Tears', *Screen*, 27, 6 (1986), pp. 6–23

An important essay explaining why we cry when watching melodramas.

Palmer, R. Barton (ed.), *Perspectives on Film Noir* (New York: G.K. Hall & Co., 1996)

This anthology republishes a representative set of French and Anglo-American essays that first identified *film noir* as a distinct style or genre of film making.

5 THE NON-FICTION FILM: FIVE TYPES OF DOCUMENTARY

What kind of world do we inhabit, with what risks and what prospects? Tales we label fiction offer imaginative answers; those we label nonfiction suggest possibly authentic ones.

Bill Nichols, *Blurred Boundaries*, p. ix

What makes a film a documentary? We can begin to answer this question by identifying some of the basic premises film spectators normally hold about documentaries:

- Firstly, the events filmed must be unstaged; that is, the events must exist above and beyond the activity of filming them. In fiction films, by contrast, events are staged for the express purpose of being filmed. The unstaged nature of the events in documentaries therefore suggest that the events have an existence independent of the cinema. This is what gives them their authenticity.
- Secondly, documentaries are conventionally understood to be non-fiction films. In other words, they must be sharply distinguished from fiction films. The world depicted in the documentary is real, not imaginary.
- Thirdly, it is often assumed that the documentary film maker simply observes and makes an objective record of real events.

In recent times, all three assumptions have come under attack. In this chapter I shall question in particular the third point. It is now commonplace to argue that the very presence of the camera influences the filmed events. Moreover, documentary film makers employ a wide variety of techniques in putting their films together; they do not simply point the camera towards their subject and let the camera roll. The documentary film maker cannot simply observe and objectively record because he or she makes technical choices – selecting the camera angle, camera lens, film stock, deciding how to edit shots together and so on. This seems to make the documentary personal and subjective. The selection and emphasis of particular events by means of film techniques seem to betray the documentary film maker's particular perspective on the filmed events. What is valorised by the *auteur* critics in relation to Hollywood fiction films is condemned in documentary films.

But by what standard of objectivity are documentary films being judged? All films necessarily involve selection and editing. No film is therefore purely objective – if by objectivity we mean that the events are seen from no particular perspective. This is an unreasonable standard by which to judge documentary films. The issue is not so much whether they are based on selection but: How do the selections made by the documentary film maker manipulate the events? Because all documentary films 'manipulate' events, then it may be better to use a more neutral term, such as 'shape' events. We can reserve the term 'manipulation' for documentaries that can be categorised as propaganda – those that hide from the spectator the processes they use in shaping events.

In the following sections, we shall see how Bill Nichols has divided up the documentary cake into five slices. Each type of documentary is defined and distinguished according to how it shapes the events being filmed by means of particular techniques selected by the film maker. This is similar to the process of genre study outlined in the previous chapter. Whereas particular genres are defined in terms of their invariant iconic and narrative attributes, types of documentary are identified according to the particular techniques they use. I shall follow Bill Nichols' theoretical discussion of the five types of documentary, although I have endeavoured to summarise and simplify his conceptual discussion and have added case studies to give substance to each category.

The five categories Nichols identifies are: the expository, observational, interactive, reflexive and the performative documentary. I shall illustrate each respective category with the following: *Coalface* (Alberto Cavalcanti, 1935), *High School* (Frederick Wiseman, 1968), *Roger and Me* (Michael Moore, 1989), *Man with a Movie Camera* (Dziga Vertov, 1928) and *The Thin Blue Line* (Errol Morris, 1988).

Expository documentary

> *Voice-of-God commentary and poetic perspectives sought to disclose information about the historical world itself and to see that world afresh, even if these views came to seem romantic and didactic.*
>
> **Bill Nichols, *Representing Reality*, pp. 32–3**

Bill Nichols' definition of expository documentary emphasises its typical characteristics: a disembodied and authoritative voiceover commentary combined with a series of images that aim to be descriptive and informative. The voiceover addresses the spectator directly, offering a series of facts or arguments that are illustrated by the image track. The voiceover either provides abstract information that the image cannot carry, or comments on those actions and events in the image that are unfamiliar or presumably unintelligible to the target audience. The aim of the expository documentary is to be descriptive and informative, or to provide a particular argument. For example, it may celebrate a set of common values, or a particular lifestyle. Below we shall see how *Coalface* celebrates a day in the life of the miner. Expository documentary is the 'classic' mode of documentary, which is now more commonly used in TV documentaries, where abstract information is conveyed via the voiceover commentary. The overall effect of the expository documentary is one of objectivity, of direct and transparent representation.

The British documentary film movement (1927–39), founded by John Grierson, made expository documentaries that were also poetic and aesthetic, rather than simply descriptive and informative. The movement operated in two government departments: firstly, the Empire Marketing Board and then, from 1933, the General Post Office. The most prestigious films of the movement include Alberto Cavalcanti's *Coalface* (1935), John Grierson's *Drifters* (1929), Humphrey Jennings' *Spare Time* (1939), Harry Watt's *North Sea* (1938), Basil Wright's *Song of Ceylon* (1939) and Watt and Wright's *Night Mail* (1936). Due to the financial restrictions imposed upon it by civil servants, the documentary film movement also made films for outside bodies, such as the gas board and the Ceylon tea company. The aim of all these documentaries was to function as a public service, to inform the 'general public' about the everyday working of the industries and corporations that shape their lives. These documentaries therefore served to improve the public image of large corporations.

The prevailing ideology of 1930s Britain in some ways resembled the ideology prevalent in 1980s Britain. In 1929 the Balfour Committee on Industry and Trade recommended that the government encourage corporate expansion, rather than State control. That is, the emphasis shifted towards unregulated capitalist expansion, rather than State intervention. The setting up of a documentary film movement, funded and regulated by the government, ran contrary to this ideology. This explains the difficulties the movement faced when it came to funding and, indeed, with its very existence. However, it also explains the rise in large corporations commissioning public relations films.

The position of the documentary film movement can be identified with centre progressive pressure groups ('middle opinion') of the 1930s, which held the following beliefs:

> *In the first place, there was a belief in the essential soundness of established society; in the second place, there was a belief in the need for State regulation and intervention, and, in the third place, there was a rejection of the option of a socialist or fascist transformation of society. These political and cultural parameters framed what some critics have described as a 'social democratic consensus', which developed in opposition to orthodox economic liberalism and marxism during the inter-war period, and which became the most influential reform movement of the period.*
>
> **Ian Aitken, *Film and Reform*, p. 168**

However, these pressure groups communicated their ideas to a middle-class audience:

> *the documentary movement was primarily dedicated to the communication of ideas to governing elites and intellectuals, and although Grierson used a rhetoric of mass communications, the reality behind the rhetoric was that the movement functioned, inevitably, as a means of minority, and not mass communication.*
>
> **Ian Aitken, *Film and Reform*, p. 173**

The middle-class bias is particularly evident in the way the movement represented the working classes. One can argue that, in films such as *Coalface* and *Spare Time*, the film makers are glorifying the working classes, exalting them by presenting them as heroic labourers, rather than exploited, degraded and poorly paid workers, living with extreme social hardships.

Coalface is an expository documentary. It consists of an authoritative voiceover that rapidly presents to the spectator statistical data on the British coal industry (the location of collieries, the amount of coal produced, the number of miners employed, injured and so on). A number of the images simply illustrate the voiceover. But others go far beyond the aim of being descriptive and informative. In a sequence depicting the miners underground, a montage of shots contrasts the half-naked bodies of the miners with the coal and the machinery. The close-ups of the miners' bodies in particular aim to represent their work as a heroic struggle against nature. This reading is strongly reinforced by the soundtrack, which consists of singing (the 'Colliers' chant' by W.H. Auden) and orchestral sound effects (the musical score was written by Benjamin Britten).

At the end of the shift, there is an extraordinary sequence of shots depicting the machinery of the pit, particularly the winding gear that brings the miners to the surface. These shots do not aim to be descriptive and informative. They are close-ups of the machinery abstracted from their surroundings, which has the effect of isolating the rhythmic movement of the machinery rather than illustrating its function. Moreover, the cutting is very quick – 32 shots are presented in only 39 seconds, which again emphasises movement and rhythm, rather than function. These shots represent an abstract film inserted into the documentary. A standard expository documentary would simply consist of a few functional shots of the winding gear. But the use of close-ups and rapid cutting in this sequence from *Coalface* creates an abstract effect that takes this sequence far beyond the merely descriptive and illustrative.

The following sequence shows the miners leaving the pit and walking home. It consists of the following shots:

- 3 shots of miners leaving the pit.
- 2 shots of a street of identical houses; the camera angle emphasises the similarity of the houses.
- 1 shot of a house situated in an open space; a washing line is to the right.
- 2 shots of chimney stacks and winding gear silhouetted against the sky; in the second shot, the camera pans left to tree branches blowing in the wind.
- 1 shot of a washing line, smoke stacks appear in the background.

- 1 shot of a coal mine; the camera pans left to a tree blowing in the wind.
- 1 shot of a ruined house, with winding gear in the background.
- 1 shot of the tree blowing in the wind; the camera pans up to the sky.

As with the previous sequence, the shots are not merely descriptive and illustrative. They evoke a number of pastoral and romantic clichés – silhouettes, the wind blowing through the trees, ruins, the 'end of the day' and so on. These shots offer a counterpoint to the voiceover, which does not talk about the wind blowing through the trees, but offers a series of statistics, or specific knowledge, such as the way the Davy lamp works. In summary, these shots do not merely depict the life of the miner; they present a pastoral, almost a mythological, image of a 'good and honest' life.

Does the film privilege the coal industry or the miners? As with the other films of the British documentary movement, *Coalface* does not attempt to present the miners as individual people, but simply as examples of a particular type of worker, together with the way they interact with their workplace and their home setting. Some critics argue that the film represents the coal industry in terms of necessity and inevitability (John Corner, *The Art of Record*, p. 61). What this means is that the coalminers' job, however harsh, is necessary. *Coalface* therefore exalts and glorifies those who carry out the work. More generally, the aesthetic approach of the British documentary movement presents a distanced view of working-class culture, a view that treats it as both exotic and strange.

The prestigious films of the documentary film movement are constructed according to a modernist or formalist aesthetics – that is, they exploit the transformative nature of film, rather than its mimetic or naturalistic potential. Grierson's philosophy consisted of using the aesthetic nature of film for social purposes. He argued that 'there is every reason to believe that industrial and commercial films require an even greater consideration of visual effects than the average dramatic film. They have indeed little else on which to subsist' (Grierson, quoted in Ian Aitken, *Film and Reform*, p. 100). This privileging of the aesthetic over the naturalistic is evident in *Coalface*.

But the centre progressive philosophy of the documentary movement is evident in its choice of subject matter. The very act of representing the intrinsic values (both positive and negative) of working-class life is radical in itself.

John Corner asks: 'How far are the two impulses [modernist aesthetics and social theme] integrated in *Coalface* and how far are they contradictory ambitions, mutually compromising each other's integrity and success?' (Corner, *The Art of Record*, p. 62). For Corner, the film combines aesthetic ambitions with public communication – to make visible to the broader public the workings of a vital national industry, and the way the lives of the ordinary workers are influenced and determined by the industry they work for. Due to these two influences, the film itself is inherently ambiguous.

Observational documentary

> *An observational mode of representation allowed the film maker to record unobtrusively what people did when they were not explicitly addressing the camera. ... But the observational mode limited the film maker to the present moment and required a disciplined detachment from the events themselves.*
>
> **Bill Nichols, *Representing Reality*, p. 33**

The observational mode of documentary is characterised by the non-intervention of the film maker in the filmed events. The observational mode is more notable for what it does not contain: there is no voice of god commentary, no intertitles and no interviews. The emphasis is to present a slice of life, or direct representation of the filmed events. The film maker attempts to be completely invisible, that is, an uninvolved bystander. The observational documentary film maker therefore aims to simply observe unfolding events. For this reason, emphasis is placed on recording events as they unfold in real time. This is why observational documentary is also called direct cinema.

In technical terms, the observational documentary tends on occasions to use long takes (where the camera is filming continuously, as described in Chapter 1). Sound is also direct and was simply recorded while the camera was rolling. These techniques are evident in the work of one of the most famous film makers of observational documentaries – Frederick Wiseman. In his documentary called *High School*, filmed in the Northeast High School in Philadelphia in 1968, Wiseman aims to observe and capture the typical, day-to-day events that take place in this school. There are no dramatic or unusual events to film here. The aim is simply to record everyday events, primarily of different classes in progress.

The observational mode establishes an 'intimate' relation to the filmed events and establishes a sense of place by refusing to manipulate or distort the events. The observational documentary is therefore attempting to persuade the spectator that the film is an accurate slice of life; that what is filmed is a transparent record of what took place in front of the camera. In other words, it is meant to be neutral and non-judgemental.

These, at least, represent the ideal of observational cinema. In practice, it is possible to discern a number of strategies that illustrate the director's intervention in the filmed events in the observational documentary – both within scenes and between scenes. Yet this intervention is played down in the observational documentary. It is possible to detect an implicit agenda at work in a number of observational documentaries. What is Frederick Wiseman's purpose in making *High School*? Did he simply want to show how schools function, or is he attempting to undermine the school by exposing the teachers as out of touch with the youth of the 1960s? We can look at the way observational documentaries intervene in the filmed events and see how this intervention reveals an implicit agenda.

As David Bordwell and Kristin Thompson point out, Wiseman only films one aspect of school life: namely, the interaction and conflict between pupils and teachers, with the teachers invariably imposing discipline. Wiseman has therefore decided to emphasise one particular event (namely, conflict) and downplay other events. Moreover, he has made definite choices about how to film these conflicts, with an emphasis on close-ups. Scene transitions may also suggest an implicit meaning. In one scene, a Spanish teacher is seen to wave her arms about, drilling the students. Wiseman then cuts to a music teacher conducting percussion musicians. The repetition of the action suggests that the students are simply being drilled, rather than taught.

Although Wiseman does not present himself as a political film maker, many political commentators detect a socialist agenda in his films – an implicit critique of American institutions such as school. But by using the observational mode, Wiseman is downplaying his own critical perspective and seems to be presenting the case that, by simply filming inside institutions such as schools and showing the power struggles that take place there, the liberal minded spectator will inevitably develop a critical attitude towards the filmed events. Because he does not attempt to intervene in the events, Wiseman would not claim responsibility for any typecast images of the people he films; he would argue that such images are already present in the events themselves. For example, the oppressive behaviour of the teachers in *High School* is a result of the American educational system, not of the presence of Wiseman's camera.

Interactive documentary

> *Interactive documentary ... arose from the ... desire to make the film maker's perspective more evident. Interview styles and interventionist tactics arose, allowing the film maker to participate more actively in present events.*
>
> **Bill Nichols, *Representing Reality*, p. 33**

The observational mode of documentary attempts to hide the presence of the film maker from the spectator. By contrast, interactive documentary makes the film maker's presence prominent, as he or she interacts with the people or events being filmed. In other words, all interactive documentaries by definition draw the filmed people and events into direct contact with the film maker. The content of the interactive documentary is based primarily on interviews, which draw out specific comments and responses from those who are filmed. An interactive documentary that is made well will allow the filmed people to express their opinions and views, and the film maker may juxtapose one opinion with a contrary opinion, therefore offering the spectator a balanced view.

Sometimes the film maker is the main person on screen, which may serve to hold the documentary together. Compare this to the expository documentary, in which the disembodied voice of the narrator holds the film together, and the observational documentary where the events themselves have to hold the film together, with a little help from the film maker who edits the shots and scenes together.

There are a number of ways in which the film maker may interact with the people he or she is filming. The film maker may appear on screen and will, formally or informally, ask the interviewee questions. Here, both film maker and interviewee share the same space and the spectator can see them interacting with one another. The film maker therefore clearly acts as a mediator between the interviewee and the spectator. Or the film maker may remain off screen, in which case we may or may not hear the questions. All we see is the interviewee addressing answers to someone just beyond the frame. Furthermore, if the film maker remains off screen, he or she has the choice of allowing the questions to be heard by the spectator; or may decide to edit out the questions altogether. Although in these examples the film maker is not seen and may not be heard, he or she still shares the same space as the interviewee, and still plays the role of mediator, but his or her presence is less evident.

Interactive documentaries show the process of interaction taking place. The act of gathering information by means of interviews is clearly shown – including the negotiation of the terms and conditions under which the interview is to take place. The result is that the spectator can see what effect the interview is having on the interviewee. Unlike expository or observational documentaries, the interactive documentary shows the process by which it is made. We must remember that in all documentaries, there is a power relation involved, between the film makers and those who are filmed. This power relation is masked by the expository and observational documentary, but is apparent in the interactive documentary (as well as the reflexive documentary, to be discussed below).

The ethical question about filming someone is made apparent in the interactive documentary. But the film maker can, nonetheless, simply use the interviews for his or her own purposes. Interaction and juxtaposition of shots and scenes, together with the use of archival footage, constitute the main tools of the interactive documentary film maker. The film maker uses these tools in order to present an argument. What is important from an ethical perspective is the manner in which the film maker presents the interviewees. How does the film maker prompt the interviewee? Is the film maker provocative? Or does the film maker allow interviewees to put their case fully? How are the interviews used in the final film? We shall begin to approach these questions by looking at one of the most controversial interactive documentaries in recent times – Michael Moore's *Roger and Me* (1989).

A description of the content of *Roger and Me* cannot convey the irony, humour and anger that the film can arouse in the spectator. But briefly, the film is about the decline of the town of Flint in Michigan, which was dependent on the continuing presence of General Motors to sustain it. But the chairman of General Motors, Roger Smith, initiated a series of closures of General Motors factories in Flint in order to move production to Mexico, where the workers are paid less than their American counterparts. The result was that Flint became one of the poorest towns in America. The film depicts Michael Moore's repeated attempts to interview Roger Smith about the closures and to invite him to Flint to see the effects his policy are having on the town. Interspersed with these repeated attempts to interview Roger Smith are Moore's interviews with various people in Flint.

Most of Moore's attempts to interview Roger Smith fail. But these moments are not left out of the film. Indeed, the process of attempting to interview Roger Smith adds humour to the film. But humour is also added by the constant presence of Michael Moore on screen as he interviews various people in a deadpan and ironic manner. *Roger and Me* is far from the observational mode of documentary. Moore is not an observer, but a participant. He therefore has no intention of remaining neutral and hidden (not least because he was born and grew up in Flint). His film represents the victims of 1980s corporate activity and he tries to make the chairman of one such corporation accountable for his actions. The difficulties Moore has in interviewing Roger Smith strengthens the film's message that chairmen of large corporations simply avoid being accountable for the social devastation that their policies bring about.

Moore conveys this strong social message by means of editing. He comments on the rich and famous people of Flint by juxtaposing interviews with them with scenes of the poor people of Flint being evicted from their homes. The first time this editing strategy is used is approximately 18 minutes into the film, where Moore interviews a number of wealthy people at the Annual *Great Gatsby* party, held at the home of one of General Motors' founding families. When Moore asks what are the positive aspects of Flint, the final interviewee replies 'Ballet, hockey. It's a great place to live'. Moore then immediately cuts to the sheriff's deputy, Fred Ross, evicting a poor family from their home.

The second time this editing strategy is used is approximately 27 minutes into the film, when Moore interviews Miss Michigan. Asked to comment on the job losses in Flint, Miss Michigan simply replies that 'I'm for employment and working in Michigan'. This is then followed by another eviction (after Moore has shown the result of the 1988 Miss America contest, which was won by Miss Michigan). The third time, approximately 49 minutes into the film, is when Moore cuts to the evictions directly after interviewing a group of upper-class women playing golf.

But the most poignant use of this editing strategy is saved for the end of the documentary, when Roger Smith is shown giving a speech on the spirit of Christmas, which Moore interacts with shots of a family in Flint being evicted from their home on Christmas eve. Moore uses the images of eviction as a form of critical commentary, to show how the rich and powerful (most notably, Roger Smith) do not understand the effect of unemployment on the poor.

Despite its strong social message, the film has been criticised for 'manipulating' and 'misrepresenting' events. In some ways, the agenda of *Roger and Me* resembles the agenda of the British documentary movement – to represent the underclasses on film, those who do not usually have a voice. But, just as the British documentary movement romanticised the lives of the working class by elevating their lifestyle, we need to see how Michael Moore has used the events in Flint for the purposes of his film.

Moore has been criticised for manipulating the chronology of events in Flint. The discrepancies in the film's chronology became apparent in an interview with Michael Moore conducted by Harlan Jacobson in the journal *Film Comment* (November/December 1989). John Corner sums up the four main discrepancies:

> **1** Ronald Reagan, depicted visiting laid-off auto workers, was a presidential candidate, not the President, when he made his visit. (The film does not describe him as president, but the assumed chronology of the scene and the projected effect of the footage works with the idea that he is.)
>
> **2** The evangelist who is depicted visiting the city after the *Great Gatsby* society party in 1987 actually visited in 1982, several years before the crucial 1986 lay-offs.
>
> **3** The three big civic development projects which are seen in the film as more or less concurrent attempts to counter the effects of the 1986–7 lay-offs (Hyatt Regency Hotel; Autoworld theme-park; Water street shopping pavilion) had all closed before these lay-offs.
>
> **4** The number of jobs lost during the 1986–7 closures seem to be far less than indicated in the film. The spread of losses from 1974 onwards is closer to the film's estimate. (The figure of 30,000 is given in an edited clip from a CBS news broadcast – which may be referring to motor industry closures of which those in Flint are only a *part*.) (John Corner, *The Art of Record*, pp. 165–6)

In the interview with Harlen Jacobson in which these discrepancies became apparent, Moore argued that the film is about a town that died in the 1980s; it is not just about the 1986–7 lay-offs. And other reviewers argued that the broader picture presented in the film (corporate greed, wasteful capital expenditure) is more important than the fine details.

However, *Roger and Me* does raise questions about the implicit boundaries that govern the making of documentaries and whether the film maker should make the spectator aware that the rules (such as sticking to the chronology of events) are being broken. For it is not immediately apparent in *Roger and Me* that the rules of documentary are being broken. However, in the fourth category of documentary, exposing the rules and conventions of documentary become the main aim of the film.

Reflexive documentary

> *Reflexive documentary arose from a desire to make the conventions of representations themselves more apparent and to challenge the impression of reality which the other three modes normally conveyed unproblematically.*
>
> **Bill Nichols, *Representing Reality*, p. 33**

In the interactive mode of documentary, we saw that the film maker on screen participates in the events being filmed. In the case of *Roger and Me*, Michael Moore interviews the people of Flint and attempts to interview Roger Smith, chairman of General Motors. In interactive documentary, therefore, the film maker does not attempt to conceal his presence, unlike the practice in expository and observational documentary.

In reflexive documentary, the film maker goes one step further than interactive documentary, attempting to expose to the spectator the conventions of documentary representation, with the effect of challenging the documentary's apparent ability to reveal the truth. Rather than focus on the events and people filmed, the reflexive documentary focuses on how they are filmed. In the reflexive documentary, the properties of the film and the film making process become the main focus of attention.

The reflexive documentary does not pretend to simply present a slice of reality, since it also tries to demonstrate to the spectator how film images are constructed. Whereas the interactive mode makes the film maker's presence known to the spectator, the reflexive documentary makes the whole process of film making known to the spectator.

Reflexive documentary challenges the documentary's status as objective and illustrates the subjective choices involved in film making. But a lack of objectivity does not necessarily reduce the significance or impact of a documentary. A documentary that acknowledges its limitations and its own perspective is more valuable than a film that pretends to be neutral and objective. Michael Moore makes no attempt to be neutral or objective and his personal involvement in the story – he was born in Flint – partly explains why he decided to make *Roger and Me*. A reflexive documentary goes much further than the interactive documentary in making the spectator aware of all the stages involved in making a documentary. One of the most celebrated examples of a reflexive documentary is Dziga Vertov's *Man with a Movie Camera* (1928).

Vertov is generally regarded to be the father of radical documentary, a type of film making that challenges normative and common-sense views of reality. Like the British documentary film movement, Vertov's work was funded by the state. But whereas the British documentaries of the 1930s reflected the opinions of centre progressive pressure groups ('middle opinion') Vertov, an iconoclast of Soviet film making during the revolutionary period, attempted to change the audience's perception of everyday reality through radical techniques that attempt to raise each spectator's consciousness.

In terms of content, *Man with a Movie Camera* is a documentary because it shows unstaged events, scenes from everyday life that add up to represent the working day – from waking up, going to work and, finally, to leisure activities. However, Vertov does not simply film these events, but transforms them by means of specific film techniques. He not only shows everyday life, but also shows how it has been filmed.

Throughout *Man with a Movie Camera*, Vertov shows the camera recording events, the editor re-arranging shots on the editing table, a film being projected and an audience in a cinema watching a film. In addition, he uses the specific qualities of film – montage, fast and slow motion, freeze frame, out of focus shots, double exposure and reverse motion – to remind us that what we see is a reconstructed reality mediated through film.

Vertov's working methods are therefore divided up into two principles: what he calls the 'Film-Truth' principle, the process of capturing life-as-it-is, and the 'Film-Eye' principle, the procedure of constructing a film out of these shots by means of the specific qualities of film. In *Man with a Movie Camera*, each shot itself is a fragment of reality. But Vertrov treats each shot as the raw material from which to make a film. Vertov calls the individual shots the bricks of film. The film makers then have a choice of building a modest house or a mansion from these bricks.

Vertov is only interested in building the filmic equivalent of a mansion. He offers us another perspective on reality, a perspective filtered through the specific qualities of film. Moreover, Vertov does not hide the fact that the view he gives the spectator is constructed, since he shows the spectator the process of construction. This is why *Man with a Movie Camera* is a reflexive documentary.

Performative documentary

> Performative *doc. (1980s–90s): stress subjective aspects of a classically objective discourse.*
> *– possible limitations: loss of referential emphasis may relegate such films to the avant-garde; 'excessive' use of style.*
>
> **Bill Nichols, *Blurred Boundaries*, p. 95**

The fifth and final category, performative documentary, has a paradoxical status because it deflects attention away from the world and towards the expressive dimension of film. That is, reference to the world is marginalised and the poetic and expressive dimensions of film are emphasised. The performative documentary does not capture the world in the same way as the other forms of documentary. It aims to represent the world indirectly.

The performative documentary evokes the mood or atmosphere traditionally found in fiction films. It aims to present its subject matter in a subjective, expressive, stylised, evocative and visceral manner. The result is that the subject matter is rendered in a vivid way that encourages the spectator to experience and feel them. But, at the same time, we have to ask ourselves whether the events become distorted as a result of the way they are represented.

The subject matter in the performative documentary remains intact, but its meaning is shown to be variable. In *The Thin Blue Line* (Errol Morris, 1988), for example, the subject matter is the murder of Dallas police officer Robert Wood in 1976. A drifter named Randall Adams was convicted of the murder, while the chief witness against him, David Harris, has been sentenced to death for another murder. Who actually shot Robert Wood, and how this event takes place, is open to question. The film is based on the testimony and memory of witnesses who purportedly saw the events. But these testimonies and memories do not add up. They are faulty and inconsistent. Morris explores these inconsistencies by re-enacting the murder. Each time a testimony reveals a new or inconsistent fact about the murder, Morris shows a re-enactment which incorporates the new or inconsistent fact. *The Thin Blue Line* is not therefore about what really happened, but about memory, lies and inconsistencies. Furthermore, these re-enactments are rendered in a vivid, stylised, and evocative manner characteristic of performance documentaries (Figure 8).

The first re-enactment of the murder takes place in the first five minutes of the film. I shall therefore describe the film's opening.

- The film begins with shots of the cityscape of Dallas at night (4 shots).
- Shot of Randall Adams talking about his journey to Dallas in 1976.
- Close-up of a police light flashing. It creates a visceral, pulsating effect.
- Shot of David Harris talking about his journey to Dallas in 1976. He talks about stealing a car and a pistol. Cut to ...
- A photograph of a pistol.
- Shot of Harris talking.
- Cityscape of Dallas at night (3 shots).
- Shot of Randall Adams. He talks about how he met David Harris (Adams's car ran out of gas and he was picked up by David Harris).
- Aerial shot of Dallas (Harris's voice appears over the image).
- Map of Dallas.
- Closer shot of the map (followed by two additional closer shots of the map, creating a jump cut effect as the camera focuses on the street in which Adams and Harris met).
- Shot of a hotel sign (motivated by the voiceover of Harris: 'I followed him [Adams] to his room').

  Interestingly, behind the motel sign is a billboard that reads 'change your life'. The events being narrated certainly changed Randall Adams's life.
- Shot of Harris speaking.

- Shot of a drive-in movie sign (Harris: 'We went to a movie that night').
- Shot of Adams. He says: 'I get up. I go to work on Saturday. Why did I meet this kid? I don't know. Why did I run out of gas at that time? I don't know. But it happened. It happened'.
- This is then followed by the re-enactment of the murder of Robert Wood. The re-enactment begins with:
- A high angle shot of a police car that has pulled up behind a car parked on the side of the road. At first, it seems that this car may be Randall Adams's car that has run out of gas. After all, in the previous shot, Adams mentions that he ran out of gas. So the editing initially links the car to Adams. This is followed by:
- An abstract shot inside the parked car. The shot consists of the rear view mirror, and a hand readjusting it. The shot is heavily backlit, turning everything in the shot into a silhouette. (The use of backlighting is a technique favoured by Hollywood directors such as Steven Spielberg.) Cut to ...
- The police car. The first police officer gets out. The police lights on top of the car shine directly into the camera as they spin round, creating a strobe lighting effect that turns the screen red at brief intervals. The lights are emphasised even more by the soundtrack which, together with Philip Glass's hypnotic music, consists of a swishing sound synchronised with the lights. The overall effect is visceral, pulsating and hypnotic.
- Close-up of a hand on the steering wheel inside the parked car. Again, it is heavily backlit.
- Shot of the police car. The second police officer gets out. She shines the torch at the parked car/in the direction of the camera. The flashing lights on the police car have the same prominence as previously.
- High-angle shot of the road, heavily backlit. The shadow of the first police officer enters from the top of the image as he walks towards the parked car.
- Extreme low shot of the parked car's back wheel, filmed from underneath the car. The police officer's feet are seen as he walks by.

- Close-up of a gun pointing towards the camera's direction. The gun is fired.
- Shot of a drawing of a hand, showing a bullet entry point.
- Shot of the gun firing.
- Shot of a drawing of a body, showing bullet entry points.
- Close-up of the gun firing.
- Another close-up of the gun, this time as it points downwards and fires a shot.
- Shot of a drawing of a body, showing bullet entry points.
- Close-up of the gun, pointing downwards and firing a shot.
- Close-up of a drawing of a body, showing bullet entry points.
- Shot of the gun being withdrawn into the car.
- Close-up of a car's pedal and the driver's foot.
- Shot of the police officer lying in the road. The car pulls away.
- Head-on shot of the police car. The second police officer enters the centre of the frame and fires her gun.
- Low shot of the car pulling away.
- Close-up of the police officer's gun, with the flashing, pulsating police lights in the background.

This re-enactment is followed by an additional drawing showing the bullet entry points, two portraits of the actual murdered police officer (one shot of him alive, one shot of him dead), two shots of his police uniform, showing the bullet entry points, a shot of a newspaper, whose headline reads 'Officer's killer sought' and, finally, three extreme close-ups of extracts from the newspaper story.

The dominant performative elements in these opening minutes include the following: the re-enactment itself; close-ups of guns, maps, newspaper headlines and pulsating police lights (whose prominence create a vivid effect that far exceeds their function); rapid editing (the jump cut effect created by the closer shots of the map; the cutting from the gun discharging to the shots of the drawings is very rapid); exaggerated camera positions (high camera angles, low camera positions); the soundtrack (Philip Glass's hypnotic music; the swishing sound synchronised with the lights, the loud gun shots). Other performative elements appear elsewhere in the film, including: the filming of some events in slow motion, together with the fact that the re-enactments are repeated on several occasions.

The performative elements of *The Thin Blue Line* create the same mood and atmosphere found in Hollywood thrillers – suspense and poised anticipation, complete with highly stylised images and soundtrack. Through these techniques Morris encourages us to experience and feel the events, rather than simply watch them from a distance. However, by doing so he also hypes the events for entertainment purposes. This raises an ethical question about Morris's manipulation of the events. Does he lose sight of the events themselves in favour of giving the spectator a thrilling experience? That is, does he lose sight of the documentary's purpose of being informative and authentic?

Despite its performative elements, Morris's film did influence the reality it filmed. *The Thin Blue Line* shows that the testimonies of the main witnesses are unreliable and inconsistent, particularly David Harris's original testimony. Indeed, at the end of the film, Harris indirectly admits to committing the murder of Robert Wood. Soon after *The Thin Blue Line* was released, Randall Adams's conviction was overturned.

I hope that this chapter has dispelled the common-sense idea that documentaries are simply objective records of real events. It may sound extreme, but it is possible to argue that the documentary film has no privileged relation to reality, since both fiction and documentary films employ the same technologies – mechanics, optics and photochemistry. A fiction film such as *The Maltese Falcon* is therefore an 'objective record' of what a group of actors, such as Humphrey Bogart, and film technicians, such as director John Huston, achieved on a Warner Bros. sound stage in 1941. What distinguishes fiction from non-fiction is the belief that the events filmed in a documentary are unstaged and therefore non-fictional. Furthermore, by using the work of Bill Nichols, I have tried to emphasise that the realm of the documentary consists of five modes or genres with their own invariant traits that distinguish them from one another.

Summary

- It is often assumed that the documentary film maker simply observes and makes an objective record of real events. But documentary film makers do not simply point the camera towards their subject and let the camera roll; they employ a wide variety of techniques in putting their films together.

- The expository documentary employs the following techniques: a disembodied and authoritative voiceover commentary, plus a series of images that aim to be descriptive and informative.
- The observational documentary tries to present a 'slice of life', or a direct representation of the filmed events. The film maker attempts to be completely invisible, that is, an uninvolved bystander.
- The interactive documentary makes the film maker's presence prominent, as he or she interacts with the people or events being filmed. These interactions primarily take the form of interviews, which draw out specific comments and responses from those who are filmed.
- The reflexive documentary attempts to expose to the spectator the conventions of documentary representation. Rather than focus on the events and people filmed, the reflexive documentary focuses on how they are filmed. The effect is that the reflexive documentary challenges the documentary's apparent ability to reveal the truth.
- Performative documentary deflects attention away from the world and towards the expressive dimension of film. That is, reference to the world is marginalised and the poetic and expressive dimensions of film are emphasised.

Further reading

Aitken, Ian, *Film and Reform* (London: Routledge, 1990)
A well-researched, in-depth study of the British documentary film movement.

Corner, John, *The Art of Record: A Critical Introduction to Documentary* (Manchester: Manchester University Press, 1996)
Accessible case studies of classic documentary films from the 1930s to the 1980s. A good starting point for anyone who wants to pursue documentary further.

Nichols, Bill, *Representing Reality: Issues and Concepts in Documentary* (Bloomington: Indiana University Press, 1989)

An important but densely written book. The chapter on documentary modes of representation has been used as the foundation for this chapter. My aim has been to make this important chapter of Nichols' book accessible to the general reader.

Nichols, Bill, *Blurred Boundaries: Questions of Meaning in Contemporary Culture* (Bloomington: Indiana University Press, 1994)
A companion volume to *Representing Reality*, offering case studies (on the Rodney King video tape, 'Reality Television', Eisenstein's *Strike*, Oliver Stone's *JFK*, and performative documentary). As with *Representing Reality*, a difficult but important book.

6 THE RECEPTION OF FILM: THE ART AND PROFESSION OF FILM REVIEWING

The role of the critic is to help people see what is in the work, what is in it that shouldn't be, what is not in it that could be. He is a good critic if he helps people understand more about the work than they could see for themselves; he is a great critic, if by his understanding and feeling for the work, by his passion, he can excite people so that they want to experience more of the art that is there, waiting to be seized. He is not necessarily a bad critic if he makes errors of judgement. (Infallible taste is inconceivable; what could it be measured against?) He is a bad critic if he does not awaken the curiosity, enlarge the interests and understanding of his audience. The art of the critic is to transmit his knowledge of and enthusiasm for art to others.

Pauline Kael, *I Lost it at the Movies*, p. 308

Film reviewing, indeed criticism in general, is commonly called professional fault finding, particularly by those whose work is frequently reviewed. My aim in this chapter is to analyse the functions and components of the film-reviewing profession and the conventions that determine how reviewers evaluate films. The first half of the chapter will outline four functions of film reviewing and its four components. The second half will consist of a comparative analysis of seven reviews of *The Lost World: Jurassic Park* (Spielberg, 1997), with the aim of charting the similarities and differences in the film's reception. In academic terms, this chapter takes a reception-studies approach to films. That is, it does not analyse films themselves (the internal approach to film studies, explored in Chapters 1–3), but investigates the way a film is received and evaluated. Reception studies explores various responses to films – both written and oral (including interviews with individual spectators). In this chapter, I have limited the responses to *The Lost World* to one privileged group of spectators, namely, professional film reviewers, who earn their living by writing on current film releases. That their work is defined as 'fault finding' is simply an outsider's view of their profession, a profession that has its own standards, conventions and rituals. My aim here is to begin to make these standards, conventions, and rituals more explicit.

The four functions of film reviewing

In this book *Making Meaning* (p. 35), David Bordwell argues that a film review can have up to four functions. It can act as:

- journalism
- advertising
- criticism
- rhetoric (writing).

As journalism, film reviewing presents to the reader news on the latest film releases and, more specifically, significant aspects of a particular film. For example, the film may have a noteworthy theme (topical subject matter, for example); it may have a significant star (an old star returning to the screen, the debut performance of a new star, or an established star taking on a significantly different role); or the production may be noteworthy. For example, the fees of the film's main stars may be very high, or the cost of production is excessive, as with *Waterworld* (Kevin Robins, 1995), which cost $175 million to produce. But this film has now been superseded by James Cameron's *Titanic* (1997), which was rumoured in the trade journal *Variety* (26 May–1 June 1997) to be budgeted at around $200 million, making it the costliest film ever.

More specifically, we can identify two types of film journalism:

- Journalism of opinion, in which the journalist presents a carefully thought-out position on a film, backed up with a set of arguments and background information;
- Journalism of taste, in which the journalist presents a simple evaluation of a film.

In-depth reviews of films combine these two types of journalism. Below I shall outline in more detail the various components of a film review.

As advertising, a review functions to publicise a film and encourages its readers to go to the cinema. Film reviewing can therefore be seen as a service industry, since it functions as a service to both the studio that financed and produced the film (by advertising their film), and as a service to film goers, by functioning as a consumer's guide to the best and worst films currently available.

Occasionally, a reviewer may write a condescending review, allowing the reader to feel superior to the film. The review therefore informs the reader of films he or she should know about, but without recommending that the reader go and see the film. Here, the review is certainly not functioning as advertising, quite the reverse. This usually applies to reviews of the summer blockbusters in the highbrow press. However, most of the summer blockbusters are review proof anyway – that is, the audience has already decided to see the film because it has a 'must-see' status attached to it and it achieves this status primarily through positive 'word of mouth'.

As criticism, a review involves the description, analysis and evaluation of films. Much of this chapter will be taken up with the task of describing film reviewing as criticism.

Finally, as writing, reviews become essays and are read for their own intrinsic literary merits, which may lead to them being republished in a single authored anthology; for example, James Agee's *Agee on Film*, Manny Farber's *Negative Space*, Pauline Kael's numerous collections, Andrew Sarris's *Confessions of a Cultist*, Jonathan Rosenbaum's *Placing Movies: The Practice of Film Criticism*, and so on.

The four components of film reviewing

Above, we saw that film journalism can be divided into a journalism of opinion (informed reviews) and a journalism of taste (which simply passes judgements). In this section we shall identify in more detail the major components that go to make up a film review.

David Bordwell (*Making Meaning*, p. 38) emphasises that a review usually consists of the following four components:

- a condensed plot synopsis
- background information
- a set of abbreviated arguments about the film
- an evaluation.

The condensed plot synopsis is simply a description of the film's plot. Most synopses tend to emphasise the big moments in the film, although it is careful not to reveal the film's ending. The background information includes genre, stars, director, anecdotes about the film's production and reception and so on (this is where the review functions as news). The set of abbreviated arguments about the film is the reviewer's main focus, as he or she analyses and comments on the film. Finally, the reviewer offers an evaluation of the film, and (implicitly or explicitly) a recommendation to see/not to see the film. The evaluation is the result of the reviewer's activity and is backed up by his or her set of abbreviated arguments and knowledge about the film's background.

> *The reviewer can arrange these components in any order, but the most common structure seems to be this: Open with a summary judgement; synopsize the plot; then supply a string of condensed arguments about the acting, story logic, sets, spectacle, or other case-centred points; lace it all with background information; and cap the review by reiterating the judgement.*
>
> **Bordwell, *Making Meaning*, p. 38**

Of course, the reviewer's judgement, writing style and decisions about how much background information and condensed arguments to give the reader, is determined by the projected readership and perceived character of the paper or magazine. A broadsheet newspaper, such as *The Observer* for example, has a projected readership that is perceived to be highly literate and knowledgeable of debates in the arts, culture and society. A film review in such a newspaper (an example from *The Observer* is printed below) will therefore be strong on background information and condensed arguments, while making an evaluative judgement implicit. It conforms to a journalism of opinion. A review in a tabloid newspaper, on the other hand, emphasises plot information and summary judgements. It is a journalism of taste. In my comparative analysis of seven reviews of *The Lost World* in the second part of this chapter, my examples from newspapers will concentrate on the more detailed reviews that appear in the broadsheet newspapers. The next section reproduces an actual film review, Philip French's review of *The English Patient* (Anthony Minghella, 1996) for *The Observer*. I then analyse this review to see how it is organised according to the four components listed above.

Philip French on *The English Patient*

> *By my reckoning, out of around 160 novels short-listed for the Booker prize since it began in 1969, 25 have been turned into films for the cinema or television. Interestingly, the three made with sizeable budgets provided by Hollywood are all set during the Second World War and their unusual perspectives make us reconsider a conflict that still overshadows our lives. The first two,*

Thomas Keneally's Schindler's List *(winner in 1982 as* Schindler's Ark*) and J.G. Ballard's* Empire of the Sun *(runner-up in 1984), are relatively straightforward chronological narratives – one biographical, the other autobiographical.*

Michael Ondaatje's **The English Patient** *(winner in 1992), however, is an immensely complex piece of storytelling, looking at the war from the viewpoints of four sharply contrasted characters living at a shattered villa in Tuscany during the months leading up to VE day in May 1945. It is a subtle meditation on history, nationality, warfare, loyalty and love, but it is also a gripping mystery story.*

Like Ondaatje, who was born in Sri Lanka, grew up in Britain and lives in Toronto, the villa's physically and psychically wounded occupants come from three continents. Hana (Juliette Binoche) is a nursing officer with the Canadian army who has lost her fiancé. When her unit moved north, she stayed behind at the villa to care for the dying English patient (Ralph Fiennes), who received appalling burns in a plane crash and is in fact Almásy, a Hungarian aristocrat educated in Britain. The third figure is Caravaggio (Willem Dafoe) a suave Canadian thief, whose criminal skills and knowledge of Italian had been employed by military intelligence, and who is in pursuit of Almásy, whom he suspects of treason. The quartet is completed by Kip (Naveen Andrews), a Sikh from India, risking his life daily as a bomb disposal officer with the Royal Engineers. Another continent enters into the story, for half of the movie takes place in Cairo and the North African desert in the Thirties where Almásy had been a member of a Royal Geographical Society cartographical expedition and had a passionate affair with Katherine (Kristin Scott Thomas), the wife of a colleague. All four have endured terrible crises and looked death in the face. Now, as the war approaches its end, they are coming to terms with its contradictions and absurdities.

Ondaatje has written poems about the cinema (his 'Late Movies With Skyler' and 'King Kong Meets Wallace Stevens' are included in my anthology The Faber Book of Movie Verse*) and his fiction is intensely cinematic. But like other novelists of whom the same can be said – Graham Greene, for instance, or Salman Rushdie – his* *work is fiendishly difficult to adapt, and the writer-director Anthony Minghella has done a remarkable job in making a coherent movie that retains the themes, motifs and density of the original.*

Moving back and forth in time from the shimmering desert to the rain-drenched Tuscan countryside, The English Patient *is a richly visual experience. Old biplanes fly over a desert landscape that looks like a woman's body. The sands of the Sahara dissolve into the crumpled sheets that cover the disfigured Almásy's bed. The thunder of approaching war in Egypt becomes the thunder of an oncoming rain storm in Tuscany. A powerful central image is the copy of Herodotus (the father of history) that Almásy has turned into a scrapbook so that it incorporates the story of his own life. The picture is also swooningly romantic and one can see what attracted the author of* Truly Madly Deeply, *another story of a transcendent love. There is grandeur in the shot of Almásy carrying the crippled Katherine, wrapped in the parachute that will be her shroud, along a mountain ledge in the desert, and there's magic in the scene where Kip hoists Hana up to the ceiling of a Tuscan church so that she can look at a Piero della Francesca fresco by the light of a flare. All the performances are first-class, with Binoche and Scott Thomas playing two of the most radiant heroines of recent cinema. Technically,* The English Patient *is a miracle. John Seale's cinematography can stand up to comparison with Freddy Young's on* Lawrence of Arabia; *Walter Murch's editing is exemplary. This thoughtful and exhilarating movie is a credit to everyone involved in its making.*

***The Observer*, Sunday, 16 March 1997**

As with many of Philip French's longer film reviews, the first paragraph of this review begins with some very general background information – in this instance, the Booker prize and the number of short-listed books that have been filmed. French notes how many books short-listed for the Booker prize have been filmed (25) and how many are set during the Second World War (three, including *The English Patient*).

In the second paragraph, French notes that *The English Patient*, winner of the Booker prize in 1992, is different from the other two Booker books set during the Second World War in that it has a complex plot structure. This paragraph, together with the third, then gives a plot synopsis of the film. This synopsis is quite long because the film's plot is long and complex.

French concentrates on the film's four main characters, together with the plot lines in which they are involved.

The final paragraph presents an analysis, or a set of abbreviated arguments about the film. These relate specifically to what French calls the film's 'richly visual experience'. In particular, French notes how the transitions from the present to the past are signified by means of sound and image: 'The sands of the Sahara dissolve into the crumpled sheets that cover the disfigured Almásy's bed. The thunder of approaching war in Egypt becomes the thunder of an oncoming rain storm in Tuscany.' French also writes about four striking scenes and shots in the film:

- the shots of the old biplanes flying over the desert (which French describes as looking like a woman's body)
- the shots of Almásy's copy of Herodotus's book on history, which Almásy also uses as a scrapbook
- the shot of Almásy carrying the crippled Katherine along a cliff ledge (Figure 9)
- the scene where Kip hoists Hana up to the ceiling of a Tuscan church so that she can see a fresco lit by a flare.

French presents two additional arguments: firstly that the performances are first-class (French singles out the acting of Juliette Binoche and Kristin Scott Thomas) and secondly, the film is technically miraculous (singling out the cinematography of John Seale and the editing of Walter Murch).

Finally, the review ends with an evaluation: the film is thoughtful and exhilarating. Yet, the rest of the review also contains brief evaluations, particularly in the adjectives and nouns that French uses. From beginning to end, the review contains the following evaluative statements (emphases added): '... a *subtle* meditation ...'; 'a *gripping* mystery story'; 'Minghella has done a *remarkable* job ...'; 'a *richly* visual experience'; 'A *powerful* central image...'; '*swooningly* romantic'; 'There is a *grandeur* in the shot ...'; 'there's *magic* in the scene ...'; 'all performances are *first-class*'; '... the most *radiant* heroines'; 'Technically, *The English Patient* is a *miracle*'; 'Murch's editing is *exemplary*'. Furthermore, it is obviously a complement for John Seale's cinematography to be compared to Freddy Young's desert cinematography in David Lean's visually stunning film *Lawrence of Arabia*.

The boundaries between the four components of French's review (indeed of most reviews) are not always clear-cut. However, French's reviews do contain all four components and they usually follow the same order – background information, condensed plot synopsis, a set of abbreviated arguments about the film and an evaluation.

Evaluation

What are reviewers looking for when they evaluate a film? Reviewers are looking for some, or all, of the following:

- the motivation of what happens in a film
- entertainment value
- social value.

Motivation

In relation to motivation, reviewers are looking for the relevance of or justification for a particular narrative event or technical skill such as an elaborate camera movement or special effects. David Bordwell (*Classical Hollywood Cinema*, p. 19) has identified four types of motivation in the cinema:

- compositional
- realistic
- intertextual
- artistic.

Compositional motivation refers to the formal structure of the film's narrative. An action or event in the narrative is motivated if it constitutes part of the film's cause-effect logic, as discussed in Chapter 2. If an action or event falls outside the cause-effect logic, it is deemed to be unmotivated. In contemporary Hollywood cinema, this usually applies to the many prolonged action sequences and special effects that appear on screen as if for no other reason than to overwhelm the audience's senses and shock their nervous system.

Realistic motivation does not necessarily mean that the action or event under question is literal or true to life. What it can also mean is that, within the world of the film's fiction, the action or event is plausible or believable. For example, in *The Lost World: Jurassic Park*, it is plausible for a T-Rex to eat Eddie (as he tries to pull the trailer up from the cliff face). But it is not plausible if the T-Rex started to talk English. However, within the context of everyday life, it is implausible for a T-Rex to eat

Eddie (or anyone else for that matter), because the T-Rex is an extinct species and has not (as yet) been brought back to life through genetic engineering. So realistic motivation not only means 'authentic', or 'corresponding to everyday life' (this only applies to the artistic movement known as Realism), but also means plausible and believable within the boundaries of the film's fiction.

Following on from realistic motivation is **intertextual motivation**, which includes the relation between the film and its source (such as a famous novel), and the relation between the film and the genre to which it belongs. If a film is based on a famous novel, reviewers will invariably look for the similarities and differences between the two. In this review *The English Patient*, Philip French writes that 'writer-director Anthony Minghella has done a remarkable job in making a coherent movie that retains the themes, motifs and density of the original [novel].' In terms of genre, conventions motivate a particular action in one film, but not in another. For example, if two characters walking along a street suddenly burst into song, accompanied by the sounds of a 50-piece orchestra, this would be motivated in a musical, but would look rather odd in a *film noir*. In the musical, the action of singing is motivated generically, whereas in the *film noir* it would be unmotivated. Sometimes a reviewer will attempt to place an unusual film within a genre in order to make sense of it. For example, *Star Wars* was described, on its initial release in 1977, as a Western in outer space, with several parallels to John Ford's *The Searchers*.

Finally, **artistic motivation** means that a particular filmic technique is motivated for aesthetic reasons. For example, an elaborate camera movement may serve the function of creating an unusual pattern, or simply to demonstrate the virtuosity of the director. Although such virtuosity is occasionally displayed in Hollywood films (as *auteur* critics argued: see Chapter 3), it is more systematically displayed in independently produced American films and in European art cinema. Reviewers who are strongly inclined to look only for compositional, realistic, or intertextual motivation will argue that such displays are simply unmotivated and pretentious. However, reviewers who appreciate independently produced American Films and European art cinema, are more sympathetic to these displays, and can justify them in terms of artistic aims and intentions.

Why is a reviewer's evaluation of a film usually guided by the search for motivation? Because motivation creates a sense of unity and coherence.

When a critic complains that a particular event or technique in a film is not motivated, he or she is arguing that it does not contribute to the overall coherence of the film, but distracts from that coherence because it appears arbitrary. A critic looking for compositional, intertextual and realistic motivation, will perceive many events and the technical virtuosity in a European art film or an American independent film as arbitrary. However, a critic familiar with the artistic intentions of European and independent American directors can see the relevance of these events and techniques – that is, will see the motivation behind such events and techniques. We can therefore distinguish critics according to the different types of motivation they are looking for in a film, which in turn determines that type of film they will evaluate positively and recommend to the reader and which they will give the thumbs down.

Critics who look only for compositional/realistic/intertextual motivation, while debunking artistic motivation, can be called conservative critics, while those who also seek out and praise artistic motivation are radical critics. Conservative critics try to cultivate commonsense rationalism, by suggesting that a film must not disturb our commonsense ideas. A good film, they argue, must have a wide appeal, and must entertain. This is a consensus view of films, a view that argues that films must simply reinforce our everyday ideas, rather than challenge us. The opposite is the case with radical critics. They champion a film that challenges our everyday assumptions and shows us the world from a new perspective. However, this opposition between conservative and radical is not clear cut. In reality, most critics fall somewhere in between; we can call these the liberal critics.

The debates in the British press over David Cronenberg's film *Crash* (1996) clearly separated the conservative critics from the radicals and the liberals. *Crash* is based on the novel by J.G. Ballard and was a controversial winner of the Special Jury Prize at the Cannes film festival in 1996. The film charts the relationship between five characters who are sexually aroused by car crashes. It depicts both the car crashes and sexual encounters between the various characters in graphic detail, while forgoing any attempt to depict character psychology or narrative motivation.

The conservative critics in the British press, such as Alexander Walker in the *London Evening Standard* and Christopher Tookey of the *Daily Mail*, believe that the film is depraved. In looking for motivation, they can only assign it to the genre of pornography. The radicals, including Suzanne

Moore, Salman Rushdie and Martin Amis (all writing in *The Independent*), together with a number of writers for *Sight and Sound* (Mark Kermode, Julian Petley and Leslie Dick), thought that it was an important piece of film art, or a social satire metaphorically commenting on the role of technology in modern society. Finally, the majority of critics (the 'liberal' critics) thought that, although many may find the film distasteful, film goers must still be given the opportunity to see it.

Entertainment value

A review that looks for entertainment value considers whether the film functions as an escapist experience for the audience. But what makes a film entertaining? Hollywood film producers would like an answer to this $64,000 question. Here I can only present some speculative ideas. Firstly, a film is entertaining if it is successful in holding audiences' attention and arousing their emotions. One important way this is achieved is by encouraging spectators to identify with a character or set of characters within the film. Under these circumstances, the character must be 'well rounded', that is, three-dimensional (rather than a two-dimensional cartoon character), with a complex psychology. A film must therefore give the time and space to express and develop a character's psychology, and needs to use techniques of narration (such as restricted narration, discussed in Chapter 2) to encourage spectators to identify with characters. Complexity and inner tensions created by complex character psychology become key in holding spectators' attention and arousing their emotions.

However, it is equally possible to answer that a film is entertaining if it takes the audience on a roller-coaster ride, offering them an experience that amazes their senses and startles their nervous system. What is important is not the film's ability to hold the audience's attention and draw out their emotions, but to overwhelm them. Complex character psychology and structures of narrative and narration are deemed unimportant, as emphasis is placed upon spectacle (extraordinary action sequences and special effects) and sound (loud explosions, stereo and surround sound, and so on).

Social value

In complete contrast to entertainment value, a film reviewer may evaluate a film positively if it depicts an important social issue. One of the all-time greats is Gillo Pontecorvo's *The Battle of Algiers* (1965), a fiction film that depicts Algeria's struggle for independence from France. Occasionally, Hollywood films depict a social issue that is not usually discussed, such as the traumas of a victim of gang rape, as in Jonathan Kaplan's *The Accused* (1988). During the mid 1990s a series of films about Northern Ireland and Irish Independence were made, including: *The Crying Game* (Neil Jordan, 1992), *In the Name of the Father* (Jim Sheridan, 1993), *Nothing Personal* (Thaddeus O'Sullivan, 1995), *Michael Collins* (Neil Jordan, 1996), and *Some Mother's Son* (Terry George, 1996).

Redemption

Now that we have considered the key influences on film evaluation, it is worth considering in passing another common practice that reviewers indulge in – namely, looking for good points in an otherwise bad film. This can be put as a question: What redeems a bad film for a reviewer?

It is very common for reviewers to criticise a film's script or, more generally, the lack of coherence of a film's narrative. Here, reviewers are looking for compositional, realistic, and/or intertextual motivation, but fail to find it. Some reviewers may even attempt to rewrite the script, making suggestions about how it could have been improved. Reviewers looking for artistic motivation may argue that the film is saved by the technical virtuosity of the camera work, editing, or set design. Auteurist critics looking only for formal similarities between a director's work may ignore the script altogether (thus following François Truffaut's lead in his essay 'A Certain Tendency of the French Cinema', discussed in Chapter 3). If the film is dealing with an important social issue, then reviewers are inclined to overlook technical mistakes, unless they are so overwhelming as to distract from the film's themes.

In a bad film, a reviewer may single out any strong acting roles, then make the point that the talent of the particular actor is wasted in this film. Finally, the set design may be the strongest point and may even be the star of the film – that is, may upstage the actors and the narrative, if they are not strong enough to compete with the lavish sets. This is the case with Paul Anderson's film *Event Horizon* (1997), in which the techno-medieval design of the interior of the Event Horizon spaceship is far superior to the acting of the characters, who are let down by a poor script. I will illustrate many of these points in more detail in the next section, when I survey reviews of *The Lost World: Jurassic Park*.

Summary

- Film reviewing can function as journalism, advertising, criticism, or writing.
- Film reviews consist of a condensed plot synopsis, background information, a set of abbreviated arguments and an evaluation.
- In evaluating a film, reviewers are looking for motivation (divided into compositional, realistic, intertextual, and artistic motivation), entertainment value (derived either from narrative or from spectacle), or social value.

Reviews of *The Lost World: Jurassic Park*

In this section we shall analyse a selection of British reviews of *The Lost World* as found in trade papers (*Screen International*), newspapers (*The Observer*, *Sunday Times*, *The Guardian*, *The Independent*) and magazines (*Empire*, *Film Review*). The following discussion assumes that you have seen *The Lost World* (Figure 10).

John Hazelton, *Screen International*, Friday 30 May 1997

John Hazelton begins his review of *The Lost World* by praising the dinosaurs and contrasts them to the poor script. At the outset, then, Hazelton is already making an evaluative judgement of the film's script and special effects. And like many other critics, he sees the lack of a good script as a problem.

Hazelton mentions that the film will do well at the box office, but probably not as much as its predecessor, *Jurassic Park*. (It is normal for sequels to make only 60 per cent box office of the original film; however, with *The Lost World*, this is probably an underestimate).

The rest of the review (four paragraphs) consists of a plot synopsis, into which Hazelton gradually introduces a set of abbreviated arguments. As for characters, he mentions only Dr Ian Malcolm (as the only substantial character to appear in both *Jurassic Park* and *The Lost World*, played both times by Jeff Goldblum) and the game hunter Roland Tembo (Pete

Postlethwaite). For Hazelton, only the latter's performance has any substance to it.

As the plot synopsis progresses, Hazelton adds more arguments. He laments the fact that the film quickly drops the conflict between the team led by Ian Malcolm and the team led by Roland Tembo, as the two teams soon join up to do battle with the dinosaurs. Finally, he adds that the final 40 minutes of the film, based in San Diego, seems to be added as an afterthought and makes the film too long, although he praises the action sequences in these final 40 minutes because they are more lively than the others.

Hazelton uses very little background information in the review and his evaluation is largely implicit, although the script, the performances and the final 40 minutes of the film eventually come under criticism. (The scenes in San Diego, in fact, last only 20 minutes). He criticises the script in particular for its lack of compositional motivation. As for other films, Hazelton only mentions *Jurassic Park*, although he does mention that the last 40 (read: 20) minutes makes a jokey reference to *Godzilla*.

Philip French, *The Observer*, Sunday 20 July 1997

Whereas Hazelton refers only briefly to other films, Philip French has written a review laced with references to other films and other background information. He begins by mentioning that Spielberg's film bears little resemblance to Michael Crichton's novel. He adds that it does, however, resemble Conan Doyle's 1912 novel of the same title and the 1925 film of that novel.

French then points out the similarities and differences between the earlier *Lost World* (1912 book/1925 film) and Spielberg's film. In doing so, French moves from background information to plot synopsis. The similarities include a remote island full of dinosaurs and the bringing back of a dinosaur to civilisation. For French, one difference is that two expeditions are evident in Spielberg's film: that of the good guys (French mentions Ian Malcolm, his girlfriend Sarah Harding (played by Julianne Moore), who are backed by the reformed Dr Hammond) and the bad guys, led by Hammond's unscrupulous nephew Peter Ludlow (played by Arliss Howard).

For French, the game hunter played by Pete Postlethwaite exists between the two opposing expeditions. He is the only complex character in the film and the only one to undergo a transformation. (In Chapter 2, I mentioned that transformation is one of the key characteristics of narrative.)

French's review then moves on to an abbreviated set of arguments. One argument concerns the relation between the film's script and special effects while the other is auteurist, referring to the superiority of Spielberg's other films. Both arguments are combined in the following sentence: 'In his obsession with special effects and spectacle, Spielberg seems to have forgotten how to develop a logical narrative, to sustain suspense and to root drama in character, the qualities that made his lean, early movies like *Duel*, *Sugarland Express* and *Jaws* so gripping'. French then charts the similarities between three scenes in *The Lost World* with three other films: the pursuit of dinosaurs by game hunters resembles scenes in Howard Hawks's safari film *Hatari*; the overhead shot of the velociraptors moving through the long grass towards the hunters resembles a famous scene in Hitchcock's *Foreign Correspondent*; and, finally, French compares *The Lost World* to *King Kong* (1933) and argues that the special effects in *The Lost World* cannot make up for the 'myth, magic, and wonder of *King Kong*'. French's review ends by mentioning that the film is unsuitable for young children, a reference to the darkness of *The Lost World*, in comparison to *Jurassic Park*.

French singles out the script for attack, particularly its lack of compositional motivation, together with the film's poor soundtrack. French also makes the point that special effects cannot compensate for the lack of script coherence. For this reason, he does not try to present a comprehensive plot synopsis. Furthermore, he names several characters and actors, together with numerous other films, including a 1925 version of Conan Doyle's *The Lost World* and *King Kong* (1933). French's negative evaluation of the film is implicit in his set of abbreviated arguments.

Tom Shone, *The Sunday Times*, Sunday 20 July 1997

Tom Shone is one of the few reviewers who is positive about *The Lost World*. The first part of his review begins with a set of abbreviated arguments that compare *The Lost World* to *Jurassic Park* and *The Lost World* evidently comes out on top. One reason is that 'The Lost World: Jurassic Park is much scarier and darker than the first film, which spent much of its time swanning around open countryside under balmy blue skies'. By contrast, most of *The Lost World* takes place at night and in the rain. Furthermore, Shone argues that in *Jurassic Park* the dinosaurs are too tame and he praises the more sinister nature of the dinosaurs in *The Lost World*.

These arguments lead Shone on to a condensed plot synopsis. He is not impressed by the way the film's narrative is hurriedly set up, or by the script's lack of coherence, for which he strongly blames Michael Crichton. However, he is impressed with the introduction of the bad guys, led by Postlethwaite, who hunt the dinosaurs, because this livens up the film. This leads Shone back to his condensed set of arguments, in which he argues that Spielberg is back on form, providing entertainment for his audience in the same way he did in *Raiders of the Lost Ark* and *Indiana Jones and the Temple of Doom*. Ultimately, Shone's evaluation of the film is grounded in the film's entertainment value achieved via spectacle, rather than via the compositional motivation of its script.

Shone then returns to comparing *The Lost World* to *Jurassic Park*. He finds only one image of significance in *Jurassic Park*: the shot of the glass of water that begins to ripple as the T-Rex approaches. This shot conforms to 'the patented Spielberg method: hunting out huge spectacle by subtle indirection, seeking out the big through the small'. Shone seems to find a variation of this image repeated in *The Lost World* (the water in a footprint left by a T-Rex begins to ripple as a T-Rex approaches; however, this shot appears only in the trailer; it does not appear in the film itself). Similarly, other scenes in *The Lost World* repeat scenes from *Jurassic Park* (particularly the action set pieces). For Shone, Spielberg has bettered himself through these variations. Shone ends on a positive evaluation of Spielberg's direction, which he finds 'relaxed and alert'.

Shone's liking of the film is based on his privileging of entertainment value via spectacle over entertainment value via compositional motivation. Much of his review is structured by an abbreviated set of arguments that compare *Jurassic Park* to *The Lost World*, in which *The Lost World* comes out on top because of its higher entertainment value.

Derek Malcolm, *The Guardian*, Friday 18 July 1997

Derek Malcolm writes a swift and deft review of *The Lost World*, making his opinion known in every sentence. The review begins by quoting the reformed Dr Hammond, who believes that the dinosaurs should now be left to roam free on site B (the second island), without human interference. Malcolm then presents a series of abbreviated arguments, concerning special effects, Spielberg's direction, the script and the motives of two characters, Ian Malcolm and Peter Ludlow (Hammond's nephew). For Malcolm, Spielberg seems to be on automatic pilot, giving the dinosaurs more character than the humans and presenting a series of clichés we have seen many times in other monster films.

Malcolm then presents a condensed plot synopsis, covering the beginning of the film, the conflict between the two teams on the island, the film's transformation into a chase movie, finally 'ending with a King Kong-like episode in America'. Malcolm then returns to his set of arguments, which are now blunt and to the point. After praising the special effects, he writes: 'The rest is amazing dross from the man who made Jaws, Close Encounters and ET – and Schindler's List'. The emphasis here is that, with *The Lost World*, Spielberg is definitely not on form: 'The film hasn't the visceral thrills of Jaws, the wonder of Close Encounters or the sweetness of ET, though there's a homage to each. It's just profoundly slick'. Malcolm ends by mentioning Ian Malcolm's daughter in the film, who is an Afro-American, and wonders what type of statement Spielberg is trying to make.

As with many other reviewers, Malcolm criticises Spielberg for privileging special effects over character and compositional motivation. He uses very little background information in this review; instead, he relies on a set of arguments. Malcolm's arguments centring on Spielberg as *auteur* leave not doubt about his evaluation of the film. However, in passing he does mention that it has high entertainment value, since he argues (quite controversially) that 'This is a bonanza for children of all ages'. Finally, he concedes that *The Lost World* does not need to be reviewed because it is already successful and well known. In other words, reviews of the film do not need to function as journalism or advertising.

Adam Mars-Jones, *The Independent*, Thursday 17 July 1997

Adam Mars-Jones's review of *The Lost World* begins with a series of arguments. The first (as with nearly all other reviewers) concerns Spielberg as *auteur*. Mars-Jones wonders why Spielberg decided to make *The Lost World*, when he decided not to make the sequel to *Jaws*, and is happy to act as executive producer on other films. Mars-Jones expresses the issue well by asking: how has Spielberg evolved as a director by making *The Lost World*? This is what other reviewers are attempting to evaluate when they discuss Spielberg as *auteur* in their reviews of *The Lost World*.

Mars-Jones then presents some background information. He informs us of the improved hydraulic systems that enabled Stan Winston's Studio to produce more live action dinosaurs for less money and that Spielberg employed a fully paid-up dinosaur consultant.

More arguments follow, concerning the script (which Mars-Jones thinks is an improvement on *Jurassic Park*), characters (with particular emphasis on Ian Malcolm) and intertextual motivation – that is, genre. Mars-Jones is troubled by the shift in genre in both *Jurassic Park* and *The Lost World*. He wonders why story material demanding to be treated as horror is presented as an adventure, then answers that Spielberg is attempting to make the material suitable for children. This shift in genre, from horror to adventure story, is less marked in *The Lost World* than in *Jurassic Park*. As for genre, then, Mars-Jones sees *The Lost World* as an improvement, because it doesn't make so many compromises as *Jurassic Park* for the sake of a young audience. In terms of genre, Mars-Jones thinks that *The Lost World* resembles *Jaws* because neither film is constructed from a child's perspective, in opposition to *Close Encounters*, *ET*, *Hook*, *Jurassic Park*, etc.

He clearly spells out the significance of this point: 'with [*Jaws*,] Spielberg was concerned not to show that he was a nice guy, but that he could deliver implacable excitement. He was actually the film director as sadistic manipulator before he was the director as big kid, and it would have been better for the *Jurassic Park* films if he had reverted wholeheartedly to the earlier set of skills'. Mars-Jones ends his review by speculating why Spielberg has made the change from a sadistic manipulator to a director as a big kid. One reason is that Spielberg is compromising his talent to the marketplace, which Mars-Jones finds extraordinary for a director who is considered one of the most powerful in the world.

Significantly, Mars-Jones does not present a plot synopsis of *The Lost World*. Instead, he simply presents fragments of plot mixed in with his arguments. In passing, he mentions that the ending of the film is 'An episode like *King Kong* without the pathos'. It is as if he is agreeing with Derek Malcolm that this film needs no reviews to present such basic information as plot. Instead, Mars-Jones presents significant arguments about the film's intertextual motivation and Spielberg as an *auteur* who has changed genre – and compromised his film-making skills – to address a younger audience (or to give his films wider appeal).

Nick Briggs, *Film Review*, August 1997

Virtually the whole of Nick Briggs's review consists of a set of condensed arguments, with one short paragraph devoted to an extremely condensed plot synopsis. Briggs begins his review by pointing out the lack of coherence between *Jurassic Park* and *The Lost World* (why, he asks, in *Jurassic Park* didn't anyone mention the second island? Why didn't Ian Malcolm mention his girlfriend?, etc.). After his plot synopsis, he praises the increased number of dinosaurs in *The Lost World* and their more sinister nature. He then moves on to criticise the lack of script and rounded characters – Ian Malcolm is an uninvolving character, and Sarah Harding isn't credible. The film fails to involve the spectators emotionally with the characters, a common criticism of Spielberg.

Yet Briggs ends by saying that this lack of script and character psychology doesn't matter too much anyway, because the film presents thrills and impressive computer graphics. In other words, for Briggs, entertainment value via spectacle is far more important than entertainment value via a solid script and three-dimensional characters. He ends his review by comparing *Jurassic Park* and *The Lost World* to the two Crichton novels on which the films are based and concludes that the films do not reproduce the energy of the novels.

Ian Nathan, *Empire*, August 1997

Ian Nathan begins his review by arguing that *The Lost World* is not as good as *Jurassic Park* and it represents Spielberg below par. He then argues that the film only loosely conforms to Crichton's novel. A few sentences follow to summarise the plot, pointing out its contrived, disjointed nature. It is only during the action sequences, Nathan argues, that we see Spielberg's signature. Nathan singles out the sequence when the T-Rexs attempt to push Ian Malcolm's trailer off the cliff and the high shot of the velociraptors running through the long grass.

In complete contrast, Nathan strongly criticises the final 40 (sic) minutes of the film. The T-Rex running rampage in San Diego simply has no compositional or intertextual motivation for Nathan, who writes that the 'lack of fundamental plot coherence leaves the great director bursting the bubble'. These scenes, he argues, are present simply to meet public demand and to make a homage to *King Kong*. Yet Nathan concludes that the film delivers when it comes to providing thrills and fun. In other words, as with Nick Briggs's review, entertainment value via spectacle is more important than entertainment value via character psychology and a strong script. Both Briggs and Nathan are encouraging their readers to see the film anyway, despite its flaws.

The last word on *The Lost World*

I could have analysed many other reviews, but they make many of the same points. Several of the above reviewers criticise *The Lost World* for its poor script – its lack of narrative coherence and its shallow character psychology. John Hazelton and Ian Nathan single out the last 40 (read: 20) minutes of the film, set in San Diego, as being particularly out of place, making the film even more unbalanced. They are looking for compositional motivation but without success. Instead, they find unmotivated special effects and action sequences. Although a number of reviewers do praise the entertainment value of the spectacles created by special effects and action sequences, they still mention the script's lack of coherence. Entertainment value via spectacle is not sufficient in itself to carry a film.

Spielberg is one of a handful of Hollywood directors to have attained star status and become a household name. For this reason, almost all reviewers take the time to discuss Spielberg and his earlier achievements. Philip French refers to Spielberg's early films (*Duel*, *Sugarland Express* and *Jaws*), which are based on logical narrative, suspense and strong character psychology, whereas Spielberg now relies on special effects and a series of dramatic action sequences that are simply strung together. Similarly, Derek Malcolm thinks that Spielberg has lost his form in *The Lost World* and argues this point by comparing it with Spielberg's successes such as *Jaws*, *Close Encounters* and *ET*. Adam Mars-Jones goes so far as to suggest that Spielberg shouldn't have directed the film, because it doesn't allow him the scope to develop as a director. Moreover, he believes that Spielberg has compromised his talent in order to appeal to a wider and younger audience. Nathan finds Spielberg making an effort only in the main action sequences and makes the same point as Mars-Jones by arguing that Spielberg has compromised too much to audience demand, by setting the final 40 (20) minutes on the mainland. Only Tom Shone thinks that Spielberg is on form.

It is possible to go on comparing and contrasting the above reviews. But instead, I shall briefly identify what the reviewers have not mentioned – namely, the social value of *The Lost World*. It may seem that this film has no obvious social value, although Mars-Jones does briefly allude to the tension between the capitalist Peter Ludlow and the environmentalist Nick Van Owen. However, Jonathan Romney in *Sight and Sound* did search more deeply for social value:

> *... in an extraordinary shot, unseen velociraptors make diagonal tracks towards their prey through a field of long grass. The film's most chilling moment, it reveals* The Lost World *for what it really is – the closest Spielberg has come to making his own Vietnam film. This is the story about an over-confident US militia moving heavy firepower into a world that's unfamiliar to them, and being outflanked by a far cannier indigenous force: the velociraptors and the disarmingly small, mobile compsognathi are the Vietcong, operating by stealth in their host terrain. Finally, InGen's militaristic initiative defeated, John Hammond makes a presidential-style address to the nation, declaring a new policy of non-intervention.*
>
> **Jonathan Romney, *Sight and Sound*, July 1997, p. 46**

We need to be cautious about Romney's truth claims – that this is what *The Lost World* is 'really' about. Instead, we simply need to take his review as an astute allegorical reading of the film, and understand his truth claims as an attempt to justify his reading.

Despite the repetition, or consensus, on a number of issues – particularly the poor nature of the script, lack of character psychology and the high technical proficiency of the special effects, the above reviewers do differ on other issues, such as what scenes and characters to single out for discussion, the relation between the film and Crichton's novel, as well as its relation to *Jurassic Park*. There are, of course, also differences in opinion between the reviewers' overall evaluation of the film. When these differences of opinion do occur, it is important not simply to side with one reviewer against another, but to take a step back and begin to consider how and why a reviewer has formulated his or her opinion. After all, as Pauline Kael points out in the quotation at the beginning of this chapter, someone 'is not necessarily a bad critic if he makes errors of judgement' because there is no absolute standard by which to judge an evaluation. Nonetheless, the framework presented in this chapter should offer sufficient guidelines to enable you to analyse the work of reviewers and appreciate the strengths and limitations of criticism in general.

Further reading

Bordwell, David, *Making Meaning: Inference and Rhetoric in the Interpretation of Cinema* (Cambridge, Mass: Harvard University Press, 1989)
An in-depth study of how films are interpreted. Bordwell spends a few pages discussing film reviewing, which I have used for this chapter.

FILM STUDIES ON THE INTERNET

No one should doubt that the internet is a valuable source of information. Gathering information is easy, once you become acquainted with using the internet. At the location box on Web client programs such as Netscape, simply type in the address (or URL – uniform resource locator) of relevant pages. Below I have listed the name and URL of a number of Web pages that I frequently use.

One of the problems with the internet is that it can yield too much information which, unlike print sources, usually remains unverified. The problem is therefore to sort the information carefully. You have to be very selective in what you choose to read. But the advantages of the internet far outweigh its disadvantages. Because it is a hypertext system (that is, a non-linear system with numerous links to other pieces of information, which are in themselves linked to numerous other pieces of information, and so on ad infinitum), then you can collect together an enormous amount of specialised information quite quickly. In fact, the internet can quickly turn you into a cinephile! The difference between a cinephile and the 'ordinary' film spectator is that, whereas the ordinary spectator simply watches movies, the cinephile loves the movies. The cinephile is a serious cineliterate film spectator – a connoisseur – who has an encyclopaedic knowledge of the movies. Such an encyclopaedic knowledge can be gained from carefully surfing the internet.

The Alfred Hitchcock Scholars/'MacGuffin' site

http://www.labyrinth.net.au/~muffin/news-home_c.html

A specialist site for those interested in Alfred Hitchcock's films, with an emphasis on serious scholarship. It is useful for its description of recent publications, an FAQ (frequently asked questions) page devoted to Hitchcock, and for long scholarly articles on specialised topics about Hitchcock's films, including: '"I never felt more alive": thoughts on

North by Northwest and its title' and 'The Gioconda smile: archetypes in/of Hitchcock's *Rear Window* (1954)'.

Chicago Reader On Film

http://www.chireader.com/movies/index.html

This site contains several valuable pages, most notably an archive of long reviews, and a list of recent films reviewed. Most of the reviews to be found in the Chicago Reader are by Jonathan Rosenbaum, a very erudite film reviewer. You will find long and detailed reviews of most contemporary films on this site.

Corona Coming Attractions

http://www.corona.bc.ca/films/main.html

This page gives you advance information about future film productions. Most of the information is in fact gossip and rumour, but it mainly comes from industry insiders who are working on these future projects, so most of the information is reliable. As with all internet sites, the information can be accessed several ways. For example, by film titles (which are listed A–Z), by genre, or by the stage of development.

The entry on each film is graded by its stage of development. For example, at the time of writing, 45 movies are listed to be at the rumour stage, including *Blade Runner 2*, *Jaws 5* and *Starship Troopers 2*. Other films are listed as being at different stages of development:

- Script Stage – the development of scripts by professional screenwriters.
- Development Hell – in which a production company commits itself to a script, and tries to find funding; stars, directors and other crew members are approached.
- In Development – the script has attracted funding and interest from stars and directors, and is therefore developed further; if a project reaches this stage, it has a good chance of being made.
- Greenlighted – the film has reached the stage of active production; all the crew and stars have been selected and principal photography begins (it is estimated that only one in ten projects actually get to this stage).

- In the Can – the film has been completed and is awaiting release.
- Vaulted – the film's release has been delayed.

By visiting this site regularly, you will gain information about what films are going to hit the movie screen long before you hear about them officially.

Daily Variety

http://www.variety.com/

The famous trade newspaper *Daily Variety* is available on-line. Non-subscribers have a limited but worthwhile access to the newspaper's stories, while subscribers have full access. As I am reluctant to pay for information on the internet, I do not know what you get by subscribing. But as a non-subscriber you receive shortened versions of news stories, reviews, and the latest information on the American box office. This is definitely one site you should visit in order to gain insider information on what's happening in Hollywood on a daily basis. Thanks to the internet, you don't need to be in California to feel that you are at the centre of Hollywood!

Documentary – Site Links

http://kali.murdoch.edu.au/~cntinuum/doco/links.htm

Documentary – Site Links is part of the Documentary site in the Culture and Communication Reading Room at Murdoch University, Australia. The aim of this site is to present hyperlinks to other sites around the world devoted to documentary. At present it contains links to 11 other sites:

- Documentary Box – a journal devoted to recent trends in making and thinking about documentaries, particularly world documentary and national documentary cinemas.
- Kilima Films – a showcase for presenting documentary films around the world via the internet; this site therefore uses the internet as an alternative medium for showing documentaries.
- The Centre for Documentary Studies at Duke University – whose aim is to make documentary skills accessible to people of all ages from all walks of life, in classrooms, lecture halls, community workshops and forums.

- Documentary Educational Resources – which is involved in the production and distribution of documentary films and videos, particularly anthropological/ethnographic films and videos.
- The American Archives of the Factual Film – a research centre dedicated to the preservation and study of 16mm non-theatrical films; that is, business, educational and documentary films that have not been shown commerically in cinemas.
- The Australian Documentary Conference – one of Australia's largest film conferences, held biennially.
- National Library of Australia: Guides to the Screen Studies Collection – a site that includes full-text notes from a series of seven programmes on documentary presented at the Humanities Research Centre at the Australian National University; the programmes were presented by Bill Nichols and Julianne Burton.
- Canadian Documentary News – an electronic newsletter for people who make documentary programmes.
- Constructing Reality: Exploring Media Issues in Documentary – this page is part of the National Film Board of Canada's site, whose aim is to produce and distribute films and other audiovisual works produced in Canada to the rest of the world.
- Video Eyeball: The 70s Documentary – a bi-monthly magazine created to provide information on little known and largely non-theatrical films which are available on video, including documentaries; part of the site looks at the The 70s Documentary.
- Critical Art Ensemble – a collective of five artists, each specialising in various areas, which is dedicated to exploring areas of cross-over between art, technology, radical politics and critical theory.

Roger Ebert, Chicago Sun Times

http://www.suntimes.com/ebert/ebert.html

The famous American film critic Roger Ebert has made accessible on the internet all his film reviews since 1985. In fact his page located at the above URL gives you six options:

1 Search Roger Ebert's Reviews
2 Current Roger Ebert Reviews
3 Roger Ebert Interviews and Essays
4 One-Minute Movie Reviews
5 Roger Ebert's The Great Movies
6 Movie Answer Man

The first option is the most comprehensive and valuable, since it consists of all of Ebert's reviews from 1985. The second option lists Ebert's reviews from the last two months, while the third lists his interviews and essays from the previous few months. Ebert's reviews are quite long, so if you don't have time to read them, then you can read the shorter reviews, usually consisting of one sentence, plus Ebert's evaluation (option 4). Option 5 covers Ebert's reviews of what he considers to be some of the greatest movies ever made, including *Casablanca*, *The Big Sleep*, *ET*, and *L'Avventura*. Finally, Ebert answers readers' questions in option 6.

Film Festivals on the World Wide Web

http://www.laig.com/law/entlaw/filmfes.htm

This site offers links to a wide range of film festivals around the world – from Asia, Europe, Canada, the United States, and Central and South America.

The Hollywood Reporter

http://www.hollywoodreporter.com/

Much of what I said about *Daily Variety* also applies to *The Hollywood Reporter*. This is another well-respected trade newspaper, which you may want to read in conjunction with *Daily Variety* in order to read about the same stories from a slightly different angle.

The International Movie Database Ltd

http://uk.imdb.com/search

This is a standard and authoritative reference site for finding out the basic information on over 130,000 movies. Search options include: Movie/TV title, cast/crew name and character name. You also have the option of advanced searches, such as two or more people working together. So, for example, you may want to see on what films Marlene Dietrich and Josef von Sternberg worked together. An advanced search yields the following results: 1. *Der Blaue Engel* (1930); 2. *Blonde Venus* (1932); 3. *The Devil Is a Woman* (1935); 4. *Dishonored* (1931); 5. *Morocco* (1930); 6. *The Scarlet Empress* (1934); and 7. *Shanghai Express* (1932).

Or you may want to do a simple search. If you admire John Seale's cinematography on *The English Patient* (1996), you may want to know what other films he has worked on. Entering his name in the search option yields the titles of the 31 films he has worked on as cinematographer – including *Witness* (1985), *The Mosquito Coast* (1986), *Gorillas in the Mist* (1988), *Dead Poets Society* (1989), *Lorenzo's Oil* (1992), *The Firm* (1993), *The Paper* (1994), *Beyond Rangoon* (1995), *The American President* (1995) and *Ghosts of Mississippi* (1996).

An advantage with looking up a movie title on this (and similar) databases is that, with more famous films at least, you will be linked to numerous pages offering reviews of the film, technical information, original release dates, awards the film has won, and availability of the film on video and laser disc. For example, by looking up *The English Patient*, you will find 22 separate links, including a link to 55 reviews – only some of which, however, are worth reading, such as those from famous magazines such as Richard Corliss's review in *Time*, or from newspapers. This demonstrates one of the problems with the internet mentioned above – too much information! The International Movie Database clearly demonstrates the limitations of using reference books, since they do not have instant hypertextual links to other information.

Screensite

http://www.tcf.ua.edu/screensite/contents.htm

Screensite is a serious and scholarly web site that focuses on both film and television studies. It is divided into four areas: Education, Research, Film/TV Production Resources, and Miscellanea. The Education page includes information on course syllabi, scholarly associations and societies, and so on. The Research page includes bibliographies, on-line journals and book abstracts. The Film/TV Production page lists numerous production companies, TV networks, festivals and competitions, screenwriting resources, and links to professional organisations such as the Directors Guild of America, Screen Actors Guild, and Writers Guild of America. Finally, Miscellanea is just that – a mix of information on video sources, on how to make stills from video, and so on.

Screen Studies – General Hotlinks

http://www.livjm.ac.uk/~mccscubi/screenlinks.html

An invaluable site maintained by Sean Cubitt at Liverpool John Moores University. This site consists of dozens of links to other sites, arranged under the following headings:

- Jobs and training
- Hollywood studios
- International film
- Scriptwriting
- Academic sites
- Cyberculture
- Communications and media
- Television
- Magazines
- Miscellaneous online resources.

Many of the sites discussed in this section can be found at this site.

Studio Briefing

http://newshare.com/sb/

This site offers a summary of business news items about the entertainment industry that appear in leading trade and general-interest papers, business publications, and TV news and talk shows. The main page is updated daily, while on another page you can search over four years of studio briefing news. By entering 'Steven Spielberg', 175 separate items were returned. This site is therefore a powerful research tool.

VFX HQ

http://www.vfxhq.com/

This site offers news and information on visual special effects. You will find discussions of recent movies that employ special effects – from *The Lost World* to *Titanic*, *Alien Resurrection*, and so on. The page on *The Lost World* is particularly detailed, and compares its special effects with those in *Jurassic Park*.

USEFUL ADDRESSES

American Film Institute
John F. Kennedy Center for the Performing Arts
Washington D.C. 20566
USA

and

P.O. Box 27999
2021 North Western Avenue
Los Angeles, CA 90027
USA

American Museum of the Moving Image
35th Avenue, at 36th Street
Astoria, Queens
New York
USA

Australian Film Institute
49 Eastern Road
South Melbourne, VIC 3205
Australia

British Film Institute (BFI)
21 Stephen Street
London WV1 4AY
England

Centre National de la Cinématographie
12 rue de Lubeck
75116 Paris
France

Cinématèque Française – Musée du Cinéma
7 Avenue Albert-de-Mun
75016 Paris
France

Cineteca Italiana
Via Palestro 16
20121 Milan
Italy

Det Danske Filmmuseum
Store Søndervoidstraede 4
1419 Copenhagen K
Denmark

Deutsches Filmmuseum
Schaumainkai 41
60596 Frankfurt/Main
Germany

Deutsches Instit für Filmkunde
Schaumainkai 41
60596 Frankfurt am Main
Germany

Dutch Film and Television Academy
Ite Boeremastraat 1
1054 PP Amsterdam
The Netherlands

European Academy for Film
and Television
Rue Verte 69
1210 Brussels
Belgium

Film Institute of Ireland
6 Eustace Street
Dublin 2
Ireland

Film Museum Jacques Ledoux
Rue Baron Horta 9
1000 Brussels
Belgium

Filmoteca Española
Carretera de la Dehesa de la Villa
s/n, 28040 Madrid
Spain

Finnish Film Foundation
Kanavakatu 12
SF-00160 Helsinki
Finland

Hong Kong Film Academy
PO Box 71311
Kowloon
Hong Kong

Hungarian Film Institute
Budakeszi út 51/b
Budapest
Hungary

Israel Film Institute
5 Yelin Mor Street
Tel Aviv 67058
Israel

Museo Nazionale del Cinema
Palazzo Chiablese
Piazza San Giovanni 2
10122 Turin
Italy

Museum of the Moving
Image/National Film Theatre
South Bank
London SE1 8XT
England

National Centre for Screen Studies
Dronningens gt. 16
N-0104 Oslo
Norway

National Museum of Photography,
Film and Television
Pictureville
Bradford
BD1 1NQ
England

Netherlands Film Museum
Vondelpark 3
1071 Amsterdam
The Netherlands

Society of Cinema Studies
c/o University of Texas Press
PO Box 7819
Austin, TX 78713-7819
USA

(see also the Society of Cinema Studies web site: http://www.CinemaStudies.org/)

Svenski Filminstitutet
Box 27126
Filmhuset
Borgvägen 1-5
S-102 52 Stockholm
Sweden

For a comprehensive list of media courses in the UK, see Lavinia Orton, *Media Courses UK* (BFI), and *A Listing of Short Courses in Film, Television, Video, and Radio* (BFI). Courses are also listed in the BFI's annual *Film and Television Handbook*. For the United States, see Ernest Pintoff, *Complete Guide to American Film Schools and Cinema and Television Courses* (Penguin books).

INDEX

Other related titles

TEACH YOURSELF

MEDIA STUDIES

Brenda Downes and Steve Miller

What is Media Studies? Why has it become the fastest growing subject area in post-16 education? How can our own experience and knowledge of the media help us when studying them?

This book provides a clear introduction for those embarking on a course of study and for those who wish to have an overview of current debates about the media.

Teach Yourself Media Studies

- explains concepts used in Media Studies
- introduces essential knowledge for 16+ examinations
- discusses issues central to the study of the media
- uses examples across a range of media technologies
- suggests relevant practical activities
- offers a guide to further study.

The authors have a wide experience of teaching media through all age ranges up to and including graduate and post-graduate level, and are currently producing educational material in a variety of media.

Other related titles

ty TEACH YOURSELF

POSTMODERNISM

Glenn Ward

One of the most fiercely disputed terms of the late twentieth century, postmodernism has had an impact in most fields, from literature and the visual arts, to cultural studies and sociology. In each of these areas, the meanings of postmodernism are flexible, but in all cases it forces us to question some of our most cherished assumptions. Postmodern debates suggest that our most ingrained ideas about the nature of history, culture, meaning and identity can no longer be taken for granted. As such, it has far-reaching implications for how we think about the world today.

This book is an indispensable guide to this sometimes demanding terrain. Aimed at readers encountering theories of postmodernism for the first time, it places the subject in a wide context. Rather than give an account of the 'postmodern condition' from a single perspective, it offers an introduction to the most important theorists in a number of different disciplines, and links theoretical questions to an eclectic range of examples, from both 'high' and 'popular' culture.

Glenn Ward is a lecturer in the Faculty of Art and Music at Bath College of Art and Design.